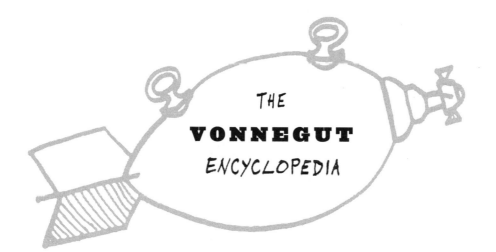

THE
VONNEGUT
ENCYCLOPEDIA

MARC LEEDS

Delacorte Press　New York

THE

VONNEGUT

ENCYCLOPEDIA

**REVISED
AND UPDATED
EDITION**

Published in the United States by Delacorte Press, an imprint of Random House,
a division of Random House LLC, a Penguin Random House Company, New York.

This is a revised edition of *The Vonnegut Encyclopedia*, originally published in 1994
by Greenwood Press, Westport, Connecticut.

Permission credits for previously published material are located on page 757.

DELACORTE PRESS and the HOUSE colophon are registered trademarks
of Random House LLC.

Library of Congress Cataloging-in-Publication Data

Leeds, Marc.
The Vonnegut Encyclopedia: revised and updated edition/Marc Leeds.
pages cm
ISBN 978-0-385-34423-4
ebook ISBN 978-0-8041-7992-8
1. Vonnegut, Kurt—Encyclopedias.   I. Title.
PS3572.O5Z756 2015
813'.54—dc23
2015001135

Printed in the United States of America on acid-free paper

randomhousebooks.com

2   4   6   8   9   7   5   3   1

Revised Edition

Book design by Liz Cosgrove

*In memory of Don Farber and in honor of his blessed union with Annie
for sixty-eight years, their friendship is spiritual.*

*For Mark Weissler, my childhood best friend. Your passing was the first real world news
I had upon waking from a coma. I awoke too late. You passed way too soon.*

For Peter Reed, my Jiminy Cricket.

For my mother, Lila Vita, who twice gave me life.

*To my daughters, Marisa and Whitney, for being more than I ever dreamed.
And to Saralyn Gold, who suffered this book's creation more greatly than did I.*

To my partner at 540.

FOREWORD TO THE FIRST EDITION

A working-class Englishman named Ned Ludd, early in the nineteenth century, smashed up some machinery that was making his skills redundant, thus giving our already rich language a word for a person wary of newfangled contraptions, such as myself, which is "Luddite." A common irony, a virtually unavoidable irony in these times, is for a Luddite to be a beneficiary of a technological advance. I myself now find my life's work as a writer, which I made with ink on bleached and flattened wood pulp, transmogrified into something as insubstantial, ephemeral, and yet immortal as the ghost of Hamlet's father on a parapet at Elsinor. Electrons. Ah me. What is one to think?

My most recent opus in the Gutenberg medium, *Fates Worse Than Death*, isn't at this writing all that recent anymore (1991). I set to work on another one, to be called *Timequake*, but I have been unable to complete it to my own satisfaction, so perhaps it will never be. Civilization will survive in any case. I hoped it to be a tragicomedy (what a language!) about the externalization in the form of compact, reasonably priced, and readily available electronic devices of all that is amusing or economically valuable about the nervous systems of human beings. Memory, given the circumstances that inspire this little essay, is the human capability that first comes to mind. Thanks to my good friend and Professor Marc Leeds, Ph.D., who fed my words to a computer, some machine will remember the two of us long after human beings have stopped giving a damn whether we lived or not.

Ha!

—Kurt Vonnegut

FOREWORD TO THE REVISED AND UPDATED EDITION

Because I watched him write when he gardened and did carpentry and everything else he did, I know how much my father would love that there is now a second edition of *The Vonnegut Encyclopedia*. He is doubled over somewhere laughing that he pulled off something much harder than the Brinks robbery. Better than cheating death.

He made something out of nothing, saved his own life in the process, and made lots of people, including me, less lonely. Lots of people.

It reads well, especially for an encyclopedia, because there was a wholeness and seriousness and earnest hard work in my father's work that resonates. There is very little, if any, tin.

I used to think he was a talented spoiled brat who got lucky and popped out a few good books. Now I'm just amazed.

Thanks, Dad.

Thanks, Marc Leeds.

Thanks to anyone anywhere who reads anything.

—Mark Vonnegut, M.D.

CONTENTS

Foreword to the First Edition *by Kurt Vonnegut*   vii

Foreword to the Revised and Updated Edition
by Mark Vonnegut, M.D.   ix

A Note About This Second Edition   xiii

Dedications   xvi

The Vonnegut Encyclopedia   **1**

Concerning Vonnegut's First Letter Home
After His POW Liberation   721

Acknowledgments   723

Index   726

A NOTE ABOUT
THIS SECOND EDITION

The first edition of this encyclopedia appeared in November 1994, when Kurt Vonnegut turned seventy-two years old. I hoped a second edition would be called for when my friend and advocate of twenty years passed the century mark, and I dreamed that there might be twice as many books for me to cover. Sadly, this was not the case. However, Kurt did add to his considerable literary legacy in the thirteen years he lived after this book's first publication.

The aim of this second edition is to broaden the original work to include all of Kurt's solo publications that appeared during his lifetime or with his explicit approval. All such works since 1994 are included here for the first time, provided they meet the criterion of Kurt's having had a direct hand in their publication. The many newly available Vonnegut manuscripts that have been made public in the past several years are not represented here because they are primarily open drafts or refused manuscripts. There is no doubt of their value for those studying Kurt's work as it developed. But my goal has always been to present Kurt's work as he approved it for publication.

However, I did fill in some entries that escaped the first edition for whatever reason, and with the republication of "Hal Irwin's Magic Lamp," I have corrected an omission that many fans brought to my attention.

Two texts present exceptional cases for consideration within this text. The first is the teleplay of *Between Time and Timbuktu*. Kurt did not write the script. He did, however, provide an introductory note to the text, and that is the only material referenced in this encyclopedia. Second, as a rule, I did not include Vonnegut interviews in this encyclopedia, even those published as books, but I made an exception for a self-interview that appears in *Palm Sunday*.

The other substantive change from the first edition is the conversion of the parenthetical page: line citations to more streamlined chapter number citations. I did so to ensure the encyclopedia's utility for all readers, whatever their edition or reading platform may be.

The works covered in this encyclopedia are (in chronological order):

Player Piano	PP	1952
The Sirens of Titan	ST	1959

Mother Night	MN	1962
Cat's Cradle	CC	1963
God Bless You, Mr. Rosewater	GBR	1965
Welcome to the Monkey House	MH	1968
Slaughterhouse-Five	SL5	1969
Happy Birthday, Wanda June	WJ	1970
Between Time and Timbuktu	TIM	1972
Breakfast of Champions	BC	1973
Wampeters, Foma & Granfalloons	WFG	1974
Slapstick	Slap	1976
Jailbird	JB	1979
Palm Sunday	PS	1981
Deadeye Dick	DD	1982
Galápagos	Gal	1985
Bluebeard	Blue	1987
Hocus Pocus	HP	1990
Fates Worse Than Death	FWD	1991
Histoire du Soldat		1993
Timequake	TQ	1997
Bagombo Snuff Box	BAG	1999
God Bless You, Dr. Kevorkian	GBK	1999
A Man Without a Country	MWC	2005
Armageddon in Retrospect	ARM	2008

Throughout the encyclopedia, type styles are governed by the following rules:

ITALICS are used for my original commentary, including original material inserted within Vonnegut quotations.

BOLD FACE is used for the title of an entry and with each of its appearances within the noted citations. Exception is made when using the referenced term within my original commentary.

QUOTATION MARKS are used for short Vonnegut quotations within my commentary and around short story or essay titles (except in citations, where such titles appear in italics). Quotation marks are also not used when the text flows from original italicized commentary into Vonnegut's words; in these cases my commentary is in italics and Vonnegut's text is in plain (roman) type.

PLACEMENT OF PARENTHETICAL CITATIONS varies. A typical entry without commentary is preceded by the citation in parentheses. In cases where original commentary flows into Vonnegut's material, the parenthetical citation comes at the end of the sentence, before the end-of-line punctuation, in accordance with Modern Language Association guidelines.

*ASTERISKS are used for footnotes (very few, indeed, since the text is self-referencing) and whenever Vonnegut uses them, principally in *Galápagos* to denote characters no longer living.

DEDICATIONS

Player Piano (1951)

For Jane—God Bless Her

Consider the lilies of the field, how they grow:
They toil not, neither do they spin;
And yet I say unto you,
That even Solomon in all his glory
Was not arrayed like one of these. . . .

Matthew 6:28

The Sirens of Titan (1959)

For Alex Vonnegut, special agent, with love

"Every passing hour brings the Solar System forty-three thousand miles closer to Globular Cluster M13 in Hercules—and still there are some misfits who insist that there is no such thing as progress."

—Ransom K. Fern

All persons, places, and events in this book are real. Certain speeches and thoughts are necessarily constructions by the author.

No names have been changed to protect the innocent, since God Almighty protects the innocent as a matter of Heavenly routine.

Mother Night (1962)
(*subtitled*) The Confessions of Howard W. Campbell, Jr.

To Mata Hari

Breathes there the man, with soul so dead,
Who never to himself hath said,
"This is my own, my native land!"
Whose heart hath ne'er within him burn'd
As home his footsteps he hath turn'd
From wandering on a foreign strand?

—Sir Walter Scott

Cat's Cradle (1963)

For Kenneth Littauer, a man of gallantry and taste.

Nothing in this book is true.

"Live by the *foma** that make you brave and kind and healthy and happy."

The Books of Bokonon I:5

**Harmless untruths*

God Bless You, Mr. Rosewater (1965)
(*subtitled*) or Pearls Before Swine

For Alvin Davis,
the telepath,
the hoodlum's friend

All persons, living and dead,
are purely coincidental,
and should not be construed.

"The Second World War was over—and there I
was at high noon, crossing Times Square with a
Purple Heart on."

— Eliot Rosewater
President, The Rosewater Foundation

Welcome to the Monkey House (1968)
A Collection of Short Works

FOR
KNOX BURGER
TEN DAYS OLDER THAN I AM.
HE HAS BEEN A VERY GOOD
FATHER TO ME.

"Beware of all enterprises
that require new clothes."

Thoreau

Slaughterhouse-Five (1969)
(*subtitled*) or The Children's Crusade

A DUTY-DANCE WITH DEATH
BY
KURT VONNEGUT
A FOURTH-GENERATION GERMAN-AMERICAN
NOW LIVING IN EASY CIRCUMSTANCES
ON CAPE COD
[AND SMOKING TOO MUCH],
WHO, AS AN AMERICAN INFANTRY SCOUT
HORS DE COMBAT, AS A PRISONER OF WAR,
WITNESSED THE FIRE-BOMBING OF
DRESDEN, GERMANY,
"THE FLORENCE OF THE ELBE," A LONG TIME
AGO,
AND SURVIVED TO TELL THE TALE.

THIS IS A NOVEL SOMEWHAT IN THE
TELEGRAPHIC
SCHIZOPHRENIC MANNER OF TALES OF THE
PLANET
TRALFAMADORE, WHERE THE FLYING
SAUCERS
COME FROM.
PEACE.

For Mary O'Hare
and Gerhard Müller

Happy Birthday, Wanda June (1970)

(*Though Vonnegut provides a lengthy introduction,
there is no specific dedication or disclaimer beyond
the normal copyright boilerplate language.*)

Breakfast of Champions (1973)
(*subtitled*) or Goodbye Blue Monday!

In Memory of Phoebe Hurty,
*who comforted me in Indianapolis —
during the Great Depression.*

When he hath tried me,
I shall come forth as gold.

—Job

Wampeters, Foma & Granfalloons (Opinions) (1974)

For
Jill
who cronkled me

I have traveled extensively in Concord.

—Henry David Thoreau

Slapstick (1976)
(*subtitled*) OR LONESOME NO MORE!

Dedicated to the memory of
Arthur Stanley Jefferson and Norvell Hardy,
two angels of my time.

"Call me but love, and I'll be new baptiz'd . . ."
—Romeo

Jailbird (1979)

For Benjamin D. Hitz,
Close friend of my youth,
Best man at my wedding.
Ben, you used to tell me about
Wonderful books you had just read,
And then I would imagine that I
Had read them, too.
You read nothing but the best, Ben,
While I studied chemistry.
Long time no see.

(*The following comes after a thirty-eight-page intro-duction and prior to the narrative.*)

Help the weak ones that cry for help, help the prosecuted and the victim, because they are your better friends; they are all the comrades that fight and fall as your father and Bartolo fought and fell yesterday for the conquest of the joy of freedom for all the poor workers. In this struggle of life you will find more love and you will be loved.
—Nicola Sacco (1892–1927)

In his last letter to his thirteen-year-old son, Dante, August, 18, 1927, three days before his execution in Charlestown Prison, Boston, Massachusetts. "Bar-tolo" was Bartolomeo Vanzetti (1888–1927), who died the same night in the same electric chair, the invention of a dentist. So did an even more forgot-ten man, Celestino Madeiros (1894–1927), who confessed to the crime of which Sacco and Vanzetti had been convicted, even while his own conviction
for another murder was being appealed. Madeiros was a notorious criminal, who behaved unselfishly at the end.

Palm Sunday (1981)
(*subtitled*) An Autobiographical Collage

For my cousins the de St. Andrés everywhere. Who has the castle now?

Deadeye Dick (1982)

For Jill

Who is Celia? What is she?
That all her swains commend her?
—Otto Waltz (1892–1960)

Galápagos (1985)

In memory of Hillis L. Howie,
(1903–1982) amateur naturalist—
A good man who
took me and my best friend Ben Hitz
and some other boys
out to the American Wild West
from Indianapolis, Indiana,
in the summer of 1938.
Mr. Howie introduced us to real Indians
and had us sleep out of doors every night
and bury our dung,
and he taught us how to ride horses,
and he told us the names of many plants
and animals,
and what they needed to do
in order to stay alive
and reproduce themselves.

One night Mr. Howie scared us half to death
on purpose,
screaming like a wildcat near our camp.
A real wildcat screamed back.

*In spite of everything, I still believe
people are really good at heart.*
                    —*Anne Frank (1929–1944)*

Bluebeard (1987)

"We are here to help each other get through this
thing, whatever it is."
                    —Dr. Mark Vonnegut, M.D.
                    (*Letter to the Author, 1985*)

BLUEBEARD
THE AUTOBIOGRAPHY OF
RABO KARABEKIAN
(1916–1988)

This book is for Circe Berman. What else can I say?
                    —R.K.

Hocus Pocus (1990)

This work of pure fiction is dedicated to the
memory of

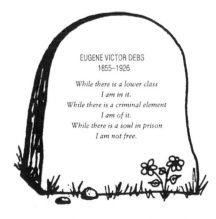

EUGENE VICTOR DEBS
1855–1926

*"While there is a lower class
I am in it.*

*While there is a criminal element
I am of it.
While there is a soul in prison
I am not free."*

(*This quote is set within Vonnegut's drawing of a
headstone.*)

Fates Worse Than Death (1991)

All persons, living and dead, are purely coincidental and should not be construed. No names have
been changed to protect the innocent, since God
Almighty protects the innocent as a matter of
Heavenly routine.

IN MEMORY OF KURT VONNEGUT (SR.)

O God who hast hitherto supported me, enable
me to proceed in this labor & in the whole task of
my present state that when I shall render up at the
last day an account of the talent committed to me
I may receive pardon for the sake of Jesus Christ.
Amen.
                    —SAMUEL JOHNSON, diary entry for
                    April 3, 1753, when he was working on his
                    *Dictionary of the English Language**

*April 3, therefore, might be called "Writer's Day."

Timequake (1997)

*Opposite the title page is Vonnegut's painting of
Kilgore Trout in front of his open and empty birdcage with the following inscription:*

Out-of-print science fiction writer Kilgore Trout in
Cohoes, New York, in 1975, having learned of the
death of his estranged son, Leon, in a Swedish
shipyard, having given his parakeet, "Cyclone
Bill," his freedom, and about to become a
vagabond.

In memory of Seymour Lawrence,
a romantic and great publisher
of curious tales told with ink
on bleached and flattened wood pulp

Bagombo Snuff Box (1999)
Uncollected Short Fiction

As in my other works of fiction:
   All persons living and dead are purely coincidental, and should not be construed. No names have been changed in order to protect the innocent. Angels protect the innocent as a matter of Heavenly routine.

In memory of my first agents,
Kenneth Littauer
and Max Wilkinson,
who taught me how to write

God Bless You, Dr. Kevorkian (1999)

Special thanks to Marty Goldenshohn of WNYC, who served as city desk editor to our roving reporter on the Afterlife, encouraging him to keep digging away at the story, and getting public radio to pay him a buck a word, which isn't bad for an out-of-the-way beat like Heaven.

A Man Without a Country (2005)

(Vonnegut's handwritten blue card two pages before the title page.)

THERE IS NO REASON
GOOD
CAN'T TRIUMPH OVER EVIL,
IF ONLY ANGELS
WILL
GET ORGANIZED
ALONG THE
LINES OF THE MAFIA.

THE
VONNEGUT
ENCYCLOPEDIA

NUMBERS

2BR02B (also **"2BR02B"**). *Kilgore Trout's novel (the alphanumeric abbreviation of Hamlet's question, "To be or not to be")* as described in God Bless You, Mr. Rosewater, *is a thematic cross between* Player Piano *and "Welcome to the Monkey House" (industrial mechanization leading to unemployment and depression combined with severe overpopulation leading to ethical suicide), complete with Ethical Suicide Parlors outfitted with pretty hostesses and Barca-Loungers.* (GBR 2) All serious diseases had been conquered. So death was voluntary, and the government, to encourage volunteers for death, set up a purple-roofed Ethical Suicide Parlor at every major intersection, right next to an orange-roofed Howard Johnson's. There were pretty hostesses in the parlor, and **Barca-Loungers**, and Muzak, and a choice of fourteen painless ways to die.

"2BR02B" is also the title of Vonnegut's short story originally appearing in the January 1962 edition of Worlds of If *and later reprinted in the 1999 collection* Bagombo Snuff Box. *"2BR02B" is another of Vonnegut's tales that ponders the personal conflicts faced by the beneficiaries of seemingly surreal medical/scientific advances in a world whose social, moral, and legal frameworks have been amended to the dictates of science. "Welcome to the Monkey House," "Tomorrow and Tomorrow and Tomorrow," and "Fortitude" are as baldly dystopian as are the worlds in* Player Piano, Cat's Cradle, *or* Hocus Pocus.

The story is set far in the future. The nation's population has stabilized at 40 million but exceedingly aged, averaging 129 years old. Ever since a cure for the effects of aging was found, people remained as youthful as they were the day they started the medication. Births, however, can occur only with the agreed-upon exchange of one soul for another—literally. In the case of thrice-blessed father-to-be Edward K. Wehling, Jr., this means needing to come up with three existing souls in exchange for those of his children.

The entirety of the story takes place in the waiting room of the famed Chicago Lying-in Hospital. Ed- ward K. Wehling, Jr., faces a rare dilemma. As the new father of triplets in a zero-sum population scheme agreed to by the nations of the world, he needs to find three people willing to die (probably by visiting an Ethical Suicide Studio) so that his children may live. His maternal grandfather has already volunteered to sacrifice himself.

Despite the seriousness of Wehling's situation, the brief story's focus is the slow exposé of both the mural and muralist at work in the waiting room. Titled "The Happy Garden of Life," The mural he was working on depicted a very neat garden. Men and women in white, doctors and nurses, turned the soil, planted seedlings, sprayed bugs, spread fertilizer. Men and women in purple uniforms pulled up weeds, cut down plants that were old and sickly, raked leaves, carried refuse to trash burners.

Never, never, never—not even in medieval Holland or old Japan—had a garden been more formal, been better tended. Every plant had all the loam, light, water, air, and nourishment it could use.

The mural is an obvious metaphor for medicine's ability to tend to all the necessities of life while gardeners in purple uniforms (like those worn by workers in the worldwide chain of Ethical Suicide Studios) prune the garden of the sick and old growth.

Responsible for the breakthrough in extending life so well, Dr. Benjamin Hitz, the hospital's chief obstetrician, a blindingly handsome man, is among the many faces being filled in by the unnamed muralist, himself a man nearly two hundred years old, though he looks no more than thirty-five thanks to the cure. (Benjamin Hitz is the name of Vonnegut's best friend from childhood; he is also mentioned in the dedication to Jailbird).

Wehling stares at a fixed spot on the wall throughout Dr. Hitz's diatribe about how much better life is for the planet now that we have advanced so far. However, Wehling displays that "thousand yard stare," a term that came about after World War II indicating one's being shell-shocked, or, in current parlance, suffering with PTSD, post-traumatic stress disorder. As Hitz winds down his impromptu lecture, Wehling very clearly knows how to resolve the dilemma of his blessings. "This child of yours—whichever one you decide to keep, Mr. Wehling," said Dr. Hitz. "He or she is going to live on a happy, roomy, clean, rich planet, thanks to population control. In a garden like in that mural there." He shook his head. "Two centuries ago, when I was a young man, it was a hell that nobody thought could last another twenty years. Now centuries of peace and plenty stretch before us as far as the imagination cares to travel."

He smiled luminously.

The smile faded when he saw that Wehling had just drawn a revolver.

Wehling shot Dr. Hitz dead. "There's room for one—a great big one," he said.

And then he shot Leora Duncan. "It's only death," he said to her as she fell. "There! Room for two."

And then he shot himself, making room for all three of his children.

Watching this macabre scene from above is the unnamed muralist. The painter sat on the top of his stepladder, looking down reflectively on the sorry scene. He pondered the mournful puzzle of life demanding to be born and, once born, demanding to be fruitful . . . to multiply and to live as long as possible—to do all that on a very small planet that would have to last forever.

It is enough to impel the old muralist to end it all. Though he picks up Wehling's smoking revolver, he decides his nerves can't handle suicide by his own hand. Instead, he calls the Federal Bureau of Termination for an appointment that afternoon. As the operator is about to finish taking the reservation, she spouts the polite boilerplate ending to all such calls, indicating just how ubiquitous was the process as well as appealing to people's sense of good citizenship. "Thank you, sir," said the hostess. "Your city thanks you, your country thanks you, your planet thanks you. But the deepest thanks of all is from future generations."

27 Bethune Street, New York, NY. *The location of Howard W. Campbell's apartment after the war, and the location of significant portions of* Mother Night.

3972 Ellis Avenue, Chicago, Illinois. *The location of the Church of Jesus Christ the Kidnapped, founded by the Right Reverend William Uranium-8 Wainwright, in* Slapstick.

4918 North Meridian Street, Indianapolis, Indiana. *The home of Mrs. Harrison C. Conners and her brother, the memorable dwarf, Newt Hoenikker. These are two of the three children of Dr. Felix Hoenikker, inventor of ice-nine, in* Cat's Cradle.

5644 North Meridian Street, Indianapolis, Indiana. *The location of the French château built by the title character in "Hal Irwin's Magic Lamp."*

"A Night for Love." *Originally published in the November 1954 edition of* The Saturday Evening Post *and reprinted in* Bagombo Snuff Box *(1999), the story's nexus is the full moon beaming down on the jealous sensibilities of the Whitman and Reinbeck families, separated by mere miles and millions of dollars. The moon is also the nexus for the two shining offspring of the Whitman and Reinbeck families, Nancy and Charlie, whose narrowed beams inside his coupe, beneath their families' jealous moon, guide them to elope.*

The more frontal subplot involves spousal jealousies long ago planted by the two early dates of Milly O'Shea Whitman and Louis C. Reinbeck. Turley is a security guard at Reinbeck Abrasives Company, and his wife, Milly, was once a beauty queen. Natalie Reinbeck, the sole wife of Louis C., the mother of young Charlie, and beneficiary of the Reinbeck lifestyle, nonetheless harbors jealousy about her husband's nearly ancient dates with Milly.

An emotional resolution reaches into the minds if not hearts of the jealous spouses, acknowledging the moon's capabilities to cause such an emotional ruckus. It is at that moment that Vonnegut serves the anti–Romeo and Juliet moment by having the offspring of social-class appositives live on rebelliously by eloping.

"A Present for Big Saint Nick." *The story first appeared in the December 1954 issue of* Argosy *magazine as "A Present for Big Nick" and later retitled by Vonnegut "A Present for Big Saint Nick" in the 1999 reprint collection entitled* Bagombo Snuff Box. *Vonnegut does not account for the minor retitling, but it does leave one to wonder why.*

Changing the title elevates the story's darkly comedic and ironic aspects. The ironic presentation of this anti-Christmas tale is evident without the change in titles. What establishes the story's power beneath its darkly comedic aspects is revealed by the otherwise mundane plight of workers, their sense of helplessness, lack of self-esteem, and absolute fear in the face of an overbearing and threatening employer.

True, not everyone works for the Mafia, but the families victimized in this story were otherwise law-abiding people who had been failing in their civilian employment before working for The Family and Big Nick. One, former middleweight boxer Bernie O'Hare, had (in a sense) been owned by Big Nick through a legal contract (establishing his rights as Bernie's manager).

The updated title allows the reader to focus on a collage of ironic twists often rendered comedically despite their dark overtones. From the outset we read of Big Saint Nick, heir to the power of Al Capone. His great power is juxtaposed by his masquerade as the altruistic one who knows who has been naughty and who has been nice, preparing the reader for some sort of comedic clowning. But Nick's Santa charade has but one purpose: to seduce the children of his employees in order to solicit from them in their moment of gratitude and peaceful Christmas greediness the rebellious, disrespectful, and perhaps disloyal sayings of their parents when they are at ease in their own homes. The parents are aware of his strategy and take great care to prepare the children. The tense struggle between Nick's ego and paranoia versus the parents' careful preparation of toddlers and grade schoolers lets hang in the balance certain disappearances at the bottom of Lake Michigan or bonus payments for well-indoctrinated answers. All are aware that lives are on the line—except for the children, who would be orphaned if their trained lies fail to convince Big Saint Nick.

Big Nick is played for the clown in the opening scene of the story. Bernie O'Hare and his family accidentally meet Mr. Pullman and his family in a jewelry store where both are looking for grotesque holiday gifts for their boss, a man all recognize as having the worst taste. While both families revel in their knowledge of Nick's low-class tastes, they delight in their search for the most horrendous cacophony of smashed-up style and substance, debased beyond all reason.

In the meantime, however, both families suffer for their intimate knowledge of Big Nick. Constant con-

tact with the great bully leaves them afraid for their lives, but it has been Nick's effect on their children that is most troubling. Young Willy O'Hare and Richard Pullman severely suffer Santa-phobia: visibly shaken and stricken with fear at the thought of seeing Santa, even department store Santas or the great and jolly fat man as a small plastic figurine. Mrs. Pullman's exasperation lets loose for all to hear, including the jewelry salesman, "It's psychosomatic," said Mrs. Pullman. "He *(her son Richard)* snuffles every time he sees a Santa Claus. You can't bring a child downtown at Christmastime and not have him see a Santa Claus somewhere. One came out of the cafeteria next door just a minute ago. Scared poor Richard half to death." *She later explains Big Saint Nick from the children's perspective.* "Why pretend?" said Mrs. Pullman. "Our Santa Claus *is* a dirty, vulgar, prying, foulmouthed, ill-smelling fake."

The clerk's eyes rolled.

Later at the party, Big Nick, dressed as Santa, abuses his position to bribe the children to get the dirt on their parents. However, direct questioning is exactly what the parents worked so hard to train their children to deflect with complimentary responses. Unfortunately, no one thought while training their children to keep them from offering what they heard other parents say, and their young minds could not grasp Nick's initial subterfuge. Unless prompted by a direct question, the children had no filters on their responses.

The children's literal-mindedness, devoid of cunning or artifice, is what begins to elevate the tension in the room. After Richard Pullman and Gwen Zerbe pass their initial interrogations and busy themselves with their gifts, Big Saint Nick turns his attention to Willy O'Hare, son of Bernie, the one-eyed bodyguard who was offered a job in a moment of true compassion by the otherwise malevolent Nick.

Having offered Big Saint Nick nothing but a well-rehearsed answer, Willy's unassuming young mind slips back to the concerns of a young boy. The situation begins to spiral out of control for everyone as the other children join in on matters they were unable to appreciate. "Willy O'Hare!" thundered Santa Claus. "Tell Santy the trut', and ya get a swell boat. What's your old man and old lady say about Big Nick?"

"They say they owe him a lot," said Willy dutifully. Santa Claus guffawed. "I guess they do, boy! Willy, you know where your old man'd be if it wasn't for Big Nick? He'd be dancin' aroun' in little circles, talking to hisself, wit'out nuttin' to his name but a flock of canaries in his head. Here, kid, here's your boat, an' Merry Christmas."

"Merry Christmas to you," said Willy politely. "Please, could I have a rag?"

"A rag?" said Santa.

"Please," said Willy. "I wanna wipe off the boat."

"Willy!" said Bernie and Wanda together.

"Wait a minute, wait a minute," said Santa. "Let the kid talk. *Why* you wanna wipe it off, Willy?"

"I want to wipe off the blood and dirt," said Willy.

"Blood!" said Santa. "Dirt!"

"Willy!" cried Bernie.

"Mama says everything we get from Santa's got blood on it," said Willy. He pointed at Mrs. Pullman. "And that lady says he's dirty."

"No I didn't, no I didn't," said Mrs. Pullman.

"Yes you did," said Richard. "I heard you."

"My father," said Gwen Zerbe, breaking the dreadful silence, "says kissing Santa Claus isn't any worse than kissing a dog."

"Gwen!" cried her father.

"I kiss the dog all the time," said Gwen, determined to complete her thought, "and I never get sick."

"I guess we can wash off the blood and dirt when we get home," said Willy.

"Why, you fresh little punk!" roared Santa Claus, bringing his hand back to hit Willy.

Though Bernie saves the day by grabbing Big Nick's hand before having the chance to wallop young Willy, all the adults in the room have their lying façades compromised. Nick assures them that knocking off everyone will come cheaply to him. Bernie follows the grab with a professional boxer's jab at his face, sending Nick into the Christmas tree, and the sight of Big Saint Nick clawing down ornaments as he fell is just the kind of slapstick comedy children cherish. As the families begin to leave, grabbing their coats and presents while Big Nick is left to yell how little he will have to pay to have them all killed, the children provide another moment of irony, singing joyfully as they leave Santa's home in sharp contrast to the fearful manner in which they arrived. The children were so happy! They danced out of the house without their coats, saying things like, "Jingle bells, you old poop," and "Eat tinsel, Santy," and so on. They were too innocent to realize that nothing had changed in the economic structure in which their parents were still embedded. In so many movies they'd seen, one punch to the face of a bad guy by a good guy turned hell into an earthly paradise.

Big Nick, embarrassed by children and employees, runs to another room to grab an armful of presents for himself sent by celebrities and others whom he assumes love him and offer their loyalty. Instead, he pulls out a gift sent all the way from Italy. He gave its red ribbon a mighty yank. The explosion not only blew off his bloody beard and fur-trimmed red hat, but removed his chin and nose as well. What a mess! What a terrible thing for the young to see, one would think, but they wouldn't have missed it for the world.

After the police left, and the corpse was carted off to the morgue, dressed like Kris Kringle from the neck down, O'Hare's wife said this: "I don't think this is a Christmas the children are going to forget very soon. I know I won't."

Their son Willy had a souvenir that would help him remember. He had found the greeting card that came with the bomb. It was in the shrubbery. It said, "Merry Christmas to the greatest guy in the world." It was signed "The Family."

There would be a rude awakening, of course. The fathers were going to have to find new jobs, ho ho.

Big Nick was as uncompromising and boorish with his Italian compatriots, so they simply resorted to assassination. They could not envision he would be dressed as Saint Nick at the moment the blast beheaded him, but that is one point of the irony emphasized by the updated 1999 title.

At a deeper level, perhaps at the level Vonnegut first considered when he wrote the story, we have the parody of a Mafia boss who is undone by the reactions of children. Moreover, the truly vulnerable in the story, families in his employ who are not themselves criminals (Pullman and Zerbe are, respectively, a lawyer and an accountant; O'Hare is just a man who lost an eye at work and needed a compassionate employer to come forward and give him a chance). All three families are appreciative that their lives before Big Nick hired them were financially unsuccessful and without much prospect for their future. Big Nick changed that. It is never indicated they are involved with criminal wrongdoing in their work for Nick, but they are aware of the ethical dilemma each lives with, and they are troubled by the compromises they make to put food on their tables. And that is very much the unvarnished truth they have to deal with as indicated by the closing line: There would be a rude awakening, of course. The fathers were going to have to find new jobs, ho ho.

As such, the focus of the story as originally titled downplays the comedic irony that is the vehicle for the tale. What we have is the eternal dilemma faced by people who often find themselves working either for absurd managers or in the production of goods and services that they know is antithetical to their own values.

Aamons, Celia. *Though Celia's maiden name is not provided in Cat's Cradle, she married Nestor Aamons when he came to San Lorenzo to design and build the House of Hope and Mercy in the Jungle for Julian Castle. Nestor and Celia are the parents of Mona.*

Aamons, Nestor. (CC 54) Nestor Aamons *(a native Finn)* was captured by the Russians, then liberated by the Germans during the Second World War. He was not returned home by his liberators, but was forced to serve in a *Wehrmacht* engineer unit that was sent to fight the Yugoslav partisans. He was captured by Chetniks, royalist Serbian partisans, and then by Communist partisans who attacked the Chetniks. He was liberated by Italian parachutists who surprised the Communists, and he was shipped to Italy.

The Italians put him to work designing fortifications for Sicily. He stole a fishing boat in Sicily, and reached neutral Portugal. *In Portugal, Nestor Aamons met Julian Castle, who persuaded him to go to San Lorenzo where he designed Castle's hospital, the House of Hope and Mercy in the Jungle,* "married a native woman named Celia, fathered a perfect daughter [Mona], and died."

A-bomb, American bomb, atomic bomb, atom-bombed, atom-bombing, atombombed, atomic weapons, hydrogen bomb, the bomb (*when clearly meaning a nuclear device*), **neutron bomb.** *Vonnegut's frequent references to nuclear devices run throughout each of his books. In* Player Piano *the supercomputer EPICAC is in charge of the technocracy's nuclear arms.* (PP XI) EPICAC could consider the merits of high-explosive bombs as opposed to **atomic weapons** for tactical support, and keep in mind at the same time the availability of explosives as opposed to fissionable materials, the spacing of enemy foxholes, the labor situation in the respective processing industries, the probable mortality of planes in the face of enemy antiaircraft technology, and on and on, if it seemed at all important, to the number of cigarettes and Cocoanut Mound Bars and Silver Stars required to support a high-morale air force.

Cat's Cradle's *narrator John/Jonah originally intends to write* an account of what important Americans had done on the day when the first **atomic bomb** was dropped on Hiroshima, Japan (CC 1). *In* Slaughterhouse-Five *Vonnegut makes frequent comparisons between the firebombing of Dresden and the destruction of Hiroshima and Nagasaki, noting that more people were killed in Dresden than in the other two cities. His point has to do with the economy of destructive forces.* (SL5 9) (British Air Marshal Sir Robert Saundby quoted in David Irving's *The Destruction of Dresden*) The advocates of nuclear disarmament seem to believe that, if they could achieve their aim, war would become tolerable and decent. They would do well to read this book and ponder the fate of Dresden, where 135,000 people died as the result of an air attack with conventional weapons. On the night of March 9th, 1945, an air attack on Tokyo by American heavy bombers, using incendiary and high explosive bombs, caused the death of 83,793 people. The **atom bomb** dropped on Hiroshima killed 71,379 people.

Similarly, Vonnegut speaks in his own voice about the bombing as a technological achievement in Palm Sunday *... and when I feel most lost in this world, I comfort myself by visiting a hardware store. I meditate there. I do not buy anything. A* hammer is still my Jesus, and my Virgin Mary is still a cross-cut saw.

But I learned how vile that religion of mine could be when the **atomic bomb** was dropped on Hiroshima. . . . There was nothing in the bombs or the airplanes, after all, which could not, essentially, be bought at a small hardware store (PS 3). *Vonnegut creates the contrast in his mind between the bombings of Dresden and Hiroshima. Dresden's conventionally engineered destruction was not beyond imagination because of its reliance on everyday materials. Hiroshima's immolation reflected a leap in materials acquisition and application.*

Colonel Looseleaf Harper in Happy Birthday, Wanda June *is said to be the pilot who dropped the bomb on Nagasaki.* Deadeye Dick *has at its core the neutron-bombing of Midland City and the suggestion that the government authorized its destruction as a test of the weapon.* (DD Epilogue) My own guess is that the American Government had to find out for certain whether the neutron bomb was as harmless as it was supposed to be. So it set one off in a small city which nobody cared about, where people weren't doing all that much with their lives anyhow, where businesses were going under or moving away. The Government couldn't test a bomb on a foreign city, after all, without running the risk of starting World War Three.

Galápagos *chronicles humanity's evolutionary return to the sea as a partial consequence of the genetically altered Hisako Hiroguchi (her mother survived the Hiroshima bombing). Warden Hiroshi Matsumoto (whose first name and first two letters of his last name spell "Hiroshima") of* Hocus Pocus *is also a survivor of the Hiroshima bombing.*

The following anecdote is one of Vonnegut's more famed references on the topic in his writing and speeches, demonstrating the relatively blurry nexus between fact and myth, between reality and fiction, between life and art—the stuff that makes ambiguity as exciting as it so often is. It also is occasion for yet another of Vonnegut's enigmatic three-word declarations, I was there. Vonnegut's famous first letter home after liberation (from POW status, repatriation to the American command, and recuperation in Le Havre) punctuates his survivorship through Dresden's fireboming and massacred civilians—piled like

cordwood for immolation—by ending successive paragraphs with a soberly delivered, But not me. *Later in* Slaughterhouse-Five, *such expressions are delivered as* So it goes *and* Poo-tee-weeet.
(TQ 2) Imagine this: A great American university gives up football in the name of sanity. It turns its vacant stadium into a **bomb** factory. So much for sanity. Shades of Kilgore Trout.

I am speaking of my alma mater, the University of Chicago. In December of 1942, long before I got there, the first chain reaction of uranium on Earth was compelled by scientists underneath the stands of Stagg Field. Their intent was to demonstrate the feasibility of an **atomic bomb**. We were at war with Germany and Japan.

Fifty-three years later, on August 6th, 1995, there was a gathering in the chapel of my university to commemorate the fiftieth anniversary of the detonation of the first **atomic bomb**, over the city of Hiroshima, Japan. I was there.

Vonnegut's tone of irony continues by the recollection of fact, not fiction. (TQ 2) Now imagine this: A man creates a **hydrogen bomb** for a paranoid Soviet Union, makes sure it will work, and then wins a Nobel Peace Prize! This real-life character, worthy of a story by Kilgore Trout, was the late physicist Andrei Sakharov.

He won his Nobel in 1975 for demanding a halt to the testing of nuclear weapons. He, of course, had already tested his. His wife was a pediatrician! What sort of person could perfect a **hydrogen bomb** while married to a child-care specialist? What sort of physician would stay with a mate that cracked?

"Anything interesting happen at work today, Honeybunch?"

"Yes. My **bomb** is going to work just great. And how are you doing with that kid with chicken pox?"

The irony of Andrei Sakharov's situation organically envelops his wife in deepening the situation's irony. (TQ 2) Andrei Sakharov was a sort of saint in 1975, a sort that is no longer celebrated, now that the Cold War is over. He was a dissident in the Soviet Union. He called for an end to the development and testing of **nuclear weapons**, and also for more freedoms for his people. He was kicked out of the USSR's Academy of Sciences.

He was exiled from Moscow to a whistlestop on the permafrost.

He was not allowed to go to Oslo to receive his Peace Prize. His pediatrician wife, Elena Bonner, accepted it for him there. But isn't it time for us to ask now if she, or any pediatrician or healer, wasn't more deserving of a Peace Prize than anyone who had a hand in creating an **H-bomb** for any kind of government anywhere?

Human rights? What could be more indifferent to the rights of any form of life than an **H-bomb**?
(TQ 3) After an **atom bomb** was dropped on Hiroshima, and then another one was dropped on Nagasaki, *Joy's Pride* was ordered to drop yet another one on Yokohama, on a couple of million "little yellow bastards." The little yellow bastards were called "little yellow bastards" back then. It was wartime. Trout described the third **atom bomb** like this: "A purple motherfucker as big as a boiler in the basement of a mid-size junior high school."
(TQ 3) No sooner had the judge restored order, though, than a huge crack opened in the floor of the Pacific Ocean. It swallowed Banalulu, courtmartial, *Joy's Pride,* unused **atom bomb** and all.
(TQ 26) In my opinion, Trout, far from giving yet another high colonic to our aborigines, is raising the question, perhaps too subtly, of whether great discoveries, such as the existence of another hemisphere, or of accessible **atomic energy**, really make people any happier than they were before.

I myself say **atomic energy** has made people unhappier than they were before, and that having to live in a two-hemisphere planet has made our aborigines a lot less happy, without making the wheel-and-alphabet people who "discovered" them any fonder of being alive than they were before.

Then again, I am a monopolar depressive descended from monopolar depressives. That's how come I write so good.
(TQ 51) In chapter 2 of this wonderful book of mine, I mention a commemoration in the chapel of the University of Chicago of the fiftieth anniversary of the **atom-bombing** of Hiroshima. I said at the time that I had to respect the opinion of my friend William Styron that the **Hiroshima bomb** saved his life. Styron was then a United States Ma-

rine, training for an invasion of the Japanese home islands, when that **bomb** was dropped.

I had to add, though, that I knew a single word that proved our democratic government was capable of committing obscene, gleefully rabid and racist, yahooistic murders of unarmed men, women, and children, murders wholly devoid of military common sense. I said the word. It was a foreign word. That word was Nagasaki.
(*BAG* Thanasphere) Maybe that was the spirit of this era of the **atom bomb**, **H-bomb**, **God-knows-what-next bomb**—to be amazed at nothing. Science had given humanity forces enough to destroy the earth, and politics had given humanity a fair assurance that the forces would be used.

Vonnegut takes the opportunity to pose an atomic bomb question to the mother of all science fiction. (*GBK* Mary Wollstonecraft Shelley) I hoped to get Mary Shelley's opinions of the **atomic bombs** we dropped on the unarmed men, women, and children of Hiroshima and Nagasaki—and promise to try again. . . . I said many ignorant people nowadays thought "Frankenstein" was the name of the monster, and not of the scientist who created him.

She said, "That's not so ignorant after all. There are two monsters in my story, not one. And one of them, the scientist, is indeed named Frankenstein."

Vonnegut's rant on human self-destructiveness may end with reference to the atomic bomb, but he places it in the legacy of man's uncontrollably destructive appetite to prosecute the wrong policies. (*MWC* 2) Evolution can go to hell as far as I am concerned. What a mistake we are. We have mortally wounded this sweet life-supporting planet—the only one in the whole Milky Way—with a century of transportation whoopee. Our government is conducting a war against drugs, is it? Let them go after petroleum. Talk about a destructive high! You put some of this stuff in your car and you can go a hundred miles an hour, run over the neighbor's dog, and tear the atmosphere to smithereens. Hey, as long as we are stuck with being homo-sapiens, why mess around? Let's wreck the whole joint. Anybody got an atomic bomb? Who doesn't have an atomic bomb nowadays?

Vonnegut pleas for perspective on our atomic precipice and the place of the H-bomb in our soci-

ety's list of anxieties. (*MWC* 7) What is radically new today is that my daughter, Lily, who has just turned twenty-one, finds herself, as do your children, as does George W. Bush, himself a kid, and Saddam Hussein and on and on, heir to a shockingly recent history of human slavery, to an AIDS epidemic, and to nuclear submarines slumbering on the floors of fjords in Iceland and elsewhere, crews prepared at a moment's notice to turn industrial quantities of men, women, and children into radioactive soot and bone meal by means of rockets and **H-bomb** warheads. Our children have inherited technologies whose byproducts, whether in war or peace, are rapidly destroying the whole planet as a breathable, drinkable system for supporting life of any kind.

Vonnegut goes on to point out the irony at the heart of the bad guessers' worldview. (*MWC* 8) Persuasive guessing has been at the core of leadership for so long, for all of human experience so far, that it is wholly unsurprising that most of the leaders of this planet, in spite of all the information that is suddenly ours, want the guessing to go on. It is now their turn to guess and guess and be listened to. Some of the loudest, most proudly ignorant guessing in the world is going on in Washington today. Our leaders are sick of all the solid information that has been dumped on humanity by research and scholarship and investigative reporting. They think that the whole country is sick of it, and they could be right. It isn't the gold standard that they want to put us back on. They want something even more basic. They want to put us back on the snake-oil standard. . . .

The more **hydrogen bomb** warheads we have, all set to go off at a moment's notice, the safer humanity is and the better off the world will be that our grandchildren will inherit.
(*MWC* 8) And if you actually are an educated, thinking person, you will not be welcome in Washington, D.C. I know a couple of bright seventh graders who would not be welcome in Washington, D.C. Do you remember those doctors a few months back who got together and announced that it was a simple, clear medical fact that we could not survive even a moderate attack by **hydrogen bombs**? They were not welcome in Washington, D.C.

Even if we fired the first salvo of **hydrogen weapons** and the enemy never fired back, the poisons released would probably kill the whole planet by and by.

What is the response in Washington? They guess otherwise. What good is an education? (*MWC* 11) "We are killing this planet as a life-support system with the poisons from all the thermodynamic whoopee we're making with **atomic energy** and fossil fuels, and everybody knows it, and practically nobody cares. This is how crazy we are. I think the planet's immune system is trying to get rid of us with AIDS and new strains of flu and tuberculosis, and so on. I think the planet should get rid of us. We're really awful animals."
See also: *MN* 17; 27; *CC* 1; 4–6; 9; 12; 15; 18; 29; 33; 34; 49; 59; 104; *SL5* 1; *MH* Report on the Barnhouse Effect; *WJ* I:1; *BC* 15; *WFG* Address to the American Physical Society; *WFG* Address to P.E.N. Conference in Stockholm, 1973; *WFG Playboy* Interview; *Slap* 16; *JB* Prologue; 6; *PS* When I Lost My Innocence; *PS* Jekyll and Hyde Updated; *DD* Preface; 6; 9; 14–16; 20; 26; Epilogue; *Gal* 1:9; 1:13; 1:17; 1:26; 1:28; *Blue* 4; 27; *HP* 7; 13; 15; 28; 32; 34; 39–40; *FWD* X; XV; *BAG* Thanasphere; Runaways; *MWC* 6; 8; 9.

"Adam" (1954). *Reprinted in* Welcome to the Monkey House *(1968), this is the short story about the birth of Peter Karl Knechtmann, the only child of Heinz and Avchen Knechtmann, both survivors of the Nazi death camps. As Heinz looks into the small face of his son, he senses the child's natural resemblance to all the family members he lost in the Holocaust. "Little Peter, little Kroll," he said softly, "little Friederich—and there's Helga in you, too. Little spark of Knechtmann, you little treasure house. Everything is saved in you." The story of the Knechtmanns' personal and cultural triumph is set against Mr. Souza's wait for a son. His wife delivers their seventh daughter.*

Adams, James Carmalt (*also* **James Carmalt Adams, Jr.**). *Vonnegut's brother-in-law, married to his sister Alice. The two died within two days of each other. He was killed September 15, 1958, in a commuter train accident (Newark Bay Rail Crash), and*

she died of cancer two days later. This episode is recounted in the prologue to Slapstick, *in* Palm Sunday, *and in* Timequake. *(TQ 25)* **Jim** had plunged them deep in debt by manufacturing a toy of his own invention. It was a corked rubber balloon with a blob of permanently malleable clay inside. It was clay with a skin!

The face of a clown was printed on the balloon. You could make it open its mouth wide with your fingers, or make its nose protrude or its eyes sink in. **Jim** called it Putty Puss. Putty Puss never became popular. Moreover, Putty Puss amassed enormous debts for its manufacture and advertising.

James Carmalt Adams, Jr., is one of the three children raised by Kurt and Jane Cox Vonnegut when his sister Alice and her husband, James Carmalt Adams, died within two days of each other. James Jr. became a goat farmer. Vonnegut recounts the realization his adopted son made about the fading memory of his parents, "tapping his forehead with his fingertips, 'It isn't the museum it should be'" (Slap Prologue). His time in the Peace Corps is briefly mentioned in Timequake.

Adams, Kurt. *One of the three children raised by Kurt and Jane Cox Vonnegut when his sister Alice and her husband, James Carmalt Adams, died within two days of each other. Kurt became a pilot for Continental Airlines.*

Adams, Steve. *One of the three children raised by Kurt and Jane Cox Vonnegut after the deaths of his sister Alice and brother-in-law, James Carmalt Adams. Steve Adams and Mark Vonnegut (Kurt's son) were the same age and became "artificial twins," as did Kurt Adams and Edith Vonnegut.*

Steve Adams is also the name of the captain of the basketball team in Deadeye Dick *who stole away Sally Freeman from Felix Waltz just before the senior prom. This prompted Felix to ask Celia Hildreth to escort him.*

In Timequake, *Vonnegut uses a personal anecdote about Steve as a sardonic illustration to Kilgore Trout's claim that "I could have written a best-seller, if I'd had the patience to create three-dimensional characters. The Bible may be the Greatest Story Ever Told, but the most popular story you can ever* tell is about a good-looking couple having a really swell time copulating outside wedlock, and having to quit for one reason or another while doing it is still a novelty" . . .

When **Steve** came home to Cape Cod for Christmas vacation from his freshman year at Dartmouth, he was close to tears because he had just read, having been forced to do so by a professor, *A Farewell to Arms*, by Ernest Hemingway. **Steve**, now a middle-aged comedy writer for movies and TV, was so gorgeously wrecked back then that I was moved to reread what it was that had done this to him. *A Farewell to Arms* turned out to be an attack on the institution of marriage. Hemingway's hero is wounded in war. He and his nurse fall in love. They honeymoon far away from the battlefields, consuming the best food and wine, without having been married first. She gets pregnant, proving, as if it could be doubted, that he is indeed all man.

She and the baby die, so he doesn't have to get a regular job and a house and life insurance and all that crap, and he has such beautiful memories. I said to **Steve**, "The tears Hemingway has made you want to shed are tears of relief! It looked like the guy was going to have to get married and settle down. But then he didn't have to. Whew! What a close shave!"

Adams, Tiger. *The pilot for Fred T. Barry, he once dated Celia Hildreth in high school, though she later married Dwayne Hoover. One evening, while* "coming in for a night landing at Will Fairchild Memorial Airport . . . he had to pull up at the last second because there was somebody out on the runway" (DD 20). *The person was Celia, whom Tiger described as looking like the Wicked Witch of the West in* The Wizard of Oz.

Adler, Ted. *In* Timequake, *Vonnegut notes that at times Kilgore Trout could be startled by the beauty of his own work, as he is when recalling his lost stories now returned to him at Xanadu, and he rhetorically asks,* How that hell did I do that (TQ 20). *Vonnegut calls this a* delightful question *that reminds him of his days on Cape Cod when handyman Ted Adler ripped down the failing ell on Vonnegut's home and, after lengthy details about the labor and engineering involved to repair the structure, the two men stand*

admiring the work when Adler asks the same question Vonnegut has Trout ask so many years later.

Adult Correctional Institution at Shepherdstown. *Located on the opposite side of Route 103 from the Quality Motor Court, the correctional facility is famous for its dentistry program and its Sexual Offenders' Wing. In* Breakfast of Champions, *the latter is the source of great fear for transvestite Harry LeSabre, the Pontiac salesman terrorized by the taunts of his employer Dwayne Hoover, though Hoover didn't know Harry's secret. Shepherdstown was also the place of incarceration for Wayne Hoobler. The institution was destroyed during the neutron-bombing of Midland City in* Deadeye Dick.

Afterlife (*see also* **blue tunnel**). *Vonnegut has always made a point of emphasizing his family's deeply felt atheism.* (FWD My Reply to a Letter) I am a fourth-generation German-American religious skeptic ("Freethinker"). Like my essentially puritanical forebears, I believe that God has so far been unknowable and hence unservable, hence the highest service one can perform is to his or her community, whose needs are quite evident. I believe that virtuous behavior is trivialized by carrot-and-stick schemes, such as promises of highly improbable rewards or punishments in an improbable afterlife. *Eugene Debs Hartke, the narrator of* Hocus Pocus, *echoes Vonnegut's own upbringing and sentiments.* (HP 1) I am in fact pretty much an Atheist like my mother's father, although I kept that to myself. Why argue somebody else out of the expectation of some sort of an **Afterlife**? (HP 24) I have looked up who the Freethinkers were. They were members of a short-lived sect, mostly of German descent, who believed, as did my Grandfather Wills, that nothing but sleep awaited good and evil persons alike in the **Afterlife**.

Nevertheless, the idea of an afterlife is at the core of Slapstick, Galápagos, *and* God Bless You, Dr. Kevorkian. *In* Slapstick *Wilbur Swain has the existence of an afterlife confirmed for him when he uses "the Hooligan" to speak with Eliza, his dearly departed twin. Swain's knowledge of the afterlife doesn't make its prospect too appealing.* (Slap Epilogue) The talkers (*on the other end of the Hooligan*) identified themselves as persons in the

afterlife. They were backed by a demoralized chorus of persons who complained to each other of tedium and social slights and minor ailments, and so on. *Prompted by all the background cackling and complaining, Swain renames the afterlife "the Turkey Farm."*

Galápagos's *narrative comes from the afterlife.* (*Gal* 2:1) I (*Leon Trout*) was painlessly decapitated one day by a falling sheet of steel while working inside the hull of the *Bahía de Darwin*, at which time I refused to set foot in the blue tunnel leading into the **Afterlife**. *Trout goes on to say that from time to time his father, the famed science fiction author Kilgore Trout, would come to the mouth of the blue tunnel to prompt him inside. Leon continuously refuses, and instead writes the ensuing text with nothing more substantial than his finger scribbling in thin air.*

Vonnegut's *speculations about an afterlife are brought into clear focus in* God Bless You, Dr. Kevorkian. *Written as a fundraising series for WNYC in New York, this work envisions an everlasting heaven without a hell, where all are accepted past the Pearly Gates by St. Peter (who proves to have quite a sense of humor). The text is predicated on a series of near-death experiences induced by Dr. Kevorkian in the Huntsville, Texas, execution chamber, during which Vonnegut travels down the blue tunnel to the afterlife for a series of brief (90-second radio spot) interviews with the famous, the nearly anonymous, and one fictional character, Kilgore Trout.*

(*TQ* 21) Humanists try to behave decently and honorably without any expectation of rewards or punishments in an **afterlife**.

(*TQ* 21) I like to sleep. I published a new requiem for old music in another book, in which I said it was no bad thing to want sleep for everyone as an **afterlife**.

(*TQ* 46) Trout had an inspiration! Instead of trying to sell the concept of free will, which he himself didn't believe in, he said this: "You've been very sick! Now you're well again. You've been very sick! Now you're well again."

That mantra worked!

Trout could have been a great advertising man. The same has been said of Jesus Christ. The basis of every great advertisement is a credible promise. Jesus promised better times in an **afterlife**. Trout

was promising the same thing in the here and now. (*BAG* Introduction) Thus encouraged, this Lazarus wrote *Slaughterhouse-Five* for Sam. That made my reputation. I am a Humanist, and so am not entitled to expect an **afterlife** for myself or anyone. But at Seymour Lawrence's memorial service at New York City's Harvard Club five years ago, I said this with all my heart: "Sam is up in Heaven now."

(*GBK* Introduction) A WORD FROM WNYC'S REPORTER ON THE **AFTERLIFE**

My first near-death experience was an accident, a botched anesthesia during a triple bypass. I had listened to several people on TV talk shows who had gone down the **blue tunnel** to the Pearly Gates, and even beyond the Pearly Gates, or so they said, and then come back to life again.

(*GBK* Introduction) About belief or lack of belief in an **afterlife**: Some of you may know I am neither Christian nor Jewish nor Buddhist, nor a conventionally religious person of any sort. I am a humanist, which means, in part, that I have tried to behave decently without any expectation of rewards or punishments after I'm dead. My German-American ancestors, the earliest of whom settled in our Middle West about the time of our Civil War, called themselves "Freethinkers," which is the same sort of thing. My great grandfather Clemens Vonnegut wrote, for example, "If what Jesus said was good, what can it matter whether he was God or not?"

(*GBK* Isaac Newton) I've met Sir Isaac Newton, who died back in 1727, as often as I've met Saint Peter. They both hang out at the Heaven end of the **blue tunnel of the Afterlife**. Saint Peter is there because that's his job. Sir Isaac is there because of his insatiable curiosity about what the **blue tunnel** is, how the **blue tunnel** works.

(*GBK* Carla Faye Tucker) Your reporter from the **Afterlife** has to sign off now. Jack and I have been asked to vacate the lethal injection facility, which must be prepared for yet another total execution. Speaking for both of us, I now say, ta-ta.

(*GBK* Isaac Asimov) "Enjoyed talking to you," he said, "but I have to get back to work now—on a six-volume set about cockamamie Earthling beliefs in an **Afterlife**."

(*MWC* 8) My parents and grandparents were humanists, what used to be called Free Thinkers. So as a humanist I am honoring my ancestors, which the Bible says is a good thing to do. We humanists try to behave as decently, as fairly, and as honorably as we can without any expectation of rewards or punishments in an **afterlife**. My brother and sister didn't think there was one, my parents and grandparents didn't think there was one. It was enough that they were alive. We humanists serve as best we can the only abstraction with which we have any real familiarity, which is our community.

See also: WFG In a Manner That Must Shame God Himself; *Slap* Prologue; 5; 8; 43; Epilogue; *Gal* 1:1; 1:14–15; 1:18; 1:21; 1:27–29; 1:35; 2:3; 2:7; *FWD* XVI; *TQ* 40; *GBK* Introduction; *GBK* Birnum Birnum; *GBK* Vivian Hallinan; *GBK* Francis Keane.

Agnes and Agnes (Barbara and Martha). *These are two barflies Ed Finnerty picks up at the bar in Homestead.* (PP IX) "Paul—I'd like you to meet my cousin **Agnes** from Detroit," said Finnerty. He rested his hand on the knee of a fat and determinedly cheerful redhead sitting next to him. "And this," he said, pointing across the table at a tall, homely brunette, "is *your* cousin **Agnes**." *They order double scotches which are actually nothing more than water. They are found out when Paul casually picks up one of their shot glasses. They are awed and resentful of Ed and Paul when they find out they are engineers from across the river,* Barbara still kept her distance from Paul and looked at him distastefully. "What are you doing over here—having a good laugh at the dumb bunnies?"

Agnew, Spiro. *Vice president Spiro Agnew is one of about forty people at a White House meeting shortly after the May 4, 1970, shooting of four students at Kent State University.* (JB 3) Vice-President **Spiro T.** **Agnew** was there. He would eventually plead *nolo contendere* to charges of accepting bribes and evading income taxes.

Aïda. (GBR 2) That evening, he *(Eliot Rosewater)* and Sylvia went to the Metropolitan Opera for the opening of a new staging of *Aïda*. . . .

Everything was fine until the last scene of the opera, during which the hero and heroine were placed in an airtight chamber to suffocate. As the doomed pair filled their lungs, Eliot called out to

them, "You will last a lot longer, if you don't try to sing." Eliot stood, leaned far out of his box, told the singers, "Maybe you don't know anything about oxygen, but I do. Believe me, you must not sing." (GBR 3) Norman Mushari learned that, on the night of *Aïda*, Eliot disappeared again, jumped out of his homeward-bound cab at Forty-second Street and Fifth Avenue.

Aiken, Conrad. *Like Vonnegut, this Pulitzer Prize winner was also the child of a suicide. In fact, Aiken's father committed a murder-suicide involving the author's mother. Aiken was the literary editor of Emily Dickinson's Selected Poems.* (PS 13) And **Conrad Aiken**, the poet, the one time I met him, told me that a child will compete with its father in an area where the father is weak, in an area where the father mistakenly believes himself to be quite accomplished. Aiken himself did this, by his own account. His father was a Renaissance man, a surgeon, an athlete, something of a musician, something of a poet, and on and on. Aiken said that he himself became a poet because he realized that his father's poetry really wasn't very good.

(*Blue* 32) He *(Terry Kitchen)* said that the poet **Conrad Aiken** had lectured at Yale when Kitchen was in law school there, and had said that sons of gifted men went into fields occupied by their fathers, but where their fathers were weak. **Aiken's** own father had been a great physician and politician and ladies' man, but had also fancied himself a poet. "His poetry was no damn good, so **Aiken** became a poet," said Kitchen. "I could never do such a thing to my old man."

Ainsworth, Dr. Mary D. (see *God Bless You, Dr. Kevorkian*).

Ainus. (HP 30) To understand how the lower ranks of guards at Athena in those days felt about White people, and never mind Black people, you have to realize that most of them were recruited from Japan's northernmost island, Hokkaido. On Hokkaido the primitive natives, the **Ainus**, thought to be very ugly because they were so pallid and hairy, were White people. Genetically speaking, they are just as white as Nancy Reagan. Their ancestors long ago had made the error, when humiliated by superior Asiatic civilizations, of shambling north instead of west to Europe, and eventually, of course, to the Western Hemisphere.

(HP 31) I misread him *(Hiroshi Matsumoto)* completely, not knowing then that the Japanese considered themselves to be as genetically discrete from other Orientals as from me or Donner or Nancy Reagan or the pallid, hairy **Ainus**, say.

air raid, air-raid, air-raid shelter, air raid siren (*also* **raid** *and* **raids** *as they refer to Dresden or to war-time bombing*). *Vonnegut took shelter during the firebombing of Dresden in an underground slaughterhouse meatlocker. Not so surprisingly, a number of his characters are forced to take refuge in similar structures.* Player Piano's *Paul Proteus is taken prisoner by the Ghost Shirt Society in an old Ilium air raid shelter. Eliot Rosewater purchases an air raid siren from Berlin for the Rosewater County volunteer fire department. Billy Pilgrim and Howard Campbell take refuge in the slaughterhouse meatlocker of* Slaughterhouse-Five. *Within that seminal text, Professor Rumfoord is hard at work on condensing the* Official History of the Army Air Force in World War Two *into one volume.* (SL5 9) The thing was, though, there was almost nothing in the twenty-seven volumes about the Dresden **raid**, even though it had been such a howling success. *This represents a fictional follow-up of Vonnegut's own search for official information about the Dresden raid which was still classified as top secret years after the event.*

Vonnegut recalls that despite whatever he was writing at the time, he was always struggling with writing a book about Dresden (SL5 1). His vision of the world became fixed during this underground episode, and aside from the explicit move to an air raid shelter by Paul Proteus, Billy Pilgrim, and Howard Campbell, other leading characters who specifically take refuge or have a transforming underground experience include:

- *Malachi Constant in the caves of Mercury (ST);*
- *John/Jonah in Papa Monzano's oubliette on San Lorenzo during the ice-nine freezing of the Earth (CC);*
- *Wilbur Swain stores his various scientific and social treatises in the underground mausoleum of his grandfather (Slap);*

- *Walter Starbuck's White House office is in its third subbasement, and he is jailed for the second time in the basement cell of a New York City police precinct before tending to the mortally wounded Mary Kathleen O'Looney in the abandoned tunnels of Grand Central Station (JB);*
- *Rudy Waltz is jailed in the basement cell of Midland City's police department after unintentionally killing Eloise Metzger (DD);*
- *Leon Trout is decapitated while constructing the hull of the* Bahía de Darwin *and refuses to enter the blue tunnel into the afterlife (Gal);*
- *Rabo Karabekian's onetime masterpiece "Windsor Blue Number Seventeen" degrades in an underground storage area due to the fatally flawed Sateen Dura-Luxe, but after retrieving the sixty-four-foot triptych, he paints his photorealistic masterpiece "Now It's the Women's Turn," the scene depicting the image Vonnegut saw when released from the German POW camp (Blue);*
- *Eugene Debs Hartke earned his silver star by going down the mouth of a Viet Cong tunnel and killing three supposed combatants, only to find out they were a mother, her child, and the child's grandmother (HP).*

(MWC 1) Total catastrophes are terribly amusing, as Voltaire demonstrated. You know, the Lisbon earthquake is funny.

I saw the destruction of Dresden. I saw the city before and then came out of an **air-raid shelter** and saw it afterward, and certainly one response was laughter. God knows, that's the soul seeking some relief.

See also: PP XXX; MN 42; GBR 7; SL5 1; MH Unready to Wear; *WJ I:6; PS* The First Amendment; Self-Interview; *DD 6; FWD X; BAG* Preface.

A. J. Topf und Sohn. *Warden Hiroshi Matsumoto purchased crematoria ovens from this German firm located in Essen, which had built the crematorium at Auschwitz during World War II. The warden needed to buy the ovens when the Mafia, using the AIDS epidemic as the reason, doubled its price for disposing of convicts' bodies. When the prisoners broke out they destroyed the facility.* (HP 32) The postwar **Topf** models all had state-of-the-art smoke scrubbers on their smokestacks, so people in Scipio, unlike the people living near Auschwitz, never knew that they had a busy corpse carbonizer in the neighborhood.

We could have been gassing and incinerating convicts over there around the clock, and who would know?

Who would care?

Ajax. *In the* Iliad, *Ajax is the son of Telamon, King of the Salamis, and second in bravery to Achilles of the Greeks who besieged Troy. Kilgore Trout wonders about the juxtaposition of such a literary reference used as the logo written across a tractor-trailer.* (BC 10, 11) Trout wondered what a child who was just learning to read would make of a message like that *(the Pyramid logo written across a tractor-trailer).*

Akbahr, Abdullah. *When Hartke meets him in the warden's waiting room, Abdullah is reading* The Protocols of the Elders of Zion. *He is part of the Black Brothers of Islam, the ruling gang at the Athena prison, and is instrumental in assisting Hartke with his prison literacy program whose principal text is* The Protocols of the Elders of Zion. *Abdullah Akbahr, a Marine veteran of the Vietnam War, was imprisoned for committing three murders as part of a drug war.* (HP 33) His name was **Abdullah Akbahr**. With my *(Eugene Debs Hartke)* encouragement, he would write several interesting short stories. One, I remember, was supposedly the autobiography of a talking deer in the National Forest who has a terrible time finding anything to eat in winter and gets tangled in barbed wire during the summer months, trying to get at the delicious food on farms. He is shot by a hunter. As he dies he wonders why he was born in the first place. The final sentence of the story was the last thing the deer said on Earth. The hunter was close enough to hear it and was amazed. This was it: "What the blankety-blank was that supposed to be all about?" (HP 33) He himself would be shot dead with buckshot and slugs after the prison break, while carrying a flag of truce, by Whitey VanArsdale, the mechanic, and Lyle Hooper, the Fire Chief.

Al. *One of the Ghost Shirt Society members who participates in the destruction of some of the physical facilities in Ilium.* (PP XXXIV) "And, by God, here'sh ol' **Al** to go with us. Where you been, y'ol' horsethief?"

"Blew up the goddam sewage 'sposal plant," said Al proudly.

Albanian Flu. *Along with the Green Death, these two plagues took many lives after the Chinese experiments destabilized gravity in* Slapstick.

Alberti, Leon Battista (1402–1472). *The Florentine Renaissance writer, architect, and humanist.* (Blue 27) She was only four blocks away—in a palazzo designed for Innocenzo "the Invisible" de Medici by **Leon Battista Alberti** in the middle of the fifteenth century.

Algonquin Hotel. *(Blue* 13) I *(Rabo Karabekian)* spent an uneventful late evening watching pornographic TV programs in my room at the *Algonquin Hotel.* I watched and didn't watch at the very same time.

Algonquins. (PP I) He *(Paul Proteus)* was showing the cat an old battlefield at peace. Here *(the Ilium Works)*, in the basin of the river bend, the Mohawks had overpowered the **Algonquins**, the Dutch the Mohawks, the British the Dutch, the Americans the British.

Algren, Nelson (1909–1981). *The Chicago novelist noted for his realistic portrayals of urban poverty. (Blue* 5) While I was at it, I asked them if they recognized the names of Jackson Pollock, Mark Rothko, or Terry Kitchen, or Truman Capote, or **Nelson Algren**, or Irwin Shaw, or James Jones, all of whom had figured not only in the history of arts and letters but in the history of the Hamptons. They did not. So much for achieving immortality via the arts and letters. *Rabo asked Celeste and her friends by the swimming pool if they knew who any of these people were as a sort of cultural quiz to satisfy his own misgivings about teenagers.*

Nelson Algren and Vonnegut met in 1965 while both were teaching at the Iowa Writers' Workshop. (FWD 2) I am able to follow the three rules for a good life set down by the late writer **Nelson Algren**, a fellow depressive, and another subject of the study of writers made at the University of Iowa. The three rules are, of course: Never eat at a place called Mom's, never play cards with a man named Doc, and most important, never go to bed with anybody who has more troubles than you do. *Vonnegut refers to Algren a number of times in* Fates Worse Than Death, *including the introduction he wrote for the 1987 reprint of Algren's* Never Come Morning.

Alice in Wonderland. (PP XXIX) "Wait until he sits in on some meetings," said Finnerty. "They're like something out of **Alice in Wonderland**, Paul." *Finnerty refers to meetings of the Ghost Shirt Society.*

In The Sirens of Titan, *Vonnegut refers to the undersized side entrance door (four and a half feet high) to the Rumfoord estate as an "Alice-in-Wonderland door" (ST 1).*

The author of the classic tale is cited by Wanda June as another resident of heaven who avidly plays shuffleboard (WJ II:2).
See also: BC 22; WFG A Political Disease; Blue *17.*

"All the King's Horses" (1953). *Reprinted in* Welcome to the Monkey House, *this Cold War short story chronicles the capture of Colonel Bryan Kelly and his wife, children, and military escort after their plane crashes in an unnamed country in Asia. Pi Ying, the sadistic outpost commander forces Kelly into a chess match using his family and captured soldiers as the chess pieces. Captured pieces are to be summarily executed. Ying is killed by his mistress, and Major Barzov, Ying's Soviet adviser, releases the captives.*

All-Night Sam. *In the short story "Next Door," in* Welcome to the Monkey House *(1968), All-Night Sam is the radio disc jockey listened to by Lemuel Harger and his mistress in the apartment adjacent to Paul Leonard's. Young Paul calls All-Night Sam to dedicate a record from Mr. Harger to his wife, Rose. Sam obliges by playing Eartha Kitt's "Somebody Bad Stole De Wedding Bell!" This drives a wedge between Harger and his mistress and brings back Rose.*

Allen, Lester (*see also* **Ginsberg**). *The former newspaperman Vonnegut knows from Cape Cod who was one of the many writing books about the murderer Tony Costa and recounted in "There's a* Maniac Loose Out There" *in* Wampeters, Foma & Granfalloons.

alter ego (*see* **Trout, Kilgore**).

"Ambitious Sophomore" (*see also* **Helmholtz, George M.**). *The short story first appeared May 1, 1954, in* The Saturday Evening Post *and was later reprinted in the 1999 collection* Bagombo Snuff Box. *Lincoln High School band director George M. Helmholtz sets his sights and personal finances, which are razor thin, on a third consecutive state title in the parade of bands. He so covets winning the thirty-pound bronze and walnut trophy to be awarded by the Chamber of Commerce that his pride and hopes for his band are balanced only by his tireless and infectiously dramatic fundraising appeals. As we learn at the end of the story, his love of music and marching band competition was to the exclusion of his ever having experienced a personal love in his life.*

The ambitious sophomore is Leroy Duggan, an unfortunately bell-shaped and highly self-conscious piccoloist. Helmholtz ordered a special uniform, in addition to the hundred new ones he originally ordered for the band, to hide Leroy's girth and help build his confidence. As it is, Leroy is prone to screwing up when marching in performance because he is self-conscious about his appearance, especially in front of girls. Helmholtz orders a uniform that has such broad shoulder pads that it still makes a V when it reaches his large waist.

Leroy enjoys a new confidence in his sartorial splendor to such an extent that he mingles with a nearby band waiting to perform, eventually cozying up to a female piccolo player. Her drum major is incensed at both Helmholtz's arrogance and Leroy's fraternization. The drum major begins taunting and then fighting with Duggan in an attempt to strip him of his band tunic and expose him as just a fat slob, thereby embarrassing him in front of his own band. It doesn't work. Leroy becomes a fighting machine, and only Helmholtz's intervention prevents Leroy from clubbing the drum major to death with his own baton. Unfortunately, the altercation ruins Leroy's uniform, so Helmholtz gives his car keys to another student to retrieve Leroy's original uniform from his trunk.

Helmholtz is crushed. He firmly believes the ill-fitting uniform will revert his star musician to his bumbling old self and assure losing. Quite the contrary. Leroy, having spoken with a girl and tearing apart the leader of a rival band, plays better than ever. Helmholtz almost cried as American flags hung in air from parachutes. Among them, like a cloudburst of diamonds, was the Sousa piccolo masterpiece. Leroy! Leroy!

With the third consecutive state championship secured, Helmholtz returns to his car to find he has a flat tire and no spare. He previously approached English department chair Harold Crane to sell for $20 his prized gold frame holding a photo of his great icon, John Philip Sousa, but they eventually struck a deal for the spare tire. (He needed the money to cover the unfunded cost of Leroy's extra uniform.)

Undeterred by being stranded, Helmholtz heads for a streetcar. His entire life is bound up in his love of music and music as competition. He is left with thoughts about Leroy's rapid evolution and remains satisfied by his own celibate life, buoyed by nothing more than the soaring spirit of music. Helmholtz thought about love as he walked back to his car alone, his arms aching with the weight of the great trophy. If love was blinding, obsessing, demanding, beyond reason, and all the other wild things people said it was, then he had never known it, Helmholtz told himself. He sighed, and supposed he was missing something, not knowing romance.

When he got to his car, he found that the left front tire was flat. He remembered that he had no spare. But he felt nothing more than mild inconvenience. He boarded a streetcar, sat down with the trophy on his lap, and smiled. He was hearing music again.

American Academy of Arts and Letters. At the time Vonnegut was elected to this prestigious organization in 1973 by its membership of 250 literary and fine artists, its full name was the American Academy and Institute of Arts and Letters. He expresses some ambivalence about the organization as he characterizes it, *It is a random matter who gets in and who doesn't, since it is loonies who do the nominating and then the voting, which is to say the artists and writers and musicians who already be-*

long. They are no good at what is primarily office work, are notoriously absentminded, are commonly either ignorant or envious of good work others may be doing, and so on. There is also a lot of logrolling, with writers saying to painters and musicians in effect, "I'll vote for somebody I never heard of in your field, if you'll vote for somebody you never heard of in mine." And so on.

Sometimes I think the American Academy and Institute of Arts and Letters shouldn't exist, since it has the power not only to honor but to insult. Look what it did to James Jones and Irwin Shaw. They couldn't help feeling like something the cat drug in whenever the Academy and Institute was mentioned. There are surely more than one hundred living American creative people of the highest excellence who feel that way this very day.

The great Hoosier humorist Kin Hubbard (never considered for membership) said that it was no disgrace to be poor, but that it might as well be. It is also no disgrace to be excluded by the Academy and Institute. But it might as well be (FWD 5).

The Academy becomes a focal point of activity in Timequake, *located next to the Manhattan homeless shelter housing Kilgore Trout. The municipal garbage can in front of the two buildings is where Trout throws out four manuscripts written during the period covered by the timequake, and where Academy security guard Dudley Prince rescues the same manuscripts.*

Amphibious Pioneers Society (*also* **Amphibians**). *An organization of the first five thousand followers of the teachings of Dr. Ellis Konigswasser in the 1953 short story "Unready to Wear," reprinted in* Welcome to the Monkey House (1968). *The amphibians have learned how to isolate their psyches and leave the physical confines of their bodies.*

Amy and Harry (*see also* **Laird, Eddie**). *In the short story "Bagombo Snuff Box," reprinted in the 1999 collection of that name, Amy is the ex-wife of inveterate liar Eddie Laird and is currently married to Harry. Eleven years earlier, for just six months during World War II, Eddie and Amy were married while he was stationed at nearby Cunningham Field. Eddie is now a potato chip salesman from Levittown, Long Island, making his first visit to the area since* his service there. Eddie calls Amy and insists on a quick visit to her home that very evening. When Eddie tells Amy on the phone about his fictional adventuresome life, she sympathetically says that they each got what they wanted in life and refers to the two of them as the eagle and the homing pigeon.

Upon Eddie's arrival, **Harry**, **Amy's** husband, a blocky man with a kind face, invited Larry in. Eddie tries to pass himself off as a world traveler, and in the process he makes Harry, a department store credit manager, feel small and sheltered, living a life of domestic entrapment with the cries of children resounding through the house along with the edgy, snappy spousal shouts from distant rooms, the call and response of worn-out lovers. The couple feel the sting and embarrassment of their own performance in front of the worldly ex-husband. When Eddie finishes recounting his false globetrotting destinations like so many bus stops, he pauses to ask his harried ex how her life has been. "And how are you, **Amy**?"

"Me?" said **Amy**. "How is any wife? Harassed."

Amy and Harry's feelings of weariness quickly disappear once Eddie trips on his own lies about the location of Ceylon. Stevie, Amy's nine-year-old son, whose eyes, frank, irreverent, and unromantic, scared him, had mistakenly thought Ceylon was off the coast of Africa, and Eddie had agreed with him. Amy knew it was off the coast of India, and this was the second lie they caught Eddie fabricating. The first was due to his own stupidity when he failed to remove the "Made in Japan" label from the Bagombo snuff box, supposed to be from Ceylon, that he brought as a gift. Stevie is Eddie's undoing on that one as well, since he turned over the box and found the label.

The family hurls sarcastic insults at Eddie as he flees in his waiting taxi. He returns to his hotel, where he calls his current wife, Selma, at home in Levittown taking care of his own four children.

"An American Family Marooned on the Planet Pluto." Vonnegut references only one line from this Kilgore Trout short story by way of meditating on his mother's great disappointment and despondency with the material misfortunes of her life. (TQ 8) My mother was addicted to being rich, to servants and unlimited charge accounts, to giving lavish dinner parties, to taking frequent first-class trips to Europe.

So one might say she was tormented by withdrawal symptoms all through the Great Depression.

She was acculturated!

Acculturated persons are those who find that they are no longer treated as the sort of people they thought they were, because the outside world has changed. An economic misfortune or a new technology, or being conquered by another country or political faction, can do that to people quicker than you can say "Jack Robinson."

As Trout wrote in his "**An American Family Marooned on the Planet Pluto**": "Nothing wrecks any kind of love more effectively than the discovery that your previously acceptable behavior has become ridiculous." He said in conversation at the 2001 clambake: "If I hadn't learned how to live without a culture and a society, acculturation would have broken my heart a thousand times."

Anderson Trailer. Among the first investments of Noel Constant, the father of Malachi, Anderson Trailer helped him complete financial transactions that demanded he invest according to stock symbols that spell out the text of the Bible. (ST 3) His very first investment was International Nitrate. After that came Trowbridge Helicopter, Electra Bakeries, Eternity Granite, Indiana Novelty, Norwich Iron, National Gelatin, Granada Oil, Del-Mar Creations, Richmond Electroplating, **Anderson Trailer**, and Eagle Duplicating.

Angela and Arthur. The sister and brother-in-law of Maude and Earl Fenton in the 1952 short story "The Package." Maude suggests to Earl that he use the false excuse of the imminent arrival of Angela, Arthur and their children for an extended stay as a way of getting out of hosting fraternity brother Dr. Charles Freeman. The ruse works. It is only after Freeman takes a taxi to a hotel that the Fentons learn they dealt badly with a true humanitarian. For more than thirty years, Freeman spent his inherited family fortune on building a hospital to service the poor in China. The Communist government eventually takes control of the hospital and jails Freeman. By the time he visits the Fentons, his appearance in a worn suit and old shoes is viewed negatively by Maude, a warning sign he may be there for a handout.

Annie. *In the short story "The Cruise of the* Jolly Roger" *(reprinted in BAG) Annie is the legal secretary who remembers small bits about the Pefkos and Major Nathan Durant's lost war buddy George. Annie fills in what she remembers when prompted by the postmistress in answering Durant's query about Pefko and the family. Annie then serves as guide, taking Durant to the square named (with a plaque) in honor of onetime resident George Pefko. While at the square, Annie prompts one of the schoolboys to explain the meaning of the day, since Durant seems rather unimpressed with what at first appears to be rote ritual. However, once young Tom speaks his heart out in reverence for the fallen, Durant comes alive to the point that he asks Annie to join him for lunch and a ride on his boat.*

Anschluss. *(JB Epilogue) In accordance with my wife's will (Ruth, Walter Starbuck's wife), incidentally, Juan and his brother, Geraldo, were receiving reparations from West Germany for the confiscation of my wife's father's bookstore in Vienna by the Nazis after the* Anschluss, *Germany's annexation of Austria in Nineteen-hundred and Thirty-eight. Juan and Geraldo are the grandsons of Walter and Ruth Starbuck.*

anthropoids. (CC 28) "Hello, fellow **anthropoids** and lily pads and paddlewheels," he (*Lyman Enders Knowles*) said to Miss Faust and me. "Yes, yes!" (*Blue* 24) The clitoris, so goes the speculation in the paper (*The New York Times*), is the last vestige of the inseminating organ of a conquered, enslaved, trivialized and finally emasculated race of weaker, but not necessarily dumber, anthro-poids!

Cancel my subscription!

anthropological, anthropologist, anthropology. *Vonnegut studied for a master's degree in anthropology at the University of Chicago and supported himself during that time by working as a police reporter for the Chicago City News Bureau. Through his thesis, he sought to graph simple tales of good and evil, but it was rejected. After publishing* Cat's Cradle, *however, the university awarded him the degree. There are two anthropology instructors in his novels: Robert Pefko returns from Korea and becomes an anthropology instructor at West Point*

(BC); *Arthur von Strelitz is Walter Starbuck's Harvard anthropology professor, and he permits his young student to use his apartment for a lovers' tryst with Mary Kathleen O'Looney.*

More importantly, the Vonnegut freethinker legacy dovetails with his understanding of anthropology and is everywhere apparent. (WFG Playboy Interview) All my books are my effort to answer that question and to make myself like life better than I do. I'm trying to throw out all the trashy merchandise adults put in my head when I was a little kid. I want to put a culture up there. People will believe anything, which means I will believe anything. I learned that in **anthropology**. I want to start believing in things that have shapeliness and harmony. (PS 5) INTERVIEWER: Did the study of **anthropology** later color your writings? VONNEGUT: It confirmed my atheism, which was the faith of my fathers anyway. Religions were exhibited and studied as the Rube Goldberg inventions I'd always thought they were. We weren't allowed to find one culture superior to any other. We caught hell if we mentioned races much. It was highly idealistic.

Vonnegut frequently mentions his mentor at the University of Chicago who strongly influenced the core of his novels, especially as they concern folk societies and extended families. (PS 5) VONNEGUT: And when I went to the University of Chicago, and I heard the head of the Department of **anthropology**, Robert Redfield, lecture on the folk society, which was essentially a stable, isolated extended family, he did not have to tell me how nice that could be. (FWD 13) When I studied **anthropology** long ago at the University of Chicago, my most famous professor was Dr. Robert Redfield . . . He said that he could describe to every fair-minded person's satisfaction one (and only one) stage every society had passed through or would pass through. He called this inevitable stage and his essay on it "The Folk Society." (FWD 2) "I hold a master's degree in **anthropology** from the University of Chicago. Students of that branch of poetry are taught to seek explanations for human comfort or discomfort — wars, wounds, spectacular diseases, and natural disasters aside — in culture, society, and history. And I have just named the villains in my books, which are never individuals. The villains again: culture, society, and history—none of them strikingly housebroken by lithium, Thorazine, Prozac, or Tofranil.

(*TQ* 32) I say in speeches in 1996, halfway through the rerun to 2001, that I became a student in the **Anthropology Department** of the University of Chicago after World War Two. I say jokingly that I never should have studied that subject, because I can't stand primitive people. They're so stupid! The real reason my interest in the study of man as an animal flagged was that my wife Jane Marie Cox Vonnegut, who would die as Jane Marie Cox Yarmolinsky, gave birth to a baby named Mark. We needed bucks.

(*TQ* 56) I know the Hindus' stock of stationery as well as they do. I didn't study **anthropology** for nothing. I find one nine-by-twelve manila envelope without assistance, remembering simultaneously a joke about the Chicago Cubs baseball team. The Cubs were supposedly moving to the Philippine Islands, where they would be renamed the Manila Folders. That would have been a good joke about the Boston Red Sox, too.

(*TQ* Epilogue) At Bernie's suggestion, GE hired me away from the Chicago City News Bureau, where I had been a beat reporter. I had worked simultaneously for a master's degree in **anthropology** at the University of Chicago.

(*BAG* Introduction) I married my childhood sweetheart Jane Marie Cox, also from Indianapolis, up in Heaven now, and enrolled as a graduate student in the **Anthropology Department** of the University of Chicago. But I didn't want to be an **anthropologist**, either.

I only hoped to find out more about human beings. I was going to be a journalist!

(*BAG* Introduction) And then the **Department of Anthropology** rejected my M.A. thesis, which proved that similarities between the Cubist painters in Paris in 1907 and the leaders of Native American, or Injun, uprisings late in the nineteenth century could not be ignored. The Department said it was unprofessional.

(*MWC* 3) Now, I don't mean to intimidate you, but after being a chemist as an undergraduate at Cornell, after the war I went to the University of Chicago and studied **anthropology**, and eventually I took a masters degree in that field. Saul Bellow was in that same department, and neither one of us ever made a

field trip. Although we certainly imagined some. I started going to the library in search of reports about ethnographers, preachers, and explorers—those imperialists—to find out what sorts of stories they'd collected from primitive people. It was a big mistake for me to take a degree in **anthropology** anyway, because I can't stand primitive people—they're so stupid. But anyway, I read these stories, one after another, collected from primitive people all over the world, and they were dead level, like the B-E axis here. So all right. Primitive people deserve to lose with their lousy stories. They really are backward. Look at the wonderful rise and fall of our stories.

(*MWC* 11) But seriously, if you keep up with current events in the supermarket tabloids, you know that a team of Martian **anthropologists** has been studying our culture for the past ten years, since our culture is the only one worth a nickel on the whole planet. You can sure forget Brazil and Argentina.

See also: PP III; *SL5* 1; *BC* 15; *WFG* There's a Maniac Loose Out There; *WFG* Address to the National Institute of Arts and Letters, 1971; *WFG Playboy* Interview; *Slap* 25; *JB* 17; *PS* The First Amendment; *Gal* 1:28; *FWD* II; V; VII; IX; XIII; XV; XIX.

anthropomorphic. (*PP* XII) "Garth's a fine man," said Paul. Garth was, too: four-square, desperate to please, and he seemed to have an **anthropomorphic** image of the corporate personality. Garth stood in relation to that image as a lover, and Paul wondered if this prevalent type of relationship had ever been given the consideration it deserved by sexologists. On second thought, he supposed that it had—the general phenomenon of a lover's devotion to the unseen—in studies of nuns' symbolic marriages to Christ. At any rate, Paul had seen Garth at various stages of his love affair, unable to eat for anxiety, on a manic crest, moved to maudlin near-crying at recollections of the affair's tender beginnings. In short, Garth suffered all the emotional hazards of a perennial game of she-loves-me, she-loves-me-not. To carry out directions from above—an irritating business for Paul—was, for Garth, a favor to please a lady. "I'd like to see him get the job."

(*Gal* 1:19) Mary used to shut up then. There would be no more **anthropomorphic** jokes.

anti-gerasone. *In the 1953 short story "Tomorrow and Tomorrow and Tomorrow," reprinted in* Welcome to the Monkey House *(1968), anti-gerasone is the anti-aging potion which allows people to seemingly live forever. Because it prevents death by natural causes, it gives rise to a severe housing shortage.*

"Any Reasonable Offer." *This short story first appeared in* Collier's *magazine (January 1952) and was later collected in* Bagombo Snuff Box *(1999). The unnamed narrator, a real estate agent vacationing in Newport, Rhode Island, tells of the middle-class woes of his industry, the clients who cut deals behind his back, and the need for more vacation time on his own. After telling about how Dennis Delahanty cheated him out of a commission, he tells the story first of Mrs. Hellbrunner and then of Mr. Hurty. The latter two are linked through the real estate agent to Colonel Bradley Peckham and his wife, Pam.*

The Peckhams are frauds. The narrator unknowingly introduces the Peckhams to the Hellbrunner and Hurty estates as potential buyers. Peckham masquerades as a troubleshooting military man temporarily on leave and working at National Steel Foundry to straighten out some things. The Peckhams like to look over estates for sale, present themselves as potential buyers, and charm their way with the owners so that they can get the feel of the place over the course of a few days. They like to get the newness out.

The narrator eventually discovers the truth about the Peckhams while telephoning National Steel to speak with the colonel, that Peckham works in the foundry's drafting department (straightening out lines) and merely vacations at these estates while posing as the colonel.

The narrator appears to have learned well from the example of the Peckhams. He is narrating this story from the Van Tuyl estate in Newport, perpetrating the same fraud as the Peckhams.

apocalyptic. (ST 10) The church, which squatted among the headstones like a wet mother dodo, had been at various times Presbyterian, Congregationalist, Unitarian, and **Universal Apocalyptic**. It was now the Church of God the Utterly Indifferent. (MN Introduction) More bombs were dropped to keep firemen in their holes, and all the little fires grew, joined one another, became one **apocalyptic** flame.

(*Gal* 1:23) And this **apocalyptic** warning so suited the wiring of the Captain's brain, even before his father came down with Huntington's chorea, that he would ever after believe that that was indeed the most likely way in which humanity would be exterminated: by meteorites. *Captain Adolf von Kleist had learned of the destructive power of meteors while a student at the United States Naval Academy.*

(TQ 38) More news of this day in August, halfway through the rerun, as yet another autumn draws near: My big brother Bernie, the born scientist who may know more about the electrification of thunderstorms than anyone, has an invariably fatal cancer, too far advanced to be daunted by the **Three Horsemen of the Oncologic Apocalypse**, Surgery, Chemotherapy, and Radiation.

Arapahos. *In* Hocus Pocus *Vonnegut uses the Arapahos as a metaphor for the inferior state of the white man in America when compared with the new elite, the dominant culture of the Japanese. Even the prison guards from Hokkaido, the white Ainus—considered the lowest strata among Japanese culture—look down upon the whites.* (HP 30) Those White people on Hokkaido had sure missed a lot. They were way behind practically everybody. And when the man who wanted to teach shop and I presented ourselves at the gate to the road that led through the National Forest to the prison, the 2 guards on duty there were fresh from Hokkaido. For all the respect our being Whites inspired in them, we might as well have been a couple of drunk and disorderly **Arapahos**.

(MWC 3) I don't think Shakespeare believed in a heaven or hell any more than I do. And so we don't know whether it's good news or bad news.

I have just demonstrated to you that Shakespeare was as poor a storyteller as any **Arapaho**.

But there's a reason we recognize Hamlet as a masterpiece: it's that Shakespeare told us the truth, and people so rarely tell us the truth in this rise and fall here [indicates blackboard]. The truth is, we know so little about life, we don't really know what the good news is and what the bad news is.

And if I die—God forbid—I would like to go to

heaven to ask somebody in charge up there, "Hey, what was the good news and what was the bad news?"

Archangel Gabriel (*also* **Gabriel horns**). *Acting as a messenger of God, one of the seven archangels, Gabriel is the angel of the Annunciation and the herald of good news and comfort.* (ST 3) The Wilburhampton Hotel was a frumpish, three-story Tudor structure across the street from the Magnum Opus Building, standing in relation to that building like an unmade bed at the feet of the **Archangel Gabriel**. Pine slats were tacked to the stucco exterior of the hotel, simulating half-timbered construction. The backbone of the roof had been broken intentionally, simulating great age. The eaves were plump and low, tucked under, simulated thatch. The windows were tiny, with diamond-shaped panes. *The Wilburhampton Hotel is where Noel Constant dreams up his "divinely inspired" investment strategy. By contrast, Winston Niles Rumfoord's estate has horns which blare for the coming of the Space Wanderer, considered a messiah by the Church of God the Utterly Indifferent. Rumfoord, acting like a God, speaks to the crowd through his estate's horns.*
(ST 10) *"Bring the Space Wanderer here!"* blatted Rumfoord's voice from the **Gabriel horns** on the walls.
(ST 10) "Welcome, Space Wanderer," blatted Rumfoord's oleomargarine tenor from the **Gabriel horns** on the wall. "How meet it is that you should come to us on the bright red pumper of a volunteer fire department. I can think of no more stirring symbol of man's humanity to man than a fire engine. . . ."
(ST 10) His voice (Rumfoord's) came not from the tree but from the **Gabriel horns** on the walls.
Eliot Rosewater, another messiah figure, tailors himself in seemingly celestial attire. (GBR 2) But he (*Eliot*) was off again in a month, carousing with firemen in Clover Lick, West Virginia, one night, and in New Egypt, New Jersey, the next. And on that trip he traded clothes with another man, swapped a four-hundred-dollar suit for a 1939 double-breasted blue chalkstripe, with shoulders like Gibraltar, lapels like the wings of the **Archangel Gabriel**, and with the creases in the trousers permanently sewed in.
(TQ 36) I consider the example set by my father's

only brother, Uncle Alex, the childless, Harvard-educated Indianapolis insurance salesman. He had me reading high-level socialist writers like Shaw and Norman Thomas and Eugene Debs and John Dos Passos when I was a teenager, along with making model airplanes and jerking off. After World War Two, Uncle Alex became as politically conservative as the **Archangel Gabriel**.

Archimedes' screw. *An ancient apparatus for moving water from one level body to another at a different level, consisting of either a spiral tube around an inclined axis, or an inclined tube containing a tightfitting, broad-threaded screw.*
Senator Rosewater mentions this ancient device to continue lecturing Eliot about the metaphorical Money River. (GBR 7) "The Money River, where the wealth of the nation flows. We were born on the banks of it—and so were most of the mediocre people we grew up with, went to private schools with, sailed and played tennis with. We can slurp from that mighty river to our hearts' content. And we even take slurping lessons, so we can slurp more efficiently. . . . From lawyers! From tax consultants! From customers' men! We're born close enough to the river to drown ourselves and the next ten generations in wealth, simply using dippers and buckets. But we still hire the experts to teach us the use of aqueducts, dams, reservoirs, siphons, bucket brigades, and the **Archimedes' screw**. And our teachers in turn become rich, and their children become buyers of lessons in slurping."

Aristotle. (ST 3) (*Ransom K.*) Fern read two books a day. It has been said that **Aristotle** was the last man to be familiar with the whole of his own culture. Ransom K. Fern had made an impressive attempt to equal **Aristotle's** achievement. He had been somewhat less successful than **Aristotle** in perceiving patterns in what he knew.
(MN 9) I (*Howard Campbell*) have at hand a clipping from the New York *Herald Tribune* of March third, about two weeks ago, in which a critic says of Kraft as a painter: Here at last is a capable and grateful heir to the fantastic inventiveness and experimentation in painting during the past hundred years. **Aristotle** is said to have been the last man to understand the whole of his culture. George Kraft

is surely the first man to understand the whole of modern art—to understand it in his sinews and bones.

(*GBR* 7) "You want me to start buying paintings for museums again? Would you be prouder of me, if I'd contributed two and a half million dollars to buy Rembrandt's *Aristotle Contemplating a Bust of Homer?*"

"Don't reduce the argument to an absurdity." *This is a piece of conversation between Eliot and his father concerning the manner in which Eliot expresses his philanthropy.*

(*FWD* 11) They said, as most of them do today, that the country was falling apart because the young people were no longer required to read Plato and **Aristotle** and Marcus Aurelius and St. Augustine and Montaigne and the like, whose collective wisdom was the foundation of any decent and just and productive society.

(*MWC* 8) Human beings have had to guess about almost everything for the past million years or so. The leading characters in our history books have been our most enthralling, and sometimes our most terrifying, guessers.

May I name two of them?

Aristotle and Hitler.

One good guesser and one bad one.

And the masses of humanity through the ages, feeling inadequately educated just like we do now, and rightly so, have had little choice but to believe this guesser or that one.

Arnold, General Benedict. (*Blue* 24) He (*Paul Slazinger*), incidentally, was from a very old American family. The first Slazinger on this continent was a Hessian grenadier serving as a mercenary with General John Burgoyne, the British general who was defeated by forces commanded in part by the rebel **General Benedict Arnold**, who would later desert to the British, at the second Battle of Freeman's Farm, north of Albany, two hundred years ago. Slazinger's ancestor was taken prisoner during the battle, and never went home, which was in Wiesbaden, Germany, where he had been the son of—guess what?

A cobbler.

In defense of his teaching and the scurrilous stories attributed to him at the meeting of the Board of Trustees, Eugene Debs Hartke invokes the image of the notorious traitor. (*HP* 15) "Mr. Moellenkamp, sir—" I said, "you know darn well, and so does everybody else here, that you can follow the most patriotic, deeply religious American who ever lived with a tape recorder for a year, and then prove that he's a worse traitor than **Benedict Arnold**, and a worshipper of the Devil. Who doesn't say things in a moment of passion or absentmindedness that he doesn't wish he could take back? So I ask again, am I the only one this was done to, and if so, why?"

Arthur, Chester Alan. (*Slap* 21) I (*Wilbur Swain*) was then not only a stupid Bobby Brown, but a conceited one. Though only a first-year medical student with the genitalia of an infant field mouse, I was the master of a great house on Beacon Hill. I was driven to and from school in a Jaguar—and I had already taken to dressing as I would dress when President of the United States, like a medical mountebank during the era of **Chester Alan Arthur**, say.

Ashland, Captain Bryant. *Cited as the "second man in space" by Mikhail Ivankov, father of Soviet Major Stepan Ivankov, in the 1958 short story "The Manned Missiles" (reprinted in the 1968 collection* Welcome to the Monkey House). *Both military astronauts meet their deaths in space. Ashland is sent into orbit to observe and photograph the Soviet capsule. The two spaceships get too close and crash, stranding both astronauts in space for eternity.*

Ashland, Charlene. *The twin sister of Colonel Bryant (Bud) Ashland, who dies in space in the 1958 short story "The Manned Missiles," reprinted in* Welcome to the Monkey House (1968). *She works for the telephone company in Jacksonville, Florida. Charlene asks that when her father writes to Mr. Ivankov, he tell him the story that shows Bud's humanity, conveying the humor all families enjoy repeating when they gather.* When Bud and **Charlene** were about eight, why I came home one night with a fish bowl and two goldfish. There was one goldfish for each twin, only it was impossible to tell one fish from the other one. They were exactly alike. So one morning Bud got up early, and there was one goldfish floating on top of the water dead. So Bud went and woke up **Charlene**, and he said, "Hey,

Charlene—your goldfish just died." That's the story **Charlene** asked me to tell you, Mr. Ivankov.

Ashland, Charles. *The father of Captain Bryant Ashland, one of the title characters in the 1958 short story "The Manned Missiles," reprinted in* Welcome to the Monkey House *(1968). Described as a "petroleum merchant in Titusville, Florida," he and Mikhail Ivankov, the father of Soviet Major Stepan Ivankov, exchange letters of regret and commiseration about their sons' fates, expressing hope that their sons' eternal orbits will bind mankind together and halt the arms/space race.* "May Major Stepan Ivankov and Captain Bryant Ashland serve to reproach us, whenever we look at the sky, for making a world in which there is no trust. May the two men be the beginning of trust between peoples. May they mark the end of the time when science sent our good, brave young men hurtling to meet in death."

Asimov, Dr. Isaac. (WFG Address to the American Physical Society) Good science-fiction writers of the present are not necessarily as eager as Arthur C. Clarke to found kindergartens on Jupiter, to leave the poor Maine ape and his clam rake far behind. **Isaac Asimov**, who is a great man, perceives three stages so far in the development of American science fiction, says we are in stage three now:

1. Adventure dominant
2. Technology dominant
3. Sociology dominant

I can hope that this is a prophetic outline of Earthling history, too. I interpret "sociology" broadly—as a respectful, objective concern for the cradle natures of Earthlings on Earth.

In Timequake, *Vonnegut recalls his eulogy for Asimov and manages to relate it to a Trout story mentioned in the novel.* (TQ 21) I spoke at a Humanist Association memorial service for **Dr. Asimov** a few years back. I said, "**Isaac** is up in Heaven now." That was the funniest thing I could have said to an audience of Humanists. I rolled them in the aisles. The room was like the court-martial scene in Trout's "No Laughing Matter," right before the floor of the Pacific Ocean swallowed up the third atomic bomb and *Joy's Pride* and all the rest of it.

When I myself am dead, God forbid, I hope some wag will say about me, "He's up in Heaven now."

Vonnegut refers to his eulogy in the introduction to God Bless You, Dr. Kevorkian *and uses Asimov as one of his interview subjects in the Blue Tunnel of the Afterlife. They briefly discuss the hell that is writing and the hell that is a writer's life without writing.* (GBK Isaac Asimov) When on Earth, **Isaac**, my predecessor as honorary president of the American Humanist Association, was the most prolific American writer of books who ever lived. He wrote nearly five hundred of the things—to my measly twenty so far, or to Honoré de Balzac's eighty-five. Sometimes Isaac wrote ten published volumes in a single year! These weren't only prize-winning science-fiction. Many were scholarly popularizations of Shakespeare and biochemistry and ancient Greek history, and the Bible and relativity, and on and on.

Isaac has a Ph.D. in chemistry from Columbia, and was born in Smolensk, in the former Soviet Union, but was raised in Brooklyn. He hated flying, and never read Hemingway or Fitzgerald or Joyce or Kafka, according to his obituary in the *New York Times.* "I am a stranger," he once wrote, "to twentieth-century fiction and poetry."
See also: GBK Introduction; GBK My Career in Post-Mortem Journalism.

"Asleep at the Switch" (*see also* **Albert Einstein, Dr. Robert Fender,** *and* **Kilgore Trout**). *In* Jailbird, *Dr. Robert Fender uses the pen name "Kilgore Trout" when publishing this short story that focuses on each person's short-sightedness as they are subject to a character audit at the reception center outside Heaven's Pearly Gates. Accountants and other business types review the records of the newly deceased who come before them, auditing how well they handled business opportunities God had afforded them while alive. They badger Albert Einstein into admitting he had been "asleep at the switch" to the opportunities presented him. Only then is he allowed to enter the Pearly Gates.*

Astor, Madelaine. *A member of the Tarkington College Board of Trustees and former graduate of the* *school, she turns out to be as dim-witted as Kimberley Wilder (another Tarkington student and daughter of Jason Wilder who acted as a spy to gather evidence against Eugene Debs Hartke).* (HP 15) But that was the only time they *(the board members)* defended me, although 1 of them had been my student, **Madelaine Astor**, née Peabody, and 5 of them were parents of those I had taught. **Madelaine** dictated a letter to me afterward, explaining that Jason Wilder had promised to denounce the college in his column and on his TV show if the Trustees did not fire me.

Atkins, Carol *(see also* **Ned Ludd***). Vonnegut's typist, mentioned in* A Man Without a Country, *illustrates the loss of personal relationships and one's place in society by a business community constantly trying to displace workers through technological advancement and the appearance of "big box" stores. He sees Carol's sweet disposition and good works as meaningless in a world striving to make people obsolete. For him, she is a modern day Ned Ludd, another loss in life's Darwinian contest between man and machine.*

Vonnegut illustrates the viciousness of such progress by first providing a sympathetic glimpse at the kind of over-the-fence banter of people who hold a genuine interest in the welfare of friends—even within an employer-employee relationship. (MWC 6) In the old days, not long ago, I used to type. And, after I had about twenty pages, I would mark them up with a pencil, making corrections. Then I would call **Carol Atkins**, who was a typist. Can you imagine? She lived out in Woodstock, New York, which you know was where the famous sex and drugs event in the '60s got its name from (it actually took place in the nearby town of Bethel and anybody who says they remember being there wasn't there). So, I would call up **Carol** and say, "Hey **Carol**. How are you doing? How is your back? Got any bluebirds?" We would chit-chat back and forth—I love to talk to people.

After a series of sincere pleasantries about family and life in general, Vonnegut gets around to asking the unassuming question about her availability to retype his pages. He praises the quality of her work and goes on to cite for the reader the circle of labor and personal relationships involved in just his work

as a writer, a one-man show who depends on goods and services found only outside his study. He goes to a stationery store for just the one envelope he needs, making small talk with the Hindu woman behind the counter and others waiting in line. From there he waits on line at the post office where he is well known and enjoys more pleasant though shallow relationships with the clerks and some of the regular patrons. Wherever Vonnegut goes on his solitary mission to effect the mailing of one set of pages, he looks forward to interacting with his neighbors as well as the regular workers he meets along the way. It is a social affair, a bonding affair, one that increases his knowledge and awareness of those in his neighborhood.

Vonnegut recognizes the contrast between his very conscious and willful employment of people for their unique positions in the chain of commerce as opposed to regular business practices that seek greater production by fewer workers. This leads him to surmise Carol Atkins's vulnerability in the computer age. (MWC 6) And so, she is a Ned Ludd now. Her typing is worthless. *He sees his neighborhood rounds as antithetical to the trends of our increasingly technologized society.*

(MWC 6) And I go home. And I have had one hell of a good time.

Electronic communities build nothing. You wind up with nothing. We are dancing animals. How beautiful it is to get up and go out and do something. We are here on Earth to fart around. Don't let anybody tell you any different.

Atkins, Fire Chief Stanley. *In the 1952 short story "Poor Little Rich Town," collected in* Bagombo Snuff Box *(1999), Atkins is chief of the Spruce Falls Volunteer Fire Department and one of its leading voices for rolling out the red carpet for Newell Cady, the efficiency expert and new vice president of the Federal Apparatus Corporation who is renting (with an option to buy) one of the old mansions in the village. Atkins hopes the town will become the center for the corporation's high level executives and that they will buy up the rundown mansions and inject the town with some much needed income. At Atkins's urging, the fire department holds a special meeting to vote in Cady as a full member of the department and head judge of the town's annual Hobby Show. However, as Cady's various schemes for efficiency* take hold and he leads the movement against purchasing a new firetruck, Atkins begins to have second thoughts about their esteemed new resident. By the time Cady speaks against the highly ornamental, long-awaited replacement firetruck, Atkins smiled sweetly, as though he'd just been shot in the stomach. Atkins lives in an eighteen-room mansion, purchased by his father, and can't wait to unload the burden it has become.

At the story's conclusion, Atkins leads the fire department in a vote against Cady's membership because their previous vote violated their charter. New members must be residents for three years before being considered for membership. In this way, the town is able to rebuff Cady's recommendations while still being polite and orderly, hoping that Spruce Falls will still be a residential destination for executives from Federal Apparatus Corporation.

Atlas, Charles. Vonnegut and Bokonon were both alumni of the Charles Atlas physical fitness program operating on the principle of "dynamic tension" (WFG Playboy Interview). In Cat's Cradle Bokonon takes Charles Atlas's idea of pitting opposing muscle groups in tension against each other to describe the social theory he and Corporal McCabe employ to coax the people of San Lorenzo into positive activities. (CC 47) It was the belief of **Charles Atlas** that muscles could be built without bar bells or spring exercisers, could be built by simply pitting one set of muscles against another.

It was the belief of Bokonon that good societies could be built only by pitting good against evil, and by keeping the tension between the two high at all times.
(WFG Playboy Interview) VONNEGUT: Right. I was a preposterous kind of flamingo. And the present the coach gave me was a **Charles Atlas course**. And it made me sick. I considered going out and slashing the coach's tires, I thought it was such an irresponsible thing for an adult to do to a kid. But I just walked out of the dance and went home. The humiliation was something I never forgot. And one night last year, I got on the phone and called Indianapolis information and asked for the number of the coach. I got him on the phone and told him who I was. And then I reminded him about the present and said, "I want you to know that my body

turned out all right." It was a neat unburdening. It certainly beats psychiatry.
See also: CC 80.

Augustus, Caesar. Referred to by Senator Lister Ames Rosewater in his famous and often used speech on the Golden Age of Rome. The senator appreciates Caesar Augustus as a "great humanitarian" for his ruthless measures intended to regain control over the moral decline of Rome. Through Senator Rosewater, Vonnegut creates an analogy between ancient Rome and modern America that predates the hard-line Republican Party rhetoric of the late 1970s and early 1980s. (GBR 2) I should like to speak of the Emperor Octavian, of **Caesar Augustus**, as he came to be known. This great humanitarian, and he was a humanitarian in the profoundest sense of the word, took command of the Roman Empire in a degenerate period strikingly like our own. Harlotry, divorce, alcoholism, liberalism, homosexuality, pornography, abortion, venality, murder, labor racketeering, juvenile delinquency, cowardice, atheism, extortion, slander, and theft were the height of fashion. Rome was a paradise for gangsters, perverts, and the lazy working man, just as America is now. As in America now, forces of law and order were openly attacked by mobs, children were disobedient, had no respect for their parents or their country, and no decent woman was safe on any street, even at high noon! And cunning, sharp-trading, bribing foreigners were in the ascendency everywhere. And ground under the heels of the big city moneychangers were the honest farmers, the backbone of the Roman Army and the Roman soul.

What could be done? Well, there were softheaded liberals then as there are bubble-headed liberals now, and they said what liberals always say after they have led a great nation to such a lawless, self-indulgent, polyglot condition: "Things have never been better! Look at all the freedom! Look at all the equality! Look how sexual hypocrisy has been driven from the scene! Oh boy! People used to get all knotted up inside when they thought about rape or fornication. Now they can do both with glee!"

And what did the terrible, black-spirited, non-fun-loving conservatives of those happy days have to say? Well, there weren't many of them left. They were dying off in ridiculed old age. And their children had been turned against them by the liberals, by the purveyors of synthetic sunshine and moonshine, by the something-for-nothing political strip-teasers, by the people who loved everybody, including the barbarians, by people who loved the barbarians so much they wanted to open all the gates, have all the soldiers lay their weapons down, and let the barbarians come in!

That was the Rome that **Caesar Augustus** came home to, after defeating those two sex maniacs, Antony and Cleopatra, in the great sea battle of Actium. And I don't think I have to re-create the things he thought when he surveyed the Rome he was said to rule. Let us take a moment of silence, and let each think what he will of the stews of today. . . .

And what methods did **Caesar Augustus** use to put this disorderly house in order? He did what we are so often told we must never, ever do, what we are told will never, ever work: he wrote morals into law, and he enforced those unenforceable laws with a police force that was cruel and unsmiling. He made it illegal for a Roman to behave like a pig. Do you hear me? It became illegal! And Romans caught acting like pigs were strung up by their thumbs, thrown down wells, fed to lions, and given other experiences that might impress them with the desirability of being more decent and reliable than they were. Did it work? You bet your boots it did! Pigs miraculously disappeared! And what do we call the period that followed this now-unthinkable oppression? Nothing more nor less, friends and neighbors, than The Golden Age of Rome.

Aurelius, Marcus. (*MN* 20) (*Werner*) Noth's house, said Westlake, had been demolished by Russian artillery, but Noth had continued to live in one undamaged room in the back. Westlake took an inventory of the room, found it to contain a bed, a table, and a candlestick. On the table were photographs of Helga, Resi, and Noth's wife.

There was a book. It was a German translation of *The Meditations of Marcus Aurelius.*

Auschwitz. (*MN* 1) Andor (*Gutman*) is a sleepy, not very bright Estonian Jew. He spent two years in the extermination camp at **Auschwitz**.

(*MN* 2) Sonderkommando means special detail. At **Auschwitz** it meant a very special detail indeed—one composed of prisoners whose duties were to shepherd condemned persons into gas chambers, and then to lug their bodies out. When the job was done, the members of the Sonderkommando were themselves killed.

(*MN* 2) He went away for a little while, after having confessed that. And he thought about **Auschwitz**, the thing he liked least to think about. *Gutman could never understand why he joined the Sonderkommando and he wonders out loud about this to Campbell while on guard in the Old Jerusalem basement jail.*

(*MN* 4) Mengel (*Bernard Mengel, another of Campbell's jailers*) was speaking of Rudolf Franz Hoess, the commandant of the extermination camp at **Auschwitz**. In his tender care, literally millions of Jews were gassed.

(*MN* 5) I, too, knew Rudolf Hoess, Commandant of **Auschwitz**. I (*Howard Campbell*) met him at a New Year's Eve party in Warsaw during the war— the start of 1944.

(*MN* 8) *Dr. Epstein complains about anyone's reminiscence of Nazi horrors.* "They should fade, said young Dr. Epstein. They belong to a period of insanity that should be forgotten as quickly as possible."

"**Auschwitz**," said his mother.

"Forget **Auschwitz**," said Dr. Epstein.

"Do you know what **Auschwitz** was?" his mother asked me.

"Yes," I said.

(*MN* 29) Do you feel that you're guilty of murdering six million Jews I (*Campbell*) said.

"Absolutely not," said the architect of **Auschwitz**, the introducer of conveyor belts into crematoria, the greatest customer in the world for the gas called Cyklon-B.

Campbell's explanation for Hoess's war crimes and all such nightmarish crimes was schizophrenia, which he likened to a "cuckoo clock in Hell." (*MN* 30) That was how Rudolf Hoess, Commandant of **Auschwitz**, could alternate over the loudspeakers of **Auschwitz** great music and calls for corpse-carriers—

(*MN* 44) When I reached the landing outside the door of young Dr. Abraham Epstein, a man who had spent his childhood in **Auschwitz**, the stench stopped me. . . .

"I'd like to surrender to an *Auschwitzer*," I said. This made him mad.

"Then find one who thinks about **Auschwitz** all the time!" he said. "There are plenty who think about nothing else. I never think about it!" (MN 44) "This is not the first time you've seen eyes like that," she said to her son in German, "not the first man you've seen who could not move unless someone told him where to move, who longed for someone to tell him what to do next, who would do anything anyone told him to do next. You saw thousands of them at **Auschwitz**."

(MN 44) What she crooned was this, a command she had heard over the loudspeakers of **Auschwitz**—had heard many times a day for years.

"*Leichentrager zu Wache*," she (*Mrs. Epstein, the doctor's mother*) crooned.

In Cat's Cradle *Julian Castle tells John/Jonah,* After death, the body turns black—coals to Newcastle in the case of San Lorenzo. When the plague was having everything its own way, the House of Hope and Mercy in the Jungle looked like **Auschwitz** or Buchenwald. We had stacks of dead so deep and wide that a bulldozer actually stalled trying to shove them toward a common grave (CC 73).

(CC 83) He (*Dr. Schlichter von Koenigswald*) was in the S.S. for fourteen years. He was a camp physician at **Auschwitz** for six of those years.

(CC 106) Dr. von Koenigswald, the humanitarian with the terrible deficit of **Auschwitz** in his kindliness account, was the second to die of ice-nine.

(WFG Biafra: A People Betrayed) I admire Miriam, though I am not grateful for the trip she gave me. It was like a free trip to **Auschwitz** when the ovens were still going full blast. I now feel lousy all the time.

(PS 12) He was right. It was impossible for her to think coherently about assholes or **Auschwitz** or anything else that might be upsetting to a little girl. *After returning from World War II, Vonnegut had a discussion with his father about one of their relations who had married a German officer before the war and had come to identify with the plight of the Germans over her native America.*

(PS 13) "There is this psychiatrist, you see. He is a colonel in the German SS in Poland during World War Two. His name is Vonnegut. That is a good German name. Colonel Vonnegut is supposed to look after the mental health of SS people in his area, which includes the uniformed staff at **Auschwitz**."

(PS 13) "Lieutenant Dampfwalze, who could be played by Peter O'Toole, feels that he can't cut the mustard anymore on the railroad platform at **Auschwitz**, where boxcars of people are unloaded day after day. He is sick and tired of it, but he has the wisdom to seek professional help. Dr. Vonnegut is an eclectic worker in the field of mental health, incidentally, a pragmatic man. He is a little bit Jungian, a little bit Freudian, a little bit Rankian— and so on. He has an open and inquiring mind."

Eugene Debs Hartke muses about the state of mankind: (HP 32) And the worst flaw is that we are just plain dumb. Admit it!

You think **Auschwitz** was intelligent?

(HP 32) My body, as I understand it, is attempting to contain the TB germs inside me in little shells it builds around them. The shells are calcium, the most common element in the walls of many prisons, including Athena. This place is ringed by barbed wire. So was **Auschwitz**.

(HP 32) There wasn't a Japanese manufacturer of crematoria, so Warden Matsumoto bought one from A. J. Topf und Sohn in Essen, Germany. This was the same outfit that had made the ovens for **Auschwitz** in its heyday.

The postwar Topf models all had state-of-the-art smoke scrubbers on their smokestacks, so people in Scipio, unlike the people living near **Auschwitz**, never knew that they had a busy corpse carbonizer in the neighborhood. *The crematoria were bought to incinerate the bodies of convicts who died from AIDS.*

(HP 39) I remember a lecture Damon Stern gave about his visit with several Tarkington students to **Auschwitz**, the infamous Nazi extermination camp in Poland during the Finale Rack. Stern used to make extra money taking trips to Europe with students whose parents or guardians didn't want to see them over Christmas or during the summertime. He caught a lot of heck for taking some to **Auschwitz**. He did it impulsively and without asking permission from anyone. It wasn't on the schedule, and some of the students were very upset afterward. (*HP* 39) The buildings (*of Auschwitz*) had been put up years before World War I, he said, as a comfortable outpost for soldiers of the Austro-Hungarian Empire. Among the many titles of that Emperor, he said was Duke of **Auschwitz**.

Referring to elements in his unpublished manuscript entitled SS Psychiatrist, *Vonnegut recalls:* "This was about an MD who had been psychoanalyzed, and he was stationed at **Auschwitz**. His job was to treat the depression of those members of the staff who did not like what they were doing there. Talk therapy was all he or anybody had to offer back then. This was before the days of—Never mind" (*FWD* 2).

(*FWD* 3) "And could any moralist have called for a more appropriate reaction by painters to World War II, to the death camps and Hiroshima and all the rest of it, than pictures without persons or artifacts, without even allusions to the blessings of Nature? A full moon, after all, had come to be known as a 'bomber's moon.' Even an orange could suggest a diseased planet, a disgraced humanity, if someone remembered, as many did, that the Commandant of **Auschwitz** and his wife and children, under the greasy smoke from the ovens, had had good food every day."

(*FWD* 8) "The United States of America had human slavery for almost one hundred years before that custom was recognized as a social disease and people began to fight it. Imagine that. Wasn't that a match for **Auschwitz**? What a beacon of liberty we were to the rest of the world when it was perfectly acceptable here to own other human beings and treat them as we treated cattle. Who told you we were a beacon of liberty from the very beginning? Why would they lie like that?"

(*FWD* 10) "When I was liberated in May, I was in the Russian zone. I spent some time with concentration camp survivors and heard their stories before returning to the American lines. I have since visited **Auschwitz** and Birkenau and have seen the collections there of human hair and children's shoes and toys and so on. I know about the Holocaust. Elie Wiesel and I are friends."

(*FWD* 12) "Hitler dreamed of killing Jews, Gypsies, Slavs, homosexuals, Communists, Jehovah's Witnesses, mental defectives, believers in democracy,

and so on, in industrial quantities. It would have remained only a dream if it hadn't been for chemists as well educated as my brother, who supplied Hitler's executioners with the cyanide gas known as Cyklon-B. It would have remained only a dream if architects and engineers as capable as my father and grandfather hadn't designed extermination camps— the fences, the towers, the barracks, the railroad sidings, and the gas chambers and crematoria—for maximum ease of operation and efficiency. I recently visited two of those camps in Poland, **Auschwitz** and Birkenau. They are technologically perfect. There is only one grade I could give their designers, and that grade is A-plus. They surely solved all the problems set for them."

(*FWD* 17) "As I say, color the people in old photographs of **Auschwitz** all shades of brown and black and you will be looking at what he sees every day." *Vonnegut wrote this for a piece about Mozambique.*

(*MWC* 1) When I'm being funny, I try not to offend. I don't think much of what I've done has been in really ghastly taste. I don't think I have embarrassed many people, or distressed them. The only shocks I use are an occasional obscene word. Some things aren't funny. I can't imagine a humorous book or skit about **Auschwitz**, for instance.

(*MWC* 1) I saw the destruction of Dresden. I saw the city before and then came out of an air-raid shelter and saw it afterward, and certainly one response was laughter. God knows, that's the soul seeking some relief.

Any subject is subject to laughter, and I suppose there was laughter of a very ghastly kind by victims in **Auschwitz**.

(*MWC* 2) In 1968, the year I wrote *Slaughterhouse-Five*, I finally became grown up enough to write about the bombing of Dresden. It was the largest massacre in European history. I, of course, know about **Auschwitz**, but a massacre is something that happens suddenly, the killing of a whole lot of people in a very short time. In Dresden, on February 13, 1945, about 135,000 people were killed by British firebombing in one night.

Auschwitzer. (*MN* 44) "I'd like to surrender to an *Auschwitzer*," I said. *Howard Campbell is speaking to Dr. Abraham Epstein who, along with his mother, survived Auschwitz.*

Auschwitzian. (PS 14) In *Gulliver's Travels*, Swift sets such high standards for unsentimentality about human beings that most of us can meet those standards only in wartime, and only briefly even then. He shrinks us, urinates on us, expands us and peers into all our nauseating apertures, encourages us to demonstrate our stupidity and mendaciousness, makes us hideously old. On paper he subjects us to every humiliating test that imaginative fiction can invent. And what is learned about us in the course of these **Auschwitzian** experiments? Only this, according to Swift's hero, Captain Gulliver: that we are disgusting in the extreme.

Averageman, John. *In the morality play performed at the engineers' annual retreat to the Meadows in* Player Piano, *John Averageman is the pawn caught in the cross-examination by the Radical and the Young Engineer. The Radical attempts to show that John's purchasing power, standard of living, and employment status have all been compromised by the engineers. The Young Engineer counters by showing John that he has more creature comforts and health protection than Caesar, Napoleon, Henry VIII, or Charlemagne.*

Avondale. *Vonnegut created two Avondale communities, one outside Rosewater, Indiana, and the other outside of Midland City, Ohio. In* God Bless You, Mr. Rosewater, *Avondale is where the few highly paid agronomists, engineers, brewers, accountants and administrators who did all that needed doing lived in a defensive circle of expensive ranch homes in another cornfield near New Ambrosia, a community named, for no reason whatsoever, "Avondale." All had gas-lit patios framed and terraced with railroad ties from the old Nickel Plate right-of-way (GBR 4). When Eliot and Sylvia went to live in Indiana, all the Avondale residents—employees of the Rosewater Corporation—tried to court the Rosewaters but their efforts were rebuffed. The Rosewater became enraged, grew snobbish, and behaved disrespectfully toward their neighbors.*

In Deadeye Dick, *Avondale is an inexpensive community of tract homes developed by Marco and Gino Maritimo. After Otto Waltz passes away in 1960, Rudy and his mother are given a terrific deal by the Maritimo brothers on one of the model homes. Rudy frequently calls Avondale a "jumble of little shitboxes." Their house had an ornate concrete mantelpiece built with radioactive cement from the Manhattan Project in Oak Ridge, Tennessee. Mrs. Waltz eventually dies from exposure to radiation emitted by the concrete. Vonnegut adds that Avondale had once been John Fortune's dairy farm and later became a testing ground for tanks produced by Fred T. Barry.*

B

B-1. (*FWD* 14) "A word about appeasement, something World War II, supposedly taught us not to practice: I say to you that the world has been ruined by appeasement. . . . Appeasement of the compulsive war-preparers. I can scarcely name a nation that has not lost most of its freedom and wealth in attempts to appease its own addicts to preparations for war.

"And there is no appeasing an addict for very long: 'I swear, man, just lay enough bread on me for twenty multiple-reentry vehicles and a fleet of **B-1** bombers, and I'll never bother you again.'"

B-17. (*HP* 4) When I (*Eugene Debs Hartke*) was 2 years old, we moved to Midland City, Ohio, where a washing-machine company named Robo-Magic Corporation was beginning to make bomb-release mechanisms and swivel mounts for machine guns on **B-17** bombers. The plastics industry was then in its infancy, and Father was sent to Robo-Magic to determine what synthetic materials from Du Pont could be used in the weapons systems in place of metal, in order to make them lighter.

B-36. (*WJ* III) HAROLD . . . Looseleaf delivered a lecture on maintenance procedures for the hydraulic system of a **B-36**.

B-36 Mother. *Aside from being numbered in the same manner as the famed* WWII *aircraft, this is also the designation of the mother of the eponymously named* "The Sisters B-36," *the Kilgore Trout short story in* Timequake. *Nothing much is said about her except that she is the wealthy mother of the three sisters, and that the evil sister got money from her very rich mom to manufacture and market these satanic devices, which made imaginations redundant* (*TQ* 5).

B-52. (*HP* 29) "A **B-52**. . . . Gore and guts everywhere." *Eugene Debs Hartke uses the image of the* **B-52** *bomber to describe the kind of destruction wrought by those on high in the administration of* Tarkington College. (*HP* 32) If the Trustees were bad, the convicts were worse. I would be the last person to say otherwise. They were devastators of their own communities with gunfights and robberies and rapes, and the merchandising of brain-busting chemicals and on and on.

But at least they saw what they were doing, whereas people like the Trustees had a lot in common with **B-52 bombardiers** way up in the stratosphere. They seldom saw the devastation they caused as they moved the huge portion of this country's wealth they controlled from here to there.

Babel (*also* **Tower of Babel**). *The discovery of the chrono-synclastic infundibula halted the launching of the* Whale, *built by Malachi Constant's Galactic Spacecraft Corporation. Since the appearance of the chrono-synclastic infundibulum indicated that all that ever will be, already was—the question it poses for man is* "What makes you think you're going anywhere?" (*ST* 1) *This offers the opportunity to look at the space program in larger, biblical terms, and, as the narrator goes on to describe, draw a parallel between the efforts necessary for space exploration and the Tower of Babel.* (*ST* 1) It was a situation made to order for American fundamentalist preachers. They were quicker than philosophers or historians or anybody to talk sense about the truncated Age of Space. Two hours after the firing of *The Whale* was called off indefinitely, the Reverend Bobby Denton shouted at his Love Crusade in Wheeling, West Virginia:

"'And the Lord came down to see the city and the tower, which the children of men builded. And the Lord said, "Behold, the people is one, and they have all one language; and this they begin to do; and *now nothing will be restrained from them, which they have imagined to do.* Go to, let us go down, and there confound their language, that they may not understand one another's speech." So the Lord scattered them abroad from thence upon the face of all the earth; and they left off to build the city.

Therefore is the name of it called **Babel**; because the Lord did there confound the language of all the earth: and from thence did the Lord scatter them abroad upon the face of the earth.'"

Bobby Denton spitted his audience on a bright and loving gaze, and proceeded to roast it whole over the coals of its own iniquity. "Are these not Bible times?" he said. "Have we not builded of steel and pride an abomination far taller than the **Tower of Babel** of old? And did we not mean, like those builders of old, to get right into Heaven with it? And haven't we heard it said many times that the language of scientists is international? They all use the same Latin and Greek words for things, and they all talk the language of numbers. . . .

"So why should we cry out in surprise and pain now when God says to us what He said to the people who built the **Tower of Babel**: 'No! Get away from there! You aren't going to Heaven or anywhere else with that thing! Scatter, you hear? Quit talking the language of science to each other! Nothing will be restrained from you which you have imagined to do, if you all keep on talking the language of science to each other, and I don't want that! I, your Lord God on High want things restrained from you, so you will quit thinking about crazy towers and rockets to Heaven, and start thinking about how to be better neighbors and husbands and wives and daughters and sons! Don't look to rockets for salvation—look to your homes and churches!'"

Babylon, Babylonian. (CC 81) My hair stood on end, as though Angela were rolling on the floor, foaming at the mouth, and babbling fluent **Babylonian**. *This is John/Jonah's reaction to hearing Angela Hoenikker play the clarinet.*

(GBR 1) And Noah begat Samuel, who married Geraldine Ames Rockefeller. Samuel became even more interested in politics than his father had been, served the Republican Party tirelessly as a king-maker, caused that party to nominate men who would whirl like dervishes, bawl fluent **Babylonian**, and order the militia to fire into crowds whenever a poor man seemed on the point of suggesting that he and a Rosewater were equal in the eyes of the law.

(MH The Foster Portfolio) And then Herbert Foster, looking drab and hunted, picked his way through the crowd. His expression was one of disapproval, of a holy man in **Babylon**. He was oddly stiff-necked and held his arms at his sides as he pointedly kept from brushing against anyone or from meeting any of the gazes that fell upon him. There was no question that being in the place was absolute, humiliating hell for him.

(WFG Excelsior! We're Going to the Moon! Excelsior!) I used to talk to G.E. scientists sometimes about exciting stuff I had read in *Scientific American*. I was reading it regularly in those days. I thought it was part of my job—to keep up. If the article I was discussing wasn't related to my listener's field, he would doze. I might as well have been speaking **Babylonian**.

(JB Prologue) The chief cast his spell. His shouted words bounced off the buildings, warred with their own echoes, and sounded like **Babylonian** by the time they reached Alexander's ears. *This is Walter Starbuck's description of that moment just before the Cuyahoga Massacre when the Cleveland chief of police read the Riot Act to the striking workers.*

(HP 24) Darius, King of Persia, he told me, crucified 3,000 people he thought were enemies in **Babylon**. *After viewing the mutilated body of Tex Johnson, Eugene Debs Hartke has an informative discussion about crucifixion with the State Police forensic medicine specialist.*

Bach, Johann Sebastian. *Vonnegut uses Bach to score a scene in* Slaughterhouse-Five *which, in retrospect for Billy Pilgrim, gains new significance because of its Tralfamadorian fourth-dimensionality.* (SL5 2) One time on maneuvers Billy was playing "A Mighty Fortress Is Our God," with music by **Johann Sebastian Bach** and words by Martin Luther. It was Sunday morning. Billy and his chaplain had gathered a congregation of about fifty soldiers on a Carolina hillside. An umpire appeared. There were umpires everywhere, men who said who was winning or losing the theoretical battle, who was alive and who was dead.

The umpire had comical news. The congregation had been theoretically spotted from the air by a theoretical enemy. They were all theoretically dead now. The theoretical corpses laughed and ate a hearty noontime meal.

Remembering this incident years later, Billy was

struck by what a Tralfamadorian adventure with death that had been, to be dead and to eat at the same time.

(*MWC* 11) Might not it be possible, then, that the Second World War was a cause of the first one? Otherwise, the first one remains inexplicable nonsense of the most gruesome kind. Or try this: Is it possible that seemingly incredible geniuses like **Bach** and Shakespeare and Einstein were not in fact superhuman, but simply plagiarists, copying great stuff from the future?

bacteria, bacterium. (*SL5* 4) The Americans' clothes were meanwhile passing through poison gas. Body lice and **bacteria** and fleas were dying by the billions. So it goes.

(*MH* Report on the Barnhouse Effect) As a weapon, then, dynamopsychism has an impressive advantage over **bacteria** and atomic bombs, beyond the fact that it costs nothing to use: it enables the professor to single out critical individuals and objects instead of slaughtering whole populations in the process of maintaining international equilibrium.

(*Gal* 1:33) If people can swim as fast and far as fur seals now, what is to prevent their swimming all the way back to the mainland, whence their ancestors came? Answer: nothing.

Plenty have tried it or will try it during periods of fish shortages or overpopulation. But the **bacterium** which eats human eggs is always there to greet them.

(*Blue* 2) And I told Mrs. Berman this about my mother: "She died when I was twelve—of a tetanus infection she evidently picked up while working in a cannery in California. The cannery was built on the site of an old livery stable, and tetanus **bacteria** often colonize the intestines of horses without hurting them, and then become durable spores, armored little seeds, when excreted. One of them lurking in the dirt around and under the cannery was somehow exhumed and sent traveling. After a long, long sleep it awakened in Paradise, something we would all like to do. Paradise was a cut in my mother's hand."

(*Blue* 32) So I could not bring myself to put them (*Karabekian's art collection*) in the barn, which was then a musty place, having been home for so long for nothing but potatoes and the earth and **bacteria** and fungi which so loved to cling to them.

(*HP* 24) He (*the mortician Norman Updike*) went on to tell me with bow-wow cheerfulness back in 1987 that people were generally mistaken about how quickly things rot, turn into good old dirt or fertilizer or dust or whatever. He said scientists had discovered well-preserved meat and vegetables deep in city dumps, thrown away presumably years and years ago. Like Hermann and Sophia Shultz, these theoretically biodegradable works of Nature had failed to rot for want of moisture, which was life itself to worms and fungi and **bacteria**.

(*GBK* Kilgore Trout) As is now the case with **Mycobacterium** tuberculosis, there is a new strain of the ethnic-cleansing **bacterium** that makes conceivable remedies of the past seem pathetic or even absurd. In every case nowadays: Too late! The victims are practically all dead or homeless by the time they are first mentioned on the six o'clock news.

All that good people can do about the disease of ethnic cleansing, now always a fait accompli, is to rescue the survivors. And watch out for Christians!

This is Kurt Vonnegut, signing off.

See also: TQ 14.

Baer (*see also* **Kroner**). *Baer is chief engineer of the Eastern Division of the National Industrial, Commercial, Communications, Foodstuffs, and Resources ruling technocracy.* (*PP* I) It was Kroner and **Baer** who would decide who was to get the most important job in their division, a job left vacant two weeks ago by death—the managership of the Pittsburgh Works.

Kroner always appears to reserve his comments, making him hard to read, yet Baer is no political slouch, though his outward appearance borders on buffoonery. (*PP* V) The other, **Baer**, slight and nervous, noisily and unconvincingly extroverted, laughed, nudged, and clapped shoulders, and maintained a continuous commentary on whatever was being said: "Fine, fine, right, sure, sure, wonderful, yes, yes, exactly, fine, good."

(*PP* V) **Baer** was a social cretin, apparently unaware that he was anything but suave and brilliant in company. Someone had once mentioned his running commentary on conversations to him, and he hadn't known what they were talking about. Technically, there wasn't a better engineer in the East, including Finnerty. There was little in the Division that hadn't been master-minded by **Baer**, who here seemed to Kroner what a fox terrier seems to a St. Bernard. Paul *(Proteus)* had thought often of the peculiar combination of Kroner and **Baer**, and wondered if, when they were gone, higher management could possibly duplicate it. **Baer** embodied the knowledge and technique of industry; Kroner personified the faith, the near-holiness, the spirit of the complicated venture. Kroner, in fact, had a poor record as an engineer and had surprised Paul from time to time with his ignorance or misunderstanding of technical matters; but he had the priceless quality of believing in the system, and of making others believe in it, too, and do as they were told.

(PP IX) The civic managers were the career administrators who ran the city. They lived on the same side of the river as the managers and engineers of the Ilium Works, but the contact between the two groups was little more than perfunctory and, traditionally, suspicious. The schism, like so many things, dated back to the war, when the economy had, for efficiency's sake, become monolithic. The question had arisen: who was to run it, the bureaucrats, the heads of business and industry, or the military? Business and bureaucracy had stuck together long enough to overwhelm the military and had since then worked side by side, abusively and suspiciously, but, like Kroner and **Baer**, each unable to do a whole job without the other.

(PP XIX) Paul reflected that **Baer** was possibly the most just, reasonable, and candid person he'd ever known—remarkably machinelike in that the only problems he interested himself in were those brought to him, and in that he went to work on all problems with equal energy and interest, insensitive to quality and scale.

"Bagladies" (*see* **Pamela Ford Hall**).

Bagnialto (*see also* **Barring-gaffner**). (BC 14) Kilgore Trout was suddenly woozy with déjà vu. The truck driver was reminding him of the premise of a book he hadn't thought about for years. The driver's toilet paper in Libertyville, Georgia, had been *The Barring-gaffner of Bagnialto, or This Year's Masterpiece*, by Kilgore Trout.

The name of the planet where Trout's book took place was **Bagnialto**, and a "Barring-gaffner" there was a government official who spun a wheel of chance once a year. Citizens submitted works of art to the government, and these were given numbers, and then they were assigned cash values according to the Barring-gaffner's spins of the wheel.

"Bagombo Snuff Box." *The title of the 1999 collection of short story reprints as well as the title of the October 1954 story first appearing in* Cosmopolitan *magazine, this is the tale of Eddie Laird, a romantic dreamer once stationed during World War II at Cunningham Field. Though only twenty-two at the time, it was there he met and married eighteen-year-old Amy. The marriage lasted only six months, but now, eleven years later, while on his first return to town, Eddie feels the urge to phone and then visit his ex-wife.*

Eddie is a dreamer of exotic adventures, something Amy knew about him from long ago, but his quick catalogue of travels over the phone with her leaves her impressed and a bit down by comparison. "I just blew in from Ceylon, by way of Baghdad, Rome, and New York."

"Good heavens," said Amy. "What a shock. I didn't even know if you were alive or dead."

Laird laughed. "They can't kill me, and by heaven, they've sure tried."

"What have you been up to?"

"Ohhhhh—a little bit of everything. I just quit a job flying for a pearling outfit in Ceylon. I'm starting a company of my own, prospecting for uranium up around the Klondike region. Before the Ceylon deal, I was hunting diamonds in the Amazon rain forest, and before that, flying for a sheik in Iraq."

"Like something out of *The Arabian Nights*," said Amy. "My head just swims."

"Well, don't get any glamorous illusions," Laird said. "Most of it was hard, dirty, dangerous work." He sighed. "And how are you, Amy?"

"Me?" said Amy. "How is any housewife? Harassed."

Eddie insists on a quick visit to Amy's home that evening. Upon arrival, Eddie is greeted at the door by Harry, Amy's second husband with whom she has the nine-year-old Stevie and another young baby. Eddie first passes himself off as having been a captain in the Air Force during the war and that he now serves in the Reserves as a major. Lie after lie begins to pile up, but it is the young Stevie who proves to be Eddie's undoing.

Stevie's eyes, frank, irreverent, and unromantic, scared him (Eddie). And well they should. It is Stevie who turns over Eddie's gift from Ceylon, the Bagombo snuff box, only to find a "Made in Japan" sticker that prompts Eddie to fabricate yet another lie about why it is there. A short while later, Eddie makes the mistake of agreeing with Stevie about the location of Ceylon off the African coast. Amy knows that it is off the coast of India, and this causes Eddie to make a straight shot for his waiting taxi to escape any further embarrassment. Once Eddie's lies are laid bare, the bit of domestic chaos we see in Amy's home begins to pale and her family unites in hurling insults at Eddie as he makes his escape.

The close of the story has Eddie in his hotel room making a call to Selma, his housewife taking care of their four children at home in Levittown, Long Island. Levittown is forever symbolic of the American Dream of home ownership for the broad range of the rising middle class. Eddie, the inveterate liar and romantic dreamer is seen as equally trapped by working-class concerns. He is, after all, a potato chip salesman traveling up and down the East Coast trying to make a living, often leaving the chaos of his own home and family concerns to the loving care of Selma, the mother of Arthur (whose teachers believe is just lazy, not dull), Dawn (in need of braces), and an unnamed set of twins. After senselessly causing Amy's family to feel small and closed in with their own domestic tensions, Eddie seeks the solace of his own brood, even if by a long distance phone call while trying to eke out his own living.

Bahía de Darwin. Spanish for "Darwin Bay," this is the cruise ship built for trips to the Galápagos Islands. Captained by Adolf von Kleist, it was scheduled for "the Nature Cruise of the Century" on Friday, November 28, 1986. It winds up as the last refuge for the remaining biped humans.

During the construction of the ship in Malmö, Sweden, Leo Trout, the son of Kilgore Trout, is decapitated by a sheet of falling steel. His ghost is the narrator of Galápagos.

Mary Wait nicknames the doomed ship the "Walloping Window Blind," taken from the Charles Carryl rhyme (Gal 2:13).

bakemaster. Another of the doppelgängers at the Timequake clambake. (TQ 60) The cast party afterward was a clambake on the beach at Xanadu. As in the last scene of 8½, the motion picture by Federico Fellini, tout le monde was there, if not in person, then represented by look-alikes. . . . The **bakemaster**, a local man who is paid to stage such parties in the summertime, resembled my late publisher Seymour Lawrence (1926–1993), who rescued me from certain oblivion, from smithereens, by publishing Slaughterhouse-Five, and then bringing all my previous books back into print under his umbrella.

Baku. In Player Piano, these are mud and straw figures once made by the now extinct Surrasi, considered an infidel tribe by the Shah of Bratpuhr. Viewed as false gods, the Shah equates America's faith in EPICAC with the Surrasis' faith in Baku.

Baltra. One of the first sights of conflict leading to the end of mankind as we know it, also one of the islands in the Galápagos chain. (Gal 1:32) It was at about that time that Peru declared war on Ecuador. Two of Peru's fighter bombers were then over Ecuadorian territories, one with its rocket tuned to the radar signals coming from Guayaquil International Airport, and the other with its rocket tuned to radar signals coming from the naval base on the Galápagos Island of **Baltra**, lair of a sail training ship, six Coast Guard ships, two oceangoing tugs, a patrol submarine, a dry dock, and, high and dry in the dry dock, a destroyer. The destroyer was the largest ship in the Ecuadorian Navy, save for one—the Bahía de Darwin.
(Gal 2:4) If they had ever reached **Baltra**, which they never did, they would have found it devastated and depopulated by yet another airmailed package of dagonite.

Bane, Joe. In the short story "Souvenir," collected in Bagombo Snuff Box (1999), this is the slothful pawnbroker visited by Eddie (the farmer) in hopes of getting $500 for his unique bit of war booty. Joe listens to Eddie's wartime recollection but remains committed to making a deal. He is unmoved after listening to Eddie's tale, remaining as first described. **Joe Bane** was a pawnbroker, a fat, lazy, bald man, whose features seemed pulled to the left by his lifetime of looking at the world through a jeweler's glass. He was a lonely, untalented man and would not have wanted to go on living had he been prevented from playing every day save Sunday the one game he played brilliantly—the acquiring of objects for very little, and the selling of them for a great deal more. He was obsessed by the game, the one opportunity life offered him to best his fellow men. The game was the thing, the money he made a secondary matter, a way of keeping score.

The Bannister. *The Midland City movie theater is first mentioned in* Breakfast of Champions, *though there is no direct connection with George Hickman Bannister's family. In* Deadeye Dick, *Rudy Waltz recalls that the building was originally Midland City's opera house but became a movie theater in 1927. When the downtown area became a haven for the homeless and local businesses moved out, the building was taken over by the Empire Furniture Company—controlled by gangsters.*

Bannister, George Hickman (*also* **Bannister Memorial Fieldhouse**). *The Midland City high school football player killed in the 1924 Thanksgiving Day game. Buried in Calvary Cemetery, his grave is marked by a sixty-two-foot obelisk funded by contributions from the community. A city ordinance makes it illegal for any structure to be built taller than Bannister's commemorative obelisk. The only change in that law comes as a result of the need to construct a radio tower for a local station. The new fieldhouse, which is under construction at the time of his death, is named in his honor. Bannister's family moved from Midland City before the obelisk is erected. Though most of the references to Bannister are made in* Breakfast of Champions, *in* Deadeye Dick *Rudy Waltz visits the grave after the neutron-bombing of Midland City, just before Hippolyte Paul De Mille's resurrection of the nearby interred aviator Will Fairchild.*

Bannister, Lucy. *In* Breakfast of Champions, *the sister of George Hickman Bannister and her parents*

leave Midland City before the commemorative sixty-two-foot obelisk is erected by the townspeople in honor of her brother.

baptism, baptismal, Baptist, baptized, baptizing. *When Malachi/Unk creates an explosive diversion to seek out Bea and Chrono, Boaz is left by himself.* (ST 6) As they stood, Boaz stood, too. "God damn, buddy," he said, "I guess we done had a **baptism** of fire."

(MN 7) I, Howard W. Campbell, Jr., was born in Schenectady, New York, on February 16, 1912. My father, who was raised in Tennessee, the son of a **Baptist** minister, was an engineer in the Service Engineering Department of the General Electric Company.

(GBR 1) It was common gossip in the office that the very first president of the Foundation, Eliot Rosewater, the Senator's son, was a lunatic. This characterization was a somewhat playful one, but as Mushari knew, playfulness was impossible to explain in a court of law. Eliot was spoken of by Mushari's co-workers variously as "The Nut," "The Saint," "The Holy Roller," "**John the Baptist**," and so on.

The following is a telephone conversation between an anonymous caller and Eliot Rosewater after the former called the Rosewater hotline. (GBR 7) "But what are you anyway—some kind of religion?"

"**Two-Seed-in-the-Spirit Predestinarian Baptist**."

"What?"

"That's what I generally say when people insist I must have a religion. There happens to be such a sect, and I'm sure it's a good one. Foot-washing is practiced, and the ministers draw no pay. I wash my feet, and I draw no pay."

"I don't get it," said the caller.

"Just a way of trying to put you at ease, to let you know you don't have to be deadly serious with me. You don't happen to be a **Two-Seed-in-the-Spirit Predestinarian Baptist**, do you?"

"Jesus, no."

"There are two hundred people who are, and sooner or later I'm going to say to one of them what I've just said to you." Eliot took a drink. "I live in dread of that moment—and it's sure to come."

In a conversation between Eliot Rosewater and his wife, Sylvia, Norman Mushari listens in on an extension phone and hears the following. (GBR 7) "Congratulate Mary Moody on her twins."

"I will, I'll be **baptizing** them tomorrow."

"**Baptizing**?" This was something new. . . .

Mushari did not register disappointment. The **baptism** would hold up very well in court as evidence that Eliot thought of himself as a Messiah.
(GBR 8) And George begat Abraham, who became a Congregationalist minister. Abraham went as a missionary to the Congo, where he met and married Lavinia Waters, the daughter of another missionary, an Illinois **Baptist**.
(SL5 1) *Now, in 1760, Dresden underwent siege by the Prussians. On the fifteenth of July began the cannonade. The Picture-Gallery took fire. Many of the paintings had been transported to the Konigstein, but some were seriously injured by splinters of bombshells,—notably Francia's "Baptism of Christ."*

In an unnamed Kilgore Trout novel, Delmore Skag was a bachelor in a neighborhood where everyone had large families. Skag was also a scientist and invented a way to reproduce himself by shaving cells from his right hand and mixing them with chicken soup exposed to cosmic rays. (BC 2) Pretty soon, Delmore was having several babies a day, and inviting his neighbors to share his pride and happiness. He had mass **baptisms** of as many as a hundred babies at a time. He became famous as a family man.
(*Slap* Epigraph) "Call me but love and I'll be new **baptiz'd**. . . ."—ROMEO
(JB 4) I myself was nothing. My father had been secretly **baptized** a Roman Catholic in Poland, a religion that was suppressed at the time. He grew up to be an agnostic. My mother was **baptized** a Greek Orthodox in Lithuania, but became a Roman Catholic in Cleveland. Father would never go to church with her. I myself was **baptized** a Roman Catholic, but aspired to my father's indifference, and quit going to church when I was twelve. When I applied for admission to Harvard, old Mr. McCone, a **Baptist**, told me to classify myself as a Congregationalist, which I did.
(FWD 16) My second wife is another Episcopalian, and like my first one thinks that I have no religion and am a spiritual cripple on that account. When

Jill's and my daughter Lily was **baptized** by the Bishop of New York in the biggest Gothic church in the world (in a neighborhood so poor that the Bishop couldn't get cable service for his TV), I did not attend. (There is a sound reason for hating me right there, but I think the main reason is cigarettes.) (*BAG* Hal Irwin's Magic Lamp) Mary had another house to go to, which was her widowed father's farm outside the town of Crawfordsville. The only place Ella Rice could think of to go with her baby was the black church where the baby had been **baptized**. Mary went there with them.

Barber, Kensington. *The Provost of Tarkington College suspected by Eugene Debs Hartke of killing Letitia Smiley, the winner of the 1922 Women's Barefoot Race and crowned Lilac Queen for her effort. Hartke's imprisonment allows him to research the events surrounding the Lilac Queen's disappearance and concludes that Barber had probably impregnated Letitia and killed her the night of her victory. Barber is quoted in newspaper articles from the period that* "Letitia had been deeply troubled by a stormy romance with a much older man down in Scipio" (HP 24). *He sent his family on their scheduled European vacation without him that summer so he could assist with the investigation. Barber experienced a nervous breakdown toward the end of the summer and was committed to the State Hospital for the Insane in Batavia.*

Barca-Lounger, Barcalounger. *Though most memorable as the seat of last repose for those entering the Ethical Suicide Parlors in the short story "Welcome to the Monkey House," in* Welcome to the Monkey House *(1968), the Barca-Lounger is referred to in other tales, as well. In* Slaughterhouse-Five *the Tralfamadorians anesthetize Billy Pilgrim and strap him to a yellow barcalounger they stole from Sears & Roebuck and later use to furnish his dome on their planet* (SL5 4).

Kilgore Trout's novel 2BR02B, *a thematic cross between* Player Piano *and "Welcome to the Monkey House," also has Ethical Suicide Parlors outfitted with pretty hostesses and Barca-Loungers.* (GBR 2) All serious diseases had been conquered. So death was voluntary, and the government, to encourage volunteers for death, set up a purple-roofed

Ethical Suicide Parlor at every major intersection, right next to an orange-roofed Howard Johnson's. There were pretty hostesses in the parlor, and **Barca-Loungers**, and Muzak, and a choice of four-teen painless ways to die.

In a sense, Rudy Waltz's mother met her death as she sat in her Barcalounger in front of the fireplace that had been built with radioactive cement from the Manhattan Project. (DD 27) So we did not panic *(while men from the Nuclear Regulatory Commission dressed in space suits took all sorts of readings of the house and neighborhood).* Good citizens don't. We waited calmly for Fred T. Barry. I was at the picture window, peering out at the street between slats of the Venetian blinds. Mother was reclining in the **Barcalounger** my brother Felix had given her three Christmases ago. She was vibrating almost imperceptibly, and a reassuring drone came from underneath her. She had the massage motor turned on low.

Barker, General Honus. *General Barker is one of the ranking officers and chaperones for Professor Barnhouse during Operation Brainstorm, a test of the professor's dynamo psychic abilities intended to destroy a number of practice targets scattered throughout the Western Hemisphere. General Barker later warns Congress that it is impossible to defend against the Barnhouse Effect. This all occurs in the 1950 short story "Report on the Barnhouse Effect,"* reprinted in Welcome to the Monkey House (1968).

Barkley, Ben. *Dr. Remenzel's black chauffeur is also a good friend of Remenzel's son, Eli, in the 1962 short story "The Lie," reprinted in* Welcome to the Monkey House (1968). *Barkley drives both to the Whitehill School for Boys, a private prep school in North Marston, Mass.*

Barlow, Frank X. (*see also* **Kilgore Trout**). *In Jailbird, one of the pseudonyms attributed to Dr. Bob Fender, a veterinarian who writes science fiction while incarcerated at Finletter Air Force Base with Walter Starbuck. Another of his pseudonyms is Kilgore Trout.*

Barnhouse, Professor Arthur (*also* **The First Church of Barnhouse;** *see also* **dynamopsych-**

ism). *In Vonnegut's 1950 short story "Report on the Barnhouse Effect,"* in Welcome to the Monkey House (1968), *thirty-nine-year-old Professor Arthur Barnhouse accidentally discovers that one's mental powers of concentration (what Barnhouse terms "dynamopsychism") can be developed into the most powerful weapon on earth. The press preferred to use the term "Barnhouse Effect." Barnhouse first realized he possessed such powers while playing his initial game of craps with other enlisted men in his barracks. He rolled "sevens" ten times in a row. Without his participation or endorsement, the First Church of Barnhouse is established in Los Angeles.* There is an understandable tendency to look upon **Professor Barnhouse** as a supernatural visitation. **The First Church of Barnhouse** in Los Angeles has a congregation numbering in the thousands. He is godlike in neither appearance nor intellect. The man who disarms the world is single, shorter than the average American male, stout, and averse to exercise. His I.Q. is 143, which is good but certainly not sensational. He is quite mortal, about to celebrate his fortieth birthday, and in good health. If he is alone now, the isolation won't bother him too much. He was quiet and shy when I knew him, and seemed to find more companionship in books and music than in his associations at the college.

Barnhouse uses this ability to demand universal disarmament. Those nations who fail to agree face destruction of their arms. Consequently, most governments—including the United States—seek to get rid of him. At one time he offered his services to the Secretary of State, but he eventually changed his mind when he felt universal disarmament would serve a better purpose. "Gentlemen," I read aloud, "As the first superweapon with a conscience, I am removing myself from your national defense stockpile. Setting a new precedent in the behavior of ordnance, I have humane reasons for going off. A. Barnhouse."

Barnstable, Barnstable First Church of God the Utterly Indifferent, West Barnstable, West Barnstable Volunteer Fire Department. *Vonnegut wrote many of his early novels while living on Cape Cod in West Barnstable, Massachusetts. The location is used a number of times throughout his work.*

In The Sirens of Titan, *the Reverend C. Homer Redwine leads the Barnstable First Church of God the Utterly Indifferent, also known as the Church of the Weary Space Wanderer. Winston Niles Rumfoord had prophesied* a lone straggler from the Army of Mars would arrive at Redwine's church some day (ST 10). *It is where Malachi Constant/Unk/the Weary Space Wanderer arrives before being sent off to Titan as a symbolic religious sacrifice (accompanied by Beatrice and Chrono). (ST 10) The church . . . had been at various times Presbyterian, Congregationalist, Unitarian, and Universal Apocalyptic. The town's volunteer fire department is comprised mostly of Redwine's followers.*

The short story "Welcome to the Monkey House" *takes place in Barnstable County, and Frank Wirtanen, captain of the Kennedy yacht Marlin in* "Brief Encounters on the Inland Waterway" *(reprinted in* Wampeters, Foma & Granfalloons)*, is a resident of West Barnstable. Also in* Wampeters, *Vonnegut notes that serial killer Antone Costa is jailed in the Barnstable County House of Correction in his essay* "There's a Maniac Loose Out There."

Vonnegut mentions in his prologue to Timequake *that his family was living in Barnstable at the time Hemingway published* The Old Man and the Sea (1952), *trying to make it as a writer while also owning Cape Cod's only Saab dealership. Vonnegut comically associates Hemingway's heroic tale of Santiago, trying and failing to bring ashore an enormous marlin before the sharks eat it all, with the obvious solution to his own ten-year struggle with completing this novel:* Filet the fish. Throw the rest away. *He later goes on to recall* The ashes of my Indianapolis wife Jane Marie Cox are mixed with the roots of a flowering cherry tree, unmarked, in **Barnstable Village**, Massachusetts (TQ 34).

In the chapter entitled "I Used to Be the Manager" (MWC), *Vonnegut again recalls his time in Barnstable as a Saab dealer and takes a moment to poke fun at the quirky engineering of the car—perhaps emblematic of the Swedes as a people.*

(TQ Prologue) I was living in **Barnstable Village** on Cape Cod when the story appeared (Hemingway's The Old Man and the Sea). I asked a neighboring commercial fisherman what he thought of it. He said the hero was an idiot. He should have hacked off the best chunks of meat and put them in the bottom of the boat, and left the rest of the carcass for the sharks.

It could be that the sharks Hemingway had in mind were critics who hadn't much liked his first novel in ten years, *Across the River and into the Trees,* published two years earlier. As far as I know, he never said so. But the marlin could have been that novel.

(TQ 34) Our last conversation was intimate. Jane asked me, as though I knew, what would determine the exact moment of her death. She may have felt like a character in a book by me. In a sense she was. During our twenty-two years of marriage, I had decided where we were going next, to Chicago, to Schenectady, to Cape Cod. It was my work that determined what we did next. She never had a job. Raising six kids was enough for her.

I told her on the telephone that a sunburned, raffish, bored but not unhappy ten-year-old boy, whom we did not know, would be standing on the gravel slope of the boat-launching ramp at the foot of Scudder's Lane. He would gaze out at nothing in particular, birds, boats, or whatever, in the harbor of **Barnstable**, **Cape Cod**.

(TQ 39) So there was Roger Downs of Indianapolis in Colorado. Here am I, of Indianapolis, on the South Fork of Long Island. The ashes of my Indianapolis wife Jane Marie Cox are mixed with the roots of a flowering cherry tree, unmarked, in **Barnstable Village**, **Massachusetts**. The branches of that tree can be seen from the ell that Ted Adler rebuilt from scratch, after which he asked, "How the hell did I do that?"

(MWC 12) I used to be the owner and manager of an automobile dealership in **West Barnstable**, **Massachusetts**, called Saab Cape Cod. It and I went out of business thirty-three years ago. The Saab then, as now, was a Swedish car, and I now believe my failure as a dealer so long ago explains what would otherwise remain a deep mystery: Why the Swedes have never given me a Nobel Prize for Literature. Old Norwegian proverb: "Swedes have short dicks but long memories."

barracks humor (see **humor**).

Barring-gaffner. *The Barring-gaffner of Bagnialto, or This Year's Masterpiece. The Kilgore Trout novel used as toilet paper in a Libertyville, Georgia, jail by a truck driver who offers a ride to the hitchhiking author. As the driver speaks, Trout becomes aware that the story—used as the driver's toilet paper—was his own.* (BC 14) The name of the planet where Trout's book took place was Bagnialto, and a "**Barring-gaffner**" there was a government official who spun a wheel of chance once a year. Citizens submitted works of art to the government, and these were given numbers, and then they were assigned cash values according to the **Barring-gaffner's** spins of the wheel.

The viewpoint of the character of the tale was not the **Barring-gaffner**, but a humble cobbler named Gooz. Gooz lived alone, and he painted a picture of his cat. It was the only picture he had ever painted. He took it to the **Barring-gaffner**, who numbered it and put it in a warehouse crammed with works of art.

The painting by Gooz had an unprecedented gush of luck on the wheel. It became worth eighteen thousand lambos, the equivalent of one billion dollars on Earth. The **Barring-gaffner** awarded Gooz a check for that amount, most of which was taken back at once by the tax collector. The picture was given a place of honor in the National Gallery, and people lined up for miles for a chance to see a painting worth a billion dollars.

There was also a huge bonfire of all the paintings and statues and books and so on which the wheel had said were worthless. And then it was discovered that the wheel was rigged, and the **Barring-gaffner** committed suicide.

Barry, Fred T. *Appearing in* Breakfast of Champions *and* Deadeye Dick, *Fred T. Barry is chairman of the Midland City Arts Festival, the wealthiest man in Midland City, exactly the same age as Kilgore Trout, founder and chairman of the board of Barrytron, Ltd.—his successor company to Robo-Magic, and sole benefactor of the Mildred Barry Memorial Center for the Arts.* (BC 3) **Fred T. Barry**, incidentally, was exactly the same age as Trout. They had the same birthday. But they certainly didn't look anything alike. **Fred T. Barry**

didn't even look like a white man anymore, even though he was of pure English stock. As he grew older and older and happier and happier, and all his hair fell out everywhere, he came to look like an ecstatic old Chinaman.

(BC 21) People who had horrible jobs during the week used to call Monday "Blue Monday" sometimes, though, because they hated to return to work after a day of rest. When **Fred T. Barry** made up the Robo-Magic motto as a young man ("*Goodbye Blue Monday*"), he pretended that Monday was called "Blue Monday" because doing the laundry disgusted and exhausted women.

(BC 21) **Fred T. Barry** wrote these ads himself, and he predicted at the time that Robo-Magic appliances of various sorts would eventually do what he called "all the Nigger work of the world," which was lifting and cleaning and cooking and washing and ironing and tending children and dealing with filth.

(DD 20) I keep wanting to say that **Fred T. Barry** was the grandest neuter I ever saw. He certainly had no sex life. He didn't even have friends. It was all right with him if life ended at any time, obviously, since this was a suicidal flight we were on *(into Midland City after the great snow storm).*

Barry, Mildred (also **the Mildred Barry Memorial Center for the Arts**). *The mother of Fred T. Barry and the namesake of Midland City's Mildred Barry Memorial Center for the Arts,* a translucent sphere on stilts, and it was illuminated from the inside. . . . (BC 6) *It sat above Sugar Creek and served as the home for the Midland City Symphony Orchestra.*

Barry, Roland. *Roland Barry has a 100 percent disability pension for the nervous breakdown he suffered ten minutes after being sworn into the Army, when he was told to take a shower with a hundred other men. He visits Eliot Rosewater daily, but Eliot doesn't remember him from one meeting to the next. Barry is indebted to Eliot because he was the only one not to think what happened to him was funny. Just before Eliot leaves Rosewater, Roland Barry gives him this poem:* (GBR 13) "Lakes, carillons, / Pools and bells, / Fifes and freshets, / Harps and wells; / Flutes and rivers, / Streams, bassoons, / Geysers, trumpets, / Chimes, lagoons. / Hear the music, / Drink the water, / As we poor lambs / All go to slaughter. / I love you Eliot. / Good-bye. I cry. / Tears and violins. / Hearts and flowers, / Flowers and tears. / Rosewater, good-bye."

Barrytron. *First appearing in* Breakfast of Champions, *Barrytron Limited (an electronics firm in Midland City involved in secret weapons work) was originally called the Midland City Ordnance Company and later the Robo-Magic Corporation. Barrytron, Ltd. was founded in its present form by Fred T. Barry, the chairman of the board. Though Barrytron is a publicly held company in* Breakfast of Champions *(Dwayne Hoover holds stock in it and Kilgore Trout receives a single stock certificate as part of his honorarium), in* Deadeye Dick *it is wholly owned by Fred T. Barry. In* Hocus Pocus, *Eugene Debs Hartke's father worked for Barrytron through World War II. It was later bought by Du Pont.*

(BC 20) The company was manufacturing a new anti-personnel bomb for the Air Force. The bomb scattered plastic pellets instead of steel pellets, because the plastic pellets were cheaper. They were also impossible to locate in the bodies of wounded enemies by means of x-ray machines.

Barrytron had no idea it was dumping this waste into Sugar Creek. They had hired the Maritimo Brothers Construction Company, which was gangster-controlled, to build a system which would get rid of the waste. . . . **Barrytron** would be absolutely sick when it learned what a polluter it had become. Throughout its history, it had attempted to be a perfect model of corporate good citizenship, no matter what it cost.

(HP 4) By the time the war was over, the company had gotten out of the washing-machine business entirely, had changed its name to **Barrytron, Limited**, and was making weapons, airplanes, and motor vehicle parts composed of plastics it had developed on its own. My father had become the company's Vice-President in Charge of Research and Development.

Barus, Alice (*see also* **Albert Lieber**). *Vonnegut's maternal grandmother, the first wife of Albert Lieber. A discrepancy exists in Vonnegut's texts about*

the passing of Alice Barus. While writing the "Roots" chapter to Palm Sunday, *Vonnegut heavily relies on the narrative of his family written by John G. Rauch. Vonnegut writes in that text that his grandmother died of pneumonia but the timing of her death is not provided. In* Timequake, *Vonnegut says that his grandmother died while giving birth to her third child. One event does not preclude the other; it is just not stated within the texts that she died of pneumonia while giving birth.*

(PS 2) AND Professor Karl Barus the musician, and his wife Alice begat another **Alice Barus**, who, according to Uncle John, "is said to have been the most beautiful and accomplished young lady in Indianapolis. She played the piano and sang; also composed music, some of which was published." She was my mother's mother.

(PS 2) This Edwardian sport married the beautiful and musical **Alice Barus** in 1885. They had three children. My mother was the oldest. And then **Alice Barus** died of pneumonia when Mother was six.

(TQ 41) I will say for the record that my grandfather Albert Lieber's first wife, **Alice**, née **Barus**, namesake of my sister Allie, died giving birth to her third child, who was Uncle Rudy. Mother was her first. The middle child was Uncle Pete, who flunked out of MIT, but who nonetheless sired a nuclear scientist, my cousin Albert in Del Mar, California. Cousin Albert reports that he has just gone blind.

Barus, Carl. *Vonnegut's great-uncle and a professor at Brown University, Barus received the American Academy of Arts and Sciences Rumford Prize in 1900 for his research on heat. Brown named their physics building in his honor. Vonnegut uses his great-uncle in a manner reminiscent of Nim-nim's (from "The Sisters B-36") penchant for making people feel low about themselves.* (TQ 55) Listen: **Uncle Carl**, in 1900 or thereabouts, experimented with the effects of X rays and radioactivity on condensation in a cloud chamber, a wooden cylinder filled with a fog he himself had concocted. He concluded and published as a certainty that ionization was relatively unimportant in condensation.

At about the same time, friends and neighbors, the Scottish physicist Charles Thomson Rees Wilson performed similar experiments with a cloud chamber made of glass. The canny Scot proved that ions produced by X rays and radioactivity had a lot to do with condensation. He criticized **Uncle Carl** for ignoring contamination from the wood walls of his chamber, for his crude method of making clouds, and for not shielding his fog from the electrical field of his X-ray apparatus.

Wilson went on to make paths of electrically charged particles visible to the naked eye by means of his cloud chamber. In 1927, he shared a Nobel Prize for Physics for doing this. **Uncle Carl** must have felt like something the cat drug in!

Barus, Karl (*also* **Carl**). *One of Kurt Vonnegut's great-grandparents. Noted by John Rauch in* Palm Sunday *as* "'Professor' Karl Barus, 'the first real professional teacher of voice, violin, and piano in the city,' according to Uncle John, and his wife, Alice Mollman. . . . He was well educated and a definite intellectual. He never engaged in trade or business but made a good income by his teaching and lived well. **Professor Barus** originally settled in Cincinnati in the early fifties, where he was appointed Musical Director of the Cincinnati Sangverein.

"In 1858 **Dr**. **Barus** was invited to come to Indianapolis to conduct the mixed chorus of German singing societies from Indianapolis, Louisville, Cincinnati, and Columbus, Ohio, at a great Musical Festival. In 1882 he was invited by Das Deutsche Haus to come to Indianapolis to be musical director of the Maennerchor, in which position he remained until 1896" (*PS* 2).

(*PS* 2) And Professor **Karl Barus** the musician, and his wife Alice begat another Alice Barus, who, according to Uncle John, "is said to have been the most beautiful and accomplished young lady in Indianapolis. She played the piano and sang; also composed music, some of which was published."

She was my mother's mother.

(*TQ* 55) Put this in your pipe and smoke it: My maternal great-uncle **Carl Barus** was a founder and president of the American Physical Society. A building at Brown University is named in his honor. **Uncle Carl Barus** was a professor there for many years. I never met him. My big brother did. Until this summer of 1996, Bernie and I had thought of him as a serene contributor to modest but tidy increases in human understanding of the laws of Nature. . . .

Listen: **Uncle Carl**, in 1900 or thereabouts, experimented with the effects of X rays and radioactivity on condensation in a cloud chamber, a wooden cylinder filled with a fog he himself had concocted. He concluded and published as a certainty that ionization was relatively unimportant in condensation.

At about the same time, friends and neighbors, the Scottish physicist Charles Thomson Rees Wilson performed similar experiments with a cloud chamber made of glass. The canny Scot proved that ions produced by X rays and radioactivity had a lot to do with condensation. He criticized **Uncle Carl** for ignoring contamination from the wood walls of his chamber, for his crude method of making clouds, and for not shielding his fog from the electrical field of his X-ray apparatus.

Wilson went on to make paths of electrically charged particles visible to the naked eye by means of his cloud chamber. In 1927, he shared a Nobel Prize for Physics for doing this. **Uncle Carl** must have felt like something the cat drug in!

(*TQ* 62) My children and grandchildren weren't there (*at the* Timequake *clambake*). That was OK, perfectly understandable. It wasn't my birthday, and I wasn't a guest of honor. The heroes that evening were Frank Smith and Kilgore Trout. My kids and my kids' kids had other fish to fry. Perhaps I should say my kids and my kids' kids had other lobsters and clams and oysters and potatoes and corn on the cob to steam in seaweed.

Whatever!

Get it right! Remember **Uncle Carl Barus**, and get it right!

Barzov, Major. *The Soviet army military observer assisting Pi Ying, a Far Eastern Communist guerrilla chief in the 1953 short story "All the King's Horses," reprinted in* Welcome to the Monkey House (1968). *Barzov stands by while Pi Ying prepares to have a chess match with Colonel Kelly involving the sixteen captured Americans as Kelly's chess pieces. When Kelly's "pieces" are taken, they are condemned to death. To Pi Ying's right, indistinct in the shadows, stood* **Major Barzov**, *the taciturn Russian military observer. He acknowledged Kelly's stare with a slow nod. Kelly continued to stare fixedly. The arrogant, bristle-haired major became restless, folding and unfolding his arms, re-*

peatedly rocking back and forth in his black boots. "I wish I could help you," he said at last.

During the course of the game Pi Ying is killed, and Barzov takes over for him. **Major Barzov** wasn't above the kind of entertainment Pi Ying had found so diverting. But Kelly sensed the difference between the major's demeanor and that of the guerrilla chief. The major was resuming the game, not because he liked it, but because he wanted to prove that he was one hell of a bright fellow, and that the Americans were dirt. Apparently, he didn't realize that Pi Ying had already lost the game. Either that, or Kelly had miscalculated.

In an ominous geopolitical metaphor, the Soviet major expresses the kind of cold war notion that continued to nag the West until the fall of the Soviet Union. "There will be others like Pi Ying eager to play you with live men, and I hope I will again be privileged to be an observer." He smiled brightly. "When and where would you like it to be?"

basement (*see also* **air-raid shelter, cellar,** *and* **subbasement**). *In a curious plot repetition, Vonnegut places a number of major characters and incidents in basements and other underground dwellings.* In a number of passages throughout his work, Vonnegut recalls taking refuge in the underground meatlocker in Dresden during its firebombing. He usually includes his participation in "corpse mining" after the attack (digging bodies and valuables out of charred basements). Among the many textual citations, there are some passages in the fiction of particular note. In* Player Piano *Paul Proteus is kidnapped by the Ghost Shirt Society and secreted in an abandoned Ilium air raid shelter. He is later captured by the ruling technocracy and held for trial in the basement cell of the Ilium Police Headquarters.*

In The Sirens of Titan, *Boaz and Unk are caught deep within the caves of Mercury. Once the two realize that the only way out of the caves is to reorient their ship's sense of up and down, Boaz remains behind with his loving Harmoniums while Unk escapes the cave by essentially having the ship navigate downward in order to actually go up.*

---

* See the author's doctoral dissertation "What Goes Around Comes Around: The Naive, Schizophrenic, Resurrected Cycle in the Novels of Kurt Vonnegut" (1987).

Mother Night's Howard Campbell *writes his memoirs from the basement cell of an Old Jerusalem jail. Earlier in the text the Soviet plot to kidnap Campbell from the basement of Dr. Jones's building is foiled by his Blue Fairy Godmother, Colonel Frank Wirtanen.*

Cat's Cradle's Franklin Hoenikker *lived in the basement of Jack's Hobby Shop where he built a scale model of an island society (foreshadowing his impact on San Lorenzo). He also had a long-term love affair with Jack's wife down in his basement apartment.*

In God Bless You, Mr. Rosewater, *Fred Rosewater goes down to his basement and finds the Merrihue Rosewater account of the family's history which prompts him to plot his own suicide. Back in Rosewater County, the Dresden fire alarm ("the loudest fire alarm in the Western Hemisphere") prompts Bella of Bella's Beauty Nook to suffer a mild heart attack in her basement shop.*

In Slaughterhouse-Five, *Vonnegut recalls his early days as a news reporter and having to report on the gruesome death of a veteran who was squashed to death by an elevator headed to the basement when he got his wedding ring stuck in the door. Within the text's story, Billy Pilgrim writes from his basement rumpus room about his time-tripping experiences in a letter addressed to the* Ilium News Leader. *Science fiction writer Kilgore Trout is said to live in a basement apartment two miles from Pilgrim's house in Ilium, New York. In* Breakfast of Champions *Trout lives in a basement apartment in Cohoes, New York.*

Jailbird's Walter Starbuck *is jailed in the basement cell of a New York City police station. Having once ignorantly implicated Leland Clewes of un-American activities (just prior to the McCarthy hearings in the 1950s), Starbuck later visits Leland and Sarah Clewes in their Tudor City basement apartment. Mary Kathleen O'Looney dies in a subbasement of Grand Central Station after having been struck by a taxi.*

Deadeye Dick's Rudy Waltz *is placed in the basement holding cage of the Midland City Police Department. It is there that patrolman Anthony Squires nicknames him "Deadeye Dick" for killing Eloise Metzger. Other officers brought curious gawkers to view the young sniper until they cleared the room for a visit by the grieved George Metzger. Later, after the tremendous snowstorm which nearly wiped out Midland City, Rudy locates his mother in a hastily arranged ward in the hospital's basement— near the morgue which once held Eloise Metzger.*

Bluebeard's Rabo Karabekian often took his meals in the basement while an apprentice to Dan Gregory. Later, Rabo stored sixty-three gallons of the unstable Sateen Dura-Luxe in his Long Island basement. In his later years, Rabo was asked to reclaim the remains of "Windsor Blue Number Seventeen," his sixty-four-foot Abstract Expressionist triptych which fell victim to the faulty paint. The painting was stored in the third subbasement of the GEFFCo Building. After cleaning the canvases, Rabo painted his masterpiece "Now It's the Women's Turn."

In Hocus Pocus, Eugene Debs Hartke's father informs his son in their basement that he will enter him in the school science fair and proceeds to take full control of his project's development. The duplicity of the father and the unwitting, uncaring obedience of the son result in an odd series of events leading to Eugene's admission to West Point, the start of his long and distinguished military career. (TQ 3) Trout described the third atom bomb like this: "A purple motherfucker as big as a boiler in the **basement** of a mid-size junior high school."

It was too big to fit inside the bomb bay. It was slung underneath the plane's belly, and cleared the runway by a foot when *Joy's Pride* took off into the wild blue yonder.

(TQ 14) "My father murdered my mother," said Kilgore Trout, "when I was twelve years old."

"Her body was in our **basement**," said Trout, "but all I knew was that she had disappeared. Father swore he had no idea what had become of her. He said, as wife-murderers often do, that maybe she had gone to visit relatives. He killed her that morning, after I left for school. . . ."

(BAG Any Reasonable Offer) Old Mrs. Hellbrunner called right after Delahanty. Her house has been on the market for three years, and it represents about all that's left of the Hellbrunner family's fortune. Twenty-seven rooms, nine baths, ballroom, den, study, music room, solarium, turrets with slits for crossbowmen, simulated drawbridge and portcullis, and a dry moat. Somewhere

in the **basement**, I suppose, are racks and gibbets for insubordinate domestics.

(BAG Hal Irwin's Magic Lamp) Hal Irwin built his magic lamp in his **basement** in Indianapolis, in the summer of 1929. . . . Like many husbands back then, he had a workshop in the **basement**.

(MWC TWO) It was pure nonsense, pointless destruction. The whole city was burned down, and it was a British atrocity, not ours. They sent in night bombers, and they came in and set the whole town on fire with a new kind of incendiary bomb. And so everything organic, except my little POW group, was consumed by fire. It was a military experiment to find out if you could burn down a whole city by scattering incendiaries over it.

Of course, as prisoners of war, we dealt hands-on with dead Germans, digging them out of **basements** because they had suffocated there, and taking them to a huge funeral pyre. And I heard—I didn't see it done—that they gave up this procedure because it was too slow and, of course, the city was starting to smell pretty bad. And they sent in guys with flamethrowers.

See also: PP I; III; XXIX; XXXI; *MN* 21–24; 29; *CC* 17; 35; 43; *GBR* 6; 13; *SL5* 1–2; 5; 8; *MH* The Foster Portfolio; *MH* More Stately Mansions; *WJ* I:4; *BC* 2–34; 8; 15; 18; 21; Epilogue; *JB* 20; Epilogue; *PS* from "Roots—Account of the Ancestry of Kurt Vonnegut, Jr., by an Ancient Friend of His Family"—formal essay by the late John G. Rauch of Indianapolis; *PS* Self-Interview; *PS* Playmates; *DD* 2; 12–14; 21–23; 26; *Blue* 4; 7; 10–11; 13–15; 21–22; 26; 31; 34; *HP* 3–4; 14; 38; *WFG* Brief Encounters on the Inland Waterway; *TQ* 30; *BAG* The Package; *BAG* Poor Little Rich Town; *BAG* The Boy Who Hated Girls.

Bassett, Earnest S. *Doctor Bassett was the manager of the Pittsburgh Works who passed away, setting in motion the jockeying for his replacement. Kroner uses the Meadows (q.v.) and the old oak tree as a setting for a brief eulogy.* (PP XIX) "Ernie was manager of the Philadelphia Works for five years, of the Pittsburgh Works for seven. He was my friend; he was *our* friend: a great American, a great engineer, a great manager, a great pioneer at the head of the procession of civilization, opening new, undreamed-of doors to better things, for better living, for more people, at less cost. . . . He gave himself unstintingly engineeringwise, managershipwise, personalitywise, Americanwise, and—" Kroner paused to look impressively from face to face. Again he talked to the clouds—"heartwise."

Batavia. *In* Hocus Pocus, *the small city in Western New York where Eugene Debs Hartke's wife and mother-in-law are confined in a "lunatic asylum" after his imprisonment. It is also the home of Clarence Daffodil-11 Johnson, the chief of police of Batavia, New York, a relative of Wilbur Swain's by government decree* (Slapstick).

Batsford, Ted. *In the short story "Poor Little Rich Town," this longtime Spruce Falls resident submits his extraordinarily large ball of string in the "string-saving class" of the town's annual Hobby Show. As Fire Chief Atkins explains to efficiency expert Newell Cady,* "It's **Ted Batsford**'s string. Can you believe it—the very first bit he ever started saving, right in the center of this ball, he picked up during the second Cleveland administration." *Cady is dismayed that such pedestrian pursuits are so highly prized by Spruce Falls but is cut short uttering a sarcastic observation when Upton Beaton distracts the conversation by taking note of Mrs. Dickie's flower arrangement entry.*

Batten, Barton, Durstine & Osborn. *In* Deadeye Dick, *Felix Waltz's soon-to-be employers, a large multinational advertising agency which actually does exist in New York City. It is among the most awarded agencies, according to the Gunn Report.*

Battle Hymn of the Republic. (GBK John Brown) "I want to get this straight," I said. "Are you saying that Thomas Jefferson, possibly our country's most beloved founding father, after George Washington, was an evil man?"

"Let that, while my body lies a-molderin' in the grave," said John Brown, "be my truth which goes marchin' on."

(Choral rendition of one stanza of "**Battle Hymn of the Republic**.")

Battle of Boca Raton. *In* The Sirens of Titan, *the battle in which Sergeant Brackman of Unk and*

Boaz's Martian assault team was badly wounded. He was the only Martian survivor—twenty-three others were killed.

Battle of the Bulge. *The final great assault of the German Army in December 1944, during which Vonnegut and his friend Bernard V. O'Hare were taken prisoner. They were eventually sent to work in Dresden, where they witnessed the famous firebombing. Billy Pilgrim endures this central episode in* Slaughterhouse-Five *and the events leading up to Vonnegut's actual capture are recounted in various places in* Fates Worse Than Death.

(TQ 19) Goebbels remembers that his kids have brought the game of Bingo with them. It was captured intact from American troops during the **Battle of the Bulge** some four months earlier. I myself was captured intact during that battle. . . . and because the grownups in the bunker have been so busy during the rise of Hitler, and now his fall, the Goebbels kids are the only ones who know how the game is played. They learned from a neighbor kid, whose family owned a prewar Bingo set.

There is this amazing scene in the story: A boy and a girl, explaining the rules of Bingo, become the center of the Universe for Nazis in full regalia, including a gaga Adolf Hitler.

(BAG Preface) This collection includes stories that draw on Vonnegut's World War Two experiences. The events on which *Slaughterhouse-Five* was based are by now widely known: how Vonnegut was captured by the Germans at the **Battle of the Bulge**, was held as a prisoner of war in Dresden, was sheltered in an underground meat storage room when that city was incinerated in massive air raids, and after the Nazi defeat wandered briefly in a Germany awash in refugees before he was reunited with American forces. "Der Arme Dolmetscher," "Souvenir," and "The Cruise of the *Jolly Roger*" treat the aftermath of war with a varying mix of humor and poignancy.

Battle of the Somme. (TQ 23) When Trout was zapped back to a line outside a blood bank in San Diego, California, in 1991, he could remember how his story about the guy with his head between his legs and his ding-dong atop his neck, "Albert Hardy," would end. But he couldn't write that finale for ten years, until free will kicked in again. Albert Hardy would be blown to pieces while a soldier in the **Second Battle of the Somme** in World War One.

Battola, Will. *In the short story "Lovers Anonymous," collected in* Bagombo Snuff Box *(1999), Battola is among a group of young men attending Sheila Hinckley's wedding who came to call themselves Lovers Anonymous. The unnamed narrator recalls Battola's words as the group drinks and sifts through their imaginations of what could have been had Sheila looked twice in their direction. But as* **Will Battola,** *the plumber, said one time, "Sheila Hinckley is now a spare whitewall tire on the Thunderbird of my dreams."*

　　Later in the story when some of the members of Lovers Anonymous meet for lunch in the local drug store, Battola remarks that Herb White's intentions to turn the ell of his home into a separate, full apartment with bathroom and kitchen, increases curiosity among the group about what is happening in Herb's marriage. Battola particularly points out the odd coincidence that Herb White has managed to make sure everyone working on his remodeling project is part of Lovers Anonymous. Most of the group are now local business owners in North Crawford, New Hampshire.

Bauerbeck, Nelson. *Bauerbeck is the old art teacher who rejects taking on Rabo Karabekian as a student at the Art Students League in New York, on the basis of his technically correct, but passionless, portfolio. (Blue 23) "On the basis of the very first picture in your portfolio," he said. "It told me, 'Here is a man without passion.' And I asked myself what I now ask you: 'Why should I teach him the language of painting, since there seems to be absolutely nothing which he is desperate to talk about?'"*

Bavaria. *In* God Bless You, Mr. Rosewater, *Eliot Rosewater's first nervous breakdown occurs after bayoneting three volunteer firemen in a smoke-filled clarinet factory in Bavaria. He was led to believe the building was filled with S.S. troops.*

Bay State Progressive. *As a Harvard student, Walter Starbuck was cochairman of this radical weekly newspaper. While working there he first met* Mary Kathleen O'Looney who volunteered her services and was put to work as the circulation manager, "handing out the paper at factory gates and along breadlines and so on" (JB 14). When Alexander Hamilton McCone found out about Starbuck's participation with the paper, he cut him off from support. Starbuck was able to graduate because McCone had already paid the year's tuition.

Beagle, Her Majesty's Ship (also **The Voyage of the Beagle**). *The vessel upon which Charles Darwin sailed as the unpaid naturalist during its voyage to the Galápagos Islands. Based on that excursion Darwin wrote* The Voyage of the Beagle, *the text in which he first set down his theory of evolution. The ship, Darwin, and his text are all frequently cited in* Galápagos.

Beame, Timothy. *The onetime assistant secretary of agriculture under Franklin Delano Roosevelt and Harvard alum who berates Walter Starbuck for his failure to protect the powers above him during the Watergate scandals. Beame is a former Rhodes Scholar and still actively running the law firm of Beame, Mearns, Weld and Weld. (JB 7)* "You ninny, you Harvard abortion, you incomparably third-rate little horse's ass," he said, and he arose from his chair. "You and Clewes have destroyed the good reputation of the most unselfish and intelligent generation of public servants this country has ever known! My God—who can care about you now, or about Clewes? Too bad he's in jail! Too bad we can't find another job for you! . . . The most important thing they teach at Harvard," he said, "is that a man can obey every law and still be the worst criminal of his time."

Bearden, Miss. *In the short story "Ambitious Sophomore," collected in* Bagombo Snuff Box *(1999), Miss Bearden is Lincoln High School's athletic office secretary, who watches in awe as sophomore piccoloist Leroy Duggan marches up and down the hall in his new and huge band uniform. Band director George M. Helmholtz prompts his young student for information about her reaction to his uniform that makes him look almost like a superhero sporting enormous shoulders and athletic waist.* "Did **Miss Bearden** like the uniform?" *said Helmholtz.*

"I don't know," said Leroy. "She didn't say anything. She just looked and looked."

Bearse, Alfy. (*BC* 12) When he (*Kilgore Trout*) lived on Cape Cod, for instance, the only person he could greet warmly and by name was **Alfy Bearse**, who was a one-armed albino. "Hot enough for you, **Alfy**?" he would say. "Where you been keeping yourself, **Alfy**?" he'd say. "You're a sight for sore eyes, **Alfy**," he'd say.

Beaton, Upton. *In the short story "Poor Little Rich Town," collected in* Bagombo Snuff Box *(1999), Upton Beaton is one of the old-line descendants of the Spruce Falls wealthy class. He is at once the voice of reason, the one most expressive of the town's values, and the one who very coyly plays along with Newell Cady's compulsiveness to streamline virtually every institution in town, calmly knowing that in the end Cady's plans will be rejected by the town once they realize what his changes have wrought.*

Beaton's introduction to the story lays out some of the conflicts and pitfalls facing efficiency expert Newell Cady's entrance versus the cultural stakes for the town. In response to Fire Chief Atkins's enthusiastic endorsement of making Cady a member of the volunteer fire department as well as the head judge of the Hobby Show, Beaton chimes in with his bit of wisdom. "Audaces fortuna juvat!" *said* **Upton Beaton**, *who was a tall, fierce-seeming sixty-five. He was the last of what had been the first family of Spruce Falls.* "Fortune," *he translated after a pause,* "favors the bold, that's true. But gentlemen—" *and he paused again, portentously, while Chief Atkins looked worried and the other members of the fire department shifted about on their folding chairs. Like his forebears,* **Beaton** *had an ornamental education from Harvard, and like them, he lived in Spruce Falls because it took little effort for a* **Beaton** *to feel superior to his neighbors there. He survived on money his family had made during the short-lived boom.*

"But," **Beaton** *said again, as he stood up,* "is this the kind of fortune we want? We are being asked to waive the three-year residence requirement for membership in the fire department in Mr. Cady's case, and thereby all our memberships are cheapened. If I may say so, the post of judge of the Hobby

Show is of far greater significance than it would seem to an outsider. In our small village, we have only small ways of honoring our great, but we, for generations now, have taken pains to reserve those small honors for those of us who have shown such greatness as it is possible to achieve in the eyes of a village. I hasten to add that those honors that have come to me are marks of respect for my family and my age, not for myself, and are exceptions that should probably be curtailed."

He sighed. "If we waive this proud tradition, then that one, and then another, all for money, we will soon find ourselves with nothing left to wave but the white flag of an abject surrender of all we hold dear!" He sat, folded his arms, and stared at the floor. . . .

"What is a village profited if it shall gain a real estate boom and lose its own soul?"

For all his warnings to the assembled volunteer firefighters and Chief Atkins in particular, Beaton plays a most interesting part in the story in that he becomes a constant companion to Newell Cady, providing all sorts of information that Cady then obsessively redesigns for more efficient outcomes. "**Beaton**'s function is to provide Cady with the facts and figures behind village activities and then to endorse outrageously Cady's realistic suggestions for reforms, which followed facts and figures as the night the day." *This is part of Beaton's passive-aggressive strategy to undo Cady's influence. He provides enough rope to Cady to doom his plans.*

Cady undoes the egalitarian spirit of the Hobby Show and later, in a most tactless and unselfconscious moment, suggests the town move to rural free delivery of their mail instead of dealing with the inefficient ways of postmistress Mrs. Dickie, all the while thinking he has the advantage of an outsider to see things others do not. "One-eyed man in the land of the blind, you might say." *To which Beaton responds sharply.* "A one-eyed man might as well be blind," *declared* **Upton Beaton**, "if he doesn't watch people's faces and doesn't give the blind credit for the senses they do have."

"What on earth are you talking about?" said Cady.

"If you'd looked at Mrs. Dickie's face instead of how she was doing her work, you would have seen she was crying," said **Beaton**. "Her husband died in a fire, saving some of these people around the village you call blind. You talk a lot about wasting time, Mr. Cady—for a really big waste of time, walk around the village someday and try to find somebody who doesn't know he can have his mail brought to his door anytime he wants to."

Once the town realizes its error in too quickly adopting Cady as one of their own and having him overturn their traditions, it is Beaton who wishes to moderate the tone of the room, exhibiting the same generosity of spirit for Cady as the townspeople expected of each other. "He's a brilliant man, and I'm sure he'll see the wisdom in the residence requirement. A village isn't like a factory, where you can walk in and see what's being made at a glance, and then look at the books and see if it's a good or bad operation. We're not manufacturing or selling anything. We're trying to live together. Every man's got to be his own expert at that, and it takes years."

When the avaricious real estate salesman arrives at the end of the story to see how the town is getting ready for their change in fortune, Beaton very calmly and sincerely expresses the wishes of Spruce Falls, "We've decided to wait and see how Mr. Cady adapts himself, before we put anything else on the market. He's having a tough time, but he's got a good heart, I think, and we're all rooting for him."

Beelzebub. *The Devil, also known as Lord of the Flies. The great series of bowls outside the Rumfoord mansion are described in such comparative terms, and the largest of the Lutz Carillon bells at Tarkington College is named for him. Franklin Hoenikker is also compared to him for the power he possesses over his trapped bugs.* (CC 37) And then, one day, one Sunday, I found out where the fugitive from justice, the model-maker, the Great God Jehovah and **Beelzebub** of bugs in Mason jars was—where Franklin Hoenikker could be found.
See also: ST 1; HP 7–8; FWD XIX.

Beethoven (also **Beethoven's Ninth Symphony**). *In* God Bless You, Mr. Rosewater, *the clingy and classless Caroline Rosewater plays an endless rack of Beethoven records at a much higher speed than is required.*

Breakfast of Champions's *Rabo wears a*

Beethoven *sweatshirt to the bar in the Holiday Inn prior to the Midland City Arts Festival.*

Beethoven is frequently referred to in Galápagos *not simply as the measure of creative genius, but as the hallmark of "oversized brains." The common refrain at the passing of a number of characters is, "Oh, well—he wasn't going to write Beethoven's Ninth Symphony anyway." First uttered by Hjalmar Arvid Bostrom at the funeral of Per Olaf Rosenquist and later at the funeral for the decapitated Leon Trout, Trout goes on to mark the passing of dogs and people with the same pronouncement. Near the end of Trout's one thousand millennia walking the earth, when humanity has evolved into nothing more cunning than sea lions, he looks forward to entering the "blue tunnel" to the afterlife* (Gal 2:8) Nothing ever happens around here anymore that I haven't seen or heard so many times before. Nobody, surely, is going to write **Beethoven's Ninth Symphony**—or tell a lie, or start a Third World War.
(FWD VI) (Speaking of composers: My sister Alice asked our father when she was about ten years old if he and Mother used to dance to **Beethoven**.)

In Timequake, Beethoven *becomes an emotional fulcrum held in a loosening grip by Zoltan, already on the edge of his masculinity and intellect.* (TQ 9) Monica and Zoltan were talking in her office at the Academy that Christmas Eve, 2000. Zoltan was crying and laughing simultaneously. They were the same age, forty, which made them baby boomers. They didn't have any kids. Because of her, his dingdong didn't work anymore. Zoltan was crying and laughing about that, certainly, but mostly about a tone-deaf kid next door, who had composed and orchestrated an acceptable, if derivative, string quartet in the manner of **Beethoven**, with the help of a new computer program called Wolfgang.

Nothing would do but that the father of the obnoxious kid show Zoltan the sheet music his son's printer had spit out that morning and ask him if it was any good or not.

Later in Timequake, *Dr. Fleon Sunoco engages in late-night, unauthorized medical research on cadavers in a manner reminiscent of early medical lore, looking for proof that the greatest minds on earth evolved in a manner that recalls current scientific discussion about bionic improvements to organic matter. Beethoven is again used as among the heights of human genius. (TQ 27)* At night, though, with nobody around, he slices up high-IQ brains, looking for little radios. He doesn't think Mensa members had them inserted surgically. He thinks they were born with them, so the receivers have to be made of meat. Sunoco has written in his secret journal: "There is no way an unassisted human brain, which is nothing more than a dog's breakfast, three and a half pounds of blood-soaked sponge, could have written 'Stardust,' let alone **Beethoven's Ninth Symphony**."

(BAG Coda to My Career) No artist from anywhere, however, not even Shakespeare, not even **Beethoven**, not even James Whitcomb Riley, has changed the course of so many lives all over the planet as have four hayseeds in Ohio, two in Dayton and two in Akron. How I wish Dayton and Akron were in Indiana! Ohio could have Kokomo and Gary.

begat, beget, begetting. *In Vonnegut's own playful way, he describes the births of various fictional characters, machines, explosives, and his own ancestors in biblical terms. (GBR 1)* And Noah **begat** Samuel, who married Geraldine Ames Rockefeller. *(GBR 1)* And Samuel **begat** Lister Ames Rosewater, who married Eunice Eliot Morgan. *(GBR 1)* That he *(Senator Lister Ames Rosewater)* is or ever was an Indiana person is a tenuous political fiction. And Lister **begat** Eliot. *(GBR 1)* And Eliot became a drunkard, a Utopian dreamer, a tinhorn saint, an aimless fool.

    Begat he not a soul.

(GBR 8) And George **begat** Abraham, who became a Congregationalist minister. . . . In the jungle, Abraham **begat** Merrihue. *(GBR 8)* But, before he did that *(Merrihue Rosewater, the parson's son who shot out his brains)*, he wrote a family history and he **begat** poor Fred, the insurance man. *(Slap Epilogue)* The boy **begat** Melody at the age of fourteen. *(PS 2)* AND Professor Karl Barus the musician, and his wife Alice **begat** another Alice Barus, who, according to Uncle John, "is said to have been the most beautiful and accomplished young lady in Indianapolis. She played the piano and sang; also composed music, some of which was published."

She was my mother's mother. . . .

Yes, and Peter Lieber, the limping war veteran, and his wife Sophia **begat** Albert Lieber, who became an Indianapolis brewer and bon vivant.

He was my mother's father. . . .

Henry Schnull, the merchant and banker, and his wife Matilda **begat** Nanette Schnull, who, according to Uncle John, "was a very beautiful woman in her prime, and had a lovely speaking and singing voice. She often sang in public. She laughed readily, enjoyed people, and was greatly admired by a host of friends."

She was my father's mother. . . .

And Clemens Vonnegut, the Free Thinker and founder of the Vonnegut Hardware Company, and his wife Katarina **begat** Bernard Vonnegut, who, Uncle John says, "was from earliest youth artistic." *(Gal 1:13)* *Zenji Hiroguchi **begat** Gokubi one million and five years ago, and then, one million years ago, this young genius **begat** Mandarax. Yes, and at the time of his **begetting** of Mandarax, his wife was about to give birth to his first human child. *(Gal 1:13) The only human being *Zengi Hiroguchi would ever **beget** was a darling but furry daughter (Akiko) he would never see.*

(Gal 1:38) Glacco **begat** dagonite, so to speak, and both were descendants of Greek fire and gunpowder and dynamite and cordite and TNT.

beginning, middle . . . and end. *(PP XVIII)* "Descent into the Maelstrom, II" he thought wearily, and closed his eyes, and gave himself over to the one sequence of events that had never failed to provide a **beginning**, **a middle**, and **a satisfactory end**. *The descent Proteus thinks of is his sexual relationship with Anita.*

(MN 32) "I admire form," I *(Howard W. Campbell)* said. "I admire things with a **beginning**, **a middle**, **an end**—and, whenever possible, a moral, too."

(SL5 5) "There are no telegrams on Tralfamadore. But you're right: each clump of symbols is a brief, urgent message—describing a situation, a scene. We Tralfamadorians read them all at once, not one after the other. There isn't any particular relationship between all the messages, except that the author has chosen them carefully, so that, when seen all at once, they produce an image of life that is beautiful and surprising and deep. There is **no be-**

ginning, **no middle**, **no end**, no suspense, no moral, no causes, no effects. What we love in our books are the depths of many marvelous moments seen all at one time." *The Tralfamadorians explain to Billy the nature of their narrative texts.*
(BC 19) I had no respect whatsoever for the creative works of either the painter or the novelist. I thought Karabekian with his meaningless pictures had entered into a conspiracy with millionaires to make poor people feel stupid. I thought Beatrice Keedsler had joined hands with other old-fashioned storytellers to make people believe that life had leading characters, minor characters, significant details, insignificant details, that it had lessons to be learned, tests to be passed, and **a beginning, a middle, and an end**. *Vonnegut makes these remarks after he enters the text and watches his characters discuss art in the bar of the Midland City Holiday Inn.*

Begum, Arjumand Banu. (DD 22) It *(the Taj Mahal)* was a memorial to something Fred T. Barry never had, and which I have never had, which is a wife. Her name was **Arjumand Banu Begum**. She died in childbirth. Her husband, who ordered the Taj Mahal to be built at any cost, was the Mogul emperor Shah Jahan.

belfry *(see also* **cupola** *and* **tower***). Aside from references to characters having "bats in their belfries," such structures have plot significance in* Jailbird, Deadeye Dick, *and* Hocus Pocus. *In* Jailbird, *it was from the belfry of the Cuyahoga Bridge and Iron Company that Daniel McCone was joined by his sons Alexander and John to watch on Christmas morning as their hired thugs and the civil authorities put down a peaceful union demonstration, resulting in the Cuyahoga Massacre.*

An errant shot from the cupola of Rudy Waltz's home winds up killing Eloise Metzger a number of blocks away and is the reason Rudy is tagged with the eponymous nickname. Vonnegut admits that he pulled off the same stunt when he was a young child but without a tragic outcome.

In Hocus Pocus, *the belfry high atop the library on the Tarkington campus offers college president Tex Johnson the opportunity to snipe at the marauding convicts who escaped the prison across the lake*

in Scipio. Johnson is eventually captured by the convicts and crucified for the many deaths he caused.

In an early short story entitled "This son of Mine," collected in Bagombo Snuff Box (1999), *Vonnegut uses the term to describe a scene of the debauched nouveau riche, reminiscent of* The Great Gatsby. But Franklin didn't. He got as far as the country club's parking lot, then didn't go in.

Suddenly he didn't want to see his friends—the killers of their fathers' dreams. Their young faces were the faces of old men hanging upside down, their expressions grotesque and unintelligible. Hanging upside down, they swung from bar to ballroom to crap game, and back to bar. No one pitied them in that great human **belfry**, because they were going to be rich, if they weren't already. They didn't have to dream, or even lift a finger.

Franklin went to a movie alone. The movie failed to suggest a way in which he might improve his life. It suggested that he be kind and loving and humble, and Franklin was nothing if he wasn't kind and loving and humble.
See also: JB Prologue; *HP* 3; 7; 9; 20; 28; 37.

belief. *The sincere as well as arbitrary nature of various belief systems is a frequent theme of Vonnegut's work. In* Player Piano, *members of the latter-day Ghost Shirt Society commit fraud by addressing Paul Proteus as an apparent coconspirator in a letter from the Ghost Shirt Society reaffirming their belief in the need for a society with purposeful human activity at its core.* (PP XXX) "You perhaps disagree with the antique and vain notion of Man's being a creation of God.

"But I find it a far more defensible **belief** than the one implicit in intemperate faith in lawless technological progress—namely, that man is on earth to create more durable and efficient images of himself, and, hence, to eliminate any justification at all for his own continued existence.

"Faithfully yours,
"Doctor Paul Proteus"
The central philosophy of Bokononist teaching is encapsulated in this short analogy: (CC 47) It was the **belief** of Charles Atlas that muscles could be built without bar bells or spring exercisers, could be built by simply pitting one set of muscles against another.

It was the **belief** of Bokonon that good societies could be built only by pitting good against evil, and by keeping the tension between the two high at all times.

In 1972 at the Republican National Convention, Vonnegut made this observation. (WFG In a Manner That Must Shame God Himself) That may not really be the message in the *(William F.)* Buckley smile. But I guarantee you that it was the monolithic **belief** that underlay the Republican National Convention in Miami Beach, Florida, in 1972. *Vonnegut phrases that belief as follows:* "Yes, oh yes, my dear man—I understand what you have said so clumsily. But you know in your heart what every Winner knows: that one must behave heartlessly toward Losers, if one hopes to survive."

Vonnegut takes such a simple view of his own belief system that he is bewildered anyone would find him threatening. (PS The People One Knows) The **beliefs** I have to defend are so soft and complicated, actually, and, when vivisected, turn into bowls of undifferentiated mush. I am a pacifist, I am an anarchist, I am a planetary citizen, and so on.

(PS Religion) How proud I became of our **belief** *(his family's legendary belief in freethinking atheism)*, how pigheadedly proud, even, is the most evident thing in my writing, I think. Haven't I already attributed the breakup of my first marriage in part to my wife's failure to share my family **belief** with me?

(PS Religion) "I have said that one guess is as good as another, but that is only roughly so. Some guesses are crueler than others—which is to say, harder on human beings, and on other animals as well. The **belief** that God wants heretics burned to death is a case in point. Some guesses are more suicidal than others. The **belief** that a true lover of God is immune to the bites of copperheads and rattlesnakes is a case in point. Some guesses are greedier and more egocentric than others. **Belief** in the divine right of kings and presidents is a case in point."

(FWD XX) It is my serious **belief** that those of us who become humorists (suicidal or not) feel free (as most people do not) to speak of life itself as a dirty joke, even though life is all there is or ever can be.

*We do, doodily do, doodily do, doodily do
What we must, muddily must, muddily must,
     muddily must:
Muddily do, muddily must, muddily do, muddily must,
Until we bust, bodily bust, bodily bust, bodily bust.*

This refrain first appears thirty-two years earlier in The Sirens of Titan, *but Vonnegut doesn't make mention of that when repeating it here.*

(TQ 7) He asked what relatives of mine had been wounded in wars. As far as I knew, only one. That was my great-grandfather Peter Lieber, an immigrant who became a brewer in Indianapolis after being wounded in one leg during our Civil War. He was a Freethinker, which is to say a skeptic about conventional religious **beliefs**, as had been Voltaire and Thomas Jefferson and Benjamin Franklin and so on. And as would be Kilgore Trout and I.

(TQ 45) The optimism that infused so much of our writing was based on our **belief** that after Magna Carta, and then the Declaration of Independence, and then the Bill of Rights, and then the Emancipation Proclamation, and then Article XIX of the Constitution, which in 1920 entitled women to vote, some scheme for economic justice could also be devised. That was the logical next step.

(BAG Preface) Many of the stories offer fascinating insights into attitudes and preoccupations of Americans in the fifties. At General Electric the motto was "Progress is our most important product," a slogan that sums up the decade's optimism and the extension of the wartime can-do spirit. There was widespread **belief** in the ability of science and technology to go on improving everyday life. The assumption of a stable society that could offer the average family a happy home, financial advancement, and living conditions made easier and more glamorous by ever better gadgetry provides the context for these stories.

(GBK Introduction) About **belief** or lack of **belief** in an afterlife: Some of you may know I am neither Christian nor Jewish nor Buddhist, nor a conventionally religious person of any sort. I am a humanist, which means, in part, that I have tried to behave decently without any expectation of rewards or punishments after I'm dead. My German-American ancestors, the earliest of whom settled in our Middle West about the time of our Civil War, called themselves "Freethinkers," which is the same sort of thing. My great grandfather Clemens Vonnegut wrote, for example, "If what Jesus said was good, what can it matter whether he was God or not?"

(*GBK* Isaac Asimov) I asked him if he was still writing, and he said, "All the time! If I couldn't write all the time, this would be hell for me. Earth would have been a hell for me if I couldn't write all the time. Hell itself would be bearable for me, as long as I could write all the time."

"Thank goodness there is no Hell," I said.

"Enjoyed talking to you," he said, "but I have to get back to work now—on a six-volume set about cockamamie Earthling **beliefs** in an Afterlife."

See also: PP X; XII; XXIX; *ST* 10; *CC* 47; 57; *SL5* 2; 9; *BC* 2; 4; 18; *JB* 1–2; *PS* Preface; *PS* The People One Knows; *PS* Religion; *DD* 13; Epilogue; *Gal* 28; 32; *Blue* 5; 19; *HP* 19; *FWD* VII; XI; XII; XVII; *BAG* Poor Little Rich Town.

Bella (*also* **Bella's Beauty Nook**). *In* God Bless You, Mr. Rosewater, *Bella was the child of a Nickel Plate Railroad brakeman, weighed 314 pounds, and founded Bella's Beauty Nook in the cellar of the Rosewater County Courthouse, one of the rare successful enterprises in town. She suffers a mild heart attack when Eliot sets off "the loudest fire alarm in the Western Hemisphere" atop the volunteer fire department at high noon.*

Bellevue Hospital. (*FWD* XIX) Dr. Robert Maslansky, who treats every sort of addict at **Bellevue Hospital** in New York City, and in the jails, too, is a saint. (When we take walks together many homeless people greet him by name.) Tris Coffin and his wife Margaret, who get out a four-page weekly called *The Washington Spectator*, are saints. (I told Tris and Margaret a month ago that I considered them saints. They said they were too old to protest very vehemently.)

This very summer, I asked the novelist William Styron in a Chinese restaurant how many people on the whole planet had what we had, which was

lives worth living. Between the two of us, we came up with seventeen percent.

(*TQ* 42) The next day I took a walk in midtown Manhattan with a longtime friend, a physician who treats every sort of addict at **Bellevue Hospital**. Many of his patients are homeless and HIV positive as well. I told him about Styron's and my figure of seventeen percent. He said it sounded about right to him.

As I have written elsewhere, this man is a saint. I define a saint as a person who behaves decently in an indecent society.

I asked him why half his patients at **Bellevue** didn't commit suicide. He said the same question had occurred to him. He sometimes asked them, as though it were an unremarkable part of a diagnostic routine, if they had thoughts of self-destruction. He said that they were almost without exception surprised and insulted by the question. An idea that sick had never entered their heads!

It was about then that we passed an ex-patient of his who was toting a plastic bag filled with aluminum cans he had gathered. He was one of Kilgore Trout's "sacred cattle," somehow wonderful despite his economic uselessness.

"Hi, Doc," he said.

Bergeron, Bruce. *In* Hocus Pocus, *a graduate of Tarkington's Class of 1985 and the son of Ed Bergeron, a Trustee of Tarkington College. The homosexual Bruce became a chorus boy for the Ice Capades. He often went over to Eugene Debs Hartke's home to dance with his crazy mother-in-law. Bruce was found dead, strangled and stabbed to death in a motel outside Dubuque, Iowa.*

When Bruce had Hartke as his music appreciation teacher at Tarkington, he set to music his experience as a child when he was caught in an elevator at Bloomingdale's with his Haitian nanny. Since they were stuck for such a long time and he was just a small child, he imagined he was at the center of an important national happening. When the elevator was freed and no one from Bloomingdale's or the media was there to greet the captives' release, he felt sullen and disappointed, and the nanny made him promise never to tell where they had been since she wasn't supposed to have been there. Hartke told him his musical description perfectly described his own return from Vietnam.

Bergeron, Ed. *In* Hocus Pocus, *a member of Tarkington College's Board of Trustees, though he resigned after his friend Eugene Debs Hartke was fired and before the prison breakout which overran the college, and father of Bruce Bergeron—the homosexual ice skater strangled and bludgeoned to death in Dubuque, Iowa.*

Hartke considered Ed his "doomsday pal" since they often spoke about the economic and environmental plight of the earth. Bergeron often debated Jason Wilder, the conservative talk show host who was eventually killed by the prisoners who took over the college. (HP 17) *His wealth was as old as the Moellenkamps', and was based on ancestral oil fields and coal mines and railroads which he had sold to foreigners in order to devote himself full-time to nature study and conservation. He was President of the Wildlife Rescue Federation, and his photographs of wildlife on the Galápagos Islands had been published in* National Geographic. (HP 17) **Bergeron**'s *epitaph for the planet, I remember, which he said should be carved in big letters in a wall of the Grand Canyon for the flying-saucer people to find, was this:*

> WE COULD HAVE SAVED IT,
> BUT WE WERE TOO DOGGONE
>   CHEAP.

Only he didn't say "doggone."
(HP 17) *One thing he used to say to me* (Hartke), *and to a class of mine he spoke to one time, was that man was the weather now. Man was the tornadoes, man was the hailstones, man was the floods. So he might have said that Scipio was Pompeii, and the escapees were a lava flow.*

The two misfortunes that forced Ed Bergeron's resignation were financial and personal. (HP 17) *A company he inherited made all sorts of products out of asbestos, whose dust proved to be as carcinogenic as any substance yet identified, with the exception of epoxy cement and some of the radioactive stuff accidentally turned loose in the air and aquifers around nuclear weapons factories and power plants. He felt terrible about this, he* told me, although he had never laid eyes on any of the factories that made the stuff. He sold them for practically nothing, since the company in Singapore that bought them got all the lawsuits along with the machinery and buildings, and an inventory of finished materials which was huge and unsalable in this country. The people in Singapore did what **Ed** couldn't bring himself to do, which was to sell all those floor tiles and roofing and so on to emerging nations in Africa. *Shortly after this episode his son Bruce, a chorus boy in the Ice Capades, is strangled and stabbed to death in a motel outside Dubuque.*

Bergeron, George and Hazel. *The parents of the outlaw Harrison Bergeron, in the story of that name reprinted in* Welcome to the Monkey House (1968). *They watch his execution on television but are barely aware of it owing to the incessant government manipulation of their minds.* **Hazel** had a perfectly average intelligence, which meant she couldn't think about anything except in short bursts. And **George**, while his intelligence was way above normal, had a little mental handicap radio in his ear. He was required by law to wear it at all times. It was tuned to a government transmitter. Every twenty seconds or so, the transmitter would send out some sharp noise to keep people like **George** from taking unfair advantage of their brains.

Bergeron, Harrison. *The title character of the short story of that name reprinted in* Welcome to the Monkey House (1968), *Harrison had been jailed by the Handicapper General's office for "suspicion of plotting to overthrow the government." The story takes place in 2081, when all people have been made equal due to the imposition of constitutionally mandated handicaps on all who were above average intellectually or physically. Though only fourteen years old and described as an underhandicapped genius and athlete, Harrison escapes from jail and breaks into a television studio where a ridiculous ballet of lead-weighted ballerinas is airing. He encourages one of the dancers to be his dance partner without the government-issued weights, bullies the orchestra to remove its handicaps in order to play its best, and declares* "Even as I stand here—" he bellowed, "crippled, hobbled, sickened—I am a greater ruler than any man who ever lived! Now watch me become what I *can* become!"

Harrison tore the straps of his handicap harness like wet tissue paper, tore straps guaranteed to support five thousand pounds.

Harrison's scrap-iron handicaps crashed to the floor.

Harrison thrust his thumbs under the bar of the padlock that secured his head harness. The bar snapped like celery. **Harrison** smashed his headphones and spectacles against the wall.

He flung away his rubber-ball nose, revealed a man that would have awed Thor, the god of thunder.

Handicapper General Diana Moon Glampers then breaks into the studio and kills Harrison and his partner with a double-barreled ten-gauge shotgun.

His father George views all this while watching television, but the head-splitting radio waves transmitted to his handicap receiver wipe out any recognition of exactly what he sees.

Bergler, Dr. Edmund. (*BAG* Introduction) The late American psychiatrist **Dr. Edmund Bergler**, who claimed to have treated more professional writers than any other shrink, said in his book *The Writer and Psychoanalysis* that most writers in his experience wrote to please one person they knew well, even if they didn't realize they were doing that. It wasn't a trick of the fiction trade. It was simply a natural human thing to do, whether or not it could make a story better. . . . **Dr. Bergler** said it commonly required psychoanalysis before his patients could know for whom they had been writing. But as soon as I finished his book, and then thought for only a couple of minutes, I knew it was my sister Allie I had been writing for. She is the person the stories in this book were written for. Anything I knew Allie wouldn't like I crossed out. Everything I knew she would get a kick out of I left in.

Allie is up in Heaven now, with my first wife Jane and Sam Lawrence and Flannery O'Connor and **Dr. Bergler**, but I still write to please her. Allie was funny in real life. That gives me permission to be funny, too. Allie and I were very close.

Berman, Abe. In Bluebeard, *the brain surgeon husband of Circe Berman. He dies six months before she*

meets Rabo Karabekian. Circe is the author of romance novels, and she tells Rabo that what gives her books a ring of authenticity for her readers is that she always wrote to her husband's tastes.

Berman, Circe. *Rabo Karabekian dedicates his memoirs,* Bluebeard, *to Circe Berman. She is the forty-three-year-old fabulously successful romance novelist (using the pen name Polly Madison) who becomes Karabekian's housemate in the Hamptons on Long Island. Her husband died six months before she met Rabo. He was Abe Berman, a brain surgeon who died of a cerebral hemorrhage. Circe is the daughter of a suicide—her father hanged himself after his clothing factory went bankrupt. It is because of Circe's prodding that Rabo decides to write his memoirs and to pick up painting again. Rabo credits her with his resurrection.* (Blue 37) "Twice now I've been a Lazarus," I said. "I died with Terry Kitchen, and Edith brought me back to life again. I died with dear Edith, and **Circe Berman** brought me back to life again."

In Greek mythology, Circe is a minor goddess of magic, an enchantress, and the daughter of Helios and Perse. She is best known for turning Odysseus' men into pigs after enticing them to feast on delicacies laced with a magical potion.

Berman, Gil (also ***If God Were Alive Today***). *Vonnegut balances chapter 11 of A Man Without a Country between two narrative alter egos whose voices and contexts stem from a wizened awareness of his own legacy. While the second half of the chapter is the province of the seemingly ever-present Kilgore Trout, the first half is given to Gil Berman, whose narrative portrait is as close to the real Vonnegut as is any critic's parallel drawn between Vonnegut and Trout. He specifically refers to Berman's concerns, all matters of his own interest in numerous literary settings.*

Beginning with a tale about Martians on Earth who eat the homeless, pee gasoline, and defecate uranium, his themes touch upon becoming a sexual neuter, atheism, the hypocrisy of some Roman Catholic clergy, and fads designed to make money from those insecure about their body images and sexual prowess.

The endpoint of Martian interest comes amidst

their scrambled departure from Earth. The female, mauve-colored Martian commander of their landing party summarizes the extent of their understanding by offering the provocative punchline, "What is it, what can it possibly be about blow jobs and golf?" Vonnegut inscribes these words in a bit of artwork (MWC 11) *facing the chapter's opening page and rephrased a few pages later.*

That is stuff from a novel I've been working on for the past five years, about **Gil Berman**, thirty-six years my junior, a standup comedian at the end of the world. It is about making jokes while we are killing all the fish in the ocean, and touching off the last chunks or drops or whiffs of fossil fuel. But it will not let itself be finished.

Its working title—or actually, its nonworking title—is *If God Were Alive Today*. And hey, listen, it is time we thanked God that we are in a country where even the poor people are overweight. But the Bush diet could change that.

And about the novel I can never finish, *If God Were Alive Today*, the hero, the stand-up comedian on Doomsday, not only does he denounce our addiction to fossil fuels and the pushers in the White House, because of overpopulation he is also against sexual intercourse. **Gil Berman** tells his audiences:

I have become a flaming neuter. I am as celibate as at least fifty percent of the heterosexual Roman Catholic clergy. And celibacy is no root canal. It's so cheap and convenient. Talk about safe sex! You don't have to do anything afterwards, because there is no afterward.

And when my tantrum, which is what I call my TV set, flashes boobs and smiles in my face, and says everybody but me is going to get laid tonight, and this is a national emergency, so I've got to rush out and buy a car or pills, or a folding gymnasium that I can hide under my bed, I laugh like a hyena. I know and you know that millions and millions of good Americans, present company not excepted, are not going to get laid tonight.

And we flaming neuters vote! I look forward to a day when the President of the United States, no less, who probably isn't going to get laid tonight ei-

ther, decrees a National Neuter Pride Day. Out of our closets we'll come by the millions. Shoulders squared, chins held high, we'll go marching up Main Streets all over this boob-crazed democracy of ours, laughing like hyenas.

What about God? If He were alive today? **Gil Berman** says, "God would have to be an atheist, because the excrement has hit the air-conditioning big time, big time" (MWC 11).

Berringer, Fred and Dave. *A subordinate of Paul Proteus at the Ilium Works, Fred Berringer challenges his boss's checkers championship with his father's invention, the robot "Checker Charley." Dave Berringer is considered one of the top "computer-machine" men in the country. Fred's ignorance about his father's invention leads to its undoing. Ed Finnerty notices some of Checker Charley's connections are loose, and they eventually cause the robot to fail, allowing Paul to retain his championship.* (PP V) **Fred Berringer**, a short, heavy, slit-eyed blond, seemed to be their leader. He was a wealthy, extroverted, dull boy from a good family of engineers and managers in Minneapolis. He had squeaked through college, and was just barely acceptable to the personnel machines. Ordinarily, nobody would have hired him. But Kroner, who knew his bloodlines, had taken him on anyway and sent him to Ilium to be trained. The break had done anything but teach him humility. He took it as evidence that his money and name could beat the system any time and, paraphrased, he'd said as much. The hell of it was that his attitude won grudging admiration from his fellow engineers, who had got their jobs the hard way. Paul supposed, gloomily, that beaters of systems had always been admired by the conventional. At any rate, Kroner still believed in the boy, so Paul had no choice but to keep him on, and to pair a smarter man with him to backstop his mental apparatus. *Fred Berringer is also present in court when Paul is tried for treason.*

Bert (*see also* **Bert Quinn; Bert Wright**). *The Nova Scotian captain of the yacht* Charity Anne Browning. (WFG Brief Encounters on the Inland

Waterway) He was sixty years old, had bright blue eyes and the complexion of a used footlocker. He was master of the *Charity Anne Browning,* a sixty-eight-foot yawl. . . . **Bert** kept the ship immaculate inside by the simple expedient of not letting anybody use anything. He kept us off the couch. I made the mistake of using an ashtray, and he took it away immediately, washed it, and put it carefully into a cupboard.

When the Charity Anne Browning *is tied up at dock overnight, Bert and his crew are seen using the toilets in the marina rather than dirty their own.*

Beryllium. *In* Slapstick, *an unnamed member of the Beryllium clan is killed while attempting to deliver a letter to Wilbur Swain. The letter from Wilma Pachysandra-17 von Peterswald, wife of the inventor of* The Hooligan *(a device to speak with the dead), tells Wilbur about her many conversations with his dead sister Eliza who expresses a great desire to communicate with him. The Beryllium is killed by Byron Hatfield on the new border between Tennessee and West Virginia. Hatfield mistook the Beryllium for Newton McCoy, a hereditary enemy. The Beryllium agreed to deliver the letter while on his way to join his clan in Maryland. Hatfield abides by his dying wish to deliver the letter to Wilbur.*

Beskudnikov. *In* Bluebeard, *Beskudnikov is an engraver of currency plates for Imperial bonds and paper money in Russia. He and his wife took in the five-year-old Dan Gregory. Gregory became his apprentice and was forced to prove his technical competence by copying Beskudnikov's engraving plates. The master engraver torments his apprentice by destroying copies Gregory worked on for months and years because he said they were deficient. Eventually, Gregory fools his master by offering him the genuine article rather than his copy.*

Gregory later torments the young Rabo Karabekian by having him create a photo-realistic painting of Gregory's attic.

Betelgeuse (*also* **Betelguese**). *A bright red star 527 light-years from Earth in the constellation Orion.* (ST 1) *Winston Niles Rumfoord had run his private space ship right into the heart of an un-* charted chrono-synclastic infundibulum two days out of Mars. Only his dog had been along. Now Winston Niles Rumfoord and his dog Kazak existed as wave phenomena—apparently pulsing in a distorted spiral with its origin in the Sun and its terminal in **Betelgeuse**. . . .

(ST 1) Winston Niles Rumfoord and his dog Kazak were wave phenomena—pulsing in distorted spirals, with their origins in the Sun and their terminals in **Betelgeuse**. Whenever a heavenly body intercepted their spirals, Rumfoord and his dog materialized on that body.

(HP 4) *Imagine the same sort of thing happening on a huge rocket ship bound for* **Betelgeuse**. *This is Hartke's idle wondering about the human waste disposal problem posed by the prison break at Scipio. The state's response was to annex Tarkington College in part for its toilet facilities.*
See also: ST 7.

Bethlehem (*also* **Star of Bethlehem**). *Kilgore Trout's explanation that God is not necessarily a benign overseer is illustrated by his analogy to the Star of Bethlehem—the example itself goes against Christian theology.* (BC 1) "I realize . . . that God wasn't any conservationist, so for anybody else to be one was sacrilegious and a waste of time. You ever see one of His volcanoes or tornadoes or tidal waves? Anybody ever tell you about the Ice Ages he arranges for every half-million years? How about Dutch Elm disease? There's a nice conservation measure for you. That's God, not man. Just about the time we got our rivers cleaned up, he'd probably have the whole galaxy go up like a celluloid collar. That's what the **Star of Bethlehem** was, you know."

In Vonnegut's "Address to the National Institute of Arts and Letters," reprinted in Wampeters, *he takes this same example and repeats it to reinforce his biochemical-anthropological theory of cosmic existence. It (the sun) will wish to collapse even more, but the atomic nuclei will prevent this. An irresistible force will meet an immovable object, so to speak. There will be a tremendous explosion. Our sun will become a supernova, a flash such as the* **Star of Bethlehem** *is thought to have been. Earth Day cannot prevent this.*

Bethune. Mother Night's *Howard W. Campbell, Jr.'s residence in the United States after the war is 27 Bethune Street, New York City.*

Biagini, Salvatore (*see* ***God Bless You, Dr. Kevorkian***).

BIBEC. *In* Jailbird, *a rising new international conglomerate based in Monaco but suspected of being Soviet in origin, BIBEC purchases American Telephone and Telegraph Company, which had just hired away Arpad Leen, the president and chairman of the board of the RAMJAC Corporation. The United States had begun liquidating RAMJAC to cover the nation's short-term economic problems.*

Bierce, Ambrose. (*Gal* 1:14) If Mandarax were still around, it would have had mostly unpleasant things to say about matrimony, such as:

> *Marriage: a community consisting of a master a mistress, and two slaves, making in all, two.*
> Ambrose Bierce (1842–?)

(*FWD* 19) "My generalization is happily or unhappily confirmed in a book called *Punchlines* (Paragon House, 1990) by William Keough of the English Department of Fitchburg State College in Massachusetts. The subtitle is *The Violence of American Humor.* Mr. Keough, by means of essays on Mark Twain, Ring Lardner, **Ambrose Bierce**, myself, comedians in the movies (both silents and talkies), and radio and TV and nightclub comics right up to the present, persuades me that the most memorable jokes by Americans are responses to the economic and physical violence of this society. 'How often does it seem that the American humorist, having set out daringly and lightly as an amused observer of the American spectacle of violence and corruption, ends up mouthing sardonic fables in a bed of gloom,' he writes.

"So guess what: My latest novel, *Hocus Pocus,* to be published in September, is a sardonic fable in a bed of gloom."

(*BAG* Introduction) Short stories can have greatness, short as they have to be. Several knocked my socks off when I was still in high school. Ernest

Hemingway's "The Short Happy Life of Francis Macomber" and Saki's "The Open Window" and O. Henry's "The Gift of the Magi" and **Ambrose Bierce**'s "An Occurrence at Owl Creek Bridge" spring to mind. But there is no greatness in this or my other collection, nor was there meant to be.

My own stories may be interesting, nonetheless, as relics from a time, before there was television, when an author might support a family by writing stories that satisfied uncritical readers of magazines, and earning thereby enough free time in which to write serious novels. When I became a full-time freelance in 1950, I expected to be doing that for the rest of my life.

I was in such good company with a prospectus like that.

(*MWC* 2) Do you know what a twerp is? When I was in Shortridge High School in Indianapolis 65 years ago, a twerp was a guy who stuck a set of false teeth up his butt and bit the buttons off the back seats of taxicabs. (And a snarf was a guy who sniffed the seats of girls' bicycles.)

And I consider anybody a twerp who hasn't read the greatest American short story, which is "Occurrence at Owl Creek Bridge," by **Ambrose Bierce**. It isn't remotely political. It is a flawless example of American genius, like "Sophisticated Lady" by Duke Ellington or the Franklin stove.

The Big Board. *Billy Pilgrim finds this Kilgore Trout novel in a Times Square bookstore while on a trip to appear as a guest on a New York radio show. After skimming its opening, Billy realizes he has read it earlier while rooming with Eliot Rosewater in a Veterans Administration hospital.* (*SL5* 9) It was about an Earthling man and woman who were kidnapped by extra-terrestrials. They were put on display in a zoo on a planet called Zircon-212.

These fictitious people in the zoo had a **big board** supposedly showing stock market quotations and commodity prices along one wall of their habitat, and a news ticker, and a telephone that was supposedly connected to a brokerage on Earth. The creatures on Zircon-212 told their captives that they had invested a million dollars for them back on Earth, and that it was up to the captives to manage it so that they would be fabulously wealthy when they were returned to Earth.

The telephone and the **big board** and the ticker were all fakes, of course. They were simply stimulants to make the Earthlings perform vividly for the crowds at the zoo—to make them jump up and down and cheer, or gloat, or sulk, or tear their hair, to be scared shitless or to feel as contented as babies in their mothers' arms.

The Earthlings did very well on paper. That was part of the rigging, of course. And religion got mixed up in it, too. The news ticker reminded them that the President of the United States had declared National Prayer Week, and that everybody should pray. The Earthlings had had a bad week on the market before that. They had lost a small fortune in olive oil futures. So they gave praying a whirl.

It worked. Olive oil went up.

big eye. (ST 12) The Earthlings behaved at all times as though there were a **big eye** in the sky—as though that big eye were ravenous for entertainment.

The **big eye** was a glutton for great theater. The **big eye** was indifferent as to whether the Earthling shows were comedy, tragedy, farce, satire, athletics, or vaudeville. Its demand, which Earthlings apparently found as irresistible as gravity, was that the shows be great. . . .

The **big eye** was the only audience that Earthlings really cared about. The fanciest performances that Salo had seen had been put on by Earthlings who were terribly alone. The imagined **big eye** was their only audience. . . .

Salo, with his diamond-hard statues, had tried to preserve some mental states of those Earthlings who had put on the most interesting shows for the imagined **big eye**.

Big Nick. *The eponymous Chicago Mafia boss in "A Present for Big Saint Nick," which is Vonnegut's retitling of the story in the 1999 collection* Bagombo Snuff Box, *first appearing in* Argosy *magazine's December 1954 issue as "A Present for Big Nick."* **Big Nick** was said to be the most recent heir to the power of Al Capone. He refused to affirm or deny it, on the grounds that he might tend to incriminate himself.

He bought whatever caught his fancy, a twenty-three-room house outside Chicago, a seventeen-room house in Miami, racehorses, a ninety-foot yacht, one hundred fifteen suits, and among other things, controlling interest in a middleweight boxer named Bernie O'Hare, the Shenandoah Blaster.

Big Nick's primary traits are his legendary ruthlessness, limitless mistrust and loathing for his employees, exhibited by his badgering tone as well as his bribery and trickery of his employees' children while dressed as Saint Nick during his annual Christmas party. The toll his behavior takes on the children is palpable. Gwen Zerbe, Willy O'Hare, and Richard Pullman all exhibit Santa-phobia at the thought of attending the party or even when seeing Santa in a store—including small plastic figurines. As Mrs. Pullman boldly says of the children's otherwise inexplicable fear of Santa, "Our Santa Claus is *a dirty, vulgar, prying, foulmouthed, ill-smelling fake." Their parents have to coach them to answer his prying questions with equanimity, but they are small, unsophisticated, and cringing.*

The focus of his bribery upon the children is to have them reveal in confidence to his Santa facade the nasty, disloyal remarks he assumes his employees make when they are home. Toward the close of the story, Big Nick raises his hand in frustration and is about to slap young Willy when Bernie saves his son by grabbing Big Nick's hand and soon after punching him in the face.

Big Nick's tirade about having them all killed for next to nothing is followed by his bringing out an armful of presents sent to him to show how much he is appreciated. One of the boxes bears Italian postmarks. This gift from his Italian counterparts apparently expresses their feelings about his legendary ruthless behavior. Now **Saint Nicholas** showed off another pretty package. "Here's one comes all the way from a friend in Italy." He gave its red ribbon a mighty yank. The explosion not only blew off his bloody beard and fur-trimmed red hat, but removed his chin and nose as well. What a mess! What a terrible thing for the young to see, one would think, but they wouldn't have missed it for the world.

After the police left, and the corpse was carted off to the morgue, dressed like Kris Kringle from the neck down, O'Hare's wife said this: "I don't think this is a Christmas the children are going to forget very soon. I know I won't."

Their son Willy had a souvenir that would help

him remember. He had found the greeting card that came with the bomb. It was in the shrubbery. It said, "Merry Christmas to the greatest guy in the world." It was signed "The Family."

"The Big Space Fuck" (1972). *Reprinted in the "Obscenity" chapter of* Palm Sunday, *this science fiction short story is set against the July 4, 1989, launch of the spaceship* Arthur C. Clarke *filled with eight hundred pounds of dried sperm and heading for the Andromeda Galaxy. The mission is an attempt to ensure the survival of humanity, which was living in an increasingly polluted—if not toxic—environment. Society had also lost all decorum. Profanity was so common that even the president called the operation "The Big Space Fuck." Sperm donors needed a 115 IQ to qualify.*

The main part of the story concerns Elk Harbor, Ohio, residents Dwayne and Grace Hoobler, who were being sued by their daughter June for being lousy parents and ruining her prospects as an adult. At the close of the story, Dwayne, Grace, and the sheriff are all eaten by an overgrown lamprey, which had to leave its Great Lakes environs because of pollution.

Bigley, Homer and Clara. *Homer is the barbershop proprietor in* Player Piano *who gets to cut the hair of the Shah of Bratpuhr. Homer and Clara are childless. (PP XX) While Halyard brooded,* **Homer Bigley**, *with the reflexes born of a life of barbering, selected his scissors, clicked them in air about the sacred head, and, as though his right hand were serviced by the same nerve as the diaphragm and voicebox, he began to cut hair and talk—talked to the uncomprehending Shah after the fashion of an extroverted embalmer with a corpse.*

Bijou Theater. *In* Bluebeard, *Rabo Karabekian's father dies in the Bijou Theater in San Ignacio, California, in 1938.*

Bikini Atoll. *The South Pacific site of atomic bomb testing conducted in the late 1940s and early 1950s. In* Galápagos, *Roy Hepburn, suffering from inoperable brain cancer, imagines that he had been a victim of the United States' atomic bomb tests at Bikini*

Atoll, preventing his having children with his wife, Mary. He also believes he helped tie up all sorts of exotic animals in preparation for the bomb tests. (Gal 1:9) To hear him tell it, he had tethered peacocks and snow leopards and gorillas and crocodiles and albatrosses to the stakes. In his big brain, **Bikini** *became the exact reverse of Noah's ark. Two of every sort of animal had been brought there in order to be atom-bombed.*

Bill (*Kilgore Trout's parakeet, also known as Cyclone Bill*). *Bill is Kilgore Trout's faithful companion with whom Trout discusses his trepidation about the fate of the planet. Trout's theory that the atmosphere would soon become unbreathable prompts some macabre musings (comparable to Vonnegut's view of writers as canaries in a coal mine—those sensitive souls serve as early warning devices to those who pay attention). (BC 2) Trout supposes that when the atmosphere became poisonous,* **Bill** *would keel over a few minutes before Trout did. He would kid* **Bill** *about that. "How's the old respiration,* **Bill**?" *he'd say, or, "Seems like you've got a touch of the old emphysema,* **Bill**," *or, "We never discussed what kind of a funeral you want,* **Bill**. *You never even told me what your religion is." And so on.*

Trout recognizes the power he possesses over Bill's life. When he understands that the fungi eating his tuxedo mindlessly know what they want, he plays with Bill by offering the parakeet his freedom. When Bill resists flying out of his open cage and out the open window, Trout sees this as true wisdom. (BC 3) Trout closed the door of the cage and latched it. "That's the most intelligent use of three wishes I ever heard of," he told the bird. "You made sure you'd still have something worth wishing for—to get out of the cage."

Trout sees the lure of the Midland City Arts Festival as a wish he should avoid to save his fantasy—much as he understood Bill's reticence to leave his cage. (BC 3) Trout shook his head. "I'm not going, **Bill**. *I don't want out of my cage. I'm too smart for that. Even if I did want out, though, I wouldn't go to Midland City to make a laughing stock of myself—and my only fan."*

Trout confides in Bill his uneasiness about the nature of the universe, that he just may be the fic-

tional whim of someone else. (BC 21) Trout was aware of me *(Vonnegut)*, too, what little he could see of me. I made him even more uneasy than Dwayne did. The thing was: Trout was the only character I ever created who had enough imagination to suspect that he might be the creation of another human being. He had spoken of this possibility several times to his parakeet. He had said, for instance, "Honest to God, **Bill**, the way things are going, all I can think of is that I'm a character in a book by somebody who wants to write about somebody who suffers all the time."

In the frontispiece to Timequake, *Vonnegut provides one of his multi-eyed portraits of Kilgore Trout with an open birdcage in the background and the caption reads,* Out-of-print science fiction writer Kilgore Trout in Cohoes, New York, in 1975, having learned of the death of his estranged son, Leon, in a Swedish shipyard, having given his parakeet, "**Cyclone Bill**," his freedom, and about to become a vagabond.

Billy the Poet. *In the short story "Welcome to the Monkey House," the notorious "nothinghead" who attempts to seduce Ethical Suicide Parlor hostesses by preventing them from taking their ethical birth control pills, allowing normal sexual urges to return. Though Billy agrees with the world's rulers that overpopulation endangers world stability, he points out that reproduction and sexuality should not be confused. After weaning the hostesses from their ethical birth control pills, Billy shares a "traditional wedding night" with them—complete with silk pajamas. He leaves them with birth control pills that prevent reproduction but that do not interfere with one's sexuality.*

biochemical-anthropological, anthropology and biology, biochemistry, biochemists. (WFG Address to the National Institute of Arts and Letters, 1971) I can be as serious as anyone here, with a few obvious exceptions. And I will prove it. I will speak of happiness it's true—but I speak of **anthropology and biochemistry** and unhappiness as well.

I wish in particular to call your attention to the work of Dr. M. Sydney Margoles, a Los Angeles endocrinologist, who is able to distinguish between male homosexuals and heterosexuals by means of urinalysis. He doesn't have to meet them. What other sweet mysteries of life are chemicals? All of them, I believe. **Biochemistry** is everything. The speculations of artists about the human condition are trash.

(WFG Address to the National Institute of Arts and Letters, 1971) As I have said before, I can explain *everything* in terms of this **biochemical-anthropological** theory of mine.

(PS When I Lost My Innocence) "I eventually wound up on academic probation. I was accelerating my course at the time—because of the war. My instructor in organic chemistry was my lab partner in **biochemistry**. He was fit to be tied."

(PS Playmates) No offense intended, but it would never occur to me to look for the best minds in any generation in an undergraduate English department anywhere. I would certainly try the physics department or the music department first—and after that **biochemistry**.

(FWD II) "He *(Mark Vonnegut)* isn't as enthusiastic about megavitamins as he used to be, before he himself became a doctor. He still sees a whole lot more hope in **biochemistry** than in talk.

(FWD X) The Class of 1940 of Shortridge High School had its Fiftieth Reunion recently, and those in charge sent out a list of members who vanished entirely as far as Indianapolis was concerned. I was able to report back that one of them was anything but a ghost to fellow **biochemists** in Boston, where he was an expert on the aging process.

In an appendix to Fates Worse Than Death, *Vonnegut includes the updated afterword his son Mark wrote for his critically acclaimed account of his own breakdown.* (FWD What My Son Mark Wanted Me to Tell the Psychiatrists in Philadelphia, Which Was Also the Afterword to a New Edition of His Book *The Eden Express*) The events described in *The Eden Express* took place nearly twenty years ago. Some things have changed. The notion that mental illness has a large **biochemical** component is no longer radical. Things have come full circle, to the point where it's unusual to hear anyone say that mental illness is all mental. The view that going crazy is caused by bad events in childhood and that talk and understanding offer the hope for a cure seems very out of date. This is a change for the better, although it has by no means brought an end to the shame, blame, and guilt which continue to compound the suffering of the mentally ill and their families.

(*TQ* 21) I am Honorary President of the American Humanist Association, whose headquarters in Amherst, New York, I have never seen. I succeeded the late author and **biochemist** Dr. Isaac Asimov in that functionless capacity.

(*TQ* 51) A friend told me he was at a wedding where the minister said at the climax of the ceremony: "You were sick, but now you're well again, and there's work to do. I now pronounce you man and wife."

Another friend, a **biochemist** for a cat food company, said she was staying at a hotel in Toronto, Canada, and she asked the front desk to give her a wake-up call in the morning. She answered her phone the next morning, and the operator said, "You were sick, but now you're well again, and there's work to do. It's seven a.m., and the temperature outside is thirty-two degrees Fahrenheit, or zero Celsius."

The doppelgänger for Vonnegut's first wife is in attendance at the Timequake *clambake and utters a variant of her favorite saying.* (*TQ* 62) Jane's unknowing stand-in, a pert young woman who teaches **biochemistry** at Rhode Island University, over at Kingston, said within my hearing, and apropos of nothing more than that day's theatrical performance and the setting sun: "I can't wait to see what's going to happen next."

(*GBK* Isaac Asimov) When on Earth, Isaac, my predecessor as honorary president of the American Humanist Association, was the most prolific American writer of books who ever lived. He wrote nearly five hundred of the things—to my measly twenty so far, or to Honoré de Balzac's eighty-five. Sometimes Isaac wrote ten published volumes in a single year! These weren't only prize-winning science-fiction. Many were scholarly popularizations of Shakespeare and **biochemistry** and ancient Greek history, and the Bible and relativity, and on and on. *See also: TQ publication data page.*

biochemistry professor. *Among the doppelgängers in attendance at the* Timequake *clambake*

is one representing Vonnegut's first wife, Jane Cox Vonnegut. (*TQ* 62) Jane's unknowing stand-in, a pert young woman who teaches biochemistry at Rhode Island University, over at Kingston, said within my hearing, and apropos of nothing more than that day's theatrical performance and the setting sun: "I can't wait to see what's going to happen next."

biodegradable. (*HP* 24) Like Hermann and Sophia Shultz, these theoretically **biodegradable** works of Nature (*meat and vegetables found in landfills*) had failed to rot for want of moisture, which was life itself to worms and fungi and bacteria.

Birch (**John Birch Society**). *Billy Pilgrim's father-in-law belongs to this right-wing political group. Billy's Cadillac El Dorado Coupe de Ville is decorated with bumper stickers given to him by his father-in-law.* (*SL5* 3) "Support Your Police Department," said another. There was a third. "Impeach Earl Warren," it said. The stickers about the police and Earl Warren were gifts from Billy's father-in-law, a member of the **John Birch Society**.

bird, birdhouses, birdlike (*see also* **Titanic Bluebird**). *Birds and bird imagery appear throughout Vonnegut's work. Perhaps the most memorable occurrences appear in* Slaughterhouse-Five, *in which birds offer a rather stultifying commentary on man's inhumanity to man.* (*SL5* 1) Everything is supposed to be very quiet after a massacre, and it always is, except for the **birds**.

And what do the **birds** say? All there is to say about a massacre, things like "*Poo-tee-weet?*"

Upon emerging from the oubliette after ice-nine freezes the planet, John/Jonah writes, I was recalled from this dream by the cry of a darting **bird** above me. It seemed to be asking me what had happened. "Poo-tee-phweet?" it asked.

We all looked up at the **bird**, and then at one another (*CC* 116).

Hiroshi Matsumoto, the Japanese prison warden and Hiroshima bombing victim, expresses his frustration over man's inability to act without malice when he declares "I wish I had been born a **bird** instead. . . . I wish we had all been born **birds** instead" (*HP* 40).

Vonnegut's views about the social utility of authors is phrased within his "canary in a coal mine vision." *(WFG Playboy Interview)* Writers are specialized cells doing whatever we do, and we're expressions of the entire society.... And when a society is in great danger, we're likely to sound the alarms. I have the **canary-bird-in-the-coal-mine theory of the arts.** You know, coal miners used to take **birds** down into the mines with them to detect gas before men got sick. The artists certainly did that in the case of Vietnam. They chirped and keeled over. But it made no difference whatsoever. Nobody important cared. But I continue to think that artists—all artists—should be treasured as alarm systems.

Birds become emblematic of a freedom separating one from the horrors of mankind as well as the embodiment of that which is most glorious in the human spirit. When Walter Starbuck first meets Ruth, a victim of the Nazi concentration camps and his future bride, he notes that Her plan was to roam alone and out-of-doors forever, from nowhere to nowhere in a demented sort of religious ecstasy. "No one ever touches me," she said, "and I never touch anyone. I am like a **bird** in flight. It is so beautiful. There is only God—and me" *(JB 2).*
(JB 7) It may be that Ruth protected herself from dread of the gathering storm, or, more accurately, from dread of the gathering silence, by reverting during the daytime, when I was at work, to the Ophelialike elation she had felt after her liberation—when she had thought of herself as a **bird** all alone with God.
(FWD VIII) I am even more offended, though, by his *(George H. W. Bush's)* failure to take notice of the most beautiful and noble and brilliant and poetical and sacred accomplishment by Americans to date. I am speaking about the exploration of the Solar System by the camera-bearing space probe *Voyager 2.* This gallant **bird** (so like Noah's dove) showed us all the outer planets and their moons! We no longer had to guess whether there was life on them or not, or whether our descendants might survive on them! (Forget it.) As *Voyager 2* departed the Solar System forever ("My work is done"), sending us dimmer and dimmer pictures of what we were and where we were, did our President invite us to love it and thank it and wish it well? No. He

spoke passionately instead of the necessity of an Amendment to the Constitution (Article XXVII?) outlawing irreverent treatment of a piece of cloth, the American flag. Such an Amendment would be on a nutty par with the Roman Emperor Caligula's having his horse declared a Consul.

Vonnegut also uses birds as admirable emblems of loyalty. Boaz terms his relationship with Unk as the happiness of two birds, "'And there they go, happy as two **birds!**'" He chuckled and cooed about the happy, **birdlike** pair *(ST 5). The Titanic Bluebirds (comparable in size to eagles) accept the teenaged Chrono into their community as one of their own. While Malachi buries his beloved Beatrice,* the sky was filled with **Titanic Bluebirds.** There must have been ten thousand, at least, of the great and noble **birds.**

Not one **bird** cried out *(ST Epilogue).*
Chrono finds sanctuary with the Titanic Bluebirds in part because the only other beings on Titan are his parents. Earlier, in Player Piano, *Edgar Rice Burroughs Hagstrohm seeks to be free from his perfectly average surroundings—and a bird sanctuary offers him a way out of his predicament. (PP XXVII)* "Hagstrohm cut up his M-17 home in Chicago with a blowtorch, went naked to the home of Mrs. Marion Frascati, the widow of an old friend, and demanded that she come to the woods with him. Mrs. Frascati refused, and he disappeared into the **bird** sanctuary bordering the housing development. There he eluded police, and is believed to have made his escape dropping from a tree onto a passing freight—"

Another bird sanctuary appears in the 1962 short story "The Lie" *(reprinted in the 1968 collection* Welcome to the Monkey House), *donated to the exclusive private school Whitehill by the generous Remenzel family. In the short story* "The Big Space Fuck" *(reprinted in* Palm Sunday), *one romantic and hopeful soul who aligns himself with birds sees his efforts worthy of a very special recognition. Amateur birdhouse maker Dwayne Hoobler (his specialty was houses made from Clorox bottles) hopes his apparent humanitarianism would qualify him along with the world's genius population to contribute sperm for the spaceship* Arthur C. Clarke, *headed for interstellar intercourse.*

Birds become the manna of mankind in Galápagos *as narrator Leon Trout recalls.* (*Gal* 1:19) These **birds** (*blue-footed boobies*) would later become crucial to the survival of the little human colony on Santa Rosalia. If those **birds** hadn't been so stupid, so incapable of learning that human beings were dangerous, the first settlers would almost certainly have starved to death.

If the multitude of bird imagery is to be fully appreciated, one must consider Vonnegut's account of the mixed messages his foreign readers encounter. (*FWD* XVIII) The trouble I caused translators by naming a book *Jailbird* is worth an essay by itself. It turns out that countries older than my own have no word for persons who find themselves locked up again and again, since the penitentiary system, an invention of American Quakers, is so new. The closest European languages could come was with their words "**gallows bird**." This failed to describe the habitual criminal I had written about, since a person cannot be hanged again and again.

(*TQ* 15) Trout characterized the sort of work he was able to get back then (*during the Great Depression*) as "cleaning **birdshit** out of cuckoo clocks."

In one of the most touching moments, Vonnegut describes for Jane (his first wife; at her behest) the idyllic moment that would grace her passing from this earth. (*TQ* 34) I told her on the telephone that a sunburned, raffish, bored but not unhappy ten-year-old boy, whom we did not know, would be standing on the gravel slope of the boat-launching ramp at the foot of Scudder's Lane. He would gaze out at nothing in particular, **birds**, boats, or whatever, in the harbor of Barnstable, Cape Cod. . . .

I told Jane that this boy, with nothing better to do, would pick up a stone, as boys will. He would arc it over the harbor. When the stone hit the water, she would die.

(*TQ* 48) Kilgore Trout was born in a hospital in Bermuda, near where his father, Raymond, was gathering material for a follow-up on his doctoral dissertation on the last of the **Bermuda Erns**. The sole remaining rookery of those **great blue birds**, the largest of all pelagic raptors, was on Dead Man's Rock, an otherwise uninhabited lava steeple in the center of the notorious Bermuda Triangle. Trout was in fact conceived on Dead Man's Rock during his parents' honeymoon.

What was particularly interesting about these **erns** was that the female **birds**, and not anything people had done, so far as anybody could tell, were to blame for the rapidly dwindling population. In the past, and presumably for thousands of years, the females had hatched their eggs, and tended the young, and finally taught them to fly by kicking them off the top of the steeple.

But when Raymond Trout went there as a doctoral candidate with his bride, he found that the females had taken to bowdlerizing the nurturing process by kicking the eggs off the top of the steeple.

(*TQ* 48) Dr. Trout expected to film nothing more than ordinary **Dalhousies**, indistinguishable from other **Dalhousies**, but pecking at the backs of deer and moose instead of tree trunks. Such simple pictures would have been exciting enough, showing that lower animals were capable of cultural as well as biological evolution. One might have extrapolated from them the supposition that one **bird** in the flock was a sort of Albert Einstein, so to speak, having theorized and then proved that blackflies were as nutritious as anything that could be dug out of a tree trunk.

Was Dr. Trout ever in for a surprise, though! Not only were these **birds** obscenely fat, and thus easy prey for predators. They were exploding, too! Spores from a tree fungus growing near **Dalhousie** nests found an opportunity to become a new disease in the intestinal tracts of the overweight **birds**, thanks to certain chemicals in the bodies of blackflies.

The new life-style of the fungus inside the **birds** at one point triggered the sudden release of quantities of carbon dioxide so copious that the **birds** blew up! One **Dalhousie**, perhaps the last veteran of the Disappointment Lake experiment, would explode a year later in a park in Detroit, Michigan, setting off the second-worst race riot in the Motor City's history.

(*TQ* 49) Kilgore Trout, the ornithologist's son wrote in *My Ten Years on Automatic Pilot*: "**The Fiduciary is a mythological bird**. It has never existed in Nature, never could, never will."

Trout is the only person who ever said a fiduciary was any sort of **bird**. The noun (from the Latin fiducia, confidence, trust) in fact identifies a sort of Homo sapiens who will conserve the property, and nowadays especially paper or computer representations of wealth, belonging to other people, including the treasuries of their governments.

He or she or it cannot exist, thanks to the brain and the ding-dong, et cetera. So we have in this summer of 1996, rerun or not, and as always, faithless custodians of capital making themselves multimillionaires and multibillionaires, while playing beanbag with money better spent on creating meaningful jobs and training people to fill them, and raising our young and retiring our old in surroundings of respect and safety.

For Christ's sake, let's help more of our frightened people get through this thing, whatever it is. (BAG Unpaid Consultant) There was a stir in the restaurant. In the doorway stood Celeste, a **bird** of paradise, creating a sensation. (BAG 2BR02B) The zero in the telephone number he pronounced "naught."

The number was 2BR02B.

It was the telephone number of an institution whose fanciful sobriquets included "Automat," "**Birdland**," "Cannery," "Catbox," "Delouser," "Easy Go," "Good-bye, Mother," "Happy Hooligan," "Kiss Me Quick," "Lucky Pierre," "Sheepdip," "Waring Blender," "Weep No More," and "Why Worry?"

"To Be or Not to Be" was the telephone number of the municipal gas chambers of the Federal Bureau of Termination. *See also: PP* XII; XVII; *ST* 1; 2; 8; 10; 12; Epilogue; *MN* 24; *CC* 9; 66; 81; 95; 117; 120; 123; *GBR* 10; 14; *SL5* 5; 10; *MH* Where I Live; *MH* Welcome to the Monkey House; *MH* The Lie; *MH* The Kid Nobody Could Handle; *WJ* Act 3; *BC* 3; 4; 10; 15; 22; Epilogue; *WFG* Brief Encounters on the Inland Waterway; *WFG* Fortitude; *WFG* Excelsior! We're Going to the Moon! Excelsior!; *WFG* The Mysterious Madame Blavatsky; *WFG* Biafra: A People Betrayed; *WFG* Address to P.E.N. Conference in Stockholm, 1973; *Slap* 6; 13; 19; 33; 42; Epilogue; *JB* 4; 7; 8; 12; 15; 16; *PS* The First Amendment; *PS* Obscenity, containing the short story "The Big Space Fuck"; *PS* Jekyll and Hyde Updated; *DD* 3; 16; 20; 25; *Gal* 1:7; 1:9; 1:17; 1:19; 1:20; 1:24; 1:38; 2:1; 2:7; 2:8; *Blue* 1; 34; *HP* 6; 25; *FWD* XV; XVII; XX; *TQ* 46; 50; 53; 63; *BAG* Unpaid Consultant, This Son of Mine, Coda to My Career; *GBK* Harold Epstein; *MWC* 1.

Birnum, Birnum (*see* **God Bless You, Dr. Kevorkian**).

birth (*see also* **ethical birth control**). *Vonnegut's birth imagery provides a constant source of speculation about matters social, psychological, and literary. Perhaps his most memorable and imaginative application occurs in the science fiction short story "Welcome to the Monkey House," reprinted in* Welcome to the Monkey House. *J. Edgar Nation, a Grand Rapids pharmacist, has invented the ethical birth control pill as a partial response to overpopulation. The pills make people numb from the waist down and are a legal requirement of all sexually mature individuals. In order to control population growth, ethical birth control pills are paired with institutionalized Ethical Suicide Parlors. One pronging was the encouragement of ethical suicide, which consisted of going to the nearest Suicide Parlor and asking a Hostess to kill you painlessly while you lay on a Barcalounger. The other pronging was compulsory* **ethical birth control**.

In Breakfast of Champions, *Dwayne Hoover's mother dies during his birth (perhaps symbolic of Vonnegut's own feelings as the child left behind a mother's suicide), and this is the same book in which Vonnegut squares off with images of his father and his own psyche.*

In Deadeye Dick, *the book which makes a criminal act of Rudy Waltz's errant shot from the family home's cupola window (an act Vonnegut himself committed as a youngster but without such grave consequences), birth is termed a "peephole" interrupting an eternity. While at the Midland City Police Department after the shooting of Eloise Metzger, Rudy was taken to a much smaller cellblock on the top floor, the third floor, which was reserved for women and for children under the age of sixteen. There was only one other prisoner up there, a black woman from out of town, who had been taken off a Greyhound bus after beating up the white driver. She was from the Deep South, and she was the one who introduced me to the idea of* **birth's** *being an opening peephole, and of death's being when that peephole closes again (DD 12).*

A more conventional but no less meaningful birth image occurs when aspiring artist Rabo Karabekian travels cross country by train to become an apprentice to world famous illustrator Dan Gregory. (Blue 8) Yes, and when the Twentieth Century Limited from Chicago plunged into a tunnel under New York City, with its lining of pipes and wires, I was out of the womb into the **birth** canal.

Vonnegut's concern for and exploration of an individual's psychological development is at the core of Mother Night. *The following material highlights his interest in the inextricable nature of good and evil, the inextricable nature of our futures bound to our past, and the need to start life with positive models.* (MN Ed Note) The title of the book is Campbell's. It is taken from a speech by Mephistopheles in Goethe's *Faust.* As translated by Carlyle F. MacIntyre (New Directions, 1941), the speech is this:

I am a part of the part that at first was all, part of the darkness that gave **birth** to light, that supercilious light which now disputes with Mother Night her ancient rank and space, and yet can not succeed; no matter how it struggles, it sticks to matter and can't get free.

(MN 1) I (*Howard Campbell*) am an American by **birth**, a Nazi by reputation, and a nationless person by inclination.

(MN 45) My own feeling is that a child should start experimenting with real people and real communities from the moment of **birth**, if possible. If, for some reason, these materials are not available, then playthings must be used.

Vonnegut frequently writes about writing and art as giving birth to the imagination. (WFG Preface) If a person with a demonstrably ordinary mind, like mine, will devote himself to giving **birth** to a work of the imagination, that work will in turn tempt and tease the ordinary mind into cleverness.

(PS The People One Knows) To accept a new myth about ourselves is to simplify our memories—and to place our stamp of approval on what might become an epitaph for our era in the shorthand of history. This, in my opinion, is why critics often condemn our most significant books and poems and plays when they first appear, while praising fee-

bler creations. The **birth** of a new myth fills them with primitive dread, for myths are so effective.

(Blue 9) Let me (*Rabo Karabekian*) put it yet another way: life, by definition, is never still. Where is it going? From **birth** to death, with no stops on the way. Even a picture of a bowl of pears on a checkered tablecloth is liquid, if laid on canvas by the brush of a master. Yes, and by some miracle I was surely never able to achieve as a painter, nor was Dan Gregory, but which was achieved by the best of the Abstract Expressionists, in the paintings which have greatness **birth** and death are always there.

Birth and death were even on that old piece of beaverboard Terry Kitchen sprayed at seeming random so long ago. I don't know how he got them in there, and neither did he.

I sigh. "Ah, me," says old Rabo Karabekian.

(TQ Prologue) So now my last book is done, with the exception of this preface. Today is November 12th, 1996, about nine months, I would guess, from its publication date, from its emergence from the **birth** canal of a printing press. There is no rush.

(TQ 12) In no time, Sodium predicted, every human ailment, including acne and jock itch, would be not only incurable but fatal. "All humans will die," said Sodium, according to Trout. "As they were at the **birth** of the Universe, all elements will be free of sin again."

Iron and Magnesium seconded Sodium's motion. Phosphorus called for a vote. The motion was passed by acclamation.

(TQ 17) The inspiration for what Mrs. Wilkerson did to young Zoltan Pepper was of course *The Scarlet Letter* by Nathaniel Hawthorne. In that one, a woman has to wear a big A for *adultery* on her bosom because she let a man not her husband ejaculate in her **birth** canal. She won't tell what his name is. He's a *preacher*!

(TQ 18) "In my entire career as a writer," said Trout in the former Museum of the American Indian, "I created only one living, breathing, three-dimensional character. I did it with my ding-dong in a **birth** canal. Ting-a-ling!" He was referring to his son Leon, the deserter from the United States Marines in time of war, subsequently decapitated in a Swedish shipyard.

(*TQ* 20) Trout wrote of Eva Braun, "Her only crime was to have allowed a monster to ejaculate in her **birth** canal. These things happen to the best of women."

(*TQ* 22) As Trout would point out to me when I read that marker in 2001: "Warren G. Harding sired an illegitimate daughter by ejaculating in the **birth** canal of a stenographer in a broom closet at the White House."

(*TQ* 27) During regular working hours, he (*Dr. Fleon Sunoco*) does what he is paid to do, which is develop a **birth control pill** that takes all the pleasure out of sex, so teenagers won't copulate.

(*TQ* 32) The real reason my interest in the study of man as an animal flagged was that my wife Jane Marie Cox Vonnegut, who would die as Jane Marie Cox Yarmolinsky, gave **birth** to a baby named Mark. We needed bucks.

(*TQ* 41) I will say for the record that my grandfather Albert Lieber's first wife, Alice, née Barus, namesake of my sister Allie, died giving **birth** to her third child, who was Uncle Rudy.

(*TQ* 59) That the only descendant of the most egomaniacal and destructive villain in American history should bear that name did not become supremely ironical until, exactly two years from the night Booth ejaculated in Julia's **birth** canal while she was massively sedated, Booth sent a wad of lead into Lincoln's dog's breakfast, into Lincoln's brain.

(*BAG* 2BR02B) One bright morning in the Chicago Lying-In Hospital, a man named Edward K. Wehling, Jr., waited for his wife to give **birth**. He was the only man waiting. Not many people were born each day anymore.

Wehling was fifty-six, a mere stripling in a population whose average age was one hundred twenty-nine.

(*MWC* Author's Note) Yes, and last July (2004) there was an exhibition of Joe's and my stuff, arranged by Joe, at the Indianapolis Art Center in the town of my **birth**. But there was also a painting by my architect and painter grandfather Bernard Vonnegut, and two by my architect and painter father Kurt Vonnegut, and six apiece by my daughter Edith and my son the doctor Mark.

See also: PP V; XVIII; *CC* 10; 85; *GBR* 1; 2; 5; 8; *SL5* 2; 5; 8; 9; *MH* Welcome to the Monkey House; *WJ* I:6; *BC* 4; 15; 19; *WFG* Good Missiles, Good Manners, Good Night; *WFG* Address to Graduating Class at Bennington College; *Slap* Prologue; 2; 6; 10; *JB* 2; 6; *PS* Roots; *PS* The People One Knows; *PS* Religion; *PS* A Nazi Sympathizer Defended at Some Cost; *PS* The Sexual Revolution; *PS* In the Capital of the World; *DD* 4; 15; *Gal* 1:13; 1:15; 1:17; 1:18; 1:22; 1:26; 1:27; 1:33; 1:37; 2:3; *Blue* 2; 9; 24; 27; 36; *HP* 1; 4; 11; 34; 39; 40; *FWD* I; III; V; VIII; IX; X; XI; XII; XIII; XIX; XXI.

Black Brothers of Islam. *The leading prison gang at the Athena prison in* Hocus Pocus. *Headed by Abdullah Akhbahr, the gang's literacy program is based on the anti-Semitic* Protocols of the Elders of Zion, *hundreds of copies of which are supplied by their Libyan supporters.*

Black Cat Café. *Considered a whorehouse by the Tarkington College crowd, the Black Cat Café is a well-respected, tightly protected community business. Owned and operated by Lyle Hooper,* "he would never admit that the availability of prostitutes in his parking lot accounted in large measure for the business he did in liquor and snacks, and for the condom machine in the men's room" (*HP* 28).

Eugene Debs Hartke tries to pass on to Tarkington freshmen the importance and position of the bar in local circles, "I had told them, too, that they were never to go into the **Black Cat Café**, which the townspeople considered their private club. It was one place they could go and not be reminded of how dependent they were on the rich kids on the hill, but I didn't say that. Neither did I say that freelance prostitutes were sometimes found there, and in the past had been the cause of outbreaks of venereal disease on campus" (*HP* 13).

Black Garterbelt (*see also* **Plague on Wheels**). *The pornographic magazine that publishes Kilgore Trout's short stories as filler for their photographs. Before traveling to the Midland City Arts Festival in* Breakfast of Champions, *Trout rummages through the old book and magazine bin of a Times Square book store and purchases the April 1962 edition containing his short story "Plague on Wheels." He wasn't aware it had been published.*

In Hocus Pocus, *Jack Patton gives a copy of the porn magazine to Eugene Debs Hartke as a gift*

while the two serve in Vietnam. Hartke stores it, unopened, in his footlocker. Sixteen years after fleeing Vietnam on the last helicopter to leave the American embassy in Saigon, Hartke and his army footlocker are reunited by United Parcel Service. Upon opening the long-lost footlocker and its contents, Hartke finally had a chance to read the short story "The Protocols of the Elders of Tralfamadore." Though no mention of the author is made, its science fiction motif and references to Tralfamadore are similar to other Kilgore Trout stories.
See also: BC 5; HP 15; 18; 20–22.

black humor (*see* **humor**).

Black Panthers (*see* **Lincoln High School**).

Blackbeard. *Philip Castle's book* San Lorenzo: The Land, the History the People *reveals that Bokonon's grandfather discovered* one quarter of a million dollars in buried pirate treasure, presumably a treasure of **Blackbeard** (*Edward Teach*).

    Blackbeard's treasure was reinvested by Bokonon's family in asphalt, copra, cacao, livestock, and poultry (CC 48).

Blake, William (1757–1827). *Howard Campbell borrows from Blake for the epigraph to his* Memoirs of a Monogamous Casanova. *(MN 23) It is a poem by* **William Blake** *called "The Question Answered":* What is it men in women do require? / The lineaments of Gratified Desire. / What is it we do in men require? / The lineaments of Gratified Desire.

    On the stairway of the volunteer fire department in Rosewater, Eliot and his father exchange Blake's poetry on the walls. (GBR 5) Eliot had painted out the messages (from the dentist who previously occupied the space). He had written a new one, a poem by **William Blake.** *This was broken up so as to fit twelve risers:* The Angel / that presided / o'er my / birth said, / "little creature, / form'd of / Joy & Mirth, / Go love / Without the / help of / any Thing / on Earth."

    At the foot of the stairs, written in pencil on the wall, by the Senator himself, was the Senator's rebuttal, another poem by **Blake:** Love seeketh only Self to please, / To bind another to Its delight, / Joys

in another's loss of ease, / And builds a Hell in Heaven's despite.

(SL5 5) One thing Trout said that Rosewater liked very much was that there really *were* vampires and werewolves and goblins and angels and so on, but that they were in the fourth dimension. So was **William Blake**, Rosewater's favorite poet, according to Trout. So were heaven and hell.

(PS Self-Interview) VONNEGUT: My education was as a chemist at Cornell and then an anthropologist at the University of Chicago. Christ—I was thirty-five before I went crazy about **Blake**, forty before I read *Madame Bovary*, forty-five before I'd even heard of Céline. Through dumb luck, I read *Look Homeward, Angel* exactly when I was supposed to.

(GBK Mary Wollstonecraft Shelley) This incredibly precocious writer's mother was a famous writer, too. Some of her books were illustrated by none other than **William Blake**! Imagine having one's book illustrated by **William Blake**! Her most passionate subject: the right of women to be treated as the equals of men.

(GBK Mary Wollstonecraft Shelley) My mystery dead person's father was a writer, too, an anti-Calvinist preacher who wrote, most memorably, "God himself has no right to be a tyrant."

    Who were the friends of such distinguished parents? **William Blake** and Thomas Paine, and William Wordsworth to name a few.

Blank, Katarina. *She was a café waitress when she married Clemens Vonnegut in 1852. Together they had Bernard Vonnegut, Kurt's grandfather. (PS Roots) She was one of seven children of a German immigrant family of peasants who came from Urloffen in Baden and settled on a farm in Wayne Township, Marion County, just west of Indianapolis. They were struggling to get their farm to be productive after felling the forest trees and draining the land.*

Blankenship, Dr. Martin Peale. *In* Hocus Pocus, *the Rhodes Scholar and University of Chicago economist is scheduled to be the graduation speaker at Tarkington College. His niece in the graduating class is Hortense Mellon. Blankenship is also close* *friends with talk show host and conservative newspaper columnist Jason Wilder.*

BLINC System. *The Blast Interval Normalization Computer, derived from the Robo-Magic washing machine and that becomes the essential component in the bomb sight release mechanism the company produces during World War II.* (BC 22) The Robo-Magic dream was interrupted by World War Two. . . . All that survived of the Robo-Magic itself was its brain, which had told the rest of the machine when to let the water in, when to let the water out, when to slosh, when to rinse, when to spin dry, and so on.

That brain became the nerve center of the so-called "**BLINC System**" during the Second World War. It was installed on heavy bombers, and it did the actual dropping of bombs after a bombardier pressed his bright red "bombs away" button. The button activated the **BLINC System**, which then released the bombs in such a way as to achieve a desired pattern of explosions on the planet below. "**BLINC**" was an abbreviation of "**Blast Interval Normalization Computer.**"

blivit. *This is Vonnegut's tongue-in-cheek introductory description of the collection composing* Palm Sunday. *He likens the broad range of material covered in that text to his brother's adolescent radio experiments which could be detected across all the radio frequencies in Indianapolis.* (PS Introduction) THIS is certainly that kind of masterpiece, and a new name should be created for such an all-frequencies assault on the sensibilities. I propose the name *blivit.* This is a word which during my adolescence was defined by peers as "two pounds of shit in a one-pound bag."

I would not mind if books simpler than this one, but combining fiction and fact, were also called **blivits**. This would encourage *The New York Times Book Review* to establish a third category for best sellers, one long needed, in my opinion. If there were a separate list for **blivits**, then authors of **blivits** could stop stepping in the faces of mere novelists and historians and so on. . . .

THIS book is not only a **blivit** but a collage. It began with my wish to collect in one volume most of the reviews and speeches and essays I had written since the publication of a similar collection, *Wampeters, Foma & Granfalloons,* in 1974. But as I arranged those fragments in this order and then that one, I saw that they formed a sort of autobiography, especially if I felt free to include some pieces not written by me. To give life to such a golem, however, I would have to write much new connective tissue. This I have done.

Blue Fairy Godmother (*see also* **Frank Wirtanen**). *Howard W. Campbell calls Harold J. Sparrow, alias Colonel Frank Wirtanen, his Blue Fairy Godmother because no one believes he was an American agent recruited and maintained by Colonel Wirtanen. The U.S. government neither confirms nor denies Wirtanen's existence.*

In Slaughterhouse-Five *there is another Blue Fairy Godmother. The red-headed British POW who beats up Paul Lazzaro also plays the part of Cinderella's Blue Fairy Godmother in a production by the British prisoners. His silver-painted airman's boots are taken by Billy Pilgrim when he, Lazzaro, and Edgar Derby are quartered in the barracks with the stage set.*

Blue Mill. *In the short story "A Night for Love," this is the one memorable restaurant Milly Whitman dines in with a young Louis C. Reinbeck, twenty years before the action of the tale.*

blue tubing, blue tunnel (*also* **tunnel** *and* **tube** *when used to mean the* **blue tunnel of the Afterlife;** *see also* **Afterlife, funnel,** *and* **God Bless You, Dr. Kevorkian**). *Throughout* Galápagos, *the narrator, Leon Trout, informs the reader about what awaits each new person as they pass away.* (Gal 2:1) I *(Leon Trout)* was painlessly decapitated one day by a falling sheet of steel while working inside the hull of the *Bahía de Darwin,* at which time I refused to set foot in the **blue tunnel** leading into the Afterlife.

(Gal 1:14) When the first Santa Rosalia marriage was performed by Kamikaze and Akiko in the year 2027, all of the original colonists had long since vanished into the sinuous **blue tunnel** which leads into the Afterlife.

(*Gal* 2:7) The question the **blue tunnel** implies by appearing is one only I can answer: Have I at last exhausted my curiosity as to what life is all about? If so, I need only step inside what I liken to a vacuum cleaner. If there is indeed suction within the **blue tunnel**, which is filled with a light much like that cast off by the electric stoves and ovens of the *Bahía de Darwin*, it does not seem to trouble my late father, the science fiction writer Kilgore Trout, who can stand right in the nozzle and chat with me.

(*GBK* Introduction) My first near-death experience was an accident, a botched anesthesia during a triple bypass. I had listened to several people on TV talk shows who had gone down the **blue tunnel** to the Pearly Gates, and even beyond the Pearly Gates, or so they said, and then come back to life again. But I certainly wouldn't have set out on such a risky expedition on purpose, without first having survived one, and then planned another in cooperation with Dr. Jack Kevorkian and the staff at the state-of-the-art lethal injection execution facility at Huntsville, Texas.

(*GBK* Introduction) There will be no more round trips for me, barring another accident. For the sake of my family, I am trying to reinstate my health and life insurance policies, if possible. But other journalists, and perhaps even tourists, will surely follow the safe two-way path I pioneered. I beg them to be content, as I learned to be, with interviews they are able to conduct on the hundred yards or so of vacant lot between the far end of the **blue tunnel and the Pearly Gates**.

To go through the **Pearly Gates**, no matter how tempting the interview on the other side, as I myself discovered the hard way, is to run the risk that crotchety Saint Peter, depending on his mood, may never let you out again. Think of how heartbroken your friends and relatives would be if, by going through the Pearly Gates to talk to Napoleon, say, you in effect committed suicide.

(*GBK* Dr. Mary D. Ainsworth) on my near death experience this morning, I found out what becomes of people who die while they're still babies. Finding that out was accidental, since I'd gone down the **blue tunnel** to interview Dr. Mary D. Ainsworth, who died last March 21, age eighty-five, in Char-

lottesville, Virginia. She was a retired but active-to-the-end developmental psychologist. . . . It turns out that there are nurseries and nursery schools and kindergartens in Heaven for people who died when they were babies. Volunteer surrogate mothers, or sometimes the babies' actual mothers, if they're dead, bond like crazy with the little souls. Cuddle, cuddle, cuddle, Kiss, kiss, kiss. Don't cry, little baby. Your mommy loves you. Bet you have to burp. I'll bet that's the trouble. There. Feel better? Time to go sleepy-bye. Goo, goo, goo.

And the babies grow up to be angels. That's where angels come from!

(*GBK* Salvatore Biagini) this morning, thanks to a controlled near-death experience, I was lucky enough to meet, at the far end of the **blue tunnel**, a man named Salvatore Biagini. Last July 8th, Mr. Biagini, a retired construction worker, age seventy, suffered a fatal heart attack while rescuing his beloved schnauzer, Teddy, from an assault by an unrestrained pit bull named Chele, in Queens. . . . I asked this historic pet lover how it felt to have died for a schnauzer named Teddy. Salvador Biagini was philosophical. He said it sure as heck beat dying for absolutely nothing in the Viet Nam War.

(*GBK* Birnum Birnum) after this morning's controlled near death experience I am almost literally heartbroken that there was no way for me to take a tape recorder down the **blue tunnel** to Heaven and back again. Never before had there been a New Orleans–style brass band, led by the late Louis Armstrong, to greet a new arrival with a rousing rendition of "When the Saints Come Marching In." The recipient of this very rare and merry honor, accorded to only one in ten million newly dead people, I'm told, was an Australian Aborigine, with some white blood, named Birnum Birnum. . . . Only in 1967, practically the day before yesterday, were the surviving Australian Aborigines granted citizenship, thanks to demonstrations led by Birnum Birnum. He was the first of his people to attend law school.

(*GBK* Roberta Gorsuch Burke) They married four years later. If past performance is any indication, they will surely stay married there at the far end of the **blue tunnel** throughout all eternity. She said to me, "Why fool around?" President Clinton told her at her husband's funeral, when she still had a year to live, "You have blessed America with your service and set an example not only for navy wives today, and to come, but for all Americans."

The simple epitaph Roberta Gorsuch Burke chose for her tombstone here on Earth: "A Sailor's Wife."

(GBK Eugene Victor Debs) And then, guess what, yesterday afternoon none other than Eugene Victor Debs, organizer and leader of the first successful strike against a major American industry, the railroads, was waiting for me at the far end of the **blue tunnel**. . . . I thanked him for words of his, which I quote again and again in lectures: "As long as there is a lower class, I am in it. As long as there is a criminal element, I am of it. As long as there is a soul in prison, I am not free."

(GBK Clarence Darrow) On this morning's trip down the **blue tunnel to the pearly gates**, Clarence Darrow, the great American defense attorney, dead for sixty years now, came looking for me.

(GBK Isaac Newton) during my controlled near-death experiences, I've met Sir Isaac Newton, who died back in 1727, as often as I've met Saint Peter. They both hang out at the Heaven end of the **blue tunnel of the Afterlife**. Saint Peter is there because that's his job. Sir Isaac is there because of his insatiable curiosity about what the **blue tunnel** is, how the **blue tunnel** works.

(GBK William Shakespeare) I asked him if he had love affairs with men as well as women, knowing how eager my WNYC audience was to have this matter settled. His answer, however, celebrated affection between animals of any sort:

"We were as twinn'd lambs that did frisk in the sun, and bleat the one at the other: what we chang'd was innocence for innocence." By changed he meant exchanged: "What we exchanged was innocence for innocence." That has to be the softest core pornography I ever heard.

And he was through with me. In effect, he told your reporter to go screw himself. "Get thee to a nunnery!" he said, and off he went.

I felt like such a fool as I made my way back to the **blue tunnel**.

(GBK Carla Faye Tucker) it is late in the afternoon of February 3, 1998. I have just been unstrapped

from a gurney following another controlled near-death experience in this busy execution chamber in Huntsville, Texas.

For the first time in my career, I was actually on the heels of a celebrity as I made my way down the **blue tunnel to Paradise**. She was Carla Faye Tucker, the born again murderer of two strangers with a pick-axe. Carla Faye was completely killed here, by the State of Texas, shortly after lunch time.

Two hours later, on another gurney, I myself was made only three-quarters dead. I caught up with Carla Faye in the **tunnel**, about a hundred fifty yards from the far end, near the **Pearly Gates**. Since she was dragging her feet, I hastened to assure her that there was no Hell waiting for her, no Hell waiting for anyone. She said that was too bad because she would be glad to go to Hell if only she could take the governor of Texas with her. "He's a murderer, too," said Carla Faye. "He murdered me."

See also: Gal 1:15; 1:18; 1:21; 1:25; 1:27; 1:28; 1:29; 1:30; 1:35; 2:3; 2:7; 2:8.

Bluebeard, *Bluebeard* (see **Rabo Karabekian** for *a more complete discussion of the novel*). *Rabo Karabekian titles his memoirs* Bluebeard *by drawing this analogy.* (Blue 5) So: **Bluebeard** is a fictitious character in a very old children's tale, possibly based loosely on a murderous nobleman of long ago. In the story, he has married many times. He marries for the umpteenth time, and brings his latest child bride back to his castle. He tells her that she can go into any room but one, whose door he shows her.

Bluebeard is either a poor psychologist or a great one, since all his new wife can think about is what might be behind the door. So she takes a look when she thinks he isn't home, but he really *is* home.

He catches her just at the point she is gazing aghast at the bodies of all his former wives in there, all of whom he has murdered, save for the first one, for looking behind the door. The first one got murdered for something else.

So—of all the people who know about my locked potato barn, the one who finds the mystery most intolerable is surely Circe Berman. She is after me all the time to tell her where the six keys are, and I tell her again that they are buried in a golden casket at the foot of Mount Ararat.

I said to her the last time she asked, which was about five minutes ago:

"Look: think about something else, anything else. I am **Bluebeard**, and my studio is my *forbidden chamber* as far as *you're* concerned."

(FWD III) I would eventually write a book about a painter, *Bluebeard*. I got the idea for it after *Esquire* asked me for a piece about the Abstract Expressionist Jackson Pollock. The magazine was putting together a fiftieth anniversary issue to consist of essays on fifty native-born Americans who had made the biggest difference in the country's destiny since 1932. I wanted Eleanor Roosevelt but Bill Moyers already had her.

(FWD III) The Franklin Library asked me to provide a special preface to its expensive edition of **Bluebeard** (illustrated by my daughter Edith Squibb). So I blathered on some more about painting, which my father and I both did badly.

(FWD III) Our guards had disappeared, and the Russian Army had not yet arrived, and we found ourselves in the valley I describe at the end of my novel **Bluebeard** (called **Bluebird** in the meticulously edited *New York Times*). *The scene is recreated by Rabo Karabekian in his 8' x 64' triptych "Now It's the Women's Turn."*

(FWD XVII) (In my novel **Bluebeard** I describe a valley full of refugees at the end of WW II. It wasn't imaginary. It was real. O'Hare and I were there.)

(FWD What Bernard V. O'Hare Said) In my novel **Bluebeard** I described the valley we have just left behind. It is being stripped of everything edible, as though by a locust plague, by liberated prisoners of war like ourselves, by convicts, lunatics, concentration camp victims, and slave laborers, and by armed German soldiers.

(TQ 25) I say in my novel **Bluebeard**, "Beware of gods bearing gifts." I think I had Allie in mind when I wrote that, and Allie in mind again when, in *Timequake One*, I had Monica Pepper spray-paint "FUCK ART!" in orange and purple across the steel front door of the Academy. Allie didn't know there was such an institution as the Academy, I'm almost sure, but she would have been happy to see those words emblazoned anywhere.

(TQ 35) Here's the thing: For a few days after Germany surrendered, on May 7th, 1945, having been directly or indirectly responsible for the deaths of maybe forty million people, there was a pocket of anarchy south of Dresden, near the Czech border, which had yet to be occupied and policed by troops of the Soviet Union. I was in it, and have described it some in my novel **Bluebeard**. Thousands of prisoners of war like myself had been turned loose there, along with death camp survivors with tattooed arms, and lunatics and convicted felons and Gypsies, and who knows what else.

See also: BAG Preface by Peter Reed.

Bluebird Farm. *In* Breakfast of Champions, *the location of Sacred Miracle Cave, once owned by the maternal ancestors of ambulance driver Eddie Key and later owned by Dwayne Hoover in partnership with the twins Lyle and Kyle Hoover.*

Boaz. *The twenty-three-year-old Private, First Class, who is one of the eight hundred real commanders of the Army of Mars in* The Sirens of Titan. *Boaz is fourteen when recruited for the Army of Mars. He and Unk (Malachi Constant) are paired together as part of the buddy system. In Boaz's right front trouser pocket is a control box capable of transmitting all sorts of signals to the antennas placed in the skulls of the Martian forces. As one of the real commanders, Boaz did not have his mind erased. He was in charge of one-tenth of the force assigned to attack the United States. He and Unk avoid the massacre awaiting the others in his command who fall in the Battle of Boca Raton. Rumfoord's alteration of the automatic pilot on their ship takes them to the caves of Mercury, where Boaz falls in love with the gentle harmoniums who inhabit them. He decides to stay with the harmoniums rather than leave with Unk because he feels he can do good deeds for them, whereas he doesn't know how to behave well with people nor do others know how to treat him well.*

Bob (*see* **Wild Bob**).

Bob & Ray. *Comedians Bob Goulding and Ray Elliott are among Vonnegut's all-time favorite comedians. The nature of his affinity for them and the* *similarity of their work with his is revealed in this passage reprinted in* Palm Sunday. *(PS The People One Knows)* And here is what I said about my friends **Bob Elliott** and **Ray Goulding**, perhaps the most significant and ridiculous American comedy team alive today, as an introduction to their book *Write If You Get Work: The Best of Bob & Ray* (Random House, 1975):

> It is the truth: Comedians and jazz musicians have been more comforting and enlightening to me than preachers or politicians or philosophers or poets or painters or novelists of my time. Historians in the future, in my opinion, will congratulate us on very little other than our clowning and our jazz. . . .
>
> It occurs to me, too, as I look through this marvelous book, that **Bob and Ray's** jokes are singularly burglar-proof. They aren't like most other comedians' jokes these days, aren't rooted in show business and the world of celebrities and news of the day. They feature Americans who are almost always fourth-rate or below, engaged in enterprises which, if not contemptible, are at least insane.
>
> And while other comedians show us persons tormented by bad luck and enemies and so on, **Bob and Ray's** characters threaten to wreck themselves and their surroundings with their own stupidity. There is a refreshing and beautiful innocence in **Bob's and Ray's** humor.
>
> Man is not evil, they seem to say. He is simply too hilariously stupid to survive.
>
> And this I believe.
>
> Cheers.

Bockman, Dr. Fred and Marion. *The physicist from Wyandotte College and his wife in the 1951 short story "The Euphio Question," reprinted in* Welcome to the Monkey House *(1968). He develops a radio telescope that transmits a pleasantly incapacitating hiss from empty areas of space. Bockman is asked to be a guest on Lew Harrison's radio talk show when he first airs the sounds from space. The sociology professor who got the two men together develops the term "Bockman's Euphoria" to* describe the cosmic hiss. He develops the euphoriaphone ("euphio") at the urging of Harrison, who sees the opportunity to cash in on one's conscious incapacitation.*

Bodovskov, Stepan. *The Russian corporal and interpreter is among the first troops to enter Berlin in* Mother Night. *He finds Howard Campbell's theater trunk full of unpublished poems, plays, and one novel. Bodovskov publishes the poems and gains fame with the theater production of* The Goblet, *a particular favorite of Stalin's.*

The novel in the trunk is Memoirs of a Monogamous Casanova, *Campbell's homage to the love he shared with his wife, Helga, and this becomes a widely distributed and often-translated underground classic.*

Despite a magnificent career as a professional plagiarist, Bodovskov is eventually executed for writing an original satire of the Red Army. George Kraft / Iona Potapov turns him in once his friendship with Howard Campbell convinces him Bodovskov is a fraud. Bodovskov's home is searched and the offending original material brings about his execution. This is an interesting and rather excessive end for a failed writer who steals the words of another.

Bohn, Arthur. (PS Roots) "Returning to Indianapolis in 1883, he engaged in the practice of architecture, first in his own office and later with **Arthur Bohn** in what became the well-known firm of Vonnegut & **Bohn**, whose successors are in practice today. This firm designed and supervised construction of many fine residences and public buildings in Indianapolis, including the first Chamber of Commerce, the Athenaeum, the John Herron Art Museum, the L.S. Ayres store, the Fletcher Trust Building, and many others."
(PS Roots) "At the age of nineteen he was well prepared in a solid foundation of secondary education, and was admitted to the Massachusetts Institute of Technology, where he studied architecture and took his degree of Bachelor of Science in 1908 — the year in which his father died. He then went with his widowed mother and his sister, Irma, to Berlin, and continued his architectural studies with the best masters. He returned to Indianapolis in

1910, and joined his father's surviving partner, **Arthur Bohn**, in the well-established firm of Vonnegut & **Bohn**. He was thus launched upon what promised to be a comfortable and successful career. His family had a prominent position in the community. They had plenty of money."

boko-maru, boko-maruing (*see also* **Bokononism**). (CC 72) What I had seen, of course, was the Bokononist ritual of *boko-maru*, or the mingling of awarenesses.

We Bokononists believe that it is impossible to be sole-to-sole with another person without loving the person, provided the feet of both persons are clean and nicely tended.

The basis for the foot ceremony is this "Calypso": We will touch our feet, yes, / Yes, for all we're worth, / And we will love each other, yes, / Yes, like we love our Mother Earth.

Dr. Julian Castle is convinced he can't operate his House of Hope and Mercy in the jungle without aspirin and boko-maru.

Bokonon. *The black founder and prophet of Bokononism whose real name is Lionel Boyd Johnson, the youngest of six children born and educated in the Episcopalian schools of Tobago. His family's wealth is based on one of Blackbeard's treasures found by his grandfather.*

In 1911 Johnson sets sail alone for London in the sloop Lady's Slipper, *in search of higher education. By his own admission he was a carouser and womanizer in his youth, prompting his own analogy between his later role as a religious leader with the admissions of Saint Augustine.* (CC 48) When I was young, / I was so gay and mean, / And I drank and chased the girls / Just like young St. Augustine. / Saint Augustine, / He got to be a saint. / So, if I get to be one, also, / Please, Mama, don't you faint.

In 1922 Johnson and Corporal Earl McCabe set sail in the Lady's Slipper *for Tobago, but are shipwrecked and wash ashore on San Lorenzo. When they see how impoverished the people are despite the wealth of Castle Sugar and the Catholic Church, they seek to reform the political power structure of the country.*

Castle Sugar withdraws since their dreams of cultivating the hard clay simply fail. McCabe overhauls

the economy and civil laws, and Bokonon designs a new religion. (CC 58) I wanted all things / To seem to make some sense, / So we all could be happy, yes, / Instead of tense. / And I made up lies / So that they all fit nice, / And I made this sad world par-a-dise.

The lies, "foma," Bokonon made up are included in his ongoing tract The Books of Bokonon. *Bokonon and McCabe base their plan of development for San Lorenzo on the theory of "Dynamic Tension," which Bokonon learned from ads for Charles Atlas's fitness and muscle building system. Bokonon was, in fact, an alumnus of the Charles Atlas program.* (CC 47) It was the belief of Charles Atlas that muscles could be built without bar bells or spring exercisers, could be built by simply pitting one set of muscles against another.

It was the belief of **Bokonon** that good societies could be built only by pitting good against evil, and by keeping the tension between the two high at all times.

The illustration facing page 1 in A Man Without a Country *is from* Cat's Cradle. *The Bokonon calypso reads in all caps:*

OH, A LION HUNTER
IN THE JUNGLE DARK,
AND A SLEEPING DRUNKARD
UP IN CENTRAL PARK,
AND A CHINESE DENTIST
AND A BRITISH QUEEN
ALL FIT TOGETHER
IN THE SAME MACHINE.
NICE, NICE,
SUCH VERY DIFFERENT
PEOPLE IN THE SAME DEVICE!
　　　　　—BOKONON

(MWC 2) And I consider anybody a twerp who hasn't read the greatest American short story, which is "Occurrence at Owl Creek Bridge," by Ambrose Bierce. *The illustration on the facing page is also from Bokonon and reads in all caps:*

I WANTED ALL
THINGS TO SEEM TO
MAKE SOME SENSE,
SO WE COULD ALL BE

HAPPY, YES, INSTEAD
OF TENSE. AND I
MADE UP LIES, SO
THEY ALL FIT NICE,
AND I MADE THIS
SAD WORLD A
PARADISE.

(MWC 9) The Chinese also gave us, via Marco Polo, pasta and the formula for gunpowder.
The opposing page is illustrated in all caps with the following:

WE DO, DOODLEY DO,
DOODLEY DO, DOODLEY DO,
WHAT WE MUST,
MUDDILY MUST,
MUDDILY MUST,
MUDDILY MUST,
UNTIL WE BUST,
BODILY BUST,
BODILY BUST,
BODILY BUST.

—BOKONON

(MWC 12) I used to be the owner and manager of an automobile dealership in West Barnstable, Massachusetts, called Saab Cape Cod. It and I went out of business thirty-three years ago. The Saab then, as now, was a Swedish car, and I now believe my failure as a dealer so long ago explains what would otherwise remain a deep mystery: Why the Swedes have never given me a Nobel Prize for Literature. Old Norwegian proverb *(illustrated on facing page):*

PECULIAR
TRAVEL SUGGESTIONS
ARE
DANCING LESSONS
FROM GOD

—BOKONON

"Swedes have short dicks but long memories."

Bokononism, Bokononist. *The outlawed religion conceived by Lionel Boyd Johnson and Earl*

McCabe, practiced exclusively on the island of San Lorenzo. Practitioners of the religion run the risk of death on the hook. The truth is that everyone on San Lorenzo is a Bokononist. Johnson (Bokonon) and McCabe develop the religion as part of their theory of dynamic tension. (CC 1) We **Bokononists** believe that humanity is organized into teams, teams that do God's Will without ever discovering what they are doing. Such a team is called a *karass* by **Bokonon**, and the instrument, the *kan-kan*, that brought me into my own particular karass was the book I never finished, the book to be called *The Day the World Ended.*
(CC 4) The first sentence in *The Books of Bokonon* is this:
"All of the true things I am about to tell you are shameless lies."
My **Bokononist** warning is this:
Anyone unable to understand how a useful religion can be founded on lies will not understand this book either.
(CC 24) Which brings me to the **Bokononist** concept of a *wampeter*.
A *wampeter* is the pivot of a *karass*. No karass is without a *wampeter*, **Bokonon** tells us, just as no wheel is without a hub.
Anything can be a *wampeter*: a tree, a rock, an animal, an idea, a book, a melody, the Holy Grail. Whatever it is, the members of its *karass* revolve about it in the majestic chaos of a spiral nebula. The orbits of the members of a *karass* about their common *wampeter* are spiritual orbits, naturally. It is souls and not bodies that revolve. As **Bokonon** invites us to sing:

Around and around and around we spin,
With feet of lead and wings of tin. . . .

And *wampeters* come and *wampeters* go, **Bokonon** tells us.
At any given time a *karass* actually has two *wampeters*—one waxing in importance, one waning. (CC 31) As a **Bokononist**, of course, I would have agreed gaily to go anywhere anyone suggested. As **Bokonon** says: "Peculiar travel suggestions are dancing lessons from God."
(CC 32) *Busy, busy, busy,* is what we **Bokononists** whisper whenever we think of how complicated

and unpredictable the machinery of life really is. (*CC* 34) It was in the tombstone salesroom that I had my first *vin-dit*, a **Bokononist** word meaning a sudden, very personal shove in the direction of **Bokononism**, in the direction of believing that God Almighty knew all about me, after all, that God Almighty had some pretty elaborate plans for me.

The following excerpt is a reference to Bokononism as part of the grand theory of dynamic tensions: (*CC* 47) And, in Castle's book, I read my first **Bokononist** poem, or "Calypso." It went like this: "Papa" Monzano, he's so very bad, / But without bad "Papa" I would be so sad; / Because without "Papa's" badness, / Tell me, if you would, / How could wicked old **Bokonon** / Ever, ever look good? (*CC* 72) What I had seen, of course, was the **Bokononist** ritual of *boko-maru*, or the mingling of awarenesses.

We **Bokononists** believe that it is impossible to be sole-to-sole with another person without loving the person, provided the feet of both persons are clean and nicely tended. (*CC* 85) I learned some things, but they were scarcely helpful. I learned of the **Bokononist** cosmogony, for instance, wherein *Borasisi*, the sun, held *Pabu*, the moon, in his arms, and hoped that would bear him a fiery child.

But poor *Pabu* gave birth to children that were cold, that did not burn; and *Borasisi* threw them away in disgust. These were the planets, who circled their terrible father at a safe distance.

Then poor *Pabu* herself was cast away, and she went to live with her favorite child, which was Earth. Earth was *Pabu's* favorite because it had people on it; and the people looked up at her and loved her and sympathized.

And what opinion did **Bokonon** hold of his own cosmogony? "Foma! Lies!" he wrote. "A pack of *foma!*"

(*CC* 89) "Do you know anybody who *might* want the job?" Fran was giving a classic illustration of what **Bokonon** calls *duffle*. *Duffle*, in the **Bokononist** sense, is the destiny of thousands upon thousands of persons when placed in the hands of a *stuppa*. A *stuppa* is a fogbound child. (*CC* 90) All things conspired to form one cosmic *vin-dit*, one mighty shove into **Bokononism**, into

the belief that God was running my life and that He had work for me to do.

And, inwardly, I *sarooned*, which is to say that I acquiesced to the seeming demands of my *vin-dit*.

Inwardly, I agreed to become the next President of San Lorenzo.

(*CC* 94) "What *is* sacred to **Bokononists**?" I asked after a while.

"Not even God, as near as I can tell."

"Nothing?"

"Just one thing."

I made some guesses. "The ocean? The sun?"

"Man," said Frank. "That's all. Just man."

(*CC* 98) "I (*Dr. von Koenigswald*) agree with one **Bokononist** idea. I agree that all religions, including **Bokononism**, are nothing but lies."

(*CC* 106) "Pain, ice, Mona—everything. And then 'Papa' said, 'Now I will destroy the whole world.'"

"What did he mean by that?"

"It's what **Bokononists** always say when they are about to commit suicide."

(*CC* 125) When I hadn't been writing, I'd been poring over *The Books of Bokonon*, but the reference to midgets had escaped me. I was grateful to Newt for calling it to my attention, for the quotation captured in a couplet the cruel paradox of **Bokononist** thought, the heartbreaking necessity of lying about reality, and the heartbreaking impossibility of lying about it.

> Midget, midget, midget, how he struts and
>   winks,
> For he knows a man's as big as what he
>   hopes and thinks!

Bolivar. *San Lorenzo's capital and only city. Despite the flattering advertising of Bolivar as a modern city, Bolivar is a third-world mess complete with a useless state-of-the-art hotel amidst the squalor of tin can and wooden crate abodes.* (*CC* 60) **Bolivar** had had many names: Caz-ma-cas-ma, Santa Maria, Saint Louis, Saint George, and Port Glory among them. It was given its present name by Johnson and McCabe in 1922, was named in honor of **Simón Bolívar**, the great Latin-American idealist and hero.

When Johnson and McCabe came upon the city, it was built of twigs, tin, crates, and mud-rested on the catacombs of a trillion happy scavengers, catacombs in a sour mash of slop, feculence, and slime.

That was pretty much the way I *(John/Jonah)* found it, too, except for the new architectural false face along the water front.

Böll, Heinrich. *(TQ 12)* I asked the late great German novelist **Heinrich Böll** what the basic flaw was in the German character. He said, "Obedience."

bomb, bomb proof, bomb shelter, bombed, bombed-out, bombing, bombproof, bomb-shells, timebomb. *(These bomb references are only for non-nuclear devices. See **A-bomb** for all other references to nuclear bombs.) Vonnegut's introduction to* Mother Night *includes his most direct account of what it was like in the slaughterhouse meatlocker during the firebombing of Dresden. (MN Introduction)* But high explosives were dropped on Dresden by American and British planes on the night of February 13, 1945, just about twenty-one years ago, as I now write. There were no particular targets for the **bombs**. The hope was that they would create a lot of kindling and drive firemen underground.

And then hundreds of thousands of tiny incendiaries were scattered over the kindling, like seeds on freshly turned loam. More **bombs** were dropped to keep firemen in their holes, and all the little fires grew, joined one another, became one apocalyptic flame. Hey presto: fire storm. It was the largest massacre in European history, by the way. And so what?

We didn't get to see the fire storm. We were in a cool meat-locker under a slaughterhouse with our six guards and ranks and ranks of dressed cadavers of cattle, pigs, horses, and sheep. We heard the **bombs** walking around up there. Now and then there would be a gentle shower of calcimine. If we had gone above to take a look, we would have been turned into artifacts characteristic of fire storms: seeming pieces of charred firewood two or three feet long—ridiculously small human beings, or jumbo fried grasshoppers, if you will.

The reality of this episode is offset by Billy Pilgrim's Tralfamadorian vision of the war in reverse while watching a war movie on late night television.

(SL5 4) The formation flew backwards over a German city that was in flames. The bombers opened their **bomb** bay doors, exerted a miraculous magnetism which shrunk the fires, gathered them into cylindrical steel containers, and lifted the containers into the bellies of the planes. The containers were stored neatly in racks. The Germans below had miraculous devices of their own, which were long steel tubes. They used them to suck more fragments from the crewmen and planes. But there were still a few wounded Americans, though, and some of the bombers were in bad repair. Over France, though, German fighters came up again, made everything and everybody as good as new.

Vonnegut creates the contrast between Dresden's conventionally engineered destruction (which relied on ordinary materials) and Hiroshima's immolation (reflecting a leap in materials acquisition and application). (PS When I Lost My Innocence) But I learned how vile that religion of mine could be when the atomic bomb was dropped on Hiroshima. . . . Only six months before, as a captured American foot soldier, I had been in Dresden when it was burned to the ground by a purposely set fire storm. I was still innocent after that. Why? Because the technology which created that fire was so familiar to me. . . . There was nothing in the **bombs** or the airplanes, after all, which could not, essentially, be bought at a small hardware store.

Vonnegut has the decorated Vietnam veteran Eugene Debs Hartke comment on the insanity of vengeful warfare. (HP 6) When I married Margaret, their mother seemed perfectly OK still, except for a mania for dancing, which was a little scary sometimes, but harmless. Dancing until she dropped wasn't nearly as loony as wanting to **bomb** North Vietnam back to the Stone Age, or **bombing** anyplace back to the Stone Age. *And in this exchange between Hartke and Hiroshima bombing victim Hiroshi Matsumoto, Hartke fills the silence between them with more blank commentary. (HP 40)* "I was in Hiroshima when it was **bombed**," he said.

I am sure there was an implied equation there: The **bombing** of Hiroshima was as unforgivable and as typically human as the Rape of Nanking.

Hartke also calls special attention to the unique difference between the effectiveness of the infantry as opposed to the firepower of an air attack. (HP 6)

What a foot-soldier can do to a body with his pip-squeak technology is nothing, of course, when compared with the ordinary, unavoidable, perfectly routine effects of aerial **bombing** and artillery. One time I saw the severed head of a bearded old man resting on the guts of an eviscerated water buffalo, covered with flies in a **bomb** crater by a paddy in Cambodia. The plane whose **bomb** made the crater was so high when it dropped it that it couldn't even be seen from the ground. But what its **bomb** did, I would have to say, sure beat the ace of spades for a calling card.

Vonnegut recalls an incident while speaking at the National Air and Space Museum on the topic of "The Legacy of Strategic Bombing." (FWD 16) During the question-and-answer period following my speech. . . . I was asked what being **bombed** strategically had done to my personality. I replied that the war had been a great adventure for me, which I wouldn't have missed for anything, and that the principal shapers of my personality were probably neighborhood dogs when I was growing up.

Within Fates Worse Than Death *Vonnegut goes on to relate the sentiments of his longtime friend and fellow Dresden survivor Bernard V. O'Hare.* (FWD 11) I said to him, "What did you learn?" The future DA O'Hare replied, "I will never again believe my Government." This had to do with our Government's tall tales of delicate surgery performed by bombers equipped with Sperry and Norden bombsights. These instruments were so precise, we had been told, that a bombardier could drop his billets-doux down the chimney of a factory if ordered to. There were solemn charades performed for newsreels in which military policemen with drawn .45 automatics escorted bombardiers carrying bombsights to their planes. That was how desperate the Germans and the Japanese were (so went the message) to learn and make use of the secret of our **bombings'** diabolical accuracy themselves.

The notion of a bomb is not completely negative for Vonnegut, as this book review indicates. (MH New Dictionary) And now I have this enormous and beautiful new **bomb** from Random House. I don't mean "**bomb**" in a pejorative sense, or in any dictionary sense, for that matter. I mean that the book is heavy and pregnant, and makes you think.

(*BAG A Present for Big Saint Nick*) Their son Willy had a souvenir that would help him remember. He had found the greeting card that came with the **bomb**. It was in the shrubbery. It said, "Merry Christmas to the greatest guy in the world." It was signed "The Family."

(*MWC 2*) In 1968, the year I wrote *Slaughterhouse-Five*, I finally became grown up enough to write about the **bombing** of Dresden. It was the largest massacre in European history. I, of course, know about Auschwitz, but a massacre is something that happens suddenly, the killing of a whole lot of people in a very short time. In Dresden, on February 13, 1945, about 135,000 people were killed by British **firebombing** in one night.

It was pure nonsense, pointless destruction. The whole city was burned down, and it was a British atrocity, not ours. They sent in night **bombers**, and they came in and set the whole town on fire with a new kind of incendiary **bomb**. And so everything organic, except my little POW group, was consumed by fire. It was a military experiment to find out if you could burn down a whole city by scattering incendiaries over it.

See also: PP VIII; XI; XIX; XXI; XXX; XXXIV; *ST* 2; *MN* 21; 30; 32; 42; *CC* 36; 102; 115; 117; *GBR* 9; 13; *SL5* 1; 3; 5; 6; 7; 8; 9; 10; *MH* Welcome to the Monkey House; *MH* All the King's Horses; *MH* The Manned Missiles; *BC* 1; 4; 12; 20; 21; *WFG* Brief Encounters on the Inland Waterway; *WFG* Yes, We Have No Nirvanas; *WFG* There's a Maniac Loose Out There; Address to the American Physical Society; Torture and Blubber; In a Manner That Must Shame God Himself; Thinking Unthinkable, Speaking Unspeakable; Address to P.E.N.; Conference in Stockholm, 1973; *Playboy* Interview; *JB* 2; *PS* When I Lost My Innocence; Roots; Self-Interview; Jonathan Swift Misperceived; *PS* Jekyll and Hyde Updated; *DD* 20; 21; 24; *Gal* 1:26; 1:32; *Blue* 30; *HP* 4; 7; 15; 32; 34–36; 39; *FWD* IX–XI; XV; XVI; What Bernard V. O'Hare Said About Our Friendship on My Sixtieth Birthday; *MWC* Author's Note.

bombardier. (*BC* 21) That brain became the nerve center of the so-called "BLINC System" during the Second World War. It was installed on heavy bombers, and it did the actual dropping of bombs after a **bombardier** pressed his bright red "bombs away" button.

(*PS When I Lost My Innocence*) "When I was a freshman here, I didn't know or care where the life of Ginger Rogers ended and the life of General Douglas MacArthur began. The senior senator from California was Mickey Mouse, who would serve with great distinction as a **bombardier** in the Pacific during the Second World War. Commander Mouse dropped a bomb down the smokestack of a Japanese battleship. The captain of the battleship was Charlie Chan. Boy, was he mad.

(*PS Self-Interview*) VONNEGUT: There was all this hokum about the Norden bombsight. You'd see a newsreel showing a **bombardier** with an MP on either side of him holding a drawn 45. That sort of nonsense, and hell, all they were doing was just flying over cities, hundreds of airplanes, dropping everything.

(*Blue* 35) "He (*a figure within Rabo Karabekian's "Now It's the Women's Turn"*) is a Canadian **bombardier** who was shot down over an oil field in Hungary. He doesn't know who I am. He can't even see my face. All he can see is a thick fog which isn't there, and he's asking me if we are home yet. . . .

"That is a concentration-camp guard who threw away his SS uniform and stole the suit from a scarecrow," I said. I pointed out a group of concentration camp victims far away from the masquerading guard. Several of them were on the ground and dying, like the Canadian **bombardier**. . . .

This was Rabo's response to Circe's question about his 64-foot painting, "How many of these are portraits of actual people?" (*Blue* 36) "The **bombardier** clinging to my leg: that's his face, as I remember it. These two Estonians in German uniforms are Laurel and Hardy. This French collaborator here is Charlie Chaplin. These two Polish slave laborers on the other side of the tower from me are Jackson Pollock and Terry Kitchen."

(*HP* 32) But at least they (*the convicts*) saw what they were doing, whereas people like the Trustees had a lot in common with B-52 **bombardiers** way up in the stratosphere. They seldom saw the devastation they caused as they moved the huge portion of this country's wealth they controlled from here to there.

(*TQ* 3) Trout said in "No Laughing Matter" that the pilot and his **bombardier** had felt somewhat godlike on previous missions, when they had had nothing more than incendiaries and conventional high explosives to drop on people. "But that was godlike with a little g" he wrote. "They identified themselves with minor deities who only avenged and destroyed. Up there in the sky all alone, with the purple motherfucker slung underneath their plane, they felt like the Boss God Himself, who had an option which hadn't been theirs before, which was to be merciful."

bombardment. (*SL5* 9) *Rumfoord has a copy of* The Destruction of Dresden *with him and includes this quote by Ira C. Eaker, Lieutenant General, U.S.A.F. retired: That the bombing of Dresden was a great tragedy none can deny. . . . cruel, though it may well be that they were too remote from the harsh realities of war to understand fully the appalling destructive power of air* **bombardment** *in the spring of 1945.*

(*WFG Biafra: A People Betrayed*) General Ojukwu described a typical Nigerian attack for us: "They pound a position with artillery for twenty-four hours, then they send forward one armored car. If anybody shoots at it, it retreats, and another twenty-four hours of **bombardment** begins. When the infantry move forward, they drive a screen of refugees before them."

bombenfest. (*SL5* 1) *The devastation of Dresden was boundless. When Goethe as a young student visited the city, he still found sad ruins:* "Von der Kuppel der Frauenkirche sah ich diese leidigen Trummer zwischen die schone stadtische Ordnung hineingesat; da ruhmte mir der Kuster die Kunst des Baumeisters, welcher Kirche und Kuppel auf einen so unerwunschten Fall schon eingerichtet und **bombenfest** erbaut hotte. Der gute Sakristan deutete mir alsdann auf Ruinene nach allen Seiten und sagte bedenklich lakonisch: Das hat der Feind gethoan!" (*as quoted from Mary Endell's* Dresden, History, Stage, and Gallery).

bomber, fighter bomber, fighter-bomber (*see also* **fighter plane**). (*ST* 7) . . . the only Martians left free and standing on the face of the Earth were the Parachute Ski Marines. . . . They were told by loudspeaker that their situation was hopeless, that **bombers** were overhead.

(SL5 4) He *(Billy Pilgrim)* came slightly unstuck in time, saw the late movie backwards, then forwards again. It was a movie about American **bombers** in the Second World War and the gallant men who flew them. . . .

Over France, a few German fighter planes flew at them backwards, sucked bullets and shell fragments from some of the planes and crewmen. They did the same for wrecked American **bombers** on the ground, and those planes flew up backwards to join the formation.

The formation flew backwards over a German city that was in flames. The **bombers** opened their bomb bay doors, exerted a miraculous magnetism which shrunk the fires, gathered them into cylindrical steel containers, and lifted the containers into the bellies of the planes. . . . But there were still a few wounded Americans, though, and some of the **bombers** were in bad repair. Over France, though, German fighters came up again, made everything and everybody as good as new.

When the **bombers** got back to their base, the steel cylinders were taken from the racks and shipped back to the United States of America, where factories were operating night and day, dismantling the cylinders, separating the dangerous contents into minerals.

(SL5 7) The city was blacked out because **bombers** might come, so Billy didn't get to see Dresden do one of the most cheerful things a city is capable of doing when the sun goes down, which is to wink its lights on one by one.

(SL5 9) When she *(Valencia)* arrived at the hospital, people rushed to the windows to see what all the noise was. The Cadillac, with both mufflers gone, sounded like a heavy **bomber** coming in on a wing and a prayer.

(SL5 9) I deeply regret that British and U.S. **bombers** killed 135,000 people in the attack on Dresden, but I remember who started the last war and I regret even more the loss of more than 5,000,000 Allied lives in the necessary effort to completely defeat and utterly destroy nazism. *(Vonnegut includes this excerpt from the foreword to* The Destruction of Dresden.)

(SL5 9) *The advocates of nuclear disarmament seem to believe that, if they could achieve their aim, war would become tolerable and decent . . . On the night of March 9th, 1945, an air attack on Tokyo by American heavy* **bombers** *using incendiary and high explosive bombs, caused the death of 83,793 people. The atom bomb dropped on Hiroshima killed 71,379 people.* (This excerpt is from British Air Marshal Sir Robert Saundby as quoted in *The Destruction of Dresden.*)

(*MH* Miss Temptation) "He's out west, ma—with the Strategic Air Command," said Fuller. The little dining room became as lonely as a **bomber** in the thin, cold stratosphere.

(*MH* Report on the Barnhouse Effect) "One hundred and twenty of them! At the same time, ten V-2s are being readied for firing in New Mexico, and fifty radio-controlled jet **bombers** are being equipped for a mock attack on the Aleutians. Just think of it!" Happily he reviewed his orders. "At exactly 1100 hours next Wednesday, I will give you the order to *concentrate*; and you, professor, will think as hard as you can about sinking the target ships, destroying the V-2s before they hit the ground, and knocking down the **bombers** before they reach the Aleutians! Think you can handle it?"

The television screens showed, from left to right, the stretch of desert which was the rocket target, the guinea-pig fleet, and a section of the Aleutian sky through which the radio-controlled **bomber** formation would roar.

Ninety minutes before H-hour the radios announced that the rockets were ready, that the observation ships had backed away to what was thought to be a safe distance, and that the **bombers** were on their way. . . .

"**Bombers** sighted!" cried the Aleutian observers. . . .

The Aleutian sky was streaked with the smoke trails of **bombers** screaming down in flames (*MH* Report on the Barnhouse Effect).

(*BC* 21) That brain became the nerve center of the so-called "BLINC System" during the Second World War. It was installed on heavy **bombers** and it did the actual dropping of bombs after a bombardier pressed his red "bombs away" button.

(*WFG* Good Missiles, Good Manners, Good

Night) My newest book was about utterly pitiful things that happened to unarmed human beings on the ground when our **bombers** went about their technical duties in the sky.

(*WFG* Biafra: A People Betrayed) The Russians were helpful in a lot of ways: They gave the Nigerians Ilyushin **bombers** and MIGs and heavy artillery.

(*PS* Self-Interview) British mosquito **bombers** attacked us at night a few times.

(*PS* Self-Interview) VONNEGUT: It was a fancy thing to see, a startling thing. It was a moment of truth, too, because American civilians and ground troops didn't know American **bombers** were engaged in saturation bombing.

(*PS* The People One Knows) The company that made a movie out of Joseph Heller's first novel, *Catch-22*, had to assemble what became the 11th or 12th largest **bomber** force on the planet at the time.

(*Gal* 1:22) "If Mrs. Onassis were to go there now," said Donoso, "people would receive her as though she were a rescuer, a worker of miracles. She would be expected to summon ships laden with food to Guayaquil—and to have United States **bombers** drop cereal and milk and fresh fruit for the children by parachute!"

(*Gal* 1:26) One thing which made the Air Force such a high morale unit was that its equipment, bought on credit and delivered before the bankruptcy, was so up to date. It had eight new French **fighter-bombers** and each of these planes, moreover, was equipped with an American air-to-ground missile with a Japanese brain which could home in on radar signals, or on heat from an engine, depending on instructions from the pilot.

(*Gal* 1:32) Two of Peru's **fighter bombers** were then over Ecuadorian territories, one with its rocket tuned to the radar signals coming from Guayaquil International Airport, and the other with its rocket tuned to radar signals coming from the naval base on the Galápagos Island of Baltra, lair of a sail training ship, six Coast Guard ships, two oceangoing tugs, a patrol submarine, a dry dock, and, high and dry in the dry dock, a destroyer.

(*Gal* 1:34) There was this Peruvian pilot a million years ago, a young lieutenant colonel who had his **fighter-bomber** skipping from wisp to wisp of finely

divided matter at the very edge of the planet's atmosphere. His name was Guillermo Reyes. . . .

(*Gal* 1:35) If he had let them run long enough to get really hot, that temperature anomaly might have attracted the electronic attention of a Peruvian **fighter-bomber** in the stratosphere.

(*HP* 4) When I was 2 years old, we moved to Midland City, Ohio, where a washing-machine company named Robo-Magic Corporation was beginning to make bomb-release mechanisms and swivel mounts for machine guns on B-17 **bombers**.

(*HP* 7) He (*Ernest Hubble Hiscock*) was a Tarkington graduate who at the age of 21 was a nose-gunner on a Navy **bomber** whose pilot crashed his plane with a full load of bombs onto the flight deck of a Japanese aircraft carrier in the Battle of Midway during World War II.

(*TQ* Copyright Page) Kurt Vonnegut was born in Indianapolis in 1922 and studied biochemistry at Cornell University. During the Second World War he served in Europe and, as a prisoner of war in Germany, witnessed the destruction of Dresden by Allied **bombers**, an experience which inspired his classic novel *Slaughterhouse-5*.

(*MWC* 2) The whole city was burned down, and it was a British atrocity, not ours. They sent in night **bombers**, and they came in and set the whole town on fire with a new kind of incendiary bomb. And so everything organic, except my little POW group, was consumed by fire. It was a military experiment to find out if you could burn down a whole city by scattering incendiaries over it.

The Bombing of Germany. *In* God Bless You, Mr. Rosewater, *Hans Rumpf's text is kept in secret by Eliot Rosewater while living in Indiana. Eliot so often reads the description of the Dresden firestorms that after reading Kilgore Trout's* Pan-Galactic Three-Day Pass *on his journey to meet Sylvia, he goes catatonic and silently recalls the passage. When gazing out the bus window, he envisions Indianapolis consumed by a firestorm.*

bomb-release. (*HP* 4) When I (*Eugene Debs Hartke*) was 2 years old, we moved to Midland City, Ohio, where a washing-machine company named Robo-Magic Corporation was beginning to make

bomb-release mechanisms and swivel mounts for machine guns on B-17 bombers.

bombsight. (*PS* Self-Interview) VONNEGUT: There was all this hokum about the Norden **bombsight**. You'd see a newsreel showing a bombardier with an MP on either side of him holding a drawn 45. That sort of nonsense, and hell, all they were doing was just flying over cities, hundreds of airplanes, and dropping everything.
(*FWD* XI) The future DA O'Hare replied, "I will never again believe my Government." This had to do with our Government's tall tales of delicate surgery performed by bombers equipped with Sperry and Norden **bombsights**. These instruments were so precise, we had been told, that a bombardier could drop his billets-doux down the chimney of a factory if ordered to. There were solemn charades performed for newsreels in which military policemen with drawn .45 automatics escorted bombardiers carrying **bombsights** to their planes. That was how desperate the Germans and the Japanese were (so went the message) to learn and make use of the secret of our bombings' diabolical accuracy themselves. *Bernard V. O'Hare is Vonnegut's longtime friend from their military days and a fellow survivor of Dresden's firebombing.*

Bonesana, Cesare, Marchese di Beccaria. *The Italian philosopher, politician, and penologist whose* On Crimes and Punishment *attacks torture and the death penalty.* (*Gal* 1:31) And, as long as there was anybody on Santa Rosalia curious as to why his or her ancestors had come there—and that sort of curiosity would finally peter out only after about three thousand years—that was the story: They were driven off the mainland by a shower of meteorites.

Quoth Mandarax:
Happy is the nation without a history.
                    Cesare Bonesana,
          Marchese di Beccaria (1738–1794)

Booboo. (*see also* **"The Sisters B-36"**). *In* Timequake, *Kilgore Trout's fictional planet in the Crab Nebula in his story "The Sisters B-36."*

booby trap, booby-trap. *Vonnegut frequently alludes to the seemingly impossible task of completely innocent activity, as though the world were rigged for failure. As Rudy Waltz terms it,* I wasn't to touch anything on this planet, man, woman, child, artifact, animal, vegetable, or mineral—since it was very likely to be connected to a push-pull detonator and an explosive charge (*DD* 16).

Aside from references to physical, intentionally designed booby traps, Vonnegut frequently refers to the booby traps he views as inherent in human relationships.
(*PP* V) Paul took two more of Berringer's pieces and made his own piece a king. "This must be the trickiest **booby trap** in history," he laughed. He was enjoying himself immensely. *Fred Berringer's boastful overconfidence in using his (faulty) Checker Charley robot in challenging Paul Proteus's checker championship.*
(*PP* XXV) The lights on the **booby-trap** mirror flashed on.
(*PP* XXX) His (*Bud Calhoun's*) hands were working in air, fashioning a **booby trap** for a coke machine. "See? Take a li'l ol' coke bottle, only fill her full of nitro. Then we run a li'l ol'—"
(*BC* 15) After that, Francine followed Robert to Midland City, where Robert oversaw the manufacture of a new sort of **booby trap**. A **booby trap** was an easily hidden explosive device, which blew up when it was accidentally twiddled in some way. One of the virtues of the new type of **booby trap** was that it could not be smelled by dogs. Various armies at that time were training dogs to sniff out **booby traps**.
(*WFG* Biafra: A People Betrayed) Whenever I did something clumsy or unlucky, a Biafran was sure to say that: "Sorry, sah!" He would be genuinely sorry. He was on my side, and against a **booby-trapped** universe.
(*DD* 19) People talk a lot about all the homosexuals there are to see in Greenwich Village, but it was all the neuters that caught my eye that day. These were my people—as used as I was to wanting love from nowhere, as certain as I was that almost anything desirable was likely to be **booby-trapped**.
(*Blue* 13) It sounded good. But guess what? She was assembling a **booby trap**. *Rabo Karabekian refers to Circe Berman's suggestion that he visit New*

York City to get his creative juices flowing once more. (HP 1) The biggest **booby trap** Fate set for me, though, was a pretty and personable young woman named Margaret Patton, who allowed me to woo and marry her soon after my graduation from West Point, and then had 2 children by me without telling me that there was a powerful strain of insanity on her mother's side of the family.

(HP 1) I (*Eugene Debs Hartke*) realize that my speaking of my first and only wife as something as inhuman as a **booby trap** risks my seeming to be yet another infernal device.

(HP 6) But they (*Hartke's children*) haven't reproduced, and with their knowing what they do about their **booby-trapped** genes, I doubt that they ever will.

(HP 6) I turned to Jack Patton, who was there with his **booby-trapped** sister and mother and his normal father, and I asked him, "What do you think of us now, Lieutenant Patton?"

(FWD XVI) "And stay clear of the Ten Commandments, as do the television evangelists. Those things are **booby-trapped**, because right in the middle of them is one commandment which would, if taken seriously, cripple modern religion as show business. It is this commandment: 'Thou shalt not kill.'"

(TQ 55) Only at this very moment in 1996, as I am about to write the next sentence, have I realized how meaningless the image of a Garden of Eden must have been to my young audience, since the world was so densely populated with other secretly frightened people, and so overplanted and rigged with both natural and manmade **booby traps**.

(MWC 4) You want to talk about irresistible whoopee?

A **booby trap**.

Fossil fuels, so easily set alight! Yes, and we are presently touching off nearly the very last whiffs and drops and chunks of them. All lights are about to go out. No more electricity. All forms of transportation are about to stop, and the planet Earth will soon have a crust of skulls and bones and dead machinery.

And nobody can do a thing about it. It's too late in the game.

book-banning. (PS The First Amendment) Here is how I propose to end **book-banning** in this country once and for all: Every candidate for school committee should be hooked up to a lie-detector and asked this question:

"Have you read a book from start to finish since high school? Or did you read a book from start to finish in high school?"

If the truthful answer is "no," then the candidate should be told politely that he cannot get on the school committee and blow off his big bazoo about how books make children crazy.

Whenever ideas are squashed in this country, literate lovers of the American experiment write careful and intricate explanations of why all ideas must be allowed to live. It is time for them to realize that they are attempting to explain America at its bravest and most optimistic to orangutans. From now on, I intend to limit my discourse with dim-witted Savonarolas to this advice: "Have somebody read the First Amendment to the United States Constitution out loud to you, you God damned fool!" *Giralmo Savonarola was a Dominican priest famous for his hostility to what he called immoral art and book burning. The result of his prolonged dispute with Pope Alexander VI resulted in his arrest, torture, and execution in 1498.*

Boone, Michael. *Born Miklós Gömbös, this is the Hungarian paternal grandfather of Kentuckian Mary Hepburn in* Galápagos. *On her mother's side, she was a distant relative of Daniel Boone. Miklós changed his name when he came to America.*

Booth, John Wilkes, Junius, and Edwin. *In* Timequake, *the three Booth brothers, what remains to this day the greatest family of tragedians in the history of the English-speaking stage* (TQ 59), *star in a New York City production of* Julius Caesar (*John plays Marc Antony, Junius plays Brutus, and Edwin plays Cassius). After their performance, John Wilkes has a preplanned tryst in his hotel with Julia Pembroke, wife of Elias Pembroke, a fictitious Rhode Island naval architect who was Abraham Lincoln's Assistant Secretary of the Navy during our Civil War* (TQ 59).

Booth drugs Pembroke's champagne, impregnates her (she had been childless due to her husband's unacknowledged infertility), and she later delivers a son, Abraham Lincoln Pembroke. The child is conceived two years to the day before Booth assassinates

Abraham Lincoln. Vonnegut says this passage is a holdover from his manuscript for what he refers to as Timequake One.

Borasisi (*see also* **Bokononism**). (*CC* 85) I learned (*from the* Books of Bokonon) *of the Bokononist cosmogony, for instance, wherein* **Borasisi**, *the sun, held* Pabu, *the moon, in his arms, and hoped that* Pabu *would bear him a fiery child.*

But poor Pabu *gave birth to children that were cold, that did not burn; and* **Borasisi** *threw them away in disgust. These were the planets who circled their terrible father at a safe distance.*

Borders, Arvin. *In the short story "Find Me a Dream" reprinted in* Bagombo Snuff Box, *Borders (known in the industry as "Mr. Pipe") is the never-been-married 46-year-old manager of the Creon Works, part of the broad industrial reach of the General Forge and Foundry Company. Quite unexpectedly, Borders appears at the Pipe City Golf and Country Club holding two cocktails, one for his new fiancée, Hildy Matthews, the widowed New York actress and mother of two young children. Hildy still mourns the death of her husband, a creative soul whose name and spirit are well known by local bandleader Andy Middleton, but not by the man she is to marry. The story closes with Hildy's proposal to be Middleton's wife and muse, promising that she could only help his career.*

Borders, Lance and **Leora** (*see also* **General Pulsifer**). *Walter Starbuck's secretary at RAMJAC and her husband attend Starbuck's going away party prior to returning to prison.* (*JB* Epilogue) My devoted secretary, **Leora Borders**, and her husband, **Lance**, were there. **Lance** was just getting over a nasty mastectomy. He told me that one mastectomy in two hundred was performed on a man. Live and learn!

Boris. *The chess computer given to Walter Starbuck by Clyde Carter and Leland Clewes before he returns to prison at the close of* Jailbird. *Starbuck notes that had "Boris" existed when he was raised in the Alexander Hamilton McCone household, it is doubtful he would have been befriended by his parents' employer.* (*JB* Epilogue) I agreed to be his chess-playing machine. If **Boris** had existed in those days,

I probably would have gone to Western Reserve, and then become a tax assessor or an office manager in a lumberyard, or an insurance salesman, or some such thing. Instead, I am the most disreputable Harvard graduate since Putzi Hänfstaengl, who was Hitler's favorite pianist.

Borisoglebsk. *In* Mother Night, *the Soviet town in which George Kraft's/Iona Potapov's wife Tanya has resided for twenty-five years without him.*

Bormann, Martin. *In* Jailbird, *the Nazi war criminal tried and convicted in absentia was the commanding officer of the father of Arthur von Strelitz, the Harvard associate professor of anthropology.*

born again, born-again. (*BC* 19) And now comes the spiritual climax of this book, for it is at this point that I, the author, am suddenly transformed by what I have done so far. This is why I had gone to Midland City: to be **born again**. And Chaos announced that it was about to give birth to a new me by putting these words in the mouth of Rabo Karabekian: "*What kind of man would turn his daughter into an outboard motor?*"
(*Blue* 8) So I (*Rabo Karabekian*) went to New York City to be **born again**.
(*PS* Children) My first wife and both my daughters are **born-again** Christians now—working white magic through rituals and prayers. That's all right.

Borzoi Dance Company. *In* Cat's Cradle, *the company for which Ukrainian midget Zinka danced. Quickly wooed by Newt Hoenikker, she claims political asylum to remain in the United States, but one week later appears at the Russian embassy wanting to return home. Zinka, as it turns out, is a Soviet agent trying to get hold of ice-nine.*

Boström, Hjalmar Arvid. *In* Galápagos, *the Swedish ship welder credited by Leon Trout with perpetuating the saying, "Oh, well—he wasn't going to write Beethoven's Ninth Symphony anyway." This wry comment on how little most of us were likely to accomplish in life, no matter how long we lived* (*Gal* 2:6), *was passed down from his World War I German grandfather in charge of burying the dead on the Western Front. . . . It was common for sol-*

diers new to that sort of work to wax philosophical over this corpse or that one, into whose face he was about to shovel dirt, speculating about what he might have done if he hadn't died so young. There were many cynical things a veteran might say to such a thoughtful recruit, and one of those was: "Don't worry about it. He wasn't going to write Beethoven's Ninth Symphony anyway" (Gal 2:6). *These are also the words Boström utters at the funeral of Leon Trout, his co-worker in the Swedish shipyard.*

Bowen, Julius King. *Proclaimed by President Warren G. Harding as the* Laughter Laureate of the United States, Master of Darky Dialects, *and* Heir to the Crown of King of Humor Once Worn by Mark Twain, **Bowen** lived in his mansion called Xanadu, from 1922 until he died 1936. A foundation in his name endows the writer's retreat at his seaside home, which has since become a resort with suites named after various writers. Monica Pepper of the American Academy of Arts and Letters administers the funds for the writer's retreat. The clambake at the close of the novel is held on the beach at Xanadu (TQ 22).

Boyden, Hay. *In "The Hyannis Port Story," reprinted in* Welcome to the Monkey House *(1968), Boyden is a building mover who chastises Robert Taft Rumfoord for bad-mouthing the Kennedys. Boyden had also purchased a bathtub enclosure from the story's narrator and installs it himself to save $7.50. Unfortunately, he does a poor job, and his dining room ceiling collapses. The resulting conversation with the narrator leads to his meeting with Commodore Rumfoord, Robert's father.*

In the short story "Lovers Anonymous," reprinted in Bagombo Snuff Box *(1999), Boyden is among a group of young, disappointed men at the wedding of Sheila Hinckley and Herb White. Each member of the group in their own way carries a small torch for the intellectually promising and adorable Sheila. One of the boozy young men (the unnamed narrator) addresses the group with ceremonial hyperbole reminiscent of olden times. "*Gentlemen, friends, brothers, I'm sure we wish the newlyweds nothing but happiness. But at the same time I have to say that the pain in our hearts will never die. And I pro-

pose that we form a permanent brotherhood of eternal sufferers, to aid each other in any way we can, though Lord knows there's very little anybody can do for pain like ours."

The crowd thought that was a fine idea. *At this point Hay Boyden steps in with his small contribution to the gathering, maintaining the verbose style and tone of his drunken friend.* **Hay Boyden,** who later became a house mover and wrecker, said we ought to call ourselves the Brotherhood of People Who Were Too Dumb to Realize That Sheila Hinckley Might Actually Want to Be a Housewife. *This prompts the drunken narrator to offer the shorter appellation for the group—Lovers Anonymous.*

Boyer, Richard O. *Along with coauthor Herbert M. Morais, Boyer wrote* Labor's Untold Story, *the text used by Vonnegut in* Jailbird *to quote Judge Thayer's comments as presiding judge at the trial of Sacco and Vanzetti.*

Boyle, Raymond. *The name Raymond Boyle appears in "The Hyannis Port Story," reprinted in* Welcome to the Monkey House *(1968), and later in* God Bless You, Mr. Rosewater. *In the short story, Boyle is a Secret Service Agent attached to the Kennedy household in Hyannis Port and is known as the resident Rumford Specialist, "or Ambassador to Rumfoordiana." It is Boyle's duty to call "Commodore" William Rumfoord and inform him that his son was caught trying to use the Kennedy yacht Marlin for a love tryst with President Kennedy's fourth cousin Sheila, from Ireland. The Rumfoords are Goldwater Republicans.*

In God Bless You, Mr. Rosewater, *Sergeant Raymond Boyle is the central figure of Kilgore Trout's novel* Pan-Galactic Three-Day Pass. *Boyle is the lone Earthling on an expedition of voyagers from two hundred galaxies. Boyle serves as an English teacher, since the other races use telepathy to communicate. The commanding officer, a Tralfamadorian, and the chaplain from Glinko-X-3, have the sad duty of telling Boyle that the Milky Way died.*

This apocalyptic tale is read by Eliot Rosewater while on a bus to Indianapolis and is connected in his mind with the Hans Rumpf book The Bombing of Germany. *The next thing Eliot sees/imagines is Indianapolis engulfed in a firestorm.*

Brackman, Sergeant Henry. *In* The Sirens of Titan, *Unk's (Malachi Constant's) platoon leader in the Martian Army. His real name is Private Francis J. Thompson and he was abducted from Fort Bragg while walking his post around the motor pool. He was the sole Martian survivor of the Battle of Boca Raton. Later, he has the concession booth next to Bee and Chrono outside the Rumfoord estate. He sells $17 replicas of the estate's famous ascending-bowls fountain.*

Brainard (*see* **Bullard**).

Braun, Eva. *Adolf Hitler's mistress, a cyanide suicide moments after their Berlin bunker marriage, and a character in Kilgore Trout's short story "Bunker Bingo Party."* (TQ 20) Trout wrote of **Eva Braun,** "Her only crime was to have allowed a monster to ejaculate in her birth canal. These things happen to the best of women."

Braun is also briefly mentioned in Vonnegut's interview in the afterlife with Adolf Hitler, in God Bless You, Dr. Kevorkian (*GBK Adolf Hitler).*

Braxton, Carter. *Historically, Carter Braxton was one of the representatives from Virginia who signed the Declaration of Independence. In* Galápagos, *Leon Trout explains his relationship to Braxton on his mother's side of the family.*

Brayton, Hal. *Though rarely seen in the short story "Poor Little Rich Town," collected in* Bagombo Snuff Box (1999), *Hal Brayton is owner of the small Spruce Falls grocery store. He reflects the shifting attitudes of the townspeople as they are first swayed by Newell Cady's talent for making efficiency the highest goal of man to turning more uncertain about systems that devalue personal interactions. It is not that Brayton mistrusts Cady, it is just that he and the town become more certain about their own values.*
The Spruce Falls annual Hobby Show took place in the church basement three weeks after Newell Cady's election to the fire department. During the intervening twenty-one days, **Hal Brayton,** the grocer, had stopped adding bills on paper sacks and bought an adding machine, and had moved his counters around so as to transform his customer space from a jammed box canyon into a racetrack.

Mrs. Dickie, the postmistress, had moved her leafy children and their table out of her cage and had had the lowest tier of mailboxes raised to eye level. The fire department had voted down scarlet and blue capes for the band as unnecessary for firefighting. And startling figures had been produced in a school meeting proving beyond any doubt that it would cost seven dollars, twenty-nine cents, and six mills more per student per year to maintain the Spruce Falls Grade School than it would to ship the children to the big, efficient, centralized school in Ilium.

He *(the real estate agent)* opened the soft drink cooler and let the lid fall shut again. "What's the matter—this thing broken? Everything's warm."

"No, **Brayton** just hasn't gotten around to plugging it in since he moved things back the way they used to be."

"You said he's the one who doesn't want to sell his place?"

"One of the ones," said Beaton.

"Who else?"

"Everybody else."

"Go on!"

"Really," said Beaton. "We've decided to wait and see how Mr. Cady adapts himself, before we put anything else on the market. He's having a tough time, but he's got a good heart, I think, and we're all rooting for him."

Breakfast of Champions (1973). *The narrative structures of Vonnegut's first six novels are modeled after autobiographical experiences giving rise to his own unique awareness of the forces at work within and around us (the interaction of one's biochemical composition in conjunction with the external environment: the intersection of nature and nurture).* Breakfast of Champions *marks a break with previous narratives by concentrating on a single character's odyssey. Vonnegut squares off with himself, alternately examining that secret part of himself which fears insanity and his more public character as a writer presenting seemingly rational explanations for our collective state of being.* (BC 1) This is a tale of a meeting of two lonesome, skinny, fairly old white men on a planet which was dying fast. . . . One of them was a science-fiction writer named Kilgore Trout. . . . The man he met was an automobile dealer, a *Pontiac* dealer named Dwayne Hoover. Dwayne Hoover was on the brink of going insane.

Rounding out their planned meeting in Midland City, Ohio, is Vonnegut, who had come to the Arts Festival incognito. I was there to watch a confrontation between two human beings I had created: Dwayne Hoover and Kilgore Trout. *Hoover and Trout harbor very specific motives for attending the festival. Together, they represent some of Vonnegut's various views of himself. To be sure, Vonnegut is the protagonist.*

Hoover wants to avoid going crazy the way his wife, Celia, did (committing suicide by eating Drano), in much the same way Vonnegut fears schizophrenia and the legacy of his own mother's suicide. (BC 18) Dwayne was hoping that some of the distinguished visitors to the Arts Festival, who were all staying at the Inn, would come into the cocktail lounge. He wanted to talk to them, if he could, to discover whether they had truths about life which he had never heard before. Here is what he hoped new truths might do for him: enable him to laugh at his troubles, to go on living, and to keep out of the North Wing of the Midland County General Hospital, which was for lunatics.

Prior to presenting Hoover and the nature of his own purpose in the text, Vonnegut muses on his own vexation. (BC 18) There in the cocktail lounge, peering out through my leaks *(mirrored sunglasses)* at a world of my own invention, I mouthed this word: *schizophrenia.*

The sound and appearance of the word had fascinated me for many years. It sounded and looked to me like a human being sneezing in a blizzard of soapflakes.

I did not and do not know for certain that I have that disease. This much I knew and know: I was making myself hideously uncomfortable by not narrowing my attention to details of life which were immediately important, and by refusing to believe what my neighbors believed.

Vonnegut refuses to believe in the isolation of experience. As already explained in Slaughterhouse-Five, "All moments, past, present and future, always have existed, always will exist. . . . It is just an illusion we have here on Earth that one moment follows another one, like beads on a string, and that

once a moment is gone it is gone forever" (SL5 2). *Though Vonnegut doesn't offer Hoover this particular explanation of the structured moment, he still maintains that as for himself,* "I had come to the conclusion that there was nothing sacred about myself or about any human being, that we were all machines, doomed to collide and collide and collide. For want of anything better to do, we became fans of collision" (BC 19).

As an exponent of Vonnegut's sense of fatalism, it falls to Kilgore Trout to inform Hoover of this mechanistic philosophy. (BC 12) . . . his head no longer sheltered ideas of how things could be and should be on the planet, as opposed to how they really were. There was only one way for the Earth to be, he thought: the way it was.

Everything was necessary. He saw an old white woman fishing through a garbage can. That was necessary. He saw a bathtub toy, a little rubber duck, lying on its side on the grating over a storm sewer. It *had* to be there.

And so on.

The limitations of such a world view may preclude hope, but it does allow Trout to admit that all artists don't necessarily find truth (or even satisfying explanations). He accepts the invitation to the festival because he wishes to point out to the organizers that perhaps there is failure in art. (BC 3) "I'm going out there to show them what nobody has ever seen at an arts festival before: a representative of all the thousands of artists who devoted their entire lives to a search for truth and beauty—and didn't find doodley-squat!"

Though Trout may think his mechanistic philosophy is bleak, his literature is appreciated in some quarters for the tribulations suffered to produce his vision. Milo Maritimo, the gay clerk at the Holiday Inn who has read much of Trout's work, greets Trout with the same longing that compels Dwayne Hoover to seek out the arts. (BC 20) Oh, Mr. Trout, teach us to sing and dance and laugh and cry. We've tried to survive so long on money and sex and envy and real estate and football and basketball and automobiles and television and alcohol—on sawdust and broken glass!

Trout, spiritual guru of Eliot Rosewater, Billy Pilgrim, and Milo Maritimo, rejects such adoration as falsely believing in the same empty symbols he wishes to strip bare. Just as Vonnegut frequently rejects his status as a cult figure for the flower children of the 1960s, Trout protests that his truths may do no more than prolong Midland City's desolation and desperation. Even so, Maritimo sees in Trout a man who is terribly wounded—because he had dared to pass through the fires of truth to the other side, which we have never seen. And then he has come back again—to tell us about the other side (BC 20). Everything Vonnegut writes comes from the far side of the fires of Dresden.

There in the lounge of the Holiday Inn, Vonnegut sets up yet another collision. Only this time, instead of fabled enemies or ancient institutions, the crash dummies are Vonnegut's psychic surrogates: Dwayne Hoover and Kilgore Trout. In response to Dwayne's desire for truth, which he desperately hopes will prevent him from going insane, Vonnegut supplies him with Trout's novel Now It Can Be Told. It is the same unsatisfying, mechanistic philosophy Trout/Vonnegut laments, Dear Sir, poor sir, brave sir. . . . You are an experiment of the Creator of the Universe. You are the only creature in the entire Universe who has free will. You are the only one who has to figure out what to do next—and why. Everybody else is a robot, a machine.

You are pooped and demoralized. . . . Why wouldn't you be? Of course it is exhausting, having to reason all the time in a universe which wasn't meant to be reasonable. . . .

You are surrounded by loving machines, hating machines, greedy machines, brave machines, cowardly machines, truthful machines, funny machines, solemn machines. . . . Their only purpose is to stir you up in every conceivable way, so the Creator of the Universe can watch your reactions (BC 23).

As sincerely as Milo Maritimo expects Trout to show him truth, Dwayne Hoover interprets Trout's novel as defining his personal existence. Outraged over the depressing knowledge that there exists no spiritual bond among men, that all the sufferings and sacrifices throughout history were for the enlightenment of a supposedly benignant Creator, Hoover assaults a number of people before he is finally subdued.

Beyond the obvious confrontation Vonnegut presents between Hoover and Trout is his own purpose for entering the text. He, too, rejects a mechanistic view that puts man in the center of a rat's maze to be observed and judged by a supposedly paternalistic and loving God. (BC 19). And now the spiritual climax of this book, for it is at this point that I, the author, am suddenly transformed by what I have done so far. This is why I had gone to Midland City: to be born again. He owes his rebirth to another surrogate artist, Abstract Expressionist painter Rabo Karabekian.

Karabekian's philosophy of art disregards any considerations of the eternal collisions of man, of the mechanistic view described by Trout that makes man subject to the awareness of a Creator. Instead, man's awareness of his own circumstances is all that can be appreciated. His $50,000 painting of Saint Anthony, nothing more than a single vertical band of luminescent color, raises the ire of the locals, but his explanation modifies Vonnegut's uneasiness. (BC 19) I now give you my word of honor . . . that the picture your city owns shows everything about life which truly matters, with nothing left out. It is a picture of the awareness of every animal. It is the immaterial core of every animal—the 'I am' to which all messages are sent. . . . Our awareness is all that is alive and maybe sacred in any of us. Everything else about us is dead machinery. Karabekian's (Vonnegut's) message is clear: whatever the state of one's existence, accepting those circumstances is easier if unencumbered by wishes for divine intervention.

For Trout, the collision of his life occurs when his creator, Vonnegut, exposes himself. (BC Epilogue) "Mr. Trout—Kilgore—I hold in my hand a symbol of wholeness and harmony and nourishment. It is Oriental in its simplicity, but we are Americans, Kilgore, and not Chinamen. We Americans require symbols which have not been poisoned by great sins our nation has committed, such as slavery and genocide and criminal neglect, or by tinhorn commercial greed and cunning."

"Look up, Mr. Trout," I said, and I waited patiently. "Kilgore—?"

The old man looked up, and he had my father's wasted face when my father was a widower—when my father was an old old man.

He saw that I held an apple in my hand.

The apple Vonnegut extends to Trout is a symbol

of knowledge that satisfies our demands for intellectual freedom (especially when confronted with Trout's mechanistic theory, or the chrono-synclastic infundibulum of The Sirens of Titan), *yet it simultaneously implies the liability and consequence of discovery, of knowledge (particularly as it is pursued in* Cat's Cradle). *Trout understands this symbol and the consequent legacy of intellectual freedom, and he shrinks from the offering by wishing for youthful renewal,* "Make me young, make me young, make me young!" *as if there were refuge in a pre-lapsarian state* (BC Epilogue). *Youth only awaits becoming old; it is all part of a larger continuum.*

After Trout's plea, the novel ends with "ETC." because Vonnegut acknowledges the inability to escape into youth, as well as the irrelevance of thinking of youth as somehow protected from the mythical archetypes man creates for himself. Indeed, it is during childhood that myths are presented and perpetuated. ETC is an expression of the inevitable. For Vonnegut, writing about the inevitable requires associating the forces around and within us in terms that have prior significance: the events of life which symbolize our most identifiable concerns. Vonnegut forever returns to his youth and beyond for those moments which enable an orderly discussion of the present.

Breed, Dr. Asa. *In* Cat's Cradle, *the vice president in charge of the Research Laboratory of the General Forge and Foundry Company—and Felix Hoenikker's boss. John/Jonah, the narrator of the text, makes an appointment with Dr. Breed to help research his proposed text,* The Day the World Ended. (CC 1) **Breed** was a pink old man, very prosperous, beautifully dressed. His manner was civilized, optimistic, capable, serene. I, by contrast, felt bristly, diseased, cynical. I had spent the night with Sandra. . . . I thought the worst of everyone, and I knew some pretty sordid things about **Dr. Asa Breed**, things Sandra had told me. Sandra told me everyone in Ilium was sure that **Dr. Breed** had been in love with Felix Hoenikker's wife. She told me that most people thought **Breed** was the father of all three Hoenikker children.

During the interview, Breed explains to John/Jonah the nature of pure research. (CC 18) "It isn't looking for a better cigarette filter or a softer face tissue or a longer-lasting house paint, God help us. Everybody talks about research and practically nobody in this country's doing it. We're one of the few companies that actually hires men to do pure research. When most other companies brag about their research, they're talking about industrial hack technicians who wear white coats, work out of cookbooks, and dream up an improved windshield wiper for next year's Oldsmobile."

"But here . . . ?"

"Here, and shockingly few other places in this country, men are paid to increase knowledge, to work toward no end but that."

"That's very generous of General Forge and Foundry Company."

"Nothing generous about it. New knowledge is the most valuable commodity on earth. The more truth we have to work with, the richer we become."

Had I been a Bokononist then, that statement would have made me howl.

Breed is responsible for telling John/Jonah about the "theoretical" ice-nine, illustrating its effects with reference to cannonballs on courthouse lawns. (CC 20) That old man with spotted hands invited me to think of the several ways in which cannonballs might be stacked on a courthouse lawn, of the several ways in which oranges might be packed into a crate.

"So it is with atoms in crystals, too; and two different crystals of the same substance can have quite different physical properties."

He told me about a factory that had been growing big crystals of ethylene diamine tartrate. The crystals were useful in certain manufacturing operations, he said. But one day the factory discovered that the crystals it was growing no longer had the properties desired. The atoms had begun to stack and lock—to freeze—in a different fashion. The liquid that was crystallizing hadn't changed, but the crystals it was forming were, as far as industrial applications went, pure junk.

How this had come about was a mystery. The theoretical villain, however, was what **Dr. Breed** called "a seed." He meant by that a tiny grain of the undesired crystal pattern. The seed, which had come from God-only-knows-where, taught the atoms the novel way in which to stack and lock, to crystallize, to freeze.

"Now think about cannonballs on a courthouse lawn or about oranges in a crate again," he suggested. And he helped me to see that the pattern of the bottom layer of cannonballs or of oranges determined how each subsequent layer would stack and lock. "The bottom layer is the seed of how every cannonball or every orange that comes after is going to behave, even to an infinite number of cannonballs or oranges."

"Now suppose," chortled **Dr. Breed**, enjoying himself, "that there were many possible ways in which water could crystallize, could freeze. Suppose that the sort of ice we skate upon and put into highballs—what we might call *ice-one*—is only one of several types of ice. Suppose water always froze as *ice-one* on Earth because it had never had a seed to teach it how to form *ice-two, ice-three, ice-four* . . . ? And suppose," he rapped on his desk with his old hand again, "that there were one form, which we will call *ice-nine*—a crystal as hard as this desk—with a melting point of, let us say, one-hundred degrees Fahrenheit, or, better still, a melting point of one-hundred-and-thirty degrees."

"All right, I'm still with you," I said.

Breed, Marvin and Avram. (CC 31) **Marvin Breed** was a sleek and vulgar, a smart and sentimental man. *Marvin is the brother of Asa Breed, Felix Hoenikker's supervisor in* Cat's Cradle. *Marvin is the tombstone salesman in Ilium who runs the Avram Breed and Sons establishment, the great-great grandfather of the scientist and the salesman. While John/Jonah interviews Marvin, he learns that Emily Hoenikker had been his girlfriend until Asa wooed her away, and then she hooked up with Felix—much to Marvin's bewilderment.*

John/Jonah also has his first Bokononist experience while with Marvin. The narrator is taken with a stone angel decorated with mistletoe and Christmas lamps. Old Avram Breed had carved the image for John/Jonah's ancestor. (CC 34) It was in the tombstone salesroom that I had my first *vin-dit*, a Bokononist word meaning a sudden, very personal shove in the direction of Bokononism, in the direction of believing that God Almighty knew all about me, after all, that God Almighty had some pretty elaborate plans for me.

The vin-dit had to do with the stone angel under the mistletoe. (CC 34) "It was never *paid* for. The story goes: this German immigrant was on his way West with his wife, and she died of smallpox here in Ilium. So he ordered this angel to be put up over her, and he showed my great-grandfather he had the cash to pay for it. But then he was robbed. Somebody took practically every cent he had. All he had left in this world was some land he'd bought in Indiana, land he'd never seen. So he moved on—said he'd be back later to pay for the angel."

"But he never came back?" I asked.

"Nope." **Marvin Breed** nudged some of the boughs aside with his toe so that we could see the raised letters on the pedestal. There was a last name written there. "There's a screwy name for you," he said. "If that immigrant had any descendants, I expect they Americanized the name. They're probably Jones or Black or Thompson now."

"There you're wrong," I murmured. . . .

"You know some people by that name?"

"Yes."

The name was my last name, too.

Breedlove, Don. *The ironically named gas-conversion unit installer who rapes Patty Keene outside the Bannister Memorial Fieldhouse at the County Fairgrounds after the Regional High School Basketball Playoffs. She never reported it to the police. She never reported it to anybody, since her father was dying at the time (BC 15).*

Vonnegut provides the dimensions of Breedlove's penis: five and seven-eighths inches long and one and seven-eighths inches in diameter (BC 15).

Breedlove impregnates Gloria Browning, leaving her to endure a botched abortion followed by a hysterectomy. Later, while repairing a defective gas oven in the Holiday Inn, he is victimized by Dwayne Hoover, who first grasps his hand in a handshake and then slams him in the ear, making him deaf on one side.

To say Breedlove is not well liked is putting it mildly. One of the neighborhood children dumps maple sugar in the gas tank of his Pontiac Ventura.

Brentner, Mr. and Mrs. *In the short story "Runaways," collected in* Bagombo Snuff Box *(1999),* *these are the parents of sixteen-year-old Rice Brentner, who twice runs away with his girlfriend, Annie Southard, the daughter of Indiana governor Jesse K. Southard. The Brentners' first appearance in the story occurs after Rice's return from his initial attempt to run away with Annie. They tag-team the young man for the scruffy look of his first mustache: insultingly, unreasonably, loudly and without paying too much attention to Rice's meager defense. This all happens while, outside their house,* The boy and his father and his mother did not hear the reporters knocking. The television set in the living room and the radio in the kitchen were both on, blatting away, and the family was having a row in the dining room, halfway between them.

The row was actually about everything in creation, but it had for its subject of the moment the boy's mustache. He had been growing it for a month and had just been caught by his father in the act of blacking it with shoe polish.

Aside from the Brentners' humiliation at the negative publicity of their son's hijinks, they suffer two additional slights. The incident brings reporters from all over Indiana to their front door, a stark contrast from the notable grandeur of the governor's mansion. Eight miles away, eight miles due south, through the heart of town and out the other side, reporters were clumping onto the front porch of the boy's father's house.

It was old, cheap, a carpenter's special, a 1926 bungalow. Its front windows looked out into the perpetual damp twilight of a huge front porch. Its side windows looked into the neighbors' windows ten feet away. Light could reach the interior only through a window in the back. As luck would have it, the window let light into a tiny pantry.

The second slight is more deeply felt by Mr. Brentner. One of the newspapers published the fact that he was a supply clerk for the school system, earning $89.62 per week. He had reason to resent the thoroughness of the reporter who had dug that figure from the public records. The sixty-two cents galled him in particular. "An eighty-nine-dollar-and-sixty-two-cent-a-week supply clerk has an I-don't-know-what-it-is for a son," he said. "The **Brentner** family is certainly covered with glory today."

Once the young lovers abscond a second time, this time toward Cleveland, the governor summons the Brentners to the governor's mansion so the four parents could unite on a plan of action to bring home their children and avoid yet a third occurrence. However, the governor's harsh response to Mr. Brentner about his inability to control his son, nearly a man, causes a verbal exchange with Mrs. Brentner that speaks well of her quick-wittedness while giving the governor some of the guff he is obviously used to dishing out. "By heaven, he would if you'd have the guts to lay down the law to him and make it stick!" said the governor with hot righteousness.

Rice's mother now did the most courageous thing in her life. She was boiling mad about having all the blame put on her son, and she now squared the governor of Indiana away. "Maybe if we'd raised our son the way you raised your daughter," she said, "maybe then we wouldn't have the trouble we have today."

The governor looked startled. He sat down at his desk. "Well said, madam," he said. He turned to his wife. "We should certainly give our child-rearing secret to the world."

Mr. Brentner reminds the others that their children are not so young anymore. He leaves open the possibility they really are in love and should be left alone. Despite the governor's initial incredulous response to Brentner's suggestion, it is clear in the final scene that they decide to go with the old reverse psychology ploy. The Ohio policeman who finds the runaways relays their parents' message, "The message is this," said the trooper, keeping his face blankly official, "you are to come home in your own car whenever you feel like it. When you get home, they want you to get married and start being happy as soon as possible."

Annie and Rice crept home in the old blue Ford, with baby shoes dangling from the rearview mirror, with a pile of comic books on the burst backseat. They came home on the main highways. Nobody was looking for them anymore.

The Brentners get back their son, the Southards their daughter.

Brentner, Rice. *In the short story "Runaways," collected in* Bagombo Snuff Box *(1999), Rice is the ex-*

reform school kid, a kid who ran a lawn mower service at the governor's country club, ran off with the governor's daughter. *Rice is the sixteen-year-old who twice runs away with his girlfriend, Annie Southard, daughter of Indiana governor Jesse K. Southard. Alienated from his parents' trivial concerns (e.g. Rice's month-old gossamer mustache that his father catches him trying to fill in with shoe polish), he is as self-involved, attention-starved, and misunderstood as Annie. However, their conversations are more rightly simultaneous monologues about their individual alienation from family. Von-negut uses Rice's unusual name to highlight their lack of shared knowledge and awareness.* The fact was that **Rice** had told her about a dozen times why he was named **Rice**, but she never really listened to him. For that matter, **Rice** never really listened to her, either. Both would have been bored stiff if they had listened, but they spared themselves that.

So their conversations were marvels of irrelevance. There were only two subjects in common—self-pity and something called love.

The runaways do share the usual teenage grudge against their parents' generation handling of everything from parenting to politics. In Chicago she and the boy had lectured reporters and police on love, hypocrisy, persecution of teenagers, the insensitivity of parents, and even rockets, Russia, and the hydrogen bomb.

Rice's family inhabits a starkly different version of the American Dream than the Southards. Eight miles away, eight miles due south, through the heart of town and out the other side, reporters were clumping onto the front porch of the boy's father's house.

It was old, cheap, a carpenter's special, a 1926 bungalow. Its front windows looked out into the perpetual damp twilight of a huge front porch. Its side windows looked into the neighbors' windows ten feet away. Light could reach the interior only through a window in the back. As luck would have it, the window let light into a tiny pantry.

Rice's stint in reform school came about from a week-long car-stealing spree involving 16 cars. He was 13 at the time and had a clean record until then. Together they drive in Rice's own Ford, complain about their individual slights by their parents, seldom listen to each other, but the circuitous na-

ture of their complaints returns them to the familiar teenager's refrain of alienation and discontent with their elders. The rock n' roll lyrics blaring from the Ford's radio deliver the modern equivalent of a Greek chorus commenting upon the action of the two protagonists.

Breslaw. *The University of Pennsylvania buys Bres-law, the University of Wisconsin football star, for $43,000 in one of the many Ivy League attempts to knock down the PE-003 rating of Cornell's coach, Doctor Roseberry, in* Player Piano.

Brewer, Ansel (*also* **Irving Buchanon** *and* **Eddie McCarty**). *Howard W. Campbell is attacked in front of his brownstone in Greenwich Village when the New York* Daily News *picks up the story about his whereabouts from* The White Christian Min-uteman. *Brewer, Buchanon, and McCarty are used as the reason for violent retribution by an unnamed New Yorker on Campbell.* (MN 20) And then a bald, bristly fat man carrying a shopping bag came in. He shouldered Resi and me away from the mailboxes with a hoarse, unapologetic bully's apology. . . . The man hit me right through the newspaper before I could comment. . . .

"That one was for Private **Irving Buchanon**," he said.

"Is that who you are?" I said.

"**Buchanon** is dead," he said. "He was the best friend I ever had. Five miles in from Omaha Beach, the Germans cut his nuts off and hung him from a telephone pole."

He kicked me in the ribs, holding Resi off with one hand. "That's for **Ansel Brewer**," he said, "run over by a Tiger tank at Aachen."

He kicked me again. "That's for **Eddie McCarty**, cut in two by a burp gun in the Ardennes," he said. "**Eddie** was gonna be a doctor."

briquet. *In* Mother Night, *Campbell's prison guard Andor Gutman uses this term to describe those Jews who seemingly went to the gas chambers without making any attempts to fight back and save themselves. He avoided becoming a "briquet" by getting false papers, joining the Hungarian SS, and killing off as many Nazis as he could without being re-vealed.*

Brokenshire, Dr. David. *In* Deadeye Dick, *the British doctor imprisoned by the Japanese but who previously discovers John Fortune in his last days in Nepal. Before dying of double pneumonia, Fortune gives Brokenshire a letter that is only forwarded to the* Midland City Bugle-Observer *long after his death. Brokenshire writes a book about Fortune and includes a map of Katmandu and the location of Fortune's grave.*

Brokenshire travels through Nepal, Tibet, Burma, and China, where the Japanese imprison him under suspicion of espionage. When Rudy Waltz writes a play about John Fortune, one of the characters is Dr. David Brokenshire.

Bromley, Milford S. (General of the Armies). *In* Player Piano, *one of the dignitaries accompanying the Shah of Bratpuhr. He is constantly distressed by the Shah's characterization of Americans, civilians and military personnel alike, as "Takaru"—slaves. Bromley tries to explain that Americans work hard because they are motivated by patriotism.*

Bronk, Mr. *Alfred Moorhead remembers this highly important General Electric contact by rigorously cycling his memory through his mnemonics training.* (BAG Mnemonics) He *(Moorhead)* reached the pencil and pad, and exhaled. The picture was fogging, but it was still there. Alfred considered the ladies one by one, wrote down their messages, and allowed them to dissolve. As their numbers decreased, he began to slow their exits in order to savor them. Now Ann Sheridan, the next-to-the-last in line, astride a western pony, tapped him on the forehead with a lightbulb to remind him of the name of an important contact at General Electric—**Mr. Bronk.** She blushed under his gaze, dismounted, and dissolved.

Brown, Betty and Bobby. *In* Slapstick, *Eliza and Wilbur Swain's stupendous intellect is effective only when they touch their heads together. Whenever separated, they each feel as dim-witted as the other. When this happens, they think of themselves in the third person, as "Betty and Bobby Brown." Before dying in the Martian avalanche, Eliza asks that her tombstone read "HERE LIES BETTY BROWN."*

Among the many theoretical papers they wrote together, one was a manual on childrearing, which they signed as Betty and Bobby Brown. The original title was The Cry of the Nocturnal Goatsucker, *but that was conceived in one of their fits of creativity. Later, when Wilbur is a practicing pediatrician in Vermont, he renames it* So You Went and Had a Baby, *under the pseudonym Dr. Eli W. Rockmell, M.D.*

Brown, Dr. Ed. (GBR 4) Sylvia was placed in a private mental hospital in Indianapolis, was taken there by Eliot and Charley Warmergran, the Fire Chief. They took her in the Chief's car, which was a red Henry J with a siren on top. They turned her over to a **Dr. Ed Brown,** a young psychiatrist who later made his reputation describing her illness. In the paper, he called Eliot and Sylvia "*Mr. and Mrs. Z,*" and he called the town of Rosewater "*Hometown, U.S.A.*" He coined a new word for Sylvia's disease, "*Samaritrophia,*" which he said meant, "*hysterical indifference to the troubles of those less fortunate than oneself.*"
(GBR 4) I *(Dr. Brown)* made it the goal of my treatments, then, to keep her conscience imprisoned, but to lift the lid of the oubliette ever so slightly, so that the howls of the prisoner might be very faintly heard. Through trial and error with chemotherapy and electric shock, this I achieved. I was not proud, for I had calmed a deep woman by making her shallow. I had blocked the underground rivers that connected her to the Atlantic, Pacific, and Indian Oceans, and made her content with being a splash pool three feet across, four inches deep, chlorinated, and painted blue.

Dr. Brown also treats Eliot in the insane asylum and is present for the final scene along with Eliot, Kilgore Trout, Senator Rosewater, and Thurmond McAllister.

Brown, John (see *God Bless You, Dr. Kevorkian*).

Brown, Payton. *In* Breakfast of Champions, *the fifteen-year-old black teenager who dies in the electric chair at Shepherdstown. Dwayne Hoover tries to save him though his efforts are not enumerated. He mentions Payton Brown while bragging to parolee Wayne Hoobler about the advancements he sought* for black people as County Executive for the Boy Scouts of America.

Browning, Gloria. *In* Breakfast of Champions, *the twenty-five-year-old cashier at Dwayne Hoover's Exit Eleven Pontiac Village who fills in at Francine Pefko's desk while she and Dwayne go for an afternoon rendezvous at a local motel. Don Breedlove raped her years earlier, and Gloria required a hysterectomy after enduring a botched abortion at the Green County Ramada Inn.*

Buchanon, Eddie (*see* **Brewer, Ansel**).

Buchenwald. *The German concentration camp is referred to (particularly for piles of dead bodies) in* Cat's Cradle (73), Slaughterhouse-Five (9), *and the 1951 short story* "The Euphio Question," *collected in* Welcome to the Monkey House (1968).

Buffalo Works. *In* Player Piano, *one of the main industrial centers of the ruling technocracy. The manager of the plant is Fred Garth. The Buffalo Works is one of many sites that suffers sabotage during the failed uprising against the technocracy.*

bugger, buggered, buggery. (*PP* XXX) "Well, it just don't seem like nobody feels he's worth a crap to nobody no more, and it's a hell of a screwy thing, people gettin' **buggered** by things they made theirselves."
(*GBR* 2) And so on. The Senator said that the carrot and the stick had been built into the Free Enterprise System, as conceived by the Founding Fathers, but that do-gooders, who thought people shouldn't ever have to struggle for anything, had **buggered** the logic of the system beyond all recognition.
(*MH* Preface) I have already put the question to a college professor, who, climbing down into his Mercedes-Benz 300SL gran turismo, assured me that public relations men and slick writers were equally vile, in that they both **buggered** truth for money.
(*MH* EPICAC) I had hoped to sleep late the next morning, but an urgent telephone call roused me before eight. It was Dr. von Kleigstadt, EPICAC's designer, who gave me the terrible news. He was on the verge of tears. "Ruined! *Ausgespielt*! Shot!

Kaput! **Buggered**!" he said in a choked voice. He hung up.
(*SL5* 9) In the window there were hundreds of books about fucking and **buggery** and murder, and a street guide to New York City, and a model of the Statue of Liberty with a thermometer on it. Also in the window, speckled soot and fly shit, were four paperback novels by Billy's friend, Kilgore Trout.
(*WJ* I:2) SHUTTLE: She's my date tonight. What do you want her to do—bring the poor old jaguars back to life with a bicycle pump? **Bugger** off! Ask Paul what he thinks.
(*BC* 16) So the Earthlings infiltrated the ad agency which had the shazzbutter account, and they **buggered** the statistics in the ads. They made the average for everything so high that everybody on the planet felt inferior to the majority in every respect.
(*BC* 17) Listen: Bunny Hoover went to Prairie Military Academy for eight years of uninterrupted sports, **buggery** and fascism. **Buggery** consisted of sticking one's penis in somebody else's asshole or mouth, or having it done to one by somebody else. Fascism was a fairly popular political philosophy which made sacred whatever nation and race the philosopher happened to belong to. It called for an autocratic, centralized government, headed up by a dictator. The dictator had to be obeyed, no matter what he told somebody to do.
(*BC* 22) Let's see: I have already explained Dwayne's uncharacteristic ability to read so fast. Kilgore Trout probably couldn't have made his trip from New York City in the time I allotted, but it's too late to **bugger** around with that. Let it stand, let it stand!
(*BC* 22) Trout made no reply. He had hoped to get through what little remained of his life without ever having to touch another human being again. Dwayne's chin on his shoulder was as shattering as **buggery** to Trout.
(*WFG* Fortitude) FRANKENSTEIN (to LITTLE): You keep her right there. I'm gonna check things over. Maybe there's been a little huggery **buggery**. (To GLORIA) How would you like to be in court for attempted murder, eh?
(*Slap* Epilogue) "**Bugger** . . . defecate . . . semen . . . balls," said the boy. *The boy is David Daffodil-11 von Peterswald, a victim of Tourette's Disease.*
(*DD* 19) There was a young man from Dundee, /

Who **buggered** an ape in a tree. / The results were most horrid, / All ass and no forehead, / Three balls and a purple goatee.

Bugle-Observer (also **Midland City Bugle-Observer**). *The main newspaper of Midland City mentioned in both* Breakfast of Champions *and* Deadeye Dick. *In* Deadeye Dick *the paper's city editor is George Metzger, husband of Eloise Metzger, the victim of Rudy Waltz's mindless shooting from his home's cupola.*

Building 58 Suite. *Paul Proteus's perception of the machinery's rhythm in Thomas Edison's old laboratory at the Ilium Works. The music intoxicates him, separates him from his anxieties. Paul enchants himself with thinking the machinery is representative of a time when technological innovation was due to man's direct involvement and signaled a triumph of spirit and intellect, representative of an era less tainted by technology's direct impact on society.* (PP I) At the door, in the old part of the building once more, Paul paused for a moment to listen to the music of Building 58. He had had it in the back of his mind for years to get a composer to do something with it—the **Building 58 Suite**. It was wild and Latin music, hectic rhythms, fading in and out of phase, kaleidoscopic sound. He tried to separate and identify the themes. There! The lathe groups, the tenors: "Furrazz-ow-ow-ow-ow-ow-ak! ting! Furr-azz-ow-ow . . ." The welders, the baritones: "Vaaaaaaa-zuzip! Vaaaaaaa-zuzip!" And, with the basement as a resonating chamber, the punch presses, the basses: "Aw-grumph! tonka-tonka. Aw-grump! tonka-tonka . . ." It was exciting music, and Paul, flushed, his vague anxieties gone, gave himself over to it.

Members of the Ghost Shirt Society drug Paul before his interrogation. Dreamily retreating into the rhythms of the Building 58 Suite, Paul projects himself at the center of an erotic ballet with his wife, Anita, who eventually lays amidst a nest of electrical wires with Kroner and Shepherd. Paul awakens from his drug-induced haze by Ed Finnerty, his Ghost Shirt interrogator.

Bullard, Dr. Brainard Keyes. *The president of Wyandotte College, who, in the 1953 short story "To-*morrow and Tomorrow and Tomorrow" (reprinted in the 1968 collection* Welcome to the Monkey House), *says* "most of the world's ills can be traced to the fact that Man's knowledge of himself has not kept pace with his knowledge of the physical world."

Bullard, Harold K. *One of the two old men in the short story "Tom Edison's Shaggy Dog," in* Welcome to the Monkey House *(1968). He and his Labrador retriever go searching for new acquaintances in a Tampa, Florida, park each day. He longs to tell everyone about the five fortunes he made and lost throughout his life,* "Two in real estate, one in scrap iron, and one in oil and one in trucking."

However, Bullard becomes the butt of his unnamed companion's ire, and he tells Bullard a story about his days with Thomas Edison when Edison was trying to figure out the proper material to use for a lightbulb filament. As the man explains, Edison's dog, Sparky, told him to use carbonized cotton thread. When eavesdropping dogs hear Sparky reveal the true intelligence of dogs, threatening the subservient relationship they had cultivated with humans, they tear Sparky to shreds. Bullard apparently swallows the entire story.

Bunker, Archie. *The racist patriarch of the TV sitcom* All in the Family. *Using Archie as the American Everyman, Vonnegut reveals the source of the subtitle for* Slapstick. (WFG *Playboy* Interview) PLAYBOY: If you had been the Democratic nominee (in the 1972 election), how would you have campaigned against Nixon?
VONNEGUT: I would have set the poor against the rich. I would have made the poor admit that they're poor. **Archie Bunker** has no sense of being poor, but he obviously is a frightened, poor man. I would convince **Archie Bunker** that he was poor and getting poorer, that the ruling class was robbing him and lying to him. I was invited to submit ideas to the McGovern campaign. Nothing was done with my suggestions. I wanted Sargent Shriver to say, "You are not happy, are you? Nobody in this country is happy but the rich people. Something is wrong. I'll tell you what's wrong. We're lonesome!"

Mary Kathleen O'Looney, the eccentric and secretive philanthropic owner of the RAMJAC Corpo-

ration, *appreciates America's passion for the views of Archie Bunker and other media stars, but she understands their actions and philosophies to be in opposition to the public good and acts accordingly.* (JB 16) "It's all such crap," she said. "I find this magazine called *People* in garbage cans," she said, "but it isn't about people. It's about crap. . . . Jackie Onassis and Frank Sinatra and the Cookie Monster and **Archie Bunker** make their moves," she said, "and then I study what they have done, and then I decide what Mary Kathleen O'Looney had better do."

"Bunker Bingo Party." *One of the four Kilgore Trout stories retrieved from the trash receptacle outside the American Academy of Arts and Letters by security guard Dudley Prince in* Timequake. *It focuses on the post-marital activities of Adolph Hitler and Eva Braun moments before their deaths in their Berlin bunker as Russian troops surround their position. The story provides a metafictional moment for Vonnegut and an unusual moment of self-appreciation by Kilgore Trout as a writer.*

Once the excitement dies down over the hasty marriage between Hitler and his mistress and spirits refocus on their dire condition, Goebbels tries to reinvigorate the group of high-ranking Nazis in the bunker. (TQ 19) Goebbels remembers that his kids have brought the game of **Bingo** with them. It was captured intact from American troops during the Battle of the Bulge some four months earlier. I myself was captured intact during that battle. Germany, to conserve its resources, has stopped making its own **Bingo** games. Because of that, and because the grownups in the bunker have been so busy during the rise of Hitler, and now his fall, the Goebbels kids are the only ones who know how the game is played. They learned from a neighbor kid, whose family owned a prewar **Bingo** set.

There is this amazing scene in the story: A boy and a girl, explaining the rules of **Bingo**, become the center of the Universe for Nazis in full regalia, including a gaga Adolf Hitler.

In another metafictional moment within the text, Vonnegut recalls how Trout spoke about the story when he sees a copy of it again at the Xanadu writers' retreat, prior to that evening's clambake. (TQ

20) By his own account to me, Trout riffled through the scruffy pages with distaste, while seated tailor-fashion and naked on his king-size bed in the Ernest Hemingway Suite. The day was hot. He was fresh from his Jacuzzi.

But then his gaze fell upon the scene in which two anti-Semitic children teach **Bingo** to high-ranking Nazis in their madly theatrical uniforms. In amazed admiration for something brilliant he himself had written, and Trout had never thought of himself as worth a hill of beans as a writer, he praised the scene as an echo of this prophecy from the Book of Isaiah:

"The wolf also shall dwell with the lamb, and the leopard shall lie down with the kid; and the calf and the young lion and the fatling together; and a little child shall lead them."

(TQ 20) In "**Bunker Bingo Party**," the Nazis participate in **Bingo**, with the Minister of Propaganda, arguably the most effective communicator in history, calling out the coordinates of winning or losing squares on the players' cards. The game proves as analgesic for war criminals in deep doodoo as it continues to be for harmless old biddies at church fairs. . . .

To return to Trout's roman à clef: As though there were a God in Heaven after all, it is Der Führer who shouts "BINGO!" Adolf Hitler wins! He says incredulously, in German, of course, "I can't believe it. I've never played this game before, and yet I've won, I've won! What can this be but a miracle?" He is a Roman Catholic.

He rises from his chair at the table. His eyes are still fixed on the winning card before him, according to Trout, "as if it were a shred from the Shroud of Turin." This prick asks, "What can this mean but that things aren't as bad as we thought they were?"

Eva Braun spoils the moment by swallowing a capsule of cyanide. Goebbels's wife gave it to her for a wedding present. *Moments later, with Russian artillery targeting Hitler's bunker, Der Fuehrer wracks his brains for a proper last set of words to say before blowing out his brains, Trout tells Vonnegut that* Hitler still hasn't lost his sense of humor. He says, "How about 'BINGO'?"

But he is tired. He puts a pistol to his head. Everybody says, "Nein, nein, nein." He convinces everyone that shooting himself is the dignified thing to do. What should his last words be? He says, "How about 'I regret nothing'?" Goebbels replies that such a statement would be appropriate, but that the Parisian cabaret performer Edith Piaf has made a worldwide reputation by singing those same words in French for decades. "Her sobriquet," says Goebbels, "is 'Little Sparrow.' You don't want to be remembered as a little sparrow, or I miss my guess."

Bunting, Arthur J. *In the short story "Unpaid Consultant," collected in* Bagombo Snuff Box *(1999), Bunting is the third-generation proprietor of a catchup factory who recently sold his business, prompting him to call the unnamed narrator to determine if he may be the right sort of financial adviser to help with his vastly increased wealth. It promises to be the narrator's largest account if he can land it.*

The narrator's prospects for Bunting's business are initially dashed by Harry when invited to attend a lunch meeting with the narrator and Bunting. The narrator did not know at that point that Harry had been only pretending to be a valued unpaid consultant to the industry. It was Harry's ruse to keep himself interesting to his wife, Celeste. Harry is unaware of who the other party will be at lunch. The old gentleman is mortified by Harry's ignorant and loud rantings about the catchup industry while simply being conducted to their table.

Apart from his dignified appearance, **Mr. Bunting** *was a splendid old gentleman, stout, over six feet tall, with the white mustache and fierce eyes of an old Indian fighter. He is filled with personal angst at selling his family's catchup business, so Harry's words cut deeply.*

Bunting proves to be an honorable, discreet, and forgiving confidant. When Harry calls to apologize for so ignorantly and unintentionally bruising his ego, explaining how he had been trying to keep himself interesting to Celeste as her career blossomed, Bunting agrees to keep the matter between themselves. Harry takes it upon himself to make the apology in a private call and further reveals both his own pretensions and Bunting's honorable reception of him in his confession to the narrator at the close of

the story. Once the narrator knows both sides of the story, Bunting proves his discretion and gentlemanly nature by not holding the incident against the narrator. **Mr. Bunting** *called the next day to say that he had accepted Harry's apology.*

"He made a clean breast of how he got into catchup," said **Mr. Bunting**, "and he promised to get out. As far as I'm concerned, the matter is closed." *Presumably, the narrator is again in the good graces of Bunting and may go forward with their business.*

Buntline, Amanita. *In* God Bless You, Mr. Rosewater, *Amanita is the mother of Lila and wife of Stewart Buntline. She is also the "Lesbian friend" of Caroline Rosewater. She passes down her old clothes and accessories to Caroline and buys her all sorts of nonsensical gifts simply because she can, including a $17 toilet paper cover from Mexico.*

Buntline, Castor. *The great-grandfather of Stewart Buntline and founder of the company that produced the Buntline Union Beacon Broom, Castor Buntline did not serve in the military during the Civil War. His intentions to employ disabled veterans were egocentric and mercenary. The disabled General George Rosewater went to work for Buntline and became the namesake of the "General George Rosewater" whiskbroom.* (GBR 8) **Buntline** perceived correctly that blind veterans would make very agreeable employees, that **Buntline** himself would gain a place in history as a humanitarian, and that no Northern patriot, for several years after the war, anyway, would use anything but a *Buntline Union Beacon Broom.* Thus was the great **Buntline** fortune begun. And, with broom profits, **Castor Buntline** and his spastic son Elihu went carpetbagging, became tobacco kings.

Castor Buntline also founded an orphanage in Pawtucket in 1878, and he wrote the oath of service for the "fortunate" few. (GBR 11) When it was founded, the **Buntlines** required three things: That all orphans be raised as Christians, regardless of race, color, or creed, that they take an oath once a week, before Sunday supper, and that, each year, an intelligent, clean female orphan enter domestic service in a **Buntline** home . . . in order to learn about the better things in life, and perhaps to be inspired to climb a few rungs of the ladder of culture and social grace.

The oath of service is as follows: (GBR 11) I do solemnly swear that I will respect the sacred private property of others, and that I will be content with whatever station in life God Almighty may assign me to. I will be grateful to those who employ me, and will never complain about wages and hours, but will ask myself instead, "What more can I do for my employer, my republic, and my God?" I understand that I have not been placed on Earth to be happy. I am here to be tested. If I am to pass the test, I must be always unselfish, always sober, always truthful, always chaste in mind, body, and deed, and always respectful to those to whom God has, in His Wisdom, placed above me. If I pass the test, I will go to joy everlasting in Heaven when I die. If I fail, I shall roast in hell while the Devil laughs and Jesus weeps.

Buntline, Elihu. *In* God Bless You, Mr. Rosewater, *Elihu is the spastic son of Castor Buntline, founder of the Buntline Union Beacon Broom company. He and his father invest their earnings and make a fortune in tobacco. He is also Stewart Buntline's grandfather.*

Buntline, Lila. *In* God Bless You, Mr. Rosewater, *Stewart and Amanita Buntline's daughter is the celebrated thirteen-year-old sailor at the Pisquontuit Yacht Club as well as the pornography and fireworks peddler to the wealthy youth in Newport, Rhode Island. She buys the latest erotic novels from the local news store and sells them at huge profits to her friends. She is so good at this that a local civic club commends the store for apparently not stocking smut, when in reality, Lila has scooped up the stock.*

Buntline, Stewart. *Just shy of forty, the husband of Amanita and father of Lila is a depressed rich man whose sole interest, however slight, is in studying the Civil War. In some ways Stewart is afflicted with the same anxieties as Eliot Rosewater: orphaned at sixteen and the benefactor of a $14-million tobacco fortune (currently earning over $800K per year) under the conservatorship of Reed McAllister, senior partner in the law firm McAllister, Robjent, Reed and*

McGee—*the same firm representing the Senator and Eliot Rosewater.*

Twenty years earlier in the story, he went to Old McAllister feeling ashamed of all his unearned wealth, asking how he could put his money to use for the poor. McAllister chastised him for his naïveté, apologized for the lack of real-world education he received at Harvard, and explained that it was Stewart's duty and sole source of personal fulfillment to cherish the fortune. Old McAllister tells him, (GBR 10) I have to offer what is perhaps an insult. Here it is, like it or not: Your fortune is the most important single determinant of what you think of yourself and of what others think of you. Because of the money, you are extraordinary. Without it, for example, you would not now be taking the priceless time of a senior partner in McAllister, Robjent, Reed and McGee. . . .

"Cling to your miracle, Mr. Buntline. Money is dehydrated Utopia. This is a dog's life for almost everybody, as your professors have taken such pains to point out. But, because of your miracle, life for you and yours can be a paradise! Let me see you smile! Let me see that you already understand what they do not teach at Harvard until the junior year: That to be born rich and to stay rich is something less than a felony."

Bunty. *This yacht belongs to Stewart and Amanita Buntline in* God Bless You, Mr. Rosewater.

Burch, Captain Arnold. *The nominal company commander of Boaz and Unk (Malachi Constant) while serving in the Martian Army, Burch is actually under Boaz's control. It is during his appearance in their barracks that Vonnegut first explains the remote control box Boaz has in his pants.* (ST 5) Only one man was slow about coming to attention. That man was Boaz. And when he did come to attention, there was something insolent and loose and leering about the way he did it.

Captain Burch, finding Boaz's attitude profoundly offensive, was about to speak to Boaz about it. But the captain no sooner got his mouth open than pain hit him between the eyes.

The captain closed his mouth without having made a sound.

Under the baleful gaze of Boaz, he came smartly

to attention, did an about-face, heard a snare drum in his head, and marched out of the barrack in step with the drum. . . . He *(Boaz)* had a small control box in his right front trouser pocket that could make his squadmates do just about anything. The box was the size of a one-pint hip flask. Like a hip flask, the box was curved to fit a body curve. Boaz chose to carry it on the hard, curved face of his thigh.

Burger, Knox. *Vonnegut's dedication page in the short story collection* Welcome to the Monkey House *reads,* For Knox Burger, Ten days older than I am. He has been a very good father to me. *Indeed, Burger was a Cornell classmate of Vonnegut's and rose to become a literary editor at* Collier's *magazine. Burger is responsible for publishing Vonnegut's first short story, "Report on the Barnhouse Effect," in 1950. Burger is also responsible for getting Vonnegut his first literary agent, Kenneth Littauer.*
(PS Self-Interview) When I was working for General Electric I wrote a story, "Report on the Barnhouse Effect," the first story I ever wrote. I mailed it off to *Collier's*. **Knox Burger** was fiction editor there. **Knox** told me what was wrong with it and how to fix it. I did what he said, and he bought the story for seven hundred and fifty dollars, six weeks' pay at G.E. I wrote another, and he paid me nine hundred and fifty dollars, and suggested that it was perhaps time for me to quit G.E. Which I did. I moved to Provincetown. Eventually, my price for a short story got up to twenty-nine hundred dollars a crack. Think of that. And **Knox** got me a couple of agents who were as shrewd about storytelling as he was—Kenneth Littauer, who had been his predecessor at *Collier's*, and Max Wilkinson, who had been a story editor for MGM. And let it be put on the record here that **Knox Burger**, who is about my age, discovered and encouraged more good young writers than any other editor of his time. I don't think that's ever been written down anywhere. It's a fact known only to writers, and one that could easily vanish, if it isn't somewhere written down.

In the preface to Breakfast of Champions, *Vonnegut recalls a conversation with Burger that gives rise to another Vonnegut alter ego, one less well known than Kilgore Trout—Philboyd Studge.* (BC Preface) What do I myself think of this particular

book? I feel lousy about it, but I always feel lousy about my books. My friend **Knox Burger** said one time that a certain cumbersome novel ". . . read as though it had been written by Philboyd Studge." That's who I think I am when I write what I am seemingly programmed to write."

Closing the text's preface is Vonnegut's oft re-peated sentiments in the voice of Philboyd Studge. (BC Preface)

> Armistice Day has become Veterans' Day.
>   Armistice Day was sacred. Veterans' Day
>   is not.
> So I will throw Veterans' Day over my shoul-
>   der. Armistice Day I will keep. I don't
>   want to throw away any sacred things.
> What else is sacred? Oh, Romeo and Juliet,
>   for instance.
> And all music is.
>
> —PHILBOYD STUDGE

Burger is one of the dearly departed souls brought back by Vonnegut to appear at the Timequake *clambake.*

burgomaster. *In the short story "Der Arme Dol-metscher," collected in* Bagombo Snuff Box (1999), *the unnamed narrator, foolishly selected to serve as the battalion's translator, is sent to keep watch on the local burgomaster (mayor). Since the Americans had recently taken over the area and were about to launch an offensive, the narrator explains* I was to be stationed with the **burgomaster** to make sure he didn't try to pull a fast one. *The burgomaster plays a prominent role in the narrator's brief, sleepless fan-tasy (see **burgomaster's daughter**) before the narra-tor packs his duffel, straightens out his bedroom and slips away under cover of darkness to return to head-quarters.*

burgomaster's daughter. *When the unnamed narrator of "Der Arme Dolmetscher" (Bag) tries to settle in for some sleep at his new post in the burgo-master's home, he is woefully unsuccessful. He fanta-sizes a romantic tryst with his host's daughter. All the lines in this brief fantasy are taken from two sources: the translation of Heinrich Heine's "Die Lorelei" and the interrogation questions in the torn military* *pamphlet given to the narrator by the three Pennsyl-vania Dutch soldiers he met while catching a ride to the burgomaster's home.*

The basic irony of the story concerns the narra-tor's selection to be the battalion's translator based on his having memorized Heine's poem, once learned from a school classmate. He neither speaks nor un-derstands German, but he is able to pass the anxiety of the moment by reciting it over and over within earshot of his colonel. The colonel, a rather poor judge of events despite his civilian work as a hotel detective, is persuaded that being able to at least mimic the language qualifies the narrator to keep a watchful eye on the burgomaster.

The more subtle irony of the moment, the fanta-sized tryst with the burgomaster's daughter, has to do with the fact that this portion of the scene is spoken with only the words from Heine's poem. The irony is that Heine's poem is about a siren perched atop a rock named Lorelei, and from that position at the narrowest part of a curve on the river Rhine, she mes-merizes sailors who lose their lives as they ignore the navigational dangers inherent to that position. In the narrator's fantasy, just as he carries the young lady up to his room and positions her on his bed, her father steps from the shadows pointing a Luger at the the him, declaring that he and his daughter are working for the Nazis and that he is their prisoner.

The language in the fantasy switches immedi-ately upon the father's appearance to the military phrases in the G.I. manual. The narrator turns the tables on his captors in his fantasy when he reaches for his gun beneath the pillow. The fantasy/playlet finishes out in the military language from the man-ual. Upon snapping out of his oddly meshed linguis-tic reverie, the narrator tidies up his room, makes the bed, and slips out into the dark to make his way back to his headquarters—just in time to act as his colo-nel's translator when they are forced to surrender to four Tiger tanks and a unit of German infantry.

Burgoyne, General John. *In* Bluebeard, *the com-manding officer of Paul Slazinger's first ancestor in America, a Hessian soldier from Wiesbaden, Ger-many, serving as a mercenary with the British.*

Burke, Roberta Gorsuch (*see* ***God Bless You, Dr. Kevorkian***).

Butler, Nicholas Murray. *In* Deadeye Dick, *the president of Columbia University is a visiting celeb-rity in Midland City, and since there was next to nothing of interest to see or do there at the time, such cultured luminaries were usually taken for a tour of Otto Waltz's in-home art studio. During the visit, Butler gets to meet a very young Rudy Waltz, years before his shooting of Eloise Metzger.*

Buzzer. *In the short story* "Souvenir," *collected in* Bagombo Snuff Box (1999), *Buzzer is Eddie's best friend and a fellow POW. The frame tale focuses on the day of their unceremonious release from a Sude-tenland prison camp. In the course of the day they fall in with some drunken Canadian soldiers cele-brating their freedom. A short time later they are met by a Nazi general and his aide trying to make their way to the American lines for surrender rather than risk capture by advancing Soviet armored divisions.*

Eddie tells pawnbroker Joe Bane the ugly details of that day and how he came to possess the general's bejeweled pocket watch, and that necessarily in-cluded the details of Buzzer's death. Eddie's fond-ness for Buzzer is evident throughout his narrative, and retelling his story eventually convinces him that despite needing money for his family, he simply can't part with that last physical tie he shares with Buzzer. As Eddie begins his story about the watch, he begins with his recollection of Buzzer. "My best buddy **Buzzer** and me," said the farmer, "were prisoners of war together in some hills in Germany—in Sude-tenland, somebody said it was. One morning, **Buzzer** woke me up and said the war was over, the guards were gone, the gates were open."

Eddie's sense of kinship with and apparent simi-larities to Buzzer are evident in the omniscient nar-rator's characterization, as if to say from an authorial level that their fates were not dissimilar at that point. The young farmer, whose name was Eddie, and his best buddy **Buzzer** walked out into peace and free-dom skinny, ragged, dirty, and hungry, but with no ill will toward anyone. They'd gone to war out of pride, not bitterness. Now the war was over, the job done, and they wanted only to go home. They were a year apart, but as alike as two poplars in a wind-break.

As the general and his aide persuade Eddie and Buzzer to go behind a nearby wall to sell their uni-

forms for the watch, the true aim of the fleeing Nazis becomes evident at the very moment Soviet tanks begin to rumble the earth and fill the skies with a shrieking artillery barrage. But it was now impossible for anybody to say any more funny stuff and still be heard. The earth shook, and the air was ripped to shreds as armored vehicles from the victorious Soviet Union, thundering and backfiring, came up the road. Everybody who could got out of the way of the juggernaut. Some were not so lucky. They were mangled. They were squashed.

Eddie and **Buzzer** and the old man and the blond found themselves behind the wall where the blond had said the Americans could swap their uniforms for the watch and civilian clothes. In the uproar, during which anybody could do anything, and nobody cared what anybody else did, the blond shot **Buzzer** in the head. He aimed his pistol at Eddie. He fired. He missed.

That had evidently been the plan all along, to kill Eddie and **Buzzer**. But what chance did the old man, who spoke no English, have to pass himself off to his captors as an American? None. It was the blond who was going to do that. And they were both about to be captured. All the old man could do was commit suicide.

Eddie went back over the wall, putting it between himself and the blond. But the blond didn't care what had become of him. Everything the blond needed was on **Buzzer**'s body. When Eddie peered over the wall to see if Buzzer was still alive, the blond was stripping the body. The old man now had the pistol. He put its muzzle in his mouth and blew his brains out.

The blond walked off with **Buzzer**'s clothes and dog tags. **Buzzer** was in his GI underwear and dead, without ID. On the ground between the old man and **Buzzer**, Eddie found the watch. It was running. It told the right time. Eddie picked it up and put it in his pocket.

Cady, Newell. *In the 1952 short story "Poor Little Rich Town," first published in the October 1952* Collier's *magazine and later reprinted in the 1999 collection* Bagombo Snuff Box, *Newell Cady is the efficiency expert and vice president of Federated Apparatus Corporation, designated as the company's director for their relocation from New York City to the depressed central New York town of Ilium. As is common in many of Vonnegut's stories, Cady represents industry's unbridled impulse for progress at the expense of comforting neighborliness.*

Cady rents with an option to buy an old mansion in the nearby town of Spruce Falls, where all the story's action occurs. Spruce Falls is as economically depressed as Ilium, but its housing stock has great curb appeal because of fifteen mansions built in the second decade of the twentieth century, mansions built when the town started to prosper due to its therapeutic waters, much as had been the case with Saratoga. However, many of the mansions are sorely in need of repair and updating since the town's original inhabitants fell on hard times when a Manhattan dermatologist erroneously diagnosed "Spruce Falls disease" as a result of their healing baths. The medical scare was enough to undo the town's economy, so Cady's rental and his company's plan to move their headquarters to nearby Ilium unrealistically lifts the spirits of the town.

Initially, Cady's move to Spruce Falls sets up hope for the town's economy, and the people do their best to lavish him with honors. Fire Chief Stanley Atkins arranges for his corps of volunteer firemen to vote Cady in as a full member of the department, and they go so far as to name him head judge of the annual Hobby Show.

However, it quickly becomes clear that Cady's efficiency suggestions make opponents of Mrs. Dickie, the postmistress, as well as Fire Chief Atkins. That is assured once Cady tries to streamline the sorting operation in the post office and his analysis that the town does not need to go into debt to purchase a new, updated firetruck when the one they have is perfectly useful. Cady's attempts to reorganize the traf-

fic flow in Hal Brayton's grocery store are also poorly received, and the same is true of his plan to close the local school and bus the children to nearby Ilium.

Cady's approach to the efficiency of local institutions lacks consideration for the people who run them and their patrons. Disappointing Fire Chief Atkins about the new fire truck is one thing, but suggesting the town switch to the more efficient rural free delivery for mail is a shattering faux pas. Cady's suggestion jeopardizes both the livelihood of Mrs. Dickie, a revered woman whose twenty-five-year tenure as postmistress followed her husband's heroic death as a volunteer firefighter in the process of saving an unknown number of townspeople. It would deprive the townspeople the opportunity to visit the post office, pay their respects to Mrs. Dickie, and generally assure her that she remained a vital part of their community. Upton Beaton's verbal exchange with Cady informs him of his errors and points out that his desire to make all things efficient undercuts the human value often at stake in our daily interactions. "It's a great advantage, coming into situations from the outside, the way I do," said **Cady**. "People inside of situations are so blinded by custom. Here you people were, supporting a post office, when you could get much better service for just a fraction of the cost and trouble." He chuckled modestly, as Atkins shut the post office door behind him. "One-eyed man in the land of the blind, you might say."

"A one-eyed man might as well be blind," declared Upton Beaton, "if he doesn't watch people's faces and doesn't give the blind credit for the senses they do have."

"What on earth are you talking about?" said **Cady**.

"If you'd looked at Mrs. Dickie's face instead of how she was doing her work, you would have seen she was crying," said Beaton. "Her husband died in a fire, saving some of these people around the village you call blind. You talk a lot about wasting time, **Mr. Cady**—for a really big waste of time, walk around the village someday and try to find somebody who doesn't know he can have his mail brought to his door anytime he wants to."

Cady also makes a tremendous mistake in changing the nature and substance of the annual Hobby Show. Intended as an opportunity for anyone in town to share their interest and expertise in any particular oddity or skillful practice, Cady is taken aback by the practice of each entrant having an exclusive category, resulting in everyone's receiving a blue ribbon for their efforts. He declares just a single winner, oblivious to the shame this brings the townspeople. Those few nonparticipants who dropped in at the church to see the exhibits, and who hadn't heard about the judging, were amazed to find one lonely object, a petit-point copy of the cover of a woman's magazine, on view. Pinned to it was the single blue ribbon awarded that day. The other exhibitors had angrily hauled home their rejected offerings, and the sole prizewinner appeared late in the evening, embarrassed and furtive, to take her entry home, leaving the blue ribbon behind.

As the downside to all of Cady's suggestions becomes clear, the town works to undo its initial rush to bestow honorific titles on their new resident. They realize that voting him fire department membership violated its bylaws because one needs to be a resident for three years before consideration. However, true to their roots in judging people for their intentions, they realize that Cady is well-meaning but misguided in thinking the town should run with the same efficiency quotient as a company. In uninviting him from the fire department, the following exchange expresses their measured response to Cady the human being, not a thing to be engineered for efficiency. "The motion's been carried, then," said Chief Atkins in a loud voice. "Mr. Beaton is to be a committee of one to inform **Mr. Cady** that his fire department membership, unfortunately, is in violation of the by-laws, which call for three years' residence in the village prior to election."

"I will make it clear to him," said Beaton, also speaking loudly, "that this is in no way a personal affront, that it's simply a matter of conforming to our by-laws, which have been in effect for years."

"Make sure he understands that we all like him," said Ed Newcomb, "and tell him we're proud an important man like him would want to live here."

"I will," said Beaton. "He's a brilliant man, and I'm sure he'll see the wisdom in the residence requirement. A village isn't like a factory, where you can walk in and see what's being made at a glance, and then look at the books and see if it's a good or bad operation. We're not manufacturing or selling anything. We're trying to live together. Every man's got to be his own expert at that, and it takes years."

Cahoun, Kitty (*see* **Krummbein, Otto and Falloleen;** *also* **"Custom-Made Bride"**).

calcimine. (*PP* 1) It soothed him (*Paul Proteus*) to look up at the wooden rafters (*of Building 58*), uneven with ancient adze marks beneath flaking **calcimine**, and at the dull walls of brick soft enough for men—God knows how long ago—to carve their initials in· "KTM," "DG," "GP," "BDH," "HB," "NNS."
(*MN* 2) We heard the bombs walking around up there. Now and then there would be a gentle shower of **calcimine**.
(*MN* 32) A bomb crashed down close by, shook loose from the ceiling a snowfall of **calcimine**, brought the woman to her feet shrieking, and her husband with her.
(*SL5* 8) The meat locker was a very safe shelter. All that happened down there was an occasional shower of **calcimine**.
(*TQ* 20) A Communistic 240-millimeter howitzer shell explodes atop the bunker. Flakes of **calcimine** from the shaken ceiling shower down on the deafened occupants. Hitler himself makes a joke, demonstrating that he still has his sense of humor. "It snows," he says. That is a poetic way of saying, too, it is high time he killed himself, unless he wants to become a caged superstar in a traveling freak show, along with the bearded lady and the geek.

Caldwell Foundation. *In* Slapstick, *the foundation sponsors the 1959 playwriting contest won by Rudy Waltz's "Katmandu." The play is brought to the Theatre de Lys in Greenwich Village and closes in one night (the same theater which produced Vonnegut's "Happy Birthday, Wanda June"). The actors and sponsors are so infuriated by Rudy's inability to explain the play that the foundation never sponsors another playwriting contest.*

Calhoun, Doctor Bud. *Though the manager of the petroleum terminal in Ilium, Calhoun is a subordinate of Paul Proteus's. The sweet-talking Georgian spends his spare time on the couch in the reception area of Proteus's office flirting with Dr. Katharine Finch, Paul's secretary. Bud is a single-minded inventor and this passage captures Paul's appreciation of Calhoun's talents and place within a historical scheme.* (PP I) Paul sometimes wondered if he wouldn't have been more content in another period of history, but the rightness of **Bud**'s being alive now was beyond question. **Bud**'s mentality was one that had been remarked upon as being peculiarly American since the nation had been born—the restless, erratic insight and imagination of a gadgeteer. This was the climax, or close to it, of generations of **Bud Calhouns**, with almost all of American industry integrated into one stupendous Rube Goldberg machine.

*Calhoun is so accomplished at inventing new labor-saving devices that he invents himself and seventy-two other people out of their jobs. Faced with unemployment, Bud joins the Ghost Shirt Society and is valued for the technical expertise he provides to the fledgling revolutionaries. Paul doesn't understand Bud's involvement with the group, since **Bud** wasn't at all interested in political action and was without capacity for resentment. As **Bud** had said of himself, "All Ah want is time an' equipmen' to faht around with, and Ah'm happy as a pig in mud"* (PP XXX). *The truth of this statement is later borne out when Bud and one of the road workers from the "Reeks and Wrecks" repair the nearly destroyed Orange-O machine, a symbol of man's growing inability to feed itself.* (PP XXXV) The man (*Bud*) had been desperately unhappy then. Now he was proud and smiling because his hands were busy doing what they liked to do best, Paul supposed—replacing men like himself with machines. He hooked up the lamp behind the Orange-O sign. "There we are."

Calvary Cemetery (*see also* **Golgotha**). *Among the many references to Calvary Cemetery, named to commemorate the place of Christ's crucifixion, one is particularly interesting. At the close of* Deadeye Dick, *the Haitian hotel chef Hippolyte Paul De Mille visits Midland City's Calvary Cemetery and* resurrects the ghost of Will Fairchild, the barnstorming aviator killed when he forgot to wear his parachute. Both of Rudy's parents are buried there as well. (DD 22) Father was buried in **Calvary Cemetery**, not all that far from Eloise Metzger. We buried him in a painter's smock, and with his left thumb hooked through a palette. Why not?

(*DD* Epilogue) Felix and I had run into the same sort of ignorance when it was time to bury Mother next to Father in **Calvary Cemetery**. People refused to believe that she herself wasn't radioactive. They were sure that she would make all the other bodies glow in the dark, and that she would seep into the water supply and so on.

(*DD* Epilogue) At the end of our third day in Midland City, Felix became tearful and risked the displeasure of Captain Julian Pefko by asking him if we could please, on the way to the main gate, have our purple school bus make a slight detour past **Calvary Cemetery**, so we could visit our parents grave.

(*DD* Epilogue) **Calvary Cemetery** has never been any comfort to me, so I almost stayed in the purple school bus.

Calvary Cemetery is also where Felix Waltz and Bucky Morissey go for some unauthorized target shooting. (DD 9) I wasn't about to say so, but I had some doubts at that point about the gun safety habits of Felix, and of his friend Bucky Morissey, too—the son of the chief of police. For the past couple of years, anyway, Felix and Bucky, without Father's knowledge, had been helping themselves to various weapons in the gun room, and had picked off crows perched on headstones in **Calvary Cemetery**, and had cut off telephone service to several farms by shooting insulators along the Shepherdstown Turnpike, and had blasted God-only-knows how many mailboxes all over the county, and had actually loosed a couple of rounds at a herd of sheep out near Sacred Miracle Cave.

In Breakfast of Champions, *Vonnegut writes about one particular Midland City luminary.* (BC 15) The Bannister Memorial Fieldhouse was named in honor of George Hickman Bannister, a seventeen-year-old boy who was killed while playing high school football in 1924. George Hickman Bannister had the largest tombstone in **Calvary Cemetery**, a sixty-two-foot obelisk with a marble football on top.

(*BC* 15) **Calvary Cemetery**, where George Hickman Bannister was at rest, was named in honor of a hill in Jerusalem, thousands of miles away. Many people believed that the son of the Creator of the Universe had been killed on that hill thousands of years ago.

Calvin, Ned. *One of the many ill and poverty stricken residents of Rosewater County whose name is invoked by Diana Moon Glampers as proof of Eliot's curative powers in the hope he will remain in town.* (GBR 5) **Ned Calvin** had that twitch in his eye since he was a little boy, and you (*Eliot*) made it stop.

Calypso. *The name of the Bokononist poems that make up most of the writings of* The Books of Bokonon, *in* Cat's Cradle.

Campbell, Archibald. *Archibald possesses an ignominious place in Rosewater family lore as recounted in Merrihue Rosewater's* A History of the Rosewaters of Rhode Island. *(GBR 11) The Old World home of the Rosewaters was and is in the Scilly Islands, off Cornwall. The founder of the family there, whose name was John, arrived on St. Mary Island in 1645, with the party accompanying the fifteen-year-old Prince Charles, later to become Charles the Second, who was fleeing the Puritan Revolution. The name Rosewater was then a pseudonym. Until John chose it for himself, there were no Rosewaters in England. His real name was John Graham. He was the youngest of the five sons of James Graham, Fifth Earl and First Marquis of Montrose. There was need for a pseudonym, for James Graham was a leader of the Royalist cause and the Royalist cause was lost. James, among other romantic exploits, once disguised himself, went to the Scotch Highlands, organized a small, fierce army, and led it to six bloody victories over the far greater forces of the Lowland Presbyterian Army of* **Archibald Campbell**, *the Eighth Earl of Argyll. James was also a poet. So every Rosewater is in fact a Graham, and has the blood of Scotch nobility in him. James was hanged in 1650. Though Vonnegut notes this was the Eighth Earl of Argyll, it seems this Campbell was more likely to have been the Ninth Earl of Argyll.*

Campbell, Howard W., Jr. *The main character of* Mother Night *also appears in* Slaughterhouse-Five. Mother Night *is Campbell's confessional text, revealing a severe lack of any sincere commitment outside his "nation of two," his passionate love relationship with his wife, Helga Noth. His rededication of the text is to himself,* a man who served evil too openly and good too secretly, the crime of his times (MN Ed Note).

Born an only child in Schenectady, New York, on February 16, 1912, the grandson of a Tennessee Baptist minister and the son of an engineer working for General Electric's Service Engineering Department. Campbell's family moves to Berlin, Germany, when GE transfers his father. Only eleven years old at the time of the move, Campbell is sent to German public schools and becomes bilingual. He becomes a playwright—writing in German—and marries the German actress Helga Noth, the elder daughter of Werner Noth, Berlin's chief of police. In 1939, Campbell's parents leave Germany when war in Europe breaks out.

Prior to America's entry into World War II, Harold J. Sparrow (alias Frank Wirtanen, alias Blue Fairy Godmother) propositions Campbell to become a secret agent for the United States. His silent agreement to pass along information is facilitated by becoming a writer and broadcaster of Nazi propaganda to the English-speaking world. I was the leading expert on American problems in the Ministry of Popular Enlightenment and Propaganda (MN 7). *Campbell's method of transmitting information to the "enemy" includes a series of coughs and verbal cues in his radio broadcasts. However, he never knows what information he is disclosing, including the information about his own wife's death in the Crimea. Seven women who fed him information are eventually found out and executed.*

Neither a Nazi nor an acknowledged American patriot, Campbell is captured by Lieutenant Bernard B. O'Hare near Hersfeld on April 12, 1945. Only President Roosevelt and Campbell's Blue Fairy Godmother know his true identity and contribution to the war effort. (SL5 8) **Campbell** was the inventor and commander of the unit (*the Free American Corps*), which was supposed to fight only on the Russian front. *Since his venomous radio broadcasts make him such a widely known and hated individ-*

ual, the most that could be done for him is a quiet release into the civilian sector.

Campbell settles in Greenwich Village and is befriended by George Kraft, a sleeper Russian agent whose real name is Iona Potapov. Kraft/Potapov arranges for Campbell's kidnapping to the Soviet Union by notifying the American Legion—and former lieutenant O'Hare—of his whereabouts, arranging for Resi Noth's impersonation of her older sister, and encouraging Campbell to leave the country since he found his wife and would never be accepted by America. The plot is foiled when the Blue Fairy Godmother learns of Kraft's involvement.

The duplicity of the people and events in his life leads Campbell to surrender to the Israeli authorities. Unsure of his crimes against humanity, Campbell is quite convinced about his "crimes against himself." He leaves the text intimating he will commit suicide, an event confirmed by his appearance in Slaughterhouse-Five.

Canadian POWs. *In the short story "Souvenir," a group of newly freed and drunken Canadian POWs come across newly freed American POWs Eddie and Buzzer. The latter pair join in the festivities and are drunk by the time they have their tragic meeting with General Heinz Guderian and his escort.*

canary, canary-in-the-coal-mine, canary-bird-in-the-coal-mine. *Vonnegut's theory about writers acting as society's proverbial canary-in-the-coal-mine is clarified in two essays.* (WFG Address to the American Physical Society) Many of you are physics teachers. I have been a teacher, too. I have taught creative writing. I often wondered what I thought I was doing, teaching creative writing, since the demand for creative writers is very small in this vale of tears. I was perplexed as to what the usefulness of any of the arts might be, with the possible exception of interior decoration. The most positive notion I could come up with was what I call the **canary-in-the-coal-mine** theory of the arts. This theory argues that artists are useful to society because they are so sensitive. They are supersensitive. They keel over like **canaries in coal mines** filled with poison gas, long before more robust types realize that any danger is there.

(WFG *Playboy* Interview) PLAYBOY: What *is* in control?
VONNEGUT: Mankind's wish to improve itself.
PLAYBOY: In a Darwinian sense?
VONNEGUT: I'm not very grateful for Darwin, although I suspect he was right. His ideas make people crueler. . . . But forget Darwin. Writers are specialized cells doing whatever we do, and we're expressions of the entire society—just as the sensory cells on the surface of your body are in the service of your body as a whole. And when a society is in great danger, we're likely to sound the alarms. I have the **canary-bird-in-the-coal-mine** theory of the arts. You know, coal miners used to take birds down into the mines with them to detect gas before men got sick. The artists certainly did that in the case of Vietnam. They chirped and keeled over. But it made no difference. Whatsoever. Nobody important cared. But I continue to think that artists—all artists—should be treasured as alarm systems.
See also: ST 7; WFG There's a Maniac Loose Out There.

Canby, Sarah Horne. *The author of the fourth most popular book in the days of the chrono-synclastic infundibula. The text is a children's book entitled* Unk and Boaz in the Caves of Mercury. (ST 9) The publisher's bland analysis of **Mrs. Canby**'s book's success appears on the dust jacket: "What child wouldn't like to be shipwrecked on a space ship with a cargo of hamburgers, hot dogs, catsup, sporting goods, and soda pop?"

Capone, Al. (BC 20) As it happened, the only other person in the lobby at the time was the beautiful young desk clerk, Milo Maritimo. . . . He was the homosexual grandson of Guillermo "Little Willie" Maritimo, a bodyguard of the notorious Chicago gangster, **Al Capone**.
(JB 19) **Al Capone**, the famous Chicago gangster, thought Sacco and Vanzetti should have been executed. He, too, believed that they were enemies of the American way of thinking about America. He was offended by how ungrateful to America these fellow Italian immigrants were.

Carlsbad Caverns (*also* **cavern**). *The home of EPICAC, the computer that controls the industrial* *output of society in* Player Piano. *In the 1950 short story "EPICAC," reprinted in* Welcome to the Monkey House *(1968), the computer is housed on the fourth floor of the physics building of Wyandotte College.*

(PP I) Shepherd, who was sick today, would then set the controls for a new batch of refrigerator backs—however many backs EPICAC, a computing machine in **Carlsbad Caverns**, felt the economy could absorb.

(PP XI) The Shah of Bratpuhr, looking as tiny and elegant as a snuffbox in one end of the vast **cavern**, handed the *Sumklish* bottle back to Khashdrahr Miasma. He sneezed, having left the heat of summer above a moment before, and the sound chattered along the walls to die whispering in bat roosts deep in **Carlsbad Caverns**.

(PP XI) Through the war, and through the postwar years to the present, EPICAC's nervous system had been extended outward through **Carlsbad Caverns**—intelligence bought by the foot and pound and kilowatt.

(PP XI) The Shah dropped to his knees on the platform and raised his hands over his head. The small, brown man suddenly seemed to fill the entire **cavern** with his mysterious, radiant dignity, alone there on the platform, communing with a presence no one else could sense.

(PP XI) President Lynn squinted at the **cavern** roof thoughtfully.

(PP XVII) The request (*the Shah of Bratpuhr had asked to visit "the home of a typical Takaru". . . . an "average man"*) had been made as they were passing through Chicago from **Carlsbad Caverns**, and Halyard had stopped off at the local personnel office for the name of a representative American in the neighborhood.

(PP XX) The letter, from the personnel officer of the State Department, had pursued him from New York to Utica to Niagara Falls to Camp Drum to Indianapolis to St. Louis to Fort Riley to Houston to Hollywood to the Grand Canyon to **Carlsbad Caverns** to Hanford to Chicago to Miami Beach.

In Slaughterhouse-Five, *Billy Pilgrim time-trips to his family's excursion to the famous caverns, a terrifying experience during which he feared the ceiling would fall in.* (SL5 5) And Billy took a very short trip through time, made a peewee jump of only ten

days, so he was still twelve, still touring the West with his family. Now they were down in **Carlsbad Caverns**, and Billy was praying to God to get him out of there before the ceiling fell in.

A ranger was explaining that the **Caverns** had been discovered by a cowboy who saw a huge cloud of bats come out of a hole in the ground.

Carlsbad Caverns is also a suspected hideout for Professor Barnhouse in the short story bearing his name. (MH Report on the Barnhouse Effect) During last week alone, three publications carried articles proving variously that he was hiding in an Inca ruin in the Andes, in the sewers of Paris, and in the unexplored lower chambers of **Carlsbad Caverns**.

In Jailbird, *Mary Kathleen O'Looney's hideaway is in the great subbasements of Grand Central Station. Walter Starbuck recalls that* Mary Kathleen opened the iron door on an iron staircase going down, down, down. There was a secret world as vast as **Carlsbad Caverns** below. It was used for nothing anymore. It might have been a sanctuary for dinosaurs. It had in fact been a repair shop for another family of extinct monsters—locomotives driven by steam (JB 15).

(JB 22) His voice came to me as though from the place where I was going next, the great **cavern** under Grand Central Station. "No problem," he said.

(JB 23) The next thing I knew, I, all alone, having made certain that no one was following me, was descending the iron staircase into the **cavern**.

(Gal 1:3) Darwin continued: "The entire surface. . . . seems to have been permeated, like a sieve, by the subterranean vapours: here and there the lava, whilst soft, had been blown into great bubbles; and in other parts, the tops of **caverns** similarly formed have fallen in, leaving circular parts with steep sides."

(TQ 43) "There are virtually no respected paintings made by persons about whom we know zilch.

We can even surmise quite a bit about the lives of whoever did the paintings in the **caverns** underneath Lascaux, France."

The Carlyle Hotel. *A RAMJAC hotel in* Jailbird.

Caroline. *In the short story "The Hyannis Port Story," reprinted in* Welcome to the Monkey House

(1968), *a Caroline is a waffle with a scoop of ice cream served at the First Family Waffle Shop.*

Caroline Islands. *In the 1950 short story* "Report on the Barnhouse Effect," *reprinted in* Welcome to the Monkey House *(1968), 120 target ships are towed to the islands as part of Operation Brainstorm, a test of Professor Barnhouse's dynamopsychic abilities.*

Carpathia. *The title of the novel by Felicia Tarkington, youngest daughter of Aaron Tarkington, about a headstrong, high-born young woman in the Mohiga Valley who fell in love with a half-Indian locktender on that same canal (HP 2), the Onondaga Canal.*

Carroll, Madeleine. *The movie actress with whom Rabo Karabekian compares his first impressions of Marilee Kemp. (Blue 18) One thing, surely, which* prevented my being effusive, was my sense of my own homeliness and powerlessness and virginity. I was unworthy of her, since she was as beautiful as **Madeleine Carroll**, the most beautiful of all movie stars. *When Rabo later establishes himself as a working artist, he has an opportunity to use his photorealistic painting skills to portray the actress stepping from a Cord automobile in front of the ocean liner* Normandie.

Carson, Johnny. *In* Galápagos, *the* Tonight Show *host interviews Captain von Kleist and learns the Ecuadorian navy has four submarines that never surface, maintaining constant radio silence.*

Carter, Clyde. *(JB 5)* He was one of the few friends I had made in prison. Our chief bond was that we had taken the same correspondence course in bartending from a diploma mill in Chicago, The Illinois Institute of Instruction, a division of The RAMJAC Corporation. On the same day and in the same mail each of us had received his Doctor of Mixology degree. **Clyde** had then surpassed me by taking the school's course in air conditioning, as well. **Clyde** was a third cousin to the President of the United States, Jimmy Carter. He was about five years younger than the President, but was otherwise his perfect spit and image. He had the same nice

manners, the same bright smile. *Mary Kathleen O'Looney rewards Carter's friendship with Starbuck by making him a vice president of the Chrysler Air Temp Division of RAMJAC. He and Leland Clewes chip in for the chess-playing computer Boris as a going-away gift for Starbuck upon his return to prison. Aside from briefly mentioning Claudia's presence, there is no description of her.*

Carver, George Washington; George Washington Carver High School. *The second high school built in Midland City after World War II intended to serve mostly the black population. As a character in his own text, Vonnegut makes a mental note to explain to Kilgore Trout the significance of the high school jackets he will see in the emergency room of the hospital after Dwayne Hoover goes on a rampage. (BC 22)* And when another Nigger high school was built after the Second World War, it was named after **George Washington Carver**, a black man who was born into slavery, but who became a famous chemist anyway. He discovered many remarkable new uses for peanuts.

But the black people wouldn't call that school by its proper name, either. On the day it opened, there were already young black people wearing jackets with the inscription "Peanut University" on their backs.

Casa Mona. *The one hotel on San Lorenzo owned by Philip Castle and named in honor of Mona Aamons Monzano. H. Lowe Crosby derisively calls it "the Pissant Hilton" before demanding quarters in the American embassy. John/Jonah recalls:* My room was a pleasant one. It faced, as did all the rooms, the Boulevard of the Hundred Martyrs to Democracy, Monzano Airport, and Bolivar harbor beyond. The **Casa Mona** was built like a bookcase, with solid sides and back and with a front of blue-green glass. The squalor and misery of the city, being to the sides and back of the **Casa Mona**, were impossible to see.

My room was air-conditioned. It was almost chilly. And, coming from the blamming heat into that chilliness, I sneezed.

There were fresh flowers on my bedside table, but my bed had not yet been made. There wasn't even a pillow on the bed. There was simply a bare, brand-new Beautyrest mattress. And there weren't any coat hangers in the closet; and there wasn't any toilet paper in the bathroom (CC 72).

When John/Jonah meets Bokonon at the end of the novel, the prophet is wearing a blue and white bedspread imprinted with the words "Casa Mona."

Casey, Dwight. *The Tarkington College English teacher who hates his department chair so much that when Eugene Debs Hartke is fired from his physics position, he asks the board for a transfer to fill the slot. That allows Muriel Peck to take Casey's position and she subsequently dies during the prison break. Casey's own fortunes are quite different.* (HP 35) **Dwight Casey** is still alive, I think. His wife came into a great deal of money soon after he replaced me. He quit at the end of the academic year and moved to the south of France.

His wife's family was big in the Mafia. She could have taught but didn't. She had a Master's Degree in Political Science from Rutgers. All he had was a BS in Hotel Management from Cornell.

Castle, Dr. Julian. *John/Jonah's original focus for the magazine article that takes him to San Lorenzo is sixty-year-old Dr. Julian Castle, an American sugar millionaire who had, at the age of forty, followed the example of Dr. Albert Schweitzer by founding a free hospital in a jungle, by devoting his life to miserable folk of another race.*

Castle's hospital was called the House of Hope and Mercy in the Jungle. Its jungle was on San Lorenzo, among the wild coffee trees on the northern slope of Mount McCabe. . . .

In his selfish days he had been as familiar to tabloid readers as Tommy Manville, Adolf Hitler, Benito Mussolini, and Barbara Hutton. His fame had rested on lechery, alcoholism, reckless driving, and draft evasion. He had had a dazzling talent for spending millions without increasing mankind's stores of anything but chagrin (CC 40).

As a draft dodger living in Portugal during World War II, *he met the Finnish architect Nestor Aamons and invited him on his journey to San Lorenzo to design the House of Hope and Mercy in the Jungle.*

Upon first meeting him years later, John/Jonah notes that **Castle** wore a baggy white linen suit and a string tie. He had a scraggly mustache. He was bald. He was scrawny. He was a saint, I think (CC 75). *He runs the hospital by relying on aspirin and boko-maru, and he provides this analysis of just how and why Bokononism works,* when it became evident that no governmental or economic reform was going to make the people much less miserable, the religion became the one real instrument of hope. Truth was the enemy of the people, because the truth was so terrible, so Bokonon made it his business to provide the people with better and better lies (CC 78). *Julian's one offspring is Philip Castle.*

Castle, Dr. Morris N. *In* The Sirens of Titan, *the physician on Mars who serves as the Director of Mental Health, responsible for wiping out the memory of new recruits. He is proud to make the pronouncement that* "We can make the center of a man's memory virtually as sterile as a scalpel fresh from the autoclave. But grains of new experience begin to accumulate on it at once. These grains in turn form themselves into patterns not necessarily favorable to military thinking. Unfortunately, this problem of recontamination seems insoluble" (ST 5).

Castle, Philip. *The son of Julian Castle, the great-grandson of the founder of Castle Sugar, and the manager and owner of Casa Mona, San Lorenzo's one hotel, as well as Castle Transportation, Inc., a hearselike 1939 Chrysler limousine with jump seats* (CC 67). *Philip authors the text* San Lorenzo: The Land, the History, the People. *The text chronicles the role Castle Sugar has had on the island as well as the impact brought about by Bokonon's appearance.*

Castle Sugar, Incorporated. *The multinational corporation owned by millionaire Julian Castle, who also builds the House of Hope and Mercy in the Jungle. The San Lorenzo branch opens in 1916 by Julian's grandfather who sought to capitalize on the sugar demands brought about by World War I. When Bokonon and McCabe arrive on the island in 1922, anything worth owning on San Lorenzo was already owned either by the Catholic Church or Castle Sugar. As Bokonon says in his calypsos,* "Oh, a very sorry people, yes, / Did I find here. / Oh, they had no music, / And they had no beer. / And, oh, everywhere / Where they tried to perch / Belonged to

Castle Sugar, Incorporated, / Or the Catholic church" (*CC* 56).

The brutal imperialism wielded by Castle Sugar at its zenith is further elaborated by Philip Castle in San Lorenzo: The Land, the History, the People, "The form of government was anarchy, save in limited situations wherein **Castle Sugar** wanted to own something or to get something done. In such situations the form of government was feudalism. The nobility was composed of **Castle Sugar**'s plantation bosses, who were heavily armed white men from the outside world. The knighthood was composed of big natives who, for small gifts and silly privileges, would kill or wound or torture on command. The spiritual needs of the people caught in this demoniacal squirrel cage were taken care of by a handful of butterball priests" (*CC* 56).

catacombs. (*CC* 60) When Johnson and McCabe came upon the city, it was built of twigs, tin, crates, and mud—rested on the **catacombs** of a trillion happy scavengers, **catacombs** in a sour mash of slop, feculence, and slime.
(*SL5* 10) Somewhere in there the poor old high school teacher, Edgar Derby, was caught with a teapot he had taken from the **catacombs**. He was arrested for plundering. He was tried and shot.
(*JB* 12) Little did I dream that I would soon be scuttling through the **catacombs** beneath the station, and that I would learn the secret purpose of The RAMJAC Corporation down there.
(*JB* 15) And then out of the **catacombs** we climbed. (*Mary Kathleen O'Looney and Walter Starbuck exiting Grand Central Station.*)
(*FWD* XVI) "I will say that you (*Unitarian Universalists*), in terms of numbers, power, and influence, and your spiritual differences with the general population, are analogous to the earliest Christians in the **catacombs** under Imperial Rome. I hasten to add that your hardships are not the same, nor are you in any danger. Nobody in the power structure thinks children of the Age of Reason amount to a hill of beans. That is the extent of your discomfort. That sure beats being crucified upside down or being fed to the carnivorous menagerie at the Circus Maximus.
(*FWD* XVI) "When I say that the Unitarian Universalists, the people who know pure baloney when

they hear it, are something like the early Christians in the **catacombs**, am I suggesting that contempt for baloney will someday be as widespread as Christianity is today? Well the example of Christianity is not encouraging, actually, since it was nothing but a poor people's religion, and servant's religion, a slave's religion, a woman's religion, a child's religion, and would have remained such if it hadn't stopped taking the Sermon on the Mount seriously and joined forces with the vain and rich and violent. I can't imagine that you would want to do that, to give up everything you believe in order to play a bigger part in world history."

Cathcart, Sally. *The dim-witted Judy Garland look-alike cheerleader and girlfriend of Jerry Rivers, president of the student body, in the play* The Chemistry Professor. *She doubles as the streetwalker in the* Dr. Jekyll *play-within-the-play.*

Cat's Cradle (1963) (*see also* **John/Jonah**). *Vonnegut's first three novels are principally concerned with the psychological hardships endured by pivotal characters whose fates are largely determined by the compelling tug of historical and cosmic forces. In the name of the ruling governmental technocracy, Kroner and Baer* (Player Piano) *dissociate Paul Proteus from his father's legacy. He, in turn, is forced to stage his own turnabout in an attempt to establish a moral foundation for civilizing communal activities among men—one more significant than simply facilitating technological and economic "progress." The compounding of governmental and industrial power is seen as an inevitable evolution as man develops a community based on manufacturing efficiency and national security. The historical precedents in* Player Piano (*especially the Ghost Shirt Society*) *provide an understanding of the eternal conflicts that Vonnegut works out on a more global scale. The conflict predetermined; the future is captive to the past's inertia.*

In The Sirens of Titan, *Vonnegut validates the captivity of the future to a historical past by creating the chrono-synclastic infundibulum. While Winston Niles Rumfoord is split in time and simultaneously inhabits two points in space, Malachi Constant, subject to the designs of Tralfamadore, is forced to assume three different identities. The destiny of man* is at the mercy of powers unseen, poorly understood, and forever in motion.

Vonnegut continues his emphasis on the individual's response to the competing and compelling historical forces in Mother Night. "Tell them the things a man does to stay alive" expresses in simple terms Arpad Kovacs's intuitive grasp of how to survive the eternal chain of conflict that brings out the ambiguous dichotomies of nearly every character in the novel. The "things" necessary for survival turn out to be deeds perpetrated after a retreat from conditions that induce a form of schizophrenia.

The endings of all three novels dwell on individuals' final responses to their environment. Proteus weighs the historical record and decides to paint his identity with the broad mythologizing (obfuscating) brush of the revolutionary; Constant is delivered to his eternal rest under the hypnotically induced benign delusion that he is in the protective care of the murdered Stony Stevenson; Howard Campbell's despondency for crimes committed against himself (that is, for his failure to do what no one else had been capable of doing — acting without pretension or deception) brings him to the brink of suicide.

Vonnegut shifts the emphasis in Cat's Cradle from pivotal characters whose impact on each tale is profoundly impotent in its repercussions, to the writer as naive observer, waiting for a grossly ironic illumination to describe the nature of human endeavor. John/Jonah's attempt to write The Day the World Ended is a naive, unselfconscious search for dissociative symptoms among those scientists who shaped the great physical (therefore political) forces which brought World War II to a close. John was looking for the ironical backyard barbecue on the day Hiroshima was roasted. His literary search for the compelling irony of man's deeds and home life is a search for the more obviously "schizophrenic." Though relinquishing his original research into the men behind "the bomb," John discovers the roots of human conflict on the island of San Lorenzo, where necessarily dissociative types attempting to promote a new communal order create artificial factions among men. The discomforting truths and lies of Bokononism reveal the schizophrenia of all creative — and destructive — elements in society.

Whereas Mother Night chronicles the crippling effects of schizophrenia as the sole method of survival, Cat's Cradle bares the civilizing influence as nothing more than a grander manifestation of the same dissociative symptoms. This leaves John/Jonah in a cataleptic trance analogous to that of Howard Campbell but with one major difference. Declining any consideration of suicide, John's trance is manifested in the narrative by use of "∴" before each chapter. This symbol is the mathematical expression meaning "therefore." Since ∴ is the first word of the text (along with every chapter), the effect creates a spherical closure of the narrative placing the end of the world (after ice-nine) at the beginning. The recapitulation of the tale as the logical outcome of the events contained therein establishes a time-looped scenario with finite boundaries similar to Billy Pilgrim's journey. The narrative-in-the-round is another manifestation of Vonnegut's structured moment theory.

John's destiny is to be a chronicler of the events that unfold (have already unfolded) in the text. As he says shortly before the opening ∴, somebody or something has compelled me to be certain places at certain times, without fail. Conveyances and motives, both conventional and bizarre, have been provided. And, according to plan, at each appointed second, at each appointed place this Jonah was there (CC 1).

John's preface to the story results from his meeting with Bokonon at the close of the novel. As the fate of the Earth becomes enveloped in ice-nine, staggered by his knowledge of the people behind this latest apocalypse, John cries out at his inability to place himself within the current of events. (CC 126) "Here it is, the end of the world; and here I am, almost the very last man; and there it is, the highest mountain in sight. I know now what my karass has been up to, Newt. It's been working night and day for maybe half a million years to get me up that mountain." I wagged my head and nearly wept. "But what, for the love of God, is supposed to be in my hands?"

Bokonon quickly answers his question, telling him that "If I were a younger man, I would write a history of human stupidity." (CC 127) It is at this point Vonnegut has John make the crossover from witness to reporter-with-a-cause. (It could be argued that Vonnegut's Dresden experience turned him into a writer with a cause: discounting any faith in man-made establishments of peace, avoiding any belief in a beneficent supernatural being paternalistically caring for man's eternity either on Earth or in a mythical heaven.)

Wishing to reorganize the communal (primarily economic) relationships among men, Bokonon and McCabe help establish Vonnegut's premise that the foundations of power are schizophrenically conceived. Exposing this symbol is John's task. Before Cat's Cradle, Vonnegut saw schizophrenia as a learned survival skill among those tossed by the great entropizing forces (nationalism/ethnocentrism) in our century. Part of Cat's Cradle's importance is that Vonnegut characterizes the formation of power (both religious and political) as an act requiring dissociation.

Though John journeys to San Lorenzo to write a travel piece, what he finds is a society structured on the principle of "dynamic tensions," bodybuilding entrepreneur Charles Atlas's theory that muscles could be built by pitting one set of muscles against another without the use of barbells or spring exercisers. It was the belief of Bokonon that good societies could be built only by pitting good against evil, and by keeping the tension between the two high at all times (CC 47).

The culmination of John's revelations is that schizophrenia is the engine of activity (both creative and destructive): that the nature of power is schizophrenic, and that schizophrenia is the revealed state of powerful forces. Bokonon's appearance in the final chapter draws to a close The Books of Bokonon with this: If I were a younger man, I would write a history of human stupidity; and I would climb to the top of Mount McCabe and lie down on my back with my history for a pillow; and I would take from the ground some of the bluewhite poison that makes statues of men; and I would make a statue of myself, lying on my back, grinning horribly, and thumbing my nose at You Know Who (CC 127).

Striking such a theatrical pose for posterity may seem comical, but it is the measure of a refined vision gained at great personal expense. As Bokonon had written earlier, "Maturity . . . is a bitter disappointment for which no remedy exists, unless laughter can be said to remedy anything" (CC 88). The history he advises John (and any other Bokononists) to

write is one that would deny the cosmic paternalism of religion and, by implication, any benevolent paternalistic constructions designed by man. This is precisely the history John had been writing all along.

Together with Bokonon's closing directive, John's revelation brings about a poised state of insight and impotence expressed by the cataleptic "∴". Stuck in his moment of time, his lot in life has been and forever will be to delineate the ambiguous explanations concerning the nature of power and the whimsy of science that forms—and takes—life. The narrative is the revelation of a naive journalist confronted by awful truths—and lies—about the establishment of power and the motivations of communal man. As it turns out, man is seen as reactive, unable to create goodness without a corresponding evil.

Vonnegut recalls the essence of the novel's plot and the genesis for its idea in Wampeters, Foma & Granfalloons and Palm Sunday. (WFG Address to the American Physical Society) It is about an old-fashioned scientist who isn't interested in people. In the midst of a terrible family argument, he asks a question about turtles. Nobody has been talking about turtles. But the old man suddenly wants to know: When turtles put in their heads, do their spines buckle or contract?

This absentminded old man, who doesn't give a damn for people, discovers a form of ice which is stable at room temperature. He dies, and some idiots get possession of the substance, which I call Ice-9. The idiots eventually drop some of the stuff into the sea, and the waters of the earth freeze—and that is the end of life on earth as we know it.

I got this lovely idea while I was working as a public relations man at General Electric. I used to write publicity releases about the research laboratory there, where my brother worked. While there, I heard a story about a visit H. G. Wells had made to the laboratory in the early Thirties.

General Electric was alarmed by the news of his coming, because they did not know how to entertain him. The company told Irving Langmuir, who was a most important man in Schenectady, the only Nobel Prize winner in private industry, that he was going to have to entertain Wells. Langmuir didn't want to do it, but he dutifully tried to imagine diversions that would delight Mr. Wells. He made up a science-fiction story he hoped Mr. Wells would want to write. It was about a form of ice which was stable at room temperature. Mr. Wells was not stimulated by the story. He later died, and so did Langmuir. After Langmuir died, I thought to myself, well, I think maybe I'll write a story. While I was writing that story about Ice-9, I happened to go to a cocktail party where I was introduced to a crystallographer. I told him about this ice which was stable at room temperature. He put his cocktail glass on the mantelpiece. He sat down in an easy chair in the corner. He did not speak to anyone or change expression for half an hour. Then he got up, came back over to the mantelpiece, and picked up his cocktail glass, he said to me, "Nope." Ice-9 was impossible.

Be that as it may, other scientific developments have been almost that horrible. The idea of Ice-9 had a certain moral validity at any rate, even though scientifically it had to be pure bunk.

(*PS* Self-Interview) INTERVIEWER: Did the study of anthropology later color your writings?

VONNEGUT: It confirmed my atheism, which was the faith of my fathers anyway. Religions were exhibited and studied as the Rube Goldberg inventions I'd always thought they were. We weren't allowed to find one culture superior to any other. We caught hell if we mentioned races much. It was highly idealistic.

INTERVIEWER: Almost a religion?

VONNEGUT: Exactly. And the only one for me. So far.

INTERVIEWER: What was your dissertation?

VONNEGUT: *Cat's Cradle*.

INTERVIEWER: But you wrote that years after you left Chicago, didn't you?

VONNEGUT: I left Chicago without writing a dissertation—and without a degree. All my ideas for dissertations had been rejected, and I was broke, so I took a job as a P.R. man for General Electric in Schenectady. Twenty years later, I got a letter from a new dean at Chicago, who had been looking through my dossier. Under the rules of the university, he said, a published work of high quality could be substituted for a dissertation, so I was entitled to an M.A. He had shown *Cat's Cradle* to the Anthropology Department, and they had said it was half-

way decent anthropology, so they were mailing me my degree. Class of 1972 or so. . . .

INTERVIEWER: Some of the characters in *Cat's Cradle* were based on people you knew at G.E., isn't that so?

VONNEGUT: Dr. Felix Hoenikker, the absent-minded scientist, was a caricature of Dr. Irving Langmuir, the star of the G.E. Research Laboratory. I knew him some. My brother worked with him. Langmuir was wonderfully absent-minded. He wondered out loud one time whether, when turtles pulled in their heads, their spines buckled or contracted. I put that in the book. One time he left a tip under his plate after his wife served him breakfast at home. I put that in. His most important contribution, though, was the idea for what I called "Ice-9," a form of frozen water that was stable at room temperature. He didn't tell it directly to me. It was a legend around the Laboratory about the time H.G. Wells came to Schenectady. That was long before my time. I was just a little boy when it happened—listening to the radio, building model airplanes.

INTERVIEWER: Yes?

VONNEGUT: Anyway—Wells came to Schenectady, and Langmuir was told to be his host. Langmuir thought he might entertain Wells with an idea for a science-fiction story—about a form of ice that was stable at room temperature. Wells was uninterested, or at least never used the idea. And then Wells died, and then, finally, Langmuir died. I thought to myself: "Finders, keepers—the idea is mine." Langmuir, incidentally, was the first scientist in private industry to win a Nobel Prize.

The title is also the central image of this apocalyptic novel. Early in the text Dr. Felix Hoenikker takes the string from a manuscript, makes the traditional cat's cradle string formation, and tries to convince Newt that he should see the cradle where the little cat sleeps. Later, in the cave beneath the waterfall on San Lorenzo, Newt explains to John/Jonah that his mostly black abstract painting is a cat's cradle. (CC 74) "Hello," I said. "I like your painting."

"You see what it is?"

"I suppose it means something different to everyone who sees it."

"It's a **cat's cradle**."

"Aha," I said. "Very good. The scratches are string. Right?"

"One of the oldest games there is, **cat's cradle**. Even the Eskimos know it."

"You don't say."

"For maybe a hundred thousand years or more, grownups have been waving tangles of string in their children's faces."

"Um."

Newt remained curled in the chair. He held out his painty hands as though a **cat's cradle** were strung between them. "No wonder kids grow up crazy. A **cat's cradle** is nothing but a bunch of X's between somebody's hands, and little kids look and look and look at all those X's.

"And?"

No damn cat, and no damn cradle."

(*TQ* 11) I wrote a letter to an old friend last spring about why I evidently couldn't write publishable fiction anymore, after trying and failing to do that for many years. He is Edward Muir, a poet and advertising man my age living in Scarsdale. In my novel *Cat's Cradle*, I say that anybody whose life keeps tangling up with yours for no logical reason is likely a member of your *karass*, a team God has formed to get something done for Him. Ed Muir is surely a member of my *karass*.

cave, cave dweller, Cro-Magnon. *Along with basements, subbasements, and underground meatlockers, caves have a prominent role to play in many of Vonnegut's tales. The Sirens of Titan has two distinctive references. The first is the description of Malachi Constant's physical appearance, which is repeated by Vonnegut when describing Malachi's new incarnation as Unk.* (ST 1) The freshening sea breeze ruffled Constant's blue-black hair. He was a well-made man—a light heavyweight, dark-skinned, with poet's lips, with soft brown eyes in the shaded eaves of a **Cro-Magnon** brow-ridge. He was thirty-one.

(*ST* 4) Unk was a well-made man—a light heavyweight, dark-skinned, with poet's lips, with soft brown eyes in the shaded eaves of a **Cro-Magnon** brow ridge. Incipient baldness had isolated a dramatic scalplock.

The second reference is a major plot element. Winston Niles Rumford arranges to strand Unk and

Boaz in the caves of Mercury for three years as part of the grand Tralfamadorian scheme to deliver a crucial replacement part for Salo's spaceship. While Unk struggles to discover a way out of the caves, Boaz becomes entranced by the ever-present harmoniums. (*ST* 8) The harmonium is a **cave-dweller**. A more gracious creature would be hard to imagine. —A *Child's Cyclopedia of Wonders and Things to Do.*

(*ST* 8) There are creatures (*harmoniums*) in the deep **caves** of Mercury. . . . The creatures cling to the singing walls of their **caves**. . . . The **caves** of Mercury are cozily warm in their depths. . . . The walls of the **caves** in their depths are phosphorescent. They give off a jonquil-yellow light. . . . The creatures in the **caves** are translucent. When they cling to the walls, light from the phosphorescent walls comes right through them. The yellow light from the walls, however, is turned, when passed through the bodies of the creatures, to a vivid aquamarine. . . . The creatures in the **caves** look very much like small and spineless kites. They are diamond-shaped, a foot high and eight inches wide when fully mature.

Rumford arranges the colorful and translucent harmoniums to spell out various messages to the trapped pair. He finally reveals the secret to their escape, which is for them to turn the ship upside down to take advantage of the unique one-way sensors in the ship's navigational system. (*ST* 9) Thanks to a power winch and the feeble tug of gravity in the **caves** of Mercury, Unk had the ship turned over by the time Boaz got back. All that remained to be done for the trip out was to press the on button. The upside-down ship would then blunder against the **cave** floor, give up, retreat from the floor under the impression that the floor was a ceiling.

In Cat's Cradle, Franklin Hoenikker has a house beneath a waterfall, and it is here that he offers narrator John/Jonah the presidency of San Lorenzo. (*CC* 87) So we went down steps cut into a cliff and into a natural **cave** that was beneath and behind the waterfall.

(*CC* 89) And here, by God, was Secret Agent X-9, a Major General, offering to make me king. . . . in a **cave** that was curtained by a tropical waterfall.

After ice-nine is released on the world, the cave takes on a new appearance. (*CC* 122) They took me to what was left of Franklin Hoenikker's house at the head of the waterfall. What remained was the **cave** under the waterfall, which had become a sort of igloo under a translucent, blue-white dome of *ice-nine*.

In the short story "Next Door," *in* Welcome to the Monkey House *(1968), Vonnegut draws on the image of a cave to describe the fearfulness of the young hero.* Paul ran back into his apartment, jumped into bed, and pulled the covers up over his head. In the hot, dark **cave** of the bed, he cried because he and All-Night Sam had helped to kill a man. . . . Numb, Paul crept out of the hot, dark **cave**, and answered the door. Just as he did, the door across the hall opened, and there stood Mr. Harger, haggard but whole.

Sacred Miracle Cave occupies a good deal of Dwayne Hoover's attention in Breakfast of Champions. *(BC 13)* The **cave** was **Sacred Miracle Cave**, a tourist trap just south of Shepherdstown, which Dwayne owned in partnership with Lyle and Kyle *(Dwayne's younger twin stepbrothers)* . . . who lived in identical yellow ranch houses on either side of the gift shop which sheltered the entrance to the **cave**.

(BC 13) The underground stream which passed through the bowels of **Sacred Miracle Cave** was polluted by some sort of industrial waste which formed bubbles as tough as ping-pong balls. . . . The bubbles would soon engulf *Moby Dick* and invade the *Cathedral of Whispers*, which was the main attraction at the **cave**.

Vonnegut returns to cave imagery as part of another hyperbolic physical description with much the same harshness he employed in The Sirens of Titan. *(Slap 15)* I still remember what an ear, nose and throat specialist said when he looked up into Eliza's enormous sinus cavities with a flashlight. "My God, nurse—" he said, "call up the National Geographic Society. We have just discovered a new entrance to **Mammoth Cave!**"

Sacred Miracle Cave makes its return in Deadeye Dick. *Felix Waltz and Bucky Morissey had been helping themselves to various weapons in the gun room, . . . and had actually loosed a couple of rounds at a herd of sheep out near* **Sacred Miracle Cave** *(DD 9). Since the cave is outside the immediate blast area of ground zero (Midland City), Rudy and Felix Waltz and Hippolyte Paul De Mille stay* at the *Quality Motor Court near Sacred Miracle Cave.*

In Bluebeard, *Rabo Karabekian combines two of Vonnegut's favorite themes, anthropology and the arts. (Blue 9)* I think that *(one's natural talents for story-telling, singing, dancing, etc.)* could go back to the time when people had to live in small groups of relatives. . . . And evolution or God or whatever arranged things genetically, to keep the little families going, to cheer them up, so that they could all have somebody to tell stories around the campfire at night, and somebody else to paint pictures on the walls of the **caves**, and somebody else who wasn't afraid of anything and so on.

(Blue 33) If I'd lived ten thousand years ago, I might have wowed the **cave dwellers** of Lascaux, France—whose standards for draughtsmanship must have been on about the same level as those of San Ignacio.

Eugene Debs Hartke and his father are shamed into defeat at the hands of Mary Alice French, whose crystallography exhibit steals the Cleveland Science Fair. (HP 5) As it happened, she too had an exhibit about crystallography. She, however, had either grown her own or gathered specimens herself from creek beds and **caves** and coal mines within 100 kilometers of her home.

(TQ 43) "There are virtually no respected paintings made by persons about whom we know zilch. We can even surmise quite a bit about the lives of whoever did the paintings in the **caverns** underneath Lascaux, France."

See also: ST 8; 9; 11; 12; CC 87–88; Blue 16 graphic; 17; 18 graphic; 20; 24; DD Epilogue; Blue 78.

Caz-ma-cas-ma. *One of the many names for the city of Bolivar on the island of San Lorenzo, in Cat's Cradle.*

Cedar Tavern. *A popular bar with artists in New York City, and the place where Rabo Karabekian hangs out with Jackson Pollock and Terry Kitchen. Collectively, they are known as the "Three Musketeers" (Blue 18).*

Céline, Louis-Ferdinand. *Vonnegut frequently refers to Louis-Ferdinand Céline (the nom de plume of*

Louis-Ferdinand Destouches). One of the two books Vonnegut takes to read on his trip to Dresden in preparation for writing Slaughterhouse-Five *is Erika Ostrovsky's* Céline and His Vision. *(SL5* 1) **Céline** was a brave French soldier in the First World War—until his skull was cracked. After that he couldn't sleep, and there were noises in his head. He became a doctor, and he treated poor people in the daytime, and he wrote grotesque novels all night. No art is possible without a dance with death, he wrote.

The truth is death, he wrote. I've fought nicely against it as long as I could . . . danced with it, festooned it, waltzed it around . . . decorated it with streamers, titillated it. . . .
(WFG Address at Rededication of Wheaton College Library, 1973) About good and evil again— and your library. The books and the films and the records and the tapes and the pictures you have in there have come from the best part of human beings who have often, in real life, been contemptible in many ways. The best example I know of goodness from vileness is the body of humane writing produced by **Louis-Ferdinand Céline**, a French physician and novelist, who was a convicted war criminal after World War Two. **Louis-Ferdinand Céline** was his pen name. His real name was **Louis-Ferdinand Destouches**. He was the son of poor people. He spent most of his adult life as a badly paid physician who treated the poor. I read his early novels without knowing anything about his vicious anti-Semitism. He kept it out of his early books. The internal evidence of those books persuaded me, and many others, too, that I was in the presence of a great man.
(PS Self-Interview) VONNEGUT: I have other things *(than love)* I want to talk about. Ralph Ellison did the same thing in *Invisible Man*. If the hero in that magnificent book had found somebody worth loving, somebody who was crazy about him, that would have been the end of the story. **Céline** did the same thing in *Journey to the End of the Night*: He excluded the possibility of true and final love—so that the story could go on and on and on.
(PS A Nazi Sympathizer Defended at Some Cost) He considered himself at least the equal of any living writer. I am told that he once said of the Nobel

prize: "Every Vaseline-ass in Europe has one. Where's mine!"

And yet, compulsively, with no financial gain in prospect, and understanding that many people will believe that I share many of his authentically vile opinions, I continue to say that there were good things about this man. And my name is most snugly tied to his in the Penguin paperback editions of his last three books, *Castle to Castle, North*, and *Rigadoon*. My name is on each cover: "With a new introduction," it says, "by Kurt Vonnegut, Jr."
(PS A Nazi Sympathizer Defended at Some Cost) I know when he began to influence me. I was well into my forties before I read him. A friend was startled that I didn't know anything about **Céline**, and he initiated me with *Journey to the End of the Night*, which flabbergasted me. I assigned it for a course in the novel which I was giving at the University of Iowa. When it was time for me to lecture for two hours about it, I found I had nothing to say.

The book penetrated my bones, anyway, if not my mind. And I only now understand what I took from **Céline** and put into the novel I was writing at the time, which was called *Slaughterhouse-Five*. In that book, I felt the need to say this every time a character died: 'So it goes.' This exasperated many critics, and it seemed fancy and tiresome to me, too. But it somehow had to be said.

It was a clumsy way of saying what **Céline** managed to imply so much more naturally in everything he wrote, in effect: "Death and suffering can't matter nearly as much as I think they do. Since they are so common, my taking them so seriously must mean that I am insane. I must try to be saner."
(PS A Nazi Sympathizer Defended at Some Cost) There is at least one significant document by **Céline** that is out of print in English. And it would be punctilious of me to say that it was written not by **Céline** but by Dr. Destouches. It is the doctoral thesis of Destouches, "The Life and Work of Ignaz Philipp Semmelweis," for which he received a bronze medal in 1924. It was written at a time when theses in medicine could still be beautifully literary, since ignorance about diseases and the human body still required that medicine be an art.

And young Destouches, in a spirit of hero-worship, told of the futile and scientifically sound battle fought by a Hungarian physician named Semmelweis (1818–1865) to prevent the spread of childbed fever in Viennese hospital maternity wards. The victims were poor people, since persons with decent sorts of dwellings much preferred to give birth at home. . . .

The jealousy and ignorance of Semmelweis's colleagues, however, caused him to be fired, and the mortality rate went up again.

The lesson Destouches learned from this true story, in my opinion, if he hadn't already learned it from an impoverished childhood and a stretch in the army, is that vanity rather than wisdom determines how the world is run.
(*FWD* VI) (Trivia: Aldous Huxley died on the same day as John F. Kennedy. **Louis-Ferdinand Céline** died two days after Ernest Hemingway.)

. . . It (*a requiem mass for the dead*) begins and ends unobjectionably enough, "*Requiem aeternam dona eis, Domine; et lux perpetua luceat eis,*" which means in English, "Rest eternal grant them, O Lord, and let light perpetual shine upon them." (A credulous and literal-minded person might conclude from this that Huxley and Kennedy and **Céline** and Hemingway and my sister and my first wife Jane and all the rest of the dead are now trying to get some sleep with the lights on.)
(*FWD* XIX) (The French writer **Louis-Ferdinand Céline** wrote about a doctor friend who was obsessed with expiring with dignity and who died in convulsions under a grand piano.)
(*FWD* XX) **Louis-Ferdinand Céline**, the French fascist (and physician) about whom I wrote in *Palm Sunday*, may have tried to achieve a little immortality with deliberate, absolutely outrageous immorality. I was talking to Saul Steinberg about **Céline** once, and I cried out in astonishment that a writer so funny and wise and gifted would intersperse what could have been masterpieces with loathsome attacks on Jews in general and, if you can believe it, jeers at the memory of Anne Frank in particular. "Why, why, why did he have to besmirch the sublimely innocent ghost of Anne Frank?" I said.

Steinberg pointed his right index finger at my breastbone. He said, "He wanted *you* to remember him."

cell, cellblock (*see* **organism**). *Vonnegut places a number of characters in jail cells and frequently discusses the writer's place in society as part of a biological metaphor.*
(*PP* XIX) Was it chance or ignorance or some subtle plot that had put him (*Paul Proteus*) in the same **cell** with Garth, the other candidate for Pittsburgh?
(*PP* XXX) History, personified at this point in the life of Doctor Paul Proteus by Ed Finnerty and the Reverend James J. Lasher, let Paul out of his **cell** in an old Ilium air-raid shelter only in order for him to eliminate the wastes accrued in the process of his continued existence as an animal.
(*PP* XXXI) The irregular tapping came from the other side of the sheetmetal wall that separated Paul's and Harold's barred **cell** from the totally enclosed tank for desperados next door.
(*ST* 8) There is no need for a circulatory system in the creatures (*harmoniums*). They are so thin that life-giving vibrations can make all their **cells** tingle without intermediaries.
(*MN* 1) *Howard W. Campbell, Jr., observes,* And sometimes, when I look out through my **cell** window at the gay and brassy youth of the infant Republic of Israel, I feel that I and my war crimes are as ancient as Solomon's old gray stones.
(*MN* 29) About that reunion: I was locked up in Tel Aviv for twenty-four hours. On my way to my **cell** there, the guards stopped me outside Eichmann's **cell** to hear what we had to say to each other, if anything.
(*MN* 45) So here I am in Israel, of my own free will, though my **cell** is locked and my guards have guns.
(*SL5* 7) In my prison **cell** I sit, / With my britches full of shit, / And my balls are bouncing gently on the floor. / And I see the bloody snag / When she bit me in the bag. / Oh, I'll never fuck a Polack any more.
(*SL5* 7) A moment went by, and then every **cell** in Billy's body shook him with ravenous gratitude and applause. *This occurs when Billy Pilgrim sneaks a spoonful of the malt-enriched vitamin syrup while a prisoner of war.*
(*MH* Report on the Barnhouse Effect) He might have dismissed the phenomenon with a low whistle. But. . . . There was one single factor in com-

mon: on both occasions, the same thought train had flashed through his mind just before he threw the dice. It was that thought train which aligned the professor's brain **cells** into what has since become the most powerful weapon on earth.

(*MH* Tomorrow and Tomorrow and Tomorrow) Em and Lou were in adjacent four-by-eight **cells**, and were stretched out peacefully on their cots.

(*BC* 2) And Skag was a scientist, and he found a way to reproduce himself in chicken soup. He would shave living **cells** from the palm of his right hand, mix them with the soup, and expose the soup to cosmic rays. The **cells** turned into babies which looked exactly like Delmore Skag. *Delmore Skag appears in an unnamed Rabo Karabekian novel that, like so many of Trout's novels, is published with pornographic photographs.*

(*BC* 11) He (*Wayne Hoobler*) had a photograph of Dwayne in his wallet. He used to have photographs of Dwayne on the walls of his **cell** at Shepherdstown.

(*BC* 15) Dwayne forgot all about Patty Keene, but she certainly hadn't forgotten him. She would get up enough nerve that night to call him on the telephone, but Dwayne wouldn't be home to answer. He would be in a padded **cell** in the County Hospital by then.

(*BC* 16) And the experimental creature wasn't killed after the banquet. He was transferred to a virgin planet instead. Living **cells** were sliced from the palms of his hands, while he was unconscious. . . . And then the **cells** were stirred into a soupy sea on the virgin planet. *The experimental creature is the main character of Trout's novel* Now It Can Be Told.

(*WFG* Address to P.E.N. Conference in Stockholm, 1973) All artists are specialized **cells** in a single, huge organism, mankind. Those **cells** have to behave as they do, just as the **cells** in our hearts or our fingertips have to behave as they do.

We here are some of those specialized **cells**. Our purpose is to make mankind aware of itself, in all its complexity, and to dream its dreams. We have no choice in the matter. . . .

Where do these external signals come from? (*The question is prompted by Vonnegut's observation that "The best of our stuff draws information and energy and wholeness from outside ourselves."*) I think they come from all the other specialized **cells** in the organism. Those other **cells** contribute to us energy and little bits of information, in order that we may increase the organism's awareness of itself—and dream its dreams.

(*WFG Playboy* Interview) VONNEGUT: Writers are specialized **cells** in the social organism. They are evolutionary **cells**. Mankind is trying to become something else; it's experimenting with new ideas all the time. And writers are a means of introducing new ideas into the society, and also a means of responding symbolically to life. I don't think we're in control of what we do.

(*WFG Playboy* Interview) Writers are specialized **cells** doing whatever we do, and we're expressions of the entire society—just as the sensory **cells** on the surface of your body are in the service of your body as a whole.

(*WFG Playboy* Interview) Clumps of cancer **cells** are probably forming in us all the time and petering out—because the clumps are below a certain size.

(*WFG Playboy* Interview) One of my favorite cartoons—I think it was by Shel Silverstein—shows a couple of guys chained to an eighteen-foot **cell** wall, hung by their wrists, and their ankles are chained, too. Above them is a tiny barred window *that a mouse couldn't crawl through. And one of the guys says to the other, "Now here's my plan. . . ."*

(*WFG Playboy* Interview) PLAYBOY: So your books have been therapy for yourself.

VONNEGUT: Sure. That's well known. Writers get a nice break in one way, at least: They can treat their mental illnesses every day. If I'm lucky, the books have amounted to more than that. I'd like to be a useful citizen, a specialized **cell** in the body politic.

(*JB* 20) The police station was so busy that there wasn't even an ordinary **cell** for me (*Walter Starbuck*). I was given a chair in the corridor outside the **cells**. It was there that the rioters insulted me from behind bars, imagining that I would enjoy nothing so much as making love to them.

(*JB* 20) I was eventually taken to a padded **cell** in the basement. It was designed to hold a maniac until an ambulance could come for her or him.

(*JB* 20) Yes, and there in my padded **cell** I told myself a joke I had read in *The Harvard Lampoon* when a freshman. It had amazed me back then because it seemed so dirty. . . . This was it:

SHE: How dare you kiss me like that?

HE: I was just trying to find out who ate all the macaroons.

(*JB* 20) So all the **cells** were checked. I wasn't in any of them, of course. The people who had brought me in and the man who had locked me up had all gone off-duty. None of them could be reached at home.

But then the detective who was trying to placate my lawyer remembered the **cell** downstairs and decided to have a look inside it, just in case.

(*PS* Obscenity) The powder certainly didn't look like much, and Dwayne Hoobler said so—but there were several hundred million sperm **cells** in there, in suspended animation.

(*PS* Children) My own son Mark found it (*"that bed of Procrustes"*) so uncomfortable that he tried to beat his brains out on it, and had to be put in a padded **cell**.

(*PS* Jonathan Swift Misperceived) Mr. Turner tells us, for example:

"The scale of Lilliput is one inch to a foot of the ordinary world. Mogg mentions [F. Mogg, Scientific American, Vol. CLXXIX, 1948] some biological difficulties: a Lilliputian would have room for far fewer cortical **cells** (so far less intelligence) than a chimpanzee; his head would be too small to carry useful eyes; and he would need eight times as many calories per ounce of body-weight as a full-scale man needs—twenty-four meals a day instead of three."

(*DD* 12) But he was led off to **cells** in the basement of police headquarters, and I was taken to a much smaller **cellblock** on the top floor, the third floor, which was reserved for women and for children under the age of sixteen. *Rudy Waltz recounts the events following his arrest and his father's in the accidental killing of Eloise Metzger.*

(*DD* 24) There in the back of the church, I daydreamed a theory of what life was all about. I told myself that Mother and Felix and the Reverend Harrell and Dwayne Hoover and so on were **cells** in what was supposed to be one great big animal. There was no reason to take us seriously as individuals. Celia in her casket there, all shot through with Drano and amphetamine, might have been a dead **cell** sloughed off by a pancreas the size of the Milky Way.

(*DD* 24) How comical that I, a single **cell**, should take my life so seriously!

. . . To whoever might be watching our insignificant lives under an electron microscope: We **cells** have names, and, if we know little else, we know our names.

(*Gal* 1:6) But now her (*Mary Hepburn's*) own big brain was urging her to take the polyethylene garment bag from around a red evening dress in her closet there in Guayaquil, and to wrap it around her head, thus depriving her **cells** of oxygen.

(*Gal* 1:13) Gokubi and Mandarax both had pressure-sensitive buttons on their backs. . . . On the face of each was an identical screen on which images could be caused to appear, and which also functioned as a solar **cell**, charging tiny batteries which, again, were exactly the same in Gokubi and Mandarax.

(*HP* 9) At the Athena state prison, as I would discover when I went to work over there, there were 6 men to each **cell** and each **cell** had been built for 2. Each 50 **cells** had a recreation room with one Ping-Pong table and one TV.

(*HP* 33) That summer I would start a literacy program in the prison, using people like Abdullah Akbahr as proselytizers for reading and writing, going from **cell** to **cell** and offering lessons.

(*FWD* II) "I think I was invited here mostly because of what happened to my dear son Mark Vonnegut, now Dr. Vonnegut. He had a very fancy crack-up, padded-**cell** stuff, straitjacket stuff, hallucinations, wrestling matches with nurses, and all that. He recovered and wrote a book about it called *The Eden Express*, which is about to be reissued in paperback by Dell, with a new Afterword by him. You should have hired him instead of me. He would have been a heck of a lot cheaper, and he knows what he is talking about.

(*TQ* 16) The timequake was going to zap him (*Dudley Prince*) back into a solitary confinement **cell**, into the hole, within the walls and towers of the New York State Maximum Security Adult Correctional Facility at Athena, sixty miles south of his hometown of Rochester, where he used to own a little video rental store.

(*GBK* James Earl Ray) when I went looking for James Earl Ray, confessed assassin of Martin Luther King, on today's controlled near-death experience, I didn't have to wander far and wide into Paradise. James Earl Ray died of liver failure on April 23 of 1998. According to Saint Peter, though, he has so far been unwilling to take a single step into the Life Everlasting awaiting him beyond the Pearly Gates.

He's no moron: he has an IQ of 108, well above average when measured against the intelligence of the general American population. He said to me that he wasn't going to set foot into eternity until a prison **cell** was built for him. He said the only way he could feel cozy forever was in a prison **cell**. In a **cell**, he said, he wouldn't give a darn how much time was passing by. Actually, he used the "s" word, wouldn't give a good "shit" how much time was passing by.

See also: PP XXXI; XXXIV; *MN* 41; *BC* 18; 19; *Slap* Prologue; *JB* 10; 20; *DD* 12; *FWD* XXX.

cellar. *Vonnegut often recalls his corpse-mining experience in the cellars of Dresden after its firebombing.* (MN Introduction) The malt syrup factory was gone. Everything was gone but the **cellars** where 135,000 Hansels and Gretels had been baked like gingerbread men.
(SL5 1) The rabid little American I call Paul Lazzaro in this book had about a quart of diamonds and emeralds and rubies and so on. He had taken these from dead people in the **cellars** of Dresden. So it goes.
(FWD X) After the raid, the corpses, most of them in ordinary **cellars**, were so numerous and represented such a health hazard that they were cremated on huge funeral pyres, or by flamethrowers whose nozzles were thrust into the **cellars**, without being counted or identified. Many friends and relatives of refugees newly arrived in Dresden can say of them nowadays only that they somehow disappeared near the end of World War II. The town was full of Polish slave laborers. Their friends and relatives must be saying of them nowadays simply that they were taken off to Germany somewhere and never came home again.
(FWD X) "Among the unidentified, not-even-counted dead in the **cellars** of Dresden there were, without doubt, war criminals or loathsomely proud relatives of war criminals, SS and Gestapo, and so on. Whatever they got was too good for them.

Maybe most of the Germans killed in Dresden, excepting the infants and children, of course, got what was coming to them. I asked another great German writer, Heinrich Böll, what he thought the dangerous flaw in the character of so many Germans was, and he said 'Obedience.'

"But I have to say that I felt no pride or satisfaction while carrying corpses from **cellars** to great funeral pyres while friends and relatives of missing watched."

Rabo Karabekian's masterpiece, "Now It's the Women's Turn," is Vonnegut's vision of what he saw the day he was released from Dresden. The painting contains a cut-away view of a cellar used for shelter that he explains to Circe Berman. (Blue 35) We went to the extreme right end for a look. . . . There was a farmhouse down at the bottom of both ends: each one buttoned up tight like a little fort, its high gates closed, and all the animals in the courtyard. And I had made a schematic cut through the earth below them so as to show their **cellars**, too, just as a museum display might give away secrets of animals' burrows underground.

"The healthy women are in the **cellar** with the beets and potatoes and turnips," I said. "They are putting off being raped as long as possible, but they have heard the history of other wars in the area, so they know that rape will surely come."

Other significant uses of cellars include the one in the home of Mother Night's *Dr. Lionel J. D. Jones, who uses it for meetings of the Iron Guard of the White Sons of the American Constitution, headed by August Krapptauer. When Howard Campbell takes refuge there as part of the kidnap conspiracy launched by Soviet agent George Kraft/ Iona Potapov, Campbell's Blue Fairy Godmother spearheads his release and reveals the true identities of Kraft and Resi Noth. Rather than face incarceration or deportation as a (reluctant) Soviet agent, Resi commits suicide by swallowing cyanide.*

God Bless You, Mr. Rosewater's *Fred Rosewater goes down to the cellar of his Pisquontuit, Rhode Island, home where he contemplates suicide until he finds the manuscript of his ancestor Merrihue Rosewater (a suicide victim) entitled* A History of the Rosewaters of Rhode Island. *The text traces the family back to nobility in Great Britain, and though Fred is momentarily buoyed by the revelation, he again thinks about hanging himself when he turns the first few pages only to realize worms have eaten his family chronicle.*

In Breakfast of Champions, *Vonnegut recalls having his mother (another suicide) tour him around Indianapolis, an attempt to instill pride in the family history.* (BC Epilogue) I thought instead of my paternal grandfather, who had been the first licensed architect in Indiana. He had designed some dream houses for Hoosier millionaires. They were mortuaries and guitar schools and **cellar** holes and parking lots now. I thought of my mother, who drove me around Indianapolis one time during the Great Depression, to impress me with how rich and powerful my maternal grandfather had been. She showed me where his brewery had been, where some of his dream houses had been. Every one of the monuments was a **cellar** hole.

And then there is the lighter side of such an image as it comes to Billy Pilgrim. (SL5 5) Billy sniffed. His hot bed smelled like a mushroom **cellar**. He had had a wet dream about Montana Wildhack.

In Timequake, Vonnegut recalls writing a letter to his brother Bernard explaining his feelings about being forced into a science track at Cornell rather than a more befitting liberal arts major. He tries to explain that for all of Bernard's scientific accomplishments, his smaller pleasures come in an educated appreciation of the arts. (TQ 43) "You yourself are gratified by some music, arrangements of noises, and again essentially nonsense. If I were to kick a bucket down the **cellar** stairs, and then say to you that the racket I had made was philosophically on a par with *The Magic Flute*, this would not be the beginning of a long and upsetting debate. An utterly satisfactory and complete response on your part would be, 'I like what Mozart did, and I hate what the bucket did.'"

(BAG Introduction) I returned to Dresden, incidentally, the setting for *Slaughterhouse-Five*, on October 7th, 1998. I was taken down into the **cellar** where I and about a hundred other American POWs survived a firestorm that suffocated or incinerated 135,000 or so other human beings. It reduced the "Florence of the Elbe" to a jagged moonscape.

While I was down in that **cellar** again, this thought came to me: "Because I have lived so long,

I am one of the few persons on Earth who saw an Atlantis before it disappeared forever beneath the waves."

(MWC 1) While we were being bombed in Dresden, sitting in a **cellar** with our arms over our heads in case the ceiling fell, one soldier said as though he were a duchess in a mansion on a cold and rainy night, "I wonder what the poor people are doing tonight." Nobody laughed, but we were still all glad he said it. At least we were still alive! He proved it. *See also: PP* III; XV; XXVII; *MN* 17; 27–28; 30; 38–39; *GBR* 4; 8; 11; *SL5* 6; *BC* 15; *JB* 9; *DD* 1; *BAG* Any Reasonable Offer, The Package.

chaos, chaotic. (PP XI) Halyard yawned, and was annoyed to think that Lynn, who had just read "order out of **chaos**" as "order out of koze," made three times as much money as he did.

(ST 1) "Things fly this way and that, my boy," he (Rumfoord) said, "with or without messages. It's **chaos**, and no mistake, for the Universe is just being born. It's the great becoming that makes the light and the heat and the motion, and bangs you from hither to yon.

(CC 24) Anything can be a *wampeter*: a tree, a rock, an animal, an idea, a book, a melody, the Holy Grail. Whatever it is, the members of its karass revolve about it in the majestic **chaos** of a spiral nebula. The orbits of the members of a *karass* about their common *wampeter* are spiritual orbits, naturally. It is souls and not bodies that revolve. As Bokonon invites us to sing:

Around and around and around we spin,
With feet of lead and wing of tin . . .

(BC 17) Listen: Bunny's mother and my mother were different sorts of human beings, but they were both beautiful in exotic ways, and they both boiled over with **chaotic** talk about love and peace and wars and evil and desperation, of better days coming by and by, of worse days coming by and by. And both our mothers committed suicide. Bunny's mother ate Drano. My mother ate sleeping pills, which wasn't nearly as horrible.

(BC 19) Once I understood what was making America such a dangerous, unhappy nation of people who had nothing to do with real life, I resolved to shun storytelling. . . . Let others bring order to **chaos**. I would bring **chaos** to order, instead, which I think I have done.

If all writers would do that, then perhaps citizens not in the literary trades will understand that there is no order in the world around us, that we must adapt ourselves to the requirements of **chaos** instead.

It is hard to adapt to **chaos**, but it can be done. I am living proof of that: It can be done.

Adapting to **chaos** there in the cocktail lounge, I now had Bonnie MacMahon, who was exactly as important as anybody else in the Universe bring more yeast excrement to Beatrice Keedsler and Karabekian.

(*BC* 19) This is why I had gone to Midland City: to be born again. And **Chaos** announced that it was about to give birth to a new me by putting these words in the mouth of Rabo Karabekian: "What kind of man would turn his daughter into an outboard motor?"

(*WFG* In a Manner That Must Shame God Himself) I'll say this: Their religions (those of the American Indians) couldn't possibly be more **chaotic** than the Christianity reinvented every day by Dr. D. Elton Trueblood, Professor at Large.

(*PS* Religion) Our country is now jammed with human beings who say out loud that life is **chaos** to them, and that it doesn't seem to matter what anybody does next. This is worse than being seasick.

(*PS* In the Capital of the World) If any of us came up with good answers, I now have no idea what they might have been. His answer was this: "The artist says, 'I can do very little about the **chaos** around me, but at least I can reduce to perfect order this square of canvas, this piece of paper, this chunk of stone.'" *The answer is provided by Vonnegut's mentor from the University of Chicago.*

(*Gal* 1:23) I (*Leon Trout*) did not know that humanity was about to be diminished to a tiny point, by luck, and then, again by luck, to be permitted to expand again. I believed that the **chaos** involving billions of big-brained people thrashing around every which way, and reproducing and reproducing, would go on and on.

(*Gal* 1:35) The most *Siegfried hoped to find was a peaceful stopping place in **chaos**.

(*Blue* 30) I have dug one of hers (*Marilee Kemp's letters*) from the archives here. It is dated three years after our reunion, June 7, 1953, and says that we have failed to paint pictures of nothing after all, that she easily identifies **chaos** in every canvas.

I answered that letter with a cable, of which I have a copy. "NOT EVEN **CHAOS** IS SUPPOSED TO BE THERE," it reads. "WE'LL COME OVER AND PAINT IT OUT. ARE OUR FACES RED. SAINT PATRICK."

(*HP* 39) Every so often, in the midst of **chaos**, you come across an amazing, inexplicable instance of civic responsibility. Maybe the last shred of faith people have is in their firemen.

(*TQ* 46) He (*Kilgore Trout*) hung up the painting again, and even made sure it was hanging straight. "That seemed somehow important, that the picture was nice and straight," he said, "and evenly spaced from the others. At least I could make that little part of the **chaotic** Universe exactly as it should be. I was grateful for the opportunity to do that."

(*TQ* 52) When I celebrate the idea of a family and family values, I don't mean a man and a woman and their kids, new in town, scared to death, and not knowing whether to shit or go blind in the midst of economic and technological and ecological and political **chaos**. I'm talking about what so many Americans need so frantically: what I had in Indianapolis before World War Two, and what the characters in Thornton Wilder's *Our Town* had, and what the Ibos have.

In chapter 45, I proposed two amendments to the Constitution. Here are two more, little enough to expect from life, one would think, like the Bill of Rights:

Article XXX: Every person, upon reaching a statutory age of puberty, shall be declared an adult in a solemn public ritual, during which he or she must welcome his or her new responsibilities in the community, and their attendant dignities.

Article XXXI: Every effort shall be made to make every person feel that he or she will be sorely missed when he or she is gone.

Such essential elements in an ideal diet for a human spirit, of course, can be provided convincingly only by extended families.

(*BAG* Coda to My Career) Given that it is no longer possible to make a living writing short stories, and that the odds against a novel's being successful are a thousand to one, creative-writing courses could be perceived as frauds, as would pharmacy courses if there were no drugstores. Be that as it may, students themselves demanded creative writing courses while they were demanding so many other things, passionately and **chaotically**, during the Vietnam War.

What students wanted and got, and what so many of their children are getting, was a cheap way to externalize what was inside them, to see in black-and-white who they were and what they might become. I italicize cheap because it takes a ton of money to make a movie or a TV show. Never mind that you have to deal with the scum of the earth if you try to make one.
See also: GBR 7; MH The Lie; BC 14.

chaperone. *Julia Pembroke's unnamed chaperone,* the alcoholic wife of an admiral, accompanied her to New York City where Mrs. Pembroke was about to have a one-night stand with John Wilkes Booth, two years to the day before assassinating President Lincoln (TQ 59).
(TQ 59) John Wilkes gallantly kissed the hand of Julia, as though they had just met, and simultaneously slipped her a packet of chloral hydrate crystals, which would be the active ingredient in a Mickey Finn for the **chaperone.**

Chaplin, Charlie. *Vonnegut very much enjoys the work of Charlie Chaplin and in a number of instances manages to work in Chaplinesque images. In his preface to the script of* Between Time and Timbuktu *(a text he did not author), Vonnegut cites the influence Chaplin and others have had on him.* (TIM XVII) I would like to say something about American comedians: they are often as brilliant and magical as our best jazz musicians, and they have probably done more to shape my thinking than any writer. When people ask me who my culture heroes are, I express pious gratitude for Mark Twain and James Joyce and so on. But the truth is that I am a barbarian, whose deepest cultural debts are to Laurel and Hardy, Stoopnagel and Bud, Buster Keaton, Fred Allen, Jack Benny,

Charlie Chaplin, Easy Aces, Henry Morgan, and on and on.

Howard Campbell evokes the following image while walking with Helga/Resi on the streets of New York after the war. (MN 23) I was not wearing war-surplus clothing. I was wearing the clothes I had put on after seeing Berlin, after shucking off the uniform of the Free American Corps. I was wearing the cloth fur-collared impresario's cloak and blue serge suit I had been captured in. I was also carrying, for whimsy, a cane. I did marvelous things with the cane: rococo manuals of arms, **Charlie Chaplin** twirls, polo strokes at orts in the gutter.

After capturing George Kraft / Iona Potapov, an FBI officer engages Kraft in some playful, derisive banter about his long spy career coming to an end, that perhaps they could make a movie of his life. The FBI officer suggests that only Charlie Chaplin could play Kraft in the movie. (MN 30) "Who else could play a spy who was steadily drunk from 1941 until 1948? Who else could play a Russian spy who built an apparatus composed almost entirely of American agents?"

As Eliot Rosewater lapses into a trance preceding his departure from the town, he becomes a Chaplinesque caricature. (GBR 13) Something there was in Eliot, though, that watched the clock. Ten minutes before his bus was due at the Saw City Kandy Kitchen, he thawed, arose, pursed his lips, picked some lint from his suit, went out his office door. He had no surface memory of the fight with his father. His step was jaunty, that of a **Chaplinesque** *boulevardier.*

He bent to pat the heads of dogs who welcomed him to street level. His new clothes hampered him, bound him in the crotch and armpits, crackled as though lined with newspaper, reminded him of how nicely turned out he was.
(WFG Why They Read Hesse) A magic theater fantasy in which Harry Haller takes part proves, incidentally, that Hesse might have been one of the most screamingly funny men of his time. It may be that he was so anguished as he wrote *Steppenwolf* that his soul could get relief only by erupting into **Charlie Chaplin** comedy. The fantasy is about two men who climb a tree by a road. They have a rifle. They declare war on all automobiles and shoot them as they come by.

(*PS Self-Interview*) INTERVIEWER: You seem to prefer Laurel and Hardy over **Chaplin**. Is that so? VONNEGUT: I'm crazy about **Chaplin**, but there's too much distance between him and his audience. He is too obviously a genius. In his own way, he's as brilliant as Picasso, and this is intimidating to me.

Rabo Karabekian identifies some of the people he included in his final masterpiece "Now It's the Women's Turn." (*Blue* 36) "How many of these are portraits of actual people?" she said.

"The bombardier clinging to my leg: that's his face, as I remember it. These two Estonians in German uniforms are Laurel and Hardy. This French collaborator here is **Charlie Chaplin**. These two Polish slave laborers on the other side of the tower from me are Jackson Pollock and Terry Kitchen."

Charity Anne Browning. *Belonging to "a Nova Scotian named Bert," the* Charity Ann Browning *is a sixty-eight-foot yawl encountered by the skipper of the* Marlin, *Frank Wirtanen of West Barnstable, Cape Cod. He and the narrator are taking the* Marlin, *which belongs to President Kennedy, down the Inland Waterway from Hyannis Port to West Palm Beach. The* Charity Ann Browning *is used as a point of maritime comparison, one of the chief narrative devices in the story.* (WFG Brief Encounters on the Inland Waterway) The ***Charity Anne Browning*** looked from the outside like a very businesslike sailing vessel, possibly engaged in the copra trade. Below decks she was like the bridal suite in the newest motor lodge in Reno—thick carpets, three tiled baths, a fifteen-foot couch covered with panther skin and steam heat. In the owner's cabin there was a king-size bed with the covers turned back. The sheets and pillow cases were dotted with forget-me-nots.

Charlestown Prison. *The place of imprisonment and execution of Sacco and Vanzetti as recounted in* Jailbird.

Charley. *In the short play "Fortitude" reprinted in* Wampeters, Foma & Granfalloons, *Charley is the hospital technician in the control room responsible for ministering to the live head of Sylvia. When she and her medical miracle worker Dr. Frankenstein* are united as a pair of talking heads, Charley makes sure to play the Jeanette MacDonald–Nelson Eddy duet "Ah, Sweet Mystery of Life" as Frankenstein previously instructed.

Charlotte. *In the short story "Next Door" reprinted in* Welcome to the Monkey House *(1968), Charlotte is the woman with whom Lemuel K. Harger is having an affair and whose loudness plays on the conscience of young Paul next door. When Paul calls All-Night Sam to dedicate a record for Mrs. Harger in Lemuel's name, Charlotte hears the radio dedication and storms out of the apartment but not before firing three shots at Lemuel and bribing Paul with a large wad of money. Though she didn't hit Harger, Paul thought he contributed to his death. She was a big, blonde woman, all soft and awry, like an unmade bed.*

Chasens, Henry Stewart (*see also* **Newt** *and* **Catharine**). *In the short story "Long Walk to Forever," in* Welcome to the Monkey House *(1968), Chasens is the unseen fiancé of Catharine (no last name).*

Checker Charley. *In* Player Piano, *Dave Berringer, one of the top "computer-machine" men in the country, invents the checker-playing computer that Fred Berringer uses to challenge Paul Proteus's checker championship. Fred's ignorance about his father's invention leads to its undoing. Ed Finnerty notices that a couple of Checker Charley's connections are loose, eventually causing the robot to fail, allowing Paul to retain his championship.*

chemical, chemically. *Vonnegut's first protracted treatment of his concern with the volatile chemistry of humans occurs during a conversation between Howard Campbell and a New York City policeman assigned to protect his vandalized apartment. Campbell is mostly a straight man while listening to the officer.* (MN 41) "Getting down in the dumps," he said. "Isn't that what they're finding out—that a lot of that's **chemicals**?"
(MN 41) "They can give a man certain **chemicals**, and he goes crazy," he said. "That's one of the things they're working with. Maybe it's all **chemicals**. . . . Maybe it's different **chemicals** that differ-

ent countries eat that makes people act in different ways at different times. . . . It has to be **chemicals**, doesn't it?" he said. . . . "I think about **chemicals** all the time. . . . Sometimes I think I should go back to school and find out all the things they've found out so far about **chemicals**. . . . Maybe, when they find out more about **chemicals**," he said, "there won't have to be policemen or wars or crazy houses or divorces or drunks or juvenile delinquents or women gone bad or anything any more."

(*MN* 41) "Certain **chemicals** get loose, and the woman can't help but act that way. Sometimes a certain **chemical** will get loose after a woman's had a baby, and she'll kill the baby. That happened four doors down from here just last week. . . . Most unnatural thing a woman can do is kill her own baby, but she did it," he said. "Certain **chemicals** in the blood made her do it, even though she knew better, didn't want to do it at all."

"Um," I said.

"You wonder what's wrong with the world—" he said, "well, there's an important clue right there."

Vonnegut continues this discourse when thinking of his mother, extending it further to explain the suicidal impulses of Dwayne Hoover, and rambles on about the prevalence of recreational drug use. (BC Preface) I tend to think of human beings as huge, rubbery, test tubes, too, with **chemical** reactions seething inside. . . . My own mother wrecked her brains with **chemicals**, which were supposed to make her sleep. . . . So it is a temptation to me, when I create a character for a novel, to say that he is what he is because of faulty wiring, or because of microscopic amounts of **chemicals** which he ate or failed to eat on that particular day.

(*BC* 1) Dwayne's incipient insanity was mainly a matter of **chemicals**, of course. Dwayne Hoover's body was manufacturing certain **chemicals** which unbalanced his mind. But Dwayne, like all novice lunatics, needed some bad ideas, too, so that his craziness could have shape and direction. . . . Bad **chemicals** and bad ideas were the Yin and Yang of madness. Yin and Yang were Chinese symbols of harmony.

(*BC* 8) Trout wandered out onto the sidewalk of Forty-second Street. It was a dangerous place to be. The whole city was dangerous—because of **chemicals** and the uneven distribution of wealth and so

on. A lot of people were like Dwayne: they created **chemicals** in their own bodies which were bad for their heads. But there were thousands upon thousands of other people in the city who bought bad **chemicals** and ate them or sniffed them—or injected them into their veins.

(*BC* 8) Sometimes they even stuffed bad **chemicals** up their assholes. . . . People took such awful chances with **chemicals** and their bodies because they wanted the quality of their lives to improve. They lived in ugly places where there were only ugly things to do. . . . So they did their best to make their insides beautiful instead. . . . The results had been catastrophic so far—suicide, theft, murder, and insanity and so on. But new **chemicals** were coming onto the market all the time.

(*BC* 15) Dwayne certainly wasn't alone, as far as having bad **chemicals** inside of him was concerned. He had plenty of company throughout all history. In his own lifetime, for instance, the people in a country called Germany were so full of bad **chemicals** for a while that they actually built factories whose only purpose was to kill people by the millions.

Vonnegut continues to discuss his appreciation of the human chemical question outside his fiction, touching on his often-touted extended families theory. (WFG Address to the National Institute of Arts and Letters, 1971) Happiness is **chemical**. Before I knew that, I used to investigate happiness by means of questions and answers.

(WFG Address to the National Institute of Arts and Letters, 1971) And I say to you that we are full of **chemicals** which require us to belong to folk societies, or failing that, to feel lousy all the time. We are **chemically** engineered to live in folk societies, just as fish are **chemically** engineered to live in clean water—and there aren't any folk societies for us anymore.

(WFG Address to the National Institute of Arts and Letters, 1971) Here is what women really want: They want lives in folk societies, wherein everyone is a friendly relative, and no act or object is without holiness. **Chemicals** make them want that. **Chemicals** make us all want that.

(WFG Address to the National Institute of Arts and Letters, 1971) **Chemicals** make us furious when we are treated as things rather than persons. When anything happens to us which would not happen to us in a folk society, our **chemicals** make us feel like fish out of water. Our **chemicals** demand that we get back into water again. If we become increasingly wild and preposterous in modern times—well, so do fish on river banks, for a little while.

(WFG Address to the National Institute of Arts and Letters, 1971) The American Academy of Arts and Letters and the National Institute of Arts and Letters don't really give a damn for arts and letters, in my opinion. They, too, are **chemically**-induced efforts to form a superstitious, affectionate clan or village or tribe. To them I say this, "Lots of luck, boys and girls."

Moving beyond our internal chemistries, Vonnegut responds to the military-industrial complex's experiments. (PS When I Lost My Innocence) "We have discovered a brand-new method for committing suicide—family style, Reverend Jim Jones style, and by the millions. What is the method? To say nothing and do nothing about what some of our businessmen and military men are doing with the most unstable substances and the most persistent poisons to be found anywhere in the universe.

"The people who play with such **chemicals** are so *dumb!*"

Eugene Debs Hartke (whose father was a chemical engineer) refers to the explanations he had to make for military assaults made by officers intoxicated with alcohol and marijuana. (HP 4) Several of the most gruesome accidents I had to explain to the press during my last year over there were caused by people who had rendered themselves imbecilic or maniacal by ingesting too much of what, if taken in moderation, could be a helpful **chemical**.

Vonnegut frequently discusses mental illness as chemically induced, including his mother's suicide and his son Mark's breakdown. (PS Children) Schizophrenia is an internal **chemical** catastrophe. It is a case of monstrously bad genetic luck, bad luck of a sort encountered in absolutely every sort of society—including the Australian aborigines and the middle class of Vienna, Austria, before the Second World War.

(PS The Sexual Revolution) He *(Vonnegut's son Mark)* never blamed me or his mother, as I have said before. His generous wish not to blame us was so stubborn that he became almost a crank on the subject of **chemical** and genetic causes of mental illness.

(FWD II) "I made the strong suggestion in *Palm Sunday* that my mother's untreated, unacknowledged insanity was caused by bad **chemicals** she swallowed rather than created within herself, principally alcohol and unlimited quantities of prescribed barbiturates. (She did not live long enough to have a doctor pep her up with some sort of amphetamine.) I am willing to believe that her ailment was hereditary, but I have no American ancestors (fully accounted for in *Palm Sunday*) who were clinically crazy. In any case, what the heck? I didn't get to choose my ancestors, and I look upon my brain and the rest of my body as a house I inhabit which was built long before I was born."

(FWD II) "Long before Mark went crazy, I thought mental illness was caused by **chemicals**, and said so in my stories. I've never in a story had an event or another person drive a character crazy. I thought madness had a **chemical** basis even when I was a boy, because a close friend of our family, a wise and kind and wryly sad man named Dr. Walter Bruetsch, who was head of the State's huge and scary hospital for the insane, used to say that his patients' problems were **chemical**, that little could be done for them until that **chemistry** was better understood."

(FWD II) "So when my mother went crazy, long before my son went crazy, long before I had a son, and finally killed herself, I blamed **chemicals**, and I still do, although she had a terrible childhood. I can even name two of the **chemicals**: phenobarbital and booze. Those came from the outside, of course, the phenobarbs from our family doctor, who was trying to do something about her sleeplessness. When she died, I was a soldier, and my division was about to go overseas."

(FWD XIV) "The AA (*Alcoholics Anonymous*) scheme, which, again, can work only if the addicts regularly admit that this or that **chemical** is poisonous to them, is now proving its effectiveness with compulsive gamblers, who are not dependent on **chemicals** from a distillery or a pharmaceutical laboratory. This is no paradox. Gamblers, in effect, manufacture their own dangerous substances. God help them, they produce **chemicals** that elate them whenever they place a bet on simply anything. . . .

"Whether the meeting I was standing before was

of Gamblers Anonymous or Alcoholics Anonymous, I would be encouraged to testify as to how the **chemicals** I had generated within myself or swallowed had alienated my friends and relatives, cost me jobs and houses, and deprived me of my last shred of self-respect."

(FWD XIV) "I now wish to direct your attention to another form of addiction, which has not been previously identified. It is more like gambling than drinking, since the people afflicted are ravenous for situations that will cause their bodies to release **chemicals** into their bloodstreams. I am persuaded that there are among us people who are tragically hooked on preparations for war."

(FWD XIX) "Jokes work this way: The jokester frightens the listener just a little bit, by mentioning something challenging, such as sex or physical danger, or suggesting that the listener is having his or her intelligence tested. Step two: The jokester makes clear that no intelligent response is required of the listener. This leaves the listener stuck with useless fight or flee **chemicals** in his or her bloodstream, which must be gotten rid of somehow, unless the listener wants to slug the jokester or do jumping jacks.

"What the listener most likely will do is expel those **chemicals** through the lungs with quick expansions and contractions of the chest cavity, accompanied by grotesque facial expressions and barking sounds."

(TQ 12) Trout said this was the story on why AIDS and new strains of syph and clap and the blueballs were making the rounds like Avon ladies run amok: On September 1st of 1945, immediately after the end of World War Two, representatives of all the **chemical** elements held a meeting on the planet Tralfamadore. They were there to protest some of their members' having been incorporated into the bodies of big, sloppy, stinky organisms as cruel and stupid as human beings.

Elements such as Polonium and Ytterbium, which had never been essential parts of human beings, were nonetheless outraged that any **chemicals** should be so misused.

(TQ 12) Sodium said enough was enough, that any further testimony would be coals to Newcastle. It made a motion that all **chemicals** involved in medical research combine whenever possible to create

ever more powerful antibiotics. These in turn would cause disease organisms to evolve new strains that were resistant to them.

In no time, Sodium predicted, every human ailment, including acne and jock itch, would be not only incurable but fatal. "All humans will die," said Sodium, according to Trout. "As they were at the birth of the Universe, all elements will be free of sin again."

Iron and Magnesium seconded Sodium's motion. Phosphorus called for a vote. The motion was passed by acclamation.

(TQ 48) Was Dr. Trout ever in for a surprise, though! Not only were these birds obscenely fat, and thus easy prey for predators. They were exploding, too! Spores from a tree fungus growing near Dalhousie nests found an opportunity to become a new disease in the intestinal tracts of the overweight birds, thanks to certain **chemicals** in the bodies of blackflies.

The new life-style of the fungus inside the birds at one point triggered the sudden release of quantities of carbon dioxide so copious that the birds blew up! One Dalhousie, perhaps the last veteran of the Disappointment Lake experiment, would explode a year later in a park in Detroit, Michigan, setting off the second-worst race riot in the Motor City's history.

See also: ST 12; MN 41; CC 19; 106; 117; GBR 12; MH Welcome to the Monkey House; MH Deer in the Works; MH Unready to Wear; WJ III; BC 4–6; 10–11; 15; 19; 23–24; WFG Fortitude; WFG Address to the National Institute of Arts and Letters, 1971; WFG Playboy Interview; Slap 9; 33; 48; JB 5; Epilogue; PS Self-Interview; PS Jekyll and Hyde Updated; DD 23; Blue 2; 19; 30; HP 1; 4; 7; 25; 28; 32; 34; FWD XXI.

chemist (see also **chemical**). (ST 1) "God told us what we had to do on this wonderful space ship. He wrote the rules so anybody could understand them. You don't have to be a physicist or a great **chemist** or an Albert Einstein to understand them."

(MN 13) Working with a **chemist** named Dr. Lomar Horthy, Jones developed Viverine, an embalming fluid, and Gingiva-Tru, a wonderfully lifelike, gum-simulating substance for false teeth.

(*CC* 11) He then told me who Horvath was. "The famous surface **chemist**," he said, "the one who's doing such wonderful things with films."

(*BC* 20) The man who told me how to diagram a segment of a molecule of plastic was Professor Walter H. Stockmayer of Dartmouth College. He is a distinguished physical **chemist**, and an amusing and useful friend of mine.

(*BC* 22) And when another Nigger high school was built after the Second World War, it was named after George Washington Carver, a black man who was born into slavery, but who became a famous **chemist** anyway. He discovered many remarkable new uses for peanuts.

(*WFG* Address to the American Physical Society) I was a chemistry major in college. H. L. Mencken started out as a **chemist**. H. G. Wells did, too. My father said he would help to pay for my college education only if I studied something serious. . . . So I went to Cornell University, and I studied chemistry and German. . . .

Back in my days as a **chemistry** student I used to be quite a technocrat. I used to believe that scientists would corner God and photograph Him in Technicolor by 1951. I used to mock my fraternity brothers at Cornell who were wasting their energies on insubstantial subjects such as sociology and government and history. And literature. I told them that all power in the future would rest properly in the hands of **chemists** and physicists and engineers.

(*PS* When I Lost My Innocence) He (*Vonnegut's father*) and my older brother, who had become a **chemist**, urged me to study chemistry instead.

(*PS* When I Lost My Innocence) "It was not Cornell's fault that I did not like this place much. . . . It was my father's fault. He said I should become a **chemist** like my brother, and not waste my time and his money on subjects he considered so much junk jewelry—literature, history, philosophy."

(*PS* When I Lost My Innocence) "Well—I am more sentimental about this occasion than I have so far indicated. We **chemists** can be as sentimental as anybody. Our emotional lives, probably because of the A-bomb and the H-bomb, and the way we spell 'Ethel,' have been much maligned."

(*PS* Self-Interview) VONNEGUT: My education was as a **chemist** at Cornell and then an anthropologist at the University of Chicago.

(*PS* Playmates) "Until that moment of truth, I had agreed with the Nobel-prize **chemist**, the late Irving Langmuir, who once said within hearing, 'Any person who can't explain his work to a fourteen-year-old is a charlatan.'"

(*Blue* 18) The cook who had begrudgingly fed me my first supper in New York City, and who kept asking, "What next, what next?" died two weeks after I got there. That finally became what was going to happen next: she would drop dead in **Turtle Bay Chemists**, a drugstore two blocks away.

(*HP* 11) When we passed a Catholic church, I recalled, he said, "You think your dad's a good **chemist**? They're turning soda crackers into meat in there. Can your dad do that?"

(*FWD* XI) (I didn't go to the reunion. I was afraid of it because, like everybody else, I had had some really lousy times in high school. I probably would have gone anyway and had a swell time and lots of laughs. But then I was lucky enough to come down with the disease of the moment in the Hamptons, which was Lyme disease. I get sick only when it's useful, knock on wood. Viral pneumonia got me out of trying to be a **chemist** in 1942. I went briefly apeshit in the 1980s in an effort to get out of life entirely, wound up playing Eightball in a locked ward for thirty days instead.)

(*FWD* XII) "Hitler dreamed of killing Jews, Gypsies, Slavs, homosexuals, Communists, Jehovah's Witnesses, mental defectives, believers in democracy, and so on, in industrial quantities. It would have remained only a dream if it hadn't been for **chemists** as well educated as my brother, who supplied Hitler's executioners with the cyanide gas known as Cyklon-B. It would have remained only a dream if architects and engineers as capable as my father and grandfather hadn't designed extermination camps—the fences, towers, the barracks, the railroad sidings, and the gas chambers crematoria—for maximum ease of operation and efficiency. I recently visited two of those camps in Poland, Auschwitz and Birkenau. They are technologically perfect. There is only one grade I could give their designers, and that is A-plus. They surely solved all the problems set for them.

(*TQ* 39) They and I were so old that we could remember when it didn't matter all that much economically whether you did or didn't go to college.

You could still amount to something. And I told my father back then that maybe I didn't want to become a **chemist** like my big brother Bernie. I could save him a ton of money if I went to work for a newspaper instead.

(*TQ* 43) And just get a load of this: My big brother Bernie, who can't draw for sour apples, and who at his most objectionable used to say he didn't like paintings because they didn't do anything, just hung there year after year, has this summer become an artist!

I shit you not! This Ph.D. physical **chemist** from MIT is now the poor man's Jackson Pollock! He squoozles glurp of various colors and consistencies between two flat sheets of impermeable materials, such as windowpanes or bathroom tiles. He pulls them apart, et voilà!

(*TQ* 44) When I went to Cornell University to become a **chemist** fifty-six years ago, I was made a fraternity brother of a man named John Hickenlooper.

Ting-a-ling?

This was his son!

(*MWC* 2) As an undergraduate at Cornell I was a chemistry major because my brother was a big-shot **chemist**. Critics feel that a person cannot be a serious artist and also have had a technical education, which I had. I know that customarily English departments in universities, without knowing what they're doing, teach dread of the engineering department, the physics department, and the chemistry department. And this fear, I think, is carried over into criticism. Most of our critics are products of English departments and are very suspicious of anyone who takes an interest in technology. So, anyway, I was a chemistry major, but I'm always winding up as a teacher in English departments, so I've brought scientific thinking to literature. There's been very little gratitude for this.

(*MWC* 2) I became a so-called science fiction writer when someone decreed that I was a science fiction writer. I did not want to be classified as one, so I wondered in what way I'd offended that I would not get credit for being a serious writer. I decided that it was because I wrote about technology, and most fine American writers know nothing about technology. I got classified as a science fiction writer simply because I wrote about Schenectady,

New York. My first book, *Player Piano*, was about Schenectady. There are huge factories in Schenectady and nothing else. I and my associates were engineers, physicists, **chemists**, and mathematicians. And when I wrote about the General Electric Company and Schenectady, it seemed a fantasy of the future to critics who had never seen the place.

I think that novels that leave out technology misrepresent life as badly as Victorians misrepresented life by leaving out sex.

(*MWC* 3) Now, I don't mean to intimidate you, but after being a **chemist** as an undergraduate at Cornell, after the war I went to the University of Chicago and studied anthropology, and eventually I took a masters degree in that field. Saul Bellow was in that same department, and neither one of us ever made a field trip. Although we certainly imagined some. I started going to the library in search of reports about ethnographers, preachers, and explorers—those imperialists—to find out what sorts of stories they'd collected from primitive people. It was a big mistake for me to take a degree in anthropology anyway, because I can't stand primitive people—they're so stupid. But anyway, I read these stories, one after another, collected from primitive people all over the world, and they were dead level, like the B-E axis here. So all right. Primitive people deserve to lose with their lousy stories. They really are backward. Look at the wonderful rise and fall of our stories.

chemistry (*see also* **chemical** *and* **chemist**). (*WFG* Science Fiction) English majors are encouraged, I know, to hate **chemistry** and physics, and to be proud because they are not dull and creepy and humorless and war-oriented like the engineers across the quad. . . . So it is natural for them to despise science fiction.

(*WFG* Address to the American Physical Society) I've had the same formal education you people have had, more or less. I was a **chemistry** major in college. H. L. Mencken started out as a chemist. H. G. Wells did, too. My father said he would help to pay for my college education only if I studied something serious. This was in the late Thirties. *Reader's Digest* magazine was in those days celebrating the wonderful things Germans were doing with chemicals. **Chemistry** was obviously the coming thing. So was German. So I went to Cornell University, and I studied **chemistry** and German. . . .

Back in my days as a **chemistry** student I used to be quite a technocrat. I used to believe that scientists would corner God and photograph Him in Technicolor by 1951.

(*WFG Playboy* Interview) I wasn't taking a whole lot of it (*Vonnegut refers to taking Ritalin for depression*), but it puzzled me so much that I could be depressed and just by taking this damn little thing about the size of a pinhead, I would feel much better. I used to think that I was responding to Attica or to the mining of the harbor of Haiphong. But I wasn't. I was obviously responding to internal **chemistry**.

(*WFG Playboy* Interview) VONNEGUT: In this book I've just finished, *Breakfast of Champions*, the motives of all the characters are explained in terms of body **chemistry**. You know, we don't give a shit about the characters' childhoods or about what happened yesterday—we just want to know what the state of their bloodstreams is. They're up when their bloodstreams are up and they're down when their bloodstreams are down.

(*PS Self-Interview*) VONNEGUT: I'm on the New York State Council for the Arts now, and every so often some other member talks about sending notices to college English departments about some literary opportunity, and I say, "Send them to the **chemistry** departments, send them to the zoology departments, send them to the anthropology departments and the astronomy departments and physics departments, and all the medical and law schools. That's where the writers are most likely to be."

(*HP 20*) I (*Eugene Debs Hartke*) would have been dead if it weren't for that great gift to civilization from the **Chemistry** Department of Harvard, which was napalm, or sticky jellied gasoline.

(*FWD V*) My father, as I have said elsewhere ad nauseam, said I could go to college only if I studied **chemistry**. How flattered I would have been if he had said instead that I, too, should become an architect.

(*FWD XVI*) "Like the early Christians, you are part of a society dominated by superstitions, by pure baloney. During Roman Imperial times, though, pure baloney was all that was available about the size of the planet, about its place in the cosmos, about the natures of its other inhabitants, about the probable origins of life, about the causes and cures of diseases, about **chemistry**, about physics, about biology, and on and on. Everybody, including the early Christians, had no choice but to be full of baloney. That is not the case today. And my goodness, do we ever have a lot of information now, and proven techniques for creating almost anything in abundance and moderating all sorts of catastrophes.

(*FWD XX*) I am now prepared to say that suicidal persons can be divided into two sorts. Styron's sort blames the wiring and **chemistry** of his brain, which could easily fit into a salad bowl. My sort blames the Universe. (Why mess around?) I don't offer this insight as yet another joke ("Why is cream more expensive than milk?"). It is my serious belief that those of us who become humorists (suicidal or not) feel free (as most people do not) to speak of life itself as a dirty joke, even though life is all there is or ever can be.

> *We do, doodily do, doodily do, doodily do*
> *What we must, muddily must, muddily must,*
> *   muddily must:*
> *Muddily do, muddily must, muddily do, mud-*
> *   dily must,*
> *Until we bust, bodily bust, bodily bust, bodily*
> *   bust.*

(*FWD "On Literature"*) If I am apathetic about most academic critics of literature, the ennui is surely mutual. Whereas I find almost nothing of use to a working fiction writer in academic criticism, I have seldom met an academic critic interested in asking a writer why and how he does what he does. To me this is like a **chemistry** professor's being proud of snubbing the element oxygen.

(*TQ 32*) Unlike Dudley Prince, Trout hadn't even earned a High School Equivalency Certificate, but he bore at least one surprising resemblance to my big brother Bernie, who has a Ph.D. in physical **chemistry** from MIT. Bernie and Trout had both, since their earliest adolescence, played games in their heads that began with this question: "If such-and-such were the case in our surroundings, what then, what then?"

(*GBK* Isaac Asimov) Isaac has a Ph.D. in **chemistry** from Columbia, and was born in Smolensk, in the former Soviet Union, but was raised in Brooklyn. He hated flying, and never read Hemingway or Fitzgerald or Joyce or Kafka, according to his obituary in the *New York Times.* "I am a stranger," he once wrote, "to twentieth-century fiction and poetry."

(*MWC* 2) As an undergraduate at Cornell I was a **chemistry** major because my brother was a big-shot chemist. Critics feel that a person cannot be a serious artist and also have had a technical education, which I had. I know that customarily English departments in universities, without knowing what they're doing, teach dread of the engineering department, the physics department, and the **chemistry** department. And this fear, I think, is carried over into criticism. Most of our critics are products of English departments and are very suspicious of anyone who takes an interest in technology. So, anyway, I was a **chemistry** major, but I'm always winding up as a teacher in English departments, so I've brought scientific thinking to literature. There's been very little gratitude for this.

See also: PP XXVIII; *MN* 31; *CC* 15; *MH* Unready to Wear; *MH* The Kid Nobody Could Handle; *WFG* Preface; *WFG* Science Fiction; *WFG* Address to the American Physical Society; *JB* Prologue; 1; 3; 5; *PS* Roots; *PS* When I Lost My Innocence; *PS* Triage; *PS* Self-Interview; *PS* Children; *PS* Jekyll and Hyde Updated; *DD* 5; *HP* 3; 4; 26; *FWD* II; IX; XII.

"The Chemistry Professor." *Reprinted in* Palm Sunday, *Vonnegut's reworking of Robert Louis Stevenson's "Dr. Jekyll and Mr. Hyde." In this version Dr. Jekyll is a chemistry professor at Sweetbread College and concocts a potion to increase the growth of chickens as a way to raise funds for the bankrupt institution. He drinks the potion, turns into a human-sized homicidal chicken, and is shot dead by Fred Leghorn. This plotline occurs while the students are rehearsing a production of Stevenson's original story to raise funds for the college.*

Vonnegut recalls that in 1978, the Broadway producer Lee Guber asked him to write a musical update of the classic. It was never produced. Vonnegut and Guber were serving together on the New York State Council of the Arts.

Chessman, Caryl. *When prison guard Clyde Carter becomes exasperated with Walter Starbuck's "It's all right," easygoing attitude about the fact his son did not come to visit or meet him for his release, Carter likens Walter's attitude to that of Caryl Chessman.* (*JB* 5) **Caryl Chessman** was a convicted kidnapper and rapist, but not a murderer, who spent twelve years on death row in California. He made all his own appeals for stays of execution, and he learned four languages and wrote two best-selling books before he was put into an airtight tank with windows in it, and made to breathe cyanide gas.

And his last words were indeed, as Clyde said, "It's all right."

Chetniks. *During World War II Nestor Aamons, a Finnish architect and father of the much sought after Mona,* was captured by the Russians, then liberated by the Germans during the Second World War. He was not returned home by his liberators, but was forced to serve in a *Wehrmacht* engineer unit that was sent to fight the Yugoslav partisans. He was captured by **Chetniks,** royalist Serbian partisans, and then by Communist partisans who attacked the **Chetniks.** He was liberated by Italian parachutists who surprised the Communists, and he was shipped to Italy (*CC* 54).

See also: BAG Bagombo Snuff Box.

Chevy Chase, MD. *In* Jailbird, *after Walter Starbuck returns from Europe with his new wife, Ruth, they move into this Washington, D.C., suburb. Ruth eventually has a small draperies business that she runs from home. Walter has to sell the house to finance his defense for his part in the Watergate scandal.*

Chez Armando. *In the short story "Custom-Made Bride," collected in* Bagombo Snuff Box (1999), *the mere mention of Chez Armando by Falloleen Krummbein serves as a turning point in her knowledge of the financially intimate details of her husband, Otto. In this, the first month of their marriage, the chic couple spend every night out partying with friends, usually picking up the tab. Falloleen's prompting comes just as Otto discusses his financial straits with his new financial adviser, the unnamed* narrator. *She is a quick study of the situation and her good sense quickly comes out in this exchange with the narrator.* "I was thinking what fun it would be to take our whole party to **Chez Armando** for dinner," said Falloleen.

Otto looked askance at me.

"We were just talking about love and money," I said to Falloleen, "and I was saying that if a woman loves a man, how much or how little money the man spends on her makes no difference to her. Do you agree?"

Otto leaned forward to hear her answer.

"Where were you brought up?" said Falloleen to me. "On a chicken farm in Saskatchewan?"

Otto groaned.

Falloleen looked at him in alarm. "There's more going on here than I know about," she said. "I was joking. Was that so awful, what I said? It seemed like such a silly question about love and money." Comprehension bloomed on her face. "Otto," she said, "are you broke?"

"Yes," said Otto.

Falloleen squared her lovely shoulders. "Then tell the others to go to **Chez Armando** without us, that you and I want to spend a quiet evening at home for a change."

Chicago Lying-in Hospital. *In the short story "2BR02B," collected in* Bagombo Snuff Box (1999), *the famed institution is the location for the entire story, particularly the waiting room for expectant parents. Historically, Dr. Joseph Bolivar DeLee observed the lack of sterile procedures during delivery, causing a variety of complications (many fatal) for both mothers and children. He changed protocol at the hospital and gained fame for the turnaround in the drop of infant mortality numbers as well as mothers surviving childbirth. None of this is mentioned in Vonnegut's short story, but one may wonder about the alliterative connection between Dr. DeLee and Leora Duncan, the ethical suicide hostess shot dead by Edward K. Wehling, Jr., the new father of triplets.*

chimney, chimneylike. (ST 1) It was ten feet long, six feet wide, and had a ceiling, like the rest of the rooms in the mansion, twenty feet high. The room was like a **chimney.** This *"architectural accident" was the room Winston Niles Rumfoord "really*

wanted with all my heart when I was a boy—this little room."

(*ST* 1) "Well—" murmured Malachi Constant, there in the **chimneylike** room under the staircase in Newport, "it looks like the messenger is finally going to be used."

(*ST* 2) The little door had been a dreamy touch. . . . the dry fountain another and the huge painting of the touch-me-not little girl with the all white pony. . . . and the **chimneylike** room under the spiral staircase and the photograph of the three sirens on Titan and Rumfoord's prophecies. . . . and the discomfiture of Beatrice Rumfoord at the top of the stairs. . . .

(*ST* 8) It had delivered its cargo to the floor of a cave one hundred and sixteen miles below the surface of Mercury. It had threaded its way down through a tortuous system of **chimneys** until it could go no deeper. *This refers to the space ship carrying Unk/Malachi and Boaz.*

(*ST* 9) It would go up the system of **chimneys** under the impression that it was going down. And it would inevitably find the way out under the impression that it was seeking the deepest possible hole. *Since the space ship could travel only "downwards," Malachi/Unk had turned the ship upside down so its navigational system would read "up" as "down," thereby allowing him to escape the caves of Mercury.*

(SL5 5) There was this difference, though: the sheds had tin **chimneys,** and out of the **chimneys** whirled constellations of sparks. *The shed doors are about to swing open to a rousing welcome of "Hail, Hail, the Gang's All Here" from the British POWs to the new American arrivals, Billy Pilgrim included.*

(MH The Hyannis Port Story) "They (tourists) don't even get to look at a Kennedy **chimney** up above the trees. All the glamour they'll get out of this administration is an overpriced waffle named Caroline."

(MH Report on the Barnhouse Effect) By the time of his discharge in 1945, he could knock bricks loose from **chimneys** three miles away. *This describes Barnhouse's early abilities exercising dynamopsychism.*

(JB Prologue) By the end of November the **chimneys** of the factory were belching smoke again.

(JB 20) When (Kenneth) Whistler came home, there was smoke coming out of his **chimney.** There

was a hot meal waiting for him inside. *Mary Kathleen O'Looney's arrival at Whistler's home in Kentucky surprises the mine worker and union organizer.*
(PS Roots) When I published my first short story, which was "Report on the Barnhouse Effect," in *Collier's*, its hero was a man who could control dice by thinking hard about them, and who could eventually loosen bricks in **chimneys** a mile away, and so on—and Uncle John said, "Now you will hear from every nut in the country. They can all do that."

(*Blue* 10) I remembered the long table and the corner cupboard full of pewter and the rustic fireplace with a blunderbuss resting on pegs driven into its **chimney** breast, from a painting he had done of Thanksgiving at Plymouth Colony. *Rabo Karabekian reminisces about a room in Dan Gregory's home.*

(*Blue* 11) I stopped at the head of the stairs, and perceived an impossibility: six free-standing **chimneys** and fireplaces, with a coal fire glowing in the hearth of every one. *Dan Gregory had purchased three connected townhouses and removed the walls separating them.*

(*Blue* 12) *Dan Gregory tells Rabo of his rearing by Beskudnikov's wife:* "I was just one more job to do, like shoveling ashes from the stoves or cleaning the lamp **chimneys** or beating the rugs."

(FWD Preface) Here are the last words he (*Heinrich Böll*) would ever say to me in this life (and he was on two canes and still smoking like a **chimney**, and about to board a taxicab to the airport in a cold London drizzle): "Oh, Koort, it is so hard, so hard." He was one of the last shreds of native German sorrow and shame about his country's part in World War II and its prelude. He told me off camera that he was despised by his neighbors for remembering when it was time to forget.

(FWD XI) During the question-and-answer period following my great speech I found an opportunity to quote O'Hare. When a Liberty ship (the *Lucretia C. Mott*, named for a women's rights advocate) had wallowed us back to the United States through severe storms in the North Atlantic, and it was time for me and my buddy to say good-bye for a while (a condition now quite permanent), I said to him, "What did you learn?" The future DA O'Hare replied, "I will never again believe my Government."

This had to do with our Government's tall tales of delicate surgery performed by bombers equipped with Sperry and Norden bombsights. These instruments were so precise, we had been told, that a bombardier could drop his billets-doux down the **chimney** of a factory if ordered to. There were solemn charades performed for newsreels in which military policemen with drawn .45 automatics escorted bombardiers carrying bombsights to their planes. That was how desperate the Germans and the Japanese were (so went the message) to learn and make use of the secret of our bombings' diabolical accuracy themselves.

Christ; Jesus Christ (*see also* **Church of Jesus Christ the Kidnapped; Sermon on the Mount**).
(PP XII) "Garth's a fine man," said Paul. Garth was, too: four-square, desperate to please, and he seemed to have an anthropomorphic image of the corporate personality. Garth stood in relation to that image as a lover, and Paul wondered if this prevalent type of relationship had ever been given the consideration it deserved by sexologists. On second thought, he supposed that it had—the general phenomenon of a lover's devotion to the unseen—in studies of nuns' symbolic marriages to **Christ**.

(ST 2) In the year Ten Million, according to Koradubian, there would be a tremendous housecleaning. All records relating to the period between the death of **Christ** and the year One Million A.D. would be hauled to dumps and burned....

The million-year period to which the burned junk related would be summed up in history books in one sentence, according to Koradubian: *Following the death of **Jesus Christ**, there was a period of readjustment that lasted for approximately one million years.*

(MN 13) And he (*Dr. Lionel J. D. Jones*) wrote and published at his own expense a book that combined not only dentistry and theology, but the fine arts as well. The name of the book was *Christ Was Not a Jew*. He proved his point by reproducing in the book fifty famous paintings of **Jesus**. According to Jones, not one painting showed Jewish jaws or teeth.

(CC 5) "It so happens I know where the string he (*Felix Hoenikker, inventor of ice-nine*) was playing with came from.... The novel was about the end of the world in the year 2000, and the name of the book was *2000 A.D.* It told about how mad scientists made a terrific bomb that wiped out the whole world. There was a big sex orgy when everybody knew that the world was going to end, and then **Jesus Christ** Himself appeared ten seconds before the bomb went off."

(*GBR* 9) There was a photograph of Trout. He was an old man with a full black beard. He looked like a frightened, aging **Jesus**, whose sentence to crucifixion had been commuted to imprisonment for life.

(*GBR* 14) "Think of the sacrilege of a **Jesus** figure redeeming stamps." *Kilgore Trout worked at a stamp redemption center in Cohoes, New York.*

(*SL5* Preface) The cattle are lowing, / The Baby awakes. / But the little Lord **Jesus** / No crying He makes.

(*SL5* 2) He *(Billy Pilgrim)* was a valet to a preacher, expected no promotions or medals, bore no arms, and had a meek faith in a loving **Jesus** which most soldiers found putrid.

(*SL5* 5) The flaw in the **Christ** stories, said the visitor from outer space, was that **Christ**, who didn't look like much, was actually the Son of the Most Powerful Being in the Universe. Readers understood that, so, when they came to the crucifixion, they naturally thought, and Rosewater said out loud again:

Oh, boy—they sure picked the wrong guy to lynch that time!

And that thought had a brother: "*There are* right people to *lynch*." Who? People not well connected. So it goes.

The visitor from outer space made a gift to Earth of a new Gospel. In it, **Jesus** really was a nobody, and a pain in the neck to a lot of people better with connections than he had. He still got to say all the lovely and puzzling things he said in the other Gospels.

So the people amused themselves one day by nailing him to a cross and planting the cross in the ground. There couldn't possibly be any repercussions, the lynchers thought. The reader would have to think that, too, since the new Gospel hammered home again and again what a nobody **Jesus** was.

And then, just before the nobody died, the heavens opened up, and there was thunder and light-

ning. The voice of God came crashing down. He told the people that he was adopting the bum as his son, giving him the full powers and privileges of The Son of the Creator of the Universe throughout all eternity. God said this: *From this moment on, He will punish horribly anybody who torments a bum who has no connections!*

(*SL5* 9) Billy cried very little, though he often saw things worth crying about, and in that respect, at least, he resembled the **Christ** of the carol: *The cattle are lowing, / The Baby awakes. / But the little **Lord Jesus** no crying He makes.*

(*SL5* 9) Another Kilgore Trout book there in the window was about a man who built a time machine so he could go back and see **Jesus**. It worked, and he saw **Jesus** when **Jesus** was only twelve years old. **Jesus** was learning the carpentry trade from his father.

Two Roman soldiers came into the shop with a mechanical drawing on papyrus of a device they wanted built by sunrise the next morning. It was a cross to be used in the execution of a rabble-rouser.

Jesus and his father built it. They were glad to have the work. And the rabble-rouser was executed on it. . . .

So Billy moved a little farther back, but not as far as the part for adults only. He moved because of absentminded politeness, taking a Trout book with him—the one about **Jesus** and the time machine.

The time-traveler in the book went back to Bible times to find out one thing in particular: Whether or not **Jesus** had really died on the cross, or whether he had been taken down while still alive, whether he had really gone on living. The hero had a stethoscope along.

Billy skipped to the end of the book, where the hero mingled with the people who were taking **Jesus** down from the cross. The time-traveler was the first one up the ladder, dressed in clothes of the period, and he leaned close to **Jesus** so people couldn't see him use the stethoscope, and he listened. . . .

The time-traveler, whose name was Lance Corwin, also got to measure the length of **Jesus**, but not to weigh him. **Jesus** was five feet and three and a half inches long. . . .

"**Jesus Christ**, where did you find this thing?"

and so on, and he had to tell the other clerks about the pervert who wanted to buy the window dressing. *The clerk in a pornographic bookstore is shocked that Billy Pilgrim wants to buy a Kilgore Trout novel rather than one of the standard pornographic offerings.*

(SL5 10) On Tralfamadore, says Billy Pilgrim, there isn't much interest in **Jesus Christ**.

(WJ II:2) WANDA JUNE Walt Disney, who gave us Snow White and the Seven Dwarfs, plays shuffleboard. **Jesus Christ** plays shuffleboard.

VON KONIGSWALD It was almost worth the trip—to find out that **Jesus Christ** in Heaven was just another guy, playing shuffleboard. I like his sense of humor, though—you know? He's got a blue-and-gold warm-up jacket he wears. You know what it says on the back? "Pontius Pilate Athletic Club." Most people don't get it. Most people think there really is a Pontius Pilate Athletic Club.

(BC 8) The prostitutes worked for a pimp now. He was splendid and cruel. He was a god to them. He took their free will away from them, which was perfectly all right. They didn't want it anyway. It was as though they had surrendered themselves to **Jesus**, for instance, so they could live unselfishly and trustingly—except that they had surrendered to a pimp instead.

(WFG *Playboy* Interview) PLAYBOY: You speak of gentle people, but somehow all this talk of **Jesus** freaks and extended families bring Charles Manson to mind.

VONNEGUT: Yes, it does. His, of course, was an extended family. He recruited all these dim-witted girls, homeless girls, usually—girls who felt homeless, at any rate—and the family meant so much to them that they would do anything for it. They were simple and they were awfully young.

(*Slap* 1) They finally came up with an answer. Melody does most of the talking for them, and this is what she said in all seriousness: "You, and **Jesus Christ**, and Santa Claus." *This is in response to Wilbur Swain's question as to who were the three most important human beings in history.*

(JB 18) When I was a young man, I expected the story of Sacco and Vanzetti to be retold as often and as movingly, to be as irresistible, as the story of **Jesus Christ** some day. Weren't modern people, if they were to marvel creatively at their own lifetimes, I

thought, entitled to a Passion like Sacco Vanzetti's, which ended in an electric chair?

(PS In the Capital of the World) "Now, as to the verses about Palm Sunday Eve: I choose them because **Jesus** says something in the eighth verse which many people I have known have taken as proof that **Jesus** himself occasionally got sick and tired of people who needed mercy all the time. I read from the Revised Standard Bible rather than the King James, because it is easier to understand. Also, I will argue afterward that **Jesus** was only joking, and it is impossible to joke in King James English. The funniest joke in the world, if told in King James English, is doomed to sound like Charlton Heston.

"I read:

"'Six days before the Passover, **Jesus** came to Bethany, where Lazarus was, whom **Jesus** had raised from the dead. There they made him a supper; Martha served, but Lazarus was one of those at table with him.

"'Mary took a pound of costly ointment of pure nard and anointed the feet of **Jesus** and wiped his feet with her hair; and the house was filled with the fragrance of the ointment.

"'But Judas Iscariot, one of his disciples (he who was to betray him) said, "Why was this ointment not sold for three hundred denarii and given to the poor?" This he said, not that he cared for the poor but because he was a thief, and as he had the money box he used to take what was put into it. **Jesus** said, "Let her alone, let her keep it for the day of my burial. The poor you always have with you, but you do not always have me."'

"Thus ends the reading, and although I have promised a joke, there is not much of a chuckle in there anywhere. The reading, in fact, ends with at least two quite depressing implications: That **Jesus** could be a touch self-pitying, and that he was, with his mission to earth about to end, at least momentarily sick and tired of hearing about the poor."

(PS In the Capital of the World) Mary begins to massage and perfume the feet of **Jesus Christ** with an ointment made from the spike plant. **Jesus** has the bones of a man and is clothed in the flesh of a man—so it must feel awfully nice, what Mary is doing to his feet. Would it be heretical of us to suppose that **Jesus** closes his eyes? . . .

"To which **Jesus** replies in Aramaic: 'Judas, don't worry about it. There will still be plenty of poor people left long after I'm gone.' . . .

"If **Jesus** did in fact say that, it is a divine black joke, well suited to the occasion. It says everything about hypocrisy and nothing about the poor. It is a Christian joke, which allows **Jesus** to remain civil to Judas, but to chide him about his hypocrisy all the same.

"'Judas, don't worry about it. There will still be plenty of poor people left long after I'm gone.'"
(*Blue* 15) "I brought you back to life," she said (*Circe Berman*). "You're my Lazarus. All **Jesus** did for Lazarus was bring him back to life—I got you writing your autobiography."
(*Blue* 24) Slazinger, high as a kite, says that every successful revolution, including Abstract Expressionism, the one I took part in, had that cast of characters at the top—Pollock being the genius in our case, Lenin being the one in Russia's, **Christ** being the one in Christianity's.
(*HP* 1) From the time I (*Eugene Debs Hartke*) was 21 until I was 35 I was a professional soldier, a Commissioned Officer in the United States Army. During those 14 years I would have killed **Jesus Christ** Himself or Herself or Itself or Whatever, if ordered to do so by a superior officer. . . .

During that war (*Vietnam*), which was about nothing but the ammunition business, there was a microscopic possibility, I suppose, that I called in a white-phosphorus barrage or a napalm air strike on a returning **Jesus Christ**.
(*HP* 11) "I heard you said **Jesus Christ** was un-American," she said, her tape recorder running all the time. *Hartke explains that his socialist Grandfather Wills had quoted Marx to him, "From each according to his abilities, to each according to his needs," and continued on by saying, "What could be more un-American Gene, than sounding like the Sermon on the Mount?"*
(*HP* 32) Think again about the crucifixions of **Jesus** and the 2 thieves, and the 6,000 slaves who followed the gladiator Spartacus. *Hartke says this as an analogy to all societies that believe their punitive measures are designed to protect the welfare of the state and preserve property.*
(*FWD* Epigraph) O God who hast hitherto supported me, enable me to proceed in this labor & in the whole task of my present state that when I shall render up at the last day an account of the talent committed to me I may receive pardon for the sake of **Jesus Christ**. Amen.

> —SAMUEL JOHNSON diary entry for April 3, 1753, when he was working on his Dictionary of the English Language*

(*FWD* VIII) The first story of mine which got into trouble with the sincerely Christian far right was about time-travelers who went back to Bible times and discovered that **Jesus Christ** was five feet, two inches tall. I think I liked **Jesus** more than the story's naysayers did, since I was asserting that I didn't care how tall or short He was.
(*FWD* XVI) "How tragic it is, then, that the major impulses in this and several other societies nowadays should be in the direction of the pure baloney and cruel entertainments of thousands of years ago, which almost inevitably lead to the antithesis of beauty and the good life and Christianity as taught by **Jesus Christ**, which is war."
(*FWD* XIX) I mentioned Abbie Hoffman in that piece about books as mantras for meditation. I realize that most people nowadays don't know who he was or what he did. He was a clowning genius, having come into the world that way, like Lenny Bruce and Jack Benny and Ed Wynn and Stan Laurel and W. C. Fields and the Marx Brothers and Red Skelton and Fred Allen and Woody Allen and so on. He was a member of my children's generation. He is high on my list of saints, of exceptionally courageous, unarmed, unsponsored, unpaid souls who have tried to slow down even a little bit state crimes against those **Jesus Christ** said should inherit the Earth someday.
(*FWD* My Reply to a Letter) I am a fourth generation German American religious skeptic ("Freethinker"). Like my essentially puritanical forebears, I believe that God has so far been unknowable and hence unservable, hence the highest service one can perform is to his or her community, whose needs are quite evident. I believe that virtuous behavior is trivialized by carrot-and-stick schemes, such as promises of highly improbable rewards or punishments in an improbable afterlife. (The pun-

---

* April 3, therefore, might be called "Writer's Day."

ishment for counterfeiting in Henry VIII's reign, incidentally, was being boiled alive in public.) The Bible is a useful starting point for discussions with crowds of American strangers, since so many of us know at least a little something about it. It has the added virtue of having for contributors at least two geniuses Moses and **Christ**.

(*TQ* 1) **Jesus** said how awful life was, in the Sermon on the Mount: "Blessed are they that mourn," and "Blessed are the meek," and "Blessed are they which do hunger and thirst after righteousness."

(*TQ* 10) The minds of children in intellectually humble American homes back then weren't swamped with countless stories from TV sets. They heard or read only a few stories, and so could remember them, and maybe learn something from them. Everywhere in the English-speaking world, one of those was "Cinderella." Another was "The Ugly Duckling." Another was the story of Robin Hood.

And another, as disrespectful of established authority as the story of Robin Hood, which "Cinderella" and "The Ugly Duckling" are not, is the life of **Jesus Christ** as described in the New Testament.

(*TQ* 20) The sheetrock was the last step. I myself would do the exterior and interior painting. I told Ted I wanted to do at least that much, or he would have done that, too. When he himself had finished, and he had taken all the scraps I didn't want for kindling to the dump, he had me stand next to him outside and look at my new ell from thirty feet away.

And then, he asked it: "How the hell did I do that?"

That question remains for me in the summer of 1996 one of my three favorite quotations. Two of the three are questions rather than good advice of any kind. The second is **Jesus Christ**'s "Who is it they say I am?"

The third is from my son Mark, pediatrician and watercolorist and sax player. I've already quoted him in another book: "We are here to help each other get through this thing, whatever it is."

(*TQ* 46) Trout could have been a great advertising man. The same has been said of **Jesus Christ**. The basis of every great advertisement is a credible promise. **Jesus** promised better times in an afterlife. Trout was promising the same thing in the here and now.

(*GBK* Introduction) My German-American ancestors, the earliest of whom settled in our Middle West about the time of our Civil War, called themselves "Freethinkers," which is the same sort of thing. My great grandfather Clemens Vonnegut wrote, for example, "If what **Jesus** said was good, what can it matter whether he was God or not?"

I myself have written, "If it weren't for the message of mercy and pity in **Jesus**' Sermon on the Mount, I wouldn't want to be a human being. I would just as soon be a rattlesnake."

(*MWC* 8) How do humanists feel about **Jesus**? I say of **Jesus**, as all humanists do, "If what he said is good, and so much of it is absolutely beautiful, what does it matter if he was God or not?"

But if **Christ** hadn't delivered the Sermon on the Mount, with its message of mercy and pity, I wouldn't want to be a human being.

I'd just as soon be a rattlesnake.

(*MWC* 9) "Do unto others what you would have them do unto you." A lot of people think **Jesus** said that, because it is so much the sort of thing **Jesus** liked to say. But it was actually said by Confucius, a Chinese philosopher, five hundred years before there was that greatest and most humane of human beings, named **Jesus Christ**.

(*MWC* 9) But back to people like Confucius and **Jesus** and my son the doctor, Mark, each of whom have said in their own way how we could behave more humanely and maybe make the world a less painful place. One of my favorite humans is Eugene Debs, from Terre Haute in my native state of Indiana.

Get a load of this. Eugene Debs, who died back in 1926, when I was not yet four, ran five times as the Socialist Party candidate for president, winning 900,000 votes, almost 6 percent of the popular vote, in 1912, if you can imagine such a ballot. He had this to say while campaigning:

> As long as there is a lower class, I am in it.
> As long as there is a criminal element, I'm of
> it.
> As long as there is a soul in prison, I am not
> free.

Doesn't anything socialistic make you want to throw up? Like great public schools, or health insurance for all?

When you get out of bed each morning, with the roosters crowing, wouldn't you like to say, "As long as there is a lower class, I am in it. As long as there is a criminal element, I am of it. As long as there is a soul in prison, I am not free."

How about **Jesus**' Sermon on the Mount, the Beatitudes?

> Blessed are the meek, for they shall inherit the Earth.
> Blessed are the merciful, for they shall obtain mercy.
> Blessed are the peacemakers, for they shall be called the children of God.

And so on.

Not exactly planks in a Republican platform. Not exactly George W. Bush, Dick Cheney, or Donald Rumsfeld stuff.
See also: PP IX; XI; XXIII; XXVI–XXVIII; XXXIII; ST 4; MN 1; 9; 11; 24; 29; CC 33; 37; 42; 46; 59; 76; 84; GBR 7; 11–12; SL5 1–2; 5–6; 9; WJ I:1; I:3–I:4; II:1; III; BC 6; 12; 14; 19; WFG Yes, We Have No Nirvanas; WFG Why They Read Hesse; WFG Playboy Interview; Slap 5; 24; 26; 38–39; 47; Epilogue; JB Prologue; 3–4; 20; PS When I Lost My Innocence; PS Self-Interview; PS The People One Knows; PS Mark Twain; PS Religion; PS Jekyll and Hyde Updated; PS In the Capital of the World; DD 10; 13; 20; 26; Epilogue; Gal 1:37; Blue 2; 11; 27; 33; 35–36; HP 1; 11; 20; 24; FWD VI; IX–X; XIV; XVI–XVII; XX; Translation of Latin Mass; TQ 20; 25; 47; 57; BAG Thanasphere; MWC 8–9.

christen. *The following is a conversation held by Resi Noth and Howard Campbell about the new identities they will assume once escaping the United States.* (MN 30) "Have you decided on a name yet?" she said.

"Name?" I said.

"Your new name—the name of the new writer whose beautiful works come mysteriously out of Mexico," she said. "I will be Mrs.—"

"*Señora*—" I said.

"*Señora* who?" she said. "*Señor* and *Señora* who?"

"**Christen** us," I said.
(CC 48) He (*Bokonon*) was **christened** Lionel Boyd Johnson.
(MH Preface) She was **christened** "Alice," but she used to deny that she was really an Alice. I agreed. Everybody agreed. Sometime in a dream maybe I will find out what her real name was. *Vonnegut refers to his sister, Alice.*
(MH The Manned Missiles) You are lucky you have a son left, Mr. Ivankov. Hazel and I don't. Bryant was the only son Hazel and I had. We didn't call him Bryant after he was **christened**. We called him Bud.
(*Slap* 2) I was born right here in New York City. I was not then a *Daffodil*. I was **christened** Wilbur *Rockefeller* Swain. . . .

We were **christened** in a hospital rather than in a church, and we were not surrounded by relatives and our parents' friends. The thing was: Eliza and I were so ugly that our parents were ashamed.
(TQ 59) Julia returned to Pembroke, Rhode Island, a town named in honor of an ancestor of her husband's, to have the kid. She was scared to death that the upper rims of the kid's ears would be like those of John Wilkes Booth, pointed like a devil's, instead of curved. But the kid had normal ears. It was a boy. It was **christened** Abraham Lincoln Pembroke.
(BAG The Cruise of the *Jolly Roger*) With a deep scar across his (*Major Nathan Durant's*) cheek, with the lobe of his right ear gone, with a stiff leg, he limped into a boatyard in New London, the port nearest the hospital, and bought a secondhand cabin cruiser. He learned to run it in the harbor there, **christened** the boat *The Jolly Roger* at the suggestion of some children who haunted the boatyard, and set out arbitrarily for Martha's Vineyard.
(BAG Hal Irwin's Magic Lamp) The baby was **christened** in a black church, and Mary was there. Hal wasn't. He and Mary were hardly speaking. Ella named the baby Irwin, in honor of the people who were so good to her. His last name was the same as hers. He was Irwin Rice.
See also: TQ 52.

Christian (*also* **Young Men's Christian Association, Christian Scientists;** *see also* **The White**

Christian Minuteman). (*MN* 11) I opened the newspaper first, found it to be *The White Christian Minuteman*, a scabrous, illiterate, anti-Semitic, anti-Negro, anti-Catholic hate sheet published by the Reverend Doctor Lionel J. D. Jones, D.D.S.

(*CC* 1) The book was to be an account of what important Americans had done on the day when the first atomic bomb was dropped on Hiroshima, Japan.

It was to be a **Christian** book. I was a **Christian** then. I am a Bokononist now.

(*GBR* 10) "Every year at least one young man whose affairs we manage comes into our office, wants to give his money away. He has completed his first year at some great university. It has been an eventful year! He has learned of unbelievable suffering around the world. He has learned of the great crimes that are at the roots of so many family fortunes. He has had his **Christian** nose rubbed, often for the very first time, in the Sermon on the Mount." *The speaker is Mr. McAllister, Stewart Buntline's attorney.*

(*SL5* 5) It (*Kilgore Trout's* Gospel from Outer Space) was about a visitor from outer space, shaped very much like a Tralfamadorian, by the way. The visitor from outer space made a serious study of **Christianity**, to learn, if he could, why **Christians** found it so easy to be cruel.

(*WFG* Yes, We Have No Nirvanas) He suggested that Jesus might have been onto something like Transcendental Meditation, but that it was garbled and lost by his followers. A few moments later he said that Jesus and the early **Christian** saints had mistakenly allowed their minds to wander. "You must have control," he said. The wandering minds of Jesus and the saints had led to what Maharishi called "an absurdity," an emphasis on faith.

(*JB* 2) My late wife Ruth, the grandmother of these children, was born in Vienna. Her family owned a rare-book store there before the Nazis took it away from them. . . . She herself was hidden by a **Christian** family, but was discovered and arrested, along with the head of that family, in Nineteen-hundred and Forty-two.

(*JB* 4) This is it: "Depart from me, you cursed, into the eternal fire prepared for the devil and his Angels" (*Emil Larkin quotes Matthew 25:41*).

These words appalled me then, and they appall me now. They are surely the inspiration for the notorious cruelty of **Christians**.

(*PS* Mark Twain) "I now quote a previous owner of this house: 'When I find a well-drawn character in fiction or biography, I generally take a warm personal interest in him, for the reason that I have known him before—met him on the river.'

"I submit to you that this is a profoundly **Christian** statement, an echo of the Beatitudes. It is constructed, as many jokes are, incidentally, with a disarmingly pedestrian beginning and an unexpectedly provoking conclusion."

(*PS* Religion) "I have spoken of the long tradition of religious skepticism in my family. One of my two daughters has recently turned her back on all that. Living alone and far from home, she has memorized an arbitrary **Christian** creed, Trinitarianism, by chance. She now has her human dignity regularly confirmed by the friendly nods of a congregation. I am glad that she is not so lonely anymore. This is more than all right with me.

"She believes that Jesus was the Son of God, or perhaps God Himself—or however that goes. I have had even more trouble with the Trinity than I had with college algebra. I refer those who are curious about it to what is known about the Council of Nicea, which took place in anno Domini 325. It was there that the Trinity was hammered into its present shape. Unfortunately, the minutes have been lost. It is known that the emperor Constantine was there, and probably spoke a good deal. He gave us the first **Christian** army. He may have given us the Holy Ghost as well.

No matter. I do not argue with my **Christian** daughter about religion at all. Why should I?

(*PS* Children) My first wife and both my daughters are born-again, **Christians** now—working white magic through rituals and prayers. That's all right. I would be a fool to say that the Free Thinker ideas of Clemens Vonnegut remain as enchanting and encouraging as ever—not after the mortal poisoning of the planet, not after two world wars, with more to come.

(*PS* Jonathan Swift Misperceived) His motives were invariably serious, however, and I now suggest that *Gulliver's Travels* can be read as a series of highly responsible sermons, delivered during a crisis in **Christian** attitudes, one that is far from over yet. The crisis is this, in my opinion: It simply will not do for adult **Christians** to think of themselves as God's little lambs anymore.

(*HP* 15) So I happened to sit in on a class where he talked about Hitler's being a devout Roman Catholic. He said something I hadn't realized before, something I have since discovered most **Christians** don't want to hear: that the Nazi swastika was intended to be a version of a **Christian** cross, a cross made out of axes. Stern said that **Christians** had gone to a lot of trouble denying that the swastika was just another cross, saying it was a primitive symbol from the primordial ooze of the pagan past.

(*FWD* V) "It seems to me now that Algren's pessimism about so much of earthly life was **Christian**. Like Christ, as we know Him from the Bible, he was enchanted by the hopeless, could not take his eyes off them, and could see little good news for them in the future, given what they had become and what Caesar was like and so on, unless beyond death there awaited something more humane."

(*FWD* VII) When I was new at such discussions I insouciantly asked a fundamentalist **Christian** opponent ("Oh, come on now, Reverend") if he knew of anyone who had been ruined by a book. (Mark Twain claimed to have been ruined by salacious parts of the Bible.)

. . . The books he and his supporters wanted out of the schools, one of mine among them, were not pornographic, although he would have liked our audience to think so. (There is the word "motherfucker" one time in my *Slaughterhouse-Five*, as in "Get out of the road, you dumb motherfucker." Ever since that word was published, way back in 1969, children have been attempting to have intercourse with their mothers. When it will stop no one knows.) The fault of *Slaughterhouse-Five*, James Dickey's *Deliverance*, J. D. Salinger's *Catcher in the Rye*, several books by Judy Blume, and so on, as far as the Reverend was concerned, was that neither their authors nor their characters exemplified his notion of ideal **Christian** behavior and attitudes.

(*FWD* VIII) The first story of mine which got into trouble with the sincerely **Christian** far right was about time-travelers who went back to Bible times and discovered that Jesus Christ was five feet, two inches tall. I think I liked Jesus more than the story's naysayers did, since I was asserting that I didn't care how tall or short He was.

(*FWD* XVI) "I was an Infantry Private during World War II and fought against the Germans in Europe. My religion as well as my blood type was stamped into my dogtags. The Army decided my religion was P, for 'Protestant.' There is no room on dogtags for footnotes and a bibliography. In retrospect, I think they should have put S on my dogtags, for 'Saracen,' since we were fighting **Christians** who were on some sort of utterly insane Crusade. They had crosses on their flags and uniforms and all over their killing machines, just like the soldiers of the first **Christian** Emperor Constantine. And they lost, of course, which has to be acknowledged as quite a setback for **Christianity**."

(*FWD* XVI) The **Christian** quick trip from love to hate and murder is our principal entertainment. We might call it 'Christianity Fails Again,' and how satisfying so many of us have been trained to find it when it fails and fails.

(*FWD* XVI) And should any **Christian** be sorry that we killed Qaddafi's baby daughter? Well—Jerry Falwell should speak to this issue, since he knows all the verses in the Bible which make murder acceptable. My own theory is that the little girl, by allowing herself to be adopted by a dark-skinned Muslim absolutely nobody watching American television could love, in effect committed suicide.

(*TQ* 7) I told Trout that Peter Lieber's Anglo-American company commander gave his men, all Freethinkers from Germany, **Christian** religious tracts for inspiration. Trout responded by giving his own revision of the Book of Genesis.

Fortunately, I had a tape recorder, which I turned on.

(*TQ* 18) The only people next door, actually, of course, were Monica and Zoltan Pepper, and the threeman day shift of armed guards, headed by Dudley Prince. Monica had given her office and janitorial staffs the day off for last-minute Christmas shopping. As it happened, they were all **Christian** or agnostic or apostate.

The night shift of armed guards would be entirely Muslim. As Trout would write at Xanadu, in *My Ten Years on Automatic Pilot*: "Muslims do not believe in Santa Claus."

(*TQ* 37) Trout himself, as I've said, was neverthe-less espousing free will when he entered the Acad-emy, and was invoking the **Judeo-Christian** deity as well: "Wake up! For God's sake, wake up, wake up! Free will! Free will!"

(*TQ* 50) I of course understand that the widespread revulsion inspired even now, and perhaps forever, by the word Communism is a sane response to the cruelties and stupidities of the dictators of the USSR, who called themselves, hey presto, Com-munists, just as Hitler called himself, hey presto, a **Christian**.

(*GBK* Introduction) About belief or lack of belief in an afterlife: Some of you may know I am neither **Christian** nor Jewish nor Buddhist, nor a conven-tionally religious person of any sort. I am a human-ist, which means, in part, that I have tried to behave decently without any expectation of rewards or punishments after I'm dead. My German-American ancestors, the earliest of whom settled in our Mid-dle West about the time of our Civil War, called themselves "Freethinkers," which is the same sort of thing. My great grandfather Clemens Vonnegut wrote, for example, "If what Jesus said was good, what can it matter whether he was God or not?"

(*GBK* Adolf Hitler) "I paid my dues along with ev-erybody else," he said. It is his hope that a modest monument, possibly a stone cross, since he was a **Christian**, will be erected somewhere in his mem-ory, possibly on the grounds of the United Nations headquarters in New York. It should be incised, he said, with his name and dates 1889–1945. Under-neath should be a two-word sentence in German: "Entschuldigen Sie." Roughly translated into En-glish, this comes out, "I Beg Your Pardon," or "Ex-cuse Me."

(*GBK* Kilgore Trout) As is now the case with Myco-bacterium tuberculosis, there is a new strain of the ethnic-cleansing bacterium that makes conceivable remedies of the past seem pathetic or even absurd. In every case nowadays: Too late! The victims are practically all dead or homeless by the time they are first mentioned on the six o'clock news.

All that good people can do about the disease of ethnic cleansing, now always a fait accompli, is to rescue the survivors. And watch out for **Christians**! (*MWC* 2) "Socialism" is no more an evil word than "**Christianity**." Socialism no more prescribed Jo-

seph Stalin and his secret police and shuttered churches than **Christianity** prescribed the Spanish Inquisition. **Christianity** and socialism alike, in fact, prescribe a society dedicated to the proposi-tion that all men, women, and children are created equal and shall not starve.

(*MWC* 2) Hitler's swastika wasn't a pagan symbol, as so many people believe. It was a working person's **Christian** cross, made of axes, of tools.

(*MWC* 8) Like my distinct betters Einstein and Twain, I now give up on people, too. I am a veteran of the Second World War and I have to say this is not the first time I have surrendered to a pitiless war machine.

My last words? "Life is no way to treat an animal, not even a mouse."

Napalm came from Harvard. Veritas!

Our president is a **Christian**? So was Adolf Hitler.

What can be said to our young people, now that psychopathic personalities, which is to say persons without consciences, without senses of pity or shame, have taken all the money in the treasuries of our government and corporations, and made it all their own?

(*MWC* 9) For some reason, the most vocal **Chris-tians** among us never mention the Beatitudes. But, often with tears in their eyes, they demand that the Ten Commandments be posted in public build-ings. And of course that's Moses, not Jesus. I haven't heard one of them demand that the Sermon on the Mount, the Beatitudes, be posted anywhere.

"Blessed are the merciful" in a courtroom? "Blessed are the peacemakers" in the Pentagon? Give me a break!

(*MWC* 9) I was once asked if I had any ideas for a really scary reality TV show. I have one reality show that would really make your hair stand on end: "C-Students from Yale."

George W. Bush has gathered around him upper-crust C-students who know no history or ge-ography, plus not-so-closeted white supremacists, aka **Christians**, and plus, most frighteningly, psy-chopathic personalities, or PPs, the medical term for smart, personable people who have no con-sciences.

To say somebody is a PP is to make a perfectly respectable diagnosis, like saying he or she has appendicitis or athlete's foot. The classic medical text on PPs is *The Mask of Sanity* by Dr. Hervey Cleckley, a clinical professor of psychiatry at the Medical College of Georgia, and published in 1941. Read it!

(*MWC* 10) Well, one wishes that those who took over our federal government, and hence the world, by means of a Mickey Mouse coup d'état, who disconnected all the burglar alarms prescribed by the Constitution, which is to say the House and Senate, and the Supreme Court, and We, the People, were truly **Christian**. But as William Shakespeare told us long ago, "The devil can cite Scripture for his purpose."

See also: PP I; XXIII; *MN* 12–14; 27; 31; *CC* 32; 43; 61–62; 65; 96–97; 102; *GBR* 1; 11; *MH* Welcome to the Monkey House; *MH* Miss Temptation; *MH* More Stately Mansions; *BC* 19; 22; *WFG* Yes, We Have No Nirvanas; *WFG* Biafra: A People Betrayed; *WFG* Address to the National Institute of Arts and Letters, 1971; *Slap* 4; 24; 41; *JB* 7; 15; *PS* Roots; *PS* Religion; *PS* Jekyll and Hyde Updated; *PS* The Sexual Revolution; *PS* In the Capital of the World; *DD* 20–21; *Blue* 27; 30; *HP* 11; 15; 31; *FWD* VII; XVI–XVII; *TQ* 17.

Christianity. (*SL5* 1) History in her solemn page informs us that the crusaders were but ignorant and savage men, that their motives were those of bigotry unmitigated, and that their pathway was one of blood and tears. Romance, on the other hand, dilates upon their piety and heroism, and portrays, in her most glowing and impassioned hues, their virtue and magnanimity, the imperishable honor they acquired for themselves, and the great services they rendered to **Christianity**. *(Vonnegut quotes Charles Mackay's* Extraordinary Popular Delusions and the Madness of Crowds.)

(*SL5* 2) He *(Roland Weary)* dilated upon the piety and heroism of "The Three Musketeers," portrayed, in the most glowing and impassioned hues, virtue and magnanimity, the imperishable honor they acquired for themselves and the great services they rendered to **Christianity**.

(*SL5* 5) . . . *The Gospel from Outer Space*, by Kilgore Trout. It was about a visitor from outer space, shaped very much like a Tralfamadorian, by the way. The visitor from outer space made a seri-

ous study of **Christianity** to learn, if he could, why Christians found it so easy to be cruel. He concluded that at least part of the trouble was slipshod storytelling in the New Testament. He supposed that the intent of the Gospels was to teach people, among other things, to be merciful, even to the lowest of the low.

(*WFG Playboy* Interview) VONNEGUT: But as far as improving the human condition goes, our minds are certainly up to that. That's what they were designed to do. And we do have the freedom to make up comforting lies. But we don't do enough of it. One of my favorite ministers was a guy named Bob Nicholson. . . . Every time one of his parishioners died, he went all to pieces. He was outraged by death. So it was up to his congregation and the relatives of the deceased to patch him up, get him pumped up on **Christianity** sufficiently to get through the funeral service. I liked that very much: Nothing he was going to say in the standard Episcopalian funeral oration was going to satisfy him. He needed better lies.

(*WFG Playboy* Interview) PLAYBOY: This longing for community may explain, at least in part, the Jesus-freak movement among young people. But why do you think they're attracted to fundamentalist **Christianity**?

VONNEGUT: Well, the choice of a core for an artificial extended family is fairly arbitrary. I've already mentioned the arts and jism and blood and spaghetti. **Christianity** is equally commonplace and harmless, and therefore good. Do you know what nucleation is? I don't, but I'll pretend I do. It has to do with how big something has to be in order to grow rather than die out. The standard example is starting a fire in a coal furnace. If the fire you start is below a certain size, it will go out. If it's larger than that, it will spread until all the fuel is on fire. Clumps of cancer cells are probably forming in us all the time and petering out—because the clumps are below a certain size. In America, it's easy to form a large clump of people who know something about **Christianity**, since there has always been so much talk about **Christianity** around. It wouldn't be easy to get a large clump of Zoroastrians, for instance. But there are very big clumps of **Christianity**. There are very big clumps of race hatred. It's easy to make either one of them grow, especially in a society as lonesome as this one is. All kinds of clumps.

PLAYBOY: So you don't admire **Christianity** any more or less than, say, a communal bowl of spaghetti every evening? Or anything else that might hold an extended family together?

VONNEGUT: I admire **Christianity** more than anything—**Christianity** as symbolized by gentle people sharing a common bowl.

(*WFG Playboy* Interview) PLAYBOY: Do you have any suggestions on how to put together healthier extended families than (*Charles*) Manson's?

VONNEGUT: Sure. Put **Christianity** or spaghetti instead of murder at their core. I recommend this for countries, too.

(*PS* Religion) "What makes me think we need a new religion? That's easy. An effective religion allows people to imagine from moment to moment what is going on and how they should behave. **Christianity** used to be like that. Our country is now jammed with human beings who say out loud that life is chaos to them, and that it doesn't seem to matter what anybody does next. This is worse than being seasick."

(*Blue* 2) Armenians, incidentally, were the first people to make **Christianity** their national religion.

(*Blue* 24) Slazinger, high as a kite, says that every successful revolution, including Abstract Expressionism, the one I took part in, had that cast of characters at the top—Pollock being the genius in our case, Lenin being the one in Russia's, Christ being the one in **Christianity's**.

(*FWD* VII) So the Reverend was not a hypocrite. He was perfectly willing to say in so many words that there was nothing sacred about the First Amendment, and that many images and ideas other than pornography should be taken out of circulation by the police, and that the official religion of the whole country should be his sort of **Christianity**. He was sincere in believing that my *Slaughterhouse-Five* might somehow cause a person to wind up in a furnace for all eternity (see the mass promulgated by Pope St. Pius V), which would be even worse (if you consider its duration) than being raped, murdered and then mutilated by a man maddened by dirty pictures.

(*FWD* XIV) Further on in the preface I went after American Eastern Seaboard prep schools again. (I am bughouse on that subject.) I said that those schools were clones of British prep schools, and that their idea of character was the so-called "**muscular Christianity**" exhibited by aristocratic imperialists in the time of Queen Victoria. (Those old-timers sure knew how to deal with monkeys without tails.) And then along comes *Masterpiece Theatre* on so-called "Public Television," dramatizing stories about the beauty and charm and wittiness not only of British imperialism but of the British class system as well. The British class system is as subversive of what the United States once hoped to be and might have been and should have been as *Das Kapital* or *Mein Kampf*. (Why is it, do you suppose, that the lower social orders don't watch more Public TV?)

(*FWD* XVI) "I was an Infantry Private during World War II and fought against the Germans in Europe. My religion as well as my blood type was stamped into my dogtags. The Army decided my religion was P 'Protestant.' There is no room on dogtags for footnotes and a bibliography. In retrospect, I think they should have put S on my dogtags, for 'Saracen,' since we were fighting Christians who were on some sort of utterly insane Crusade. They had crosses on their flags and uniforms and all over their killing machines, just like the soldiers of the first Christian Emperor Constantine. And they lost, of course, which has to be acknowledged as quite a setback for **Christianity**."

(*FWD* XVI) "So there you have my scheme for making **Christianity**, which has killed so many people so horribly, a little less homicidal: substituting the word 'respect' for the word 'love.' And as I said, I have been in actual battle with people who had crosses all over themselves. They were sure no fun.

"I have little hope that my simple reform will attract any appreciable support during my lifetime, anyway, or in the lifetimes of my children. The Christian quick trip from love to hate and murder is our principal entertainment. We might call it '**Christianity** Fails Again,' and how satisfying so many of us have been trained to find it when it fails and fails.

"In America it takes the form of the cowboy story. A goodhearted, innocent young man rides into town, with friendly intentions toward one and all. Never mind that he happens to be wearing a loaded Colt .44 on either hip. The last thing he wants is trouble. But before he knows it, this loving man is face to face with another man, who is so unlovable that he has absolutely no choice but to shoot him. **Christianity Fails Again**."

(*FWD XVI*) "Very early British versions are tales of the quests of the **Christian** knights of King Arthur's Camelot. Like Hermann Göring, they have crosses all over them. They ride out into the countryside to help the weak, an admirably **Christian** activity. They are certainly not looking for trouble."

Never mind that they are iron Christmas trees decorated with the latest in weaponry. And before they know it, they are face to face with other knights so unlovable that they have absolutely no choice but to chop them up as though they were sides of beef in a butcher shop. **Christianity Fails Again**. What fun! And I point out to you that there was an implied promise that our own government would entertain us with failures of **Christianity** when John F. Kennedy allowed his brief Presidency to be called Camelot.

(*FWD XVI*) "You are like them, as I have already said, in that you live in a time when killing is a leading entertainment form. According to the American Academy of Pediatrics, the average American child watches 18,000 TV murders before it graduates from high school. That kid has seen **Christianity** fail with pistols and rifles and shotguns and machine guns. It has seen **Christianity** fail with guillotines and gallows and electric chairs and gas chambers. That youngster has seen **Christianity** fail with fighter planes and bombers and tanks and battleships and submarines—with hatchets and clubs and chain saws and butcher knives.

(*FWD XVI*) "How tragic it is, then, that the major impulses in this and several other societies nowadays should be in the direction of the pure baloney and cruel entertainments of thousands of years ago, which almost inevitably lead to the antithesis of beauty and the good life and **Christianity** as taught by Jesus Christ, which is war."

(*FWD XVII*) (The photograph at the head of this chapter shows me in action in Mozambique, demonstrating **muscular Christianity** in an outfit that might have been designed by Ralph Lauren. The aborigines didn't know whether to shit or go blind until I showed up. And then I fixed everything.)

(*FWD My Reply to a Letter*) As for the preaching of formal **Christianity**, I am all for it.

(*MWC 2*) "Socialism" is no more an evil word than "**Christianity**." Socialism no more prescribed Joseph Stalin and his secret police and shuttered churches than **Christianity** prescribed the Spanish Inquisition. **Christianity** and socialism alike, in fact, prescribe a society dedicated to the proposition that all men, women, and children are created equal and shall not starve.

See also: CC 96; BC 119; JB 15; PS 20; 22; PS Religion; PS The Sexual Revolution; HP; FWD XV–XVI.

Chrono. *The son of Beatrice Rumfoord and Malachi Constant, Chrono is born on Mars and lives his first eight years there. Named for one of the twenty-one months in the Martian calendar, Chrono picks up a piece of scrap metal at one of the manufacturing plants on Mars, and this becomes the long awaited spare part for the Tralfamadorian messenger, Salo.*

Chrono is the best German batball player at school and is feared by the other children. He and his mother are diverted from the main part of the Martian invasion and crash-land in the Amazon Rain Forest. They are the only two survivors of the crash and are initiated into the Gumbo tribe. (ST 10) During the initiation, mother and son had been staked at the ends of tethers in the middle of the village, with **Chrono** representing the Sun and Bee representing the Moon, as the Sun and the Moon were understood by the Gumbo people.

As a result of their experiences, Bee and **Chrono** were closer than most mothers and sons.

Chrono lives out his life as the sole human being on Titan and eventually joins and gains acceptance by the Titanic bluebirds. (ST Epilogue) At the age of seventeen, young **Chrono** had run away from his palatial home to join the Titanic bluebirds, the most admirable creatures on Titan. **Chrono** now lived among their nests by the Kazak pools. He wore their feathers and sat on their eggs and shared their food and spoke their language.

chrono-synclastic infundibula. *Vonnegut's cosmogonic theory that all things are as they once were and will be as they have always been: that all is bal-*

anced as it always will be. He wrote about this perception in his opening comments to Happy Birthday, Wanda June. *(WJ About This Play)* "This intolerable balancing of characters and arguments reflected my true feelings: I felt and I still feel that everybody is right, no matter what he says. I had, in fact, written a book about everybody's being right all the time, *The Sirens of Titan*. And I gave a name in that book to a mathematical point where all opinions, no matter how contradictory, harmonized. I called it a *chrono-synclastic infundibulum*.

"I live in one."

The primary use of the chrono-synclastic infundibulum occurs in The Sirens of Titan. *(ST 1)* CHRONO-SYNCLASTIC INFUNDIBULA— Just imagine that your Daddy is the smartest man who ever lived on Earth, and he knows everything there is to find out, and he is exactly right about everything, and he can prove he is right about everything. Now imagine another little child on some nice world a million light years away, and that little child's Daddy is the smartest man who ever lived on that nice world so far away.

And he is just as smart and just as right as your Daddy is. Both Daddies are smart, and both Daddies are right.

Only if they ever met each other they would get into a terrible argument, because they wouldn't agree on anything. Now, you can say that your Daddy is right and the other little child's Daddy is wrong, but the Universe is an awfully big place. There is room enough for an awful lot of people to be right about things and still not agree.

The reason both Daddies can be right and still get into terrible fights is because there are so many different ways of being right. There are places in the Universe, though, where each Daddy could finally catch on to what the other Daddy was talking about. These places are where all the different kinds of truths fit together as nicely as the parts in your Daddy's solar watch. We call these places **chrono-synclastic infundibula**.

The Solar System seems to be full of **chrono-synclastic infundibula**.

There is one great big one we are sure of that likes to stay between Earth and Mars. We know about that one because an Earth man and his Earth dog ran right into it.

You might think it would be nice to go to a **chrono-synclastic infundibulum** and see all the different ways to be absolutely right, but it is a very dangerous thing to do. The poor man and his poor dog are scattered far and wide, not just through space, but through time, too.

Chrono (kroh-no) means time. **Synclastic** (sin-class-tick) means curved toward the same side in all directions, like the skin of an orange. **Infundibulum** (infun-dib-u-lum) is what the ancient Romans like Julius Caesar and Nero called a funnel. If you don't know what a funnel is, get Mommy to show you one.

Because of the revelation of eternal and recurring circumstances, The discovery of the **chrono-synclastic infundibula** said to mankind in effect: "What makes you think you're going anywhere?" *(ST 1) Winston Niles Rumfoord and his dog Kazak travel through time and space by riding the wave of the chrono-synclastic infundibulum.*

In the short story "The Big Space Fuck," reprinted in Palm Sunday, *the plan is to aim the sperm-loaded spaceship Arthur C. Clarke directly into one of the eighty-seven known chrono-synclastic infundibulae ensuring* "the ship and its load would be multiplied a trillion times, and would appear everywhere throughout space and time.

"If there's any fecundity anywhere in the Universe," the scientist promised, "our seed will find it and bloom" *(PS Obscenity).*

Chrysler Building. *The home of RAMJAC's American Harp Company (top floor) in* Jailbird.

In Galápagos, *Bobby King, mastermind of The Nature Cruise of the Century, moved into new offices within the hollow crown of the Chrysler Building, formerly the showroom of a harp company which found itself bankrupt (Gal 1:17).*

In Bluebeard, *Rabo Karabekian considers it the most beautiful skyscraper in the world (Blue 23). Karabekian's feelings for the Chrysler Building reflect Vonnegut's personal assessment as he reveals in* Fates Worse Than Death. *(FWD Preface)* Q: What is your favorite building?
A: The **Chrysler Building** in Manhattan.

Chung, Lowell. *(HP 9)* The most successful athlete ever to come from Tarkington, arguably, was a horseman from my own time, **Lowell Chung**. He won a Bronze Medal as a member of the United States Equestrian Team in Seoul, South Korea, back in 1988. *Chung graduates with an Associate of Arts degree in 1984.*

Chung, Mrs. *In* Hocus Pocus, *Lowell's mother, a member of Tarkington's Board of Trustees and described by Eugene Debs Hartke as owning half of Honolulu without being able to read, write or do math. She speaks only Chinese and uses John W. Fedders, Jr., another Tarkington Trustee, as her interpreter for college meetings. She dies of tetanus, having never been inoculated against it in her home in China.*

Church of God the Utterly Indifferent. *Founded and presided over by Winston Niles Rumfoord in the days following the failed Martian invasion, the church has over three billion followers worldwide. Predicated on Rumfoord's knowledge of the chronosynclastic infundibulum and on the Tralfamadorians' manipulation of earth history via the Universal Will to Become,* "To us of the **Church of God the Utterly Indifferent**, there is nothing more cruel, more dangerous, more blasphemous that a man can do than to believe that—that luck, good or bad, is the hand of God!" (ST 11) *Members of the church are made to wear bags of buckshot and other handicapping devices to enforce equality, a device Vonnegut previously used in the short story "Harrison Bergeron," reprinted in* Welcome to the Monkey House *(1968).*

Church of Jesus Christ the Kidnapped. *(Slap 38)* "... a tiny cult in Chicago, but destined to become the most popular American religion of all time."

In a leaflet about the new sect, Wilbur Swain reads the following: At the very top of the leaflet was a primitive picture of Jesus, standing with His Body facing forward, but with His face in profile—like a one-eyed jack in a deck of playing cards.

He was gagged. He was handcuffed. One ankle was shackled and chained to a ring fixed to the floor. There was a single perfect tear dangling from the lower lid of His Eye.
QUESTION: What is your name?
ANSWER: I am the Right Reverend William Ura-

nium-8 Wainwright, Founder of the **Church of Jesus Christ the Kidnapped** at 3972 Ellis Avenue, Chicago, Illinois.
QUESTION: When will God send us His Son again?
ANSWER: He already has. Jesus is here among us.
QUESTION: Why haven't we seen or heard anything about Him?
ANSWER: He has been kidnapped by the Forces of Evil.
QUESTION: What must we do?
ANSWER: We must drop whatever we are doing, and spend every waking hour in trying to find Him. If we do not, God will exercise His Option.
QUESTION: What is God's Option?
ANSWER: He can destroy Mankind so easily, any time he chooses to (*Slap* 38).

Upon Wilbur's return to the Empire State Building, he sees a painting of Jesus Christ the Kidnapped in the lobby.

Churchill, Winston. *The British wartime prime minister serves as an exemplar for Eugene Debs Hartke as proof that even those in supremely responsible positions sometimes behave in seemingly irresponsible ways. Hartke does this as a way of defending his own high school behavior, which included smoking marijuana when he should have been paying attention to more important matters.* (HP 4) I make no apologies for having been zapped during my darkest days in high school. **Winston Churchill** was bombed out of his skull on brandy and Cuban cigars during the darkest days of World War II.

Eugene Debs Hartke later invokes Churchill as being one of the many people who regularly walks around with one drug habit or another. (HP 12) When you dare to think about how huge the illegal drug business is in this country, you have to suspect that practically everybody has a steady buzz on, just as I did during my last 2 years in high school, and just as General Grant did during the Civil War, and just as **Winston Churchill** did during World War II.

Cincinnati Bengals. *In* Bluebeard *Rabo Karabekian owns one-quarter share of the Cincinnati Bengals, an inheritance from his wife, Edith.*

Cinderella. *"Cinderella" is an important image as well as concept for Vonnegut. Upon arrival at the POW camp, Billy Pilgrim and the other newly captured Americans are treated to a roughhouse performance of the play by British POWs. When midnight strikes in the play and Cinderella exclaims, "Goodness me, the clock has struck— / Alackday, and fuck my luck," Billy falls into hysterics and is led from the barracks to a hospital where he is shot up with morphine (SL5 5).*

Edgar Derby cares for Billy in the hospital. Paul Lazzaro joins them when knocked unconscious by the Blue Fairy Godmother of the play. As a result, they are the only three Americans not included in dividing the camp's provisions among the allied prisoners. Consequently, they are forced to sleep on the stage, and it is there Billy finds Cinderella's slippers and appropriates them for himself. (SL5 6) **Cinderella's** slippers, which were airman's boots painted silver, were capsized side by side under a golden throne. . . . Billy, curled in his azure nest, found himself staring at **Cinderella's** silver boots under a throne. . . . And then he remembered that his shoes were ruined, that he *needed* boots. He hated to get out of his nest, but he forced himself to do it. He crawled to the boots on all fours, sat, tried them on.

The boots fit perfectly. Billy Pilgrim was **Cinderella**, and **Cinderella** was Billy Pilgrim.

In Breakfast of Champions, *Vonnegut again creates a Cinderella of sorts when Patty Keene senses that Dwayne Hoover could be her Blue Fairy Godmother because he could solve all her money worries. She lives under the burden of paying for her father's medical bills as he dies of cancer (BC 15).*

Celia Hildreth is sarcastically characterized as another incarnation of Cinderella when Felix Waltz asks her to the prom, only to be later victimized by the antics of Otto Waltz. (DD 6) But miracles do happen. A new **Cinderella** *is born every minute. One of the richest, cutest boys in town, and the president of the senior class, no less, invited her to the senior prom.*

Overriding the relative importance of these references within his fiction is Vonnegut's appreciation of Cinderella's narrative structure. In his "Self-Interview" reprinted in Palm Sunday, *Vonnegut defends simple plots like Cinderella's by saying, "I guarantee you that no modern story scheme, even plotlessness, will give a reader genuine satisfaction, unless one of those old fashioned plots is smuggled in somewhere. I don't praise plots as accurate representations of life, but as ways to keep readers reading. . . . When you exclude plot, when you exclude anyone's wanting anything, you exclude the reader, which is a mean-spirited thing to do" (PS 5). This is a later reflection of Vonnegut's rejected master's thesis in anthropology at the University of Chicago.*

In "The Sexual Revolution," also reprinted in Palm Sunday, *Vonnegut recounts his graphical appreciation of the tale with other similar tales. (PS 18) But then I had another look at a graph I had drawn of Western civilization's most enthusiastically received story, which is "* **Cinderella** *." At this very moment, a thousand writers must be telling that story again in one form or another. This very book is a* **Cinderella** *story of a kind.*

I confessed that I was daunted by the graph of "**Cinderella**," and was tempted to leave it out of my thesis, since it seemed to prove that I was full of shit. It seemed too complicated and arbitrary to be a representative artifact—lacked the simple grace of a pot or a spearhead. . . .

The steps, you see, are all the presents the fairy godmother gave to **Cinderella**, the ball gown, the slippers, the carriage, and so on. The sudden drop is the stroke of midnight at the ball. **Cinderella** is in rags again. All the presents have been repossessed. But then the prince finds her and marries her, and she is infinitely happy ever after. She gets all the stuff back, and *then* some. A lot of people think the story is trash, and, on graph paper, it certainly looks like trash.

But then I said to myself, Wait a minute—those steps at the beginning look like the creation myth of virtually every society on earth. And then I saw that the stroke of midnight looked exactly like the unique creation myth in the Old Testament. And then I saw that the rise to bliss at the end was identical with the expectation of redemption as expressed in primitive Christianity.

The tales were identical.

I was thrilled to discover that years ago, and I am just as thrilled today.

The apathy of the University of Chicago is repulsive to me.

They can take a flying fuck at the mooooooo-ooooooooon.

(*TQ* 10) The minds of children in intellectually humble American homes back then weren't swamped with countless stories from TV sets. They heard or read only a few stories, and so could remember them, and maybe learn something from them. Everywhere in the English-speaking world, one of those was "**Cinderella**." Another was "The Ugly Duckling." Another was the story of Robin Hood.

And another, as disrespectful of established authority as the story of Robin Hood, which "**Cinderella**" and "The Ugly Duckling" are not, is the life of Jesus Christ as described in the New Testament.

(*BAG* Unpaid Consultant) "I feel like **Cinderella**," said Celeste. "One day, Harry and I were struggling along on his pay from Joe's Greasing Palace, and the next day, everything I touched seemed to turn to gold."

(*BAG* A Night for Love) About twenty minutes after that, the telephones in both houses rang. The burden of the messages was that Charlie Reinbeck and Nancy Whitman were fine. They had, however, put their own interpretation on the moonlight. They'd decided that **Cinderella** and Prince Charming had as good a chance as anybody for really living happily ever after. So they'd married.

(*MWC* 3) Now there's a Franz Kafka story [begins line D towards bottom of G-I axis]. A young man is rather unattractive and not very personable. He has disagreeable relatives and has had a lot of jobs with no chance of promotion. He doesn't get paid enough to take his girl dancing or to go to the beer hall to have a beer with a friend. One morning he wakes up, it's time to go to work again, and he has turned into a cockroach [draws line downward and then infinity symbol]. It's a pessimistic story. (*Opposing page has graph of good and ill fortune and Cinderella.*)

(*MWC* 3) The question is, does this system I've devised help us in the evaluation of literature? Perhaps a real masterpiece cannot be crucified on a cross of this design. How about *Hamlet*? It's a pretty good piece of work I'd say. Is anybody going to argue that it isn't? I don't have to draw a new line, because Hamlet's situation is the same as **Cinderella**'s, except that the sexes are reversed.

His father has just died. He's despondent. And right away his mother went and married his uncle, who's a bastard. So Hamlet is going along on the same level as **Cinderella** when his friend Horatio comes up to him and says . . .

(*MWC* 3) Neither good news nor bad news. Hamlet didn't get arrested. He's prince. He can kill anybody he wants. So he goes along, and finally he gets in a duel, and he's killed. Well, did he go to heaven or did he go to hell? Quite a difference. **Cinderella** or Kafka's cockroach? I don't think Shakespeare believed in a heaven or hell any more than I do. And so we don't know whether it's good news or bad news.

civic, civic managers, civics, junior civics. (*PP* IX) The **civic managers** were the career administrators who ran the city. They lived on the same side of the river as the managers and engineers of the Ilium Works, but the contact between the two groups was little more than perfunctory and, traditionally, suspicious. The schism, like so many things, dated back to the war, when the economy had, for efficiency's sake, become monolithic.

(*WFG Playboy* Interview) PLAYBOY: Do you consider yourself a radical in any sense?

VONNEGUT: No, because everything I believe I was taught in **junior civics** during the Great Depression at School 43 in Indianapolis, with full approval of the school board. School 43 wasn't a radical school. America was an idealistic, pacifistic nation at that time. I was taught in the sixth grade to be proud that we had a standing Army of just over a hundred thousand men and that the generals had nothing to say about what was done in Washington. I was taught to be proud of that and to pity Europe for having more than a million men under arms and spending all their money on airplanes and tanks. I simply never unlearned **junior civics**. I still believe in it. I got a very good grade.

(*PS* Roots) "Aside from his attachment to his profession, Bernard (*Vonnegut's paternal grandfather*) took little participation in the social or **civic** life of the community."

(*PS* Self-Interview) INTERVIEWER: You just laughed about something.

VONNEGUT: It was something dumb I remembered about high school. It doesn't have anything to do with writing.

INTERVIEWER: You care to share it with us anyway?

VONNEGUT: Oh—I just remembered something that happened in a high school course on **civics**, on how our government worked. The teacher asked each of us to stand up in turn and tell what we did after school . . . a guy name J. T. Alburger . . . kept nudging me, urging me, daring me to tell the truth about what I did after school. He offered me five dollars to tell the truth. He wanted me to stand up and say, "I make model airplanes and jerk off."

(*PS Jekyll and Hyde Updated*) Dr. Jekyll played by JERRY comes out of his house, the image of **civic** decency, and is recognized and adored by all. He is trying to get into his secret lab without being observed. While biding his time, he performs acts of **civic** virtue which are noted and admired by one and all.

(*HP* 39) Every so often, in the midst of chaos, you come across an amazing, inexplicable instance of **civic** responsibility. Maybe the last shred of faith people have is in their firemen.

See also: PP XXXIII; *MN* 41; *MH* Where I Live; *PS* Roots.

Claessen. *Dan Gregory's Belgium canvas supplier. Marilee Kemp regularly sends Rabo Karabekian supplies from Dan Gregory's own stockpile while he is away in San Ignacio. (Blue 7) "No other artist west of the Rockies had such priceless art supplies!"*

Claggett, Noble. *The student of Mary Hepburn's who writes a poem for extra credit about the courtship dance of the blue-footed boobies after viewing a film of their mating rituals. Though later killed in Vietnam, his poem is memorized by Mary and later taught to Mandarax. This is what he had to say about the blue-footed boobies: Of course I love you, / So let's have a kid / Who will say exactly / What its parents did; / "Of course I love you, / So let's have a kid / Who will say exactly / What its parents did; / 'Of course I love you, / So let's have a kid/ Who will say exactly / What its parents did—'" / Et cetera.* **Noble Claggett** (1947–1966) (*Gal* 1:20).

clan. (*WFG* Address to the National Institute of Arts and Letters, 1971) The American Academy of Arts and Letters and the National Institute of Arts

and Letters don't really give a damn for arts and letters, in my opinion. They, too, are chemically-induced efforts to form a superstitious, affectionate **clan** or village or tribe. To them I say this, "Lots of luck, boys and girls."

(*PS* 2) The marriage (*of Edith and Kurt Sr., on November 22, 1913*) was approved by both families; but the Schnull-Vonnegut **clan** was slightly condescending. In the pecking order in the social hierarchy of the community, and particularly in the German group it was generally understood that the Schnull-Vonnegut **clan** ranked ahead of the Lieber-Barus **clan**.

(*PS* Roots) The couple (*Vonnegut's parents, Edith and Kurt Sr.*) were married by the Reverend Frank S. C. Wicks, a Unitarian clergyman, in an evening ceremony in the First Unitarian Church attended by members of the two families—Lieber and Vonnegut—and a bevy of lovely bridesmaids and handsome ushers. But these families in three generations were then numerous and both **clans** had many friends. The Liebers and the Vonneguts with the Hollwegs, Mayers, Severeins, Schnulls, Rauchs, Frenzels, Pantzers, Haueisens, Kipps, Kuhns, Metzgers, and Kothes were the leading German families of the city. . . . And they loved to celebrate weddings, particularly between congenial **clans** of a common heritage and cultural background. The nuptials qualified to be celebrated in accordance with the best German traditions: food, drink, dancing, music, and song.

(*PS* Roots) "In addition to the numerous relatives of the Lieber-Vonnegut **clans** Albert had a host of friends, a rigid selection of whom had to be invited. About six hundred of them came."

(*PS* Religion) "We thought we could do without tribes and **clans**. Well, we can't."

(*FWD* VII) (I had studied anthropology, after all, and so knew in my bones that human beings can't like life very much if they don't belong to a **clan** associated with a specific piece of real estate.)

The Attorney General's Commission on Pornography, a traveling show about dirty books and pictures put on the road during the administration of Ronald Reagan, was something else again. At least a couple of the panel members would later be revealed as having been in the muck of financial or sexual atrocities. There was a **clan** feeling, to be sure, but the family property in this case was the White House, and an amiable, sleepy, absent-minded old movie actor was its totem pole.

Clarke, Arthur C. *Influenced by Olaf Stapledon, Arthur Charles Clarke, author of many seminal science fiction works such as* 2001: A Space Odyssey, Childhood's End, The City and the Stars, The Exploration of Space, *and* Voices from the Sky, *is noted for blending hard science and evolutionary mysticism. Trained in physics and mathematics and twice chairman of the British Interplanetary Society, Clarke's expansive expertise ranges from space flight to underwater research. Vonnegut refers to him in a number of instances and names a space ship in his honor in the short story "The Big Space Fuck."*
(*WFG* Excelsior! We're Going to the Moon! Excelsior!) We have spent something like $33 billion on space so far. We should have spent it on cleaning up our filthy colonies here on earth. There is no urgency whatsoever about getting somewhere in space, much as **Arthur C. Clarke** wants to discover the source of the terrific radio signals coming from Jupiter. It isn't as though we aren't already going somewhere in space. Every passing hour brings the whole solar system 43,000 miles closer to Globular Cluster M13 in Hercules. . . .

Brilliant space enthusiasts like **Arthur C. Clarke** are treasures, of course, to the thousands of persons in the enormously profitable spaceship trade. He speaks more enchantingly than they do. His art and their commercial interests coincide. "The discovery that Jupiter is quite warm and has precisely the type of atmosphere in which life is believed to have arisen on Earth may be the prelude to the most significant biological findings of this century," he wrote recently in *Playboy*.
(*WFG* Excelsior! We're Going to the Moon! Excelsior!) "The Earth is our cradle, which we are about to leave," says **Arthur C. Clarke**. "And the Solar System will be our kindergarten." Most of us will never leave this cradle, of course, unless death turns out to be a form of astronautics.
(*WFG* Excelsior! We're Going to the Moon! Excelsior!) Good science-fiction writers of the present are not necessarily as eager as **Arthur C. Clarke** to found kindergartens on Jupiter, to leave the poor Maine ape and his clam rake far behind.

(*PS* Funnier on Paper Than Most People) "Perhaps you have read the novel *Childhood's End* by **Arthur C. Clarke**, one of the few masterpieces in the field of science fiction. All of the others were written by me. In **Clarke's** novel, mankind suddenly undergoes a spectacular evolutionary change. The children become very different from the parents, less physical, more spiritual—and one day they form up into a sort of column of light which spirals out into the universe, its mission unknown. The book ends there."
(*PS* Obscenity) This was a period of great permissiveness in matters of language, so even the President was saying shit and fuck and so on, without anybody's feeling threatened or taking offense. It was perfectly OK. He called the Space Fuck a Space Fuck and so did everybody else. It was a rocket ship with eight hundred pounds of freeze-dried jizzum in its nose. It was going to be fired at the Andromeda Galaxy, two million light years away. The ship was named the *Arthur C. Clarke*, in honor of a famous space pioneer.
(*PS* Obscenity) "The way I understand it," the sheriff replied, "I'd have to sit there for more than two million years. My old lady might wonder what's become of me." He was a lot smarter than Dwayne. He had jizzum on the *Arthur C. Clarke*, and Dwayne didn't. You had to have an I.Q. of over 115 to have your jizzum accepted.
(*PS* Obscenity) There were at least eighty-seven chrono-synclastic infundibulae, time warps, between Earth and the Andromeda Galaxy. If the *Arthur C. Clarke* passed through any one of them, the ship and its load would be multiplied a trillion times, and would appear everywhere throughout space and time.
(*PS* Obscenity) While all the human beings were in their houses, watching the Big Space Fuck, lampreys were squirming out of the ooze and onto land. Some of them were nearly as long and thick as the *Arthur C. Clarke*.
(*HP* 23) This wasn't **Arthur C. Clarke**, the science fiction writer who wrote all the books about humanity's destiny in other parts of the Universe. This was Arthur K. Clarke, the billionaire speculator and publisher of magazines and books about high finance.
(*HP* 40) Subtract the title of the science fiction

movie based on a novel by **Arthur C. Clarke** *(2001: A Space Odyssey)* which I saw twice in Vietnam. Do not panic. This will give you a negative number, but Arabs in olden times taught us how to deal with such. *This is part of the math riddle Hartke weaves throughout the text to reveal the number of people he knowingly killed in war, which is equal to the number of women with whom he has made love.*

Clarke, Arthur K. *This Arthur Clarke is more like the late Malcolm Forbes, publisher of* Fortune *magazine, than the science fiction novelist.* (HP 23) It was a motorcade of highly successful Americans, most on motorcycles, but some in limousines, led by **Arthur Clarke**, the fun-loving billionaire. He himself was on a motorcycle, and on the saddle behind him, holding on for dear life, her skirt hiked up to her crotch, was Gloria White, the 60-year-old lifelong movie star!
(HP 23) This wasn't Arthur C. Clarke, the science fiction writer who wrote all the books about humanity's destiny in other parts of the Universe. This was **Arthur K. Clarke**, the billionaire speculator and publisher of magazines and books about high finance.
(HP 23) **Arthur K. Clarke** was coming to Tarkington to get an honorary Grand Contributor to the Arts and Sciences Degree.
(HP 23) Everybody knew **Arthur Clarke** was going to get a meaningless certificate. But only Tex Johnson and the campus cops and the Provost had advance warning of the spectacular entrance he planned to make. It was a regular military operation. The motorcycles, and there were about 30 of them, and the balloon had been trucked into the parking lot behind the Black Cat Café at dawn.
(HP 23) **Clarke's** big arrival wasn't a half-bad dress rehearsal for Judgment Day. St. John the Divine in the Bible could only imagine such an absolutely knockout show with noise and smoke and gold and lions and eagles and thrones and celebrities and marvels up in the sky and so on. But **Arthur K. Clarke** had created a real one with modern technology and tons of cash!
(HP 23) **Arthur Clarke**, astride his bike, was looking in my direction. That was because great pals of his on the Board of Trustees were waving to him from the building right behind me. I found myself

deeply offended by his proof that big money could buy big happiness.
(HP 27) I parked the bike in plain view in front of the Black Cat Café, noting several champagne corks on the sidewalk and in the gutter. . . . This was where **Arthur K. Clarke** had formed up his motorcycle gang for its unopposed assault on Tarkington.
(HP 29) **Arthur K. Clarke** had provided everything but water and toilets. So Muriel *(Peck)* had dared to ask some of them who they were and what they did.
(HP 29) So **Arthur K. Clarke**, along with all his other activities, was a whimsical people-collector. He invited people he didn't really know, but who had caught his eye for 1 reason or another, to his parties, and they came, they came.

Claycomb, Judge and Moon. *The Indianapolis judge entertained by Powers Hapgood the morning before Vonnegut meets the famous labor leader at lunch with his Uncle Alex and his father, as recounted in the preface to* Jailbird. *Moon Claycomb was a high school classmate of Vonnegut's. After listening all morning to labor union war stories from Powers Hapgood, Judge Claycomb, enthralled with Hapgood's tales, asked* "why would such a man from such a distinguished family and with such a fine education choose to live as you do?"

"Why?" said Hapgood, according to Hapgood. "Because of the Sermon on the Mount, sir."

And **Moon Claycomb**'s father said this: "Court is adjourned until two P.M." *(JB Prologue) Vonnegut uses this anecdote to explain the significance of the Sermon on the Mount and how it relates to the events at the Cuyahoga Massacre.*

Cleckley, Dr. Hervey. *Vonnegut explores his visceral disgust for George W. Bush by referencing a standard medical text, Dr. Cleckley's* The Mask of Sanity, *explaining psychopathic personalities.*

I was once asked if I had any ideas for a really scary reality TV show. I have one reality show that would really make your hair stand on end: "C-Students from Yale."

George W. Bush has gathered around him upper-crust C-students who know no history or geography, plus not-so-closeted white supremacists, aka Christians, and plus, most frighteningly, psychopathic personalities, or PPs, the medical term for smart, personable people who have no consciences.

To say somebody is a PP is to make a perfectly respectable diagnosis, like saying he or she has appendicitis or athlete's foot. The classic medical text on PPs is *The Mask of Sanity* by **Dr. Hervey Cleckley**, a clinical professor of psychiatry at the Medical College of Georgia, and published in 1941. Read it!

Some people are born deaf, some are born blind or whatever, and this book is about congenitally defective human beings of a sort that is making this whole country and many other parts of the planet go completely haywire nowadays. These were people born without consciences, and suddenly they are taking charge of everything.

PPs are presentable, they know full well the suffering their actions may cause others, but they do not care. They cannot care because they are nuts. They have a screw loose! (MWC 9).

Cleveland Science Fair. *In* Hocus Pocus, *the place of humiliation for Eugene Debs Hartke and his father when the judges quickly determine Eugene's crystal display is the work of his father. However, this is also where Eugene meets Sam Wakefield, who recruits him for West Point and later hires him to teach at Tarkington College.*

Clewes, Dr. Alan. (*HP* 3) The Episcopalian priest, **Dr. Alan Clewes**, a graduate of Harvard, would teach Latin, Greek, Hebrew, and the Bible (*at the Mohiga Valley Free Institute, eventually to become Tarkington College*).
(*HP* 3) One week before the first class was held, which was in Latin, taught by the Episcopalian priest **Alan Clewes**, Andre Lutz the Belgian arrived at the mansion with 3 wagons carrying a very heavy cargo, a carillon consisting of 32 bells.

Clewes, Leland and Sarah (*see also* **Sarah Wyatt**). *Walter Starbuck first meets Leland Clewes as an opponent when the two row crew for Harvard and Yale at the Henley Regatta—Starbuck a coxswain and Clewes a bowman. They meet again years later in adjoining work cubicles at the Department of Agriculture. They become tennis buddies, but their*

friendship halts when Clewes marries Sarah Wyatt. He and Sarah have a daughter (unnamed in the text) three years older than Starbuck's son.

During the heyday of McCarthyism, the then congressman Richard Nixon questions Starbuck for the names of known members of the Communist Party who worked for the U.S. government. (*JB* 4) I named a number of men who were known to have been communists during the Great Depression, but who had proved themselves to be outstanding patriots during World War Two. On that roll of honor I included the name of **Leland Clewes**.

Clewes at first denies having been a Communist and insists on testifying before Congress. (*JB* 4) Two horrible years later **Leland Clewes** was convicted on six counts of perjury. He became one of the first prisoners to serve his sentence in the then new Federal Minimum Security Adult Correctional Facility on the edge of Finletter Air Force Base—thirty-five miles from Atlanta, Georgia.

Clewes and his wife eventually appreciate the positive effects brought out by the prison experience. As they later explain to Starbuck, "**Sarah** and I have often talked about what we would like to say most to you. . . . And it's this:" he said, "'Thank you very much, Walter. My going to prison was the best thing that ever happened to **Sarah** and me.' I'm not joking. Word of honor: It's true."

I was amazed. "How can that be?" I said.

"Because life is supposed to be a test," he said. "If my life had kept going the way it was going, I would have arrived in heaven never having faced any problem that wasn't as easy as pie to solve. Saint Peter would have had to say to me, 'You never lived, my boy. Who can say what you are?'"

"I see," I said.

"**Sarah** and I not only have love," he said, "but we have love that has stood up to the hardest tests" (*JB* 13).

For the wrong Starbuck commits against Clewes and for the magnanimous manner by which he rebounds, Mary Kathleen O'Looney makes Clewes a vice president in the Diamond Match Division of the RAMJAC Corporation.

Before Starbuck is sent back to jail, Leland and Sarah host a going-away party in his honor. (*JB* Epilogue) *They have not moved out of their basement apartment in Tudor City, nor has* **Sarah** *given* up private nursing, although **Leland** is now pulling down about one hundred thousand dollars a year at RAMJAC. Much of their money goes to the Foster Parents Program, a scheme that allows them to support individual children in unfortunate circumstances in many parts of the world. They are supporting fifty children, I think they said. They have letters and photographs from several of them, which they passed around. *He and Clyde Carter buy Walter "Boris," a chess-playing computer, as a going-away gift. Leland and Sarah live in the basement apartment of the same Tudor City building as Starbuck's son.*

Clinton, President. *In* God Bless You, Dr. Kevorkian, *Vonnegut recalls the words of President Clinton to Roberta Gorsuch Burke at the funeral of her husband, Admiral Burke.* (GBK Roberta Gorsuch Burke) **President Clinton** told her at her husband's funeral, when she still had a year to live, "You have blessed America with your service and set an example not only for navy wives today, and to come, but for all Americans."

Clinton Street. *In* Galápagos, *Clinton Street is the main street in Ilium, New York. In* Hocus Pocus, *Clinton Street is the name of the main street in both Scipio and Athena, New York. The name is a common one in New York because of the high esteem held for Governor DeWitt Clinton (1817–1822), a prime political force in the construction of the Erie Canal.*

Clough and Higgins. *The accounting firm for Noel Constant's Magnum Opus Corporation in* The Sirens of Titan.

Clowes, Henry. (DD Preface) This is fiction, not history, so it should not be used as a reference book. I say, for example, that the United States Ambassador to Austria-Hungary at the outbreak of the First World War was **Henry Clowes**, of Ohio. The actual ambassador at that time was Frederic Courtland Penfield of Connecticut.

In 1914 Otto Waltz is trying to gain an art education in Europe and is so taken with the seeming romanticism of German militarism that he asks friends if they could secure him a post in the Hungarian

Life Guard, whose officers' uniforms included a panther skin. . . .

He was summoned by the American Ambassador to the Austro-Hungarian Empire, **Henry Clowes**, who was a Cleveland man and an acquaintance of Father's parents. Father was then twenty-two years old. **Clowes** told Father that he would lose his American citizenship if he joined a foreign army, and that he had made inquiries about Father, and had learned that Father was not the painter he pretended to be, and that Father had been spending money like a drunken sailor, and that he had written to Father's parents, telling them that their son had lost all touch with reality, and that it was time Father was summoned home and given some honest work to do (DD 2).

Clowes informs Otto Waltz that his parents are aware of his waywardness and have threatened to cut him off if he fails to return to Midland City. Waltz returns home.

Club Cybernetics. *In* Player Piano, *Dr. Ewing J. Halyard is in Club Cybernetics when he witnesses what he thinks to be unbecoming behavior on the part of Cornell football coach Doctor Roseberry and other members of the team. Halyard sends his letter to Cornell president Doctor Albert Herpers. Halyard eventually pays for this tattling when he returns to Cornell to make up a missing physical education course.*

Coates, Arnold. *After Rabo Karabekian receives a telegram signed by Dan Gregory (though in actuality surreptitiously sent by Marilee Kemp) to come to New York as his apprentice, Rabo reveals his good luck to Arnold Coates.* (Blue 8) The first person I told about this magnificent opportunity was the old newspaper editor for whom I had been drawing cartoons. His name was **Arnold Coates**, and he said this to me:

"You really are an artist, and you have to get out of here or you'll shrivel up like a raisin. Don't worry about your father. He's a perfectly contented, self-sufficient zombie, if you'll pardon my saying so.

"New York is just going to be a stopover for you," he went on. "Europe is where the real painters are, and always will be."

He was wrong about that.

cocoon. (*ST* 12) The spiral telescoped slightly, making a curtsey. And then it began to revolve around Rumfoord, spinning a continuous **cocoon** of green light. . . .

"All I can say," said Rumfoord from the **cocoon**, "is that I have tried my best to do good for my native Earth while serving the irresistible wishes of Tralfamadore." *This sounds similar to Howard Campbell's "serving good too secretly and evil too openly." The spiral is the chrono-synclastic infundibulum about to take Rumfoord out of the Solar System.*
(*ST* 12) The green **cocoon** left the ground, hovered over the dome. "Remember me as a gentleman of Newport, Earth, and the Solar System," said Rumfoord. He sounded serene again, at peace with himself, and at least equal to any creature that he might encounter anywhere.

"In a punctual way of speaking," came Rumfoord's glottal tenor from the **cocoon**, "good-by."

The **cocoon** and Rumfoord disappeared with a *pft.* . . .

Old Salo came bounding into the courtyard just as Rumfoord and his **cocoon** disappeared. . . .

He looked up at the place where the **cocoon** had hovered.
(*MN* 11) And the thick, bristly, olive-drab **cocoon** I (*Howard Campbell*) had built for myself was frayed a little, was weakened enough to let some pale light in.
(*Gal* 2:1) When young Mary stuck her head out of her **cocoon**, out of her sleeping bag, she saw rotting logs and an undammed stream. . . .

The bird call was coming from a thicket of briars and sumac fifty paces away. She was glad for this alarm clock, for it had been her intention when she went to sleep to awake this early, and to think of her sleeping bag as a **cocoon**, and to emerge from it sinuously and voluptuously, as she was now doing, a vivacious adult.

"Coda to My Career as a Writer for Periodicals." *This final section of* Bagombo Snuff Box *(1999) does not deliver the keys to the kingdom of writing for periodicals as the title suggests. It begins with an explanation that three of the stories are not what they were originally, that the publishers prodded him to significantly revise them before declaring that this collection represents literary fossils. Reread-*ing three of them so upset me, because the premise and the characters of each were so promising, and the denouement so asinine, that I virtually rewrote the denouement before I could stop myself. Some "editing"! They are "The Powder-Blue Dragon," "The Boy Who Hated Girls," and "Hal Irwin's Magic Lamp." As fossils, they are fakes on the order of Piltdown Man, half human being, half the orangutan I used to be.

With his apologia out of the way, Vonnegut goes on to laud the golden age of short story publishing, decrying its passing as newer artists have fewer outlets for their work and to practice their craft. He then goes on to criticize the expansion of creative writing courses since it is a rare writer who can make a living from the craft. But Vonnegut is sensitive to the essential reason for one's insistence on writing. What the heck, practicing an art isn't a way to earn money. It's a way to make one's soul grow.

Bon voyage.

Vonnegut returns to the theme of pursuing art to make one's soul grow in his anecdote about writing (for free) for NUVO, *the Indianapolis alternative weekly paper. In answer to NUVO's prompt reflecting on what it is like to be a native midwesterner, Vonnegut cites Sir Walter Scott:* "Breathes there the man, with soul so dead, who never to himself has said, this is my own, my native land!" (*Vonnegut previously used this reference in* Mother Night.) *He defends midwesterners by citing such heroes as Abraham Lincoln, Eugene V. Debs, and James Whitcomb Riley, not to mention Cole Porter, Hoagy Carmichael, Frank Lloyd Wright, and Louis Sullivan, Twyla Tharp and Bob Fosse, Ernest Hemingway and Saul Bellow, Mike Nichols and Elaine May. Toni Morrison!*

Larry Bird!

Closing his remarks about being a virtually landlocked midwesterner, even one who transplanted himself for long periods to Cape Cod and New York City, Vonnegut ends this text with sincere awe about his origins, using the R-word in a completely secular manner but one which nonetheless evokes the same spiritual appreciation. What geography can give all Middle Westerners, along with the fresh water and topsoil, if they let it, is awe for a fertile continent stretching forever in all directions.

Makes you religious. Takes your breath away.

Vonnegut offers neither a checklist for authors nor a guarantee of success, but his "Coda to My Career" comes down to practicing that which helps us grow regardless of geography, that the land of one's origin presents a variety of experiences from which to draw upon, and that one must be open to the mystical awesomeness of life in all its varieties.

Coggin's Pond. *The retirement home of Colonel Harold J. Sparrow—alias Frank Wirtanen, and referred to by Howard W. Campbell as his Blue Fairy Godmother, in* Mother Night. *It is from this location, "six miles west of Hinkleyville, Maine," that he offers his oath to Israeli authorities that Campbell's public wartime persona was part of his covert work for the United States.*

Cohen, Abe. (*BC* 21) **Abe Cohen**, the jeweler, said to Karabekian, "If artists would explain more, people would like art more. You realize that?"
(*BC* 23) Only one person noticed her sufficiently to comment out loud. He was **Abe Cohen**, the jeweler. He said this about Mary Alice (*Mary Alice Miller, the Women's Breast Stroke Champion of the World and Queen of the Midland City Arts Festival*), despising her sexlessness and innocence and empty mind: "Pure tuna fish!"

Cohen, Isadore Raspberry-19. (*Slap* 1) I (*Wilbur Swain*) inhabit the first floor of the Empire State Building with my sixteen-year-old granddaughter, who is Melody Oriole-2 von Peterswald, and with her lover, **Isadore Raspberry-19 Cohen**. The three of us have the building all to ourselves.

Cohen, Israel (*also* **Cohen Rink**). (*HP* 9) In my time, students didn't skate on the lake anymore, but on an indoor rink given in 1971 by the **Israel Cohen** Family. But they still had sailboat races and canoe races on the lake.
(*HP* 9) That morning, with the phones dead and the electricity cut off, with unburied bodies everywhere, and with all the food in Scipio already consumed as though by a locust plague, he (*Alton Darwin*) had gone up to **Cohen Rink** and put on ice skates for the first time in his life. After a few tottering steps, he had found himself gliding around and around, and around and around.

Cohn, Roy. *Senator Joe McCarthy's legal assistant and chief counsel to the Senate Permanent Investigating Committee. When only a child, Norman Mushari idolizes Cohn.* (*GBR* 2) Little Norman Mushari was only twelve in those troubled days, was assembling plastic model airplanes, masturbating, and papering his room with pictures of Senator Joe McCarthy and **Roy Cohn**.
(*JB* Prologue) There is another minor character, whom I call "**Roy M. Cohn**." He is modeled after the famous anticommunist and lawyer and businessman named, straightforwardly enough, one would have to say, **Roy M. Cohn**. I include him with his kind permission, given yesterday (January 2, 1979) over the telephone. I promised to do him no harm and to present him as an appallingly effective attorney for either the prosecution or the defense of anyone. *When Walter Starbuck is arrested for possession of stolen clarinet parts, the RAMJAC Corporation hires Cohn to defend him.*

Cohoes (*also* **Cohoes High School**). (*BC* 2) In 1972, Trout lived in a basement apartment in **Cohoes**, New York. He made his living as an installer of aluminum combination storm windows and screens.

In Galápagos, *Leon Trout remembers growing up in Cohoes.* (*Gal* 1:27) When I was a child in **Cohoes**, my mother took me to see the circus in Albany one time, although we could not afford it and Father did not approve of circuses.
(*Gal* 1:28) When I was a little boy in **Cohoes**, and could detect nothing in the life of our little family about which I could be proud, my mother told me that I had the blood of French noblemen flowing in my veins.
(*Gal* 2:7) Oh, yes, and there was one other thing I could be proud of, and this really counted for something in **Cohoes**: My father had been a United States Marine.
(*Gal* 2:7) I was then flunking every course but art at school. Nobody flunked art at **Cohoes High School**. That was simply impossible. And I ran away to find my mother, which I never did.

coil. (*PP* VIII) Paul returned to the garage, **coiled** the siphon hose in the glove compartment, and drove off.

(*WFG* There's a Maniac Loose Out There) In his (*Antone "Tony" C. Costa's*) closet in the rooming house where he helped Patricia Walsh and Mary Ann Wysocki with their luggage, police found a **coil** of stained rope.

(*MH* EPICAC) "Is this poetry?" he asked. He began clicking away. . . . EPICAC had found himself. The spool of paper ribbon was unwinding at an alarming rate, feeding out **coils** onto the floor. I asked him to stop, but EPICAC went right on creating.

(*MH* EPICAC) The ceiling over EPICAC was blackened with smoke, and my ankles were tangled in **coils** of paper ribbon that covered the floor.

(*MH* EPICAC) Oblivious to all else around me, I reeled up the tangled yards of paper ribbon from the floor, draped them in **coils** about my arms and neck, and departed for home.

(*BC* 15) Dwayne mimicked her cruelly in a falsetto voice: "'I don't even know what you think I asked you for,'" he said. He looked about as pleasant and relaxed as a **coiled** rattlesnake now. It was his bad chemicals, of course, which were compelling him to look like that.

(*Slap* 17) Mother did not say anything at first. But she had clearly become subhuman in the finest sense. She was a **coiled** female panther suddenly willing to tear the throats out of any number of childrearing experts—in defense of her young.

(*Gal* 2:8) There were still ten meters of stern line, of white nylon umbilical cord, **coiled** by a cleat on the main deck. The Captain tied knots in this, and then he and Mary climbed down it to the shoal, and waded ashore to gather eggs and kill lower animals who had no fear of them.

(*HP* 20) "'To die, to sleep; to sleep: perchance to dream: ay, there's the rub; for in that sleep of death what dreams may come when we have shuffled off this mortal **coil**, must give us pause.'" *Eugene Debs Hartke recites Shakespeare's lines as he prepares to defiantly leave the meeting of Tarkington's Board of Trustees, convened to dismiss him.*

college humor (*see* **humor**).

Collier's. In 1950, Collier's *magazine published Vonnegut's first short story, "Report on the Barnhouse Effect," later reprinted in* Welcome to the Monkey House *(1968). The fiction editor was Knox Burger, and he introduced Vonnegut to the literary agents Kenneth Littauer and Max Wilkinson.*

(*FWD* I) "I sold my first story to **Collier's**. Received my check ($750 minus a 10% agent's commission) yesterday noon. It now appears that two more of my works have a good chance of being sold in the near future." *This is part of a letter Vonnegut wrote to his father concerning his first paycheck as a writer.*

colonel. *The colonel in charge of the American battalion in the short story "Der Arme Dolmetscher," collected in* Bagombo Snuff Box *(1999), has a history of questionable decision-making as implied by the unnamed narrator when recalling his commanding officer's impulsive order to make him a translator stationed in the house of a local Belgian burgomaster. He did not trust the burgomaster who, though recently freed from German occupation, was viewed as a security risk.*

In civilian life, the colonel is employed as a hotel detective in Mobile, Alabama. The narrator does not fail to let slip his sense of irony noting that his commanding officer, presumably a worldly and highly trained professional whose job it was to detect the subtleties of behavior across a wide swath of people and cultures, fails to recognize the obvious language limitations of the would-be translator as well as having his own difficulty detecting the spoken language of his battlefield enemies. The narrator's criticisms of the colonel's abilities are further ridiculed by being cast in the vernacular of his speech. While a student, I had learned the first stanza of Heinrich Heine's "Die Lorelei" by rote from a college roommate, and I happened to give those lines a dogged rendition while working within earshot of the battalion commander. The **Colonel** *(a hotel detective from Mobile) asked his Executive Officer (a dry-goods salesman from Knoxville) in what language the lyrics were. The Executive withheld judgment until I had bungled through "Der Gipfel des Berges foounk-kelt im Abendsonnenschein."*

"Ah believes tha's Kraut, **Cuhnel**,*" he said.*

My understanding in English of the only Ger-

man I knew was this: "I don't know why I am so sad. I can't get an old legend out of my head. The air is cool and it's getting dark, and quiet flows the Rhine. The peak of the mountain twinkles in evening sunshine."

The **Colonel** felt his role carried with it the obligation to make quick, headstrong decisions. He made some dandies before the Wehrmacht was whipped, but the one he made that day was my favorite. "If tha's Kraut, whassat man doin' on the honey-dippin' detail?" he wanted to know. Two hours later, the company clerk told me to lay down the buckets, for I was now battalion interpreter.

Colson, Charles W. *The Watergate coconspirator who eventually serves time and later dedicates his life to Jesus Christ, Walter Starbuck refers to Colson as a fellow jailbird. The fictional Colson is also attributed with nicknaming Starbuck "the Geek" (JB 4).*

The Columbia Conserve Company. *As described in* Jailbird, *the company was established in 1903 and sold off in 1953, though it struggled for survival after 1931—the victim of economics during the Great Depression. It was a cannery specializing in tomato soup, chili, and catsup. Created by brothers Norman, William, and Hutchins Hapgood, it was their "experiment in industrial democracy" in that it had a seven-member council of workers advising on wages and working conditions. The company developed a retirement plan, sick pay, and stock-bonus plans. Vonnegut catalogues this information in the text's prologue, taking great pains to state that the three brothers who attempted this noble experiment were all Harvard men, as were Starbuck, McCone, and so many of the Watergate criminals.*

column. (PP 1) Gingerly, Paul pressed a button on the steering **column.** A motor purred, gears grumbled softly, and the two front seats lay down side by side like sleepy lovers.
(ST 1) "Yes," said Constant from below, "that Mr. Constant is still here." He was in plain view, leaning against a **column** in the arch that opened onto the foyer. But he was so low in the composition, so lost in architectural details as to be almost invisible.
(ST 10) The rube made a show of being a judicious

shopper. He compared the toy with the real article it was supposed to represent. The real article was a Martian space ship on top of a **column** ninety-eight feet tall. The **column** and space ship were inside the walls of the Rumfoord estate—in the corner of the estate where the tennis courts had once been.

Rumfoord had yet to explain the purpose of the space ship, whose supporting **column** had been built with the pennies of school children from all over the world. The ship was kept in constant readiness. What was reputedly the longest free-standing ladder in history leaned against the **column**, led giddily to the door of the ship.
(ST 10) The Space Wanderer's gaze climbed the ladder to the tiny door of the space ship on top of the **column.**
(ST 12) Rumfoord stood bolt upright, his eyes popping, a fiery **column.**
(MN 32) "There is every chance," I said, "that I would have become a sort of Nazi Edgar Guest, writing a daily **column** of optimistic doggerel for daily papers around the world. And, as senility set in—the sunset of life, as they say—I might even come to believe what my couplets said: that everything was probably all for the best."
(MN 42) While the **column** of air enclosed by the stairs had carried in the past a melancholy freight of coal dust and cooking smells and the sweat of plumbing, that air was cold and sharp now. . . . All warm gases had been whisked up the stairwell and out my windows, as though up a whistling flue.
(CC 120) I wasn't half so curious about the living, probably because I sensed accurately that I would first have to contemplate a lot of dead. I saw no **columns** of smoke from possible camp fires; but they would have been hard to see against an horizon of worms.
(GBR 4) The town of Rosewater was in the dead center of the county. In the dead center of town was a Parthenon built of honest red brick, **columns** and all. Its roof was green copper.
(GBR 13) As the many fires broke through the roofs of the burning buildings, a **column** of heated air rose more than two and a half miles high and one and a half miles in diameter. . . . This **column** was turbulent, and it was fed from its base by in-rushing cooler ground-surface air. One and one and a half

miles from the fires this draught increased the wind velocity from eleven to thirty-three miles per hour. *Vonnegut notes he is quoting from Hans Rumpf's* The Bombing of Germany.

(*GBR* 13) Eliot, rising from his seat in the bus, beheld the firestorm of Indianapolis. He was awed by the majesty of the **column** of fire, which was at least eight miles in diameter and fifty miles high. The boundaries of the **column** seemed absolutely sharp and unwavering, as though made of glass. Within the boundaries, *helixes* of dull red embers turned in stately harmony about an inner core of white. The white seemed holy.

(*SL5* 2) The woman and the pony were posed before velvet draperies which were fringed with deedlee-balls. They were flanked by **Doric columns**. In front of one **column** was a potted palm. . . . Le Fevre argued that the picture was fine art, and that his intention was to make Greek mythology come alive. He said the **columns** and the potted palm proved that. *Vonnegut's description of what is supposed to be the first pornographic photograph—a daguerrotype.*

(*MH* Welcome to the Monkey House) The view was blocked by the backside of a mocked-up thermometer twenty feet high, which faced the street. It was calibrated in billions of people on Earth, from zero to twenty. The make-believe **column** of liquid was a strip of translucent red plastic. It showed how many people there were on Earth. Very close to the bottom was a black arrow that showed what the scientists thought the population ought to be.

(*BC* Preface) She was rich (*Phoebe Hurty—to whom* Breakfast of Champions *is dedicated*), but she had gone to work every weekday of her adult life, so she went on doing that. She wrote a sane and funny advice-to-the-lovelorn **column** for the Indianapolis *Times.*

(*WFG* There's a Maniac Loose Out There) Here is what she (*Evelyn Lawson*) wrote in her **column** after the district attorney held a sensational press conference about the bodies.

(*WFG* Biafra: A People Betrayed) The worst sufferers there were the children of refugees, driven from their homes, then driven off the roads and into the bush by MIGs and armored **columns**.

(*WFG* In a Manner That Must Shame God Himself) Art Buchwald said he came to the convention

in order to see his pals, mostly other news people. He told our table about a **column** he had just written. The comical premise was that the Republican party had attracted so many campaign contributions that it found itself with two billion dollars it couldn't spend. It decided to buy something nice for the American people. Here was the gift: a free week's bombing of Vietnam.

(*WFG* Address at Rededication of Wheaton College Library, 1973) William F. Buckley said in a recent **column** that I would be overjoyed by Nixon's political defeat, since I had made a career of despising America. That proves he hasn't read me much.

(*Slap* 37) The news **columns** told of triumphs by various relatives, and warned against others who were child molesters or swindlers and so on. *The news columns appear in government-sponsored family newspapers recounting the exploits of various government established extended families.*

(*JB* 3) We named our son Walter F. Starbuck, Jr. Little did we dream that the name would become as onerous as Judas Iscariot, Jr., to the boy. He would seek legal remedy when he turned twenty-one, would have his name changed to Walter F. Stankiewicz, the name that appears over his **columns** in *The New York Times.*

(*JB* 3) The President himself (*Richard Nixon*) at last noticed the **column** of smoke rising from my place (*Walter Starbuck's*), and he stopped all business to stare at me. He had to ask Emil Larkin who I was.

(*JB* 16) So there Mary Kathleen and I were—among all those harps. They are very strange-looking instruments, now that I think about them, and not very far from poor Ruth's idea of civilization even in peacetime—impossible marriages between Greek **columns** and Leonardo da Vinci's flying machines.

(*JB* Epilogue) If you can believe the gossip **columns**, there is to be a talent search for an actress to play the Irish immigrant girl.

(*PS* The People One Knows) He (*William F. Buckley*) can do a **column** in 20 minutes, he tells us, and turn out 150 a year. . . .

(*PS* Funnier on Paper Than Most People) "Perhaps you have read the novel *Childhood's End* by Arthur C. Clarke, one of the few masterpieces in the field of science fiction. All of the others were written by me. In Clarke's novel, mankind suddenly undergoes a spectacular evolutionary change. The children become very different from the parents, less physical, more spiritual—and one day they form up into a sort of **column** of light which spirals out into the universe, its mission unknown. The book ends there."

(*DD* 22) According to a gossip **column** Mother and I *(Rudy Waltz)* read, he and his fourth wife had divided the penthouse in half with a line of chairs. Neither one was supposed to go in the other one's territory.

Felix was also due to be fired any day, according to the same **column** because the ratings of NBC prime time television shows were falling so far behind those of the other networks.

(*Gal* 1:21) There were forty-two of them, counting mates or companions who were nonentities, but they had organized themselves into a few dinner parties, duly reported in gossip **columns** that day, in order to pass pleasantly the hours remaining until limousines came to cushion and muffle them away to Kennedy International Airport—

(*Blue* 8) Nowadays, of course, just about our only solvent industry is the merchandising of death, bankrolled by our grandchildren, so that the message of our principal art forms, movies and television and political speeches and newspaper **columns**, for the sake of the economy, simply has to be this: War's hell, all right, but the only way a boy can become a man is in a shoot-out of some kind, preferably, but by no means necessarily, on a battlefield.

(*Blue* 27) She was only four blocks away *(Marilee, Countess Portomaggiore—the coal miner's daughter responsible for bringing Rabo Karabekian to Dan Evans's attention)*—in a palazzo designed for Innocenzo "the Invisible" de Medici by Leon Battista Alberti in the middle of the fifteenth century. It was a cruciform structure whose four wings abutted on a domed rotunda twelve meters in diameter and in whose walls were half embedded eighteen Corinthian **columns** four and a half meters high. Above the capitals of the **columns** was a clerestory, a wall pierced with thirty-six windows. Above this was the dome—on whose underside was an epiphany, clouds almighty and Jesus and the Virgin Mary and angels looking down through clouds, painted by Paolo Uccello.

(*Blue* 27) The second puzzle was this: Why were the vast rectangles between the encircling **columns** at ground level blank?

(*Blue* 30) She said that our unexpected reunion was a stroke of luck for since she thought I might have brought the solution to an interior decorating problem which had been nagging at her for many years, namely: what sort of pictures, if any, should she put on the inane blanks between the **columns** of her rotunda? "I want to leave some sort of mark on this place while I have it," she said, "and the rotunda seems the place to do it."

(*HP* 11) I thought she *(Kimberley Wilder)* had noted her father's conviction, often expressed as **columns** and on his TV show, and no doubt at home, that a few teachers who secretly hated their country were making young people lose faith in its future and leadership.

(*HP* 13) I knew who he *(Jason Wilder)* was, of course, and something of how his mind worked, having read his newspaper **column** and watched his television show from time to time.

(*HP* 13) I read your **columns** and watch your TV show regularly.

(*HP* 15) Madelaine *(Astor)* dictated a letter to me afterward, explaining that Jason Wilder had promised to denounce the college in his **column** and on his TV show if the Trustees did not fire me.

(*HP* 34) As I say, every **column** adds up to 3,888. *This is a reference to a war chart noting vital statistics of Churchill, Hitler, Roosevelt, Il Duce (Mussolini), Stalin, and Tojo.*

(*BAG* Preface by Peter Reed) Vonnegut began writing short stories in the late 1940s, while employed in public relations at General Electric in Schenectady, New York. Earlier, he had cut his teeth on journalism: while attending Shortridge High School in Indianapolis (1936–1940), he had been a regular contributor to and managing editor of its daily newspaper, *The Shortridge Echo*, and in college he worked on *The Cornell Daily Sun*. In his **columns** he creates characters, and one begins to see the humor and witty social iconoclasm evident in the mature work. The war intervened, with the dramatic circumstances that would be the stuff of his masterpiece, *Slaughterhouse-Five*, yet Vonnegut's course to becoming a writer had already been set.

(*BAG* Thanasphere) Groszinger paused in a patch of sunlight on the laboratory building's steps, and read again the front-page news story, which ran fancifully for a **column**, beneath the headline "Mystery Radio Message Reveals Possible Will Fraud." The story told of two radio amateurs, experimenting illegally on the supposedly unused ultra-high-frequency band, who had been amazed to hear a man chattering about voices and a will.

(*BAG* Souvenir) The **column** had been moving more and more slowly, growing more packed. Now it came to a muttering halt. . . .

From far down the road came an exchange of shouts like a distant surf. Restless, anxious moments later, the cause of the trouble was clear: The **column** had met another, fleeing in terror from the opposite direction. The Russians had the area surrounded. Now the two **columns** merged to form an aimless whirlpool in the heart of a small village, flooding out into side lanes and up the slopes on either side.

(*BAG* Souvenir) The noise of a tank **column** of the Red Army grew louder.

(*BAG* Unpaid Consultant) I could see the firelight playing over the **columns** of figures, *The Wall Street Journal*, the prospectuses and graphs. I could hear Celeste and her husband Harry murmuring about the smell of new-mown hay, American Brake Shoe preferred, moonlight on the Wabash, Consolidated Edison three-percent bonds, cornbread, and Chicago, Milwaukee, St. Paul, and Pacific common.

(*BAG* Der Arme Dolmetscher) Chief among these was the mutilated pamphlet. I examined each of its precious pages in turn, delighted by the simplicity of transposing English into German. With this booklet, all I had to do was run my finger down the left-hand **column** until I found the English phrase I wanted, and then rattle off the nonsense syllables printed opposite in the right-hand **column**. "How many grenade launchers have you?" for instance, was Vee feel grenada vairfair habben zee? Impeccable German for "Where are your tank **columns**?" proved to be nothing more troublesome than Vo zint eara pantzer shpitzen?

(*BAG* Der Arme Dolmetscher) DOLMETSCHER: What unit are you from? (BURGOMASTER remains sullen, silent. BURGOMASTER'S DAUGHTER goes to his side, weeps softly. DOL-

METSCHER confronts BURGOMASTER'S DAUGHTER.) Where have you hidden your motorcycle? (Turns again to BURGOMASTER.) Where are your howitzers, eh? Where are your tank **columns**? How many grenade launchers have you? (*BAG* Der Arme Dolmetscher) I ran my eye down the left-hand **columns** of my pamphlet until I found the phrase that most fairly represented our sentiments.

"Don't shoot," I said.

A German tank officer swaggered in to have a look at his catch. In his hand was a pamphlet, somewhat smaller than mine. "Where are your howitzers?" he said.

Combat Respiratory Rations (*also called* **CRRs** *or* **goofballs**). *Enriched oxygen pills needed by recruits of the Martian army every six hours.* (ST 6) The bloodstream takes on this oxygen through the wall of the small intestine rather than through the lungs. *Beatrice Rumfoord taught the proper use of the goofballs in conjunction with the Schliemann Breathing method.*

comedians. *Vonnegut's great appreciation for comedy's comforts, structure, and cultural significance is encapsulated in the following excerpts:* (PS Self-Interview) And I want to say, too, that humorists are very commonly the youngest children in their families. When I was the littlest kid at our supper table, there was only one way I could get anybody's attention, and that was to be funny. I had to specialize. I used to listen to radio **comedians** very intently, so I could learn how to make jokes. And that's what my books are, now that I'm a grownup—mosaics of jokes.

(PS The People One Knows) It is the truth: **Comedians** and jazz musicians have been more comforting and enlightening to me than preachers or politicians or philosophers or poets or painters or novelists of my time. Historians in the future, in my opinion, will congratulate us on very little other than our clowning and our jazz.

Though Vonnegut did not write Between Time and Timbuktu, *he did provide a preface to its publication.* (TIM XVII) I would like to say something about American **comedians**: they are often as brilliant and magical as our best jazz musicians, and they have probably done more to shape my thinking than any writer. When people ask me who my culture heroes are, I express pious gratitude for Mark Twain and James Joyce and so on. But the truth is that I am a barbarian, whose deepest cultural debts are to Laurel and Hardy, Stoopnagel and Bud, Buster Keaton, Fred Allen, Jack Benny, Charlie Chaplin, Easy Aces, Henry Morgan, and on and on.

They made me hilarious during the Great Depression, and all the lesser depressions after that. When Bob Elliot and Ray Goulding agreed to work on this TV show, I nearly swooned.

(*FWD* XI) (Except that the minister and I would become good friends, and he would invite me to say a few words during a Christmas Eve service along with the **comedian** Joey Adams, and he and the congregation would eventually come to a parting of the ways, and one of his offenses, supposedly, was having lent the pulpit to a known atheist, who was me and not Joey Adams.)

(*FWD* XIX) "My generalization is happily or unhappily confirmed in a book called *Punchlines* (Paragon House, 1990) by William Keough of the English Department of Fitchburg State College in Massachusetts. The subtitle is *The Violence of American Humor*. Mr. Keough, by means of essays on Mark Twain, Ring Lardner, Ambrose Bierce, myself, **comedians** in the movies (both silents and talkies), and radio and TV and nightclub comics right up to the present, persuades me that the most memorable are responses to the economic and physical violence of this society."

(*FWD* XXI) (The second funniest clean joke in the world was told to me personally by the great **comedian** Rodney Dangerfield. We were in a movie together. He said he had a great uncle who was admired for his cleanliness. He was the talk of the neighborhood. This old man took six, seven, eight, sometimes as many as twelve baths or showers every day. After he died, his whole funeral cortege went through a car wash on the way to the cemetery.)

(*TQ* Epilogue) He (*Bernard Vonnegut*) was funnier than I am in conversation. During the Great Depression, I learned as much about jokes while tagging after him as I did from the **comedians** in movies and on the radio. I was honored that he found me funny, too. It turned out that he had ac-

cumulated a small portfolio of my stuff that had amused him. One item was a letter I had written to our uncle Alex when I was twenty-five. (*Vonnegut sends his Uncle Alex a fraudulent GE letter in response to his having sent money through the mail for a copy of the photograph used in an article about Bernard Vonnegut. It is reprinted in full in* Timequake, *page 248. Vonnegut's reply, signed by Guy Fawkes, sarcastically mocks the money sent to cover the piddling photo costs of his request to a company as large as General Electric, and further berates the imposition on their time in complying with his request. Uncle Alex was none too amused when first receiving the reply, but the Vonnegut brothers thought is was hilarious.*)

(*MWC* 1) I grew up at a time when comedy in this country was superb—it was the Great Depression. There were large numbers of absolutely top **comedians** on radio. And without intending to, I really studied them. I would listen to comedy at least an hour a night all through my youth, and I got very interested in what jokes were and how they worked.

When I'm being funny, I try not to offend. I don't think much of what I've done has been in really ghastly taste. I don't think I have embarrassed many people, or distressed them. The only shocks I use are an occasional obscene word. Some things aren't funny. I can't imagine a humorous book or skit about Auschwitz, for instance. And it's not possible for me to make a joke about the death of John F. Kennedy or Martin Luther King. Otherwise I can't think of any subject that I would steer away from, that I could do nothing with. Total catastrophes are terribly amusing, as Voltaire demonstrated. You know, the Lisbon earthquake is funny.

(*MWC* 1) There is a superficial sort of laughter. Bob Hope, for example, was not really a humorist. He was a **comedian** with very thin stuff, never mentioning anything troubling. I used to laugh my head off at Laurel and Hardy. There is terrible tragedy there somehow. These men are too sweet to survive in this world and are in terrible danger all the time. They could be so easily killed.

(*MWC* 11) That is stuff from a novel I've been working on for the past five years, about Gil Berman, thirty-six years my junior, a standup **comedian** at the end of the world. It is about making jokes while we are killing all the fish in the ocean, and touching off the last chunks or drops or whiffs of fossil fuel. But it will not let itself be finished.

Its working title—or actually, its nonworking title—is *If God Were Alive Today*. And hey, listen, it is time we thanked God that we are in a country where even the poor people are overweight. But the Bush diet could change that.

And about the novel I can never finish, *If God Were Alive Today*, the hero, the stand-up **comedian** on Doomsday, not only does he denounce our addiction to fossil fuels and the pushers in the White House, because of overpopulation he is also against sexual intercourse. Gil Berman tells his audiences:

I have become a flaming neuter. I am as celibate as at least fifty percent of the heterosexual Roman Catholic clergy. And celibacy is no root canal. It's so cheap and convenient. Talk about safe sex! You don't have to do anything afterwards, because there is no afterward.

And when my tantrum, which is what I call my TV set, flashes boobs and smiles in my face, and says everybody but me is going to get laid tonight, and this is a national emergency, so I've got to rush out and buy a car or pills, or a folding gymnasium that I can hide under my bed, I laugh like a hyena. I know and you know that millions and millions of good Americans, present company not excepted, are not going to get laid tonight. (MWC Author's Note) And since we first met, Joe (*Petro III*) has beguiled others into sending him pictures for him to do with what he so much loves to do. Among them are the **comedian** Jonathan Winters, an art student long ago, and the English artist Ralph Steadman, whose accomplishments include the appropriately harrowing illustrations for Hunter Thompson's Fear and Loathing books. And Steadman and I have come to know and like each other on account of Joe.
See also: TQ 45.

common decency. (BC 2) "And then Earthlings discovered tools. Suddenly agreeing with friends could be a form of suicide or worse. But agreements went on, not for the sake of **common** sense or **decency** or self-preservation, but for friendliness."
(*Slap* Prologue) I have had some experiences with love, or think I have, anyway, although the ones I have liked best could easily be described as "**common decency.**" I treated somebody well for a little while, or maybe even for a tremendously long time, and that person treated me well in turn. Love need not have had anything to do with it.
(*Slap* Prologue) I wish that people who are conventionally supposed to love each other would say to each other, when they fight, "Please—a little less love, and a little more **common decency.**"

. . . My longest experience with **common decency**, surely, has been with my older brother, my only brother, Bernard, who is an atmospheric scientist in the State University of New York at Albany. (*Slap* Prologue) It is lucky, too, for human beings need all the relatives they can get—as possible donors or receivers not necessarily of love, but of **common decency.**
(PS Mark Twain) Only a genius (*Mark Twain*) could have misrepresented our speech and our wittiness and our common sense and our **common decency** so handsomely to ourselves and the outside world.
(GBK Introduction) Whereas formal religions surely comfort many members of the WNYC staff, that staff's collective effect on its community is humanism—an ideal so Earthbound and unmajestic that I never capitalize it. As I have used it here, "humanist" is nothing more supernatural than a handy synonym for "good citizenship and **common decency.**"

I wish one and all long and happy lives, no matter what may become of them afterwards. Use sunscreen! Don't smoke cigarettes.

cone, cone-shaped, conical. (PP XXI) An old man, with a white beard reaching to his waist, wearing a long white robe and golden sandals and a blue **conical** hat speckled with golden stars, sits atop an extraordinarily tall stepladder. *The old man is the Sky Manager in the annual summer play produced at the Meadows (q.v.).*
(ST 1) The fountain itself was . . . a **cone** described by many stone bowls of decreasing diameters. The bowls were collars on a cylindrical shaft forty feet high.
(ST 8) He imagined a remarkable fountain, a **cone** described by descending bowls of increasing diameters. It wouldn't do.

(*MH* Where I Live) To get bass, one follows the birds, looks for **cone-shaped** formations of them, casts his lure to the place where the cone points. Bass will be feeding there.

(*BC* 1) There were pictures and statues of this supposed imaginary beacon for children to see. It was sort of an ice-cream **cone** on fire.

(*JB* 5) "When they are very young," Dr. Fender writes in the persona of Frank X. Barlow, "barnacles can drift or creep whence-so-ever they hanker, anywhere in the seven seas and the brackish estuaries thereof. Their upper bodies are encased in **cone-shaped** armor. Their little tootsies dangle from the **cones** like clappers from dinnerbells.

"But there comes a time for every barnacle, at childhood's end, when the rim of its **cone** secretes a glue that will stick forever to whatever it happens to touch next. So it is no casual thing on Earth to say to a pubescent barnacle or to a homeless soul from Vicuna, 'Sit thee doon, sit thee doon.'" *Here, Vonnegut echoes "The Rime of the Ancient Mariner."*

(*JB* Epilogue) Israel Edel gave me a rubber ice-cream **cone** with a squeaker in it—a plaything for my little dog, who is a female Lhasa apso, a golden dustmop without a handle. . . . *Vonnegut's next book,* Palm Sunday, *has a cover photograph of him with his Lhasa apso.*

I have never bred her, but now, according to the veterinarian, Dr. Howard Padwee, she is experiencing a false pregnancy and believes the rubber ice-cream **cone** to be a puppy. . . .

I observe how profoundly serious Nature has made her about a rubber ice-cream **cone**—brown rubber **cone**, pink rubber ice cream. I have to wonder what equally ridiculous commitments to bits of trash I myself have made. . . . The human condition in an exploding universe would not have been altered one iota if, rather than live as I have, I had done nothing but carry a rubber ice-cream **cone** from closet to closet for sixty years.

(*DD* 2) I do not believe he would have stayed in Midland City, if it weren't for what remained of his childhood home, which was its fanciful carriage house. It was hexagonal. It was stone. It had a **conical** slate roof.

(*DD* 2) A hexagonal loft encircled and overhung the great chamber. This was partitioned off into bedrooms and bathrooms and a small library.

Above that was an attic under the **conical** slate roof. Father had no immediate use for the attic, so it was left in its primitive condition.

(*DD* 3) They *(the Maritimo brothers)* could either await death, or they could invent something to do. They invented. They saw a **conical** slate roof on the other side of the river, and they walked toward that. In order to keep putting one foot in front of the other, they pretended that it was of utmost importance that they reach that structure and no other.

(*DD* 20) It was the **conical** slate roof of my childhood home, only a few blocks away. The peak of the **cone**, where the cupola used to be, was capped with very light gray tar roofing, with bits of sand stuck to it. In the light of a full moon, it was glittering white—like snow.

(*DD* 20) We had circled over the city, so we approached the **conical** roof from the north. Wind had piled snow halfway up the big north window.

(*Gal* 1:1) A million years later, they *(the Galápagos Islands)* do possess white beaches and blue lagoons. But when this story begins, they were still ugly humps and domes and **cones** and spires of lava, brittle and abrasive, whose cracks and pits and bowls and valleys brimmed over not with rich topsoil or sweet water, but with the finest, driest volcanic ash.

Conestoga. *As chronicled in* Hocus Pocus, *westward pioneers often chose these covered wagons named for the location of their original construction, the Conestoga Valley of Pennsylvania. Eugene Debs Hartke points out one myth that grew from the ubiquitous land rovers: the cigars transported by the pioneers picked up the name "stogies" as representative of the Conestoga wagon. He also points out that By 1830, the sturdiest and most popular of these wagons were in fact made by the Mohiga Wagon Company right here in Scipio, New York (HP 2). The founder of the company is the dyslexic inventor and manufacturer Aaron Tarkington.*

Conners, Harrison C. *Once a laboratory assistant to Felix Hoenikker in* Cat's Cradle, *Conners goes to Indianapolis where he is the founding president of Fabri-Tek, a company dealing in weapons technology. After his old mentor passes away, he returned to Hoenikker's home, speaks with Angela about old* *times, and two weeks later they wed. Conners proves to be a lousy husband, a drunk, and womanizer.*

conspiracy. (*PP* XXXII) "Doctor Proteus," said the prosecutor nastily. The television cameras closed in on his sneer and panned to the beads of sweat on Paul's forehead. "You have pleaded guilty to **conspiracy** to advocate the commission of sabotage, isn't that so? . . .

"This **conspiracy**, of which you are the head, has as its method, and I quote from your famous letter, 'We are prepared to use force to end the lawlessness, if other means fail.' Those are your words, Doctor?"

(*MN* 11) It was dumb luck that brought us together. No **conspiracy** was involved at first. It was I who knocked on his door, invaded his privacy. If I hadn't carved that chess set, we never would have met. *Campbell speaks about his meeting George Kraft, also known as Soviet agent Colonel Iona Potapov.*

(*MN* 12) Howard W. Campbell, Jr., a great writer and one of the most fearless patriots in American history, now lives in poverty and loneliness in the attic of 27 Bethune Street. Such is the fate of thinking men brave enough to tell the truth about the **conspiracy** of international Jewish bankers and international Jewish Communists who will not rest until the bloodstream of every American is hopelessly polluted with Negro and/or Oriental blood. *This is from an item printed in* The White Christian Minuteman.

(*BC* 19) I had no respect whatsoever for the creative works of either the painter or the novelist. I thought Karabekian with his meaningless pictures had entered into a **conspiracy** with millionaires to make poor people feel stupid. I thought Beatrice Keedsler had joined hands with other old-fashioned storytellers to make people believe that life had leading characters, minor characters, significant details, insignificant details, that it had lessons to be learned, tests to be passed, and a beginning, a middle, and an end.

(*WFG* Hello, Star Vega) Let me hasten to say: They are quite certain that we are not being visited now. (*Carl*) Sagan served this year on a committee that reviewed the handling by the Air Force of UFO reports, and he is able to state:

The saucer myths represent a neat compromise between the need to believe in a traditional paternal God and the contemporary pressures to accept the pronouncements of science. . . . Repeated sightings of UFOs and the persistence of the United States Air Force and members of the responsible scientific community in explaining the sightings away have suggested to some that a **conspiracy** exists to conceal from the public the true nature of the UFOs. But precisely because people desire so intensely that unidentified flying objects be of a benign, intelligent, and extraterrestrial origin, honesty requires that . . . we accept only the most rigorous logic and the most convincing evidence.

(*WFG* The Mysterious Madame Blavatsky) Colonel Olcott was for a while so respected for his soundness of mind that he was made a member of an elite committee of three, whose purpose was to discover the extent of the **conspiracy** that led to the death of Abraham Lincoln.

(*WFG* Playboy Interview) PLAYBOY: You said it was sexual. *The interviewer refers to Vonnegut's sense of the space program.*

VONNEGUT: It's a tremendous space fuck, and there's some kind of **conspiracy** to suppress that fact. That's why all the stories about launches are so low-key. The never give a hint of what a visceral experience it is to watch a launch. How would the taxpayers feel if they found out they were buying orgasms for a few thousand freaks within a mile of the launch pad? And it's an extremely satisfactory orgasm. I mean, you are shaking and you do take leave of your senses. And there's something about the sound that comes shuddering across the water. I understand that there are certain frequencies with which you can make a person involuntarily shit with sound. So it does get you in the guts.

(*HP* 28) The Townies protected the image he (*Lyle Hooper*) had of himself, in spite of State Police raids and visits from the County Health Department, as a family man who ran a place of refreshment whose success depended entirely on the quality of the drinks and snacks he served. This kindly **conspiracy** protected Lyle's son Charlton, as well. Charlton grew to be 2 meters tall, and was a New York State High School All-Star basketball center in his senior year at Scipio High School, and all he ever had to say about his father was that he ran a restaurant (*the Black Cat Café*).

conspiratorial. (*PP* IX) "I love *you*, Anita. Good-bye." He looked up at Finnerty. "O.K., let's go." He felt somehow **conspiratorial**, and got a small lift from the feeling. Being with Finnerty had often had that effect. Finnerty had an air of mysteriousness about him, an implication that he knew of worlds unsuspected by anyone else—a man of unexplained absences and shadowy friends. Actually, Finnerty let Paul in on very little that was surprising, and only gave him the illusion of sharing in mysteries—if, indeed, there were any. The illusion was enough. It filled a need in Paul's life, and he went gladly for a drink with the odd man.
(*PP* XIV) "Paul, about this Finnerty and Lasher business—" His (*Dr. Kroner's*) playfully **conspiratorial** tone implied that the proposed prosecution of these two was sort of a practical joke. "Just wanted to tell you that I called Washington about it, to let them in on what we're going to do, and they say we should hold off for a while. They say the whole thing ought to be well planned at the top level. It's apparently bigger stuff than I thought." His voice dropped to a whisper. "It's beginning to look like a problem nationwise, not just Iliumwise."

conspirators. (*PP* V) The others laughed like **conspirators**. Apparently something special had been cooked up, and one or two of the older engineers seemed to be sharing in the high expectations. *Berringer and his engineer friends taunt Proteus about a proposed championship match with Checker Charlie.*
(*PP* XXX) It wasn't a brilliant-looking aggregation of **conspirators**, on the whole, but a righteous and determined one.
(*ST* Epilogue) The **conspirators** presumably fled. *The "sleeper" in the house nearby Malachi's bus stop on the outskirts of Indianapolis presumes he chased away some dangerous prowlers when he hears Salo's ship lift off.*
(*FWD* I) He told us about the time he emptied a New York subway car in three stops by boarding it with a large number of friends who pretended to be strangers to one another. This was in the wee hours following New Year's Eve. Each **conspirator** was carrying a copy of the *Daily News* with the bold headline: HOOVER OUT, ROOSEVELT IN. Troy had saved the papers from Roosevelt's landslide victory

about a year before. (That would have been back at the very start of 1934, I guess, when I was eleven years old, the fourth year of the Great Depression.)

conspire. (*PP* XXVII) She'd (*Anita Proteus*) have to leave New York State, of course, since the only grounds for divorce there were adultery, and incitement to **conspire** to advocate sabotage. A case could be made for either, he supposed, but not with dignity.
(*PP* XXXII) Paul had pleaded guilty to **conspiring** to advocate the commission of sabotage, but was now being tried for treason, three weeks after his arrest.
(*ST* 3) His situation, working for Noel Constant and then Malachi, **conspired** nicely to make almost anything he might say bitterly funny—for he was superior to Constant *pere* and *fils* in every respect but one, and the respect excepted was the only one that really mattered. The Constants—ignorant, vulgar, and brash—had copious quantities of dumb luck.
(*ST* 6) The fielders and Miss Fenstermaker dodged the ball as though it were a red-hot cannonball. When the ball came to a stop of its own accord, the fielders went after it with a sort of ritual clumsiness. Clearly, the point of their efforts was not to hit Chrono with the ball, was not to put him out. The fielders were all **conspiring** to increase the glory of Chrono by making a show of helpless opposition.
(*ST* 12) Rumfoord held his hands high, and his fingers were spread. Streaks of pink, violet, and pale green Saint Elmo's fire streamed from his fingertips. Short streaks of pale gold fizzed in his hair, **conspiring** to give him a tinsel halo.
The following is a list of indictments against Dr. Lionel J. D. Jones, D.D.S., D.D. and twenty-seven others: **Conspiring** to destroy the morale and faith and confidence of the members of the military and naval forces of the United States and the people of the United States in their public officials and republican form of government; **conspiring** to seize upon and use and misuse the right of freedom of speech and of the press to spread their disloyal doctrines, intending and believing that any nation allowing its people the right of freedom of speech is powerless to defend itself against enemies masquerading as patriotic; and seeking to obstruct, impede,

break down and destroy the proper functioning of its republican form of government under the guise of honest criticism; **conspiring** to render the Government of the United States bereft of the faith and confidence of the members of the military and naval forces and of the people, and thereby render that government powerless to defend the nation or the people against armed attack from without or treachery from within (*MN* 11).

(*CC* 90) All things **conspired** to form one cosmic *vin-dit*, one mighty shove into Bokononism, into the belief that God was running my life and that He had work for me to do.

(*SL5* 4) The American fliers turned in their uniforms, became high school kids. And Hitler turned into a baby, Billy Pilgrim supposed. That wasn't in the movie. Billy was extrapolating. Everybody turned into a baby, and all humanity, without exception, **conspired** biologically to produce two perfect people named Adam and Eve, he supposed. *Billy had become "slightly unstuck in time," watching a war movie on television—backwards.*

Constant, Benjamin. (*ST* 3) The family could trace its line back through an illegitimacy to **Benjamin Constant**, who was a tribune under Napoleon from 1799 to 1801, and a lover of Anne Louise Germaine Necker, Baronne de Stael-Holstein, wife of the then Swedish ambassador to France.

Constant, Malachi. *The son of Noel Constant and Florence Whitehill, Malachi is chairman of Magnum Opus, Inc., when Beatrice Rumfoord invites him (at her husband's request) to the Rumfoord estate for one of Winston Niles Rumfoord's chronosynclastic infundibulated materializations. Malachi had been thrown out of the University of Virginia in his freshman year, but was still the richest American—and a notorious rakehell (MN 4).*

Malachi's name means "constant messenger," and he believes he is destined for some great use. But when he is told he will visit Mars and Titan, mate with Beatrice Rumfoord and sire a son, Malachi goes on a nearly two-month alcohol binge, losing all his father's financial legacy.

He is subject to all of Rumfoord's predictions and at various times is known as Malachi, Unk, or the Space Wanderer. He and Boaz are trapped in a cave on a moon, and when he finally extricates himself and returns to Earth, he is hailed as the long-prophesied Space Wanderer—only to become the object of scorn and ritual religious sacrifice to Rumfoord and his Church of God the Utterly Indifferent. All this is predetermined by the plotting Tralfamadorians who seek to get a spare part to their intergalactic messenger, Salo. Malachi's son, Chrono, is the unknowing guardian of the part, nothing more than a piece of sheet metal he carries as his good luck charm.*

Malachi dies at a bus stop on the outskirts of Indianapolis, under a blanket of snow and in the midst of a posthypnotic illusion suggested by Salo. In a complete transformation from his former hedonism, he wants to end his life in Indianapolis because it "is the first place in the United States of America where a white man was hanged for the murder of an Indian. The kind of people who'll hang a white man for murdering an Indian—" said **Constant**, "that's the kind of people for me" (*ST* Epilogue).

Constant, Noel. *The founder of Magnum Opus and father of Malachi Constant. A native of New Bedford, Massachusetts, he was a traveling salesman of copper-bottomed cookware. At the age of thirty-nine, while in room 223 of the Wilburhampton Hotel, he devises his unique method of investment. In the dresser of the hotel room was a Gideon Bible and a fourteen-year-old newspaper page with stock market quotations.* (*ST* 3) Magnum Opus was built with a pen, a check book, some check-sized Government envelopes, a Gideon Bible, and a bank balance of eight thousand, two hundred and twelve dollars. The bank balance was **Noel Constant**'s share in the estate of his anarchist father. The estate had consisted principally of Government bonds.

And **Noel Constant** had an investment program. It was simplicity itself. The Bible would be his investment counselor . . . he increased his fortune to a million and a quarter.

Noel Constant did it without genius and without spies. His system was so idiotically simple that some people can't understand it, no matter how often it is explained. The people who can't understand it are people who have to believe, for their own peace of mind, that tremendous wealth can be produced only by tremendous cleverness.

This was **Noel Constant**'s system:

He took the Gideon Bible that was in his room, and he started with the first sentence in Genesis.

The first sentence in Genesis, as some people may know, is: "In the beginning God created the heaven and the earth." **Noel Constant** wrote the sentence in capital letters, put periods between the letters, divided the letters into pairs, rendering the sentence as follows: "I.N., T.H., E.B., E.G., I.N., N.I., N.G., G.O., D.C., R.E., A.T., E.D., T.H., E.H., E.A., V.E., N.A., N.D., T.H., E.E., A.R., T.H."

And then he looked for corporations with those initials, and bought shares in them. His rule at the beginning was that he would own shares in only one corporation at a time, would invest his whole nest-egg in it, and would sell the instant the value of his shares had doubled.

Noel Constant has an infrequent but regular affair with Florence Whitehill, who gives birth to their son Malachi. At his one and only meeting with his son, he advises him in terms more blunt than Polonius's advice to his son: "My father gave me only two pieces of advice," he said, "and only one of them has stood the test of time. They were: 'Don't touch your principal,' and 'Keep the liquor bottle out of the bedroom.'" (ST 3).

Constant, Sylvanus. *The father of Noel Constant and grandfather of Malachi was* a loom fixer in the New Bedford Mills of the Nattaweena Division of the Grand Republic Woolen Company. He was an anarchist, though he never got into any trouble about it, except with his wife (ST 3). *The eight thousand dollars Noel uses to begin Magnum Opus is his inheritance earned by his anarchist father through investments in government bonds.*

Converse, Lou. *The building contractor for Earl and Maude Fenton in the 1952 short story "The Package" (reprinted in* Bagombo Snuff Box), *Lou returns to the home on the first day the Fentons take ownership. He needs to explain all the remote controls built into the estate's state-of-the-art electronics.*

This first day becomes quite busy since Dr. Charley Freeman pays an unanticipated visit to Earl, his fraternity brother from long ago, simultaneous with the photographer Slotkin and a writer sent by Home Beautiful *magazine to do a feature story on the new feature-rich home. While Earl and Maude change clothes to be photographed in each of the home's many rooms and beautiful gardens, it is Lou who has a meaningful conversation with the visiting Dr. Freeman and learns of his humanitarian work in China, having used his medical degree and family fortune for the past thirty years to open a hospital for the poor. The Communist Chinese government seized Freeman's hospital and jailed him before eventually throwing him out of the country, robbing him of a lifetime's worth of philanthropic endeavors.*

Freeman's appearance at the Fentons' is less than impressive in his threadbare suit and worn-out shoes. Maude's judgment of his appearance leads her to believe he is after a handout or is hatching a scheme to get money from Earl.

It falls to Lou at the end of the evening to reveal Freeman's story to the Fentons. However, as the third party in the room, Lou waits to say anything until Maude successfully clears out the beggar she imagines stands before her.

Maude concocts a story about her sister's family coming to stay the night, leading to Freeman's gracious departure in a cab for a hotel in the city. Earl is overcome with personal guilt and his own lack of humanitarianism. He is last seen mindlessly pressing the buttons on the remote control, asking Lou which one will start the day over again so he can act less selfishly.

Cooley, Franklin. *In* Bluebeard, *this father of six sits astride a riding lawn mower, prompting Rabo Karabekian to wonder if he has any idea about the cultural revolution Rabo was carrying on in his potato barn as he transformed the fatally flawed "Windsor Blue Number Seventeen" into "Now It's the Women's Turn." Regardless, by the time Rabo is prepared to show Circe Berman the painting, they can only reach the barn by following the path cut out by Cooley.*

Cooper, Oveta, and Mary Selwyn Kirk. *In* Slapstick, *these are the caring nurses providing sincere attention to the malformed but brilliant twins Wilbur and Eliza Swain at the family's Vermont estate. Once the twins are older and agree to show the world they are indeed intelligent, they first reveal their true* characters to Oveta Cooper, assuring her all the staff would remain employed for all the kindness they showed over the years.

Corbett, General William K. *The camp commander who plays host to the visiting Shah of Bratpuhr (PP VII).*

Cordiner, Dr. Cordelia Swain. *The world-renowned psychologist hired to test the intelligence of Wilbur and Eliza Swain. She recommends the twins be permanently separated. She has three doctoral degrees and heads a private testing firm responsible for billings of three billion dollars per year. In remembering the impact Dr. Cordiner had on him, Wilbur cites Dostoyevsky and extrapolates even further.* (Slap 16) "One sacred memory from childhood is perhaps the best education." I can think of another quickie education: Meeting a human being who is tremendously respected by the adult world, and realizing that that person is actually malicious.
(Slap 16) **Dr. Cordelia Swain Cordiner** was invariably impressive and gracious when in the presence of grownups. She was elaborately dressed the whole time she was in the mansion—in high-heeled shoes and fancy dresses and jewelry. . . .

When she got Eliza and me alone, though, she seethed with paranoia.

"None of your tricks, no more of your snotty little kid millionaire tricks with me," she would say.

Dr. Cordiner insists on testing the twins separately to prevent Wilbur and Eliza from using their mental telepathy. They test poorly and insist they take the test again—together. Their mother also insists Dr. Cordiner retests them. Upon retesting, they answer every question correctly, but the physical frenzy brought on by their telepathy drives away their parents and causes the doctor to faint.

cork, corkscrew-shaped, corkscrews. (ST 10) The man who had the booth next to Bee's was Harry Brackman. . . . He had a **cork** leg and a stainless steel right hand.
(MH Where I Live) The course was built on the lawn of what had once been an American Legion Post—and, right in the middle of the cunning little bridges and granulated **cork** fairways was a Sherman tank, set there in simpler and less enterprising

days as a memorial to the veterans of World War Two.
(MH Next Door) "If I could hear Harger pulling a **cork**, he can certainly hear you," said his father.
(BC Preface) Those people *(syphilitics)* were infested with carnivorous little **corkscrews** which could be seen only with a microscope. The victims' vertebrae were welded together after the **corkscrews** got through with the meat between. . . .

Here was his problem: his brains, where the instructions to his legs originated, were being eaten alive by **corkscrews**. The wires which had to carry the instructions weren't insulated anymore, or were eaten clear through. Switches along the way were welded open or shut. *Vonnegut recollects a childhood moment he witnessed at the Indianapolis intersection called "the Crossroads of America," the corner of South Meridian and Washington Street, where the famous Ayres clock designed by his father still hangs two stories above the intersection.*
(BC 9) Around the toilet seat was a band of paper. . . . This loop of paper *(marked sanitary)* guaranteed Dwayne that he need have no fear that **corkscrew-shaped** little animals would crawl up his asshole and eat up his wiring. That was one less worry for Dwayne.
(WFG Address at Rededication of Wheaton College Library, 1973) Here I am, due to become fifty years old two days from now. I have imagined during most of that half century that I was responding to life around me as a just and sensitive man, blowing my **cork** with good reason from time to time. Only recently, with the help of a physician, have I realized that I have blown my **cork** every twenty days, no matter what is really going on.
(WFG *Playboy* Interview) PLAYBOY: Do you experience manic periods as well depressive ones?
VONNEGUT: Until recently, about every twenty days, I blew my **cork**. I thought for a long time that I had perfectly good reasons for these periodic blowups; thought people around me had it coming to them. But only recently have I realized that this has been happening regularly since I've been six years old.
(*Blue* 20) Marilee Kemp wasn't the only one who was trapped like Nora in *A Doll's House* before Nora blew her **cork**. I (*Rabo Karabekian*) was another one.

(TQ 25) Jim *(Adams)* had plunged them *(himself and his wife, Alice, Vonnegut's sister)* deep in debt by manufacturing a toy of his own invention. It was a **corked** rubber balloon with a blob of permanently malleable clay inside. It was clay with a skin!

Cormody. *A screw machine operator occupying booth 7 in the 1955 short story "Deer in the Works," reprinted in* Welcome to the Monkey House *(1968).*

Cornell University *(also **Cornell Daily Sun**). Vonnegut often speaks of the two years he spent at Cornell before going into the army shortly after the attack on Pearl Harbor. The "Roots" chapter in* Palm Sunday *contains John Rauch's history of the Vonnegut family complete with his father's instructions to study the sciences, especially chemistry. By his own admission, Vonnegut was not a good student. While at Cornell he wrote a humor column for the* Cornell Daily Sun *and was a member of the Delta Upsilon fraternity.*

Throughout his fiction Vonnegut sprinkles Cornellians. In Player Piano *the pompous real estate agent Dr. Pond holds a Doctor of Realty degree from Cornell's graduate school. All of Dr. Ewing J. Halyard's Cornell degrees are temporarily rescinded because a degree audit reveals he did not complete his undergraduate physical education requirement. Cornell football coach Dr. Harold Roseberry was the subject of a nasty letter Halyard wrote five years earlier, and Roseberry is given the opportunity to exact revenge by Cornell president Dr. Albert Herpers, who passes along the note before Halyard's make-up exam.*

Cat's Cradle's narrator John/Jonah is a Cornell alum as well as a member of Delta Upsilon. Through the course of the novel he learns that H. Lowe Crosby is his fraternity brother and fellow Cornell graduate, and Newt Hoenikker was a DU pledge when he flunked out of Cornell.

God Bless You, Mr. Rosewater's Norman Mushari is a graduate of Cornell's law school. Slapstick's Professor Elihu Swain is credited with starting Cornell's Department of Civil Engineering at the age of twenty-two.

Galápagos's Siegfried von Kleist is another graduate of the Cornell Hotel School, as is Hocus Pocus's Dwight Casey, a Tarkington College English teacher.

Tarkington is depicted as one of Cornell's athletic rivals.

(TQ 25) The best Jane *(Vonnegut's first wife)* could do, and it was a time of panic for unmarried women, was a guy who came home a PFC, who had been flunking all his courses at **Cornell** when he went off to war, and who didn't have a clue as to what to do next, now that free will had kicked in again.

(TQ 44) OK, how about the fact that the name of the owner of the Wynkoop Brewing Company, a guy about Joe's age, was John Hickenlooper? So what? Only this: When I went to **Cornell University** to become a chemist fifty-six years ago, I was made a fraternity brother of a man named John Hickenlooper.

Ting-a-ling?

(TQ 62) Only the dead had doppelgängers at that party *(the clambake)* back in 2001. Arthur Garvey Ulm, poet and Resident Secretary of Xanadu, an employee of the American Academy of Arts and Letters, was short and had a big nose, like my war buddy Bernard V. O'Hare.

My wife Jill was among the living, thank goodness, and was there in the flesh, as was Knox Burger, a **Cornell** classmate of mine.

(BAG Preface by Peter Reed) Earlier, he had cut his teeth on journalism: while attending Shortridge High School in Indianapolis (1936–1940), he had been a regular contributor to and managing editor of its daily newspaper, The Shortridge Echo, and in college he worked on **The Cornell Daily Sun**. In his columns he creates characters, and one begins to see the humor and witty social iconoclasm evident in the mature work. . . .

The late forties and early fifties were still a largely television-free era, with a steady demand for entertaining reading material. In 1949, Vonnegut sent "Report on the Barnhouse Effect" to Collier's. Knox Burger, who was fiction editor there, recognized the author's name from **Cornell**, where Burger had been editor of the campus humor magazine, *The Widow*, and gave the story his attention.

(BAG This Son of Mine) "Look at him, Rudy!" said Merle, lashing the merriment onward. "Foot taller'n his old man, and president of what at **Cornell**?"

"Interfraternity Council," murmured Franklin,

embarrassed. He and Karl avoided looking at each other. Their fathers had taken them hunting together maybe a hundred times. But the boys had hardly spoken to each other, had exchanged little more than humorless nods and head shakes for hits and misses.

"And how many fraternities at **Cornell**?" said Merle.

"Sixty-two," said Franklin, more softly than before.

(MWC 2) As an undergraduate at **Cornell** I was a chemistry major because my brother was a big-shot chemist. Critics feel that a person cannot be a serious artist and also have had a technical education, which I had. I know that customarily English departments in universities, without knowing what they're doing, teach dread of the engineering department, the physics department, and the chemistry department. And this fear, I think, is carried over into criticism. Most of our critics are products of English departments and are very suspicious of anyone who takes an interest in technology.

(MWC 3) Now, I don't mean to intimidate you, but after being a chemist as an undergraduate at **Cornell**, after the war I went to the University of Chicago and studied anthropology, and eventually I took a masters degree in that field. *This is another of Vonnegut's self-deprecating remarks before explaining his graphs of iconic plot types.*

Corpus Christi. (HP 15) His (Tex Johnson's) father, whose name certainly wasn't Johnson, was a Lithuanian second mate on a Russian freighter who jumped ship when it put in for emergency repairs at **Corpus Christi**. Zuzu told me that Tex's father was not only an illegal immigrant but the nephew of the former Communist boss of Lithuania.

(HP 16) I wonder if his father would have jumped ship in **Corpus Christi** if he had known what an unhappy end his only son would come to under American Free Enterprise.

(TQ 3) Joy's Pride itself was perfectly OK, and in a hangar there on Banalulu. It was named in honor of the pilot's mother, Joy Peterson, a nurse in obstetrics in a hospital in **Corpus Christi**, Texas.

Cortes, Hernando. (CC 57) **Hernando Cortes** was the first man to have his sterile conquest of San

Lorenzo recorded on paper. **Cortes** and his men came ashore for fresh water in 1519, named the island, claimed it for Emperor Charles the Fifth, and never returned. Subsequent expeditions came for gold and diamonds and rubies and spices, found none, burned a few natives for entertainment and heresy, and sailed on.

Cortez, Major Ricardo. *The Peruvian jet pilot in* Galápagos *who mistakenly destroys the Colombian freighter* San Mateo, *thinking it is the* Bahía de Darwin.

Corwin, Lance. *When Billy Pilgrim visits a pornographic bookstore in New York's Times Square, he comes upon a Kilgore Trout novel about a man who built a time machine so he could go back and see Jesus. . . . The time-traveler in the book went back to Bible times to find out one thing in particular: Whether or not Jesus had really died on the cross, or whether he had been taken down while still alive, whether he had really gone on living. The hero had a stethoscope along.*

Billy skipped to the end of the book, where the hero mingled with the people who were taking Jesus down from the cross. The time-traveler was the first one up the ladder, dressed in clothes of the period, and he leaned close to Jesus so people couldn't see him use the stethoscope, and he listened.

There wasn't a sound inside the emaciated chest cavity. The Son of God was dead as a doornail.

So it goes.

The time-traveler, whose name was **Lance Corwin**, also got to measure the length of Jesus, but not to weigh him. Jesus was five feet and three and a half inches long (SL5 9).

Cosby, Janet. *Vonnegut's lecture agent is a guest at the closing clambake in* Timequake.

Costa, Antone C. *The subject of Vonnegut's essay "There's a Maniac Loose Out There." Costa killed four women on Cape Cod, and Edith Vonnegut's acquaintance with him is enough for Vonnegut to unveil his shock and fear in this revealing understatement.* (WFG) My nineteen-year-old daughter Edith knows **Tony Costa**. She met him during a crazy summer she spent on her own in Provincetown, knew him well enough to receive and decline an invitation he evidently extended many girls: "Come and see my marijuana patch."

Cotuit Harbor. *In* God Bless You, Mr. Rosewater, *Eunice Morgan Rosewater drowns in the harbor when her son, Eliot, accidentally knocks her overboard with the boom of their sailboat.*

Coulomb, Marc. *Once Rabo Karabekian is no longer Dan Gregory's apprentice, he earns money drawing caricatures of people in Central Park. (Blue 23)* When he struck up a conversation with me in Central Park, **Marc Coulomb** was only twenty-five, and had been sent from Paris to find an advertising agency to make his family's services better known in the U.S.A. *Coulomb is a Bulgarian-Armenian whose original name, Marktich Kouyoumdjian, is later "Frenchified." Coulomb Frères et Cie is the family business.*
(Blue 23) Purely on the basis of race prejudice, I think, one Armenian taking care of another, he bought me a suit, a shirt, a necktie, and a new pair of shoes, and took me to the advertising agency he liked best, which was Leidveld and Moore. He told them they could have the **Coulomb** account if they would hire me as an artist. Which they did.

When Germany invades France, Coulomb Frères et Cie goes out of business and the advertising agency releases Karabekian. Karabekian then joins the U.S. Army, specializing in camouflage techniques.

While in the process of writing his memoirs, Rabo reads Coulomb's obituary in The New York Times. *(Blue 23)* He was a hero of the French Resistance, they say, and was, at the time of his death, chairman of the board of **Coulomb Frères et Cie**, the most extensive travel organization in the world.

Counsel, Bob. *In the short story* "Runaways," *collected in* Bagombo Snuff Box (1999), **Counsel** *was the son of a man who had gotten very rich on coin-operated laundries. He spent most of his time at the country club. He was in love with Annie.*
The mere mention of Bob Counsel's name over the phone invigorates Mary Southard, despondent over her daughter Annie's recent attempt to run away with her boyfriend Rice (the son of a school supply clerk). Mrs. Southard's highly offended sense of class

consciousness is buoyed by the interest she believes is expressed by the voice on the phone. However, Mrs. Southard talks nonstop, blurting apologies for Annie's behavior while hoping Counsel is a harbinger of better days. "Oh, she'll be so glad to hear from you, **Bob**—to know she's still got her old friends, her real friends to fall back on. Hearing your voice," *said the governor's wife,* "our Annie will know everything's going to get back to normal again." *Mrs. Southard's monopolization of the call, barely listening to a briefly acknowledged grunt on the other end, symbolizes the essence of poor parenting. Bob Counsel is not on the other end of the call. It is Rice. The call is a setup to have Annie meet up later with Counsel at the country club for tennis, but it will really be Rice in his Ford at a corner gas station before they run away again.*

Count Dracula. *In what Wilbur describes as his mother's temporary fit of insanity on the eve of the twins' fifteenth birthday, she declares,* "How can I love **Count Dracula** and his blushing bride?"— *meaning Eliza and me (Slap 10).*
Rabo Karabekian describes his trip with Floyd Pomerantz from Manhattan to East Hampton in Pomerantz's stretch Cadillac limousine as "coffinlike"—which he says is better than "womblike." Rabo goes to New York at the prodding of Circe Berman who insists he go to prove he was still a healthy man, in no way in need of assistance, in no way an invalid. So Floyd Pomerantz's chauffeur delivered me to the first flagstone of my doorpath. I clambered out of our fancy casket like **Count Dracula**, blinded by the setting sun. I groped my way to my front door and entered *(Blue 14). It is only after Rabo's return that he finds out about the early demise of his "Windsor Blue Number Seventeen" and eventually repaints the canvas with his masterpiece, "Now It's the Women's Turn."*
Vonnegut takes intense pleasure describing the service people in his New York neighborhood of Turtle Bay, particularly the woman in the postal center. (TQ 57) Because she works sitting down, and because of the counter and the smock she wears, all I have ever seen of her is from the neck up. That's enough! From the neck up she is like a Thanksgiving dinner! I don't mean she looks like a plateful of turkey and sweet potatoes and cranberry sauce. I

mean she makes me feel like that is what has just been set before me. Dig in! Dig in!

Unadorned, I believe, her neck, and face and ears and hair would still be Thanksgiving dinner. Every day, though, she hangs new dingle-dangles from her ears and around her neck. Sometimes her hair is up, sometimes it's down. Sometimes it's frizzy, sometimes it's straight. What she can't do with just her eyes and lips! One day I'm buying a stamp from **Count Dracula**'s daughter! The next day she's the Virgin Mary.

This time she's Ingrid Bergman in *Stromboli*.

counter-clockwise, counterclockwise. (*ST* 1) She was behaving like an invalid—tottering, blinking hard, making her voice like wind in the treetops. She wore a long white dressing gown whose soft folds formed a **counter-clockwise** spiral in harmony with the white staircase. The train of the gown cascaded down the top riser, making Beatrice continuous with the architecture of the mansion. (*ST* 6) The child's hair was jet black, bristly—and the black bristles grew in a violently **counterclockwise** swirl. *This is the beginning of a longer description of Chrono, the son of Malachi and Beatrice.* (*CC* 84) He pointed them out, **counterclockwise**. "House of Hope and Mercy in the Jungle, 'Papa's palace,' and Fort Jesus." *Frank Hoenikker points out some of the significant establishments on San Lorenzo.*

Cowper, William. (*DD* 15) When we heard about that fatal flash back home, in fact, I had quoted the words of **William Cowper**, which a sympathetic English teacher had given me to keep from killing myself when I was young: God moves in a mysterious way / His wonders to perform; / He plants his footsteps in the sea, / And rides upon the storm.

Cox, Riah and Harvey. *The parents of Vonnegut's first wife, Jane Marie Cox. Though Vonnegut reveals nothing about Harvey, he has this eloquent description of his mother-in-law that is as informative as it is stylistically consistent with his depictions of fictional characters,* **RIAH Fagan Cox** was a gallant and pretty little woman from Columbia City, Indiana, which is in the northeast corner of the state,

about halfway between Fort Wayne and Winona Lake. She was born into a so-called "good family," but her father was an alcoholic. He could not hold a job.

So, although little more than a child, **Riah** set out to rescue herself and her brother and eventually their descendents [*sic*] from want and obscurity. She sent herself to the University of Wisconsin, and took a master's degree in the classics. Her thesis was a high school textbook on the Latin and Greek roots of common words in English. It was adopted by many school systems all over the country, and earned enough money to enable **Riah** to put her brother through medical school. He set up practice in Hollywood, and became the beloved obstetrician of many famous movie stars.

She married a lawyer in Indianapolis who did not make much money. She took jobs teaching Latin and Greek and English, and became the Indianapolis representative for touring lecturers and musicians. She also sold silly, witty short stories to magazines from time to time. Thus was she able to send her son and daughter to the best private schools, even during the Great Depression. Her daughter became a Phi Beta Kappa at Swarthmore.

She died three years ago, and is buried in Crown Hill Cemetery in Indianapolis, somewhere between John Dillinger, the bank robber, and James Whitcomb Riley, the "Hoosier Poet." I liked her a lot. She was a good friend of mine. She was my first mother-in-law.

I mention her in this chapter on obscenity because she imagined that I used certain impolite words in my books in order to cause a sensation, in order to make the books more popular. She told me as a friend that the words were having the opposite effect in her circle of friends, at least. Her friends could not bear to read me anymore (*PS Obscenity*). (*TQ* 25) During the Great Depression, financial sacrifices were made to send Allie to school with Hoosier heiresses at Tudor Hall, School for Girls, or *Two-Door Hell, Dump for Dames*, four blocks south of Shortridge High School, where she could have received what I received, a free and much richer and more democratic and madly heterosexual education.

The parents of my first wife Jane, **Harvey and Riah Cox**, did the same thing: sent their only daughter to Tudor Hall, and bought her rich girls' clothes, and maintained for her sake membership in the Woodstock Golf and Country Club they could ill afford, so she could marry a man whose family had money and power.

Craig, David. *(TQ 23)* I told Trout in 2001 about a redheaded boyhood friend of mine, **David Craig**, now a builder in New Orleans, Louisiana, who won a Bronze Star in our war for knocking out a German tank in Normandy. He and a buddy came upon this steel monster parked all alone in a woods. Its engine wasn't running. There wasn't anybody outside. A radio was playing popular music inside.

    Dave and his buddy fetched a bazooka. When they got back, the tank was still there. A radio was still playing music inside. They shot the tank with the bazooka. Germans didn't pop out of the turret. The radio stopped playing. That was all. That was it.

    Dave and his buddy skedaddled away from there.

Crane, Harold. *In the short story "Ambitious Sophomore," collected in* Bagombo Snuff Box *(1999), Harold Crane is the head of the English department at Lincoln High School and an acquaintance of marching band director George M. Helmholtz. When Helmholtz has to cover the $20 beyond the band's budget for a new, custom-designed uniform for piccoloist Leroy Duggan, he tries to sell the gold picture frame gracing his treasured picture of John Philip Sousa. Crane turns down the deal, but they cut another for Helmholtz's spare tire. Crane needs the tire but really makes the deal only because Helmholtz insists it is for the band. At the close of the state band competition,* When he *(Helmholtz) got to his car, he found that the left front tire was flat. He remembered that he had no spare. But he felt nothing more than mild inconvenience. He boarded a streetcar, sat down with the trophy on his lap, and smiled. He was hearing music again.*

Crawfordsville, Indiana. *In the short story "Hal Irwin's Magic Lamp," Mary Irwin returns home to her (unnamed) father's leaking farmhouse in Crawfordsville after the stock market crash, her husband's suicide, and delivering Ella Rice and her baby to the loving arms of a black church congregation.*

Creative Playthings, Inc. *Toward the close of* Mother Night, *New York lawyer Alvin Dobrowitz forwards Howard Campbell's mail to his Jerusalem jail cell. Creative Playthings's educational catalogue is one of the pieces forwarded to Campbell. He is on their mailing list ever since filling out applications to teach German language in the public schools.*

    Campbell takes the company's catalogue and its underlying educational philosophy to task for aiming to teach the wrong lessons. He believes he speaks with as much authority as a teaching lifer for having experienced from the inside the blind delirium of World War II. Campbell appreciates the catalogue's offerings as so many toys to simply keep children busy when they are not in school, but he sees a critical lack in the company's philosophical focus. (MN 45) Such toys help the child work off aggressions. . . . To which I reply:

Dear Friends: As one who has experienced extensively with life in the home and community, using real people in true-to-life situations, I doubt that any playthings could prepare a child for one millionth of what is going to hit him in the teeth, ready or not.

    My own feeling is that a child should start experimenting with real people and real communities from the moment of birth, if possible. If, for some reason, these materials are not available, then playthings must be used.

    But not bland, pleasing, smooth, easily manipulated playthings like those in your brochure, friends. Let there be nothing harmonious about our children's playthings, lest they grow up expecting peace and order, and be eaten alive.

    As for children's working off aggressions, I'm 100% against it. They are going to need all the aggressions they can contain for ultimate release in the adult world. Name one great man in history who did not go boiling and bubbling through childhood with a lashed-down safety valve.

    Let me tell you that the children in my charge for an average of twenty-five hours a week are not likely to lose their keen edge during the forty-five hours they spend with their parents. They aren't moving hand-carved animals on and off a Noah's Ark, believe me. They are spying on real grownups all the time, learning what they fight about, what they're greedy for, how they satisfy their greed, why and how they lie, what makes them go crazy, the different ways they go crazy, and so on.

I cannot predict the fields in which these children of mine will succeed, but I guarantee success for them without exception, anywhere in the civilized world.

Yours for realistic pedagogy,
Howard W. Campbell, Jr.

Creon, PA. *In the short story "Find Me a Dream,"* collected in Bagombo Snuff Box (1999), *Creon is another in the link of small industrial towns tied to the General Forge and Foundry Company. GFF owns the Creon Works, the world's largest pipe producer characterized by Vonnegut's Cold-War rhetoric this way:* If the Communists ever expect to overtake the democracies in sewer pipe production, they are certainly going to have to hump some—because just one factory in **Creon**, **Pennsylvania**, produces more pipe in six months than both Russia and China put together could produce in a year. That wonderful factory is the **Creon Works** of the General Forge and Foundry Company.

As Works manager, Arvin Borders told every rookie engineer, "If you don't like sewer pipe, you won't like **Creon**." Borders himself, a forty-six-year-old bachelor, was known throughout the industry as "Mr. Pipe."

Creon Pipe-Dreamers. *In the short story "Find Me a Dream," collected in* Bagombo Snuff Box *(1999), clarinetist Andy Middleton leads the Creon Pipe-Dreamers, a supper-club jazz band.*

Crimea. *In* Mother Night, *Helga Noth dies in the Crimea when the Russians recapture it from the Nazis. Howard Campbell is unaware of her death though he transmits the news in code to his American contacts. When Resi Noth poses as her sister, she claims to have been captured in the Crimea and raped by Russian soldiers before being sent to the Ukraine.*

Crispus Attucks High School (*also* **Innocent Bystander H.S.**). *Vonnegut makes a mental note to*

explain to Kilgore Trout the significance of the high school jackets he will see in the hospital after being victimized in Dwayne Hoover's rampage. This is yet another example of Vonnegut's using fiction to provoke new ironies for the reader about history and the development of culture—forever the anthropologist. (BC 22) Let's see, let's see. Oh, yes—I have to explain a jacket Trout will see at the hospital. *The jacket bears the inscription "INNOCENT BYSTANDER H.S."*

Here is the explanation: There used to be only one Nigger high school in Midland City, and it was an all Nigger high school still. It was named after **Crispus Attucks**, a black man who was shot by British troops in Boston in 1770. There was an oil painting of this event in the main corridor of the school. Several white people were stopping bullets, too. **Crispus Attucks** himself had a hole in his forehead which looked like the front door of a birdhouse.

But the black people didn't call the school *Crispus Attucks High School* anymore. They called it *Innocent Bystander High*.

Undoubtedly, Vonnegut appropriated the name of the institution from the Indianapolis high school of his youth that was the only one open to the city's African American students.

Crocker, Harry. *The plumber in the 1962 short story "Go Back to Your Precious Wife and Son," reprinted in* Welcome to the Monkey House *(1968), who chides the narrator for not personally measuring the movie starlet Gloria Hilton for her customized shower door.*

Crocker, Pete. *In the short story "Welcome to the Monkey House," Crocker is sheriff of Barnstable County, participating in the manhunt for the* "notorious nothinghead named Bill the Poet."

Crocker, Virginia. (MN 7) My *(Howard Campbell's)* mother was the former **Virginia Crocker**, the daughter of a portrait photographer from Indianapolis. She was a housewife and an amateur cellist. She played cello with the Schenectady Symphony Orchestra, and she once had dreams of my playing the cello, too.

Crone, Joe (*see also* **Billy Pilgrim**). *In Fates Worse Than Death, Vonnegut reveals that Joe Crone was his model for* Slaughterhouse-Five's *Billy Pilgrim. (FWD XI)* The fellow ex-Dresden PW at my National Air and Space Museum lecture was Tom Jones, who had paired off (as ordered) in his 106th Division platoon with **Joe Crone**, the model for Billy Pilgrim, the leading character in *Slaughterhouse-Five*. Jones said, in a letter I got only yesterday, "I remember Crone in Camp Atterbury. When we went on a forced march I had to walk behind him and pick up all the utensils falling out of his backpack. He could never do it right.

"I bunked with him when he died. One morning he woke up and his head was swollen like a watermelon and I talked him into going on sick call. By midday word came back that he had died. You remember we slept two in a bunk so I had to shake **Crone** several times a night and say, 'Let's turn over.' I recall how in the early morning hours the slop cans at the end of the barracks overflowed. Everyone had the shits, and it flowed down the barracks under everyone's bunk. The Germans never would give us more cans."

Joe Crone is buried somewhere in Dresden wearing a white paper suit. He let himself starve to death before the firestorm. In *Slaughterhouse-Five* I have him return home to become a fabulously well-to-do optometrist. (Jones and **Crone** were stockpiled college kids like O'Hare and me. We all read a lot at Camp Atterbury.)

Vonnegut sent a letter to the editor dated April 13, 1995, containing a photostat of Edward Reginald Crone, Jr., who died of malnutrition and despair on April 11th, 1945, while a prisoner of war in Dresden, Germany. He was the model for the character Billy Pilgrim in the novel "Slaughterhouse-Five" [sic] by Kurt Vonnegut, a fellow prisoner. The photostat has additional information and bears the image of Crone as well as the official stamp of the 106th Infantry Division.

Crosby, H. Lowe and Hazel. *The Chicago bicycle manufacturer and his wife travel to San Lorenzo in hopes of opening a new manufacturing plant. He is a Cornell graduate and she is from Indiana, both sources of great pride and granfalloonery. The Cros-bys take refuge in a palace oubliette along with Frank and Newt Hoenikker when the presidential palace is attacked and the outbreak of ice-nine ensues. Hazel instantly becomes fond of John/Jonah, insisting he call her "Mom." They are among the few survivors at the close of* Cat's Cradle.

Crown Hill Cemetery. *The Indianapolis cemetery where the Vonnegut family plot holds his parents and his sister, Alice, as well as the remains of John Dillinger, James Whitcomb Riley, and his first mother-in-law.*

(TQ 10) Allie died in New Jersey. She and her husband, Jim, also a native Hoosier, are buried whole in **Crown Hill Cemetery** in Indianapolis. So is James Whitcomb Riley, the *Hoosier Poet*, a never-married lush. So is John Dillinger, the beloved bank robber of the 1930s. So are our parents, Kurt and Edith, and Father's kid brother Alex Vonnegut, the Harvard-educated life insurance salesman who said, whenever life was good, "If this isn't nice, what is?" So are two previous generations of our parents' forebears: a brewer, an architect, merchants and musicians, and their wives, of course.

Full house!

(TQ 38) It is much too early to talk about, but when he dies, God forbid, I don't think his ashes should be put in **Crown Hill Cemetery** with James Whitcomb Riley and John Dillinger, who belonged only to Indiana. Bernie *(Kurt's brother)* belongs to the World.

Bernie's ashes should be scattered over the dome of a towering thunderhead.

(TQ 39) Why did so many of us bug out of a city built by our ancestors, where our family names were respected, whose streets and speech were so familiar, and where, as I said at Butler University last June, there was indeed the best and worst of Western Civilization?

Adventure!

It may be, too, that we wanted to escape the powerful pull, not of gravity, which is everywhere, but of **Crown Hill Cemetery**.

Crown Hill got my sister Allie. It didn't get Jane. It won't get my big brother Bernie. It won't get me.

See also: JB 10; PS Roots; Obscenity; TQ 41.

crucifix. (*SL5* 2) Billy, after all, had contemplated torture and hideous wounds at the beginning and the end of nearly every day of his childhood. Billy had an extremely gruesome **crucifix** hanging on the wall of his little bedroom in Ilium. A military surgeon would have admired the clinical fidelity of the artist's rendition of all Christ's wounds—the spear wound, the thorn wounds, the holes that were made by the iron spikes. Billy's Christ died horribly. He was pitiful. . . .

Billy wasn't a Catholic, even though he grew up with a ghastly **crucifix** on the wall. His father had no religion. His mother was a substitute organist for several churches around town. She took Billy with her whenever she played, taught him to play a little, too. She said she was going to join a church as soon as she decided which one was right.

She never *did* decide. She did develop a terrific hankering for a **crucifix**, though. And she bought one from a Santa Fe gift shop during a trip the little family made out West during the Great Depression. Like so many Americans, she was trying to construct a life that made sense from things she found in gift shops.

And the **crucifix** went up on the wall of Billy Pilgrim.

(*WFG* Yes, We Have No Nirvanas) I went outside the hotel after that, liking Jesus better than I had ever liked Him before. I wanted to see a **crucifix**, so I could say to it, "You know why You're up there? It's your own fault. You should have practiced Transcendental Meditation, which is easy as pie. You would also have been a better carpenter."

(*HP* 24) But I would tell him now (*Damon Stern*), if he hadn't been killed while trying to save the horses, that the most important message of a **crucifix**, to me anyway, was how unspeakably cruel supposedly sane human beings can be when under orders from a superior authority.

(*TQ* 27) As for how little he (*Kilgore Trout*) was affected by the rerun, as compared with the hell it had been for most of the rest of us, he wrote in *My Ten Years on Automatic Pilot:* "I didn't need a timequake to teach me being alive was a crock of shit. I already knew that from my childhood and **crucifixes** and history books."

crucifixion, crucify, crurifragium (*also* **"Crucifixion in Rome"**). (*GBR* 9) There was a photograph of Trout. He was an old man with a full black beard. He looked like a frightened, aging Jesus, whose sentence to **crucifixion** had been commuted to imprisonment for life.

(*SL5* 5) The flaw in the Christ stories, said the visitor from outer space, was that Christ, who didn't look like much, was actually the Son of the Most Powerful Being in the Universe. Readers understood that, so, when they came to the **crucifixion**, they naturally thought, and Rosewater read out loud again:

Oh, boy—they sure picked the wrong guy to lynch this time!

(*WJ* III) WOODLY Oh—look at the poor, **crucified** violin, would you?

HAROLD It died for your sins.

WOODLY This little corpse is intended as a lesson?

(*JB* 7) I told my poor wife during those first months of unemployment that, yes, that was certainly an option we held, in case all else failed: that I could at any time raise my arms like a man **crucified**, so to speak, and fall backward into General Motors or General Electric or some such thing.

(*PS* Religion) "Now a rich Roman tourist, a man, a successful speculator in Mesopotamian millet futures, comes upon the scene. I make him rich, because everybody hates rich people so much. He is blase about **crucifixions**, since he has seen so many strangers **crucified** all over the Roman Empire. Crosses then were as common as lampposts are today."

(*PS* The Sexual Revolution) Anyone can graph a simple story if he or she will **crucify** it, so to speak, on the intersecting axes.

(*DD* Preface) There really was a John Rettig, and his painting in the Cincinnati Art Museum, "Crucifixion in Rome," is as I have described it.

(*DD* 20) Joseph brought the goblet to the **crucifixion**, and some of Christ's blood fell into it. Joseph was arrested for his Christian sympathies. He was thrown into prison without food or water, but he survived for several years. He had the goblet with him, and every day it filled up with food and drink.

(*DD* 21) One of the ten greatest paintings in the world, as far as he (*Rudy's father*) was concerned, was "**Crucifixion in Rome**," by John Rettig, which he had bought for a song in Holland, during his student days. It now hangs in the Cincinnati Art Museum.

"**Crucifixion in Rome**," in fact, was one of the few successes in the art marketplace, or in any sort of marketplace, which Father experienced in his threescore years and eight. . . .

But the only painting anybody wanted was "**Crucifixion in Rome**." The Cincinnati Art Museum bought it for not much money, and the museum wanted it not because its greatness was so evident, I'm sure, but because it had been painted by a native of Cincinnati. It was a tiny thing, about the size of a shirt cardboard—about the size of Father's work in progress, the nude in his Vienna studio.

(*DD* 21) "**Crucifixion in Rome**" is signed "John Rettig," and it is dated 1888. So it was painted four years before Father was born. Father must have bought it in 1913 or so. Felix thinks there is a possibility that Hitler was with Father on that skylarking trip to Holland. Maybe so.

"**Crucifixion in Rome**" is indeed set in Rome, which I have never seen. I know enough, though, to recognize that it is chock-a-block with architectural anachronisms.

(*Blue* 33) I had better explain to young readers that the *Shroud of Turin* is a linen sheet in which a dead person has been wrapped, which bears the imprint of an adult male who has been **crucified**, which the best scientists of today agree may indeed be two thousand years old. It is widely believed to have swaddled none other than Jesus Christ, and is the chief treasure of the Cathedral of San Giovanni Battista in Turin, Italy.

(*Blue* 35) Mrs. Berman told me a legend about Gypsies I had never heard before: "They stole the nails from the Roman soldiers who were about to **crucify** Jesus," she said.

(*HP* 4) I remained philosophical, thanks to marijuana and alcohol, while the community decided whether to **crucify** me as a fraud or to crown me as a genius. *Hartke speaks of the governing body authorities at the Cleveland Science Fair.*

(*HP* 8) Even though he (*Tex Johnson, the president of Tarkington College*) was dead when the convicts got to him, they were so outraged that they **cruci-**

fied him in the loft of the stable where the students used to keep their horses, at the foot of Musket Mountain.

So a President of Tarkington, my mentor Sam Wakefield, blew his brains out with a Colt .45. And his successor, although he couldn't feel anything, was **crucified**.

(*HP* 12) I think I felt what could be called love for Zuzu Johnson, whose husband was **crucified**.

(*HP* 16) In the folder was a report by a private detective hired by Wilder to investigate my sex life. . . . He didn't miss a thing Zuzu and I did during the second semester. There was only 1 misunderstood incident: when I went up into the loft of the stable, where the Lutz Carillon had been stored before there was a tower and where Tex Johnson was **crucified** 2 years ago. *The misunderstood incident involves Hartke and the architect aunt of a student who visited the tower with him to review the beam work. The detective mistakenly assumes they make love in the tower.*

(*HP* 16) He (*Tex Johnson*) was a cuckold in the present, and **crucifixion** awaited him in the future.

(*HP* 22) The joke was that Tex Johnson, the College President, having seen one too many motorcycle movies, believed that the campus might actually be assaulted by Hell's Angels someday. This fantasy was so real to him that he had bought an Israeli sniper's rifle, complete with a telescopic sight, and ammunition for it from a drugstore in Portland, Oregon. . . . That was the same weapon which would eventually get him **crucified**.

(*HP* 24) He was especially fascinated by Tex Johnson's body. He had seen almost everything in his line of work, he told me, but never a man who had been **crucified**, with spikes through the palms and feet and all.

He told me one thing I'd never realized: that the Jews, not just the Romans, also **crucified** their idea of criminals from time to time. Live and learn!

Darius, King of Persia, he told me, **crucified** 3,000 people he thought were enemies in Babylon. After the Romans put down the slave revolt led by Spartacus, he said, they **crucified** 6,000 of the rebels on either side of the Appian Way! . . .

As I said at the beginning of this book, if I had been a professional soldier back then, I probably would have **crucified** people without thinking much about it, if ordered to do so.

(*HP* 24) I might have taught recruits who had never had anything to do with **crucifixions**, who maybe had never even seen one before, a new word from the vocabulary of military science of that time. The word was *crurifragium*. . . .

It is a Latin word for "breaking the legs of a **crucified** person with an iron rod in order to shorten his time of suffering." But that still didn't make **crucifixion** a country club.

(*HP* 26) In the story, the Elders of Tralfamadore were indifferent, to say the least, to all the suffering going on. When 6,000 rebellious slaves were **crucified** on either side of the Appian Way back in good old 71 B.C., the elders would have been delighted if a **crucified** person had spit into the face of a centurion, giving him pneumonia or TB.

(*HP* 27) I straddled the banana-shaped saddle, which turned out to be surprisingly considerate of my sensitive crotch and hindquarters. Sailing down a hill on that bicycle in the sunshine wasn't anything like being **crucified**.

(*HP* 28) When I visited Lyle up there, he knew the story of those holes, knew the sniper had been **crucified** in the stable loft.

(*HP* 32) Think again about the **crucifixions** of Jesus and the 2 thieves, and the 6,000 slaves who followed the gladiator Spartacus.

(*HP* 39) I also supervised the exhumation of the bodies next to the stable. They had been buried for only a few days, but then the Government, personified by a Coroner and the Medical Examiner from the State Police who knew so much about **crucifixions**, ordered us to dig them up again.

(*HP* 40) That must have been for him like walking down the Appian Way back in 71 B.C., when 6,000 nobodies had just been **crucified** there. Some little kid or maybe a lot of little kids may have walked down that road back then. What could a little kid say on such an occasion? "Daddy, I think I have to go to the bathroom"?

(*FWD* XIV) (Even Jesus Christ, if He hadn't been **crucified**, would have started repeating Himself.)

(*FWD* XIV) "But suppose we foolishly got rid of our nuclear weapons, our Kool-Aid, and an enemy came over here and **crucified** us. **Crucifixion** was the most painful thing the ancient Romans ever

found to do to anyone. They knew as much about pain as we do about genocide. They sometimes **crucified** hundreds of people at one time. That is what they did to all the survivors of the army of Spartacus, which was composed mostly of escaped slaves. They **crucified** them all. There were several miles of crosses."

(*FWD* XIV) "We know of one person who was **crucified** in olden times, who was supposedly as capable as we or the Russians are of ending life everywhere. But He chose to endure agony instead. All He said was, 'Forgive them, Father—they know not what they do.'"

(*FWD* XIV) "I don't believe that we *are* about to be **crucified**. No potential enemy we now face has anywhere near enough carpenters. Not even people at the Pentagon at budget time have mentioned **crucifixion**. I am sorry to have to put that idea into their heads. I will have only myself to blame if, a year from now, the Joint Chiefs of Staff testify under oath that we are on the brink of being **crucified**."

(*FWD* XIV) "So I haven't had much luck, have I, in identifying fates worse than death? **Crucifixion** is the only clear winner so far, and we aren't about to be **crucified**. We aren't about to be enslaved, either, to be treated the way white Americans used to treat black Americans. And no potential enemy that I have heard of wants to come over here to treat all of us the way we still treat American Indians."

(*FWD* XVI) "I will say that you, in terms of numbers, power, and influence, and your spiritual differences with the general population, are analogous to the earliest Christians in the catacombs under Imperial Rome. I hasten to add that your hardships are not the same, nor are you in any danger. Nobody in the power structure thinks children of the Age of Reason amount to a hill of beans. That is the extent of your discomfort. That sure beats being **crucified** upside down or being fed to the carnivorous menagerie at the Circus Maximus."

(*TQ* 1) It appears to me that the most highly evolved Earthling creatures find being alive embarrassing or much worse. Never mind cases of extreme discomfort, such as idealists' being **crucified**. Two important women in my life, my mother and my only sister, Alice, or Allie, in Heaven now, hated life and said so. Allie would cry out, "I give up! I give up!"

(*MWC* 3) The question is, does this system I've devised help us in the evaluation of literature? Perhaps a real masterpiece cannot be **crucified** on a cross of this design. How about *Hamlet*? It's a pretty good piece of work I'd say. Is anybody going to argue that it isn't? I don't have to draw a new line, because Hamlet's situation is the same as Cinderella's, except that the sexes are reversed. (MWC 12) REQUIEM

> The **crucified** planet Earth,
> should it find a voice
> and a sense of irony,
> might now well say
> of our abuse of it,
> "Forgive them, Father,
> They know not what they do."

cruciform. (*Blue* 27) She (*Marilee Kemp*) was only four blocks away—in a palazzo designed for Innocenzo "the Invisible" de Medici by Leon Battista Alberti in the middle of the fifteenth century. It was a **cruciform** structure whose four wings abutted on a domed rotunda twelve meters in diameter and in whose walls were half embedded eighteen Corinthian columns four and a half meters high. Above the capitals of the columns was a clerestory, a wall pierced with thirty-six windows.

"The Cruise of the *Jolly Roger*." *First appearing in the April 1953 issue of* Cape Cod Compass, *and later collected in* Bagombo Snuff Box (1999), *"The Cruise of the* Jolly Roger" *is the patriotically sentimental tale of retired Army Major Nathan Durant as he journeys around Martha's Vineyard, Cape Cod, and New London, Connecticut. A homeless child of the Great Depression with no details concerning family history, regional origins, or simple likes and dislikes, Nathan Durant finds a home in the Army as well as an all-pervasive soldier's view of the world.* During the Great Depression, Nathan Durant was homeless until he found a home in the United States Army. He spent seventeen years in the Army, thinking of the earth as terrain, of the hills and valleys as enfilade and defilade, of the horizon as something a man should never silhouette himself against, of the houses and woods and thickets as cover. It was a good life, and when he—got tired of thinking about war, he got himself a girl

and a bottle, and the next morning he was ready to think about war some more.

When he was thirty-six, an enemy projectile dropped into a command post under thick green cover in defilade in the terrain of Korea, and blew Major Durant, his maps, and his career through the wall of his tent.

Durant is so completely enmeshed with military life that he has no goals beyond being a soldier. While recuperating in a Veteran's hospital, Durant silently adopts the goal of his injured roommate and upon release buys a cabin cruiser. Just as he had no such thought of buying a boat before meeting the other injured veteran, Durant also has no idea what to name his new vessel. However, at the suggestion of some children hanging around the boatyard, Durant agrees to name her The Jolly Roger *and sets off for Martha's Vineyard.*

Martha's Vineyard proves too sedate for Durant, a man of action at home with conflict. He continues on to Chatham, the elbow of Cape Cod, and finds a beautiful woman. However, without his uniform, Durant is no longer that appealing or enticingly mysterious to women. Had he been in his old uniform, seeming as he'd liked to seem in the old days, about to leave on a dangerous mission, he and the woman might have strolled off together. . . . But the woman looked away without interest. He was nobody and nothing. The spark was gone.

Durant's disappointment leads him back to his cruiser where he takes off for Provincetown, a noted artists community. No sooner does he step ashore than he is accosted by a young couple with a camera hoping to take photos of artists who may eventually be famous. Durant disappoints them by saying he is simply a retired Army officer.

Durant then comes upon a group of four artists named Marion, Ed, Teddy, and Lou. Marion sketches Durant, clearly capturing the veteran's pain and directionless disposition developed through the Great Depression and now continuing in his restless first days as a civilian with no clear mission in mind. What Durant saw was a big, scarred, hungry man, hunched over and desolate as a lost child. "Do I really look that bad?" he said, managing to laugh.

"Do you really feel that awful?"

Durant joins the four artists for lunch. Once

Marion realizes the artists have been monopolizing the conversation, they prompt Durant to tell about his military experience. This act of recalling his service is new to him, resulting in the honest, spontaneous assessment of war by a career soldier who presumably has seen it all. He had never tried to tell the tale before, and now, in his eagerness to be glib and urbane, he found himself including details, large and small, as they occurred to him, until his tale was no tale at all, but a formless, unwieldy description of war as it had really seemed: a senseless, complicated mess that in the telling was first-rate realism but miserable entertainment. *Marion expresses compassion for all Durant endured but uses her sentiments as an opportunity to gather her friends and wish him well as they leave.*

Left again to his own amusement, Durant returns to the Jolly Roger *without much incentive to go on owning the boat. Looking for the chart to lead him back to New London, Connecticut, to sell the boat, Durant realizes he is only a few miles from the hometown of his late war buddy George Pefko. When he first arrives at Pefko's hometown, no one is able to remember him or such a family, including the longtime postmistress. However, Annie, a secretary from a nearby law office, remembers the Pefkos rented the summer home of Paul Eldredge throughout a winter season nearly fifteen years earlier. Vonnegut intimates that George Pefko was as rootless and without purpose before joining the Army as was Durant.*

Though Pefko was a transient resident who happened to enlist from that location, the town accorded him the same honor as other fallen soldiers from the area. They named a small square in his honor with a plaque on a rock at its center. Durant is accompanied by Annie as he searches for Pefko's square. This occurs on the day before Memorial Day, the day schoolchildren marched to each of the squares named in honor of the fallen soldiers. As the children lay flowers by Pefko's plaque, Annie and the unnamed school teacher prompt young Tom to explain to Major Durant why they are doing what they are doing. "He died fighting so we could be safe and free. And we're thanking him with flowers, because it was a nice thing to do." He looked up at Annie, amazed that she should ask. "Everybody knows that."

These simple words from one so young are terribly

moving for the old soldier. He finds himself renewed in his patriotism, bonded again with George Pefko, and appealing enough to Annie that one is left believing that he may just have found another home, another reason to live. "It's true, isn't it," murmured Durant. "It's so damn simple, and so easy to forget." Watching the innocent marchers under the flowers, he was aware of life, the beauty and importance of a village at peace. "Maybe I never knew—never had any way of knowing. This is what war is about, isn't it. This."

Durant laughed. "George, you homeless, horny, wild old rummy," he said to George Pefko Memorial Square, "damned if you didn't turn out to be a saint."

The old spark was back. Major Durant, home from the wars, was somebody.

"I wonder," he said to Annie, "if you'd have lunch with me, and then, maybe, we could go for a ride in my boat."

Cruz, Hernando. *The first mate on the* Bahía de Darwin, *Cruz is an experienced seaman having made fifty cruises to the Galápagos Islands. He is part of the skeleton crew sailing the* Bahía de Darwin *from Sweden and supervises its outfitting in Guayaquil. His wife is expecting their twelfth child when he decides to walk away from his ship and return to his family. According to the story's narrator, Leon Trout, Cruz's decision is a momentous one for humanity.* (Gal 1:25) That left Adolf von Kleist completely in charge, although he did not know shit from Shinola about navigation, the Galápagos Islands, or the operation and maintenance of a ship that size.

The combination of the Captain's incompetence and the decision of **Hernando Cruz** to go to the aid of his own flesh and blood, although the stuff of low comedy at the time, has turned out to be of incalculable value to present-day humankind. So much for comedy. So much for supposedly serious stuff. Leon Trout characterized the relationship between Captain von Kleist and **Hernando Cruz** as a common symbiotic pairing of politesse and practicality. Trout surmises that had **Cruz** stayed aboard ship it would never have been run aground by von Kleist which, as it turns out, was the saving grace of humanity.

The Cry of the Nocturnal Goatsucker. *Written pseudonymously under the names Betty and Bobby Brown, this childrearing text is the result of one of the telepathic binges of Eliza and Wilbur Swain in* Slapstick. *When Wilbur later becomes a pediatrician, he publishes it under the pseudonym Dr. Eli W. Rockmell, M.D., an amalgamation of his and his sister's name. The publisher retitles the text* So You Went and Had a Baby.

cuckold, cuckolding. (*ST* 11) He (*Winston Niles Rumfoord*) was so well supplied with great material that he could actually let his voice trail off as he announced that the one-eyed, gold-toothed woman was his wife, and that he had been **cuckolded** by Malachi Constant.
(*GBR* 4) Avondale's clammy respect for the monarchy turned to incredulous contempt, and then to savagery. Yahooism, drinking, **cuckolding**, and self-esteem all took sharp upturns.
Rabo writes of his affair with Marilee Kemp, The man we were about to **cuckold** (*Dan Gregory*) or whatever was fifty-three, with only seven more years to go, a mere stripling in retrospect (*Blue* 21).
(*HP* 16) He (*Tex Johnson*) was a **cuckold** in the present, and crucifixion awaited him in the future.

cuckoo clock in Hell (*also* **totalitarian mind**). (*MN* 38) I have never seen a more sublime demonstration of the **totalitarian mind**, a mind which might be likened unto a system of gears whose teeth have been filed off at random. Such a snaggle-toothed thought machine, driven by a standard or even by a substandard libido, whirls with the jerky, noisy, gaudy pointlessness of a **cuckoo clock in Hell.** . . .
Jones wasn't completely crazy. The dismaying thing about the classic **totalitarian mind** is that any given gear, though mutilated, will have at its circumference unbroken sequences of teeth that are immaculately maintained, that are exquisitely machined.
Hence the **cuckoo clock in Hell**—keeping perfect time for eight minutes and twenty-three seconds, jumping ahead fourteen minutes, keeping perfect time for six seconds, jumping ahead two seconds, keeping perfect time for two hours and one second, then jumping ahead a year.

The missing teeth, of course, are simple, obvious truths, truths available and comprehensible even to ten-year-olds, in most cases.
The willful filing off of gear teeth, the willful doing without certain obvious pieces of information—
That was how a household as contradictory as one composed of Jones, Father Keeley, Vice-Bundesfuehrer Krapptauer, and the Black Fuehrer could exist in relative harmony—
That was how my father-in-law could contain in one mind an indifference toward slave women and love for a blue vase—
That was how Rudolf Hoess, Commandant of Auschwitz, could alternate over the loudspeakers of Auschwitz great music and calls for corpse-carriers—
That was how Nazi Germany could sense no important differences between civilization and hydrophobia—
That is the closest I can come to explaining the legions, the nations of lunatics I've seen in my time. And for me to attempt such a mechanical explanation is perhaps a reflection of the father whose son I was. *Am.* When I pause to think about it, which is rarely, I am, after all, the son of an engineer.

The Culver Citizen. (*TQ* 39) I knew Mr. Johnson pretty well. Father and I used to go hunting for rabbits and birds with him down in Brown County, before Allie cried so much we had to give it up. He asked me there in his office, leaning back in his swivel chair, his eyes slits, how I planned to begin my career as a journalist.
"Well, sir," I said, "I thought maybe I could get a job on ***The Culver Citizen*** and work there for three or four years. I know the area pretty well." Culver was on Lake Maxincuckee in northern Indiana. We used to have a summer cottage on that lake.

Culver Military Academy. *Wilbur Swain travels to Indiana for a summit meeting of sorts with the King of Michigan and Stewart Oriole-2 Mott in a setting drawn from Vonnegut's childhood.* (*Slap* 5) My interview with the King took place, incidentally, in his palace on Lake Maxinkuckee, in northern Indiana, where **Culver Military Academy** had once stood. I was still nominally the President of the United States of America, but I had lost control of everything. There wasn't any Congress any more, or any system of Federal Courts, or any Treasury or Army or any of that.

(FWD 4) "She asked me on our honeymoon what influence **Culver Military Academy**, which I haven't even mentioned, had on my thinking when I was a child. It was at the head of the lake, after all, and was the principal employer of the town, which is also called Culver. It was like a little West Point and Annapolis combined, with a Cavalry troop and a big fleet of sailboats and noisy parades and so on. They fired a cannon every night at sunset.

cupola (see also **belfry** and **tower**). (GBR 5) When a fire call came in, Eliot would push a red button mounted on the wall under his commission as a Notary Public. The button activated a doomsday bullhorn under the **cupola** on top of the firehouse. Eliot had paid for the horn, and the **cupola**, too.

(SL5 3) A siren went off, scared the hell out of him. He was expecting World War Three at any time. The siren was simply announcing high noon. It was housed in a **cupola** atop a firehouse across the street from Billy's office. *The siren shriek from the firehouse cupola prompts another jump in time for Billy Pilgrim.*

(DD 3) After they (*the Maritimo brothers*) had eaten, he took them up into the attic above the loft, the future gun room. There were two old cots up there. Light and air came from windows in a **cupola** at the peak of the roof. A ladder, its bottom bolted to the center of the attic floor, led up into the **cupola**. Father told the brothers that they could make the attic their home, until they found something better.

(DD 4) Father and Mother also bought the enormous weather vane from the gatehouse of the von Furstenberg estate, and put it atop their **cupola** back home, making the studio taller than anything in the county, except for the dome of the county courthouse, a few silos, the Fortunes' dairy barn, and the Midland County National Bank.

(DD 9) I (*Rudy Waltz*) liked it so much, and it liked me so much, since I had fired it so well that morning, that I took it with me when I climbed the lad-

der up into the **cupola**. I wanted to sit up there for a while, and look out over the roofs of the town, supposing that my brother might be going to his death, and hearing and feeling the tanks in the street below. Ah, sweet mystery of life.

(DD 10) Father came upstairs to find out if I was all right. I was better than that. I was at one with the universe. I heard him coming, but I was unconcerned—even though I was still at an open window in the **cupola** with the Springfield in my arms.

(DD 10) I took my own sweet time about descending from the **cupola**. Firing the Springfield over the city was now part of my treasure-house of memories.

(DD 10) Father knew exactly where it had come from. He had heard the bang. He had seen me at the top of the ladder in the **cupola**, with the Springfield in my arms.

(DD 11) Father ascended the ladder into the **cupola**, where I had been so recently. He there accomplished what Marco Maritimo later said should have been impossible for one man with such small and inappropriate tools. He cut away the base of the **cupola**, and he capsized it. It twisted free from its last few feeble moorings, and it went bounding down the slate roof, and it went crashing, weather vane and all, onto Chief Morissey's police car in the driveway below.

(DD 12) They (*Gino and Marco Maritimo*) had received the obscene invitation (*to view Rudy in jail*), offered as though nothing could be more civilized, soon after capping the hole in our roof where the **cupola** had been.

(DD 14) His headlights picked out a strange broken form in the driveway. It hadn't been there on the previous morning. It was of course the wreckage of the **cupola** and the famous weather vane. It had been pulled off the top of the police chief's car and left there in the driveway.

(DD 20) Guess what it was. It was the conical slate roof of my childhood home, only a few blocks away. The peak of the cone, where the **cupola** used to be, was capped with very light gray tar roofing, with bits of sand stuck to it. In the light of a full moon, it was glittering white—like snow. *Rudy tells of a Japanese person new to Midland City who asks him to come out from the pharmacy into the night air to see* *the image which reminds him of* "Fujiyama. . . . the sacred volcano of Japan."

(*DD* 26) In this case, the government was about as careless as a half-wit boy up in a **cupola** with a loaded Springfield rifle—on Mother's Day. *Rudy compares his carelessness with the government's negligence in knowingly selling radioactive cement as war surplus. Exposure to the cement eventually kills his mother.*

(*HP* 3) The 1 bell that was going to get to sing at once was installed in the **cupola** of the mansion, with its rope running all the way down to the first floor. It would call people to classes and, if need be, also serve as a fire alarm. . . .

The rest of the bells, it turned out, would slumber in the loft for 30 years, until 1899, when they were hanged as a family, the 1 from the **cupola** included, on axles in the belfry of the tower of a splendid library given to the school by the Moellenkamp family of Cleveland.

"Custom-Made Bride." *Originally published in the March 27, 1954, edition of* The Saturday Evening Post *and reprinted in 1999's* Bagombo Snuff Box, *the story focuses on the financial difficulties of designer Otto Krummbein and Falloleen, his wife of one month, whose real name is Kitty Cahoun.*

Otto's commercial success and willful ignorance about money are matched only by his shallow appreciation for the exterior beauty of all things, including his wife. Having neglected to ever pay income taxes, his newly arrived bill from the Internal Revenue Service prompts him to contact attorney Hal Murphy who then contacts the unnamed narrator.

The unnamed narrator is a customer's man for an investment counseling firm, charged in his new task with assessing Krummbein's assets and devising a repayment schedule that will keep the designer out of jail. The ensuing story takes place at the coldly modern Krummbein home, a rectangular glass structure sitting atop a cylinder with a spiral staircase outside the curved base leading up to the main level. There is also a spiral staircase within the cylinder that leads down to Otto's windowless home office.

Krummbein made a relative fortune by designing new facades of common objects. Otto Krummbein is a genius, designer of the Krummbein Chair, the Krummbein Di-Modular Bed, the body of the Marittima-Frascati Sports Racer, and the entire line of Mercury Kitchen Appliances.

He is so engrossed in beauty that his mental development in money matters is that of a chickadee.

Krummbein views the landscape of current design technology as part of the reason for modern man's psychological problems, and that is why we have all the unrest, this running to psychiatrists, broken homes, wars. We haven't learned to design our living for our own times. Our lives clash with our times.

As the story unfolds, Krummbein badly miscalculates the importance of external beauty over one's internal virtues. Though married to Kitty for only a month, he has turned her into his own design experiment, going so far as to call her Falloleen instead of Kitty. When the narrator appears at their home, he first meets Falloleen dressed in a tightly fitting leopard print leotard and heavy makeup. As Krummbein proudly declares, Did you ever see a woman who fitted so well into surroundings like this—who seems herself to be designed for contemporary living?

However, when the honeymooners are left together while the narrator tries to make financial sense of their records, it is clear they have nothing to speak about and that Kitty is unhappy being his design experiment. As she tells the narrator about her background and her real name, "It's a Krummbein original," said Falloleen. "Kitty Cahoun didn't go with the decor." She hung her head. "Love—" she said, "don't ask me any more silly questions about love."

When Otto recalls that his latest design project, moonlight-engineered cosmetics, is the result of looking at Kitty without seeing her in the best light possible, she explodes and this eventually leads to fixing their relationship. "I'm sick of being Falloleen and the style show that never ends!" Her voice dropped to a whisper. "She's dull and shallow, scared and lost, unhappy and unloved." *She concedes that she went along with Otto's ideas because she loves him, but she has had enough. Otto admits that compared with Kitty, Falloleen* "was a crashing bore when she wasn't striking a pose or making a dramatic entrance or exit. I lived in terror being left alone with her." *They agree that Otto will continue to design for Falloleen but that Kitty will maintain her personal-*

ity and not be buried by the clothes, the makeup, or the stylizations of Otto.

To round things out, Krummbein gives the narrator free reign to correct his financial affairs. After all, having a professional money manager is the modern way for Otto to assure himself that he can work without getting into financial trouble.

Krummbein's highly prized sense of style and fortunate marketing decisions made him a wealthy man, but he apparently lacked the discipline required for running the back-office needs of his business. Kitty appears to have just the right sense of practicality to help rescue her husband from his own deficiencies.

"Custom-Made Bride" serves as a double entendre: Falloleen Krummbein (née Kitty Cahoun) first appears as the seemingly shallow, highly made-up, and chic incarnation of her avant-garde designer husband's vision, but she also possesses the good sense and discipline to enforce the financial austerity measures recommended by their new financial adviser, the unnamed narrator. As such, the story is a confirmation of Vonnegut's sense of the innate practicality of women and their frequently unappreciated capabilities due to sexist stereotypes.

Cuthrell, William K. *The State Department representative who patronizingly responds to Professor Barnhouse's estimation of the potential peaceful uses for dynamopsychism. Cuthrell sides with General Barker's sense of realism and hopes Barnhouse will, too.* (MH Report on the Barnhouse Effect) "Unfortunately, the general is right in his own way," he said. "I wish to heaven the world were ready for ideals like yours, but it simply isn't. We aren't surrounded by brothers, but by enemies. It isn't a lack of food or resources that has us on the brink of war—it's a struggle for power. Who's going to be in charge of the world, our kind of people or theirs?"

Cuyahoga Bridge and Iron Company. *Founder Daniel McCone grows his company until it becomes the single largest employer in Cleveland by 1913. The neighborhood around the company, the shops and homes, all belong to Cuyahoga Bridge. It becomes the sight of the Cuyahoga Massacre in 1894 after a long and bitter strike.* (JB 1) **Cuyahoga Bridge and Iron**, incidentally, lost its identity, save

in labor history, long ago. It was absorbed by Youngstown Steel shortly after the Second World War, and Youngstown Steel itself has now become a mere division of The RAMJAC Corporation.

Cuyahoga Massacre. (JB Prologue) There is mentioned in this book a violent confrontation between strikers and police and soldiers called the **Cuyahoga Massacre**. It is an invention, a mosaic composed of bits taken from tales of many such riots in not such olden times.

After a long dissertation about the political favors called in by Daniel McCone to put down the strikers and vivid descriptions of the unprofessional behavior by the National Guard, the impressions of the incident left on McCone's heir are simple and ominous. (JB Prologue) Years later Alexander McCone, when asked by Starbuck what he thought the principal cause of the **Cuyahoga Massacre** had been, would reply: "American am-am-am-amateurism in muh-muh-matters of luh-life and duh-duh-duh-death." (JB 1) . . . the man who sent me to Harvard, Alexander Hamilton McCone, watched it *(the massacre)* from the factory clock tower in the company of his father and his older brother John. That was when he ceased to be a slight stammerer and became, when the least bit anxious about anything, a bubbling booby of totally blocked language instead.

Cyclone Bill (*see* **Bill**, *Kilgore Trout's parakeet*)**.**

cylinder, cylindrical. (PP VIII) On the long grade past the golf course, the engine seemed to be hitting on no more than three **cylinders**, and a squad from the Reconstruction and Reclamation Corps, putting in a spruce windbreak to the north of the clubhouse, turned to watch the car's enervated struggle with gravity.
(ST 1) The mower's swath skirted a dry fountain. The man who ran the mower had become creative at this point, had made the path fork. Constant could choose the side of the fountain on which he preferred to pass. Constant stopped at the fork, looked up. The fountain itself was marvelously creative. It was a cone described by many stone bowls of decreasing diameters. The bowls were collars on a **cylindrical** shaft forty feet high.
(ST 5) He (*Unk—Malachi Constant*) found an alu-

minum **cylinder** with a screw cap. Inside the **cylinder** was a very long letter written in pencil. *The letter is written by Unk to himself after having had his memory wiped clean a series of times prior to the Martian invasion of Earth. His brainwashing is not totally successful. He writes the letter to himself in order to piece together the small bits of information he still has rattling around inside.*

(CC 97) Around his *(Papa Monzano's)* neck hung a chain with a **cylinder** the size of a rifle cartridge for a pendant. I supposed that the **cylinder** contained some magic charm. I was mistaken. It contained a splinter of *ice-nine.*

(CC 105) "He took it! Whatever was in that **cylinder**, 'Papa' took—and now he's dead."

I remembered the **cylinder** "Papa" had hung around his neck, and I made an obvious guess as to its contents. "Cyanide?" . . .

That he had died of the contents of the **cylinder** around his neck was obvious. One hand held the **cylinder** and the **cylinder** was uncapped. And the thumb and index finger of the other hand, as though having just released a little pinch of something, were stuck between his teeth.

(SL5 4) The formation flew backwards over a German city that was in flames. The bombers opened their bomb bay doors, exerted a miraculous magnetism which shrunk the fires, gathered them into **cylindrical** steel containers, and lifted the containers into the bellies of the planes. . . .

When the bombers got back to their base, the steel **cylinders** were taken from the racks and shipped back to the United States of America, where factories were operating night and day, dismantling the **cylinders**, separating the dangerous contents into minerals. Touchingly, it was mainly women who did this work. The minerals were then shipped to specialists in remote areas. It was their business to put them into the ground, to hide them cleverly, so they would never hurt anybody ever again.

(SL5 4) The saucer was one hundred feet in diameter, with portholes around its rim. . . . It came down to hover over Billy, and to enclose him in a **cylinder** of pulsing purple light.

(MH The Manned Missiles) Stepan made pleasant jokes about his little house in the sky. He said it was a **cylinder** ten meters long and four meters in diameter. It could be very cozy.

(BC 15) There was a sexual revolution going on in the country, and women were demanding that men pay more attention to women's pleasure during sexual intercourse, and not just think of themselves. The key to their pleasure, they said, and scientists backed them up, was the clitoris, a tiny meat **cylinder** which was right above the hole in women where men were supposed to stick their much larger **cylinders**.

(WFG Address to the National Institute of Arts and Letters, 1971) I began with physical anthropology. I was taught how to measure the size of the brain of a human being who had been dead a long time, who was all dried out. I bored a hole in his skull, and I filled it with grains of polished rice. Then I emptied the rice into a graduated **cylinder**. I found this tedious.

(WFG Address to the National Institute of Arts and Letters, 1971) Dr. Redfield is dead now. Perhaps some physical anthropologist of the future will fill his skull with grains of polished rice, and empty it out again—into a graduated **cylinder**.

(Slap 19) Be that as it may, our hands were busy—which is often the case with the hands of dying people. We had brought what we thought were the best of our writings with us. We rolled them into a **cylinder**, which we hid in an empty bronze funerary urn. *These are the treatises written by Eliza and Wilbur Swain that would eventually lead to a disruption in the Earth's gravitational force when the Chinese base their experiments on the stolen documents.*

(DD 7) The engine *(on the 1932 Keedsler touring car)* had sixteen **cylinders**, and the two spare tires were mounted in shallow wells in the front fenders.

(TQ 55) Listen: Uncle Carl, in 1900 or thereabouts, experimented with the effects of X rays and radioactivity on condensation in a cloud chamber, a wooden **cylinder** filled with a fog he himself had concocted. He concluded and published as a certainty that ionization was relatively unimportant in condensation.

At about the same time, friends and neighbors, the Scottish physicist Charles Thomson Rees Wilson performed similar experiments with a cloud chamber made of glass. The canny Scot proved that ions produced by X rays and radioactivity had a lot to do with condensation. He criticized Uncle

Carl for ignoring contamination from the wood walls of his chamber, for his crude method of making clouds, and for not shielding his fog from the electrical field of his X-ray apparatus.

Wilson went on to make paths of electrically charged particles visible to the naked eye by means of his cloud chamber. In 1927, he shared a Nobel Prize for Physics for doing this. Uncle Carl must have felt like something the cat drug in!

(*BAG* Custom-Made Bride) Otto's home and place of business is thirty miles from town, in a wilderness by a waterfall. It looks, roughly, like a matchbox resting on a spool. The upper story, the matchbox, has glass walls all the way around, and the lower story, the spool, is a windowless brick **cylinder**. . . . She was making spiral motions with her hand, and I understood at last that I was to climb the spiral ramp that wound around the brick **cylinder**.

(*BAG* Custom-Made Bride) His (*Otto Krummbein's*) studio was inside the brick **cylinder**, and he led me through a door and down another spiral ramp into it. There were no windows. All light was artificial.

(*BAG* Ambitious Sophomore) Helmholtz was lighting pieces of punk with Haley's lighter, blowing on them, and passing them on to every fourth man, who had a straight, **cylindrical** firework under his sash.

D

"D.P." (1953) (*see also* **Karl Heinz**). *The short story reprinted in* Welcome to the Monkey House *(1968) about six-year-old Karl Heinz, the offspring of a black American soldier and a German woman, according to Peter, an older orphan living in the same Karlswald orphanage. Karl lives in the hope that among the American military stationed nearby, someone will reunite him with his father.*

D'Arthanay, Barbara. *Vonnegut's daughter-in-law by her marriage to his inherited son/nephew, James Adams.* (PS Children) He (James Adams) is married to a former New England schoolteacher who lived and worked with him for several years on his goat farm on a mountaintop in Jamaica. They are as uninterested in social rank and property as was Henry David Thoreau.

The Daffy-nition. *The privately published newspaper for those in the extended family of Daffodils.* (*Slap* 37) There were editorials calling for family health insurance programs and sports teams and so on. There was one interesting essay, I remember, either in *The Daffy-nition* or *The Coober Gossip*, which said that families with high moral standards were the best maintainers of law and order, and that police departments could be expected to fade away.

Daggett, Bill. *In the short story "The Powder-Blue Dragon," collected in* Bagombo Snuff Box *(1999), Daggett is the owner of two sports car dealerships, one in New York City and another in a New England seaside* village that had once been a whaling port. Now its natives served the owners and renters of mansions on the beachfront. *He employs Kiah Higgins (for cash—no benefits) as an hourly worker. Daggett, a portly New Yorker who operated his branch showroom only in the summer, is one of a string of characters in the story who pays little attention to Kiah beyond his employment.*

Daggett contributes to Kiah's sense of ignored anonymity, a point driven home once more when he feels compelled to call for bank verification of Kiah's check for $5,651, the full purchase price of the Marittima-Frascati sports car Daggett has at his city dealership. Upon delivery of the car to Kiah, Daggett explains in great detail the precise manufacturer recommendations for breaking in the car before trying to hit its top speed rating of 130 mph. Having gone through the exercise of educating the young man about the car, Daggett does not understand why Kiah intentionally burns up the engine on his first day of ownership.

dagonite. *Vonnegut—through Leon Trout—discusses the ancestry of this explosive as another means of discussing the interconnectedness of all activity.* (*Gal* 1:38) The happy Colombianos were chewing and swallowing some of that poor cow's meat when they were blown to bits by the latest advance in the evolution of high explosives, which was called "**dagonite**." **Dagonite** was the son, so to speak, of a considerably weaker explosive made by the same company, and called "glacco." Glacco begat **dagonite**, so to speak, and both were descendants of Greek fire and gunpowder and dynamite and cordite and TNT.

So it might be said that the Colombianos had treated the cow abominably, but that retribution had been swift and terrible, thanks largely to the big-brained inventors of **dagonite**.
(*Gal* 1:38) The detonation of **dagonite**, son of glacco, direct descendant of noble dynamite, caused a tidal wave in the estuary, which was six meters high when it swept the bus off the wharf at the Guayaquil waterfront and drowned Siegfried von Kleist, who wanted to die anyway.

Daily Pancreas. *The Sweetbread College newspaper in the play* The Chemistry Professor *(PS Jekyll and Hyde Updated).*

"The Dancing Fool." *This Kilgore Trout short story is printed in a 1962 edition of* Black Garterbelt *magazine, a pornographic publication that uses any text* *as filler between pictures of naked women. Trout finds the magazine while browsing through an adult bookstore in Times Square. Unaware this story was ever picked up for publication, Trout was looking for materials he previously published to prepare himself for the Midland City Arts Festival. As seen in the reference below from* Fates Worse Than Death, *Vonnegut had other—more political—ambitions for the story's theme.* (BC 5) As for the story itself, it was entitled "**The Dancing Fool**." Like so many Trout stories, it was about a tragic failure to communicate.

Here was the plot: A flying saucer creature named Zog arrived on Earth to explain how wars could be prevented and how cancer could be cured. He brought the information from Margo, a planet where the natives conversed by means of farts and tap dancing.

Zog landed at night in Connecticut. He had no sooner touched down than he saw a house on fire. He rushed into the house, farting and tap dancing, warning the people about the terrible danger they were in. The head of the house brained Zog with a golfclub.

(FWD What My Son Mark Wanted Me to Tell the Psychiatrists in Philadelphia, Which Was Also the Afterword to a New Edition of His Book *The Eden Express*) Because the most visible of the antiwar protestors, who included many returned Vietnam veterans, were so young, all they stood for could be dismissed by their enemies as symptoms of immaturity. They were attempting to save lives and resources, but their appearance and manners (and music, and excitement and confusion about sex) made them unfit, so went the argument, for such a serious role.

I memorialized this prejudice in a plot scheme for a short story (never written) to be called "**The Dancing Fool**." I included the plot in a novel.

Dane, Lieutenant General Franklin. *The military's top officer of Project Cyclops in the short story "Thanatos." It is Dane's decision to try jamming radio transmissions from Major Rice to keep the public from either panicking or simply losing interest in earthly matters if they should learn the truth about where human souls go after death, that they in fact can be contacted if man can reach the Thanasphere, as accomplished by the major.*

Darlington, Edward Seward. *In* The Sirens of Titan, *the halfwit stable boy at the Rumfoord Mansion during Winston's childhood. He is teamed with the Japanese gardener and his daughter against Winston, the butler, and Miss MacKenzie for games of German batball.*

Darrow, Clarence (*see* **God Bless You, Dr. Kevorkian**).

Darwin, Alton. *Alton Darwin leads the prison revolt in* Hocus Pocus. *Befriended by Eugene Debs Hartke, Darwin's complex character provokes Hartke's comparisons to both Jack Patton and himself. Darwin is killed by a sniper's bullet while ice skating at night on the frozen lake between the college and the prison. Darwin's story has an enigmatic hold on Hartke.* (HP 9) When I later went to work at the prison, I encountered a mass murderer named **Alton Darwin** who also could do arithmetic in his head. He was Black. Unlike Claudia Roosevelt, he was highly intelligent in the verbal area. The people he had murdered were rivals or deadbeats or police informers or cases of mistaken identity or innocent bystanders in the illegal drug industry. His manner of speaking was eloquent and thought-provoking.

(HP 9) **Alton Darwin** was the first example I had ever seen of leadership in the raw. He was a man without any badges of rank, and with no previously existing organization or widely understood plan of action. He had been a modest, unremarkable man in prison. The moment he got out, though, sudden delusions of grandeur made him the only man who knew what to do next, which was to attack Scipio, where glory and riches awaited all who dared to follow him.

(HP 9) **Alton Darwin** had the same untightened screw (*as Jack Patton*). He was a convicted mass murderer, but never showed any remorse that I could see.

(HP 9) **Alton Darwin**, and this was true of Jack Patton, too, spoke of trivial and serious matters in the same tone of voice, with the same gestures and facial expressions. Nothing mattered more or less than anything else. . . .

So I was pondering the desertion problem when **Alton Darwin** said with exactly the same intensity, "I can skate on ice. Do you believe that?"

(*HP* 10) SOMETIMES **Alton Darwin** would talk to me about the planet he was on before he was transported in a steel box to Athena. "Drugs were food," he said. "I was in the food business. Just because people on one planet eat a certain kind of food they're hungry for, that makes them feel better after they eat it, that doesn't mean people on other planets shouldn't eat something else. On some planets I'm sure there are people who eat stones, and then feel wonderful for a little while afterwards. Then it's time to eat stones again."

(*HP* 19) I have long had a sort of ballpark figure in my head. I am quite sure that I killed more people than did my brother-in-law. I hadn't been working as a teacher at Athena very long before it occurred to me that I had almost certainly killed more people than had the mass murderer **Alton Darwin** or anybody else serving time in there. That didn't trouble me, and still doesn't. I just think it is interesting.

(*HP* 25) The convicts didn't create a new flag. They flew the Stars and Stripes from the bell tower (*of Tarkington College*). **Alton Darwin** said they weren't against America. He said, "We are America."

(*HP* 36) "STAR Wars," said **Alton Darwin**.

He was alluding to Ronald Reagan's dream of having scientists build an invisible dome over this country, with electronics and lasers and so on, which no enemy plane or projectile could ever penetrate. **Darwin** believed that the social standing of his hostages was an invisible dome over Scipio.

Darwin, Charles (*also* **Darwinian, Darwinism,** *and* **Darwinists**).

Vonnegut injects the father of evolutionary theory a number of times throughout his work, perhaps nowhere more continuously than in Galápagos.

After Vonnegut strings together the deaths of Robert Kennedy, Martin Luther King, Jr., the government's body counts in Vietnam, and the natural death of his father, he continues with this passage. (*SL5* 10) On Tralfamadore, says Billy Pilgrim, there isn't much interest in Jesus Christ. The Earthling figure who is most engaging to the Tralfamadorian mind, he says, is **Charles Darwin**—who taught that those who die are meant to die, that corpses are improvements. So it goes.

The same general idea appears in "The Big Board" by Kilgore Trout. The flying saucer creatures who capture Trout's hero ask him about Darwin. They also ask him about golf.

(*WFG* In a Manner That Must Shame God Himself) And looking at one day's news or a few days' news or a few years' news is a lot like staring at the radiator ornament of a Stutz Bearcat, it seems to me. Which is why so many of us would love to have a visitor from another planet, who might have a larger view of our day-to-day enterprises, who might be able to give us some clue as to what is really going on.

He would tell us, I think, that no real Winner fears God or believes in a punitive afterlife. He might say that Earthlings put such emphasis on truthfulness in order to be believed when they lie. President Nixon, for instance, was free to lie during his acceptance speech at the convention, if he wanted to, because of his famous love for the truth. And the name of the game was "Survival." Everything else was hokum.

He might congratulate us for learning so much about healing the planet, and warn us against wounding the planet so horribly during our real estate dealings, that it might never heal.

The visitor might say by way of farewell what **Charles Darwin** seemed to say to us, and we might write his words in stone, all in capital letters, like the words of the mayor of Birmingham: THE WINNERS / ARE AT WAR / WITH THE LOSERS, / AND THE FIX / IS ON. / THE PROSPECTS / FOR PEACE ARE / AWFUL.

Vonnegut muses that if he were a visitor from another planet, he would like to address earthlings based on his observations. (*WFG* In a Manner That Must Shame God Himself) I would say, "The two real political parties in America are the *Winners* and the *Losers*. The people do not acknowledge this. They claim membership in two imaginary parties, the *Republicans* and the *Democrats*, instead.

"Both imaginary parties are bossed by Winners. When Republicans battle Democrats, this much is certain: Winners will win.

"The Democrats have been the larger party in the past because their leaders have not been as openly contemptuous of Losers as the Republicans have been.

"Losers can join imaginary parties. Losers can vote.

"Losers have thousands of religions, often of the

bleeding heart variety," I would go on. "The single religion of the Winners is a harsh interpretation of **Darwinism**, which argues that it is the will of the universe that only the fittest should survive.

"The most pitiless **Darwinists** are attracted to the Republican party, which regularly purges itself of suspected bleeding hearts. It is in the process now of isolating and ejecting Representative Paul N. McCloskey, for instance, who has openly raged and even wept about the killing and maiming of Vietnamese."

(*WFG Playboy* Interview) PLAYBOY: What *is* in control?

VONNEGUT: Mankind's wish to improve itself.

PLAYBOY: In a **Darwinian** sense?

VONNEGUT: I'm not very grateful for **Darwin**, although I suspect he was right. His ideas make people crueler. **Darwinism** says to them that people who get sick deserve to be sick, that people who are in trouble most deserve to be in trouble. When anybody dies, cruel **Darwinists** imagine we're obviously improving ourselves in some way. And any man who's on top is there because he's a superior animal. That's the social **Darwinism** of the last century, and it continues to boom. But forget **Darwin**. . . .

(*Gal* 1:3) **Darwin Bay** was named in honor of the great English scientist **Charles Darwin**, who had visited Genovesa and several of its neighbors for five weeks back in 1835—when he was a mere stripling of twenty-six, nine years younger than *(James)* Wait. **Darwin** was then the unpaid naturalist aboard Her Majesty's Ship *Beagle*, on a mapping expedition that would take him completely around the world and would last five years.

In the cruise brochure, which was intended to delight nature-lovers rather than the pleasure-seekers, **Darwin**'s own description of a typical Galápagos Island was reproduced, and was taken from his first book, *The Voyage of the* Beagle:

"Nothing could be less inviting than the first appearance. A broken field of black basaltic lava, thrown into the most rugged waves, and crossed by great fissures, is everywhere covered by stunted, sun-burnt brushwood, which shows little signs of life. The dry and parched surface, being heated by the noon-day sun, gave to the air a close and sultry feeling, like that from a stove: we fancied even that the bushes smelt unpleasantly."

Darwin continued: "The entire surface . . . seems to have been permeated, like a sieve, by the subterranean vapours: here and there the lava, whilst soft, had been blown into great bubbles; and in other parts, the tops of caverns similarly formed have fallen in, leaving circular parts with steep sides." He was vividly reminded, he wrote, ". . . of those parts of Staffordshire, where the great iron foundries are most numerous."

(*Gal* 1:4) The Anglo-Saxon **Charles Darwin**, underspoken and gentlemanly, impersonal and asexual and blankly observant in his writings, was a hero in teeming, passionate, polyglot Guayaquil because he was the inspiration for a tourist boom. If it weren't for **Darwin**, there would not have been a Hotel El Dorado or a *Bahía de Darwin* to accommodate James Wait. There would have been no boutique to clothe him so comically.

If **Charles Darwin** had not declared the Galápagos Islands marvelously instructive, Guayaquil would have been just one more hot and filthy seaport, and the islands would have been worth no more to Ecuador than the slag heaps of Staffordshire.

Darwin did not change the islands, but only people's opinion of them. That was how important mere opinions used to be back in the era of great big brains.

(*FWD* Preface) Q: What is the trait you most deplore in others?

A: **Social Darwinism**.

(*FWD* XV) "If you go to the Galápagos Islands, and see all the strange creatures, you are bound to think what **Charles Darwin** thought when he went there: How much time Nature has in which to accomplish simply anything. If we desolate this planet, Nature can get life going again. All it takes is a few million years or so, the wink of an eye to Nature."

(*FWD* XVI) Bishop Moore, as I've said, went to war a religious skeptic and came out of it a profoundly convinced Trinitarian. He told me he had a vision during the fighting on Guadalcanal. He went on from his vision (although he was born rich and had a rich Anglo-Saxon's education and tastes and friends) to minister to the poor in parishes where the prosperous had fled to the suburbs, to speak loathingly of social **Darwinists** (Neo-Cons, the

FBI, the CIA, humorless, anal-retentive Republicans, and so on).

(*TQ* 27) "The smarties had to be getting outside help," Trout said to me at Xanadu. While impersonating the mad Sunoco, Trout himself seemed convinced that there was a great big computer somewhere, which, by means of radio, had told Pythagoras about right triangles, and Newton about gravity, and **Darwin** about evolution, and Pasteur about germs, and Einstein about relativity, and on and on.

"That computer, wherever it is, whatever it is, while pretending to help us, may actually be trying to kill us dummies with too much to think about," said Kilgore Trout.

(*TQ* 27) I did not ask, but the surgical metaphor could not have been unfamiliar to him. Furthermore, life being the **Darwinian** experiment, or "crock of shit," as Trout liked to call it, Roger himself had surely departed more than one tennis tournament having, like Skip, undergone a colostomy to his self-regard.

(*TQ* 47) Listen: A Harvard education for my Uncle Alex wasn't the trophy of a micromanaged **Darwinian** victory over others that it is today. His father, the architect Bernard Vonnegut, sent him there in order that he might become *civilized*, which he did indeed become, although fabulously henpecked, and nothing more than a life insurance salesman.

I am eternally grateful to him, and indirectly to what Harvard used to be, I suppose, for my knack of finding in great books, some of them very funny books, reason enough to feel honored to be alive, no matter what else may be going on.

(*TQ* 48) But when Raymond Trout went there (*Bermuda*) as a doctoral candidate with his bride, he found that the females had taken to bowdlerizing the nurturing process by kicking the eggs off the top of the steeple.

Thus did Kilgore Trout's father providentially become a specialist, thanks to the female Bermuda Erns' initiative, or whatever you want to call it, in evolutionary mechanisms governing fates of species, mechanisms other than the Occam's Razor of **Darwin's Natural Selection**.

(*TQ* 49) I asked my big brother Bernie in the American Museum of Natural History in New York, and this was long before the period of the rerun, whether he believed in **Darwin's** theory of evolution. He said he did, and I asked how come, and he said, "Because it's the only game in town."

Bernie's reply is the tag line of yet another joke from long ago, like "Ting-a-ling, you son of a bitch!" It seems a guy is off to play cards, and a friend tells him the game is crooked. The guy says, "Yeah, I know, but it's the only game in town."

I am too lazy to chase down the exact quotation, but the British astronomer Fred Hoyle said something to this effect: That believing in **Darwin's** theoretical mechanisms of evolution was like believing that a hurricane could blow through a junkyard and build a Boeing 747.

No matter what is doing the creating, I have to say that the giraffe and the rhinoceros are ridiculous.

And so is the human brain, capable, in cahoots with the more sensitive parts of the body, such as the ding-dong, of hating life while pretending to love it, and behaving accordingly: "Somebody shoot me while I'm happy!"

(*GBK* Isaac Newton) It isn't enough for Newton that during his eighty-five years on Earth he invented calculus, codified and quantified the laws of gravity, motion, and optics, and designed the first reflecting telescope. He can't forgive himself for having left it to **Darwin** to come up with the theory of evolution, to Pasteur to come up with the germ theory, and to Albert Einstein to come up with relativity.

"I must have been deaf, dumb, and blind not to have come up with those myself," he said to me. "What could have been more obvious?"

(*GBK* Mary Wollstonecraft Shelley)
never before
have i been
a tease
about a dead person I've interviewed, but now is the time. Let's see how smart you are about the history of big ideas.

For starters: This former Earthling, although not quite twenty, published an idea as persistent in the minds of thinking people today as Pasteur's germ theory, say, or **Darwin's** theory of evolution, or Malthus's dread of overpopulation.

Das Reich der Zwei. *Translated as* "The **Nation of Two**," *this is the play Howard Campbell thinks of writing about his relationship with Helga Noth.* (MN 9) It was going to be about the love my wife and I had for each other. It was going to show how a pair of lovers in a world gone mad could survive by being loyal only to a nation composed of themselves—a **nation of two**.
(MN 10) *Das Reich der Zwei*, the **nation of two** my Helga and I had—its territory, the territory we defended so jealously, didn't go much beyond the bounds of our great double bed.

While contemplating the play and sitting on a park bench, Campbell is approached by his soon-to-be Blue Fairy Godmother and asked to become an American agent. His double-agent status eventually makes Campbell a "stateless schizophrenic." (MN 10) And when that **nation** ceased to be, I became what I am today and what I always will be, a stateless person.

This image of a "nation of two" is also used in Slapstick *when Wilbur and Eliza decide to bring true their mother's wish for any sign of intelligence among the twins. They paint a sign on a bedsheet telling their parents they can be as smart or dumb as the world wants them to be. This prompts the intelligence testing conducted by Dr. Cordelia Swain Cordiner and the twins' eventual separation.* (Slap 11) THUS did Eliza and I destroy our Paradise—our **nation of two**.

Davenport Spot-welding Company (*also* **Davenport Wire and Cable Company**). *In* "Mnemonics," *Vonnegut's second published short story, originally appearing in the April 1951 issue of* Collier's *magazine and later reprinted in the 1999 collection* Bagombo Snuff Box, *these two companies have confused billing problems that Alfred Moorhead sorts out with the assistance of his mnemonics training and naturally gifted memory.*

Davis, Alvin. *The subject of Vonnegut's dedication to* God Bless You, Mr. Rosewater. *For Alvin Davis, / the telepath, / the hoodlums' friend. He is more fully remembered in* Timequake *after Kilgore Trout declares that Hemingway, O'Neill, Sinclair Lewis, and John Steinbeck were examples of literary heroes who were alcoholics. Vonnegut adds the following*

about William Saroyan and Alvin Davis. (TQ 8) Gambling ruined William Saroyan. A combination of booze and gambling did in the journalist **Alvin Davis**, a much-missed friend of mine. I asked **Al** one time what was the biggest kick he got from games of chance. He said it came after he had lost all his money in an around-the-clock poker game.

He went back after a few hours with money he had gotten wherever he could get it, from a friend, from hocking something, from a loan-shark. And he sat down at the table and said, "Deal me in."

Davis, Benjamin. *Toward the close of* Breakfast of Champions, *Vonnegut admits to a lack of attention that prompts him to reveal that in an earlier version of the book, Benjamin Davis took care of Kazak, the Doberman pinscher guarding the supply yard of the Maritimo Brothers Construction Company. In that previous version, Vonnegut explains that Benjamin Davis is the husband of Lottie Davis, Dwayne Hoover's maid. Aside from training Kazak to be mean and turning him loose at sundown, Davis is also first trumpet with the Midland City Symphony Orchestra—without pay. In the text as it finally appears, Benjamin Davis is outside the story except as Vonnegut chronicles this false allusion (see BC 285–86).*

Davis, Lottie. *Dwayne Hoover's black housekeeper, married to Benjamin Davis. Lottie appears in both* Breakfast of Champions *and* Deadeye Dick. *Aside from Dwayne Hoover, Lottie is the only other person to cry at Celia Hoover's funeral in* Deadeye Dick.
(BC 2) Dwayne had a black servant named **Lottie Davis**. She cleaned his house every day. Then she cooked his supper for him and served it. Then she went home. She was descended from slaves.

Lottie Davis and Dwayne didn't talk much, even though they liked each other a lot.
(BC Epilogue) In an earlier version of this book, I had Benjamin Davis, the black husband of **Lottie Davis**, Dwayne Hoover's maid, take care of Kazak.
(DD 27) The service started quietly enough. I heard only one person crying, and she was way up front, and I think it was **Lottie Davis**, the Hoovers' black maid. She and Dwayne were the only people there to do a whole lot of crying, since practically

nobody else had seen Celia for seven years—since she had starred in *Katmandu*.

The Day the World Ended (see also Cat's Cradle).

The title of John/Jonah's opening chapter to his memoirs reveals the unlikely start of his journey toward enlightenment and the frozen apocalypse. (CC 1) When I was a much younger man, I began to collect material for a book to be called **The Day the World Ended**.

The book was to be factual.

The book was to be an account of what important Americans had done on the day when the first atomic bomb was dropped on Hiroshima, Japan.

It was to be a Christian book. I was a Christian then. I am a Bokononist now.

I would have been a Bokononist then, if there had been anyone to teach me the bittersweet lies of Bokonon. But Bokononism was unknown beyond the gravel beaches and coral knives that ring this little island in the Caribbean Sea, the Republic of San Lorenzo.

We Bokononists believe that humanity is organized into teams, teams that do God's Will without ever discovering what they are doing. Such a team is called a *karass* by Bokonon, and the instrument, the *kan-kan*, that brought me into my own particular *karass* was the book I never finished, the book to be called **The Day the World Ended**.

While in Ilium researching the legacy of Dr. Felix Hoenikker, John/Jonah considers using a picture of the scientist's tombstone for a cover shot. The irony is that John/Jonah thought he was looking at the tomb of one of the principal participants in constructing the atom bomb, yet the moment foreshadows the ice-nine destruction of the planet. (CC 29) Sleet was still coming down, acid and gray. I thought the old man's tombstone in all that sleet might photograph pretty well, might even make a good picture for the jacket of **The Day the World Ended**.

de la Madrid, Dr. Jose Sepulveda.

In Galápagos, *the president of Ecuador who plans a state breakfast and parade in honor of the many luminaries expected to arrive for the "Nature Cruise of the Century." The event is canceled when nearly all the expected celebrities fail to attend.*

de Medici, Innocenzo.

A fictional member of the famed de Medici family, Innocenzo "the Invisible" was a banker and first owner of the palatial estate Marilee Kemp lives in when she becomes the Countess Portomaggiore. Designed by Leon Battista Alberti (a historically accurate character) in the fifteenth century, It was a cruciform structure whose four wings abutted on a domed rotunda twelve meters in diameter and in whose walls were half embedded eighteen Corinthian columns four and a half meters high. Above the capitals of the columns was a clerestory, a wall pierced with thirty-six windows. Above this was the dome—on whose underside was an epiphany, God Almighty and Jesus and the Virgin Mary and angels looking down through clouds, painted by Paolo Uccello *(another historically accurate character)*. The terrazzo floor, its designer unknown, but almost surely a Venetian, was decorated with the backs of peasants planting and harvesting and cooking and baking and making wine and so on (*Blue* 27).

De Mille, Hippolyte Paul.

The Creole-speaking Haitian headwaiter at the Grand Hotel Oloffson in Port au Prince, Haiti, who becomes an employee of Rudy and Felix Waltz when they purchase the resort. De Mille claims to be eighty years old and counts fifty-nine descendants. More importantly, he practices voodoo, swearing he can make spirits rise and haunt their surroundings.

De Mille accompanies Rudy and Felix on their trip back to the neutron-bombed Midland City. After visiting the graves of their parents and Celia Hildreth Hoover in Mount Calvary Cemetery, De Mille argued that we owed it both to the past and to the future to raise some sort of representative ghost which would haunt the city, no matter who lived there, for generations to come. . . . So he raised the ghost of Will Fairchild. The old barnstormer was wearing goggles and a white silk scarf and a black leather helmet and all, but no parachute (*DD* Epilogue).

Rudy tells the reader the ghost of Will Fairchild will haunt Midland City looking for the parachute he failed to wear. In his amazement over the voodoo resurrection, Rudy comes to understand that differences in culture should not be feared, that the amount we don't know about the capabilities of vari-

ous cultures should cease to amaze us. In an apparent reference to the mysteries of his own culture, which he believes neutron-bombed his hometown as a test in the name of national security, Rudy leaves the text with the cryptic line, You want to know something? We are still in the Dark Ages. The Dark Ages—they haven't ended yet *(DD Epilogue).*

de Stael-Holstein, Baronne. *(ST 3) The family (Malachi Constant's) could trace its line back through an illegitimacy to Benjamin Constant, who was a tribune under Napoleon from 1799 to 1801, and a lover of Anne Louise Germaine Necker (a historical figure),* **Baronne de Stael-Holstein**, *wife of the then Swedish ambassador to France.*

de Sucre, Antonio Jose. *Vonnegut weaves yet another true figure from history into the anthropological tracings of present narratives. (Gal 1:7) A similar decay in imagined value was happening to the British pound and the French and Swiss francs and the West German mark. The Ecuadorian sucre, meanwhile, named in honor of* **Antonio Jose de Sucre** *(1795–1830), a national hero, had come to be worth less than a banana peel.*
(Gal 1:21) Without knowing anything about naval architecture, he (Bobby King) had made a ship more attractive by persuading its owners not to call it, as they were about to do, the **Antonio Jose de Sucre**, *but the Bahía de Darwin. He had transformed what was to have been a routine, two-week trip out to the islands and back into the nature cruise of the century. How had he worked such a miracle? By never calling it anything but "the Nature Cruise of the Century."*

de Wet, Mrs. Marthinus. *The 1924 graduate of Tarkington College who writes a letter taking exception to any retooling or tuning of the great Lutz Carillon bells. Having married the owner of a gold mine in South Africa, she senses her financial sway with the school's trustees.*
For Eugene Debs Hartke, her overly romantic views about the project typify the objections forwarded by some alumni. Her concern for the school's loss of history—the bells were formed from discarded Civil War weapons—is put into ironic contrast by Hartke: If my Socialist grandfather, nothing but a

gardener at Butler University, could read the letter from **Mrs. de Wet** *and note its South African return address, he would be grimly gratified. There was a clear-as-crystal demonstration of a woman living high on profits from the labor of black miners, overworked and underpaid (HP 8).*
One interesting aspect of this incident is that Vonnegut frequently writes of the dangers of losing one's sense of history. In this case the clash of ironies is as correctly juxtaposed as is the universal correctness described as a property of the chrono-synclastic-infundibulum.

Deadeye Dick. *The nickname patrolman Anthony Squires gives to Rudy Waltz after shooting to death Eloise Metzger. As long as Rudy remains in Midland City, someone somewhere would utter the nickname. He receives nightly phone calls at Schramm's Pharmacy asking if he really is "the" Deadeye Dick.*
While visiting New York for the production of "Katmandu," Rudy comes to understand his fascination with John Fortune. (DD 19) I no longer cared about the play. It was **Deadeye Dick**, tormented by guilt in Midland City, who had found old John Fortune's quite pointless death in Katmandu, as far away from his hometown as possible, somehow magnificent. He himself yearned for distance and death.

Deadeye Dick (1982) *(see also* **Rudy Waltz***). Institutionalized schizophrenia and a jury-rigged world are central concerns in* Deadeye Dick. *The narrative revolves around a series of four murders. Two of the murders are accidental, the other two not so much. As a group, they tend to point out the hypocrisy and schizophrenic tendencies of those in power to retain power.*
Rudy Waltz, the "neutered" pharmacist known as "Deadeye Dick" for his accidental murder of Mrs. Eloise Metzger and her unborn child, writes this memoir which includes: the accidental murder of August Gunther by Midland City Police Chief Morissey, the radiation death of Rudy's mother whose fireplace was constructed with contaminated cement from the Manhattan project and sold by the Nuclear Regulatory Commission, and the neutron-bombing of Midland City, Ohio. Chief Morissey accidentally blows off the head of August Gunther while on a hunting trip with Rudy's father, Morissey's

son, and John Fortune. They are standing next to each other when Morissey's shotgun inexplicably fires. None of his hunting buddies thinks it would be fair to crucify Morissey for an accident that could have happened to anybody, tragic though it was. Together they conspire to protect Morissey by letting Gunther's body drift down Sugar Creek.

Rudy's mother is the victim of a more calculated plot. Apparently, bureaucrats at the NRC believed selling off contaminated cement to building contractors would make the Manhattan Project more cost effective than just the mere avoidance of invading the Japanese mainland.

The only evidence linking Emma Waltz's brain tumors to the fireplace is the accidental exposure of a pack of film left in the house by Cliff McCarthy (in real life a friend of Vonnegut's and an art professor at Ohio University). Rudy and his brother Felix successfully sue the government, the Maritimo Brothers Construction Company, and the Ohio Valley Ornamental Concrete Company.

As for the neutron-bombing of Midland City, there are two primary theories about its occurrence. The government claims the bomb accidentally exploded when falling off a truck transporting it to an unnamed western state's destination. However, the farmers in surrounding communities hire a university professor to study the blast configuration using the pattern of livestock deaths to determine the outer perimeter of the bomb.

The professor determines that the blast occurred sixty feet above the pavement. The farmers envision an elaborate government conspiracy, convinced this was the purposeful act of unnamed forces that are forever in motion. Lawyer Bernard Ketchum asks the farmers who they think nuked the city. (DD Epilogue) This was the answer he got: "They don't want us to know their name, so they don't have a name. You can't fight back against something that don't have a name."

"The military-industrial complex?" said Ketchum archly. "The Rockefellers? The international conglomerates? The CIA? The Mafia?"

And the farmer said to him, "You like any of them names? Just help yourself. Maybe that's who it is, maybe it ain't. How's a farmer supposed to find out? It's whoever it was shot President Kennedy and his brother—and Martin Luther King."

So there we had it—the ever-growing ball of American paranoia, the ball of string a hundred miles in diameter, with the unsolved assassination of John F. Kennedy at its core.

"You mention the Rockefellers," said the farmer. "If you ask me, they don't know any more'n I do about who's really running things, what's really going on."

As for Rudy, My own guess is that the American Government had to find out for certain whether the neutron bomb was as harmless as it was supposed to be. So it set one off in a small city which nobody cared about, where people weren't doing all that much with their lives anyhow, where businesses were going under or moving away. The Government couldn't test a bomb on a foreign city, after all, without running the risk of starting World War Three.

There is even a chance that Fred T. Barry, with all his contacts high in the military, could have named Midland City as the ideal place to test a neutron bomb (DD Epilogue).

Rudy's own tale of murder takes place on Mother's Day 1944 (the same day Vonnegut's mother committed suicide). Though only twelve years old at the time, Rudy is given the key to the gun room and told to clean some of the weapons. Feeling at one with himself and the Springfield 30-06, Rudy loads the weapon while surveying Midland City from the attic gun room. Though knowing better, he fires off one round without any thought of aiming. Eight blocks away Mrs. Eloise Metzger goes down with a bullet between the eyes. Rudy recalls, So this was Mother's Day to most people, but to me it was the day during which, ready or not, I had been initiated into manhood (DD 9).

Rudy believes the world is cruel and duplicitous. (DD 16) I wasn't to touch anything on this planet, man, woman, child, artifact, animal, vegetable, or mineral—since it was likely to be connected to a push-pull detonator and an explosive charge.

Despite ominous speculations about the neutron-bombing and Rudy's incredulity about the possibilities for innocent personal activity, Vonnegut manages a voodoo resurrection denouement with hope as its message. Rudy's chef from his hotel in Haiti, Hippolyte Paul De Mille, is capable of resurrecting the dead. Together they stand in Midland

City's Calvary Cemetery while Hippolyte raises the spirit of Will Fairchild. Fairchild was a stunt flyer who died in an air show, though he could have been saved had he been wearing his parachute. His spirit roams the empty city looking for his chute. In the midst of all he concocts, Vonnegut looks to undo irrational and fatal impulses in a search for survival.

Deal, Borden. *Among the lost friends Vonnegut wants to have at the* Timequake *clambake is Borden Deal. His remembrance is filled with humor and a literary history lesson before lapsing into a longing to see his old friend.* (TQ 63) This is not a Gothic novel. My late friend **Borden Deal**, a first-rate southern novelist, so southern he asked his publishers not to send review copies north of the Mason-Dixon line, also wrote Gothic novels under a feminine nom de plume. I asked him for a definition of a Gothic novel. He said, "A young woman goes into an old house and gets her pants scared off."

Borden and I were in Vienna, Austria, for a congress of PEN, the international writers' organization founded after World War One, when he told me that. We went on to talk about the German novelist Leopold von Sacher-Masoch, who in print found humiliation and pain so delectable at the end of the previous century. Because of him, modern languages have the word masochism.

Borden not only wrote serious novels and Gothics. He wrote country music. He had his guitar back in his hotel room, and was working, he said, on a song called "I Never Waltzed in Vienna." I miss him. I want a look-alike for **Borden** at the clambake, and two luckless fishermen in a little rowboat right offshore, dead ringers for the saints Stanley Laurel and Oliver Hardy.

So be it.

Deal, Selena. *At the time we meet this young, upstairs maid in* God Bless You, Mr. Rosewater, *Selena has been working for Amanda and Stewart Buntline for only a month of her one-year commitment.*

Her connection to the Buntlines provides another irony of Christian charity starting in a pure state and morphing with the generations into an abusive prop of a twisted capitalist and religious philosophy.

She was raised by Wilfred Parrot in an orphanage founded by Castor Buntline, Stewart's great-grandfather, and bound by his oath mixing capitalism and predestination. (GBR 11) I do solemnly swear that I will respect the sacred private property of others, and that I will be content with whatever station in life God Almighty may assign me to. I will be grateful to those who employ me, and will never complain about wages and hours, but will ask myself instead, "What more can I do for my employer, my republic, and my God?" I understand that I have not been placed on Earth to be happy. I am here to be tested. If I am to pass the test, I must be always unselfish, always sober, always truthful, always chaste in mind, body, and deed, and always respectful to those to whom God has, in His Wisdom, placed above me. If I pass the test, I will go to joy everlasting in Heaven when I die. If I fail, I shall roast in hell while the Devil laughs and Jesus weeps.

Selena is far more knowledgeable about cultural matters than are her employers and is forever vexed by Amanda's inappropriate corrections. In a letter to Mr. Parrot, Selena unleashes her frustrations and provides the basis for the novel's subtitle. (GBR 11) What gets me most about these people, Daddy, isn't how ignorant they are, or how much they drink. It's the way they have of thinking that everything nice in the world is a gift to the poor people from them or their ancestors. The first afternoon I was here, Mrs. Buntline made me come out on the back porch and look at the sunset. So I did, and I said I liked it very much, but she kept waiting for me to say something else. I couldn't think of what else I was supposed to say, so I said what seemed liked a dumb thing. "Thank you very much," I said. That was exactly what she was waiting for. "You're entirely welcome," she said. I have since thanked her for the ocean, the moon, the stars in the sky, and the United States Constitution.

Maybe I am just too wicked and dumb to realize how wonderful Pisquontuit really is. Maybe this is a case of pearls before swine, but I don't see how. I am homesick. Write soon. I love you.

Deal, Selma. *In the short story "Lovers Anonymous," collected in* Bagombo Snuff Box (1999), *Selma is the waitress behind the lunch counter at* *the drugstore when a loose collection of men self-nicknamed Lovers Anonymous come in as part of their normal lunch routine. The group is widely known, and Selma does not miss the opportunity to joke with the unnamed narrator when he enters.* "Well, you great lover, got a quorum now. What you gonna vote about?"

Debs, Eugene Victor (*see also* **Sermon on the Mount** *and* **God Bless You, Dr. Kevorkian**). *The labor leader from Terre Haute, Indiana, for whom Vonnegut names two of his characters: Eugene Debs Hartke, the narrator of* Hocus Pocus, *and Eugene Metzger—the son of Eloise and George Metzger in* Deadeye Dick.

Vonnegut dedicates Hocus Pocus *to Debs with the inscription,* This work of pure fiction is dedicated to the memory of

EUGENE VICTOR DEBS
1855–1926
"While there is a lower class I am in it,
  While there is a criminal element
I am of it. While there is a soul in prison I
  am not free."

(*HP* 1) **Debs** was a Socialist and a Pacifist and a Labor Organizer who ran several times for the Presidency of the United States of America, and got more votes than has any other candidate nominated by a third party in the history of this country.
(*TQ* 36) In the waning summer of 1996, I ask myself if there were ideas I once held that I should now repudiate. I consider the example set by my father's only brother, Uncle Alex, the childless, Harvard-educated Indianapolis insurance salesman. He had me reading high-level socialist writers like Shaw and Norman Thomas and **Eugene Debs** and John Dos Passos when I was a teenager, along with making model airplanes and jerking off. After World War Two, Uncle Alex became as politically conservative as the Archangel Gabriel.

But I still like what O'Hare and I said to German soldiers right after we were liberated: That America was going to become more socialist, was going to try harder to give everybody work to do, and to ensure that our children, at least, weren't hungry or cold or illiterate or scared to death.

Lotsa luck!

Vonnegut goes on to express his appreciation for Eugene Debs in terms he usually holds only for the Sermon on the Mount. (*TQ* 36) I still quote **Eugene Debs** (1855–1926), late of Terre Haute, Indiana, five times the Socialist Party's candidate for President, in every speech:

"While there is a lower class I am in it, while there is a criminal element I am of it; while there is a soul in prison, I am not free."

In recent years, I've found it prudent to say before quoting **Debs** that he is to be taken seriously. Otherwise many in the audience will start to laugh. They are being nice, not mean, knowing I like to be funny. But it is also a sign of these times that such a moving echo of the Sermon on the Mount can be perceived as outdated, wholly discredited horsecrap.

Which it is not.
(*TQ* 50) Yes, and the word *Socialist* was the second S in *USSR*, so good-bye, *Socialism* along with *Communism*, good-bye to the soul of **Eugene Debs** of Terre Haute, Indiana, where the moonlight's shining bright along the Wabash. From the fields there comes the breath of new-mown hay.

"While there is a soul in prison, I am not free." (*BAG* Coda to My Career) I might have added that some of the greatest words ever spoken in American history were uttered with just such a Jew's-harp twang, including the Gettysburg Address of Abraham Lincoln of Illinois and these by **Eugene V. Debs** of Terre Haute, Indiana: "While there is a lower class I am in it, while there is a criminal element I am of it; while there is a soul in prison, I am not free."

I would have kept to myself that the borders of Indiana, when I was a boy, cradled not only the birthplace of **Eugene V. Debs**, but the national headquarters of the Ku Klux Klan.

Debs is also the subject of one of Vonnegut's interviews in the Blue Tunnel to the Afterlife in God Bless You, Dr. Kevorkian. (*GBK* Eugene Victor Debs) During what has been almost a year of interviewing completely dead people, while only half-dead myself, I asked Saint Peter again and again if I could meet a particular hero of mine. He is my fellow Hoosier, the late **Eugene Victor Debs** of Terre Haute, Indiana. He was five times the Socialist

Party's candidate for president back when this country still had a strong Socialist Party.

And then, guess what, yesterday afternoon none other than **Eugene Victor Debs**, organizer and leader of the first successful strike against a major American industry, the railroads, was waiting for me at the far end of the blue tunnel. We hadn't met before. This great American died in 1926 at the age of seventy-one when I was only four years old.

I thanked him for words of his, which I quote again and again in lectures: "As long as there is a lower class, I am in it. As long as there is a criminal element, I am of it. As long as there is a soul in prison, I am not free."

He asked me how those words were received here on Earth in America nowadays. I said they were ridiculed. "People snicker and snort," I said. He asked what our fastest growing industry was. "The building of prisons," I said.

"What a shame," he said. And then he asked me how the Sermon on the Mount was going over these days. And then he spread his wings and flew away.
(MWC 2) That wage earners, without social position or higher education or wealth, are of inferior intellect is surely belied by the fact that two of the most splendid writers and speakers on the deepest subjects in American history were self-taught workmen. I speak, of course, of Carl Sandburg the poet from Illinois, and Abraham Lincoln of Kentucky, then Indiana, and finally Illinois. Both, may I say, were continental, freshwater people like me. Another freshwater person and splendid speaker was the Socialist Party candidate **Eugene Victor Debs**, a former locomotive fireman who had been born to a middle-class family in Terra Haute, Indiana.

Hooray for our team!
(MWC 2) I never met Carl Sandburg or **Eugene Victor Debs**, and I wish I had. I would have been tongue-tied in the presence of such national treasures.

I did get to know one socialist of their generation—Powers Hapgood of Indianapolis. He was a typical Hoosier idealist. Socialism is idealistic. Hapgood, like **Debs**, was a middle-class person who thought there could be more economic justice in this country. He wanted a better country, that's all.

(MWC 9) But back to people like Confucius and Jesus and my son the doctor, Mark, each of whom have said in their own way how we could behave more humanely and maybe make the world a less painful place. One of my favorite humans is **Eugene Debs**, from Terre Haute in my native state of Indiana.

Get a load of this. **Eugene Debs**, who died back in 1926, when I was not yet four, ran five times as the Socialist Party candidate for president, winning 900,000 votes, almost 6 percent of the popular vote, in 1912, if you can imagine such a ballot. He had this to say while campaigning:

> As long as there is a lower class, I am in it.
> As long as there is a criminal element, I'm
> of it.
> As long as there is a soul in prison, I am not
> free.

"Deer in the Works" (1955). *Originally appearing in* Esquire *and reprinted first in* Canary in a Cathouse *and later in* Welcome to the Monkey House (1968), *the story focuses on the chaos caused by the unexpected entrance of a deer into the Ilium Works of the Federal Apparatus Corporation—very similar to the Ilium Works in* Player Piano.

On David Potter's first day as a public relations writer for the facility (an echo of Vonnegut's time as a public relations writer for General Electric), he is assigned to cover the massive deer hunt by security personnel. When the photographer flashes a few pictures before Lou Flammer prepares to give the orders to shoot, the deer bolts toward Potter, who opens the gate, letting the deer escape. His actions are taken as a sign of compassion and humanity in the midst of an overly technologized and desensitized society— and most unappreciated by the stunned posse.

Deer Park, Long Island. *In* Hocus Pocus, *the location of the New York State prison for Orientals* (HP 12).

Deerfield Academy. *In* Hocus Pocus, *the Massachusetts prep school attended by Eugene Debs Hartke, Jr., contemptuously recalled by Vonnegut in his nonfiction.* (FWD X) In Indianapolis back then, it was only the really dumb rich kids who got sent away to prep school. (I knew some of them, and after they graduated from Andover or Exeter or St. Paul's or wherever, they were *still* dumb and rich.) So I was astonished and annoyed, when I took up permanent residence in the East, to meet so many people who thought it only common sense that they be allowed to set the moral and intellectual tone for this country because they had been to prep school. (It was my personal misfortune that so many of them had become literary critics. I'm about to be judged by **Deerfield Academy**? Deerfield *Academy?* Give me a break!)

Del Prado Hotel. *The Ilium hotel where the narrator of* Cat's Cradle *stays while researching for his book* The Day the World Ended (CC 10, 12).

Delahanty, Dennis. *In the short story "Any Reasonable Offer," first appearing in Collier's magazine (January 1952) and later collected in* Bagombo Snuff Box *(1999), Dennis Delahanty is the first example used by the unnamed real estate agent narrator to convey the sleazy experiences and odd behaviors someone in his profession regularly witnesses. The narrator readily provides a serious prospective buyer after viewing Delahanty's property soon after the owner calls for his services. Later that evening, Delahanty cuts a deal with the buyer and tries getting out of paying the narrator's commission. According to the narrator, Delahanty never did pay.*

Delaney, Ed. *In the 1952 short story "The No-Talent Kid," collected in* Bagombo Snuff Box *(1999), band director George Helmholtz grows weary of Walter Plummer's delusions about his clarinet talents. As the last chair in the C Band, Plummer challenges perhaps the best musician in A Band, the first clarinet seat held by Flammer. Mr. Helmholtz cleared his throat. "I admire your spirit, Plummer, but isn't that rather ambitious for the first of the year? Perhaps you should start out with, say, challenging* **Ed Delaney**." **Delaney** *held down the last chair in the B Band.*

Delbert. *The tourist outside the Rumfoord Mansion wearing a Robin Hood hat with Rumfoord's picture on it and embroidered with his own name.* *He is browsing at Sergeant Brackman's booth while awaiting the materialization (ST 10).*

Delgado, Private Geraldo. *The Ecuadorian soldier who kills Andrew MacIntosh and Zenji Hiroguchi. He breaks into a souvenir shop looking for food amid the chaos expanding across South America. He is an eighteen-year-old paranoid schizophrenic who thought his big problem was enemies with little radios (Gal 1:27). He kills the two men when he sees Hiroguchi playing with Mandarax, which Delgado mistakes for a radio.*

Delgado's break-in establishes a pathway for the cruise passengers to make it to safety in the hotel. Leon Trout points out that if not for Delgado, the next million years of history would take place without any human beings.

Delicto, Flagrante (*see also* **The Wrinkled Old Family Retainer**). *The groom in Kilgore Trout's only play,* The Wrinkled Old Family Retainer, *written shortly after his return from World War II and briefly mentioned in* Timequake.

The Latin phrase from which this character's name derives is in flagrante delicto, meaning "in a blazing offense," colloquially used to mean "getting caught red-handed."

Delicto's bride is Mirabile Dictu, translated from the Latin as "wonderful to tell." (TQ 46) The Wrinkled Old Family Retainer *is about a wedding. The bride is Mirabile Dictu, a virgin. The groom is* **Flagrante Delicto**, *a heartless womanizer.*

Delta Upsilon. *Vonnegut's Cornell fraternity, which can also claim among its members Buck Young (the football player sought after by Cornell coach Doctor Roseberry in* Player Piano*), John/ Jonah (the narrator of* Cat's Cradle*), Newt Hoenikker (though he is only a pledge before flunking out of Cornell), and bicycle manufacturer H. Lowe Crosby (also in* Cat's Cradle*).*

In Timequake, *Vonnegut recalls speaking in Denver with the son of his late fraternity brother, both named John Hickenlooper. The son is the current governor of Colorado. (TQ 44) OK, how about the fact that the name of the owner of the Wynkoop Brewing Company, a guy about Joe's age, was John Hickenlooper? So what? Only this: When I went to*

Cornell University to become a chemist fifty-six years ago, I was made a fraternity brother of a man named John Hickenlooper.

Ting-a-ling?

This was his son! My fraternity brother had died when this son was only seven. I knew more about him than his own son did! I was able to tell this young Denver brewer that his dad, in partnership with another **Delta Upsilon** brother, John Locke, sold candy and soft drinks and cigarettes out of a big closet at the top of the stairs on the second floor of the fraternity house.

They christened it *Hickenlooper's Lockenbar*. We called it *Lockenlooper's Hickenbar*, and *Barkenhicker's Loopenlock*, and *Lockenbarker's Loopenhick*, and so on.

Happy days! We thought we'd live forever.

Denny, Kyle. *Walter Starbuck's football-playing Harvard classmate from Philadelphia, who* died in a fall in his bathtub on the day the Japanese bombed Pearl Harbor. He cracked his head open on a faucet (JB 9). *He had also dated Sarah Wyatt.*

Denton, the Reverend Bobby. *The holy man conducting his Love Crusade in Wheeling, West Virginia, and who sees the construction of the spacecraft* the Whale *and man's search of the heavens as analogous to the biblical Tower of Babel. The discovery of the chrono-synclastic infundibula halts that search as God had dispersed the nations of man for building the tower.* (ST 1) "Are these not Bible times?" he said. "Have we not builded of steel and pride an abomination far taller than the Tower of Babel of old? And did we not mean, like those builders of old, to get right into Heaven with it? And haven't we heard it said many times that the language of scientists is international? They all use the same Latin and Greek words for things, and they all talk the language of numbers."

"Der Arme Dolmetscher." *Translated as "The Army Interpreter," the story first appeared in the July 1955 issue of* The Atlantic Monthly *and was later reprinted in* Bagombo Snuff Box *(1999).*

The 1944 setting of the story is a short distance from the German defensive position known as the Siegfried Line. As the narrator recalls, I qualified for the position while waiting to move from France into the front lines. While a student, I had learned the first stanza of Heinrich Heine's "Die Lorelei" by rote from a college roommate, and I happened to give those lines a dogged rendition while working within earshot of the battalion commander. *(The poem is a ballad about a siren perched atop the Lorelei rock at one of the narrowest points on the eastern bank of the Rhine.)*

The colonel has his executive officer station the soldier at the home of a nearby Belgian burgomaster. Since the Americans only recently seized the area, the colonel wants to make sure the town's mayor has no part to play in relaying information back to the Germans. The would-be interpreter protests that he really is unfit for the task, but his colonel (in civilian life, a hotel detective from Mobile, Alabama) and his executive officer (a dry goods salesman from Knoxville) are unswayed. Those in authority were too harried to hear my declarations of incompetence. "You talk Kraut good enough foah us," said the Executive Officer. . . . "Besides," the Executive concluded, "theah ain't nobody else can talk Kraut at all."

The narrator catches a ride on a farm truck headed toward the burgomaster's home when he meets a small group of American soldiers, three disgruntled Pennsylvania Dutchmen who applied for interpreters' jobs months earlier. When I made it clear that I was no competition for them, and that I hoped to be liquidated within twenty-four hours, they warmed up enough for me to furnish the interesting information that I was a **Dolmetscher**. They also decoded "Die Lorelei" at my request. This gave me command of about forty words (par for a two-year-old), but no combination of them would get me so much as a glass of cold water.

Additionally, the Pennsylvanians give the narrator a pamphlet purporting to make German easy for the man in the foxhole.

"Some of the first pages are missing," the donor explained as I jumped from the truck before the burgomaster's stone farmhouse. "Used 'em for cigarette papers," he said. *Those first few pages had all the translations for simple, polite conversation. The remaining pages had to do with actual interrogatories to be used on captured soldiers, such as* Where are your tank columns?

Armed with no other language facility than the bit of Heine in translation and a series of militarily important questions, the sleepless narrator lay in his bed at the burgomaster's home and worries himself into a fantasy (a brief play within the tale) involving himself, the burgomaster, the burgomaster's daughter, and a guard (see **burgomaster's daughter**). *He envisions a romantic tryst with the young maiden, using Heine as their script. He carries her to his bedroom and finds his script switching from Heine to the military pamphlet, softly asking her to* surrender her charms *to him.*

Her father suddenly appears armed with a Luger and demands Hands up! *The language of the players is now completely composed of the terse commands and questions memorized from the torn military instruction manual. The narrator imagines himself reaching beneath his pillow for his gun, forcing the burgomaster to surrender in fear for his life and his daughter's. The three Pennsylvania Dutch soldiers arrive just in time to hear the father and daughter admit to being German spies dropped by parachute behind the American lines.*

The fantasy is so dispiriting for the narrator that he resolves to leave. He tidies up his room, makes the bed, packs his duffel, and quietly slips past the blackout curtains as he makes his return to battalion headquarters. He tells the colonel and executive officer that his talents were worthless at the burgomaster's home since they spoke a low dialect of German and he spoke only high German. The officers are mildly amused by the narrator's return, and the colonel insists he stay put to act as his personal interpreter since German tanks have surrounded their position.

The final irony of the story comes in the wake of the Americans' yielding their position to the Germans, apparently as ill-equipped to bridge the language barrier as the narrator. Twenty minutes later I was in the thick of dolmetsching again. Four Tiger tanks drove up to the front door of Headquarters, and two dozen German infantrymen dismounted to round us up with submachine guns.

"Say sumpin'," ordered the Colonel, spunky to the last.

I ran my eye down the left-hand columns of my pamphlet until I found the phrase that most fairly represented our sentiments.

"Don't shoot," I said.

A German tank officer swaggered in to have a look at his catch. In his hand was a pamphlet, somewhat smaller than mine. "Where are your howitzers?" he said.

Derby, Edgar. *The forty-four-year-old Indianapolis high school teacher who is captured at the Battle of the Bulge and sent to a POW camp on the same train with Billy Pilgrim. While digging bodies out of the ashen rubble of Dresden, German soldiers summarily execute him for looting. He had innocently picked up a Dresden china teapot. In the first chapter of* Slaughterhouse-Five, *Vonnegut muses that Derby's death should be the fitting ironic conclusion.* (SL5 1) "I think the climax of the book will be the execution of poor old **Edgar Derby**," I said. "The irony is so great. A whole city gets burned down, and thousands and thousands of people are killed. And then this one American foot soldier is arrested in the ruins for taking a teapot. And he's given a regular trial, and then he's shot by a firing squad."

Derby tries to protect Billy Pilgrim, standing up to the bullying of Paul Lazzaro and speaking out against the preachings of Howard Campbell while taking shelter in the slaughterhouse on the night of the firebombing. Derby has a son in the Marines serving in the Pacific theater.

Derby, Howard. *The hospital mail clerk in the play* Fortitude, *reprinted in* Wampeters, Foma & Granfalloons.

Destouches, Louis-Ferdinand (*see* **Céline**).

Di Capistrano, Paulo. *In* Breakfast of Champions, *when Wayne Hoobler is picked up for suspicious behavior outside the back gate of Barrytron, Ltd., the police find di Capistrano's Playboy membership card on him. Hoobler got it out of the garbage cans behind the Holiday Inn* (BC 19).

di Sanza, Dr. Carlo. *In* Jailbird, *the convicted felon serving his time at Finletter Air Force Base holds a doctorate in law from the University of Naples.* (JB 5) He was a naturalized American citizen and was serving his second term for using the mails to promote a Ponzi scheme. He was ferociously patriotic. *This reference to the nature of di Sanza's crimes allows Starbuck to explain what a Ponzi scheme is and create an analogy between this and the operation of government. (JB 5)* "In America I have been a millionaire two times," he said, "and I will be a millionaire again."

"I'm sure of it," I said, and I was. He would simply start up his third Ponzi scheme—consisting, as before, of offering fools enormous rates of interest for the use of their money. As before, he would use most of the money to buy himself mansions and Rolls-Royces and speedboats and so on, but returning part of it as the high interest he had promised. More and more people would come to him, having heard of him from gloatingly satisfied recipients of his interest checks, and he would use their money to write more interest checks—and on and on.

I am now convinced that **Dr. di Sanza**'s greatest strength was his utter stupidity. He was such a successful swindler because he himself could not, even after two convictions, understand what was inevitably catastrophic about a Ponzi scheme. . . .

I am now moved to suppose, with my primitive understanding of economics, that every successful government is of necessity a Ponzi scheme. It accepts enormous loans that can never be repaid. How else am I to explain to my polyglot grandchildren what the United States was like in the nineteen-thirties, when its owners and politicians could not find ways for so many of its people to earn even the most basic necessities, like food and clothes and fuel. It was pure hell to get shoes!

And then, suddenly, there were formerly poor people in officers' clubs, beautifully costumed and ordering filets mignon and champagne. There were formerly poor people in enlisted men's clubs, serviceably costumed and clad and ordering hamburgers and beer. A man who two years before had patched the holes in his shoes with cardboard suddenly had a Jeep or a truck or an airplane or a boat, and unlimited supplies of fuel and ammunition. He was given glasses and bridgework, if he needed them, and he was immunized against every imaginable disease. No matter where he was on the planet, a way was found to get hot turkey and cranberry sauce to him on Thanksgiving and Christmas.

What had happened?
What could have happened but a Ponzi scheme?

Dickie, Mrs. *In the 1952 short story "Poor Little Rich Town," collected in* Bagombo Snuff Box *(1999), Mrs. Dickie is representative of the small-town kindnesses that are tolerable, even welcome, because they put people and their harmless ways ahead of any other concerns. She has been the postmistress of Spruce Falls for twenty-five years, a position she inherited when her husband died. He was a volunteer firefighter and heroically died while saving an unspecified number of lives in a house fire.*

Mrs. Dickie runs the post office in her own idiosyncratic fashion. The layout of her facility suits her comfort and ease and is therefore not a model of efficiency. When Newell Cady introduces himself to Mrs. Dickie, his obsessive desire to make all things more efficient overtakes him, charming his way past her postal cage and showing her new ways to hold mail while also altering the layout of the sorting bins. She is amazed at his thoroughness and begins to think there is something valuable in his assistance.

By the end of the story it is clear that Mrs. Dickie's twenty-five years of ingrained habits have gotten the better of her. She is in fact less productive because she can not adapt to Cady's methodologies. Adding insult to injury, Cady enters the post office and proclaims to those on line what a wasteful hardship it is for him to go eight-tenths of a mile out of his way to pick up his mail every day, ignoring the fact that Mrs. Dickie can hear him. He goes on to boast what he learned about the availability of rural free delivery and that that would avoid having to drop by the post office to receive mail—but not before taking the time to turn and absentmindedly remonstrate Mrs. Dickie for falling back to her old inefficient ways of holding the mail while sorting it.

Upton Beaton takes it upon himself to instruct Newell Cady on the error of his ways, on his lack of understanding the personal stakes we have in each other's lives, on giving people credit for making an effort at life. "A one-eyed man might as well be blind," declared Upton Beaton, "if he doesn't watch people's faces and doesn't give the blind credit for the senses they do have.

"If you'd looked at **Mrs. Dickie**'s face instead of

how she was doing her work, you would have seen she was crying," said Beaton. "Her husband died in a fire, saving some of these people around the village you call blind. You talk a lot about wasting time, Mr. Cady—for a really big waste of time, walk around the village someday and try to find somebody who doesn't know he can have his mail brought to his door anytime he wants to."

On a smaller point, Mrs. Dickie is awarded a ribbon at the Hobby Show for her flower arrangement, but this is just another nicety in town. Everyone wins ribbons and no one enters anyone else's category. The categories are established according to one's entry, assuring uniqueness without competition. The entire point of the tradition is to give people credit for their efforts. The Hobby Show respected each person's effort. It was never intended as an actual competition of skills, as Cady tried to reform it.

Dictu, Mirabile (*see also* **The Wrinkled Old Family Retainer**). *In* Timequake, *the bride of Flagrante Delicto in Kilgore Trout's only play, written shortly after World War II. The Latin translation of her name is "wonderful to tell" (TQ 46).*

Dillon University. *In* God Bless You, Mr. Rosewater, *Caroline Rosewater's alma mater in Dodge City, Kansas. She graduated Phi Beta Kappa in philosophy.*

Dina and Donna. *Originally from Kokomo, Indiana, these identical twins are out joyriding when Deadeye Dick's Felix Waltz drives into their car, sending Donna through the windshield. Though severely scarred by the accident, Donna and Felix later marry.*

District Attorney. *In* Timequake, *the unscrupulous and politically ambitious prosecutor responsible for incarcerating Dudley Prince eventually meets an ugly fate.* (TQ 16) He (Dudley Prince) knew that in seven years he would be exonerated by DNA tests of dried ejaculate material on the victim's panties. This exculpatory evidence would again be found languishing in a glassine envelope in the walk-in vault of the **District Attorney** who had framed him in the hopes of being nominated for Governor.

And, oh yes, that same **DA** would be found wearing cement overshoes on the bottom of Lake Cayuga in just six more years.

Divine, Celeste and Harry. *In the short story "Unpaid Consultant," collected in* Bagombo Snuff Box (1999), *this very-much-in-love couple knew the unnamed narrator back in high school, but it was seventeen years before they reached out to him. For good reason, too, since just two years earlier, the happy couple was struggling on Harry's income from Joe's Greasing Palace while Celeste worked at developing her singing talents. Then Celeste hit it big.* "I feel like Cinderella," said **Celeste**. "One day, **Harry** and I were struggling along on his pay from Joe's Greasing Palace, and the next day, everything I touched seemed to turn to gold."

Celeste calls the narrator because they knew he had become a financial adviser. He was used to being called in to review the portfolios of past acquaintances, but this was the largest one of all. Celeste holds a steady spot on a weekly television show. As the narrator recalls when she welcomes him at the door, Her hair is black and curly, her eyes large and brown, her lips full and glistening. Painted and spangled and sheathed in gold lamé, **Celeste** is before the television cameras for one hour each week, making love to all the world. For this public service she gets five thousand dollars a week.

By contrast, Harry (whose last name is never disclosed) senses his own purposelessness once Celeste is able to provide for them in ways they never could have imagined. For fifteen years they scraped by on his mechanic's earnings and managed to stay deeply attached. His own labors held them afloat, but that all changed as he reveals in his confession to the narrator. "**Harry**, you're working as a mechanic," I said.

"Not half an hour ago," said **Harry**, "a man with a broken fuel pump thanked God for me. Have a seat."

"What about the catchup business?" I said.

"It saved my marriage and it saved my life," said **Harry**. "I'm grateful to the pioneers, like the Buntings, who built it."

"And now you've quit, just like that?" I snapped my fingers.

"I was never in it," said **Harry**. "Bunting has promised to keep that to himself, and I'd appreciate it if you'd do the same."

"But you know so much about catchup!" I said.

"For eighteen months after **Celeste** struck it rich and we moved here," said **Harry**, "I walked the streets, looking for a job suitable for the husband of the famous and beautiful **Celeste**."

Remembering those dark days, he rubbed his eyes, reached for the catchup. "When I got tired, cold, or wet," he said, "I'd sit in the public library, and study all the different things men could do for a living. Making catchup was one of them."

He shook the bottle of catchup over his hamburger, violently. The bottle was almost full, but nothing came out. "There—you see?" he said. "When you shake catchup one way, it behaves like a solid. You shake it another way, and it behaves like a liquid." He shook the bottle gently, and catchup poured over his hamburger. "Know what that's called?"

"No," I said.

"Thixotropy," said **Harry**. He hit me playfully on the upper arm. "There—you learned something new today."

Harry's confession to catchup manufacturer Arthur J. Bunting softens the depth of the insults hurled during his falsely macho and ignorant rantings at the restaurant. The two were being put together by the narrator who thinks they are an obvious match, perhaps proof to Bunting that he could be entrusted to guide his considerable investment portfolio.

Harry researched the catchup industry so he could pass himself off to Celeste as something more than just a mechanic. He wanted to show her his growth over their years together as she was suddenly thrust into stardom. It is a false bravura that endangers the narrator's financial practice, bruises the ego of an industry tycoon, and threatens to expose himself as a fraud to his beloved Celeste.

Arthur J. Bunting, for his part, proves to be a sympathetic and gracious gentleman in keeping Harry's secret. The narrator, too, appears unwilling to upset Harry's world. As for Harry, he promises Bunting to drop the catchup charade. Instead, he has already established himself as an expert, unpaid consultant to the birdseed industry, managing to keep secret his day job as a mechanic. By honoring Harry's secret, the unnamed narrator and Bunting hold a bond between them that may prompt new business for the financial consultant.

This midday meeting between the narrator and Harry presents a stark contrast compared to their first meeting when Harry was drunkenly swilling martinis on his living room floor, loudly complaining about the catchup industry while gently asking Celeste for more to drink. Having exposed his secret first to Bunting and now the narrator, Harry is comfortable in his coveralls and grease-encrusted fingernails—though he maintains the importance of his new pretensions to keep Celeste interested in him as her husband, her devoted lover, and a valued unpaid consultant.

Dobrowitz, Alvin. *Howard Campbell's Israeli lawyer who earnestly tries to defend him against the allegations of war crimes. (MN 45) Hope springs eternal, they say, in the human breast. It springs eternal, at any rate, in the breast of* **Dobrowitz***, which is, I suppose why he costs so much.*

Dodge, Dr. Ned. *The manager of Chicago's Proteus Park, a postwar development of three thousand dream houses for three thousand families with presumably identical dreams (PP XVII). He anxiously guides the Shah of Bratpuhr on a tour through the home of Edgar and Wanda Hagstrohm, which is filled with dozens of electrical appliances intended to instantaneously perform menial household chores.*

"Dog's Breakfast." *This episode may be the most comical metafictional moment in all of Vonnegut's work. Kilgore Trout channels his own suspicions about human intelligence through the character of Dr. Fleon Sunoco in his retelling of "Dog's Breakfast" to Kurt Vonnegut while attending the writers retreat at Xanadu. Sunoco becomes a victim of his own introspection. (TQ 27)* The first story Trout had to rewrite after the timequake zapped him back to 1991, he told me, was called "**Dog's Breakfast**." It was about a mad scientist named Fleon Sunoco, who was doing research at the National Institutes of Health in Bethesda, Maryland. Dr. Sunoco believed really smart people had little radio receivers in their heads, and were getting their bright ideas from somewhere else.

"The smarties *had to be getting outside help*," Trout said to me at Xanadu. While impersonating the mad Sunoco, Trout himself seemed convinced that there was a great big computer somewhere, which, by means of radio, had told Pythagoras about right triangles, and Newton about gravity, and Darwin about evolution, and Pasteur about germs, and Einstein about relativity, and on and on.

"That computer, wherever it is, whatever it is, while pretending to help us, may actually be trying to *kill* us dummies with too much to think about," said Kilgore Trout.
(*TQ* 27) At night, though, with nobody around, he (*Sunoco*) slices up high-IQ brains, looking for little radios. He doesn't think Mensa members had them inserted surgically. He thinks they were *born* with them, so the receivers have to be made of meat. Sunoco has written in his secret journal: "There is no way an unassisted human brain, which is nothing more than a **dog's breakfast**, three and a half pounds of blood-soaked sponge, could have written 'Stardust,' let alone Beethoven's Ninth Symphony."

Dr. Sunoco is at first so taken with his own discovery that he assumes he will surely be awarded a Nobel Prize. Even before publishing his findings, he buys a formal set of tails for his expected presentation in Stockholm. (*TQ* 27) Trout said: "Fleon Sunoco jumped to his death into the National Institutes of Health parking lot. He was wearing his new suit of tails, which would never get to Stockholm.

"He realized that his discovery proved that he didn't deserve credit for making it. He was hoisted by his own petard! Anybody who did anything as wonderful as what he had done couldn't possibly have done it with just a human brain, with nothing but the **dog's breakfast** in his braincase. He could have done it only with outside help."

Dole, Dr. Helen. *The unmarried twenty-six-year-old candidate to fill Hartke's physics position at Tarkington College. She expresses the same depth of social understanding as Hartke and would probably approve of the politics of his own namesake, Eugene Victor Debs.*
(*HP* 37) She was born in South Korea, and had grown up in what was then West Berlin. She held a Doctorate in Physics from the University of Berlin. Her father had been a Master Sergeant in the Quartermaster Corps of the Regular Army, serving in Korea and then in our Army of Occupation in Ber-

lin. When her father retired after 30 years, to a nice enough little house in a nice enough little neighborhood in Cincinnati, and she saw the horrible squalor and hopelessness into which most black people were born there, she went back to what had become just plain Berlin and earned her Doctorate.

Tarkington's Board of Trustees asks Dr. Dole to promise never to discuss politics, history, economics, or sociology. She becomes infuriated and called them a bunch of European planters.

She asserted that Europeans like them were robbers with guns who went all over the world stealing other people's land, which they then called their plantations. And they made the people they robbed their slaves. She was taking a long view of history, of course. Tarkington's Trustees certainly hadn't roamed the world on ships, armed to the teeth and looking for lightly defended real estate. Her point was that they were heirs to the property of such robbers, and to their mode of thinking, even if they had been born poor and had only recently dismantled an essential industry, or cleaned out a savings bank, or earned big commissions by facilitating the sale of beloved American institutions or landmarks to foreigners. . . .

"Now," she said to them, "you are selling this plantation because the soil is exhausted, and the natives are getting sicker and hungrier every day, begging for food and medicine and shelter, all of which are very expensive. The water mains are breaking. The bridges are falling down. So you are taking all your money and getting out of here" (*HP* 37).

This is Hartke's revelation when he finally gets to assess Dr. Dole. (*HP* 37) So she and I, working independently, had noticed the same thing: That even our natives, if they had reached the top or been born at the top, regarded Americans as foreigners. That seems to have been true, too, of people at the top in what used to be the Soviet Union: to them their own ordinary people weren't the kinds of people they understood and liked very much.

Domesday Book. *Eliot Rosewater's ledger in which he keeps coded information on all the Foundation's operations in Rosewater, Indiana. In the back of the* Domesday Book *is an unfinished novel Eliot started years before. The novel is about rein-*

carnation. (GBR 7) Heaven is the bore of bores, *Eliot's novel went on,* so most wraiths queue up to be reborn—and they live and love and fail and die, and they queue up to be reborn again. They take pot luck, as the saying goes. They don't gibber and squeak to be one race or another, one sex or another, one nationality or another, one class or another. What they want and what they get are three dimensions—and comprehensible little packets of time—and enclosures making possible the crucial distinction between inside and outside.

Don. *The astronaut dreamed up by Kilgore Trout while sitting in a pornographic movie house. Don travels to a planet where all the animal and plant life had been killed by pollution, except for humanoids. The humanoids ate food made from petroleum and coal* (BC 5). *His hosts manage to scrape together a feast in his honor, and their discussions turn to pornography and censorship on their respective planets. They take Don to a pornographic movie house where he views films of humanoids salivating and slobbering over a feast of food.*
(BC 5) When **Don** and his friends left the theater, they were accosted by humanoid whores, who offered them eggs and oranges and milk and butter and peanuts and so on. The whores couldn't actually deliver these goodies, of course.

The humanoids told **Don** that if he went home with a whore, she would cook him a meal of petroleum and coal products at fancy prices.

And then, while he ate them, she would talk dirty about how fresh and full of natural juices the food was, even though the food was fake.

Donald. *The golden retriever roaming around Ilium and adopted by Roy and Mary Hepburn in Galápagos. Donald makes Roy very happy as he lies dying of cancer.*

Donna. *A Manhattan slave of Vera Chipmunk-5 Zappa who brings Wilbur a fancy candlestick for his birthday, in* Slapstick *(43). He is, after all, known lovingly as the King of Candlesticks.*

Donner, John (*also* **Donner Party**). *Donner is the shop teacher who drives Eugene Debs Hartke from*

Scipio to the prison in Athena so both can apply for teaching jobs. Donner proudly speaks of his appearance on the Donahue *show concerning people who were raised in foster homes and frequently beaten. Hartke doesn't believe this was a real "Donner," because he didn't know about* the infamous **Donner Party**, which got caught in a blizzard back in 1846 while trying to cross the Sierra Nevada Mountains in wagons to get to California. Their wagons were very likely made right here in Scipio. . . .

Those who survived the blizzard did so by becoming cannibals. The final tally, and several women and children were eaten, was 47 survivors out of 87 people who had begun the trip (HP 31). Hartke claims to have known several Donners including two unrelated Tarkington students as well as a sergeant in Vietnam. Hartke's experience indicated that all Donners related to their infamous ancestors knew the legacy attached to their name.

Donnini, Jim. *In the caption accompanying a photograph in* Fates Worse Than Death *(in the chapter "What Bernard V. O'Hare Said"), Vonnegut reveals that Jim Donnini is one of the POWs with whom he was released at the end of World War II. In the photograph, Donnini sits on a bench playing a harmonica while Vonnegut rests with his head against the rear of a wagon.*

Until the publication of FWD, *however, Jim Donnini was better known as the Chicago youth being brought up by his uncle Bert Quinn in the 1955 short story "The Kid Nobody Could Handle," reprinted in* Welcome to the Monkey House *(1968). Though Quinn recalls the tough times lived so far by a young Jim, he feels incapable of setting him on a better path. However, under the tough love tutelage of high school band director George M. Helmholtz, the close of the story promises Jim's redemption.*

As Quinn describes Jim, "His mother's dead. His old man married my sister, walked out on her, and stuck her with him. Then the court didn't like the way she was raising him, and put him in foster homes for a while. Then they decided to get him clear out of Chicago, so they stuck me with him." He shook his head. "Life's a funny thing, Helmholtz."

"Not very funny, sometimes," said Helmholtz. He pushed his eggs away.

"Like some whole new race of people coming up," said Quinn wonderingly. "Nothing like the kids we got around here. Those boots, the black jacket—and he won't talk. He won't run around with the other kids. Won't study. I don't think he can even read and write very good."

Helmholtz reforms Jim Donnini by first shaming him (taking away his tough-guy boots) and then offering him John Philip Sousa's trumpet. After a long silence, Helmholtz picked up the trumpet. He kissed the cold mouthpiece and pumped the valves in a dream of a brilliant cadenza. Over the bell of the instrument, Helmholtz saw **Jim Donnini**'s face, seemingly floating in space—all but deaf and blind. Now Helmholtz saw the futility of men and their treasures. He had thought that his greatest treasure, the trumpet, could buy a soul for **Jim**. The trumpet was worthless. *Helmholtz destroys the instrument, thinking he had failed, that Jim was already beyond reach. However, at the close of the story, Jim sits in the band room with the repaired trumpet, waiting for practice to begin.*

Donoso, Dr. Teodoro. *The one Ecuadorian official in the United States with whom Bobby King closely consults about the Nature Cruise of the Century.* (Gal 1:21) And the last call King made before leaving his office was to a man who had become a very close friend during the past ten months, who was **Dr. Teodoro Donoso**, a poet and physician from Quito, who was Ecuador's ambassador to the United Nations. He earned his medical degree at Harvard.

Donoso recognizes that economic failure of the entire region is a foregone conclusion. Ironically, Donoso had been preparing an elegy to "The Last Kanka-bono," unaware that the Kanka-bonos would eventually help restock humanity with the help of Mary Hepburn.

Donovan, General. *In* Mother Night, *General Donovan is one of only three people who knows about the espionage work conducted by Howard Campbell. The other two are Harold J. Sparrow (Campbell's Blue Fairy Godmother) and President Franklin Delano Roosevelt.*

Doris. *The daughter of the genetically mutated Akiko Hiroguchi, the first human to be born with a furry coat similar to a seal's. Akiko has a number of children but it is not clear where in the birth order Doris falls. However, Leon Trout says,* The father of Akiko's daughter was the oldest of the Captain's children, Kamikaze, only thirteen years old (Gal 1:13). *Akiko names her daughter after Doris Wojciehowitz, whom she learned about from the real-life romance stories told by Mary Hepburn.*

Dornberger, General Walter. *It is at the general's birthday party that Howard Campbell meets Werner von Braun in* Mother Night. *Historically speaking, Dornberger had been in charge of a number of Nazi rocket programs during World War II.*

Dorset. *The small town ten miles from Ilium that is home to David Potter and his family in the short story "Deer in the Works." Potter owns the Dorset newspaper, which could have been put out of business if even one of the surrounding small town papers printed a one-page Dorset supplement. This small example is another of Vonnegut's commentaries about the tenuous nature of livelihoods devoted to the sincerely romantic quest of writers in general and journalists in particular.*

Dostoevski, Feodor. *One of Vonnegut's favorite authors and one whom he frequently writes into his work. They share the same birthday, though 101 years apart.* (SL5 5) Rosewater said an interesting thing to Billy one time about a book that wasn't science fiction. He said that everything there was to know about life was in *The Brothers Karamazov*, by **Feodor Dostoyevsky**. "But that isn't enough any more," said Rosewater.

Vonnegut finds kinship with Dostoyevsky in their shared sense of the interdependence of all activities. (BC 20) The proper ending for any story about people it seems to me, since life is now a polymer in which the Earth is wrapped so tightly, should be that same abbreviation, which I now write large because I feel like it, which is this one:
ETC.

"It's all like an ocean!" cried **Dostoevski**. I say it's all like cellophane.
(WFG Excelsior! We're Going to the Moon! Excelsior!) "One sacred memory from childhood is perhaps the best education," said **Feodor Dostoevski**. I

believe that, and hope that many Earthling children will respond to the first human footprint on the moon as a sacred thing. We need sacred things. The footprint could mean, if we let it, the Earthlings have done an unbelievable difficult and beautiful thing which the Creator, for Its own reasons, wanted Earthlings to do.
(*Slap* 16) **Fedor Mikhailovich Dostoevski**, the Russian novelist, said one time that, "One sacred memory from childhood is perhaps the best education." I *(Wilbur Swain)* can think of another quickie education for a child, which, in its way, is almost as salutary: Meeting a human being who is tremendously respected by the adult world, and realizing that that person is actually a malicious lunatic.

Dougie. *Mentioned as one of Corporal Fuller's long-lost friends serving with the Strategic Air Command in the short story "Miss Temptation," in* Welcome to the Monkey House *(1968).*

Downs, Roger. *Vonnegut uses the memory of his high school classmate (who in later years competed on the Senior Men's Tennis Circuit) to illustrate a basic lesson of life,* No matter what a young person thinks he or she is really hot stuff at doing, he or she is sooner or later going to run into somebody in the same field who will cut him or her a new asshole, so to speak. *Vonnegut then goes on to relate how their classmate William H. C. "Skip" Failey admits after playing Downs that* Roger cut me a new asshole (*TQ* 38). *Vonnegut sees a natural alignment between his accomplished friend's experience and Kilgore Trout's basic view of life.* (*TQ* 38) . . . life being the Darwinian experiment, or "crock of shit," as Trout liked to call it, **Roger** himself had surely departed more than one tennis tournament having, like Skip, undergone a colostomy to his self-regard.

"Dr. Schadenfraude." *Estimated by Vonnegut to be Kilgore Trout's 2,500th story, written while he was living in the Manhattan homeless shelter that once housed the Museum of the American Indian, situated aside the American Academy of Arts and Letters,* It was set in the office of a psychiatrist in St. Paul, Minnesota.
    The name of the shrink was the name of the story, too, which was "**Dr. Schadenfreude**." This

doctor had his patients lie on a couch and talk, all right, but they could ramble on only about dumb or crazy things that had happened to total strangers in supermarket tabloids or on TV talk shows.
    If a patient accidentally said "I" or "me" or "my" or "myself" or "mine," **Dr. Schadenfreude** went ape.
    He leapt out of his overstuffed leather chair. He stamped his feet. He flapped his arms. He put his livid face directly over the patient. He snarled and barked things like this: "When will you ever learn that nobody cares anything about you, you, you, you boring, insignificant piece of poop? Your whole problem is you think you matter! Get over that, or sashay your stuckup butt the hell out of here!" (*TQ* 17).

Drano. *Celia Hoover commits suicide by eating Drano, prompting Vonnegut's comparisons between her suicide and his mother's. Though Rudy Waltz suggests Celia's abuse of amphetamines caused her to eat Drano, Vonnegut suggests that it was simply the will of each woman to take her own life, and he does so with consistency of character through* Breakfast of Champions *and* Deadeye Dick.
(*BC* 6) He *(Dwayne)* even forgot that his wife Celia had committed suicide, for instance, by eating **Drano**—a mixture of sodium hydroxide and aluminum flakes, which was meant to clear drains. Celia became a small volcano, since she was composed of the same sorts of substances which commonly clogged drains.
(*BC* 17) Listen: Bunny's mother and my mother were different sorts of human beings, but they were both beautiful in exotic ways, and they both boiled over with chaotic talk about love and peace and wars and evil and desperation, of better days coming by and by, of worse days coming by and by. And both our mothers committed suicide. Bunny's mother ate **Drano**. My mother ate sleeping pills, which wasn't nearly as horrible.
(*BC* 23) "All you robots want to know why my wife ate **Drano**?" Dwayne asked his thunderstruck audience. "I'll tell you why: She was that kind of machine!"
(*DD* 12) Celia knew the arts center was going to open, and the newspaper and the radio station and the politicians and so on all said what a difference

it was going to make in the quality of life in Midland City. But there was the can of **Drano**, with all its dire warnings, and she just couldn't wait around anymore.

(DD 24) I would be glad to attempt a detailed analysis of Celia Hoover's character, if I thought her character had much of anything to do with her suicide by **Drano**. As a pharmacist, though, I see no reason not to give full credit to amphetamine. *Rudy Waltz contemplates the seeming inevitability of self-destruction while attending Celia's funeral.* (DD 24) The corpse was a mediocrity who had broken down after a while. The mourners were mediocrities who would break down after a while.

The city itself was breaking down. Its center was already dead.

Everybody shopped at the outlying malls. Heavy industry had gone bust. People were moving away.

The planet itself was breaking down. It was going to blow itself up sooner or later anyway, if it didn't poison itself first. In a manner of speaking, it was already eating **Drano**.

In Palm Sunday, *Vonnegut describes the desperation in a friend's voice on the phone who, together with Vonnegut, was asked to write a blurb for the dust jacket of a book by one of their friends. After reading the book Vonnegut declined to write a blurb, but the other writer* called me up in the middle of the night, long distance and sounding as though he had just swallowed **Drano**. "My God," he said, "you just can't leave me on that book jacket all alone" (PS The Sexual Revolution).

Dresden. *Undoubtedly, the single most influential moment of Vonnegut's life occurs while a POW assigned to a work camp in Dresden, Germany. In one way or another, Dresden is brought up in* Mother Night, God Bless You, Mr. Rosewater, Slaughterhouse-Five, Wampeters, Foma & Granfalloons, Slapstick, Palm Sunday, Bluebeard, Timequake, Bagombo Snuff Box, *and* A Man Without a Country. *His most dispassionate account of the incident appears in the introduction to* Mother Night. (MN Introduction) After a while the war came, and I was in it, and I was captured, so I got to see a little of Germany from the inside while the war was still going on. I was a private, a battalion scout, and, under the terms of the Geneva Convention, I had to work for my keep, which was good, not bad. I didn't have to stay in prison all the time, somewhere out in the countryside. I got to go to a city, which was **Dresden**, and to see the people and the things they did.

There were about a hundred of us in our particular work group, and we were put out as contract labor to a factory that was making a vitamin-enriched malt syrup for pregnant women. It tasted like thin honey laced with hickory smoke. It was good. I wish I had some right now. And the city was lovely, highly ornamented, like Paris, and untouched by war. It was supposedly an "open" city, not to be attacked since there were no troop concentrations or war industries there.

But high explosives were dropped on **Dresden** by American and British planes on the night of February 13, 1945, just about twenty-one years ago, as I now write. There were no particular targets for the bombs. The hope was that they would create a lot of kindling and drive firemen underground.

And then hundreds of thousands of tiny incendiaries were scattered over the kindling, like seeds on freshly turned loam. More bombs were dropped to keep firemen in their holes, and all the little fires grew, joined one another, became one apocalyptic flame. Hey presto: fire storm. It was the largest massacre in European history, by the way. And so what?

We didn't get to see the fire storm. We were in a cool meat-locker under a slaughterhouse with our six guards and ranks and ranks of dressed cadavers of cattle, pigs, horses, and sheep. We heard the bombs walking around up there. Now and then there would be a gentle shower of calcimine. If we had gone above to take a look, we would have been turned into artifacts characteristic of fire storms; seeming pieces of charred firewood two or three feet long—ridiculously small human beings, or jumbo fried grasshoppers, if you will.

The malt syrup factory was gone. Everything was gone but the cellars where 135,000 Hansels and Gretels had been baked like gingerbread men. So we were put to work as corpse miners, breaking into shelters, bringing bodies out. And I got to see many German types of all ages as death had found them, usually with valuables in their laps. Sometimes relatives would come to watch us dig. They were interesting, too.

(FWD II) "Elie Wiesel made his reputation with a

book called *Night*, which is about the horrors of the holocaust as witnessed by the boy he used to be. I made my reputation with a book called *Slaughterhouse-Five*, which is about a British and American response to that Holocaust, which was the firebombing of **Dresden** as witnessed by the young American Infantry Private First Class I used to be. We both have German last names. . . .

"The Holocaust explains almost everything about why Elie Wiesel writes what he writes and is what he is. The firebombing of **Dresden** explains absolutely nothing about why I write what I write and am what I am. I am sure you are miles ahead of me in thinking of a thousand clinical reasons for this being true. I didn't give a damn about **Dresden**. I didn't know anybody there. I certainly hadn't had any good times there before they burned it down. I had seen some **Dresden** china back home in Indianapolis, but I thought then and still think now that it's mostly kitsch. . . . And **Dresden** china isn't made in **Dresden** anyway. It's made in Meissen. That's the town they should have burned down. . . .

"Before I was a soldier I was a journalist, and that's what I was in **Dresden**—a voyeur of strangers' miseries. I was outside the event. Elie Wiesel, seeing what he saw—and he was just a boy, and I was a young man—was the event itself. The firebombing of **Dresden** was quick, was surgical, as the military scientists like to say, fitting the Aristotelian ideal for a tragedy, taking place in less than twenty-four hours. The Holocaust ground on and on and on."

(*FWD* X) The firebombing of **Dresden** was an emotional event without a trace of military importance. The Germans purposely kept the city free of major war industries and arsenals and troop concentrations so that it might be a safe haven for the wounded and refugees. There were no air-raid shelters to speak of and few antiaircraft guns. It was a famous world art treasure, like Paris or Vienna or Prague, and about as sinister as a wedding cake. I will say again what I have often said in print and in speeches, that not one Allied soldier was able to advance as much as an inch because of the firebombing of **Dresden**. Not one prisoner of the Nazis got out of prison a microsecond earlier. Only one person on earth clearly benefited, and I am

that person. I got about five dollars for each corpse, counting my fee tonight.

(*FWD* X) "Among the unidentified, not-even-counted dead in the cellars of **Dresden** there were, without doubt, war criminals or loathsomely proud relatives of war criminals, SS and Gestapo, and so on. Whatever they got was too good for them. Maybe most of the Germans killed in **Dresden**, excepting the infants and children, of course, got what was coming to them. I asked another great German writer, Heinrich Böll, what he thought the dangerous flaw in the character of so many Germans was, and he said, 'Obedience.'"

(*FWD* X) The firebombing of **Dresden**, which had no military significance, was a work of art. It was a tower of smoke and flame to commemorate the rage and heartbreak of so many who had had their lives warped or ruined by the indescribable greed and vanity and cruelty of Germany. The British and Americans who built the tower had been raised, like me, and in response to World War I, to be pacifists.

(*TQ* 35) Here's the thing: For a few days after Germany surrendered, on May 7th, 1945, having been directly or indirectly responsible for the deaths of maybe forty million people, there was a pocket of anarchy south of **Dresden**, near the Czech border, which had yet to be occupied and policed by troops of the Soviet Union. I was in it, and have described it some in my novel *Bluebeard*. Thousands of prisoners of war like myself had been turned loose there, along with death camp survivors with tattooed arms, and lunatics and convicted felons and Gypsies, and who knows what else.

(*BAG* Preface by Peter Reed) This collection includes stories that draw on Vonnegut's World War Two experiences. The events on which *Slaughterhouse-Five* was based are by now widely known: how Vonnegut was captured by the Germans at the Battle of the Bulge, was held as a prisoner of war in **Dresden**, was sheltered in an underground meat storage room when that city was incinerated in massive air raids, and after the Nazi defeat wandered briefly in a Germany awash in refugees before he was reunited with American forces. "Der Arme Dolmetscher," "Souvenir," and "The Cruise of the *Jolly Roger*" treat the aftermath of war with a varying mix of humor and poignancy. (*BAG* Introduction) I returned to **Dresden**, incidentally, the setting for *Slaughterhouse-Five*, on October 7th, 1998. I was taken down into the cellar where I and about a hundred other American POWs survived a firestorm that suffocated or incinerated 135,000 or so other human beings. It reduced the "Florence of the Elbe" to a jagged moonscape.

While I was down in that cellar again, this thought came to me: "Because I have lived so long, I am one of the few persons on Earth who saw an Atlantis before it disappeared forever beneath the waves."

(*BAG* Introduction) Slowly but surely, Fate, which had spared my life in **Dresden**, now began to shape me into a fiction writer and a failure until I was a bleeding forty-seven years of age! But first I had to be a publicity hack for General Electric in Schenectady, New York.

(*MWC* 1) I saw the destruction of **Dresden**. I saw the city before and then came out of an air-raid shelter and saw it afterward, and certainly one response was laughter. God knows, that's the soul seeking some relief.

(*MWC* 1) True enough, there are such things as laughless jokes, what Freud called gallows humor. There are real-life situations so hopeless that no relief is imaginable.

While we were being bombed in **Dresden**, sitting in a cellar with our arms over our heads in case the ceiling fell, one soldier said as though he were a duchess in a mansion on a cold and rainy night, "I wonder what the poor people are doing tonight." Nobody laughed, but we were still all glad he said it. At least we were still alive! He proved it.

(*MWC* 2) In 1968, the year I wrote *Slaughterhouse-Five*, I finally became grown up enough to write about the bombing of **Dresden**. It was the largest massacre in European history. I, of course, know about Auschwitz, but a massacre is something that happens suddenly, the killing of a whole lot of people in a very short time. In **Dresden**, on February 13, 1945, about 135,000 people were killed by British firebombing in one night.

It was pure nonsense, pointless destruction. The whole city was burned down, and it was a British

atrocity, not ours. They sent in night bombers, and they came in and set the whole town on fire with a new kind of incendiary bomb. And so everything organic, except my little POW group, was consumed by fire. It was a military experiment to find out if you could burn down a whole city by scattering incendiaries over it.

(*MWC* 2) I was a writer in 1968. I was a hack. I'd write anything to make money, you know. And what the hell, I'd seen this thing, I'd been through it, and so I was going to write a hack book about **Dresden**. You know, the kind that would be made into a movie and where Dean Martin and Frank Sinatra and the others would play us. I tried to write, but I just couldn't get it right. I kept writing crap.

So I went to a friend's house—Bernie O'Hare, who'd been my pal. And we were trying to remember funny stuff about our time as prisoners of war in **Dresden**, tough talk and all that, stuff that would make a nifty war movie. And his wife, Mary O'Hare, blew her stack. She said, "You were nothing but babies then."

And that is true of soldiers. They are in fact babies. They are not movie stars. They are not Duke Wayne. And realizing that was the key, I was finally free to tell the truth. We were children and the subtitle of *Slaughterhouse-Five* became *The Children's Crusade*.

Why had it taken me twenty-three years to write about what I had experienced in **Dresden**? We all came home with stories, and we all wanted to cash in, one way or another. And what Mary O'Hare was saying, in effect, was, "Why don't you tell the truth for a change?"

Ernest Hemingway wrote a story after the First World War called "A Soldier's Home" about how it was very rude to ask a soldier what he'd seen when he got back home. I think a lot of people, including me, clammed up when a civilian asked about battle, about war. It was fashionable. One of the most impressive ways to tell your war story is to refuse to tell it, you know. Civilians would then have to imagine all kinds of deeds of derring-do.

See also: FWD V; X–XI; What Bernard V. O'Hare Said About Our Friendship on My Sixtieth Birthday; From "The Bomber's Baedeker" (*Guide to the*

Economic Importance of German Towns and Cities, 1944).

Dresden, History, Stage and Gallery (*see* **Mary Endell**).

Dresser, Paul. *According to Eugene Debs Hartke in* Hocus Pocus, *Henry Moellenkamp and Paul Dresser teamed up to write the ballad "Mary, Mary, Where Have You Gone?" Henry brought the words to Dresser to be set to music, then Henry rewrote the lyrics into Tarkington's alma mater (HP 3). Dresser wrote "On the Banks of the Wabash" (the state song of Indiana) and "My Gal Sal," and he was the brother of the author Theodore Dreiser.*

druggist. *In the short story "The Powder-Blue Dragon," collected in* Bagombo Snuff Box (1999), *Kiah Higgins goes into the drugstore to cash a $5 check to himself, the first check he has written from his account. He wanted to make sure a check written by him was really money, would really work. The seventy-year-old druggist engages Kiah in small talk about his many jobs and his love of foreign cars. The druggist views Kiah's obsession with foreign cars as shallow, wondering why he doesn't ever speak about American cars. Kiah's belief that foreign cars have class strikes the druggist as too great a reach for a young man scratching his way through life, assuming that as hardworking as Kiah is, such dreams should be beyond his concerns.* "Class! Listen who's talking about class all the time. He sweeps floors, polishes cars, waits tables, pumps gas, and he's got to have class or nothing."

"You dream your dreams, I'll dream mine," Kiah said.

"I dream of being young like you in a village that's as pretty and pleasant as this one is," said the **druggist**. "You can take class and—"

drupelets. *Vonnegut describes the overpopulation problem that precipitated such measures as Ethical Suicide Parlors and ethical birth control pills at the beginning of the short story "Welcome to the Monkey House," in* Welcome to the Monkey House (1968). *This was at a time when the population of Earth was 17 billion human beings. That was far too many mammals that big for a planet that small.* The people were virtually packed together like **drupelets**.

Drupelets *are the pulpy little knobs that compose the outside of a raspberry.*

Later in the story, we are told that There were 80 miles of sewers under Greater Hyannis, which had a population of 400,000 **drupelets**, 400,000 souls.

In the short story "2BR02B," in Welcome to the Monkey House (1968), *Dr. Hitz illustrates the dilemma faced by the world (and science) in the face of overpopulation using a drupelet as illustration.* "A **drupelet**, Mr. Wehling, is one of the little knobs, one of the little pulpy grains, of a blackberry," said Dr. Hitz. "Without population control, human beings would now be packed on the surface of this old planet like **drupelets** on a blackberry! Think of it!"

Wehling continued to stare at the spot on the wall.

"In the year 2000," said Dr. Hitz, "before scientists stepped in and laid down the law, there wasn't even enough drinking water to go around, and nothing to eat but seaweed—and still people insisted on their right to reproduce like jackrabbits. And their right, if possible, to live forever."

"I want those kids," said Wehling. "I want all three of them."

"Of course you do," said Dr. Hitz. "That's only human."

"I don't want my grandfather to die, either," said Wehling.

At that point Wehling resolves to make sure all his triplets would survive as people, not to be illustrated as impersonal druplelets. He shoots to death Dr. Hitz, the ethical suicide hostess Leora Duncan, and himself.

DSM (Dog Story of the Month). *One of the smaller book clubs established by the National Council of Arts and Letters authorized by the ruling technocracy in* Player Piano.

Duchamp, Marcel. *In the closing Author's Note to* A Man Without a Country, *Vonnegut speaks about the art he makes and has silkscreened by his collaborator Joe Petro III. As for his artistic influences, he confides that* Most of our stuff has been my knockoffs of Paul Klee and **Marcel Duchamp** and so on.

duffle (*see also* **Bokononism**). (CC 89) "Do you know anybody who might want the job?" Frank was giving a classic illustration of what Bokonon calls **duffle**. *Duffle*, in the Bokononist sense, is the destiny of thousands upon thousands of persons when placed in the hands of a *stuppa*. A *stuppa* is a fog-bound child.

Duggan, Leroy. *In the short story "Ambitious Sophomore," collected in* Bagombo Snuff Box (1999), *Duggan is the star sophomore piccoloist upon whom band director George M. Helmholtz pins all his hopes for a third consecutive state championship. The young man first appears shy and clumsy, nearly unable to stay in line or perform in uniform when girls are nearby. It does not help that he is a shy, droll, slope-shouldered sophomore. Leroy was so self-conscious that when anyone turned to look at him he did a sort of fan dance with his piccolo case and portfolio, hiding himself as well as he could behind them.*

The bell-shaped young man is nearly unsightly when dressed in his conventionally fitting marching band tunic. As such, Helmholtz spends more than regularly charged to get his young star a heavily padded, custom-fit tunic that transforms his appearance into a larger-than-life, triangular and heroic silhouette, just the effect Helmholtz envisions for Duggan's soaring piccolo solo in "The Stars and Stripes Forever" during the state competition. More than Duggan's appearance is transformed.

While in the staging area for the band competition, the sartorial masquerade that Duggan slips on his shoulders also shrouds his spirit in a previously unseen confidence. He begins to mingle with a nearby band and engages a competing piccolo player into the conventional one teen's pickup of another. When the competing drum major, who has just been put in his place by the sardonic Helmholtz, sees the otherwise paunchy piccoloist fraternize with one of his own, he makes the mistake of picking on Duggan, daring him—embarrassing him in front of his heart's desire—to remove the tunic and reveal what a misshapen fatty he really is. They fight, and though Duggan's tunic is ruined, he manages to violently beat the drum major to the ground and is prepared to club him with his own marching baton. Helmholtz and others intervene before the drum major is further humiliated or hurt.

Changing back into his original marching band uniform, turning him back into a bell-shaped schlub, does not remove Duggan's newfound self-confidence. Surprisingly, Helmholtz almost cried as American flags hung in air from parachutes. Among them, like a cloudburst of diamonds, was the Sousa piccolo masterpiece. Leroy! Leroy! Having once worn his spiritually uplifting custom tunic in romance and battle, Duggan continues to feel as though he is still riding the crest of popularity and confidence. Proof is later provided when, after the award ceremony, Duggan is seen once again engaged in warm conversation with the pretty blonde piccoloist from the other band. Duggan's actions earn him the nicknames "Blabbermouth Duggan" and "Casanova Duggan" from Assistant Principal Stewart Haley.

Duke of Oklahoma. *In* Slapstick, *one of the military leaders at war with Stewart Oriole-2 Mott, the King of Michigan. The Duke had executed the "Urbana Massacre," unknowingly killing the father of Melody Oriole-2 von Peterswald.*

Dumas, Alexandre (1802–1870). *The French novelist and dramatist whose works include such historical romances and swashbucklers as* The Count of Monte Cristo, The Three Musketeers, *and* The Black Tulip. *(Gal 1:13) If you punched out on its back 1802, for example, the year of Charles Darwin's birth, Mandarax would tell you that **Alexandre Dumas** and Victor Hugo were also born then, and that Beethoven completed his Second Symphony, and that France suppressed a Negro rebellion in Santo Domingo.*

Dun Roamin. *Winston Niles Rumfoord's home on Titan, which was a reproduction of India's Taj Mahal. (ST 12) It was Rumfoord's wry fancy to call his Titan home* **Dun Roamin**.

Duncan, Leora. *In the short story "2BR02B," collected in* Bagombo Snuff Box (1999), A coarse, formidable woman strode into the waiting room on spike heels. Her shoes, stockings, trench coat, bag, and overseas cap were all purple, a purple the painter called "the color of grapes on Judgment Day."*

The medallion on her purple musette bag was

the seal of the Service Division of the Federal Bureau of Termination, an eagle perched on a turnstile.

Leora Duncan has been an Ethical Suicide Suite hostess for five years and shows the telltale signs of one who's been ingesting the cure for overpopulation. The woman had a lot of facial hair—an unmistakable mustache, in fact. A curious thing about gas chamber hostesses was that no matter how lovely and feminine they were when recruited, they all sprouted mustaches within five years or so.

Leora admires the work and vision of Dr. Benjamin Hitz. The unnamed muralist, whose views are well skewed from the predominant position in the world, uses her naiveté to have her pick a character in the mural that represents her sense of self in the painting so that he could paint her portrait into place. She is honored to be so closely positioned to the hero who prevented overpopulation, It was the portrait of a tanned, white-haired, omnipotent Zeus, two hundred forty years old. "Who doesn't admire him?" she said again. "He was responsible for setting up the very first gas chamber in Chicago."

Dunkel, Stan. A grinning, bald, big-toothed man, wearing a badge that said, "Stan Dunkel, Sales," *tries to sell David Potter an X-ray Spectrogoniometer (MH Deer in the Works). Potter is the recently hired public relations man at the Ilium Works of the Federal Apparatus Corporation who is sent to cover the story of a deer that has strayed onto the grounds, and who releases the deer when given the chance.*

duprass. *In Bokononist terms, a duprass is a karass composed of only two people.* (CC 41) "A true **duprass**," Bokonon tells us, "can't be invaded, not even by children born of such a union." *Members of a duprass always die within a week of each other.* (CC 55) A **duprass**, Bokonon tells us, is a valuable instrument for gaining and developing, in the privacy of an interminable love affair, insights that are queer but true. The Mintons' cunning exploration of indexes was surely a case in point. A **duprass**, Bokonon tells us, is also a sweetly conceived establishment. The Mintons' establishment was no exception.

Durant, Major Nathan. *In the short story "The Cruise of the* Jolly Roger," *collected in* Bagombo Snuff Box *(1999), Major Nathan Durant, a child of the Great Depression with no particular locale to call home, leaves the service after recuperating from an injury received in the Korean War. After serving seventeen years, Durant has no family or personal philosophy about life except to see the world as instructed by the Army: to remember that life is a series of vulnerabilities to assess.* During the Great Depression, **Nathan Durant** was homeless until he found a home in the United States Army. He spent seventeen years in the Army, thinking of the earth as terrain, of the hills and valleys as enfilade and defilade, of the horizon as something a man should never silhouette himself against, of the houses and woods and thickets as cover. It was a good life, and when he got tired of thinking about war, he got himself a girl and a bottle, and the next morning he was ready to think about war some more.

When he was thirty-six, an enemy projectile dropped into a command post under thick green cover in defilade in the terrain of Korea, and blew **Major Durant**, his maps, and his career through the wall of his tent.

Void of ambition in his civilian life and without a set of goals, Durant adopts his veterans' hospital roommate's desire to own a boat and simply set sail. Durant purchases a cabin cruiser but is bereft at the thought of naming his new vessel. Some local boys hanging around the marina give him the ominous name for her.

Durant's first stop at Martha's Vineyard proves too sedate, so he heads to Chatham and then Provincetown on Cape Cod. After meeting up with a group of artists at Provincetown, where Marion sketches him (to his chagrin at what it betrays), Durant decides to head to New London, Connecticut, to sell his boat. However, before heading for New London, Durant realizes he is near the hometown of George Pefko, a friend during World War II who was killed in combat.

Durant first learns that almost no one has any recollection of George or any Pefkos. It is not until Annie, a legal secretary in a nearby law firm, overhears Durant's conversation with the postmistress that she remembers the Pefkos were a large family who were last in town nearly fifteen years ago. At first they had the summer rental home belonging to Paul Eldredge, but they decided to take the place through the winter, too. They seemed as rootless as Durant.

Durant's visit to the town is one day before Memorial Day, when the town's students march with their band from one memorial square to the other, placing flowers near the commemorative plaques. He first sees this as a fairly mindless exercise that takes place everywhere, often without giving much thought to what or whom people were memorializing. His sense at that point is very much that soldiers are forgotten once disconnected from service to their country. When Annie and the unnamed school teacher prompt young Tom to explain the meaning of his school's participation in their Memorial Day ritual, Durant is spiritually restored by the young boy's appreciation as he stands by George Pefko's plaque. "He died fighting so we could be safe and free. And we're thanking him with flowers, because it was a nice thing to do." He looked up at Annie, amazed that she should ask. "Everybody knows that."

. . . "It's true, isn't it," murmured **Durant**. "It's so damn simple, and so easy to forget." Watching the innocent marchers under the flowers, he was aware of life, the beauty and importance of a village at peace. "Maybe I never knew—never had any way of knowing. This is what war is about, isn't it. This."

Durant laughed. "George, you homeless, horny, wild old rummy," he said to George Pefko Memorial Square, "damned if you didn't turn out to be a saint."

The old spark was back. **Major Durant**, home from the wars, was somebody.

"I wonder," he said to Annie, "if you'd have lunch with me, and then, maybe, we could go for a ride in my boat."

Dürer, Albrecht. *Walter Starbuck claims to have been the first to ask for a sculpted rendition of Dürer's drawing of two hands held in prayer.* (JB 3) My wedding gift to Ruth was a wood carving commissioned by me. It depicted hands of an old person pressed together in prayer. It was a three-dimensional rendering of a drawing by **Albrecht Dürer**, a sixteenth-century artist, whose house Ruth and I had visited many times in Nuremberg, during our courting

days. That was my invention, so far as I know, having those famous hands on paper rendered in the round. Such hands have since been manufactured by the millions and are staples of dim-witted piety in gift shops everywhere. *Ruth loved the sculpture to the extent that it influenced their decision about which house to purchase when they moved to Chevy Chase, Maryland. She thought the mantelpiece was a "perfect resting place for her hands."*

As an aside to Circe Berman in Bluebeard, *Rabo Karabekian modestly speaks of his considerable drawing talent by saying that he "wasn't an* **Albrecht Dürer**" *(Blue 33).*

The Dutch. *The Ithaca bar that serves as a gathering spot for Cornell fans in* Player Piano. *It is there that Dr. Roseberry, Cornell's football coach, and the State Department's Dr. Ewing J. Halyard meet prior to Halyard's attempted makeup for his lacking physical education course requirement.*

Duty-Dance, A Duty-Dance with Death. *The term denotes an obligatory commitment, and the title page of Vonnegut's masterpiece reads:*

Slaughterhouse-Five

or

THE CHILDREN'S CRUSADE

A DUTY-DANCE WITH DEATH
BY
Kurt Vonnegut, Jr.
A FOURTH-GENERATION GERMAN-
   AMERICAN
NOW LIVING IN EASY CIRCUM-
   STANCES
ON CAPE COD
[AND SMOKING TOO MUCH],
WHO, AS AN AMERICAN INFANTRY
   SCOUT
HORS DE COMBAT,
WITNESSED THE FIRE-BOMBING OF
   DRESDEN, GERMANY,
"THE FLORENCE OF THE ELBE,"
A LONG TIME AGO,

AND SURVIVED TO TELL THE TALE.
THIS IS A NOVEL
SOMEWHAT IN THE TELEGRAPHIC
   SCHIZOPHRENIC
MANNER OF TALES
OF THE PLANET TRALFAMADORE,
WHERE THE FLYING SAUCERS
   COME FROM.
PEACE.

The subtitle is extracted from a book Vonnegut takes with him on his return to Dresden in preparation for writing the text. (SL5 1) My other book was Erika Ostrovsky's Céline and His Vision. Céline was a brave French soldier in the First World War—until his skull was cracked. After that he couldn't sleep, and there were noises in his head. He became a doctor, and he treated poor people in the daytime, and he wrote grotesque novels all night. No art is possible without **a dance with death**, *he wrote.*

The truth is death, he wrote. I've fought nicely against it as long as I could . . . danced with it, festooned it, waltzed it around . . . decorated it with streamers, titillated it. . . .

Time obsessed him.

Duveneck, Frank. *Duveneck taught at the Cincinnati School of Art and was part of the American expatriate group of artists touring Europe prior to World War I. Vonnegut notes in the preface to* Deadeye Dick, *There really was a* **Frank Duveneck**, *and I in fact own a painting by him, "Head of a Young Boy." It is a treasure left to me by my father. I used to think it was a portrait of my brother Bernard, it looks so much like him (DD Preface).*

Within the text Cliff McCarthy tells Rudy over the phone that Otto Waltz was mentioned in Duveneck's diary. According to McCarthy, "**Duveneck** heard about this wonderful studio a young painter was building in Midland City, and on March 16, 1915, he went and had a look at it" *(DD 26). When Rudy presses McCarthy for Duveneck's opinion about his father, McCarthy relents and reads the entry. (DD 26)* "'. . . Otto Waltz should be shot. He should be shot for seeming to prove the last thing that needs to be proved in this part of the world: that an artist is a person of no consequence.'"

Dynamic Tension (CC 47).

. . . Midgets are, after all, diversions for silly or quiet times, and I was serious and excited about Bokonon's theory of what he called "**Dynamic Tension**," his sense of a priceless equilibrium between good and evil.

When I first saw the term "**Dynamic Tension**" in Philip Castle's book, I laughed what I imagined to be a superior laugh. The term was a favorite of Bokonon's, according to young Castle's book, and I supposed that I knew something that Bokonon didn't know: that the term was one vulgarized by Charles Atlas, a mail-order muscle-builder. . . .

It was the belief of Charles Atlas that muscles could be built without bar bells or spring exercisers, could be built by simply pitting one set of muscles against another.

It was the belief of Bokonon that good societies could be built only by pitting good against evil, and by keeping the tension between the two high at all times.

And, in Castle's book, I read my first Bokononist poem, or "Calypso."

It went like this: "Papa" Monzano, he's so very bad, / But without bad "Papa" I would be so sad; / Because without "Papa's" badness, / Tell me, if you would, / How could wicked old Bokonon / Ever, ever look good?

dynamopsychic, dynamopsychism (*see also* **Barnhouse**). (*MH* Report on the Barnhouse Effect) The name he (*Dr. Barnhouse*) chose for the phenomenon was "*dynamopsychism*," or force of the mind. . . .

Their total energy can be brought to bear on any single point the professor chooses, and that energy is undiminished by distance. As a weapon, then, **dynamopsychism** has an impressive advantage over bacteria and atomic bombs, beyond the single fact that it costs nothing to use: it enables the professor to single out critical individuals and objects instead of slaughtering whole populations in the process of maintaining international equilibrium.

There is talk of screening the population for men potentially as powerful **dynamopsychically** as the professor . . . so another costly armaments race, with a new twist, has begun. . . .

Popularly, the "Age of Barnhouse" is said to have

begun a year and a half ago, on the day of Operation Brainstorm. That was when **dynamopsychism** became significant politically. Actually, the phenomenon was discovered in May, 1942, shortly after the professor turned down a direct commission in the Army and enlisted as an artillery private. Like X-rays and vulcanized rubber, **dynamopsychism** was discovered by accident. . . .

In time, he came to recognize another startling feature of **dynamopsychism**: *its strength increased with use. . . .*

It was then that he told me of **dynamopsychism**. He knew only that there was such a force; he could not explain it. "It's me and me alone—and it's awful."

Dyot. *In the San Lorenzan dialect this means God (in* Cat's Cradle*).*

dyslexia. *The disease suffered by Mohiga Valley Free Institute founder Aaron Tarkington. Though he overcame the resulting handicap and his own four children were unaffected by being carriers, the marriages of his descendants endangered a broad spectrum of the wealthy and powerful.* (HP 2) All 3 of Aaron Tarkington's daughters married into prosperous and enterprising families in Cleveland, New York, Wilmington, Delaware—innocently making the threat of **dyslexia** pandemic in an emerging ruling class of bankers and industrialists, largely displaced in my time by Germans, Koreans, Italians, English, and, of course, Japanese. *Because a Mollenkamp married one of Aaron Tarkington's daughters, the families' common descendants suffered eleven times over from the disorder. All eleven* had gone to college in Scipio, since no other institution of higher learning would take them.

The first Moellenkamp to graduate from here was Henry, who enrolled in 1875, when he was 19, and when the school was only 6 years old. It was at that time that its name was changed to Tarkington College (HP 3). *The narrator presumes the name change came about because Henry's grandfather was a trustee of the Mohiga Valley Free Institute, as were other men whose families married Tarkingtons and suffered from dyslexia, and that it sounded too* much like a poorhouse or a hospital. It is my guess that he would not have minded having the place sound like a catchment for the poor, if only he had not suffered the misfortune of having his own grandson go there (HP 3).

Hartke goes on to muse that if not for the birth of Henry Mollenkamp, the Mohiga Valley Free Institute would have succumbed to the economic depression that eventually hit the rest of the region, that the 800,000-volume library would not have been built, that the Lutz Carillon would never have been hung in the bell tower, and that there would have been no one in Scipio for the ten thousand prisoners at Athena to terrorize after escaping.

Eagle-l (*see* **Captain Bernard O'Hare**).

Eaker, Ira C., Lieutenant General, U.S.A.F. *Professor Rumfoord cites Eaker as one of his friends and a contributor to David Irving's* The Destruction of Dresden. *Vonnegut freely quotes some of Eaker's remarks as follows: (SL5 9) I find it difficult to understand Englishmen or Americans who weep about enemy civilians who were killed but who have not shed a tear for our gallant crews lost in combat with a cruel enemy. . . . I think it would have been well for Mr. Irving to have remembered, when he was drawing the frightful picture of the civilians killed at Dresden, that V-1's and V-2's were at that very time falling on England, killing civilian men, women, and children indiscriminately, as they were designed and launched to do. It might be well to remember Buchenwald and Coventry, too. . . .*

I deeply regret that British and U.S. bombers killed 135,000 people in the attack on Dresden, but I remember who started the last war and I regret even more the loss of more than 5,000,000 Allied lives in the necessary effort to completely defeat and utterly destroy Nazism.

Eastman, George. *The inventor of the Kodak camera and founder of the Rochester based Eastman Kodak company, who committed suicide in 1932. According to Eugene Debs Hartke in* Hocus Pocus, *Eastman's suicide note said nothing more than "My work is done." Hartke notes that his mentor, Sam Wakefield, retired Lieutenant General and President of Tarkington College, committed suicide in 1978 and left the same note. In* Fates Worse Than Death, *Vonnegut uses the phrase to mark the occasion of Voyager 2's leaving our Solar System.*

echolalia. *Also called "echophrasia," this is the involuntary repetition of words or phrases uttered by others. It is a symptom of both schizophrenia and autism, among other diseases. Professor Rumfoord believes Billy Pilgrim suffers from it when they share*

a hospital room after Billy's plane crash. (SL5 9) **Echolalia** *is a mental disease which makes people immediately repeat things that well people around them say. But Billy didn't really have it. Rumfoord simply insisted, for his own comfort, that Billy had it. Rumfoord was thinking in a military manner: that an inconvenient person, one whose death he wished for very much, for practical reasons, was suffering from a repulsive disease. Despite Vonnegut's doubting words about Billy's possible affliction,* Slaughterhouse-Five *is "a novel somewhat in the telegraphic schizophrenic manner of tales of the planet Tralfamadore."*

In Breakfast of Champions, *Dwayne Hoover's echolalia precedes his violent outburst in Midland City.*

Eddie (**the farmer**). *In the short story "Souvenir,"collected in* Bagombo Snuff Box (1999), *Eddie is the interior narrator to this frame tale about indifferent greed and naive luck burdened by a long memory. Pressured for money to support his family only a few years after the war, Eddie's nearly final resolve is to sell for $500 his one bit of war booty, a jeweled pocket watch with a German inscription that he came to possess upon release from his Sudetenland POW camp. Retelling the particulars of the tale, necessarily recalling the details of his best friend Buzzer's death, finally persuades Eddie to take back the watch from pawnbroker Joe Bane's counter. The $500 is not worth Eddie's parting with his last connection to Buzzer.* No sooner had Bane hung up his coat and hat and umbrella, taken off his rubbers, turned on the lights, and settled his great bulk on a stool behind a counter than a lean young man in overalls, shy and dark as an Indian, plainly poor and awed by the city, walked in to offer him a fantastic pocketwatch for five hundred dollars.

Eddie snatched the watch from under the pawnbroker's nose. "Thanks for letting me know what it's worth," he said. "Makes more sense to keep it for a souvenir."

Edel, Israel and Norma. *In* Jailbird, *Israel Edel is the slovenly thirty-year-old night clerk at the Hotel Arapahoe when Walter Starbuck arrives in Manhattan after his first imprisonment at the Finletter Federal Prison facility in Georgia. Edel holds a Ph.D. in history from Long Island University, graduated summa cum laude, and is a member of Phi Beta Kappa, but he can't find an academic appointment. After making small talk with Starbuck, Edel is counted among those who showed him kindness and is rewarded for his deed by Mary Kathleen O'Looney, who makes him the vice president in charge of purchasing for Hospitality Associates, Ltd., a RAMJAC subsidiary. Despite Edel's Ph.D. in history, Starbuck is dismayed by Edel's lack of knowledge about Sacco and Vanzetti, as he confuses them with "thrillkillers" Leopold and Loeb.*

Norma is Israel's black wife who suffered the miscarriage of twins. She dislikes Starbuck, which he supposes is part of the hormonal legacy of her miscarriage. Once Israel becomes a RAMJAC executive, they buy and renovate a brownstone in Brooklyn Heights, an area ripe for yuppie gentrification.

Edison, Thomas. *Edison is a revered figure by Paul Proteus in* Player Piano *and maintains his memory by keeping intact Edison's elaborate laboratory. Proteus is so enamored by Edison's achievements that he refers to the whir of the lab's machinery as the* Building 58 Suite.

Edison is a central figure in Vonnegut's "Tom Edison's Shaggy Dog," collected in Welcome to the Monkey House. *Edison is seen in his Menlo Park, New Jersey, laboratory in the process of looking for a filament for his new invention, the electric light bulb. After a series of failures and an accidental meeting with his neighbor Harold K. Bullard and his faithful dog Sparky, Edison hooks up Sparky to another invention—the intelligence analyzer.* "And the last words that Sparky ever spoke were to **Thomas Edison**. 'Try a piece of carbonized cotton thread,' he said. Later, he was torn to bits by a pack of dogs that had gathered outside the door, listening."

Vonnegut also makes mention of Edison in "The Mysterious Madame Blavatsky," *collected in* Wampeters, Foma & Granfalloons, *as a notable*

member of the Theosophical Society. In Slapstick, Professor Swain died of his fatness in the mansion, at a dinner he gave in honor of Samuel Langhorne Clemens and **Thomas Alva Edison** (*Slap* 4).

(TQ 9) Founders of the Academy at the turn of the century were contemporaneous with **Thomas Alva Edison**, inventor of, among other things, sound recordings and motion pictures. Before World War Two, though, these schemes for holding the attention of millions all over the world were only squawking or flickering lampoons of life itself.

Edison Park. *A public park at the edge of Homestead in* Player Piano. *Both locations are on the opposite side of the river from the Ilium Works.*

Ehrens, Kurt and Heinrich. *The brothers whom Heinz Schildknecht's unnamed wife reveres as models of success and upward mobility, constantly berating Heinz for his comparatively low station in the new Nazi order. Heinz, of course, is an undercover Israeli agent prepared to testify against his best friend, Howard Campbell, Jr. Campbell sees Mrs. Schildknecht's appreciation of the Ehrens brothers as typically totalitarian and twisted.* (MN 21) As for the kind of woman Heinz's wife had been: I knew her only slightly, though I saw her fairly often. She was a nonstop talker, which made her hard to know, and her theme was always the same: successful people, people who saw opportunities and grasped them firmly, people who, unlike her husband, were important and rich.

"Young **Kurt Ehrens**—" she would say, "only twenty-six, and a full colonel in the S.S.! And his brother **Heinrich**—he can't be more than thirty-four, but he has eighteen thousand foreign workers under him, all building tank traps. **Heinrich** knows more about tank traps than any man alive, they say, and I used to dance with him."

On and on she would talk this way, with poor Heinz in the background, smoking his brains out. And one thing she did to me was make me deaf to all success stories. The people she saw as succeeding in a brave new world were, after all, being rewarded as specialists in slavery, destruction, and death. I don't consider people who work in those fields successful.

Eichmann, Adolf. *The "bureaucratic Genghis Khan" of Nazi Germany, "the architect of Ausch- witz, the introducer of conveyor belts into cremato- ria, the greatest customer in the world for the gas called Cyklon-B," was kidnapped in South America by the Israeli secret service, convicted for war crimes and executed in 1961. He and Howard Campbell, Jr., briefly met once in Germany while having their official portraits photographed by Arndt Klopfer, and are later jailed together for a short period in Tel Aviv. Eichmann is serene about his incarceration, telling Campbell,* Life is divided up into phases. . . . Each one is very different from the others, and you have to be able to recognize what is expected of you in each phase. That's the secret of successful living (MN 29).

Eichmann is dumbfounded by Campbell's guess that he will plead innocent to his charges on the grounds he was simply following orders. (MN 29) This man *(Eichmann)* actually believed that he had invented his own trite defense, though a whole nation of ninety some-odd million had made the same defense before him. Such was his paltry un- derstanding of the God-like human act of inven- tion. *This prompts Campbell to compare the nature of Eichmann's crimes to his own and make the fol- lowing judgment.* (MN 29) The more I think about **Eichmann** and me, the more I think that he should be sent to the hospital, and that I am the sort of person for whom punishments by fair, just men were devised.

As a friend of the court that will try **Eichmann,** I offer my opinion that **Eichmann** cannot distinguish between right and wrong—that not only right and wrong, but truth and falsehood, hope and despair, beauty and ugliness, kindness and cruelty, comedy and tragedy, are all processed by **Eichmann**'s mind indiscriminately, like birdshot through a bugle.

My case is different. I always know when I tell a lie, am capable of imagining the cruel conse- quences of anybody's believing my lies, know cru- elty is wrong. I could no more lie without noticing it than I could unknowingly pass a kidney stone.

If there is another life after this one, I would like very much, in the next one, to be the sort of person of whom it could truly be said, "Forgive him—he knows not what he does."

This cannot be said of me now.

As evidence of Eichmann's detachment, he later has a note smuggled to Campbell's Old Jerusalem cell asking if he thought it necessary to have a liter- ary agent. Campbell replies it is if one plans to suc- cessfully cope with book clubs and movie rights.

Vonnegut's continuing interest in society's loss of historical perspective prompts him to wonder why, in his review of Webster's New International Diction- ary, *is the memory of John Dillinger perpetuated, while of* **Adolf Eichmann** there is neither gibber nor squeak? (MH New Dictionary)

Einstein, Albert. *Vonnegut uses Einstein as an ob- ject of comparison for extremely intelligent people to express their disgust over being asked to perform me- nial chores. Slapstick's Dr. Cordelia Swain Cordiner and Dr. Jekyll of "Jekyll and Hyde Revisited" ex- claim, "That's like asking Einstein to balance a checkbook." The title rabbit in Kilgore Trout's "The Smart Bunny" is compared to Einstein and Shake- speare* (Breakfast of Champions).

Vonnegut admires both Einstein's intelligence and humanity as expressed by Walter Starbuck and as he steps into the narrative. (JB 9) I had been to the Arapahoe once before—in the autumn of Nineteen-hundred and Thirty-one. Fire had yet to be domesticated. **Albert Einstein** had predicted the invention of the wheel, but was unable to de- scribe its probable shape and uses in the language of ordinary women and men. *This is a satirically oblique reference to nuclear fission.*
(JB 19) During their deliberations, they received thousands of telegrams, some in favor of the execu- tions, but most opposed. Among the telegraphers were Romain Rolland, George Bernard Shaw, **Al- bert Einstein,** John Galsworthy, Sinclair Lewis, and H. G. Wells. *This is in reference to those nota- bles who telegraphed their opposition to the execu- tions of Sacco and Vanzetti.*

Einstein is the major character in Kilgore Trout's short story "Asleep at the Switch," whose premise is that before anyone is permitted past heaven's gates, God's auditors give them an IRS-type interrogation. (JB 20) "Asleep at the Switch" was quite a sacrile- gious story. The hero was the ghost of **Albert Ein- stein.** He himself was so little interested in wealth that he scarcely heard what his auditor had to say to him. It was some sort of balderdash about how he could have become a billionaire, if only he had gotten a second mortgage on his house in Bern, Switzerland, in Nineteen-hundred and Five, and invested the money in known uranium deposits before telling the world that E = Mc^2.

"But there you were—asleep at the switch again," said the auditor.

"Yes," said **Einstein** politely, "it does seem rather typical."

"So you see," said the auditor, "life really was quite fair. You did have a remarkable number of opportunities, whether you took them or not."

"Yes, I see that now," said **Einstein**.

"Would you mind saying that in so many words?" said the auditor.

"Saying what?" said **Einstein**.

"That life was fair."

"Life was fair," said **Einstein**.

"If you don't really mean it," said the auditor, "I have many more examples to show you. For instance, just forgetting atomic energy: If you had simply taken the money you put into a savings bank when you were at the Institute for Advanced Studies at Princeton, and you had put it, starting in Nineteen-hundred and Fifty, say, into IBM and Polaroid and Xerox—even though you had only five more years to live—" The auditor raised his eyes suggestively, inviting **Einstein** to show how smart he could be.

"I would have been rich?" said **Einstein**.

"'Comfortable,' shall we say?" said the auditor smugly. "But there you were again—" And again his eyebrows went up. (JB 20) All the auditing stories that **Einstein** heard were told by Americans. He had chosen to settle in the American part of heaven. Understandably, he had mixed feelings about Europeans, since he was a Jew. (JB 20) It was in character for **Einstein** to be offended first by the mathematics of the system the auditors wanted everybody to be so grateful for. He calculated that if every person on Earth took full advantage of every opportunity, became a millionaire and then a billionaire and so on, the paper wealth on that one little planet would exceed the worth of all the minerals in the universe in a matter of three months or so. Also: There would be nobody left to do any useful work. . . .

The story ended abruptly. **Einstein** did not get to see God. But God sent out an archangel who was boiling mad. He told **Einstein** that if he continued to destroy ghosts' respect for the audits, he was going to take **Einstein**'s fiddle away from him for all eternity. So **Einstein** never discussed the audits with anybody ever again. His fiddle meant more to him than anything.

Einstein is also one of heaven's active shuffleboard aficionados in Happy Birthday, Wanda June.

For both Bernard Vonnegut and Kurt, Jr., Einstein holds a mystical place as recalled in Timequake. *They are taken by the philosophical/ religious implications of Einstein's mathematical perceptions as they relate to the incalculable creations of humankind.* (TQ Epilogue). We were luckier with Bernard. He died the beloved, sweet, funny, highly intelligent old geezer he deserved to become. He was enraptured at the very end by a collection of sayings of **Albert Einstein**. Example: "The most beautiful thing we can experience is the mysterious. It is the source of all true art and science." Another: "Physical concepts are free creations of the human mind, and are not, however it may seem, uniquely determined by the external world."

Most famously, **Einstein** is reputed to have said, "I shall never believe that God plays dice with the world." Bernard was himself so open-minded about how the universe might be dealt with that he thought praying would help, possibly, in drastic situations. When his son Terry had cancer of the throat, Bernie, ever the experimentalist, prayed for his recovery. Terry indeed survived.

Vonnegut again lauds Einstein's ethos when pairing the scientist with Mark Twain, his literary idol, as they each seemingly saw good reason for abandoning all hope for humanity. Vonnegut uses the unimpeachable sensibilities of these iconic figures to support his own resignation from humanity. (MWC 8) **Albert Einstein** and Mark Twain gave up on the human race at the end of their lives, even though Twain hadn't even seen the First World War. War is now a form of TV entertainment, and what made the First World War so particularly entertaining were two American inventions, barbed wire and the machine gun.

Shrapnel was invented by an Englishman of the

same name. Don't you wish you could have something named after you?

Like my distinct betters **Einstein** and Twain, I now give up on people, too. I am a veteran of the Second World War and I have to say this is not the first time I have surrendered to a pitiless war machine.

My last words? "Life is no way to treat an animal, not even a mouse."
See also: ST 1; WJ II:2; BC 20; Slap 16; JB 20; PS Jekyll and Hyde Revisited; MWC 11.

El Greco. In God Bless You, Mr. Rosewater, Eliot authorizes the family foundation purchase of an El Greco painting for Tampa, Florida. In Breakfast of Champions, Eliot loans his own El Greco painting of Saint Sebastian to the Midland City Arts Festival. In Hocus Pocus, Tarkington College benefactor Robert Moellenkamp loses all his possessions including an El Greco, when he is bankrupt by the failure of Microsecond Arbitrage. (BC 19) Mary Alice was smiling at a picture of Saint Sebastian, by the Spanish painter **El Greco**. It had been loaned to the Festival by Eliot Rosewater, the patron of Kilgore Trout. Saint Sebastian was a Roman soldier who had lived seventeen hundred years before me and Mary Alice Miller and Wayne and Dwayne and all the rest of us. He had secretly become a Christian when Christianity was against the law.
See also: GBR 2; BC 3; HP 19.

Eldredge, Paul. Though Eldredge is unseen in the short story "The Cruise of the Jolly Roger," collected in Bagombo Snuff Box (1999), his summer rental home in New London serves as temporary home for George Pefko's transient family. It is from here that Pefko enlists in the army and serves with Major Nathan Durant in World War II before being killed in action. "And they did live out on the dunes, too. Goodness, that was a long time ago—ten or fifteen years. Remember that big family that talked **Paul Eldredge** into letting them live in one of his summer cottages all winter? About six kids or more. That was the Pefkos. A wonder they didn't freeze to death, with nothing but a fireplace for heat. The old man came out here to pick cranberries, and stayed on through the winter."

Ellen. In "Mnemonics," Vonnegut's second published short story originally appearing in the April 1951 issue of Collier's magazine and later reprinted in Bagombo Snuff Box (1999), Ellen is the secretary to Alfred Moorhead, a recent workshop participant who learns new memory tricks to help improve his workplace productivity. His particular application of what he learns includes the use of the names of contemporary Hollywood Starlets. Both Ellen and Alfred suppress their emotions for each since their first day working together. At the end of the story, Alfred cannot juggle all the starlets' names and his confusion leads him to mindlessly and literally fall into a close moment with Ellen. The veil of his feelings is gone and Ellen, likewise, voices her own emotions for Alfred.

Emmy. Vonnegut mentions his cousin Emmy, among other family and friends, to illustrate just how widely spread the family became after generations of living in Indianapolis. (TQ 39) My boyhood pal David Craig, who made a radio in a German tank stop playing popular music during World War Two, is a builder in New Orleans. My cousin **Emmy**, whose dad told me I was a man at last when I came home from war, and who was my lab partner in physics class at Shortridge High School, lives only about thirty miles east of Dave in Louisiana.

"Empire State." Vonnegut recalls Kilgore Trout's short story to punctuate another metafictional moment in Timequake, this time touching on Vonnegut's often repeated sentiments that not all scientific progress is . . . progress—and that sometimes religion can offer a welcome salve. (TQ 31) My daughter Nanny has a son, Max, who is twelve now, in 1996, halfway through the rerun. He will be seventeen when Kilgore Trout dies. This past April, Max wrote for school a really swell report on Sir Isaac Newton, a superman so ordinary in appearance. It told me something I hadn't known before: That Newton was advised by those who were his nominal supervisors to take time out from the hard truths of science to brush up on theology.

I like to think they did this not because they were foolish, but to remind him of how comforting and encouraging the make-believe of religion can be for common folk.

To quote from Kilgore Trout's story "**Empire State**," which is about a meteor the size and shape of the Manhattan skyscraper, approaching Earth point-first at a steady fifty-four miles an hour: "Science never cheered up anyone. The truth about the human situation is just too awful."

Empire State Building. *The landmark Manhattan skyscraper where* Mother Night's *Howard Campbell is taken after being arrested in Dr. Jones's basement. Though he is quickly released, once in front of the building he has a quiet discussion with a policeman about the role chemicals have on human behavior.*

Eliot Rosewater moves the Rosewater Foundation into the building. (GBR 2) *He hired a suite of offices in the* **Empire State Building**. *He had them painted lime, burnt-orange and oyster white. He proclaimed them the headquarters for all the beautiful, compassionate and scientific things he hoped to do.*

Wilbur Swain lives in the landmark building once it's abandoned after the Green Death, the Albanian Flu, and unstable gravity destroys present geopolitical structures. This is where Wilbur writes his memoirs and is joined by his granddaughter and her lover, Melody Oriole-2 von Peterswald and Isadore Raspberry-19 Cohen. It is here that Swain dies in a funeral scene that includes a thousand candles lit along the great lobby of the building.

Endell, Mary. *The author of the 1908 book* Dresden, History, Stage and Gallery. *In the opening chapter of* Slaughterhouse-Five, *Vonnegut recounts that when he visited his old wartime buddy Bernard V. O'Hare and his wife Mary, she placed the book in his bedroom. Among the several paragraphs Vonnegut pastes into his text is the following:* It is hoped that this little book will make itself useful. It attempts to give to an English-reading public a bird's-eye view of how Dresden came to look as it does, architecturally; of how it expanded musically, through the genius of a few men, to its present bloom; and it calls attention to certain permanent landmarks in art that make its Gallery the resort of those seeking lasting impressions (SL5 1).

enlaced. (*Slap* Epilogue) Melody's candlestick depicted a nobleman's flirtation with a shepherdess at the foot of a treetrunk **enlaced** in flowering vines.

Enlightened Self-interest, enlightening, enlightenment. (CC 103) "When a man becomes a writer, I (*John/Jonah*) think he takes on a sacred obligation to produce beauty and **enlightenment** and comfort at top speed."
(GBR 4) In the sweet silence (*when in the throes of Samaritrophia—q.v.*), the mental processes look about for a new leader, and the leader most prompt to appear whenever the conscience is stilled, **Enlightened Self-interest**, does appear. **Enlightened Self-interest** gives them a flag, which they adore on sight.
(PS The People One Knows) It is the truth: Comedians and jazz musicians have been more comforting and **enlightening** to me than preachers or politicians or philosophers or poets or painters or novelists of my time.
(HP 26) One author wrote a series of side-splitting satires about Tralfamadorians arriving on other planets with the intention of spreading **enlightenment**.
See also: MN 29; PS A Nazi Sympathizer Defended at Some Cost.

entombed. (*Slap* 2) Our parents did not hide us in a private hospital for cases such as ours. They **entombed** us instead in a spooky old mansion which they had inherited—in the midst of two hundred acres of apple trees on a mountaintop, near the hamlet of Galen, Vermont.
(JB Epilogue) I had **entombed** the will itself in a safe-deposit box of Manufacturers Hanover Trust Company, a division of RAMJAC.
(Blue 34) They (*the peeling canvases of "Windsor Blue Number Seventeen"*) were found **entombed** in a locked chamber in the bottommost of the three basement floors under the Matsumoto Building, formerly the GEFFCo Building.

EPICAC. *The supercomputer originally appearing in the 1950 short story that bears its name (reprinted in the 1968 collection* Welcome to the Monkey House) *and later in* Player Piano. *In both cases it was de-*

signed to control military strategy as well as armaments. In the novel it becomes the central organ of the National Industrial, Commercial, Communications, Foodstuffs, and Resources Board. The scope of its mission covers all aspects of life, standing as the grand designer of society's material and human development. (PP XI) . . . the oldest section of the computer . . . what had been the whole of EPICAC I, but what was now little more than an appendix or tonsil of EPICAC XIV. Yet, EPICAC I had been intelligent enough, dispassionate enough, retentive enough to convince men that he, rather than they, had better do the planning for the war that was approaching with stupefying certainty. The ancient phrase used by generals testifying before appropriation committees, "all things considered," was given some validity by the ruminations of EPICAC I, more validity by EPICAC II, and so on, through the lengthening series. EPICAC could consider the merits of high-explosive bombs as opposed to atomic weapons for tactical support, and keep in mind at the same time the availability of explosives as opposed to fissionable materials, the spacing of enemy foxholes, the labor situation in the respective processing industries, the probable mortality of planes in the face of enemy antiaircraft technology, and on and on, if it seemed at all important, to the number of cigarettes and Cocoanut Mound Bars and Silver Stars required to support a high-morale air force. Given the facts by human beings, the war-born EPICAC series had offered the highly informed guidance that the reasonable, truth-loving, brilliant, and highly trained core of American genius could have delivered had they had inspired leadership, boundless resources, and two thousand years.

(PP XI) And it was EPICAC XIV who would decide for the coming years how many engineers and managers and research men and civil servants, and of what skills, would be needed in order to deliver the goods; and what I.Q. and aptitude levels would separate the useful men from the useless ones, and how many Reconstruction and Reclamation Corps men and how many soldiers could be supported at what pay level and where, and . . .

Vonnegut uses EPICAC to illustrate Norbert Wiener's prediction of a Third Industrial Revolution.

Paul Proteus's preparation of a speech includes this exchange with his secretary: "It seemed very fresh to me—I mean that part where you say how the First Industrial Revolution devalued muscle work, then the second one devalued routine mental work. I was fascinated.

"Norbert Wiener, a mathematician, said all that way back in the nineteen-forties. It's fresh to you because you're too young to know anything but the way things are now. . . . In a way, I guess the third one's been going on for some time, if you mean thinking machines. That would be the third revolution, I guess—machines that devaluate human thinking. Some of the big computers like EPICAC do that all right, in specialized fields" (PP I).

Despite the authority bestowed upon EPICAC by the ruling technocracy, the Shah of Bratpuhr is convinced it is not the wise conscience it is meant to be since it can't answer the question, "What are people for?"

EPICAC's original short story appearance is consistent with the military application alluded to in Player Piano, but it self-destructs because it can't become human. As the creation of Dr. Ormand von Kleigstadt, EPICAC sprawls over an acre of floor space in the physics building of Wyandotte College. The unnamed narrator of the story is a mathematician who discovers that EPICAC is capable of creating original love poetry. He has the computer focus its poetic efforts on Pat Kilgallen, another mathematician at work on the computer. The narrator doesn't possess the capacity for romantic expression so he has EPICAC create the work and he signs his name to it. Pat and the narrator fall in love and marry. When he and EPICAC argue about the computer's inability to have an actual loving relationship with Pat, EPICAC burns itself out in a fit of poetic passion. The text he leaves behind is enough poetry for the narrator to give his wife for their next five hundred wedding anniversaries.

Epstein, Dr. Abraham and his mother. The Jewish physician and his mother who live on the second floor of Campbell's Greenwich Village apartment building. They are survivors of Auschwitz. Dr. Epstein is a self-confessed anti-Zionist who has no interest in seeking retaliation against Nazi war criminals. Mrs. Epstein remembers the Nazi legacy of Howard Campbell the radio propagandist. Dr. Epstein is there to declare August Krapptauer dead after heroically trying to carry up the bags of Resi Noth, and he is there to repair Campbell's broken ribs after a beating by irate war veteran Bernard B. O'Hare. In a mildly catatonic episode, Campbell surrenders himself to Epstein so that he may be tried for his alleged war crimes. He wants to surrender to "an Auschwitzer." Though the doctor wants no part of Campbell's humiliation, his mother insists they cooperate and give him what he wants, someone to take him into custody for the Israeli authorities. In a bizarre twist, Mrs. Epstein seeks to fulfill Campbell's fate in a manner reminiscent of Auschwitz. (MN 11) "He *has* to go," said his mother. And then she leaned closer to me, across the kitchen table. She crooned something in German, made it sound like a fragment of a ditty remembered from a happy childhood.

What she crooned was this, a command she had heard over the loudspeakers of Auschwitz—had heard many times a day for years.

"*Leichenträger zu Wache*," she crooned. A beautiful language, isn't it?

Translation?

"Corpse-carriers to the guardhouse." That's what that old woman crooned to me.

Epstein, Harold (*see* **God Bless You, Dr. Kevorklan**).

equilibrium. (WFG Preface) I keep losing and regaining my **equilibrium**, which is the basic plot of all popular fiction. And I myself am a work of fiction. . . .

I happen to have my **equilibrium** just now. I received a note from a twelve-year-old this morning. He had read my latest novel, *Breakfast of Champions*, and he said, "Dear Mr. Vonnegut: Please don't commit suicide." God love him. I have told him I am fine.

This book is dedicated to a person (*the photographer Jill Krementz, Vonnegut's second wife*) who helped me to regain my **equilibrium**. I say she cronkled me.

See also: CC 47; *MH* Report on the Barnhouse Effect; *WFG* Preface.

The Era of Hopeful Monsters. *The Kilgore Trout novel brought to mind by Leon Trout who, in reflecting on the broad range of human foibles presented by the text's main characters, recalls:* It was about a planet where the humanoids ignored their most serious survival problems until the last possible moment. And then, with all the forests being killed and all the lakes being poisoned by acid rain, and all the groundwater made unpotable by industrial wastes and so on, the humanoids found themselves the parents of children with wings or antlers or fins, with a hundred eyes, with no eyes, with huge brains, with no brains, and on and on. These were Nature's experiments with creatures which might, as a matter of luck, be better planetary citizens than the humanoids. Most died, or had to be shot, or whatever, but a few were really quite promising, and they intermarried and had young like themselves.

I will now call my own lifetime a million years ago "the Era of Hopeful Monsters," with most of the monsters novel in terms of personality rather than body type. And there are no such experiments, either with bodies or personalities, going on at the present time (*Gal* 1:16).

Erie Coal and Iron. *In* Jailbird, *workers from this Buffalo company went to Cleveland to support the striking workers at Cuyahoga Bridge and Iron.*

ethical birth control, ethical birth-control pills, ethical suicide. (*MH* Welcome to the Monkey House) So the World Government was making a two-pronged attack on overpopulation. One was the encouragement of **ethical suicide**, which consisted of going to the nearest Suicide Parlor and asking a Hostess to kill you painlessly while you lay on a Barcalounger. The other pronging was compulsory **ethical birth control**.

. . . He was referring to the fact that **ethical birth-control pills**, the only legal form of birth control, made people numb from the waist down.

So Nancy had to sit down there in the booth, to pretend to marvel at the freshness of the yarn the old man told, a story everybody knew, about how J. Edgar Nation happened to experiment with **ethical birth control**.

Ethical Suicide Parlor. *The federally sponsored purple-roofed facilities instituted to help stem the overpopulation problem.* (GBR 2) So death was voluntary, and the government, to encourage volunteers for death, set up a purple-roofed **Ethical Suicide Parlor** at every major intersection, right next door to an orange-roofed Howard Johnson's. . . . The **suicide parlors** were busy places, because so many people felt silly and pointless, and because it was supposed to be an unselfish, patriotic thing to do, to die.

The hostesses were all over six feet and virgins. Billy the Poet, the protagonist of the story, specializes in kidnapping and deflowering the hostesses. There was a Howard Johnson's next door to every **Ethical Suicide Parlor**, and vice versa. The Howard Johnson's had an orange roof and the **Suicide Parlor** had a purple roof, but they were both the Government.

Every fifteen minutes his *(the average citizen's)* television would urge him to vote intelligently or consume intelligently, or worship in the church of his choice, or love his fellow men, or obey the laws—or pay a call to the nearest **Ethical Suicide Parlor** and find out how friendly and understanding a Hostess could be.

Vonnegut also uses the construct of ethical suicide parlors in the short story "2BR02B," reprinted in Bagombo Snuff Box *(1999).* "Nobody's really happy about taking a close relative to the Catbox," said Dr. Hitz sympathetically.

"I wish people wouldn't call it that," said Leora Duncan.

"What?" said Dr. Hitz.

"I wish people wouldn't call it the Catbox, and things like that," she said. "It gives people the wrong impression."

"You're absolutely right," said Dr. Hitz. "Forgive me." He corrected himself, gave the municipal gas chambers their official title, a title no one ever used in conversation. "I should have said 'Ethical Suicide Studios,'" he said.

Ethical Suicide Service (**E.S.S.**). *In the short story "Welcome to the Monkey House," in* Welcome to the Monkey House *(1968), this is the branch of government service responsible for conducting "ethical suicides" at parlors next to Howard Johnson restau-*rants. *Members of the organization are all good-looking female virgins whose job it is to talk the undecided into committing suicide.*

Ethical Suicide Studio (*see also* **Ethical Suicide Parlor**). *In the short story "2BR02B," reprinted in* Welcome to the Monkey House *(1968), Ethical Suicide Studios are ubiquitous the world over. In the United States, they are regulated by the Federal Bureau of Termination, whose phone number is eponymously represented as 2BR02B. The hostesses wear purple outfits.* The medallion on her *(Leora Duncan's)* purple musette bag was the seal of the Service Division of the Federal Bureau of Termination, an eagle perched on a turnstile.

"The Euphio Question" (1951). *Reprinted in Vonnegut's short story collection* Welcome to the Monkey House *(1968), this tale focuses on the Federal Communications Commission testimony of an unnamed sociology professor from Wyandotte College speaking against radio announcer Lew Harrison's license application to broadcast sounds from space transmitted through a euphoriaphone, an invention of Wyandotte physics professor Dr. Fred Bockman. The sounds evoke a blissful, mind-numbing euphoria that can last for days. The sociology professor sees great potential harm in letting Lew Harrison's avarice control such a powerful instrument. At the close of his testimony, Harrison pumps the hearing room full of the sounds from space and gets the committee to approve his application.*

euphoriaphone. *The device Lew Harrison wants to market for people to tune into the mind-numbing sounds from outer space.* (MH The Euphio Question) "We'll make a little amplifier with a transmitter and an aerial on it. Shouldn't cost over fifty bucks to make, so we'd price it in the range of the common man—five hundred bucks, say. We make arrangements with the phone company to pipe signals from your antenna right into the homes of people with these sets. The sets take the signal from the phone line, amplify it, and broadcast it through the houses to make everybody in them happy. See? Instead of turning on the radio or television, everybody's going to want to turn on the happiness. No casts, no stage sets, no expensive cameras—no nothing but that hiss."

Evelyn and Her Magic Violin. *A statue on Titan made from Titanic peat.* (ST 12) The statue was of a nude woman playing a slide trombone. It was entitled, enigmatically, **Evelyn and Her Magic Violin**.

Everett, Norman. *He and Hartke's grandfather were both Tarkington College campus gardeners.* (HP 12) He had a son who had been paralyzed from the waist down by a mine in Vietnam and was a permanent resident in a Veterans Administration hospital over in Schenectady.

Ewald, Lincoln. *The Nazi sympathizer who uses a* short wave transmitter during the war in order to tell the Germans what was being produced by the Rosewater Saw Company every day, which was paratroop knives and armor plate. His first message, and the Germans hadn't asked him for any messages at all, was to the effect that, if they could bomb Rosewater, the entire American economy would shrivel and die. He didn't ask for money in exchange for the information. He sneered at money, said that that was why he hated America, because money was king. He wanted an Iron Cross, which he requested be sent in a plain wrapper (GBR 13). *His transmissions are intercepted by game wardens in Turkey Run State Park. They turn the information over to the FBI. Ewald is subsequently sent to a mental institution for the remainder of the war.*

Long after the war he runs a small stand that sold shoelaces, razorblades, soft drinks, and copies of *The American Investigator. . . .* His sinister little leper's booth there in the ruin of a great civilization was easy to miss (GBR 13). *He still greeted people with a bitter but sincere "Heil Hitler."*

executive officer. *In the short story "Der Arme Dolmetscher" collected in* Bagombo Snuff Box *(1999), the executive officer is second in command to the colonel and dutifully follows his orders, even those that seem inexplicable such as when he appoints the unnamed narrator to be battalion translator. Vonnegut attempts to capture the Tennessee roots of the executive officer, a dry goods salesman*

from Knoxville before the war. When the would-be interpreter protests that he really is unfit for the task, he punctuates his recollection of the moment by emphasizing the Southern drawl of the executive officer, as if to match the stupidity of the order with a familiar regional prejudice against those sounding Southern. Those in authority were too harried to hear my declarations of incompetence. "You talk Kraut good enough foah us," said the Executive Officer. . . . "Besides," the Executive concluded, "theah ain't nobody else can talk Kraut at all."

extended family. *Anthropology professor Dr. Robert Redfield at the University of Chicago first introduced Vonnegut to this concept, which he goes on to discuss at great length in* Wampeters, Foma & Granfalloons, Palm Sunday, *and* Fates Worse Than Death. *It is a major narrative device in* Slapstick, *a creation of Wilbur and Eliza Swain, and briefly alluded to by Rabo Karabekian in* Bluebeard. *The concept is also included in* Timequake, God Bless You, Dr. Kevorkian, *and* A Man Without a Country, *a final trio of books intended to look back, assess, praise and pan.*

(WFG Preface) My longer-range schemes have to do with providing all Americans with artificial **extended families** of a thousand members or more.

(WFG *Playboy* Interview) VONNEGUT: Well, the choice of a core for an artificial **extended family** is fairly arbitrary. I've already mentioned the arts and jism and blood and spaghetti. Christianity is equally commonplace and harmless, and therefore good.

(Slap Prologue) But, because of the sorts of minds we were given at birth, and in spite of their disorderliness, Bernard (Vonnegut) and I belong to artificial **extended families** which allow us to claim relatives all over the world. . . . It is lucky, too, for human beings need all the relatives they can get—as possible donors or receivers not necessarily of love, but of common decency.

(Slap 32) "An ideal **extended family**," Eliza and I had written so long ago, "should give proportional representation to all sorts of Americans, according to their numbers. The creation of ten thousand such families, say, would provide America with ten thousand parliaments, so to speak, which would discuss sincerely and expertly what only a few hypocrites now discuss with passion, which is the welfare of all mankind."

(*PS* Self-Interview) VONNEGUT: And if my father's and grandfather's ghosts haunt that town (*Indianapolis*), they must be wondering where all their buildings have gone to. . . . They must be wondering where all their relatives went, too. They grew up in a huge **extended family** which is no more. . . . And when I went to the University of Chicago, and I heard the head of the Department of Anthropology, Robert Redfield, lecture on the folk society, which was essentially a stable, isolated **extended family**, he did not have to tell me how nice that could be.

(*PS* Religion) "We should return to **extended families** as quickly as we can, and be lonesome no more, lonesome no more. . . .

"Let me beguile you just a little bit more about **extended families**. Let us talk about divorce, and the fact that one out of every three of us here has been or will be divorced. When we do it, we will very likely wrangle and wail and weep formlessly about money and sex, about treachery, about outgrowing one another, about how close love is to hate, and so on. Nobody ever gets anywhere close to the truth, which is this: The nuclear family doesn't provide nearly enough companionship. . . ."

(*Blue* 22) I (*Rabo Karabekian*), born in America far from any other Armenians, save for my parents, eventually became a member of two artificial **extended families** which were reasonably respectable, although surely not the social equals of Harvard or Yale:

1. The Officer Corps of the United States Army in time of war,
2. The Abstract Expressionist school of painting after the war.

(*FWD* II) "But I am surely a great admirer of Alcoholics Anonymous, and Gamblers Anonymous, and Cocaine Freaks Anonymous, and Shoppers Anonymous, and Gluttons Anonymous, and on and on. And such groups gratify me as a person who studied anthropology, since they give to Americans something as essential to health as vitamin C, something so many of us do not have in this particular civilization: an **extended family**. Human beings have almost always been supported and comforted and disciplined and amused by stable lattices of many relatives and friends until the Great American Experiment, which is an experiment not only with liberty but with rootlessness, mobility, and impossibly tough-minded loneliness.

(*FWD* II) "All of you, I am sure, when writing a prescription for mildly depressed patients, people nowhere as sick as my mother or my son were, have had a thought on this order: 'I am so sorry to have to put you on the outside of a pill. I would give anything if I could put you inside the big, warm life-support system of an **extended family** instead.'" *Vonnegut was speaking to the American Psychiatric Association meeting in Philadelphia.*

(*FWD* III) "All vigorous schools of art, it would seem, start with artificial **extended families**. What bonded Pollock's particular family was not agreement as to what, generally, a picture should look like. Its members were unanimous, though, as to where inspiration should come from: the unconscious, that part of the mind which was lively, but which caught no likenesses, had no morals or politics, and had no tired old stories to tell yet again."

(*FWD* XIII) A vitamin or mineral deficiency always has bad effects. A Folk Society deficiency (hereafter "FSD") quite often does. The trouble begins when a person suffering from FSD stops thinking, in order to become a member of an artificial **extended family** which happens to be crazy. The homicidal "family" of Charles Manson springs to mind. Or what about the cult of the Reverend Jim Jones in Guyana, whose members on his advice ("Tonight you will be with me in Paradise") fed the kids Kool-Aid laced with cyanide and then drank it themselves. (The Reverend Jones, like Manson, was from Indianapolis. . . .)

(*FWD* XIII) Every cockamamie artificial **extended family** of FSD sufferers resembles Redfield's Folk Society to this extent: it has a myth at its core. The Manson family pretended to believe (the same thing as believing) that its murders would be blamed on blacks. Los Angeles would then be purified somehow by a race war. The myth at the core of the political family which calls itself "Neo-Conservatives" isn't that explicit, but I know what it is, even if most of them can't put it into words. This is it: They are British aristocrats, graduates of Oxford or Cambridge, living in the world as it was one hundred years ago.

(FWD XXI) I am only sorry that the mostly German American Freethinker movement did not survive the obliteration, since it might have become an **extended family** for the millions of good Americans who find all the big questions about life unanswered, save by ancient baloney of human manufacture. Before World War I, the Freethinkers had cheerful congregations, and picnics, too, in many parts of this country. If not God, what was there for them to serve during their short stay on Earth? Only one thing was left to serve under such circumstances, which was their community. Why should they behave well (which they did), quite certain as they were that neither Heaven nor Hell awaited them? Virtue was its own reward.

(TQ 4) When excellent German novelist and graphic artist Günter Grass heard that I was born in 1922, he said to me, "There are no males in Europe your age for you to talk to." He himself was a kid during Kilgore Trout's and my war, as were Elie Wiesel and Jerzy Kosinski and Milos Forman, and on and on. I was lucky to be born over here instead of over there, and white and middle-class, and into a house full of books and pictures, and into a large **extended family**, which exists no more.

(TQ 24) I say in lectures in 1996 that fifty percent or more of American marriages go bust because most of us no longer have **extended families**. When you marry somebody now, all you get is one person.

I say that when couples fight, it isn't about money or sex or power. What they're really saying is, "You're not enough people!"

Sigmund Freud said he didn't know what women wanted. I know what women want. They want a whole lot of people to talk to.

(TQ 49) Yes, and any dream of taking better care of our people might as well be a transvestite hermaphrodite without some scheme for giving us all the support and companionship of **extended families**, within which sharing and compassion are more plausible than in an enormous nation, and a *Fiduciary* may not be as mythical as the *Roc* and the *Phoenix* after all.

(TQ 52) Yes, and Trout harped on the human need for **extended families**, and I still do, because it is so obvious that we, because we are human, need them

as much as we need proteins and carbohydrates and fats and vitamins and essential minerals.

I have just read about a teenage father who shook his baby to death because it couldn't control its anal sphincter yet and wouldn't stop crying. In an **extended family**, there would have been other people around, who would have rescued and comforted the baby, and the father, too.

If the father had been raised in an **extended family**, he might not have been such an awful father, or maybe not a father at all yet, because he was still too young to be a good one, or because he was too crazy to ever be a good one.

I was in southern Nigeria in 1970, at the very end of the Biafran War there, on the Biafran side, the losing side, the mostly Ibo side, long before the rerun. I met an Ibo father of a new baby. He had four hundred relatives! Even with a losing war going on, he and his wife were about to go on a trip, introducing the baby to all its relatives.

(TQ 52) In chapter 45, I proposed two amendments to the Constitution. Here are two more, little enough to expect from life, one would think, like the Bill of Rights:

Article XXX: Every person, upon reaching a statutory age of puberty, shall be declared an adult in a solemn public ritual, during which he or she must welcome his or her new responsibilities in the community, and their attendant dignities.

Article XXXI: Every effort shall be made to make every person feel that he or she will be sorely missed when he or she is gone.

Such essential elements in an ideal diet for a human spirit, of course, can be provided convincingly only by **extended families**.

(TQ 60) There were of course many club members who had no parts in Abe Lincoln in Illinois, who would have liked at least to blow that big brass rooster, once they saw it and then heard it blown by the plumber himself during dress rehearsal. But the club most of all wanted Trout to feel that he was home at last, and a vital member of an **extended family**.

Not merely the club and the household staff at Xanadu, and the chapters of Alcoholics Anonymous and Gamblers Anonymous, which met in the ballroom there, and the battered women and children and grandparents who had found shelter there, were grateful for his healing and encouraging mantra, which made bad times a coma: You were sick, but now you're well again, and there's work to do. The whole world was.

(*GBK* Introduction) What do men want? They want a lot of pals, and they wish people wouldn't get so mad at them.

Why are so many people getting divorced today? It's because most of us don't have **extended families** anymore. It used to be that when a man and a woman got married, the bride got a lot more people to talk to about everything. The groom got a lot more pals to tell dumb jokes to.

A few Americans, but very few, still have **extended families**. The Navahos. The Kennedys.

But most of us, if we get married nowadays, are just one more person for the other person. The groom gets one more pal, but it's a woman. The woman gets one more person to talk to about everything, but it's a man.

When a couple has an argument, they may think it's about money or power or sex, or how to raise the kids, or whatever. What they're really saying to each other, though, without realizing it, is this:

"You are not enough people!"

(*GBK* Introduction) I met a man in Nigeria one time, an Ibo who had six hundred relatives he knew quite well. His wife had just had a baby, the best possible news in any **extended family**.

They were going to take it to meet all its relatives, Ibos of all ages and sizes and shapes. It would even meet other babies, cousins not much older than it was. Everybody who was big enough and steady enough was going to get to hold it, cuddle it, gurgle to it, and say how pretty it was, or handsome.

Wouldn't you have loved to be that baby?

(*MWC* 5) A husband, a wife and some kids is not a family. It's a terribly vulnerable survival unit.

I met a man in Nigeria one time, an Ibo who had six hundred relatives he knew quite well. His wife had just had a baby, the best possible news in any **extended family**.

They were going to take it to meet all its relatives, Ibos of all ages and sizes and shapes. It would even meet other babies, cousins not much older than it was. Everybody who was big enough and steady enough was going to get to hold it, cuddle it, gurgle to it, and say how pretty or how handsome it was.

Wouldn't you have loved to be that baby?

I sure wish I could wave a wand, and give every one of you an **extended family**, make you an Ibo or a Navaho—or a Kennedy.

Now, you take George and Laura Bush, who imagine themselves as a brave, clean-cut little couple. They are surrounded by an enormous **extended family**, what we should all have—I mean judges, senators, newspaper editors, lawyers, bankers. They are not alone. That they are members of an **extended family** is one reason they are so comfortable. And I would really, over the long run, hope America would find some way to provide all of our citizens with **extended families**—a large group of people they could call on for help.

See also: WFG Preface; *WFG Playboy* Interview; *Slap* Prologue; 19; 32; 36; 37; 41; 46; 48; *PS* Funnier on Paper Than Most People; *PS* Religion; *Blue* 22; *FWD* VII.

Fabri-Tek (also **Fabritek**). *In* Cat's Cradle, *the Indianapolis electronics firm specializing in defense technology founded by Harrison C. Conners, the onetime laboratory assistant to Franklin Hoenikker and the unfaithful husband of Angela Hoenikker.*

Failey, Bonnie. *In* Jailbird, *among the many children caught in the crossfire during the Christmas morning Cuyahoga Massacre at the Cuyahoga Bridge and Iron Company is the infant Bonnie Failey. She becomes immortalized in the labor song bearing her name composed by Henry Niles Whistler.*

Failey, Dr. *The family doctor for the Leonards in the short story "Next Door," reprinted in* Welcome to the Monkey House.

Failey, William. (PS Self-Interview) *In reference to his short story "The Big Space Fuck," Vonnegut recalls,* Which reminds me of my good Indianapolis friend, about the only Indianapolis friend I've got left—**William Failey.** When we got into the Second World War, and everybody was supposed to give blood, he wondered if he couldn't give a pint of jizzum instead.

In his final novel, Vonnegut uses the memory of his lifelong friend to illustrate a basic lesson of life, No matter what a young person thinks he or she is really hot stuff at doing, he or she is sooner or later going to run into somebody in the same field who will cut him or her a new asshole, so to speak. *Failey's declaration after losing at table tennis (Ping-Pong) to another friend:* Roger cut me a new asshole (TQ 38).

Fairbanks, Charles Warren. *Once a U.S. senator from Indiana who later served as Theodore Roosevelt's vice president, Fairbanks is cited by Rabo Karabekian as an ancestor of Richard Fairbanks, Jr., Edith's husband prior to her marriage to Rabo, in* Bluebeard.

Fairbanks, Richard, Jr. *Edith Taft's first husband prior to her marrying Rabo Karabekian in Blue-*

beard. Fairbanks descends from Charles Warren Fairbanks, a former U.S. senator and Theodore Roosevelt's vice president. Richard was a Cincinnati sportsman and investment banker who did very little in the later years of his life. Karabekian first engages the couple when he rents their Long Island potato barn for use as a studio. Rabo and Edith become a couple only after Fairbanks passes away. Edith and Richard were childless, and her inheritance, which eventually becomes Rabo's, includes a share in the Cincinnati Bengals football team.

Fairchild, Will. *There are two quite distinct references to Will Fairchild. The character appears in both* Breakfast of Champions *and* Deadeye Dick *with drastically different outcomes. In* Breakfast, *Fairchild is the maternal uncle of Beatrice Keedsler who lives at the enormous Keedsler mansion. In 1926, Fairchild, a World War 1 aviation hero with the Lafayette Escadrille, went to the Keedsler estate with a Springfield rifle,* shot and killed five relatives, three servants, two policemen, and all the animals in the Keedsler's private zoo. Then he shot himself through his heart. . . .

When an autopsy was performed on him, a tumor the size of a piece of birdshot was found in his brain. This was what *caused* the murders (BC Epilogue).

The town already commemorated his wartime heroics in a number of significant ways. Fairchild Heights is the most desirable neighborhood in Midland City and home to Dwayne Hoover; Fairchild Boulevard runs in front of the county hospital, and it is the street on which Vonnegut confronts Kilgore Trout; the Fairchild Hotel was once a fashionable downtown establishment but fell victim to urban blight, became home to Ye Old Rathskeller, Midland City's transvestite bar, and was home to the homosexual Bunny Hoover, Dwayne's son; across the street from the hotel was Fairchild Park, where fifty-six murders occurred in two years. There was also Fairchild High School.

In Deadeye Dick, *Fairchild's death is not the re-*

sult of a murder-suicide. The war hero makes a living as an aviation barnstormer and dies in a crash in the 1922 Midland City air show. He fails to wear his parachute. Buried at Mount Cavalry Cemetery beneath a bronze propeller inscribed with the Lafayette Escadrille's "Gone West" (which, to the American aviators in Europe, meant going home), the spirit of Will Fairchild is risen in a voodoo resurrection by Hippolyte Paul De Mille. Rudy Waltz remarks Fairchild will roam the neutron-bombed city looking for his parachute.

Farber, Don and Anne. *Don and Anne Farber celebrated their sixty-fourth wedding anniversary in 2012, including more than forty years of friendship and business ties with Kurt Vonnegut. Don Farber served as Vonnegut's lawyer, agent, and confidant, eventually serving as executor of Vonnegut's literary estate. Vonnegut acknowledges their relationship by having the Farbers attend the* Timequake *clambake.* (*TQ* 62) My closest business associate, **Don Farber**, lawyer and agent, was there with his dear wife, **Anne**.

Sidney Offit, Vonnegut's proclaimed closest friend, recalls in his foreword to the posthumously published Look at the Birdie, With his signature gentle but mordant wit, Kurt participated in family celebrations, meetings of writers' organizations, and our gab and laugh sessions with Morley Safer and **Don Farber**, George Plimpton and Dan Wakefield, Walter Miller and Truman Capote, Kevin Buckley and Betty Friedan.

Farmers of Southwestern Ohio for Nuclear Safety. *The neutron-bombing of Midland City turns the farmers on the outskirts of the flash area into grassroots activists. The organization hires an outside investigator whose findings yield clues to an ominous conspiracy that directly contradicts the government's explanation. One of the farmers (Rudy Waltz supposes him to be named Osterman) hands out leaflets and speaks about various conspiracy theories he finds credible.* (DD Epilogue) But that didn't weaken the argument of their leaflet, to wit: that the United States of America was now ruled, evidently, by a small clique of power brokers who believed that most Americans were so boring and ungifted and small time that they could be slain by

the tens of thousands without inspiring any long-term regrets on the part of anyone. "They have now proved this with Midland City," said the leaflet, "and who is to say that Terre Haute or Schenectady will not be next?"

That was certainly the most inflammatory of their beliefs—that Midland City had been neutron-bombed on purpose, and not from a truck, but from a missile site or a high-flying airplane. They had hired a mathematician from, they said, "a great university," to make calculations independent of the Government's, as to where the flash had originated. The mathematician could not be named, they said, for fear that retaliatory action would be taken against him, but it was his opinion, based largely on the pattern of livestock deaths on the outer perimeter of the flash, that the center of the flash was near Exit 11 on the Interstate, all right, but at least sixty feet above the pavement. That certainly suggested a package which had arrived by air.

Either that, or a truck had been hauling a neutron bomb in an enormous pop-up toaster.

Bernard Ketchum asked the farmer who had given us our leaflets to name the clique which had supposedly neutron-bombed Midland City. This was the answer he got: "They don't want us to know their name, so they don't have a name. You can't fight back against something that don't have a name."

"The military-industrial complex?" said Ketchum archly. "The Rockefellers? The international conglomerates? The CIA? The Mafia?"

And the farmer said to him, "You like any of them names? Just help yourself. Maybe that's who it is, maybe it ain't. How's a farmer supposed to find out? It's whoever it was shot President Kennedy and his brother—and Martin Luther King."

So there we had it—the ever-growing ball of American paranoia, the ball of string a hundred miles in diameter, with the unsolved assassination of John F. Kennedy at its core.

"You mention the Rockefellers," said the farmer. "If you ask me, they don't know any more'n I do about who's really running things, what's really going on."

Farmer Osterman hypothesizes it was all part of a plan to bring back slavery. Neutron-bombing small cities would alleviate unemployment and provide cheap housing for boatloads of people fleeing places like Haiti and Jamaica.

Farrow, Dudley and Grace. *Two characters in Kilgore Trout's novel* The Smart Bunny, *who destroy the lead character.* (BC 20) She led a normal female rabbit's life, despite her ballooning intellect. She concluded that her mind was useless, that it was a sort of tumor, that it had no usefulness within the rabbit scheme of things.

So she went hippity-hop, hippity-hop toward the city, to have the tumor removed. But a hunter named **Dudley Farrow** shot and killed her before she got there. **Farrow** skinned her and took out her guts, but then he and his wife **Grace** decided that they had better not eat her because of her unusually large head. They thought what she had thought when she was alive—that she must be diseased.

fascism, fascist. (MN Introduction) My personal experience with Nazi monkey business was limited. There were some vile and lively native American **Fascists** in my home town of Indianapolis during the thirties, and somebody slipped me a copy of *The Protocols of the Elders of Zion*, I remember, which was supposed to be the Jews' secret plan for taking over the world.
(MN 29) *Howard W Campbell, Jr., recalls,* My clothes had been ruined in the beating I'd taken. So, from the resources of Jones' household, I was given other clothes. I was given a pair of shiny black trousers by Father Keeley, a silver-colored shirt by Dr. Jones, a shirt that had once been part of the uniform of a defunct American **Fascist** movement called, straightforwardly enough, "The Silver Shirts."
(BC 17) Listen: Bunny Hoover went to Prairie Military Academy for eight years of uninterrupted sports, buggery and **fascism**. Buggery consisted of sticking one's penis in somebody else's asshole or mouth, or having it done to one by somebody else. **Fascism** was a fairly popular political philosophy which made sacred whatever nation and race the philosopher happened to belong to. It called for an autocratic, centralized government, headed up by a dictator. The dictator had to be obeyed, no matter what he told somebody to do.

(*Slap* 23) "**Fascists** are inferior people who believe it when somebody tells them they're superior," she said. *Eliza is speaking to her brother Wilbur.*
(PS The People One Knows) *Catch-22* is now the dominant myth about Americans in the war against **fascism**.
See also: PP XXI; MN 17; 29; 34; *Slap* 23; JB 16; *Blue* 18.

father . . . son. (ST 3) The only person Noel Constant ever told was his son, Malachi. On Malachi's twenty-first birthday. That birthday party of two took place in Room 229 of the Wilburhampton. It was the first time **father and son** had ever met. *It was during that meeting that Noel told Malachi about using successive letters in the Bible as his only guide to investment.*
(ST 3) Old Noel saw young Malachi looking at the picture, and was confused and embarrassed by the whole thing about **fathers and sons**. He ransacked his mind for something good to say, and found almost nothing. *The picture is Noel's only photograph of young Malachi, at the beach with his mother.*
(MN 1) Arnold *(Marx)* is studying to be a lawyer. The avocation of Arnold and of his father, a gunsmith, is archaeology. **Father and son** spend most all their spare time excavating the ruins of Hazor.
(MN 38) That is the closest I can come to explaining the legions, the nations of lunatics I've seen in my time. And for me to attempt such a mechanical explanation is perhaps a reflection of the **father whose son** I was. *Am.* When I pause to think about it, which is rarely, I am, after all, the son of an engineer. *Campbell refers to his "cuckoo clock in Hell" theory of the dissociated, totalitarian mind. He notes that as the son of a General Electric engineer, his metaphor is one of mutilated gears and "other teeth . . . stripped by the clutchless shifts of history."*
(CC 103) The Castles, **father and son**, stood separate from the rest of the company. Long unwelcome at "Papa's" palace, they were curious as to why they had now been invited there.
(CC 104) "How do you think the people of San Lorenzo would take to industrialization?" I asked the Castles, **father and son**.
(GBR 5) McAllister indicated with a tired smile that he wasn't about to apologize for the design of the Foundation. It had, after all, done exactly what

it was meant to do, had handed the fortune from **father to son**, without the tax collector's getting a dime.

(*GBR* 7) Eliot took a drink of Southern Comfort, was uncomforted. He coughed, and his father coughed, too. This coincidence, where **father and son** matched each other unknowingly, inconsolable hack for hack, was heard not only by Sylvia, but by Norman Mushari, too.

(*DD* 9) At dawn on Mother's Day, while Mother was still asleep, Father and Felix and I went out to the rifle range of the Midland County Rod and Gun Club, as we had done at least a hundred times before. It was a Sunday morning ritual, this discharging of firearms. Although I was only twelve, I had fired rifles and pistols and shotguns of every kind. And there were plenty of other **fathers and sons**, blazing away and blazing away.

(*HP* 1) I resigned my commission in 1975, after the excrement hit the air-conditioning, not failing, however, to **father a son** on my way home, unknowingly, during a brief stopover in the Philippines. I thought surely that the subsequent mother, a young female war correspondent for *The Des Moines Register*, was using foolproof birth control.

(*FWD* I) He died eventually, and in an act of Freudian cannibalism, I dropped the "Jr." from my name. (Thus in lists of my works do I appear to be both my **father and my son**, Kurt Vonnegut and Kurt Vonnegut, Jr.)

(*BAG* This Son of Mine) "Look at him, Rudy!" said Merle, lashing the merriment onward. "Foot taller'n his old man, and president of what at Cornell?"

"Interfraternity Council," murmured Franklin, embarrassed. He and Karl avoided looking at each other. Their **fathers** had taken them hunting together maybe a hundred times. But the **boys** had hardly spoken to each other, had exchanged little more than humorless nods and head shakes for hits and misses.

(*BAG* This Son of Mine) "You're the only one—do you know that?" choked Merle.

"The only one—I swear!"

"The only one what, sir?" said Franklin.

"**The only son who's sticking with what his father or his grandfather or sometimes even his great-grandfather built**." Merle shook his head

mournfully. "No Hudson in Hudson Saw," he said. "I don't think you can even cut cheese with a Hudson saw these days. No Flemming in Flemming Tool and Die. No Warner in Warner Street. No Hawks, no Hinkley, no Bowman in Hawks, Hinkley, and Bowman."

Merle waved his hand westward. "You wonder who all the people are with the big new houses on the west side? Who can have a house like that, and we never meet them, never even meet anybody who knows them? They're the ones who are taking over instead of the sons. The town's for sale, and they buy. It's their town now—people named Ferguson from places called Ilium.

"What is it about the **sons**?" said Merle. "They're your friends, boy. You grew up with them. You know them better than their **fathers** do. What is it? All the wars? Drinking?"

"I don't know, Father," said Franklin, taking the easiest way out. He folded his napkin with a neat finality. He stood. "There's a dance out at the club tonight," he said. "I thought I'd go."

"You do that," said Merle.

But Franklin didn't. He got as far as the country club's parking lot, then didn't go in.

Suddenly he didn't want to see **his friends—the killers of their fathers' dreams**. Their young faces were the faces of old men hanging upside down, their expressions grotesque and unintelligible. Hanging upside down, they swung from bar to ballroom to crap game, and back to bar. No one pitied them in that great human belfry, because they were going to be rich, if they weren't already. They didn't have to dream, or even lift a finger.

Franklin went to a movie alone. The movie failed to suggest a way in which he might improve his life. It suggested that he be kind and loving and humble, and Franklin was nothing if he wasn't kind and loving and humble.

(*BAG* This Son of Mine) It was now Karl's turn to work the trap. As he and Franklin changed places, Franklin hit him on the arm and gave him a cynical smile. Franklin put everything into that blow and the smile—**fathers and sons**, young dreams and old dreams, bosses and employees, cold feet, boredom, and gunpowder.

(*BAG* This Son of Mine) With the moment to think about, to puzzle him pleasantly, Franklin found that the music wasn't speaking anymore of just Rudy and Karl. It was speaking of all **fathers and sons**. It was saying what they had all been saying haltingly, sometimes with pain and sometimes with anger and sometimes with cruelty and sometimes with love: that **fathers and sons** were one.

It was saying, too, that a time for a parting in spirit was—no matter how close anyone held anyone, no matter what anyone tried.

Faust. *In Vonnegut's "Editor's Note" to* Mother Night, *he records that Howard Campbell bestowed the title on his memoirs by taking it from Goethe's* Faust. (MN Ed Note) I am a part of the part that at first was all, part of the darkness that gave birth to light, that supercilious light which now disputes with Mother Night her ancient rank and space, and yet can not succeed; no matter how it struggles, it sticks to matter and can't get free. Light flows from substance, makes it beautiful; solids can check its path, so I hope it won't be long till light and the world's stuff are destroyed together.

Faust, Naomi. *Dr. Asa Breed's longtime secretary at the Ilium Works, research home of Dr. Felix Hoenikker, the father of ice-nine. She escorts John/Jonah, the narrator of* Cat's Cradle, *through Hoenikker's well-preserved laboratory. It is there the narrator finds photographs of cannonballs stacked in various patterns, early visual studies in preparation for the development of ice-nine. Her discussions with Dr. Breed about the true nature of Hoenikker indicate to the narrator that Miss Faust was moving along the same inexorable path of self-awareness as the narrator.* (CC 25) "Dr. Breed keeps telling me the main thing with Dr. Hoenikker was truth."

"You don't seem to agree."

"I don't know whether I agree or not. I just have trouble understanding how truth, all by itself, could be enough for a person."

Miss Faust was ripe for Bokononism.

February 13, 1944. *The date of the Dresden fire-bombing. The firestorm kept Vonnegut in the slaughterhouse meatlocker until the following day, Valentine's Day.*

February 13, 1976, is the death date of Slaughterhouse-Five's *Billy Pilgrim.*

February 14, 1960, marks the Greenwich Village opening and closing of Rudy Waltz's "Katmandu" in Deadeye Dick. *The gently falling snowflakes in New York City appear to breathe life into Rudy, but they are the remnants of a midwestern blizzard that kills his father and nearly wipes out Midland City.*

(TQ Prologue) I had the timequake zap everybody and everything in an instant from **February 13th**, 2001, back to February 17th, 1991. Then we all had to get back to 2001 the hard way, minute by minute, hour by hour, year by year, betting on the wrong horse again, marrying the wrong person again, getting the clap again. You name it!

Though the timequake occurs on February 13, time skips ahead to February 17th before everyone relives the 10 years of the timequake. (TQ 3) In *Timequake One*, Kilgore Trout wrote a story about an atom bomb. Because of the timequake, he had to write it twice. The ten-year rerun following the timequake, remember, made him and me, and you, and everybody else, do everything we'd done from **February 17th**, 1991, to February 12th, 2001, a second time.

(TQ 16) "The timequake of 2001 was a cosmic charley horse in the sinews of Destiny. At what was in New York City 2:27 p.m. on **February 13th** of that year, the Universe suffered a crisis in self-confidence. Should it go on expanding indefinitely? What was the point?

"It fibrillated with indecision. Maybe it should have a family reunion back where it all began, and then make a great big BANG again.

"It suddenly shrunk ten years. It zapped me and everybody else back to **February 17th**, 1991, what was for me 7:51 a.m., and a line outside a blood bank in San Diego, California."

(TQ 22) I forget what I was doing on the afternoon of **February 13th**, 2001, when the timequake struck. It couldn't have been much. I sure as heck wasn't writing another book. I was seventy-eight, for heaven's sakes! My daughter Lily was eighteen!

(TQ 22) Zoltan had the limo that afternoon. He was on his way to pick up Monica. She was awaiting Zoltan's arrival when the timequake struck. He would get as far as ringing the Academy doorbell before he was zapped back to **February 17th**, 1991. He would be ten years younger and whole again!

(TQ 28) And then, on what was the afternoon of

February 13th, 2001, in New York City, way-the-hell-and-gone up on West 155th Street, and everywhere, free will had all of a sudden kicked in again. (*TQ* 32) . . . A Study of History by the English historian Arnold Toynbee, who is up in Heaven now. He wrote about challenges and responses, saying that various civilizations persisted or failed depending on whether or not the challenges they faced were just too much for them. He gave examples.

The same might be said for individuals who would like to behave heroically, and most strikingly in the case of Kilgore Trout on the afternoon and evening of **February 13th**, 2001, after free will kicked in. If he had been in the area of Times Square, or near the entrance or exit of a major bridge or tunnel, or at an airport, where pilots, as they had learned to do during the rerun, had expected their planes to take off or land safely of their own accord, the challenge would have been too much not only for Trout but for anyone else.

(*TQ* 50) What matters now is that, on the afternoon of **February 13th**, 2001, Kilgore Trout roused Dudley Prince from his Post-Timequake Apathy. Trout urged him to speak, to say anything, no matter how nonsensical. Trout suggested he say, "I pledge allegiance to the flag," or whatever, to prove to himself thereby that he was again in charge of his own destiny.

Prince spoke groggily at first. He didn't pledge allegiance, but indicated instead that he was trying to understand everything Trout had said to him so far. He said, "You told me I had something."

"You were sick, but now you're well, and there's work to do," said Trout.

"Before that," said Prince. "You said I had something."

"Forget it," said Trout. "I was all excited. I wasn't making sense."

"I still want to know what you said I had," said Prince.

"I said you had free will," said Trout.

"Free will, free will, free will," echoed Prince with wry wonderment. "I always wondered what it was I had. Now I got a name for it."

"Please forget what I said," said Trout. "There are lives to save!"

"You know what you can do with free will?" said Prince.

"No," said Trout.

"You can stuff it up your ass," said Prince. (*TQ* 51) On the afternoon of **February 13th**, 2001, alone, and then during the next two weeks or so, Kilgore's Creed did as much to save life on Earth as Einstein's E equals mc squared had done to end it two generations earlier.

(*TQ* 54) For the Mbuti, the rain forest Pygmies of Zaire, Africa, **February 13th**, 2001, was in all probability a day neither more nor less amazing than any other day, unless a rogue airplane happened to land on top of one of them after the rerun stopped. (*MWC* 2) In 1968, the year I wrote *Slaughterhouse-Five*, I finally became grown up enough to write about the bombing of Dresden. It was the largest massacre in European history. I, of course, know about Auschwitz, but a massacre is something that happens suddenly, the killing of a whole lot of people in a very short time. In Dresden, on **February 13**, 1945, about 135,000 people were killed by British firebombing in one night.

It was pure nonsense, pointless destruction. The whole city was burned down, and it was a British atrocity, not ours. They sent in night bombers, and they came in and set the whole town on fire with a new kind of incendiary bomb. And so everything organic, except my little POW group, was consumed by fire. It was a military experiment to find out if you could burn down a whole city by scattering incendiaries over it.

"The Febs." *In* Slaughterhouse-Five, *the barbershop quartet composed of optometrists (hence, their name is an acronym for "Four-eyed Bastards"), who perform at the wedding anniversary of Billy and Valencia Pilgrim and on board the ill-fated charter flight that crashes in Vermont.*

Fedders, John W., Jr. *In* Hocus Pocus, *Fedders is a Tarkington College alumnus and trustee who grows up in Hong Kong and later serves as an interpreter for Mrs. Chung at board meetings. Fedders's father was an importer of ivory and rhinoceros horns, and was suspected of dealing in large quantities of opium. Though the younger Fedders survives captivity at the hands of the escaped prisoners from Athena, he did suffer a heart attack. Under the stress of the ordeal, Fedders spoke only Chinese.*

Federal Apparatus Corporation. *In "Poor Little Rich Town," originally published in the October 1952 issue of* Collier's *magazine and later reprinted in the 1999 collection* Bagombo Snuff Box, The Federal Apparatus Corporation *plans to relocate its company headquarters from New York City to Ilium. It sends their new vice president and efficiency expert Newell Cady to oversee the move. He settles into the nearby town of Spruce Falls, a village of long-neglected small mansions and quaint, small town institutions and traditions that are at odds with his modern corporate mindset to streamline all personal and institutional activities.*

Federal Bureau of Termination. *In the short story "2BR02B," collected in* Bagombo Snuff Box (1999), *the Federal Bureau of Termination is the administrative arm that schedules appointments for the Ethical Suicide Suites. The title of the story is the hotline number to the bureau. The medallion on her (Leora Duncan's) purple musette bag was the seal of the Service Division of the* **Federal Bureau of Termination**, *an eagle perched on a turnstile.*

Federal Minimum Security Adult Correctional Facility, Finletter Air Force Base. *The place of incarceration for convicted Watergate coconspirator Walter F. Starbuck as well as Leland Clewes and Dr. Robert Fender, in* Jailbird.

Fender, Dr. Robert. *In* Jailbird, *the veterinarian who was the only American convicted for treason during the Korean War and serves his life sentence at the Finletter Federal Prison where Walter Starbuck is also imprisoned. Fender is the prison's supply room clerk, but he earns a living as a science fiction writer using the names Frank X. Barlow and Kilgore Trout.*

Fender's offense isn't as nefarious as the crime may seem. While serving in Osaka as a meat inspector for the military, he fell in love with Izumi, a Japanese Edith Piaf impersonator. As it turns out, she is a North Korean agent, though Fender did not know this at the time. He took pity on Izumi based on her stories of deprivation. He was caught trying to bribe a sailor from New Zealand into stowing her away from Japan.

Fender is kind to all who enter or leave the prison, going so far as to mend the cigarette burns in Star-buck's suit upon his release. Though Mary Kathleen O'Looney tries to repay Fender's kindness to Starbuck with a vice presidency in RAMJAC, his conviction for treason is too great a crime to overcome.

Among the stories he is credited with writing as Kilgore Trout and Frank X. Barlow are "Asleep at the Switch" and an untitled reference to a story about creatures from the planet Vicuna who survive by entering the bodies of human beings, and another about a planet where the greatest crime was ingratitude. Fender welcomes Starbuck back to prison with a telegram that says ting-a-ling, which in the story about Vicuna means both hello and good-bye.

Fenstermaker, Isabel. *In* The Sirens of Titan, *Miss Fenstermaker is the seventy-three-year-old certified public school teacher from Minnesota who is swept away by a Martian agent in Duluth when she tries to sell him a copy of the Jehovah's Witness publication* The Watchtower. *On Mars, after her memory is cleaned, she teaches school and umpires German batball games. It is she who takes young Chrono's class on a field trip to a flamethrower factory, where he picks up a piece of scrap steel strapping in the packaging department. It is that piece of metal that is delivered to Salo on Titan so that he can continue his Tralfamadorian journey across the galaxy.*

Fenstermaker, Lowell. *In* Hocus Pocus, *the wealthy meat packer who marries Harriet Gummer, the Des Moines Register correspondent who becomes pregnant by Eugene Debs Hartke during their one-night stand in the Philippines. Fenstermaker raises Gummer's son, Rob Roy, as his own, giving him his own name and bequeathing to him all his wealth.*

Fenstermaker, Rob Roy. *The child of Eugene Debs Hartke and Harriet Gummer, conceived during their one-night stand in the Philippines. He is named for the sweet alcoholic drink they had at the bar when they met. Rob Roy is later given the surname of his adoptive father, Lowell Fenstermaker, graduates from Yale, and inherits his stepfather's wealth.*

Rob Roy is at first embarrassed about his inherited wealth, particularly because he feels troubled in a non-sequitur manner by the cruelties inflicted on other living beings (such as milk-fed veal calves). However, he reveals to Hartke that he felt differently about his wealth after being arrested for molesting children. He goes to Tarkington to meet his birth father and tell him he is leaving the country.

In the course of their meeting, Rob Roy tells Hartke some fanciful lies concocted by his mother to explain why his birth parents were never married and to fill in a lost family history. Gummer told him Hartke's high school sweetheart was hit by a car and paralyzed from the waist down one day before their senior prom, but he felt committed to marrying her anyway; that Hartke's father was blinded from his wounds as a World War II flying ace; and that Hartke had a brother named Bob who died from spinal meningitis after being invited for a tryout with the New York Yankees.

Fenton, Earl and Maude. The newly minted millionaires and proud parents of Dr. Earle Fenton, Jr., and Ted Fenton, Esq., in the 1952 short story "The Package." Earl Fenton is also the college fraternity brother of Dr. Charley Freeman, his surprise visitor on the very day the Fentons return from an around-the-world cruise and move in to their new estate, a pushbutton wonder of luxury living. The trip is a celebratory vacation after having sold the manufacturing plant that made them millions. Earl is justly proud of his extravagant home, having worked his way through college only to rise to the heights of the American Dream.

On this glorious day of the Fentons' completion of their dream trip, capped off by taking possession of their new home, they unexpectedly play host to Charley Freeman while Home Beautiful sends their photographer, Slotkin, and an unnamed female reporter to do a story about the couple's Xanadu moment. With the focus of the day naturally on documenting the wonders of the home and its proud owners, there is little time for Earl to have any meaningful conversation with Freeman despite not having seen each other for more than thirty years. However, while Earl and Maude spend the day changing outfits to suit the themes of various rooms, the couple begin to chatter about Earl's money-strapped college days, having to wait on tables for his wealthy fraternity brothers, including Charley Freeman. Earl remembers his own sense of inadequacy and shame,

sure that some of his frat brothers must have shot him glances of indifference or treated him rudely as a result of not being a trust fund baby as were so many others in their circle. Tellingly, Earl is unable to recall a single specific instance of such treatment by his frat brothers, and this is especially true of his guest, Charley Freeman.

Nonetheless, Maude is suspicious that Freeman should show up out of the blue just as they are markedly moving up in society. It does not help that Freeman is attired in a well-worn suit in need of replacement and shoes with souls worn thin. She believes Freeman will try to ask Earl for money for one scheme or another, and she turns Charley's discomfiting and hazy college recollections as the opportunity for him to get back at, or at least protect themselves from, the wiles of the idle rich, a class the Fentons believe breeds only scheming snobs who maintain their class by shady dealings. Maude persuades Earl to uninvite Charley to stay the night by saying that her sister Angela and her family were coming to stay the night. Charley takes the hint and leaves by taxi for a hotel.

It is only when Lou Converse, the Fentons' house contractor who is in attendance most of the day to explain all the remote control devices, speaks to Earl after Charley's leaving that Freeman's story comes out and shames Earl for his hubris in chasing the material aspects of the American Dream while his once rich fraternity brother took a decidedly different route. Freeman became a doctor after college and lived the next thirty years in China, spending the bulk of his family's fortune on building a hospital to treat the poor. He returned to the United States only after the Communist government in China seized his hospital and tossed him in jail before eventually deporting him from the country. This is when Earl, in a trancelike daze, asks Lou to show him the remote control button that will allow him to replay the day. Earl's American Dream turned into a moment of self-loathing.

Fenton, Earl Jr., M.D., and Ted, Esq. The unseen and highly accomplished young sons of Earl and Maude Fenton as mentioned by Earl, Sr., during a conversation with the unnamed narrator, in Vonnegut's 1952 Collier's short story "The Package" (reprinted in BAG, 1999).

Ferguson, Guy. *In the short story "This Son of Mine" (The Saturday Evening Post, August 1956; reprinted in the 1999 collection Bagombo Snuff Box), Ferguson is the unseen agent from Ilium's General Forge and Foundry who offers Merle Waggoner $2 million for his pump company. He is used as a symbol of the impersonal, increasing conglomeration of American industry voraciously taking over smaller companies.*

When Franklin first tells his father he does not want to take over his father's business, Merle responds, "I'll call up General Forge and Foundry, and tell them we accept their offer." He ran his finger down his calendar pad until he found a name and telephone number. "If we want to sell, I'm to call somebody named **Guy Ferguson** *at something called extension five-oh-nine at something called the General Forge and Foundry Company at someplace called Ilium, New York." He licked his lips. "I'll tell him he and his friends can have Waggoner Pump."*

Toward the story's close, Merle congratulates his son on reconsidering his inheritance, continuing not only the business he built but going against the tide of impersonal business transactions that will eventually swallow the local history and lore of American entrepreneurship. Merle waved his hand westward. "You wonder who all the people are with the big new houses on the west side? Who can have a house like that, and we never meet them, never even meet anybody who knows them? They're the ones who are taking over instead of the sons. The town's for sale, and they buy. It's their town now—people named **Ferguson** *from places called Ilium."*

Fern, Ransom K. (*printed as* Ransom K. Ferm *in the epigraph to* The Sirens of Titan). *Fern is the sixty-year-old president of Magnum Opus, the company founded by Noel Constant. Noel describes the physical appearance of his money manager: A butt like two beebees. . . .* **Ransom K. Fern** *is like a camel who has burned up both his humps, and now he's burning up everything else but his hair and eyeballs (ST 3).*

At the age of twenty-two, Fern was working for the Internal Revenue Service when he became familiar with the tremendous wealth of Noel Constant. In a manner similar to that of Norman Mushari in Von-

negut's later novel God Bless You, Mr. Rosewater, *Fern learns how to look for great wealth while a student. (ST 3) "I had a professor in the Harvard Business School," said young* **Fern** *to Noel Constant, "who kept telling me that I was smart, but that I would have to find my boy, if I was going to be rich. He wouldn't explain what he meant. He said I would catch on sooner or later. I asked him how I could go looking for my boy, and he suggested that I work for the Bureau of Internal Revenue for a year or so.*

"When I went over your tax returns, Mr. Constant, it suddenly came to me what it was he meant. He meant I was shrewd and thorough, but I wasn't remarkably lucky. I had to find somebody who had luck in an astonishing degree—and so I have." Fern proposes Magnum Opus to Constant, emphasizing that it would protect Constant's great wealth from the IRS, and that included snowing them with so much paperwork they would never be able to trace the company for more funds.

Fernandina Island. (Gal 1:14) *The last human marriage in the Galápagos Islands, and thus the last one on Earth, was performed on* **Fernandina Island** *in the year 23,011.*

Fieser, Dr. Louis. *The Harvard professor and inventor of napalm prominently mentioned in Vonnegut's "Address to the American Physical Society." After receiving a letter from a former student of Fieser's who informed Vonnegut he doubted Fieser would even be aware of a demonstration against weapons research, Vonnegut tells his APS audience:* This letter helped me to see that **Dr. Fieser** and other old-fashioned scientists like him were and are as innocent as Adam and Eve. There was nothing at all sinful in **Dr. Fieser**'s creation of napalm. Scientists will never be so innocent again. Any young scientist, by contrast, when asked by the military to create a terror weapon on the order of napalm, is bound to suspect that he may be committing modern sin. God bless him for that (WFG Address to the American Physical Society).

fighter plane, fighter-plane (*see also* **bomber**). *Fighter planes destroy Papa Monzano's seaside castle, sending his frozen body and shards of ice-nine to the waters below in* Cat's Cradle.

In Jailbird, *the constant shriek of jet fighters taking off precipitates Walter Starbuck's recollection of dirty limericks.*

In Hocus Pocus, *Hartke explains his wartime infantry exploits in visual terms.* (HP 15) I said to Pamela what I had said to Harriet: "If I were a **fighter plane** instead of a human being, there would be little pictures of people painted all over me."

. . . So I barged into a group of students sitting in front of the great fireplace in the main lounge. . . . I got between the students and the fire, so there was no way they could ignore me, and I said to them, "If I were a **fighter plane** instead of a human being, there would be little pictures of people painted all over me."

(HP 39) I was back in bed with a voluptuous female war correspondent from *The Des Moines Register*, whose lips were like sofa pillows, telling her that, if I had been a **fighter plane**, I would have had little pictures of people painted all over me.
See also: CC 63; 66; *SL5* 8; *JB* 1–3; 8; *FWD* XI; XVI.

The Fighting Danes. *After Eliot Rosewater escapes the performance of* Aïda, *he travels around the country, stopping briefly in Elsinore, California, always keeping in touch with Sylvia through letter writing.* (GBR 3) The name of the place set him off on a new line of speculation about himself, to the effect that he was a lot like Shakespeare's Hamlet.

Dear Ophelia—

Elsinore isn't quite what I expected, or maybe there's more than one, and I've come to the wrong one. The high school football players here call themselves "**The Fighting Danes**." In the surrounding towns they're known as "The Melancholy Danes." In the past three years they have won one game, tied two, and lost twenty-four. That's what happens, I guess, when Hamlet goes in as quarterback.

(TQ 3) The crewmen aboard *Joy's Pride*, at any rate, told the pilot on the intercom that they felt much as he did. They were all alone up there in the sky. They didn't need a **fighter escort**, since the Japanese didn't have any airplanes left. The war was over, except for the paperwork, arguably the situation even before *Enola Gay* cremated Hiroshima.

To quote Kilgore Trout: "This wasn't war any-more, and neither had been the obliteration of Nagasaki. This was 'Thanks to the Yanks for a job well done!' This was *show biz* now."

Finale Rack. *Eugene Debs Hartke learns this term by reading the anonymously published short story* "The Protocols of the Elders of Tralfamadore," *printed in* Black Garterbelt *magazine.* (HP 26) This was apparently from the vocabulary of pyrotechnicians, specialists in loud and bright but otherwise harmless nighttime explosions for climaxes of patriotic holidays. A **Finale Rack** was a piece of milled lumber maybe 3 meters long and 20 centimeters wide and five centimeters thick, with all sorts of mortars and rocket launchers nailed to it, linked in series by a single fuse.

When it seemed that a fireworks show was over, that was when the Master Pyrotechnician lit the fuse of the **Finale Rack**. *The author of these protocols calls World War II the "Finale Rack." Hartke leads us to believe this is only the beginning of the end of "the show," civilization and culture as we know it.*

Finch, Dr. Katharine. *The only woman in* Player Piano's *Ilium Works is Paul Proteus's secretary. Though secretarial labor had been automated out of existence, she is retained as a matter of deference to Paul's rank as manager of the works. After Paul marries Anita, his previous secretary, Katharine succeeds her as Paul's secretary. Her boyfriend is Dr. Bud Calhoun, the real brains behind the Ilium Works.*

"Find Me a Dream." *Originally appearing in the February 1961 issue of* Cosmopolitan *(reprinted in the 1999 collection* Bagombo Snuff Box*), the short story "Find Me a Dream" opens with a bit of Cold War rhetoric establishing the setting of bucolic plenty, Creon, Pennsylvania, where American muscular industrialism becomes the odd meeting ground for the beautiful, romantic, and widowed Hildy Matthews; the uninspiring and culturally ignorant industrial nouveau riche (Arvin Borders and his ilk—and the women who marry them); and jazz musician Andy Middleton, who steers straight toward his devoted siren, the same Hildy, a woman driven to be a muse. It is Hildy who proposes to Middleton at the end of the story despite the fact that she is newly* *affianced to Borders. She is the mother of two and widow of a highly revered jazzman, but whereas her fiancé can't keep his name straight, Andy Middleton knows the name and revered spirit of the man. She sincerely does not want to be the cause of Arvin Borders's career stagnating because she is not the kind of woman approved of by the parent company. She offers herself in marriage to Andy Middleton as his loving muse, one who could only improve his fortunes.*

Finkelstein, Isadore and Rachel. *There are two Izzy Finkelsteins and both are tailors by trade. In* Deadeye Dick, *Finkelstein is Otto Waltz's tailor in Midland City. Finkelstein had to endure Otto's spontaneous cries of "Heil Hitler" before the war.*

In Bluebeard, *Isadore had a tailor shop above the Cedar Tavern in Manhattan where Rabo Karabekian and his Abstract Expressionist friends drank and talked about painting. Finkelstein clothed the threadbare artists and was paid by Rabo who was repaid by his friends with original paintings. Finkelstein was a tank gunner in General Patton's Third Army during the war. When not tailoring or hanging out with Rabo's group, Isadore makes representational paintings much appreciated by Rabo when he sees them at the one-man show displayed in the tailor shop by Rachel Finkelstein after her husband's sudden stroke and death in 1953.*

Finnerty, Edward Francis. *Paul Proteus's slovenly best friend, the Irish-whisky-drinking renegade engineer who rose far above his family's own humble beginnings to secure a position with the National Industrial Planning Board, far above the feared duo of Kroner and Baer. Finnerty returns to the Ilium Works where he and Paul started thirteen years earlier, to visit Proteus and tell him he was quitting his exalted position. When the two go drinking in Homestead, Finnerty decides to stay with Rev. Lasher, a member of the Ghost Shirt Society. Paul leaves Finnerty in the Homestead Bar, where he is the only one to manually play the player piano, the central image of the text. Finnerty eventually joins the neo-Luddite revolutionary organization. Paul sees the stark differences between Finnerty and himself and often wonders about the comparative depth of his friend's innate intelligence. (PP IV) Paul envied* **Finnerty's** *mind, for* **Finnerty** *could be anything he*

wanted to be, and be brilliant at it. Whatever the times might have called for, **Finnerty** *would have been among the best. If this had been the age of music,* **Finnerty** *would have been, and in fact was, a top-flight pianist—or he might have been an architect or physician or writer. With inhuman intuition,* **Finnerty** *could sense the basic principles and motives of almost any human work, not just engineering. It is Finnerty who balks at Kroner's laundry list of the technocrats' material accomplishments by reminding everyone that at the same time dope addiction, alcoholism, and suicide went up proportionately. . . . And organized vice and divorce and juvenile delinquency, all parallel the growth of the use of vacuum tubes (PP V).*

Finnerty is responsible for the shame brought to Fred Berringer during Paul's championship match with Checker Charley. He noticed some of the robot's connections were loose but failed to reveal this to Berringer. This was his way of asserting the dominance of people over machines. Later, when Paul is a Ghost Shirt captive in the underground shelter, Finnerty tells him their sole purpose is to "get back to basic values, basic virtues! . . . Men doing men's work, women doing women's work. People doing people's thinking" (PP XXX). These sentiments are far removed from the days when he, Paul, and Lawson Shepherd devised a machine to replicate the labor of lathe operator Rudy Hertz.

Finnerty, Noyes. *In* God Bless You, Mr. Rosewater, *Noyes Finnerty sweeps floors in the Rosewater Volunteer Fire Department. Despite the glory brought by centering the 1933 and 1934 undefeated Noah Rosewater Memorial High School basketball teams, Noyes is better known for strangling to death his unfaithful sixteen-year-old wife in 1934. Eliot Rosewater manages to arrange parole from his life sentence after reading about the case in back issues of* The Rosewater County Clarion Call. *Noyes never thanks Eliot. Drawing on his prison experience and his own criminal neuroses, Finnerty associates Eliot's dissociative split with Charley Warmergram. Of greater note is Finnerty's careful observations about an essential change in character stemming from an inexplicable break with reality. (GBR 13)* **Noyes Finnerty** *spoke up. "All he hears is the big click." He came forward for a closer examination of Eliot.*

His approach was not sympathetic. It was clinical. Eliot's response was clinical, too, as though a nice doctor were shining a bright light in his eyes, looking for something. "He heard that *click*, man. Man, did he ever hear that *click*. . . . It ain't a thing that happens just in prison. In prison, though, you get to listening for things more and more. You stay there long enough, you go blind, you're all ears. The click is one thing you listen for. . . . You get to know a man, and down deep there's something bothering him bad, and maybe you never find out what it is, but it's what makes him do like he does, it's what makes him look like he's got secrets in his eyes. And you tell him, 'Calm down, calm down, take it easy now.' Or you ask him, 'How come you keep doing the same crazy things over and over again, when you know they're just going to get you in trouble again?' Only you know there's no sense arguing with him, on account of it's the thing inside that's making him go. It says, 'Jump,' he jumps. It says, 'Steal,' he steals. It says, 'Cry,' he cries. Unless he dies young, though, or unless he gets everything all his way and nothing big goes wrong, that thing inside of him is going to run down like a wind-up toy. You're working in the prison laundry next to this man. You've known him twenty years. You're working along, and all of a sudden you hear this *click* from him. You turn to look at him. He's stopped working. He's all calmed down. He looks real dumb. He looks real sweet. You look in his eyes, and the secrets are gone. He can't even tell you his own name right then. He goes back to work, but he'll never be the same. That thing that bothered him so will never click on again. It's dead, it's *dead*. And that part of that man's life where he had to be a certain crazy way, that's *done!*"

Firehouse Harris (*see* **"The Foster Portfolio"**).

The First District Court of Thankyou. *Eliot Rosewater is instrumental in securing the prison release of Noyes Finnerty, once the star center on the championship Noah Rosewater Memorial High School basketball teams of 1933 and 1934. Finnerty had been serving a life sentence for strangling his sixteen-year-old wife in 1934. Vonnegut points out that Finnerty's cynicism and lack of gratitude was a common experience. (GBR 13) He (Eliot) was used*

to ingratitude. One of his favorite Kilgore Trout books dealt with ingratitude and nothing else. It was called ***The First District Court of Thankyou***, which was a court you could take people to, if you felt they hadn't been properly grateful for something you had done. If the defendant lost his case, the court gave him a choice between thanking the plaintiff in public, or going into solitary confinement on bread and water for a month. According to Trout, eighty per cent of those convicted chose the black hole.

Fishbein, Mrs. *Code-named X-229, Mrs. Fishbein is the seamstress sewing together all the ghost shirts for the rebellious forces in* Player Piano. *In stark contrast to the mass production techniques in the rest of society, Mrs. Fishbein has already prepared 758 shirts before her developing cataracts put her six weeks behind in production.*

Fitzgerald, Bernard. *A distant relative of John F. Kennedy's (they have a common great-grandfather), Fitzgerald is the eighty-year-old Roman Catholic priest responsible for saving six young Kankabono girls, in* Galápagos. *They are eventually artificially impregnated with the sperm of Captain von Kleist through the scientific know-how of Mary Hepburn.*

Flammer. *In the 1952 short story "The No-Talent Kid," Flammer is the undisputed first seat clarinetist in George Helmholtz's "A" band at Lincoln High School. He becomes the challenge target of Walter Plummer, the band's worst musician, as part of his delusions about his own abilities. What Plummer desires more than beating out Flammer is earning a band sweater with a varsity letter.*

Flammer, Lou. *Flammer is the fat, thirtyish publicity director at the Ilium Works of the Federal Apparatus Corporation in the 1955 short story "Deer in the Works," reprinted in* Welcome to the Monkey House *(1968). He is an ideal company man, prepared at a moment's notice to lecture visiting Boy Scouts about the positive values Scouting imparts to young men in preparation for becoming corporate managers (56 percent of the managers were Eagle Scouts). Earlier in his life, Flammer became disenchanted with the financial headaches of running his* *own weekly newspaper. He also grew disappointed trying to save parts of his community that seemed fated to destruction by the sprawling corporations. By selling out to a national chain, something his protégé David Potter was contemplating, Flammer prospered and consistently hawked the positive company line. It is Flammer who assigns Potter, the new PR man, the task of covering the story of the stray deer that enters the Works.*

Flemming, Pearl. *One of the physically afflicted citizens in Rosewater County (she needed crutches to get around), Pearl was seemingly miraculously cured by Eliot in* God Bless You, Mr. Rosewater.

Flemming, Willard and Mary (*see also* **James Wait** *and* **Mary Hepburn**). *In* Galápagos, *James Wait travels with the name Willard Flemming on his fake Canadian passport. As Flemming, he proposes to Mary Hepburn, who is posing as Mary Kaplan. Mary agrees to marry "Willard" when he is near death on the* Bahía de Darwin. *Married by Captain von Kleist, "Flemming" dies only minutes after the wedding.*

"Flocka Butt" (*see* **Dr. Stewart Rawlings Mott**).

Florio, General Lucas. *In* Hocus Pocus, *the commander of the Rainbow Division, the 42nd Division of the National Guard in Schenectady, New York, who is ordered to quell the prison riot in Athena. His division is all white as a result of the resegregation of the military, though there are some Asians classified as Honorary White People.*

Florio drafts Eugene Debs Hartke to act as the new warden once the riot is silenced. Florio later claims Tarkington College for the government in order to use the college's and Scipio's state-of-the-art sanitary facilities. Despite Florio's respect for Hartke, political hacks force him to arrest Hartke for insurrection. Florio is aware that his political patrons require him to find a scapegoat and an opportunity to turn the uprising to their political advantage.

folk society, FSD (*see also* **extended family**). (WFG Address to the National Institute of Arts and Letters, 1971) Dr. Redfield is dead now. . . . While he lived, he had in his head a lovely dream which he called "**The Folk Society**." He published this dream in *The American Journal of Sociology,* Volume 52, 1947, pages 293 through 308. *Vonnegut goes on to paraphrase Redfield's idea by stating that folk societies were so small that everybody knew everybody well, and associations lasted for life. The members communicated intimately with one another, and very little with anybody else.*

(WFG Address to the National Institute of Arts and Letters, 1971) Moreover [Dr. Redfield goes on], in the **folk society** much besides human beings is treated personally. The pattern of behavior which is first suggested by the inner experience of the individual—his wishes, fears, sensitivities, and interests of all sorts—is projected into all objects with which he comes in contact. Thus nature, too, is treated personally; the elements, the features of the landscape, the animals, and especially anything in the environment which by its appearance or behavior suggests the attributes of mankind—to all these are attributed qualities of the human person. [I (Vonnegut) stop quoting now.]

And I say to you that we are full of chemicals which require us to belong to **folk societies,** or failing that, to feel lousy all the time. We are chemically engineered to live in **folk societies,** just as fish are chemically engineered to live in clean water—and there aren't any **folk societies** for us anymore.

(PS Religion) "Channing grew up in what the late anthropologist Robert Redfield called a **folk society,** a relatively isolated community of like-thinking friends and relatives, a stable extended family of considerable size. Redfield said that we were all descended from persons who lived in such societies, and that we were likely to hanker to live in one ourselves from time to time. A **folk society,** in his imagination and in our imaginations, too, is an ideal scheme within which people can take really good care of one another, can share fairly, and can distribute honors to one and all."

(FWD XIII) When I studied anthropology long ago at the University of Chicago, my most famous professor was Dr. Robert Redfield. The idea that all societies evolved through similar, predictable stages on their way to higher (Victorian) civilization, from polytheism to monotheism, for instance, or from the tom-tom to the symphony orchestra, had by then been ridiculed into obscurity. It was generally agreed that there was no such ladder as cultural evolution. But Dr. Redfield said in effect, "Wait just a minute." He said that he could describe to every fair-minded person's satisfaction one (and only one) stage every society had passed through or would pass through. He called this inevitable stage and his essay on it "**The Folk Society**."

First of all, a **Folk Society** was isolated, and in an area it considered organically its own. It grew from that soil and no other. The break between the living and the dead was indistinct, and bonds of kinship crisscrossed every which way. There was such general agreement as to what life was all about and how people should believe in every conceivable situation that very little was debatable. (*FWD XIII*) A **Folk Society deficiency** (hereafter "**FSD**") quite often does (*have a chemical imbalance*). The trouble begins when a person suffering from **FSD** stops thinking, in order to become a member of an artificial extended family which happens to be crazy. The homicidal "family" of Charles Manson springs to mind. Or what about the cult of the Reverend Jim Jones in Guyana, whose members on his advice ("Tonight you will be with me in Paradise") fed the kids Kool-Aid laced with cyanide and then drank it themselves. *See also:* WFG Address to the National Institute of Arts and Letters, 1971; *PS* Self-Interview; *PS* Religion; *FWD* XIII; XVI.

foma (*see also* **Bokononism**). (*CC* Dedication) Nothing in this book is true.

> "Live by the *foma** that make you brave and kind and healthy and happy."
> *The Books of Bokonon* 1:5

(*CC* 85) I learned some things, but they were scarcely helpful. I learned of the Bokononist cosmogony, for instance, wherein *Borasisi*, the sun, held *Pabu*, the moon, in his arms, and hoped that *Pabu* would bear him a fiery child.

But poor *Pabu* gave birth to children that were cold, that did not burn; and *Borasisi* threw them away in disgust. These were the planets, who circled their terrible father at a safe distance.

Then poor *Pabu* herself was cast away, and she went to live with her favorite child, which was Earth. Earth was *Pabu's* favorite because it had people on it; and the people looked up at her and loved her and sympathized.

And what opinion did Bokonon hold of his own cosmogony? "*Foma!* Lies!" he wrote. "A pack *of foma!*"
(*CC* 64) I turned to *The Books of Bokonon*, still sufficiently unfamiliar with them to believe that they contained spiritual comfort somewhere. I passed quickly over the warning on the title page of *The First Book:*

"Don't be a fool! Close this book at once! It is nothing but **foma**!"

Foma, of course, are lies.
(*WFG* Preface) DEAR READER: The title of this book is composed of three words from my novel *Cat's Cradle*. A *wampeter* is an object around which the lives of many otherwise unrelated people may revolve. The Holy Grail would be a case in point. *Foma* are harmless untruths, intended to comfort simple souls. An example: "Prosperity is just around the corner." A *granfalloon* is a proud and meaningless association of human beings. Taken together, the words form as good an umbrella as any for this collection of some of the reviews and essays I have written, a few of the speeches I have made. Most of my speeches were never written down.

Ford, Henry. *In* Hocus Pocus, *Eugene Debs Hartke credits the famed industrialist with accepting the virulently anti-Semitic* Protocols of the Elders of Zion *to the extent that he provided financial support for its publication in the United States.*

Ford's involvement with publishing the forged tract is well delineated in Carol Gelderman's Henry Ford: The Wayward Capitalist *(Dial Press, 1981). In 1919 Ford purchased the Dearborn Independent, a small rural weekly newspaper at the time. Ford appointed his friend and fellow anti-Semite Ernest Liebold general manager. The two men shared the belief that international Jewish bankers, particularly the Rothschilds and Warburgs, manipulated geopolitical relations for their own financial benefit. In 1920 the Dearborn Independent published a series entitled "The International Jew: The World's Problem." Soon after the series went into*

---

* Harmless untruths

production, Liebold established a private detective agency dedicated to finding scandal in the private lives of Jews or suspected Jews and to the acquisition of anti-Semitic writings. The agency acquired The Protocols of the Wise Men of Zion *in 1920 and had them translated for publication in the* Independent. *Despite the fact that international scholars had already established the text's false and fabricated background, excerpts were continually published through December* 1921.

Though the Independent *was a small rural weekly when Ford bought it, he used his automobile dealers to sell subscriptions to their customers. Ford's* Independent *quickly grew to three-quarters of a million subscribers while the anti-Semitic articles were appearing in the paper.*

Ford, Rose Aldrich. (*Slap* 28) Somewhere in there I (*Wilbur Swain*) married an equally wealthy woman, actually a third cousin of mine, whose maiden name was **Rose Aldrich Ford**. She was very unhappy, because I did not love her, and because I would never take her anywhere. I have never been good at loving. We had a child, Carter Paley Swain, whom I also failed to love.

Fort Belvoir. (*Blue* 25) I (*Rabo Karabekian*) was a master sergeant at **Fort Belvoir** (*Fairfax County, Virginia*) when I read of the deaths of Dan Gregory and Fred Jones in Egypt.

Fort Benjamin Harrison. *Located outside Indianapolis, it is there that Roland Barry in* God Bless You, Mr. Rosewater *suffers a nervous breakdown when—ten minutes after being sworn—he is ordered to take a shower with a hundred other men.*

Fort Benjamin Harrison is also where Bluebeard's *Rabo Karabekian has surgical repairs made to his orbital socket from the war wound that took his eye. Rabo chooses not to endure all the surgery required to make the socket hold a glass eye, so he is left wearing an eye patch.*

Fort Benning. (WFG Address to Graduating Class at Bennington College, 1970) I demand that the administration of Bennington College establish an R.O.T.C. unit here. It is imperative that we learn more about military men, since they have so much

of our money and power now. It is a great mistake to drive military men from college campuses and into ghettos like **Fort Benning** and Fort Bragg. Make them do what they do so proudly in the midst of men and women who are educated.

In Deadeye Dick, *Felix Waltz completes his basic training at Fort Benning, Georgia, before Rudy kills Mrs. Metzger. While at Fort Benning, Felix never finds out about the tragedy.*

In Bluebeard, *Rabo Karabekian earns the Soldier's Medal for saving the lives of two soldiers while an instructor at Fort Benning. (Blue 27)* In 1941, I was giving a course in camouflage techniques to officer candidates at **Fort Benning**, Georgia. I saw a barracks on fire, and I gave the alarm, and then went in twice, without regard for my own safety, and carried out two unconscious enlisted men.

Fort Bragg. *The army base from which Private Francis J. Thompson is abducted only to become Sergeant Brackman after his memory is wiped clean by Rumfoord's Martian forces in* The Sirens of Titan.

In the short story "Long Walk to Forever," reprinted in Welcome to the Monkey House *(1968), Newt (not Newt Hoenikker from* Cat's Cradle) *goes AWOL from Fort Bragg to be with his best friend, Catharine. He realizes he loves her and leaves Fort Bragg to propose marriage, only to find out she is engaged to someone else.*

In Breakfast of Champions, *Francine Pefko, Dwayne Hoover's secretary, lives at Fort Bragg after her husband, Robert, graduates from West Point and goes to parachute school in South Carolina.*

In Hocus Pocus, *while Eugene Debs Hartke is in Vietnam, his family lives at Fort Bragg. Eventually his wife moves the family so they could live at her mother's house while she pursues a degree in physical therapy at Johns Hopkins University.*

Fort Jesus. *The training camp for the soldiers of San Lorenzo in* Cat's Cradle.

"Fortitude" (1968). *The short play in which the medical genius Dr. Norbert Frankenstein uses an advanced computer to mechanically control the biochemical status of Sylvia Lovejoy, the one-hundred-year-old widow of a billionaire. All that remains of Sylvia is her head, which sits atop miles of* electrical cables and tubes. She longs to kill herself but her mechanical arms are built to guard against such an incident. Her hairdresser takes pity on her and smuggles a gun to her room, but because she can't kill herself she instead shoots Dr. Frankenstein. His wounds would have been fatal if not for the quick-thinking medical team, which removes his head and attaches it to a device similar to Sylvia's. Such was his wish if his own death were imminent, along with the playing of the Jeanette MacDonald–Nelson Eddy recording of "Ah, Sweet Mystery of Life" upon waking next to Sylvia.

Fortune, John. In Deadeye Dick, dairy farmer John Fortune was Otto Waltz's best friend when both were in their twenties. Fortune served as Otto's best man at his wedding. While helping Otto do some household construction, John dropped an oak timber on Otto's foot and the resulting injury kept him from military service in World War I. John went to war and received numerous medals. Like Waltz, Fortune was also of German heritage and his name was an anglicized version of the German word for luck—cluck.

In 1916, Fortune is among the group of hunters (including Otto Waltz, Police Chief Morissey, his son Bucky, and August Gunther) when Chief Morissey's shotgun accidentally fires, decapitating August Gunther. All conspire to keep the killing a secret.

John Fortune deeply disagrees with Otto Waltz's affection for Adolf Hitler and this causes an irrevocable split in their friendship.

After Fortune's wife passes away, he casts about for something to keep himself going. He becomes deeply influenced by James Hilton's 1933 imaginary Shangri-La as described in Lost Horizon. He goes to Asia, searches for tranquility, and dies in 1938. His last words to those he leaves behind in Midland City are recorded from his last postcard and printed in the Bugle-Observer: "To all my friends and enemies in the buckeye state. Come on over. There's room for everybody in Shangri-La" (DD 17). The message didn't reach Midland City until 1944 when adventurer Dr. Brokenshire finally gets around to mailing the note along with a map of Fortune's burial place.

Young Rudy Waltz, only six when Fortune dies in Nepal, grows up thinking this is the most admirable person in Midland City and writes an essay to that effect for his teacher, Mrs. Shoup. She is so impressed that Rudy forever thinks of doing more with the story. Eventually, he turns it into the play "Katmandu," and in 1959 he wins the Caldwell Foundation playwriting contest. The prize is a professional production of the play at the Theatre de Lys in Greenwich Village (the same theater that produced Vonnegut's Wanda June).

"The Foster Portfolio" (1951) (also **Herbert and Alma Foster** and **Firehouse Harris**). In this short story, reprinted in Welcome to the Monkey House (1968), Herbert is the secretly wealthy working man (two jobs almost all the time) who struggles with living dichotomously as the pious, reverent, and committed family man while sneaking away three nights a week to play piano jazz in a low-class local bar, as did his unfaithful and deserting father. The family was supported by the grandfather after Herbert's father left. Grandfather Foster left Herbert an estate of stocks and bonds worth $850,000.

However, Herbert kept his wealth a secret from his wife, Alma, for fear it would disrupt the honest, hardworking life they have created, one in which it pleases them to earn all their smallest pleasures. For her part, Alma is dutiful and respectful of all the effort Herbert puts into earning a living, playing piano for the church choir, and volunteering in the fire department. She is totally unaware of Herbert's secret life. My client, **Herbert Foster**, hadn't had a new suit in three years; he had never owned more than one pair of shoes at a time. He worried about payments on his secondhand car, and ate tuna and cheese instead of meat, because meat was too expensive. His wife made her own clothes, and those of **Herbert, Jr.**, and the curtains and slipcovers—all cut from the same bargain bolt. **The Fosters** were going through hell, trying to choose between new tires or retreads for the car; and television was something they had to go two doors down the street to watch. Determinedly, they kept within the small salary Herbert made as a bookkeeper for a wholesale grocery house.

And then **Herbert Foster**, looking drab and

hunted, picked his way through the crowd. His expression was one of disapproval, of a holy man in Babylon. He was oddly stiff-necked and held his arms at his sides as he pointedly kept from brushing against anyone or from meeting any of the gazes that fell upon him. There was no question that being in the place was absolute, humiliating hell for him.

I called to him, but he paid no attention. There was no communicating with him. **Herbert** was in a near coma of see-no-evil, speak-no-evil, hear-no-evil. . . .

Herbert dusted off the piano bench with his handkerchief, and sat down gingerly. He took a cigarette from his breast pocket and lighted it. And then the cigarette started to droop slowly from his lips; and, as it drooped, **Herbert** hunched over the keyboard and his eyes narrowed as though he were focusing on something beautiful on a faraway horizon.

Startlingly, **Herbert Foster** disappeared. In his place sat an excited stranger, his hands poised like claws. Suddenly he struck, and a spasm of dirty, low-down, gorgeous jazz shook the air, a hot, clanging wraith of the twenties.

. . . Nobody could do anything for **Herbert**. **Herbert** already had what he wanted. He had had it long before the inheritance or I intruded. He had the respectability his mother had hammered into him. But just as priceless as that was an income not quite big enough to go around. It left him no alternative but—in the holy names of wife, child, and home—to play piano in a dive, and breathe smoke, and drink gin, to be **Firehouse Harris**, his father's son, three nights out of seven.

Foust, Senator Warren. *When the power of dynamopsychism is revealed, Senator Foust seeks federal funds to screen the population for men who may possess the potential weapon, declaring:* He who rules the Barnhouse Effect rules the world! (*MH* Report on the Barnhouse Effect).

Francis, Dick. *In* Timequake, *Vonnegut recalls meeting the British former steeplechase champion and highly successful crime author noting that he expected him to be smaller, perhaps because of the*

usually diminutive jockeys in American horse racing. Vonnegut uses Francis and the horse industry to compare how young adults in America are approaching their early adulthood, and then he extends the illustration to include a favorite topic: self-respect.
(*TQ* 55) I said he was a bigger man than I had expected. He replied that it took a big man to "hold a horse together" in a steeplechase. This image of his remained in the forefront of my memory so long, I think, because life itself can seem a lot like that: a matter of holding one's self-respect together, instead of a horse, as one's self-respect is expected to hurdle fences and hedges and water.

My dear thirteen-year-old daughter Lily, having become a pretty adolescent, appears to me, as do most American adolescents, to be holding her self-respect together the best she can in a really scary steeplechase.
(*TQ* 55) I should have told them (*the Butler University graduating class Vonnegut addressed on May 11, 1996, Butler's 139th commencement, in his hometown of Indianapolis*) they were like **Dick Francis** when **Dick Francis** was young, and astride an animal full of pride and panic, in the starting gate for a steeplechase.

More: If a steed balks again and again at hazards, it is put out to pasture. The self-respects of most middle-class American people my age or older, and still alive, are out to pasture now, not a bad place to be. They munch. They ruminate.

If self-respect breaks a leg, the leg can never heal. Its owner has to shoot it. My mother and Ernest Hemingway and my former literary agent and Jerzy Kosinski and my reluctant thesis advisor at the University of Chicago and Eva Braun all come to mind.

Francis X. Donovan Post of the American Legion in Brookline. *The fictitious name Campbell gives the American Legion Post to which Bernard B. O'Hare belongs and where Kraft/Potapov sends news of Campbell's whereabouts, in* Mother Night.

Frank, Anne. *The martyred author of* The Diary of Anne Frank. *Vonnegut uses a line from her diary as the epigraph of* Galápagos—*a story about humanity's bizarre and cruel mishandling of technology that* *brings an end to the human species as we know it.* In spite of everything, I still believe people are really good at heart. —*Anne Frank (1929–1944)*

Frankenstein, Dr. Norbert. *The sixty-five-year-old physician in the play* Fortitude *who has kept Sylvia alive for thirty-six years (and seventy-eight operations). The remarkable aspect is that only Sylvia's head survives, connected to all sorts of pumps, filters, and electronic gear. He busily shows Dr. Elbert Little the marvels he has wrought through the unique combination of his medical and technological expertise. Frankenstein is determined to keep her alive for all eternity. He has limited the range of motion on Sylvia's mechanical arms so she can't kill herself. When she is smuggled a gun for just that purpose and realizes she can't commit suicide, she shoots Frankenstein instead. He is saved by Dr. Little, who connects Frankenstein's head to a second set of identical apparatuses next to Sylvia's bed. For as long as technologically feasible, the two bodiless wonders will remain alive subject to the amphetamine-and-barbiturate-induced states prescribed by the medical team.*

Frankenstein, Dr. (**Victor**, *as well as references to* **Dr. Frankenstein's creature, the monster**). *Aside from the obvious allusion Vonnegut makes in creating Dr. Norbert Frankenstein as part of his play* Fortitude, *Vonnegut's great admiration of Mary Wollstonecraft Shelley's literary creation and legacy may be found in his brief interview with her from the Blue Tunnel to the Afterlife in* God Bless You, Dr. Kevorkian.

Other references to Dr. Frankenstein or his monster are detailed below.

(*Slap* 26) When (*Norman*) Mushari came to my house to tell me (*Wilbur Swain*) about Eliza's prospective move to Peru, a week after the orgy, he confessed that he himself had become severely disoriented while tied to a diningroom chair.

"You looked more and more like **Frankenstein monsters** to me," he said. "I became convinced that there was a switch somewhere in the house that controlled you. I even figured out which switch it was. The minute I untied myself, I ran to it and tore it out by the roots."

It was Mushari who had ripped the thermostat from the wall.

(*JB* 18) I thought to myself, "My goodness—these waitresses and cooks are as unjudgmental as the birds and lizards on the Galápagos Islands, off Ecuador." I was able to make the comparison because I had read about those peaceful islands in prison, in a *National Geographic* loaned to me by the former lieutenant governor of Wyoming. The creatures there had had no enemies, natural or unnatural, for thousands of years. The idea of anybody's wanting to hurt them was inconceivable to them.

So a person coming ashore there could walk right up to an animal and unscrew its head, if he wanted to. The animal would have no plan for such an occasion. And all the other animals would simply stand around and watch, unable to draw any lessons for themselves from what was going on. A person could unscrew the head of every animal on an island, if that was his idea of business or fun.

I had the feeling that if **Frankenstein's monster** crashed into the coffee shop through a brick wall, all anybody would say to him was, "You sit down here, Lambchop, and I'll bring you your coffee right away.'

(*FWD* XII) "Which brings us to the differences between men and women. Feminists have won a few modest successes in the United States during the past two decades, so it has become almost obligatory to say that the differences between the two sexes have been exaggerated. But this much is clear to me: Generally speaking, women don't like immoral technology nearly as much as men do. This could be the result of some hormone deficiency. Whatever the reason, women, often taking their children with them, tend to outnumber men in demonstrations against schemes and devices which can kill people. In fact, the most effective doubter of the benefits of unbridled technological advancement so far was a woman, Mary Wollstonecraft Shelley, who died 134 years ago. She, of course, created the idea of the **Monster of Frankenstein**.

"And to show you how fruity, how feminine I have become in late middle age: If I were the President of MIT, I would hang pictures of Boris Karloff as the **Monster of Frankenstein** all over the institution. Why? To remind students and faculty that humanity now cowers in muted dread, expecting to be killed sooner or later by **Monsters of Frankenstein**. Such killing goes on right now, by the way, in many other parts of the world, often with our sponsorship — hour after hour, day after day.

"What should be done? You here at MIT should set an example for your colleagues everywhere by writing and then taking an oath based on the Hippocratic Oath, by which medical doctors have been bound for twenty-four centuries. Do I mean to say that no physician in all that time has violated that oath? Certainly not. But every doctor who has violated it has been correctly branded a scumbag. (*TQ* 51) When I liken Trout there in the entrance hall of the American Academy of Arts and Letters, awakening Dudley Prince from PTA, to **Dr. Frankenstein**, I am alluding of course to the antihero of the novel *Frankenstein — or, The Modern Prometheus*, by Mary Wollstonecraft Shelley, second wife of the English poet Percy Bysshe Shelley. In that book, the scientist **Frankenstein** puts a bunch of body parts from different corpses together in the shape of a man.

Frankenstein jazzes them with electricity. The results in the book are exact opposites of those since achieved in real-life American state penitentiaries with real-life electric chairs. Most people think **Frankenstein** is **the monster**. He isn't. **Frankenstein** is the scientist.

Prometheus in Greek mythology makes the first human beings from mud. He steals fire from Heaven and gives it to them so they can be warm and cook, and not, one would hope, so we could incinerate all the little yellow bastards in Hiroshima and Nagasaki, which are in Japan. (*TQ* 53) The **monster** in *Frankenstein — or, The Modern Prometheus* turns mean because he finds it so humiliating to be alive and yet so ugly, so unpopular. He kills **Frankenstein**, who, again, is the scientist and not **the monster**. And let me hasten to say that my big brother Bernie never has been a **Frankenstein**-style scientist, never has worked nor would have worked on purposely destructive devices of any sort. He hasn't been a Pandora, either, turning loose new poisons or new diseases or whatever.

According to Greek mythology, Pandora was the first woman. She was made by the gods who were angry with Prometheus for making a man out of mud and then stealing fire from them. Making a woman was their revenge. They gave Pandora a box. Prometheus begged her not to open it. She opened it. Every evil to which human flesh is heir came out of it.

The last thing to come out of the box was hope. It flew away.

I didn't make that depressing story up. Neither did Kilgore Trout. Ancient Greeks did.

This is the point I want to make, though: **Frankenstein's monster** was unhappy and destructive, whereas the people Trout energized in the neighborhood of the Academy, although most of them wouldn't have won any beauty contests, were by and large cheerful and public spirited. *See also: PS* Jekyll and Hyde Revisited.

Franklin, Benjamin. (*ST* 6) The person responsible for the heavy emphasis on German batball on Mars was, of course, Winston Niles Rumfoord, who was responsible for everything on Mars.

Howard W. Sams proves in his *Winston Niles Rumfoord, Benjamin Franklin, and Leonardo da Vinci* that German batball was the only team sport with which Rumfoord was at all familiar as a child. Sams shows that Rumfoord was taught the game, when a child, by his governess, a Miss Joyce MacKenzie. (*PS* Roots) "But he (*Clemens Vonnegut*) was a very model of Victorian asceticism, lived frugally, and eschewed excesses of any kind," says Uncle John. I try. I don't drink anymore, but I smoke like a house afire. I am monogamous, but I have married twice.

"He greatly admired **Benjamin Franklin**, whom he called an American saint, and named his third son after him instead of naming him for one of the saints on the Christian calendar." I myself have named my only son after Mark Twain, another American Saint.

Vonnegut cites Franklin as part of a comical counterpoint showing how Captain von Kleist's bumbling actually saves mankind. (*Gal* 1:26) One emergency plan the Captain didn't consider there in the shower was that he himself take full charge of the ship, with only Mary Hepburn to help him—and that he run it aground on Santa Rosalia, which would become the cradle of all humankind.

Here is a quotation well known to Mandarax:

> *A little neglect may breed great mischief . . . for want of a nail the shoe was lost; for want of a shoe the horse was lost; for want of a horse the rider was lost.*
> Benjamin Franklin (1706–1790)

Yes, and a little neglect can breed good news just as easily. For want of Hernando Cruz aboard the *Bahía de Darwin,* humanity was saved. Cruz would never have run the ship aground on Santa Rosalia. (TQ 7) He *(Trout)* asked what relatives of mine had been wounded in wars. As far as I knew, only one. That was my great-grandfather Peter Lieber, an immigrant who became a brewer in Indianapolis after being wounded in one leg during our Civil War. He was a Freethinker, which is to say a skeptic about conventional religious beliefs, as had been Voltaire and Thomas Jefferson and **Benjamin Franklin** and so on. And as would be Kilgore Trout and I. (TQ 21) Are we enemies of members of organized religions? No. My great war buddy Bernard V. O'Hare, now dead, lost his faith as a Roman Catholic during World War Two. I didn't like that. I thought that was too much to lose.

I had never had faith like that, because I had been raised by interesting and moral people who, like Thomas Jefferson and **Benjamin Franklin,** were nonetheless skeptics about what preachers said was going on. But I knew Bernie had lost something important and honorable.

Again, I did not like that, did not like it because I liked him so much. (BAG This Son of Mine) The factory made the best centrifugal pumps in the world, and Merle Waggoner owned it. He'd started it. He'd just been offered two million dollars for it by the General Forge and Foundry Company. He didn't have any stockholders and he didn't owe a dime. He was fifty-one, a widower, and he had one heir—a son. The boy's name was Franklin. The boy was named for **Benjamin Franklin.**

Frascati, Marion and Lou. *Marion and Lou were friends with Edgar Rice Burroughs Hagstrohm and his wife, Wanda, in* Player Piano. *One month after Lou passes away, Edgar and Marion begin an affair. For Hagstrohm, the guilt of his secret life and the absolute dreariness of life on the assembly line pushes him over the edge. One night he cuts up his Chicago home with a blowtorch and runs naked to Marion's house, imploring her to flee to the woods with him. She refuses and he eludes police, escaping into the bird sanctuary bordering their housing development.*

Free American Corps. *The creation of Howard W. Campbell in* Mother Night, *the organization is also mentioned in* Slaughterhouse-Five *when Campbell makes a recruitment trip to Dresden, arriving in time to take cover with the American POWs in the meatlocker during the firebombing.* (MN 18) The **Free American Corps** was a Nazi daydream—a daydream of a fighting unit composed mainly of American prisoners of war. It was to be a volunteer organization. It was to fight only on the Russian front. It was to be a high-morale fighting machine, motivated by a love of western civilization and a dread of the Mongol hordes.

When I call this unit a Nazi daydream, incidentally, I am suffering an attack of schizophrenia—because the idea of the **Free American Corps** began with me. I suggested its creation, designed its uniforms and insignia, wrote its creed.

freethinker, free thinker (often capped) (*see also* **Clemens Vonnegut**). *Vonnegut's perspectives on religion are due in large measure to the German freethinker legacy passed down from his great-grandfather Clemens Vonnegut. Among his fictional characters, Vonnegut calls Ed Finnerty a freethinker* (Player Piano), *Hartke's grandfather Wills, and Hermann and Sophia Shultz* (Hocus Pocus). *Beatrice Rumfoord* (Sirens) *dreamed of a freethinking companion.* (PS Religion) And it is to suggest to her *(Jane Vonnegut)* and to some others why it was painful that I chose for this book's epigraph a quotation from a thin book, *Instruction in Morals,* published in 1900 and written by my **Free Thinker** great-grandfather Clemens Vonnegut, then seventy-six years old: "Whoever entertains liberal views and chooses a consort that is captured by superstition risks his liberty and his happiness."

(*PS Children*) My first wife and both my daughters are born-again Christians now—working white magic through rituals and prayers. That's all right. I would be a fool to say that the **free thinker** ideas of Clemens Vonnegut remain as enchanting and encouraging as ever—not after the mortal poisoning of the planet, not after two world wars, with more to come.

(*HP 24*) I (*Eugene Debs Hartke*) have looked up who the **Freethinkers** were. They were members of a short-lived sect, mostly of German descent, who believed, as did my Grandfather Wills, that nothing but sleep awaited good and evil persons alike in the Afterlife, that science had proved all organized religions to be baloney, that God was unknowable, and that the greatest use a person could make of his or her lifetime was to improve the quality of life for all in his or her community.

(*FWD XVI*) "There was a newspaper humorist named Kin Hubbard in my hometown of Indianapolis, where my ancestors were **Freethinkers** and then Unitarians or not much of anything as far as religious labels go. Kin Hubbard attended a graduation ceremony out there in Indiana. He commented afterward on the graduation address to the departing seniors. He said it might be better to spread out the really important stuff over four years instead of saving it all up until the very end."

(*FWD My Reply to a Letter*) I am a fourth generation German American religious skeptic ("**Freethinker**"). Like my essentially puritanical forebears, I believe that God has so far been unknowable and hence unservable, hence the highest service one can perform is to his or her community, whose needs are quite evident. I believe that virtuous behavior is trivialized by carrot-and-stick schemes, such as promises of highly improbable rewards or punishments in an improbable afterlife. (The punishment for counterfeiting in Henry VIII's reign, incidentally, was being boiled alive in public.) The Bible is a useful starting point for discussions with crowds of American strangers, since so many of us know at least a little something about it. It has the added virtue of having for contributors at least two geniuses, Moses and Christ.

(*TQ 7*) He (*Trout*) asked what relatives of mine had been wounded in wars. As far as I knew, only one. That was my great-grandfather Peter Lieber, an immigrant who became a brewer in Indianapolis after being wounded in one leg during our Civil War. He was a **Freethinker**, which is to say a skeptic about conventional religious beliefs, as had been Voltaire and Thomas Jefferson and Benjamin Franklin and so on. And as would be Kilgore Trout and I.

I told Trout that Peter Lieber's Anglo-American company commander gave his men, all **Freethinkers** from Germany, Christian religious tracts for inspiration. Trout responded by giving his own revision of the Book of Genesis.

(*MWC 8*) My parents and grandparents were humanists, what used to be called **Free Thinkers**. So as a humanist I am honoring my ancestors, which the Bible says is a good thing to do. We humanists try to behave as decently, as fairly, and as honorably as we can without any expectation of rewards or punishments in an afterlife.

(*GBK Introduction*) About belief or lack of belief in an afterlife: Some of you may know I am neither Christian nor Jewish nor Buddhist, nor a conventionally religious person of any sort. I am a humanist, which means, in part, that I have tried to behave decently without any expectation of rewards or punishments after I'm dead. My German-American ancestors, the earliest of whom settled in our Middle West about the time of our Civil War, called themselves "**Freethinkers**," which is the same sort of thing. My great grandfather Clemens Vonnegut wrote, for example, "If what Jesus said was good, what can it matter whether he was God or not?"

I myself have written, "If it weren't for the message of mercy and pity in Jesus' Sermon on the Mount, I wouldn't want to be a human being. I would just as soon be a rattlesnake."

See also: PP V; ST 10; PS Roots; PS Religion; HP 24; FWD XXI.

free will, free-willed (*see also **Now It Can Be Told***). (*SL5 4*) "You sound to me as though you don't believe in **free will**," said Billy Pilgrim.

"If I hadn't spent so much time studying Earthlings," said the Tralfamadorian, "I wouldn't have any idea what was meant by '**free will**.' I've visited thirty-one inhabited planets in the universe, and I have studied reports on one hundred more. Only on Earth is there any talk of **free will**."

(*BC* 1) Only Dwayne Hoover had **free will**. *This is the message Dwayne derives from Kilgore Trout's novel* Now It Can Be Told.

Trout did not expect to be believed. He put the bad ideas into a science-fiction novel, and that was where Dwayne found them. The book wasn't addressed to Dwayne alone. Trout had never heard of Dwayne when he wrote it. It was addressed to anybody who happened to open it up. It said to simply anybody, in effect, "Hey guess what: You're the only creature with **free will**. How does that make you feel?" And so on.

See also: PP XXXIII; *ST* 5; 10; *MN* 45; *CC* 36; *BC* 5; 8; 16; 22–24; *HP* 38; *TQ* Prologue; 3; 6; 8; 13; 16; 21–23; 25; 27–29; 31–32; 37; 45–46; 50–52; 54.

Freeman, Dr. Charley. *In the 1952 short story "The Package," collected in* Bagombo Snuff Box *(1999), Freeman is the unanticipated houseguest of Earl and Maude Fenton on their first day in their new scientifically state-of-the-art palatial estate. Freeman and Earl Fenton were fraternity brothers in college. Charley went on to become a physician in 1916 as Earl became an industrialist.*

Though friends from college, they had occupied distinctly different social classes and this was a long dormant sore spot for Earl. Earl waited on tables to help pay his way through college, often waiting on his wealthy fraternity brothers (such as Charley), and long felt that they harbored bad feelings for their brothers not born to wealth.

After college Charley uses his medical degree and the bulk of his family's fortune to open a hospital in China for the poor and lives there for more than thirty years. Having depleted his personal fortune, losing control of his hospital to the Communist Chinese government, being arrested and thrown into jail in China, Charley is eventually expelled from the country. With a threadbare wardrobe he finds himself in town on the same day his old fraternity brother Earl returns from his triumphal around-the-world trip in celebration of having sold his manufacturing plant for millions. Ironically, when briefly recalling college memories about their old college friends, Charley acknowledges their insensitivity to people of lesser social standing by stating in all seriousness, "God help them if they didn't outgrow the ridiculous social values of college days."

Charley falls victim to the snootiness of Maude Fenton, who believes Earl's old friend is there for a handout, an act of chutzpah after all Earl told her of his inferior feelings in college when dealing with his well-heeled fraternity brethren. It finally falls to Lou Converse, the Fentons' building contractor, to set them straight about the humanitarian efforts of their friend, but it is too late. They had already reneged on their offer to have him stay the night by lying about a visit from Maude's sister's family. By then, Charley has left in a taxi for a hotel, and Earl, ashamed of his own behavior, is left mindlessly pressing buttons on his remote-control for the new home's many electronic tricks, and almost trancelike, Earl is searching for the button that will allow him to start the day again, for a chance to be less occupied by his materialism and more concerned about Charley.

Freeman, Sally. *Felix Waltz's high school girlfriend in* Deadeye Dick *who dumps him just before the senior prom in favor of basketball captain Steve Adams. Instead, Felix asks the beautiful but socially outcast Celia Hildreth. What should have been a proud moment for Felix and Sally turns into one of the most shameful for Felix and Celia when they are forced to endure the shenanigans of Otto Waltz. (Steve Adams is the name of one of the nephews Vonnegut adopted after the deaths of his sister and brother-in-law.)*

French, Mary Alice. *After the judges at the Ohio State Science Fair discover that Eugene Debs Hartke had next to nothing to do with his crystallography display, they award first place to Mary Alice French for her original crystallography display. Though the Mayor of Cincinnati declared a "Mary Alice French Day," she loses in the national competition held in Washington, D.C. Hartke's revaluation of his life causes him some pain when considering the impact he and his father may have had on Mary Alice's life.* (*HP* 5) I have to wonder now, with so much time in which to think about people I've hurt, if Father and I didn't indirectly help set up **Mary Alice French** for her terrible disappointment in Washington.

There is a good chance that the judges in Cleveland gave her First Prize because of the moral contrast between her exhibit and ours.

Friedmann, Tuvia. *Howard Campbell writes his* Mother Night *memoirs at the behest of Tuvia Friedmann, Director of the Haifa Institute for the Documentation of War Criminals. Friedmann promises Campbell all the help he needs while he sits in his Old Jerusalem jail cell. He even provides Campbell with a Third Reich era typewriter complete with the twin lightning bolts of the S.S., the Schutzstaffel. Friedmann was a real individual and held the office cited by Vonnegut in the novel.*

fubar. *(Blue ?)* During that war we had a word for extreme man-made disorder which was **fubar**, an acronym for "fucked up beyond all recognition." Well—the whole planet is now **fubar** with postwar miracles, but, back in the early 1960s, I *(Rabo Karabekian)* was one of the first persons to be totally wrecked by one—an acrylic wall-paint whose colors, according to advertisements of the day, would ". . . outlive the smile on the 'Mona Lisa.'"

Fuller, Norman. *In the short story "Miss Temptation" (reprinted in* Welcome to the Monkey House*), Corporal Norman Fuller has just returned from service in the Korean War and is bitter about almost everything in his life. When he sees Susanna, a breathtakingly beautiful actress visiting the rural community to perform in a summer stock theater group, Fuller loudly shames her as a temptress. In reality, Susanna is tempting no one; Fuller sees in her all his disappointing experiences with women. He fails to sense she is as full of feelings as he, and she prepares to leave town and not go on with the theater group. When he is sent to her apartment to deliver her newspaper, Susanna shames him by showing him how hurt she was by his outrageous conduct and by others like him who never seem to appreciate that beautiful people are frequently degraded by those who fail to approach and learn how normal they are. Fuller apologizes by escorting Susanna through downtown, a sign of public penance.*

funnel, funnel-shaped *(see also* **blue tunnel***).* *(ST 1)* Infundibulum (infun-dib-u-lum) is what the ancient Romans like Julius Caesar and Nero called a **funnel**. If you don't know what a **funnel** is, get Mommy to show you one. *(From Dr. Cyril Hall's* A Child's Cyclopedia of Wonders and Things to Do.*) (Gal 1:29)* He didn't tell Wait about it, but his big brain put on quite a movie for him while he was unconscious. It showed him one end of a writhing piece of blue tubing, about five meters in diameter, big enough to drive a truck through, and lit up inside like the **funnel** of a tornado. It did not roar like a tornado, however.
(WJ III) MILDRED I never saw a tornado when I was alive, and I grew up in Oklahoma. There's this big, black, **funnel-shaped** cloud. Sounds like a railroad train without the whistle. I had to come to Heaven to see a thing like that.

G

Gabriel (*see* **Archangel Gabriel**).

Galápagos (1985; *see also* **Leon Trout, Bahía de Darwin**). *At the close of* Deadeye Dick, *the resurrected spirit of Will Fairchild is left to walk the plains of Midland City. Vonnegut seems to have so well liked the idea of a risen phantom in search of survival that this next novel is narrated by another phantom, the decapitated spirit of Vietnam veteran and deserter Leon Trout, son of science fiction writer Kilgore Trout.*

Leon writes his tale one million years in the future about the time back in 1986 when Homo sapiens *were embarking on their next evolutionary epoch. Man's newest development returned him to the sea in a manner resembling sea lions and, just as importantly, man's capacity for reason declined and gave way to instinct. Though not explicitly stated, the narrative assumption is that man had managed to temporarily destroy the environment to the extent that it would no longer sustain humanity in its present form. Though offered the opportunity to step through the "blue tunnel to the afterlife" and reunite with his father, Leon decides to roam the earth to satisfy his curiosity about what life is all about.*

Not surprisingly, Vonnegut traces the root cause of humanity's ills to our large and well-developed brains. (Gal 1:14) *That cumbersome computer could hold so many contradictory opinions on so many different subjects all at once, and switch from one opinion or subject to another one so quickly, that a discussion between a husband and wife under stress could end up like a fight between blindfolded people wearing roller skates.*

According to the ensuing scheme of existence, which Leon traces back to an aborted cruise bound for the Galápagos Islands, artificial constructs of wealth and twentieth-century man's belief in the perfectibility and preferability of machines in place of man yield to a more harmonious placement of the species within the great chain of being (reminiscent of Player Piano). *By contrast, writing one million*

years in the future, Leon notes that People have no such illusions today. They learn very early what kind of a world this really is, and it is a rare adult indeed who hasn't seen a careless sibling or parent eaten alive by a killer whale or shark (Gal 1:22).

In refusing immediate admission to the afterlife, Leon seeks the vision afforded Tralfamadorians in Sirens *and* Slaughterhouse. (Gal 2:7) I had chosen to be a ghost because the job carried with it, as a fringe benefit, license to read minds, to learn the truth of people's pasts, to see through walls, to be many places all at once, to learn in depth how this or that situation had come to be structured as it was, and to have access to all human knowledge.

But he hadn't really learned more by sticking around for an extra million years. His own life experiences should have been enough to satisfy his curiosity (particularly since he was a participant in a war atrocity similar to My Lai as well as his father's unwitting coconspirator in driving his mother from their home). However, in the new scheme, man no longer suffers the pain of living with the mental associations of community. Less gray matter means less unhappiness. No pain—the comforting final realization of Alice Vonnegut as she waited for death to claim her (see MH XIV).

Despite Vonnegut's insistence that humanity will eventually destroy itself, the evolutionary leap back into the water (a move that saves the species from annihilation) is made possible by the product of man's destructive will. The sperm of the nearly sexless German American Captain Adolf von Kleist is used to artificially inseminate Akiko Hiroguchi, the daughter of a Hiroshima bombing victim whose genes mutated due to radiation exposure. Vonnegut seems to be saying that within the seeds of our destruction lays the promise of our salvation.

Galápagos Islands. *In the novel named for the islands made famous by Charles Darwin, the Galápagos Islands becomes the center of man's next great evolutionary step as small-brained, sea lion–type* *creatures. This is made possible by the artificial insemination of the genetically deformed daughter of a Hiroshima bombing victim with the sperm from a German American sea captain.*

Galen, Vermont. *In* Slapstick, *the town closest to the mansion of Professor Elihu Swain, where local people raise Wilbur and Eliza out of their parents' heartbroken and horrified sight.*

gallows humor (*see* **humor**).

Garland, Dorothy Daffodil-7. *In* Slapstick, *of all the thousands in attendance when Wilbur Swain goes to Indianapolis for a Daffodil family reunion, this eleven-year-old African-American girl wins the drawing to chair the meeting.*

Garr, Vernon and Mary. *Vernon is a mechanic at the Sunoco station next to Dwayne Hoover's Pontiac dealership in* Breakfast of Champions. *Vernon's wife is schizophrenic and thinks he is trying to turn her brain into plutonium. Vernon and Dwayne are on friendly terms, and in an ironic twist, Garr takes solace in discussing with Dwayne the problems of living with a schizophrenic; Dwayne is soon to experience his own schizophrenic breakdown.*

Garth, Dr. Fred (*and his children* **Brud**, **Alice**, *and little* **Ewing**). *Fred Garth is first introduced as Paul Proteus's competition for the Pittsburgh Works position. As competitors, they are distinctly different characters. While at the Meadows corporate retreat, Garth shares a bunk with Paul and despondently speaks about the General Classification Tests facing his children and the effect on him as a parent worrying about their performance.* (PP XIX) "It's a trial, though, watching your kids grow up, wondering if they've got what it takes, seeing 'em just about killing themselves before the General Classification Tests, then waiting for the grades—" *The sentence ended in a sigh.* "I've just gone through that GCT business with my oldest, **Brud**, and I've got to live through the whole nightmare twice more still, with **Alice** and little **Ewing**."
(PP XII) "**Garth**'s a fine man," *said Paul.* **Garth** *was, too: four-square, desperate to please, and he*

seemed to have an anthropomorphic image of the corporate personality. **Garth** *stood in relation to that image as a lover, and Paul wondered if this prevalent type of relationship had ever been given the consideration it deserved by sexologists. On second thought, he supposed that it had—the general phenomenon of a lover's devotion to the unseen—in studies of nuns' symbolic marriages to Christ. At any rate, Paul had seen* **Garth** *at various stages of his love affair, unable to eat for anxiety, on a manic crest, moved to maudlin near-crying at recollections of the affair's tender beginnings. In short,* **Garth** *suffered all the emotional hazards of a perennial game of she-loves-me, she-loves-me-not. To carry out directions from above—an irritating business for Paul—was, for* **Garth**, *a favor to please a lady.*

Paul and Garth eventually share a basement cell in police headquarters along with "a small, elegant young Negro named Harold, who was in jail for petty sabotage." *It is there that Paul has Garth confirm that it was he who torched the sacred oak tree at the Meadows. He did it because his son Brud had again done poorly on the GCT's and* "cracked up." *Garth felt betrayed by the system he had worshipped.*

Gates, Bill. (MWC 6) **Bill Gates** *says,* "Wait till you can see what your computer can become." *But it's you who should be doing the becoming, not the damn fool computer. What you can become is the miracle you were born to be through the work that you do.*

Garu, Krishna (*also* **Krishna Gatu**). *Among the many Earthlings conscripted for the Army of Mars in* The Sirens of Titan, *this Indian typesetter is captured during the invasion of India only after his gun blows up. He later sells trinkets to pilgrims from The Church of God the Utterly Indifferent outside the Rumfoord mansion. He has outstanding warrants in Calcutta for bigamy, pandering, and nonsupport.*
(PP XIX) *A single, badly scorched man named* **Krishna Garu** *attacked all of India with a double-barreled shotgun. Though there was no one to radio-control him, he did not surrender until his gun blew up.*
(PP XXVIII) *And down the line of booths from*

Brackman and Chrono and Bee were Martian husks who had been identified as Myron S. Watson, an alcoholic, who had disappeared from his post as a wash room attendant at Newark Airport . . . as Charlene Heller, assistant dietitian of the cafeteria of Stivers High School in Dayton, Ohio . . . as **Krishna Garu**, a typesetter still wanted, technically, on charges of bigamy, pandering, and nonsupport in Calcutta, India . . . as Kurt Schneider, also an alcoholic, manager of a failing travel agency in Bremen, Germany.

Gatch. *The Gatch brothers (no first names are offered) once worked for the Maritimo Brothers Construction Company in* Deadeye Dick. *One of them had a shoplifting daughter (vaguely remembered by Rudy Waltz as either Mary, Martha, or Marie), who tried to make new friends by making presents of the stolen items. One of the Gatch brothers was working as a floor-waxer at the Midland City airport when Celia Hoover appears in a drugged stupor on the runway. A Gatch goes out to get her and returns Celia to her home.*

GCT (General Classification Tests). *The aptitude tests given to young teenagers in* Player Piano. *The results of the tests determine the extent to which one is permitted to pursue education or career goals. One's entire future is shaped by the test, and it is, therefore, dreaded by most.*

GEFFCo. *First mentioned in* Galápagos *as Ilium's primary industry and employer of Roy Hepburn, and appearing later in* Bluebeard *as the owner of Rabo Karabekian's ill-fated "Windsor Blue Number Seventeen."*

Roy's employment with GEFFCo comes to an end when the Japanese Matsumoto company is called in to modernize the plant's facilities. Nearly the entire workforce below the management level is laid off. Matsumoto makes it possible to run the facility with only twelve workers. With GEFFCo's employment opportunities so severely curtailed, Ilium loses nearly all its young families. The 1986 graduating class of Ilium High School would be its last.

In Bluebeard, *GEFFCo purchases Karabekian's eight-panel abstract painting to hang in the lobby of their Park Avenue headquarters. By the time Kara-*

bekian receives notification of the painting's deterioration in the third subbasement of the building, Matsumoto had purchased GEFFCo and renamed the building for themselves.

Gelhorne, Dr. Francis Eldgrin (*also* **Gelhorne Enterprises**). *The recipient of numerous honorary doctorates but never one earned by his own academic efforts, Dr. Gelhorne succeeds George Proteus in becoming the second National Industrial, Commercial, Communications, Foodstuffs, and Resources Director. It is he who presents the ruling technocracy's scheme to have Paul Proteus infiltrate the fledgling Ghost Shirt Society. He coins the oft-repeated phrase "God smiles on the Meadows." (PP XXII)* His spherical bulk was enclosed in a double-breasted, dark-blue suit. His single concession to the Meadows' tradition of informality was an unbuttoned collar and the sliding of his necktie knot a fraction of an inch below where it should have been. Though he was seventy, his hair was as thick and black as a twenty-year-old Mexican's. His fatness was turned into something impressive rather than comical by his perpetual I-smell-excrement expression.

The head of the ruling technocracy is an anomaly in that he had none of the qualifications for employment and responsibility programmed into EPICAC's computerized specifications. (PP XXII) He had no college degree of any kind, other than bouquets of honorary doctorates that had come to him in his late fifties and sixties.

He'd had nothing to do with industry, in fact, until he was thirty. Before that, he'd pulled a mail-order taxidermy business out of bankruptcy, sold his interest in it, and bought a trailer truck. He'd built his fleet to five trucks when he received a hot market tip, sold his business, invested the proceeds, and tripled his wealth. With this bonanza, he'd bought the largest, yet failing, ice-cream plant in Indianapolis, and put the business in the black inside of a year by building ice-cream routes servicing Indianapolis manufacturing plants during the lunch hour. In another year, he had his trucks carrying sandwiches and coffee along with ice cream. In another year, he was running plant cafeterias all over town, and the ice-cream business had become a minor division of **Gelhorne Enterprises**.

He'd found that many of the manufacturing firms were owned by third or fourth-generation heirs who, by some seeming law of decay, didn't have the nerve or interest the plants' founders had had. **Gelhorne**, half playfully at first, had offered these heirs advice, and found them amazingly eager to surrender responsibility. He'd bought in, watched and learned, and, discovering nerve was as valuable as special knowledge, he'd become manager and part owner of a dozen small plants.

There he'd come to the attention of Paul's father in Washington, and Paul's father had made **Gelhorne** his general executive manager when the whole economy had been made one flesh. When Paul's father died, **Gelhorne** had taken over.

It could never happen again. The machines would never stand for it.

General Forge and Foundry Company. *The major employer of Ilium in* Cat's Cradle *and* Slaughterhouse-Five. *According to Dr. Asa Breed, vice-president in charge of the Research Laboratory at General Forge and Franklin Hoenikker's former supervisor, there are more than 30,000 workers on the day shift at the plant. The company was stingy when it came to compensating its scientists for their inventions. They paid a $45 bonus for every patent they produced. In* Slaughterhouse-Five *it is noted that because GF&F has 68,000 employees, Billy Pilgrim and the other optometrists made good money providing all the required safety glasses.*

In the short story "This Son of Mine," collected in Bagombo Snuff Box *(1999), Ilium, New York's General Forge and Foundry has an outstanding buyout offer of $2,000 for Merle Waggoner's centrifugal pump company, but he is making them wait for a decision while trying to persuade his son to take over when he retires. Waggoner's contact at the Ilium-based company is Guy Ferguson. For proprietor Merle Waggoner, Ilium is a symbol of the modern era's corporate consolidation, conglomeratization, and the loss of America's regionalist heritage.* Merle waved his hand westward. "You wonder who all the people are with the big new houses on the west side? Who can have a house like that, and we never meet them, never even meet anybody who knows them? They're the ones who are taking over instead of the sons. The town's for sale, and they buy. It's

their town now—people named Ferguson from places called Ilium.

In the short story "Find Me a Dream," collected in Bagombo Snuff Box *(1999), General Forge and Foundry Company is the parent company of the Creon Works, the world's largest pipe producer.*

generation gap. (WFG Why They Read Hesse) Students of the famous **Generation Gap** might ponder this: Two of the leading characters in *Steppenwolf* are Johann Wolfgang von Goethe (1749–1832) and Wolfgang Amadeus Mozart (1756–1791), who appear as ghosts in dreams.
(WFG Address to the National Institute of Arts and Letters, 1971) The **generation gap** is an argument between those who believe folk societies are still possible and those who know they aren't.
(BAG Runaways) "Oh Bob, oh Bob, oh Bob—you dear boy," she said. "How nice, how awfully nice of you to call. It was what I was praying for! She has to talk to somebody her own age. Oh, her father and I have talked to her, and I guess she heard us, but there's such a **gap between the generations** these days."

genesis, Genesis Gang (*also* **Book of Genesis**). (ST 3) This comes very close to describing the **genesis** of Magnum Opus. The materials with which Noel Constant built his fortune were hardly more nourishing in themselves than calendar dates and bedsprings. . . .

He took the Gideon Bible that was in his room, and he started with the first sentence in **Genesis**.

The first sentence in **Genesis**, as some people may know, is: "In the beginning God created the heaven and the earth." *Noel Constant divided the sequence of letters as they appeared in the Bible as his investment guide, starting with Genesis.*
(WFG Preface) One tip of the string is forever vanishing. Its neighboring loop is forever retreating from extinction. The other end is forever growing. Its neighboring loop is forever pursuing **Genesis**. *This is Vonnegut's sense of the universe, which he depicts* as straight as a string, except for a loop at either end.
(WFG In a Manner That Must Shame God Himself) And one thing that fascinated me about the Super Realtors' Worship Service on Sunday (*the*

1972 *Republican National Convention in Miami)* was that Colonel Frank Borman was on the bill. He looked as tired of space opera as Abbie Hoffman was of clowning. He did his bit, which was to read about the Creation from **Genesis**, and that was that.

(PS Religion) "The Book of **Genesis** is usually taken to be a story about what happened a long time ago. The beginning of it, at least, can also be read as a prophecy of what is going on right now. It may be that Eden is this planet. If that is so, then we are still in it. It may be that we, poisoned by all our knowledge, are still crawling toward the gate. . . ."

The "Genesis Gang" is the nickname given to Rabo Karabekian and all his Abstract Expressionist friends by Marilee Kemp, then the Countess Portomaggiore. (Blue 30) She said that we should call ourselves the "**Genesis Gang**," since we were going right back to the beginning, when subject matter had yet to be created. . . .

I have dug one of hers *(Marilee's letters)* from the archives here . . . says that we have failed to paint pictures of nothing after all, that she easily identifies chaos in every canvas. This is a pleasant joke, of course. "Tell that to the rest of the **Genesis Gang**," she says.

In Timequake, *Vonnegut uses the story of his great-grandfather Peter Lieber, an immigrant from Germany, a freethinker, and a soldier in the Union Army during the Civil War, as a jumping-off point for Kilgore Trout to spout an impromptu, oral, revised version of the Book of Genesis. It casts God's creation as inherently chaotic and violent while Satan (as a woman) tries to help humanity avoid boredom and experience pleasure. Trout/Vonnegut manages a swipe at the pharmaceutical industry by way of analogy with Satan's original intent. (TQ 7)* Fortunately, I had a tape recorder, which I turned on.

"Please stop eating and pay attention," he said. "This is important. . . .

"In the beginning there was absolutely nothing, and I mean nothing" he said. "But nothing implies something, just as up implies down and sweet implies sour, as man implies woman and drunk implies sober and happy implies sad. I hate to tell you this, friends and neighbors, but we are teensy-weensy implications in an enormous implication. If you don't like it here, why don't you go back to where you came from?

"The first something to be implied by all the nothing," he said, "was in fact two somethings, who were God and Satan. God was male. Satan was female. They implied each other, and hence were peers in the emerging power structure, which was itself nothing but an implication. Power was implied by weakness.

"God created the heaven and the earth," the old, long-out-of-print science fiction writer went on. "And the earth was without form, and void, and darkness was upon the face of the deep. And the spirit of God moved upon the face of the waters. Satan could have done this herself, but she thought it was stupid, action for the sake of action. What was the point? She didn't say anything at first.

"But Satan began to worry about God when He said, 'Let there be light,' and there was light. She had to wonder, 'What in heck does He think He's doing? How far does He intend to go, and does He expect me to help Him take care of all this crazy stuff?'

"And then the shit really hit the fan. God made man and woman, beautiful little miniatures of Him and her, and turned them loose to see what might become of them. The Garden of Eden," said Trout, "might be considered the prototype for the Colosseum and the Roman Games.

"Satan," he said, "couldn't undo anything God had done. She could at least try to make existence for His little toys less painful. She could see what He couldn't: To be alive was to be either bored or scared stiff. So she filled an apple with all sorts of ideas that might at least relieve the boredom, such as rules for games with cards and dice, and how to fuck, and recipes for beer and wine and whiskey, and pictures of different plants that were smokable, and so on. And instructions on how to make music and sing and dance real crazy, real sexy. And how to spout blasphemy when they stubbed their toes.

"Satan had a serpent give Eve the apple. Eve took a bite and handed it to Adam. He took a bite, and then they fucked.

"I grant you," said Trout, "that some of the ideas in the apple had catastrophic side effects for a minority of those who tried them." Let it be noted here that Trout himself was not an alcoholic, a junkie, a gambler, or a sex fiend. He just wrote.

"All Satan wanted to do was help, and she did in

many cases," he concluded. "And her record for promoting nostrums with occasionally dreadful side effects is no worse than that of the most reputable pharmaceutical houses of the present day."

geodesic dome. *In the short story "Welcome to the Monkey House," Billy the Poet kidnaps Nancy the suicide parlor hostess and hides her beneath the geodesic dome sheltering the Kennedy Compound Museum in Hyannis Port.*

In Slaughterhouse-Five, Billy Pilgrim and Montana Wildhack are housed in a geodesic dome on Tralfamadore, protecting them from the cyanide atmosphere of the planet. Billy is later murdered in a Chicago geodesic dome by fellow former POW Paul Lazzaro. At the time of Billy's death, the United States had been Balkanized into twenty small nations, Chicago had been hydrogen-bombed by the Chinese, and the geodesic dome provided an artificial atmosphere capable of sustaining life.

George. *(last name not supplied, so it is indeterminate whether this is the brother of Earl Fenton or of Maude Fenton). In Vonnegut's 1952 Collier's short story "The Package," collected in* Bagombo Snuff Box *(1999), George is briefly mentioned in a dialogue aside in which Earl Fenton discusses the fortunate and presumably well-earned accomplishments of his sons. ". . . . young Earl's a doctor now, got a big house in Santa Monica, and Ted's just passed his bar exams and gone in with his* **Uncle George—**"

George. *In "The Powder-Blue Dragon," the disbelieving car dealer Bill Daggett calls George at the bank in the next village to verify the check written by Kiah Higgins to purchase his dream car, the Marittima-Frascati.*

German batball. *The national sport of Mars as well as the chief sport of the Army of Mars, a game played with particular excellence by the eight-year-old Chrono, son of Malachi Constant and Beatrice Rumfoord. (ST 6) The game of* **German batball** *is played with a flabby ball the size of a big honeydew melon. The ball is no more lively than a ten-gallon hat filled with rain water. The game is something like baseball, with a batter striking the ball into a field of opposing players and running around bases;*

and with the fielders attempting to catch the ball and frustrate the runner. There are, however, only three bases in **German batball**—first, second, and home. And the batter is not pitched to. He places the ball on one fist and strikes the ball with his other fist. And if a fielder succeeds in striking the runner with the ball when the runner is between bases, the runner is deemed *out*, and must leave the playing field at once.

The person responsible for the heavy emphasis on **German batball** *on Mars was, of course, Winston Niles Rumfoord, who was responsible for everything on Mars.*

(ST 6) *Howard W. Sams proves in his* Winston Niles Rumfoord, Benjamin Franklin, and Leonardo da Vinci *that* **German batball** *was the only team sport with which Rumfoord was at all familiar as a child. Sams shows that Rumfoord was taught the game, when a child, by his governess, a Miss Joyce MacKenzie.*

Back in Rumfoord's childhood in Newport, a team composed of Rumfoord, Miss MacKenzie, and Earl Moncrief the butler, used to play **German batball** *regularly against a team composed of Watanabe Wataru the Japanese gardener, Beverly June Wataru the gardener's daughter, and Edward Seward Darlington the half-wit stable boy. Rumfoord's team invariably won.*

German tank officer. *In the final scene of the short story "Der Arme Dolmetscher," collected in* Bagombo Snuff Box *(1999), German tanks surround the American battalion headquarters in France, leaving the linguistically deficient unnamed narrator (the official translator of the unit) thumbing through his tattered pamphlet of military phrasing for just the right response to the four Tiger tanks appearing at their door. As if the entire war had come to a halt while the search for just the right words ensued, I ran my eye down the left-hand columns of my pamphlet until I found the phrase that most fairly represented our sentiments.*

"Don't shoot," I said.

A **German tank officer** swaggered in to have a look at his catch. In his hand was a pamphlet, somewhat smaller than mine. "Where are your howitzers?" he said. *So ends this story, with its theme of the irony of linguistic ineptitude in times of war.*

Gettysburg Address (*also* **Gettysburg**). *Howard Campbell records in his* Mother Night *memoirs that he was preparing to write a pageant entitled "Last Full Measure," an homage to the German soldier, but the idea was shelved. He told Goebbels the title comes from Lincoln's famous address. When Hitler reads the text of the Gettysburg Address, he writes to Campbell,* Some parts of this . . . almost made me weep. All northern peoples are one in their deep feelings for soldiers. It is perhaps our greatest bond (MN 5).

Vonnegut sees in Lincoln's Gettysburg Address the poetry and humane center of both the president and the traditions of his own midwestern expression. He sees Lincoln as a kindred spirit, closely aligning himself with Lincoln's assertion of core American values and sense of decency—certainly more admirable than what passes for patriotism today. As such, Vonnegut engages Lincoln's essential Americanness as a defense of his own positions.
(PS Children) "When I thought I was going to talk about reference points, I had in mind the fixtures in a simpler and more stable civilization than what we have today. Examples: Shakespeare's *Hamlet*, Beethoven's Fifth Symphony, Leonardo's Mona Lisa, Lincoln's **Gettysburg Address**, Mark Twain's *Huckleberry Finn*—the Great Wall of China, the Leaning Tower of Pisa, the Sphinx. These few works of art used to be enormous monuments in the minds of public school graduates in every corner of this country. They have now been drowned in our minds, like Atlantis, if you will, by the latest sensations on television and radio, and in our motion picture palaces and *People* magazine.

Vonnegut's concerns are core American concerns, and the soul of Lincoln's words and example are used as a benchmark to denigrate stereotypical right wing responses of the day. (MWC 7) The most intelligent and decent prayers ever uttered by a famous American, addressed To Whom It May Concern, and following an enormous man-made calamity, were those of Abraham Lincoln at **Gettysburg**, Pennsylvania, back when battlefields were small. They could be seen in their entirety by men on horseback atop a hill. Cause and effect were simple. Cause was gunpowder, a mixture of potassium nitrate, charcoal, and sulfur. Effect was flying metal. Or a bayonet. Or a rifle butt.

Abraham Lincoln said this about the silenced killing grounds at **Gettysburg**:

We cannot dedicate—we cannot consecrate—we cannot hallow this ground. The brave men, living and dead, who struggled here have consecrated it far above our poor power to add or detract.

Poetry! It was still possible to make horror and grief in wartime seem almost beautiful. Americans could still have illusions of honor and dignity when they thought of war. The illusion of human you-know-what. That is what I call it: "The you-know-what."

And may I note parenthetically that I have already in this section exceeded by a hundred words or more the whole of Lincoln's **Gettysburg Address**. I am windy.

(BAG Coda to My Career) About that accent: When I was in the Army during the Second World War, a white Southerner said to me, "Do you have to talk that way?"

I might have replied, "Oh, yeah? At least my ancestors never owned slaves," but the training session at the rifle range at Fort Bragg in North Carolina seemed neither the time nor the place to settle his hash.

I might have added that some of the greatest words ever spoken in American history were uttered with just such a Jew's-harp twang, including the **Gettysburg Address** of Abraham Lincoln of Illinois and these by Eugene V. Debs of Terre Haute, Indiana: "While there is a lower class I am in it, while there is a criminal element I am of it; while there is a soul in prison, I am not free."
(GBK Introduction) This rambling introduction is four times as long as the most efficient, effective piece of writing in the history of the English-speaking world, which was Abraham Lincoln's address on the battlefield at **Gettysburg**.
(MWC 7) Abraham Lincoln. He always steals the show. I am about to quote him again.

More than a decade before his **Gettysburg Address**, back in 1848, when Lincoln was only a Congressman, he was heartbroken and humiliated by our war on Mexico, which had never attacked us.

James Polk was the person Representative Lincoln had in mind when he said what he said. Abraham Lincoln said of Polk, his president, his armed forces' commander-in-chief:

> Trusting to escape scrutiny, by fixing the public gaze upon the exceeding brightness of military glory—that attractive rainbow, that rises in showers of blood—that serpent's eye, that charms to destroy he plunged into war.

Holy shit! And I thought I was a writer!
(*HP* 3) One week before the first class was held, which was in Latin, taught by the Episcopalian priest Alan Clewes, Andre Lutz the Belgian arrived at the mansion with 3 wagons carrying a very heavy cargo, a carillon consisting of 32 bells. He had cast them on his own time and at his own expense in the wagon factory's foundry. They were made from mingled Union and Confederate rifle barrels and cannonballs and bayonets gathered up after the **Battle of Gettysburg**. They were the first bells and surely the last bells ever to be cast in Scipio.
(*HP* 8) One letter is from an old bellpuller, very likely dead by now, a member of the Class of 1924 who had married a man named Marthinus de Wet, the owner of a gold mine in Krugersdorp, South Africa. She knew the history of the bells, that they had been made from weapons gathered up after the **Battle of Gettysburg**. She did not mind that the bells would soon be played electrically. The bad idea, as far as she was concerned, was that the sour bells, Pickle and Lemon and Big Cracked John and Beelzebub, were going to be turned on lathes in Belgium until they were either in tune or on the scrap heap.

"Are Tarkington students no longer to be humanized and humbled as I was day after day," she asked, "by the cries from the bell tower of the dying on the sacred, bloodsoaked grounds of **Gettysburg**?"
See also: MH Welcome to the Monkey House; FWD XVI; *HP* 2; 4; 11; 35; *BAG* The No-Talent Kid; *MWC* 7.

Ghost Shirt Society. *In* Player Piano, *many disgruntled engineers and workers of all levels join this rebellion that is a cross between a Luddite uprising and a desperate cry for revitalizing man's spirit through meaningful labor, thereby restoring his sense of worth and humanity. The Reverend James J. Lasher begins the group and draws on the symbolism of the American Indian holy man Wovoka (Jack Wilson) and his message of respect for all humanity, including the holy duty of each person to live in peace and harmony with others while pursuing one's individual goals.*

Historically, Wovoka spread his word through ritualized dance circles introduced to the Nevada Paiute in 1889. It was the Sioux who added the talismanic shirt to protect them in battle from bullets and other wounds. As such, the Sioux practice went beyond the message and peaceful intentions Wovoka preached.

Within Vonnegut's novel, the Ghost Shirt Society very much frightens the leaders of the ruling technocracy. Most people have been removed from pursuing meaningful work due to advances in technology. Vonnegut draws their relevance to current times through Reverend Lasher. (PP XXIX) "Toward the end of the nineteenth century," said Lasher, "a new religious movement (*the Ghost Shirt Society*) swept the Indians in this country, Doctor. . . .

"With the game and land and ability to defend themselves gone," said Lasher, "the Indians found out that all the things they used to take pride in doing . . . were going or gone . . . Great religious leaders could no longer show that the old religious beliefs were the way to victory and plenty. . . .

"And the **Ghost Dance** religion," said Lasher, "was that last, desperate defense of the old values. . . ."

It is left to the ruling engineers to determine for themselves if automating all manner of production is a healthy and sane thing to do to people since they are left without artisanal pursuits, hopes of a better future, and advancement based on merit. The question is easily answered by the Reeks and Wrecks, but it splits engineers into different camps resulting in a nefarious plot to infiltrate the Ghost Shirt Society via Paul Proteus.

Drs. Gelhorne, Kroner, and Baer hatch the plot to infiltrate the Ghost Shirt Society while simultaneously testing the loyalty of Paul Proteus who, because his father was the legendary George Proteus, is a logical and popular candidate to take over the Pitts-

burgh Plant and eventual leadership positions in the ruling technocracy. Their plot pits the religious zeal of the original Ghost Shirt movement against the current regime's faith in technology. Together with their inventions, George and Paul Proteus form the new trinity: the father, the son, and the ghost in the machine. George is father of technocracy's first regime; Paul is the son of EPICAC's first guardian and himself the creator and overseer of lifeless machines that contain the working essence of once productive human spirits.

For all Paul's intellectual achievements and rapid advancement in the ruling technocracy (nepotism notwithstanding), his conflict lies in a growing awareness that the system designed to relieve man from physical and mental labor also strips people of their dignity. Developing this awareness is as much the result of his own sheltered experiences becoming juxtaposed with the Homesteaders and the misgivings of Finnerty and Lasher, as it is the result of diabolical scheming on the part of Gelhorne, Kroner, and Baer. By the time Gelhorne springs the plan on Proteus at the Meadows retreat, Paul already decided to quit the technocracy.

Paul stands at the center of the scheme developed by the technocrats, a scheme requiring Paul's public resignation so that he could infiltrate the upstart Ghost Shirt Society. At the same time, those in the Ghost Shirt movement seek to use Paul's name regardless of his true allegiance. Neither side is particularly interested in his true convictions. Moreover, the leadership characterizes their own meetings by recognizing the fantastical basis of their quest. (PP XXIX) "Wait until he sits in on some meetings," said Finnerty. "They're like something out of Alice in Wonderland, Paul."

Proteus's decision to claim leadership of the Ghost Shirt Society enables him to climb atop Vonnegut's soapbox (specifically, the witness stand in his treason trial). Citing the obvious polarities of life in the technocratic age, Paul reasons that not Every new piece of scientific knowledge is a good thing for humanity, and that The main business of humanity is to do a good job of being human beings . . . not to serve as appendages to machines, institutions, and systems (PP XXXII).

Paul pays a steep personal price for his decision since it results in the breakdown of his marriage.

Anita eventually pairs off with Paul's nemesis, Shepherd, a brown-nosing corporate climber. Having lost his wife to one conspiracy, Paul loses control of his own convictions when leaders of the Ghost Shirt Society sign his name to a protest letter. Within that letter lay the beliefs of the Ghost Shirt Society as rendered by their chief public information officer, Professor Ludwig von Neumann. The letter asserts that technology is, indeed, an overall benefit to humanity; however, when society abdicates self-governance in favor of designs determined by inanimate entities, the result goes against natural law.

"Again, let me say we are all in this together, but the rest of us, for what we perceive as good, plain reasons, have changed our minds about the divine right of machines, efficiency, and organization, just as men of another age changed their minds about the divine right of kings, and about the divine rights of many other things.

"During the past three wars, the right of technology to increase in power and scope was unquestionably, in point of national survival, almost a divine right. Americans owe their lives to superior machines, techniques, organization, and managers and engineers. For these means of surviving the wars, the **Ghost Shirt Society** and I thank God. But we cannot win good lives for ourselves in peacetime by the same methods we used to win battles in wartime. The problems of peace are altogether more subtle.

"I deny that there is any natural or divine law requiring that machines, efficiency, and organization should forever increase in scope, power, and complexity, in peace as in war. I see the growth of these now, rather, as the result of a dangerous lack of law.

"The time has come to stop the lawlessness in that part of our culture which is your special responsibility. . . .

"I propose that men and women be returned to work as controllers of machines, and that the control of people by machines be curtailed. I propose, further, that the effects of changes in technology and organization on life patterns be taken into careful consideration, and that the changes be withheld or introduced on the basis of this consideration.

"These are radical proposals, extremely difficult to put into effect. But the need for their being put into effect is far greater than all of the difficulties, and infinitely greater than the need for our national holy trinity, Efficiency, Economy, and Quality.

"Men, by their nature, seemingly, cannot be happy unless engaged in enterprises that make them feel useful. They must, therefore, be returned to participation in such enterprises.

"I hold, and the members of the **Ghost Shirt Society** hold.

"That there must be virtue in imperfection, for Man is imperfect, and Man is a creation of God.

"That there must be virtue in frailty, for Man is frail, and Man is a creation of God.

"That there must be virtue in inefficiency, for Man is inefficient, and Man is a creation of God.

"That there must be virtue in brilliance followed by stupidity, for Man is alternately brilliant and stupid, and Man is a creation of God.

"You perhaps disagree with the antique and vain notion of Man's being a creation of God.

"But I find it a far more defensible belief than the one implicit in intemperate faith in lawless technological progress—namely, that man is on earth to create more durable and efficient images of himself, and, hence, to eliminate any justification at all for his own continued existence.

"Faithfully yours,

"Doctor Paul Proteus" (PP XXX)

The professor and the other leaders of the rebellion are more understanding about the benign benefits of technology than is the great mass of rebels. He pays for this understanding by getting struck in the head by a rioter wielding the Sacred Mace of the Order of the Aurora Borealis while trying to prevent the destruction of a radio tower. Paul thinks of von Neumann as the consummate academician. (PP XXXV) He had been less interested in achieving a premeditated end than in seeing what would happen with given beginnings.

As the Ghost Shirt leadership looks out over the ruins of Ilium and prepares to surrender, von Neumann concludes, "This isn't the end, you know. . . . Nothing ever is, nothing ever will be— not even Judgment Day" (PP XXXV). The leadership knew theirs was a doomed cause, but they needed to try.

Reverend Lasher compares the limited and short-lived victory of the modern-day Ghost Shirt Society over the ruling technocracy to that one Indian triumph, however hollow it would inevitably prove to be. (PP XXXV) "This is like the Indians' massacre of Custer and his men," said Lasher reflectively. "The **Little Bighorn**. One isolated victory against an irresistible tide. More and more whites where Custer came from; more and more machines where these came from. But we may win yet." *The Ghost Shirt leadership knew the ruling technocracy would recover in the short run and maintain power, but they recognize it as a necessary first step in the rebellion.*

Gibney, Peter. *In* Jailbird, *the musical composer and Harvard classmate of Walter Starbuck's who turns on Starbuck once he testifies against Leland Clewes. As Starbuck recalls,* **Gibney** *sent me a picture postcard, so that my wife and the postman could read the message, too.*

"Dear shithead, it said, why don't you crawl back under a damp rock somewhere?" *The picture was of the Mona Lisa, with that strange smile of hers (JB 12).*

"Gilgongo." *The name of the short story Kilgore Trout was imagining while hitchhiking to the Midland City Arts Festival in* Breakfast of Champions. *It was an anti-conservation story about a planet where new species are constantly being created. Because the planet was becoming so crowded, the story opens with a party in honor of a man who wiped out a species of panda bears. "Gilgongo" meant extinct in the native language of the planet. The planet was finally overcome by a blanket of life one hundred feet thick.*

Gingiva-Tru and **Viverine.** *Together with Dr. Lomar Horthy, the Reverend Dr. Lionel J. D. Jones co-invented both the gum-simulating substance for false teeth and the embalming fluid. By the time Jones is paroled in 1950 from his conviction for sedition, both inventions dominate their respective markets and make Jones a wealthy man. He earns enough wealth to republish* The White Christian Minuteman, *which led him to his fateful meeting with Mother Night's Howard Campbell.*

Ginsberg, Allen. *The prominent poet from the Beat Movement whose "bardic improvisations" are largely* *attributed to his experimentation with hallucinogenic drugs, the teachings of Zen Buddhism, and the influence of William Blake.* (PS Obscenity) "**Allen Ginsberg** and I were inducted into the National Institute of Arts and Letters in the same year, 1973. Somebody from *Newsweek* called me up to ask what I had to say about two such antiestablishment writers being embraced by such a conservative organization.

I said this, and I meant it, and my comment was not printed: "My goodness, if **Mr**. **Ginsberg** and I aren't already members of the establishment, I don't know who is." *This anecdote is repeated from an earlier telling by Vonnegut in the "Playboy Interview" included in* Wampeters.

Glampers, Diana Moon. *Originally appearing as the authoritarian Handicapper General of the United States in the short story "Harrison Bergeron," reprinted in* Welcome to the Monkey House *(1968), she is probably better remembered as the neurotic domestic servant employed by Senator Rosewater to maintain the family home in Rosewater, Indiana. In* "Harrison Bergeron" *she shoots to death both the title character and the ballerina who dared to remove their government-issued handicap bags full of lead balls.*

In God Bless You, Mr. Rosewater, *Diana Moon Glampers is quite a different character. She is an illiterate sixty-eight-year-old virgin who, by almost anybody's standards, was too dumb to live. . . . No one had ever loved her. There was no reason why anyone should. She was ugly, stupid, and boring. On the rare occasions when she had to introduce herself, she always said her full name, and followed that with the mystifying equation that had thrust her into life so pointlessly:*

"My Mother was a Moon. My father was a Glampers" (GBR 5).

Deathly afraid of lightning, Diana Moon Glampers calls Eliot whenever it storms. During one storm she rattles off a number of "miracles" wrought by Eliot, the savior of Rosewater. (GBR 5) "Dawn Leonard had boils for ten years, and you cured 'em. Ned Calvin had that twitch in his eye since he was a little boy, and you made it stop. Pearl Flemming came and saw you, and she threw her crutch away.

And now my kiddleys have stopped hurting, just hearing your sweet voice."

"I'm glad."

"And the thunder and lightning's stopped."

It was true. There was only the hopelessly sentimental music of rainfall now.

Glinko-X-3. In God Bless You, Mr. Rosewater, *the home planet of the chaplain in Kilgore Trout's Pan-Galactic Three-Day Pass who has to break the news of the Milky Way's death to the earthling Sergeant Boyle. It was this story that sends Eliot Rosewater into a catatonic trance, imagining that he sees Indianapolis going up in a firestorm.*

Globular Cluster M13. (ST Epigraph) "Every passing hour brings the Solar System forty-three thousand miles closer to **Globular Cluster Ml3** in Hercules—and still there are some misfits who insist that there is no such thing as progress." —RANSOM K. FERM [*sic*]
(WFG Excelsior! We're Going to the Moon! Excelsior!) We have spent something like $33 billion on space so far. We should have spent it on cleaning up our filthy colonies here on earth. There is no urgency whatsoever about getting somewhere in space, much as Arthur C. Clarke wants to discover the source of the terrific radio signals coming from Jupiter. It isn't as though we aren't already going somewhere in space. Every passing hour brings the whole solar system 43,000 miles closer to **Globular Cluster M13** in Hercules.

Gloria. *The beautiful beautician in the play* Fortitude *who befriends Sylvia, the one-hundred-year-old woman whose head alone remains of her body. Sylvia is connected to a roomful of machines and watched over by Dr. Frankenstein. Gloria takes pity on Sylvia and smuggles a handgun into her room so her friend can commit suicide. However, Sylvia's mechanical arms are positioned to prevent just such an occurrence. Instead, Sylvia shoots Dr. Frankenstein, who winds up connected to a roomful of machines as well.*

Glossbrenner, Uncle Dan (*né* **Daniel Independence Glossbrenner;** *see also* **Alex Vonnegut**).

Vonnegut's "Uncle" Dan is mentioned by name only once in A Man Without a Country, but it is an anecdote he often shared in conversation, and he does so without directly naming him in Timequake (45). Vonnegut prefaces his usual laudatory comments about Uncle Alex and his advice to take conscious note of the beautiful moments in one's life with his rather one-dimensional take on Uncle Dan. (MWC 12) When I got home from the Second World War, my **Uncle Dan** clapped me on the back, and he said, "You're a man now." So I killed him. Not really, but I certainly felt like doing it. **Dan**, that was my bad uncle, who said a male can't be a man unless he'd gone to war.

As Richard Vonnegut recalls in a June 2012 email, There aren't that many **Dan**'s [*sic*] in or near the Vonnegut line.

The only **Dan** who—I can think—would have been close to K was **Daniel Independence Glossbrenner** who married Edna Schnuell (without the umlaut, the u becoming a diphthong with an e).

Edna Schnuell was one of 3 daughters of Gustav Schnuell, who was the brother of Nanette Schnuell Vonnegut, K's grandmother, and wife of Bernard V. the architect.

Thus Kurt Sr would have been a first cousin to Edna Schnuell, and thus K would have been a first cousin, by marriage, once removed to **D.I.G.** He was in both wars, a Colonel, and active with the Military (42nd, Rainbow Division) between the wars. (Since The Colonel was like Teddy Roosevelt, very pro military, I could see his logic—and K's hating this pro-war, pro-patriot logic.)

An interesting story is that Irma Vonnegut Lindener, Kurt Sr's sister, and K's Aunt ("Taunte" auf Deutsch), married Kurt (another) Lindener about 1920.

They lived in Germany before and during the war. Irma suffered through numerous bomb attacks. Near the end, The Colonel, who had a jeep, a chauffeur, and some supplies at his discretion personally delivered supplies, beyond the lines, to Aunt Irma, thus supporting Edna's first cousin.

(Even I called Irma "Aunt," although she was two generations removed and a cousin line over from me. Interesting how certain words slide, particularly the family titles of aunte [*sic*] and uncle.)

Despite my ramblings, let me see if my Cousin Cathy can confirm.

Richard

Cathy Cale's response provides more confirmation about the likelihood that this "Uncle" Dan is the same as Richard Vonnegut recalls, but her information contributes to a greater appreciation of Dan Glossbrenner.
Yes—He most certainly was **Uncle Dan**. Kurt lived at Rainbow Farm at some point—maybe after his Mother's suicide (not sure), spent many summers there, and shared Maxinkuckee with **Dan**, Emmy, Catey, and Meg.

I do know **Uncle Dan** & Aunt Edna were there for him after he suffered the loss of his Mother—they were very close then.

Kurt came to the Farm after his war experience and had a difficult time sharing his horror of war with his **Uncle Dan** as **Dan** was the Colonel with the mindset of the consummate soldier.

I do not have detailed accounts, but Aunt Jane Cozier, and Aunt Meg Batchelor could certainly be resources. I am finding some amazing things as I go through Mom's boxes which pertain to KV.

Cathy

Gluck, Werner. *The sixteen-year-old German guarding Billy Pilgrim and Edgar Derby. Together they looked like three wartime fools:* And there in the doorway were **Gluck** and Derby and Pilgrim—the childish soldier and the poor old high school teacher and the clown in his toga and silver shoes (SL5 7). *Pilgrim and Gluck never find out they are* *distant cousins. They both get their first glimpse of completely nude women when Werner mistakenly leads them to a shower where refugee girls from Breslau are cleaning themselves. Werner grew up in Dresden and presumably dies in the firestorm.*

"Go Back to Your Precious Wife and Son"

(1962). *The short story, reprinted in* Welcome to the Monkey House *(1968), narrated by the unnamed New Hampshire vendor and installer of storm windows and bathtub enclosures. He relates the tale of the movie star Gloria Hilton and her fifth husband, the screenwriter George Murra, who left his wife to be with Hilton. She loses patience with him because he has failed to produce a screenplay for her and because he deeply misses his son, who needs close guidance. Eventually, Gloria Hilton leaves Murra; he reclaims his relationship with his son and returns to his wife. Murra is left with the custom shower door with Hilton's image etched in glass.*

The Goblet (also The Snow Rose and Seventy Times Seven).

Howard Campbell's play, which is stolen by the Soviet plagiarist Stepan Bodovskov and becomes a favorite of Stalin's. Frank Wirtanen reminds Campbell of the plot when he breaks the news to him about George Kraft / Iona Potapov. (MN 35) "A blindingly pure young maiden . . . guards the Holy Grail. She will surrender it only to a knight who is as pure as herself. Such a knight comes along, and is pure enough to win the Grail.

"By winning it, he causes the girl to fall in love with him, and he falls in love with her. . . .

"The knight and the girl—" said Wirtanen, continuing the tale, "they begin to have impure thoughts about each other, tending, involuntarily, to disqualify themselves from any association with the Grail. The heroine urges the hero to flee with the Grail, before he becomes unworthy of it. The hero vows to flee without the Grail, leaving the heroine worthy of continuing to guard it.

"The hero makes their decision for them . . . since they have both become impure in thought. The Holy Grail disappears. And, stunned by this unanswerable proof of their depravity, the two lovers confirm what they firmly believe to be their damnation with a tender night of love.

"The next morning, confident of hell-fire, they promise to give each other so much joy in life that hell-fire will be a very cheap price to pay. The Holy Grail thereupon appears to them, signifying that Heaven does not despise love like theirs. And then the Grail goes away again, forever, leaving the hero and the heroine to live happily ever after."

As a sign of Campbell's success, The Goblet was running in Dresden and Berlin simultaneously, and The Snow Rose was also playing in Berlin. Rather than resting with such good fortune, Campbell finishes Seventy Times Seven *as his other plays continue playing. (MN 9) All three plays were medieval romances, about as political as chocolate éclairs.*

God Bless You, Dr. Kevorkian. *This brief collection of twenty-one fictional interviews is a transcription of ninety-second radio spots Vonnegut wrote and read for airing as part of a fundraising drive for National Public Radio's WNYC. Published by Seven Stories Press in 1999, the premise is to use Dr. Jack Kevorkian's death-inducing machine for Vonnegut's controlled trips down the blue tunnel to the Afterlife. Once there, he conducts a series of interviews with the famous, the infamous, and the seemingly ordinary.*

The only exception to this scheme is Vonnegut's interview with a very much alive Kilgore Trout, also the only interview with a fictitious individual. Vonnegut squeezes in this one "live" subject when Kevorkian has to take a break to attend to his own legal problems. Vonnegut carries on in order not to leave WNYC with dead air.

Vonnegut outlines the premise as resulting from a botched anesthesia during a triple bypass, sending him down the blue tunnel to the Afterlife to the Pearly Gates . . . and then come back to life again (GBK Introduction). Having survived this near-death experience, he gets the agreement of the state of Texas and Dr. Jack Kevorkian to use the Huntsville death chamber for additional near-death experiences to interview selected people who already took their one and only trip down the blue tunnel.

Vonnegut begins by anticipating the usual objections from those who often mistakenly believe he is anti-religion. He pieces together bits of himself often scattered throughout his work in an attempt to define his arms-length relationship with conventional religion, finishing with sentiments that no religious person could deny while invoking (though not by name) the memorable sentiments of Clemens Vonnegut. (GBK Introduction) About belief or lack of belief in an afterlife: Some of you may know I am neither Christian nor Jewish nor Buddhist, nor a conventionally religious person of any sort. I am a humanist, which means, in part, that I have tried to behave decently without any expectation of rewards or punishments after I'm dead. My German-American ancestors, the earliest of whom settled in our Middle West about the time of our Civil War, called themselves "Freethinkers," which is the same sort of thing. My great grandfather Clemens Vonnegut wrote, for example, "If what Jesus said was good, what can it matter whether he was God or not?"

I myself have written, "If it weren't for the message of mercy and pity in Jesus' Sermon on the Mount, I wouldn't want to be a human being. I would just as soon be a rattlesnake."

Despite Vonnegut's disbelief in a mythical Afterlife, he often enjoys joking about it. In a number of cases throughout this book as well as other places, Vonnegut repeats the joke he made at the memorial for science fiction writer, friend, and his predecessor as honorary president of the American Humanists Association, Dr. Isaac Asimov. (GBK Introduction) "Isaac is up in Heaven now." That was the funniest thing I could have said to an audience of humanists. It rolled them in the aisles. Mirth! Several minutes had to pass before something resembling solemnity could be restored.

As for Vonnegut's own sense of what lies beyond this life, he combines the words of his dying sister, Alice, with a thankful acknowledgment that, all in all, he had suffered far fewer indignities than others. (GBK Introduction) My epitaph in any case? "Everything was beautiful. Nothing hurt." I will have gotten off so light, whatever the heck it is that was going on.

Participating in a fundraiser for WNYC is seen as a fit activity for a humanist since the station's mission and its employees (religious or not) contribute to the humanist ideal. (GBK Introduction) Humanists . . . are content to serve as well as they can, the only abstraction with which they have some familiarity: their communities. . . . WNYC satisfies the

people's right to know—as contrasted with, as abject slaves of high-roller publicists and advertisers, keeping the public vacantly diverted and entertained. . . . As I have used it here, "humanist" is nothing more supernatural than a handy synonym for "good citizenship and common decency."

Vonnegut calls on the memory of his famed Uncle Alex to point out that there are plenty of enjoyable moments here on earth—even heavenly—if only we would take a moment of appreciation by remarking out loud, "If this isn't nice, what is?" (GBK Introduction)

His introduction goes on to hit familiar concerns and quips: the need for extended families (using the Ibo tribe as a familiar touchstone); the different needs between the sexes and his assessment that a major cause of divorce is the natural limitations of one individual's relationship with another. (GBK Introduction) When a couple has an argument, they may think it's about money or power or sex, or how to raise the kids, or whatever. What they're really saying to each other, though, without realizing it, is this:

"You are not enough people!"

Vonnegut paints a playful picture of Saint Peter both in the introduction and throughout the interviews. (GBK Introduction) To go through the Pearly Gates, no matter how tempting the interview on the other side, as I myself discovered the hard way, is to run the risk that crotchety Saint Peter, depending on his mood, may never let you out again. Think of how heartbroken your friends and relatives would be if, by going through the Pearly Gates to talk to Napoleon, say, you in effect committed suicide.

Vonnegut begins the introduction hoping that other journalists will follow his lead for interviews down the blue tunnel to the Afterlife. His choice of subjects falls on a scale that broadly includes epitomes of good and evil that one may not have imagined on their own. The number of purely anonymous spirits is encouraging for the depth of their stories. What he seems to want most, however, is for the reader (and fellow writers) to understand the extent of human potential (good and bad) and the epiphanic Uncle Alex moment when we can see the present before us and say, "If this isn't nice, what is?" Appreciating the goodness in life should be ac-

knowledged, evil recognized for its effects, and the Afterlife as purely inconsequential (at least in the eyes of humanists).

Vonnegut's cavalcade meeting him in the blue tunnel to the Afterlife is more akin to Chaucer's pilgrims as described in the General Prologue to the Canterbury Tales. There is a mixture of evil, nobility, piety, and hypocrites to keep one forever wondering about the reaches of human comprehension and motivation.

VONNEGUT'S AFTERLIFE CAVALCADE

The collection's subjects and order of appearance have their own thematic logic, a fairly tight ebb and flow presenting an accounting of Vonnegut's hallmark concerns. The bulleted information below is meant to provide a shorthand understanding of those movements as presented by the order of the interviews. After the bulleted schema is a deeper exploration of Vonnegut's interview subjects (marked with asterisks) focusing on their lives as interpreted through his own philosophical concerns.

- Dr. Ainsworth's interview addresses the most innocent of all in anyone's worldview, those with nothing more than an instinctive need for uncritical and constant loving care: babies.
- Salvatore Biagini's blind heroism for man's best friend is in keeping with Vonnegut's love of animals (dogs especially), while providing political commentary about lives sacrificed for pointless political pursuits.
- Birnum Birnum is the Aboriginal contemporary of Dr. Martin Luther King, Jr. The doubly named Birnum is a model both of human rights activism and of the sad eternal human pursuit of genocide as a colonization tool; and if those attempts fail, the least that will stem from them will be the diminution of indigenous people.
- John Brown's interview provides another portrait of a heroic human rights activist, this one executed by then Colonel Robert E. Lee of the United States Marines, who, of course, would later commit treason by commanding the armies of the Confederacy.
- Interviewing Roberta Gorsuch Burke, the widow of naval legend Admiral Arleigh Burke, is a respectful testament to fidelity, both to one's spouse and to one's commitment to public service.

- Vonnegut then turns from loyalty to spouse and country to broader commitments addressing human rights, civil rights, workers' rights, and opposition to the death penalty. He does so by having the legendary attorney Clarence Darrow seek out Vonnegut's microphone so that he may bless the fairly recent practice of greater media access to court proceedings as a check on the biased or otherwise unjust administration of law.
- Vonnegut's interview with Eugene Victor Debs reasserts his own commitment to social justice while reaffirming the primacy of sentiments found in the Sermon on the Mount (despite his heralded opposition to blind religious faith).
- Reclaimed from expected death followed by a lifelong Edenic love spent exploring the world's great gardens and parks, Harold and Esta Epstein personify Vonnegut's Cat's Cradle description of a duprass: (CC 55) A duprass, Bokonon tells us, is a valuable instrument for gaining and developing, in the privacy of an interminable love affair, insights that are queer but true. The Mintons' cunning exploration of indexes was surely a case in point. A duprass, Bokonon tells us, is also a sweetly conceived establishment. Vonnegut-the-interviewer establishes the idealism of such a relationship in his brief description. It hazards no complexity, no closeted scandals, and bares only the outlines of love in an endless garden.
- Vivian and Vincent Hallinan present a similarly loving couple, but their abiding passion for social justice leads to a series of arrests for his courtroom demeanor and her activities on behalf of civil rights. In 1964, Vivian and her five sons are arrested during a civil rights demonstration. The father purposely remains away from the event to bail out the family. Their leftist politics are supported by the financial fortune Mr. Hallinan amassed during the Great Depression by using his cash (he was not a holder of stocks) to buy apartment buildings in San Francisco. They left a family legacy supporting progressive causes. Their son Terrence Hallinan served as the district attorney of San Francisco (1996–2004) and supported a broad diversity of liberal causes.
- Starkly contrasting with Vivian Hallinan's humanism and her family's struggle for social justice is the troubling interview Vonnegut records

with the most infamous figure in modern history, Adolf Hitler. Hitler asks forgiveness while admitting to nothing more than the possibility that his actions may have indirectly led to the deaths of millions. The pathology of his totalitarian mind (Mother Night) has him identify with the victims of World War II, hoping for the installation of a monument to him at the United Nations complete with a cross indicating his Christian faith and the inscription "Entschuldigen Sie." As Vonnegut translates, "I Beg Your Pardon," or "Excuse Me."

- The John Wesley Joyce interview returns to Vonnegut's concern about the life of the writer. So many of his own narrators are writers or artists that it is natural for him to think about the pairings between those who pursue a creative life with alcohol, one of his own famous habits.

- If alcohol is the fuel of writers, then their success as monogamous lovers is always an unfair measure of their success as human beings. Frances Keane is one such academic and literary artist whose New York Times obituary, noting that her three marriages ended in divorce, strikes Vonnegut as removing the cherry from atop an otherwise beautiful dessert. Her parting words with her interviewer politely tell him to get lost.

- Sir Isaac Newton's interview highlights the scientist's eternal desire to understand the workings of everything, in this case the blue tunnel to the Afterlife. It also draws attention to the inadequacy of religious or purely literary explanations, neat as they may be in a romanticized context. At its core, however, is the very human need to know how things work as well as our inability to know everything.

- Peter Pellegrino was a pioneering military pilot in World War I who eventually turned to a life of silence and wonder among the clouds by becoming an avid hot air balloonist. Unlike Newton, who needed to know the essence of the universe as a way of engineering the future, Pellegrino takes the reverse tack. He simplifies man's experience with the science of flight as a way of touching the sky, knowing heaven in ways almost indescribable but most assuredly only as part of life on earth. His exchange with an eavesdropping, objecting, and interrupting Saint Peter emphasizes that life on

earth is filled with greater wonders than the mysteries of the Afterlife.

- James Earl Ray's interview illustrates that bigotry and mindless hatred are eternal; that killing the messenger does not kill the message; and that Vonnegut sees life everlasting behind the Pearly Gates as a myth, since even history's most heinous actors are welcome. In essence, if evil zealots need fear no final punishment, the living have no hope.

- The great revelation in Vonnegut's Shakespeare interview comes when Saint Peter confirms that there is no Hell. Vonnegut casts Shakespeare as ambiguous in his answers (about his authorship and suspected bisexuality) and disdainful toward his interviewer's use of the midwestern vernacular.

- The final words of Vonnegut's Shakespeare interview repeat Hamlet's famous ontological question To be or not to be. It is not surprising, therefore, that his next interviewee is Mary Wollstonecraft Shelley, author of Frankenstein—or, The Modern Prometheus. For all the humane principles her parents stood for and wrote about, Shelley's creation is the one that poses the question about man's ability to assume the power and responsibility of creation by exploring science without regard to outcomes. This is a constant concern of Vonnegut's throughout his career. Shelley's clarification of the confusion caused by people's erroneously referring to Frankenstein as the monster in effect equates the creator with his creation. As she says, There are two monsters in my story, not one. And one of them, the scientist, is indeed named Frankenstein (GBK Mary Wollstonecraft Shelley). Unbridled scientific application becomes, quite literally, horrifying.

- By contrast, Vonnegut's interview with Dr. Philip Strax illustrates the selflessness and humor of a life dedicated to alerting humanity to early warning signs of our mortality. The inventor of the mammogram and author of three books of poetry (showcasing at times a wise and ribald humor) speaks with Vonnegut just beyond the preening throng of angels hoping for Joe DiMaggio's autograph on their wings. Strax is the kind of ethical scientist who stands in relative anonymity to pop culture figures but whose positive contributions to humanity are far more significant than those of *the legends of sport. As so often happens in life and literature, the painful ironies of life eventually drove him to invent the device that would save millions of lives. It was the death of his wife from breast cancer at the age of thirty-nine that motivated Strax in his research. Strax's resolve in the face of tragedy, while expressing himself humorously through literature, makes him the kind of figure Vonnegut finds admirable and truly heroic.*

- *The innate goodness, talent, and resolve so evident in Dr. Strax are turned on their head in Vonnegut's following interview, with the pickaxe killer Carla (Karla) Faye Tucker. Despite her prison conversion to Christianity (she married her prison chaplain), she was a killer born to all the disadvantages predicted by poverty, parental strife, and prepubescent drug use with elders. Vonnegut's interview with Tucker takes place before she even gets to the Pearly Gates, since her execution on February 3, 1998, precedes his own Kevorkian-guided trip by only two hours. Resolved to go to God and bear judgment, she is displeased to learn from Vonnegut that there is no Hell, since she would gladly go there if it also meant taking the Texas governor with her for denying her clemency. She claimed that he, too, was a murderer—hers. That governor was George W. Bush, who would later draw Vonnegut's constant ire when he became president.*

- *Vonnegut's interview with his literary alter ego, Kilgore Trout, puts yet another metafictional twist on an already metafictional premise. Presented as the only interview in the series with a living person, it is therefore not held in the blue tunnel to the Afterlife. Dr. Kevorkian has his own legal troubles, so Vonnegut substitutes this Trout interview to continue his fundraising efforts on behalf of WNYC. Trout's speech addresses the wholesale physical destruction of society through the revival of ethnic cleansing: nothing more than homicidal xenophobic paranoia. Trout compares this trend with the efficiency of genetic mutations in human disease: As is now the case with Mycobacterium tuberculosis, there is a new strain of the ethnic-cleansing bacterium that makes conceivable remedies of the past seem pathetic or even absurd. In every case nowadays: Too late! The victims are practically all dead or homeless*

by the time they are first mentioned on the six o'clock news.

Trout's only response is similar to his take on the resumption of free will in Timequake: *Take care of the living—and beware the myth makers who too often lead us into contemptible actions. All that good people can do about the disease of ethnic cleansing, now always a* fait accompli, *is to rescue the survivors. And watch out for Christians!*

- *If interviewing Kilgore Trout gives Vonnegut the opportunity to mouth off once again about genocides, the unrelenting myth-based vendettas that destroy people and the hallmarks of civilization, then his parting interview with Isaac Asimov helps explain the positive channels Vonnegut (and Asimov) employ to remain true to themselves and their human-first agenda. As Asimov says, "If I couldn't write all the time, this would be hell for me. Earth would have been a hell for me if I couldn't write all the time. Hell itself would be bearable for me, as long as I could write all the time."*

Asimov continues to add to his oeuvre even from behind the Pearly Gates, remaining reverently humanistic in his topic, a six-volume set about cockamamie Earthling beliefs in the Afterlife.

For both Asimov and Vonnegut, writing offers an escape from the hell of other people, the myth makers who rule our lives, the pious who use religion as a club. The seclusion of writing, its self-imposed isolation, is the writer's only refuge when faced with the inhumanity of others.

The interviews within God Bless You, Dr. Kevorkian:

Dr. Mary D. Ainsworth

Vonnegut begins his series of interviews by focusing on the most innocent souls of all, those who happen to die as babies. He weaves a tapestry based on the very significant work of the developmental psychologist Dr. Mary D. Ainsworth and his own romantic fantasy.

Ainsworth's long career (she remained active until her death at the age of eighty-five) examines the bonding (or lack thereof) between mother and child in the first year of life. Vonnegut ends his interview with the good doctor having learned the comforting fact that in the Afterlife, babies who die are the source of all the angels in the world. Moreover, upon their arrival at the Pearly Gates, they are well cared for and bond quickly with surrogate mothers (or their own if also deceased).

Though such fabrication in Cat's Cradle would be declared foma, Vonnegut (the author—not the interviewer) provides a very comforting myth that respects and extends the primary importance of a nurturing environment.

Salvatore Biagini

The retired seventy-year-old Queens construction worker suffered a fatal heart attack while saving his schnauzer, Teddy, from certain death in the jaws of Chele, a neighborhood pit bull. Biagini's interview from the Afterlife is notable for his comfort with the meaning of his death, as he explains to Vonnegut. I asked this historic pet lover how it felt to have died for a schnauzer named Teddy. **Salvador Biagini** was philosophical. He said it sure as heck beat dying for absolutely nothing in the Viet Nam War.

Birnum Birnum

Welcomed to heaven by Louis Armstrong leading a New Orleans brass band, Birnum Birnum, an Australian Aborigine from Tasmania, is heralded for helping gain the independence of his people in 1967. As Vonnegut writes, the Aborigines and Tasmanians had the simplest and most primitive cultures of any people then on Earth. They were regarded as vermin, with no more minds and souls than rats, say. They were shot; they were poisoned. Only in 1967, practically the day before yesterday, were the surviving Australian Aborigines granted citizenship, thanks to demonstrations led by **Birnum Birnum**. He was the first of his people to attend law school.

There were no survivors on Tasmania. I asked him for a sound bite about the Tasmanians to take back to WNYC. He said they were victims of the only completely successful genocide of which we know.

John Brown

Vonnegut follows the Birnum interview with that of another civil rights activist, the martyred American abolitionist John Brown, who argues Thomas Jefferson was an evil man as measured by his own words within the Declaration of Independence.

Brown's heavenly attire is as he left the world, wearing a hangman's noose for a necktie. When asked by his interviewer about it, Brown says he expects all saved souls to exhibit such garb, much as religious penitents bear their faith for all to see. His eyes were glowing like coins. "Without shedding of blood," he said, "there is no remission of sin." It turns out that's in the New Testament, Hebrews 9:22.

I congratulated him on what he'd said on his way to be hanged before a gleeful, jeering throng of white folks. I quote: "This is a beautiful country." In only five words, he had somehow encapsulated the full horror of the most hideous legal atrocities committed by a civilized nation until the Holocaust.

Brown earned his noose for his famous 1859 attack on the armory at Harper's Ferry, and his military executioner was then Colonel Robert E. Lee of the United States Marines. At the head of a force of only eighteen other anti-slavery fanatics, he captured the virtually unguarded Federal Armory at Harper's Ferry, Virginia. His plan? To pass out weapons to slaves, so they could overthrow their masters. Suicide.

Law-abiding citizens opened fire from all sides, killing eight of his men, two of them his sons.

Vonnegut sees the fervor and sincerity in Brown, who likewise looks into the words of Jefferson and sees a prophet. He said there was a Virginian, Thomas Jefferson, who had actually encapsulated God in only six words: "All men are created equal." (Math does not count. This is Vonnegut's text.) Brown goes on to cast Jefferson's paradox. "This perfect gentleman, sophisticated, scientific, wise," **John Brown** went on, "was able to write those incomparable sacred words while owning slaves. Tell me: Am I really the only person to realize that he, by his example, made our beautiful country an evil society from the very first, where subservience of persons of color to white people was deemed in perfect harmony with the natural law?"

"I want to get this straight," I said. "Are you saying that Thomas Jefferson, possibly our country's most beloved founding father, after George Washington, was an evil man?"

"Let that, while my body lies a-molderin' in the grave," said **John Brown**, "be my truth which goes marchin' on."

Vonnegut-the-interviewer recalls that as Brown finishes his remarks, a heavenly chorus sings a stanza of "The Battle Hymn of the Republic."

Roberta Gorsuch Burke

Mrs. Burke's official obituary lists her as a "Navy legend" who was "affectionately known as 'the first lady of the United States Navy.'" Vonnegut correctly cites her epitaph at the bottom of the headstone marking both her and her husband's graves. She died last January at the age of ninety-eight. Admiral Burke, by then retired of course, died a year before that at the age of ninety-nine. They met on a blind date in 1919, when he was in his first year at the Naval Academy. On that date, she was a last minute substitute for her older sister. Fate.

They married four years later. If past performance is any indication, they will surely stay married there at the far end of the blue tunnel throughout all eternity. She said to me, "Why fool around?" President Clinton told her at her husband's funeral, when she still had a year to live, "You have blessed America with your service and set an example not only for navy wives today, and to come, but for all Americans."

The simple epitaph **Roberta Gorsuch Burke** *chose for her tombstone here on Earth: "A Sailor's Wife."*

Among other notable military assignments, Admiral Burke served on President Kennedy's Bay of Pigs Study Group. Vonnegut creates a familiar diminutive out of Admiral Burke's first name, Arly, though the actual spelling is Arleigh. Despite his legendary naval record, his own epitaph is simply "Sailor."

Clarence Darrow

Vonnegut recalls that his fifteenth pursuit of an interview is a bit different from the others. The legendary defense attorney (and one of Vonnegut's all-time heroes) Clarence Darrow goes looking for Vonnegut because he wants WNYC's listeners to hear his opinions of television cameras in courtrooms. He goes on to explain why he is so encouraged by media presence in the courtroom: "The presence of those cameras finally acknowledges," he said to me, "that justice systems anywhere, anytime, have never cared whether justice was achieved or not. Like Roman games, justice systems are ways for unjust governments—and there is no other sort of government—to be enormously entertaining with real lives at stake."

Vonnegut goes on to thank Mr. Darrow for having made American history much more humane than it would have been otherwise, with his eloquent defenses . . . of early organizers of labor unions, of teachers of unpopular scientific truths, and for his vociferous contempt for racism, and for his loathing of the death penalty. And the late, great lawyer **Clarence Darrow** *said only this to me: "I did my best to entertain."*

Eugene Victor Debs

Unlike Clarence Darrow, who sought out Vonnegut, Debs waits at the far end of the blue tunnel for Vonnegut's arrival, as the author requested through Saint Peter. Vonnegut notes here and elsewhere that the Hoosier from Terre Haute is a particular hero of mine. This five-time Socialist Party presidential candidate is responsible for one of Vonnegut's most often repeated and heartfelt sentiments (also the epigraph to Hocus Pocus): As long as there is a lower class, I am in it. As long as there is a criminal element, I am of it. As long as there is a soul in prison, I am not free.

Hearing Vonnegut quote his own words back to him prompts Debs to ask how those words were received here on Earth in America nowadays. I said they were ridiculed. "People snicker and snort," I said. He asked what our fastest growing industry was. "The building of prisons," I said.

"What a shame," he said. And then he asked me how the Sermon on the Mount was going over these days. And then he spread his wings and flew away.

Harold Epstein

Vonnegut paints a touching portrait of a rare couple, Harold and Esta Epstein of Larchmont, New York. At the time of the interview, only Harold had passed through the blue tunnel to the Afterlife at the age of ninety-four. Thirty-four years earlier, the certified public accountant had suffered a heart attack. The couple took to gardening for therapy. These two love birds, **Harold** and **Esta Epstein**, traveled around the world four times, seeking, and often finding, wonderful new plants for American gardens, although neither one of them had any formal training as a horticulturalist. At the time **Harold**'s soul traded his old flesh for new flesh in Heaven, he was president emeritus of the American Rock Garden Society, the Greater New York Orchid Society, and the Northeast Region of the American Rhododendron Society.

When asked for some parting words to offer the WNYC *listeners,* He *said,* "My only regret is that everybody couldn't be as happy as we were." The late **Harold Epstein** said that the first thing he did after he got to Heaven, after picking a flower he'd never seen before, was to thank God for the priceless gift of garden insanity.

Vivian Hallinan

If the Epsteins present an idyllic idealization of a love tightly binding two people to each other and to nature, Vivian and Vincent Hallinan are similarly bonded to each other, but their external passion is the welfare of others. So moved is Vonnegut by reading Vivian's inspiring New York Times *obituary that he opens his WNYC interview declaring that* today I fell in love with a dead woman! Her name is **Vivian Hallinan**.

According to Vonnegut's effusive summary of her obituary, her husband built a real estate fortune during the Great Depression by purchasing apartment buildings in San Francisco. However, it is what they did with their money in politics that causes Vonnegut to fall in love. Vivian abides by a similar philosophy to that of Eugene Victor Debs, one of Vonnegut's heroes, but she has the money to support her causes. So while Vincent, the 1952 Progressive Party presidential candidate, a leftist lawyer and avowed socialist, went to jail for his obstreperous defense of labor leader Harry Bridges . . . accused of being a Communist during the McCarthy era, *Vivian involved herself in a series of diverse social causes. Arrested for marching in a civil rights demonstration in 1964, she was accompanied to jail by her five sons, who had participated in the demonstration as well. Her husband waited outside the jail with bail. Nearly twenty years later she funneled money to the Nicaraguan Sandinistas.*

Vonnegut closes his admiring interview with Vivian with this remembrance of her in the blue tunnel. **Vivian Hallinan** *has chosen to be eternally twenty-four, an utter knockout! I asked her how she felt about being called "colorful." She said she would rather have been called what Franklin D. Roosevelt was called by his enemies: "A traitor to her class."*

Adolf Hitler

As brief as all these interviews are (ninety-second spoken format), the Hitler interview disturbs for various reasons, including the very idea of Hitler in heaven and his request to be remembered with a monument bearing a cross to indicate his Christian background. Vonnegut has Hitler deliver an empty, no-fault, modern-day political apology intended to express remorse for the "possibility" that his actions may have been wrong, and if so, he certainly did not intend for all those millions to die. I was gratified to learn that he now feels remorse for any actions of his, however indirectly, which might have had anything to do with the violent deaths suffered by thirty-five million people during World War II.

Hitler goes on to make it seem as if both he and Eva Braun were also victims caught up in the catastrophe of World War II. "I paid my dues along with everybody else," *he said.* He closes his remarks to Vonnegut by relating a dream that indicates just how pathologically dissociative he is. This is reminiscent of Vonnegut's description of the totalitarian mind in Mother Night: It is his hope that a modest monument, possibly a stone cross, since he was a Christian, will be erected somewhere in his memory, possibly on the grounds of the United Nations headquarters in New York. . . . Underneath should be a two-word sentence in German: "Entschuldigen Sie."

Roughly translated into English, this comes out, "I Beg Your Pardon," or "Excuse Me."

John Wesley Joyce

In one of the briefest of all the interviews, Vonnegut turns to speak with John Wesley Joyce, owner of the Lion's Head Bar in Greenwich Village, famed for being in its time (1966–1996) the country's most famous hangout for heavy-drinking, non-stop-talking writers in America. One wag described the clientele as "drinkers with writing problems." This is an old line about writers in the twentieth century, perhaps most famously attributed to the Irish poet Brendan Behan.

The Joyce interview refocuses Vonnegut on the act of writing, the development of intellect, and the pursuit of self-expression.

Frances Keane

Celebrated by Vonnegut for her noted expertise as a romance languages expert and writer of children's books, *succumbing to pancreatic cancer at the age of eighty-five. Vonnegut is troubled by the implications left open by the language of her* New York Times *obituary.* It seemed to me that her generally laudatory obit in the *New York Times* cut her off at the knees at the very end with this stark sentence: "Her three marriages ended in divorce." *When Vonnegut asks about the short shrift given to her marital life, Keane answers with indifference and indignation—in three languages.*

"Así es la vida," she said.

"C'é la vita," she said.

"C'est la vie," she said.

And then: "Go fly a kite!"

Sir Isaac Newton

Ever curious, Sir Isaac Newton turns the tables on his interviewer. He wants to know from Vonnegut about the composition of the blue tunnel to the Afterlife. Before that question, however, Vonnegut notes that this is not the first time he has gone down the tunnel and noticed Newton. Both Newton and Saint Peter hang out at the Heaven end of the blue tunnel of the Afterlife. Saint Peter is there because that's his job. **Sir Isaac** *is there because of his insatiable curiosity about what the blue tunnel is, how the blue tunnel works.*

After Vonnegut briefly lists Newton's many achievements, the great scientist's ego gets the better of him. He can't forgive himself for having left it to Darwin to come up with the theory of evolution, to Pasteur to come up with the germ theory, and to Albert Einstein to come up with relativity. "I must have been deaf, dumb, and blind not to have come up with those myself," he said to me. "What could have been more obvious?"

Returning to the subject of the tunnel's composition, Vonnegut is at a loss to provide a satisfactory answer, and Saint Peter is quick to offer an equally unsatisfactory answer. I tell him that it's made of whatever dreams are made of, which leaves him monumentally unsatisfied.

Saint Peter quoted Shakespeare to him: There are more things in Heaven and Earth, Horatio, than are dreamt of in your philosophy.

Peter Pellegrino

The founder of the Balloon Federation of America and first American to balloon across the Alps, Pellegrino's enthusiasm for the sport has him urging Vonnegut to try it before he dies. For the intrepid balloonist, floating on clouds is his idea of heaven. (GBK Peter Pellegrino) "For God's sake, man—get a tank of propane and a balloon while you've still got time, or you'll never know what Heaven is!"

Saint Peter is none too happy with Pellegrino, insisting "this is Heaven!" *The guardian at the Pearly Gates is included in this interview because Vonnegut is no longer allowed through the gates for his interviews. He is warned that the next time he passes the gates will be his last.*

Saint Peter shows a sense of sarcastic humor in addressing both his uninspired resident, Pellegrino, and Vonnegut. Pellegrino goes for the last word in this exchange. Saint Peter said to me, "Not only do you still have time to go ballooning. You might also write a book with the title, 'Heaven and Its Discontents.'" He said to **Pellegrino**, ironically of course, "If you'd had crack cocaine on Earth, I suppose Heaven would also be a disappointment."

"Bingo!" said **Pellegrino**.

Pellegrino closes the interview waxing rhapsodic about the wonder of ballooning after his experiences with military aviation. "But I felt like an invader, an alien up there, tearing up the sky with my propellers, dirtying it up with my noise and exhaust," he went on. "I didn't go up in a balloon until I was thirty-five. That was a dream come true. That was Heaven, and I was still alive.

"I became the sky."

James Earl Ray

Whereas Vonnegut's interview with Adolf Hitler reveals a psychopathic mass murderer who finds remorse only by identifying himself among the victims of World War II, James Earl Ray is further embit-

tered that the results of his evil ran counter to what he had hoped. In assassinating the Reverend Dr. Martin Luther King, Jr., Ray did not realize the civil rights movement and his words would advance as far as they have. He killed the messenger, not the message. Vonnegut recalls, He said he never would have shot "the big n," meaning Dr. King, if he'd known the bullet would make what "the big n" said and fought for so effing famous all over the effing world. "Because of me," he said, "little white children are being taught that 'the big n' was some kind of American hero, like George effing Washington. Because of my little old bullet," he said, "the shit 'the big n' said has been carved into marble monuments and inlaid with effing gold, I hear."

Ray refuses to pass through the Pearly Gates until he can be guaranteed a prison cell. If not a sign of his acclimation to institutionalization, perhaps this is a sign of his sense of guilt for inadvertently advancing the cause of civil rights. He never fully explains.

Although Ray refuses to enter Life Everlasting, Saint Peter still has to put up with an earful of his dreadful racism. In another sign that either Saint Peter has a sense of humor or that Vonnegut-the-interviewer liberally paraphrases, this is how we are to understand the strains put on the eternal guardian of the Afterlife: His conversation is still liberally sprinkled with the "n" word for African-Americans, despite Saint Peter's pleas that he, for the love of God, pipe the hell down.

William Shakespeare

Vonnegut's interview with Shakespeare is both humbling and revelatory. Vonnegut's naturally self-deprecating assessment takes a further beating from Shakespeare's disdain. The particular midwestern voice Vonnegut has always been proud to claim is laid low by the Bard. We did not hit it off. He said the dialect I spoke was the ugliest English he had ever heard, "fit to split the ears of groundlings." He asked if it had a name, and I said, "Indianapolis."

After being rejected for congratulating Shakespeare on the Oscar-winning movie Shakespeare in Love (declaring both the Oscars and Romeo and Juliet to be "A tale told by an idiot, full of sound and fury, signifying nothing"), Vonnegut presses two unsettled issues: the truth of his authorship and his sexuality.

Shakespeare's responses to both instances are ambiguous and treated sarcastically by Vonnegut. I asked him point-blank if he had written all the plays and poems for which he'd been given credit. "That which we call a rose by any other name would smell as sweet," he said. "Ask Saint Peter!" Which I would do.

I asked him if he had love affairs with men as well as women, knowing how eager my WNYC audience was to have this matter settled. His answer, however, celebrated affection between animals of any sort:

"We were as twinn'd lambs that did frisk in the sun, and bleat the one at the other: what we chang'd was innocence for innocence." By changed he meant exchanged: "What we exchanged was innocence for innocence." That has to be the softest core pornography I ever heard.

And he was through with me. In effect, he told your reporter to go screw himself. "Get thee to a nunnery!" he said, and off he went. . . . The beaut about exchanging innocence for innocence was from The Winter's Tale.

The revelation within this interview comes from Saint Peter, not Shakespeare: there is no eternal punishment. I at least remembered to ask Saint Peter if **Shakespeare** had written **Shakespeare**. He told me that nobody arriving in Heaven, and there was no Hell, had claimed authorship for any of it. Saint Peter added, "Nobody, that is, who was willing to submit to my lie-detector test."

Vonnegut signs off the interview humorously acknowledging his own value before the Bard while also raising the eternal ontological question. This is your tongue-tied, humiliated, self-loathing, semi-literate Hoosier hack Kurt Vonnegut, signing off with this question for today: "To be or not to be?"

Mary Wollstonecraft Shelley

If Vonnegut is overly deferential to Shakespeare, he is in genuine awe of the literary heritage and creativity of the mother of modern science fiction, Mary Wollstonecraft Shelley, author of Frankenstein—or, The Modern Prometheus. Vonnegut offers perspective for those unfamiliar with the depth of her creation, noting that although not quite twenty, [she] published an idea as persistent in the minds of thinking people today as Pasteur's germ theory, say, or Darwin's theory of evolution, or Malthus's dread of overpopulation.

In praising Mary's parents' legacy, Vonnegut takes note of her mother's seminal publication, A Vindication of the Rights of Woman: Her most passionate subject: the right of women to be treated as the equals of men.

As for her father, William Godwin, Vonnegut recounts that he was an anti-Calvinist preacher who wrote, most memorably, "God himself has no right to be a tyrant." The echo of Saint Peter's words in the previous interview coincide with Godwin's sentiments.

As for Mary Shelley's great masterpiece, Vonnegut has nothing but the highest praise for her vision and treatment of Shakespeare's ontological question in the previous interview. I spoke in Heaven today to **Mary Wollstonecraft Shelley**, author, again before she was twenty, of the most prescient and influential science fiction novel of all times: *Frankenstein: Or the Modern Prometheus.* That was in 1818, a full century before the end of the First World War—with its Frankensteinian inventions of poison gas, tanks and airplanes, flame throwers and land mines, and barbed-wire entanglements everywhere.

Vonnegut tries to pose a similar question to Shelley as was pursued by the narrator of Cat's Cradle, *John/Jonah, who wants to ask the Hoenikkers what old man Hoenikker was doing on the day the atomic bomb was dropped. In this case,Vonnegut hoped to get* **Mary Shelley***'s opinions of the atomic bombs we dropped on the unarmed men, women, and children of Hiroshima and Nagasaki—and promise to try again. She ignores the question and instead speaks only about family and friends.*

Shelley avoids speculating about events she never saw come to pass. She instead offers a correction to a common confusion, the conundrum caused by the eponymous title. Vonnegut begins by prompting Shelley. I said many ignorant people nowadays thought "Frankenstein" was the name of the monster, and not of the scientist who created him.

She said, "That's not so ignorant after all. There are two monsters in my story, not one. And one of them, the scientist, is indeed named Frankenstein."

Dr. Philip Strax

Vonnegut's next interview subject illustrates the flip side of Shelley's jaundiced view of man's dominion over creation. Rather than using advancing scientific technology without a clear and useful purpose, and without regard to outcomes, Dr. Philip Strax models the practical application of science in addressing our painful mortality without redefining man's place in the great chain of being.

Vonnegut's portrait of Dr. Strax is framed by the doctor's ribald literary humor while emphasizing his relative anonymity through the happenstance of sharing Joe DiMaggio's death date. Vonnegut speaks to Dr. Strax without notice by others, overlooked by the throng of agitated angels vying to have their wings autographed by the Yankee Clipper.

The relatively unknown three volumes of poetry penned by Dr. Strax (certainly more a personal triumph than a hitting streak shared by millions of fans) and his nearly anonymous creation of the mammogram is news to the common reader—though its consequences for the health of women is legendary and more widely known than the legends of sport.

But all this belies the pain that drove Dr. Strax's medical inventiveness. Though himself a radiologist, he lost his wife to breast cancer when she was only thirty-nine. He thereafter dedicated his efforts toward the early radiological detection of this life-threatening disease. He did so with humor and wisdom penned in verse throughout a long and successful life—however anonymous he may appear next to Joltin' Joe.

Vonnegut praises the good doctor's literary efforts by quoting the following.

'Tis better to have love and lust
Than let our apparatus rust.

Let us remind our poor men folk in deed
   and song:
There are two types of men in this womanly
   world:
Those who know they are weak,
Those who think they are strong.

Carla Faye Tucker

(Commonly misspelled. Her birth name is Karla.) Vonnegut launches down the blue tunnel only hours after pickaxe killer Carla Faye Tucker's execution, interviewing her before she learns the secrets beyond

the Pearly Gates. She enters the blue tunnel having been denied clemency by the governor, having long accepted Jesus as her Lord and Savior, having married her prison chaplain: still, a killer born to all the disadvantages predicted by poverty, parental strife, and prepubescent drug use with her elders.

Tucker was never loved enough to have someone care about the options that should have been open to her as a young innocent. She certainly never had the preparation for life that allowed Dr. Strax to overcome his tragedies, to have a comically humane way of looking at ourselves. For Carla Faye, her refocused religiosity comes too late and is not appreciated as genuine by the born-again Christian, recovering alcohol and cocaine abuser, then Texas governor George W. Bush.

Tucker has no fear of burning forever in the Afterlife because she is prepared for any final judgment, provided it is the same hellish end for the governor. I caught up with **Carla Faye** in the tunnel, about a hundred fifty yards from the far end, near the Pearly Gates. Since she was dragging her feet, I hastened to assure her that there was no Hell waiting for her, no Hell waiting for anyone. She said that was too bad because she would be glad to go to Hell if only she could take the governor of Texas with her. "He's a murderer, too," said **Carla Faye**. "He murdered me."

Kilgore Trout

As Vonnegut nears the end of his postmortem journalism due to Dr. Kevorkian's own legal troubles, he uses these last two interviews for expressions that are closest to the core of his own experiences and narrative concerns. The first of the two puts still more metafictional twists into a set of interviews that is already metafictional. It is also the only interview in the series with a person said to still be alive, Vonnegut's alter ego, Kilgore Trout, and held on terra firma rather than in the blue tunnel.

As Kilgore Trout's dental plate continually drops out of place, garbling his words beyond direct transcription for anyone who wasn't there, Vonnegut takes it upon himself to synthesize Trout's words from memory and the poor-quality tape. Vonnegut's creation, Kilgore Trout, is quoted by Vonnegut as an independent authority. Perhaps this is Vonnegut comically telling us in other words, "You had to be there."

When prompted for a comment about Kosovo, Serbia, Trout takes off on a diatribe for nearly two pages, all of which Vonnegut says he is repeating in his own voice owing to the garbled nature of the tape. What follows is an indictment against:

• the wholesale destruction of civilian structures and cities. The infrastructure of the Serb tyranny should have been left unharmed in order to support justice and sanity, should they return. All cities and even little towns are world assets. For NATO to make one unliveable is to cut off its nose to spite its face, so to speak.

• the historic trending of ethnic cleansing that is proceeding at an ever more rapid pace due to our scientific developments and mental deficiencies. The homicidal paranoia and schizophrenia of ethnic cleansing does its worst quickly now, almost instantly, like a tidal wave or volcano or earthquake—in Rwanda and now Kosovo, and who knows where else? The disease used to take years. One thinks of the Europeans killing off the Aborigines in the Western Hemisphere, and in Australia and Tasmania, and the Turks' elimination of Armenians from their midst—of course the Holocaust, which ground on and on from 1933 to 1945. The Tasmanian genocide, incidentally, is the only one of which I've heard which was one-hundred-percent successful. Nobody on the face of the Earth has a native Tasmanian as a forebear!

Trout (through Vonnegut) finishes with the only remaining humanist's response to the chaos of man's own myth making, one that focuses on people while rejecting faith in a deity as a solution. All that good people can do about the disease of ethnic cleansing, now always a *fait accompli,* is to rescue the survivors. And watch out for Christians!

Isaac Asimov

Dr. Jack Kevorkian's legal troubles bring Vonnegut's career as a postmortem journalist to an end, but not before one last Afterlife interview, this time with his good friend Isaac Asimov. With irony Vonnegut notes the obvious about his work with Kevorkian (This purported murderer has saved my life more than a dozen times!) and his loving humanist's sarcastic joke in presenting Asimov. Forgive my mixed emotions, then, as I mourn the misery of one friend, Jack, who is still alive, while rejoicing in the relative well-being of another—**Isaac Asimov**, who died of kidney and heart failure, age seventy-two, eight years ago.

Vonnegut lauds the many accomplishments of the Russian-born, Brooklyn-raised Ph.D. chemist from Columbia University (certainly fitting the mold Kurt Vonnegut, Sr., and older brother Bernard planned for Kurt Jr.) whose lifelong bibliography totals more than five hundred books. These weren't only prize-winning science-fiction. Many were scholarly popularizations of Shakespeare and biochemistry and ancient Greek history, and the Bible and relativity, and on and on. *When prompted, Asimov asserts that he is still writing:* "All the time! If I couldn't write all the time, this would be hell for me. Earth would have been a hell for me if I couldn't write all the time. Hell itself would be bearable for me, as long as I could write all the time."

Though Vonnegut informs Asimov that there is no Hell, Asimov tries to end the conversation by telling Vonnegut that he has to get back to writing his latest work, a six-volume set about cockamamie Earthling beliefs in the Afterlife.

Their final banter explains why Asimov was able to be so productive (aside from having something to say). **Isaac Asimov** replied with but a single word: "Escape." And then he appended a famous statement by the similarly prolific French writer Jean-Paul Sartre:

"Hell is other people."

For both authors, writing offers an escape from the hell of other people. Like Asimov, Vonnegut continued writing long past the time he said anyone his age would produce a masterpiece. His practice, his insistence on writing well past the time he said he would or should may be explained by the order produced in his own brain in response to the cacophony of cruel, domineering myths.

God Bless You, Mr. Rosewater (subtitled *Pearls Before Swine;* 1965) (*see also* **Eliot Rosewater, Kilgore Trout, Samaritrophia, uncritical love**). *Eliot Rosewater seeks to reestablish communal ties in his ancestral home (Rosewater County) not by pitting people or ideologies in opposition to each other as in* Cat's Cradle, *but by providing for people's needs as they ask for assistance. And unlike* Player Piano's *insistence that man continually step back from labor because of automation's economy and a desire to avoid the drudgery of repetitious and menial activities, Eliot sees the need for human participation in production if for no other reason than it keeps people involved with living. Kilgore Trout comes to Eliot's aid and phrases Eliot's views in ways that even Senator Rosewater understands.* (GBR 14) "Poverty is a relatively mild disease for even a very flimsy American soul, but uselessness will kill strong and weak souls alike, and kill every time.

"We must find a cure."

At the close of Cat's Cradle, *the history Bokonon advises John/Jonah to write would deny the cosmic paternalism of religion and, by implication, any benevolent constructions designed by man. Considering Eliot by this measure, we are left with a series of magnanimous gestures, yet we have to doubt the efficacy of his paternalism. Without direction and foresight, the rich orphans of Rosewater County could be as dangerous as Felix Hoenikker or as degenerate as the idle rich in Pisquontuit. As a literary product of the mid-1960s, Rosewater's backdrop appears to concern itself with an historical guilt among the "haves" in relation to the "have-nots." Bequeathing gobs of money to the poor doesn't settle the more pressing problem of uselessness (as evidenced by Vonnegut's satire of the wealthy on Cape Cod).*

Goebbels, Paul Joseph. *In* Mother Night, *Reichsleiter Dr. Paul Joseph Goebbels, Head of the German Ministry of Popular Enlightenment and Propaganda, is also Howard Campbell's boss. It is Goebbels's idea to have Campbell write "The Last Full Measure" (whose title is taken from Lincoln's Gettysburg Address), a pageant in honor of the German soldiers who lost their lives in the Jewish uprising in the Warsaw Ghetto. The project is abandoned before Campbell can complete it.*

In Timequake, *Goebbels and his family play a central role in Kilgore Trout's short story "Bunker Bingo Party." His children teach Hitler and the others to play bingo while taking refuge in Hitler's Berlin bunker. This happens moments before Hitler marries Eva Braun and their dual suicide.*

Gokubi. *The first generation of simultaneous language translators invented by Zenji Hiroguchi, an employee of Matsumoto in Galápagos. Capable of translating ten languages, Gokubi was eventually succeeded by Mandarax.*

The Golden House of the Roman Emperor Nero. *The Tralfamadorians use their Universal Will to Become to send messages concerning the status of the replacement part for Salo's spaceship. The messages are conveyed in great architectural monuments on Earth that could be monitored by Salo. (ST 12)* **The Golden House of the Roman Emperor Nero** *meant: "We are doing the best we can."*

"Golden Wedding." *Another of the Kilgore Trout stories in* Timequake *rescued from the trash receptacle outside the American Academy of Arts and Letters by security guard Dudley Prince. "Golden Wedding" provides a new concept of time as proposed by a commercially minded couple. (TQ 24)* I thank Trout for the concept of the man-woman hour as a unit of measurement of marital intimacy. This is an hour during which a husband and wife are close enough to be aware of each other, and for one to say something to the other without yelling, if he or she feels like it. Trout says in his story **"Golden Wedding"** that they needn't feel like saying anything in order to credit themselves with a man-woman hour.

"Golden Wedding" is another story Dudley Prince rescues from the trash receptacle before the timequake. It is about a florist who tries to increase his business by convincing people who both work at home, or who spend long hours together running a Ma-and-Pa joint, that they are entitled to celebrate several wedding anniversaries a year.

He calculates that an average couple with separate places of work logs four man-woman hours each weekday, and sixteen of them on weekends. Being sound asleep with each other doesn't count. This gives him a standard man-woman week of thirty-six man-woman hours.

He multiplies that by fifty-two. This gives him, when rounded off, a standard man-woman year of eighteen hundred man-woman hours. He advertises that any couple that has accumulated this many man-woman hours is entitled to celebrate an anniversary, and to receive flowers and appropriate presents, even if it took them only twenty weeks to do it!

If couples keep piling up man-woman hours like that, as my wives and I have done in both my marriages, they can easily celebrate their Ruby Anniversary in only twenty years, and their Golden in twenty-five!

Goldwater, Barry. *In "The Hyannis Port Story," reprinted in* Welcome to the Monkey House *(1968), the Rumfoord estate has a garishly displayed portrait of Barry Goldwater facing the Kennedy family compound.* On a second-floor balcony was a huge portrait of **Barry Goldwater**. It had bicycle reflectors in the pupils of its eyes. Those eyes stared right through the Kennedy gate. There were floodlights all around it, so I could tell it was lit up at night. And the floodlights were rigged with blinkers.

Golgotha (*see also* **Calvary Cemetery**). *The site of Jesus Christ's crucifixion (SL5 6)* Billy dozed, awakened in the prison hospital again. The sun was high. Outside were **Golgotha** sounds of strong men digging holes for upright timbers in hard, hard ground. Englishmen were building themselves a new latrine. They had abandoned their old latrine to the Americans—and their theater, the place where the feast had been held, too.
(JB 18) As for the last days of Sacco and Vanzetti as a modern Passion: As on **Golgotha**, three lower-class men were executed at the same time by a state. This time, though, not just one of the three was innocent. This time two of the three were innocent.

Gömbos, Miklós (*see* **Boone**).

Gomburg, Crowther. *The author of* Primordial Scales, *a chronicle of Noel Constant's Magnum Opus, Inc., predicates his text on the notion that Magnum Opus was a product of a complex of inabilities to love. Reading between the lines of* **Gomburg***'s book, it is increasingly clear that* **Gomburg** *is himself unloved and unable to love (ST 3).*

The Goober Gossip. *The privately published newspaper for those in the extended family of Peanuts.*

(*Slap* 37) There were editorials calling for family health insurance programs and sports teams and so on. There was one interesting essay, I remember, either in *The Daffy-nition* or **The Goober Gossip**, which said that families with high moral standards were the best maintainers of law and order, and that police departments could be expected to fade away.

goofballs (*see* **Combat Respiratory Rations**).

Gooz. *A central character in Kilgore Trout's* The Barring-gaffner of Bagnialto, or This Year's Masterpiece, *Gooz is a cobbler who paints a picture of his cat, offers it to the Barring-gaffner, and through the luck of the wheel, the painting is valued at one billion dollars.* (BC 14) The Barring-gaffner awarded **Gooz** a check for that amount, most of which was taken back at once by the tax collector. The picture was given a place of honor in the National Gallery, and people lined up for miles for a chance to see a painting worth a billion dollars.

Göring, Reichsmarschall Hermann. Jailbird's *Walter Starbuck records that he and Ruth were married on October* 15, 1946 *(and he assumes that was the day they conceived their one child), the same day Reichsmarschall Hermann Göring committed suicide.*

Gorky, Arshile (1904–1948). (*Blue* 36) "Yup," I said. "We were extricating ourselves from Happy Valley, and returning to real life. The melancholy roll-call of real-life suicides among the Abstract Expressionists again: (*Arshile*) **Gorky** by hanging in 1948, Pollock and then almost immediately Kitchen, by drunken driving and then pistol in 1956 and then Rothko with all possible messiness by knife in 1970."

The Gospel from Outer Space (*also* **Gospels**). *In* Slaughterhouse-Five, *after his charter plane crashes, Billy Pilgrim shares a hospital room with Eliot Rosewater. Rosewater tells Billy a Kilgore Trout tale.* (SL5 5) It was about a visitor from outer space, shaped very much like a Tralfamadorian, by the way. The visitor from outer space made a serious study of Christianity, to learn, if he could, why

Christians found it so easy to be cruel. He concluded that at least part of the trouble was slipshod storytelling in the New Testament. He supposed that the intent of the **Gospels** was to teach people, among other things, to be merciful, even to the lowest of the low.

But the **Gospels** actually taught this:
Before you kill somebody, make absolutely sure he isn't well connected. So it goes.

The flaw in the Christ stories, said the visitor from outer space, was that Christ, who didn't look like much, was actually the Son of the Most Powerful Being in the Universe. Readers understood that, so, when they came to the crucifixion, they naturally thought, and Rosewater read out loud again:
Oh, boy—they sure picked the wrong guy to lynch that time!

And that thought had a brother: "*There are right people to lynch.*" Who? People not well connected. So it goes.

The visitor from outer space made a gift to Earth of a new **Gospel**. In it, Jesus really was a nobody, and a pain in the neck to a lot of people with better connections than he had. He still got to say all the lovely and puzzling things he said in the other **Gospels**.

So the people amused themselves one day by nailing him to a cross and planting the cross in the ground. There couldn't possibly be any repercussions, the lynchers thought. The reader would have to think that, too, since the new **Gospel** hammered home again and again what a nobody Jesus was.

And then, just before the nobody died, the heavens opened up, and there was thunder and lightning. The voice of God came crashing down. He told the people that he was adopting the bum as his son, giving him the full powers and privileges of The Son of the Creator of the Universe throughout all eternity. God said this: *From this moment on, He will punish horribly anybody who torments a bum who has no connections!*

Gossett, George and Nancy (*see* **Grand Triumvirate**).

Gottlieb, Adolph. *Part of Karabekian's huge collection of Abstract Expressionist paintings includes Gottlieb's "Frozen Sounds Number Seven."* (*Blue*

24) Slazinger was a lamb when they unswaddled him. "Just put me to bed," he said. He named the room he wanted to be put in, the one on the second floor with **Adolph Gottlieb**'s "Frozen Sounds Number Seven" over the fireplace and a bay window looking across the dunes to the ocean.

Gottwald's estate. *Gottwald's estate in* Player Piano *promises a pastoral refuge for Paul and Anita Proteus from an overly technologized society. The farm is completely without motorized farming implements or electricity. Gottwald had long since passed away. The farm was on the market for fourteen years by the time Proteus brings Anita to see where he plans to spend his years after quitting the Ilium Works. Gottwald originally bought the farm from old Mr. Haycox. Haycox's son was guaranteed the right to run the farm until he passed away. Along with help from the Reeks and Wrecks, the now aged younger Mr. Haycox is adamant about remaining caretaker of the estate.*

Grace Daffodil-13 (Cousin Grace). *At the Daffodil family meeting in Indianapolis, "Cousin Grace" is a mentally unbalanced woman whom Wilbur uses to prove the viability of his and Eliza's scheme for large, artificially extended families.* (Slap 46) What was more: She was a menace only to herself, so nobody was particularly mad at her. Her children had wandered off to better-run houses almost as soon as they were able to walk, I was told. That was surely one of the most attractive features of Eliza's and my invention, I think: Children had so many homes and parents to choose from.

Graham, Jack (*see also* **Mary Kathleen O'Looney**). *In* Jailbird, *Graham was born a multimillionaire, became a mining engineer, and took control of the RAMJAC Corporation (then a small company), which became the nation's dominating economic entity. He met Mary Kathleen O'Looney in the streets of a Kentucky coal-mining town when she fled her cabin in fear of drunken union organizer Kenneth Whistler. Jack Graham becomes a recluse and dies in 1952, survived only by his wife, Mary Kathleen.*

Graham, James and John (**Fifth Earl and First Marquis of Montrose**). *Fred Rosewater learns* *about the establishment of the family name and the founder of his family by reading* A History of the Rosewaters of Rhode Island, *by Merrihue Rosewater.* (GBR 11) The Old World home of the Rosewaters was and is in the Scilly Islands, off Cornwall. The founder of the family there, whose name was John, arrived on St. Mary Island in 1645, with the party accompanying the fifteen-year-old Prince Charles, later to become Charles the Second, who was fleeing the Puritan Revolution. The name Rosewater was then a pseudonym. Until John chose it for himself, there were no Rosewaters in England. His real name was **John Graham**. He was the youngest of the five sons of **James Graham**, Fifth Earl and First Marquis of Montrose. There was need for a pseudonym, for **James Graham** was a leader of the Royalist cause, and the Royalist cause was lost. James, among other romantic exploits, once disguised himself, went to the Scotch Highlands, organized a small, fierce army, and led it to six bloody victories over the far greater forces of the Lowland Presbyterian Army of Archibald Campbell, the Eighth Earl of Argyll. James was also a poet. So every Rosewater is in fact a **Graham**, and has the blood of Scotch nobility in him. James was hanged in 1650.

Grand Hotel Oloffson. (*DD* Preface) There is a real hotel in this book, the **Grand Hotel Oloffson** in Port au Prince, Haiti. I love it, and so would almost anybody else. My dear wife Jill Krementz and I have stayed there in the so-called "James Jones Cottage," which was built as an operating room when the hotel was headquarters for a brigade of United States Marines, who occupied Haiti, in order to protect American financial interests there, from 1915 until 1934.

The exterior of that austere wooden box has subsequently been decorated with fanciful, jigsaw gingerbread, like the rest of the hotel. *Vonnegut has the Waltz brothers purchase the hotel with the settlement they receive for their mother's wrongful death from radiation exposure. They are at the hotel when Midland City is neutron-bombed.*

Grand Triumvirate. *This group of college friends represents a sore spot of remembrance for the title character of "Hal Irwin's Magic Lamp," collected in*

Bagombo Snuff Box (1999), *who brings them up in a fit of pique when his wife, Mary, protests she does not need a cook.* Mary wanted to cry. Here she thought she'd been making Hal feel better, and she'd been making him feel worse instead.

"What do you think I think when I see Bea Muller or Nancy Gossett downtown in their fur coats, buying out the department stores?" Hal said. "I think about you, stuck in this house. I think, Well, for crying out loud, I used to be president of their husbands' fraternity house! For crying out loud, me and Harve Muller and George Gossett used to be the **Grand Triumvirate**. That's what they used to call the three of us in college—the **Grand Triumvirate**! We used to run the college, and I'm not kidding. We founded the Owl's Club, and I was president.

"Look where they live, and look where we live," Hal went on. "We oughta be right out there with 'em at Fifty-seventh and North Meridian! We oughta have a cottage right next to 'em at Lake Maxinkuckee! Least I can do is get my wife a cook."

granfalloon. *In Bokononist terms, a* granfalloon *is a false* karass. *(CC 42)* Hazel's *(Crosby)* obsession with Hoosiers around the world was a textbook example of a false *karass,* of a seeming team that was meaningless in terms of the ways God gets things done, a textbook example of what Bokonon calls a *granfalloon.* Other examples of *granfalloons* are the Communist party, the Daughters of the American Revolution, the General Electric Company, the International Order of Odd Fellows—and any nation, anytime, anywhere.

As Bokonon invites us to sing along with him:

If you wish to study a *granfalloon*,
Just remove the skin of a toy balloon.

(WFG Preface) DEAR READER: The title of this book is composed of three words from my novel *Cat's Cradle.* A *wampeter* is an object around which the lives of many otherwise unrelated people may revolve. The Holy Grail would be a case in point. *Foma* are harmless untruths, intended to comfort simple souls. An example: "Prosperity is just around the corner." A *granfalloon* is a proud and meaningless association of human beings. Taken together,

the words form as good an umbrella as any for this collection of some of the reviews and essays I have written, a few of the speeches I have made. Most of my speeches were never written down.

Grant, Robert. *In* Jailbird, *Vonnegut cites the retired probate judge as one of three men assigned to review the convictions and death sentences for Sacco and Vanzetti. Along with Harvard President A. Lawrence Lowell and MIT President Samuel W. Stratton, the committee agreed with Judge Thayer's sentence.*

Grass, Günter. *In* Fates Worse Than Death, *Vonnegut recalls a brief conversation he has with author and graphic artist Günter Grass and then repeats the same anecdote in* Timequake. *(FWD X)* The great German writer **Günter Grass**, who was a boy during World War II, asked me one time in what year I was born. I told him 1922. He said that there were no males my age still alive in Germany, Austria, or the Soviet Union. That was only a slight exaggeration *(see also TQ XIII).*

Grasso, Elmer Glenville. *The skeptical voter attending a political rally during Wilbur Swain's campaign for president. Wilbur explains to Grasso how a society would function with his proposed artificially extended families. Grasso is concerned about the possibility of being artificially connected to relatives he doesn't like, and this prompts Wilbur to lecture him about how that could be different than having unpleasant biological relatives. (Slap 33)* "Mr. **Grasso**," I said, "I personally will be very disappointed, if you do not say to artificial relatives you hate, after I am elected, 'Brother or Sister or Cousin,' as the case may be, 'why don't you take a flying fuck at a rolling doughnut? Why don't you take a flying fuck at the mooooooooooooon?'

"You know what relatives you say that to are going to do, Mr. **Grasso**?" I went on. "They're going to go home and try to figure out how to be better relatives!"

great becoming. *(ST 1)* "Things fly this way and that, my boy," he *(Rumfoord)* said, "with or without messages. It's chaos, and no mistake, for the Universe is just being born. It's the **great becoming** that makes the light and the heat and the motion, and bangs you from hither to yon."

Great Wall of China. *The Tralfamadorians use their Universal Will to Become to send messages concerning the status of the replacement part for Salo's spaceship. The messages are conveyed in great architectural monuments on Earth that could be monitored by Salo.* (ST 12) **The Great Wall of China** means in Tralfamadorian, when viewed from above: *"Be patient. We haven't forgotten about you."*

Greathouse, Virgil (*also* **Greathouse and Smiley**). *The former Secretary of Health, Education, and Welfare and one of the richest men in the country arrives to serve his Watergate sentence at the Finletter Minimum Security Adult Correctional Facility on the same day Walter Starbuck is being released. Greathouse was a Quaker, as was his boss Richard Nixon.* (JB 4) I knew **Greathouse** mainly by sight—and of course by reputation. He was a famous tough guy, the founder and still majority stockholder in the public relations firm of **Greathouse and Smiley**, which specialized in putting the most favorable interpretations on the activities of Caribbean and Latin American dictatorships, of Bahamian gambling casinos, of Liberian and Panamanian tanker fleets, of several Central Intelligence Agency fronts around the world, of gangster-dominated unions such as the International Brotherhood of Abrasives and Adhesives Workers and the Amalgamated Fuel Handlers, of international conglomerates such as RAMJAC and Texas Fruit, and on and on.

He was bald. He was jowly. His forehead was wrinkled like a washboard. He had a cold pipe clamped in his teeth, even when he sat on a witness stand. I got close enough to him one time to discover that he made music on that pipe. It was like the twittering of birds. He entered Harvard six years after I graduated, so we never met there. We made eye-contact only once at the White House—at the meeting where I made a fool of myself by lighting so many cigarettes. I was just a little mouse from the White House pantry, as far as he was concerned. He spoke to me only once, and that was after we were both arrested. We came together accidentally in a courthouse corridor, where we were facing

separate arraignments. He found out who I was and evidently thought I might have something on him, which I did not. So he put his face close to mine, his eyes twinkling, his pipe in his teeth, and he made me this unforgettable promise: "You say anything about me, Buster, and when you get out of jail you'll be lucky to get a job cleaning toilets in a whorehouse in Port Said."

It was after he said that, that I heard the birdcalls from his pipe.

Greathouse was a Quaker, by the way—and so was Richard M. Nixon, of course. This was surely a special bond between them, one of the things that made them best of friends for a while.

(JB 4) Emil Larkin, the Presbyterian, and **Virgil Greathouse**, the Quaker, had been thick as thieves back in the good old days. They had not only dominated the burglaries and the illegal wiretaps and the harassment of enemies by the Internal Revenue Service and so on, but the prayer breakfasts, as well.

The Green Death. *In* Slapstick, *while the rest of the country has to deal with the Albanian Flu, those on Manhattan Island are forced to contend with "The Green Death." The plague is so deadly that all crossing points to Manhattan are cut off.* (Slap 43) They (*the Raspberry family*) discovered the antidote through dumb luck. They ate fish without cleaning them, and the antidote, probably pollution left over from olden times, was somewhere in the guts of the fish they ate.

(Slap Epilogue) **The Green Death**, on the other hand, was caused by microscopic Chinese, who were peace-loving and meant no one any harm. They were nonetheless invariably fatal to normal sized human beings when inhaled or ingested.

Wilbur is saved when kidnapped by the Raspberries and force-fed a small trapezoid of what seemed to be a tasteless sort of peanut-brittle. It was in fact boiled and dried fish guts, which contained the antidote to **The Green Death** (*Slap* Epilogue). *Wilbur was captured so he could care for the ill patriarch of the family, Hiroshi Raspberry-20 Yamashiro. Yamashiro survived his bout with pneumonia and from among the many gifts brought to Wilbur for curing him, he chose only a single brass candlestick. From then on he became known as the King of Candlesticks.*

Green Diamond Plow. *In* Deadeye Dick, *the tank-producing facility near Midland City that brings Eleanor Roosevelt to town for a morale boosting visit. While there she visits the famous studio of Otto Waltz and leaves only hours before Rudy accidentally kills the pregnant Eloise Metzger.*

Green River Cemetery. *The Long Island cemetery in* Bluebeard *where Edith Karabekian, Rabo's wife, is buried. He plans to be buried there next to her, not far from the graves of Jackson Pollock and Terry Kitchen.*

Green Team. *The team at the Meadows executive retreat and competition festival captained by Dr. Lawson Shepherd, Paul Proteus's college friend and longtime associate who served as his second in command at the Ilium Works.* (PP XIV) *Well, if one cared about such things,* **Green** *was the lowest in the unofficial hierarchy of teams. It was one of those things that was understood without anyone's saying anything about it.*

Greenfield Bank and Trust Company. *The two lieutenants of the National Guard unit sent to put down the strike at the Cuyahoga Bridge and Iron Company are twin sons of the president of the Greenfield Bank and Trust Company.* (JB Prologue) *The postmaster and the banker had both done local favors for the governor. The commissions were their rewards. And the officers, in turn, had rewarded those who had pleased them in some way by making them sergeants or corporals.*

Gregory, Dan. *Born Daniel Gregorian in Moscow, he came to the United States in 1907 and became an* illustrator of magazine stories and advertisements, and of books for young people (*Blue* 6). *He became one of the most well paid artists in American history and frequently abused his live-in girlfriend, Marilee Kemp. She was once sent by Gregory to have an abortion. Gregory unwillingly accepted Rabo Karabekian as an apprentice after the aspiring artist accepted Marilee's invitation (in Gregory's name) to travel to New York. Gregory's own talents developed while an apprentice for Beskudnikov, an engraver for the Czar of plates for paper currency and bonds. Beskudnikov and his wife cared for Gregory from the* time he was five years old, but it wasn't until he began his art training that Gregory fell victim to Beskudnikov's tormenting. Gregory mimics his old master's nasty ways when Karabekian comes to study with him.

Rabo Karabekian makes the following assessment of his old mentor. (*Blue* 9) But let's forget me for the moment, and focus on the works of **Gregory**. They were truthful about material things, but they lied about time. He celebrated moments, anything from a child's first meeting with a department store Santa Claus to the victory of a gladiator at the Circus Maximus, from the driving of the golden spike which completed the transcontinental railroad to a man's going on his knees to ask a woman to marry him. But he lacked the guts or the wisdom, or maybe just the talent, to indicate somehow that time was liquid, that one moment was no more important than any other, and that all moments quickly run away.

Let me put it another way: **Dan Gregory** was a taxidermist. He stuffed and mounted and varnished and mothproofed supposedly great moments, all of which turn out to be depressing dust-catchers, like a moosehead bought at a country auction or a sailfish on the wall of a dentist's waiting room.

Clear?

Let me put it yet another way: life, by definition, is never still. Where is it going? From birth to death, with no stops on the way. Even a picture of a bowl of pears on a checkered tablecloth is liquid, if laid on canvas by the brush of a master. Yes, and by some miracle I was surely never able to achieve as a painter, nor was **Dan Gregory**, but which was achieved by the best of the Abstract Expressionists, in the paintings which have greatness birth and death are always there.

Gregory's best friend was Fred Jones and both were great admirers of Benito Mussolini. He and Jones asked permission to accompany in uniform the Italian Army and both were killed around December seventh of 1940 at Sidi Barrani, Egypt. . . . (*Blue* 13)

Gregory's photorealistic style and sentiments made him rage at Abstract Expressionism. When he saw Marilee and Rabo exiting the Museum of Modern Art he became livid. (*Blue* 21) "I don't give a hoot what pictures you look at," he said. "All I asked was that you not pay your respects to an institution which thinks that the smears and spatters and splotches and daubs and dribbles and vomit of lunatics and degenerates and charlatans are great treasures we should all admire."

The largest collection of Dan Gregory paintings and illustrations is in a private museum in Lubbock, Texas.

GRIOT™. *In* Hocus Pocus, *the Parker Brothers computer game that projects the outcome of one's life based on a series of demographic and life experience questions. Eugene Debs Hartke frequently uses the device and, in so doing, realizes the game's programming is based on a series of stereotypes generally held to be true by major media. When Hartke tells* GRIOT™ *about his life experiences up to Vietnam,* It made me a burned-out case, on the basis of my length of service over there, I think. It had me becoming a wife-beater and an alcoholic, and winding up all alone on Skid Row *(HP 12).*

Though the game's programmers supposedly updated the software every three months with the latest demographic trends for various ethnic groups, its synthesized futures usually reflected worst-case scenarios for minority groups and optimistic outcomes for whites. Hartke's skepticism about the efficacy of GRIOT™ *is underscored by Parker Brothers' change in ownership.* (HP 12) There is some question now, I've heard, about whether **GRIOT™** is as deep and up-to-date as it used to be, since Parker Brothers, the company that makes it, has been taken over by Koreans. The new owners are moving the whole operation to Indonesia, where labor costs next to nothing. They say they will keep up with American news by satellite.

One wonders.

Groszinger, Dr. Bernard. *The youthful rocket scientist in charge of the billion dollar, top secret project called Project Cyclops in the short story "Thanasphere." The project is intended to place into orbit a senior officer who will act as a weather spotter in the event the Cold War turns into a shooting match between nuclear powers. Flight commander Major Rice presents unlikely reports that he hears voices above the stratosphere, forcing Dr. Groszinger to face an unexpected clash of science and faith. It is eventually learned the voices are real, that the dead* spirits congregate far above the earth and are still involved with people they left behind. This causes Dr. Groszinger to question his place in science when faced with the spiritual questions posed by this new awareness. *(BAG* Thanasphere*)* He was trying to imagine the world of the future—a world in constant touch with the spirits, the living inseparable from the dead. It was bound to come. Other men, probing into space, were certain to find out. Would it make life heaven or hell? Every bum and genius, criminal and hero, average man and madman, now and forever part of humanity—advising, squabbling, conniving, placating. . . . What discovery of the dead would do to humanity he didn't know, but the impact would be terrific. Now, like the rest, he would have to wait for the next wild twist of history.

Guayaquil, Ecuador. *The city due east of the Galápagos Islands serves as the embarkation point for passengers planning to take "the Nature Cruise of the Century."*

Guderian, General Heinz (Hitler's chief of the Army General Staff). *In the short story "Souvenir," collected in* Bagombo Snuff Box *(1999), General Guderian (most often referred to in the narrative as "the old man") is accompanied by an unnamed blond German escort as they try to escape the Sudetenland in the face of advancing Soviet armored forces. The two realize that their war is soon to be over and desperately want to surrender to American forces rather than the brutally vengeful Soviet troops. The general offers Eddie and Buzzer (who that day had been released from their captivity as POWs) his bejeweled pocket watch in exchange for their uniforms and some assistance in getting to the American lines. However, once the Germans persuade the naive Americans to make the exchange,* Eddie and Buzzer and **the old man** and the blond found themselves behind the wall where the blond had said the Americans could swap their uniforms for the watch and civilian clothes. In the uproar, during which anybody could do anything, and nobody cared what anybody else did, the blond shot Buzzer in the head. He aimed his pistol at Eddie. He fired. He missed.

That had evidently been the plan all along, to

kill Eddie and Buzzer. But what chance did **the old man**, who spoke no English, have to pass himself off to his captors as an American? None. It was the blond who was going to do that. And they were both about to be captured. All **the old man** could do was commit suicide.

Eddie went back over the wall, putting it between himself and the blond. But the blond didn't care what had become of him. Everything the blond needed was on Buzzer's body. When Eddie peered over the wall to see if Buzzer was still alive, the blond was stripping the body. **The old man** now had the pistol. He put its muzzle in his mouth and blew his brains out.

It should be noted that while Guderian (1888–1954) was an important military leader and innovator of armored warfare, in real life he did not commit suicide.

guesser. *Vonnegut's only use of this word in the following context appears in* A Man Without a Country. *It comes as a bridge in chapter 8. Vonnegut knits his belief system in this long transitional section fringed by the humanity of Christ's Sermon on the Mount on one end and the currency of today's myths that continue to run both our individual lives and the global realpolitik. (The closest Vonnegut comes to this in earlier work is in* Cat's Cradle: foma; *things that make us happy and healthy—if not also ignorant.)*

But if Christ hadn't delivered the Sermon on the Mount, with its message of mercy and pity, I wouldn't want to be a human being.

I'd just as soon be a rattlesnake.

* * *

Human beings have had to **guess** about almost everything for the past million years or so. The leading characters in our history books have been our most enthralling, and sometimes our most terrifying, **guessers**.

May I name two of them?

Aristotle and Hitler.

One good **guesser** and one bad one.

And the masses of humanity through the ages, feeling inadequately just like we do now, and rightly so, have had little choice but to believe this **guesser** or that one (MWC 8).

What follows is a list of global woes paired with myths historically offered to soften our understanding; responding to the unreasonable, the unanswerable, with belief in yet another circumlocuting myth. Vonnegut ties such guessers to the worst of our historical and probable future declines. The guessers are sick of science interfering with every discussion about our moving forward culturally and politically. For them, there is no historical, scientific, or purely compassionate reason to improve the world beyond what it has become. (For some, they want to turn back the clock, a humorously Vonnegutian narrative technique.)

We must acknowledge that persuasive **guessers**, even Ivan the Terrible, now a hero in the Soviet Union, have sometimes given us the courage to endure extraordinary ordeals which we had no way of understanding. Crop failures, plagues, eruptions of volcanoes, babies being born dead—the **guessers** often gave us the illusion that bad luck and good luck were understandable and could somehow be dealt with intelligently and effectively. Without that illusion, we all might have surrendered long ago.

But the **guessers**, in fact, knew no more than the common people and sometimes less, even when, or especially when, they gave us the illusion that we were in control of our destinies.

Persuasive **guessing** has been at the core of leadership for so long, for all of human experience so far, that it is wholly unsurprising that most of the leaders of this planet, in spite of all the information that is suddenly ours, want the **guessing** to go on. It is now their turn to **guess** and **guess** and be listened to. Some of the loudest, most proudly ignorant **guessing** in the world is going on in Washington today. Our leaders are sick of all the solid information that has been dumped on humanity by research and scholarship and investigative reporting. They think that the whole country is sick of it, and they could be right. It isn't the gold standard that they want to put us back on. They want something even more basic. They want to put us back on the snake-oil standard (MWC 8).

Vonnegut ends this discussion about guessers by appealing to his readers to do the unpopular, the dangerous, the necessary individual action to keep from becoming myth-keepers, guessers all. He asks that we avoid accepting the uninformed myths of leadership that is sure to do two things: make the planet unin-habitable by our own myths; and ensure that one's opposition based on science and reason will be re-warded with ostracism or worse.

And if you actually are an educated, thinking person, you will not be welcome in Washington, D.C. I know a couple of bright seventh graders who would not be welcome in Washington, D.C. Do you remember those doctors a few months back who got together and announced that it was a sim-ple, clear medical fact that we could not survive even a moderate attack by hydrogen bombs? They were not welcome in Washington, D.C.

Even if we fired the first salvo of hydrogen weap-ons and the enemy never fired back, the poisons released would probably kill the whole planet by and by.

What is the response in Washington? They **guess** otherwise. What good is an education? The boisterous **guessers** are still in charge—the haters of information. And the **guessers** are almost all highly educated people. Think of that. They have had to throw away their educations, even Harvard or Yale educations.

If they didn't do that, there is no way their unin-hibited **guessing** could go on and on and on. Please, don't you do that. But if you make use of the vast fund of knowledge now available to educated persons, you are going to be lonesome as hell. The **guessers** outnumber you—and now I have to **guess**—about ten to one (MWC 8).

It is notable that Vonnegut's next bit of fringe to this line of thinking concerns the nation's historical shame of slavery and its attendant plague of racism. In this case he cites the presidential election of 2000 to illustrate the bad guessers' past tactics to main-tain power through inherently racist appeals. For Vonnegut, the distasteful outcome results in our na-tional image mirroring the bad guessers, yet one more reason to become a man without a country. (MWC 8) In case you haven't noticed, as the result of a shamelessly rigged election in Florida, in which thousands of African Americans were arbi-trarily disenfranchised, we now present ourselves to the rest of the world as proud, grinning, jut-jawed, pitiless war-lovers with appallingly powerful weaponry—who stand unopposed.

Guggenheim. *Vonnegut traveled back to Dresden in 1967 with a Guggenheim Foundation grant to research* Slaughterhouse-Five.

In Bluebeard, *Rabo Karabekian's "Hungarian Rhapsody Number Six" was bought by the Guggen-heim Museum and, as happened with all his paint-ings made with Sateen Dura-Luxe, it was flaking apart.*

Guido. *At the Mafia-run crematoria behind the Meadowdale Cinema Complex in* Hocus Pocus, *Guido has the black market concession on gasoline in the post-prison-riot period.*

Gumbo. *The Gumbo tribe saves Beatrice Rumfoord and her son Chrono after the failed Martian inva-sion of Earth. (ST 10) Bee's upper front teeth were gold, and her skin, like the skin of her son, was the color of golden oak.*

Bee had lost her upper front teeth when the space ship in which she and Chrono had ridden from Mars crash-landed in the **Gumbo** region of the Amazon Rain Forest. She and Chrono had been the only survivors of the crash, and had wan-dered through the jungles for a year.

The color of Bee's and Chrono's skins was per-manent, since it stemmed from a modification of their livers. Their livers had been modified by a three-month diet consisting of water and the roots of the salpa-salpa or Amazonian blue poplar. The diet had been a part of Bee's and Chrono's initia-tion into the **Gumbo** tribe.

During the initiation, mother and son had been staked at the ends of tethers in the middle of the village, with Chrono representing the Sun and Bee representing the Moon, as the Sun and the Moon were understood by the **Gumbo** people.

As a result of their experiences, Bee and Chrono were closer than most mothers and sons. (ST 10) The good-luck piece had probably saved Chrono's and Bee's lives in the jungle. The **Gumbo** tribesmen had recognized the piece of metal as an object of tremendous power. Their respect for it had led them to initiate rather than eat its owners.

Gummer, Harriet. *In* Hocus Pocus, The Des Moines Register *correspondent who has a child from her brief sexual encounter with Eugene Debs Hartke* *after he escapes from the American embassy in Saigon on the last day of the war. Hartke is unaware that their brief moment in Manila produced a son, Rob Roy. She later marries Lowell Fenstermaker, the owner of a meat packing company, who adopts Rob Roy as his son.*

Gumps, Andy. *Vonnegut uses this term in reference to the appearance his brother Bernard and he must have struck as they flew to Indianapolis for the funeral of their Uncle Alex. (Slap Prologue)* We were both over six feet tall. We still had most of our hair, which was brown. We had identical mustaches— duplicates of our late father's mustache.

We were harmless looking. We were a couple of nice old **Andy Gumps**.

Andy Gump was a comics character from Vonnegut's youth, whose everyman appeal stems from the comedy stereotypical of middle-aged, middle-class males. Physically, there is a broad resemblance between the Vonneguts and Gump including tousled curly hair, mustaches, and noticeably weak chins.

Gunther. *In the short story "Brief Encounters on the Inland Waterway," Gunther is the unhappy Swedish captain of the* Golden Hind VI, *an ocean liner among yachts.*

Gunther, August. *The best friend of Rudy's father, Otto Waltz, Gunther is decapitated by an accidental shotgun blast discharged by Francis X. Morissey, Midland City's chief of police, while on a geese hunting trip with Otto, Francis Morissey, and John Fortune. They all agree it was an honest accident that could only ruin more lives if the identity of the killer is revealed. They decide to send the decapitated body of August Gunther floating down Sugar Creek.*

Rudy Waltz's grandmother hired a rapscallion German cabinetmaker, who had studied art in Berlin in his youth, to give Father drawing and painting lessons on weekends and after school.

It was a sweet racket for both teacher and pupil. The teacher's name was **August Gunther**, and his peephole must have opened in Germany around 1850. Teaching paid as well as cabinetmaking, and, unlike cabinetmaking, allowed him to be as drunk as he pleased.

After Father's voice changed, moreover, **Gun-**ther could take him on overnight visits by rail to Indianapolis and Cincinnati and Louisville and Cleveland and so on, ostensibly to visit galleries and painters' studios. The two of them also managed to get drunk, and to become darlings of the fanciest whorehouses in the Middle West (DD 1). *Gunther is eventually fired and blacklisted by Otto's parents and is later suspected of setting fire to their mansion.*

Gunther, Grace. *The only child of the soon-to-be decapitated August Gunther, in* Deadeye Dick.

The Gutless Wonder. *(SL5 8)* "What are you?" Trout asked the boy scornfully. "Some kind of **gutless wonder**?"

This, too, was the title of a book by Trout, **The Gutless Wonder**. It was about a robot who had bad breath, who became popular after his halitosis was cured. But what made the story remarkable, since it was written in 1932, was that it predicted the widespread use of burning jellied gasoline on human beings.

It was dropped on them from airplanes. Robots did the dropping. They had no conscience, and no circuits which would allow them to imagine what was happening to the people on the ground.

Trout's leading robot looked like a human being, and could talk and dance and so on, and go out with girls. And nobody held it against him that he dropped jellied gasoline on people. But they found his halitosis unforgivable. But then he cleared that up, and he was welcomed to the human race.

Gutman, Andor. *In* Mother Night, *Gutman is an Estonian Jew who survived two years at Auschwitz and now guards Howard Campbell from noon to six p.m. each day in the basement confines of an Old Jerusalem prison. For reasons unknown to himself during the war, he joined the* Sonderkommando, *corpse-carrying inmates, just as Himmler prepares to close down the camp's ovens. The* Sonderkommando *responds to the frequent call over the loudspeakers,* "Leichtenträger zu Wache," *meaning "Corpse-carriers to the guardhouse." This is the same phrase Auschwitz survivor Mrs. Epstein murmurs to the catatonic Campbell when he seeks to turn himself in to the Israelis. Gutman is ashamed for having volunteered for the detail, and* *he reveals to Campbell the tragic paradox he faced in the concentration camp.* (MN 2) "There were loudspeakers all over the camp," he said, "and they were never silent for long. There was much music played through them. Those who were musical told me it was often good music—sometimes the best."

"That's interesting," I said.

"There was no music by Jews," he said. "That was forbidden."

"Naturally," I said.

"And the music was always stopping in the middle," he said, "and then there was an announcement. All day long, music and announcements."

"Very modern," I said.

He closed his eyes, remembered gropingly. "There was one announcement that was always crooned, like a nursery rhyme. Many times a day it came. It was the call for the Sonderkommando."

"Oh?" I said.

"*Leichenträger zu Wache,*" he crooned, his eyes still closed.

Translation: "Corpse-carriers to the guard-house." In an institution in which the purpose was to kill human beings by the millions, it was an understandably common cry.

"After two years of hearing that call over the loudspeakers, between the music," **Gutman** said to me, "the position of corpse-carrier suddenly sounded like a very good job."

"I can understand that," I said.

"You can?" he said. He shook his head. "I can't," he said. "I will always be ashamed. Volunteering for the Sonderkommando—it was a very shameful thing to do."

"I don't think so," I said.

"I do," he said. "Shameful," he said. "I never want to talk about it again."

H

Hacketts, Elmo C., Jr. *In* Player Piano, *Pfc. Elmo Hacketts is the unintended object of scrutiny by the Shah of Bratpuhr, who declares Hacketts to be a Takaru—a slave. His commanders insist citizens in America become soldiers out of a sense of duty and patriotism. However, the thoughts of this two-year veteran are to serve out the next twenty-three years and retire to Evanston, Illinois, so he could hang out with his friends and have no employment commitments. He knew his only two choices were between the Army and the Reconstruction and Reclamation Corps, and decidedly felt the Army was the preferable fate. He longed for overseas duty so he could get a real weapon with live ammunition and feel more like a soldier.*

Paul Proteus rides a train through upstate New York and overhears a conversation among members of Hacketts's old Army unit. Proteus knows well the limited options open to such people, and when he hears that Hacketts's request for overseas duty was granted, that he was on his way to Tamanrasset in the Sahara, Vonnegut has this to say about Paul's silent conclusion: Paul sighed for **Hacketts,** born into a spiritual desert, now being shipped to where the earth was sterile, too *(PP XXVI).*

Haggedorn, Elbert. *In the 1953 short story "Tomorrow and Tomorrow and Tomorrow," reprinted in* Welcome to the Monkey House *(1968), Haggedorn is the focus of a televised news story from Council Bluffs, Iowa. The content of the story is interrupted by squabbling in the Schwartz home, but we do learn that Haggedorn is 183 years old and wedged into something requiring two hundred workers to dig him out.*

Hagstrohm, Delores and Edgar, Jr. *The children of Edgar and Wanda Hagstrohm, all residents of Proteus Park in Chicago. While eating dinner with the Shah of Bratpuhr, Delores and Edgar, Jr., fall all over themselves with conflicting stories about their father's supposed bowling date with Joe Prince. Edgar was having an affair, and his son tries to protect his secret though he hates him for it. (PP XVII)* "I remember now he said he was going bowling with Pop. Sis got it all wrong, Mom." *His hands were trembling, and, clumsily, he knocked over his milk glass. Both he and his father jumped to their feet to catch it before it toppled all the way. Young* **Edgar** *caught it, and when his eyes met old Edgar's they were full of hate.* "Guess I'm too tired to go to the ball game after all," *he said.* "Guess I'll stay home and watch television with Mom."

Hagstrohm, Edgar Rice Burroughs *(and his wife,* **Wanda***). The Shah of Bratpuhr requested a visit at the home of a typical family, and the Hagstrohms were chosen by computer. The Shah arrives while Edgar is rereading a Tarzan story and just before he was going to tell his wife, Wanda, about the long and deeply felt affair he was having with Marion Frascatti, the widow of his best friend, Lou. (PP XVII)* EDGAR R. B. HAGSTROHM, *thirty-seven, R&R-131313, Undercoater First Class, 22nd Surface Preserving Battalion, 58th Maintenance Regiment, 110th Building and Grounds Division, Reconstruction and Reclamation Corps, had been named after his father's favorite author, the creator of Tarzan—Tarzan, who, far away from the soot and biting winter of the* **Hagstrohms'** *home town, Chicago, made friends with lions and elephants and apes, and swung through trees on vines, and was built like a brick outhouse with square wheels and Venetian blinds, and took what he wanted of civilization's beautiful women in tree houses, and left the rest of civilization alone.* E.R.B. Hagstrohm *liked Tarzan as much as his father had, and hated being a little man and being in Chicago ten times as much.*

(PP XVII) The personnel machines had considered the problem and ejected the card of **Edgar R. B. Hagstrohm,** *who was statistically average in every respect save for the number of his initials: his age (36), his height (5' 7"), his weight (148 lbs.), his years of marriage (11), his I.Q. (83), the number of his children (2: 1 m., 9; 1 f., 6), the number of his*

bedrooms (2), his car (3 yr. old Chev. 2 dr. sed.), his education (h.s. grad, 117th in class of 233; maj. in business practice; 2nd string f'ball, b'k'tb'l; soc. comm., sen'r play; no coll.), his vocation (R&R), his avocations (spec'r sports, TV, softb'l, f'sh'g), and his war record (5 yrs., 3 ov'sea; T-4 radioman; 157th Inf. Div.; battle stars: Hjoring, Elbesan, Kabul, Kaifen, Ust Kyakhta; wounded 4 times; P'ple H't, 3 cl.; Silv. Star; Br'ze Star, 2 cl.; G'd Condo Med.).

The stress of Hagstrohm's average existence proves too much for him to endure. He becomes an outlaw and seeks to escape into a world much like the fictional one created by his namesake. (PP XXVII) The portrait emerged from a slit in the top of the machine bit by bit—first the hair, then the brows, on line with the word WANTED, and then, on line with the large, fey eyes, the name: **Edgar Rice Burroughs Hagstrohm**, R&R-131313. **Hagstrohm**'s sordid tale emerged along with his nose: "**Hagstrohm** cut up his M-17 home in Chicago with a blowtorch, went naked to the home of Mrs. Marion Frascati, the widow of an old friend, and demanded that she come to the woods with him. Mrs. Frascatti refused, and he disappeared into the bird sanctuary bordering the housing development. There he eluded police, and is believed to have made his escape dropping from a tree onto a passing freight—"

Haifa Institute for the Documentation of War Criminals.
Under the direction of Tuvia Friedmann, the institute is responsible for providing Howard Campbell with the means and research assistance to write his Mother Night *memoirs. The institute made it a practice to collect statements from accused war criminals to fill out their own documentation of the Holocaust.*

"Hal Irwin's Magic Lamp."
This story has an enigmatic publishing history. First appearing in the June 1957 issue of Cosmopolitan *magazine and later in the 1961 collection* Canary in a Cat House, *it was then dropped from that text's retitled 1968 reprint,* Welcome to the Monkey House. *The story resurfaces in the 1999 collection* Bagombo Snuff Box, *but not before Vonnegut revises what he says was so asinine about its original version* (BAG Coda to My Career).

Vonnegut's 1999 version of "Hal Irwin's Magic Lamp" melds O. Henry's legendary twist of sentimentality with the politics of one of his favorite political figures, Eugene Victor Debs. He presents the failed efforts at compatibility of the fatally coupled, fortune hoarding stockbroker (though domestically well meaning) and his bride of two years, a devoted wife who sees with compassion those for whom it should be natural to offer Christian charity. Hal and Mary Irwin are as mismatched in their material values as they are in their spirituality.

At ten years older than Mary, it was easy for him to buffalo her about a lot of things, and one of the things was money. While Hal gives her a pittance to run their home, causing Mary to believe they are poor, he made a half million dollars on the stock market, and nobody knew it. Not even his wife.

Hal's actions may be odd but his intentions are romantically noble. The kitschy magic lamp Hal makes is just his sense of humor finding an interesting way of telling his very humble wife that they are rich and that their new home is a French château he had built on North Meridian Street, far from their shotgun house and soot on Seventeenth and Illinois Streets.

For her part, Mary was perfectly happy with their relatively obscure, hardscrabble lives. Vonnegut presents Mary's purity of spirit and devotion through her religious lens and sincere practice of a simple life in stark contrast to Hal's primary focus. That girl was as wholesome as a peach and a glass of milk. Being poor gave her room to swing her religion around. When the end of the month came, and they'd eaten pretty well, and she hadn't asked Hal for an extra dime, she felt like a little white lamb. And she thought Hal was happy, even though he was broke, because she was giving him a hundred million dollars' worth of love.

There was only one thing about being poor that really bothered Mary, and that was the way Hal always seemed to think she wanted to be rich. She did her best to convince him that wasn't true.

Hal's false projection onto Mary of his own material desires backfires on multiple accounts. His racial insensitivity has him involve Ella Rice as a prop (playing the jinni) *in his contrived magic lamp show. Ella works as a domestic servant for a friend of Hal's. However, Ella becomes more than a prop on a special evening in the Irwin house. Mary is com-*

pletely taken by the pregnant but unmarried Ella and has her move in with them in their new regal home. What Hal hadn't counted on, though, was that Mary would find Ella so likable, but so pitiful, not a cook, but a fellow human being in awful trouble. He had expected them to go to the kitchen to talk about this and that, what Hal liked to eat, and so on. But Mary asked Ella about her pregnancy, which was obvious. Ella, who was no actress, and at the end of her rope in any case, burst into tears. The two women, one white, one black, stayed in the living room and talked about their lives instead.

The devotion Hal shows toward mammonism and Mary's Christian purity are tested by the inevitable Wall Street crash of 1929. Aligning himself with those of later legend who pitched themselves from the windows of brokerage offices, Hal sees the loss of his dearly amassed paper fortune as the end of his existence. The stocks Hal had bought on margin became worthless. All of a sudden, everybody thought they were too expensive at any price. So what Hal Irwin owed to his brokerage, and what his brokerage owed to a bank in turn, was more than everything he owned—the new house, the unsold old house, the furniture, the car, and on and on. You name it!

He wasn't loved at home even in good times, so Hal went out a seventh-story window without a parachute. *In Hal Irwin's most destitute and desperate moment, he fails to trust in or turn to his steadfast wife, Mary, a spiritual soul as devoid of greed as she is filled with grace. Vonnegut introduces the reader to Hal through the eccentricity required to maintain the secrecy of his wealth. In the end, Hal sees his life's work become as worthless as the proverbial paper on which his fortune had been printed. His refusal to face his future makes a clear statement—Hal is disabled from imagining a future starting with nothing more than Mary's love, stoic devotion, and pragmatism.*

Widowed, foreclosed, and without prospects, Mary Irwin accompanies Ella Rice to the black church that baptized her newborn son, Irwin Rice. It's the only place Ella could think of to go, and they are met there by throngs of other desperate victims of the Great Depression. Mary slips away from the church only after Ella settles in, eats, and nurses young Irwin. She then heads for Crawfordsville, *where her widowed father lives in his leaky old house that no longer has electricity because he can no longer pay the bill. Vonnegut closes the story with a warm moment between the impoverished father and daughter that contrasts with the weakness of Hal in facing the future with Mary—while also noting that those without resources will always have primary concern for those around them. . . .* her father took her in. How could he not? She told him about the homeless people in the black church. She asked him what he thought would become of them in such awful times.

"The poor take care of the poor," he said.

It is not the encyclopedist's job to prefer one version of a story to another. Suffice it to say that unless there is a broad call for republishing the original 1957 version, the 1999 one will stand if for no other reason than its general accessibility. Also, one has to respect the author's claim to the last editorial hand on his own work. Regardless of the reason for the update, the two versions offer a glimpse of Vonnegut working under the demands of a specific readership, publisher, personal demands, and modes of expression in the 1950s as opposed to different parameters and sense of personal legacy afforded the 1999 version. Having staked out that editorial stance, the following notable differences can be readily understood by reading the original. They are offered here only because there are two existing versions of the text.

- *The circumstances by which Ella comes to live with the Irwins is marginally different.*
- *Ella's last name in the original is Washington, not Rice.*
- *Ella names her son Grand Triumvirate Washington in honor of Hal Irwin's facetious request.*
- *Whereas Mary is childless in the 1999 version, she manages to overcome her diagnosis of barrenness and have a daughter in the 1957 original.*
- *Hal is shamed by his wife's reaction to all their newfound wealth and asks her to make one final wish on the lamp to make her happy.*
- *Mary's wish results in their losing all their material wealth, including their new château, but the $5,000 college fund gift she insisted upon helped Ella's son become Dr. Grand Triumvirate Washington.*
- *Hal does not pitch himself out a seventh-floor window because of the Wall Street crash of 1929;*

instead, the unnamed narrator's final line of the story jokingly refers to Mary's final magic lamp wish: Personally, I never forgave her for the Depression.

- Hal and Mary enjoy a long, loving marriage, eventually blessed with their own daughter and proud of their effect on Ella's family.
- The dialectic between a blinding mammonism and Christian charity in the fairly dark 1999 version is considerably glossed over in the earlier version, as illustrated by the happy outcome for readers of Cosmopolitan in 1957.

Haley, Stewart. *In the short story "Ambitious Sophomore," collected in* Bagombo Snuff Box (1999), *Lincoln High School's assistant principal, Stewart Haley, is responsible for overseeing the marching band budget, a task that means trying to control the room when discussing band business with George M. Helmholtz, the band's director who spends his funds as fast as he raises them. While Haley is aware of Helmholtz's wildly demonstrative defense of his band, Helmholtz is aware of Haley's attempt to control the situation, and the result is a comical, close-corner battle of wills.* Whenever it was necessary for **Haley** to discuss band finances with Helmholtz, **Haley** tried to corner the bandmaster where he couldn't march and swing his arms.

Helmholtz knew this, and felt trapped when **Haley** appeared in the door of the bandmaster's small office, brandishing a bill for ninety-five dollars.

Haley is accompanied by an unnamed boy delivering a custom band uniform intended for star sophomore piccoloist Leroy Duggan, but the $95 bill that comes with it is $20 more than is in the band's account. Haley objects to Helmholtz's purchase of yet another uniform after having just purchased a hundred new ones. Helmholtz writes a personal check to soothe Haley's concerns and to satisfy Mr. Kornblum, the uniform supplier. Vonnegut uses the exchange between Haley and Helmholtz as an opportunity to describe the latter's concerns about Leroy who lacks all confidence when marching in public, especially when girls are in the area.

Haley exclaims that when Leroy tries on the oversized and heavily padded uniform that he looks like champion boxer Rocky Marciano. When Haley sees

Helmholtz in his own grandiose band master's uniform at the marching band competition, his private, derisive comment is that he looks like a Bulgarian rear admiral. Haley is also the one who spots Leroy chatting up a female piccolo player from an opposing band and calls the otherwise shy and receding piccoloist Blabbermouth Duggan and then Casanova Duggan.

As sarcastic as Haley is in all his appearances within the story, he is the first to rush out of the stands to shake Helmholtz's hand when Lincoln High wins the competition, and he then turns effusive in his awe at Leroy's solo performance during "The Star-Spangled Banner" while contradicting Helmholtz's explanation of why he was able to achieve such grandeur. That wasn't school spirit— that was the love song of a full-bodied American male. Don't you know anything about love?

It is that final comment that makes Helmholtz reflect for a quick moment that he never experienced the love of a woman in his life. Music always held Helmholtz in ecstasy. He quickly lets the thought pass as his head again fills with music while holding his trophy.

Hall, Dr. Cyril (*see also* **chrono-synclastic infundibula**). *The author of the entry on the chrono-synclastic infundibula in* A Child's Cyclopedia of Wonders and Things to Do, *in* The Sirens of Titan.

Hall, Pamela Ford. *Tarkington College's visiting Artist in Residence, a sculptress who works in polyurethane. She is a childless divorcée and alcoholic with a preference for blackberry brandy. Hall and Eugene Debs Hartke have a brief physical affair. During their first night together, he got drunk on brandy and they made love in her art studio. She got him to talk about his killing in Vietnam, and the brandy made him so maudlin he went to the student union and cried about it in front of the students.*

Pamela Ford Hall's one-woman show of her polyurethane sculptures at the Hanson Centre for the Arts in Buffalo is also the museum's inaugural installation. Entitled "Bagladies," the figures are no bigger than a shoe box. When the founder of the museum makes her late arrival and all the entryway doors are thrown open, the lightweight polyurethane figures blow off their pedestals and against the base-

board heating system. They melted and gave off a terrific stench.

Hall had deep feelings for Hartke though she knew about his womanizing. Once, while drunk and depressed, Pamela provides a magnificently complex insight to Hartke's emotional capabilities. (HP 24) "You know what you ought to say to any woman dumb enough to fall in love with you?" she asked me. Her gaze was on Musket Mountain, not on me.

"No," I said.

And she said, "Welcome to Vietnam."

Hallinan, Vivian (*see* **God Bless You, Dr. Kevorkian**).

Halporn, Amy. *A friend of Anita Proteus. (PP I)* "**Amy Halporn** said this morning she'd heard something about you *(Paul)* and Pittsburgh. Her husband was with Kroner today, and Kroner had the impression that you didn't want to go to Pittsburgh."

Halyard, Dr. Ewing J. *In* Player Piano, *Halyard is the State Department's guide assigned to escort the Shah of Bratpuhr on his tour of the United States. He continually battles the Shah's labeling of Americans as slaves. Halyard's exalted position within the government is jeopardized when an audit of academic credentials reveals Halyard neglected to complete a physical education requirement while an undergraduate at Cornell University. He is instructed to report to Doctor Roseberry to make up the deficiency. Roseberry is Cornell's athletic director and head football coach. Unfortunately for Halyard, Roseberry possesses a damning letter written by Halyard to Cornell President Herpers about the bad behavior displayed by the coach and his team while in a public restaurant. Halyard fails his physical education make-up test, is stripped of his Ph.D., and faces unemployment just as he and the Shah are caught in the Ghost Shirt uprising in Ilium.*

Hamilton, Alexander. *The author of* The Federalist Papers *and first Secretary of the Treasury (1789–1795). An elitist, he lacked faith in the abilities of the common man, advocated a strong centralized government, and recommended the creation of a national bank. Hamilton was killed in a duel by political foe Aaron Burr. (GBR 2)* "I ask him *(Eliot)* what

he dreams about," the doctor continued, "and he tells me, 'Samuel Gompers, Mark Twain, and **Alexander Hamilton**.' I ask him if his father ever appears in his dreams, and he says, 'No, but Thorsten Veblen often does.'"

Hamlet. *While Eliot Rosewater aimlessly travels across America, he stops for a time in Elsinore, California, and the name of the location provides him an opportunity to examine himself and see parallels with the tragic character. Addressing the letter to his wife Sylvia as "Dear Ophelia," Eliot goes on to say:* The last thing you said to me before I got out of the taxicab was that maybe we should get a divorce. I did not realize that life had become that uncomfortable for you. I do realize that I am a very slow realizer. I still find it hard to realize that I am an alcoholic, though even strangers know this right away.

Maybe I flatter myself when I think that I have things in common with **Hamlet**, that I have an important mission, that I'm temporarily mixed up about how it should be done. **Hamlet** had one big edge on me. His father's ghost told him exactly what he had to do, while I am operating without instructions. But from somewhere something is trying to tell me where to go, what to do there, and why to do it. Don't worry, I don't hear voices. But there is this feeling that I have a destiny far away from the shallow and preposterous posing that is our life in New York. And I roam.

And I roam *(GBR 3). Eliot signs the letter in Hamlet's name.*

Years later, Vonnegut uses the narrative structure of the lead characters in Hamlet *and "Cinderella" to make a point about the predictability of culturally acceptable plot lines in literature, the core of his (rejected) anthropology master's thesis at the University of Chicago.(MWC 3)* The question is, does this system I've devised help us in the evaluation of literature? Perhaps a real masterpiece cannot be crucified on a cross of this design. How about *Hamlet*? It's a pretty good piece of work I'd say. Is anybody going to argue that it isn't? I don't have to draw a new line, because **Hamlet**'s situation is the same as Cinderella's, except that the sexes are reversed.

His father has just died. He's despondent. And right away his mother went and married his uncle,

who's a bastard. So **Hamlet** is going along on the same level as Cinderella when his friend Horatio comes up to him and says, "**Hamlet**, listen there's this thing up in the parapet, I think maybe you'd better talk to it. It's your dad." So **Hamlet** goes up and talks to this, you know, fairly substantial apparition there. And this thing says, "I'm your father, I was murdered, you gotta avenge me, it was your uncle did it, here's how."
(opposing page has graph of good and ill fortune and Kafka)
(MWC 3) To this day we don't know if that ghost was really **Hamlet**'s father. . . . So we don't know whether this thing was really **Hamlet**'s father or if it was good news or bad news. And neither does **Hamlet**. But he says okay, I got a way to check this out. I'll hire actors to act out the way the ghost said my father was murdered by my uncle, and I'll put on this show and see what my uncle makes of it. So he puts on this show. And it's not like Perry Mason. His uncle doesn't go crazy and say, "I—I—You got me, you got me, I did it, I did it." It flops. Neither good news nor bad news. After this flop **Hamlet** ends up talking with his mother when the drapes move, so he thinks his uncle is back there and he says, "All right, I am so sick of being so damn indecisive," and he sticks his rapier through the drapery. Well, who falls out? This windbag, Polonius. This Rush Limbaugh. And Shakespeare regards him as a fool and quite disposable.

You know, dumb parents think that the advice that Polonius gave to his kids when they were going away was what parents should always tell their kids, and it's the dumbest possible advice, and Shakespeare even thought it was hilarious.

"Neither a borrower nor a lender be." But what else is life but endless lending and borrowing, give and take?

"This above all, to thine own self be true." Be an egomaniac!

Neither good news nor bad news. **Hamlet** didn't get arrested. He's prince. He can kill anybody he wants. So he goes along, and finally he gets in a duel, and he's killed. Well, did he go to heaven or did he go to hell? Quite a difference. Cinderella or Kafka's cockroach? I don't think Shakespeare believed in a heaven or hell any more than I do. And so we don't know whether it's good news or bad news.

I have just demonstrated to you that Shakespeare was as poor a storyteller as any Arapaho. (MWC 3) But there's a reason we recognize **Hamlet** as a masterpiece: it's that Shakespeare told us the truth, and people so rarely tell us the truth in this rise and fall here [indicates blackboard]. The truth is, we know so little about life, we don't really know what the good news is and what the bad news is.

And if I die—God forbid—I would like to go to heaven to ask somebody in charge up there, "Hey, what was the good news and what was the bad news?" *(opposing page has graph of good and ill fortune and* Hamlet*)*
See also: FWD III.

Handy, Fred. *In* Hocus Pocus, *the college roommate of Eugene Debs Hartke's father who also trained as a chemical engineer. Handy left engineering and became a highly successful junk bond broker. After Barrytron lays off Hartke's father, Handy invites him on a cruise down the Inland Waterway to his estate in Palm Beach. When Hartke sees all the plastic jugs and bottles floating along the route, all the while realizing how much he contributed to the development of those plastics that would survive a thousand years, he begins to feel that he had indeed prostituted his intellect.*

Hanfstaengl, Putzi. Jailbird's *Walter Starbuck compares himself with (Ernst) "Putzi" Hanfstaengl, Hitler's favorite pianist, in an effort to properly express the extent to which he had disgraced Harvard by implicating Leland Clewes in the congressional hearings about Communists in the government.*

Hansels and Gretels. (MN Introduction) *Everything was gone but the cellars where 135,000* **Hansels and Gretels** *had been baked like gingerbread men. This is Vonnegut's description of the people lost in the Dresden firebombing.*

Hanson, Miss (*also* **Hanson Centre for the Arts**). *In* Hocus Pocus, *the aged Miss Hanson is a Rockefeller heir and resident of Buffalo, New York, who establishes as a gift to the city the Hanson Centre for the Arts. The inaugural art exhibit is a series of polyurethane sculptures entitled "Bagladies" by*

Tarkington College Artist in Residence Pamela Ford Hall. When three sets of entryway doors are simultaneously thrown open to allow the late-arriving Miss Hanson free access in her wheelchair, the Lake Erie winds sweep the lightweight sculptures off their pedestals and bring them to rest against the baseboard heating system, where they melt down into a stinking mess.

The Hapgoods, Three Earnest Brothers. *Vonnegut refers to this 1977 book by Michael D. Maraccio in* Jailbird's *prologue to round out the legacy of the Hapgoods, William, Norman, and Hutchins. All three graduated from Harvard and their sense of social justice was so strong that William, one of the founders of The Columbia Conserve Company, helped institute all sorts of workers' benefits that would eventually lead to employee ownership of the company. The Great Depression finished the company as an economic justice experiment, though it did not get sold off until 1953. Uncle Alex Vonnegut was a Harvard classmate of William's son, Powers Hapgood.*

As Vonnegut recalls, Alex had nothing politically in common with Powers; he arranged a luncheon with Kurt Jr. and his father because the young soldier was thinking of a career in the unions. Powers was vice president of the CIO Indianapolis chapter at the time and a radical celebrity for his unionization efforts and loudly leading protests against the executions of Sacco and Vanzetti. Vonnegut uses Powers as the model for Jailbird's *Kenneth Whistler.*

Powers Hapgood was late to lunch due to his extended testimony that morning before Judge Claycomb, the father of Vonnegut's high school classmate Moon Claycomb. Powers regaled the lunch group with his fawning reception by the Judge that morning, and it forever made an impact on Vonnegut's writing. (JB Prologue) It turned out that he had been telling stories all morning in court, too. The judge was fascinated, and almost everybody else in court was, too—presumably by such unselfish high adventures. The judge had encouraged **Hapgood**, I gathered, to go on and on. Labor history was pornography of a sort in those days, even more so in these days. In public schools in the homes of nice people it was and remains pretty much taboo to tell tales of labor's sufferings and derring-do. . . .

Moon Claycomb's father, according to **Powers Hapgood**, asked him this final question just before lunch: "**Mr. Hapgood**," he said, "why would a man from such a distinguished family with such a fine education choose to live as you do?"

"Why?" said **Hapgood**, according to **Hapgood**. "Because of the Sermon on the Mount, sir."

And Moon Claycomb's father said this: "Court is adjourned until two P.M."

In A Man Without a Country, *Vonnegut recounts the luncheon story but this time puts more humanity in it by coloring in sympathetic and true details about Hapgood's life and works.* (MWC 2) I did get to know one socialist of their generation—**Powers Hapgood** of Indianapolis. He was a typical Hoosier idealist. Socialism is idealistic. **Hapgood**, like Debs, was a middle-class person who thought there could be more economic justice in this country. He wanted a better country, that's all.

After graduating from Harvard, he went to work as a coal miner, urging his working-class brothers to organize in order to get better pay and safer working conditions. He also led protesters at the execution of the anarchists Nicola Sacco and Bartolomeo Vanzetti in Massachusetts in 1927.

Happy Birthday, Wanda June (1970) (*see also* **June, Wanda**). *Loosely based on Odysseus' return from the Trojan War in the last book of Homer's Odyssey, this play is Vonnegut's response to what he saw as Odysseus' "cruelly preposterous" actions when he finds his wife, Penelope, surrounded by suitors. Harold Ryan is Vonnegut's Odysseus in whom he seeks to portray all the worst characteristics of an Ernest Hemingway–like character. Penelope is courted by the pacifist physician Dr. Norbert Woodly as well as the vacuum salesman and weight lifter Herb Shuttle. The latter is more taken with wooing the wife of the famous warrior and hunter.*

Harold Ryan and his companion Colonel Looseleaf Harper return eight years after mysteriously disappearing on a hunting trip. Harper is credited with piloting the bomber that atom-bombed Nagasaki. Their return falls on Ryan's birthday, and without any warning of his arrival they hastily buy a leftover birthday cake intended for Wanda June, who was killed when run over by an ice-cream truck.

Ryan challenges Woodly for Penelope. Woodly

fails and admits his cowardice, something Penelope admires over her husband's bullying bravura. However, Woodly retreats, having to rethink his life's meaning. Herb Shuttle was more easily dispatched by Ryan since he was really most interested in serving a legendary character—he lacked his own identity.

The ghosts of Wanda June and Nazi Major von Konigswald (himself killed by Ryan after a long career of brutality and atrocity) wear pink jackets emblazoned with the words "Harold Ryan Fan Club."

Hardy, Albert. *The title character in a Kilgore Trout short story retold in* Timequake. *Trout is in the middle of writing the story when the timequake hits, making it impossible for him to complete the story for ten years when free will kicks in again. Vonnegut compares his own activities on the day of that fictional event with those of his alter ego.* (TQ 22, 23) I forget what I was doing on the afternoon of February 13th, 2001, when the timequake struck. It couldn't have been much. I sure as heck wasn't writing another book. I was seventy-eight, for heaven's sakes! My daughter Lily was eighteen!

Old Kilgore Trout was still writing, though. Seated on his cot at the shelter, where everybody thought his name was Vincent van Gogh, he had just begun a story about a working-class Londoner, **Albert Hardy**, also the name of the story. **Albert Hardy** was born in 1896, with his head between his legs, and his genitalia sprouting out of the top of his neck, which looked "like a zucchini."

Albert's parents taught him to walk on his hands and eat with his feet. That was so they could conceal his private parts with trousers. The private parts weren't excessively large like the testicles of the fugitive in Trout's father's Ting-a-ling parable. That wasn't the point. . . .

When Trout was zapped back to a line outside a blood bank in San Diego, California, in 1991, he could remember how his story about the guy with his head between his legs and his ding-dong atop his neck, "**Albert Hardy**," would end. But he couldn't write that finale for ten years, until free will kicked in again. **Albert Hardy** would be blown to pieces while a soldier in the Second Battle of the Somme in World War One.

Albert Hardy's dogtags wouldn't be found. His body parts would be reassembled as though he had been like everybody else, with his head atop his neck. He couldn't be given back his dingdong. To be perfectly frank, his ding-dong wouldn't have been what you might call the subject of an exhaustive search.

Albert Hardy would be buried under an Eternal Flame in France, in the Tomb of the Unknown Soldier, "normal at last."

Harger, Lemuel K. and Rose. *In the short story "Next Door," reprinted in* Welcome to the Monkey House (1968), *while Rose is out of the apartment, her husband, Lemuel, uses it for a rendezvous with another woman. Paul Leonard, the young boy who lives next door, is horrified by all he hears through the paper-thin walls. He calls the late night radio disc jockey All-Night Sam (q.v.) and dedicates a song from Lemuel to his wife. Harger and his lover hear the radio dedication and break up in a rage. Rose returns, and Lemuel couldn't feel any better.*

Hari, Mata. *Howard Campbell originally dedicates* Mother Night *to the famous spy, surmising:* She whored in the interest of espionage, and so did I. *Upon reconsideration he decides to dedicate it to himself:* I would prefer to dedicate it to one familiar person, male or female, widely known to have done evil while saying to himself, "A very good me, the real me, a me made in heaven, is hidden deep inside" (MN Editor's Note).

harmonium. *In* The Sirens of Titan, *the only indigenous life-form on the planet Mercury, dwelling deep in its caves. Their only nourishment had been Mercury's naturally vibrating hum until the arrival of Unk and Boaz. Their thin, translucent, kite-shaped physiology allows the colors of the cave walls to shine through them. They have no circulatory system; their four suction-cup-type organs are used to attach themselves to sound-emitting sources that directly feed the entire creature. Each harmonium is capable of reproduction; their young look no more substantial than dandruff. Their communication is limited to two telepathic phrases,* "Here I am, here I am, here I am," *and* "So glad you are, so glad you are, so glad you are" (ST 8).

Winston Niles Rumfoord uses the harmoniums to spell out different messages to the stranded space travelers. Through them he provides an answer to the problem of how to extricate their spaceship from the cave. By turning the ship upside down, they can fool the automatic navigation device, which can only determine how to go down. Despite their newfound realization that the harmoniums weren't really communicating their messages to Unk and Boaz, the latter refuses to leave. He knows he can provide what the harmoniums need and they give Boaz his much-wanted attention.

Harper, Alice. The former wife of Colonel Looseleaf Harper in Happy Birthday, Wanda June, Alice couldn't stand her husband's job as a test pilot. He eventually gave up flying for her and briefly sold insurance. Alice does not appear in the play, though she frequently comes to Colonel Harper's mind when he speaks of his many frustrations.

Harper, Colonel Looseleaf. Harold Ryan's war buddy and constant hunting companion in Happy Birthday, Wanda June. Retired from the Army Air Corps, Harper is cited as the pilot who dropped the atom bomb on Nagasaki that killed 74,000 people. After the war he and Ryan crash-land in a light plane in the Amazon Rain Forest in quest of diamonds. Ryan recalls Harper lost his little toe to piranha fish while taking shelter in a treetop during a flash flood.

In Breakfast of Champions, Colonel Harper is the charter airplane pilot who delivers Eliot Rosewater to the Midland City Arts Festival.

Harrell, the Reverend Charles. The minister who eulogizes Celia Hoover and who had played the role of John Fortune opposite Celia's role as his wife in Rudy Waltz's play "Katmandu." At Celia's funeral service he publicly forgives Rudy for shooting Eloise Metzger. To say the least, the minister did not inspire confidence about religious matters. (DD 24) I daydreamed at Celia's funeral. There was no reason to expect that anything truly exciting or consoling would be said. Not even the minister, the **Reverend Charles Harrell**, believed in heaven or hell. Not even the minister thought that every life had a meaning, and that every death could startle us into learning something important, and so on. The corpse was a mediocrity who had broken down after a while. The mourners were mediocrities who would break down after a while.

Harrington, Herb. Vonnegut recalls his own unsettling shift while observing large scale human slaughter during an African trip he took as an assignment for PEN. Having experienced Dresden, Vonnegut went on to see Biafra and then Mozambique in their horribly cruel civil wars. Barbarity is one of humanity's disturbing constants—absolutes—but the changes it makes to surviving witnesses provides a partial explanation for how such trends continue throughout time. Often spoken of as the process of desensitization, Vonnegut shares his experience with an old Shortridge High classmate who testifies to bearing similar witness in China during the war. (FWD VII) I ran into an old friend from Shortridge High School, a great inventor and mechanical engineer named **Herb Harrington**, while I was writing my dry-eyed piece about Mozambique. I confessed that something had happened to me since Biafra, that Mozambique had impressed me intellectually but not emotionally. I told **Herb** that I had seen little girls about the age of my own precious Lily drifting off to death, having been in the bush too long before reaching a refugee center, but that I felt hardly anything afterward. He said that the same thing had happened to him when he was in the Army during World War II, with a small crew installing radio stations along the coast of China. Wagonloads of Chinese who had starved to death were a common sight, and he soon (in less than a week) no longer noticed them.

Harrison, Dr. Edmund L. (also **Edmond**). The young engineer from the Ithaca Works befriended by Paul Proteus at the Meadows (q.v.). They take a sincere liking of each other, and when Proteus is supposedly thrown out of the ruling technocracy in a move to infiltrate the Ghost Shirt Society, Kroner sends Harrison to meet Paul at the docks with a drink and words of encouragement. Proteus advises Harrison to make a clear decision about whether he wants to live within the technology-driven society or make a go of life through his own hard work. Later in the text, Harrison has an opportunity to express these same choices to Buck Young, the much-sought-after Cornell football recruit.

Harrison, Lew. *In the 1951 short story "The Euphio Question," reprinted in* Welcome to the Monkey House *(1968), Harrison is the radio announcer who first interviews Wyandotte College's Dr. Fred Bockman upon his invention of the euphoriaphone, a receiver and amplifier to listen to the sounds of space. It is Harrison's idea to develop a marketing scheme for the euphoriaphone. The machine makes people's minds go numb and open to subliminal suggestions. So scheming and unethical is Harrison that the narrator (in testimony before a congressional committee), finishes with the following:* In closing, I'd like to point out that **Lew Harrison**, the would be czar of euphio, is an unscrupulous person, unworthy of public trust. It wouldn't surprise me, for instance, if he had set the clockwork on this sample euphio set so that its radiations would addle your judgments when you are trying to make a decision. In fact, it seems to be whirring suspiciously at this very moment, and I'm so happy I could cry. I've got the swellest little kid and the swellest bunch of friends and the swellest old wife in the world. And good old **Lew Harrison** is the salt of the earth, believe me. I sure wish him a lot of good luck with his new enterprise.

"Harrison Bergeron" (1961) (*see* **Bergeron**).

Harry (*see* **Amy and Harry** *and* **Laird, Eddie**).

Harry (*see* **Celeste and Harry Divine** *and* **"Unpaid Consultant"**).

Hartke, Eugene Debs. *The narrator of* Hocus Pocus *who sits in the library of Tarkington Prison, formerly Tarkington College, writing his memoirs on irregularly sized slips of paper, which accounts for the solid black lines studded throughout the narrative. Hartke taught at Tarkington College for twenty-five years, starting just after the end of the Vietnam War. He claims to have been the last American to leave Saigon in the helicopter evacuation from the U.S. embassy when the city fell to the North Vietnamese. Hartke was a lieutenant colonel and winner of the Silver Star at the time he resigned. He received the medal for killing with a hand grenade five Vietnamese hiding in enemy tunnels. Among them were a grandmother, mother, and baby.*

Hartke makes a point of avoiding all profanity in his memoirs, going so far as to substitute euphemisms for the language of others, as well. He always conducts himself this way because, as he tells his troops in Vietnam, clear communication could mean the difference between life and death for all. For this he is forever known as "The Preacher." Despite this pastoral nicknaming, Hartke admits to a large number of sexual affairs as well as legitimate killings (during his Vietnam service). In the course of writing, Hartke realizes the astonishing coincidence that the number of his 100-percent-legal military kills and . . . adulteries is exactly the same and is also the number he would like to have engraved on his tombstone (HP 40). *Rather than come out and tell the number, Hartke frequently alludes to it and makes a riddle for the reader to decipher. Here is how the riddle breaks down:*

RUNNING TOTAL		
Eugene Debs' death date	1926	1926
subtract title of Arthur C. Clarke's science fiction movie	-2001	-75
add year of Hitler's birth	+1889	1814
add gestation period of opossum	+12	1826
divide by square root of 4	(divide by) 2	913
subtract 100 x 9	-900	13
add most children by one woman	+69	82
TOTAL		82

Hartke closes out the riddle and his memoir with a statement undercutting all the cunning and inventiveness which marks humanity's achievements while also reflecting the decline in human development signified by (among other things) the cruel application of technology in Vietnam, the Japanese colonization of America, and the prison break at Athena. (HP 40) Just because some of us can read and write and do a little math, that doesn't mean we deserve to conquer the Universe.

Hartke is the second of three Vonnegut characters named for Indiana labor leader Eugene Victor Debs. The first is Eugene Debs Metzger, son of the ill-fated Eloise Metzger killed by Rudy Waltz in Deadeye Dick. *The third character so named is Hartke's son, Eugene Debs Hartke, Jr.*

Hartke Sr. marries Margaret Patton, sister of his West Point classmate Jack Patton. Upon Hartke's return from Vietnam and rejection from M.I.T., he finds out from a Patton family acquaintance that Margaret's family has a strong strain of hereditary insanity whose onset begins in middle age. Shortly thereafter, his wife and mother-in-law fall to the disease and become his full-time responsibility while teaching at Tarkington.

Hartke was recruited for West Point by then Lieutenant Colonel Sam Wakefield while in attendance at the Cleveland Science Fair. Hartke and his father were roundly criticized and all but disqualified by the judges for the crystal display that was clearly not Eugene's work. Hartke is later recruited by former Major General Sam Wakefield, now President of Tarkington College, to teach physics and play the Lutz Carillon at the school in the Finger Lakes region of New York. He is eventually fired from his teaching post for repeating anti-American and anti-Christian historical anecdotes first uttered by his good friend and fellow teacher Damon Stern. He takes employment with the prison in Athena, teaching basic literacy skills to the inmates. After the prison break, Hartke is falsely imprisoned on the allegation he helped plan the bloody escape.

Aside from the children he raises with Margaret (Eugene Debs, Jr. and Melanie), he had an illegitimate child with Des Moines Register *reporter Harriet Gummer, conceived in the Philippines on his way home from Vietnam. Harriet named their son after the mixed drink they had when they met, Rob Roy. His own children came to hate both their parents for having children despite the hereditary insanity. In Hartke's defense, he didn't know about the genetic disorder until after his return from war.*

Hartke, Melanie and Eugene, Jr. *The bitterly resentful children of Eugene and Margaret Hartke. When Margaret Patton's family secret of hereditary insanity comes out, the children are furious with their parents for having had children who would be forced to wait for their biological time bombs to go off.* (HP 10) **Melanie** was 21, and studying mathematics at Cambridge University in England. **Eugene Jr.** was completing his senior year at Deerfield Academy in Massachusetts, and was 18, and had

his own rock-and-roll band, and had composed maybe 100 songs by then.

But **Melanie** would have spoiled our tableau on the beach. Like my mother until she went to Weight Watchers, she was very heavy. That must be hereditary. If she had kept her back to the convicts, she might at least have concealed the fact that she had a bulbous nose like the late, great, alcoholic comedian W. C. Fields. **Melanie**, thank goodness, was not also an alcoholic.

But her brother was.

And I could kill myself now for having boasted to him that on my side of the family the men had no fear of alcohol, since they knew how to drink in moderation. We were not weak and foolish where drugs were concerned.

At least **Eugene Jr.** was beautiful, having inherited the features of his mother. When he was growing up in this valley, people could not resist saying to me, with him right there to hear it, that he was the most beautiful child they'd ever seen.

I have no idea where he is now. He stopped communicating with me or anybody in this valley years ago.

He hates me.

So does **Melanie**, although she wrote to me as recently as 2 years ago.

She was living in Paris with another woman. They were both teaching English and math in an American high school over there.

My kids will never forgive me for not putting my mother-in-law into a mental hospital instead of keeping her at home, where she was a great embarrassment to them. They couldn't bring friends home. If I had put Mildred into a nuthouse, though, I couldn't have afforded to send **Melanie** and **Eugene Jr.** to such expensive schools. I got a free house at Tarkington, but my salary was small.

Also, I didn't think Mildred's craziness was as unbearable as they did.

In the Army I had grown used to people who talked nonsense all day long. Vietnam was 1 big hallucination. After adjusting to that, I could adjust to anything.

What my children most dislike me for, though, is my reproducing in conjunction with their mother. They live in constant dread of suddenly going as batty as Mildred and Margaret. Unfortunately, there is a good chance of that.

Hatfield, Byron. *In* Slapstick, *the frontiersman who kills the courier carrying a letter from Wilma von Peterswald, wife of the inventor of* The Hooligan *(a device for communicating with the dead), to Wilbur Swain. He mistook the man for Newton McCoy, a hereditary enemy of his family's.*

Hausmännin, Walpurga. *In Eliot Rosewater's unfinished novel about reincarnation that he writes at the back of his* Domesday Book *(the ledger recording transactions of the Rosewater Foundation in Rosewater County), Walpurga Hausmännin is the most recent incarnation of the now bodiless spirit who recalls why she refuses to come back to life in another body. She speaks as a free spirit, literally, existing in a kind of bodiless purgatory without any rewards or punishments.* (GBR 7) Uncomfortable as it is here, however, there are a few of us who do not care to be reborn. I am among that number. I have not been on Earth since 1587 A.D., when, riding around in the meat of one **Walpurga Hausmännin,** I was executed in the Austrian village of Dillingen. The alleged crime of my meat was witchcraft. When I heard the sentence, I certainly wanted out of that meat. I was about to leave it anyway, having worn it for more than eighty-five years. But I had to stay right with it when they tied it astride a sawhorse, put the sawhorse on a cart, took my poor old meat to the Town Hall. There they tore my right arm and left breast with red-hot pincers. Then we went to the lower gate, where they tore my right breast. Then they took me to the door of the hospital, where they tore my right arm. And then they took me to the village square. In view of the fact that I had been a licensed and pledged midwife for sixty-two years, and yet had acted so vilely, they cut off my right hand. And then they tied me to a stake, burned me alive, and dumped my ashes into the nearest stream.

As I say, I haven't been back since.

Haycox. *Old Mr. Haycox is a direct descendant of the original owners of the farm that came to be known as the Gottwald estate in* Player Piano. *Ac-*cording to the deed his father constructed prior to selling out, his son was to be caretaker of the land for as long as he lived or as long as he wished. After Paul Proteus is shown the property by the snobbish Dr. Pond (whose degree is in real estate), Haycox's contempt for a society which displaces people by creating Ph.D.s for every imaginable walk of life is clearly shown when he proclaims himself to be a* doctor of cowshit, pigshit, and chickenshit. . . . When you doctors figure out what you want, you'll find me out in the barn shoveling my thesis *(PP XV). After Proteus purchases the estate, Haycox refuses to carry out his orders to prepare the house for Anita's arrival. It isn't until Paul's wishes are expressed as favors that Haycox goes out of his way to make everything perfect for Anita's first appearance at the farm. Not surprisingly, Haycox later appears as a member of the Ghost Shirt Society when Proteus is held captive by the rebels in an abandoned bomb shelter.*

Hazor. *As the eighteen-year-old prison guard Arnold Marx explains to Howard Campbell in* Mother Night, *Hazor was a Canaanite city in northern Palestine that existed at least nineteen hundred years before Christ. About fourteen hundred years before Christ, Arnold tells me, an Israelite army captured* **Hazor,** *killed all forty thousand inhabitants, and burned it down* (MN 1). *Arnold and his father were amateur archaeologists who spent their spare time as part of an excavation team at Hazor. Arnold's fascination with the city stems not from the Israeli victory, but from the succeeding Israeli settlement there that was destroyed by "the Assyrian," Tiglath-pileser the Third, in 732 B.C.*

Heath, Durling. *The red-headed Cockney midget and shoe repairman in Cohoes, New York, with whom Kilgore Trout had enjoyed a friendly relationship in* Breakfast of Champions. *Heath grows weary of Trout's polite but meaningless conversation and finally screams at the writer to leave him alone.*

Hederich, Oberdienstleiter Karl. *In* Mother Night, *the ping-pong-playing doubles partner of Reichsleiter Goebbels, Howard Campbell's boss at the Ministry of Propaganda and Popular Enlightenment. Hederich and Goebbels are roundly defeated* *by Campbell and his best friend Heinz Schildknecht, then a member of the underground anti-Nazi movement and an Israeli agent after the war.*

Heinz, Karl (*also known as* **Joe Louis** *and* **Brown Bomber**). *In the 1953 short story "D.P.," reprinted in* Welcome to the Monkey House (1968). *Karl Heinz is a six-year-old American German, fathered by a black American soldier in World War II. He lives in a Catholic orphanage run by nuns in the village of Karlswald in the American zone of occupation. It is with great affection that the village carpenter gives him the nickname "Joe Louis," after the most highly regarded black man he knew. Young Karl eventually becomes aware of a black American sergeant serving nearby with the occupation forces and steals away one evening to seek him out. The military unit showers him with the traditional chocolates and the sergeant gives him his own watch, promising that he will try to visit again. Karl tells one of the boys at the orphanage that the soldier promised to return and take him back to America.*

Heliogabalus. *When Kilgore Trout senses the public is closing in on him because of his invitation to the Midland City Arts Festival in* Breakfast of Champions, *he likens it to his theory that the atmosphere would eventually become unbreathable. He tells Bill, his parakeet, that they would all become Heliogabalus. Vonnegut informs the reader that Heliogabalus was the Roman emperor who would imprison an individual inside a sculpted bull and have a fire lit beneath it. The last sounds of the dying individual would be heard through the bull's mouth.*

helix (*see also* **spiral**). (MN 43) The railing stopped O'Hare, and he gazed down the stairwell, down a beckoning **helix** to the patch of sure death below.
(GBR 14) Eliot, rising from his seat in the bus, beheld the firestorm of Indianapolis. He was awed by the majesty of the column of fire, which was at least eight miles in diameter and fifty miles high. The boundaries of the column seemed absolutely sharp and unwavering, as though made of glass. Within the boundaries, **helixes** of dull red embers turned in stately harmony about an inner core of white. The white seemed holy.
(Blue 20) He (Fred Jones) must have felt like (Terry)

Kitchen again when he fired his machine guns up in the wild blue yonder, and saw a plane in front of him draw a **helix** of smoke and flame—ending in a sunburst far below.

Hellbrunner, Mrs. *In the short story "Any Reasonable Offer," first appearing in* Collier's *magazine (January 1952) and later collected in* Bagombo Snuff Box (1999), *Mrs. Hellbrunner is the second example used by the unnamed narrating real estate agent to convey the odd behaviors and expectations someone in his profession regularly witnesses. As her remaining asset of what had once been a very large Hellbrunner family fortune, all* Twenty-seven rooms, nine baths, ballroom, den, study, music room, solarium, turrets with slits for crossbowmen, simulated drawbridge and portcullis, and a dry moat *had to be explained to her as appealing only to a very small set of customers. Mrs. Hellbrunner knows of the quick Delahanty sale once the narrator got involved, so she is initially dismayed that her home has been on the market for three years. She had been holding firm for a $100,000 offer.*

Eventually, the narrator shows the Hellbrunner estate to the Peckhams, the vacation-defrauding couple who use it for daily recreation for four days and evenings before Mrs. Hellbrunner tries to force the issue of the sale. The Peckhams decline citing his new assignment to begin shortly in Bangkok.

It is Hellbrunner's desperation to unload the property at 70 percent of her previous asking price that leads the narrator to contact "Colonel" Peckham at National Steel Foundry, only to then realize that Peckham had misrepresented himself and with his wife was a serial fraud looking for nothing more than freeloading on opulent estates as a way of vacationing.

Heller, Charlene. *A veteran of the Army of Mars who has a concession booth outside the Rumfoord estate, down the line from Bea's and Chrono's booth. Prior to her Martian Army days she had been an assistant dietitian of the cafeteria of Stivers High School in Dayton, Ohio* (ST 10).

Helmholtz, George M. *The first of the Lincoln High School band director's various caring and mercurial literary characterizations occurs in the 1952* short story "The No-Talent Kid," *first printed in the October issue of* The Saturday Evening Post *and collected in* Bagombo Snuff Box (1999). *Helmholtz's Black Panthers marching band are licking their wounds, having finished second after winning the previous ten state championships. In his initial magazine rendition, Helmholtz feels he lost to Johnstown High School because of their eye-popping seven-foot-diameter bass drum.*

Vonnegut's broad descriptions of Helmholtz indicate obsessive egotism, a penchant for innovations that kept his teams winning, his recriminating disappointment in defeat, and his elitist finger-pointing at inadequate judges. **Mr**. **Helmholtz**, a man of forty, who believed that his great belly was a sign of health, strength, and dignity, smiled angelically, as though he were about to release the most exquisite sounds ever heard by human beings. Down came his baton.

The football team lost half its games and the basketball team lost two-thirds of theirs, but the band, in the ten years **Mr**. **Helmholtz** had been running it, had been second to none until this past June. It had been the first in the state to use flag twirlers, the first to use choral as well as instrumental numbers, the first to use triple-tonguing extensively, the first to march in the breathtaking double time, the first to put a light in its bass drum. Lincoln High School awarded letter sweaters to the members of the A Band, and the sweaters were deeply respected, and properly so. The band had won every statewide high school band competition for ten years—save the showdown in June.

The following is thought by Helmholtz at the beginning of the next school year but after his defeat by Johnstown High while listening to band class C, a notably unaccomplished group of musicians but also fairly young. Most hope they will transition to B band and perhaps find a coveted spot on the A band. While members of the C Band dropped out of the waltz, one by one, as though mustard gas were coming out of the ventilation, **Mr**. **Helmholtz** continues to smile and wave his baton for the survivors, and to brood inwardly over the defeat his band had sustained in June, when Johnstown High School had won with a secret weapon, a bass drum seven feet in diameter. The judges, who were not musicians but politicians, had had eyes and ears for

nothing but this Eighth Wonder of the World, and since then **Mr**. **Helmholtz** had thought of little else.

Helmholtz becomes more spare in expression when, toward the end of the tale, he has to make peace with his second nemesis, C band's miserable last chair clarinetist Walter Plummer. Plummer, by his own account, is there to earn a prized sweater with the band's varsity letter—musicianship be damned. This final discussion is an arrangement that bothers no one's conscience. "If the school gets that drum, whoever's pulling it will be as crucial and valued a member of the A Band as the first-chair clarinet. What if it capsized?"

"He'd win a band letter if it didn't capsize?" said Plummer.

And **Mr**. **Helmholtz** said this: "I don't see why not."

In the short story "Ambitious Sophomore," appearing in the May 1, 1954, issue of The Saturday Evening Post *and later reprinted in* Bagombo Snuff Box (1999), *Helmholtz sets his sights and personal finances, which are razor thin, on a third consecutive state title in the parade of bands. He so covets winning the colossal thirty-pound trophy to be awarded by the Chamber of Commerce that his pride and hopes for his band are balanced only by his tireless and infectiously dramatic fundraising appeals. As we learn at the end of the story, his love of music and marching band competition was to the exclusion of his ever having experienced a personal love in his life. He so lavishly spends his band's budget on excessive props and uniforms that competing band directors derisively refer to Helmholtz as "The Plunger" and "Diamond Jim." Beyond Helmholtz's constant fundraising and bloated budgeting is his hubris:* When he was called forward to receive the trophy, the bandmaster crossed the broad square to the accompaniment of a snare drum and a piccolo. As he returned with thirty pounds of bronze and walnut, the band played "Lincoln's Foes Shall Wail Tonight," words and music by **George M**. **Helmholtz**.

Vonnegut opens "Ambitious Sophomore" with a jibe at Helmholtz's girth, tempered by genuine appreciation for his dedication to craft. **George M**. **Helmholtz**, head of the music department and director of the band of Lincoln High School, was a good, fat man who saw no evil, heard no evil, and spoke no evil, for wherever he went, the roar and boom and blast of a marching band, real or imagined, filled his soul. There was room for little else, and the Lincoln High School Ten Square Band he led was, as a consequence, as fine as any band on earth.

The irony of the story and title is that the rotund Helmholtz (two-time state champion band director in this story) and his sophomore piccoloist Leroy Duggan are physically similar, and both of them hear and produce music at a virtuoso level, but the loveless band director unknowingly bestows courage upon his shy protégé by ordering a custom-fit marching tunic for the large, bell-shaped star (who turns into a super-human-sized triangle of symmetrical muscularity) scheduled to play the soaring piccolo solo in "The Stars and Stripes Forever."

Before the band's competition performance, Duggan's self-confidence soars so high that he strikes up a casual conversation with an opposing band's female piccolo player. The sartorial excess of Duggan's silhouette catches the eye of the opposing band's drum major, who makes the mistake of prodding Duggan to take off the uniform to show everyone how misshapen and fat he is. In the process of embarrassing Duggan, the drum major also ruins the star performer's new uniform. Duggan badly beats up the drum major; Helmholtz steps in only when the young sophomore grabs his foe's marching baton and prepares to club his fallen bully.

In the end, Duggan wears his old, unflattering tunic, plays his solo beautifully—like a cloudburst of diamonds—and gets the girl piccoloist from the other band, while Helmholtz gets his state trophy, loving only his statuesque symbol of triumph while imagining beautiful music in his head—quite a different portrait from that of his smitten, sophomore protégé.

Helmholtz is struck dumb by the evening. **Helmholtz** thought about love as he walked back to his car alone, his arms aching with the weight of the great trophy. If love was blinding, obsessing, demanding, beyond reason, and all the other wild things people said it was, then he had never known it, **Helmholtz** told himself. He sighed, and supposed he was missing something, not knowing romance. . . . He boarded a streetcar, sat down with the trophy on his lap, and smiled. He was hearing music again.

In the 1955 short story "The Kid Nobody Could Handle," reprinted in Welcome to the Monkey House *(1968), Helmholtz is the caring head of the music department at Lincoln High School, responsible for turning around the wayward Jim Donnini.*

Helmholtz is probably best remembered for his part in recruiting Malachi Constant for the Army of Mars in Vonnegut's 1959 novel (his second), The Sirens of Titan. *He is one-half of a recruiting team of agents seeking volunteers for Rumfoord's Army of Mars. Helmholtz poses as a former high school bandmaster teamed with Roberta Wiley, supposedly a former algebra teacher and an apparent male cross-dresser. Moments after Malachi Constant reads his father's letter in the Wilburhampton Hotel, Helmholtz and Wiley enter the room and offer him a way out of his earthly mess. (ST 3)* Your situation on Earth is hopeless. Your wife is a beast. Moreover, our intelligence informs us that here on Earth you will not only be made penniless by civil suits, but that you will be imprisoned for criminal negligence as well.

In addition to a pay scale and privileges well above those accorded lieutenant-colonels in Earthling armies, we can offer you immunity from all Earthling legal harassment, and an opportunity to see a new and interesting planet, and an opportunity to think about your native planet from a fresh and beautifully detached viewpoint.

Hemingway, Ernest. *Vonnegut opens the prologue to* Timequake *(a metafictional text in which Vonnegut both as character and author tries to recall what it is like to salvage his book that was ten years in the making) referencing the heroic efforts of Santiago, the Cuban fisherman in Hemingway's* The Old Man and the Sea *who heroically tries and fails to bring ashore the enormous marlin lashed to the side of his small boat before the sharks eat it all. Vonnegut hits upon the solution that eluded Santiago but that is squarely within his own writerly insight:* Filet the fish. Throw the rest away. *Vonnegut considers how much past his artistic prime he must be (mentioning the toils of Hemingway, Brahms, and his worn out architect father, Kurt Sr.) and likens* Timequake *to Santiago's marlin,* My great big fish, which stunk so, was entitled *Timequake. Let us think of it as* Timequake One. *And let us think of this one, a stew made from its best parts mixed with* thoughts and experiences during the past seven months or so, as *Timequake Two*.

Kilgore Trout, A hobo for much of his life, he died in luxury in the **Ernest Hemingway Suite** of the writers' retreat Xanadu in the summer resort village of Point Zion, Rhode Island. That's nice to know (*TQ* Prologue).

It is in the Ernest Hemingway Suite on the afternoon preceding the text's climactic clambake that Trout tells Vonnegut about the night his father—the man who had killed his mother—woke him and told him the slightly ribald "ting-a-ling" story concerning an escaped fugitive who had his testicles whacked by a policeman's billy club (TQ 4).

The Ernest Hemingway Suite is also the site where Dudley Prince turns over to Trout the four stories he thought he had thrown into the garbage receptacle outside the American Academy of Arts and Letters (TQ 5).

Vonnegut goes on to point out that among other things, neither he nor Hemingway had ever killed another being. However, as the topics of suicide, age, and fraternity frequently reappear in the text, Vonnegut opines, If self-respect breaks a leg, the leg can never heal. Its owner has to shoot it. My mother and **Ernest Hemingway** and my former literary agent and Jerzy Kosinski and my reluctant thesis advisor at the University of Chicago and Eva Braun all come to mind.

But not Kilgore Trout. His indestructible self-respect is what I loved most about Kilgore Trout. Men loving men can happen, in peacetime as well as war. I also loved my war buddy Bernard V. O'Hare (*TQ* 13).

In the introduction to Bogombo Snuff Box, *Vonnegut admires the short story writers who moved him as a young reader and takes pride in having published in some of the same magazines early in his career that other literary luminaries had:* Short stories can have greatness, short as they have to be. Several knocked my socks off when I was still in high school. **Ernest Hemingway's** "The Short Happy Life of Francis Macomber" and Saki's "The Open Window" and O. Henry's "The Gift of the Magi" and Ambrose Bierce's "An Occurrence at Owl Creek Bridge" spring to mind. But there is no greatness in this or my other collection, nor was there meant to be (*BAG* Introduction).

(*MWC* 1) **Ernest Hemingway** wrote a story after the First World War called "A Soldier's Home" about how it was very rude to ask a soldier what he'd seen when he got back home. I think a lot of people, including me, clammed up when a civilian asked about battle, about war. It was fashionable. One of the most impressive ways to tell your war story is to refuse to tell it, you know. Civilians would then have to imagine all kinds of deeds of derring-do.

Vonnegut's very close friend Sidney Offit notes in his foreword to the posthumously published Look at the Birdie *that Vonnegut took great pride in having published in the same magazines as had so many of America's great writers—including Hemingway.*

Hepburn, Mary and Roy. *In* Galápagos, *the childless Hepburns are lifelong Iliumites. Roy is a millwright at GEFFCo, Ilium's largest employer. For twenty-five years Mary is a much-loved high school biology teacher. So well loved is she that for twelve consecutive years the students voted her the most popular teacher. Her nickname among the students is "Mother Nature Personified" and the high school's last graduating class dedicated their yearbook to her.*

After years of service to GEFFCo and then to its successor Matsumoto, Roy is summarily discharged along with hundreds of other workers. Matsumoto had so well computerized the manufacturing process that only twelve workers were needed to run the mill. On the day of his discharge, Roy signs them up for "the Nature Cruise of the Century." They were the very first people to sign on for the trip. Shortly thereafter, Roy's brain tumor is detected and he dies August 3, 1986, at the age of fifty-nine. Mary, then fifty-one, keeps her promise to him and travels down to Ecuador for the cruise.

A distant relative of Daniel Boone, Mary becomes the midwife to the next evolutionary step for Homo sapiens. She secretively uses the sperm from Captain Adolf von Kleist to inseminate the Kankabono girls. One of the sons from this union pairs off with the furry Akiko, the product of genetic mutation due to radiation fallout at Hiroshima, and the human race is well on its way to returning to the sea as something closely resembling sea lions.

Though deeply devoted to her husband, Roy, Mary has a brief affair with Robert Wojciehowitz, head of the English Department at Ilium High

School. Later, while on board the Bahía de Darwin, *she takes pity on the dying con artist James Wait (posing as Willard Flemming), and marries him just before he dies. She lives with Adolf von Kleist for ten years after being stranded, breaking up only after he finds out about her use of his sperm. She dies at the age of eighty-one when eaten by a shark.*

Herald, Randy. *The showgirl whose picture is on the cover of* The Investigator *with the headline "I WANT A MAN WHO CAN GIVE ME A GENIUS BABY!" (GBR 8) Insurance salesman Fred Rosewater uses the headline as an opportunity to launch into a life insurance pitch to the few customers in the coffee shop.*

Herpers, Dr. Albert. *In* Player Piano, *the president of Cornell University and the recipient of a five-year-old letter from Doctor Ewing J. Halyard, highly critical of the school's football program. Doctor Herpers shares the letter with football coach Roseberry, who gladly exacts revenge upon Halyard when a computer check finds that Halyard is short a physical education class and will have to return to Cornell or lose his advanced degrees.*

Herrick, Cleota. *Despite being dubbed "the ugliest woman in Indiana," Noah Rosewater married her because she had four hundred thousand dollars. With her money he expanded the factory and bought more farms, all in Rosewater County. He became the largest individual hog farmer in the North. And, in order not to be victimized by meat packers, he bought controlling interest in an Indianapolis slaughterhouse. In order not to be victimized by steel suppliers, he bought controlling interest in a steel company in Pittsburgh. In order not to be victimized by coal suppliers, he bought controlling interest in several mines. In order not to be victimized by money lenders, he founded a bank (GBR 1). Cleota is the great-grandmother of Eliot Rosewater. She gives birth to Samuel Rosewater, who becomes a Republican Party king-maker.*

Hertz, Rudy. *In* Player Piano, *the aging lathe operator at the Ilium Works whose work motion is immortalized on a computer tape by Paul Proteus, Ed Finnerty, and Lawson Shepherd. The tape is then used to develop computerized manufacturing machines that replicate the operations of master workers. The three young engineers' experiments greatly contribute to automating blue-collar workers out of employment.*

Hickenlooper, John, Jr. and Sr. *In* Timequake, *Vonnegut recalls going out to Denver for an art show of his prints with artistic collaborator Joe Petro III. As an homage to Vonnegut, Wynkoop Brewing Company, under the ownership of local microbrewer (and later Denver mayor) John Hickenlooper, Jr., creates Kurt's Mile-High Malt from the recipe of his maternal grandfather Albert Lieber. (TQ 38) The secret ingredient in the beer that won a Gold Medal for the Indianapolis Brewery at the Paris Exposition of 1889 was coffee!*

Ting-a-ling!

That still wasn't enough fun out there in Denver? OK, how about the fact that the name of the owner of the Wynkoop Brewing Company, a guy about Joe's age, was **John Hickenlooper**? So what? Only this: When I went to Cornell University to become a chemist fifty-six years ago, I was made a fraternity brother of a man named **John Hickenlooper**.

Ting-a-ling?

This was his son! My fraternity brother had died when this son was only seven. I knew more about him than his own son did! I was able to tell this young Denver brewer that his dad, in partnership with another Delta Upsilon brother, John Locke, sold candy and soft drinks and cigarettes out of a big closet at the top of the stairs on the second floor of the fraternity house.

They christened it *Hickenlooper's Lockenbar.* We called it *Lockenlooper's Hickenbar,* and *Barkenhicker's Loopenlock,* and *Lockenbarker's Loopenhick,* and so on.

Happy days! We thought we'd live forever.

Old beer in new bottles. Old jokes in new people.

* * *

I told young **John Hickenlooper** a joke his dad taught me. It worked like this: His dad would say to me, no matter where we were, "Are you a member of the Turtle Club?" I had no choice but to bellow at the top of my lungs, "YOU BET YOUR ASS I AM!"

I could do the same thing to his dad. On some particularly solemn and sacred occasion, such as the swearing in of new fraternity brothers, I might whisper to him, "Are you a member of the Turtle Club?" He would have no choice but to bellow at the top of his lungs, "YOU BET YOUR ASS I AM!"

Higgins, Kiah. *In the short story "The Powder-Blue Dragon," collected in* Bagombo Snuff Box (1999), *the orphaned Kiah Higgins diligently saves his money from various and simultaneous hourly jobs with one goal in mind—buying the legendary and seemingly mystical Marittima-Frascati sports car. With such a car, Kiah would gain a presence, an importance for being someone of note, something that so escapes him in his everyday life that he blends into the background. His sense of ignored anonymity is so great that he feels compelled to point out to his local druggist, someone who knows him long and well, that his name is printed on the $5 check he wants to cash.*

Kiah writes a check for the Marittima-Frascati's full purchase price of $5,651 and hands it over to his employer, car dealer Bill Daggett. In shocked disbelief, Daggett calls George, a banker in the next town, only to learn that Kiah's check is indeed good. When delivering the car to Kiah, Daggett explains in great detail how to break in its engine, a process that will take thousands of miles before the owner should think about testing its top speed rating of 130 mph. Kiah has other plans.

On his first day of ownership, Kiah coyly plays cat and mouse with a beautiful stranger driving a Cadillac convertible. Her name turns out to be Marion. Kiah decides to follow Marion off the turnpike and turns in at the same cocktail lounge where she has plans to meet Paul, her fiancé. Kiah hopes to strike up a conversation with her. He hopes that some of the car's class will rub off on him and remove the specter of anonymity. Such is not the case. She knows little about cars. The beginning of her brief conversation with Kiah displays her quick wit through double entendre (she takes his reference to her Cadillac with a quick quip and cutting revelation about herself and her views of the men in her life) while also dismissing him with tactless honesty.

"Hello," he said to the girl, with more assurance than he thought possible. "How's the Cad treating you?"

She laughed. "My car, my fiancé, or my father?"

"Your car," **Kiah** said, feeling stupid for not having a snappier retort.

"Cads always treat me nicely. I remember you now. You were in that darling little blue thing with yellow seats. I somehow didn't connect you with the car. You look different."

Similar to Marion's disbelief that Kiah owns the sports car, bartender Ralph and fiancé Paul are also suspicious that Kiah's car could be as powerful as he says it is or that he is the owner. Neither asks for his name, leaving Kiah, for all practical purposes, anonymous.

Marion and Paul take off in his British Hampton, and Kiah soon passes them in his Marittima-Frascati, flipping them the bird. But Kiah senses that the car will not resolve his invisibility. He deliberately runs the speedometer to 144 mph before the engine ceases, turning the car into a burned-out worthless heap of metal.

When Kiah was orphaned at the age of sixteen because his parents died in a head-on crash (determined by officials to be their fault), his sense of anonymity only increases as a boardinghouse tenant. His hope that owning a classy automobile would make him known (at least for his extravagance) did not play out. Killing the car as he did—an exotic sports car taken beyond its limits on its first day of ownership by an obsessed young man with nothing else to his name—well, perhaps that would be the one act of his that would make people curious about his name. As he tells a befuddled Daggett once he makes his way back to the dealership, "That's one dead sports vehicle. You'll have to send the tow truck."

"My God, boy, why would you do such a thing?"

"Call me **Kiah**."

"**Kiah**," echoed Daggett, convinced he was dealing with a lunatic.

"Who knows why anybody does anything?" said **Kiah**. "I don't know why I killed it. All I know is I'm glad it's dead."

In killing the Marittima-Frascati, Kiah asserts his identity (echoing Melville's opening line, "Call me Ishmael," as well as Vonnegut's draft opening of

Cat's Cradle, *"Call me Jonah," penned in the 1950s, though the novel did not appear in print until 1963). Kiah will forever be known in the old whaling village as the man who killed his prized possession on his first day of ownership.*

Higgins, Mr. and Mrs. *In the short story "The Powder-Blue Dragon," collected in* Bagombo Snuff Box (1999), *His (Kiah's) father had worked for a landscape contractor, his mother as a chambermaid at the Howard Johnson's out on the turnpike. They were killed in a head-on collision in front of the Howard Johnson's when Kiah was sixteen. The police had said the crash was their fault. His parents had no money, and their secondhand Plymouth Fury was totaled, so they didn't even have a car to leave him.*

Hildreth, Celia (*see* **Celia Hoover**).

Hildreth, Gerald. *The sixty-year-old owner of an immaculately kept taxicab on eastern Long Island, whose local roots go back three hundred years. Bluebeard's Rabo Karabekian points out that when Hildreth was with the Rescue Squad, he found Jackson Pollock's body sixty feet from the tree his car hit and only weeks later was picking up the pieces of Terry Kitchen's head.*

Hildreth, Shirley. *In* Deadeye Dick, *Celia Hildreth Hoover's sister who left Midland City and was never heard from again, though she was rumored to have been seen as an extra in the remake of* King Kong.

Hilton, Gloria. *The movie star wife of the writer George Murra in the 1962 short story "Go Back to Your Precious Wife and Son," reprinted in* Welcome to the Monkey House (1968). *Her previous four husbands were a motorcycle policeman, a sugar millionaire, a Tarzan movie star, and her agent. The couple moved from Los Angeles to New Hampshire so Murra could be closer to his son (from his first marriage), who was attending a private high school. The unnamed narrator of the story is a bathtub enclosure salesman and installer who witnesses the breakup of Hilton and Murra. She has grown weary of Murra, who has failed to write a word since their*

move. The bathtub man is there to install a custom-made shower door with a glass etching of Gloria Hilton's head. At the height of the marital spat she tells Murra to go back to his wife and son.

Hilyer, Tom. *The middle-class Whitehill School classmate of the wealthy Dr. Remenzel, both of whom are escorting their sons to the ritzy private school for their own first day. Hilyer and his son were both scholarship students, meaning their parents didn't have the means to send them. They earned their way into Whitehill on academic merit, the primary criterion for admission. Remenzel's son, Eli, has not told his parents that he failed to meet the strict academic requirements for admission, and this is why the short story is called "The Lie." (See also entry for Remenzel.)*

Hinkley, Bearse. *The seventy-two-year-old pharmacist in the short story "Miss Temptation" (reprinted in* Welcome to the Monkey House) *who kindly prepares Susanna's New York newspapers for her alluring and barefoot arrival each afternoon. When the recently returned Corporal Fuller demeans Susanna for her bohemian appearance, she decides to leave the summer stock theater troop. Hinkley convinces Fuller that he must deliver Susanna's newspapers and apologize for his jealousy.*

Hiroguchi, Akiko. *The daughter of Zenji and Hisako Hiroguchi, Akiko's genetic code is altered by her mother's exposure to radiation during the atomic bombing of Hiroshima. She was born on the "northern-most extremity of the Galápagos Islands." The result is that Akiko and Kamikaze (Captain von Kleist's son by one of the Kankabono women made possible by Mary Hepburn's unauthorized use of von Kleist's sperm), give rise to an entirely new, furry version of humans. Thus, Hiroshima's atomic bombing and an unwitting German American provide the basis for man's return to the sea—a salvation of sorts considering the fate of the Earth from Leon Trout's perspective across a million years in the future. (Gal 1:13) When* **Akiko** *became an adult on Santa Rosalia, she would be very much like her mother on the inside, but in a different sort of skin . . .* **Akiko** *was protected from sunburn, and from the chilly water when she swam, and the abrasiveness of lava when* she chose to sit or lie down—whereas her mother's bare skin was wholly defenseless against these ordinary hazards of island life.

Hiroguchi, Hisako. *The wife of Zenji Hiroguchi and the mother of Akiko, the furry progenitor of humanity as it moves back to the oceans. Hisako's mother survives the atomic-bombing of Hiroshima, but her genetic code is altered so that when Hisako gives birth to Akiko, she was covered with a fine fur coat.*

Hisako taught ikebana, the Japanese art of flower arranging. She became infuriated with Zenji when she learned he had programmed Mandarax to teach ikebana in hundreds of languages.

After the paranoid schizophrenic deserter Private Geraldo Delgado kills Zenji during a looting spree, Hisako pairs off with the blind Selena MacIntosh. Together they die in a suicide pact thirty-one years after being stranded on Galápagos. Hisako suffered deep depression for her last twenty years.

Hiroguchi, Zenji. *In* Galápagos, *the husband of Hisako and father of Akiko, this twenty-nine-year-old computer genius creates Gokubi and then Mandarax. Though an acknowledged computer genius, he is a salary worker for Matsumoto, and this allows Andrew MacIntosh to approach Hiroguchi about opening his own company. MacIntosh invites Zenji and Hisako to visit his Mexican villa and then join him for "the Nature Cruise of the Century" in the hope he could get Hiroguchi to leave Matsumoto. The Hiroguchis travel to Mexico under the name Kenzaburo, listing Zenji's occupation as a veterinarian. The paranoid schizophrenic deserter Private Geraldo Delgado, who had been looting a store down on the docks of Guayaquil, shoots Hiroguchi and MacIntosh in the backs of their heads.*

Hiscock, Ernest Hubble. (HP 7) He was a Tarkington graduate who at the age of 21 was a nose-gunner on a Navy bomber whose pilot crashed his plane with a full load of bombs onto the flight deck of a Japanese aircraft carrier in the Battle of Midway during World War II. *His divorced parents took up a collection to repair and mechanize the Lutz Carillon. This had been a source of displeasure for some alumni, who felt modernization took away*

from the college's tradition. Without the need for students to swing on the bell ropes, the bells could be played by keyboard, which is exactly what gave Eugene Debs Hartke so much pleasure years later.

Hitler, Adolf (*also* **Adolph**; *see also* **God Bless You, Dr. Kevorkian**). Vonnegut mentions Hitler in Mother Night, Cat's Cradle, Slaughterhouse-Five, Wanda June, Jailbird, Deadeye Dick, Galápagos, Bluebeard, Hocus Pocus, Bagombo Snuff Box, God Bless You, Dr. Kevorkian, *and* Armageddon in Retrospect.

In Timequake, *Hitler's final moments in his besieged Berlin bunker are imagined in Kilgore Trout's short story "Bunker Bingo Party."* (TQ 23) A Communistic 240-millimeter howitzer shell explodes atop the bunker. Flakes of calcimine from the shaken ceiling shower down on the deafened occupants. **Hitler** himself makes a joke, demonstrating that he still has his sense of humor. "It snows," he says. That is a poetic way of saying, too, it is high time he killed himself, unless he wants to become a caged superstar in a traveling freak show, along with the bearded lady and the geek.

He puts a pistol to his head. Everybody says, "Nein, nein, nein." He convinces everyone that shooting himself is the dignified thing to do. What should his last words be? He says, "How about 'I regret nothing'?"

Goebbels replies that such a statement would be appropriate, but that the Parisian cabaret performer Edith Piaf has made a worldwide reputation by singing those same words in French for decades. "Her sobriquet," says Goebbels, "is 'Little Sparrow.' You don't want to be remembered as a little sparrow, or I miss my guess."

Hitler still hasn't lost his sense of humor. He says, "How about 'BINGO'?"

But he is tired. He puts the pistol to his head again. He says, "I never asked to be born in the first place."

The pistol goes "BANG!"

In God Bless You, Dr. Kevorkian, *a rather truculent Hitler is one of Vonnegut's interviewees in the blue tunnel to the Afterlife.* (GBK Adolf Hitler) I was lucky enough on this trip to interview none other than the late **Adolf Hitler**.

I was gratified to learn that he now feels remorse

for any actions of his, however indirectly, which might have had anything to do with the violent deaths suffered by thirty-five million people during World War II. He and his mistress Eva Braun, of course, were among those casualties, along with four million other Germans, six million Jews, eighteen million citizens of the Soviet Union, and so on.

"I paid my dues along with everybody else," he said.

It is his hope that a modest monument, possibly a stone cross, since he was a Christian, will be erected somewhere in his memory, possibly on the grounds of the United Nations headquarters in New York. It should be incised, he said, with his name and dates 1889–1945. Underneath should be a two-word sentence in German: "Entschuldigen Sie."

Roughly translated into English, this comes out, "I Beg Your Pardon," or "Excuse Me."

In Man Without a Country, *Vonnegut talks about the virtues of "freshwater people" (people from the landlocked interior of a country) and charismatic speakers. He segues from praising Carl Sandburg, Abraham Lincoln, and Eugene Victor Debs to considerations of social organizations along the lines of religious and political doctrines. In short order Vonnegut reveals the limitations of such pride. (MWC 2)* "Socialism" is no more an evil word than "Christianity." Socialism no more prescribed Joseph Stalin and his secret police and shuttered churches than Christianity prescribed the Spanish Inquisition. Christianity and socialism alike, in fact, prescribe a society dedicated to the proposition that all men, women, and children are created equal and shall not starve.

Adolf Hitler, incidentally, was a two-fer. He named his party the National Socialists, the Nazis. **Hitler**'s swastika wasn't a pagan symbol, as so many people believe. It was a working person's Christian cross, made of axes, of tools.

Hitz, Benjamin D. (*JB* Dedication) For **Benjamin D. Hitz**, / Close friend of my youth, / Best man at my wedding. / Ben, you used to tell me about / Wonderful books you had just read, / And then I would imagine that I / Had read them, too. / You read nothing but the best, Ben, / While I studied chemistry. / Long time no see.

Hitz is also mentioned in the dedication of Galápagos as one of Vonnegut's companions on a trip out west with Hillis L. Howie.

In Timequake, *Vonnegut provides this update on* **Benjamin Hitz**, The Best Man at Jane's and my wedding in Indianapolis, **Benjamin Hitz** of Indianapolis, is a widower now in Santa Barbara, California. **Ben** dated an Indianapolis cousin of mine several times this spring. She is a widow on the seacoast of Maryland (*TQ* 45).

In the short story "2BR02B," collected in Bagombo Snuff Box (1999), *Vonnegut keeps the memory alive of his childhood best friend and best man at his first wedding by using his name for that of the physician at the Chicago Lying-in Hospital in charge of both obstetrics and the facility's adherence to the strict population rules. He is, after all, the inventor of Ethical Suicide Studios. He holds a prominent place and flattering rendition in "The Happy Garden of Life," the mural being painted by the nearly two-hundred-year-old artist whose experiences have him doubting the ethics and fairness of the entire population control premise. He was referring to one of the male figures in white, whose head was a portrait of* **Dr. Benjamin Hitz**, *the hospital's chief obstetrician. Hitz was a blindingly handsome man.*

His advancements in science cause the suicide hostess Leora Duncan to fawn over the artist's rendering. "Who doesn't admire him?" she said, worshipping the portrait of **Hitz**. *It was the portrait of a tanned, white-haired, omnipotent Zeus, two hundred forty years old. "Who doesn't admire him?" she said again. "He was responsible for setting up the very first gas chamber in Chicago."*

"Nothing would please me more," said the painter, "than to put you next to him for all time. Sawing off a limb—that strikes you as appropriate?"

"That is kind of like what I do," she said. She was demure about what she did. What she did was make people comfortable while she killed them.

And while Leora Duncan was posing for her portrait, into the waiting room bounded **Dr. Hitz** *himself. He was seven feet tall, and he boomed with importance, accomplishments, and the joy of living.*

Because Leora Duncan does not glean the sarcasm of the muralist, she is more than happy to have her portrait so closely situated to that of Dr. Hitz.

Hitz is eventually killed by Edward K. Wehling, Jr., the new father of triplets. Wehling also kills Leora Duncan before committing suicide to satisfy the law's needs for three older souls in exchange for any new ones born into the world.

Hitz, Lowell W. *The twenty-five millionth child born in the Chicago Lying-in Hospital, according to a news report in the life-without-aging short story* "Tomorrow and Tomorrow and Tomorrow," *published in 1953 and reprinted in* Welcome to the Monkey House *(1968).*

Hobby Show prizewinner. *In the short story* "Poor Little Rich Town," *collected in* Bagombo Snuff Box *(1999), the Spruce Falls Annual Hobby Show is an opportunity for anyone in town to submit an entry based on their own particular interest, provided the entry is completely unique to the entire show. In effect, there are as many prize categories as there are entrants. Hence, everyone becomes a blue ribbon winner. Everyone goes home feeling good about themselves, affirmed that they are being recognized for their unique effort at living a meaningful life.*

All that changes when the efficiency expert Newell Cady from the Federal Apparatus Corporation moves to town and objects to such a scheme. He is from the corporate world where there are very clearly winners and losers. He convinces the show's other judges that only a single winner should be selected. The effect of this on the townspeople is quite clear. Those few nonparticipants who dropped in at the church to see the exhibits, and who hadn't heard about the judging, were amazed to find one lonely object, a petit-point copy of the cover of a woman's magazine, on view. Pinned to it was the single blue ribbon awarded that day. The other exhibitors had angrily hauled home their rejected offerings, and the sole **prizewinner** appeared late in the evening, embarrassed and furtive, to take her entry home, leaving the blue ribbon behind.

Hocus Pocus *(1990) (see also* **Eugene Debs Hartke, Tarkington College, Hiroshi Matsumoto**). *Vonnegut uses the magicians' famous phrase in reference to man's ability to rationalize new, often misleading explanations of history. Outside of the novel named for such a "big-brained" skill, its only other occurrence is early in* Breakfast of Champions. *In that novel's opening pages, when Vonnegut debunks the myths we are taught as youngsters in elementary school, he says,* It was as though the country were saying to its citizens, *"In nonsense is strength."*

A lot of the nonsense was the innocent result of playfulness on the part of the founding fathers of the nation of Dwayne Hoover and Kilgore Trout. The founders were aristocrats, and they wished to show off their useless education, which consisted of the study of **hocus-pocus** from ancient times (BC 1).

Considering Vonnegut's usage for the term, it is surprising it doesn't reappear until the novel Hocus Pocus. *Eugene Debs Hartke uses it to describe the tirades he would employ to encourage his troops in Vietnam to be the best, most ruthless soldiers they could be.* (HP 19) In Vietnam, though, I really was the mastermind. Yes, and that still bothers me. During my last year there, when my ammunition was language instead of bullets, I invented justifications for all the killing and dying we were doing which impressed even me! I was a genius of lethal **hocus pocus**!

. . . If my list of women isn't to include high school or prostitutes, then my list of those whose lives I took shouldn't include possibles and probables, or those killed by artillery or air strikes called in by me, and surely not all those, many of them Americans, who died as an indirect result of all my **hocus pocus**, all my blah blah blah.

When Hartke reflects on the murder mystery of Letitia Smiley, he understands the college's position in relation to the investigation based on his Vietnam experience. (HP 24) I have to wonder, too, in light of my own experiences in public-relations **hocus pocus** and the recent history of my Government, if there weren't a lot of people back in 1922 *(the year of Vonnegut's birth)* who could put 2 and 2 together as easily as I have now. For the sake of the reputation of what had become Scipio's principal business, the college, there could have been a massive cover-up.

As much as anything else, Hocus Pocus *is about the loss of history and culture. These memoirs of Eugene Debs Hartke, written in the library of what was Tarkington College and now part of the New York*

State prison system, include considerations of parental fraud, the legacy of genetic disabilities, and the loss of a traditionally dynamic relationship and communal bond held by the wealthy in common with the working classes (this harkens back to themes in God Bless You, Mr. Rosewater). Captivated by the search for a worthy perpetual-motion machine and his concern for those with learning disabilities, Elias Tarkington established the Mohiga Valley Free Institute in 1869. In 1875 the school's name was changed but its mission remained. Over time it became a beacon for learning-disabled children of wealthy families from around the world. The list of college benefactors includes historical figures noted for their brutality (Pahlavi, the family of the former Shah of Iran; Somoza, the former Central American dictator) and fictitious characters such as Jason Wilder, a William F. Buckley type whose extreme conservatism is the driving force behind Hartke's 1991 dismissal for "teaching pessimism."

Vonnegut uses the time frame of the novel, from the rise of The Mohiga Wagon Company to the takeover of Tarkington College, to show the roots of American wealth and cultural dominance as well as its demise. Scipio and Tarkington prospered as long as people maintained meaningful occupations. Once America achieved such a high standard of living that people did not want to work as hard as they once did, industry closed its domestic plants and reopened abroad, resulting in a shift of wealth. America became a consumer rather than a producer, eventually losing its ability to handle such central functions as maintaining its prison systems. Any idea of an enduring American Dream is doomed from the hocus pocus it inflicts on its people in the false pursuit of maintaining its culture.

Hoenikker, Angela. The oldest of Felix Hoenikker's three children, Angela is the source for most of Little Newt's childhood memories of his father. When she was sixteen her mother died while giving birth to Newt, leaving Angela to care for her father and brothers. She and her brothers each had chips of ice-nine from their father's first experiment, the one that killed him and the family's dog. It was she who found their father dead on Christmas Eve, and it was she who helped John/Jonah clean up the shards of ice-nine splintered from the frozen sink full of water attached to the equally stone-frozen body of Dr. von Koenigswald.

Newt provides an important historical footnote about Angela. (CC 6) "**Angela** was one of the unsung heroines of the atom bomb, incidentally, and I don't think the story has ever been told. Maybe you can use it. After the turtle incident (Dr. Hoenikker wondered whether their spines buckled or contracted), Father got so interested in turtles that he stopped working on the atom bomb. Some people from the Manhattan Project finally came out to the house to ask **Angela** what to do. She told them to take away Father's turtles. So one night they went into his laboratory and stole the turtles and the aquarium. Father never said a word about the disappearance of the turtles. He just came to work the next day and looked for things to play with and think about, and everything there was to play with and think about had something to do with the bomb. . . . Father was all she had. She didn't have any boy friends. She didn't have any friends at all. She had only one hobby. She played the Clarinet."

John/Jonah is crude in his initial description of her. (CC 51, 53) **Angela** was the horse-faced platinum blonde I had noticed earlier.

. . . And then **Angela**, a woman to whom God had given virtually nothing with which to catch a man, showed me a picture of her husband (Harrison C. Conners, onetime lab assistant to her father and now president of Fabri-Tek in Indianapolis). Angela's marriage is a complete failure according to Newt, who tells John/Jonah how cruel and unfaithful Conners is to his sister.

While having drinks on San Lorenzo with Newt, Julian Castle, and John/Jonah, Angela gets sentimentally sloppy and resentful of how little monetary compensation her father received for his scientific achievements. Newt asks her to play her clarinet for them since that always calms and pleases him. Newt sees this as a way of settling down Angela more than anything else. The ensuing scene startlingly reveals the true depth and talent of this hideous giant for John/Jonah. (CC 81) I did not know what was going to come from **Angela**'s clarinet. No one could have imagined what was going to come from there.

I expected something pathological, but I did not expect the depth, the violence, and the almost intolerable beauty of the disease.

Angela moistened and warmed the mouthpiece, but did not blow a single preliminary note. Her eyes glazed over, and her long, bony fingers twittered idly over the noiseless keys. . . .

Meade Lux Lewis played four bars alone—and then **Angela Hoenikker** joined in.

Her eyes were closed. I was flabbergasted. She was great.

She improvised around the music of the Pullman porter's son, went from liquid lyricism to rasping lechery to the shrill skittishness of a frightened child, to a heroin nightmare.

Her glissandi spoke of heaven and hell and all that lay between.

Such music from such a woman could only be a case of schizophrenia or demonic possession.

My hair stood on end, as though **Angela** were rolling on the floor, foaming at the mouth, and babbling fluent Babylonian.

When the music was done, I shrieked at Julian Castle, who was transfixed, too, "My God—life! Who can understand even one little minute of it?"

"Don't try," he said. "Just pretend you understand."

"That's—that's very good advice." I went limp.

Angela's death was an equally moving scene for John/Jonah. (CC 126) And I saw magnificence in the way poor **Angela** had died, too. She had picked up a clarinet in the ruins of Bolivar and had begun to play it at once, without concerning herself as to whether the mouthpiece might be contaminated with ice-nine.

"Soft pipes, play on," I murmured huskily.

Hoenikker, Celia. *In* Cat's Cradle, *Dr. Felix Hoenikker's unseen sister who lives on Shelter Island, New York, raising giant schnauzers.*

Hoenikker, Dr. Felix. *The Nobel Prize winner for physics and father of ice-nine in* Cat's Cradle. *He stole away the heart of Emily from his future boss Dr. Marvin Breed, when both were students at M.I.T. A short man, Hoenikker sired a giantess, Angela, and a midget, Newton (Little Newt). Franklin was the middle child. There were rumors that Dr. Breed actually fathered Emily's children.*

The narrator of the text makes a research trip to Ilium as part of his research for his book The Day the World Ended, *a chronicle of the activities conducted by the scientists responsible for the atom bomb on the day it was dropped on Hiroshima. In a sense, he was looking for the ironic Sunday family barbecue on the day the bomb was dropped. The narrator later learns from Newton that on that fateful day, Dr. Hoenikker was in his pajamas and bathrobe, smoking a cigar, and playing "cat's cradle" with a piece of string. What he finds at the Research Laboratory of the General Forge and Foundry Company is Hoenikker's legacy of playful absentmindedness. Ice-nine became a reality after a Marine general complained about all the mud the Marines traditionally had to get through.*

Hoenikker died of an apparent heart attack at his Cape Cod home on Christmas Eve after telling his children about his invention. He was busy melting down the sliver of ice-nine when he took a break, sat in his wicker chair, and died. The children returned, cleaned up the puddles of water in the kitchen, and when the family dog licked the towel he froze into a furry stone. The children then split up the remaining ice-nine between them.

Vonnegut's inspiration for Dr. Hoenikker is recounted in the "Playboy Interview," reprinted in Palm Sunday. *(PS Self-Interview)* VONNEGUT: **Dr. Felix Hoenikker**, the absent-minded scientist, was a caricature of Dr. Irving Langmuir, the star of the G.E. Research Laboratory. I knew him some. My brother worked with him. Langmuir was wonderfully absent-minded. He wondered out loud one time whether, when turtles pulled in their heads, their spines buckled or contracted. I put that in the book. One time he left a tip under his plate after his wife served him breakfast at home. I put that in. His most important contribution, though, was the idea for what I called "Ice-9," a form of frozen water that was stable at room temperature. He didn't tell it directly to me. It was a legend around the Laboratory about the time H. G. Wells came to Schenectady. That was long before my time. I was just a little boy when it happened—listening to the radio, building model airplanes.

Hoenikker, Emily. *The wife of Felix Hoenikker and mother of Franklin, Angela, and Newt. She dies during the birth of Newt because of a previously crushed pelvis suffered after driving Felix's Marmon. She was* driving his car because Felix snapped one day and left his car in traffic.

Before meeting Felix, Emily and Marvin Breed, the tombstone carver and salesman, were starting to become good friends while still in high school. They were cochairs of the Class Colors Committee. Breed gives up football to take violin lessons because Emily is such a well-accomplished musician on a number of instruments. When Asa Breed comes home from M.I.T. with schoolmate Felix Hoenikker, Emily breaks Marvin's heart.

Emily's unusual tombstone is described as an alabaster phallus twenty feet high and three feet thick (CC 29).

Hoenikker, Franklin. *The middle child of Emily and Dr. Felix Hoenikker, Frank grows up a solemn and solitary child. On the day of Hiroshima's bombing, he is busy putting red and black ants in a jar to see them fight. In high school he gets a job at Jack's Hobby Shop, where he spends all his earnings on constructing a realistic, small-scale depiction of an entire country. Unknown to Jack, Frank was also having a sexual affair with his wife. Because he spent all his afternoon and evening time in the hobby shop, he often fell asleep in school and is derisively called "Secret Agent X-9" by the other students, who universally look at him as an oddball.*

Frank leaves Ilium during the graveside funeral service for his father and hitches his way down to Sarasota, Florida. There he goes to work at a model shop, which turns out to be a front for running stolen cars to Cuba. Two years after the death of his father, the Treasury Department secures a warrant for his arrest, but he flees the country in a boat that just makes it to San Lorenzo before sinking. Though at first placed under arrest by the authorities, when Papa Monzano finds out he is the son of Felix Hoenikker, he releases him from prison and makes him a Major General and Minister of Science and Progress in the Republic of San Lorenzo. In exchange, Frank gives him the sliver of ice-nine he had since his father died. Frank is twenty-six at the time.

Hoenikker, Newton. *The youngest child of Emily and Dr. Felix Hoenikker, Little Newt is literally the midget of the family. The narrator of Cat's Cradle*

contacts Newt once he finds out he is pledging the Delta Upsilon fraternity. The narrator was a Cornell alumnus and a DU brother. (Vonnegut attended Cornell before the war and became a DU brother as well.) Little Newt had planned to major in pre-med, but he flunks out and is forced to resign his DU pledge. Along with his brother and sister, Newt receives one-third of the remaining ice-nine after his father's death.

After only a brief acquaintance, Newt marries Zinka, a Ukrainian midget and dancer with the Borzoi Dance Company performing in Indianapolis. Shortly after their honeymoon, Zinka steals Newt's chip of ice-nine and returns to the Soviet Union. She claims to be twenty-three, but Newt later finds out she is forty-two.

Little Newt's birth causes the death of his mother. She had previously crushed her pelvis in a car accident. She was not used to driving her husband's Marmon, which she retrieved from downtown Ilium when he abandoned it in traffic one morning.

Hoenikker, Rudolph. *Dr. Felix Hoenikker's identical twin. He lives in Zurich and manufactures music boxes. As with their sister Celia, Rudolph is mentioned but not seen in* Cat's Cradle.

Hoess, Rudolf Franz. *The Commandant of Auschwitz who was hanged in 1947 with the assistance of Bernard Mengel, one of Howard Campbell's Jerusalem prison guards in* Mother Night. *Campbell credits Hoess with organizing the Sonderkommando, the corpse-carrying volunteers from the Auschwitz inmates. Campbell further cites Hoess as one of the prime illustrations of the "cuckoo-clock in hell"—his description of the totalitarian mind.*

Hoffman, Abbie. *Vonnegut cites the famous antiwar activist Abbie Hoffman with only the highest esteem.* (FWD XIX) "I was willing to believe back in the 1960s that deep meditation as practiced in India might be a way to achieve happiness and wisdom which had not been previously available to people of European and African stock. The Beatles also believed this for a while. I doubt that the late, great (I mean it) **Abbie Hoffman** ever believed it. He wasn't about to give up his frenzied sense of humor, the

sanest thing in this country during the Vietnam War, in exchange for personal, inner peace."
(*FWD* XIX) I mentioned **Abbie Hoffman** in that piece about books as mantras for meditation. I realize that most people nowadays don't know who he was or what he did. He was a clowning genius, having come into the world that way, like Lenny Bruce and Jack Benny and Ed Wynn and Stan Laurel and W. C. Fields and the Marx Brothers and Red Skelton and Fred Allen and Woody Allen and so on. He was a member of my children's generation. He is high on my list of saints, of exceptionally courageous, unarmed, unsponsored, unpaid souls who have tried to slow down even a little bit state crimes against those Jesus Christ said should inherit the Earth someday.

He did this with truth, anger, and ridicule.

I doubt that **Abbie Hoffman**'s clowning shortened the Vietnam War by as much as a microsecond; nor did protests by anyone but the enemy. At a meeting of writers (P.E.N.) in Stockholm, when that war still had about a year to go, I said that almost all American artists of every sort were opposed to the war, forming a sort of laser beam of moral outrage. The power of this beam, I reported, turned out to be equivalent to that of a banana cream pie three feet in diameter when dropped from a stepladder four feet high.

Vonnegut sees in Hoffman the natural and historically doomed choreography of leftists arrayed against a more mean-spirited conservative enemy, one expert at ridiculing progressives. (WFG In a Manner That Must Shame God Himself) I now glimpsed **Abbie Hoffman**, the clowning revolutionary. He had been stopped for perhaps the dozenth time that day by security men, who looked just like Dr. Ellsberg. He was a weary clown by now. His press credentials were in order. He was gathering material for a book.

"Who you representing?" he was asked.

"Field and Stream," he said.

I had the feeling he wasn't going to be clowning much more. A lot of naturally funny people who want to help Losers aren't going to clown anymore. They have caught on that clowning doesn't throw off the timing or slow down cruel social machinery. In fact, it usually serves as a lubricant.

Every so often somebody tells me that it is a delicious fact of history that clowns have often been the most effective revolutionaries. That isn't true. Cruel social machines in the past have needed clowns for lubrication so much that they have often manufactured them. Consider the Spanish Inquisition.

When the Inquisition was about to burn somebody alive in a public square, it shaved that person from head to foot. It tortured the person to the point of babbling idiocy, fitted him out with a dunce cap and a lurid paper cloak. His or her face was painted or masked.

Hey presto! A clown!

The idea, of course, was to make the victim comical rather than pitiful. Pity is like rust to a cruel social machine.

* * *

I do not say that America's Winners are about to burn America's Losers in public squares—although, if they did, it would be nothing new. I say that the Winners are avid to neglect the Losers, which is cruelty too.
(*FWD* What My Son Mark Told Me to Tell the Psychiatrists in Philadelphia, Which Was Also the Afterword to a New Edition of His Book *The Eden Express*) Mark's (*Vonnegut's son*) only crime against his government, and the only crime committed by **Abbie Hoffman** and so many others of that generation during the Vietnam War, was a sublimely Jeffersonian form of treason. It was disrespect. . . . If **Abbie Hoffman** had been my son, I would have told him that he was doing the right thing while the Vietnam War was going on. I would have warned him, too, that he was putting his life on the line for his countrymen.

In response to a fan's letter about the absurdity of some of the increased security measures at airports after the terrorist attacks of 9/11, Vonnegut finds in Hoffman the kind of tactical brilliance found only in such saintly clowns. (MWC 10) The shoe thing at the airports and Code Orange and so on are world-class practical jokes, all right. But my all-time favorite is one the holy, anti-war clown **Abbie Hoffman** (1936–1989) pulled off during the Vietnam War. He announced that the new high was banana peels taken rectally. So then FBI scientists stuffed banana peels up their asses to find out if this was true or not. Or so we hoped.

Holdermann, Bill. *The engineer and manager from the Indianapolis Works who writes the morality play performed at the Meadows executive retreat in* Player Piano.

Holderness, Marvin Sharpe. *While serving a prison sentence for murdering his brother, Holderness sends a manuscript of his novel* 2000 A.D. *to Dr. Felix Hoenikker, asking his advice about what type of explosive to write into his tale. The string used to hold together the manuscript is the same used by Hoenikker to play "cat's cradle" on the morning of the Hiroshima bombing. Hoenikker never read the manuscript. Little Newt did and he told John/Jonah the following:* The novel was about the end of the world in the year 2000, and the name of the book was 2000 A.D. It told about how mad scientists made a terrific bomb that wiped out the whole world. There was a big sex orgy when everybody knew that the world was going to end, and then Jesus Christ Himself appeared ten seconds before the bomb went off *(CC 5).*

Holiday Inn (*"The World's Innkeeper"*). *The Holiday Inn of the mythical Midland City, Ohio, is the center of activity in* Breakfast of Champions, *serving as the forum for Dwayne Hoover's announcement that his wife, Celia, committed suicide as well as his violent rampage after reading Kilgore Trout's novel* Now It Can Be Told. *Wearing mirrored sunglasses purchased at the Holiday Inn outside Ashtabula, Ohio, Vonnegut walks into the bar of Midland City's franchise to become a part of the confrontation involving Kilgore Trout, Dwayne Hoover, and Rabo Karabekian.*
(BC 6) He went past his principal place of business, which was *Dwayne Hoover's Exit Eleven Pontiac Village*, and he turned into the parking lot of the new **Holiday Inn** next door. Dwayne owned a third of the Inn partnership with Midland City's leading orthodontist, Dr. Alfred Maritimo, and Bill Miller, who was Chairman of the Parole Board at the Adult Correctional Institution at Shepherdstown, among other things. *Dwayne's homosex-*

ual son Bunny, né George, played piano in the hotel's bar.

In Slaughterhouse-Five, *Billy Pilgrim owns one-fifth of a Holiday Inn in Ilium, New York. One of Billy's business partners is the physician who gives Valencia Pilgrim a hysterectomy.*

Midland City's Holiday Inn is also ground zero for the neutron-bombing in Deadeye Dick.
See also: BC 18; 20; WFG Playboy *Interview; PS* Playmates.

Home Sweet Home Moving and Storage. *In* Bluebeard, *Rabo Karabekian uses the company to store his great collection of abstract expressionist paintings. He also employs them to retrieve his decaying mural "Windsor Blue Number Seventeen" from the basement of the GEFFCo building in Manhattan.*

Homestead. *The southern part of Ilium, New York, across the river from both the Ilium Works and the neighborhood lived in by the employed Ph.D.s, in* Player Piano. *It is where the unemployed and the Reeks and Wrecks live.*

Homo sapiens. (GBR 10) "They *(the poor)* stand today as a monumental caricature of **Homo sapiens**, the harsh and horrible reality created by us out of our own misguided pity. They are also, if we continue our present course, the living prophecy of what a great percentage of the rest of us will become." *This is from "A Rift Between Friends in the War of Ideas," a pamphlet sent to Stewart Buntline from Reed McAllister, lawyer to both Buntline and the Rosewater estate, to help undo Stewart's socialist notions, which he had long ago abandoned, though unknown to McAllister.*

homosexual, homosexuality. *As contentious as this subject is for many, Vonnegut never deals contemptuously with homosexuals in his stories. His notable homosexual characters include:*
• *The fawning, obsequious Bunny Weeks (owner of the dockside restaurant The Weir in* God Bless You, Mr. Rosewater) *is ill-mannered and rude to all but his wealthy patrons. His cutting remarks, however, are based on economic class distinctions and have nothing to do with his homosexuality.*

- *Dwayne Hoover's homosexual son Bunny (né George) is the kindly piano player in the Tally-ho Room of the Midland City Holiday Inn* (Breakfast of Champions *and* Deadeye Dick).
- *Milo Maritimo is the Holiday Inn's night desk clerk* (Breakfast of Champions), *grandson of Guillermo "Little Willie" Maritimo, one of Al Capone's bodyguards.*
- *James Wait is a misled and slightly twisted homosexual prostitute* (Galápagos).
- *Marilee Kemp marries Count Portomaggiore, Mussolini's minister of culture and head of British Intelligence in Italy during the war* (Bluebeard). *He took a wife to avoid any suspicion of espionage, but he was eventually executed for being a homosexual pedophile.*
- *Bruce Bergeron is the homosexual Ice Capades chorus boy — Tarkington class of 1985 — befriended by Andrea Wakefield, the college president's wife who enjoys him as a skating partner. He is eventually killed by someone presumed to hate gays.*
- *Kilgore Trout's* Plague on Wheels (Breakfast of Champions) *has a spaceship from Lingo-three carrying Kago and a crew of Zeltoldimarians, all homosexual.*
- *Mrs. Lyle Hooper leaves her husband, the owner of Scipio's Black Cat Café, whose parking lot was used for prostitution, when she becomes aware of her lesbianism.*

Aside from these notable instances, Vonnegut makes a few references to homosexuality undercutting society's ambiguous appreciations of maleness and gayness. (PP IX) He *(Ed Finnerty)* had a candor about his few emotional attachments that Paul found disquieting. He used words to describe his feelings that Paul could never bring himself to use when speaking of a friend: love, affection, and other words generally consigned to young and inexperienced lovers. It wasn't **homosexual**; it was an archaic expression of friendship by an undisciplined man in an age when most men seemed in mortal fear of being mistaken for pansies for even a split second.
(CC 55) "You know why Castle will never marry the girl, even though he loves her, even though she loves him, even though they grew up together?" he whispered.

"No, sir, I don't."
"Because he's a **homosexual**," whispered Minton. "She can tell that from an index, too." *Ambassador Minton speaking to John/Jonah about Philip Castle and Mona Aamons Monzano. Mrs. Minton used to index books and claimed all sorts of revelations could be gleaned from one's method on indexing.*
(SL5 5) The Tralfamadorians tried to give Billy clues that would help him imagine sex in the invisible dimension. They told him that there could be no Earthling babies without male **homosexuals**. There could be babies without female homosexuals. There couldn't be babies without women over sixty-five years old. There could be babies without men over sixty-five. There couldn't be babies without other babies who had lived an hour or less after birth. And so on.
(BC 17) The armed forces knew he *(Bunny Weeks)* was a **homosexual**, that he was certain to fall in love with other fighting men, and the armed forces didn't want to put up with such love affairs.
(WFG Address to the National Institute of Arts and Letters, 1971) I wish in particular to call your attention to the work of Dr. M. Sydney Margoles, a Los Angeles endocrinologist, who is able to distinguish between male **homosexuals** and heterosexuals by means of urinalysis. He doesn't ever have to meet them. What other sweet mysteries of life are chemicals? All of them, I believe. Biochemistry is everything. The speculations of artists about the human condition are trash.
(DD 15) I think I am a **homosexual**, but I can't be sure. I have never made love to anyone. *The private musings of Rudy Waltz.*
(FWD II) "A rule we used to be able to extrapolate from cultural history, one which doesn't seem to work anymore, is that an American writer had to be an alcoholic in order to win a Nobel Prize. Sinclair Lewis, Eugene O'Neill, John Steinbeck, the suicide Ernest Hemingway. That rule no longer works, in my opinion, because artistic sensibilities are no longer regarded in this country as being characteristic of females. I no longer have to arrive at this lectern drunk, having slugged somebody in a bar last night, in order to prove that I am not what was a loathsome creature not long ago, which is to say a **homosexual**."

See also: ST 12; GBR 2; 9; BC 2; 6; 15; 17; 20; 23; WFG There's a Maniac Loose Out There; WFG In a Manner That Must Shame God Himself; JB 10; 16; DD 19; 22–23; Gal 1:3; 1:29; Blue 20; 29; HP 17; 22; FWD V; XII; XX.

Hoobler. *The original family name of Dwayne Hoover's stepparents.* (BC 14) Dwayne Hoover's stepparents had come from . . . West Virginia to Midland City during the First World War, to make big money at the Keedsler Automobile Company, which was manufacturing airplanes and trucks. When they got to Midland City, they had their name changed legally from *Hoobler* to *Hoover*, because there were so many black people in Midland City named **Hoobler**.

As Dwayne Hoover's stepfather explained to him one time, "It was embarrassing. Everybody up here naturally assumed **Hoobler** was a *Nigger* name."

Hoobler, Cynthia. *Briefly hired by Rudy Waltz to care for his parents while he went to New York for the production of "Katmandu," Cynthia is the daughter of Mary Hoobler.*

Hoobler, Dwayne, Grace, and Wanda June. *In the short story "The Big Space Fuck," reprinted in the section of* Palm Sunday *entitled "Obscenity," the Hooblers are being sued by their daughter Wanda June. She was the head of a shoplifting ring and The only way she could avoid prison was to prove that everything she was and did was her parents' fault* (PS Obscenity).

Dwayne and Grace live in Elk Harbor, Ohio, on the shore of what used to be Lake Erie. Lake Erie was almost solid sewage now. There were man-eating lampreys in there thirty-eight feet long. **Dwayne** was a guard in the Ohio Adult Correctional Institution, which was two miles away. His hobby was making birdhouses out of Clorox bottles. He went on making them and hanging them around his yard, even though there weren't any birds any more (PS Obscenity). *Dwayne had an IQ under 115 and was therefore disqualified from contributing sperm to be carried aboard the spaceship* Arthur C. Clarke *on its way to Andromeda.*

Wanda June's charges against her parents were based on normal parental discipline and/or slovenli-ness. (PS Obscenity) **Dwayne** was reading charges against himself, so he didn't ask **Grace** what awful thing she was supposed to have done when **Wanda June** was only four, but here it was: Poor little **Wanda June** drew pretty pictures with a crayon all over the new living-room wallpaper to make her mother happy. Her mother blew up and spanked her instead. Since that day, **Wanda June** claimed, she had not been able to look at any sort of art materials without trembling like a leaf and breaking out into cold sweats. "Thus was I deprived," **Wanda June**'s lawyer had her say, "of a brilliant and lucrative career in the arts."

Dwayne meanwhile was learning that he had ruined his daughter's opportunities for what her lawyer called an "advantageous marriage and the comfort and love there from." **Dwayne** had done this, supposedly, by being half in the bag whenever a suitor came to call. Also, he was often stripped to the waist when he answered the door, but still had on his cartridge belt and his revolver. She was even able to name a lover her father had lost for her: John L. Newcomb, who had finally married somebody else. He had a very good job now. He was in command of the security force at an arsenal out in South Dakota, where they stockpiled cholera and bubonic plague.

Hoobler, Josephus. *In* Breakfast of Champions, *the former slave who goes north to Midland City after receiving liberation from his master. He settles on a piece of land called Bluebird Farm. His descendants lose the farm in the Great Depression when the Midland County Merchants Bank forecloses on the mortgage. Due to the many black families in the area bearing his name, Dwayne Hoover's stepfather changes his name from Hoobler when he arrives from West Virginia.*

In 1937, after Dwayne's stepfather takes possession of Bluebird Farm in an insurance settlement, Dwayne discovers what is later called Sacred Miracle Cave.

Hoobler, Mary. *The cook for the Waltz family in* Deadeye Dick, *the source of Rudy Waltz's culinary textual interludes (including recipes for corn bread, barbecue sauce, and chitlins). She claims that Eleanor Roosevelt's visit to the Waltz's was the highlight* *of her life. Rudy spends a great deal of time with Mary in the kitchen and learns how to cook and clean from her.*

Hoobler, Wayne. *A descendant of Josephus Hoobler, Wayne is paroled from The Adult Correctional Institution at Shepherdstown on the authority of Parole Board Chair Don Miller, father of Mary Alice Miller, Queen of the Arts Festival. He goes straight to Dwayne Hoover's Exit Eleven Pontiac Village because he has a strong desire to work for Dwayne Hoover. Wayne was without any social awareness and actually longed for the safer confines of Shepherdstown. (BC 18) He missed the clash of steel doors. He missed the bread and the stew and the pitchers of milk and coffee. He missed fucking other men in the mouth and the asshole, and being fucked in the mouth and the asshole, and jerking off—and fucking cows in the prison dairy, all events in a normal sex life on the planet, as far as he knew. Vonnegut suggests the appropriate epitaph for Wayne should read,* BLACK JAILBIRD—HE ADAPTED TO WHAT THERE WAS TO ADAPT TO *(BC illustration).*

"The Hooligan." *The invention of Dr. Felix Bauxite-13 von Peterswald, which allows one to speak with the dead in* Slapstick. *It wasn't invented for this purpose. Francis Iron-7 Hooligan, a janitor in the doctor's laboratory, accidentally discovers its remarkable ability. When von Peterswald listens to the sounds from the other side, he describes it as sounding like a poor phone connection to a badly run turkey farm. Wilbur Swain uses the device to speak with his dead sister Eliza.*

Hooligan, Francis Iron-7. *In* Slapstick, *the janitor at work in Dr. von Peterswald's office who stores away the doctor's invention intended for use with a particle-accelerator that is shut down for lack of electricity. In the process of putting the pieces away atop a file cabinet, Hooligan discovers he is listening to voices of the dead. Wilbur Swain later uses the device to speak with his dead sister Eliza.*

Hooper, Charlton. *The son of Lyle Hooper, owner of the Black Cat Café, notary public, and chief of*

the Scipio Volunteer Fire Department. Despite the fact his father's café is really a whorehouse, Lyle is so well liked and respected that it never stigmatized Charlton. (HP 28) This kindly conspiracy protected Lyle's son **Charlton***, as well.* **Charlton** *grew to be 2 meters tall, and was a New York State High School All-Star basketball center in his senior year at Scipio High School, and all he ever had to say about his father was that he ran a restaurant. Charlton is such a good athlete that the New York Knicks invite him for a tryout. He turns down basketball, becomes a physicist at the Supercollider in Waxahachie, Texas, leaves when funds dry up and returns to Western New York to teach at Hobart College in Geneva. He returns to Scipio only to claim his father's body after the prison break.*

Hooper, Lyle. *Chief of the Volunteer Fire Department, notary public, father of all-star basketball center Charlton Hooper, and owner of the Black Cat Café in Scipio, Hooper is eventually shot in the back of the head during the prison break at Athena. The Black Cat Café is openly known as a whorehouse of sorts. The prostitutes did their business out back in parked vans. The townspeople loved Lyle Hooper and never called his bar a whorehouse, but the trustees of the college are adamant about its true nature.*

Hooper's wife leaves him when she discovers her Sapphic side. She runs off to Bermuda with the town's female high school gym teacher and earns a living giving sailing lessons.

Lyle Hooper and Whitey VanArsdale ambush and kill three escaped convicts after the prison break, including one named Abdullah, who had been flying white pillowcases from broomsticks. VanArsdale is killed immediately, but Hooper is taken prisoner and held in the bell tower. He is ceaselessly taunted by being called "pimp." Before his execution he admits his restaurant really is a whorehouse. This prompts Hartke to paraphrase Hooper's lesson about life in general. (HP 29) **LYLE Hooper***'s last words, I think we can say with the benefit of hindsight in the year 2001, might serve as an apt epitaph for a plurality of working adults in industrialized nations during the 20th Century. How could they help themselves, when so many of the jobs they or their mates could get had to do with large-scale deceptions, legal thefts from public treasuries, or the wrecking of the* food chain, the topsoil, the water, or the atmosphere?

Hoover, Bunny (*né* **George**). *In* Breakfast of Champions, *Bunny Hoover is the son of Dwayne and Celia Hoover, though we are led to believe by a later reference in* Galápagos *that he was fathered by James Wait during a one-time sexual liaison with Celia. Like Vonnegut, Bunny is the son of a suicide. When only ten years old, Bunny is sent to military school because he tells his father* he wished he were a woman instead of a man, because what men did was so often cruel and ugly. **Bunny Hoover** went to Prairie Military Academy for eight years of uninterrupted sports, buggery and fascism. Buggery consisted of sticking one's penis in somebody else's asshole or mouth, or having it done to one by somebody else. Fascism was a fairly popular political philosophy which made sacred whatever nation and race the philosopher happened to belong to. It called for an autocratic, centralized government, headed up by a dictator. The dictator had to be obeyed, no matter what he told somebody to do (BC 17).

After military school, Bunny becomes the piano player in the cocktail lounge of his father's Holiday Inn. He lives in the Fairchild Hotel in the most dangerous part of Midland City. Despite working for his father, they have not spoken to each other in years.

Hoover, Celia. *Born Celia Hildreth, she first appears in* Breakfast of Champions *as Dwayne Hoover's wife and later in* Deadeye Dick *where she is variously seen as Felix Waltz's prom date, the starring actress in Rudy's play "Katmandu," and as a drug addict partial to amphetamines prior to her suicide with Drano. She and Dwayne are the parents of George—better known as Bunny, the homosexual piano player in the Tally-Ho room of the Holiday Inn. However, in* Galápagos *we are told that George is the result of a one-time sexual encounter between Celia and James Wait.*

Vonnegut draws some parallels between Celia and his own mother. (BC 17) **Celia Hoover** was crazy as a bedbug.

My mother was, too.

Listen: Bunny's mother and my mother were different sorts of human beings, but they were both beautiful in exotic ways, and they both boiled over with chaotic talk about love and peace and wars and evil and desperation, of better days coming by and by, of worse days coming by and by. And both our mothers committed suicide. Bunny's mother ate Drano. My mother ate sleeping pills, which wasn't nearly as horrible.

And Bunny's mother and my mother had one really bizarre symptom in common: neither one could stand to have her picture taken. They were usually fine in the daytime. They usually concealed their frenzies until late at night. But, if somebody aimed a camera at either one of them during the daytime, the mother who was aimed at would crash down on her knees and protect her head with her arms, as though somebody was about to club her to death. It was a scary and pitiful thing to see.

Celia's first mention in Deadeye Dick *fills in her family history. Felix Waltz was the high school class president and had just been dumped by his girlfriend who was going to the prom with the captain of the football team.* (DD 6) Felix executed a sociological master stroke. He invited a girl who was at the bottom of the social order, whose parents were illiterate and unemployed, who had two brothers in prison, who got very poor grades and engaged in no extracurricular activities, but who, nonetheless, was one of the prettiest young women anybody had ever seen.

Her family was white, but they were so poor that they lived in the black part of town. Also: The few young men who had tried to trifle with her, despite her social class, had spread the word that, no matter what she looked like, she was as cold as ice.

This was **Celia Hildreth**.

After being scared from Felix's home by his father's outrageous greeting, we later see Celia with Dwayne Hoover, then a civilian inspector for the Army Air Corps, coming to view Rudy in jail after killing Eloise Metzger. After the blizzard that wipes out most of Midland City, Rudy again meets Celia as she works behind the counter in the hospital assisting people in locating their displaced relatives. She directs Rudy to the basement of the hospital where his mother is recovering.

Celia's death occurs in 1970, a few months before the opening of the Mildred Barry Memorial Arts

Center. Vonnegut takes a shot at the medical community through the grief expressed by Dwayne after Celia's suicide. (DD 24) The word was all over town of how in need of support he was, of how vocally ashamed he was to have been such a bad husband that his wife had committed suicide. He had been quoted to me as having made a public announcement in the Tally-ho Room of the new Holiday Inn, the day after **Celia** killed herself: "I take half the blame, but the other half goes to that son-of-bitching Doctor Jerry Mitchell. Watch out for the pills your doctor tells your wife to take. That's all I've got to say."

Hoover, Dwayne. *The Midland City entrepreneur who begins life as an adopted orphan. He marries Celia Hildreth who commits suicide in 1970 by swallowing Drano. Their one child is the homosexual piano player George, better known as Bunny, though in* Galápagos *we are given to believe George is the issue of a one-time sexual encounter between Celia and James Wait.* Breakfast of Champions *is primarily focused on the mental breakdown of Dwayne Hoover. What pushes Dwayne over the edge is Kilgore Trout's novel* Now It Can Be Told. **Dwayne**'s incipient insanity was mainly a matter of chemicals, of course. **Dwayne Hoover**'s body was manufacturing certain chemicals which unbalanced his mind. But **Dwayne**, like all novice lunatics, needed some bad ideas, too, so that his craziness could have shape and direction. . . .

The bad ideas were delivered to **Dwayne** by Kilgore Trout. . . . Here was the core of the bad ideas which Trout gave to **Dwayne**: Everybody on Earth was a robot, with one exception—**Dwayne Hoover**. . . .

Trout did not expect to be believed. He put the bad ideas into a science-fiction novel, and that was where **Dwayne** found them. The book wasn't addressed to **Dwayne** alone. Trout had never heard of **Dwayne** when he wrote it. It was addressed to anybody who happened to open it up. It said to simply anybody, in effect, "Hey guess what: You're the only creature with free will. How does that make you feel?" (BC 1)

Dwayne has an ongoing affair with Francine Pefko, his secretary from his Exit Eleven Pontiac Village. Aside from his automobile dealership, Dwayne owns one-third of the Holiday Inn, three Burger Chefs, too, and five coin-operated car washes, and pieces of the Sugar Creek Drive-In Theatre, Radio Station WMCY, the Three Maples Par-Three Golf Course, and seventeen hundred shares of common stock in Barrytron, Limited, a local electronics firm. He owned dozens of vacant lots. He was on the Board of Directors of the Midland County National Bank (BC 6).

In 1937 Dwayne discovers Sacred Miracle Cave and explores it with his stepfather. He gains one-third ownership of the cave when he and his stepbrothers inherit it from his stepfather who had been awarded it as part of a legal judgment for a car accident.

Dwayne is briefly seen in Deadeye Dick *when he is invited to view Rudy Waltz sitting in jail. Dwayne is accompanied by Celia Hildreth as they walk past the cage. Rudy recalls that Dwayne somehow avoided serving in the military during the war, serving instead as a civilian inspector of the Army Air Corps.*

Hoover, Lyle and Kyle. *Dwayne Hoover's younger twin stepbrothers who take care of their joint ownership of Sacred Miracle Cave in* Breakfast of Champions. *They live in identical yellow ranch homes on opposite sides of the cave. In 1954 Lyle had his nose broken in a fight over a woman at the Roller Derby. Since that time, Lyle did most of the speaking for the twins. Dwayne shows a true and deep affection for his brothers, who come to his car dealership to inform him about the chemical contamination threatening the Sacred Miracle Cave.*

Though Dwayne's parents adopted him after long years of trying to conceive their own children, Mrs. Hoover conceived the twins soon after he joined them.

Horthy, Dr. Nilsak. *The chemist who teams with the Rev. Dr. Lionel J. D. Jones in* Mother Night *to develop the highly successful embalming fluid Viverine as well as Gingiva-Tru, a gum-simulating substance for false teeth.*

Horton. *The Cincinnati resident and owner of Schramm's pharmacy in Midland City where Rudy Waltz works as a pharmacist in* Deadeye Dick.

Horvath, Dr. Nilsak. *A surface chemist at the Research Laboratory of the General Forge and Foundry Company in* Cat's Cradle. *Francine Pefko is his secretary.*

Hotchner, A. E. *(TQ 12)* I asked **A. E. Hotchner,** a friend and biographer of the late Ernest Hemingway, if Hemingway had ever shot a human being, not counting himself. **Hotchner** said, "No."

Hotel Arapahoe (*see also* **Algonquin Hotel**). *The Hotel Arapahoe is the scene for one of the more embarrassing moments of the youthful Walter Starbuck as well as his refuge when newly released from federal prison. It is there he finds a drawer full of stolen clarinet parts and is rearrested when he tries to sell them.*

The Arapahoe is owned by the RAMJAC Corporation. Starbuck's first appearance at the Arapahoe is in the company of Sarah Wyatt. (JB 10) I was flabbergasted. I might have been peering into the twinkling prisms of a time machine. On the other side of the French doors was the famous dining room of the **Hotel Arapahoe** in pristine condition, complete with a Gypsy fiddler—almost atom for atom as it must have been in the time of Diamond Jim Brady. A thousand candles in the chandeliers and on the tables became billions of tiny stars because of all the silver and crystal and china and mirrors in there.

Later in its life, the Arapahoe has a distinctly different appearance and clientele. (JB 10) No one ever made a reservation at the **Arapahoe** anymore. The only way to arrive there was unexpectedly, in response to some misfortune. As Israel said to me only the other day, when we happened to meet in an elevator, "Making a reservation at the **Arapahoe** is like making a reservation in a burn ward."

Hotel El Dorado. *Wilhelm and Gottfried von Kleist, paternal uncles of Siegfried and Captain Adolf von Kleist, own this Ecuadorian hotel, the planned collection point for passengers of "The Nature Cruise of the Century,"* a brand-new, five-story tourist accommodation—built of unadorned cement block. It had the proportions and mood of a glass-front bookcase, high and wide and shallow. Each bedroom had a floor-to-ceiling wall of glass

looking westward—toward the waterfront for deep-draft vessels dredged in the delta three kilometers away (Gal 1:3).
See also: Gal 1:4.

House of Hope and Mercy in the Jungle (*see* **Dr. Julian Castle**).

Hovanessian, Kevork (*also* **Hovanissian**). *Bluebeard's Rabo Karabekian proudly lists Hovanessian among the many Armenians to have done well after their families immigrated to the United States. According to Rabo, Hovanessian owns the former J. P. Morgan estate in Southampton, recently sold his ownership of Twentieth Century-Fox, and offers Karabekian $3 million for all the art treasures in his potato barn without seeing them. The offer comes after Hovanessian reads an article stating Rabo was holding on to a large collection of Abstract Expressionist masterpieces to drive up their value.*

How You Doin'? *When Kilgore Trout hitches a ride in a Ford Galaxie driven by a traveling salesman, Vonnegut recalls this Trout novel.* (BC 15) Trout wrote a novel one time which he called ***How You Doin'?*** and it was about national averages for this and that. An advertising agency on another planet had a successful campaign for the local equivalent of Earthling peanut butter. The eye-catching part of each ad was the statement of some sort of average—the average number of children, the average size of the male sex organ on that particular planet—which was two inches long, with an inside diameter of three inches and an outside diameter of four and a quarter inches—and so on. The ads invited the readers to discover whether they were superior or inferior to the majority, in this respect or that one—whatever the respect was for that particular ad.

The ad went on to say that superior and inferior people alike ate such and such brand of peanut butter. Except that it wasn't really peanut butter on that planet. It was *Shazzbutter.*

And so on.

CHAPTER 16
And the peanut butter–eaters on Earth were preparing to conquer the shazzbutter-eaters on the planet

in the book by Kilgore Trout. By this time, the Earthlings hadn't just demolished West Virginia and Southeast Asia. They had demolished everything. So they were ready to go pioneering again.

They studied the shazzbutter-eaters by means of electronic snooping, and determined that they were too numerous and proud and resourceful ever to allow themselves to be pioneered.

So the Earthlings infiltrated the ad agency which had the shazzbutter account, and they buggered the statistics in the ads. They made the average for everything so high that everybody on the planet felt inferior to the majority in every respect.

And then the Earthling armored space ships came in and discovered the planet. Only token resistance was offered here and there, because the natives felt so below average. And then the pioneering began.

Vonnegut goes on at various points to describe people according to their dimensions in relationship to national averages.

Howard Johnson's. *The orange-roofed restaurant chain that is next door to every purple-roofed Ethical Suicide Parlor in the 1968 short story "Welcome to the Monkey House." It was previously mentioned in the exact same context in Kilgore Trout's "2BR02B" and referred to in* God Bless You, Mr. Rosewater. *Those who came in for ethical suicides were entitled to a final free meal at Howard Johnson's.*

Huie, William Bradford. *The author of* The Execution of Private Slovik, *a copy of which is found beneath a seat cushion and read by Billy Pilgrim while in the waiting room of the Pine Knoll nursing home. He is waiting to see his mother.*

In 1993, Vonnegut wrote a new libretto to Igor Stravinsky's 1917 composition An American Soldier's Tale, Histoire du Soldat, *commemorating Private Slovik.*

Humana, Dr. Vox. *"Papa" Monzano's Christian minister who seems more ready for mystical sacrifices than traditional Christian ministry. He waits outside "Papa's" bedroom prepared to deliver last rites complete with a brass dinner bell, a tranquilized chicken in a hatbox, a Bible, and a butcher knife. He explains to* Cat's Cradle's *narrator that along with*

Bokononism, Christianity and Protestantism had been outlawed for years.

He received his doctorate from the Western Hemisphere University of the Bible of Little Rock, Arkansas. Their motto is "Make Religion Live!" Since there is no way for him to understand traditional Catholic practices, he takes it upon himself to make up things as needed. When "Papa" calls for last rites, he throws out Dr. Humana and insists on Bokononist last rites.

Dr. Humana is also a talented artist. He drew the target posters of all the Communist and Fascist leaders to be shot at during the great celebration.

He was named for the organ stop that struck his mother when the San Lorenzo Cathedral was dynamited in 1923.

humane. (*GBR* 2) I tell you, boys, I used to belong to a volunteer fire department, and I'd belong to one now, if there were such a human thing, such a **humane** thing, in New York City.

(*BC* Preface) I have no culture, no **humane** harmony in my brains. I can't live without a culture anymore.

(*BC* 1 illustration) The American Academy of Arts and Sciences caused a monument to be erected over his ashes. Carved in its face was a quotation from his last novel, his two-hundred-and-ninth novel, which was unfinished when he died. *The monument read,*

Kilgore Trout
1907-1981
"WE ARE HEALTHY ONLY TO THE EXTENT THAT
OUR IDEAS ARE **HUMANE**."

(*WFG* Address at Rededication of Wheaton College Library, 1973) The best example I know of goodness from vileness is the body of **humane** writing produced by Louis-Ferdinand Céline, a French physician and novelist, who was a convicted war criminal after World War Two.

(*WFG Playboy* Interview) VONNEGUT: Several years ago, Norbert Wiener, the MIT mathematician, wrote in *Atlantic* that he wasn't going to give any more information to industry or the Government, because they weren't gentle people, because they don't have **humane** uses for things.

(*WFG* Address to P.E.N. Conference in Stockholm, 1973) We will become influential when those who have listened to our myths have become influential. Those who rule us now are living in accordance with myths created for them by writers when *they* were young. It is perfectly clear that our rulers do not question those myths for even a minute during busy day after busy day. Let us pray that those terribly influential writers who created those our leaders were **humane**.

(*FWD* V) "Hemingway was unquestionably an artist of the first rank, with an admirable soul, the size of Kilimanjaro. His choice of subject matter, though, bullfighting and nearly forgotten wars and shooting big animals for sport, often makes him a little hard to read nowadays. Conservation and **humane** treatment of animals and contempt for the so-called arts of war rank high on most of our agendas nowadays."

(*GBK* Clarence Darrow) I thanked Mr. Darrow for having made American history much more **humane** than it would have been otherwise, with his eloquent defenses in the court of early organizers of labor unions, of teachers of unpopular scientific truths, and for his vociferous contempt for racism, and for his loathing of the death penalty. And the late, great lawyer Clarence Darrow said only this to me: "I did my best to entertain."

(*MWC* 7) Many years ago I was so innocent I still considered it possible that we could become the **humane** and reasonable America so many members of my generation used to dream of. We dreamed of such an America during the Great Depression, when there were no jobs. And then we fought and often died for that dream during the Second World War, when there was no peace.

But I know now that there is not a chance in hell of America becoming **humane** and reasonable. Because power corrupts us, and absolute power corrupts us absolutely. Human beings are chimpanzees who get crazy drunk on power. By saying that our leaders are power-drunk chimpanzees, am I in danger of wrecking the morale of our soldiers fighting and dying in the Middle East? Their morale, like so many lifeless bodies, is already shot to pieces. They are being treated, as I never was, like toys a rich kid got for Christmas.

(*MWC* 9) "Do unto others what you would have them do unto you." A lot of people think Jesus said that, because it is so much the sort of thing Jesus liked to say. But it was actually said by Confucius, a Chinese philosopher, five hundred years before there was that greatest and most **humane** of human beings, named Jesus Christ.

(*MWC* 9) But back to people like Confucius and Jesus and my son the doctor, Mark, each of whom have said in their own way how we could behave more **humanely** and maybe make the world a less painful place.

See also: GBR 5; *MH* Report on the Barnhouse Effect; *WFG* Hello, Star Vega; *WFG* Address to Graduating Class at Bennington College, 1970; *WFG Playboy* Interview; *Slap* 2; 36; *JB* 16; 18; *PS* The First Amendment; *PS* Self-Interview; *PS* Religion; *PS* Children; *PS* Jekyll and Hyde Updated; *FWD* V; VIII; X; XIX.

humanism, humanist. (*WFG* Hello, Star Vega) "Thus," says Sagan the **humanist**, "the characteristic signs of life on Earth which may be detectable over interstellar distance include the baleful contents of many American television programs." It is a sobering thought that Gomer Pyle and the Beverly Hillbillies may be among our chief interstellar emissaries.

(*WFG* Address to the American Physical Society) There was a safety officer in the laboratory who called on him regularly, begging him to clean up the death traps all around the room. One day my brother said to him, "If you think this is a mess, you should see what it's like up here." And my brother pointed to his own head. I loved him for that. We love each other very much, even though I am a **humanist** and he is physicist.

I am charmed that you should call me in your program notes here a **humanist**. I have always thought of myself as a paranoid, as an overreactor, and a person who makes a questionable living with his mental diseases. Fiction writers are not customarily persons in the best of mental health. . . .

You have called me a **humanist**, and I have looked into **humanism** some, and I have found that a **humanist** is a person who is tremendously interested in human beings. My dog is a **humanist**.

(*WFG* Address to the American Physical Society) One of the things that I tell beginning writers is this: "If you describe a landscape, or a cityscape, or a seascape, always be sure to put a human figure somewhere in the scene. Why? Because readers are human beings, mostly interested in human beings. People are **humanists**. *Most* of them are **humanists**, that is."

(*JB* 3) Soon after our marriage I *(Walter Starbuck)* was transferred to Wiesbaden, Germany, outside of Frankfurt am Main, where I was placed in charge of a team of civilian engineers, which was winnowing mountains of captured German technical documents for inventions and manufacturing methods and trade secrets American industry might use. . . . There was nothing that a **humanist** could not supervise—or so it was widely believed at the time.

(*TQ* 21) I am Honorary President of the **American Humanist Association**, whose headquarters in Amherst, New York, I have never seen. I succeeded the late author and biochemist Dr. Isaac Asimov in that functionless capacity. That we have an organization, a boring business, is to let others know we are numerous. We would prefer to live our lives as **Humanists** and not talk about it, or think more about it than we think about breathing.

Humanists try to behave decently and honorably without any expectation of rewards or punishments in an afterlife. The creator of the Universe has been to us unknowable so far. We serve as well as we can the highest abstraction of which we have some understanding, which is our community.

(*TQ* 21) I spoke at a **Humanist Association** memorial service for Dr. Asimov a few years back. I said, "Isaac is up in Heaven now." That was the funniest thing I could have said to an audience of **Humanists**. I rolled them in the aisles. The room was like the court-martial scene in Trout's "No Laughing Matter," right before the floor of the Pacific Ocean swallowed up the third atomic bomb and *Joy's Pride* and all the rest of it.

When I myself am dead, God forbid, I hope some wag will say about me, "He's up in Heaven now."

(*TQ* 21) Yesterday, Wednesday, July 3rd, 1996, I received a well-written letter from a man who never asked to be born in the first place, and who has been a captive of our nonpareil correctional facilities, first as a juvenile offender and then as an adult offender, for many years. He is about to be released

into a world where he has no friends or relatives. Free will is about to kick in again, after a hiatus of a good deal more than a decade. What should he do?

I, Honorary President of the **American Humanist Association**, wrote back today, "Join a church." I said this because what such a grown-up waif needs more than anything is something like a family.

I couldn't recommend **Humanism** for such a person. I wouldn't do so for the great majority of the planet's population.

The German philosopher Friedrich Wilhelm Nietzsche, who had syphilis, said that only a person of deep faith could afford the luxury of religious skepticism. **Humanists**, by and large educated, comfortably middle-class persons with rewarding lives like mine, find rapture enough in secular knowledge and hope. Most people can't.

Voltaire, French author of *Candide*, and therefore the **Humanists'** Abraham, concealed his contempt for the hierarchy of the Roman Catholic Church from his less educated, simpler-minded, and more frightened employees, because he knew what a stabilizer their religion was for them.

(*BAG* Introduction) Thus encouraged, this Lazarus wrote *Slaughterhouse-Five* for Sam. That made my reputation. I am a **Humanist**, and so am not entitled to expect an afterlife for myself or anyone. But at Seymour Lawrence's memorial service at New York City's Harvard Club five years ago, I said this with all my heart: "Sam is up in Heaven now."

(*GBK* Introduction) I am honorary president of the **American Humanist Association**, having succeeded the late, great, spectacularly prolific writer and scientist, Dr. Isaac Asimov in that essentially functionless capacity. At an **A.H.A.** memorial service for my predecessor I said, "Isaac is up in Heaven now." That was the funniest thing I could have said to an audience of **humanists**. It rolled them in the aisles. Mirth! Several minutes had to pass before something resembling solemnity could be restored.

I made the joke, of course, before my first near-death experience—the accidental one.

So when my own time comes to join the choir invisible or whatever, God forbid, I hope someone will say, "He's up in Heaven now." Who really knows? I could have dreamed all this.

My epitaph in any case? "Everything was beautiful. Nothing hurt." I will have gotten off so light, whatever the heck it is that was going on.

(*GBK* Introduction) **Humanists**, having received no credible information about any sort of God, are content to serve as well as they can, the only abstraction with which they have some familiarity: their communities. They don't have to join the **A.H.A.** to be one.

Yes, and this booklet of my conversations with the dead-and-buried was created in the hope that it would earn a little bit of money—not for me, but for the National Public Radio Station WNYC in downtown Manhattan. WNYC enhances the informed wit and wisdom of its community and mine. It does what nocommercial radio or TV station can afford to do any more. WNYC satisfies the people's right to know—as contrasted with, as abject slaves of high-roller publicists and advertisers, keeping the public vacantly diverted and entertained.

Whereas formal religions surely comfort many members of the WNYC staff, that staff's collective effect on its community is **humanism**—an ideal so Earthbound and unmajestic that I never capitalize it. As I have used it here, "**humanist**" is nothing more supernatural than a handy synonym for "good citizenship and common decency."

I wish one and all long and happy lives, no matter what may become of them afterwards. Use sunscreen! Don't smoke cigarettes.

(*GBK* Introduction) My late Uncle Alex Vonnegut, my father's kid brother, a Harvard-educated life insurance agent in Indianapolis who was well read and wise, was a **humanist** like all the rest of the family. What Uncle Alex found particularly objectionable about human beings in general was that they so seldom noticed it when they were happy.

He himself did his best to acknowledge it when times were sweet. We could be drinking lemonade in the shade of an apple tree in the summertime, and Uncle Alex would interrupt the conversation to say, "If this isn't nice, what is?"

(*GBK* Isaac Asimov) When on Earth, Isaac, my predecessor as honorary president of the **American Humanist Association**, was the most prolific American writer of books who ever lived. He wrote nearly five hundred of the things—to my measly twenty so far, or to Honoré de Balzac's eighty-five. Sometimes Isaac wrote ten published volumes in a single year! These weren't only prize-winning science-fiction. Many were scholarly popularizations of Shakespeare and biochemistry and ancient Greek history, and the Bible and relativity, and on and on.

Isaac has a Ph.D. in chemistry from Columbia, and was born in Smolensk, in the former Soviet Union, but was raised in Brooklyn. He hated flying, and never read Hemingway or Fitzgerald or Joyce or Kafka, according to his obituary in the *New York Times*. "I am a stranger," he once wrote, "to twentieth-century fiction and poetry."

(*GBK* Isaac Asimov) I asked him if he was still writing, and he said, "All the time! If I couldn't write all the time, this would be hell for me. Earth would have been a hell for me if I couldn't write all the time. Hell itself would be bearable for me, as long as I could write all the time."

"Thank goodness there is no Hell," I said.

"Enjoyed talking to you," he said, "but I have to get back to work now—on a six-volume set about cockamamie Earthling beliefs in an Afterlife."

"I myself would cheerfully settle for sleep," I said.

"Spoken as a true **humanist**," he said, becoming more antsy by the second.

"One last question," I begged. "To what do you attribute your incredible productivity?"

Isaac Asimov replied with but a single word: "Escape." And then he appended a famous statement by the similarly prolific French writer Jean-Paul Sartre:

"Hell is other people."

(*MWC* 8) Do you know what a **humanist** is?

My parents and grandparents were **humanists**, what used to be called Free Thinkers. So as a **humanist** I am honoring my ancestors, which the Bible says is a good thing to do. We **humanists** try to behave as decently, as fairly, and as honorably as we can without any expectation of rewards or punishments in an afterlife. My brother and sister didn't think there was one, my parents and grandparents didn't think there was one. It was enough that they were alive. We **humanists** serve as best we can the only abstraction with which we have any real familiarity, which is our community.

I am, incidentally, Honorary President of the **American Humanist Association**, having succeeded the late, great science fiction writer Isaac Asimov in that totally functionless capacity. We had a memorial service for Isaac a few years back, and I spoke and said at one point, "Isaac is up in heaven now." It was the funniest thing I could have said to an audience of **humanists**. I rolled them in the aisles. It was several minutes before order could be restored. And if I should ever die, God forbid, I hope you will say, "Kurt is up in heaven now." That's my favorite joke.

How do **humanists** feel about Jesus? I say of Jesus, as all **humanists** do, "If what he said is good, and so much of it is absolutely beautiful, what does it matter if he was God or not?"

humanistic physicist. *Vonnegut recalls a letter sent to him by Professor George F. Norwood, Jr., from the University of Miami in Coral Gables.* (WFG Address to the American Physical Society) "I saw with interest the announcement of the talk entitled 'The Virtuous Scientist,' to be delivered by you and Eames and Drexler . . . Unfortunately, I will not be present at the New York meeting this year. However, as a **humanistic physicist**, I would very much appreciate receiving a copy of the talk."

If Professor Norwood really is a **humanistic physicist**, then he is exactly my idea of what a virtuous physicist should be. A virtuous physicist is a **humanistic physicist**. Being a **humanistic physicist**, incidentally, is a good way to get two Nobel Prizes instead of one. What does a **humanistic physicist** do? Why, he watches people, listens to them, thinks about them, wishes them and their planet well.

humanitarian, humanitarianism. (CC 106) Dr. von Koenigswald, the **humanitarian** with the terrible deficit of Auschwitz in his kindliness account, was the second to die of *ice-nine.*
(WFG In a Manner That Must Shame God Himself) But there was a Pavlovian thing going on, and it has been going on for many years now: The wishes of the hostile crowds were invariably **humanitarian**, and the crowds weren't even hostile most of the time. But wherever they went, armies of policemen went to—to protect nice people from them. . . . (*The "hostile crowds" of humanitarians*

were the protesters attending the 1972 Republican National Convention in Miami.)

So a Pavlovian connection has been made in the minds of people who are really awfully nice: When more than two people show up with a **humanitarian** idea, the police should be called.

If the police don't act immediately, and if the **humanitarians** behave in a manner that is dignified or beautiful or heartbreaking, there is still something nice people can do.

They can ignore the **humanitarians**.
(*Gal* 1:26) This new explosive was regarded as a great boon to big-brained military scientists. As long as they killed people with conventional rather than nuclear weapons, they were praised as **humanitarian** statesmen.
See also: CC 102; GBR 2; 8; JB 7.

humanity. (*PP* V) "It was practically his life—away from the laboratory," said Berringer. He was shocked and scared. "Years and years. Why did it have to happen?" It was one more hollow echo to the question **humanity** had been asking for millenniums, the question men were seemingly born to ask. *Berringer is speaking after the demise of the robot Checker Charlie.*
(*PP* XXI) Their eyes had met, and an inexpressibly sweet sense of eternal tragedy had passed between them, between their generations—a legacy of *Weltschmerz* as old as **humanity**. *Paul Proteus thinks back to the first time his father brought him to the Meadows and he saw the morality play intended to sanctify the role of engineers and the ruling technocracy.*
(*PP* XXXII) "The witness will please tell what he considers to be a lie," said the judge.

"Every new piece of scientific knowledge is a good thing for **humanity**," said Paul. . . .

"Now a truth," said the judge.

"The main business of **humanity** is to do a good job of being human beings," said Paul, "not to serve as appendages to machines, institutions, and systems."
(*ST* 10) "I (*Winston Niles Rumfoord*) can think of no more stirring symbol of man's **humanity** to man than a fire engine."
(*MN* 8) I (*Howard Campbell*) committed high treason, crimes against **humanity**, and crimes against

my own conscience, and I got away with them until now.

(*MN* 14) Keeley was unfrocked, and Pope Pius sent a long letter to the American Hierarchy in which he said, among other things: "No true Catholic will take part in the persecution of his Jewish compatriots. A blow against the Jews is a blow against our common **humanity**."

(*CC* 1) We Bokononists believe that **humanity** is organized into teams, teams that do God's Will without ever discovering what they are doing.

(*MH* Report on the Barnhouse Effect) As though the pointlessness of my work were not bad enough, the professor annoyed me further with irrelevant questions. His favorites were: "Think: we should have dropped the atomic bomb on Hiroshima?" and "Think every new piece of scientific information is a good thing for **humanity**?"

(*BC* 2) He (*Kilgore Trout*) told Bill that **humanity** deserved to die horribly, since it had behaved so cruelly and wastefully on a planet so sweet.

Vonnegut recalls a favorite quote of his from Guy Murchie's Music of the Spheres. (*WFG* Excelsior! We're Going to the Moon! Excelsior!) I sometimes wonder whether **humanity** has missed the real point in raising the issue of mortality and immortality—in other words, whether mortality itself may be a finite illusion, being actually immortality and, even though constructed of just a few "years," that those few years are all the time there really is, so that, in fact, they can never cease.

(*WFG* Address to Graduating Class at Bennington College, 1970) I beg you to believe in the most ridiculous superstition of all: that **humanity** is at the center of the universe, the fulfiller or the frustrator of the grandest dreams of God Almighty.

(*Gal* 1:23) I (*Leon Trout*) did not know that **humanity** was about to be diminished to a tiny point, by luck, and then, again by luck, to be permitted to expand again. I believed that the chaos involving billions of big-brained people thrashing around every which way, and reproducing and reproducing, would go on and on. It did not seem likely that an individual could be significant in such an unplanned uproar.

(*Gal* 1:38) And the *Bahía de Darwin* wasn't just any ship. As far as **humanity** was concerned, she was the new Noah's ark.

(*Gal* 2:7) "Leon! Leon! Leon!" he implored. "The more you learn about people, the more disgusted you'll become. I would have thought that your being sent by the wisest men in your country, supposedly, to fight a nearly endless, thankless, horrifying, and, finally, pointless war (*in Vietnam*), would have given you sufficient insight into the nature of **humanity** to last you throughout all eternity!" *Kilgore Trout implores his son Leon to enter the blue tunnel into the Afterlife.*

(*HP* 26) I did not realize at the time how much that story ("*The Protocols of the Elders of Tralfamadore*") affected me. . . . But down deep the story was beginning to work like a buffered analgesic. What a relief it was, somehow, to have somebody else confirm what I had come to suspect toward the end of the Vietnam War, and particularly after I saw the head of a human being pillowed in the spilled guts of a water buffalo on the edge of a Cambodian village, that **Humanity** is going somewhere really nice was a myth for children under 6 years old, like the Tooth Fairy and the Easter Bunny and Santa Claus.

(*FWD* XI) "If flying-saucer creatures or angels or whatever were to come here in a hundred years, say, and find us gone like the dinosaurs, what might be a good message for **humanity** to leave for them, maybe carved in great big letters on a Grand Canyon wall?

"Here is this old poop's suggestion:

WE PROBABLY COULD HAVE SAVED
  OURSELVES,
BUT WERE TOO DAMNED LAZY TO
  TRY VERY HARD.

"We might well add this:
AND TOO DAMN CHEAP."

(*FWD* XII) "My brother got his doctorate in 1938, I think. If he had gone to work in Germany after that, he would have been helping to make Hitler's dreams come true. If he had gone to work in Italy, he would have been helping to make Mussolini's dreams come true. If he had gone to work in Japan, he would have been helping to make Tojo's dreams come true. If he had gone to work in the Soviet Union, he would have been helping to make Stalin's dreams come true. He went to work for a bottle manufacturer in Butler, Pennsylvania, instead. It can make quite a difference not just to you but to **humanity**: the sort of boss you choose, whose dreams you help come true."

(*FWD* XII) "And to show you how fruity, how feminine I have become in late middle age: If I were the President of MIT, I would hang pictures of Boris Karloff as the Monster of Frankenstein all over the institution. Why? To remind students and faculty that **humanity** now cowers in muted dread, expecting to be killed sooner or later by Monsters of Frankenstein. Such killing goes on right now, by the way, in many other parts of the world, often with our sponsorship—hour after hour, day after day."

(*FWD* XIX) "My Lord, I think I even said in fact I know I said that **humanity** itself had become an unstoppable glacier made of hot meat, which ate up everything in sight and then made love, and then doubled in size again. I topped that off with a stage aside to the effect that the Pope in Rome was of no help when it came to slowing down the meat."

(*TQ* 28) This was one heck of a moment for anyone operating a form of self-propelled transportation, or who was a passenger in one, or who stood in the path of one. For ten years, machinery, like people, had been doing whatever it had done the first time through the decade, often with fatal results, to be sure. As Trout wrote in *My Ten Years on Automatic Pilot*: "Rerun or not, modern transportation is a game of inches." The second time through, though, the hiccuping Universe, not **humanity**, was responsible for any and all fatalities. People might look as though they were steering something, but they weren't really steering. They couldn't steer.

Quoting Trout again: "The horse knew the way home." But when the rerun ended, the horse, which might actually have been anything from a motor scooter to a jumbo jet, didn't know the way home anymore. People were going to have to tell it what to do next, if it wasn't going to be an utterly amoral plaything of Newton's Laws of Motion.

(*BAG* Thanasphere) Perhaps his secretary would react as he himself had reacted, with a shrug. Maybe that was the spirit of this era of the atom bomb, H-bomb, God-knows-what-next bomb—to be amazed at nothing. Science had given **humanity** forces enough to destroy the earth, and politics

had given **humanity** a fair assurance that the forces would be used. There could be no cause for awe to top that one. But proof of a spirit world might at least equal it. Maybe that was the shock the world needed, maybe word from the spirits could change the suicidal course of history.

(*BAG* Thanasphere) He (*Groszinger*) was trying to imagine the world of the future—a world in constant touch with the spirits, the living inseparable from the dead. It was bound to come. Other men, probing into space, were certain to find out. Would it make life heaven or hell? Every bum and genius, criminal and hero, average man and madman, now and forever part of **humanity**—advising, squabbling, conniving, placating . . .

(*BAG* Thanasphere) He (*Groszinger*) didn't want to be the one to tell the world. He wished he had had nothing to do with sending Rice out into space. What discovery of the dead would do to **humanity** he didn't know, but the impact would be terrific. Now, like the rest, he would have to wait for the next wild twist of history.

(*MWC* 8) And the masses of **humanity** through the ages, feeling inadequately educated just like we do now, and rightly so, have had little choice but to believe this guesser or that one.

(*MWC* 8) Some of the loudest, most proudly ignorant guessing in the world is going on in Washington today. Our leaders are sick of all the solid information that has been dumped on **humanity** by research and scholarship and investigative reporting. They think that the whole country is sick of it, and they could be right. It isn't the gold standard that they want to put us back on. They want something even more basic. They want to put us back on the snake-oil standard.

Loaded pistols are good for everyone except inmates in prisons or lunatic asylums.

Millions spent on public health are inflationary.

That's correct.

Billions spent on weapons will bring inflation down.

That's correct.

Dictatorships to the right are much closer to American ideals than dictatorships to the left.

That's correct.

The more hydrogen bomb warheads we have, all set to go off at a moment's notice, the safer humanity is and the better off the world will be that our grandchildren will inherit.

That's correct.

Industrial wastes, and especially those that are radioactive, hardly ever hurt anybody, so everybody should shut up about them.

That's correct.

Industries should be allowed to do whatever they want to do: Bribe, wreck the environment just a little, fix prices, screw dumb customers, put a stop to competition, and raid the Treasury when they go broke.

That's correct.

That's free enterprise.

And that's correct.

The poor have done something very wrong or they wouldn't be poor, so their children should pay the consequences.

That's correct.

The United States of America cannot be expected to look after its own people.

That's correct.

The free market will do that.

That's correct.

The free market is an automatic system of justice.

That's correct.

I'm kidding.

(MWC 8) Subsequently, it might be said that he (*Dr. Semmelweis*) has saved millions of lives—including, quite possibly, yours and mine. What thanks did Semmelweis get from the leaders of his profession in Viennese society, guessers all? He was forced out of the hospital and out of Austria itself, whose people he had served so well. He finished his career in a provincial hospital in Hungary. There he gave up on **humanity**—which is us, and our information-age knowledge—and on himself.

One day, in the dissecting room, he took the blade of a scalpel with which he had been cutting up a corpse, and he stuck it on purpose into the palm of his hand. He died, as he knew he would, of blood poisoning soon afterward.

The guessers had had all the power. They had won again. Germs indeed. The guessers revealed something else about themselves, too, which we should duly note today. They aren't really interested in saving lives. What matters to them is being

listened to—as, however ignorantly, their guessing goes on and on and on. If there's anything they hate, it's a wise human.

So be one anyway. Save our lives and your lives, too. Be honorable.

See also: PP IX; XXXII; *ST* 11; *MN* 9; 44; *SL5* 4; *MH* Tom Edison's Shaggy Dog; *MH* Report on the Barnhouse Effect; *MH* Unready to Wear; *WFG* Thinking Unthinkable, Speaking Unspeakable; *WFG Playboy* Interview; *Gal* 1:6; 1:9; 1:14; 1:16; 1:23; 1:26; 1:28; 1:32; 1:33; 1:35; 2:4; *HP* 5; 23; *FWD* III; X; XIV–XV.

humankind. *With rare exception, this is a term Vonnegut reserves for speaking about the continuation of the species in* Galápagos *or when speculating about the future after recalling his visit to the Galápagos Islands.*

(*Gal* 1:23) So without any idea that he was going to be the sire of all **humankind**, I got into the head of Captain Adolf von Kleist as he rode in a taxicab from Guayaquil International Airport to the *Bahía de Darwin*.

(*Gal* 1:27) They (*the Kankabono girls*) would grow to womanhood on Santa Rosalia, where, along with Hisako Hiroguchi, they would become the mothers of all modern **humankind**.

(*Gal* 1:33) But I have yet to see an octopus, or any sort of animal, for that matter, which wasn't entirely content to pass its time on earth as a food gatherer, to shun the experiments with unlimited greed and ambition performed by **humankind**.

(*Blue* 35) While there were notorious disputes in Europe as to which races and subraces were vermin, all Europeans could agree that the thieving, fortune-telling, child-stealing Gypsies were the enemies of all decent **humankind**. So they were hunted down everywhere.

(*HP* 18) I argued that it was a teacher's duty to speak frankly to students of college age about all sorts of concerns of **humankind**, not just the subject of a course as stated in the catalogue. "That's how we gain their trust, and encourage them to speak up as well," I said, "and realize that all subjects do not reside in neat little compartments, but are continuous and inseparable from the one big subject we have been put on Earth to study, which is life itself."

(*FWD* XV) "If you go to the Galápagos Islands, and see all the strange creatures, you are bound to think what Charles Darwin thought when he went there: How much time Nature has in which to accomplish simply anything. If we desolate this planet, Nature can get life going again. All it takes is a few million years or so, the wink of an eye to Nature.

"Only **humankind** is running out of time.

"My guess is that we will not disarm, even though we should, and that we really will blow up everything by and by. History shows that human beings are vicious enough to commit every imaginable atrocity, including the construction of factories whose only purpose is to kill people and burn them up.

"It may be that we were put here on Earth to blow the place to smithereens. We may be Nature's way of creating new galaxies. We may be programmed to improve and improve our weapons, and to believe that death is better than dishonor.

"And then, one day, as disarmament rallies are being held all over the planet, *ka-blooey!* A new Milky Way is born."
(*MWC* 2) Evolution can go to hell as far as I am concerned. What a mistake we are. We have mortally wounded this sweet life-supporting planet—the only one in the whole Milky Way—with a century of transportation whoopee. Our government is conducting a war against drugs, is it? Let them go after petroleum. Talk about a destructive high! You put some of this stuff in your car and you can go a hundred miles an hour, run over the neighbor's dog, and tear the atmosphere to smithereens. Hey, as long as we are stuck with being homo sapiens, why mess around? Let's wreck the whole joint. Anybody got an atomic bomb? Who doesn't have an atomic bomb nowadays?

But I have to say this in defense of **humankind**: In no matter what era in history, including the Garden of Eden, everybody just got here. And, except for the Garden of Eden, there were already all these games going on that could make you act crazy, even if you weren't crazy to begin with. Some of the crazymaking games going on today are love and hate, liberalism and conservatism, automobiles and credit cards, golf, and girls' basketball.
See also: Gal 1:15; 1:23–28; 1:32; 1:35–36; 2:4; *FWD* XII.

humanness. (*Slap* 10) "I would give anything, Caleb, for the faintest sign of intelligence, the merest flicker of **humanness** in the eyes of either twin." (*TQ* 43) "I dare to suggest that no picture can attract serious attention without a particular sort of human being attached to it in the viewer's mind. If you are unwilling to claim credit for your pictures, and to say why you hoped others might find them worth examining, there goes the ball game.

"Pictures are famous for their **humanness**, and not for their pictureness."

humanoid (*see also* **Don** *and* ***Era of Hopeful Monsters***). *Vonnegut's few references to humanoids are associated with science fiction stories written by Kilgore Trout except for the one in* Hocus Pocus. *Though "The Protocols of the Elders of Tralfamadore" is not specifically attributed to Trout, it appears in* Black Garterbelt, *a porn magazine that frequently published Trout's stories as filler for the photographs.* (*Gal* 1:16) I am reminded of one of my father's novels, *The Era of Hopeful Monsters.* It was about a planet where the **humanoids** ignored their most serious survival problems until the last possible moment.
(*HP* 26) The Elders, incidentally, had given up on influencing the **humanoids** of Tralfamadore, who were right below where they were meeting. The Tralfamadorians had senses of humor and so knew themselves for the severely limited lunkers, not to say crazy lunkers, they really were. They were immune to the kilovolts of pride the Elders jazzed their brains with.
See also: BC 5.

humor, humorist (**American, barracks, black, college, gallows, Hoosier, Jewish, middle-European, white**). (*CC* 56) By contrast (*with the natives of San Lorenzo*), Johnson and McCabe had the glittering treasures of literacy, ambition, curiosity, gall, irreverence, health, **humor**, and considerable information about the outside world.
(*SL5* 5) (*The following is read by a German major from one of Howard W. Campbell, Jr.'s, monographs.*) *America is the wealthiest nation on Earth, but its people are mainly poor, and poor Americans are urged to hate themselves. To quote the American* **humorist** *Kin Hubbard, "It ain't no disgrace to be*

poor, but it might as well be." It is in fact a crime for an American to be poor, even though America is a nation of poor.

(WJ II:2) VON KONIGSWALD It was almost worth the trip—to find out that Jesus Christ in Heaven was just another guy, playing shuffleboard. I like his sense of **humor**, though—you know? He's got a blue-and-gold warm-up jacket he wears. You know what it says on the back? "Pontius Pilate Athletic Club." Most people don't get it. Most people think there really is a Pontius Pilate Athletic Club.

(WFG Why They Read Hesse) Hesse is no **black humorist**. **Black humorists**' holy wanderers find nothing but junk and lies and idiocy wherever they go. A chewing-gum wrapper or a used condom is often the best they can do for a Holy Grail. Not so with the wanderers of Hesse; they always find something satisfying—holiness, wisdom, hope.

(WFG *Playboy* Interview) PLAYBOY: Another way of dealing with sadness, of coming to terms with problems you can't solve, is through **humor**. Is that your way?

VONNEGUT: Well, I try. But laughter is a response to frustration, just as tears are, and it solves nothing, just as tears solve nothing. Laughing or crying is what a human being does when there's nothing else he can do. Freud has written very soundly on **humor**—which is interesting, because he was essentially such a **humorless** man. The example he gives is of the dog who can't get through a gate to bite a person or fight another dog. He digs dirt. It doesn't solve anything, but he has to do *something*. Crying or laughing is what a human being does instead.

(WFG *Playboy* Interview) VONNEGUT: So the biggest laughs are based on the biggest disappointments and the biggest fears.

PLAYBOY: Is that what's called **black humor**? Or is all **humor black**?

VONNEGUT: In a sense, it probably is. Certainly, the people Bruce Jay Friedman named as **black humorists** weren't really very much like one another. I'm not a whole lot like J. P. Donleavy, say, but Friedman saw some similarity there and said we were both **black humorists**. So critics picked up the term because it was handy. All they had to do was say **black humorists** and they'd be naming twenty writers. It was a form of shorthand. But

Freud had already written about **gallows humor**, which is **middle-European humor**. It's people laughing in the middle of political helplessness. **Gallows humor** had to do with people in the Austro-Hungarian Empire. There were Jews, Serbs, Croats—all these small groups jammed together into a very unlikely sort of empire. And dreadful things happened to them. They were powerless, helpless people, and so they made jokes. It was all they could do in the face of frustration. The **gallows humor** that Freud identifies is what we regard as **Jewish humor** here: It's **humor** about weak, intelligent people in hopeless situations. And I have customarily written about powerless people who felt there wasn't much they could do about their situations.

(PS The People One Knows) Mr. (*Joseph*) Heller is a first-rate **humorist** who cripples his own jokes intentionally—with the unhappiness of the characters who perceive them.

(PS The People One Knows) And while other comedians show us persons tormented by bad luck and enemies and so on, Bob and Ray's characters threaten to wreck themselves and their surroundings with their own stupidity. There is a refreshing and beautiful innocence in Bob's and Ray's **humor**.

(PS Funnier on Paper Than Most People) "When I was a boy in Indianapolis, there was a **humorist** there named Kin Hubbard. He wrote a few lines for *The Indianapolis News* every day. Indianapolis needs all the **humorists** it can get. He was often as witty as Oscar Wilde. He said, for instance, that Prohibition was better than no liquor at all. He said that whoever named near-beer was a poor judge of distance. He said that it was no disgrace to be poor, but that it might as well be. He went to a graduation ceremony one time, and he said afterward that he thought it would be better if all the really important stuff was spread out over four years instead of being saved up for the very end."

(FWD V) "The last time I was in Boise, also as a lecturer, I met a nice woman with a wry sense of **humor** about men. Her husband was then out hunting with heavy-duty equipment and pals. She laughed about that. She said men had to get out of doors and drink and kill things before they could show how much they loved each other. She thought it was ridiculous that they had to go to so much trouble and expense before they could express something as simple and natural as love."

(*FWD* XI) "In the children's fable *The White Deer*, by the late American **humorist** James Thurber, the Royal Astronomer in a medieval court reports that all the stars are going out. What has really happened is that the astronomer has grown old and is going blind. That was Thurber's condition, too, when he wrote his tale. He was making fun of a sort of old poop who imagined that life was ending not merely for himself but for the whole universe. Inspired by Thurber, then, I choose to call any old poop who writes a popular book saying that the world, or at least his own country, is done for, a 'Royal Astronomer' and his subject matter 'Royal Astronomy.'"

(*FWD* XIX) "For whatever reason, **American humorists** or satirists or whatever you want to call them, those who choose to laugh rather than weep about demoralizing information, become intolerably unfunny pessimists if they live past a certain age. If Lloyd's of London offered policies promising to compensate comical writers for loss of sense of **humor**, its actuaries could count on such a loss occurring, on average, at age sixty-three for men, and for women at twenty-nine, say."

"My generalization is happily or unhappily confirmed in a book called *Punchlines* (Paragon House, 1990) by William Keough of the English Department of Fitchburg State College in Massachusetts. The subtitle is *The Violence of **American Humor***. Mr. Keough, by means of essays on Mark Twain, Ring Lardner, Ambrose Bierce, myself, comedians in the movies (both silents and talkies), and radio and TV and nightclub comics right up to the present, persuades me that the most memorable jokes by Americans are responses to the economic and physical violence of this society. 'How often does it seem that the **American humorist**, having set out daringly and lightly as an amused observer of the American spectacle of violence and corruption, ends up mouthing sardonic fables in a bed of gloom,' he writes.

"So guess what: My latest novel, *Hocus Pocus* . . . is a sardonic fable in a bed of gloom."

(*FWD* XIX) "As a good friend pointed out to me one time, my ideas have everything but originality. That was my fate. So I came up with the wholly unoriginal idea of writing a *Don Quixote* set in modern times. There might be a certain amount of freshness to my tale, I hoped, if I gave an affectionate razzing to what had long been my dream of an ideal citizen. Although Mr. Keough doesn't say so, I think all **American humorists**, when saying how flawed American citizens really are, would not be interested in doing that if they did not have clear images in their heads of what American citizens ought to be. Dreams of ideal citizens are as essential to our **humorists**, in my opinion, as they were to Karl Marx and Thomas Jefferson."

(*FWD* XX) ". . . suicidal persons can be divided into two sorts. Styron's sort blames the wiring and chemistry of his brain, which could easily fit into a salad bowl. My sort blames the Universe. (Why mess around?) I don't offer this insight as yet another joke ("Why is cream more expensive than milk?"). It is my serious belief that those of us who become **humorists** (suicidal or not) feel free (as most people do not) to speak of life itself as a dirty joke, even though life is all there is or ever can be.

(*FWD* XXI) Many people feel that **humor** (professorial drolleries excepted) is a scheme of self defense which only members of famously maligned and oppressed minorities should be allowed to use. (Mark Twain cast himself as poor white trash.) It must seem very wrong to them that I, an educated, middle class person of German descent, should joke all the time. As far as they are concerned, I might as well be singing "Ol' Man River" with tears in my eyes.

The following passage is from Bernard V. O'Hare's comments on his friendship with Vonnegut in honor of his sixtieth birthday. (*FWD* What Bernard V. O'Hare Said About Our Friendship on My Sixtieth Birthday) In some reviews Kurt has been characterized as a **black humorist**. Those reviewers wouldn't know **black humor** from Good Friday. They don't know that what they read is only his reaction to the sight of the world gone mad and rushing headlong toward Dresden to the hundredth power.

And they miss his message, in which he pleads that world governments found their rule on something more akin to the Sermon on the Mount than the preachings of those who lead the world to Armageddon.

There is certainly nothing wrong with a man like that. And if such thinking constitutes **black humor**, it's too bad there is not an epidemic of it. (*TQ* 20) A Communistic 240-millimeter howitzer shell explodes atop the bunker. Flakes of calcimine from the shaken ceiling shower down on the deafened occupants. Hitler himself makes a joke, demonstrating that he still has his sense of **humor**. "It snows," he says. That is a poetic way of saying, too, it is high time he killed himself, unless he wants to become a caged superstar in a traveling freak show, along with the bearded lady and the geek.

(*TQ* 20) He puts a pistol to his head. Everybody says, "Nein, nein, nein." He convinces everyone that shooting himself is the dignified thing to do. What should his last words be? He says, "How about 'I regret nothing'?" Goebbels replies that such a statement would be appropriate, but that the Parisian cabaret performer Edith Piaf has made a worldwide reputation by singing those same words in French for decades. "Her sobriquet," says Goebbels, "is 'Little Sparrow.' You don't want to be remembered as a little sparrow, or I miss my guess."

Hitler still hasn't lost his sense of **humor**. He says, "How about 'BINGO'?"

But he is tired. He puts the pistol to his head again. He says, "I never asked to be born in the first place."

The pistol goes "BANG!"

(*TQ* 22) A cast-iron historical marker on the border between Point Zion's public beach and Xanadu said the mansion had been Bowen's home and place of work from 1922 until his death in 1936. It said President Warren G. Harding had proclaimed Bowen "Laughter Laureate of the United States, Master of Darky Dialects, and Heir to the Crown of King of **Humor** Once Worn by Mark Twain."

(*TQ* 45) The Indianapolis **humorist** Kin Hubbard said about: Prohibition that it was "better than no liquor at all." Intoxicating liquors did not become lawful again until 1933. By then, the bootlegger Al Capone owned Chicago, and Joseph P. Kennedy, father of a murdered-President-to-be, was a multimillionaire.

(*BAG* Preface by Peter Reed) As popular fiction, these stories are accomplished in their energy, **humor**, and insight. It is important that the twenty-odd known stories not collected in *Monkey House*

be preserved in book form, for they have their place in the Vonnegut canon as surely as his acclaimed novels. It is in these stories where he honed his skills that we see evolve the range of Vonnegut's talents, and the topics and techniques further developed in his later work. . . .

Earlier, he had cut his teeth on journalism: while attending Shortridge High School in Indianapolis (1936–1940), he had been a regular contributor to and managing editor of its daily newspaper, *The Shortridge Echo*, and in college he worked on *The Cornell Daily Sun*. In his columns he creates characters, and one begins to see the **humor** and witty social iconoclasm evident in the mature work. The war intervened, with the dramatic circumstances that would be the stuff of his masterpiece, *Slaughterhouse-Five*, yet Vonnegut's course to becoming a writer had already been set.

(*BAG* Preface by Peter Reed) . . . where Burger had been editor of the campus **humor** magazine, *The Widow*, and gave the story his attention. After some revisions, "Barnhouse" became Vonnegut's first story to be accepted for publication. Burger was helpful also in introducing Vonnegut to Kenneth Littauer and Max Wilkinson, two agents with long experience in guiding aspiring writers. . . .

"Der Arme Dolmetscher," "Souvenir," and "The Cruise of the *Jolly Roger*" treat the aftermath of war with a varying mix of **humor** and poignancy. (*BAG* Preface by Peter Reed) Several stories rely on a convenient narrator, someone like a storm window salesman or a financial advisor, with access to many different social settings. Such a person can enter the homes of rich celebrities, as happens in "Custom-Made Bride" and "Unpaid Consultant," and deliver matter-of-fact observations. These narrators lend the immediacy of an intimate voice, a presence who, by virtue of being there, authenticates the account. Often theirs is the perspective of sound common sense that keeps the bizarre grounded in the everyday, and their wry commentary or ironic tone is a source of **humor**.

Vonnegut's **humorous** stories fit that American tradition of the tall tale epitomized by Mark Twain. "Tom Edison's Shaggy Dog," which appears in *Welcome to the Monkey House*, is the classic example of the form. Both "Mnemonics" and "Any Reasonable Offer" in this collection rise to an abrupt joke ending. Untraditional is Vonnegut's use of **humor** in science fiction stories. He characteristically seizes on the comic possibilities of the otherworldly settings and bizarre events typical of science fiction. "Thanasphere" belongs in the category of comic science fiction, the story combining space travel (then only an exciting prospect) and conventional notions of the spirits of the dead being "up there." If the story's **humor** is tinged with poignancy, that, too, is characteristic of Vonnegut. *Player Piano* and *The Sirens of Titan*, novels cast in the science fiction mode, abound in plot developments that are at once comic and painful, as does the classic short story "EPICAC," which appears in *Welcome to the Monkey House*.

(MWC 1) Any subject is subject to laughter, and I suppose there was laughter of a very ghastly kind by victims in Auschwitz.

Humor is an almost physiological response to fear. Freud said that **humor** is a response to frustration—one of several. A dog, he said, when he can't get out a gate, will scratch and start digging and making meaningless gestures, perhaps growling or whatever, to deal with frustration or surprise or fear.

And a great deal of laughter is induced by fear. I was working on a funny television series years ago. We were trying to put a show together that, as a basic principle, mentioned death in every episode and that this ingredient would make any laughter deeper without the audience's realizing how we were inducing belly laughs.

There is a superficial sort of laughter. Bob Hope, for example, was not really a **humorist**. He was a comedian with very thin stuff, never mentioning anything troubling. I used to laugh my head off at Laurel and Hardy. There is terrible tragedy there somehow. These men are too sweet to survive in this world and are in terrible danger all the time. They could be so easily killed.

(MWC 1) True enough, there are such things as laughless jokes, what Freud called **gallows humor**. There are real-life situations so hopeless that no relief is imaginable.

While we were being bombed in Dresden, sitting in a cellar with our arms over our heads in case the ceiling fell, one soldier said as though he were a duchess in a mansion on a cold and rainy night,

"I wonder what the poor people are doing tonight." Nobody laughed, but we were still all glad he said it. At least we were still alive! He proved it.

(MWC 4) Our government's got a war on drugs. That's certainly a lot better than no drugs at all. That's what was said about prohibition. Do you realize that from 1919 to 1933 it was absolutely against the law to manufacture, transport, or sell alcoholic beverages, and the Indiana newspaper **humorist** Ken Hubbard said, "Prohibition is better than no liquor at all."

(MWC 12) **Humor** is a way of holding off how awful life can be, to protect yourself. Finally, you get just too tired, and the news is too awful, and **humor** doesn't work anymore. Somebody like Mark Twain thought life was quite awful but held the awfulness at bay with jokes and so forth, but finally he couldn't do it anymore. His wife, his best friend, and two of his daughters had died. If you live long enough, a lot of people close to you are going to die.

It may be that I am no longer able to joke—that it is no longer a satisfactory defense mechanism. Some people are funny, and some are not. I used to be funny, and perhaps I'm not anymore. There may have been so many shocks and disappointments that the defense of **humor** no longer works. It may be that I have become rather grumpy because I've seen so many things that have offended me that I cannot deal with in terms of laughter.

(MWC 12) All I really wanted to do was give people the relief of laughing. **Humor** can be a relief, like an aspirin tablet. If a hundred years from now people are still laughing, I'd certainly be pleased.

See also: PP XXX; *MN* 5; 18; *CC* 43; 86; *GBR* 13; *WFG* Teaching the Unteachable; *WFG* Biafra: A People Betrayed; *JB* 20; *PS* Roots; *PS* Self-Interview; *PS* The People One Knows; *PS* Mark Twain; *PS* Religion; *PS* In the Capital of the World; *Gal* 1:10; 1:35; 1:36; 2:8; *Blue* 31; *HP* 6; 14; 15; 26; *FWD* V; VIII; XVI; XIX.

Hundred Martyrs to Democracy. *Shortly after the official speech-making honoring the memory of San Lorenzo's lost soldiers, their inept air force misfires and hits the seaside castle of Papa Monzano, precipitating the frozen destruction of the Earth when Papa's ice-nine cadaver falls into the sea. Nar-*

rator John/Jonah recalls the American ambassador's words. (CC 65) Minton now spoke of the so-called **Hundred Martyrs to Democracy**, and he told a whopping lie. "There is not an American school-child who does not know the story of San Lorenzo's noble sacrifice in World War Two. The hundred brave San Lorenzans, whose day tomorrow is, gave as much as freedom-loving men can. The President of the United States has asked me to be his personal representative at ceremonies tomorrow, to cast a wreath, the gift of the American people to the people of San Lorenzo, on the sea."

John/Jonah gets the real truth about the martyrs from his cab driver. (CC 68, 69) I asked the driver who the **Hundred Martyrs to Democracy** had been. The boulevard we were going down, I saw, was called the **Boulevard of the Hundred Martyrs to Democracy**.

The driver told me that San Lorenzo had declared war on Germany and Japan an hour after Pearl Harbor was attacked.

San Lorenzo conscripted a hundred men to fight on the side of democracy. These hundred men were put on a ship bound for the United States, where they were to be armed and trained.

The ship was sunk by a German submarine right outside of Bolivar harbor.

"*Dose, sore,*" he said, "*yeeeara lo hoon-yera mora-toorz tut zamoocrtz-ya.*"

"Those, sir," he'd said in dialect, "are the **Hundred Martyrs to Democracy**."

Hurty, Mr. (*also* **the Hurty place**). *In the short story "Any Reasonable Offer," first appearing in* Collier's *magazine (January 1952) and later collected in* Bagombo Snuff Box *(1999), Mr. Hurty has his estate on the market at an asking price of $85,000. The home has a pool, occupied horse stables, a greenhouse, and room for a traditional English labyrinth as desired by Mrs. Peckham. Hurty made his money as the largest used-car salesman in his part of the state. He is also victimized by the fraudulent couple as they spend the better part of three afternoons and evenings trying on the estate and Hurty's patience. Hurty fails to entice the aristocratically aloof Peckhams with the fiction of a competing buyer, a retired brewer from Toledo.*

Hurty, Phoebe. *The advice-to-the-lovelorn columnist for the defunct* Indianapolis Times *and to whom Vonnegut dedicated* Breakfast of Champions. *She also wrote ads for the William H. Block Company department store and hired Vonnegut to write ads for teenage clothing. Her impact on him seems understandable from the preface.* (BC Preface) She wrote this ad for an end-of-the-summer sale on straw hats: "For prices like this, you can run them through your horse and put them on your roses. . . ."

She would talk bawdily to me and her sons, and to our girlfriends when we brought them around. She was funny. She was liberating. She taught us to be impolite in conversation not only about sexual matters, but about American history and famous heroes, about the distribution of wealth, about school, about everything.

I now make my living by being impolite. I am clumsy at it. I keep trying to imitate the impoliteness which was so graceful in **Phoebe Hurty**. I think now that grace was easier for her than it is for me because of the mood of the Great Depression. She believed what so many Americans believed then: that the nation would be happy and just and rational when prosperity came.

I never hear that word anymore: Prosperity. It used to be a synonym for Paradise. And **Phoebe Hurty** was able to believe that the impoliteness she recommended would give shape to an American paradise.

Now her sort of impoliteness is fashionable. But nobody believes anymore in a new American paradise. I sure miss **Phoebe Hurty**.

Hurty is one of many revered souls from Vonnegut's past who manage to appear at the Timequake *clambake.* (TQ 62) Among other departed souls whom I would not summon back to life, if I had had the power to do so, but who were represented by doppelgängers: nine of my teachers at Short-ridge High School, and **Phoebe Hurty**, who hired me in high school to write ad copy about teenage clothing for Blocks' Department Store, and my first wife Jane, and my mother, and my uncle John Rauch, husband to another of Father's first cousins. Uncle John provided me with a history of my family in America, which I printed in *Palm Sunday.*

"The Hyannis Port Story" (1963). *The Camelot-inspired short story, reprinted in* Welcome to the Monkey House *(1968), about the amiable but deeply divisive confrontation between Commodore Rumfoord, a staunch and lifelong Republican, and President Kennedy. Rumfoord insists on keeping a billboard-sized poster of Barry Goldwater on his front lawn, complete with floodlights—all directly across the street from the Kennedy Compound.*

Secret Service Agent Raymond Boyle informs Rumfoord that his son Robert was caught on Kennedy's yacht Marlin *preparing for a love tryst with Sheila Kennedy, the president's fourth cousin, who is visiting from Ireland. Robert and the beautiful, endearing Sheila dine with his parents, and the commodore softens to the extent that he turns off the Goldwater floodlights. The president drives by and asks Rumfoord to turn on the lights so Khrushchev's son-in-law could see them—and so he can find his own way home.*

Hyatt, Malcolm. *The pharmacist who preceded Rudy Waltz at Schramm's in* Deadeye Dick. *Hyatt was a high school classmate of Otto Waltz's and was killed by a robber with a sawed-off shotgun.*

I. G. Farben. *The name of this German corporation first appears as the buyer of RAMJAC's Down Home Records Division in* Jailbird, *and later in* Hocus Pocus *as the buyer of Du Pont (which had previously purchased Barrytron). Eugene Debs Hartke points out that Tarkington College trustee Sydney Stone brokered the deal that bought out Du Pont. Hartke also adds that I. G. Farben is* the same company that manufactured and packaged and labeled and addressed the cyanide gas used to kill civilians of all ages, including babes in arms, during the Holocaust (*HP* 4).

ice-nine. *The final creation of* Cat's Cradle's *Dr. Felix Hoenikker while working at the Research Laboratory of the General Forge and Foundry Company in Ilium. Having gathered together his children and Labrador Retriever, the Hoenikkers take a Christmas vacation to their Cape Cod cottage. On Christmas Eve Dr. Hoenikker is playing with his small quantity of ice-nine, melting it down and refreezing more water. He takes a break and suddenly dies in his wicker rocking chair. Angela, Franklin, and Newt discover their father's creation and split it up between them. Angela's sliver is eventually acquired by her husband's defense company; Little Newt's chunk is stolen by his Ukrainian wife Zinka, who returns with it to the Soviet Union; and Franklin surrenders his to "Papa" Monzano, leading the way to an icy destruction of the earth.*

Dr. Hoenikker began work on ice-nine after a Marine Corps general complained to him about all the mud his troops traditionally had to overcome. Ice-nine is a new crystal formation that turns moisture into an elongated chain of ice upon contact. It has a melting point of 114° Fahrenheit, so that when one small crystal of ice-nine comes into contact with another body of water or surface moisture, it immediately freezes.

Vonnegut's original idea for ice-nine is recorded in the Playboy *interview, reprinted in* Palm Sunday. *He notes that at the G.E. Research Laboratory where his brother worked as a physicist and Vonne-* gut *was a publicity writer, there was a legendary story about Dr. Irving Langmuir, the star of the lab, and his meeting with the visiting celebrated science fiction writer H. G. Wells. (PS Self-Interview)* VONNEGUT: Anyway—Wells came to Schenectady, and Langmuir was told to be his host. Langmuir thought he might entertain Wells with an idea for a science-fiction story—about a form of ice that was stable at room temperature. Wells was uninterested, or at least never used the idea. And then Wells died, and then, finally, Langmuir died. I thought to myself: "Finders, keepers—the idea is mine."

Ilium. *This mythical central New York community is modeled after Schenectady, New York, where Vonnegut worked as a publicity writer for General Electric before devoting himself full time to writing. Ilium is prominently featured in* Player Piano, Cat's Cradle, Slaughterhouse-Five, Galápagos, *and the short stories "The Deer in the Works" and "Poor Little Rich Town."*

In Player Piano, *Ilium is home to the Ilium Works (managed by Dr. Paul Proteus), one of the first manufacturing centers absorbed by the National Manufacturing Council. Ilium becomes the home of the Ghost Shirt Society, the neo-Luddite revolutionary group. The National Manufacturing Council tears down the building housing the Ilium Historical Society and in its place built the Ilium Atomic Reactor. The Ilium Putsch was the Ghost Shirt Society's attempt to overtake all manufacturing and governmental facilities. From the earliest point in the text, Vonnegut lays out the present state of Ilium's geographical and population divisions as well as its history, a history that is faithful to the actual development of central New York.*
(PP I) **ILIUM,** New York, is divided into three parts.

In the northwest are the managers and engineers and civil servants and a few professional people; in the northeast are the machines; and in the south, across the Iroquois River, is the area known locally as Homestead, where almost all of the people live. . . .

He (*Paul Proteus*) was showing the cat an old battlefield at peace. Here, in the basin of the river bend, the Mohawks had overpowered the Algonquins, the Dutch the Mohawks, the British the Dutch, the Americans the British. Now, over bones and rotten palings and cannon balls and arrowheads, there lay a triangle of steel and masonry buildings, a half-mile on each side—the **Ilium Works**. Where men had once howled and hacked at one another, and fought nip-and-tuck with nature as well, the machines hummed and whirred and clicked, and made parts for baby carriages and bottle caps, motorcycles and refrigerators, television sets and tricycles—the fruits of peace.

Paul raised his eyes above the rooftops of the great triangle to the glare of the sun on the Iroquois River, and beyond—to Homestead, where many of the pioneer names still lived: van Zandt, Cooper, Cortland, Stokes. . . .

The Ilium of Cat's Cradle *is home to the General Forge and Foundry Company and Dr. Felix Hoenikker. When the government recruited Hoenikker to work on the Manhattan Project, it agreed to his demands to do all his work in Ilium. It was at his research lab in Ilium that he makes his final creation, ice-nine. Vonnegut supplies more historical background by recalling Ilium was an important hub for outfitting settlers heading out to the Western territories. The present site of the Research Laboratory of the General Forge and Foundry Company was where the old stockade was and where public hangings were held.*

Slaughterhouse-Five's Billy Pilgrim was born in Ilium in 1922 (Vonnegut's birth year). He attended Ilium High School and then the Ilium School of Optometry, which was owned by his future father-in-law. Though Kilgore Trout is seen elsewhere living in Cohoes, New York, as well as Manhattan, in Slaughterhouse *he lives in Ilium. Billy leaves a tape recording chronicling his time trips to Tralfamadore and beyond death. The tape sits in a safe-deposit box at the Ilium Merchants National Bank and Trust.*

Mary and Roy Hepburn of Galápagos *are lifelong residents of Ilium. Mary worked for twenty-five years as an outstanding biology teacher at Ilium High School, and Roy worked for GEFFCo. The high school closes when the Matsumoto company of Japan purchased GEFFCo, then the largest em-* *ployer in town, and computerized its manufacturing process so no more than twelve workers were needed.*

The Ilium Works of the Federal Apparatus Corporation in the 1955 short story "The Deer in the Works" (reprinted in the 1968 collection Welcome to the Monkey House) *is not the highly computerized operation of* Player Piano, *but it is similarly intended to represent the dehumanization of society in an increasingly mechanized society. Primarily an armaments contractor, it is the second-largest industrial plant in America and is in the midst of a hiring blitz to keep up with demand.*

In the short story "Poor Little Rich Town," originally published in the October 1952 issue of Collier's magazine and later reprinted in Bagombo Snuff Box (1999), *The Federal Apparatus Corporation plans to relocate its company headquarters from New York City to Ilium. The upstate New York hamlet is near bankruptcy since its textile mills moved south after WWII. Ilium is unseen in this story while the focus of the tale is nearby Spruce Falls.*

In the short story "This Son of Mine," collected in Bagombo Snuff Box (1999), *Ilium is again home of General Forge and Foundry. Through its representative, Guy Ferguson, the company offers to buy out Waggoner Pump for $2 million. For proprietor Merle Waggoner, Ilium is a symbol of the modern era's corporate consolidation, conglomeratization, and the loss of America's regionalist heritage.* Merle waved his hand westward. "You wonder who all the people are with the big new houses on the west side? Who can have a house like that, and we never meet them, never even meet anybody who knows them? They're the ones who are taking over instead of the sons. The town's for sale, and they buy. It's their town now—people named Ferguson from places called **Ilium**."

Ilium Gazette. *In* Slaughterhouse-Five, *the sixty-two-year-old Kilgore Trout works* as a circulation man for the *Ilium Gazette,* manages newspaper delivery boys, bullies and flatters and cheats little kids (SL5 8). *Billy Pilgrim is a fan of Trout's books and when he realizes Trout lives only two miles from him, Billy seeks him out and strikes up a slight friendship. Later, when Billy prepares to go on a New York radio talk show, he tells the host he worked for the* Ilium Gazette.

Ilium Historical Society. *The society's building is torn down and replaced by the Ilium Atomic Reactor in* Player Piano.

Ilium Merchants National Bank and Trust. (SL5 6) As a time-traveler, he *(Billy Pilgrim)* has seen his own death many times, has described it to a tape recorder. The tape is locked up with his will and some other valuables in his safe-deposit box at the **Ilium Merchants National Bank and Trust**, he says.

I, Billy Pilgrim, the tape begins, *will die, have died, and always will die on February thirteenth, 1976* [italics in original]. *(This is the thirty-first anniversary of the firebombing of Dresden.)*

Ilium News Leader. *Billy Pilgrim sends a letter to the editor of his hometown newspaper explaining time travel and his experiences on Tralfamadore, in* Slaughterhouse-Five.

Ilium School of Optometry. *Billy Pilgrim's alma mater, owned and operated by his father-in-law, Lionel Merble, in* Slaughterhouse-Five.

Ilium Works (*see* **Ilium**).

incantation. (PP XXXIII) "I'm going to bat for you," his immediate superior had written, but it was, Halyard knew, an archaic **incantation** in a wilderness of metal, glass, plastic, and inert gas.
(BC 23) The person who answered this **incantation** (*"Olly-olly-ox-infreeeeeeeeeeeeeeeeeeeeeeeeeeeee"* *was shouted by Dwayne Hoover)* was a person who had never played hide-and-seek in his life. It was Wayne Hoobler who had never played hide-and-seek in his life.

Indianapolis. *Vonnegut's hometown figures prominently in a number of narratives. In* Player Piano, *the head of the National Manufacturing Council is Dr. Gelhorne, who early on increases his modest business success by purchasing the largest ice-cream plant in Indianapolis. He schedules the ice-cream truck routes to service the heavy industry manufacturing plants. He expands their services to include cafeteria items, eventually running most of the plants' in-house cafe-*

terias. The ice-cream business becomes a minor division of Gelhorne Enterprises.

In The Sirens of Titan, *Malachi Constant asks Salo to return him to Earth to live out his years in Indianapolis. Though he had never been there before, Constant remembers reading that* **Indianapolis**, Indiana . . . is the first place in the United States of America where a white man was hanged for the murder of an Indian. The kind of people who'll hang a white man for murdering an Indian . . . that's the kind of people for me (ST Epilogue).

Virginia Crocker, the mother of Mother Night's *Howard Campbell, is the daughter of an Indianapolis portrait photographer. The Soviet spy George Kraft / Iona Potapov lies to Campbell, saying he is a widower from Indianapolis and that his wife is buried there. When Kraft/Potapov circulates letters to a number of civic organizations and publications about the whereabouts of the infamous Howard Campbell, he sends a copy to* The Legion Magazine *in Indianapolis.*

Angela Hoenikker of Cat's Cradle *lives at 4918 North Meridian Street, Indianapolis, Indiana, with her husband, Harrison C. Connors. Connors owns the Indianapolis-based defense contractor Fabri-Tek, and presumably stores Angela's sliver of ice-nine at his manufacturing plant. Her brother Newt falls in love with Zinka, a Ukrainian midget and dancer with the Borzoi Dance Company performing in Indianapolis. He later sees her perform at Cornell, as well. After Zinka swipes his shard of ice-nine and flees back to the Soviet Union, Newt takes refuge in his sister's Indianapolis home.*

Noah Rosewater, the scheming entrepreneur who cons his brother out of his birthright and buys his way out of military service during the Civil War, maximized the profitability of his military contracts by purchasing the largest Indianapolis slaughterhouse to avoid being victimized by meat packers. Eliot's wife Sylvia is treated for Samaritrophia at Dr. Ed Brown's private mental institution in Indianapolis. After reading Kilgore Trout's Pan-Galactic Three-Day Pass *on a bus to Indianapolis, Eliot falls into a catatonic trance and looks up to see the city being consumed in a fire-storm. (GBR 14) Eliot, rising from his seat in the bus, beheld the fire-storm of* **Indianapolis**. He was awed by the majesty of the column of fire, which was at least eight miles in diameter and fifty miles high. The boundaries of the column seemed absolutely sharp and unwavering, as though made of glass. Within the boundaries, helixes of dull red embers turned in stately harmony about an inner core of white. The white seemed holy. *The novel's denouement takes place on a tennis court in Dr. Brown's Indianapolis asylum where Eliot is treated for a year after the bus episode.*

Slaughterhouse-Five's *Edgar Derby, whose summary execution in the ashes of Dresden for picking up a piece of unbroken china—intended to be Vonnegut's ironic climax—had been an Indianapolis high school teacher.*

Phoebe Hurty, the columnist and ad writer to whom Vonnegut dedicates Breakfast of Champions, *is noted as a witty Indianapolis widow. Also within this text, Vonnegut explains that he first suspects humans are robots of one sort or another when, as a young boy, he frequently saw men in downtown Indianapolis suffering "locomotor ataxia," a symptom of the final stages of syphilis.*

Vonnegut's prefatory note to Slapstick *reveals that while flying back to Indianapolis for a family funeral, he is forced to realize the void in his life left by his sister's early death, that she was the audience he tried to keep in mind while writing. Indianapolis is later noted as the Daffodil capitol of North America, the artificially extended family to which Wilbur Swain belongs. It is (and remains to this day) the location of the Eli Lilly Company, producer of tribenzo-Deportamil, the Tourette's syndrome medication that Wilbur relies upon for so long.*

Jailbird's *union organizer Kenneth Whistler is inspired by Indianapolis's legendary Powers Hapgood.*

Vonnegut describes Deadeye Dick's *neutron-bombing of Midland City as* the disappearance of so many people I cared about in **Indianapolis** when I was starting out to be a writer. **Indianapolis** is there, but the people are gone (DD Preface).

Bluebeard's *Rabo Karabekian has one eye removed at Fort Benjamin Harrison outside Indianapolis, after being wounded in the war.*

(HP 1) I (*Eugene Debs Hartke*) was named at the behest of my maternal grandfather, Benjamin Wills, who was a Socialist and an Atheist, and nothing but a groundskeeper at Butler University, in **Indianapolis**, Indiana, in honor of Eugene Debs of Terre Haute, Indiana. Debs was a Socialist and a Pacifist and a Labor Organizer who ran several times for the Presidency of the United States of America, and got more votes than has any other candidate nominated by a third party in the history of this country. *Hartke later learns that his wife's mother and grandmother are inpatients in the State Hospital for the Insane in Indianapolis. The old family friend who reveals this information runs an Indianapolis medical-waste company.*

For more complete information about Vonnegut's Indianapolis history, readers should consult the chapter entitled "Roots" in Palm Sunday *as well as* Fates Worse Than Death.

Indianapolis is also the locale for most of the story in "Hal Irwin's Magic Lamp."

(TQ 1) My father, Kurt Senior, an **Indianapolis** architect who had cancer, and whose wife had committed suicide some fifteen years earlier, was arrested for running a red light in his hometown. It turned out that he hadn't had a driver's license for twenty years!

You know what he told the arresting officer? "So shoot me," he said.

(TQ 4) At least I seized the opportunity this past May to thank my birthplace, as a graduation speaker at Butler University. I said, "If I had it to do all over, I would choose to be born again in a hospital in **Indianapolis**. I would choose to spend my childhood again at 4365 North Illinois Street, about ten blocks from here, and to again be a product of that city's public schools."

(TQ 7) He asked what relatives of mine had been wounded in wars. As far as I knew, only one. That was my great-grandfather Peter Lieber, an immigrant who became a brewer in **Indianapolis** after being wounded in one leg during our Civil War. He was a Freethinker, which is to say a skeptic about conventional religious beliefs, as had been Voltaire and Thomas Jefferson and Benjamin Franklin and so on. And as would be Kilgore Trout and I.

(TQ 10) Allie died in New Jersey. She and her husband, Jim, also a native Hoosier, are buried whole in Crown Hill Cemetery in **Indianapolis**. So is James Whitcomb Riley, the *Hoosier Poet*, a never-married lush. So is John Dillinger, the beloved bank robber of the 1930s. So are our parents, Kurt and Edith, and Father's kid brother Alex Vonnegut, the Harvard-educated life insurance salesman who said, whenever life was good, "If this isn't nice, what is?" So are two previous generations of our parents' forebears: a brewer, an architect, merchants and musicians, and their wives, of course.

Full house!

(*TQ* 34) I did not speak at her Episcopal obsequy. I wasn't up to it. Everything I had to say was for her ears alone, and she was gone. The last conversation we had, we two old friends from **Indianapolis**, was two weeks before she died. It was on the telephone. She was in Washington, D.C., where the Yarmolinskys had their home. I was in Manhattan, and married, as I still am, to the photographer and writer Jill Krementz.

I don't know which of us initiated the call, whose nickel it was. It could have been either one of us. Whoever it was, it turned out that the point of the call was to say good-bye.

(*TQ* 36) In the waning summer of 1996, I ask myself if there were ideas I once held that I should now repudiate. I consider the example set by my father's only brother, Uncle Alex, the childless, Harvard-educated **Indianapolis** insurance salesman. He had me reading high-level socialist writers like Shaw and Norman Thomas and Eugene Debs and John Dos Passos when I was a teenager, along with making model airplanes and jerking off. After World War Two, Uncle Alex became as politically conservative as the Archangel Gabriel.

(*TQ* 39) Why did so many of us bug out of a city built by our ancestors, where our family names were respected, whose streets and speech were so familiar, and where, as I said at Butler University last June, there was indeed the best and worst of Western Civilization?

Adventure!

(*TQ* 39) Father said I had better talk to his close friend Fred Bates Johnson, a lawyer who as a young man had been a reporter for the now defunct Democratic daily *The Indianapolis Times*.

(*TQ* 41) I don't think I missed the boat when I failed to write a novel about Albert Lieber, and how he was largely responsible for my mother's suicide on Mother's Day Eve, 1944. German-Americans in

Indianapolis lack universality. They have never been sympathetically, or even villainously, stereotyped in movies or books or plays. I would have had to explain them from scratch.

Lotsa luck!

(*TQ* 41) The point I want to make is that Mother's father, the brewer, Republican big shot, and neo-aristocratic bon vivant, married a violinist after his first wife died. She turned out to be clinically bughouse. Face it! Some women are! She hated his kids with a passion. She was jealous of his love for them. She wanted to be the whole show. Some women do!

This female bat out of hell, who could play a fiddle like nobody's business, abused Mother and Uncle Pete and Uncle Rudy so ferociously, both physically and mentally, during their formative years, before Grandfather Lieber divorced her, that they never got over it.

If there had been a significant body of potential book-buyers who might care about rich German-Americans in **Indianapolis**, it would have been a piece of cake for me to bang out a roman-fleuve demonstrating that my grandfather in fact *murdered* my mother, albeit very slowly, by double-crossing her so long ago.

"Ting-a-ling, you son of a bitch!"

Working title: Gone With the Wind.

(*TQ* 52) When I celebrate the idea of a family and family values, I don't mean a man and a woman and their kids, new in town, scared to death, and not knowing whether to shit or go blind in the midst of economic and technological and ecological and political chaos. I'm talking about what so many Americans need so frantically: what I had in **Indianapolis** before World War Two, and what the characters in Thornton Wilder's *Our Town* had, and what the Ibos have.

(*TQ* 62) Another look-alike there (*at the* Timequake *clambake*) was Rosemary Smith, Mask and Wig's costume mistress, and mother of Frank Smith, its superstar. She resembled Ida Young, grandchild of slaves, who worked for us in **Indianapolis** when I was little. Ida Young, in combination with my uncle Alex, had as much to do with my upbringing as my parents did.

(*BAG* Coda to My Career) I still write for periodicals from time to time, but never fiction, and only when somebody asks me to. I am not the dynamic self-starter I used to be. An excellent alternative weekly in **Indianapolis**, NUVO, asked me only a month ago to write an essay for no pay on the subject of what it is like to be a native Middle Westerner. I have replied as follows:

"Breathes there the man, with soul so dead, who never to himself has said, this is my own, my native land!"

This famous celebration of no-brainer patriotism by the Scotsman Sir Walter Scott (1771–1832), when stripped of jingoistic romance, amounts only to this: Human beings come into this world, for their own good, as instinctively territorial as timber wolves or honeybees. Not long ago, human beings who strayed too far from their birthplace and relatives, like all other animals, would be committing suicide.

This dread of not crossing well-understood geographical boundaries still makes sense in many parts of the world, in what used to be Yugoslavia in Europe, for example, or Rwanda in Africa. It is, however, now excess instinctual baggage in most of North America, thank God, thank God. It lives on in this country, as obsolescent survival instincts often do, as feelings and manners that are by and large harmless, that can even be comical.

Thus do I and millions like me tell strangers that we are Middle Westerners, as though we deserved some kind of a medal for being that. All I can say in our defense is that natives of Texas and Brooklyn are even more preposterous in their territorial vanity.

Nearly countless movies about Texans and Brooklynites are lessons for such people in how to behave ever more stereotypically. Why have there been no movies about supposedly typical Middle Western heroes, models to which we, too, might then conform?

All I've got now is an aggressively nasal accent. (*BAG* Coda to My Career) When I was born, in 1922, barely a hundred years after Indiana became the nineteenth state in the Union, the Middle West already boasted a constellation of cities with symphony orchestras and museums and libraries, and institutions of higher learning, and schools of music and art, reminiscent of the Austro-Hungarian Em-

pire before the First World War. One could almost say that Chicago was our Vienna, **Indianapolis** our Prague, Cincinnati our Budapest, and Cleveland our Bucharest.

To grow up in such a city, as I did, was to find such cultural institutions as ordinary as police stations or firehouses. So it was reasonable for a young person to daydream of becoming some sort of artist or intellectual, if not a policeman or fireman. So I did. So did many like me.

(*BAG* Coda to My Career) Such provincial capitals, which is what they would have been called in Europe, were charmingly self-sufficient with respect to the fine arts. We sometimes had the director of the **Indianapolis** Symphony Orchestra to supper, or writers and painters, or architects like my father, of local renown.

I studied clarinet under the first-chair clarinetist of our symphony orchestra. I remember the orchestra's performance of Tchaikovsky's 1812 Overture, in which the cannons' roars were supplied by a policeman firing blank cartridges into an empty garbage can. I knew the policeman. He sometimes guarded street crossings used by students on their way to or from School 43, my school, the James Whitcomb Riley School.

(*GBK* William Shakespeare) during my most recent controlled near-death experience, I got to interview William Shakespeare. We did not hit it off. He said the dialect I spoke was the ugliest English he had ever heard, "fit to split the ears of groundlings." He asked if it had a name, and I said, "**Indianapolis**."

(*MWC* 2) Do you know what a twerp is? When I was in Shortridge High School in **Indianapolis** 65 years ago, a twerp was a guy who stuck a set of false teeth up his butt and bit the buttons off the back seats of taxicabs. (And a snarf was a guy who sniffed the seats of girls' bicycles.)

And I consider anybody a twerp who hasn't read the greatest American short story, which is "Occurrence at Owl Creek Bridge," by Ambrose Bierce.

(*MWC* 2) I did get to know one socialist of their generation—Powers Hapgood of **Indianapolis**. He was a typical Hoosier idealist. Socialism is idealistic. Hapgood, like Debs, was a middle-class person who thought there could be more economic justice in this country. He wanted a better country, that's all.

After graduating from Harvard, he went to work as a coal miner, urging his working-class brothers to organize in order to get better pay and safer working conditions. He also led protesters at the execution of the anarchists Nicola Sacco and Bartolomeo Vanzetti in Massachusetts in 1927.

Hapgood's family owned a successful cannery in **Indianapolis**, and when Powers Hapgood inherited it, he turned it over to the employees, who ruined it.

We met in **Indianapolis** after the end of the Second World War. He had become an official in the CIO. There had been some sort of dust-up on a picket line, and he was testifying about it in court, and the judge stops everything and asks him, "Mr. Hapgood, here you are, you're a graduate of Harvard. Why would anyone with your advantages choose to live as you have?"

Hapgood answered the judge: "Why, because of the Sermon on the Mount, sir."

And again: Hooray for our team. (*MWC* Author's Note) Yes, and last July (2004) there was an exhibition of Joe's and my stuff, arranged by Joe, at the **Indianapolis** Art Center in the town of my birth. But there was also a painting by my architect and painter grandfather Bernard Vonnegut, and two by my architect and painter father Kurt Vonnegut, and six apiece by my daughter Edith and my son the doctor Mark. *See also: TQ* Title Page; 7; 28; 30; 34; 35; 45; 46; 48; 52; 54; *BAG* Preface by Peter Reed; *BAG* Introduction; *BAG* Runaways; *BAG* Hal Irwin's Magic Lamp; *GBK* Introduction; *MWC* 5; 7; 12; *MWC* Author's Note; Back Page.

instructor. *In* "Mnemonics," *Vonnegut's second published short story originally appearing in the April 1951 issue of* Collier's *magazine and later reprinted in* Bagombo Snuff Box *(1999), the instructor at the Memory Clinic encourages Alfred Moorhead to come up with a series of images that are meaningful to him and that more effectively apply the principles of mnemonics for improving a manager's productivity. Moorhead realizes his best set of images is those of contemporary Hollywood starlets including Rita Hayworth, Lana Turner, Jane Russell, Ava Gardner, and Ann Sheridan.*

Iron Guard of the White Sons of the American Constitution. *In* Mother Night, *the neo-Nazi youth group organized by August Krapptauer and that holds its meetings in the basement of a building owned by Dr. Lionel J. D. Jones. Though there are fewer than a dozen boys participating, their parents drive great distances so their children can attend.*

Iron Maiden. (*PP* XXVI) "Nope. Guess not," said Paul (*Proteus*). He filed this remark away for his next meeting with Bud Calhoun. He could see the device now—sort of an **Iron Maiden**, without the spikes, of course, and electronic, of course, that would grasp a little girl firmly at St. Louis, and eject her into the arms of relatives at Poughkeepsie. (*CC* 118 Chapter Title) The **Iron Maiden** and the Oubliette. (*CC* 118) Then he speaks (*in* The Books of Bokonon) of the rack and the peddiwinkus and the **iron maiden** and the *veglia* and the oubliette. (*SL5* 2) Weary's father once gave Weary's mother a Spanish thumbscrew in working condition—for a kitchen paperweight. Another time he gave her a table lamp whose base was a model one foot high of the famous "**Iron Maiden of Nuremburg**." The real **Iron Maiden** was a medieval torture instrument, a sort of boiler which was shaped like a woman on the outside—and lined with spikes. (*SL5* 2) Weary had told Billy Pilgrim about the **Iron Maiden**, about the drain in her bottom—and what that was for. . . .

Weary scornfully bet Billy one time that he didn't even know what a blood gutter was. Billy guessed that it was the drain in the bottom of the **Iron Maiden**, but that was wrong. (*WFG* Torture and Blubber) But it is not easy in real life to make a healthy man blubber, no matter how wicked he may be. So good men have invented appliances which make unconstrained weeping easier—the rack, the boot, the **iron maiden**, the pediwinkis, the electric chair, the cross, the thumbscrew.

Irving, David. *The publication of Irving's* The Destruction of Dresden *revealed to Vonnegut that it was* "the largest massacre in European history." *Vonnegut quotes extensively from the text in* Slaughterhouse-

Five *by having Professor Rumfoord refer to it while sharing a hospital room with airplane crash survivor Billy Pilgrim.*

Beyond the narrow confines of Vonnegut's citation of British military historian David Irving in Slaughterhouse-Five, *it should be noted that in later years Irving became an outspoken Holocaust denier. He failed in his libel suit against American historian Deborah Lipstadt who discredited aspects of his work. Irving was eventually arrested in Austria and convicted under their Verbotsgesetz law (Prohibition Act of 1947), originally instituted to suppress reviving the Nazi party and later expanded to cover the crime of Holocaust denial or minimizing Nazi war crimes. Irving went to prison in Austria from February to December 2006.*

Irwin, Hal and Mary. *The title character of the short story "Hal Irwin's Magic Lamp," collected in* Bagombo Snuff Box *(1999), is an Indianapolis stockbroker, ten years older than his wife of two years, Mary, and completely secretive about amassing a half-million-dollar fortune by short-selling stocks. The remainder of this entry is based on Vonnegut's revised 1999 version of the story for the collection* Bagombo Snuff Box. *Some of the essential differences between the two stories are outlined in the entry for "Hal Irwin's Magic Lamp."*

Throughout the brief two years of their marriage, Hal keeps secret from Mary the mechanical aspects of their financial life including his paper fortune of stocks sold short, his construction of a French chateau on North Meridian Street, his purchase of a Marmon luxury car, and his intention to keep a full-time staff for their new home. He does, however, contrive an amusing way to break the news to Mary of their changed circumstances. Until the opening of the story, Hal had been giving Mary a meager monthly allowance to run the house, but now he wanted to lovingly break the news of their changed circumstances to her with some style and comedy. **Hal Irwin** built his magic lamp in his basement in Indianapolis, in the summer of 1929. It was supposed to look like Aladdin's lamp. It was an old tin teapot with a piece of cotton stuck in the spout for a wick. **Hal** bored a hole in it for a doorbell button, which he hooked up to two flashlight batteries and

a buzzer inside. Like many husbands back then, he had a workshop in the basement.

Hal takes pains to keep up the charade of granted wishes from an Aladdin's lamp by hiring Ella Rice to play the part of a turban-headed jinni. Ella is an African American domestic worker employed by a friend of his. Hal is relieved not to be hiring a black man because he is uncomfortable in their presence. Hal is unaware until Ella's arrival that she is also near the end of her very obvious pregnancy.

Ella first meets Mary according to Hal's amateurish but romantic plot to provide his wife with a cook, a notion she takes with modest defense. However, she originally agrees to obey her husband, mindful to protest only so far, expressed by hoping that her own homemaking skills had been satisfactory to make him a warm home. What **Hal** hadn't counted on, though, was that **Mary** would find Ella so likable, but so pitiful, not a cook, but a fellow human being in awful trouble. He had expected them to go to the kitchen to talk about this and that, what **Hal** liked to eat, and so on. But **Mary** asked Ella about her pregnancy, which was obvious. Ella, who was no actress, and at the end of her rope in any case, burst into tears. The two women, one white, one black, stayed in the living room and talked about their lives instead. *The two become instant and constant companions.*

Once Hal arrives and insists they go through with the charade, it is one rich bauble after another: the Marmon, the château, Ella's admission of being hired for the part. This last bit of news shocks Mary into silence, her sensibilities offended. No sooner does Ella make this admission than they are all at the city's hospital, the only one that admitted black people. She had a healthy baby boy, and **Hal** paid for it.

Ella shows her appreciation to Hal by naming her son Irwin Rice. However, similar to the boy's natural father, Hal does not show for his christening. Vonnegut then tells us that **Mary** had never loved **Hal**, but had managed to like him. It was a job. There weren't many ways for women to earn their own money back then, and she hadn't inherited anything, and wouldn't unless **Hal** died. **Hal** was no dumber than most men she'd known. She certainly didn't want to be alone. They had a black yard man and a black laundress, and a white house-maid from Ireland, who lived in the mansion. **Mary** insisted on doing the cooking. Ella Rice offered to do it, at least for herself. But nobody except **Mary** was allowed to cook.

She hated the new house so much, and the gigantic car, which embarrassed her, that she couldn't even like **Hal** any more. This was very tough on **Hal**, extremely tough, as you can well imagine. Not only was he not getting love, or what looked like love, from the woman he'd married, but she was giving ten times more love than he'd ever gotten, and nonstop, to a baby as black as the ace of spades! *In the same way that Hal fails to realize his wife's sensibilities (either about himself, about Mary's essentially pure Christian spirit, or about Mary's displeasure with how Hal treats Ella), he fails to understand something everyone else in his industry did not understand—the worthlessness of a paper fortune.*

Having sold short into the market, the Wall Street Crash of 1929 prompts Hal Irwin to jump from his seventh-floor office window rather than face life without the wealth of his childhood dreams. Before his swan dive into the mythical history of that financially fateful day, he is aware of the ironies and failures of his life. He once stood importantly as the leader of his fraternity as well as the Grand Triumvirate (two friends from his youth who did far better than he; people he held up as financial models to emulate). He is also sensitive to the fact that he misunderstands his wife who will probably never love him. He leaves Mary—penniless and homeless. She accompanies Ella back to the church that christened little Irwin Rice. Mary then returns to her father's leaky home. She told him about the homeless people in the black church. She asked him what he thought would become of them in such awful times.

"The poor take care of the poor," he said.

Based on her father's closing words after she delivers Ella to safety, it is no wonder that Vonnegut's first introduction of Mary paints her as a socially angelic spirit. That girl was as wholesome as a peach and a glass of milk. Being poor gave her room to swing her religion around. When the end of the month came, and they'd eaten pretty well, and she hadn't asked **Hal** for an extra dime, she felt

like a little white lamb. And she thought **Hal** was happy, even though he was broke, because she was giving him a hundred million dollars' worth of love.

There was only one thing about being poor that really bothered **Mary**, and that was the way **Hal** always seemed to think she wanted to be rich. She did her best to convince him that wasn't true.

"The Island of Death." *In* Slapstick, *because of Manhattan's outbreak of the "Green Death" plague, people across the river call it "the Island of Death."*

Ivankov, Aksinia. *The wife of cosmonaut Major Stepan Ivankov, Aksinia is a pediatrician. (MH* The Manned Missiles*)* This is my letter, and I will get **Aksinia**, Stepan's widow, to read it to me to make sure Alexei has made it say exactly what I wish it to say. **Aksinia**, too, understands English very well. She is a physician for children. She is beautiful. She works very hard so she can forget sometimes her grief for Stepan.

Ivankov, Alexei. *The seventeen-year-old brother of Major Stepan Ivankov, the dead cosmonaut in the 1958 short story "The Manned Missiles," reprinted in* Welcome to the Monkey House *(1968). Alexei speaks and writes English and German, so he is chosen by his father to translate his thoughts in a letter to Charles Ashland, the father of the dead American astronaut Captain Bryant (Bud) Ashland. Mikhail Ivankov illustrates the stark differences once held by his sons but how their recently shared tragedies stopped Alexei from speaking so cavalierly.* It was not for the Soviet Union but for the beauty and truth in space, Mr. Ashland, that Stepan worked and died. He did not like to speak of the warlike uses of space. It was **Alexei** who liked to speak of such things, of the glory of spying on earth from baby moons, of guiding missiles to their targets from baby moons, of mastering the earth with weapons fired from the moon itself. . . . **Alexei** has not spoken well of war since.

Ivankov, Major Stepan. *In the 1958 short story "The Manned Missiles," reprinted in* Welcome to the Monkey House *(1968), Ivankov is the first Soviet cosmonaut in orbit. He and the American astro-*

naut Captain Bryant (Bud) Ashland are stranded in space for eternity when their ships collide. Ashland had been sent to observe and photograph the cosmonaut.

Ivankov, Mikhail. *The Ukrainian stonemason and father of cosmonaut Major Stepan Ivankov in the 1958 short story "The Manned Missiles," reprinted in* Welcome to the Monkey House *(1968). He and Charles Ashland exchange letters of condolence tinged with hope for world peace after both their sons lose their lives in a space-based Cold War confrontation. The depth of his loss is expressed in a joke he makes about Prokhor Ivanoff (below).*

Ivanoff, Prokhor. *Mikhail Ivankov, the grieving father of the dead cosmonaut Major Stepan Ivankov in the 1958 short story "The Manned Missiles," reprinted in* Welcome to the Monkey House *(1968), makes a black joke using Ivanoff to illustrate the dimensions of his loss.* I will tell you a joke, Mr. Ashland. When the second baby moon of the U.S.S.R. went up with a dog in it, we whispered that it was not really a dog inside, but **Prokhor Ivanoff**, a dairy manager who had been arrested for theft two days before. It was only a joke, but it made me think what a terrible punishment it would be to send a human being up there. I could not stop thinking about that. I dreamed about it at night, and I dreamed that it was myself who was being punished.

Izumi. *The North Korean spy posing as a nightclub singer who is wooed by the veterinarian and military meat inspector Dr. Bob Fender in* Jailbird. *Fender's fellow officers and drinking buddies lead her to believe Fender was so gloomy because he had the solemn duty of commanding an elite unit guarding atomic weapons. She persuades Fender to take her back to where he lives and works and is dismayed to find out Fender is a meat inspector. After spending a night of romance, they awaken to radio reports announcing the capture of a North Korean spy ring except for Izumi. Fender, already in love with Izumi, conceals her for eleven days. However, the two are turned in by a New Zealand sailor he failed to bribe.*

J

Jackie. *A waffle with strawberries and cream at the First Family Waffle Shop in the short story "The Hyannis Port Story,"* reprinted in Welcome to the Monkey House *(1968)*.

Jack's Hobby Shop. *The Ilium, New York, hobby shop in* Cat's Cradle *that serves as Frank Hoeniker's teenage refuge. There he works and spends most of his earnings on lifelike miniatures he uses to construct a realistic country setting on a rectangular piece of plywood in the basement, a prelude to his later work on the artificially constructed, dynamic tensions of state affairs on San Lorenzo.*

On another matter, Jack never realizes that his wife has a long-standing sexual affair with Frank.

Jackson, George Miramar. *In the short story "This Son of Mine," collected in* Bagombo Snuff Box *(1999), Jackson is the highly attentive, long-tenured parking lot security guard at Waggoner Pump who dreams of an indoor job with the company. When Franklin Waggoner leaves his father's office to visit his aunt Margaret, Jackson sees the company's young heir from a distance and hustles across the lot to deliver Franklin's sports car to save him the trouble of walking an extra fifty feet. Franklin thanks Jackson for his trouble but mistakenly calls him Harry, evidence that the reluctant heir never took a deep interest either in the company or the people who worked there. Undeterred, Jackson forgives Franklin his error and remains steadfast in his dream, "No offense, Mistuh Waggonuh, suh! Just remember next time—**George Miramar Jackson**, suh!" In George's eyes there blazed the dream of a future time, when Franklin would be boss, when a big new job would open up indoors. In that dream, Franklin would say to his secretary, "Miss So-and-So? Send for—" And out would roll the magical, magnificent, unforgettable name.*

*Franklin drove out of the parking lot without dreams to match even **George Miramar Jackson**'s.*

***Jailbird** (1979).* Jailbird *is the autobiographical saga of Walter F. Starbuck (formerly Stankiewicz),*

the Harvard-educated son of immigrant domestics in the service of Alexander Hamilton McCone. The course of Starbuck's life is largely determined by deaths that occurred long before he was born.

McCone is an heir to the Cuyahoga Bridge and Iron Company. In October 1894, McCone's father laid off large numbers of workers because they refused to take a pay cut. After a long and failing strike, the bankrupt families planned a peaceful protest on Christmas day, but old man McCone called in his political debts by assembling the Ohio National Guard to protect his factory. Since the nature of protesters is to stand firm and the nature of ill-prepared militiamen is to make fatal mistakes, or as Alexander would later recall that there were "certain instabilities inherent in the pageant," that day became known as the Cuyahoga Massacre.

Alexander withdrew from the family enterprise. He endured a childless marriage by befriending the son of his cook and chauffeur and promising that in return for his companionship (largely as a chess partner) he would send Walter to Harvard. For his part, Walter was willing to spend his childhood and youth so unnaturally for this reason (JB Prologue).

Alexander's refusal to enter the firm and instead become a famous Cleveland art patron, as well as the benefactor of an immigrant family, is his own way of making amends with his father's legacy. Walter does his part to follow the lead of his mentor, though his story reveals a mindless fealty to authority. He studies liberal arts at Harvard because McCone planned it that way. While an undergraduate, he embarrasses himself by taking Sally Wyatt to the Hotel Arapahoe for a dinner date meticulously planned by McCone, but falls victim to his own carelessness by tipping a strolling violinist with the bulk of his money.

During the McCarthy hearings in the 1950s, Walter errantly blurts out the name of an old and trusted friend, Leland Clewes, as having been a Communist. Later, while working in a subbasement office of the White House as President Nixon's special adviser on youth affairs, his own passivity leads the Watergate brain trust to stash the payoff money in Starbuck's safe. Unable to identify those responsible for framing him, and unwilling to commit the same error that landed Leland Clewes in jail, Walter takes the rap and goes to federal prison at Finletter Air Force Base in Georgia.

Regardless of the task at hand, Walter always acts in accordance with the expectations of the moment. He does little requiring forethought, and whatever intellectual insights he expresses are ideas developed by others. Walter appreciates the fiasco of his extravagant date at the Arapahoe with full candor: "I was a robot programmed to behave like a genuine aristocrat" (JB 10). He also understands that just as his future was in part determined by Alexander McCone's disgust with the type of ruthless capitalism that brought about the Cuyahoga Massacre, he was fortunate to have been born before the present era of computerization since that would have allowed McCone to indulge himself in games without the need for human competition. This realization hits Walter toward the close of the novel when he is presented with a computerized chessboard before returning to jail. (JB Epilogue) He (the computer "Boris") can even joke about the moves I make. "Really?" he will say; or, "Have you played this game before?" or, "Is this a trap?" or, "Spot me a queen."

Those are the standard chess jokes. Alexander Hamilton and I exchanged those same tired jokes endlessly when, for the sake of a Harvard education in my future, I agreed to be his chess-playing machine. If Boris had existed in those days, I probably would have gone to Western Reserve, and then become a tax assessor or an office manager, or an insurance salesman, or some such thing.

In a manner quite uncharacteristic for Vonnegut, the women in Jailbird play central roles in presenting depth and understanding; Walter adapts to their sensibilities. (JB 10). "How would I ever have got through life without women to act as my interpreters."

Sarah Wyatt fills in his French void while on their date, but more importantly, she is capable of pattering their string of one-line jokes, enabling Walter to travel back to a time less complicated with knowledge of the world.

Walter's wife is his translator in postwar Germany, and it is her talent that made him succeed

and be recognized by the Allied powers for his efforts at repatriating displaced individuals.

As for Mary Kathleen O'Looney, when Walter fumbles as a spokesman for Communism as a Harvard student, it is she who knows how to speak with members of the working class.

Walter realizes the negligible contributions he made to his own development. While awaiting release from prison for the Watergate conviction, he senses the moment as the demarcation from one life to another. Fearing his past complacency, Walter takes focused refuge in a bawdy song from his youth he thinks may really have been a way of honoring the powers of women, of dealing with the fears they inspired.

Sally in the garden,
Sifting cinders,
Lifted up her leg
And farted like a man.
The bursting of her bloomers
Broke sixteen winders.
The cheeks of her ass went—

Here the singers, in order to complete the stanza, were required to clap three times (JB 1).

For Walter, "Those three claps completed a rowdy song I had never liked, and which I had not thought about for thirty years or more. I was making my mind as blank as possible, you see, since the past was so embarrassing and the future so terrifying" (JB 1). And in a manner similar to the schizophrenic breaks of other Vonnegut characters, Starbuck describes his own status: "So there I was all alone on a bench in the middle of nowhere again. I entered a period of catatonia again—staring straight ahead at nothing, and every so often clapping my old hands three times" (JB 1).

Beyond the subbasement of the White House and the high-jinx that leads to his imprisonment is Walter's growing awareness of the historical and economic forces that have shaped his life. Cleveland Lawes, the RAMJAC chauffeur who kindly offers Walter a ride back from the prison, advises Walter that his son's toy steering wheel could illustrate a valuable lesson to the president: "He said that the President of the United States ought to be given a wheel like that at his inauguration, to remind him and everybody else that all he could do was pretend to steer" (JB 8). *Later, Walter comes to the epiphany that in the midst of the mindless engine of capitalism* "nobody who is doing well in this economy ever even wonders what is really going on. We are chimpanzees. We are orangutans" (JB 10).

His realization is set in stark relief when he encounters Mary Kathleen O'Looney in midtown Manhattan. (JB 14) Sociologically, of course, this melodrama was as gripping as *Uncle Tom's Cabin* before the Civil War. Mary Kathleen O'Looney wasn't the only shopping-bag lady in the United States of America. There were tens of thousands of them in major cities throughout the country. Ragged regiments of them had been produced accidently, and to no imaginable purpose, by the great engine of the economy. Another part of the machine was spitting out unrepentant murderers ten years old, and dope fiends and child batterers and many other bad things. People claimed to be investigating. Unspecified repairs were to be made at some future time.

Good-hearted people were meanwhile as sick about all these tragic by-products of the economy as they would have been about human slavery a little more than a hundred years before.

Mary Kathleen and Walter take temporary refuge in the uppermost offices of the Chrysler Building, home of the American Harp Company—a RAMJAC subsidiary. Just as Walter had been victimized by unknown Watergate criminals, he again falls victim to deeds of the unknown. He asks American Harp sales manager Delmar Peale if he knows of any dealers who might be interested in the clarinet parts he found in his room at the Hotel Arapahoe. The keen octogenarian remembers a police bulletin about a stolen truckload of such parts and coolly keeps Walter waiting while contacting police. Only one day since his release for crimes committed in the subbasement of the White House, Walter finds himself imprisoned in the basement padded cell of the local police precinct. None other than Roy Cohn, Senator McCarthy's chief counsel during the Communist witch hunts of the 1950s, is employed by RAMJAC to free him. Ah, fate.

After his release and his meeting with Arpad Leen, Mrs. Jack Graham's right-hand man at RAMJAC (which owns 19 percent of the United States), Walter

realizes that Mary Kathleen O'Looney is Mrs. Jack Graham, the chief executive officer of RAMJAC. He returns to Mary's haunts in the catacombs of Grand Central Station and finds her in a bathroom stall dying from injuries she received when hit by a taxi (owned by RAMJAC). She was mailing instructions to Arpad Leen commanding him to hire Walter and a host of those who had been kind to him. Before dying, Mary Kathleen absolves Walter for his historic lack of sincerity. (JB 23). "You couldn't help it that you were born without a heart. At least you tried to believe what the people with hearts believed—so you were a good man just the same."

Walter did bargain in good faith with destiny, however crude the slapstick may have become. Yet, he always lamented his lack of conviction. (JB 18) The most embarrassing thing to me about this autobiography, surely, is its unbroken chain of proofs that I was never a serious man. I have been in a lot of trouble over the years, but that was all accidental. Never have I risked my life, or even my comfort, in the service of mankind. Shame on me.

Walter realizes that pretension to goodness is merely shadowboxing. Whether or not he tried to believe in things others felt were good didn't matter. After all, societal values of goodness are neither universal nor permanent. He offers a glimpse of the dimension of the problem at a going away dinner held in his honor before returning to jail for concealing Mary Kathleen's last will and testament. (JB Epilogue) You know what is finally going to kill this planet? . . . A total lack of seriousness. Nobody gives a damn anymore about what's really going on, what's going to happen next, or how we ever got into such a mess in the first place.

Walter decries having to operate with only a limited understanding of the forces at work on life. Moreover, for Vonnegut the anthropology student, neglecting history makes the foundations of the future that much more frightening. Arnold Marx, the eighteen-year-old archaeology student / prison guard in the opening of Mother Night, *can recall the atrocities of Tiglath-pileser the Third but is ignorant of events in his own time. Vonnegut's compulsion to tell the truth of American atrocities in the early chapters of* Breakfast of Champions *is meant to mock the false history taught in the myth-making days of our earliest education/indoctrination.*

This loss of history is further punctuated by Vonnegut's reference to Sacco and Vanzetti. When Walter is most aware of his lack of seriousness, he recalls a conversation he had concerning the condemned anarchists. (JB 18) And it seems strange to me now that I have to explain who Sacco and Vanzetti were. I recently asked young Israel Edel at RAMJAC, the former night clerk at the Arapahoe, what he knew about Sacco and Vanzetti, and he told me confidently that they were rich, brilliant thrill-killers from Chicago. He had them confused with Leopold and Loeb.

Why should I find this unsettling? When I was a young man, I expected the story of Sacco and Vanzetti to be retold as often and as movingly, to be as irresistible, as the story of Jesus Christ some day. Weren't modern people, if they were to marvel creatively at their own lifetimes, I thought, entitled to a Passion like Sacco and Vanzetti's, which ended in an electric chair?

As for the last days of Sacco and Vanzetti as a modern Passion: As on Golgotha, three lower-class men were executed at the same time by a state. This time, though, not just one of the three was innocent. This time two of the three were innocent.

Sacco and Vanzetti also bargained in good faith with destiny. The irony of these two anarchists being falsely convicted and executed along with the confessed murderer is not lost in Vanzetti's last words as executioners strap him into the chair, "Never in our full life could we hope to do such work for tolerance, for justice, for man's understanding of man, as now we do by accident" (JB 19). *Lost, too, in unstudied history are Judge Thayer's remarks, also offered in good faith with his sense of destiny,* "This man, although he may not have actually committed the crime attributed to him, is nevertheless morally culpable, because he is the enemy of our existing institutions" (JB 19).

*Our willful ignorance of historical truth (whatever that may be) consigns us to continued victimization. Ignoring objective truth in the name of institutional salvation opens the way for establishment schizophrenia. As a result, people live by the designs of conspirators (the Judge Thayers) and participate in the conspiracy of design by clinging to and perpetuating the myths presented in youth. Vonnegut asserts that we have already reached this insti-*tutionalized schizophrenia. What we are missing is the common decency and respect of The Sermon on the Mount.

James, Jesse. *In* Breakfast of Champions, *Dwayne Hoover's stepfather bought a human skeleton from a doctor's estate, laid the rusted pieces of a .45 caliber revolver in its right hand, and placed the sham in Sacred Miracle Cave. They told the tourists the skeleton must have belonged to a railroad robber who took refuge in the cave and then got trapped by a rockslide.*

Jarvis, Colin and Ma. *In the prologue to* Jailbird, *Colin Jarvis is cited as the leader of the striking workers at the Cuyahoga Bridge and Iron Company, an ordinary foundryman with a gift for oratory (JB Prologue). The company resumed production with scabs and had Colin Jarvis arrested on trumped-up murder charges. His wife, Ma Jarvis, picked up the leadership banner during her husband's imprisonment. Her message to Daniel McCone was that the workers were prepared to return to work at whatever terms he dictated, but McCone was so incensed he refused to take them back.*

Jason, Ed. *In the 1955 short story "Deer in the Works" (reprinted in the 1968 collection* Welcome to the Monkey House), *Jason is David Potter's assistant at a small newspaper in Dorset, New York. Jason recently graduated from college and his father wanted to purchase the paper for him. Potter was thinking of selling because he was looking into a public relations job at the Ilium Works of the Federal Apparatus Corporation.*

Jefferson, Arthur Stanley (*see also* **Laurel and Hardy**). (*Slap* Dedication) Dedicated to the memory of **Arthur Stanley Jefferson** and **Norvell Hardy**, two angels of my time.
(TQ 63) I want a look-alike for Borden (*Deal*) at the clambake, and two luckless fishermen in a little rowboat right offshore, dead ringers for the saints **Stanley Laurel and Oliver Hardy.**
So be it.
(TQ 63) And Kilgore Trout said at the clambake, with **Laurel and Hardy** in a rowboat only fifty yards offshore, that young people liked movies with a lot

of shooting because they showed that dying didn't hurt at all, that people with guns could be thought of as "free-lance anesthetists."

(MWC 1) There is a superficial sort of laughter. Bob Hope, for example, was not really a humorist. He was a comedian with very thin stuff, never mentioning anything troubling. I used to laugh my head off at **Laurel and Hardy**. There is terrible tragedy there somehow. These men are too sweet to survive in this world and are in terrible danger all the time. They could be so easily killed.

Jefferson Observatory, Lenin Observatory, Mare Imbrium. *The Sirens of Titan's Martian invasion of Earth begins when Martian Imperial Commandos attack Earth's moon on April 23 (the year is not mentioned) and take possession of America's Jefferson Observatory, the Soviet Union's Lenin Observatory, and Holland's Mare Imbrium.*

Jekyll, Dr. Henry and Hortense. *The absent-minded chemistry professor calls his wife "Mildred."* (PS Jekyll and Hyde Updated) . . . "the venerable head of the chemistry department . . . the only faculty member with a statewide reputation" and Elbert Whitefeet's closest friend.

Jekyll concocts a growth potion for chickens (containing, among other hazardous compounds, LSD) to compete with the compound given him by Fred Leghorn, the wealthy chicken magnate. He drinks his own fowl growth potion and becomes an enormous, homicidal chicken. His dying clucks are pleas to be roasted and given to an orphanage. However, all agree it would be unchristian and ill-advised for Sweetbread College to let out any publicity on the matter, so he is buried in an unmarked grave.

Jesus (*see* **Christ**).

Jewish humor (*see* **humor**).

Johannsen, Nils (*also* **Johannsen Grinder Company**). *Jailbird's union organizer Kenneth Whistler leads a rally of striking workers against the company young Nils inherited. Johannsen's Scandinavian grandfather started the company, but Nils was running the business into the ground. Nils was asked to leave Harvard after hardly attending any classes during* his two years there. When his Harvard classmates caught him shooting craps with loaded dice, they stuck his head in a toilet bowl at the Ritz. Whistler uses his knowledge of the affair to compare Johannsen's use of the police to protect his property rights against the workers' human rights as playing with loaded dice.

John/Jonah. *Cat's Cradle's Bokononist narrator begins his tale by parodying Melville's Moby Dick.* (CC 1) Call me **Jonah**. My parents did, or nearly did. They called me **John**.

Jonah—John—if I had been a Sam, I would have been a **Jonah** still—not because I have been unlucky for others, but because somebody or something has compelled me to be certain places at certain times, without fail. Conveyances and motives, both conventional and bizarre, have been provided. And, according to plan, at each appointed second, at each appointed place this **Jonah** was there.

John/Jonah begins researching a book covering the activities of the atom bomb's inventors on the day it was dropped on Hiroshima. He plans to call it The Day the World Ended. *He is hoping to find the ironic backyard barbecue on the day Hiroshima was fried. What he finds instead is an amoral priesthood of scientists who gave little thought to the real world applications made of their newly found scientific truth. Above all he finds the legacy of Dr. Felix Hoenikker, ice-nine, which would eventually lock up all the moisture on Earth. Its boiling point: 114° Fahrenheit.*

His research takes him to Ilium's Research Laboratory of the General Forge and Foundry Company (the fictional counterpart to General Electric's Schenectady research facility where Vonnegut was a publicity writer and where he first learned of the Irving Langmuir suggestion to H. G. Wells of a storyline suggesting an ice-nine-type substance). From there John/Jonah goes to the perfectly rectangular island of San Lorenzo (mimicking Franklin Hoenikker's hobby shop construction of a society in microcosm) where he learns of the artificial dynamic tensions juxtaposing the Bokononist faith and "Papa" Monzano's dictatorship. Together they help keep the people economically underdeveloped but spiritually fulfilled.

John/Jonah starts writing the text before his trip to San Lorenzo and continues writing after ice-nine is released into the seas. He starts every chapter with the three-dot mathematical symbol for "therefore," and this may indicate that the beginning of the text presupposes its end—a true Bokononist conundrum. Though some reprints of the text dropped the three dots (presumably to save one hundred twenty-seven lines of text, roughly three and a half pages), Vonnegut assured me in a letter that those three dots included in the first edition were his. He repeated the same to me in person while having lunch in the backyard of his Sagaponack home in 1992. EDITOR'S NOTE: There is disagreement about the origination of the three-dot mathematical symbol for "therefore." When included in the first edition of this text as written above, I had not heard the apocryphal telling in publishing circles that the book's designer or compositor put in the symbol. Mark Vonnegut recently told me those dots were not in the original copy he proofed with his dad. I can only surmise that someone added those dots but can no longer assert with certainty that Vonnegut placed them there himself, simply overlooked their placement, or that the meaning is intended as indicated.

Johnson, Clarence Daffodil-H. *While thumbing through the Daffodil family directory in the Empire State Building,* Wilbur Swain *learns he is related to* **Clarence Daffodil-H Johnson,** *the Chief of Police of Batavia, New York* (Slap 37).

Johnson, Fred Bates. *In* Timequake, *Vonnegut recalls when his father first heard him say he wants to write for a newspaper:* Father said I had better talk to his close friend **Fred Bates Johnson,** a lawyer who as a young man had been a reporter for the now defunct Democratic daily *The Indianapolis Times* (153). *After Johnson politely listens to the young Vonnegut explain how he plans to work his way up from small papers until experienced enough to be worthy of working for his hometown paper, Johnson makes one phone call and lands young Kurt a job with* The Indianapolis Times, *which he soon declines in order to attend Cornell.*

In the short story "Thanasphere," collected in Bagombo Snuff Box (1999), *F. B. Johnson is the name of the Evansville chief of police who has more details about the death of Andrew Tobin in a hunting accident.*

Johnson, Henry "Tex." *The last president of Tarkington College having assumed the post after Sam Wakefield's suicide. When the prisoners break out of the prison across the lake and come to Tarkington, Tex goes to the library bell tower with his high-powered rifle and starts sniping the escaped convicts. They eventually shoot him out of the bell tower and crucify his body in the loft of the college's stables.*

Johnson previously served as Provost of Rollins College in Winter Park, Florida. He held an undergraduate degree in Business Administration from Texas Tech University. Though he claimed to have descended from one of the ill-fated soldiers at the Alamo, he was actually the son of a Lithuanian second mate on a Russian freighter who jumped ship when it put in for emergency repairs at Corpus Christi. Zuzu told me that **Tex's** *father was not only an illegal immigrant but the nephew of the former Communist boss of Lithuania* (HP 15).

Shortly after Tex and his wife, Zuzu, moved to Tarkington, she and Eugene Debs Hartke started a sexual relationship that lasted until about a month before Hartke is forced to resign by the Board of Trustees. A private investigator's report of their affair was disclosed to Tex as well as the board. Hartke had a solid friendship with Tex yet was never troubled by his duplicity. This prompts Hartke to recall that Tex was a cuckold in the present, and crucifixion awaited him in the future. I wonder if his father would have jumped ship in Corpus Christi if he had known what an unhappy end his only son would come to under American Free Enterprise (HP 16).

Johnson, Zuzu. *The wife of Tarkington College President Howard "Tex" Johnson and the longtime lover of Eugene Debs Hartke in* Hocus Pocus. *She and Hartke get together whenever Tex is out of town. At the meeting of Tarkington's Board of Trustees convened to fire Hartke, a private investigator's report indicates that in one semester the lovers had no less than thirty trysts. Though Hartke is able to separate his emotions from his lust, Zuzu can not. She eventually complains that Hartke never would act on their small talk about leaving their spouses and taking off for Venice where she would tend a flower shop and he would teach English. This leads to their final breakup.*

Zuzu is killed when the prisoners from across the lake break out and make their way to the college's campus. She and her husband are buried at the foot of Musket Mountain.

Johnstown High School. *In the 1952 short story "The No-Talent Kid," collected in* Bagombo Snuff Box (1999), *Johnstown's marching band beats out Lincoln High School's attempt for an eleventh straight state title. Lincoln band director George Helmholtz believes it was a non-musical decision based on the appearance of Johnstown's secret weapon, a bass drum seven feet in diameter.*

The judges, who were not musicians but politicians, had had eyes and ears for nothing but this eighth Wonder of the World, and since then Mr. Helmholtz had thought of little else.

Jolson, Al. *The star of the first movie with sound, the Jewish entertainer was once a close friend of Dan Gregory, in* Bluebeard. *Jolson and other notable guests argued with Gregory about Mussolini at a dinner party, and from that time forward Gregory became a pariah to them. Rabo Karabekian uses Jolson as another example of the loss of cultural memory among the young when he recalls that his cook's daughter and friends couldn't identify him.*

Jones, Fred. *The World War I flyer who lost an eye (as did Rabo Karabekian in World War II) and who serves Dan Gregory as a valet and constant male companion. They weren't homosexuals, nor was Jones treated as a servant. They were simply inseparable friends. Jones and Gregory eventually die dressed in uniforms of Mussolini's troops at Sidi Barrani, Egypt, one year before the attack on Pearl Harbor.*

Karabekian understands Jones because he is able to see him in ways that others may not appreciate. In so doing, Rabo sheds light not only on Jones but also on some of his Abstract Expressionist painter buddies. (Blue 20) His life had been all downhill since World War One, when he had discovered a gift for flying rattletrap kites which were machine-gun platforms. The first time he got his hands on the joystick of an airplane, he must have felt what Terry Kitchen felt when he gripped a spray gun. He must have felt like Kitchen again when he fired his machine guns up in the wild blue yonder, and saw a plane in front of him draw a helix of smoke and flame—ending in a sunburst far below.

What beauty! So unexpected and pure! So easy to achieve!

Fred Jones told me one time that the smoke trails of falling airplanes and observation balloons were the most beautiful things he ever expected to see. And I now compare his elation over arcs and spirals and splotches in the atmosphere with what Jackson Pollock used to feel as he watched what dribbled paint chose to do when it struck a canvas on his studio floor.

Same sort of happiness!

Except that what Pollock did lacked that greatest of all crowd pleasers, which was human sacrifice.

Jones, Lionel J. D. (the Reverend Doctor Lionel J. D. Jones, D.D.S., D.D.). *The publisher of* The White Christian Minuteman, *Jones was born in Haverhill, Massachusetts, in 1889, was raised as a Methodist (MN 13). Jones flunks out of the University of Pennsylvania Dental School in 1910, not so much because of his lack of dental knowledge but because regardless of the subject,* **Jones** *managed to go from it to a theory that was all his own—that the teeth of Jews and Negroes proved beyond question that both groups were degenerate (MN 13). His parents disown him when they become aware of his activities at school. He finds work as an apprentice embalmer with Scharff Brothers Funeral Home. At the age of twenty-four he marries the fifty-eight-year-old widowed owner of the funeral home, Hattie Scharff. She dies in 1928.*

During the marriage he teams with chemist Dr. Lomar Horthy, inventing both the embalming fluid Viverine and Gingiva-Tru, a "gum-stimulating substance for false teeth."

After his wife dies, Jones sells the funeral home and starts The White Christian Minuteman. *After fourteen issues Jones is wiped out in the 1929 stock market crash. (MN 13) In the next-to-the-last issue,* **Jones** *billed himself on the masthead as "***Dr. Lionel J. D. Jones, D.D.S.***"*

In 1939 he applies for the presidency of the Little Rock School of Embalming, and after attaining the position he marries the widowed owner of the school, Mary Alice Shoup—she was sixty-eight. Jones liquidated the funeral school and had it rechartered as

The Western Hemisphere University of the Bible. The university held no classes, taught nothing, did all its business by mail. Its business was the awarding of doctorates in the field of divinity, framed and under glass, for eighty dollars a throw (MN 13).

Jones takes one of his school's doctorates, expands the number of his titles, and revives The White Christian Minuteman *when his second wife passes away. He publishes a book entitled* Christ Was Not a Jew, *the thesis of which is that by evaluating all the artistic renditions of Jesus Christ it can be determined he was not Jewish.*

His newspaper picks up sponsorship by the Nazis. In 1942 he is arrested, tried, and convicted for sedition and serves eight years of a fourteen-year sentence. Upon his release from prison, Jones comes into great wealth from his patent on Gingiva-Tru, and in 1955 he reissues The White Christian Minuteman.

In 1960 he receives a letter from George Kraft / Iona Potapov about the whereabouts of Howard Campbell. Accompanied by his strange entourage, Jones seeks out Howard Campbell to lend whatever support he can.

In the cellar of Jones's home, August Krapptauer led the Iron Guard of the White Sons of the American Constitution. Jones's inner circle includes Krapptauer, Father Keeley, and the Black Fuehrer of Harlem.

Jorgenson, Coach. *Dubbed the* silent Swede *by Lincoln High School band director George M. Helmholtz in the short story "Ambitious Sophomore," collected in* Bagombo Snuff Box (1999), *Coach Jorgenson utters his one and only line when seeing the otherwise bell-shaped sophomore piccoloist Leroy Duggan sporting his oversized band uniform that makes him look almost like a superhero with enormous shoulders and athletic waist. As Leroy speaks to Helmholtz recalling the coach's words,* He said that only in this band-happy school would they make a piccolo player out of a man built like a locomotive.

Joseph of Arimathea. *The story of the Holy Grail is the impetus for Fred T. Barry to show off his command of obscure "facts." Here he tries to prove that Sir Galahad was Jewish.* (DD 20) According to Fred T. Barry, a Jew named **Joseph of Arimathea** took Christ's goblet when the Last Supper was over.

He believed Christ to be divine. . . . But then Sir Galahad presented himself at Camelot, and it was evident to everyone that his heart was perfectly pure. And he did find the Grail. He was not only spiritually entitled to it. He was legally entitled to it as well, since he was the last living descendant of that wandering Jew, **Joseph of Arimathea**.

journalism, New Journalism. (WFG Preface) Everything else in here shows me trying to tell the truth nakedly, without the ornaments of fiction, about this or that. Which brings us to a discussion of the place of the "**New Journalism**," as opposed to fiction, in the literature of modern times.

. . . There's some **New Journalism** in here— about Biafra, about the Republican Convention of 1972. It's loose and personal.
(WFG Preface) I have wavered some on this, but I am now persuaded again that acknowledged fiction is a much more truthful way of telling the truth than the **New Journalism** is. Or, to put it another way, the very finest **New Journalism** is fiction. . . .

And fiction is melody, and **journalism**, new or old, is noise.
(WFG A Political Disease) Insults of that sort, isolated in a review, convey the idea of **journalism** at least as contemptible as the man attacked. But in the context of such a long and passionate book, such lapses seem almost beautiful. Curiously, they are frenzied, so grotesque, that they can do no harm to *(Senator)* Eagleton. I am extremely grateful for the **New Journalism**, many responsible people are not. And what I think about it now is that it is the literary equivalent of Cubism: All rules are broken; we are shown pictures such as no mature well-trained artist ever painted before, and in the crazy new pictures we somehow see luminous new aspects, beloved old truths.
(PS Introduction) It is a marvelous new literary form. This book combines the tidal power of a major novel with the bone-rattling immediacy of front-line **journalism**—which is old stuff now, God knows, God knows.
(HP 6) There were plenty of other exits, and I should have headed for 1 of those. At that moment, every other exit led to the University of Michigan and **journalism** and music-making, and a lifetime of saying and wearing what I goshdarned pleased.

See also: MH Deer in the Works; *PS* Introduction; *BAG* Preface; *GBK* Isaac Asimov.

journalist, New Journalist. (*WFG* Preface) Thucydides is the first **New Journalist** I know anything about. He was a celebrity who put himself at the center of the truths he was trying to tell, and he guessed when he had to, and he thought it worthwhile to be charming and entertaining. He was a good teacher. He did not wish to put his students to sleep with the truth, and he meant to put the truth into strikingly human terms, so his students would remember. . . .

Am I a **New Journalist**? I guess. There's some New Journalism in here—about Biafra, about the Republican Convention of 1972. It's loose and personal.

(*WFG* Preface) The **New Journalist** isn't free to tell nearly as much as a fiction writer, to show as much. There are many places he can't take his reader, whereas the fiction writer can take the reader anywhere, including the planet Jupiter, in case there's something worth seeing there.

(*WFG* Address to P.E.N. Conference in Stockholm, 1973) **Journalists** and teachers are often bullied or fired in my country—for saying this or that. But writers of novels and plays and short stories and poems have never been hurt or hampered much. They haven't even been noticed much by federal, state, or local governments, no matter how insolent or blasphemous or treasonous those writers may be. This has been going on now for nearly two hundred years.

(*WFG* A Political Disease) I WORRY about the health of Dr. Hunter Thompson. I think I am supposed to do that. He is the most creatively crazy and vulnerable of the **New Journalists**, seemingly, and scattered throughout his dispatches are alarming reports on his health. Nor are his sicknesses imaginary. In this, his latest book, he gives the opinion of a physician: "He'd never seen anybody with as bad a case of anxiety as I had. He said I was right on the verge of a complete mental, physical, and emotional collapse."

(*WFG* A Political Disease) I can put it more gruesomely—calling attention to the way people behave under torture sometimes, the way they are likely to thrash around and say things they might not say under other circumstances: The **New Journalists** are Populists screaming in pain.

They believe that it is easy and natural for Americans to be brotherly and just. That illusion, if it is an illusion, is the standard for well-being in the **New Journalists'** minds. Any deviation from that standard is perceived as a wound or a sickness.

(*HP* 4) When Du Pont took over Barrytron, the double fence, the Dobermans, my father and all, I was a high school senior, all set to go to the University of Michigan to learn how to be a **journalist**, to serve John Q. Public's right to know.

(*BAG* Introduction) But I didn't want to be an anthropologist, either. I only hoped to find out more about human beings. I was going to be a **journalist**!
See also: MH Deer in the Works; *WFG* Playboy Interview; *JB* XVII:L18; *HP* 1; *TQ* 31; *TQ* 154; *MWC* 3.

Joy's Pride. *In Kilgore Trout's short story "No Laughing Matter,"* Joy's Pride *is the bomber named in honor of the pilot's mother, Joy Peterson, a nurse in obstetrics in a hospital in Corpus Christi, Texas* (*TQ* 3). *The bomber is equipped with the third atom bomb intended to be dropped on the Japanese at the close of World War II. This time the intended target is Yokohama. Trout describes the bomb slung beneath the craft as* A purple motherfucker as big as a boiler in the basement of a mid-size junior high school.

(*TQ* 3) The more the pilot thought about it, though, the surer he was that his sweet widowed mother could never tell reporters she was happy that her son's airplane had killed a world's record number of civilians all at once. *In addition, the pilot feels that bombing Yokohama has no tactical value at this point and with the full agreement of his crew decides to return to their base at Banalulu.*

Joyce, John Wesley (*see **God Bless You, Dr. Kevorkian**).

Joyce, Leroy. *The focus of a story told by the Holiday Inn cocktail waitress Bonnie MacMahon in* Breakfast of Champions. *Joyce was a convicted rapist on death row at the Shepherdstown Adult Correctional Institution. Bonnie's husband, Ralph, was Leroy's guard at the time, and only hours be-*

fore his scheduled execution, Joyce cut off his penis and handed it to Ralph in a coffee cup. Vonnegut interjects that though this is only a novel, he gave Bonnie the gist of a real story that occurred in Arkansas.

Judgment Day. (PP I) Objectively, Paul tried to tell himself, things really were better than ever. For once, after the great bloodbath of the war, the world really was cleared of unnatural terrors—mass starvation, mass imprisonment, mass torture, mass murder. Objectively, know-how and world law were getting their long-awaited chance to turn earth into an altogether pleasant and convenient place in which to sweat out **Judgment Day**.

(PP XXXV) Von Neumann considered Paul and then the broken glass. "This isn't the end, you know," he said. "Nothing ever is, nothing ever will be—not even **Judgment Day**."

(SL5 8) "That's right. And I'm not the only one who's listening. God is listening, too. And on **Judgment Day** he's going to tell you all the things you said and did. If it turns out they're bad things instead of good things, that's too bad for you, because you'll burn forever and ever. The burning never stops hurting." *Trout speaks with Maggie White.*

(BC 15) "On **Judgment Day**," said Francine, "when they ask me what bad things I did down here, I'm going to have to tell them, 'Well—there was a promise I made to a man I loved, and I broke it all the time. I promised him never to say I loved him.'"

(Slap 3) But there was one tremendous monument, with thick granite walls, a slate roof, and great doors, which would clearly last past **Judgment Day**. It was the mausoleum of the founder of the family's fortune and the builder of our mansion, Professor Elihu Roosevelt Swain.

(JB 1) Life goes on, yes—and a fool and his self-respect are soon parted, perhaps never to be reunited even on **Judgment Day**.

(JB 4) "Virgil Greathouse is no more and no less my brother than you or any other man," he said. "I will try to save him from hell, just as I am now trying to save you from hell." He then quoted the harrowing thing that Jesus, according to Saint Matthew, had promised to say in the Person of God to sinners on **Judgment Day**.

This is it: "Depart from me, you cursed, into the eternal fire prepared for the devil and his angels." (Matthew 25:1)

(JB 10) I speak only of Ruth as "my wife." It would not surprise me, though, if on **Judgment Day** Sarah Wyatt and Mary Kathleen O'Looney were also certified as having been wives of mine.

(PS Mark Twain) "I am moved on this occasion to put into a few words the ideal my parents and Twain and the rest held before me, and which I have now passed on. The ideal, achieved by few, is this: Live so that you can say to God on **Judgment Day**, 'I was a very good person, even though I did not believe in you.'"

". . . Religious skeptics often become very bitter toward the end, as did Mark Twain. I do not propose to guess now as to why he became so bitter. I know why I will become bitter. I will finally realize that I have had it right all along: that I will not see God, that there is no heaven or **Judgment Day**."

(Blue 4) In the imaginary galleries in the distance are my own Abstract Expressionist paintings, miraculously resurrected by the Great Critic for **Judgment Day**, and then pictures by Europeans, which I bought for a few dollars or chocolate bars or nylon stockings when a soldier, and then advertisements of the sort I had been laying out and illustrating before I joined the Army—at about the time news of my father's death in the Bijou Theater in San Ignacio came.

(Blue 25) Gregory, I remember, was bid farewell in the papers as possibly the best-known American artist in history. Fred (Jones) was sent on to **Judgment Day** as a World War One ace, which he wasn't, and an aviation pioneer.

(Blue 31) What will be found written after the name of Rabo Karabekian in the Big Book on **Judgment Day**?

"Soldier: Excellent.

"Husband and Father: Floparroo.

"Serious Artist: Floparroo." *Rabo's self-evaluation.*

(HP 3) He (Elias Tarkington) had no fewer than 27 contraptions built, which he foolishly expected to go on running, after he had given them an initial spin or whack, until **Judgment Day**.

This is Hartke's answer to his lawyer when asked why he was making up the two lists: all the women with whom he had meaningful sexual relationships and all the people he knows he has killed. (HP 19) "To speed things up on **Judgment Day**," I said. . . .

I told him I wanted to be buried with my 2 lists, so that, if there really was going to be a **Judgment Day**, I could say to the Judge, "Judge, I have found a way to save you some precious time in Eternity. You don't have to look me up in the Book in Which All Things Are Recorded. Here's a list of my worst sins. Send me straight to Hell, and no argument."

(HP 23) *(Arthur C.)* Clarke's big arrival wasn't a half-bad dress rehearsal for **Judgment Day**.

(HP 40) If there really is a big book somewhere, in which all things are written, and which is to be read line by line, omitting nothing, on **Judgment Day**, let it be recorded that I, when Warden of this place, moved the convicted felons out of the tents on the Quadrangle and into the surrounding buildings. They no longer had to excrete in buckets or, in the middle of the night, have their homes blown down. The buildings, except for this 1, were divided into cement-block cells intended for 2 men, but most holding 5.

(TQ Epilogue) Extenuating circumstance to be mentioned on **Judgment Day**: We never asked to be born in the first place.

(BAG 2BR02B) A coarse, formidable woman strode into the waiting room on spike heels. Her shoes, stockings, trench coat, bag, and overseas cap were all purple, a purple the painter called "the color of grapes on **Judgment Day**."

The medallion on her purple musette bag was the seal of the Service Division of the Federal Bureau of Termination, an eagle perched on a turnstile.

June, Wanda (*see also* **Happy Birthday, Wanda June**). *There are four incarnations of the character Wanda June. Her first appearance is in* The Sirens of Titan *as a six-year-old girl being dragged through the crowded concession stands outside the Rumford estate. Winston Niles Rumfoord and Kazak are about to materialize and banish Malachi, Beatrice, and Chrono to Titan.*

The second Wanda June is the title character of

the play. An error in the text indicates she is either eight or ten years old at the time of her death. She is killed by the drunken driver of an ice-cream truck. Wanda is happy in heaven. Her description of heaven makes it sound like a wonderful carnival. The title of the play comes from the birthday cake left at the bakery by her parents after her sudden death. Wanda's companions in heaven run the gamut from war criminals to innocents. Vonnegut sees this flaw in the play as an inherent characteristic of his literature. He recalls in its preface, Somewhere in there my father died, and one of the last things he said to me was that I had never written a story with a villain in it. That was surely one of the troubles with my play—and that remains a major trouble with it to this day. Even after we opened **Happy Birthday, Wanda June**, *we experimented shamelessly with endings. We had various people shoot Harold, including children. We had Harold shoot various people, including children. We had Harold do the world the favor of shooting himself* (WJ About This Play).

In the short story "The Big Space Fuck," reprinted in the "Obscenity" chapter of Palm Sunday, *Wanda June is the only daughter of the degenerate Dwayne and Grace Hoobler. Wanda June is suing her parents for ruining her childhood, resulting in diminished opportunities for her as an adult.*

In Hocus Pocus, Wanda June is the wife of Tarkington College Professor Damon Stern. When the Athena prison break occurs, Stern sends Wanda June and the kids to her brother's house in Lackawanna, New York. The Sterns had saved Japanese yen in a Brussels sprouts container in their freezer, and that was all she takes away from Scipio. Damon Stern stays behind to wake others in Scipio, and is eventually killed by the marauding convicts.

Juno. *In Roman mythology, Juno is the goddess of the Pantheon and sister/wife of Jupiter. In the short story "Welcome to the Monkey House," Billy the Poet derisively applies the term to Nancy McLuhan, the hostess he kidnaps from the Ethical Suicide Parlor. He plans to let her ethical birth control pills wear off and have sex with her.*

K

Kago (*see also* ***Plague on Wheels***). *In* Breakfast of Champions, *Kago is the spokesperson for the band of Zeltoldimarian space travelers who promise to keep alive the story of the automobile civilization on Lingo-Three. These are all elements in Kilgore Trout's* Plague on Wheels.

Kairys, Anna. *Walter Starbuck's mother.* (JB 1) And what was I to Mr. McCone, that I should have been born into the unhappy stillness of his mansion? My mother, born **Anna Kairys** in Russian Lithuania, was his cook. My father, born Stanislaus Stankie-wicz in Russian Poland, was his bodyguard and chauffeur. They genuinely loved him.

Kanka-bonos. *In* Galápagos, *the Ecuadorian tribe descended from native Indians and escaped African slaves. The six Kanka-bono girls cared for by Roman Catholic priest Father Bernard Fitzgerald eventually become the mothers of humanity as it evolves by returning to the sea. Through the ingenuity of Mary Hepburn, the Kanka-bonos are artificially inseminated with the sperm of Captain Adolf von Kleist. Their offspring mate with the genetically altered and furry children of Akiko Hiroguchi.*

The Kanka-bono girls are the last remaining members of their tribe when Father Fitzgerald arranges a ride for them to Guayaquil with bush pilot Eduardo Ximénez. The effects of pesticides dropped in their jungle home had orphaned the girls. Once they are in Guayaquil, Domingo Quezeda volunteers to care for them and serve as their interpreter, but he proves to be a lecherous old man who takes advantage of their naïveté.

kan-kan (*see also* **Bokononism**). (CC 1) We Boko-nonists believe that humanity is organized into teams, teams that do God's Will without ever dis-covering what they are doing. Such a team is called a *karass* by Bokonon, and the instrument, the ***kan-kan***, that brought me into my own particular *karass* was the book I never finished, the book to be called *The Day the World Ended.*

Karabekian, Dorothy (*see also* **Rabo Kara-bekian**). *Rabo's first wife, a registered nurse, who is now widowed by her second husband and lives in a beachfront condominium in Sarasota, Florida. After Rabo spent eight years in the military,* Poor **Dorothy** thought she was marrying a mature, fatherly retired military gentleman. What she got instead was an impossibly self-centered and undisciplined jerk of nineteen or so! (*Blue* 32) *She becomes despondent over Rabo's involvement with the starving Abstract Expressionist artists who pay off their loans to Rabo with their paintings. When she gets angry with Rabo about the lack of talent among his group—agreeing with the published comments of an Italian sculp-tor—he draws two portraits of their children on the blank walls of their home. She doesn't understand why he doesn't use that talent to get commissioned work. He responds, "It's just too fucking easy." When they split up, Dorothy cuts the two pieces of Sheet-rock from the wall and takes them with her.*

Karabekian, Rabo. *There are various incarnations of Rabo Karabekian. The one-eyed Armenian Ameri-can war veteran, Abstract Expressionist painter, and art collector writes his autobiography,* Bluebeard, *at the request of Circe Berman.*

Rabo first appears as one of three distinguished guests at the Midland City Arts Festival in Breakfast of Champions. *The first piece of artwork purchased for The Mildred Barry Memorial Center for the Arts is Karabekian's "The Temptation of Saint Anthony," a $50,000 acquisition.*

Introduced as a "minimal painter" as opposed to a "minimalist painter," Rabo's painting is nothing more than a single band of luminescent color on a white background. Within the text, Vonnegut fre-quently makes mention that he is in his own text to be reborn. He finds himself unexpectedly "renewed" by Rabo's interpretation of his painting. (BC 19) "I now give you my word of honor," he went on, "that the picture your city owns shows everything about life which truly matters, with nothing left out. It is a picture of the awareness of every animal. It is the immaterial core of every animal—the 'I am' to which all messages are sent. It is all that is alive in any of us—in a mouse, in a deer, in a cocktail waitress. It is unwavering and pure, no matter what preposterous adventure may befall us. A sacred picture of Saint Anthony alone is one vertical, unwavering band of light. If a cockroach were near him, or a cocktail waitress, the picture would show two such bands of light. Our awareness is all that is alive and maybe sacred in any of us. Everything else about us is dead machinery."

Though Rabo's painting is briefly alluded to in Deadeye Dick, it isn't until the appearance of Bluebeard that Rabo becomes more than the wisecracking snob he is in Breakfast of Champions. He was born in 1916 in San Ignacio, California, to Armenian refugees. He is a largely self-taught artist, though when Rabo begins a correspondence with Marilee Kemp (believing she is merely relaying information from the famed New York illustrator Dan Gregory), he is instructed to copy Gregory's illustrations as part of his training. Rabo briefly works as an illustrator for a San Ignacio newspaper but leaves for New York to become Gregory's apprentice. He is unaware that Gregory only agrees to send for him because of Gregory's assault on Marilee Kemp. Gregory suffers Rabo's presence, training his protégé in the same brutal manner as he was tutored by Beskudnikov. Rabo and Marilee become constant companions, eventually developing a brief physical relationship.

During World War II, Rabo serves in the Army Engineers, charged with using his artistry to camouflage military outposts. He loses his left eye during a shelling attack while serving in Europe. Upon returning to the United States and undergoing surgery and recuperation at Fort Benjamin Harrison outside Indianapolis, Rabo returns to New York. He takes up with a number of fledgling artists and becomes one of the founders of the Abstract Expressionist school of art. Rabo marries a registered nurse, Dorothy, and sires two sons, Terry and Henri. Dorothy becomes disturbed with the amount of time Rabo spends with the other artists and his participation in an art form that, in her view, revealed nothing and was commercially worthless. Dorothy's despondency with Rabo's friends grows as they constantly borrow money from him and repay him with their original artwork.

Though she had no way to know at the time, those repayments formed the basis of Rabo's world-class collection of Abstract Expressionist paintings.

After Dorothy takes the children and leaves their home in the village of Springs, Long Island, Rabo moves into the potato barn (six miles away on the waterfront of East Hampton), a space he previously rented from Edith and Richard Fairbanks, Jr., to store his art collection. After Edith is widowed and his own divorce becomes final, Rabo and Edith begin a relationship that leads to a twenty-five-year marriage. Rabo later learns he lost Edith the same week Marilee Kemp passed away in Italy.

Rabo goes on to live a quiet life on Long Island until he meets Circe Berman, who moves into his life and causes him to reexamine his past by writing his memoirs. He titles those memoirs Bluebeard, and it is through Rabo's recall that we learn about his disastrous decision to use Sateen Dura-Luxe paint for his Abstract Expressionist creations. He learns of the paint's peculiar and tragic defect when told his sixty-four-foot triptych "Windsor Blue Number Seventeen," has nearly completely peeled itself clean down to the underlying canvas. After retrieving its remains from the third subbasement of the Matsumoto Building in New York City, Rabo returns to the potato barn and paints "Now It's the Women's Turn." This new triptych depicts the scene Rabo saw in the meadows of Europe after its liberation. More than five thousand figures, some no larger than a cigarette, are realistically rendered. It is similar to Vonnegut's description of the scenes he saw in Europe after being liberated from his POW camp, and this is confirmed in Fates Worse Than Death. Perhaps as a reference to his own past "single-band" paintings, Rabo paints himself into the triptych. With his back to the viewer, his image is divided by the space between two canvases. Rather than a single band of luminescent color representing one's essential awareness, Rabo's single band of emptiness (the space between the canvases) takes the place of his spine.

Rabo keeps this new masterpiece locked away in the potato barn until Circe Berman persuades him to reveal it. The barn and the painting become a tourist mecca.

Karabekian, Terry and Henri. The sons of Rabo and Dorothy Karabekian in Bluebeard. They are named after Rabo's best friend Terry Kitchen and his favorite artist, Henri Matisse. After Rabo and Dorothy break up, the boys resent Rabo and have nothing to do with him. They eventually assume the name of their stepfather Roy Steel. Terry grows up to work publicity for the Chicago Bears, and Henri works for the Pentagon as a civilian contract compliance officer. Rabo feels a great deal of guilt about his failure to properly father the boys, but he decides to leave his valuable collection of Abstract Expressionist paintings to them in his will, provided they change their names back to Karabekian. Rabo does this out of respect for his mother's wishes that the family name live on.

karass (see also **Bokononism**). (CC 1) We Bokononists believe that humanity is organized into teams, teams that do God's Will without ever discovering what they are doing. Such a team is called a *karass* by Bokonon, and the instrument, the *kan-kan*, that brought me into my own particular *karass* was the book I never finished, the book to be called *The Day the World Ended.*
(CC 24) Which brings me to the Bokononist concept of a *wampeter.*

A *wampeter* is the pivot of a *karass*. No *karass* is without a *wampeter*, Bokonon tells us, just as no wheel is without a hub.

Anything can be a *wampeter*: a tree, a rock, an animal, an idea, a book, a melody, the Holy Grail. Whatever it is, the members of its *karass* revolve about it in the majestic chaos of a spiral nebula. The orbits of the members of a *karass* about their common *wampeter* are spiritual orbits, naturally. It is souls and not bodies that revolve. As Bokonon invites us to sing:

Around and around and around we spin,
With feet of lead and wings of tin. . . .

And *wampeters* come and *wampeters* go, Bokonon tells us.

At any given time a *karass* actually has two *wampeters*—one waxing in importance, one waning.

Karlswald. In the short story "D.P.," reprinted in Welcome to the Monkey House (1968), the German village on the Rhine within the American zone of occupation where the American German youngster Karl Heinz lives in an orphanage, hoping for the return of his American father. Karl is nicknamed "Joe Louis" by the village carpenter, in tribute to the most famous black man he knows.

Karpinski, Big John, Dorene, and Little John. Rabo's neighbors to the north in East Hampton. Little John is a poor student, is arrested for selling dope, joins the Army during the Vietnam War—which brings great pride to Big John—and comes back in a body bag. Though their family farm has been in operation for three generations, Big John and Dorene are preparing to sell it in six-acre parcels for a housing development.

Big John is a wounded Korean War veteran. The six-acre lot Rabo lives on was sold to his second wife, Edith, and her first husband by Big John's father. This final series of sales liquidating the Karpinski ancestral homeland brings the following insight from Karabekian. (Blue 36) **Big John** and **Dorene** will become cash millionaires in a condominium in Florida, where winter never comes. So they are losing their own sacred plot of earth at the foot of their own Mount Ararat, so to speak—without experiencing that ultimate disgrace: a massacre.

Kasabian, F. Donald. In Bluebeard, Rabo Karabekian recalls the achievements of Armenian Americans, among them F. Donald Kasabian. (Blue 4) Armenians have done brilliantly in this country during the short time they've been here. My neighbor to the west is **F. Donald Kasabian**, executive vice-president of Metropolitan Life—so that right here in exclusive East Hampton, and right on the beach, too, we have two Armenians side by side.

Katmandu (see also **John Fortune**). Rudy Waltz's play about his childhood hero, the dairy farmer John Fortune. The play has its origins in one of Rudy's high school essays. Rudy's teacher Naomi Shoup went to pieces after reading the essay and urged him to become a writer. For years Rudy continued to work on changing the essay into a play, and in 1959 he wins a contest for new playwrights. His prize includes an engagement at New York City's Theatre de Lys, the same theater where Vonnegut's Wanda June was produced.

"Katmandu" is such a disaster that it runs for just one night on February 14, 1960, fifteen years and a day after the firebombing of Dresden. The next morning, Rudy and his brother Felix fly back to the snowed-in Midland City in search of their parents, only to find out their father has died.

Rudy stays with his brother and sister-in-law in New York while the play is in rehearsal, and for the first time in his life he could separate himself from the Deadeye Dick legacy. Able to stand outside himself, Rudy realizes, I no longer cared about the play. It was Deadeye Dick, tormented by guilt in Midland City, who had found old John Fortune's quite pointless death in **Katmandu**, as far away from his hometown as possible, somehow magnificent. He himself yearned for distance and death.

So, there in Greenwich Village, looking up at my name on the marquee, I was nobody. My braincase might as well have been filled with stale ginger ale (DD 19). *The play has two more performances in 1963 at Midland City's Fairchild High School by the Midland City Mask and Wig Club.*

Kazak (*also* **Kazakh**). *There are three dogs named either Kazak or Kazakh in Vonnegut's work. The first Kazak is Winston Niles Rumfoord's "hound of space," a female mastiff traveling with her master along the same chrono-synclastic infundibulum in the novel* The Sirens of Titan. *At the end of the text an explosion on the sun causes Kazak to be transported through time and space without her master. Rumfoord is left holding his dog's choke collar. In an earlier part of the text, Rumfoord named one of the Martian months after Kazak. Later, on Titan, he names* a cluster of ninety-three ponds and lakes, incipiently a fourth sea . . . the **Kazak Pools** (ST 12).

In Breakfast of Champions, *Kazak is the Doberman pinscher patrolling the supply yard of the Maritimo Brothers Construction Company. Toward the end of the text, when Vonnegut again enters the narrative to confront Kilgore Trout, Kazak leaps toward the top of the fence to get at Vonnegut, who is standing next to his rented car. Vonnegut leaps over the hood of the car in mortal fear, though Kazak is restrained by the height of the fence.*

In Galápagos, *Kazakh is the seeing-eye German shepherd belonging to Selena Macintosh. Kazakh has been fixed and well trained to ignore her normal* canine instincts. *After being stranded on Santa Rosalia, the six Kanka-bono girls steal Kazakh while Selena is asleep. They choke Kazakh to death, cook her in the ship's oven, and eat her.*

Keane, Frances (*see* ***God Bless You, Dr. Kevorkian***).

Keedsler, Beatrice. *The Midland City native and gothic novelist invited to return home as an honored guest at the Arts Festival. Dwayne Hoover breaks Beatrice Keedsler's jaw during his violent outrage. Aviator and World War I hero Will Fairchild was Beatrice's maternal uncle. In 1926 he shot and killed five of her relatives at the Keedsler mansion.*

While sharing drinks with Rabo Karabekian in the lounge of the Midland City Holiday Inn, Keedsler echoes Vonnegut's sense that former regional distinctions in American life have become homogenized. (BC 18) **Beatrice Keedsler**, the Gothic novelist, had grown up in Midland City. "I was petrified about coming home after all these years," she said to Karabekian.

"Americans are always afraid of coming home," said Karabekian, "with good reason, may I say."

"They *used* to have good reason," said **Beatrice**, "but not anymore. The past has been rendered harmless. I would tell any wandering American now, 'Of course you can go home again, and as often as you please. It's just a motel.'"

Vonnegut's assessment of Keedsler's written works and of art in general is rather brutal when viewed through their affects on the masses. (BC 19) I had no respect whatsoever for the creative works of either the painter or the novelist. I thought Karabekian with his meaningless pictures had entered into a conspiracy with millionaires to make poor people feel stupid. I thought **Beatrice Keedsler** had joined hands with other old-fashioned storytellers to make people believe that life had leading characters, minor characters, significant details, insignificant details, that it had lessons to be learned, tests to be passed, and a beginning, a middle, and an end.

As I approached my fiftieth birthday, I had become more and more enraged and mystified by the idiot decisions made by my countrymen. And then I had come suddenly to pity them, for I understood how innocent and natural it was for them to behave so abominably, and with such abominable results: They were doing their best to live like people invented in story books. This was the reason Americans shot each other so often: It was a convenient literary device for ending short stories and books.

Keeley, Father Patrick (also **Keely**). *The seventy-three-year-old defrocked Paulist priest reclaimed from Skid Row by the Rev. Dr. Lionel J. D. Jones in* Mother Night. *Prior to World War II, Father Keeley served as the chaplain for a Detroit gun club established by Nazi agents. One of the club's fondest hopes was to shoot Jews. Keeley's involvement comes to the attention of Vatican officials when they read a newspaper's account of one of Keeley's virulently anti-Semitic benedictions. As a result, Pope Pius XI defrocks him. Keeley resorts to alcohol and is found homeless and hopeless by Dr. Jones. Howard Campbell reveals that the prayer offered by Keeley to the gun club was a paraphrase of one of his own anti-Semitic diatribes delivered on shortwave radio. Father Keeley eventually serves as Jones's secretary and chaplain for the Iron Guard of the White Sons of the American Constitution.*

Keene, Patty. *The seventeen-year-old blond waitress at Dwayne Hoover's Burger Chef restaurant in* Breakfast of Champions. *She takes the job to help pay off hospital bills accumulated by her father's fatal bout with colon cancer. She previously became pregnant when raped by Don Breedlove outside the Bannister Memorial Fieldhouse after the regional high school basketball playoffs. She decided not to report the crime because her father was dying at the time.*

Vonnegut uses Patty to comment on the manner in which some women have been trained to succeed in our society. (BC 15) **Patty Keene** was stupid on purpose, which was the case with most women in Midland City. The women all had big minds because they were big animals, but they did not use them much for this reason: unusual ideas could make enemies, and the women, if they were going to achieve any sort of comfort and safety, needed all the friends they could get.

So, in the interests of survival, they trained themselves to be agreeing machines instead of thinking machines. All their minds had to do was to discover what other people were thinking, and then they thought that, too.

Patty hoped she could entice Dwayne Hoover to take an interest in her since his wealth could solve so many of her problems. She sincerely pitied Dwayne for the suicide of his wife and his shame about having a homosexual son.

Kelly, Colonel Bryan. *In the 1953 short story "All the King's Horses," reprinted in* Welcome to the Monkey House *(1968), Colonel Kelly, his wife and twin sons, and a group of military technical specialists crash-land in an unnamed Far East Communist country while traveling to India for posting as a military attaché.*

Kelly is forced by his captor Pi Ying, and later Major Barzov, the Soviet attaché, into playing a game of chess to free his family. The bizarre twist is that all the Americans are chess pieces who will be put to death if taken during the game. Kelly precipitates the assassination of Pi Ying when he realizes he would have to sacrifice his son during the game to achieve victory. Pi Ying's mistress kills him when she realizes what is about to happen. Barzov takes over for Pi Ying and goes on to lose to Kelly's strategy. Barzov spares the life of Kelly's son.

Kelly, Margaret (and her twin sons **Jerry** and **Paul**). *The wife of Colonel Bryan Kelly and the mother of twin ten-year-old sons (Jerry and Paul) in the 1953 short story "All the King's Horses," reprinted in* Welcome to the Monkey House *(1968). In a game of chess with Pi Ying, the Kellys' captor, she is forced to play the queen, her sons are the knights, and her husband is the king and chess rival to their captor. Lost chess pieces result in the deaths of some of Colonel Kelly's soldiers.*

Kemp, Marilee. *The daughter of an illiterate West Virginia coal miner, former Ziegfeld Follies showgirl, mistress of Dan Gregory (who sends her away for an abortion while they live in Europe), and the eventual Countess Portomaggiore, Marilee is fondly remembered by* Bluebeard's *Rabo Karabekian for posing as Gregory's assistant and providing him material and spiritual support through the mail. She took it upon herself to correspond with Rabo when Gregory ignored his letters. Marilee went so far as to* *send Karabekian some of Gregory's expensive art supplies. When Gregory finds out, he beats her and throws her down a flight of stairs in his brownstone, breaking both her legs and one arm. As a result, Marilee limped for the rest of her life. While Marilee recuperates in the hospital, a temporarily remorseful Gregory promises to bring Rabo to New York City. She and Rabo, only two years apart in age, strike up a close friendship and eventually enjoy a brief physical relationship.*

Marilee reveals to Rabo that she had a series of abusive relationships with men: her father used to beat her, her junior high school football team raped her after the prom, the stage manager of the Ziegfeld Follies was sexually coercive, and Dan Gregory had thrown her down the stairs.

After Dan Gregory and Fred Jones are killed at Sidi Barrani, Marilee stays on in Italy in the company of Bruno, Count Portomaggiore, Mussolini's Oxford-educated Minister of Culture. The Count was homosexual and not physically interested in Marilee. He occasionally engages in pedophilia. Mussolini is pressured to get rid of the Count because he is viewed as a security risk, so Mussolini orders the Count to marry Marilee. She later learns that her husband was the head of British Intelligence in Italy. After the war, Marilee becomes the most high-volume Sony distributor in Europe and a great collector of American postwar modern art.

Marilee Kemp and Rabo's second wife, Edith, pass away in the same week.

Kennedy, Robert. *During Vonnegut's writing of* Slaughterhouse-Five, *Robert Kennedy was assassinated, and he includes this historical moment as well as the assassination of Martin Luther King, Jr., to chronicle the cycle of deaths and new births that occur each day. It prompts Vonnegut to see some virtue in the Tralfamadorian view of the life cycle.* (SL5 10) **Robert Kennedy,** *whose summer home is eight miles from the home I live in all year round, was shot two nights ago. He died last night. So it goes. . . .*

If what Billy Pilgrim learned from the Tralfamadorians is true, that we will all live forever, no matter how dead we may sometimes seem to be, I am not overjoyed. Still—if I am going to spend eternity visiting this moment and that, I'm grateful that so many of those moments are nice.

(BC Epilogue) Parking lots were vacant, except for night watchmen's cars which were here and there. There was no traffic on Fairchild Boulevard, which had once been the aorta of the town. The life had all been drained out of it by the Interstate and by the **Robert F. Kennedy** *Inner Belt Expressway, which was built on the old right-of-way of the Monon Railroad. The Monon was defunct.*

Kern, Shirley. *As* Hocus Pocus's *Eugene Debs Hartke begins to take account of all the women with whom he's made love, his first memory of a meaningful sexual encounter is with Shirley Kern when he was twenty.*

Kestenbaum, Stanley. *The accountant who marries Alice, the first wife of Colonel Looseleaf Harper, in* Happy Birthday, Wanda June.

Ketchum, Bernard. *In* Deadeye Dick, *Ketchum lost an eye as a child when a playmate shot him with a beebee gun. The Midland City lawyer represents Eugene Metzger, the widower of Jane who is killed by Rudy Waltz's errant shot from his attic gun room. He is later hired by Felix and Rudy Waltz to sue anyone connected with the sale of the radioactive Oak Ridge cement that caused the massive brain tumors that killed their mother. He successfully sues the Nuclear Regulatory Commission, the Maritimo Brothers Construction Company, and the Ohio Valley Ornamental Concrete Company. The Waltz brothers then buy the Hotel Oloffson in Haiti.*

Ketchum is a Harvard Law School graduate. One of his sons flunks out of his alma mater and becomes a welder in Alaska; the other son "deserted to Sweden during the Vietnam War" and worked with alcoholics. Ketchum arranges for fake affidavits enabling Hippolyte Paul De Mille, the Waltzes' Haitian chef, to accompany the group to Midland City, where he eventually conducts a voodoo resurrection at Calvary Cemetery.

Key, Eddie. *The young black ambulance driver who helps remove the wounded from the streets of Midland City after Dwayne Hoover's violent outburst. He is a direct descendant of Francis Scott Key as well as a descendant of the family that originally owned Bluebird Farm, the site of Sacred Miracle*

Cave. He knows stories about more than six hundred of his ancestors including Africans, Indians, and whites. He enjoys a heightened spiritual awareness because of his knowledge, and for this reason he is unique among Vonnegut's characters; Eddie Key lived more fully because of his appreciation of history. (BC 24) **Eddie Key** knew so much about his ancestry because the black part of his family had done what so many African families still do in Africa, which was to have one member of each generation whose duty it was to memorize the history of the family so far . . . looking out through the windshield, he had the feeling that he himself was a vehicle, and that his eyes were windshields through which his progenitors could look, if they wished to.

Francis Scott Key was only one of thousands back there. On the off-chance that **Key** might now be having a look at what had become of the United States of America so far, **Eddie** focused his eyes on an American flag which was stuck to the windshield. He said this very quietly: "Still wavin', man."

Eddie Key's familiarity with a teeming past made life much more interesting to him than it was to Dwayne, for instance, or to me, or to Kilgore Trout, or to almost any white person in Midland City that day. We had no sense of anybody else using our eyes—or our hands. We didn't even know who our great-grandfathers and great-grandmothers were. **Eddie Key** was afloat in a river of people who were flowing from here to there in time. Dwayne and Trout and I were pebbles at rest.

And **Eddie Key**, because he knew so much by heart, was able to have deep, nourishing feelings about Dwayne Hoover, for instance, and about Dr. Cyprian Ukwende, too. Dwayne was a man whose family had taken over Bluebird Farm. Ukwende, an Indaro, was a man whose ancestors had kidnapped an ancestor of **Key**'s on the West Coast of Africa, a man named Ojumwa. The Indaros sold him for a musket to British slave traders, who took him on a sailing ship named the *Skylark* to Charleston, South Carolina, where he was auctioned off as a self-propelled, self-repairing farm machine.

"The Kid Nobody Could Handle" (1955) (*see* **Jim Donnini**).

Kilgallen, Pat. *The love interest of both the unnamed narrator and the eponymous EPICAC in the 1950 short story of that name, reprinted in* Welcome to the Monkey House *(1968). Kilgallen and the narrator are mathematicians at work on EPICAC, which is housed at Wyandotte College. Kilgallen refuses the narrator's inept advances until he has EPICAC compose love poetry for her. They marry and in the wake of EPICAC's self-destruction through a poetic fury, the narrator is left with five hundred years worth of poetry for his wife.*

Kilgore's Creed. *In an attempt to rouse Dudley Prince from his post-timequake apathy, Kilgore Trout tells Prince,* You were sick, but now you're well again, and there's work to do (TQ 51). *Vonnegut goes on to describe how influential Kilgore's Creed had become, distinguishing Trout's brand of pragmatism with the destructive results of Einstein's search for scientific truth.* (TQ 51) What I find worth exclaiming about right now is the continuing applicability to the human condition, years after free will has ceased to be a novelty, of what jazzed Dudley Prince back to life, of what is now known generally as **Kilgore's Creed**: "You were sick, but now you're well again, and there's work to do."

Teachers in public schools across the land, I hear, say **Kilgore's Creed** to students after the students have recited the Pledge of Allegiance and the Lord's Prayer at the beginning of each school day. Teachers say it seems to help.

A friend told me he was at a wedding where the minister said at the climax of the ceremony: "You were sick, but now you're well again, and there's work to do. I now pronounce you man and wife."

Another friend, a biochemist for a cat food company, said she was staying at a hotel in Toronto, Canada, and she asked the front desk to give her a wake-up call in the morning. She answered her phone the next morning, and the operator said, "You were sick, but now you're well again, and there's work to do. It's seven a.m., and the temperature outside is thirty-two degrees Fahrenheit, or zero Celsius."

On the afternoon of February 13th, 2001, alone, and then during the next two weeks or so, **Kilgore's Creed** did as much to save life on Earth as Einstein's *E equals mc squared* had done to end it two generations earlier.

Kilgore's Creed is broadcast for the benefit of all in the immediate aftermath of the resumption of free will. Vonnegut uses Jerry Rivers as the messenger of the creed (the name of Sweetbread College's forever optimistic student body president in the play The Chemistry Professor, *reprinted in* Palm Sunday*).* (TQ 53) It was Jerry Rivers, the chauffeur of the Peppers' stretch limousine, however, who steered his dreamboat around wrecked vehicles and their victims, often driving on sidewalks, to reach the studios of the Columbia Broadcasting System down on West 52nd Street. Rivers awakened the staff there with, "You were sick, but now you're well again, and there's work to do." And then he got them to broadcast that same message on both radio and TV from coast to coast.

In order to get them to do that, though, he had to tell them a lie. He said everybody was recovering from a nerve gas attack by persons unknown. So the first version of **Kilgore's Creed** to reach millions in the nation, and then billions in the world, was this: "This is a CBS exclusive! There has been a nerve gas attack by persons unknown. You were sick, but now you're well again, and there's work to do. Make sure all children and senior citizens are safe indoors."

Kilyer, Tom. *Tom Kilyer was once a "scholarship boy" at the elite and expensive Whitehill School, and now his son has also been accepted on academic merit and given financial assistance in the 1962 short story "The Lie" (q.v.), reprinted in* Welcome to the Monkey House *(1968). Kilyer had written the school song, which was engraved on a school monument.*

Kimberly. *A student at Sweetbread College despondent over the institution's bankruptcy, in the play* The Chemistry Professor.

King, Bobby. *The middle-aged Manhattan publicity man who organizes "the Nature Cruise of the Century" in* Galápagos.

King of Candlesticks. *Though known as the "King of New York," Slapstick's Wilbur Swain is also called* the "The King of Candlesticks" for his huge collection of candlesticks.

Kirk, Mary Selwyn and Oveta Cooper. *The two practical nurses who kindly see to the needs of Wilbur and Eliza Swain at their Vermont estate in* Slapstick.

Kisco, Buddy. *In the corrupt world of intercollegiate athletics illustrated by Cornell's inability to buy quality football players in* Player Piano, *Buddy Kisco is emblematic of a system that exploits its athletes. In* Player Piano, *college football is operated as a professional enterprise complete with long-term, lucrative player contracts. Kisco dies while playing for Rutgers, but the system leaves his widow nothing more than a government pension.*

"Kiss Me Again." *In* Timequake, *Vonnegut makes two references to Kilgore Trout's only love story. Both references are made in relationship to the clambake. One is very early in the text and the other very late. Early in the text while amusing the guests at the clambake, Trout enthusiastically echoes Vonnegut's Uncle Alex's maxim,* If this isn't nice, what is? (TQ 22). *Vonnegut goes on to describe just how taken Trout is by all the adulation and the* man-made epiphanies like this one. . . .

He declared the corn on the cob, steamed in seaweed with lobsters and clams, to be *heavenly*. He added, "And don't all the ladies look like *angels* tonight!" He was feasting on corn on the cob and women as *ideas*. He couldn't eat the corn because the upper plate of his false teeth was insecure. His long-term relationships with women had been disasters. In the only love story he ever attempted, **"Kiss Me Again,"** he had written, "There is no way a beautiful woman can live up to what she looks like for any appreciable length of time."

The moral at the end of that story is this: "Men are jerks. Women are psychotic."

Toward the close of the novel when Vonnegut provides a more complete description of the clambake's ambience and Trout's performance, it is Trout who quotes himself from the story and closes his comment with the cryptic and multidimensional "ting-a-ling." (TQ 63) There on the beach, whatever Trout said produced laughter and applause. He couldn't believe it! He said the pyramids and Stonehenge were built in a time of very feeble gravity, when boulders could be tossed around like sofa pillows, and people loved it. They begged for more. He gave them the line from "**Kiss Me Again**": "There is no way a beautiful woman can live up to what she looks like for any appreciable length of time. Ting-a-ling?" People told him he was as witty as Oscar Wilde!

Kissinger, Henry. *Richard Nixon's secretary of state makes a series of appearances in Vonnegut's work. He and Walter Starbuck find themselves in the same White House staff meeting convened because of the National Guard shootings of students at Kent State University. Starbuck makes a fool of himself with multiply lit cigarettes during the meeting.*

In Galápagos, *Vonnegut includes Kissinger on the preliminary passenger list for "the Nature Cruise of the Century."*

In Hocus Pocus, *Kissinger is one of the revelers in the caravan accompanying Arthur Clarke on his trip to Tarkington College. Although most of Clarke's companions join him on a motorcycle ride to the college from Rochester, New York, Kissinger rides down in a limousine. Nonetheless,* Just like the people on the motorcycles . . . the people in the limousines wore gold crash helmets decorated with dollar signs *(HP 23).*

Eugene Debs Hartke recalls, Although I had been an instrument of his geopolitics, I felt no connection between him and me. His face was certainly familiar. He might have been, like Gloria White, somebody who had been in a lot of movies I had seen.

I dreamed about him once here in prison, though. He was a woman.

He was a Gypsy fortune-teller who looked into her crystal ball but wouldn't say anything *(HP 29). See also: FWD X.*

Kitchen, Terry. *Rabo Karabekian's best friend and fellow Abstract Expressionist painter in* Bluebeard. *Together with Jackson Pollock, the three of them are known as "the Three Musketeers" for their endless hours of drinking in New York's Cedar Tavern. Rabo names his first son after Kitchen; his second son is named after Terry's and Rabo's favorite painter, Henri Matisse. Unlike the first-generation Armenian*

American Rabo Karabekian, Terry Kitchen came from an old and wealthy family. A graduate of Yale Law School and clerk to Supreme Court Justice John Harlan, Kitchen was also a Silver Star winner and member of the 82nd Airborne during World War II.

Shortly after Jackson Pollock commits suicide, Rabo's wife and children leave him. Three weeks later, Kitchen blew out his brains with a pistol in his mouth. Karabekian speculates that among Kitchen's many problems, he never regained his balance after shooting his father in the shoulder during an argument. He is buried in Long Island's Green River Cemetery near Jackson Pollock and Rabo's second wife, Edith.

Kitchen introduces Rabo to his concept of the "non-epiphany." After Rabo describes the blank contentedness he felt after three hours of lovemaking to Marilee Kemp, Terry explains that the non-epiphany is "A concept of my own invention. . . . The trouble with God isn't that He so seldom makes Himself known to us. . . . The trouble with God is exactly the opposite: He's holding you and me and everybody else by the scruff of the neck practically *constantly.*"

He said he had just come from an afternoon at the Metropolitan Museum of Art, where so many of the paintings were about God's giving instructions, to Adam and Eve and the Virgin Mary, and various saints in agony and so on. "These moments are very rare, if you can believe the painters—but who was ever nitwit enough to believe a painter?" he said, and he ordered another double Scotch, I'm sure, for which I would pay. "Such moments are often called 'epiphanies' and I'm here to tell you they are as common as houseflies," he said. . . .

"'Contentedly adrift in the cosmos,' were you?" **Kitchen** said to me.

"That is a perfect description of a non-epiphany, that rarest of moments, when God Almighty lets go of the scruff of your neck and lets you be human for a little while. How long did the feeling last?"

"Oh—maybe half an hour," I said.

And he leaned back in his chair and he said with deep satisfaction:

"And there you are" *(Blue 21).*

Kitchen admits to having his own non-epiphanies only after sex and the two times he took heroin. (Blue 22) As **Terry Kitchen** *once said of a postcoital* experience of his own: "The epiphany came back, and everybody had to put on their clothes and run around again like chickens with their heads cut off."

After the war, Karabekian and Kitchen become roommates in a Union Square apartment. Kitchen attaches himself to Karabekian and wherever Rabo takes his family, Kitchen is sure to follow. When Terry helps Rabo move his art collection out to the Long Island potato barn, Kitchen has Rabo purchase a paint sprayer for him similar to the type Rabo used for camouflage during the war. He then spray paints a discarded piece of beaverboard and suddenly finds his artistic medium. Until that point, Kitchen's artwork suffered from his lack of basic artistic talent. Kitchen previously displayed enormous talents for all his endeavors, but making art was his Mount Everest, which had yet to be scaled at the time he made the characterization.

So close are Rabo and Kitchen that when the latter commits suicide, Rabo considers himself dead as well. The only other time Rabo experiences such a loss is after his wife, Edith, passes away.

Kittredge, Waltham. *Kittredge's* The American Philosopher Kings *is cited as the preeminent chronicle of America's ruling class.* (ST 1) It was **Kittredge** who proved that the class was in fact a family, with its loose ends neatly turned back into a hard core of consanguinity through the agency of cousin marriages. Rumfoord and his wife, for instance, were third cousins, and detested each other.

And when Rumfoord's class was diagramed by **Kittredge**, it resembled nothing so much as the hard, ball-like knot known as a *monkey's fist.*

Kittredge coins the term "un-neurotic courage" to describe the pure courage displayed by such acts as Rumfoord's flight straight into the known chrono-synclastic infundibulum. It is a courage without the conscious pursuit of fame or money, and without any hint of mental defect.

Klee, Paul. *In his closing Author's Note to* A Man Without a Country, *Vonnegut speaks about the art he makes and has silkscreened by his collaborator Joe Petro III. As for his artistic influences, he confides that* Most of our stuff has been my knockoffs of **Paul Klee** and Marcel Duchamp and so on.

Kleindienst, Edward Strawberry-4. *President Wilbur Swain's valet who dies of the Albanian Flu in* Slapstick.

Klinkowitz, Jerome. *Professor of English at Northern Iowa University and a most prolific literary scholar with a significant bibliography about Vonnegut, Klinkowitz is among the select few invited to attend the Timequake clambake in tandem with his onetime writing partner Asa Pieratt, a research librarian at the University of Delaware.*

Klopfer, Arndt. (MN 29) *The New York Times published a portrait of me (Howard Campbell, Jr.) as a much younger man, my official portrait as a Nazi and idol of the international airwaves. I can only guess at the year in which the picture was taken—1941, I think.*

Arndt Klopfer, the photographer who took the picture of me, did his best to make me look like a Maxfield Parrish Jesus covered with cold cream. He even gave me a halo, a judiciously placed spot of nebulous light in the background. The halo was no special effect for me alone. Everybody who went to **Klopfer** *got a halo, including Adolf Eichmann.*

I can say that for certain about Eichmann, without asking for confirmation from the Haifa Institute, because Eichmann had his picture taken just ahead of me at **Klopfer's** *studio.*

Knechtmann, Avchen, Heinz (*and various other Knechtmanns*). *In the 1954 short story "Adam," reprinted in* Welcome to the Monkey House (1968), *Avchen and Heinz are German Jews, survivors of the Nazi concentration camp terrors. Heinz is the orphaned son of Karl and Helga Knechtmann. The story's tone is set by the anxieties prompted by Helga's prospect for a troubled delivery. Those troubles are the result of the malnutrition she suffered as a child imprisoned and set to work in the camps.*

"Adam" is as much about the hope new parents hold for their children as it is about the legacy and self-imposed responsibility Holocaust survivors feel about continuing life and the culture which was the target of so many evils.

Though many critics wonder about Vonnegut's feelings toward victims of the Holocaust when he repeatedly recalls the events of Dresden and Hiroshima (notably the columnist George Will), "Adam" is early evidence of his concern for all people subject to genocidal policies and the inferno of international politics. The man he left behind, all alone now, was **Heinz Knechtmann**, a presser in a dry-cleaning plant, a small man with thin wrists and a bad spine that kept him slightly hunched, as though forever weary. His face was long and big-nosed and thin-lipped, but was so overcast with good-humored humility as to be beautiful. His eyes were large and brown, and deep-set and long-lashed. He was only twenty-two, but seemed and felt much older. He had died a little as each member of his family had been led away and killed by the Nazis, until only in him, at the age of ten, had life and the name of **Knechtmann** shared a soul. He and his wife, **Avchen**, had grown up behind barbed wire. . . .

When the numbness of weary wishing lifted momentarily during this second vigil, **Heinz**'s mind was a medley of proud family names, gone, all gone, that could be brought to life again in this new being—if it lived. **Peter Knechtmann**, the surgeon; **Kroll Knechtmann**, the botanist; **Friederich Knechtmann**, the playwright. Dimly recalled uncles. Or if it was a girl, and if it lived, it would be **Helga Knechtmann**, **Heinz**'s mother, and she would learn to play the harp as **Heinz**'s mother had, and for all **Heinz**'s ugliness, she would be beautiful. The **Knechtmann** men were all ugly, the **Knechtmann** women were all lovely as angels though not all angels. It had always been so—for hundreds and hundreds of years.

"Hello, hello, hello, little **Knechtmann**," said **Heinz** to the red prune on the other side of the glass. His voice echoed down the hard, bare corridor, and came back to him with embarrassing loudness. He blushed and lowered his voice. "Little **Peter**, little **Kroll**," he said softly, "little **Friederich**—and there's **Helga** in you, too. Little spark of **Knechtmann**, you little treasure house. Everything is saved in you."

"They couldn't kill us, could they, **Heinz**?"

"No."

"And here we are, alive as we can be."

"Yes."

"The baby, **Heinz**—" She opened her dark eyes

wide. "It's the most wonderful thing that ever happened, isn't it?"

"Yes," said **Heinz**.

The Knights of Kandahar. *A fraternal order that savagely beats the state police to wrest control of Griffin Boulevard during the Ghost Shirt rebellion in Ilium, in* Player Piano.

In the 1952 short story "The No-Talent Kid," reprinted in Bagombo Snuff Box (1999), *this local civic organization goes bankrupt, the victim of its embezzling treasurer. As part of its asset liquidation to settle accounts, the group sells its huge bass drum used for parades. It is so large that it needs a separate individual to haul the cart carrying it. The musically challenged last chair of Lincoln High School's C Band, Walter Plummer, acquires the drum just before his director George Helmholtz is able to make the deal. The two work out an agreement that Plummer will get his band sweater and varsity letter in exchange for being the one to haul the drum's cart during performances, and Helmholtz will get to pick his own percussionist to play the instrument.*

Knowles, Lyman Enders. *The enigmatic elderly elevator operator at the Research Laboratory of the General Forge and Foundry Company, the same employer of Felix Hoenikker. Knowles is notable for his odd behavior at work, often grabbing his behind and exclaiming "Yes, yes!" whenever making a witty remark. "'This here's a re-search laboratory. Re-search means* look again, *don't it? Means they're looking for something they found once and it got away somehow, and now they got to* re-search *for it? How come they got to build a building like this, with mayonnaise elevators and all, and fill it with all these crazy people? What is it they're trying to find again? Who lost what?' Yes, yes!" (CC 28)*

Knowles characterizes the Hoenikker children as "Babies full of rabies . . . Yes, yes!"

Kolhouri. *The Shah of Bratpuhr is the spiritual leader of this sect of six million members in* Player Piano.

Konigswasser, Dr. Ellis. *The mathematician in the 1953 short story "Unready to Wear," reprinted in* Welcome to the Monkey House (1968), *who "did* *all his living with his mind" and who is so distressed with caring for his body that he accidentally discovers how to separate his spiritual essence from his body. Those who follow his teachings are called amphibians. Amphibians put on bodies that they keep in storage centers for whenever they feel like doing work or dressing up.*

"Unready to Wear" is perhaps Vonnegut's earliest attempt to address demands made on humans simply because of their dependence on biology. "The mind's the only thing about human beings that's worth anything. Why does it have to be tied to a bag of skin, blood, hair, meat, bones, and tubes? No wonder people can't get anything done, stuck for life with a parasite that has to be stuffed with food and protected from weather and germs all the time. And the fool thing wears out anyway—no matter how much you stuff and protect it!"

By following the instructions in **Konigswasser**'s book for about two years, almost anybody could get out of his body whenever he wanted to. The first step was to understand what a parasite and dictator the body was most of the time, then to separate what the body wanted or didn't want from what you yourself—your psyche—wanted or didn't want. Then, by concentrating on what you wanted, and ignoring as much as possible what the body wanted beyond plain maintenance, you made your psyche demand its rights and become self-sufficient.

Nobody but a saint could be really sympathetic or intelligent for more than a few minutes at a time in a body—or happy, either, except in short spurts. I haven't met an amphibian yet who wasn't easy to get along with, and cheerful and interesting—as long as he was outside a body. And I haven't met one yet who didn't turn a little sour when he got into one.

The minute you get in, chemistry takes over—glands making you excitable or ready to fight or hungry or mad or affectionate, or—well, you never know what's going to happen next.

Koradubian, Martin. *In* The Sirens of Titan, *this Boston solar watch repairman, liar, and writer authors a magazine article for $3,000 about one of Winston Niles Rumfoord's materializations, based on his claim that he had been invited. The article is completely false.* (ST 2) **Koradubian** claimed in his

story that Rumfoord had told him about the year Ten Million A.D.

In the year Ten Million, according to **Koradubian**, there would be a tremendous house-cleaning. All records relating to the period between the death of Christ and the year One Million A.D. would be hauled to dumps and burned. This would be done, said **Koradubian**, because museums and archives would be crowding the living right off the earth.

The million-year period to which the burned junk related would be summed up in history books in one sentence, according to **Koradubian**:

"Following the death of Jesus Christ, there was a period of readjustment that lasted for approximately one million years."

Kornblum, Mr. *In the short story "Ambitious Sophomore," collected in* Bagombo Snuff Box (1999), *Mr. Kornblum is the unseen band uniform supplier to Lincoln High School and another easy mark for the histrionic antics of band director George M. Helmholtz. Kornblum sends an unnamed delivery boy to the school with the custom tunic for piccoloist Leroy Duggan, a bell-shaped sophomore and the star soloist in the upcoming state marching band competition.* "**Mr. Kornblum** said he was losing money on it as it was," said the delivery boy. "He said Mr. Helmholtz came in and started talking, and before he knew it—"

Koshevoi, Mr. *In the 1958 short story "The Manned Missiles," reprinted in* Welcome to the Monkey House (1968), *Koshevoi is the Soviet ambassador to the United Nations who publicly delivers the letter from the bereaved Mr. Ivankov to Mr. Ashland. The tale is told through an exchange of letters by the two men who lose their sons in space when Captain Bryant Ashland's capsule collides with that of Ivankov's son, a Soviet cosmonaut. Ashland was sent to observe and photograph the Soviet ship. Koshevoi at first speaks harshly about the American astronaut, but he later agrees with both nations' finding that the deaths of the two men were accidental.*

Kouyoumdjian, Marktich (*see* **Marc Coulomb**).

Kovacs, Arpad. (MN 3) The guard who relieves Andor Gutman at six each night is **Arpad Kovacs**.

Arpad is a Roman candle of a man, loud and gay. *Kovacs, one of the four Jerusalem prison guards taking shifts watching Howard Campbell, is a Hungarian Jew who joined the Nazi S.S. in order to stay alive. He is upset with the widespread image of Jews who complacently, quietly went to their deaths in the gas chambers. He calls those Jews briquets. One could make the case that Kovacs understands Campbell's apparent collaboration since he recognizes the incongruity of himself being a Jew in the Hungarian S.S., and this* fact is the basis for his sympathy with me *(Campbell)*. "Tell them the things a man does to stay alive! What's so noble about being a briquet?" (MN 3)

He is a harsh critic of Campbell's propaganda invectives, conjecturing that "Goebbels should have fired you and hired me as the radio scourge of the Jews. I would have raised blisters around the world! . . . What an Aryan I made!" *(MN 3) Despite all his bravado, Kovacs reveals that his true work for the SS allowed him to frame fourteen Nazis for execution as traitors. Eichmann personally congratulates Kovacs for ferreting out the alleged spies, though Kovacs was unaware at the time just how important Eichmann was—or else he would have killed him.*

Kraft, George. *Though Iona Potapov's true identity isn't known by the government of the United States until 1941, the Soviet spy operated in America since 1935 posing as aspiring artist George Kraft. By chance after the war, Howard Campbell settles into the same Greenwich Village apartment house as Kraft. The two strike up a friendship based upon their mutual loneliness and interest in chess. Campbell purchases a war surplus whittling kit, the product of which is a complete chess set. He introduces himself to Kraft and the two become constant companions. In 1931, Kraft beat chess Grand Master Tartakover in Rotterdam.*

Kraft's paintings become the object of much praise after he begins his sentence at the Federal Penitentiary at Fort Leavenworth, bringing as much as $10,000 each.

Kraft was a member of Alcoholics Anonymous. Despite his duplicity, he was sincere in his appreciation of the organization, frequently echoing Vonnegut's own admiration of the group. Kraft also used the A.A. meetings to make his spy contacts, which Campbell reasons was typical of his schizophrenia as a spy that he would use an institution he so admired for purposes of espionage (MN 11).

Once Kraft learns of Howard Campbell's wartime persona as a Nazi propagandist, he sets in motion a number of plots intended to extract Campbell from the U.S. and have him tried in Moscow. He notifies Moscow that Stepan Bodovskov was a plagiarist who had taken Campbell's manuscripts as war booty and published them under his own name. He also notifies a number of American publications and patriotic organizations about Campbell's whereabouts. Resi Noth was brought out of a Russian prison and sent to America to pose as her sister Helga, Campbell's wife, who was presumed dead. Exposing Campbell and reuniting him with Helga was meant to force him to flee America. Kraft arranges for them all to fly to Mexico for refuge, only he plans for a quick transfer to a flight to Moscow where Campbell would face a war crimes trial. Campbell's Blue Fairy Godmother foils Kraft's plans and arrests him for espionage.

Kraft submits a deposition to the Israelis in preparation for Campbell's war crime trials in which he declares under oath that Russian intelligence was never able to turn up any proof that I (Howard Campbell) had been an American agent. He offers the opinion that I was an ardent Nazi, but that I shouldn't be held responsible for my acts, since I was a political idiot, an artist who could not distinguish between reality and dreams (MN 45).

Kraft, Mary. *One of the two hostesses at the Ethical Suicide Parlor in the short story* "Welcome to the Monkey House," *in* Welcome to the Monkey House *(1968). Nancy (McLuhan) was a strawberry blonde.* **Mary** *was a glossy brunette. Their uniforms were white lipstick, heavy eye makeup, purple body stockings with nothing underneath, and black-leather boots. They ran a small operation—with only six suicide booths. In a really good week, say the one before Christmas, they might put sixty people to sleep. It was done with a hypodermic syringe.*

Kramm, Doris. *Delmar Peale's eighty-seven-year-old secretary at The American Harp Company's headquarters atop the Chrysler Building. (JB 15)*

Doris wept because she had had two hard blows in rapid succession. She had been notified on the previous afternoon that she was going to have to retire immediately, now that RAMJAC had taken over. The retirement age for all RAMJAC employees everywhere, except for supervisory personnel, was sixty-five. And then that morning, while she was cleaning out her desk, she got a telegram saying that her great-grandniece had been killed in a head-on collision after a high-school senior prom in Sarasota, Florida. **Doris** had no descendents [*sic*] of her own, he explained, so her collateral relatives meant a lot to her. *Mary Kathleen O'Looney cancels the RAMJAC retirement order to save Doris's job.*

Krapptauer, August. *The founder and Vice-Bundesfuehrer of the Iron Guard of the White Sons of the American Constitution, Krapptauer was in ill health and passes away shortly after he appears. His immediate cause of death could be considered chivalry, since his heart gives out after climbing up and down the stairs of Campbell's brownstone carrying Resi/Helga's luggage.* (MN 14) Jones' bodyguard was **August Krapptauer**, former Vice-Bundesfuehrer of the German-American Bund. **Krapptauer** was sixty-three, had done eleven years in Atlanta, was about to drop dead. But he still looked garishly boyish, as though he went to a mortuary cosmetologist regularly. The greatest achievement of his life was the arrangement of a joint meeting of the Bund and the Ku Klux Klan in New Jersey in 1940. At that meeting, **Krapptauer** declared that the Pope was a Jew and that the Jews held a fifteen-million-dollar mortgage on the Vatican. A change of Popes and eleven years in a prison laundry had not changed his mind. *As Campbell later reveals, he was responsible for broadcasting those lies which Krapptauer so readily accepted. Just after Campbell delivers Krapptauer's eulogy to the basement throng of the White Sons of the American Constitution, the Blue Fairy Godmother reappears to save Campbell from the kidnapping plot of Kraft/Potapov.*

Krebbs, Sherman. *The impoverished nihilistic poet, "a platinum blond Jesus with spaniel eyes," and self-professed National Chairman of Poets and Painters for Immediate Nuclear War who borrows John/Jonah's New York City apartment. Krebbs*

wrecks the apartment, kills John/Jonah's cat, runs up hundreds of dollars in long distance bills, sets the couch on fire, and uses excrement to write poetry on the floor. When John/Jonah discovers his murdered cat with a sign around its neck that says "Meow," he is convinced that Krebbs was a wrang-wrang. (CC 36) A *wrang-wrang*, according to Bokonon, is a person who steers people away from a line of speculation by reducing that line, with the example of the *wrang-wrang's* own life, to an absurdity.

I might have been vaguely inclined to dismiss the stone angel as meaningless, and to go from there to the meaninglessness of all. But after I saw what **Krebbs** had done, in particular what he had done to my sweet cat, nihilism was not for me.

Somebody or something did not wish me to be a nihilist. It was **Krebbs**'s mission, whether he knew it or not, to disenchant me with that philosophy. Well done, **Mr**. **Krebbs**, well done.

Krementz, Jill. *One of America's most noted female photographers and Vonnegut's second wife (they were married in 1979) and to whom he dedicated* Wampeters, Foma & Granfalloons *with the words* FOR / JILL / WHO CRONKLED ME.

Vonnegut writes a much simpler dedication to her in Deadeye Dick, *and notes that they stayed in the "James Jones Cottage" of Haiti's Grand Hotel Oloffson, the same hotel owned by the Waltz brothers in the text—the brothers' refuge during the neutron-bombing of Midland City.*

Ms. Krementz was a war photographer in Vietnam (The Face of Vietnam *with CBS correspondent Dean Brelis), and produced books focusing on children* (A Very Young Dancer; How It Feels When a Parent Dies; Sweet Pea: A Black Girl Growing Up in the Rural South). *Vonnegut has a great number of stories about their life together in* Fates Worse Than Death, *and it is there he reveals his nickname for her—Xanthippe (not all that flattering, since Xanthippe, though the much younger wife of Socrates, is noted as much for her shrewishness as for her devotion as wife and mother). He also includes an homage written in honor of her fiftieth birthday.* (FWD IX) The Festschrift ended with this clever sonnet, "To **Jill** Turning Fifty," by one of **Jill**'s favorite photographic subjects, the man of letters John Updike:

The comely soul of self-effacement, you
can be admired as the twinkle in
a thousand authors' eyes where you, unseen,
perform behind the camera. How do
you soften up those hardened visages,
pickled in the brine of daily words?—
Eudora, Tennessee, Anais, Kurt,
Saul, Gore, Bill, Jim, Joan, Truman, Toni,
    Liz?

And children, too, grow docile in your lens,
and stare like lilies toward your clicking sun
while how it feels to be a very young
whatever is elicited. Now ends
your fifth decade. Live henceforth, Leica
    queen,
as Jill all candle lit, the seeress seen.

Krementz is briefly mentioned in Timequake as
part of a discussion about religion Vonnegut holds
with Trout a few hours before the clambake, "He
asked if I myself had ever tried to join a church,
just for the hell of it, to find out what that was like.
He had. The closest I ever came to that, I said, was
when my second-wife-to-be, **Jill Krementz**, and
I thought it would be cute, and also ritzy, to be
married in the Little Church Around the Corner,
a Disneyesque Episcopal house of worship on
East Twenty-ninth Street off Fifth Avenue in Manhattan.

"When they found out I was a divorced person,"
I said, "they prescribed all sorts of penitent services
I was to perform before I was clean enough to be
married there" (TQ 21).

In Man Without a Country, Krementz is mentioned in passing as Vonnegut describes his own
practice of using the U.S. Postal Service as well as
his patronage of local shopkeepers, activities that
keep him grounded with his neighborhood (chapter 6, which begins with the words "I have been
called a Luddite").

Kremlin. The Tralfamadorians use their Universal
Will to Become to send messages concerning the status of the replacement part for Salo's spaceship. The
messages are conveyed in great architectural monuments on Earth that could be monitored by Salo.
(ST 12) The meaning of the **Moscow Kremlin**

when it was first walled was: "You will be on your
way before you know it."

Kroner, Anthony. One half of the Kroner and Baer
duo, Anthony Kroner is the spiritual supervisor of the
ruling technocracy in Player Piano. Along with Drs.
Baer and Gelhorne, he devises a plan to infiltrate the
Ghost Shirt Society, a Luddite group devoted to
overthrowing the technocracy that has displaced humanity as the center of societal concern in favor of
machines. At the center of the conspiracy is Paul Proteus, whom Kroner hopes to win over as part of a
loyalty test in his bid for manager of the Pittsburgh
Works.

Kroner was very close to Proteus's father, Doctor
George Proteus—"the nation's first National Industrial, Commercial, Communications, Foodstuffs,
and Resources Director, a position approached in
importance only by the presidency of the United
States." Accordingly, "**Kroner** . . . took a breeder's
interest in his engineers' bloodlines" (PP IV).

Most typically, however, Kroner is thought of in
relationship with his alter ego, Dr. Baer. (PP XXXV)
"**Kroner**'s with Baer, Baer's with **Kroner**," said
Finnerty.

(PP V) One of the older men, **Kroner**, tall, heavy
and slow, listened to the youngsters with ponderous affectionateness. The other, Baer, slight and
nervous, noisily and unconvincingly extroverted,
laughed, nudged, and clapped shoulders, and
maintained a continuous commentary on whatever was being said: "Fine, fine, right, sure, sure,
wonderful, yes, yes, exactly, fine, good."

(PP V) Baer waved and called to them in his high-
pitched voice. **Kroner** nodded almost imperceptibly, and stood perfectly still, not looking directly at
them, waiting for them to come up so that greetings
could be exchanged quietly and with dignity.

Kroner's enormous, hairy hand closed about
Paul's, and Paul, in spite of himself, felt docile,
and loving, and childlike. It was as though Paul
stood in the enervating, emasculating presence of
his father again. **Kroner**, his father's closest friend,
had always made him feel that way, and seemingly
wanted to make him feel that way. Paul had sworn
a thousand times to keep his wits about him the
next time he met **Kroner**. But it was a matter beyond his control, and at each meeting, as now, the

power and resolve were all in the big hands of the older man.

(*PP* V) Baer was a social cretin, apparently unaware that he was anything but suave and brilliant in company. Someone had once mentioned his running commentary on conversations to him, and he hadn't known what they were talking about. Technically, there wasn't a better engineer in the East, including Finnerty. There was little in the Division that hadn't been master-minded by Baer, who here seemed to **Kroner** what a fox terrier seems to a St. Bernard. Paul had thought often of the peculiar combination of **Kroner** and Baer, and wondered if, when they were gone, higher management could possibly duplicate it. Baer embodied the knowledge and technique of industry; **Kroner** personified the faith, the near-holiness, the spirit of the complicated venture. **Kroner**, in fact, had a poor record as an engineer and had surprised Paul from time to time with his ignorance or misunderstanding of technical matters; but he had the priceless quality of believing in the system, and of making others believe in it, too, and do as they were told.

The two were inseparable, though their personalities met at almost no point. Together, they made an approximately whole man.

(*PP* V) He smiled beatifically. **Kroner** was the rock, the fountainhead of faith and pride for all in the Eastern Division.

Paul is set off in stark contrast from Kroner and others who firmly believe in the ruling technocracy. (*PP* VI) **Kroner**, too, kept alive the notion that Paul could be expected to follow in his father's footsteps. This faith of **Kroner**'s had had a lot to do with Paul's getting to be manager of Ilium; and now that faith might get him the managership of Pittsburgh. When Paul thought about his effortless rise in the hierarchy, he sometimes, as now, felt sheepish, like a charlatan. He could handle his assignments all right, but he didn't have what his father had, what **Kroner** had, what Shepherd had, what so many had: the sense of spiritual importance in what they were doing; the ability to be moved emotionally, almost like a lover, by the great omnipresent and omniscient spook, the corporate personality. In short, Paul missed what made his father aggressive and great: the capacity to really give a damn.

Kroner is often seen as the great protector of the technocracy *and emblematic of the engineering mindset.* (*PP* VIII) As **Kroner** often said, eternal vigilance was the price of efficiency. And the machines tirelessly riffled through their decks again and again and again in search of foot draggers, free riders, and misfits.

(*PP* IX) The civic managers were the career administrators who ran the city. They lived on the same side of the river as the managers and engineers of the Ilium Works, but the contact between the two groups was little more than perfunctory and, traditionally, suspicious. The schism, like so many things, dated back to the war, when the economy had, for efficiency's sake, become monolithic. The question had arisen: who was to run it, the bureaucrats, the heads of business and industry, or the military? Business and bureaucracy had stuck together long enough to overwhelm the military and had since then worked side by side, abusively and suspiciously, but, like **Kroner** and Baer, each unable to do a whole job without the other.

Kroner also presents a distinct contrast from his engineering siblings, possessing an appreciation for "old world" craftsmanship and lifestyle not unlike Paul's, though Kroner's is based on luxurious creature comforts while Paul's is rooted in old-fashioned human labor (seen most graphically when Paul tries to persuade Anita to leave Homestead and retire with him to life on a working farm). (*PP* XII) The **Kroner** home, just outside Albany, was a Victorian mansion, perfectly restored and maintained down to the filigree along the eaves, and the iron spikes along the roof peak. The arch prophet of efficiency, **Kroner**, preferred it to the gracile, wipe-clean-with-a-damp-cloth steel and glass machines almost all of the engineers and managers lived in. Though **Kroner** had never accounted for his having bought the place—beyond saying that he liked lots of room—it was so in keeping with him that no one gave the anachronism more than passing thought. . . .

The mansion was one more affirmation of **Kroner**'s belief that nothing of value changed; that what was once true is always true; that truths were few and simple; and that a man needed no knowledge beyond these truths to deal wisely and justly with any problem whatsoever.

Kroner also relied on the images of power from the old era as props for his power. (*PP* XII) The fact was, **Kroner** never fired his guns. His pleasure seemed to be in owning and handling them. He also used them for props, to give an air of informality to his man-to-man talks. He announced raises and promotions, demotions and firings, and praised or warned, always in seemingly casual asides made while swabbing a bore.

Paul followed him into the dark-paneled study, and waited for him to choose his weapon from the gunrack that filled one wall. **Kroner** ran his index finger along the collection, like a stick along a picket fence. It had been a matter of speculation among **Kroner**'s underlings as to whether there was any significance in the guns he chose for a particular discussion. For a while the rumor was current that shotguns were bad news, rifles were good news. But it hadn't withstood the test of time. **Kroner** finally chose a ten-gauge shotgun, broke open the breach, and squinted through the bore at a streetlight outside.

Though generally appreciated as the spiritual head of the engineers, Kroner is often awkward in his sentimental expression. (PP XIX) **Kroner** detached himself from the crowd and walked soberly to the thick tree trunk. He turned and looked down at his hands thoughtfully. His first words were so soft, so choked with emotion, that few heard them. He inhaled deeply, threw back his shoulders, raised his eyes, and gathered strength to say them again. . . .

"It is our custom," said **Kroner**, "it is the custom here at the Meadows—our custom, our Meadows—to meet here under our tree, our symbol of strong roots, trunk, and branches, our symbol of courage, integrity, perseverance, beauty. It is our custom to meet here to remember our departed friends and co-workers."

And now he forgot the crowd, and talked to the fat cumulus clouds scudding over the blue sky. "Since last we met, Doctor Ernest S. Bassett has left our world for his reward in a better one. Ernie, as you all know, was. . . .

"Ernie was manager of the Philadelphia Works for five years, of the Pittsburgh Works for seven. He was my friend; he was our friend: a great American, a great engineer, a great manager, a great pioneer at the head of the procession of civilization, opening new, undreamed-of doors to better things, for better living, for more people, at less cost."

Now and then brokenly, **Kroner** told of Ernie Bassett as a young engineer, and he traced his career from works to works.

"He gave himself unstintingly engineeringwise, managershipwise, personalitywise, Americanwise, and—" **Kroner** paused to look impressively from face to face. Again he talked to the clouds—"heartwise."

A man stepped from the crowd to hand **Kroner** a long white box.

Kroner opened it slowly and studied it thoughtfully before showing its contents to anyone else. At last he reached in and unfurled a blue and white pennant, the Armed Forces "E" that Bassett had won during the war as manager of the Philadelphia Works.

A muted bugle played taps.

Kroner knelt at the foot of the tree and placed Ernie Bassett's pennant there.

Kroner, Janice. *Mrs. Anthony Kroner who was a fat repository of truisms, adages, and homilies, and was usually addressed by the young engineers and managers as "Mom"* (PP XII).

Kropotnik, Commissar. *The Soviet leader who fears the power of the Barnhouse Effect (q.v.) and begins a new arms race.*

Krummbein, Otto and Falloleen (*see also* **Kitty Cahoun**). *Otto is the man responsible for remaking his mate according to his tastes in the short story "Custom-Made Bride," collected in* Bagombo Snuff Box (1999). *Otto's commercial success and willful ignorance about money are matched only by his shallow appreciation for the exterior beauty of all things including his wife, Falloleen, née Kitty Cahoun.*

Otto has neglected ever to pay income tax, and his newly arrived bill from the Internal Revenue Service prompts him to contact the attorney Hal Murphy, who then contacts the unnamed narrator. When the narrator puts the question to Otto about what he wants to do with his money, the ensuing response shows he is very aware of what he has done to his wife, the artificiality of his creation, and the narrow limits of his otherwise artistic eye. When I put the question to a client named **Otto Krummbein,** *he* said he wanted to make two women happy: Kitty and Falloleen. **Otto Krummbein** is a genius, designer of the Krummbein Chair, the Krummbein Di-Modular Bed, the body of the Marittima-Frascati Sports Racer, and the entire line of Mercury Kitchen Appliances.

He is so engrossed in beauty that his mental development in money matters is that of a chickadee. When I showed him the first stock certificate I bought for his portfolio, he wanted to sell it again because he didn't like the artwork.

As for Falloleen—Kitty—"One year ago," she said, "I was a plain, brown-haired, dowdy thing, fresh out of secretarial school, starting to work as secretary to the **Great Krummbein**."

"Love at first sight?" I said.

"For me," murmured **Falloleen**. "For **Otto** it was a design problem at first sight. There were things about me that jarred him, that made it impossible for him to think straight when I was around. We changed those things one by one, and what became of **Kitty Cahoun**, nobody knows."

"**Kitty Cahoun**?" I said.

"The plain, brown-haired, dowdy thing, fresh out of secretarial school," said **Falloleen**.

"Then **Falloleen** isn't your real name?" I said.

"It's a **Krummbein** original," said Falloleen. "**Kitty Cahoun** didn't go with the decor." She hung her head. "Love—" she said, "don't ask me any more silly questions about love."

As the story unfolds, Krummbein badly miscalculates the importance of exterior beauty over one's internal virtues. Though married to Kitty for only a month, he has turned her into his own design experiment, going so far as to call her Falloleen instead of Kitty. When the narrator appears at their home, *he first meets Falloleen dressed in a tightly fitting leopard-print leotard and heavy makeup. As Krummbein proudly declares,* Did you ever see a woman who fitted so well into surroundings like this—who seems herself to be designed for contemporary living? *However, when the honeymooners are left alone together while the narrator is off to the side trying to make financial sense of their records, it is clear that they have nothing to speak about and that Kitty is unhappy being his design experiment. This is when she tells the narrator about the brevity of their relationship and her rapid transformation.*

When Otto recalls that his latest design project, moonlight-engineered cosmetics, is the result of looking at Kitty without seeing her in the best light possible, she explodes. Fortunately for them, it is the beginning of redefining their relationship. "I'm sick of being **Falloleen** and the style show that never ends!" Her voice dropped to a whisper. "She's dull and shallow, scared and lost, unhappy and unloved." *She concedes that she went along with Otto's ideas because she loves him, but she can no longer take it. Otto admits that compared with Kitty, Falloleen* "was a crashing bore when she wasn't striking a pose or making a dramatic entrance or exit. I lived in terror of being left alone with her." *They agree that Otto will continue to design for Falloleen but that Kitty will maintain her personality and not be buried by the clothes, the makeup, the stylizations of Otto.*

To round things out, Krummbein gives the narrator free rein over his financial affairs. After all, having a professional money manager is the modern way for Otto to assure himself that he can work without getting into financial trouble.

Lady's Slipper. In Cat's Cradle, *there are two boats called Lady's Slipper. Both boats are owned by Bokonon. The first takes him from his home in Tobago to England, where he studies at the London School of Economics and Political Science. On his return to the island, he is picked up by the Nazi submarine U-99, which sinks his vessel. The British naval ship Raven captures the sub, frees Bokonon, and sinks the U-99. Upon Bokonon's return to Tobago, he builds the Lady's Slipper II. Eventually, he and Corporal Earl McCabe wreck the schooner on the rocks of San Lorenzo in the middle of a storm. Lady's Slipper II's lifeboat becomes the bed of "Papa" Monzano. Eventually, "Papa" swallows ice-nine while in the bed, and when the walls of the castle crumble into the sea, the boat and "Papa" go crashing down, turning the world's water into ice-nine.*

Lafayette Escadrille. *One of Vonnegut's early literary editors was Kenneth Littauer, a veteran pilot with the Lafayette Escadrille during World War I. In* Deadeye Dick, *doomed stunt flyer Will Fairchild is also a member of the World War I outfit.*

Laird, Eddie (*also* **Selma, Arthur, and Dawn**). *In the short story "Bagombo Snuff Box," collected in* Bagombo Snuff Box *(1999), Laird is a traveling potato chip salesman from Levittown, Long Island, returning to the small town he has called home since being stationed at Cunningham Field during World War II. Though only twenty-two at the time, he marries Amy (no mention of a last name), who is only eighteen. The two are married for just six months when they split.*

Laird's return prompts him to look in on Amy to see how she made out after all this time. He tries to pass himself off as an adventuresome pilot who had flown for a pearling company in Ceylon (now Sri Lanka), hunted for diamonds in the Amazon rain forest, and flown for an Iraqi sheik. He claims to have quit the Ceylon job to pursue his own efforts in the Klondike prospecting for uranium. Though he says he was a captain and pilot during the war, and now a Major in the Reserve Air Force, by the end of the story there is no reason to believe any of his malarkey.

His grandiose stories seem familiar and believable to Amy when he first arrives for a visit at her house. Amid the chaos of her home filled with tiresome haranguing with her husband, Harry, about everyday matters concerning food, clothing, and babies, she does not question Eddie's stories. He previously passed himself off as a wandering free spirit to the unnamed bartender in town. "I just didn't want to be owned, that's all. I wanted to be able to stick my toothbrush in my hip pocket and take off whenever I felt like it. And she didn't go for that. So . . ." He grinned. "Adiós. No tears, no hard feelings."

Eddie makes Harry uncomfortable with his dashing and romantic travelogue, causing even more friction with his wife. However, Eddie's tale begins to unravel when he presents the couple with a gift from his travels to Ceylon, the Bagombo snuff box encrusted with semiprecious gems. He has failed to remove the "Made in Japan" sticker from its bottom. The label is spotted by nine-year-old Stevie, Amy and Harry's son, who challenges Eddie about it. Before long, a conversation about the location of Ceylon has Eddie agreeing with Stevie that it is off the coast of Africa, but they are both corrected by Amy, who knows it is off the coast of India. It is all Eddie can do to duck into his waiting taxi to avoid further embarrassment as the family mocks him with all the foreign gibberish he tried to pass off during his brief stay.

The story closes with Eddie calling his wife, Selma, back in Levittown, telling her how successful he has been on the trip and inquiring about his own four children: Arthur (whose teachers believe he is just lazy, not dull), Dawn (in need of braces), and an unnamed set of twins. After senselessly causing Amy's family to feel small and closed in with their own domestic tensions, Eddie seeks the solace of his own brood, even if by a long-distance phone call while trying to eke out his own living.

Lake Maxincuckee (*also* **Lake Maxinkuckee**; *see also* **Grand Triumvirate**). *The Vonnegut family summer home was on this northern Indiana lake, and its significance is fully described in* Fates Worse Than Death. *(FWD IV)* "No matter where I am, and even if I have no clear idea where I am, and no matter how much trouble I may be in, I can achieve a blank and shining serenity if only I can reach the very edge of a natural body of water. The very edge of anything from a rivulet to an ocean says to me: 'Now you know where you are. Now you know which way to go. You will soon be home now.'

"That is because I made my first mental maps of the world, in the summertime when I was a little child, on the shores of **Lake Maxincuckee**, which is in northern Indiana, halfway between Chicago and Indianapolis, where we lived in the wintertime. **Maxincuckee** is three miles long and two and a half miles across at its widest. Its shores are a closed loop. No matter where I was on its circumference, all I had to do was keep walking in one direction to find my way home again. What a confident Marco Polo I could be when setting out for a day's adventure!

"Yes, and I ask the reader of this piece, my indispensable collaborator: Isn't your deepest understanding of time and space and, for that matter, destiny shaped like mine by your earliest experiences with geography, by the rules you learned about how to get home again? What is it that can make you feel, no matter how mistakenly, that you are on the right track, that you will soon be safe and sound at home again?

"The closed loop of the lakeshore was certain to bring me home not only to my own family's unheated frame cottage on a bluff overlooking the lake, but to four adjacent cottages teeming with close relatives. The heads of those neighboring households, moreover, my father's generation, had also spent their childhood summertimes at **Maxincuckee**, making them the almost immediate successors there to the Potawatomi Indians. They even had a tribal name for themselves, which sounded like 'Epta-mayan-hoys.' Sometimes my father, when a grown man, would call out to **Maxincuckee** in general, 'Epta-mayan-hoy?' And a first cousin fishing from a leaky rowboat or a sister reading in a hammock, or whatever, would give this reply: 'Ya! Epta-mayan-

hoy!' What did it mean? It was pure nonsense from their childhoods. It was German, if not transliterated as I have done, meaning this: 'Do abbots mow hay? Yes! Abbots mow hay!'

"So what? So not very much, I guess, except that it allows me to say that after the Potawatomis came the Epta-mayan-hoys, who have vanished from **Lake Maxincuckee** without a trace. It is as though they had never been there.

"Am I sad? Not at all. Because everything about that lake was imprinted on my mind when it held so little and was so eager for information, it will be my lake as long as I live. I have no wish to visit it, for I have it all right here. I happened to see it last spring from about six miles up, on a flight from Louisville to Chicago. It was as emotionally uninvolving as a bit of dry dust viewed under a microscope. Again: That wasn't the real **Maxincuckee** down there. The real one is in my head.

"The one in my head is the one I swam across, all two and one-half miles of it, when I was eleven years old, with my sister, five years older than me, and my brother, nine years older than me, in a leaky rowboat near me, urging me on. My sister died thirty years ago. My brother, an atmospheric scientist, is still going strong, daydreaming about clouds and electricity. Times change, but my lake never will.

"If I were ever to write a novel or a play about **Maxincuckee**, it would be Chekhovian, since what I saw were the consequences of several siblings' inheriting and trying to share a single beloved property, and with their own children, once grown, moving to other parts of the world, never to return, and on and on. Our cottage, owned jointly and often acrimoniously by my father and his brother and his sister, was sold to a stranger at the end of World War II. The buyer put off taking possession for a week in order that I, just married after being discharged from the Army, might take my bride there for a honeymoon. . . .

"We went out in an old, leaky rowboat, which all my life I had called 'The Beralikur,' a mixture of my first name with those of my siblings, Bernard and Alice. But that name was not painted on the boat, which would have been redundant. Everybody who was anybody at **Maxincuckee** already knew that the name of that leaky boat was the Beralikur."

Vonnegut used the setting in Slapstick. *The King of Michigan takes over what was once the Culver Military Academy and establishes it as his palace. It is there the powerless President Wilbur Swain meets with the King. Though Swain notices a number of killed and wounded soldiers during his helicopter flight in the aftermath of the* **Battle of Lake Maxincuckee**, *families were reuniting and being kind to each other rather than fighting. He is told that since there were no more nations, the various extended families found it easier to be merciful toward each other.*

In Timequake, *Vonnegut includes a conversation he held as a teenager when interviewing for a summer internship with Mr. Johnson, a friend of his father's. His naive response to the gentleman indicates he felt comfortable enough with the Lake Maxincuckee area to work it as a fledgling reporter for the summer.* (TQ 39) "Well, sir," I said, "I thought maybe I could get a job on The Culver Citizen and work there for three or four years. I know the area pretty well." Culver was on **Lake Maxincuckee** in northern Indiana. We used to have a summer cottage on that lake.

Hal Irwin views living at Lake Maxinkuckee a true symbol of having made it in society. (BAG Hal Irwin's Magic Lamp) "Look where they live, and look where we live," Hal went on. "We oughta be right out there with 'em at Fifty-seventh and North Meridian! We oughta have a cottage right next to 'em at **Lake Maxinkuckee**! Least I can do is get my wife a cook."

lambos. *In Kilgore Trout's* The Barring-gaffner of Bagnialto, *winners of the yearly art lottery are paid in lambos.* (BC 14) The painting by Gooz had an unprecedented gush of luck on the wheel. It became worth eighteen thousand ***lambos***, the equivalent of one billion dollars on Earth. The Barring-gaffner awarded Gooz a check for that amount, most of which was taken back at once by the tax collector.

lamprey. *An eel with a jawless sucking mouth. In the short story "The Big Space Fuck," some of them have grown as large as the space ship* Arthur C. Clarke *and have slithered out of the noxious slime polluting the Great Lakes. One of them eats Dwayne and Grace Hoobler as well as the sheriff.*

Lancer. *As part of Vonnegut's musings about the nature of life and the reasons we live as we do, he describes the life of Lancer the Greyhound and compares him with the troubled ex-convict Wayne Hoobler. Lancer lived* in a one-room apartment fourteen feet wide and twenty-six feet long, and six flights of stairs above street level. His entire life was devoted to unloading his excrement at the proper time and place. There were two proper places to put it: in the gutter outside the door seventy-two steps below, with the traffic whizzing by, or in a roasting pan his mistress kept in front of the Westinghouse refrigerator.

Lancer had a very small brain, but he must have suspected from time to time, just as Wayne Hoobler did, that some kind of terrible mistake had been made (BC 18).

Landry, Cynthia. *The former childhood sweetheart of John F. Kennedy who becomes the bride of Lance Rumfoord. The newlyweds are seen honeymooning on the yacht* Scheherezade *by Billy and Valencia Pilgrim in* Slaughterhouse-Five.

Lapp, Marlin T. *In* The Sirens of Titan, *long after Winston Niles Rumfoord is caught in the chronosynclastic infundibulum and Beatrice is taken to Mars, the mortgage holders of his Newport estate lease it to Marlin T. Lapp, a showman who sold tickets to Rumfoord and Kazak's materializations.*

Larkin, Emil. *President Nixon's "most vindictive advisor and dreaded hatchet man" is convicted of obstruction of justice in the Watergate case and serves his sentence in the Adult Correctional Facility at Finletter Air Force Base.* (JB 4) This was a big man, goggle-eyed and liver-lipped, who had been a middle linebacker for Michigan State at one time. He was a disbarred lawyer now, and he prayed all day long to what he believed to be Jesus Christ. **Larkin** had not been sent out on a work detail or assigned any housekeeping task, incidentally, because of what all his praying on hard prison floors had done to him. He was crippled in both legs with housemaid's knee. *So complete and sincere is his born-again status that when RAMJAC's Heartland House Publishing Company prints Larkin's autobiography,* Brother, Won't You Pray with Me?, *he donates all his royalties to the Salvation Army.*

Lasher, the Reverend James J. *The charismatic leader of the revived Ghost Shirt Society introduces himself to Paul Proteus and Ed Finnerty in the Homestead saloon as designated by the technocracy's guidelines, evidence of the dehumanizing categorization of people by the ruling engineers.* (PP IX) "The name is **Lasher**, the **Reverend James J. Lasher**, R-127 and SS-55. Chaplain, Reconstruction and Reclamation Corps."

"The first number's for Protestant minister. What's the second, that SS thing?" said Finnerty.

"Social scientist," said **Lasher**. "The 55 designates an anthropologist with a master's degree."

"And what does an anthropologist do these days?" said Paul.

"Same thing a supernumerary minister does— becomes a public charge, a bore, or possibly a rumdum, or a bureaucrat."

Lasher voices the protesters' seminal complaints about how a centrally designed and completely efficient capitalist market (based on a wartime production model) drives society into such severe class distinctions that people have now been rendered useless, a psychologically devastating blow to their humanity and one without sufficient support from traditional biblical teachings.
(PP IX) "What was this business about the people across the river being the opposition?" said Paul. "You think they do the Devil's work, do you?"

"That's pretty strong. I will say you've shown up what thin stuff clergymen were peddling, most of them. When I had a congregation before the war, I used to tell them that the life of their spirit in relation to God was the biggest thing in their lives, and that their part in the economy was nothing by comparison. Now, you people have engineered them out of their part in the economy, in the market place, and they're finding out—most of them—that what's left is just about zero. A good bit short of enough, anyway. My glass is empty."

Lasher sighed. "What do you expect?" he said. "For generations they've been built up to worship competition and the market, productivity and economic usefulness, and the envy of their fellow men—and boom! it's all yanked out from under them. They can't participate, can't be useful anymore. Their whole culture's been shot to hell. My glass is empty."

"I just had it filled again," said Finnerty.

"Oh, so you did." **Lasher** sipped thoughtfully. "These displaced people need something, and the clergy can't give it to them—or it's impossible for them to take what the clergy offers. The clergy says it's enough, and so does the Bible. The people say it isn't enough, and I suspect they're right."
(PP IX) "Strange business," said **Lasher**. "This crusading spirit of the managers and engineers, the idea of designing and manufacturing and distributing being sort of a holy war: all that folklore was cooked up by public relations and advertising men hired by managers and engineers to make big business popular in the old days, which it certainly wasn't in the beginning. Now, the engineers and managers believe with all their hearts the glorious things their forebears hired people to say about them. Yesterday's snow job becomes today's sermon."

Lasher sums up the historical shift in establishing classes, concluding the new system is as brutal and unforgiving as the last. Finnerty sees the same and appears to be in full agreement with Lasher. (PP IX) "Things are certainly set up for a class war based on conveniently established lines of demarkation. And I must say that the basic assumption of the present setup is a grade-A incitement to violence: the smarter you are, the better you are. Used to be that the richer you were, the better you were. Either one is, you'll admit, pretty tough for the have-not's to take. The criterion of brains is better than the one of money, but"—he held his thumb and forefinger about a sixteenth of an inch apart—"about that much better."

"It's about as rigid a hierarchy as you can get," said Finnerty. "How's somebody going to up his I.Q.?"

"Exactly," said **Lasher**. "And it's built on more than just brain power—it's built on special kinds of brain power. Not only must a person be bright, he must be bright in certain approved, useful directions: basically, management or engineering."

Lasher foreshadows the coming rebellion and Paul's part in it while at the same time describing the tragic consequences people face when displaced from useful and meaningful occupation. (PP IX) "We'll give them something to sink their teeth in?" said Paul. He noticed he was getting somewhat thick of speech.

"You'll be what they'll get to sink their teeth in." **Lasher** laid his hand on Paul's shoulder.

"One more thing: I want to be sure you understand that men really do worry about what there is for their sons to live for; and some sons do hang themselves."

Later in the text when Kroner presents the plan for Paul Proteus to infiltrate the Ghost Shirt Society, particularly looking for information on Lasher and Finnerty, Paul realizes his previously unstructured thoughts on the social situation finds expression in the words and sentiments of Reverend Lasher. (PP XII) The hands on his knees tightened. Paul struggled resentfully against the urge to pour his heart out to this merciful, wise, gentle father. But his sullenness decayed. Paul began to talk.

His formless misgivings and disquiet of a week before, he realized, had shape now. The raw material of his discontent was now cast in another man's molds. He was saying what **Lasher** had said the night before, talking about the spiritual disaster across the river, about the threat of revolution, about the hierarchy that was a nightmare to most. The way he phrased it, it wasn't a condemnation, it was a plea for refutation.

At one point Anita warns Paul, "Shepherd says **Lasher** and Finnerty are being watched as potential saboteurs" (PP XVI). *She is unaware of the great schemes going on with her husband in the middle.*

Lasher goes on to give a complete history lesson to Paul as part of his explanation as to why the rebellion chose the Ghost Shirts to represent them. This is typical of the anthropology lessons Vonnegut sprinkles throughout his novels. (PP XXIX) "What's a ghost shirt?" murmured Paul between prickling lips.

"Toward the end of the nineteenth century," said **Lasher**, "a new religious movement swept the Indians in this country, Doctor."

"The Ghost Dance, Paul," said Finnerty.

"The white man had broken promise after promise to the Indians, killed off most of the game, taken most of the Indians' land, and handed the Indians bad beatings every time they'd offered any resistance," said **Lasher**.

"Poor Injuns," murmured Paul.

"This is serious," said Finnerty. "Listen to what he's telling you."

"With the game and land and ability to defend themselves gone," said **Lasher**, "the Indians found out that all the things they used to take pride in doing, all the things that had made them feel important, all the things that used to gain them prestige, all the ways in which they used to justify their existence—they found that all those things were going or gone. Great hunters had nothing to hunt. Great fighters did not come back from charging into repeating-arms fire. Great leaders could lead the people nowhere but into death in hopeless attack, or deeper into wastelands. Great religious leaders could no longer show that the old religious beliefs were the way to victory and plenty."

Paul, suggestible under the drug, was deeply disturbed by the plight of the redskins. "Golly."

"The world had changed radically for the Indians," said **Lasher**. "It had become a white man's world, and Indian ways in a white man's world were irrelevant. It was impossible to hold the old Indian values in the changed world. The only thing they could do in the changed world was to become second-rate white men or wards of the white men."

"Or they could make one last fight for the old values," said Finnerty with relish.

"And the Ghost Dance religion," said **Lasher**, "was that last, desperate defense of the old values. Messiahs appeared, the way they're always ready to appear, to preach magic that would restore the game, the old values, the old reasons for being. There were new rituals and new songs that were supposed to get rid of the white men by magic. And some of the more warlike tribes that still had a little physical fight left in them added a flourish of their own—the Ghost Shirt."

"Last Full Measure" (*see* **Howard W. Campbell**).

Laurel and Hardy. *Vonnegut dedicates* Slapstick *to the comedy team he calls* two angels of my time. *Vonnegut goes on to write,* I have called it "Slapstick" because it is grotesque, situational poetry—like the slapstick film comedies, especially those of **Laurel and Hardy**, of long ago.

It is about what life *feels* like to me.

There are all these tests of my limited agility and intelligence. They go on and on.

The fundamental joke with **Laurel and Hardy**,

it seems to me, was that they did their best with every test.

They never failed to bargain in good faith with their destinies, and were screamingly adorable and funny on that account.

There was very little love in their films. There was often the situational poetry of marriage, which was something else again. It was yet another test—with comical possibilities, provided that everybody submitted to it in good faith.

Love was never at issue. And, perhaps because I was so perpetually intoxicated and instructed by **Laurel and Hardy** during my childhood in the Great Depression, I find it natural to discuss life without ever mentioning love.

It does not seem important to me.

What does seem important? Bargaining in good faith with destiny (*Slap* Prologue).

Bluebeard's *Rabo Karabekian includes Laurel and Hardy as Estonians in German uniforms in his masterpiece "Now It's the Women's Turn."*

Eugene Debs Hartke imagines his appearance with his father at the Ohio Science Fair as something resembling the comic duo. (HP 4) Even as Father and I were setting up our exhibit, we were spotted by other contestants as a couple of comedians, as **Laurel and Hardy**, maybe, with Father as the fat and officious one and me as the dumb and skinny one. The thing was, Father was doing all the setting up, and I was standing around looking bored. All I wanted to do was go outside and hide behind a tree or something and smoke a cigarette. We were violating the most basic rule of the Fair, which was that the young exhibitors were supposed to do all the work, from start to finish. Parents or teachers or whatever were forbidden in writing to help at all.

In Timequake, *Vonnegut makes sure their presence is represented at the clambake.* (TQ 327) I want a look-alike for Borden *(Deal)* at the clambake, and two luckless fishermen in a little rowboat right off-shore, dead ringers for the saints **Stanley Laurel and Oliver Hardy**.

So be it.
(*MWC* 1) There is a superficial sort of laughter. Bob Hope, for example, was not really a humorist. He was a comedian with very thin stuff, never mentioning anything troubling. I used to laugh my head off at **Laurel and Hardy**. There is terrible tragedy there somehow. These men are too sweet to survive in this world and are in terrible danger all the time. They could be so easily killed.

Lawes, Cleveland and Eucharist ("Ukey"). *Cleveland Lawes is the black chauffeur who escorts Virgil Greathouse to the federal prison at Finletter Air Force Base. Before returning to Atlanta, Lawes becomes interested in Walter Starbuck who is passing time at a bus stop by going through his hand-clapping of the "Sally" rhyme.*

Lawes had little formal education but is self-educated, reading an average of five books a week in his limousine while waiting for his employers. Because of his initial kindness to Starbuck, Lawes later becomes personnel director of the Transico Division of the RAMJAC Corporation, a limousine, taxicab, rental car, parking lot, and garage business.

As a private in the Korean War, Lawes was taken prisoner and later befriended by the Chinese major in charge of his prison—a Harvard man. Because of the harsh treatment and cruelties Lawes experienced growing up in the American South, he accepted his captor's invitation to live in China after the war. He eventually wants to return home because he misses the church music and food of his youth. The Chinese bargain on his behalf for his return to America with only a minimal amount of punishment.

Eucharist Lawes, more frequently called "Ukey," is Cleveland's wife. Her given name means "happy gratitude."

Lawrence, Seymour. *One in a short line of Vonnegut's publishers that he held in high regard. As the dedication to* Timequake *reads,* In memory of **Seymour Lawrence**, a romantic and great publisher of curious tales told with ink on bleached and flattened wood pulp.

In Timequake, *Lawrence is represented at the climactic clambake by his doppelgänger, the unnamed Bakemaster.* (TQ 60) The bakemaster, a local man who is paid to stage such parties in the summertime, resembled my late publisher **Seymour Lawrence** (1926–1993), who rescued me from certain oblivion, from smithereens, by publishing *Slaughterhouse-Five*, and then bringing all my previous books back into print under his umbrella.

In his introduction to the 1999 collection Bagombo Snuff Box, *Vonnegut mentions his indebtedness to Lawrence for keeping his books in print in the sixties, and notes that he used the same line at Seymour Lawrence's memorial service as he used for Isaac Asimov. Vonnegut's dates for Seymour Lawrence are moved by one year on each end in difference with his* Timequake *reference.* That anything I have written is in print today is due to the efforts of one publisher, **Seymour "Sam" Lawrence** (1927–1994). When I was broke in 1965, and teaching at the Writers' Workshop at the University of Iowa all alone, completely out of print, having separated myself from my family on Cape Cod in order to support them, **Sam** bought rights to my books, for peanuts, from publishers, both hardcover and softcover, who had given up on me. **Sam** thrust my books back into the myopic public eye again.

CPR! Cardiopulmonary resuscitation of this author who was all but dead!

Thus encouraged, this Lazarus wrote *Slaughterhouse-Five* for **Sam**. That made my reputation. I am a Humanist, and so am not entitled to expect an afterlife for myself or anyone. But at **Seymour Lawrence**'s memorial service at New York City's Harvard Club five years ago, I said this with all my heart: "**Sam** is up in Heaven now."

See also: TQ 7; 62; BAG Introduction.

Lazarus. (*PS Embarrassment*) We woke up in ambulances headed for different hospitals, so to speak, and would never get together again. We were alive, yes, but the marriage was dead.

And it was no **Lazarus**.

(*PS In the Capital of the World*) " 'Six days before the Passover, Jesus came to Bethany, where **Lazarus** was, whom Jesus had raised from the dead. There they made him a supper; Martha served, but **Lazarus** was one of those at table with him. . . .

"His male companions for this supper are themselves a mockery. One is Judas, who will betray him. The other is **Lazarus**, who has recently been dead for four days. **Lazarus** was so dead that he stunk, the Bible says. **Lazarus** is surely dazed, and not much of a conversationalist—and not necessarily grateful, either, to be alive again. It is a very mixed blessing to be brought back from the dead.

"If I had read a little farther, we would have learned that there is a crowd outside, crazy to see **Lazarus**, not Jesus. **Lazarus** is the man of the hour as far as the crowd is concerned."

(*Blue 2*) It was a postwar miracle that did me in. I had better explain to my young readers, if any, that the Second World War had many of the promised characteristics of Armageddon, a final war between good and evil, so that nothing would do but that it be followed by miracles. Instant coffee was one. DDT was another. It was going to kill all the bugs, and almost did. Nuclear energy was going to make electricity so cheap that it might not even be metered. It would also make another war unthinkable. Talk about loaves and fishes! Antibiotics would defeat all diseases. **Lazarus** would never die:

How was that for a scheme to make the Son of God obsolete?

(*Blue 15*) "I brought you back to life," she said. "You're my **Lazarus**. All Jesus did for **Lazarus** was bring him back to life. I not only brought you back to life—I got you writing your autobiography."

(*Blue 37*) "Twice now I've been a **Lazarus**," I said. "I died with Terry Kitchen, and Edith brought me back to life again. I died with dear Edith, and Circe Berman brought me back to life again."

Vonnegut describes himself as a Lazarus in relation to Samuel Lawrence, his friend and publisher, who saved his writing career. (*BAG Introduction*) CPR! Cardiopulmonary resuscitation of this author who was all but dead!

Thus encouraged, this **Lazarus** wrote *Slaughterhouse-Five* for Sam. That made my reputation. I am a Humanist, and so am not entitled to expect an afterlife for myself or anyone. But at Seymour Lawrence's memorial service at New York City's Harvard Club five years ago, I said this with all my heart: "Sam is up in Heaven now."

See also: PS In the Capital of the World.

Lazzaro, Paul. *In* Slaughterhouse-Five, *the car thief from Cicero, Illinois, who promises to have Billy Pilgrim killed after the war for contributing to the frostbite death of Roland Weary. Lazzaro relishes talking about how easy it is for him to have someone killed. With equal ghoulishness he describes once killing a troublesome dog with a steak laced with the cut-up springs from a clock. In the aftermath of the Dresden firebombing when prison-*

ers are put to work as corpse miners, Lazzaro manages to steal jewelry from the dead in the burned-out cellars. He eventually kills Billy Pilgrim on the evening of February 13, 1976, thirty-one years to the day after the firebombing of Dresden.

Le Fèvre, Andre. *The photo assistant to Louis J. M. Daguerre, whom Vonnegut cites as selling one of the earliest pornographic photographs—a* woman attempting sexual intercourse with a Shetland Pony (SL5 2). *Vonnegut notes that in 1841, Le Fèvre was sentenced to six months in prison for the sale, and that he died in prison.*

In God Bless You, Mr. Rosewater, *Lila Buntline sells copies of that image to friends in Newport, Rhode Island.*

In Slaughterhouse-Five, *Roland Weary has a copy of the photograph in his coat when he is captured during the Battle of the Bulge.*

leaks. *Kilgore Trout's term for mirrors. The term also provides an illustration of the respectability Trout receives after his death.* (BC 2) It amused him to pretend that mirrors were holes between two universes.

If he saw a child near a mirror, he might wag his finger at a child warningly, and say with great solemnity, "Don't get too near that **leak**. You wouldn't want to wind up in the other universe, would you?"

Sometimes somebody would say in his presence, "Excuse me, I have to take a **leak**." This was a way of saying that the speaker intended to drain liquid wastes from his body through a valve in his lower abdomen.

And Trout would reply waggishly, "Where I come from, that means you're about to steal a mirror."

And so on.

By the time of Trout's death, of course, everybody called mirrors *leaks*.

That was how respectable even his jokes had become.

See also: BC 10; 18; 19; 20; 21.

Leech, Leonard. *Norman Mushari's old law professor who teaches him how to focus on succeeding, advice that Mushari made his credo.* (GBR 1) He recalled what his favorite professor, **Leonard Leech**,

once told him about getting ahead in law. **Leech** said that, just as a good airplane pilot should always be looking for places to land, so should a lawyer be looking for situations where large amounts of money were about to change hands.

"In every big transaction," said **Leech**, "there is a magic moment during which a man has surrendered a treasure, and during which the man who is due to receive it has not yet done so. An alert lawyer will make that moment his own, possessing the treasure for a magic microsecond, taking a little of it, passing it on. If the man who is to receive the treasure is unused to wealth, has an inferiority complex and shapeless feelings of guilt, as most people do, the lawyer can often take as much as half the bundle, and still receive the recipient's blubbering thanks."

Leeds, Marc. *The author of this text who remains appreciative for his nearly twenty-year friendship with Vonnegut. Vonnegut surprised Leeds when the latter came across the following in* Timequake. (TQ 62) Also in the flesh at the clambake were five men half my age who made me want to keep on going in my sunset years because of their interest in my work. They weren't there to see me. They wanted at long last to meet Kilgore Trout. They were Robert Weide, who in this summer of 1996 is making a movie in Montreal of *Mother Night*, and **Marc Leeds**, who wrote and had published a witty encyclopedia of my life and work, and Asa Pieratt and Jerome Klinkowitz, who have kept my bibliography up-to-date and written essays about me as well, and Joe Petro III, numbered like a World War, who taught me how to silk-screen.

Leen, Arpad. *Walter Starbuck recalls* the very public and communicative president and chairman of the board of directors of The RAMJAC Corporation. He would become my boss of bosses, and Cleveland Lawes's boss of bosses, too, when we both became corporate officers of RAMJAC. I say now that **Arpad Leen** is the most able and informed and brilliant and responsive executive under whom it has ever been my privilege to serve. He is a genius at acquiring companies and keeping them from dying afterward.

He used to say, "If you can't get along with me, you can't get along with anybody."

It was true, it was true. (*JB* 8)

Leghorn, Fred. "... shrewd hayseed king of the mechanized chicken industry" (*PS* Jekyll and Hyde Revisited). *Jerry Rivers's fifth stepfather (soon to be divorced from his mother), Leghorn asks Dr. Henry Jekyll to analyze a secret growth potion from one of his competitors. Jekyll concocts his own fowl growth potion, tests it on himself, turns into a human-sized homicidal chicken, and is shot to death by Leghorn.*

LeGrand, Pierre. *One of Eugene Debs Hartke's more emotionally troubled students, LeGrand uses his wealth to purchase expensive gifts as a way of winning friends. Debs recalls that his Mercedes was* a gift from the mother of a student of mine named **Pierre LeGrand**. His maternal grandfather had been dictator of Haiti, and had taken the treasury of that country with him when he was overthrown. That was why **Pierre**'s mother was so rich. He was very unpopular. He tried to win friends by making expensive gifts to them, but that didn't work, so he tried to hang himself from a girder of the water tower on top of Musket Mountain. I happened to be up there, in the bushes with the wife of the coach of the Tennis Team.

So I cut him down with my Swiss Army knife. That was how I got the Mercedes.

Pierre would have better luck 2 years later, jumping off the Golden Gate Bridge, and a campus joke was that now I had to give the Mercedes back (*HP* 10).

Leidveld and Moore. *In* Bluebeard, *the New York advertising agency hired by Marc Coulomb on behalf of Coulomb Frères et Cie of France, on the stipulation that they hire Rabo Karabekian.*

Lembrig, Dr. Thor. *Lembrig's one appearance indicates that, late in life, Kilgore Trout and his science fiction stories would achieve an impressive measure of exposure.* (*BC* 18) As an old, old man, Trout would be asked by **Dr. Thor Lembrig**, the Secretary-General of the United Nations, if he feared the future. He would give this reply:

"Mr. Secretary-General, it is the *past* which scares the bejesus out of me."

Lenin Observatory (*see* **Jefferson Observatory**).

Leonard, Dawn. *According to Diana Moon Glampers—and not disputed by Eliot Rosewater—Dawn Leonard's ten-year-old case of boils was cured by Eliot, further proof that Eliot was the savior of Rosewater County.*

Leonard, John. *The late and highly regarded literary critic is among Vonnegut's select gathering at the* Timequake *clambake.*

Leonard, Paul. *The eight-year-old boy in the short story "Next Door," reprinted in* Welcome to the Monkey House (1968), *who is frightened and appalled by the sounds he hears through his apartment wall as Mr. Harger and his mistress carry on while Mrs. Harger is away. Paul eventually calls "All-Night Sam," a radio disc jockey taking record dedications, and dedicates a song from Mr. Harger to his wife, Rose. When the lovers hear the dedication, they have a loud and final parting of the ways.*

LeSabre, Harry and Grace. *In* Breakfast of Champions, *Harry is the sales manager at Dwayne Hoover's Pontiac dealership. Harry's twenty-year experience with Dwayne allows him to see that Dwayne is starting to lose his mind.*

Harry is a heterosexual transvestite. He never tells Dwayne this secret, and Dwayne would never have suspected it since Harry always wore business suits in black or gray with white shirts. However, when Dwayne warns Harry to dress in a festive mood for the upcoming Hawaiian Week promotion, Harry suspects Dwayne knows his secret. He spends an entire Veterans' Day weekend worrying he would be publicly exposed. Only Grace, Harry's cigar-smoking wife, knows his secret and supports him for sharing an active and mutually pleasing sex life.

Harry invested in Xerox stock years earlier (at $8.00 per share), and Grace suggests they cash in the stock and leave Midland City for Maui, Hawaii. She deeply shares the discomfort and pain brought to Harry by the declining Dwayne. The text suggests they went to Hawaii.

Letzinger, Coach. *In the unfinished novel at the back of Eliot Rosewater's* Domesday Book, *reincarnation is very much its thematic center. It is not clear if Eliot creates Coach Letzinger or he is chronicling the exploits of a local townsman.* (GBR 7) Coeur de Lion has found himself once again taken captive during his travels, imprisoned this time in the flesh of **Coach Letzinger**, a pitiful exhibitionist and freelance garbage man in Rosewater, Indiana. **Coach**, with poor old King Richard inside, goes to Indianapolis on the Greyhound bus three or four times a year, dresses up for the trip in shoes, socks, garters, a raincoat, and a chromium-plated whistle hung around his neck. When he gets to Indianapolis, **Coach** goes to the silverware department of one of the big stores, where there are always a lot of brides-to-be picking out silver patterns. **Coach** blows his whistle, all the girls look, **Coach** throws open his raincoat, closes it again, and runs like hell to catch the bus back to Rosewater.

"The Lie" (1962) (*see* **Tom Hilyer** *or* **Dr. Remenzel**).

Lieber, Albert and wife **Alice** (*née* Barus; *see also* **Alice Barus**). *Vonnegut's maternal grandparents. Albert was the son of Vonnegut's maternal great-grandfather Peter. Vonnegut has some rather damning things to say about his grandfather as well as for his second wife (see below in the* Timequake *reference for chapter 41).*
(PS Roots) We have come now to a rascal, whose emotional faithlessness to his children, in my humble opinion, contributed substantially to my mother's eventual suicide. As I have said, he was the son of the limping Civil War Veteran. When his father retired to Dusseldorf, **Albert** remained in Indianapolis to run the brewery that his father had sold to a British syndicate. He was born in 1863.
(TQ 11) **Albert Lieber**, was then in the full tide of success as one of the town's rich men. He resided on a beautiful estate of some hundred acres just to the northwest of the city, in a large residence which he had recently constructed. . . .

The marriage was approved by both families; but the Schnull-Vonnegut clan was slightly condescending. In the pecking order in the social hierarchy of the community, and particularly in the German group it was generally understood that the Schnull-Vonnegut clan ranked ahead of the **Lieber-Barus** clan.
(TQ 26) But Peter Lieber gave the brewery to his son **Albert**, my maternal grandfather, and he went back to his original hemisphere. He decided he liked that one better.
(TQ 40) I think Mother was raised to be so useless because her father **Albert Lieber**, the brewer and speculator, believed that America was going to have an aristocracy based on the European model. Proofs of membership in such a caste over there, and so it would be over here, too, he must have reasoned, were wives and daughters who were ornamental.
(TQ 41) I don't think I missed the boat when I failed to write a novel about **Albert Lieber**, and how he was largely responsible for my mother's suicide on Mother's Day Eve, 1944. German-Americans in Indianapolis lack universality. They have never been sympathetically, or even villainously, stereotyped in movies or books or plays. I would have had to explain them from scratch.

Lotsa luck!
(TQ 41) I will say for the record that my grandfather **Albert Lieber**'s first wife, **Alice**, née **Barus**, namesake of my sister Allie, died giving birth to her third child, who was Uncle Rudy. Mother was her first. The middle child was Uncle Pete, who flunked out of MIT, but who nonetheless sired a nuclear scientist, my cousin **Albert** in Del Mar, California. Cousin **Albert** reports that he has just gone blind.
(TQ 41) The point I want to make is that **Mother's father**, the brewer, Republican big shot, and neo-aristocratic bon vivant, married a violinist after his first wife died (Ora D. Lane). She turned out to be clinically bughouse. Face it! Some women are! She hated his kids with a passion. She was jealous of his love for them. She wanted to be the whole show. Some women do!

This female bat out of hell, who could play a fiddle like nobody's business, abused Mother and Uncle Pete and Uncle Rudy so ferociously, both physically and mentally, during their formative years, before **Grandfather Lieber** divorced her, that they never got over it.

If there had been a significant body of potential book-buyers who might care about rich German-

Americans in Indianapolis, it would have been a piece of cake for me to bang out a roman-fleuve demonstrating that my grandfather in fact *murdered* my mother, albeit very slowly, by double-crossing her so long ago.

"Ting-a-ling, you son of a bitch!"

Working title: *Gone With the Wind.*

(*TQ* 44) Listen: Only three weeks ago at this writing, on September 6th, 1996, Joe and I opened a show of twenty-six of our prints in the 1/1 Gallery in Denver, Colorado. A local microbrewery, Wynkoop, bottled a special beer for the occasion. The label was one of my self-portraits. The name of the beer was Kurt's Mile-High Malt.

You think that wasn't fun? Try this: The beer, at my suggestion, was lightly flavored with coffee. What was so great about that? It tasted really good, for one thing, but it was also an homage to my maternal grandfather **Albert Lieber**, who was a brewer until he was put out of business by Prohibition in 1920. The secret ingredient in the beer that won a Gold Medal for the Indianapolis Brewery at the Paris Exposition of 1889 was coffee!

Ting-a-ling! (*See also: TQ* 45 and 63.)

See also: PS Roots.

Lieber, Albert II. (*TQ* 41) I will say for the record that my grandfather Albert Lieber's first wife, Alice, née Barus, namesake of my sister Allie, died giving birth to her third child, who was Uncle Rudy. Mother was her first. The middle child was Uncle Pete, who flunked out of MIT, but who nonetheless sired a nuclear scientist, my cousin **Albert** in Del Mar, California. Cousin **Albert** reports that he has just gone blind.

Lieber, Andy. *Kilgore Trout hitches a ride toward the Midland City Arts Festival and is picked up by Andy Lieber in his Ford Galaxie. Lieber becomes a point of departure for Vonnegut to recount the plot of Trout's novel* How You Doin'? *which "was about national averages for this and that." (BC* 17) Kilgore Trout, hitchhiking westward, ever westward had meanwhile become a passenger in a Ford *Galaxie*. The man at the controls of the *Galaxie* was a traveling salesman for a device which engulfed the rear ends of trucks at loading docks. It was a telescoping tunnel of rubberized canvas.

. . . The idea of the gadget was to allow people in a building to load or unload trucks without losing cold air in the summertime or hot air in the wintertime to the out-of-doors. (*He also sold wire, cable, rope, and Excelsior fire extinguishers.*) . . . He was his own boss, in that he represented products whose manufacturers couldn't afford salesmen of their own.

"I make my own hours, and I pick the products I sell. The products don't sell me," he said. His name was **Andy Lieber**. He was thirty-two. He was white. He was a good deal overweight like so many people in the country. He was obviously a happy man. He drove like a maniac. The *Galaxie* was going ninety-two miles an hour now. "I'm one of the few remaining free men in America," he said.

He had a penis one inch wide and seven and a half inches long.

During the past year, he had averaged twenty-two orgasms per month. This was far above the national average. His income and the value of his life insurance policies at maturity were also far above average.

Lieber, Pete. *Vonnegut's uncle, named after his own grandfather.* (*TQ* 41) I will say for the record that my grandfather Albert Lieber's first wife, Alice, née Barus, namesake of my sister Allie, died giving birth to her third child, who was Uncle Rudy. Mother was her first. The middle child was **Uncle Pete**, who flunked out of MIT, but who nonetheless sired a nuclear scientist, my cousin Albert in Del Mar, California. Cousin Albert reports that he has just gone blind.

Lieber, Peter. *One of Vonnegut's maternal grandfathers, readers are first introduced to him in* Palm Sunday. (*PS Roots*) My father and grandfathers were in no wars. Only one of my four great-grandfathers was in a war, the Civil War. This was **Peter Lieber**, born in Dusseldorf, Germany, in 1832. My mother's maiden name was Lieber. This **Peter Lieber**, who is no more real to me than to you, came to America with one million other Germans in 1848. His father was a brush manufacturer. He was living in New Ulm, Minnesota, running a general store and trading for furs with the Indians, when the Civil War broke out. When Abraham

Lincoln called for 75,000 volunteers, **Peter Lieber** joined the 22nd Minnesota Battery of Light Artillery, and served for two years until wounded and honorably discharged.

"The knee-joint of his right leg was permanently damaged, and he walked with a limp to the end of his days," according to my Uncle John Rauch (1890–1976). Uncle John was not in fact my uncle, but the husband of a first cousin of my father, Gertrude Schnull Rauch.

Rauch's history of Peter Lieber continues, a classic tale of businessman turned into a political power broker. (PS Roots) "Almost all of my ancestors delivered themselves directly from Europe to Indianapolis, except for **Peter Lieber** and Sophia de St. Andre, who had the general store in New Ulm, Minnesota. When **Peter** returned from the Civil War with a crippled leg, he was full of stories about how Indianapolis was booming. New Ulm was dead by comparison.

So **Peter**, according to Uncle John, wangled an appointment as one of the secretaries to Oliver P. Morton, the Governor of Indiana. The governor needed a German liaison secretary in his political activities. The pay was good and steady, and **Peter** remained in his office until the close of the war.

"In 1865 came an opportunity for **Peter**. The leading brewery of the city was known as Gack & Biser's. Owing to death of the proprietors, the business was offered for sale. Peter bought it and renamed it **P. Lieber & Co. Peter** knew absolutely nothing of the brewery business, but he engaged a skilled brewmaster named Geiger who did, and proceeded to brew and sell **Lieber's Beer**. It was a successful venture from the very start. **Peter** gave his principal attention to sales, at which he became adept. This involved political activity and manipulation of saloon outlets.

"**Peter** was always involved in politics. He had to be in order to get saloon licenses for his favored customers. Until 1880 he was a staunch Republican, as all the Civil War veterans were. But in that year the Republicans, at the insistence of the Methodist Church, adopted a plank in their platform recommending a restraint upon the beer and liquor trade. It was the first stirring of Prohibition. This outraged **Peter** and was a threat to his interests. He

promptly changed his politics and was thereafter a Democrat—and an aggressive, active one.

"He contributed generously to Grover Cleveland's Campaign Funds, particularly in 1892, when Cleveland was elected President for the second time. He was rewarded by being appointed Consul General of the United States to Dusseldorf in 1893."

Peter Lieber sold his brewery to a British syndicate, which was eager to have **Peter**'s oldest son, my grandfather Albert, run it for them.

Peter returned to Germany in 1893, where he bought a castle on the Rhine near Dusseldorf. He took with him President Cleveland's commission as Consul General of the United States to Dusseldorf. Uncle John says, "He hoisted the Stars and Stripes over his castle, delegated his negligible duties to subordinates, and finished his days in opulence and official grandeur."

Vonnegut quotes John G. Rauch's history of the Vonneguts to explain what happened to the brewery and family fortune first established by Civil War veteran Peter Lieber. (PS Roots) He (*Albert Lieber, Vonnegut's grandfather*), like all rich men, had a miscellaneous assortment of personal property which will be acquired not for investment but as adjuncts of abundant privileges such as miscellaneous securities, paintings, porcelains, furniture, and other art objects. Much had to be sold but he had a few securities left and his estate inventory came to $311,607.65. All that his children got out of the **Peter Lieber** fortune was a small remnant from Albert's estate and a few trust funds which **Peter** had established for them in Merchants Bank stock. And so the proverbial cycle of "shirt sleeves to shirt sleeves" was completed in three generations due for them to Prohibition and Albert's extravagance and improvidence.

In a broad conversation with Kilgore Trout that stems from discussing war and evolves into religion and Trout's alternative to the Book of Genesis, Vonnegut again recalls his great-grandfather. (TQ 7) He asked what relatives of mine had been wounded in wars. As far as I knew, only one. That was my great-grandfather **Peter Lieber**, an immigrant who became a brewer in Indianapolis after being wounded in one leg during our Civil War. He was a Freethinker, which is to say a skeptic about conventional religious beliefs, as had been Voltaire and Thomas Jefferson and Benjamin Franklin and so on. And as would be Kilgore Trout and I.

I told Trout that **Peter Lieber**'s Anglo-American company commander gave his men, all Freethinkers from Germany, Christian religious tracts for inspiration. Trout responded by giving his own revision of the Book of Genesis.

Fortunately, I had a tape recorder, which I turned on.

(TQ 26) "... a great-grandfather of mine on my mother's side switched hemispheres in time to be wounded in the leg as a soldier for the Union in our notoriously uncivil Civil War. His name was **Peter Lieber**. **Peter Lieber** bought a brewery in Indianapolis, and it prospered. A brew of his won a Gold Medal at the Paris Exposition of 1889. Its secret ingredient was coffee."

Lieber, Rudy. *Vonnegut's uncle, the younger brother of Edith Vonnegut. In* Timequake, *Vonnegut recalls that his grandmother Alice Barus Lieber died while giving birth to Rudy, her third child behind Edith and Pete.*

Linberg, Karl. *In the short story "This Son of Mine," collected in* Bagombo Snuff Box *(1999), Karl is a second-generation lathe operator at Waggoner Pump, the son of Rudy Linberg, and similar to his father, a musician (clarinetist), and sharpshooter with a rifle.* "**Karl** always did what his father wanted him to do, did it with profound love. . . . **Karl** was a carbon copy of his father. He was such a good mimic of Rudy that his joints seemed to ache a little with age. He seemed sobered by fifty-one years of life, though he'd lived only twenty. He seemed instinctively wary of safety hazards that had been eliminated from the factory by the time he'd learned to walk. **Karl** stood at attention without humility, just as his father had done."

Similar in age to Franklin Waggoner, heir to the company, the two endured an awkward friendship growing up under the tutelage of their two single fathers. When Franklin visits his father on a weekend home from Cornell, the fathers and sons go shooting one afternoon and it is only then that the reluctant

heir is told by Karl that Rudy's lifelong plan was to position his son to take over the company if Franklin should ever fail to live up to his father's expectations. Franklin has changed his mind about taking over the plant, but Karl only learns of this turn of events after revealing his father's lifelong plotting. "I'm— I'm glad you're not gonna take over the factory," said **Karl**. "That's good—that's great. Maybe, when you come through town with a show, I'll come backstage and see you. That all right? You'll remember me?"

"Remember you?" said Franklin. "Good gosh, **Karl**!" For a moment he felt like the actor he'd dreamed briefly of being.

"Get out from under your old man," said **Karl**, "that's the thing to do. I just wanted to tell you—in case you thought I was thinking something else."

"Thanks, **Karl**," said Franklin. He shook his head weakly.

"But I'm not going to be an actor. I'm going to take over when Father retires. I told him last night."

"Why?" said **Karl**. "Why?" He was angry.

"It makes the old man happy, and I don't have any better ideas."

"You can do it," **Karl** said. "You can go away. You can be anything you want!"

Franklin put his hands together, then opened them to form a flower of fatalism. "So can anybody."

Karl's eyes grew huge. "I can't," he said. "I can't! Your father doesn't just have you. He's got his big success." He turned away, so Franklin couldn't see his face. "All my old man's got is me."

"Oh, now, listen," said Franklin. "Hey, now!"

Karl faced him. "I'm what he'd rather have than the half of Waggoner Pump he could have had for two thousand dollars!" he said. "Every day of my life he's told me so. Every day!"

"Well, my gosh, **Karl**," said Franklin, "it is a beautiful relationship you've got with your father."

"With my father?" said **Karl** incredulously. "With yours—with yours. It's him I'm supposed to get to love me. He's supposed to be eating his heart out for a son like me. That's the big idea." He waved his arms. "The station wagon, the duets, the guns that never miss, the damn-fool son that works on hand signals—that's all for your father to want."

Franklin was amazed. "**Karl**, that's all in your head. You are what your own father would rather have than half of Waggoner Pump or anything!"

"I used to think so," said **Karl**.

"The plate and cube you made," said Franklin, "you gave them to my father, but they were really a present for yours. And what perfect presents from a son to a father! I never gave my father anything like that—anything I'd put my heart and soul into. I couldn't!"

Karl reddened and turned away again. "I didn't make 'em," he said. He shivered. "I tried. How I tried!"

"I don't understand."

"My father had to make 'em!" said **Karl** bitterly. "And I found out it didn't make any difference to him who made 'em, just as long as your father thought I'd made 'em."

Franklin gave a sad, low whistle.

"When my old man did that, he rubbed my nose in what the big thing was to him." **Karl** actually wiped his nose on his jacket sleeve.

"But **Karl**—" said Franklin.

"Oh, hell," **Karl** said, tired. "I don't blame him. Sorry I said anything. I'm OK—I'm OK. I'll live."

Despite Karl's apparent loss to fate and Waggoner family fortune, he tries to convince Franklin that when they return to the firing line, he is going to purposely miss so Franklin can win and make his father proud. Though Franklin nicks the target, Karl can't keep himself from firing a bulls'-eye, either to appease his father's continuing lust to position his son in the good graces of his employer or because his father's competitiveness and conniving are ingrained in his character, as well.

Linberg, Rudy. *A master lathe operator and the first employee at Merle Waggoner's centrifugal pump company in the short story "This Son of Mine," collected in* Bagombo Snuff Box *(1999). Rudy's life is propelled by jealousy and resentment at his employer's good fortune and his skittishness for passing up a partnership opportunity in the early days of the firm. Merle offered him a partnership for only $2,000, but Rudy believed the company was too shaky for the investment. "He was Merle's age, and he had the deep and narrow dignity of a man who had learned his limitations early—who had never tried to go be-*

yond them. His limitations were those of his tools, his flute, and his shotgun."

Rudy and his son Karl share a deep bond, often communicating through gesture rather than with words. Though the two are well matched as amateur musicians, Rudy on flute and Karl on clarinet, the father's rigorous metalworks training in Sweden made him a master artisan, the likes of which were unmatched by the son. Father and son share a love and closeness not enjoyed by Merle and Franklin Waggoner.

In a subtle and devious manner, Rudy grooms his son to fit in the good graces of Merle, hoping that Karl would take over the company if the indecisive and disinterested Franklin would ever walk away from his inheritance. Though Karl reveals to Franklin his father's lifelong plotting, Franklin had already changed his mind and was prepared to run the company after graduation from Cornell.

Lincoln High School (*also* **Ten Square Band** *and* **Black Panthers**). *Under the direction of George M. Helmholtz, Ten Square Band is the name of the Lincoln High School marching band, winners of multiple state championships. The mascot of the school (appearing only as an image on their banners) is the black panther. All are mentioned in three short stories: "The No-Talent Kid," "Ambitious Sophomore," and "The Boy Who Hated Girls." Lincoln High School is also mentioned in the 1955 short story "The Kid Nobody Could Handle" (reprinted in the 1968 collection* Welcome to the Monkey House).

Though unnamed by state, Lincoln High is the primary setting for the short stories "The Kid Nobody Could Handle," "The No-Talent Kid," and "Ambitious Sophomore" (the latter two reprinted in the 1999 collection Bagombo Snuff Box). *In the first story, Helmholtz reclaims the soul of the juvenile delinquent Jim Donnini, the step-nephew of Bert Quinn. In the second story, Helmholtz makes a deal with his C Band's worst clarinetist, Walter Plummer, in order to access Plummer's huge bass drum that he won with quick thinking and action during the liquidation sale of the Knights of Kandahar. Helmholtz feels the lack of such an awesomely sized instrument was the difference between winning and losing his eleventh straight state title the previous season to*

Johnstown High School. In exchange for the drum, Plummer will be responsible for hauling the drum on its own cart during performances. His reward will be what he coveted the entire time—a band sweater with varsity letter.

Lind, Jenny. *"The Swedish Nightingale" who sang at the Opera House in Midland City in 1881. She is immortalized by an historical marker in front of the building which was across from Fairchild Park, the seediest part of town in* Breakfast of Champions.

Lingamon, Cynthia Anne. *Cynthia Anne is murdered by her father Ned Lingamon because she wouldn't stop crying. She wasn't more than an infant. Her brief mention is made by Vonnegut as he extemporizes an incident on the phone in the lounge of the Midland City Holiday Inn. The passage parallels the concept of narrative control and interaction between the author and his fictional creations as seen in Kilgore Trout's novel* Now It Can Be Told. *(BC 19) He had now also committed the lowest crime which an American could commit, which was to kill his own child. Her name was* **Cynthia Anne,** *and she certainly didn't live very long before she was made dead again. She got killed for crying and crying. She wouldn't shut up.*

First she drove her seventeen-year-old mother away with all her demands, and then her father killed her.

And so on.

Lingamon, Ned. *In* Breakfast of Champions, *Midland City's most decorated Vietnam veteran (he won the Congressional Medal of Honor) calls Harold Newcomb Wilbur, the bartender at the Holiday Inn, from jail after being charged with killing his daughter, Cynthia Anne.*

Lingo-Three (*see also* ***Plague on Wheels***). *(BC 2) The words in the book, incidentally, were about life on a dying planet named* **Lingo-Three,** *whose inhabitants resembled American automobiles. (BC 2)* **Lingo-Three** *was visited by space travelers, who learned that the creatures were becoming extinct for this reason: they had destroyed their planet's resources, including its atmosphere.*

Littauer, Kenneth. *Vonnegut dedicates* Cat's Cradle *to* Littauer, a man of gallantry and taste, *and whom he credits as his literary mentor in* Palm Sunday. *Vonnegut recalls that Littauer, when only twenty-three, was a colonel in the Lafayette Escadrille during World War I and the first pilot to strafe a trench (PS 5). Littauer was a literary agent introduced to Vonnegut by Knox Burger.*

(TQ 62) **Colonel Littauer** *sold a dozen or more of my stories, several to Knox (Burger), making it possible for me to quit my job with General Electric and move with Jane and our then two kids to Cape Cod as a free-lance writer.*

(BAG Dedication) In memory of my first agents, **Kenneth Littauer** *and Max Wilkinson, who taught me how to write. (See also: Peter Reed's preface to this text, and Vonnegut's letter to Miller Harris appearing as a prefatory note in* Look at the Birdie.*)*

Little, Dr. Elbert. *In the play entitled* Fortitude, *reprinted in* Wampeters, Foma & Granfalloons, *Dr. Little is a general practitioner from Vermont (recently named Family Doctor of the Year by the* Ladies' Home Journal*) who comes to visit Sylvia, Dr. Frankenstein's experiment in life extension techniques. Sylvia's head is connected to a roomful of wires and computers. She had written to Dr. Little after reading the magazine article about him and asked him to visit and bring cyanide. He shows up without the cyanide and is initially repulsed by all he sees. When Sylvia shoots Dr. Frankenstein with her mechanical arm, Little becomes an important member of the transplant team that detaches Frankenstein's head and reattaches it to a companion set of machines so he and Sylvia can live side by side in perpetuity.*

Little, Sherman Wesley. *In* God Bless You, Mr. Rosewater, *Sherman Little appears as an entry in Eliot's Domesday Book, his ledger for recording the Indiana transactions of the Rosewater Foundation. (GBR 7) "Sherman Wesley Little," wrote Eliot. "Indy, Su-TDM-LO-V2-W3K3-K2CP-RF $300." Decoded, this meant that* **Little** *was from Indianapolis, was a suicidal tool-and-die maker who had been laid off, a veteran of the Second World War with a wife and three children, the second child suffering from cerebral palsy. Eliot had awarded him a Rosewater Fellowship of $300.*

Little Bighorn. *The site of the American Indian victory over General Custer. Reverend Lasher compares the limited and short-lived victory of the modern-day Ghost Shirt Society over the ruling technocracy to that one Indian triumph, however hollow it would inevitably prove to be.* (PP XXXV) "This is like the Indians' massacre of Custer and his men," said Lasher reflectively. "The **Little Bighorn**. One isolated victory against an irresistible tide. More and more whites where Custer came from; more and more machines where these came from. But we may win yet."

In Hocus Pocus, *Eugene Debs Hartke compares the swift dispatch of his youthful, fraudulent science fair crystal exhibition with Custer's defeat. He further compares it with other such swift and just rebukes.* (HP 4) Other people made short work of Father's and my invincible contest entry in Cleveland 43 years ago.

Generals George Armstrong Custer at the **Little Bighorn**, and Robert E. Lee at Gettysburg, and William Westmoreland in Vietnam all come to mind.

Locke, John. *In* Timequake, *while recalling his discussion with Denver brewer John Hickenlooper, Jr., Vonnegut makes a passing reference to another fraternity brother and their activities.* (TQ 44) I was able to tell this young Denver brewer that his dad, in partnership with another Delta Upsilon brother, **John Locke**, sold candy and soft drinks and cigarettes out of a big closet at the top of the stairs on the second floor of the fraternity house.

They christened it *Hickenlooper's Lockenbar.* We called it *Lockenlooper's Hickenbar,* and *Barkenhicker's Loopenlock,* and *Lockenbarker's Loopenhick,* and so on.

Happy days! We thought we'd live forever.

Lonesome No More (*see* **Slapstick** *and* **Sargent Shriver**). *The phrase is Vonnegut's campaign slogan suggestion to Sargent Shriver during his 1972 vice presidential campaign, and later became the subtitle of* Slapstick, *capturing the philosophy behind Wilbur Swain's plan for artificially extended families.*

"Long Walk to Forever" (1960) (*see* **Newt and Catharine**).

Love Crusade. *In* The Sirens of Titan, *the Christian fundamentalist revival tour headed by the Reverend Bobby Denton. His preachments center on the chrono-synclastic infundibula is analogous to the biblical story of the Tower of Babel. Those who attend the Wheeling, West Virginia, meetings are known as Love Crusaders.*

Lovejoy, Sylvia. *The one-hundred-year-old bodiless patient of Dr. Norbert Frankenstein in the play* Fortitude. *When Lovejoy was sixty-four and Frankenstein was twenty-nine, he performed his first lifesaving surgery on her. Since then she has endured seventy-eight operations, leaving her with only her head attached to a series of tubes and computers controlled by Frankenstein's around-the-clock medical team.*

She is naturally despondent with her life, but Frankenstein controls her moods through the application of drugs. At the end of the play, Gloria, Sylvia's compassionate hairdresser, brings her a pistol so she could kill herself with her mechanical arm. However, Frankenstein anticipated she might want to eventually commit suicide, so he designed the arm with a limited range of motion, effectively preventing her from succeeding. Instead, she turns the gun on her doctor and they are next seen in side-by-side hospital beds, two heads connected to a labyrinth of tubes and wires.

"Lovers Anonymous." *First published in the October 1963 issue of* Redbook *and later reprinted in the 1999 collection* Bagombo Snuff Box, *this short story is remarkable for how well it represents the poorly understood tenets of the budding women's movement occurring at the time. The unnamed narrator, an aluminum storm door and window salesman and high school admirer of Sheila Hinckley, notes that she* had been the smartest girl in high school, and had been going like a house afire at the University of Vermont, too. We'd all assumed there wasn't any point in serious courting until she'd finished college.

And then, right in the middle of her junior year, she'd quit and married Herb. *Herb White is a Korean War veteran who studies bookkeeping and taxes via correspondence courses, does the accounting for most of the population of North Crawford, New Hampshire, and shocks everyone when he marries*

Sheila, a very pretty, intelligent woman practically all the men in my particular age group had hoped to marry. *Together they have twin daughters. The narrator is speaking a little more than twenty years after Sheila married Herb.*

Sheila's lofty post–high school goals were only half-jokingly expressed by her as a caption for the yearbook. Despite her gender, the group who knew her best thought it was all possible. As the narrator recalls, Everybody was supposed to predict what kind of work he or she would go into in later life. Sheila put down that she would discover a new planet or be the first woman justice of the Supreme Court or president of a company that manufactured fire engines.

She was kidding, of course, but everybody— including Sheila, I guess—had the idea that she could be anything she set her heart on being.

Sheila's sudden departure from university and all those ambitions are swept away in her blithe replies to the narrator years before at her wedding. I asked her, "Well now, what's the fire engine industry going to do?"

And she laughed and said, "It's going to have to limp along without me. I'm taking on a job a thousand times as important—keeping a good man healthy and happy, and raising his young."

"What about the seat they've been saving for you on the Supreme Court?"

"The happiest seat for me, and for any woman worthy of the name of woman," she said, "is a seat in a cozy kitchen, with children at my feet."

"You going to let somebody else discover that planet, Sheila?"

"Planets are stones, stone-dead stones," she said. "What I want to discover are my husband, my children, and through them, myself. Let somebody else learn what she can from stones."

But this is a tale of personal growth, freedom from the lockstep of gender-based conformity largely unquestioned by society prior to the civil rights and women's movements. The impetus for such growth comes from reading Woman, the Wasted Sex, or, The Swindle of Housewifery. *Authored by an unnamed women's college president, the text challenges historical stereotypes chronicling the second-class status of women. It also points the way to brighter days for both genders by untethering women from*

the traditionally narrow pursuits of family caretaker. The book has only five sections, but their titles indicate a brief historical survey across five million years, establishing proof of its thesis before mapping out the prospects for significantly brighter days provided men and women take the conscious initiative to reorder their priorities and expectations while eschewing old stereotypes. The breadth of the text is glimpsed through the narrator's recording of the individual chapter titles. I looked inside the book and found it was divided in these five parts:

I. 5,000,000 B.C.–A.D. 1865, The Involuntary Slave Sex
II. 1866–1919, The Slave Sex Given Pedestals
III. 1920–1945, Sham Equality—Flapper to Rosie the Riveter
IV. 1946–1963, Volunteer Slave Sex—Diaper Bucket to Sputnik
V. Explosion and Utopia

(It should be noted that Betty Friedan's highly influential book The Feminine Mystique *appeared eight months before this Vonnegut short story.) Reference to Theodore Parker, a Unitarian minister famous for his pre–Civil War activities regarding abolition, women's rights, and his advocacy of a personal relationship with God rather than believing the Bible is without error, is made in both the fictitious* Woman, the Wasted Sex, or, The Swindle of Housewifery *and Betty Friedan's* The Feminine Mystique. *As the narrator read out loud:* "'The domestic function of woman does not exhaust her powers. To make one half the human race consume its energies in the functions of housekeeper, wife and mother is a monstrous waste of the most precious material God ever made.'"

Spiritually and intellectually challenged by such words, Sheila is moved to tears while watching a public television show on the origins of the cosmos. "There was this discussion going on between some college professors about the different theories of how the solar system had been born. Sheila all of a sudden burst into tears, said her brains had turned to mush, said she didn't know anything about anything anymore."

Sheila's determination to finish her degree and become a teacher compels her to arrange for separate living quarters in the ell of the house for Herb so that she has less responsibility for his space and more time to study. To his credit, Herb reads the book after Sheila and is similarly moved, so much so that he begins to feel guilty for perhaps sidetracking her from a more enlightened and productive life. In conversation with the narrator, Herb agrees with his wife's wisdom in having him establish his own living space within the house so that she can have more time to pursue her interests. "I realize now, ten years too late," he said, "that I've ruined that wonderful woman's life, had her waste all her intelligence and talent—on what?" He shrugged and spread his hands. "On keeping house for a small-town bookkeeper who hardly even finished high school, who's never going to be anything he wasn't on his wedding day."

He hit the side of his head with the heel of his hand. I guess he was punishing himself, or maybe trying to make his brains work better. "Well," he said, "I'm calling in all you anonymous lovers I can to help me put things right—not that I can ever give her back her ten wasted years. When we get the ell fixed up, at least I won't be underfoot all the time, expecting her to cook for me and sew for me and do all the other stupid things a husband expects a housewife to do.

"I'll have a little house all my own," he said, "and I'll be my own little housewife. And anytime Sheila wants to, she can come knock on my door and find out I still love her. She can start studying books again, and become an oceanographer or whatever she wants. And any handyman jobs she needs done on that big old house of hers, her handy neighbor—which is me—will be more than glad to do."

It is left to the unnamed narrator, a member of the group calling itself Lovers Anonymous, to view the physical separation in the Hinckleys' home life (he is measuring their house for windows for the ell that Herb will call home) and report that rather than thinking the couple is having marital problems, the reconfiguration of the house is actually a measure of the couple's growth and commitment to Sheila's dreams and highly regarded potential.

In high school and college, Sheila is viewed by the young men in her circle as vibrant, intelligent, *destined to do great works. Admired by these men, none thought they were good enough or smart enough to pursue her. Her unexpected decision in her junior year of college to suddenly marry Herb White leaves the young men dumbfounded. As Hay Boyden states, we ought to call ourselves the Brotherhood of People Who Were Too Dumb to Realize That Sheila Hinckley Might Actually Want to Be a Housewife. Instead, the unnamed narrator, another of Sheila's admirers and as drunk as the others assembled at her wedding, suggests to the group of jealous men that they simplify the unofficial name of their group to Lovers Anonymous. Regardless of how they refer to themselves or wish to make light of the situation, it is ironic that they should think so highly of Sheila's abilities yet be surprised by her decision to marry (especially to one so below her own intellectual accomplishments). After all, the text that is causing everyone to rethink gender-based roles (and limitations) assumes that the vast majority of humanity will assume those roles as a matter of course, that society's basic expectations will lead to conformity and (for women) intellectual repression.*

By the close of the story, the blue-collar narrator appreciates the positive changes brought about in the Hinckleys' ten-year marriage and goes so far as to encourage his own wife to read the book. However, unlike Sheila's previous academic achievements in high school or her successful though short stay in college years earlier, the narrator jokes that he will be able to keep in check his own wife's potential ambitions by slipping her old report card into the red text to be used as a bookmark. Though tinged with a bit of sexist sarcasm, it is a gentle reminder (perhaps humorously) that though the benefits are many for those who are intellectually equipped and prepared to go beyond the limiting expectations of mindlessly assigned gender-based roles, his wife never showed Sheila's kind of academic promise, so she should not let her imagination stray too far from her current role.

Lowell, A. Lawrence. *In* Jailbird, *Walter Starbuck notes that this former president of Harvard University was also chairman of the three-member committee that reviewed the death sentences for Sacco and Vanzetti. Despite the telegrams of thousands who* took issue with the sentence, the committee felt electrocuting the two would serve justice. The incident serves to further Starbuck's continued jabs at Harvard's image as the embodiment of enlightenment and a training ground for society's elite social architects.

Lubbock, Luke. *In* Player Piano, *Luke epitomizes the power of sartorial symbolism. He is first seen leading a parade bearing an enormous elephant tusk before changing uniforms and leading the Royal Parmesans in the same parade. Because the bathrooms are filled with bar patrons, Luke is forced to change costumes in the booth where Ed Finnerty, Reverend Lasher, and Paul Proteus are drinking and discussing societal divisions and the likelihood of class confrontation. As Luke begins to change costume,* Paul relaxed his vigil for an instant to glance at **Luke,** and he was shocked at the transformation.

The man was in his underwear now, ragged and drab, and none-too-clean. And **Luke** had somehow shrunk and saddened and was knobbed and scarred and scrawny. He was subdued now, talking not at all, and meeting no one's eyes. Almost desperately, hungrily, he ripped open the brown parcel and took from it a pale-blue uniform, encrusted with gold embroidery and piped in scarlet. He pulled on the trousers and black boots, and the jacket with its ponderous epaulets. **Luke** was growing again, getting his color back, and as he strapped on his saber he was talkative again—important and strong. He bundled up his other costume in the brown paper, left the parcel with the bartender, and rushed into the street, waving naked steel.

A whistle blew, and the Parmesans fell in behind him, to be led to glorious exploits in a dreamworld those on the sidewalk could only speculate about (PP IX).

At the Meadows executive retreat, Luke appears as a busboy and is later audibly heard as the lone, loudly sobbing individual during the eulogy for the manager of the Pittsburgh Works. Later, Luke appears in Ghost Shirt garb as one of Proteus's interrogators in the Ilium air raid shelter, then as one of the strategic planners of the Ghost Shirt upheaval. Luke informs the conspirators that their plan to infiltrate the upper echelons in major social organiza- tions across the country was about sixty percent successful.

Lucretia A. Mott. *In* Slaughterhouse-Five, *the freighter named for the American suffragette Lucretia Mott transports Billy Pilgrim home after his liberation from a German prison camp. Vonnegut appropriated the incident from his own experience.* (FWD XI) When a Liberty Ship (the *Lucretia C. Mott,* named for a women's rights advocate) had wallowed us back to the United States through severe storms in the North Atlantic, and it was time for me and my buddy to say good-bye for a while (a condition now quite permanent), I said to him, "What did you learn?" The future DA O'Hare replied, "I will never again believe my Government." This had to do with our Government's tall tales of delicate surgery performed by bombers equipped with Sperry and Norden bombsights.

Ludd, Ned (*see also* **Carol Atkins**). (PS When I Lost My Innocence) It is quite awful, really, to realize that perhaps most of the people around me find lives in the service of machines so tedious and exasperating that they would not mind much, even if they have children, if life were turned off like a light switch at any time. How many of your readers will deny that the movie *Dr. Strangelove* was so popular because its ending was such a happy one? I am invited to all sorts of **neo-Luddite** gatherings, of course, and am sometimes asked to speak. I had this to say between rock and roll numbers at an anti nuke rally in Washington, D.C., on May 6, 1979:

"I am embarrassed. We are all embarrassed. We Americans have guided our destinies so clumsily, with all the world watching, that we must now protect ourselves against our own government and our own industries. . . ."

Vonnegut opens chapter 6 of A Man Without a Country *acknowledging a common and too facile charge against him as being anti-technology. After broadly outlining the early 19th century history of Englishman Ned Ludd and his rebellion against advances in mechanical looms, Vonnegut laments the displacement of workers by certain mechanical and computer advances, particularly if they disrupt one's sense of community and personal growth in favor of high-volume production and low worker engagement. The losses Vonnegut fears are economic and highly personal as he frequently speaks of people losing out to technological progress, often leaving them questioning their own value both personally and societally.* (MWC 6) I have been called a **Luddite**.

I welcome it.

Do you know what a **Luddite** is? A person who hates newfangled contraptions. **Ned Ludd** was a textile worker in England at around the start of the nineteenth century who busted up a lot of new contraptions—mechanical looms that were going to put him out of work, that were going to make it impossible for him with his particular skills to feed, clothe, and shelter his family. In 1813 the British government executed by hanging seventeen men for "machine breaking," as it was called, a capital crime.

Luma County Clarion. *Rabo Karabekian's first paying job as an artist came when he drew a picture of Benito Mussolini for the editor of this San Ignacio, California, newspaper (Blue 7).*

Luma County Savings and Loan Association. *The San Ignacio bank nicknamed "El Banco Busto" because it had failed. (Blue 7)* El Banco Busto, moreover, had held the mortgage on the little building whose first floor was Father's shop and whose second story was our home. Father used to own the building, thanks to a loan from the bank. After the bank failed, though, its receivers liquidated all its assets, foreclosing all the mortgages which were in arrears, which was most of them. Guess why they were in arrears? Practically everybody had been dumb enough to entrust their savings to El Banco Busto.

Lutz, Andre. (HP 3) The chief engineer at the (Mohiga) wagon company, for example, whose name was **Andre Lutz**, was a native of Liege, Belgium, and had served as an apprentice to a bell founder there. He would teach Chemistry. His French wife would teach French and Watercolor Painting.

(HP 3) One week before the first class was held, which was in Latin, taught by the Episcopalian priest Alan Clewes, **Andre Lutz** the Belgian arrived

at the mansion with 3 wagons carrying a very heavy cargo, a carillon consisting of 32 bells. He had cast them on his own time and at his own expense in the wagon factory's foundry. They were made from mingled Union and Confederate rifle barrels and cannonballs and bayonets gathered up after the Battle of Gettysburg. They were the first bells and surely the last bells ever to be cast in Scipio. . . .

Andre Lutz gave the new college all those bells, even though there was no place to hang them. He said he did it because he was so sure that it would 1 day be a great university with a bell tower and everything. He was dying of emphysema as a result of the fumes from molten metals that he had been breathing since he was 10 years old. He had no time to wait for a place to hang the most wonderful consequence of his having been alive for a little while, which was all those bells, bells, bells.

Lutz Carillon. *The Lutz Carillon is the set of enormous bells forged by Andre Lutz and donated to the Mohiga Valley Free Institute, later becoming Tarkington College. Among other things, the bell tower is the site of composition, self-reflection, and spiritual delight for Eugene Debs Hartke.* (HP 1) The greatest stroke of luck for me *(Eugene Debs Hartke)*, the biggest chunk of manna from Heaven, was that Tarkington had need of somebody to play the **Lutz Carillon**, the great family of bells at the top of the tower of the college library, where I am writing now. . . .

The happiest moments in my life, without question, were when I played the **Lutz Carillon** at the start and end of every day.

(HP 3) If Henry Moellenkamp hadn't come out of his mother's womb dyslexic, there would never have been a tower in which to hang the **Lutz Carillon**.

(HP 7) Judging from letters to *The Musketeer*, I think the change that generated the most passionate resistance was the modernization of the **Lutz Carillon** soon after World War II, a memorial to Ernest Hubble Hiscock. He was a Tarkington graduate who at the age of 21 was a nose-gunner on a Navy bomber whose pilot crashed his plane with a full load of bombs onto the flight deck of a Japanese aircraft carrier in the Battle of Midway during World War II.

(*HP* 7) In the old days 4 of the bells were famously off-key, but beloved, and were known as "Pickle" and "Lemon" and "Big Cracked John" and "Beelzebub." The Hiscocks had them sent to Belgium, to the same bell foundry where Andre Lutz had been an apprentice so long ago. There they were machined and weighted to perfect pitch, their condition when I got to play them.

(*HP* 8) Most of the letters to *The Musketeer* protesting the modernization of the **Lutz Carillon** are from people who had somehow hung on to the wealth and power they had been born to.

(*HP* 16) In the folder was a report by a private detective hired by Wilder to investigate my sex life. . . . He didn't miss a thing Zuzu and I did during the second semester. . . . There was only 1 misunderstood incident: when I went up into the loft of the stable, where the **Lutz Carillon** had been stored before there was a tower and where Tex Johnson was crucified 2 years ago. I went up with the aunt of a student. She was an architect who wanted to see the pegged post-and-beam joinery up there. The operative assumed we made love up there. We hadn't.

Lynn, Jonathan (*see* **Alfred Planck**).

MacCleary, Lou. *The Executive Manager of National Industrial Security in* Player Piano. *His one scene is in the Council House at the Meadows executive retreat during which he, Kroner, and Gelhorne reveal their plan to Paul Proteus to use him to infiltrate the Ghost Shirt Society.*

Machu Picchu. *In* Slapstick, *Vonnegut uses Machu Picchu as a nexus joining the rise and fall of an ancient and mysterious culture to the fall of all modern culture.*

After Eliza and Wilbur Swain experience an orgasm of creativity yielding their treatise about extended families as well as their theories about relative gravity, Eliza moves to a condominium in Machu Picchu. There she is approached by Fu Manchu, a miniaturized Chinese agent sent to the ancient site in search of lost Inca secrets. She agrees to permit him access to the twins' theories stored in the family mausoleum in Vermont, provided he gets her a trip to the Mars colony established by the Chinese. After Fu Manchu secures the Swain's secrets, China's experiments destroy the planet's gravity. Wilbur recalls: And somewhere in there a night of actual bad gravity crumbled the foundations of **Machu Picchu**. The condominiums and boutiques and banks and gold bricks and jewelry and pre-Columbian art collections and the Opera House and the churches, and *all* that, sloped down the Andes, wound up in the sea.

I cried (*Slap* 39). *Wilbur's divorced wife and their son had moved to the same condominium as Eliza before the disaster.*

MacIntosh, Andrew. *This widower in* Galápagos, *whom Vonnegut describes as* an American financier of great inherited wealth (*Gal* 1:4), *is generally patterned after Malcolm Forbes. (Gal 1:15)* *Andrew MacIntosh didn't even care if he himself lived or died—as evidenced by his enthusiasms for skydiving and the racing of high-performance motor vehicles and so on.*

So I have to say that human brains back then had become such copious and irresponsible generators of suggestions as to what might be done with life, that they made acting for the benefit of future generations seem one of many arbitrary games which might be played by narrow enthusiasts—like poker or polo or the bond market, or the writing of science-fiction novels.

More and more people back then, and not just *Andrew MacIntosh, had found ensuring the survival of the human race a total bore. (Gal 1:18) *Andrew MacIntosh certainly enjoyed his exposure on talk shows. He was a welcome guest on them because he was so outrageous. He held forth about what fun life was if you had unlimited money to spend. He pitied and scorned people who weren't rich, and so on. (Gal 1:18) It is a joke to me that this man should have presented himself as an ardent conservationist, since so many of the companies he served as a director or in which he was a major stockholder were notorious damagers of the water or the soil or the atmosphere. But it wasn't a joke to *MacIntosh, who had come into this world incapable of caring much about anything. So, in order to hide this deficiency, he had become a great actor, pretending even to himself that he cared passionately about all sorts of things.

MacIntosh is the sponsor of a number of guests gathered for "the Nature Cruise of the Century" including Zenji Hiroguchi, creator of Gokubi and Mandarax. Hiroguchi and MacIntosh are shot dead by Delgado, an Ecuadorian soldier foraging for food among stores that had been separated from the general population by barbed wire. They surprise Delgado, who panics and shoots.

MacIntosh's association with Hiroguchi is used by Leon Trout, the narrator of Galápagos, *to write a metaphor applicable to humans in the 20th century as well as one million years later when humanity has returned to the sea:* What he (MacIntosh) meant to get from *Zenji, probably in Yucatan, or surely during "the Nature Cruise of the Century," was *Zenji's signature on an agreement to head a new corporation, whose stock *MacIntosh would merchandize.

Like James Wait, *MacIntosh was a fisherman of sorts. He hoped to catch investors, using for bait not a price tag on his shirt but a Japanese computer genius.

And now it appears to me that the tale I have to tell, spanning a million years, doesn't change all that much from beginning to end. In the beginning, as in the end, I find myself speaking of human beings, regardless of their brain size, as fisherfolk (Gal 1:11).

MacIntosh's constant and frantic telephoning, together with his graceless pursuit of Hiroguchi's partnership, is terribly unsettling for the Japanese inventor. The Hiroguchis' discomfort takes final form with Mandarax's diagnosis. (Gal 1:12) The Hiroguchis could no longer conceive of any good news for themselves which could be delivered by *Andrew MacIntosh. They honestly believed him to be a madman, which misconception, ironically, had been impressed upon them by *Zenji's own creation, which was Mandarax. . . . Mandarax . . . could diagnose with respectable accuracy one thousand of the most common diseases which attacked Homo Sapiens, including twelve varieties of nervous breakdown. . . .

In Yucatan, the Hiroguchis had followed such a daisy chain of questions and answers, describing for Mandarax the behavior of *Andrew MacIntosh. Mandarax had at last displayed these words in Japanese on the screen, which was about the size of a playing card: Pathological personality.

Leon Trout builds on Mandarax's diagnosis of MacIntosh and offers yet another parallel between the present state of humanity and its landed ancestors. (Gal 1:23) There is another human defect which the Law of Natural Selection has yet to remedy: When people of today have full bellies, they are exactly like their ancestors of a million years ago: very slow to acknowledge any awful troubles they may be in. Then is when they forget to keep a sharp lookout for sharks and whales.

This was a particularly tragic flaw a million years ago, since the people who were best informed

about the state of the planet, like *Andrew MacIntosh, for example, and rich and powerful enough to slow down all the waste and destruction going on, were by definition well fed.

So everything was always just fine as far as they were concerned.

MacIntosh, Selena. *When we first see Selena in Galápagos, the eighteen-year-old congenitally blind daughter of Andrew MacIntosh prepares for "the Nature Cruise of the Century." Her mother died while giving birth to Selena. Accompanied by her dog Kazakh, Selena becomes marooned on Santa Rosalia with Captain Adolf von Kleist, Hisako Hiroguchi, Mary Hepburn, and the six Kanka-bono girls. Once marooned, Selena and Hisako pair off to raise the latter's furry daughter, Akiko, born on the island. Vonnegut states that Selena and Hisako die in a suicide pact, but the details of the event are not recorded.*

MacIntyre, Carlyle F *The translator of the 1941, New Directions edition of Goethe's* Faust *cited by Vonnegut in the editor's note to the text (MN Editor's Note).*

Mackay, Charles. *When Vonnegut visited his friend Bernard V. O'Hare to jog his own memory about the bombing of Dresden when struggling with the writing of* Slaughterhouse-Five, *Mary O'Hare insists that Vonnegut not glorify the soldiers' personalities since they really were just children. This led him to think of the Crusades in relation to his own war experience. Bernard O'Hare then pulled down a copy of Mackay's 1841 book* Extraordinary Popular Delusions and the Madness of Crowds. *(SL5 1)* **Mackay** had a low opinion of *all* Crusades. The Children's Crusade struck him as only slightly more sordid than the ten Crusades for grown-ups. O'Hare read this handsome passage out loud:

History in her solemn page informs us that the crusaders were but ignorant and savage men, that their motives were those of bigotry unmitigated, and that their pathway was one of blood and tears. Romance, on the other hand, dilates upon their piety and heroism, and por-

trays, in her most glowing and impassioned hues, their virtue and magnanimity, the imperishable honor they acquired for themselves, and the great services they rendered to Christianity. . . .

Now what was the grand result of all these struggles? Europe expended millions of her treasures, and the blood of two million of her people; and a handful of quarrelsome knights retained possession of Palestine for about one hundred years!

MacKenzie, Joyce. *The governess who teaches German batball to Winston Niles Rumfoord as a young child in* The Sirens of Titan. *She regularly teams with Rumfoord and the butler Earl Moncrief against gardener Watanabe Wataru, his daughter Beverly June, and the stable boy Edward Seward Darlington.*

MacMahon, Bonnie and Ralph. *In* Breakfast of Champions, *Bonnie is the Holiday Inn cocktail waitress who serves Rabo Karabekian a martini with the greeting "Breakfast of Champions." She becomes incensed over Karabekian's flippant remarks about champion swimmer Mary Alice Miller, the Queen of the Arts Festival. Bonnie lashes out at Rabo's $50,000 painting until he explains its significance to her and the patrons at the bar.*

Rabo mockingly suggests Bonnie offer some story with local color to Beatrice Keedsler, another invited artist to the festival. Vonnegut has Bonnie tell Keedsler about Leroy Joyce, a convicted rapist who avoids electrocution by slicing off his penis while on death row at the Shepherdstown Adult Correctional Institution. Joyce put his penis in a cup and hands it to Ralph Hoover, Bonnie's husband and a guard in the Sexual Offenders' Wing of the institution. Vonnegut says this was a true story that originally happened in Arkansas.

Bonnie and Ralph lose most of their assets by investing in a failed car wash in Shepherdstown. Part of Dwayne Hoover's violent rampage includes punching Bonnie, though she succeeds in preventing Dwayne from further beating his son Bunny.

Madeiros, Celestino. *As chronicled in* Jailbird, *Madeiros is already in prison when he admits to the*

killings for which Sacco and Vanzetti had been convicted. All three were executed on the same evening in Charlestown Prison. As one of Vonnegut's many references to the deaths of innocents, he draws this pointed inversion of the traditional image of Christ's execution. (JB 18) As for the last days of Sacco and Vanzetti as a modem Passion: As on Golgotha, three lower-class men were executed at the same time by a state. This time, though, not just one of the three was innocent. This time two of the three were innocent.

Madge. *The unnamed narrator's wife in the 1953 short story "Unready to Wear," reprinted in* Welcome to the Monkey House *(1968). Both husband and wife are members of the Amphibious Pioneers Society, an association of the first five thousand people to follow the teachings of Dr. Ellis Konigswasser, the mathematician who has discovered how to separate one's spiritual essence from the body.*

Madison, Polly. *Circe Berman's pen name under which she publishes twenty-one novels, in* Bluebeard.

Magnum Opus, Incorporated. *Founded and chaired by Noel Constant in room 223 of the Wilburhampton Hotel, Magnum Opus is the holding company for all of Constant's business dealings. Ransom K. Fern (from the Bureau of Internal Revenue) calls on Constant to show him how he should have made $200 million dollars instead of the $59 million he reported. Constant agrees with Fern's assessment and makes him president of the company.* (ST 3) Fern showed him an organizational plan that had the name **Magnum Opus, Incorporated**. It was a marvelous engine for doing violence to the spirit of thousands of laws without actually running afoul of so much as a city ordinance.

The company's base of wealth was Noel Constant's investment scheme based on the Bible. (ST 3) **Magnum Opus** was built with a pen, a check book, some check-sized Government envelopes, a Gideon Bible, and a bank balance of eight thousand, two hundred and twelve dollars. The bank balance was Noel Constant's share in the estate of his anarchist father. The estate had consisted principally of Government bonds.

Constant had the Magnum Opus building constructed directly across the street from the Wilburhampton Hotel. (ST 3) The **Magnum Opus** Building was a slender, prismatic, twelve-sided shaft, faced on all twelve sides with blue-green glass that shaded to rose at the base. The twelve sides were said by the architect to represent the twelve great religions of the world. So far, no one had asked the architect to name them.

(ST 3) Those who want more detailed histories of **Magnum Opus**, Inc., can go to their public libraries and ask for either Lavina [*sic*] Waters' romantic *Too Wild a Dream?* or Crowther Gomburg's harsh *Primordial Scales.*

Mainland (*see* **Meadows**).

Mamigonian, Leo. *The son of Vartan Mamigonian, described as* an Egyptian man of mystery, believed to be an arms dealer *(Blue 27). Leo purchases the estate of Marilee Kemp, the Contessa Portomaggiore, from her late husband's second cousin. (Blue 27)* **Leo Mamigonian** bought all the contents of the palazzo, too, and so must own Marilee's collection of Abstract Expressionist paintings, which was the best in Europe, and second in the world only to mine *(Rabo Karabekian's).*

Mamigonian, Vartan. *Mamigonian is an Armenian survivor of massacre attempts predating that of Karabekian's parents. Cited as both thief and savior by Rabo's parents, Mamigonian's history is one built on predatory relationships. (Blue 2)* "Thank you, **Vartan Mamigonian**," he might say. This was the name of a great Armenian national hero, who led a losing army against the Persians in the fifth century. The **Vartan Mamigonian** Father had in mind, however, was an Armenian shoe manufacturer in Cairo, Egypt, to which polyglot metropolis my parents escaped after the massacre. It was he, a survivor of an earlier massacre, who persuaded my naive parents, who had met on a road to Cairo, that they would find the streets paved with gold, if only they could find their way to, of all places, San Ignacio, California. But that is a story I will tell at another time.

Rabo's father summed up the lessons he learned from his knowledge of Mamigonian as follows:

"Never trust a survivor," my father used to warn me, with **Vartan Mamigonian** in mind, "until you find out what he did to stay alive."

This **Mamigonian** had grown rich manufacturing military boots for the British Army and the German Army, which would soon be fighting each other in World War One. He offered my parents low-paid work of the dirtiest kind. They were fools enough to tell him, since he was a fellow Armenian survivor, about Mother's jewels and their plans to marry and go to Paris to join the large and highly cultivated Armenian colony there *(Blue 3).*

Mamigonian sought to gain the confidence of Rabo's parents in order to get the jewels his mother smuggled out in her mouth. (Blue 3) So **Mamigonian** constructed a fantasy which he proposed to trade for the jewels. He must have found San Ignacio, California, in an atlas, since no Armenian had ever been there, and since no news of that sleepy farming town could have reached the Near East in any form. **Mamigonian** said he had a brother in San Ignacio. He forged letters from the brother to prove it. The letters said, moreover, that the brother had become extremely rich in a short time there. There were many other Armenians there, all doing well. They were looking for a teacher for their children who was fluent in Armenian and familiar with the great literature in that language.

If **Mamigonian** knew a good teacher in Cairo who might be interested, this nonexistent brother wrote, **Mamigonian** was authorized to sell him the deed. This would secure the teaching job for Father, and make him one of the larger property owners in idyllic San Ignacio. *So this is how the Karabekians were swindled out of the family jewels.*

A Man Without a Country. *Originally published in 2005 by Seven Stories Press and later reprinted in 2007 by Random House,* A Man Without a Country *stitches together various autobiographical snippets intended to explain how Vonnegut comes to the conclusion that he has to give up his national identity as well as any association with humanity in general. He feels this way because those in power too often rely on misinformation or misperceptions presented as generally accepted principles. He points out the dangerous falsehoods of such views based on nothing more than guesses, myths, and poorly conceived ste-*

reotypes. *Interestingly, though he strenuously makes his case against all sorts of uninspected "isms," his Author's Note at the close of the text reaffirms his deep affection for other artists and writers engaged in soulful expression.*

Each chapter is preceded by one of Vonnegut's "samplers," aphorisms that he wrote and later had artistic collaborator Joe Petro III produce as silk-screens. Within the chapters, sections are visually cued by Vonnegut's well-known asterisk (his rendering of a rectum, the image of an asshole that he famously uses in his signature).

President George W. Bush is a frequent target for Vonnegut, emblematic of those who willingly operate with too little information or decide to take action based on the myths passed down by previous generations.

As with so much of Vonnegut's work, he abhors willful ignorance and the unquestioned belief in myths that too often make enemies of otherwise benign souls. He points out that our wars as well as the impending destruction of the planet due to climate change (the result of man's unchecked, unstudied advances in technology) are prime examples of the dangers inherent in simply following the consumerist herd and the advice of politicians whose "guesses" are often based on something other than fact.

In the end, Vonnegut finds a way to reclaim his humanity and a sense of beauty by exploring the souls of artists. What follows is a chapter by chapter review of events as well as a series of explanations that tie the construction of the essays to his larger thesis.

1. As a kid I was the youngest—

Vonnegut opens the text with a brief overview of how he developed a sense for what is humorous: the comedy inherent within tragedy (with nods to Laurel and Hardy); understanding the arc of a comic setup as learned listening to comics during the Golden Age of Radio; stating that while he considers almost all topics and tragedies open to comedic treatment, he draws the line at such things as the Holocaust and the assassinations of President Kennedy and Rev. Dr. Martin Luther King. The lessons of Vonnegut's earliest years taught him that humor can gain much wanted attention and instill a sense of belonging within his family. His humor, however, needed to be

relevant within his family of highly educated and culturally progressive elders.

2. Do you know what a twerp is?

Without specifically noting his own transition between essays, Vonnegut moves the reader from his personal record of striving to be a relevant final sibling in a family of seriously thoughtful individuals (descendants of a notable legacy in their hometown's cultural development) to the extreme opposite: a twerp.

Vonnegut's sense of a "twerp" reflects one who unintentionally lacks or purposely avoids a broad, deep, and reflective education. This wide-ranging section ties together all sorts of ignorance, willful or otherwise, as illustrated by his concerns with art, literature, science, socialism and religion.

He praises hallmarks of high art and democratic ideals including Ambrose Bierce's "Occurrence at Owl Creek Bridge" (which he regards as the greatest American short story), Duke Ellington's "Sophisticated Lady," and the Franklin stove (Franklin did not patent his stove because he wanted its technology to spread widely for the benefit of others). He continues, I consider anybody a twerp who hasn't read Democracy in America by Alexis de Tocqueville. There can never be a better book than that one on the strengths and vulnerabilities inherent in our form of government.

Want a taste of that great book? *He says, and he said it 169 years ago, that* in no country other than ours has love of money taken a stronger hold on the affections of men. Okay? (MWC 2)

Without directly addressing cultural critics who often decry thought-provoking art, Vonnegut reminds his readers all great literature . . . is all about what a bummer it is to be a human being (MWC 2).

Vonnegut extends his concern to the willful abandonment of knowledge by taking frequent swipes at climate change deniers, representatives of an ecologically unsupportable fossil fuel based transportation scheme that he believes will destroy the planet. He also forgives some of humanity's shortsightedness by reminding us that, from an evolutionary standpoint, the intellectual development of man is relatively recent.

Vonnegut again speaks with pride of his midwestern roots, particularly the Great Lakes people who *stood in the vulnerable vanguard advancing the cause of the common working man by aligning themselves with both unionized labor movements as well as a form of pure socialism.* (MWC 2) Like me, many American socialists were freshwater people. Most Americans don't know what the socialists did during the first half of the past century with art, with eloquence, with organizing skills, to elevate the self-respect, the dignity and political acumen of American wage earners, of our working class.

His defense of socialism resides in basic tenets of Christianity and by noting the misrepresentation of socialism through political fear-mongering. (MWC 2) "Socialism" is no more an evil word than "Christianity." Socialism no more prescribed Joseph Stalin and his secret police and shuttered churches than Christianity prescribed the Spanish Inquisition. Christianity and socialism alike, in fact, prescribe a society dedicated to the proposition that all men, women, and children are created equal and shall not starve.

Vonnegut's spirited defense of socialist ideals ties together his adulation of childhood hero and Indianapolis native Powers Hapgood with the core of Christian compassion. (MWC 2) We met in Indianapolis after the end of the Second World War. He had become an official in the CIO. There had been some sort of dust-up on a picket line, and he was testifying about it in court, and the judge stops everything and asks him, "Mr. Hapgood, here you are, you're a graduate of Harvard. Why would anyone with your advantages choose to live as you have?" Hapgood answered the judge: "Why, because of the Sermon on the Mount, sir."

The essay's closing portions disclose Vonnegut's pride in coming from a line of artists whose background was in fact more scientific than usual, to his usual swipe at university English departments that avoid contact with science departments, staffed by the very same literary critics who labeled him a science-fiction writer simply because his works included considerations of technology.

I did not want to be classified as one, so I wondered in what way I'd offended that I would not get credit for being a serious writer. I decided that it was because I wrote about technology, and most fine American writers know nothing about technology. I got classified as a science fiction writer simply

because I wrote about Schenectady, New York. My first book, *Player Piano*, was about Schenectady. There are huge factories in Schenectady and nothing else. I and my associates were engineers, physicists, chemists, and mathematicians. And when I wrote about the General Electric Company and Schenectady, it seemed a fantasy of the future to critics who had never seen the place.

I think that novels that leave out technology misrepresent life as badly as Victorians misrepresented life by leaving out sex (MWC 2).

Vonnegut's final reflections about the dynamic of being broadly educated (an artist reflecting the depth of his family's concerns, his regional influences and worldly experiences) yields a revelation about his success with Slaughterhouse-Five *that addresses his acceptance of the confluence of knowledge and humanitarian concerns that can only be termed serendipitous.*

But I think the Vietnam War freed me and other writers, because it made our leadership and our motives seem so scruffy and essentially stupid. We could finally talk about something bad that we did to the worst people imaginable, the Nazis. And what I saw, what I had to report, made war look so ugly. You know, the truth can be really powerful stuff. You're not expecting it.

Of course, another reason not to talk about war is that it's unspeakable (MWC 2).

3. Here is a lesson in creative writing.

Having established his bona fides as a writer, Vonnegut launches into his familiar comical refrains and witticisms against a life devoted to art and the humanities before deconstructing character development in familiar stories. Vonnegut juxtaposes the constricting formalities and commoner's scorn for academic pretentiousness against the ad hominem attacks on those in stereotypical pursuit of studying arts and humanities—those people who remind us that looking at art, living a life of self-reflection, leads to such a seminal question about the history of humanity as this: "Hey, what was the good news and what was the bad news?" (MWC 3).

Vonnegut initiates this essay with his half-serious, half-comic warning against using semicolons, sarcastically pointing out that they are grammatically superfluous, signifying no more than the author's college attendance. This bitter insight is undoubtedly tied to his displeasure with university critics who offensively labeled him a science-fiction writer. He goes on to pity the poor humanities majors whose heartfelt pursuits will no doubt bring unconsolable pain to their parents. (MWC 3) If you want to really hurt your parents, and you don't have the nerve to be gay, the least you can do is go into the arts. I'm not kidding. The arts are not a way to make a living. They are a very human way of making life more bearable. Practicing an art, no matter how well or badly, is a way to make your soul grow, for heaven's sake. Sing in the shower. Dance to the radio. Tell stories. Write a poem to a friend, even a lousy poem. Do it as well as you possibly can. You will get an enormous reward. You will have created something.

The focus of the essay quickly turns to Vonnegut's famous graphs of classical stories such as Cinderella, The Metamorphosis, *and* Hamlet. *Graphed along a vertical G-I axis (good fortune and ill fortune) and a horizontal B-E axis (beginning and end), Vonnegut reduces plot to a series of familiar outcomes. Though the resulting graphs hint only at the essential movements of major characters relative to plot development, Vonnegut points out that it is the characterizations within those spare graphical movements that determine a work's value, and that includes its often bewildering, subtly ambiguous revelations exemplified by his brief analysis of Polonius after Hamlet stages the play-within-the-play intended to catch his Uncle Claudius.*

After this flop Hamlet ends up talking with his mother when the drapes move, so he thinks his uncle is back there and he says, "All right, I am so sick of being so damn indecisive," and he sticks his rapier through the drapery. Well, who falls out? This windbag, Polonius. This Rush Limbaugh. And Shakespeare regards him as a fool and quite disposable.

You know, dumb parents think that the advice that Polonius gave to his kids when they were going away was what parents should always tell their kids, and it's the dumbest possible advice, and Shakespeare even thought it was hilarious.

"Neither a borrower nor a lender be." But what else is life but endless lending and borrowing, give and take?

"This above all, to thine own self be true." Be an egomaniac! (MWC 3).

Vonnegut's graphs of classic stories break down the common arcs of iconic stories, thematically distinct from one another but run through a critical method applicable to all of humanity's travails as told through the written story. They represent patterns of understanding that repeat themselves in all cultures because there are only so many arcs to the human story regardless of the complexity of the culture that produces a given story. In the end, we are left with a moment of self-reflection and the need to sort out the values at play in our histories.

But there's a reason we recognize *Hamlet* as a masterpiece: it's that Shakespeare told us the truth, and people so rarely tell us the truth in this rise and fall here (*indicates blackboard*). The truth is, we know so little about life, we don't really know what the good news is and what the bad news is.

And if I die—God forbid—I would like to go to heaven to ask somebody in charge up there, "Hey, what was the good news and what was the bad news?" (MWC 3).

4. I'm going to tell you some news.

This chapter is Vonnegut's indictment of our collective guilt over the worldwide transportation/fossil fuel nexus that will one day lead to our own economic and environmental catastrophes once these limited fuels are only sparingly available. His method for getting there is brief and begins with his own personal self-destructive habit: smoking. Quoting the old song "Cigarettes and Whiskey and Wild, Wild Women," he defines a smoker as A fire at one end and a fool at the other (MWC 4). Vonnegut's familiar refrain about the lies of the Brown and Williamson Tobacco Company (manufacturers of Pall Mall, his choice of cigarette since the age of twelve) stamping their packages with all sorts of dire warnings about illness and early death, simply did not come true. Vonnegut sarcastically points out Brown and Williamson's false promises to take him out of his misery with an early death meant that he has had to live long enough to witness other atrocities, that The last thing I ever wanted was to be alive when the three most powerful people on the whole planet would be named *(George W.)* Bush, Dick and Colon (MWC 4).

Vonnegut morphs his exposition moving from personal addiction to societal habits whose results are significantly more dire than the consequences of just one person's destructive habits. Requiring an inexhaustible supply of fossil fuels as well as accepting its negative environmental and social ills, the results of our current transportation technologies come chillingly close to an individual's responses to addiction—only the implications for society are writ large. (MWC 4) Here's what I think the truth is: We are all addicts of fossil fuels in a state of denial. And like so many addicts about to face cold turkey, our leaders are now committing violent crimes to get what little is left of what we're hooked on.

5. Okay, now let's have some fun.

Vonnegut titillates his reader by opening with the prospect of talk about sex, a topic he seldom writes about except by inference. However, he quickly turns the discussion not to the act of sex or even sensuality but to the differences between the sexes as a way of homing in on one of his most memorable themes, extended families.

Starting from the premise that women want many people to speak with and that men want a lot of pals, Vonnegut then provides his answer to society's increasing divorce rates.

Why are so many people getting divorced today?

It's because most of us don't have extended families anymore. It used to be that when a man and a woman got married, the bride got a lot more people to talk to about everything. The groom got a lot more pals to tell dumb jokes to.

A few Americans, but very few, still have extended families. The Navahos. The Kennedys.

But most of us, if we get married nowadays, are just one more person for the other person. The groom gets one more pal, but it's a woman. The woman gets one more person to talk to about everything, but it's a man.

When a couple has an argument nowadays, they may think it's about money or power or sex or how to raise the kids or whatever. What they're really saying to each other, though without realizing it, is this: "You are not enough people!" (MWC 5).

He briefly mentions President George W. Bush and his wife, Laura, as surrounded by an enormous extended family, what we should all have—I mean judges, senators, newspaper editors, lawyers, bankers. They are not alone. That they are members of an extended family is one reason they are so comfortable (MWC 5). *Vonnegut returns to his own example as emblematic of what was once an insulated community of German Americans who immigrated almost en masse to establish communities in America representing what they left behind. The strength of his own community's entrance to the larger American community began a long struggle to undo myths of their cultural legacy on their way to assimilation both culturally and financially. Even his own first marriage to Jane Marie Cox in 1945 is challenged by* one of her uncles *(who)* asked her if she really "wanted to get mixed up with all those Germans" (MWC 5).

Vonnegut points out that sometimes those extended families clash in unexpected ways but that the movement of first-generation immigrant groups (typically those with the closest cultural ties to their geographical past) can cause large shifts in thinking by those already here. (MWC 5) They arrived at a time when the Anglo ruling class, like our polyglot corporate oligarchs of today, wanted the cheapest and tamest workers they could find anywhere in the whole wide world. The specifications for such persons, then as now, were those listed by Emma Lazarus in 1883: "tired," "poor," "huddled," "wretched," "homeless," and "tempest-tost." And people like that had to be imported back then. Jobs couldn't, as today, be sent to them right where they were so unhappy. Yes, and they were coming here any way they could, by the tens of thousands.

But in the midst of this tidal wave of misery was what would in retrospect seem to the Anglos a Trojan horse, one filled with educated, well-fed, middle-class German businessmen and their families, who had money to invest. . . .

And these guilt-free people, speaking English at work but German at home, built not only successful businesses, most strikingly in Indianapolis and

Milwaukee and Chicago and Cincinnati, but their own banks and concert halls and social clubs and gymnasia and restaurants, and mansions and summer cottages, leaving the Anglos to wonder, with good reason, I have to say, "Who the hell's country *is* this anyway?"

6. I have been called a Luddite.

This chapter beguiles the reader by recalling the small, highly personal moments in Vonnegut's life made possible because he does not readily adapt to either the computer era or the big-box store consumerism enabling the hoarding of goods for the sake of efficiency. The placement of this chapter, one that emphasizes socialization over time-saving strategies that limit an awareness of one's community, is thematically connected to the previous chapter because both call for a personal appreciation of one's neighbors. Whether one operates within the confines of an extended family or more broadly seeks out socialization, even assimilation, with the surrounding culture, Vonnegut points out the personal gains to be made by increasing our personal presence within the community. He supports his assertion while describing his rounds to a local stationery store and the local post office. In one he takes great pleasure in describing the otherworldliness of his Hindu clerk in the store: The woman behind the counter has a jewel between her eyes. Now isn't that worth the trip? *(MWC 6). He even relishes the opportunity to describe the sensory perceptions at play in licking the seal and fixing in place the small iron clasp on a manila envelope. This part undoubtedly addresses the sensory experiences lost to those who use email.*

From stationery store to post office, where he harbors a secret love for the female postal clerk whom he sees only from above the waist, Vonnegut imagines that her daily dress and hairdo are calculated to please his polyglot neighborhood that closely borders the United Nations complex in New York. (MWC 6) But every day she will do something with herself above her waist to cheer us up. Sometimes her hair will be all frizzy. Sometimes she will have ironed it flat. One day she was wearing black lipstick. This is all so exciting and so generous of her, just to cheer us all up, people from all over the world.

So I wait in line, and I say, "Hey what was that language you were talking? Was it Urdu?" I have nice chats. Sometimes not. There is also, "If you don't like it here, why don't you go back to your little tinhorn dictatorship where you came from?" One time I had my pocket picked in there and got to meet a cop and tell him about it. Anyway, finally I get up to the head of the line. I don't reveal to her that I love her. I keep poker-faced. She might as well be looking at a cantaloupe, there is so little information in my face, but my heart is beating. And I give her the envelope, and she weighs it, because I want to put the right number of stamps on it, and have her okay it. If she says that's the right number of stamps and cancels it, that's it. They can't send it back to me. I get the right stamps and I address the envelope to Carol in Woodstock.

Carol Atkins is Vonnegut's typist, more rightly retypist. He would type his own pages, correct them by hand, and then send them to Carol Atkins for retyping. Of course he could avoid sending her such pages and correct them himself, but then he would lose the small talk and friendship of a loyal employee and friend, the chance to see his exotic stationery store clerk, miss the opportunity to feel his heart beat faster when visiting his always surprising postal clerk, and generally miss the ambience of his neighborhood. All this would be gone for the sake of using a computer and buying his stationery and stamps in bulk. He closes with a familiar Vonnegut remark. (MWC 6) Electronic communities build nothing. You wind up with nothing. We are dancing animals. How beautiful it is to get up and go out and do something. We are here on Earth to fart around. Don't let anybody tell you any different.

7. I turned eighty-two on November 11, 2004.

*Vonnegut's seventh chapter is a look backward, taking note along the way of life's big question (*What is life all about? *[MWC 7]), his appreciation of music (particularly the blues), his assessment of what foreigners think of America today, runaway technology that threatens the life support systems of the planet as reflected in our diminishing expectations for the future, the dehumanizing affects of wielding absolute power, and the poetic strains of Twain and Lincoln (the latter most notably for his rhetorical abilities indicating both the common sentiments for his time while capturing the timelessness of war's romanticized versions of bloodshed). The chapter's fu-*

sion of such seemingly disparate ideas is in fact organically connected, proving once again how easily Vonnegut manages to tie together the loose strings of life (cat's cradle, anyone?).

Dr. Mark Vonnegut answers his father's question about the purpose of life as follows. (MWC 7) Father, we are here to help each other get through this thing, whatever it is.

As for Vonnegut's reverence for the broad musical genre of American blues, his facetious response suggests a potential epitaph for his headstone: THE ONLY PROOF HE NEEDED FOR THE EXISTENCE OF GOD WAS MUSIC (MWC 7). More important, he makes the point of reminding readers that this is America's only indigenous music and that it came from the fatiguing depression and legacy of slavery. As Vonnegut notes, the priceless gift that African Americans gave the whole world when they were still in slavery was a gift so great that it is now almost the only reason many foreigners still like us at least a little bit. That specific remedy for the worldwide epidemic of depression is a gift called the blues. All pop music today—jazz, swing, be-bop, Elvis Presley, the Beatles, the Stones, rock-and-roll, hip-hop, and on and on—is derived from the blues (MWC 7).

Vonnegut transitions the discussion from the blues to personal depression (his own admitted lifelong malady), by referencing his friend and jazz historian Albert Murray. Vonnegut recounts Murray's telling him that during the era of slavery in this country—an atrocity from which we can never fully recover—the suicide rate per capita among slave owners was much higher than the suicide rate among slaves.

Murray says he thinks this was because slaves had a way of dealing with depression, which their white owners did not: They could shoo away Old Man Suicide by playing and singing the Blues. He says something else which also sounds right to me. He says the blues can't drive depression clear out of a house, but can drive it into the corners of any room where it's being played. So please remember that (MWC 7).

As for the views foreigners have of the United States, Vonnegut answers in a way that alludes to President George W. Bush's assessment that some in the world (particularly the Islamic world) hate America for its freedoms. Instead, he notes jazz as a posi-

tive entrée to American culture, denies as nonsense that those who hate us do so for our freedoms, and stresses that our military involvements around the world have earned the world's disdain for our actions. (MWC 7) Foreigners love us for our jazz. And they don't hate us for our purported liberty and justice for all. They hate us now for our arrogance.

As a corollary to Vonnegut's long-expressed belief that relatively speaking we all just got here and have little idea how to clean up the mess of past conflicts, epidemics, national enmities, and the oppression of new technologies, he offers the analysis that collectively we are heir to a shockingly recent history of human slavery, to an AIDS epidemic, and to nuclear submarines slumbering on the floors of fjords in Iceland and elsewhere, crews prepared at a moment's notice to turn industrial quantities of men, women, and children into radioactive soot and bone meal by means of rockets and H-bomb warheads. Our children have inherited technologies whose byproducts, whether in war or peace, are rapidly destroying the whole planet as a breathable, drinkable system for supporting life of any kind.

Anyone who has studied science and talks to scientists notices that we are in terrible danger now. Human beings, past and present, have trashed the joint.

The biggest truth to face now—what is probably making me unfunny now for the remainder of my life—is that I don't think people give a damn whether the planet goes on or not. It seems to me as if everyone is living as members of Alcoholics Anonymous do, day by day. And a few more days will be enough. I know of very few people who are dreaming of a world for their grandchildren (MWC 7).

The romanticism of youth held the promise that we could become the humane and reasonable America so many members of my generation used to dream of (MWC 7). Age, education, and personal experience beat the romanticism right out of him.

But I know now that there is not a chance in hell of America becoming humane and reasonable. Because power corrupts us, and absolute power corrupts us absolutely. Human beings are chimpanzees who get crazy drunk on power. By saying that our leaders are power-drunk chimpanzees, am I in danger of wrecking the morale of our soldiers fighting and dying in the Middle East? Their morale, like so many lifeless bodies, is already shot to pieces. They are being treated, as I never was, like toys a rich kid got for Christmas (MWC 7).

Vonnegut follows his assertion that our frontline soldiers have become so much fodder for a distant elite by invoking the prayerful, minimalist, poetic expression of one of his great heroes, Abraham Lincoln, at Gettysburg.

> We cannot dedicate—we cannot
> consecrate—we cannot hallow this ground.
> The brave men, living and dead, who
> struggled here have consecrated it far above
> our poor power to add or detract.

Poetry! It was still possible to make horror and grief in wartime seem almost beautiful. Americans could still have illusions of honor and dignity when they thought of war. The illusion of human you-know-what. That is what I call it: "The you-know-what" (MWC 7).

It is the melding of science, industrial technology, and the history of senseless slaughter—even massacres such as the one he witnessed in Dresden—that move Vonnegut to constantly rejigger the formula in his novels to produce the often grim outcomes he envisions. In opposition to those fans of high-tech warfare who believe their science, their knowledge, their god, and their sense of superior moral values will overcome their less enlightened and gifted enemies, Vonnegut offers his experience to debunk such hokum.

Its enthusiasts, its fans, if I may call them that, assume that leaders of political entities we find inconvenient or worse are capable of pity for their own people. If they see or at least hear about fricasseed women and children and old people who looked and talked like themselves, maybe even relatives, they will be incapacitated by weepiness. So goes the theory, as I understand it.

Anyone who believes that might as well go all the way and make Santa Claus and the tooth fairy icons of our foreign policy (MWC 7).

Having recalled his witnessing such horrors, Vonnegut apostrophizes the humanism and poetry of Twain and Lincoln on similar matters. (MWC 7) One of the most humiliated and heartbroken pieces Mark Twain ever wrote was about the slaughter of six hundred Moro men, women, and children by our soldiers during our liberation of the people of the Philippines after the Spanish-American War. Our brave commander was Leonard Wood, who now has a fort named after him. Fort Leonard Wood in Missouri.

As for Lincoln, Vonnegut reaches for his words as a congressman in 1848 concerning our war on Mexico, which had never attacked us. James Polk was the person Representative Lincoln had in mind when he spoke. Abraham Lincoln said of Polk, his president, his armed forces' commander-in-chief:

> Trusting to escape scrutiny, by fixing the public gaze upon the exceeding brightness of military glory—that attractive rainbow, that rises in showers of blood—that serpent's eye, that charms to destroy—he plunged into war.

Holy shit! And I thought I was a writer! (MWC 7)

Vonnegut further points out that slavery was illegal in Mexico and this was one of the reasons U.S. settlers in Texas fought to break away from what was legitimate Mexican territory. It was this war that also brought into the U.S. fold California, Utah, Nevada, Arizona, and parts of New Mexico, Colorado, and Wyoming (MWC 7).

Vonnegut finishes the chapter with another swipe at George W. Bush. His message is that Bush plunged us into war with the Arabs because he simply did not understand them; that his arrogant Americanism, similar to President Polk and Leonard Wood, remains a hallmark of humanity's long list of atrocities found wherever there is ignorant jingoism, fear, and an unhealthy dose of misdirected scientific know-how.

8. Do you know what a humanist is?

This chapter may be the quintessence of Vonnegut's statements concerning his familial tradition of free-thinking humanism and its relationship to Christi-

anity (the other major religion that has most affected his life). He explores how otherwise educated people cross the line to irrational thought. At best its results may be benign; at worst, it becomes a guessing game of faith, mysticism, and blue skies leading to moral straight jackets and violently jingoistic distinctions between people.

Vonnegut launches this transition at the close of the previous chapter. He points to the writings and speeches of Twain and Lincoln in the aftermath of genocidal massacres of people and language—language abused to blend both justification and glorification of the martial life. And the martial life's most heralded end is in the ultimate sacrifice, which, in the middle of the nineteenth century, often meant the melding of Muscular Christianity with muscular imperialistic policies. He does so to point out that what was once firmly held as axioms from God, those stereotypes and misreadings of the Bible that led to the most immoral official policies, would eventually be declared illegal through the Thirteenth, Fourteenth, and Fifteenth Amendments.

Twain and Lincoln are both descriptive and prescient in their analysis of the psycholinguistic jabberwocky employed to justify unimaginable horrors. They understand the neologized twisting of emotions in preparation for battling incomparable evil, a monster of fantasy. They understand the abandonment of reason, logic, and objective reality in favor of rewoven myths that encourage people to act in their own worst interests by willfully disregarding valid information.

Vonnegut links himself to the midwestern voices of Twain and Lincoln through the traditions of his parents and grandparents, part of the freethinker movement.

So as a humanist I am honoring my ancestors, which the Bible says is a good thing to do. We humanists try to behave as decently, as fairly, and as honorably as we can without any expectation of rewards or punishments in an afterlife. . . . We humanists serve as best we can the only abstraction with which we have any real familiarity, which is our community (MWC 8).

He continues with his common refrain about his presidency of the American Humanist Association, a comical one at that. The brevity and wit of his own style creates an opportunity to toy with language, yielding uncomfortable comic relief at the moment he eulogizes a likeminded friend. He then surprises critics by asking the same treatment for himself.

I am, incidentally, Honorary President of the American Humanist Association, having succeeded the late, great science fiction writer Isaac Asimov in that totally functionless capacity. We had a memorial service for Isaac a few years back, and I spoke and said at one point, "Isaac is up in heaven now." It was the funniest thing I could have said to an audience of humanists. I rolled them in the aisles. It was several minutes before order could be restored. And if I should ever die, God forbid, I hope you will say, "Kurt is up in heaven now." That's my favorite joke.

How do humanists feel about Jesus? I say of Jesus, as all humanists do, "If what he said is good, and so much of it is absolutely beautiful, what does it matter if he was God or not?"

But if Christ hadn't delivered the Sermon on the Mount, with its message of mercy and pity, I wouldn't want to be a human being.

I'd just as soon be a rattlesnake (MWC 8).

The core of Vonnegut's humanism explains his appreciation for core Christian values, values to be lived while here on earth without fear of losing the heavenly kingdom.

Vonnegut comes honestly to the tradition of the freethinkers, since that was his heritage. Having dovetailed his humanism with Christian values, the two dominant religious influences in his life, Vonnegut goes to the heart of his differences with religious belief. Such belief requires an appealing and often harmless intellectual capitulation: believing in myths requires overriding reason, science, observable fact; overriding such objective measures, surrendering one's intellect in favor of fantastical stories, allows a priesthood to rise, developing a rigid schema that separates people according to their adherence to the central myth. Once people are divided over competing myths, a cult of personality can take over (history is his proof) with catastrophic outcomes born of minor differences.

He declares that such believers in myth—their

leaders, especially—are "guessers." Aristotle, Hitler, Ivan the Terrible are all guessers in that they postulated what could not be seen, measured, or fully understood. It is here that Vonnegut transitions his very fluid argument into historic examples of good guessers and bad guessers. Among both types of guessers are persuasive guessers, the pivot step in the argument tying religion to politics—and both are considered unreliable.

Persuasive guessing has been at the core of leadership for so long, for all of human experience so far, that it is wholly unsurprising that most of the leaders of this planet, in spite of all the information that is suddenly ours, want the guessing to go on. It is now their turn to guess and guess and be listened to. Some of the loudest, most proudly ignorant guessing in the world is going on in Washington today. Our leaders are sick of all the solid information that has been dumped on humanity by research and scholarship and investigative reporting. They think that the whole country is sick of it, and they could be right. It isn't the gold standard that they want to put us back on. They want something even more basic. They want to put us back on the snake-oil standard (MWC 8).

Vonnegut's anger rises with the con game. He hates those who conspire, wrapped in the cloak of positive myths and scheming to disenfranchise the "other." He especially hates the religious and political sycophants and grifters who prey on those willing to dismiss science and critical reasoning, willfully abandoning essential knowledge and surrendering the boundaries of their humanity.

Vonnegut follows with a satirical inductive tirade pressing American hot-button issues sensitive on left and right—imponderable, if not impossible to solve geopolitical concerns. He careens from one point to the next with the timing of Henny Youngman one-liners building a litany of snake-oil standards (each presented within the myth that sells it):

- *The myth of Second Amendment insecurity (gun rights);*
- *The myth that spending on universal public healthcare is necessarily inflationary;*
- *The myth that spending on weapons systems necessarily brings down inflation;*

- *The myth that right wing dictators share American values more than left wing dictators;*
- *The myth that our last line of protection ultimately rests in stockpiling hydrogen bombs;*
- *The myth that industrial and radioactive waste pose no threat to humanity now or in the future;*
- *The myth that free enterprise can police itself against waste, fraud, and abuse; against environmental degradation; against anticompetitive manipulations of markets and governing authorities.*

Vonnegut proclaims these are the myths that manifest the free enterprise system, the basis of right wing ideology that has pushed the country to the far right. This is the country he saw while writing in 2005, the middle of the second Bush White House. He goes on to list the other myths he sees prevalent in the right wing perception:

- *The myth that the poor largely brought their problems onto themselves, that their children are meant to clean up their parents' mess as best they can;*
- *The myth that the government is not expected to care for the welfare of its people;*
- *The myth that the invisible hand of the free market will care for people;*
- *The myth that the free market is a just system.*

When looked at in light of the clear midwestern thinking of Twain and Lincoln in the previous chapter, these myths, these sound bites, are what constitute the American conversation. All of these concerns are woven into the fabric of Vonnegut's stories from his earliest publications. Twain and Lincoln stand in defense of Vonnegut's freethinker legacy, his proclamation as a humanist.

The promulgators of myth eschew fact, provide no useful information. Vonnegut uses the guesser's myth of nuclear stockpiles as a source of protection against unraveling misinformation, a lack of information, a lack of clarity, logic, and compassion. When Vonnegut looks at Bush's Washington in 2005, he describes just how it is that people can fall for such mythmaking.

What is the response in Washington? They guess otherwise. What good is an education? The boisterous guessers are still in charge—the haters of information. And the guessers are almost all highly educated people. Think of that. They have had to throw away their educations, even Harvard or Yale educations.

If they didn't do that, there is no way their uninhibited guessing could go on and on and on (MWC 8).

Vonnegut pivots on the example of the powerful who can maintain the fantasy only by ignoring information, disregarding their Ivy educations as soon as possible. Interestingly, Vonnegut says little about the mythic benefits of those Ivy educations for the population in general. However, he does appeal to his readers for critical reasoning, insisting that they neither disregard empirical evidence nor expect many others to listen to them. In wagging his finger at the reader he asks that an education based in observable, measurable dimensions never be disregarded — but like the humanities students who will forever break their parents' hearts for choosing such a major, he wants the reader to understand how isolating such exercises in intellectual engagement can be. (MWC 8) Please, don't you do that. But if you make use of the vast fund of knowledge now available to educated persons, you are going to be lonesome as hell. The guessers outnumber you — and now I have to guess — about ten to one. *As Vonnegut says elsewhere and makes into a poster appearing in the posthumously published* Armageddon in Retrospect,

> IN THE U.S.A.
> IT'S WINNERS
> VS.
> LOSERS,
> AND THE FIX
> IS
> ON.

It is easy to imagine Vonnegut holding up that poster followed by a blackout transition, Vaudevillian style, as he returns to bashing the electoral shenanigans that led to the selection of President Bush, the result of a shamelessly rigged election in Florida, in which thousands of African Americans were arbitrarily disenfranchised, we now present our-

selves to the rest of the world as proud, grinning, jut-jawed, pitiless war-lovers with appallingly powerful weaponry — who stand unopposed.

In case you haven't noticed, we are now as feared and hated all over the world as the Nazis once were (MWC 8).

Vonnegut explains that the ease with which we have been able to follow such winners, such guessers, such unelected leaders is that they have dehumanized millions and millions of human beings simply because of their religion and race. We wound 'em and kill 'em and torture 'em and imprison 'em all we want. *He further insists that we also dehumanized our own soldiers, not because of their religion or race, but because of their low social class* (MWC 8). *They become the tagline, the unreasoned solution to nearly impossible conflicts.*

Vonnegut can take no more. In a life spanning more than eight decades, a world war, his country's participation in the firebombing of a city above his head, seeing the country follow willfully false pretexts for too many wars, he declares his final liberation from the guessers-in-charge. (MWC 8) So I am a man without a country, except for the librarians and a Chicago paper called *In These Times. The willing suspension of disbelief may work for Coleridge's dictate for appreciating the theater, but Vonnegut cannot abide the willing suspension of intelligence in the public sphere. It's too dangerous. His proximate reason for resigning himself to a nationless status is that he can't accept being represented by President Bush and his policies; his willful disregard for educated, critical reasoning; his continually wrong guessing in the face of real information and real American bodies being sent home under false pretenses and in direct contradiction to valid information.*

His resignation goes further than simply nationality. Vonnegut aligns his action with Albert Einstein and Mark Twain *(who)* gave up on the human race at the end of their lives, even though Twain hadn't even seen the First World War. War is now a form of TV entertainment, and what made the First World War so particularly entertaining were two American inventions, barbed wire and the machine gun. . . . Like my distinct betters Einstein and Twain, I now give up on people, too. I am a veteran of the Second World War and I have to say this is not the first time I have surrendered to a pitiless war machine (MWC 8).

Vonnegut leaves this section of thoughtless guessers pointing out that Life is no way to treat an animal, not even a mouse *(MWC 8). In other writings, Vonnegut cites Alfred Nobel as the humanitarian who ironically funds his awards with earnings from his explosives empire. In this instance he points out that the most acclaimed of Western universities, Harvard, was the birthplace of napalm; that both Bush and Hitler claim to be Christians. Any belief system that allows those leaders to share a common heritage is enough to rip out hope.*

As the once reluctant, unappointed guru of the counterculture to whom people were flocking for answers, Vonnegut can only shrug at what has happened to his America and wonder. (MWC 8) What can be said to our young people, now that psychopathic personalities, which is to say persons without consciences, without senses of pity or shame, have taken all the money in the treasuries of our government and corporations, and made it all their own? *And this was all written just a few years before the banking crisis of 2008, the emergence of the Tea Party, Occupy Wall Street, and open reference to the 99 percent as a new touchpoint for discussing social strata.*

Despite his stateless declaration when faced with the bad guessers in charge of so much of life, Vonnegut closes this chapter with a portrait of hope. It is the idea of a truly modern hero. It is the bare bones of the life of Ignaz Semmelweis, my hero. . . . He became an obstetrician, which should make him modern hero enough. He devoted his life to the health of babies and mothers. We could use more heroes like that. There's damn little caring for mothers, babies, old people, or anybody physically or economically weak these days as we become ever more industrialized and militarized with the guessers in charge (MWC 8).

Vonnegut's facts for Semmelweis's story are sometimes a bit confused (Vienna versus Budapest; the circumstances of Semmelweis's death), but whatever poetic license he takes, the core of his presentation stays within the ironic example Semmelweis provides.

Semmelweis ran counter to the medical guessers

of his time in Budapest. After careful observation of the delivery practices at St. Rochus Hospital, he postulated that their comparatively high rate of death among delivering mothers in hospital as opposed to midwife facilities had to do with the cleanliness of the delivering physicians. He suggested that it was perhaps the physicians transferring germs from other patients as well as cadavers in the morgue. His germ theory was without the scientific proof provided twenty-five years later by the work of Louis Pasteur. Semmelweis merely asked his colleagues to wash using a chlorine-based solution.

Vonnegut casts Semmelweis as one of the guessers who had it right but was overtaken by the more powerful medical establishment of his time, much offended by Semmelweis's suggestion that physicians transported death to their patients. However, to quiet his loud public protestations, the hospital changed its practices and the death rate for delivering mothers dropped to almost zero.

Despite his success, Semmelweis is virtually ostracized by the rest of the community and has to leave. Though true, Vonnegut writes that Semmelweis's depression overcame him and he knowingly cut his hand with the scalpel he had just used on a cadaver. He did die of blood poisoning but there are other records of his death that state the blood poisoning was internal due to the beating he received when being unwillingly admitted to an asylum.

Nevertheless, Semmelweis is the hero because he sought out reliable information through logic, reason, observation. Vonnegut sees his withdrawal to a rural hospital as his expression of giving up on people. For maintaining his principles, Vonnegut groups Semmelweis along with Twain and Lincoln.

Just as Vonnegut renounces country and humanity, his example of Semmelweis illustrates the possibility of hope through the everlasting truths of verifiable, earthly, scientific proof and the integrity of individuals ready to pursue its path. Vonnegut points to Semmelweis in making his final appeal to the reader. Those warnings about being different, majoring in humanities, avoiding the guessers who rely on falsehoods and the status quo, these all lead to this one shining example who chose to embrace information rather than myth.

Beyond the guessers' dishonest use of information, Vonnegut also sees within them a Machiavel-

lian zeal for power that has nothing to do with the common welfare, that what they most hate is knowledge that lifts the veil of falsehoods. The guessers revealed something else about themselves, too, which we should duly note today. They aren't really interested in saving lives. What matters to them is being listened to—as, however ignorantly, their guessing goes on and on and on. If there's anything they hate, it's a wise human.

So be one anyway. Save our lives and your lives, too. Be honorable (MWC 8).

This chapter is a call to intellectual arms, to moral rearmament based on the realities of life instead of the myths too easily offered and too easily accepted.

9. "Do unto others what you would have them do unto you."

Along with the call to individual heroism at the close of the previous chapter, Vonnegut opens here with the Golden Rule (and correcting even well-meaning, Western-oriented guessers that the speaker is Confucius—five hundred years before Christ). The thrust of this brief chapter is twofold: maintaining that knowledge is prized above the misinforming myths of the guessers, and that socialism (particularly as articulated by Eugene Debs) is kin to the core teachings of Christianity, specifically the Beatitudes found in Christ's Sermon on the Mount.

Vonnegut seeds the chapter with commonly known phrases and references to popular culture that are either frequently misattributed or require additional materials to critically reason through the statement. Such misattribution is a sign of personal ignorance that may or may not be the legacy of the guessers who have dumbed down education and common information. In the second instance, Vonnegut points to the necessary practice of gathering relevant materials and observations to develop well-informed hypotheses that advance society (as exemplified by Semmelweis).

Vonnegut's novels consistently target the tension between earned knowledge and willful ignorance, the keys to this chapter as well. Along with the error in attribution assumed in the chapter's opening line, Vonnegut:

- *cites the irony of America's negative connotations burdening the word "socialist" when its teachings are so closely aligned with those of Christianity;*

- *illustrates the ignorance of unquestioned repetition when Christians demand that the Ten Commandments be posted in public buildings. And of course that's Moses, not Jesus. I haven't heard one of them demand that the Sermon on the Mount, the Beatitudes, be posted anywhere (MWC 9);*

- *points out that the Republican Party's conservative Christian values (as unofficially vested in George W. Bush, Dick Cheney, and Donald Rumsfeld) fail to reflect the teachings of the Beatitudes;*

- *asserts that* George W. Bush has gathered around him upper-crust C students who know no history or geography, plus not-so-closeted white supremacists, aka Christians, and plus, most frighteningly, psychopathic personalities, or PPs, the medical term for smart, personable people who have no consciences *(MWC 9);*

- *explains that documentarian Michael Moore's title for* Fahrenheit 9/11 *can't be fully appreciated without understanding its reference to Ray Bradbury's* Fahrenheit 451, *a dystopian novel whose focus is the willful abandonment—even destruction—of knowledge and imagination, the denial of access to information especially through books, the only real source of fully vetted information.*

These examples highlight the ongoing tension between the know-nothing guessers and those who believe in the free flow and cultivation of knowledge, which is why Vonnegut cites the heroism of librarians as guardians of knowledge. While on the subject of burning books, I want to congratulate librarians, not famous for their physical strength, their powerful political connections or great wealth, who, all over this country, have staunchly resisted antidemocratic bullies who have tried to remove certain books from their shelves, and destroyed records rather than have to reveal to thought police the names of persons who have checked out those titles (MWC 9).

As a corollary to the saintly actions of librarians, Vonnegut lambasts modern media for its dumbing down of information. The America I loved still exists at the front desks of our public libraries.

And still on the subject of books: Our daily news

sources, newspapers and TV, are now so craven, so unvigilant on behalf of the American people, so uninformative, that only in books do we learn what's really going on.

I will cite an example: *House of Bush, House of Saud* by Craig Unger, published in early 2004, that humiliating, shameful, blood-soaked year (MWC 9).

This chapter contains one of the rare instances when even comedy cannot be called upon to soften Vonnegut's rage. He calls many in the second Bush administration psychopathic personalities (PPs), smart people with no consciences. PPs are presentable, they know full well the suffering their actions may cause others, but they do not care. They cannot care because they are nuts. They have a screw loose! . . .

They might have felt that taking our country into an endless war was simply something decisive to do. What has allowed so many PPs to rise so high in corporations, and now in government, is that they are so decisive. They are going to do something every fuckin' day and they are not afraid. Unlike normal people, they are never filled with doubts, for the simple reason that they don't give a fuck what happens next. Simply can't. Do this! Do that! Mobilize the reserves! Privatize the public schools! Attack Iraq! Cut health care! Tap everybody's telephone! Cut taxes on the rich! Build a trillion-dollar missile shield! Fuck habeas corpus and the Sierra Club and *In These Times*, and kiss my ass! (MWC 9).

Vonnegut's argument is predicated on the soundness of the socialist agenda because it cares about people (the value most prized by his esteemed son Mark, surely one of Vonnegut's true heroes), that socialism is defended by the core concerns of Jesus as expressed in his Sermon on the Mount, and that the majority of the ruling class and media class are populated by nefarious guessers who sacrifice the prize of their educations and critical reasoning in favor of negative myth making.

10. A sappy woman from Ypsilanti sent me a letter a few years back.

Having gone through nine chapters of humor and rage at a society given over to notoriously bad guessers, Vonnegut now faces the fearful slide into chaos presented by such unthinking, insensitive leadership in opposition to many individual personal concerns. Vonnegut uses this chapter to present little more than a handful of questions, observations, and requests speculating on the governance prospects for the country since the Bush administration so brazenly tramples the civil rights of people and the integrity of sovereign nations.

Vonnegut presents part of a letter from a pregnant forty-three-year-old woman in Ypsilanti, Michigan, who has decided to give birth for the first time and is worried about bringing a child into a world full of global terrors and an American leadership that seems to be acting without the agreement of its people, taking actions that are at best constitutionally questionable. She is wary about bringing a new life into such a frightening world (MWC 10).

Vonnegut recalls the man who walked up to him in Pittsburgh with one request: "Please tell me it will all be okay" (MWC 10). *Another fan writes about the absurdity of airline security lines, particularly the need to take off shoes. He is annoyed and wonders if Vonnegut could have imagined such a reflexive and ungraceful response to terrorists. Yet another inquiry seems to agree with the Bush administration's hawkish responses to foreign policy including preemptive strikes against Iraq and al-Qaeda.*

Still another writer from Little Deer Isle, Maine, critiques President Bush by noting that the administration's lies to the public and its treatment of prisoners held in Guantánamo Bay make it virtually impossible to support such policies. As noted by the writer, And how can there ever be peace, and even trust in our leaders, if the American people aren't told the truth? (MWC 10).

A man from San Francisco writes with complete indignation asking how it is possible for the public to be so stupid as to believe the legitimacy of Bush's election. He is upset that people believe the election was settled through votes and not a Supreme Court decision whose pretext stated its decision could never be used as a precedent for other elections. The writer rejects the notion that America is necessarily safer by killing supposed enemies and destroying their countries just because we act on the fears of guessers when they say who poses a threat to the nation.

Vonnegut empathizes with his readers, though his responses are not always helpful in the direct manner they wish to hear. *In response to the pregnant woman from Ypsilanti,* Vonnegut first commiserates with her over the lack of luck for her baby born in a country without a national health plan or decent public education, a country in which the death penalty is still in use and college costs have risen past affordability for almost everyone in the country. The positive side to his message rests in his faith that there will always be individual saints trying to improve conditions for all. (MWC 10) But I replied that what made being alive almost worthwhile for me, besides music, was all the saints I met, who could be anywhere. By saints I meant people who behaved decently in a strikingly indecent society.

To Joe in Pittsburgh, he adapts Eliot Rosewater's christening speech intended for the Moody twins. (MWC 10) "Welcome to the Earth, young man," I said. "It's hot in the summer and cold in the winter. It's round and wet and crowded. At the outside, Joe, you've got about a hundred years here. There's only one rule that I know of: Goddamn it, Joe, you've got to be kind!"

To the gentleman in Seattle complaining about what he sees as the absurd response in the way we secure airliners (especially disconcerting for him is the mandate to remove one's shoes), Vonnegut agrees and points out this is standard operating procedure for the government. However, Vonnegut uses the history of government responses to perceived national threats to make fun of the rule-makers. (MWC 10) The shoe thing at the airports and Code Orange and so on are world-class practical jokes, all right. But my all-time favorite is one the holy, anti-war clown Abbie Hoffman (1936–1989) pulled off during the Vietnam War. He announced that the new high was banana peels taken rectally. So then FBI scientists stuffed banana peels up their asses to find out if this was true or not. Or so we hoped.

To the fearful man trying to equate the unknown danger posed by an individual with a loaded gun to the unimaginable dangers presented by Iraq, who sees danger all about him, Vonnegut answers with equal parts of wit and smarminess, intended to point out the absurdity of living under constant fear and suspicion of everyone around him. (MWC 10) Please, for the sake of us all, get a shotgun, preferably a 12-gauge double-barrel, and right there in your own neighborhood blow off the heads of people, cops excepted, who may be armed.

Vonnegut shares with readers the exasperated words of *a correspondent from Little Deer Isle, Maine, complaining about the union of leadership and media in promulgating the worst images of the nation's enemies, finally asking* And how can there ever be peace, and even trust in our leaders, if the American people aren't told the truth? *Aside from belittling our government and its emphasis on Christian values as we battle with the Islamic world,* Vonnegut resorts to Shakespeare to explain the disappointing circumstances prompting his forlorn fan's questions. (MWC 10) "The devil can cite Scripture for his purpose."

The final letter cited by Vonnegut is *from a San Franciscan who sees nothing but cruel irony in the war reasoning of President Bush, fantasizing that once people wised up to the rhetorical and humanitarian fallacies at the core of the Bush message, Americans would regroup and demand a sincerely humanitarian approach to our conflicts.* Vonnegut replies with a grim resignation that evil and stupidity will forever challenge humanity. As proof, he offers the central theme of Mark Twain's final and unfinished text, *The Mysterious Stranger.* (MWC 10) I told him that if he doubted that we are demons in Hell, he should read *The Mysterious Stranger,* which Mark Twain wrote in 1898, long before the First World War (1914–1918). In the title story he proves to his own grim satisfaction, and to mine as well, that Satan and not God created the planet earth and "the damned human race." If you doubt that, read your morning paper. Never mind what paper. Never mind what date.

11. Now then, I have good news for you and some bad news.

Aside from the opening gag promised in this first line, this chapter's humor is predicated on the given condition that there are some humans who pay at-

tention to all the terrible stuff we have done to the planet and each other—but there are also all the unthinking ones who either don't care what we are doing to the planet and our neighbors or are part of the deplorable guessing elite. It is certainly a natural outgrowth of the text's development, one that also enables Vonnegut to include references to an unfinished novel (If God Were Alive Today) as well as Kilgore Trout.

The chapter opens with news that Martians landed in New York and are staying at the Waldorf Astoria. In a scenario that could appeal only to the right wing's elite guessers and unthinking people everywhere, the good news is that they only eat homeless men, women, and children of all colors, and they pee gasoline *and poop uranium (MWC 11). A right-wing win-win is thwarted when the Martians decide to leave* because they know how terrible global warming was about to become (MWC 11). *The six-inch-tall unnamed leader of the Martian mission, a female who parts Earth with an observation on a couple of American activities that are simply incomprehensible to Martians, asks* "What is it . . . what can it possibly be about blowjobs and golf?" (MWC 11).

Vonnegut points out that this bit of science fiction mixed with political and environmental concerns is part of his unfinished novel, If God Were Alive Today. *It focuses on* Gil Berman, thirty-six years my junior, a standup comedian at the end of the world. It is about making jokes while we are killing all the fish in the ocean, and touching off the last chunks or drops or whiffs of fossil fuel. But it will not let itself be finished (MWC 11). *The Martians give up on Earth and humanity because of the irreversible environmental mess humans are heading for, and Gil Berman, a self-described* flaming neuter, *refuses to go along with the media's preoccupation with overt sexuality, implying that their concerns are limited to flashing sexually charged pictures across the tube or advertising goods that in one way or another are all about making one more attractive to the opposite sex. Similar to the Martians who leave the planet because they know just how bad climate change is going to be, Gil Berman says that* God would have to be an atheist, because the excrement has hit the air-conditioning big time, big time (MWC 11).

Having said his piece about humanity destroying the planet, mostly due to our unimaginative answers to alternative power sources for transportation and our generally lazy and wasteful consumer culture, Vonnegut turns his attention to one of his prime interests—time. He speculates on time as circular and recurrent. As such, events that come later in linear time can affect prior events. His interest in time affects another major interest, history.

Here Kurt calls on his alter ego, Kilgore Trout, for a discussion about President Bush's 2004 State of the Union Address. Trout phones Vonnegut to ask about the speech, and during the ensuing conversation Vonnegut cuts loose on the outlandish, self-destructive, even insane activities of mankind.

That night I got a call from my friend, the out-of-print-science-fiction writer Kilgore Trout. He asked me, "Did you watch the State of the Union address?"

"Yes, and it certainly helped to remember what the great British socialist playwright George Bernard Shaw said about this planet."

"Which was?"

"He said, 'I don't know if there are men on the moon, but if there are, they must be using the earth as their lunatic asylum.' And he wasn't talking about the germs or the elephants. He meant we the people."

"Okay."

"You don't think this is the Lunatic Asylum of the Universe?"

"Kurt, I don't think I expressed an opinion one way or the other."

"We are killing this planet as a life-support system with the poisons from all the thermodynamic whoopee we're making with atomic energy and fossil fuels, and everybody knows it, and practically nobody cares. This is how crazy we are. I think the planet's immune system is trying to get rid of us with AIDS and new strains of flu and tuberculosis, and so on. I think the planet should get rid of us. We're really awful animals. . . ."

And I said good-bye to my friend, hung up the phone, sat down and wrote this epitaph: "The good Earth—we could have saved it, but we were too damn cheap and lazy" (MWC 11).

Opposite this page is a chapter-ending Vonnegut drawing of a tombstone with the following inscrip-

tion in caps: LIFE IS NO WAY TO TREAT AN ANIMAL.

12. I used to be the owner and manager of an automobile dealership in West Barnstable, Massachusetts, called Saab Cape Cod.

Vonnegut's final numbered chapter (there are still the "Requiem" and "Author's Note"), divided into five sections separated by his trademark asterisk, ties together the two elements responsible for his artistic legacy: the humor that distinguishes his narrative voice, and the good disposition of readers who embrace his method and message.

The chapter nominally covers his youthful experience as a Saab dealer; the talk of a Nobel Prize for literature that surrounded his career ever since Slaughterhouse-Five; *the assured disappointment of each generation as it realizes the sins of their forebears; depression; technology's unintended subversion of imagination; and a model for appraising creative work as offered by friend and artist Saul Steinberg.*

Vonnegut's first section is an elaborate, self-deprecating two-and-a-half-page joke about his time as a Saab dealer and his lack of a Nobel Prize. His introduction of the topic culminates in a biting one-liner, but this is mere foreshadowing for what is to come. As he says of his Saab Cape Cod dealership, It and I went out of business thirty-three years ago. The Saab then, as now, was a Swedish car, and I now believe my failure as a dealer so long ago explains what would otherwise remain a deep mystery: Why the Swedes have never given me a Nobel Prize for Literature. Old Norwegian proverb: "Swedes have short dicks but long memories" *(MWC 12).*

What follows is an elaborate setup full of easy one-line gags including praise for the Saab's unusual engine that required all sorts of attentiveness (very frequent use of additional oil) to avoid a smoky disaster, and just the kind of ignorant guesser's belief in the myth of Swedish technical precision that so well portends a bad if not comical outcome. (MWC 12) There was this as well: As one prospective customer said to me, "They make the best watches. Why wouldn't they make the best cars, too?" I was bound to agree . . . It was the wet dream, if you like, of en-gineers in an airplane factory who's never made a car before.

Once Vonnegut has the reader bound up in the mechanical oddities of the engine (the suicide doors opening into the slipstream*) and the general geekiness of the car that failed to appeal to straight women (MWC 12)—his implication that only masculine lesbians would find the car's challenges appealing—piling one myth on top of another. The humor trap is ready to be snapped.*

But if you stayed away too long . . . the oil would separate from the gas and sink like molasses to the bottom of the tank. So when you started up again, you would lay down a smokescreen like a destroyer in a naval engagement. And I actually blacked out the whole town of Woods Hole at high noon that way, having left a Saab in a parking lot there for about a week. I am told old timers there still wonder out loud about where all that smoke could have come from. I came to speak ill of Swedish engineering, and so diddled myself out of a Nobel Prize (MWC 12).

Vonnegut's facetious explanation, this humorous trap he's created for not having won a Nobel Prize, is carefully set up in the first paragraph, then buried beneath increasingly complex layers of exotic car care minutiae, distracting implications about women in general and lesbians in particular, his own ignorant guesser's belief in common myths, and a final focus on his own legendary failure to uphold the proud tradition of Swedish engineering. Hence, no Nobel Prize for him.

This schematic of Vonnegut's joke—one that speaks to the themes of the larger text—is precisely what he wants the reader to understand as he begins the second section of the chapter with **It's damn hard** to make jokes work *(MWC 12). This section is both an explanation of the mechanics of his humor and a spirited defense of his work ethic. Vonnegut was very much aware of the popular press's disparaging charges that his texts were full of jokes woven into his complex narratives. He explains that the very short chapters of* Cat's Cradle *represent one day's work, and each one is a joke. By contrast,* If I were writing about a tragic situation, it wouldn't be necessary to time it to make sure the thing works. You can't really misfire with a tragic scene. It's bound to be moving if all the right elements are present. But a joke is like building a mousetrap from scratch. You have to work pretty hard to make the thing snap when it is supposed to snap (MWC 12).

Though humor has its own tight, demanding structure, it is only a tool. (MWC 12) Humor is a way of holding off how awful life can be, to protect yourself. Finally, you get just too tired, and the news is too awful, and humor doesn't work anymore. *He cites the example of Mark Twain, whose legendary humor could no longer effectively combat the tragedies of his life, including the deaths of his wife, two daughters, and best friend. Vonnegut senses the same impasse in his life.*

Like Twain, Vonnegut has his share of woe in his scrapbook. Having lived long enough to experience World War II, Dresden, his mother's suicide, his sister's early death coincident with her husband's death in a commuter train accident (doubling the number of children in his house almost overnight), the country's endless stream of questionable wars and society's cultural upheavals over race, gender, and the selfish politics of extremism, Vonnegut reasons that he has every right to declare himself a stateless person, one apart from the rest of world's myth-based nationalistic zeal. Empathizing with Twain, Vonnegut claims the same result of his longevity and experience. (MWC 12) It may be that I am no longer able to joke—that it is no longer a satisfactory defense mechanism. . . . There may have been so many shocks and disappointments that the defense of humor no longer works. It may be that I have become rather grumpy because I've seen so many things that have offended me that I cannot deal with in terms of laughter.

Though he understands his similarity with Twain, Vonnegut is more concerned that the thematic interests of his work and the affects of life's cruel nature have hampered his own vision of his writing future. He sees his own work as a natural, organic response to the events of the world. (MWC 12) I really don't know what I'm going to become from now on. I'm simply along for the ride to see what happens to this body and this brain of mine. I'm startled that I became a writer. I don't think I can control my life or my writing. Every other writer I

know feels he is steering himself, and I don't have that feeling. I don't have that sort of control. I'm simply becoming.

All I really wanted to do was give people the relief of laughing. Humor can be a relief, like an aspirin tablet. If a hundred years from now people are still laughing, I'd certainly be pleased.

Clearly, Vonnegut is curious about what will become of him so late in life, but he is even more interested in knowing that his body of work, his methodology and message, will outlive his late-stage writing dilemma. Vonnegut does not often wonder about his readership far into the future, at least not in print.

This casting about for his future and legacy so late in life prompts a shift to the third section of the chapter, one that presents the yin and yang of his family's concerns as well as a return to one of his most beloved and wise family members, his revered Uncle Alex.

Vonnegut frames this section against his often repeated message that the planet is in a terrible mess. But it has always been a mess. There have never been any "Good Old Days," there have just been days. And as I say to my grandchildren, "Don't look at me. I just got here" (MWC 12). *And this is where the bad guessers, the adherents of destructive myths, can be seen everywhere, eternally, including within his own family.* (MWC 12) There are old poops who will say that you do not become a grown-up until you have somehow survived, as they have, some famous calamity—the Great Depression, the Second World War, Vietnam, whatever. Storytellers are responsible for this destructive, not to say suicidal, myth. Again and again in stories, after some terrible mess, the character is able to say at last, "Today I am a woman. Today I am a man. The end."

Such fallaciousness does not escape his own family. (MWC 12) When I got home from the Second World War, my Uncle Dan clapped me on the back, and he said, "You're a man now." So I killed him. Not really, but I certainly felt like doing it.

Dan, that was my bad uncle, who said a male can't be a man unless he'd gone to war.

Vonnegut's beloved Uncle Alex presents a more humane approach to life and one's place in it. He provides a momentary antidote to depression, focusing his pleasure center on soaking up the goodness in life when it presents itself. As Vonnegut recalls of Uncle Alex, his principal complaint about other human beings was that they so seldom noticed it when they were happy. So when we were drinking lemonade under an apple tree in the summer, say, and talking lazily about this and that, almost buzzing like honeybees, Uncle Alex would suddenly interrupt the agreeable blather to exclaim, "If this isn't nice, I don't know what is" (MWC 12).

Vonnegut closes this portion of the chapter appealing to his readers as he has done with his children. Nevertheless, even his own family battles between those who promulgate destructive myths and those who want to consciously acknowledge when life is—happily—as good as it gets. The latter insist on appreciating the splendor of the moment. No one escapes the battle between the dark myths and a more enlightened (if not evolved) approach to the world, but Vonnegut emphasizes the need to appreciate those moments that fill us with wonder, filling us with a cosmic sense of thank-you for life's bounty and beauty.

In the fourth section of the chapter Vonnegut emphasizes the effort necessary for critical thinking, especially the expansive, informative outcomes resulting from broadly and liberally considering various sources. He contrasts the easy, lazy, and limiting exercise of accepting and repeating myths in opposition to the effort required to satisfy curiosity through the informed gathering of information. On one side is the ignorant acceptance of often dark myths; the other side represents the path to enlightened, educated viewpoints from which one may develop new knowledge and awareness.

Vonnegut asserts that We are not born with imagination. It has to be developed by teachers and parents (MWC 12). He goes on to consider the development of imagination through art and writing, tasks requiring some amount of skill and adherence to a few basic rules. Sometimes the rules need to be broken, as he consciously and notably breaks his own rule about semicolons.

In the end, it is the exercise of one's will to understand another, to experience something outside their own concerns, the empathy with which they approach life that establishes whether one is going to abide by the dark myths of conventionality or strike out by consciously seeking to understand the other, the outsider, the territory beyond the conventional myth.

All this culminates in the anecdote presented in the fifth and final section of the chapter. Vonnegut shares his conversation with artist and friend Saul Steinberg, a nearly coded philosophical appreciation about the disparate vagaries of artistic intent and the manner by which we respond to art. Steinberg's response addresses the essence of Vonnegut's concerns about what drives him and his potential for a valued literary legacy (despite the lack of a Nobel Prize). It is noteworthy that the manner of Vonnegut's recall of this incident is structured in a proposition followed by six alternating anaphoric paragraphs. From the writer often criticized for too easily tossing off his stories without much care, Vonnegut closes the text with a linguistic double helix; his final examination of art may be seen as free verse poetry of the sublime.

Who was the wisest person I ever met in my entire life? It was a man, but of course it needn't have been. It was the graphic artist Saul Steinberg, who like everybody else I know, is dead now. I could ask him anything, and six seconds would pass, and then he would give me a perfect answer, gruffly, almost a growl. He was born in Romania, in a house where, according to him, "the geese looked in the windows."

I said, "Saul, how should I feel about Picasso?"

Six seconds passed, and then he said, "God put him on Earth to show us what it's like to be *really* rich."

I said, "Saul, I am a novelist, and many of my friends are novelists and good ones, but when we talk I keep feeling we are in two very different businesses. What makes me feel that way?"

Six seconds passed, and then he said, "It's very simple. There are two sorts of artists, one not being in the least superior to the other. But one responds to the history of his or her art so far, and the other responds to life itself."

I said, "Saul, are you *gifted*?"

Six seconds passed, and then he growled, "No, but what you respond to in any work of art is the artist's struggle against his or her limitations" (MWC 12).

Requiem

This is the first of two pieces following the formally numbered chapters within the text. Its title comes from the Catholic funeral mass and is presented as free-verse poetry in three stanzas with a total of twenty lines. Vonnegut the apostate, the freethinker, the Unitarian, the humanist, has way too much knowledge of the Bible (Old and New Testament), and this makes his loudest detractors, usually among the most ardent believers and mythicists, feel uncomfortable within their own scripture. Vonnegut cites the words of Jesus to attack the bad guessers whose belief in dangerous myths (this time about climate change) has led to the destruction of the planet.

Using anthropomorphism, Vonnegut has the planet utter the plaintive words of the crucified Christ calling upon his father to forgive this crime of his crucifixion. "Forgive them, Father, / They know not what they do." But with Vonnegut's legacy of scientific truth within his family and his own training, he suggests that the sinners who have killed the planet knew what they were doing, The irony would be / that we know / what we are doing. After all, modern industry as well as the military-industrial complex are replete with scientists capable of modeling the downstream effects of their work. They will be held accountable along with everyone else when they successfully kill the planet.

And the earth, having suffered its relatively quick (considering the age of the planet) but nevertheless painful demise, exhales into the thinning ether, "It is done." / People did not like it here. The implication of the Requiem *is that we are at fault for disdaining science and embracing lifestyle choices that enabled our matricide of Mother Earth.*

Author's Note

The Author's Note is nothing short of a love letter barely dressed as a letter of thanks, a note of endearment for Vonnegut's association with the Kentucky artist Joe Petro III. Before getting into the details of their meeting, Vonnegut broadly paints the significance of their relationship in the most expansive and personal terms. I have to have been one of the luckiest persons alive, since I have survived for four

score and two years now. I can't begin to count all the times I should have been dead or wished I were. But one of the best things that ever happened to me, a one-in-a-billion opportunity to enjoy myself in perfect innocence, was my meeting Joe.

Vonnegut goes on to recount Petro's academic background (a zoology degree from the University of Tennessee) and his large paintings turned into posters for Greenpeace. Before he can speak of much more, he returns again to thanking Joe, this time in a short expression that seems filled with deep-seated secrets, hints of personal revelations that would never receive full expression in public, an unspoken privately held bond between men that forms the bedrock of their mutual respect and love. As he says, and it seems quite possible in retrospect that Joe Petro III saved my life. I will not explain. I will let it go at that.

Vonnegut explains that the "samplers" of his aphorisms separating each of the text's chapters are examples of some of the word-based work they did together. He does not go on to explain the great diversity of works completed with Petro, but Vonnegut's artwork spans everything extending from self-portraits to an Absolut Vodka ad (based on Cat's Cradle) *to Kilgore Trout to the view of the three wise men as seen through the eyes of the baby Jesus, and his subjects continue on from there.*

After word got out about their partnership, Petro worked with comedian Jonathan Winters and English artist Ralph Steadman (who became friends with Vonnegut). In 2004, Petro arranged an exhibition of Vonnegut's work at the Indianapolis Art Center and included work by Vonnegut's paternal grandfather Bernard (an architect and painter), his father, as well as his children Edith and Mark. The good spirits spilled over into a letter Vonnegut wrote to Ralph Steadman. "Joe Petro III staged a reunion of four generations of my family in Indianapolis, and he has made you and me feel like first cousins. Is it possible that he is God? We could do worse."*

---

* *The author of this encyclopedia was at the 1993 meeting between Vonnegut and Petro. Peter Reed and I were in attendance to interview Mr. Vonnegut for one of our books. We were graciously hosted by Ollie Lyon and his effervescent wife Billie. Mr. Lyon worked with Vonnegut in the PR department at GE and they remained good friends over the years. Mr. Lyon became a well-connected benefactor of Midway College, an all female equestrian school preparing students*

The partnership between Vonnegut and Petro is called Origami Express because of the elaborately folded packages Joe often sent to Kurt. Vonnegut reveals his inspiration from the works of Paul Klee and Marcel Duchamp. One of Vonnegut's friends out in the Hamptons was the late painter Syd Solomon. In response to Vonnegut's curiosity about how to tell a good picture from a lesser one, Solomon provides him with a bit of advice he finds invaluable and empowering. He said, "Look at a million pictures, and you can never be mistaken." *When Edith learns of Solomon's pronouncement, she agrees.* She said she "could rollerskate through the Louvre, saying, 'Yes, no, no, yes, no, yes,' and so on."

It should come as no surprise that though much of this text provides reasons for Vonnegut's withdrawal from country and humanity, he subverts his own position by expressing deep appreciation and love for likeminded artists, fans, and family members for their understanding, their shared viewpoints, and art's ability to buoy their spirits.

man-woman hour *(see* **"Golden Wedding"***).*

Manchu, Fu. *The minuscule ("diminutive" would be too large) Chinese agent in* Slapstick *who tells Wilbur Swain about the deal China made with Eliza in order to get hold of the writings she coauthored with her brother and stored in Professor Swain's mausoleum. They promised Eliza a trip to their colony on Mars in return for access to the Swain twins' theories about gravity and extended families. Fu Manchu travels by dematerialization. On the twins' fiftieth birthday, Wilbur receives birthday greetings from his sister and a letter from Fu Manchu informing him of Eliza's death in a Martian avalanche. Simultaneously on Earth, the Chinese experiments with gravity (based on the Swains' theories) cause tremendous destruction due to cataclysmic geological shifts. The consequent failure of stable natural forces eliminates geopolitical confrontations and limits political enmity to neighboring communities.*

to become horse trainers and managers within the equine community. The event was a fundraiser for a new library at the college. Joe Petro III was simply a fan at the time and saw an opportunity to contact Vonnegut to help with the publicity posters. Their relationship blossomed from there.

Mandarax. *The second generation of voice translators invented by twenty-nine-year-old Zenji Hiroguchi in* Galápagos. *The first generation was called Gokubi, which could translate ten languages. Mandarax could identify and translate more than one thousand languages, diagnose more than a thousand diseases and prescribe remedies, recall poetry from a database of classic works appropriate to any topic, recall historical events by date, and was programmable for any course of instruction from surgery to ikebana, the Japanese art of flower arranging.*

Hiroguchi planned to give a copy of Mandarax to Jackie Onassis during "the Nature Cruise of the Century," and in preparing this gift, he programmed it with his wife's lectures about ikebana. This enraged his wife, who lectured him in a manner reminiscent of other moments in Vonnegut's work that pit man's increasing technological abilities against human work. (Gal 1:14) "You, *Doctor Hiroguchi," she went on, "think that everybody but yourself is just taking up space on this planet, and we make too much noise and waste valuable natural resources and have too many children and leave garbage around. So it would be a much nicer place if the few stupid services we are able to perform for the likes of you were taken over by machinery. That wonderful **Mandarax** you're scratching your ear with now: what is that but an excuse for a meanspirited egomaniac never to pay or even thank any human being with a knowledge of languages or mathematics or history or medicine or literature or ikebana or anything?"

Contrary to Hisako Hiroguchi's tirade, Leon Trout (the text's narrator) describes the appearance of Mandarax in organic terms rather than distinguishing between humans and machinery. (Gal 1:13) When Akiko became an adult on Santa Rosalia, she would be very much like her mother on the inside, but in a different sort of skin. The evolutionary sequence from Gokubi to **Mandarax**, by contrast, was a radical improvement in the contents of a package, but with few perceptible changes in the wrapper. Akiko was protected from sunburn, and from the chilly water when she swam, and the abrasiveness of lava when she chose to sit or lie down— whereas her mother's bare skin was wholly defenseless against these ordinary hazards of island life. But Gokubi and **Mandarax**, as different as they were inside, inhabited nearly identical shells of high-impact black plastic, twelve centimeters high, eight wide, and two thick.

Any fool could tell Akiko from Hisako, but only an expert could tell Gokubi from **Mandarax**.

Maniacs in the Fourth Dimension. *The only mention of this Kilgore Trout novel occurs during a conversation between Billy Pilgrim's mother and Bertram Copeland Rosewater. Billy and Rosewater are hospital roommates. While Billy remains silent beneath his covers, this is their conversation.* (SL5 6) "He was at the top of his class when this happened," said Billy's mother.

"Maybe he was working too hard," said Rosewater. He held a book he wanted to read, but he was much too polite to read and talk, too, easy as it was to give Billy's mother satisfactory answers. The book was **Maniacs in the Fourth Dimension**, by Kilgore Trout. It was about people whose mental diseases couldn't be treated because the causes of the diseases were all in the fourth dimension, and three-dimensional Earthling doctors couldn't see those causes at all, or even imagine them.

One thing Trout said that Rosewater liked very much was that there really were vampires and werewolves and goblins and angels and so on, but that they were in the fourth dimension. So was William Blake, Rosewater's favorite poet, according to Trout. So were heaven and hell.

"The Manned Missiles" (1958) (*see also* **Ashland** *and* **Ivankov**). *This Cold War short story, published in 1958 and reprinted in* Welcome to the Monkey House *(1968), is told through an exchange of letters between the fathers of Major Stepan Ivankov and Captain Bryant Ashland. America launches Ashland into orbit to observe the Soviet cosmonaut's mission, but he accidentally loses control of his capsule and crashes into his Russian counterpart. Both vehicles are disabled in space and neither can return home. The fathers' letters express the emotions of men without political considerations. Each is a loving father seeking to comfort the other for their common loss.*

Mansfield, Dave. *In the short story "Poor Little Rich Town," Mansfield struggles to overhear a con-* *versation held by Fire Chief Atkins, Upton Beaton, and Ed Newcomb concerning the hidden and poor condition of the otherwise picturesque mansions in Spruce Falls. They eagerly desire to unload some properties on unsuspecting executives from the Federal Apparatus Corporation who will be moving to the area as a result the company's expected relocation to neighboring Ilium. The three get a little loud and uneasy about revealing these secrets when they suddenly catch themselves worrying about who else may be listening. Beaton steps in to ease their fears:* "Calm down! Nobody out there but old **Dave Mansfield**, and he hasn't heard anything since his boiler blew up."

Maori. *A member of the aboriginal people of New Zealand appears twice in Vonnegut's work. In* Slaughterhouse-Five, *a Maori soldier of unknown rank and captured at Tobruk worked side by side with Billy Pilgrim the morning after the firebombing of Dresden, digging bodies and valuables out of the rubble. After the bodies started to rot, the Maori succumbed to the stink that was like roses and mustard gas (SL5 10), developing the dry heaves and eventually dying.*

In Bluebeard, *a Maori corporal from the New Zealand Field Artillery, also captured at Tobruk, is painted into Rabo Karabekian's sixty-four-foot triptych "Now It's the Women's Turn." He is sitting on a German ammunition box with three bullets left inside, reading an anti-Semitic weekly from Latvia.* (Blue 36) It is six months old, and offers tips on gardening and home canning. The **Maori** is studying it very earnestly, in the hopes of learning what we would all like to know about ourselves: where he is, what is going on, and what is likely to happen next.

The only other time Vonnegut mentions the Maoris is in the short story "Bagombo Snuff Box," collected in Bagombo Snuff Box *(1999), in which they are used as a verbal prop by Laird while trying to impress his hosts at the beginning of some after-dinner drinks.* "Anything at all, Harry," Laird said. "I've had kava with the **Maoris**, scotch with the British, champagne with the French, and cacao with the Tupi. I'll have a rye or a beer with you. When in Rome . . ." He dipped into his pocket and brought out a snuff box encrusted with semiprecious gems.

Mare Imbrium (*see* **Jefferson Observatory**).

Margo. *The home planet of Zog, the flying saucer traveler who lands in Connecticut and is beaten to death with a golf club when trying to warn a family about a fire in their house. Tragically, Zog communicates by farting and tap dancing, so his strange appearance and attempts to tell the family about the imminent danger are simply too bizarre and frightening for the homeowner. All this takes place in Kilgore Trout's short story "The Dancing Fool," published in 1962 in* Black Garterbelt *magazine. Trout learns of its publication after buying a back issue of the porn magazine in* Breakfast of Champions.

Marion. *In the short story "The Powder Blue Dragon," collected in* Bagombo Snuff Box *(1999), Marion is the quick-witted and dismissive fiancée of Paul. She and Kiah Higgins meet on the turnpike as they flirt by passing one another: she in her convertible Cadillac; he in his Marittima-Frascati sports car. Marion appreciates the good looks of his car but barely remembers Kiah as the driver when they briefly speak moments later in the lounge where she is to meet Paul*

She is another in a string of characters in the story who sees right past Kiah, keeping him as part of the anonymous background, never asking for or receiving his name. The beginning of her brief conversation with Kiah displays her quick wit through double entendre while also dismissing him with tactless honesty. She uses his reference to her Cadillac to quip with a cutting revelation about herself and her views of the men in her life. "Hello," *he said to the girl,* with more assurance than he thought possible. "How's the Cad treating you?"

She laughed. "My car, my fiancé, or my father?"

"Your car," Kiah said, feeling stupid for not having a snappier retort.

"Cads always treat me nicely. I remember you now. You were in that darling little blue thing with yellow seats. I somehow didn't connect you with the car. You look different."

Marion is last seen driving off with Paul in his British Hampton as Kiah soars past, flipping them the bird before deciding to burn out his transmission.

Marion, Ed, Teddy, and Lou. *In the short story* "The Cruise of the Jolly Roger," *collected in* Bagombo Snuff Box *(1999), these Provincetown artists accidentally meet up with Major Nathan Durant and spend the afternoon together. Marion sketches Durant with his permission, but he is disturbed by her portrayal. What Durant saw was a big, scarred, hungry man, hunched over and desolate as a lost child.* "Do I really look that bad?" *he said, managing to laugh.*

"Do you really feel that awful?"

As the five mingle for lunch, Durant feels out of place and senses their boredom with his war stories. Marion expresses gratitude for Durant's sharing, but the artists quickly take their leave.

Maritimo, Dr. Alan. (*DD* Epilogue) Dr. Alan Maritimo, the veterinarian, and his wife (*unnamed*). Alan *was a maverick in the* Maritimo *family, who had declined to go into the building business. His entire household was killed by the flash.* "The flash," *of course, refers to the neutron-bombing of Midland City, Ohio.*

Maritimo, Dr. Alfred. (*BC* 6) Dwayne owned a third of the inn (*Holiday Inn*) partnership with Midland City's leading orthodontist, Dr. Alfred Maritimo, and Bill Miller, who was Chairman of the Parole Board at the Adult Correctional Institution at Shepherdstown, among other things.

Maritimo, Carlo. *One of the many relatives who works for the Midland City–based Maritimo Brothers Construction Company. In* Breakfast of Champions, *Carlo listens to Rabo Karabekian's explanation of his painting while in the Tally-ho Room of the Holiday Inn.*

Maritimo, Gino and Marco. *The founders and operators of Maritimo Brothers Construction Company appear in both* Breakfast of Champions *and* Deadeye Dick. *Though Marco isn't mentioned by name in* Breakfast of Champions, *Gino is noted as Midland City's premier dope dealer. It was the Maritimo brothers' guard dog, a Doberman named Kazak, who frightens Vonnegut near the end of that text when he prepares to meet an unsuspecting Kilgore Trout.*

The history of the Maritimo brothers in Midland City is recounted in Deadeye Dick. *When Gino was* eighteen and Marco was twenty, they worked as stokers aboard an Italian freighter. While loading cargo in Newport News, Virginia, they fled to avoid conscription that awaited them upon their return to Italy and because they thought they could make a better life for themselves in the United States. Assisted by members of the Newport News Italian American community, the two jump a ride on an empty railway boxcar. After being robbed at knifepoint by four hoboes, the two leave the train only to be discovered by railway detectives in Midland City.

From a distance they see the conical slate roof of Otto Waltz's home and decide to head there. They come upon Otto, dressed in one of his ornate costumes picked up on his European excursion, who offers them the chance to work for food. Otto spoke to them in Italian and offered them all the food they needed. Otto clothed them, provided shelter in the cupola gun room, and put them to work around the house. They were forever grateful to Otto and all his family.

The Maritimos became the most successful building contractors in Midland City. The night before that fateful Mothers Day when Rudy accidentally kills Mrs. Metzger, Marco and his family dine with the Waltzes to commemorate the drafting of each family's oldest son. Marco's son Julio is eventually killed in Germany.

When an enormous snowstorm hits Midland City and destroys the Waltz family home, Gino and Marco frantically drive a company bulldozer to the hospital just in time to learn of Otto's death. It is later learned they did hundreds of thousands of dollars' worth of property damage with the dozer.

Marco and Gino purchase John Fortune's dairy farm and create the Avondale development (the land was previously used as a testing ground for tanks during the war). After the Waltzes are financially ruined, Rudy and his mother move into the show unit in Avondale.

Unknown to the Maritimos was the fact that they had purchased cement from the Nuclear Regulatory Commission. The radioactive cement was used in the construction of the fireplace, eventually ruled the cause of Mrs. Waltz death. The Waltz brothers are forced to sue the Maritimo Brothers Construction Company, the Nuclear Regulatory Commission, and the Ohio Valley Ornamental Concrete Company.

Though they apparently didn't know in advance about the radioactive cement, Gino and Marco are overcome with guilt, and without any urging send workers into the home to rip out the fireplace, making it look as though a fireplace never existed.

In Breakfast of Champions, the Maritimos construct the famed Mildred Barry Memorial Center for the Arts. Marco dies of natural causes a month before Celia Hoover's suicide, and Gino is electrocuted inspecting the center's drawbridge a few months later, just prior to its opening.

Maritimo, Guillermo. A first cousin to Gino and Marco Maritimo and the grandfather of Milo Maritimo, the homosexual desk clerk at the Midland City Holiday Inn, in Breakfast of Champions. Guillermo "Little Willie" Maritimo served as one of Al Capone's bodyguards in Chicago and is not seen in the text.

Maritimo, Julio. In Deadeye Dick, the eldest son of Marco Maritimo. He and Felix Waltz are drafted into military service at the same time. Julio is killed fighting in Germany.

Maritimo, Milo. The homosexual desk clerk at the Midland City Holiday Inn, grandson of Guillermo "Little Willie" Maritimo (one of Al Capone's bodyguards), and first cousin to Gino and Marco Maritimo, owners of Maritimo Brothers Construction Company. Milo is overjoyed to be the first in town to welcome Kilgore Trout's arrival for the Arts Festival. Maritimo had taken the trouble to write to Eliot Rosewater so he could read some of Trout's work before his arrival. Rosewater lends Milo his Trout collection of forty-one novels and sixty-three short stories and is reading his novel The Smart Bunny upon arrival. The desk clerk is overjoyed that Midland City will become known as the first community to acknowledge the greatness of Trout. Much to Trout's consternation, Milo's effusive welcome indicates his high expectations for Trout's arrival. (BC 20) "We are so ready for a Renaissance, Mr. Trout! You will be our Leonardo!"

In preparation for the Arts Festival banquet, Milo makes the crown and scepter to be borne by Mary Alice Miller, Queen of the festival.
See also: BC 2.

Martha. *In* Breakfast of Champions, *Vonnegut speaks in his own voice and offers the information that his psychiatrist's name is Martha, no last name provided.* (BC 24) She gathers jumpy people together into little families which meet once a week. It's a lot of fun. She teaches us how to comfort one another intelligently. She is on vacation now. I like her a lot.

Marx, Arnold. *The eighteen-year-old, red-headed, Israeli-born amateur archaeologist and law student, one of Howard Campbell, Jr.'s, four prison guards at the opening of* Mother Night. *Arnold and his father, a gunsmith by trade, excavate the ruins of Hazor under the direction of Yigael Yadin. Marx provides Campbell with an interesting object lesson concerning the interpretation of history and its all-too-frequent misapplications, foreshadowing Campbell's "cuckoo-clock in hell" theory.* (MN 1) Hazor, **Arnold** tells me, was a Canaanite city in northern Palestine that existed at least nineteen hundred years before Christ. About fourteen hundred years before Christ, **Arnold** tells me, an Israelite army captured Hazor, killed all forty thousand inhabitants, and burned it down.

"Solomon rebuilt the city," said Arnold, "but in 732 B.C. Tiglath-pileser the Third burned it down again." *Campbell receives this lesson as Arnold's way of informing him about an ancient ruler whom he perceives to be one of the most vicious criminals in history—Tiglath-pileser the Third—though he never considers those forty thousand people killed by the ancient Israelis. When Campbell mentions his own boss, the Nazi war criminal Paul Joseph Goebbels, Arnold has no idea who that is. Campbell resigns himself to the sweep of history and the relative obscurity both he and his alleged crimes will eventually suffer.* (MN 1) And I felt the dust of the Holy Land creeping in to bury me, sensed how thick a dust-and-rubble blanket I would one day wear. I felt thirty or forty feet of ruined cities above me; beneath me some primitive kitchen middens, a temple or two—and then—

Tiglath-pileser the Third.

Mary. *The forty-foot fishing boat belonging to Harry Pena on which he made his living with sons Manny and Kenny.* (GBR 10) She was a gray, lapstreak tub

whose purpose was to wallow home in all weather with tons of fresh fish on board. There wasn't any shelter on her, except for a wooden box to keep the big new Chrysler dry. The wheel and the throttle and the clutch were mounted on the box. All the rest of the *Mary* was a bare-boned tub.

Mashtots, Mesrob. *Among the many notable Armenians proudly recorded by Rabo Karabekian is Mesrob Mashots,* the inventor of the Armenian alphabet, unlike any other, about four hundred years before the birth of Christ. . . . There are about six million of us now, including my two sons and three grandchildren, who know nothing and care nothing about **Mesrob Mashtots** (Blue 2). *Rabo estimates the number of Armenians when he writes his memoirs and believes they are all stigmatized by the Turkish massacre of Armenians.*

Masters, Barbara. (WFG Good Missiles, Good Manners, Good Night) I WENT to high school in Indianapolis with a nice girl named **Barbara Masters**. Her father was an eye doctor in our town. She is now the wife of our Secretary of Defense (Melvin Laird).

Matheson. *Ilium's pompous manager in charge of testing and placement for the General Classification Test, in* Player Piano.

Matsumoto, Hiroshi. *The lifelong employee of the Sony Corporation is also Warden of the New York State Maximum Security Adult Correctional Facility at Athena and serves as Vonnegut's voice on some matters economic and social. Previous to his appointment at Athena (New York State had contracted with Sony to run their correctional facilities), Matsumoto served Sony as the manager of a "for profit" hospital in Lexington, Kentucky, a position that deeply vexed him because he was forced to turn away indigent patients.*

When only eight years old, Matsumoto survived the atomic bombing of Hiroshima, understandably leaving him with some indelible memories. He leads a solitary existence with almost no hint of close friends. However, to some small extent he befriends Eugene Debs Hartke after hiring him to teach at the prison.

Matsumoto is chased away from the commotion at Athena during the prison break and winds up lost in the nearby forest. Two days later he emerges from the forest frozen and demoralized. His feet require amputation due to frostbite and gangrene. Matsumoto returns to Hiroshima where he eventually takes his life by committing hara-kiri.

Matsumoto's experience as an atomic bomb survivor and a lifelong employee of Sony provides a unique perspective on the economic and social ties binding Japan and the United States, and he conveys these thoughts to Hartke, who heartily agrees with him. (HP 32) He *(Matsumoto)* said, "I only wish our Chairman of the Board back in Tokyo could have spent just one hour with me in our emergency room, turning away dying people because they could not afford our services."

"You had a body count in Vietnam, I believe?" he said. It was true. We were ordered to count how many people we killed so that higher headquarters, all the way back to Washington, D.C., could estimate how much closer, even if it was only a teeny-weeny bit closer, all our efforts were bringing us to victory. There wasn't any other way to keep score.

"So now we count dollars the way you used to count bodies," he said.

"What does that bring us closer to? What does it mean? We should do with those dollars what you did with the bodies. Bury and forget them! You were luckier with your bodies than we are with all our dollars."

"How so?" I said.

"All anybody can do with bodies is burn them or bury them," he said. "There isn't any nightmare afterwards, when you have to invest them and make them grow.

"What a clever trap your Ruling Class set for us," he went on. "First the atomic bomb. Now this."

"Trap?" I echoed wonderingly.

"They looted your public and corporate treasuries, and turned your industries over to nincompoops," he said. "Then they had your Government borrow so heavily from us that we had no choice but to send over an Army of Occupation in business suits. Never before has the Ruling Class of a country found a way to stick other countries with all the responsibilities their wealth might imply,

and still remain rich beyond the dreams of avarice! No wonder they thought the comatose Ronald Reagan was a great President!"

Hartke uses Matsumoto's sentiments to explain the decayed social conditions resulting from economic hedonism and the general lack of faith in the economic traditions that built small communities through local investment. Such a system thrived on the interdependence of the upper and working classes in a community, the very model that originally built Scipio and Tarkington College. (HP 32) What Warden **Matsumoto** had said about people like them *(the rich in general, though Hartke makes specific reference here to members of the Tarkington Board of Trustees)* was accurate. They had managed to convert their wealth, which had originally been in the form of factories or stores or other demanding enterprises, into a form so liquid and abstract, negotiable representations of money on paper, that there were few reminders coming from anywhere that they might be responsible for anyone outside their own circle of friends and relatives.

They *(the board members)* didn't rage against the convicts. They were mad at the Government for not making sure that escapes from prison were impossible. The more they ran on like that, the clearer it became that it was their Government, not mine or the convicts' or the Townies'. Its first duty, moreover, was to protect them from the lower classes, not only in this country but everywhere.

Were people on Easy Street ever any different?

Think again about the crucifixions of Jesus and the 2 thieves, and the 6,000 slaves who followed the gladiator Spartacus.

Matsumoto Corporation. *This corporation appears in both* Galápagos *and* Bluebeard. *In both instances, Vonnegut makes reference to Matsumoto's takeover of GEFFCo. In* Galápagos, *Matsumoto's modernization of GEFFCo's Ilium manufacturing plant results in the loss of hundreds of jobs, since they can run the plant with only twelve workers. Ilium is driven into bankruptcy due to the loss of its largest workforce. One of the laid-off workers is Roy Hepburn. Matsumoto is also the employer of Zenji Hiroguchi, creator of Gokubi and Mandarax.*

In Bluebeard, *Matsumoto assumes ownership of GEFFCo's Manhattan office building as well as its* art collection, including Rabo Karabekian's "Windsor Blue Number Seventeen." One of their security guards calls Karabekian about the demise of his painting and offers him the opportunity to retrieve its remains.

Matthews, Hildy. *In the short story "Find Me a Dream," collected in* Bagombo Snuff Box *(1999), Hildy is a minor New York actress and the widowed mother of two young children. She is tied romantically and artistically to her jazzman husband's needs* even though he was the worst husband a woman could have. That's how good I am at loving. *The story presents her at a crossroads: marry Arvin Borders for the financial and material peace he promises, or go with her whimsically artistic heart by proposing to Andy Middleton, being both wife and muse to a soul (with a solid middle-class income) who is already akin to the spirit of her old romance while promising at least life without an eternal struggle for material peace. Hildy opts for art, for Middleton. All this is settled for Hildy in just one night on the greens at the Pipe City Golf and Country Club in self-reflection and conversation with Andy. She does not want to ruin Borders's career chances by an unpopular marriage, so despite her engagement, she proposes to Middleton, promising to love him and help fulfill his dreams.*

mausoleum. *Wilbur and Eliza Swain use the mausoleum of Professor Elihu Roosevelt Swain, founder of the family fortune, as a childhood escape and as the repository for their treatises on gravity and artificially extended families. As children they take refuge there to read books and sing songs (especially "We're Off to See the Wizard" from* The Wizard of Oz*). Later, Wilbur retrieves the gravity treatise for the Chinese at the request of a message sent by his sister. (Slap 3)* It was actually possible for Eliza and me, for example, to vanish into a huge grandfather clock in the ballroom at the top of the northernmost tower, and to emerge almost a kilometer away—through a trap door in the floor of the **mausoleum** of Professor Elihu Roosevelt Swain.
(Slap 4) There were thousands of books in the mansion. By the time we were ten, we had read them all by candlelight, at naptime or after bed-

time—in secret passageways, or often in the **mausoleum** of Elihu Roosevelt Swain.
(Slap 30) The exterior doors to the **mausoleum** had been welded shut. So Fu Manchu and I had to enter the secret passageways, the alternative universe of my childhood, and come up through the **mausoleum's** floor.
See also: Slap 3; 7; 19; 29; 30; 32; 42.

Max. *Vonnegut mentions his grandson Max as a way of introducing yet another Kilgore Trout maxim, this time about science. (TQ 31)* My daughter Nanny has a son, **Max,** who is twelve now, in 1996, halfway through the rerun. He will be seventeen when Kilgore Trout dies. This past April, **Max** wrote for school a really swell report on Sir Isaac Newton, a superman so ordinary in appearance. It told me something I hadn't known before: That Newton was advised by those who were his nominal supervisors to take time out from the hard truths of science to brush up on theology.

I like to think they did this not because they were foolish, but to remind him of how comforting and encouraging the make believe of religion can be for common folk.

To quote from Kilgore Trout's story "Empire State," which is about a meteor the size and shape of the Manhattan skyscraper, approaching Earth point-first at a steady fifty-four miles an hour: "Science never cheered up anyone. The truth about the human situation is just too awful."

McAllister, Reed. *This may be an internal inconsistency of Vonnegut's in* God Bless You, Mr. Rosewater. *Vonnegut refers to Reed McAllister as "Old McAllister" (GBR 10), the attorney from McAllister, Robjent, Reed and McGee representing Stewart Buntline of Newport, Rhode Island. It seems unlike Vonnegut to have two closely associated characters sharing the same last name, a first name which is part of the law firm, and a reference to "Old McAllister" when he doesn't mean the senior partner, Thurmond McAllister.*

In any case, Reed McAllister is responsible for transforming Stewart Buntline from an idealistic youth possessed of great inheritance to a conservative middle-aged man of wealth. McAllister is forever forwarding Buntline capitalist tracts such as "A Rift

Between Friends in the War of Ideas," long after Buntline became comfortable with his wealth.

McAllister, Thurmond (*also* **McAllister, Robjent, Reed and McGee**). *The seventy-six-year-old senior partner in the Washington, D.C., law firm McAllister, Robjent, Reed and McGee, representing the Indiana Rosewaters and Stewart Buntline of Rhode Island, in* God Bless You, Mr. Rosewater. *It is the senior partner who first suggests establishing the Rosewater Foundation as a way of avoiding inheritance taxes. Norman Mushari is hired by the firm as an aide to the senior partner in the hope of toughening the softening old lawyer.*

McBundy, Hortense Muskellunge-13. *The private secretary of President Wilbur Swain dies of the Albanian Flu in* Slapstick.

McCabe, Earl. *Corporal Earl McCabe is the "idealistic Marine deserter" stationed in Port-au-Prince, Haiti, who steals his outfit's recreation fund and gives five hundred dollars to new friend Lionel Boyd Johnson (later Bokonon) to purchase a schooner so the two could sail back to the United States. Gale-force winds shipwreck the pair on the coastal rocks of San Lorenzo. In comparison to the diseased and impoverished natives,* Johnson and **McCabe** had the glittering treasures of literacy, ambition, curiosity, gall, irreverence, health, humor, and considerable information about the outside world (CC 56). *They arrive in 1922 and announce they are taking charge of the island, and Castle Sugar quickly withdraws.*

Johnson and McCabe try to reform San Lorenzan society. Johnson invents a new religion, Bokononism, and McCabe tackles the economy and legal system. McCabe tries socialism, but there wasn't any real wealth to redistribute. Johnson asks McCabe to outlaw Bokononism so there would be a new and vital "dynamic tension" created among the people. The two friends are trapped by their own creation. Bokonon needs to live as a saint, and McCabe has to repress all his natural goodness so he could carry out his side of the artificial struggle between the government and Bokononism. As Julian Castle recalls, "The drama was very tough on the souls of the two main actors, **McCabe** and Bokonon. As young men, they had been pretty much alike, had both been half-angel, half-pirate.

"But the drama demanded that the pirate half of Bokonon and the angel half of **McCabe** wither away. And **McCabe** and Bokonon paid a terrible price in agony for the happiness of the people—**McCabe** knowing the agony of the tyrant and Bokonon knowing the agony of the saint. They both became, for all practical purposes, insane" (CC 79). *Castle is so convinced about the effects of this personality split that he believes it eventually causes McCabe's death. (CC 83)* "Unrelieved villainy just wore him out, is my guess."

Johnson and McCabe rename the capital of San Lorenzo to Bolivar, and the highest peak on the island is named Mount McCabe.

McCarthy, Cliff. *The Ohio University art professor who was viewed by Vonnegut on a local PBS documentary series about Ohio artists. He and Vonnegut enjoyed a long friendship and correspondence. McCarthy is introduced in the preface to* Deadeye Dick *and later becomes fictionally important as a teller of documented truth about Otto Waltz's status in the art community as well as crimes of the military-industrial complex.*

McCarthy is among those in attendance at the Timequake *clambake.*

(DD Preface) **Cliff McCarthy** is about my age and from my part of America, more or less. When he went to art school, it was drummed into him that the worst sort of painter was eclectic; borrowing from here and there. But now he has had a show of thirty years of his work, at Ohio University, and he says, "I notice that I have been eclectic." It's strong and lovely stuff he does. My own favorite is "The Artist's Mother as a Bride in 1917." His mother is all dressed up, and it's a warm time of year, and somebody has persuaded her to pose in the bow of a rowboat. The rowboat is in a perfectly still, narrow patch of water, a little river, probably, with the opposite bank, all leafy, only fifty yards away. She is laughing.

McCarthy's painting is later used by Vonnegut as a photograph of Rudy's mother. While she lay dying, imagining herself on a spaceship to Mars, she recalls "That picture," . . . *and she would smile and give my* hand a squeeze. I was supposed to know which of all the pictures in the world she meant. I thought for a while that it was Father's unfinished masterpiece from his misspent youth in Vienna. But in a moment of clarity, she made it clear that it was a scrapbook photograph of her in a rowboat on a small river somewhere, maybe in Europe. Then again, it could have been Sugar Creek. The boat is tied to shore. There aren't any oars in place. She isn't going anywhere. She wears a summer dress and a garden hat. Somebody has persuaded her to pose in the boat, with water around her and dappled with shade. She is laughing. She has just been married, or is about to be married.

She will never be happier. She will never be more beautiful (*DD* 27).

McCarthy plays a key role in unravelling the mystery of what killed Mrs. Waltz. (*DD* 26) We probably never would have found out that it was the mantelpiece that killed her, if it weren't for an art historian from Ohio University over at Athens. His name was **Cliff McCarthy**. He was a painter, too. And **Cliff McCarthy** never would have got involved in our lives, if it hadn't been for all the publicity Mother received for objecting to the kind of art Fred T. Barry was buying for the arts center. He read about her in *People* magazine. Then again, Mother almost certainly wouldn't have become so passionate about taking Fred T. Barry on in the first place, if it hadn't been for little tumors in her brain, which had been caused by the radioactive mantelpiece.

Wheels within wheels!

People magazine described Mother as the widow of an Ohio painter.

Cliff McCarthy had been working for years, financed by a Cleveland philanthropist, on a book which was to include every serious Ohio painter, but he had never heard of Father. So he visited our little shitbox, and he photographed Father's unfinished painting over the fireplace. That was all there was to photograph, so he took several exposures of that with a big camera on a tripod. He was being polite, I guess.

But the camera used flat packs of four-by-five film, and he had exposed some of it elsewhere, so he got several packs out of his camera bag.

He accidentally left one behind—on the mantelpiece. One week later he swung off the Interstate, on his way to someplace else, and he picked up the pack.

Three days after that, he called me on the telephone to say that the film in the pack had all turned black, and that a friend of his who taught physics had offered the opinion that the film had been close to something which was highly radioactive.

He gave me another piece of news on the telephone, too. He had been looking at a diary kept by the great Ohio painter Frank Duveneck at the end of his life. He died in 1919, at the age of seventy-one. Duveneck spent his most productive years in Europe, but he returned to his native Cincinnati after his wife died in Florence, Italy.

"Your father is in the diary!" said **McCarthy**. "Duveneck heard about this wonderful studio a young painter was building in Midland City, and on March 16, 1915, he went and had a look at it."

"What did he say?" I asked.

"He said it was certainly a beautiful studio, such as any artist in the world would have given his eyeteeth to have."

"I mean, what did he say about Father?" I said.

"He liked him, I think," said **McCarthy**.

"Look, I said,—I'm aware that my father was a fraud, and Father knew it, too. Duveneck was probably the only really important painter who ever saw Father's masquerade. No matter how cutting it is, please tell me what Duveneck said."

"Well—I'll read it to you," said **McCarthy**, and he did: "'Otto Waltz should be shot. He should be shot for seeming to prove the last thing that needs to be proved in this part of the world: that an artist is a person of no consequence.'"

McCarthy, Kevin. *The late actor starred as Harold Ryan in* Happy Birthday, Wanda June *and is often referred to by Vonnegut as his favorite actor. McCarthy is among the guests at the* Timequake *clambake.*

McCarthy, Senator Joseph. *The infamous focal point in the search for Communist sympathizers in the U.S. government during the 1950s is frequently mentioned in Vonnegut's work.*

In Cat's Cradle, *Ambassador Minton loses his*

post after his wife's letter to The New York Times *attracts the attention of congressional powers.*

In God Bless You, Mr. Rosewater, *a young Norman Mushari is pictured papering his room with photos of the senator and his assistant, Roy Cohn.*

In Jailbird, *Ben Shapiro, Walter Starbuck's best man and the one who delivers the Starbucks' first child, loses his promotion to full colonel when McCarthy learns Shapiro was a Communist before the war. Later in the same text, RAMJAC hires Roy Cohn, McCarthy's chief counsel of the Senate Permanent Investigating Committee, to defend Starbuck.*

McCarty, Eddie (*see* **Brewer, Ansel**).

McClellan, Grace and George, and their neighbors **Anne** and her husband (unnamed). *In the short story "More Stately Mansions," reprinted in* Welcome to the Monkey House *(1968), Anne and her unnamed husband, the narrator of the story, are subjected to the interior decorating schemes of the desperate Grace McClellan. Grace's husband, George, had suffered one financial setback after another, and Grace's dreams of becoming a remodeling contractor worked themselves out on her unsuspecting neighbors. Though Grace is obnoxiously aggressive in her criticism and advice about such matters, Anne and her husband come to realize the McClellans' sad plight and decide to humor them. When Grace falls seriously ill, George comes into an inheritance from a distant relative and is assisted by Anne and her husband in directing a remodel of the McClellans' house before Grace returns from the hospital. The small inconsistencies in the execution of her design mildly disturb Grace, but they become a source of inspiration for her to continue her interest and dreams of large-scale remodeling.*

McCone, Alexander Hamilton and Clara. *The younger son of Daniel McCone, Alexander graduates without distinction from Harvard in 1894 and is notable for befriending Walter F. Starbuck, the son of his cook and chauffeur. McCone is forty-one when Walter is born into his mansion on Cleveland's Euclid Avenue. Though McCone is married to Alice Rockefeller and the father of their daughter, Clara, his wife and child are so embarrassed by his terrible stammering that they spend most of their time in Eu-*

rope. Alexander McCone promises Walter a Harvard education if he would be his companion, and so begins Walter's lifelong affection for chess, the game he learned at the knee of McCone.

Alexander feels morally committed to the family firm, the Cuyahoga Bridge and Iron Company, "I then believed that a rich man should have some understanding of the place from which his riches came. That was very juvenile of me. Great wealth should be accepted unquestioningly, or not at all" (JB Prologue).

Alexander was present at the Cuyahoga Massacre. After witnessing the assassins hired by his father to help quell the union strikers, with blank affect and an abject complicity due to family relationships, he declares the event was the result of American am-am-am-amateurism in muh-muh-matters of luh-life and duh-duh-duh-death *(JB Prologue).*

McCone, Daniel and John. *Daniel McCone is the founder and owner of the Cuyahoga Bridge and Iron Company, which becomes Cleveland's largest employer by the time of Walter Starbuck's birth.* (JB Prologue) McCone was a hard-bitten and brilliant little mechanical engineer, self-educated, born of working-class parents in Edinburgh, Scotland.

In October 1894, McCone demands his workers take a ten percent pay cut. They refuse, go out on strike, and in December McCone and his two sons watch from the factory windows while the authorities first advocated compliance with the riot act and quickly followed those orders with an armed charge on the strikers and their families. (JB Prologue) Old **Daniel McCone** would say to his sons as he looked out over the battlefield, vacant now except for bodies, "Like it or not, boys, that's the sort of business you're in."

(JB 2) **Daniel McCone** had two sons, Alexander Hamilton McCone, then twenty-two, and **John**, twenty-five. Alexander had graduated without distinction from Harvard in the previous May. He was soft, he was shy, he was a stammerer. **John**, the elder son and the company's heir apparent, had flunked out of the Massachusetts Institute of Technology in his freshman year, and had been his father's most trusted aide ever since.

Starbuck records that McCone held some severe theories about race. (JB 18) My parents were recruited at once by an agent of the Cuyahoga Bridge and Iron Company in Cleveland. He was instructed to hire only blond Slavs, **Mr. McCone** once told me, on his father's theory that blonds would have the mechanical ingenuity and robustness of Germans, but tempered with the passivity of Slavs. The agent was to pick up factory workers, and a few presentable domestic servants for the various **McCone** households, as well. Thus did my parents enter the servant class.

McCoy, Newton. *In Slapstick, Byron Hatfield mistakenly shoots a Beryllium messenger sent by Wilma Pachysandra-17 von Peterswald to deliver a message to President Wilbur Swain. Hatfield thought he was shooting at his old nemesis, Newton McCoy.*

The McGarvey Family. *In the 1953 short story "Tomorrow and Tomorrow and Tomorrow," reprinted in* Welcome to the Monkey House *(1968), The McGarvey Family is a television series that has been in production for at least one hundred twelve consecutive years.*

McLuhan, Nancy. *In the short story "Welcome to the Monkey House," Nancy McLuhan is the virginal Ethical Suicide Parlor hostess kidnapped by Billy the Poet (originally disguised as the Foxy Grandpa). Taken to the Hyannis Port Kennedy Compound, now a national monument underneath a geodesic dome, Nancy is subdued with drugs administered by deflowered former hostesses. In a drugged haze, Nancy admits to being sixty-three and a virgin. She is kept on the dry-docked Kennedy yacht* Marlin, *until her ethical birth control pills wear off.*

McSwann, Ross L. *The swaggering Mayor of Boca Raton, Florida, who mockingly pleads "Send us more Martians" after the failed Martian invasion (ST 7). The townspeople hang twenty-three from lampposts, shoot dead another eleven, and take Sergeant Brackman prisoner. McSwann goes on to become a United States Senator.*

Meadow Lark (see **Queen of the Meadows**).

Meadows. (PP IV) The **Meadows** was a flat, grassy island in the St. Lawrence, in Chippewa Bay,

where the most important men, and the most promising men ("Those whose development within the organization is not yet complete," said the Handbook) in the Eastern and Middle-Western Divisions spent a week each summer in an orgy of morale building—through team athletics, group sings, bonfires and skyrockets, bawdy entertainment, free whisky and cigars; and through plays, put on by professional actors, which pleasantly but unmistakably made clear the nature of good deportment within the system, and the shape of firm resolves for the challenging year ahead.

The Meadows is where the ruling technocracy hatches their plan to have Paul Proteus infiltrate the Ghost Shirt Society. Of course, by the time Paul arrives at the Meadows, he had planned on quitting.

A central feature of the Meadows experience was the morality play repeated each year. (PP XXI) The play was virtually the same play that had begun every **Meadows** *session, even before the war, when the island had belonged to a steel company. Twenty years ago, Paul's father had brought him up here, and the play's message had been the same: that the common man wasn't nearly as grateful as he should be for what the engineers and managers had given him, and that the radicals were the cause of the ingratitude.*

Fred Garth, a competitor of Paul's for manager of the Pittsburgh Works, becomes disaffected with the stringent social design of the ruling technocracy when one of his children does poorly on the all-important General Classification Tests. He takes out his frustration by peeling the bark off the Great Oak of the Meadows and setting it on fire.

Complementing the Meadows is the Mainland, a camp for wives and children, and women employees whose development wasn't yet complete, across the water from the **Meadows**, *the island where the men went (PP XIV).*

Mellon, Hortense. *The graduating Tarkington student and harpist whose uncle, the University of Chicago economist Dr. Martin Peale Blankenship, is invited to deliver the keynote speech in* Hocus Pocus. *Eugene Debs Hartke remembers Hortense for her false teeth, the result of a violent mugging she endured after leaving a party at the Waldorf Astoria. Her parents are among the many Tarkington parents* *who lost fortunes in the stock-swindling Microsecond Arbitrage fiasco.*

Melrose, Mr. *In the short story "Any Reasonable Offer," first appearing in* Collier's *magazine (January 1952) and later collected in* Bagombo Snuff Box *(1999), Mr. Melrose is an office worker at National Steel Foundry who plays interoffice phone tag by relaying out loud the call for Mr. Peckham in Drafting: the imposter, middle-class cubicle worker about to be found out by the unnamed narrating real estate agent.*

Memoirs of a Monogamous Casanova. *Howard Campbell's homage to the love he shares with his wife, Helga, celebrating their passion and sexuality. The Russian plagiarist Stepan Bodovskov has this work printed anonymously and benefits handsomely from its Eastern Bloc bestseller status. Campbell doesn't understand how it could have been printed in those countries, but Frank Wirtanen explains the odd appeal it enjoyed. (MN 35)* "**Memoirs of a Monogamous Casanova** is a curious little chapter in Russian history," said Wirtanen. "It could hardly be published with official approval in Russia—and yet, it was such an attractive, strangely moral piece of pornography, so ideal for a nation suffering from shortages of everything but men and women, that presses in Budapest were somehow encouraged to start printing it—and those presses have, somehow, never been ordered to stop." Wirtanen winked at me. "One of the few sly, playful, harmless crimes a Russian can commit at no risk to himself is smuggling home a copy of **Memoirs of a Monogamous Casanova**. And for whom does he smuggle it? To whom is he going to show this hot stuff? To that salty old crony, his wife.

"For years," said Wirtanen, "there was only a Russian edition. But now, it is available in Hungarian, Rumanian, Latvian, Estonian, and, most marvelous of all, German again."

Howard Campbell recalls the text's epigraph is a poem by William Blake called "The Question Answered":

What is it men in women do require?
The lineaments of Gratified Desire.

What is it women do in men require?
The lineaments of Gratified Desire.
   (MN 23)

Inspired to love again by Resi Noth impersonating Campbell's wife, Helga, Howard adds a final 643rd chapter and prints it directly in Mother Night *(MN 23).*

Memory Clinic. *In "Mnemonics," Vonnegut's second published short story originally appearing in the April 1951 issue of* Collier's *magazine and later reprinted in* Bagombo Snuff Box *(1999), the Memory Clinic is a two-day company-sponsored event for middle-management in an attempt to improve productivity. It is there that Alfred Moorhead is able to more capably apply his already remarkable memory through the use of mnemonics. By the end of the story, despite being well suited to memory games, Alfred falters, but in doing so he reveals his long suppressed love for his secretary Ellen, and she lets her own suppressed feelings slip through as well.*

Mencken, Barbira. *In* Bluebeard, *the former screen star and ex-wife of Paul Slazinger living in the Turtle Bay section of Manhattan, near Greta Garbo and Katharine Hepburn. (Blue 13)* This woman came out of the brownstone with the duplex and triplex. She was old and trembly, but her posture was good, and it was easy to see that she had been very beautiful at one time. I locked my gaze to hers, and a flash of recognition went off in my skull. I knew *her* but she didn't know *me*. We had never met. I realized that I had seen her in motion pictures when she was much younger. A second later, I came up with her name. She was **Barbira Mencken**, the ex-wife of Paul Slazinger.

Mendoza, Jose. *In* Breakfast of Champions, *Mendoza is the Puerto Rican gang member who paints the insignia of the Pluto Gang on the backs of members' jackets. The Pluto Gang hopes to rid their neighborhood of drug dealers so the government would be more inclined to provide social services.*

Mengel, Bernard. *One of four guards assigned to Howard Campbell in the Old Jerusalem basement* jail cell. Mengel is a *Polish Jew who* once saved his own life in the Second World War by playing so dead that a German soldier pulled out three of his teeth without suspecting that Mengel was not a corpse (MN 3).

Mengel helped hang Auschwitz commandant Rudolf Franz Hoess by tying his legs together with a leather strap. (MN 4) "After we finished hanging Hoess . . . I packed up my clothes to go home. The catch on my suitcase was broken, so I buckled it shut with a big leather strap. Twice within an hour I did the very same job—once to Hoess and once to my suitcase. Both jobs felt about the same."

Mengel later tells Campbell that judging from the way he sleeps compared with the other Nazi prisoners, he must have a very guilty conscience about his war activities. After a period of routine and familiarity, Mengel tells Campbell that he observes his sleep constantly breaks from restlessness with frantic cries into the night. His other Nazi prisoners sleep perfectly soundly.

Merble, Lionel. *The owner of the Ilium School of Optometry and father-in-law of Billy Pilgrim in* Slaughterhouse-Five. *After his death in the charter flight that crashes in the Sugarbush Mountains, Billy becomes the school's proprietor.*

Merganthaler, Corporal. *The corporal is the central figure in a war story told by a sergeant about how he received the Silver Star. Paul Proteus overhears the story while riding on a train through upstate New York. The story highlights the importance of technology over individual acts of bravery. The sergeant says his unit was about to have its perimeter overrun when he sent Merganthaler back for help.* (PP XXVI) So over they come, screamin' bloody murder, and us with nothing but our goddamn rifles and bayonets workin'. Looked like a tidal wave comin' over at us. . . . Just then, up comes **Merganthaler** with a truck and generator he's moonlight-requisitioned from the 57th. We hooked her into our lines, cranked her up, and my God, I wish you could of seen it. The poor bastards fryin' on the electric fence, the proximity mines poppin' under 'em,' the microwave sentinels openin' up with the remote-control machine-gun nests, and the fire-control system swiveling the guns and flamethrowers around as long as anything was quiverin' within a mile of the place. And that's how I got the Silver Star."

Merrihue, Faith. (GBR 8) And blind George *(General George Rosewater)* was given a fourteen-year-old girl, an orphan named **Faith Merrihue**, who was to be his eyes and his messenger. When she was sixteen, George married her. *She later gives birth to Abraham Rosewater.*

Messiah. *Paul Proteus (the Ghost Shirt Society), Eliot Rosewater, and Kilgore Trout are all cast as messiahs, though none ever tries to pose as such. Proteus is the victim of the scheming Ghost Shirt Society, which seeks to reclaim human dignity in a world full of technomania. Eliot Rosewater's benevolence is ignorantly though innocently inflated by Diana Moon Glampers and Mary Moody, while Norman Mushari is quick to exploit his kindness. Billy Pilgrim views Kilgore Trout as one of the many holy men he saw go to waste in Dresden.*
(PP IX) "You figure to be the new **Messiah**?" said Finnerty. *Ed Finnerty is speaking with Reverend Lasher.*

"Sometimes I think I'd like to be—if only in self-defense. Also, it'd be a swell way to get rich. Trouble is, I can be sold or unsold on anything too easily. I enjoy being talked into something. Pretty shaky outlook for a **Messiah**. Besides, who ever heard of a short, fat, middle-aged **Messiah** with bad eyesight? And I haven't got that common touch. Frankly, the masses give me a pain in the tail, and I guess I show it." He made clucking sounds with his tongue. "I'm going to get myself a uniform, so I'll know what I think and stand for."
(PP X) If his attempt to become the new **Messiah** had been successful, if the inhabitants of the north and south banks had met in the middle of the bridge with Paul between them, he wouldn't have had the slightest idea of what to do next. He knew with all his heart that the human situation was a frightful botch, but it was such a logical, intelligently arrived-at botch that he couldn't see how history could possibly have led anywhere else.
(PP XXIX) "And the Ghost Dance religion," said

Lasher, "was that last, desperate defense of the old values. **Messiahs** appeared, the way they're always ready to appear, to preach magic that would restore the game, the old values, the old reasons for being. There were new rituals and new songs that were supposed to get rid of the white men by magic. And some of the more warlike tribes that still had a little physical fight left in them added a flourish of their own—the Ghost Shirt."

(GBR 7) Mushari did not register disappointment. The baptism would hold up very well in court as evidence that Eliot thought of himself as a **Messiah**.

(SL5 8) Trout's paranoid face was terribly familiar to Billy, who had seen it on the jackets of so many books. But, coming upon that face suddenly in a home-town alley, Billy could not guess why the face was familiar. Billy thought maybe he had known this cracked **messiah** in Dresden somewhere. Trout certainly looked like a prisoner of war.

(PS Religion) "It may be that moral simplicity is not possible in modern times. It may be that simplicity and clarity can come only from a new **messiah**, who may never come. We can talk about portents, if you like. I like a good portent as much as anyone. What might be the meaning of the comet Kahoutek [sic], which was to make us look upward, to impress us with the paltriness of our troubles, to cleanse our souls with cosmic awe? Kahoutek was a fizzle, and what might this fizzle mean?"

See also: PP IX; XXX; XXXIV.

Metzger, Eloise. In Deadeye Dick, the ill-fated pregnant woman who is vacuuming her home when Rudy Waltz unthinkingly fires a shot from the upstairs gunroom of his home. She was the wife of George Metzger, city editor of the Bugle-Observer, and the mother of Eugene Debs Metzger and Jane Addams Metzger.

Metzger, Eugene Debs and Jane Addams. The children of George and Eloise Metzger. (DD 15) **Eugene** and **Jane** were named . . . for Eugene V. Debs, the labor hero from Terre Haute, Indiana, and Jane Addams, the Nobel prize–winning social reformer from Cedarville, Illinois.

(DD 15) **Eugene Debs Metzger**, it turned out,

lived in Athens, Greece, and owned several tankers, which flew the flag of Liberia.

His sister, **Jane Addams Metzger**, who found her mother dead and vacuum cleaner still running so long ago, a big, homely girl, as I recall, and big and homely still, according to Ketchum, was living with a refugee Czech playwright on Molokai, in the Hawaiian Islands, where she owned a ranch and was raising Arabian horses.

Metzger, George. The widowed husband of Eloise Metzger and the editor of the Midland City Bugle-Observer. (DD 13) He was bald on top. He was skinny, and his posture was bad, and he was dressed like almost no other man in Midland City—in gray flannel trousers and a tweed sport coat, what I would recognize much later at Ohio State as the uniform of an English professor. All he did was write and edit at the Bugle-Observer all day long. . . . He was a newspaper gypsy. He had been hired away from the Indianapolis Times. It would come out at legal proceedings later on that he was born to poor parents in Kenosha, Wisconsin, and had put himself through Harvard, and that he had twice worked his way to Europe on cattle boats. The adverse information about him, which was brought out by our lawyer, was that he had once belonged to the Communist party, and had attempted to enlist in the Abraham Lincoln Brigade during the Spanish Civil War.

Metzger was sickened by the behavior of the police officers that bring him to the jail in the hope he would beat Rudy Waltz for killing his wife. Instead, he leaves the station and forgives Rudy in a Bugle-Observer editorial. (DD 13) "My wife has been killed by a machine which should never have come into the hands of any human being. It is called a firearm. It makes the blackest of all human wishes come true at once, at a distance: that something die.

"There is evil for you.

"We cannot get rid of mankind's fleetingly wicked wishes. We can get rid of the machines that make them come true.

"I give you a holy word: DISARM."

Metzger hires Bernard Ketchum to sue Otto Waltz and succeeds in taking most of the family's assets. He leaves for Florida and buys a weekly newspaper in Cedar Key, investing the rest of the Waltz family wealth in "two thousand acres of open land near Orlando." He makes a fortune when Disney purchases the land for development.

Aside from the weekly Metzger purchases, he tries and fails to produce a newspaper expressing his exotic views on war and firearms and the brotherhood of man and so on (DD 15).

Miasma, Khashdrahr. The nephew of and interpreter for the Shah of Bratpuhr in Player Piano. His name appears in this quite different context. (BC 24) The two physicians on the disaster vehicle named Martha were Cyprian Ukwende, of Nigeria, and **Khashdrahr Miasma**, from the infant nation of Bangladesh. Both were parts of the world that were famous from time to time for having the food run out. Both places were specifically mentioned, in fact, in Now It Can Be Told, by Kilgore Trout. Dwayne Hoover read in that book that robots all over the world were constantly running out of fuel and dropping dead, while waiting around to test the only free-willed creature in the Universe, on the off-chance that he should appear.

Microsecond Arbitrage, Inc. The center of a major stock swindle that leaves a number of Tarkington benefactors, and Tarkington College itself, nearly penniless. (HP 13) That swindle claimed to be snapping up bargains in food and shelter and clothing and fuel and medicine and raw materials and machinery and so on before people who really needed them could learn of their existence. And then the company's computers, supposedly, would get the people who really needed whatever it was to bid against each other, running profits right through the roof. It was able to do this with its clients' money, supposedly, because its computers were linked by satellites to marketplaces in every corner of the world.

The computers, it would turn out, weren't connected to anything but each other and their credulous clients like Tarkington's Board Chairman.

Board Chairman Robert W. Moellenkamp is so excited about Microsecond Arbitrage that he authorizes the sale of all the college's property in Scipio (including the old wagon factory, brewery, and

land), to a Japanese company, preferring to invest the cash in the fraudulent firm.

middle-European humor (see **humor**).

Middleton, Andy. In the short story "Find Me a Dream," Andy Middleton is the clarinet player and leader of the Creon Pipe-Dreamers, a supper-club jazz band. While taking a short break from playing at Creon's Pipe City Golf and Country Club, he strolls out to the golf course where he meets Hildy Matthews, the widowed mother of two young children. She is all set to marry Arvin Borders, but she sees in Middleton the kind of musical spirituality and material security that makes her more comfortable. After all, she lives to fulfill others' dreams. She does not want to ruin Border's career prospects, so despite her engagement, she asks Middleton to marry her, promising to love him and help fulfill his dreams.

Midland City. The locus of activity in both Breakfast of Champions and Deadeye Dick. In Breakfast of Champions, Vonnegut uses it as the meeting ground for Kilgore Trout, Dwayne Hoover, and himself during the October 1972 Midland City Arts Festival commemorating the opening of the Mildred Barry Memorial Center for the Arts. Trout is invited to take part in a symposium entitled "The Future of the American Novel in the Age of McLuhan." In Deadeye Dick, Midland City is where Rudy Waltz fires the errant and fateful shot that kills the pregnant Eloise Metzger. The blizzard of February 14, 1960, devastates the town. It is later neutron-bombed, and Hippolyte Paul De Mille resurrects the ghost of the World War I ace Will Fairchild at Calvary Cemetery.

Many view Midland City as Vonnegut's stand-in for his hometown of Indianapolis. He borrowed the name of the real Crispus Attucks High School of Indianapolis and placed it in Midland City, and the tragic death of Mrs. Metzger occurs on Mother's Day 1944, the same day Vonnegut's mother committed suicide.

Midland City is also the hometown of Galápagos's James Wait, the product of a dysfunctional family in that his father and sister had an incestuous relationship and left town to live together. James *studied auto mechanics in high school before going to New York City to become a male prostitute.* Hocus Pocus's *Eugene Debs Hartke, Jr., moved there with his family when only two years old so his father could work for Robo-Magic Corporation.*

Vonnegut's description of the sensibilities of Midland City residents sounds remarkably similar to his description of the totalitarian mind as understood through his cuckoo clock in Hell analogy. (BC 15) It *didn't matter much what most people in* **Midland City** *said out loud, except when they were talking about money or structures or travel or machinery—or other measurable things. Every person had a clearly defined part to play—as a black person, a female high school drop-out, a Pontiac dealer, a gynecologist, a gas-conversion burner installer. If a person stopped living up to expectations, because of bad chemicals or one thing or another, everybody went on imagining that the person was living up to expectations anyway.*

That was the main reason the people in **Midland City** *were so slow to detect insanity in their associates. Their imaginations insisted that nobody changed much from day to day. Their imaginations were flywheels on the ramshackle machinery of the awful truth.*

Notable Midland City events and institutions in Breakfast of Champions:
Adult Correctional Institution at Shepherdstown (nearby)
Blizzard of 1960 (February 14, the night of Rudy's opening/closing of "Katmandu" in Greenwich Village)
Crispus Attucks High School (Innocent Bystander High)
Dwayne Hoover's Exit Eleven Pontiac Village
Fairchild Hotel
Fairchild Boulevard—main street of town
George Washington Carver High School
Holiday Inn (site of the Trout-Hoover-Vonnegut confrontation)
John F. Kennedy High School
Keedsler Automobile Company
Maharishi Mahesh Yogi once visited
Maritimo Brothers Construction (BC, DD)
Mildred Barry Memorial Center for the Arts (BC, DD)

Midland City Arts Festival, October 1972
Midland City Association of Women's Clubs
Midland City Bugle-Observer
Midland City Chamber of Commerce
Midland County General Hospital
Midland County National Bank (BC, DD)
The Opera House, home of the Midland City Symphony Orchestra, eventually becomes a movie house called the Bannister, and later becomes the home of the Empire Furniture Company
Prairie Mutual
Radio Station WMCY
Robo-Magic Corporation of America, later becoming the Midland City Ordnance Company and eventually Barrytron, Limited. In the end, Du Pont buys out Barrytron. (HP)
Sacred Miracle Cave
Saint Christopher High School, later changed to Saint Athanasius
Sugar Creek
Tomb of George Hickman Bannister
The violent emotional breakdown of Dwayne Hoover, and in the same week a fourteen-year-old boy shoots his parents because he didn't want to show them his bad report card.
Western Electric

Notable Midland City events and institutions in Deadeye Dick:
Avondale, a suburb of Midland City developed by the Maritimo Brothers Construction Co. and where Emma Waltz dies of exposure to radioactivity from cement used during the Manhattan Project.
Calvary Cemetery (BC, DD)
Fairchild High School, where Celia Hildreth starred in the local production of Rudy Waltz's "Katmandu"
Fairchild Park
Farmers of Southwestern Ohio for Nuclear Sanity
Liederkranz cheese invented by a local dairy around 1865
Midland County Fair (1922) during which World War I ace Will Fairchild of the Lafayette Escadrille crashes during an exhibition. He wasn't wearing a parachute. Hippolyte Paul De Mille resurrects Fairchild's spirit at Calvary cemetery at the close of Deadeye Dick.

Midland County Mask and Wig Club
Midland County Rod and Gun Club
Mothers Day 1944, Rudy kills Eloise Metzger and
    her fetus
The Quality Motor Court
Rudy Waltz — born in 1932
Schramm's Drugstore (where Rudy Waltz works as
    the night-shift pharmacist)
Tally-ho Room
YMCA

The Midland City Ordnance Co. *The base of Dwayne Hoover's financial nest egg enabling him to purchase his car agency, Dwayne Hoover's Exit Eleven Pontiac Village.* (BC 4) Here is where Dwayne got the money to buy the agency: He borrowed it from the *Midland County National Bank.* For collateral, he put up stock he owned in a company which was then called the **Midland City Ordnance Company**. It later became *Barrytron, Limited*. When Dwayne first got the stock, in the depths of the Great Depression, the company was called *The RoboMagic Corporation of America*.

The name of the company kept changing through the years because the nature of its business changed so much. But its management hung on to the company's original motto — for old time's sake. The motto was this:

GOODBYE, BLUE MONDAY.

Midland County Mask and Wig Club. In Deadeye Dick, *the community theater fulfills the wishes of Fred T. Barry to perform an all-Ohio revival of Rudy Waltz's "Katmandu."*

Midland County Merchants Bank. *The bank that forecloses on ex-slave Josephus Hoobler's Bluebird Farm, in* Breakfast of Champions. *Dwayne Hoover's father (descendant of Josephus) is later awarded the farm in an insurance settlement for a car accident. Bluebird Farm is the location of Sacred Miracle Cave.*

Midnight Pussycats. *The pornographic magazine features a cover story about the fate of Montana Wildhack. The editors suspect she is at the bottom of San Pedro Bay, the victim of a gangland-style mur-*

der. (SL5 9) Billy *(Pilgrim)* wanted to laugh. The magazine, which was published for lonesome men to jerk off to, ran the story so it could print pictures taken from blue movies which Montana had made as a teen-ager. Billy did not look closely at these. They were grainy things, soot and chalk. They could have been anybody.

Midway College. *If Vonnegut's maxim is true that Peculiar travel suggestions are dancing lessons from God* (MWC 11), *then Midway College qualifies as the ballroom mambo he danced to the end.* (MWC Author's Note) Here's the thing: Back in 1993, almost eleven years ago now, I was scheduled to lecture on November 1 at **Midway College**, a women's school on the edge of Lexington. Well in advance of my appearance, a Kentucky artist, Joe Petro III, son of the Kentucky artist Joe Petro II, asked me to do a black-and-white self-portrait, which he could then use in silk-screen posters to be used by the school. So I did and he did. Joe was only thirty-seven back then, and I was a mere spring chicken of only seventy-one, not even twice his age.

Their collaborative efforts in transferring Vonnegut's art to silkscreened prints occupied much of Vonnegut's interest in his later years. The Midway College connection came through Vonnegut's longtime friend and former General Electric public relations associate Ollie Lyons. The event was remarkable for a number of reasons.

It was the reunion of old friends who made genuine time for each other over the years.

It was the beginning of Vonnegut's long partnership with Joe Petro III.

It was another opportunity for Vonnegut to meet with Peter Reed, his first major academic supporter, who was there with Marc Leeds to photograph and interview the author for contributions to two books edited by them.

Midway College did very well with their fundraiser.

Mihalich, Jeff. In Timequake, *Vonnegut mentions getting a letter from this physics major attending the University of Illinois at Urbana, confiding that despite his stellar performance in the subject as a high school student, he was having terrible difficulties with it at the university and losing his enthusiasm for the* *subject. Vonnegut takes the opportunity to address his quandary in two ways, the first with a preview of what he plans to write in reply to Mihalich and the other as a general warning to all.* (TQ 38) "You might want to read the picaresque novel *The Adventures of Augie March* by Saul Bellow. The epiphany at the end, as I recall, is that we shouldn't be seeking harrowing challenges, but rather tasks we find natural and interesting, tasks we were apparently born to perform. . . ." *The second Vonnegut advisory leads in to a longer story about always having others around us who are simply better at any given activity.* (TQ 38) To put it another way: No matter what a young person thinks he or she is really hot stuff at doing, he or she is sooner or later going to run into somebody in the same field who will cut him or her a new asshole, so to speak.

Mildred Peasely Bangtree Memorial Theater. *In the play* Jekyll and Hyde Updated, *reprinted in* Palm Sunday, *the Sweetbread College theater where a student production of* Dr. Jekyll and Mr. Hyde *is rehearsing to raise funds for the bankrupt institution. The college's real-life Dr. Jekyll dies from gunshots onstage after having been transformed into a human-sized chicken.*

Miller, Bill (**Don?**). *Mary Alice Miller's father is inexplicably named both Bill and Don. Bill/Don is a one-third owner of Midland City's Holiday Inn and chairman of the Parole Board at the Adult Correctional Institution at Shepherdstown.* (BC 6) Dwayne owned a third of the inn partnership with Midland City's leading orthodontist, Dr. Alfred Maritimo, and **Bill Miller**, who was Chairman of the Parole Board at the Adult Correctional Institution at Shepherdstown, among other things.
(BC 23) Mary Alice's father, **Don Miller**, was, among other things, Chairman of the Parole Board at Shepherdstown. It was he who had decided that Wayne Hoobler, lurking among Dwayne's used cars again, was fit to take his place in society.
(BC 23) Mary Alice Miller's father, **Don Miller**, was in his car near Dwayne, waiting for Mary Alice to come back with her crown and scepter, but he never saw anything of the show Dwayne put on. . . . **Don** was lying on his back, with his head well below window level, resting, staring at the ceil-

ing. He was trying to learn French by means of listening to lessons recorded on tape.

Miller, Lydia and Verne (*also* **Miller's Hardware Store**). *In the short story* "Who Am I This Time?" (*in* Welcome to the Monkey House), *Verne owns Miller's Hardware Store and employs Harry Nash, the introvert who miraculously changes into character when performing on stage with the North Crawford Mask and Wig Club. Lydia often plays in the community theater, and she tries to warn Helene Shaw, a newcomer to the troupe, not to be seduced by Nash's onstage persona.*

Miller, Mary Alice. *The fifteen-year-old Women's Two Hundred Meter Breast Stroke Champion of the World, Mary Alice is the cover girl on the program for the Midland City Arts Festival and also Queen of the Festival.* (BC 19) The cover of the program showed her in a white bathing suit, with her Olympic Gold Medal hanging around her neck. . . . **Mary Alice** was smiling at a picture of Saint Sebastian, by the Spanish painter El Greco. It had been loaned to the Festival by Eliot Rosewater, the patron of Kilgore Trout. . . .
(BC 19) The picture **Mary Alice** smiled at with such uncritical bliss showed a human being who was so full of arrows that he looked like a porcupine. . . . (Her father), a member of the Parole Board out at Shepherdstown, had taught **Mary Alice** to swim when she was eight months old, and that he had made her swim at least four hours a day, every day, since she was three.

Mary Alice's legacy is defamed by Rabo Karabekian in the bar at the Holiday Inn, while Milo Maritimo hopes Midland City's fortunes will rise through the Arts Festival along with Mary Alice's fame. (BC 20) "No longer will Midland City be known merely as the home of **Mary Alice Miller**, the Women's Two Hundred Meter Breast Stroke Champion of the World. It will also be the city which first acknowledged the greatness of Kilgore Trout."

Ministry of Popular Enlightenment and Propaganda (*see* **Howard W. Campbell, Jr.**).

"The Minorite Church of Vienna." *When Rudy Waltz's father was an aspiring art student in Europe,* *he befriended another failing artist, Adolf Hitler. Rudy's father bought Hitler's watercolor of "The Minorite Church of Vienna," which hung for years over his parents' bed. At the time, it was the only money Hitler had earned in quite a while. When Hitler becomes chancellor of Germany, Otto Waltz sends his congratulations and the painting back to his old art buddy. Hitler invited the Waltzes to be his guests for a visit. Only Rudy stayed behind.*

Minot, Dr. Frank. *The author of* Are Adults Harmoniums? *takes issue with the popularity of Sarah Horne Canby's* Unk and Boaz in the Caves of Mercury *because he believes she romanticizes their exploits.* (ST 9) **Dr. Frank Minot** . . . sees something more sinister in the love children have for the book. "Dare we consider," he asks, "how close Unk and Boaz are to the everyday experience of children when Unk and Boaz deal solemnly and respectfully with creatures that are in fact obscenely unmotivated, insensitive, and dull?" **Minot**, in drawing a parallel between human parents and harmoniums, refers to the dealings of Unk and Boaz with harmoniums. The harmoniums spelled out for Unk and Boaz a new message of hope or veiled derision every fourteen Earthling days—for three years.

Minton, Horlick and Claire. *Horlick Minton is the new American ambassador to San Lorenzo and travels to the island republic on the same plane as bicycle manufacturer H. Lowe Crosby and John/Jonah, the text's narrator. He and his wife are described as a "duprass"—"a karass built for two." Claire had been a professional book indexer.*

Horlick was once fired by the State Department during the McCarthy era "for pessimism. Communism had nothing to do with it," as Crosby had intimated in his loud barroom baiting (CC 44). *Both Mintons acknowledged it was Claire's letter to* The New York Times *that cost Horlick his job.* (CC 44) "'Americans,'" he said, quoting his wife's letter to the *Times*, "'are forever searching for love in forms it never takes, in places it can never be. It must have something to do with the vanished frontier. . . .'"

"What was so awful about the letter?" I *(John/Jonah)* asked.

"The highest possible form of treason," said **Minton**, "is to say that Americans aren't loved wherever they go, whatever they do. **Claire** tried to make the point that American foreign policy should recognize hate rather than imagine love."

"I guess Americans *are* hated a lot of places."

"*People* are hated a lot of places. **Claire** pointed out in her letter that Americans, in being hated, were simply paying the normal penalty for being people, and that they were foolish to think they should somehow be exempted from that penalty. But the loyalty board didn't pay any attention to that. All they knew was that **Claire** and I both felt that Americans were unloved."

The Mintons die together as the walls of the presidential palace crumble into the sea when the San Lorenzan Air Force misfires at the target ships during a national celebration.

Miss Canal Zone. *Malachi Constant's most recent conquest. There was no question about it—the girl in the photograph was staggeringly beautiful. She was* **Miss Canal Zone**, *a runner-up in the Miss Universe Contest—and in fact far more beautiful than the winner of the contest. Her beauty had frightened the judges* (ST 1).

Constant uses her photograph to convince Rumfoord that he has no reason to accept his fate as a space traveler. Rumfoord tries to entice him with tales of the beautiful women to be had on Titan, and when he returns Malachi's photograph, he slips in another with the image of the three sirens of Titan. (ST 1) *Within the margins lay shimmering depths. The effect was much like that of a rectangular glass window in the surface of a clear, shallow, coral bay. At the bottom of that seeming coral bay were three women—one white, one gold, one brown. They looked up at Constant, begging him to come to them, to make them whole with love.*

Their beauty was to the beauty of **Miss Canal Zone** *as the glory of the Sun was to the glory of a lightning bug.*

"Miss Temptation" (1956) (*see* **Norman Fuller**).

Mitchell, Allison. *In the opening chapter of* Slaughterhouse-Five, *Vonnegut speaks about those accompanying him when he goes to see his old war buddy Bernard V. O'Hare.* (SL5 1) I took two little girls with me, my daughter, Nanny, and her best friend, **Allison Mitchell**. They had never been off Cape Cod before. When we saw a river, we had to stop so they could stand by it and think about it for a while.

Mitchell, Dr. Jerome. (*DD* 21) **Dr. Jerome Mitchell** was married to the former Barbara Squires, the younger sister of Anthony Squires. Anthony Squires was the policeman who had given me the nickname Deadeye Dick. *When in high school, Mitchell and Felix Waltz are bitter enemies. Mitchell is believed to sadistically torture dogs and cats all the while claiming to perform scientific experiments. He builds his practice by prescribing painkillers for anyone who wants them. He and his wife live next door to Dwayne and Celia Hoover and encourages his wife and Celia to take amphetamines. At Celia's funeral service, Dwayne Hoover loudly blames Dr. Mitchell for his part in turning her into a suicide.*

"Mnemonics." *Vonnegut's second short story, published in the April 1951 issue of* Collier's *magazine and reprinted in* Bagombo Snuff Box *(1999), concerns a love delayed. The addle-brained and disorganized businessman Alfred Moorhead seeks help at the Memory Clinic to learn new strategies to improve his faulty ways. His device for remembering clients' needs involves the visualization of steamy movie actresses from the 1940s and '50s. His fantasized relationships with these starlets is severely stressed when Moorhead's boss Ralph L. Thriller gives him a complex set of tasks requiring one too many actresses to remember. Confused and unconscious of his actions, Moorhead reaches out to the imaginary starlet before him, trying to remember her name and the client contact information he associates with her, and instead mistakenly and modestly grabs hold of his secretary, Ellen, for whom he has long since suppressed his desire. Her surprise pierces her own long-suppressed desires as her coy response ends the story.* "Oh, gosh!" said Alfred, freeing her. "Ellen—I'm sorry, I forgot myself."

"Well, praise be, you finally remembered me."

Moakely, George Minor. *Dr. Breed informs* Cat's Cradle's *narrator that on the site of the Ilium Re-search Laboratory there once stood the town stockade complete with gallows. In 1782 mass murderer George Minor Moakley suffered public hanging for killing twenty-six people. The narrator quietly appreciates the irony that escapes Dr. Breed, who finds it mind-boggling that Moakely went to his death unrepentant. Of course, the site of his execution is the same location where Dr. Hoenikker once worked on the Manhattan Project and later developed ice-nine.*

Mobutu, President. *In* Hocus Pocus, *Zaire's President Mobutu purchases a San Diego ice-cream company which then lays off Jerry Peck. He and wife Muriel return to the family's eastern roots in Scipio, New York.*

Moby Dick. *The great white whale is recalled four times in Vonnegut's work. In* Breakfast of Champions *Moby Dick is a huge painted boulder in Sacred Miracle Cave. Dan Gregory illustrates an edition of Melville's book in* Bluebeard, *and in* Hocus Pocus *the library display of bell clappers from the Lutz Carillon takes on mythic proportions*, it became a college tradition for upperclasspersons to tell incoming freshmen that the clappers were the petrified penises of different mammals. The biggest clapper, which had once belonged to Beelzebub, the biggest bell, was said to be the penis of none other than **Moby Dick**, the Great White Whale (*HP* 8). *In* A Man Without a Country, *Vonnegut uses Melville's great work to be counted as one of many with a similar comment on the human condition.* (*MWC* 2) Do you realize that all great literature—**Moby Dick**, Huckleberry Finn, A Farewell to Arms, The Scarlet Letter, The Red Badge of Courage, The Iliad *and* The Odyssey, Crime and Punishment, The Bible, *and* "The Charge of the Light Brigade"—are all about what a bummer it is to be a human being? (Isn't it such a relief to have somebody say that?)

Moellenkamp, Henry. *In* Hocus Pocus, *the nineteen-year-old dyslexic student graduates from Tarkington College in 1875, the school's sixth year of operation and the year its name changes from the Mohiga Valley Free Institute. Henry's grandfather was a board member and son-in-law of the institu-*

tion's founder, Aaron Tarkington. He sought the name change for fear his grandson's alma mater would sound like a poorhouse or hospital.

The Moellenkamp family remains great benefactors of the college. They donate the library, which Eugene Debs Hartke points out becomes the second best small private school library in the country. The family also constructs the bell tower housing the school's Lutz Carillon. The bell tower later houses Hartke as he turns memoirist. Hartke believes that without Henry's attendance and his family's great generosity, the school would long ago have failed along with the rest of Scipio.

Henry Moellenkamp graduates with honors and goes on to Oxford University, subsequently becoming a congressman and then a six-term United States senator from Ohio. At the turn of the century, Henry writes the lyrics to "Mary, Mary, Where Have You Gone?" a ballad composed by his friend and Indiana-born Paul Dresser, the brother of novelist Theodore Dreiser.

Moellenkamp, Robert W. In Hocus Pocus, Robert W. Moellenkamp is the last chairman of the Board of Trustees of Tarkington College. He is a descendant of Tarkington's founder, previous board members, and father of two Tarkingtonians. He presides over the board meeting that ousts Eugene Debs Hartke, though he is unaware that at that moment the Microsecond Arbitrage stock swindle was becoming public knowledge. He loses his family's ancient fortune and is responsible for the financial failure of the college. As were many other members of the Tarkington and Moellenkamp families, Robert is illiterate due to extreme dyslexia. However, he is also gifted with Aaron Tarkington's superior ability to memorize after listening to material read aloud two or three times.

Mohiga Ice Cream Emporium (see **Jerry and Muriel Peck**).

Mohiga Valley Free Institute (see **Tarkington College**).

Mohiga Wagon Company. Founded by the illiterate and dyslexic Aaron Tarkington in Hocus Pocus, the company prospers by building the "Conestoga"

wagon, the name commonly used to describe the covered wagons used by settlers heading to the western frontier. Aaron's son Elias stipulates in his last will and testament that the Mohiga Valley Free Institute should be established and financially endowed with his shares in the family-owned wagon company, carpet company, and brewery.

Moncrief, Earl. Winston Niles Rumfoord's butler in his Newport, Rhode Island, mansion, and a trusted friend from the time they played German batball together in Winston's youth. Moncrief is an integral part of Rumfoord's scheme to recruit people for the Army of Mars and their eventual invasion of Earth. While Rumfoord is split in time and space, The man who managed the Martian investments, headed the Martian Procurement Program and the Martian Secret Service on Earth, the man who took orders directly from Rumfoord, was **Earl Moncrief**, the ancient Rumfoord butler. **Moncrief**, given the opportunity at the very close of his servile life, became Rumfoord's ruthless, effective, and even brilliant Prime Minister of Earthling Affairs (ST 7).

At Rumfoord's direction, **Earl Moncrief**, the butler, built his financial, procurement, and secret service organizations with the brute power of cash and a profound understanding of clever, malicious, discontented people who lived behind servile facades.

It was such people who took the Martian money and the Martian orders gladly. They asked no questions. They were grateful for the opportunity to work like termites on the sills of the established order (ST 7).

It was Moncrief's responsibility to parcel out the schematics of Salo's spaceship to different manufacturers around the world and energize them with Universal Will to Become from Salo's ship.

Monzano, Miguel "Papa." The self-educated septuagenarian dictator of San Lorenzo in Cat's Cradle, and the first human being to die of ice-nine poisoning. Years earlier he spares the life of Franklin Hoenikker, who fled to San Lorenzo to avoid prosecution in Florida for smuggling cars to Cuba. "Papa" is so enamored to know that Franklin is the son of Felix Hoenikker that he makes him the Minister of Science and Progress.

"Papa" is part of the charade established by Bokonon and McCabe to make Bokononism taboo while working toward civil development of the island.

Despite publicly professing to be a Christian, "Papa" is a Bokononist to the very end, receiving the Bokononist Last Rites of boko-maru from Dr. Schlichter von Koenigswald. Monzano falls ill and is laid out in his bed, the converted dinghy from Bokonon's schooner the Lady's Slipper, the same boat that delivered Bokonon and Corporal Earl McCabe to San Lorenzo when their schooner sank. Now, the dinghy is plated with gold. It is here that "Papa" takes the vial from around his neck and ingests the chip of ice-nine given to him by Franklin Hoenikker when he first arrived on the island. When the walls of the castle begin to crumble, the dinghy and the body slip into the water below, turning all the world's water into crystalline ice-nine.

Monzano, Mona Aamons. The xylophone-playing blond negro beauty in Cat's Cradle, Mona is the daughter of Finnish architect Nestor Aamons and an unnamed San Lorenzan. Nestor dies shortly after completing Julian Castle's House of Hope and Mercy in the Jungle, leading "Papa" to adopt Mona when she is orphaned.

Philip Castle names the island's one hotel Casa Mona in her honor.

After "Papa" Monzano slips into the sea during the catastrophic commemoration of the Hundred Martyrs of Democracy, Mona and John/Jonah take refuge in an oubliette prepared for "Papa" in case of emergency. When they emerge three days later, they find hundreds of bodies in the frozen base of what was a waterfall. John/Jonah sees misery and deceit wrought by Bokonon's suicidal suggestions to the throngs, but Mona sees those suicides as a simple way to solve so much for so many. She then touches her finger to the ground and lifts the specks of ice-nine to her lips.

Moody, Mary (also **Foxcroft** and **Melody**). Mary Moody is descended from a long line of Rosewater County natives well know for arson and bearing twins. Mary was a suspected arsonist, convicted shoplifter, and a five-dollar whore (GBR 12).

In the course of the novel, Mary gives birth to twin daughters, Foxcroft and Melody. Long before Norman Mushari persuades Mary to file a false pa-

ternity suit against Eliot, she asks Eliot to baptize the twins. This, too, would be used by Mushari in legal action to wrest control of the Rosewater Foundation. In a phone conversation with Sylvia, Eliot says he reluctantly agreed to the ceremony despite having no clerical authority. (GBR 7) "What will you say? What will you do?"

"Oh—I don't know." Eliot's sorrow and exhaustion dropped away for a moment as he became enchanted by the problem. A birdy little smile played over his lips. "Go over to her shack, I guess. Sprinkle some water on the babies, say, 'Hello, babies. Welcome to Earth. It's hot in the summer and cold in the winter. It's round and wet and crowded. At the outside, babies, you've got about a hundred years here. There's only one rule that I know of, babies—:

"'God damn it, you've got to be kind.'"

Eliot sent each of the twins his usual present for children born in the county: a share of IBM stock.

Moon, Fletcher. Noah Rosewater paid to have Fletcher Moon take his place in the company of Indiana riflemen raised by his brother George for service in the Civil War. Moon's short service to the cause prompts an exchange of letters between the brothers that reveals the dry wit, greed, and lack of sentimentality so characteristic of their descendant, Senator Lister Ames Rosewater. (GBR 8) **Moon** was blown to hamburger by Stonewall Jackson's artillery at Second Bull Run.

During the retreat through the mud toward Alexandria, Captain Rosewater took time out to write his brother Noah this note:

Fletcher Moon kept up his end of the deal to the utmost of his ability. If you are put out about your considerable investment in him being used up so quickly, I suggest you write General Pope for a partial refund. Wish you were here.

George

To which Noah replied:

I am sorry about **Fletcher Moon**, but, as the Bible says, "A deal is a deal." Enclosed find some routine legal papers for you to sign. They empower me to run your half of the farm and the saw factory until your return, etc., etc. We are undergoing great privations here at home. Everything is going to the troops. A word of appreciation from the troops would be much appreciated.

Noah.

MoonMist Tobacco, Ltd. *In* The Sirens of Titan, *Malachi Constant tries to avoid the future as outlined by Winston Niles Rumfoord by selling his shares in Galactic Spacecraft and putting all the proceeds into MoonMist Tobacco. The most memorable advertisement for the company* was the picture of the three sirens of Titan. There they were—the white girl, the golden girl, and the brown girl.

The fingers of the golden girl were fortuitously spread as they rested on her left breast, permitting an artist to paint in a **MoonMist** Cigarette between two of three. The smoke from her cigarette passed beneath the nostrils of the brown and white girls, and their space-annihilating concupiscence seemed centered on mentholated smoke alone (ST 2).

As it turns out, MoonMist assists in the collapse of Constant's empire. The Journal of the American Medical Association *publishes an article indicating that MoonMist is the principal cause for sterility in both sexes. Ransom K. Fern, manager of Magnum Opus, conservatively approximates Constant's financial exposure to be around $5 billion.*

The image of the three sirens stays with Malachi though his memory is nearly wiped clean on Mars. Malachi eventually sees statues of the three sirens in a pool on Titan, placed there by Salo.

Moorhead, Alfred. *In* "Mnemonics," *Vonnegut's second published short story, originally appearing in the April 1951 issue of* Collier's *magazine and later reprinted in* Bagombo Snuff Box (1999), *Moorhead is the multitasking middle manager whose confidence in his own newly acquired memory skills, learned at a company-sponsored two day Memory Clinic, accidentally contributes to the unveiling of his suppressed love for his secretary, Ellen:* . . . since he had attended the company's two-day Memory Clinic, names, facts, and numbers clung to his memory like burdocks to an Airedale. The clinic had, in fact, indirectly cleared up just about every major problem in his uncomplicated life, save one—his inability to break the ice with his secretary, Ellen, whom he had silently adored for two

years. . . . *She is shocked by his momentary break in character and she has apparently also held suppressed emotions for her boss.*

Moorhead's memory success hinges on his use of mnemonics learned at a company workshop. His particular application of the system involves anchoring points of business information to the names of contemporary Hollywood starlets, which means from the 1940s and '50s, particularly Rita Hayworth, Lana Turner, Jane Russell, Ava Gardner, and Ann Sheridan.

It is while utilizing mnemonics to solve the confusing billing dilemma of closely named Davenport companies that Moorhead's suppressed love for his secretary, Ellen, comes out in a pained personal confession that he first commits in writing; he then— just as rashly and quickly—covers over those feelings. **Alfred** sighed and picked up a sheaf of invoices. The first was addressed to the **Davenport Spot-welding Company**. He closed his eyes and a shimmering tableau appeared. He had composed it two days previous, when Mr. Thriller had given him special instructions. Two davenports faced each other. Lana Turner, sheathed in a tight-fitting leopard skin, lay on one. On the other was Jane Russell, in a sarong made of telegrams. Both of them blew kisses to **Alfred**, who contemplated them for a moment, then reluctantly let them fade.

He scribbled a note to Ellen: Please make sure *Davenport Spot-welding Company* and *Davenport Wire and Cable Company* have not been confused in our billing. Six weeks before, the matter would certainly have slipped his mind. I love you, he added, and then carefully crossed it out with a long black rectangle of ink.

mopery. (TQ 17) Mrs. Wilkerson suspected plagiarism. Zoltan (*Pepper*) confessed, thinking it was a funny rather than a serious thing he'd done. To him, plagiarism was what Trout would have called a ***mopery***, "indecent exposure in the presence of a blind person of the same sex."

moral, moralist, morality, moralize, morally. (ST 1) Winston Niles Rumfoord was something else again—**morally**, spatially, socially, sexually, and electrically.

(ST 3) One night in Los Angeles, at any rate, Noel

Constant got it into his head to become a speculator. He was thirty-nine at the time, single, physically and **morally** unattractive, and a business failure.

(ST 11) At the height of his good luck, Malachi Constant was worth more than the states of Utah and North Dakota combined. Yet, I daresay, his **moral** worth was not that of the most corrupt little fieldmouse in either state.

(MN Introduction) This is the only story of mine whose **moral** I know. I don't think it's a marvelous **moral**; I simply happen to know what it is: We are what we pretend to be, so we must be careful about what we pretend to be.

. . . There's another clear **moral** to this tale, now that I think about it: When you're dead you're dead.

And yet another **moral** occurs to me now: Make love when you can.

It's good for you.

(MN 25) "That **Moral** Rearmament movement," he said, "believes in absolute honesty, absolute purity, absolute unselfishness, and absolute love." *A barfly has a conversation with Howard Campbell.*

In a conversation with Frank Wirtanen, his Blue Fairy Godmother, Howard Campbell begins, "I admire form," I said. "I admire things with a beginning, a middle, an end—and, whenever possible, a **moral**, too."

"If I'd killed myself when you expected me to kill myself," I said, "maybe a **moral** would have occurred to you. . . ."

"I'm not used to things having form—or **morals**, either," he said. "If you'd died, I probably would have said something like, 'Goddamn, now what'll we do?' A **moral**? It's a big enough job just burying the dead, without trying to draw a **moral** from each death," he said. "Half the dead don't even have names. I might have said you were a good soldier" (MN 32).

(MN 35) "*Memoirs of a Monogamous Casanova* is a curious little chapter in Russian history," said Wirtanen. "It could hardly be published with official approval in Russia—and yet, it was such an attractive, strangely **moral** piece of pornography, so ideal for a nation suffering from shortages of everything but men and women, that presses in Budapest were somehow encouraged to start printing it—and those presses have, somehow, never been

ordered to stop." *The depth of its passion and sensuality was made moral by its subject matter—the relationship between a husband and wife.*

(MH Preface) I used to be a public relations man for General Electric, and then I became a freelance writer of so-called "slick fiction," a lot of it science fiction. Whether I improved myself **morally** by making that change I am not prepared to say.

(MH Welcome to the Monkey House) "He didn't have the slightest idea his pills would be taken by human beings someday," said the Foxy Grandpa. "His dream was to introduce **morality** into the monkey house at the Grand Rapids Zoo. Did you realize that?" he inquired severely. *Foxy Grandpa is actually "Billy the Poet," the outlaw specializing in kidnapping and deflowering Ethical Suicide Parlor hostesses.*

(SL5 5) "There are no telegrams on Tralfamadore. But you're right: each clump of symbols is a brief, urgent message—describing a situation, a scene. . . . There is no beginning, no middle, no end, no suspense, no **moral**, no causes, no effects. What we love in our books are the depths of many marvelous moments seen all at one time."

(WFG Address to the American Physical Society) I have already called the fictitious inventor of the fictitious Ice-9 an old-fashioned sort of scientist. There used to be a lot of **morally** innocent scientists like him. No more. Younger scientists are extremely sensitive to the **moral** implications of all they do. My fictitious old-time scientist asked, among other things, this question: "What is sin?" He asked that question mockingly as though the concept of sin were as obsolete as plate armor. Young scientists, it seems to me, are fascinated by the idea of sin.

(WFG Address to the American Physical Society) I have never seen a more depressed audience leaving a theater. *The Diary of Anne Frank* was a lighthearted comedy when compared with Lilienthal's performance for that particular audience, on that particular night, in that particular city, where science was king. The young scientists and their young wives had learned something which most scientists now realize: that their bosses are not necessarily sensitive or **moral** or imaginative men. Ask Wernher Von Braun. His boss had him firing rockets at London.

The old-fashioned scientist I described in *Cat's Cradle* was the product of a great depression and of World War Two and some other things, of course. The mood of technical people in World War Two can be expressed in slogans such as "Can do!" and "The difficult we do right away; the impossible takes a little longer!"

The Second World War was a war against pure evil. I mean that seriously. There was never any need to **moralize**. Nothing was too horrible to do to any enemy that vile. This **moral** certainty and the heartlessness it encouraged did not necessarily subside when the war was won. Virtuous scientists, however, stopped saying "Can do!"

I don't find this particularly congenial, **moralizing** up here. **Moralizing** hasn't really been my style up to now. But people, university people in particular, seem to be demanding more and more that persons who lecture to them put **morals** at the end of their lectures.
(WFG Address to the American Physical Society) I asked one of my hosts in what way I had offended the audience. He replied that they had hoped I would **moralize**. They had hired me as a **moralist**.

So now when I speak to students, I do **moralize**. I tell them not to take more than they need, not to be greedy. I tell them not to kill, even in self-defense. I tell them not to pollute water or the atmosphere. I tell them not to raid the public treasury. I tell them not to work for people who pollute water or the atmosphere, or who raid the public treasury. I tell them not to commit war crimes or to help others to commit war crimes. These **morals** go over very well. They are, of course, echoes of what the young say themselves.
(WFG *Playboy* Interview) VONNEGUT: But my brother has always tried to be alert to the violent uses of what he might turn up, and it saddened him to find out that silver iodide had been used in warfare. So scientists *have* become concerned about the **morality** of what they're doing. It's been happening for some time. Several years ago, Norbert Wiener, the MIT mathematician, wrote in *Atlantic* that he wasn't going to give any more information to industry or the Government, because they weren't gentle people, because they don't have humane uses for things.
(JB 19) He told the jury, "This man, although he may not have actually committed the crime attributed to him, is nevertheless **morally** culpable, because he is the enemy of our existing institutions." *Vonnegut quotes Judge Webster Thayer's remarks at the murder trial of Sacco and Vanzetti. He cites the quote from* Labor's Untold Story, *written by Richard O. Boyer and Herbert M. Morais.*
(PS Epigraph)

> Whoever entertains liberal views
> and chooses a consort that is captured
> by superstition risks his liberty
> and his happiness.
> —CLEMENS VONNEGUT
> (1824–1906) *Instruction in Morals* (The Hollebeck Press, Indianapolis, 1900)

(PS Religion) Toward the end of our marriage, it was mainly religion in a broad sense that Jane and I fought about. She came to devote herself more and more to making alliances with the supernatural in her need to increase her strength and understanding—and happiness and health. This was painful to me. She could not understand and cannot understand why that should have been painful to me, or why it should be any of my business at all.

And it is to suggest to her and to some others why it was painful that I chose for this book's epigraph a quotation from a thin book, *Instruction in Morals*, published in 1900 and written by my Free Thinker great-grandfather Clemens Vonnegut, then seventy-six years old:

> "Whoever entertains liberal views and chooses a consort that is captured by superstition risks his liberty and his happiness."

(PS Religion) Socrates told us that the unexamined life wasn't worth living. The Louds demonstrated that the **morally** unstructured life is a clunker, too. *The Louds were the subject of a film documentary on average American family life.*
(PS Religion) "If I have offended anyone here by talking of the need of a new religion, I apologize. I am willing to drop the word religion, and substitute for it these three words: *heartfelt moral code*. We

sure need such a thing, and it should be simple enough and reasonable enough for anyone to understand. The trouble with so many of the **moral** codes we have inherited is that they are subject to so many interpretations. . . .

"If we were to try to grow recent strains of hypocrisy in the laboratory, what would we grow them in? I think they would grow like Jack's beanstalk in a mulch of ancient **moral** codes.

"It may be that **moral** simplicity is not possible in modern times. It may be that simplicity and clarity can come only from a new messiah, who may never come."

(*PS Religion*) "As an ordinary person, appalled as I am by the speed with which we are wrecking our topsoil, our drinking water, and our atmosphere, I will suggest an idea about good and evil which might fit into a modern and simple **moral** code. Evil disgusts us. Good fills us with joy and brings a sparkle to our eyes. That much remains the same. . . .

"But the worst thing about my **moral** code is that it invites people to have the fun of being glamorously wicked at first, which many of us feel is sexy, and then becoming almost swooningly virtuous at the end. This comes close to being the biography of Saint Augustine, and of several other famous holy men."

(*PS Religion*) "At any rate, I don't think anybody ever dreaded hell as much as most of us dread the contempt of our fellowmen. Under our new and **heartfelt moral code**, we might be able to horrify would-be evildoers with just that: the contempt of their fellowmen. . . .

"For that contempt to be effective, though, we would need cohesive communities, which are about as common as bald eagles these days. And it is curious that such communities should be so rare, since human beings are genetically such gregarious creatures. They need plenty of like-minded friends and relatives almost as much as they need B-complex vitamins and a **heartfelt moral code**."

(*Blue* 17) "Painters—and storytellers, including poets and playwrights and historians," he said. "They are the justices of the Supreme Court of Good and Evil, of which I am now a member, and to which you may belong someday!" (*Spoken by Dan Gregory.*)

How was *that* for delusions of **moral** grandeur! (*TQ* 6) In the only love story he *(Kilgore Trout)* ever attempted, "Kiss Me Again," he had written, "There is no way a beautiful woman can live up to what she looks like for any appreciable length of time."

The **moral** at the end of that story is this: "Men are jerks. Women are psychotic."

(*TQ* 21) Are we *(humanists)* enemies of members of organized religions? No. My great war buddy Bernard V. O'Hare, now dead, lost his faith as a Roman Catholic during World War Two. I didn't like that. I thought that was too much to lose.

I had never had faith like that, because I had been raised by interesting and **moral** people who, like Thomas Jefferson and Benjamin Franklin, were nonetheless skeptics about what preachers said was going on. But I knew Bernie had lost something important and honorable.

Again, I did not like that, did not like it because I liked him so much.

There is a poignant moment from the play within Timequake *when Vonnegut has Trout backstage awaiting his one train-whistle moment but totally caught up within the sentiments of another of his midwestern heroes, Abraham Lincoln. His acceptance of history and fate is tempered by optimism for the present.* (*TQ* 61) "Perhaps we have come to the dreadful day of awakening, and the dream is ended. If so, I am afraid it must be ended forever. I cannot believe that ever again will men have the opportunity we have had. Perhaps we should admit that, and concede that our ideals of liberty and equality are decadent and doomed. I have heard of an eastern monarch who once charged his wise men to invent him a sentence which would be true and appropriate in all times and situations. They presented him the words, 'And this too shall pass away.'

"That is a comforting thought in time of affliction—'And this too shall pass away.' And yet let us believe that it is not true! Let us live to prove that we can cultivate the natural world that is about us, and the intellectual and **moral** world that is within us, so that we may secure an individual, social and political prosperity, whose course shall be forward, and which, while the earth endures, shall not pass away. . . .

"I commend you to the care of the Almighty, as

I hope that in your prayers you will remember me. . . . Good-bye, my friends and neighbors."

An actor playing the bit part of Kavanagh, an Army officer, said, "Time to pull out, Mr. President. Better get inside the car."

Lincoln gets into the car as the crowd sings "John Brown's Body."

Another actor, cast as a brakeman, waved his lantern.

That was when Trout was supposed to blow the whistle, and he did.

As the curtain descended, there was a sob backstage. It wasn't in the playbook. It was ad lib. It was about beauty. It came from Kilgore Trout.

Vonnegut directly pairs his appreciation for Lincoln and Twain as midwestern voices that managed to focus attention on the most important issues. (MWC 7) Where are Mark Twain and Abraham Lincoln now when we need them? They were country boys from Middle America, and both of them made the American people laugh at themselves and appreciate really important, really **moral** jokes. Imagine what they would have to say today.

In A Man Without a Country, *Vonnegut includes a letter from a fan who is as upset with the immoral leadership of George W. Bush as he is. Vonnegut comments with a brief statement about the eternal nature of such creatures.* (MWC 10) But as William Shakespeare told us long ago, "The devil can cite Scripture for his purpose."

Or as a man from San Francisco put it in a letter to me:

How can the American public be so stupid? People still believe that Bush was elected, that he cares about us and has some idea of what he is doing. How can we "save" people by killing them and destroying their country? How can we strike first on the belief that we will soon be attacked? No sense, no reason, no **moral** grounds have gotten through to him. He is nothing but a moron puppet leading us all over the precipice. Why can't people see that the military dictator in the White House has no clothes?

I told him that if he doubted that we are demons in Hell, he should read *The Mysterious Stranger,* which Mark Twain wrote in 1898, long before the First World War (1914–1918). In the title story he proves to his own grim satisfaction, and to mine as well, that Satan and not God created the planet earth and "the damned human race." If you doubt that, read your morning paper. Never mind what paper. Never mind what date.

See also: PP III; VIII; XXVIII–XXIX; *ST* 1; 11; *MN* 25; 31–32; *CC* 113; *GBR* 1–2; 5; 7; *SL5* 5; *MH* Welcome to the Monkey House; *MH* The Foster Portfolio; *MH* New Dictionary; *WFG* Address to the American Physical Society; *WFG* Address at Rededication of Wheaton College Library, 1973; *Slap* 37; 44; *JB* Prologue; 23; *PS* Roots; *PS* The People One Knows; *PS* Religion; *PS* Children; *PS* Jekyll and Hyde Updated; *DD* 21; *Gal* 1:3; 1:13; 1:32–1:33; *HP* 5; 18; 20.

morale, morale-builders. (*PP* IV) The Meadows was a flat, grassy island in the St. Lawrence, in Chippewa Bay, where the most important men, and the most promising men ("Those whose development within the organization is not yet complete," said the Handbook) in the Eastern and Middle-Western Divisions spent a week each summer in an orgy of **morale** building—through team athletics, group sings, bonfires and skyrockets, bawdy entertainment, free whisky and cigars; and through plays, put on by professional actors, which pleasantly but unmistakably made clear the nature of good deportment within the system, and the shape of firm resolves for the challenging year ahead.

(*PP* V) Kroner and Baer seemed delighted. They were forever suggesting that teams be formed and games be played as a method for building **morale** in the Eastern Division's family.

(*PP* VI) Finnerty was a magical name again; Paul's feelings about him had swung a full circle. **Morale** and *esprit de corps*, which Paul hadn't felt in any undertaking for years, had sprung up between them in the course of the exhilarating humiliation of Checker Charley.

(*ST* 6) Boaz had arranged things so that he and Unk would be on board the company mother ship for the invasion. . . . It was meant to carry only two men, the rest of the space being taken up by candy, sporting goods, recorded music, canned hamburgers, board games, goofballs, soft drinks, Bibles, note paper, barber kits, ironing boards, and other **morale-builders**.

(*MN* 13) He (*Dr. Jones*) wasn't arrested until July in 1942, when he was indicted with twenty-seven others for: Conspiring to destroy the **morale** and faith and confidence of the members of the military and naval forces of the United States and the people of the United States in their public officials and republican form of government. . . .

(*PS* When I Lost My Innocence) I, for one, now know what is really going on, so I can plan more shrewdly and be less open to surprise. But my **morale** has been lowered a good deal, so I am probably not any stronger than I used to be.

(*PS* Religion) "Sermons deeply rooted in local history and sociology and politics are by and large harmless, and perhaps even charming in a relatively closed and isolated community. Why shouldn't a preacher in such a society raise the **morale** of his parishioners by implying they are better servants of God than strangers are? That is a very old type of sermon—very old indeed. As old as the hills. Read the Old Testament."

(*DD* 9) She was none other than Eleanor Roosevelt, the wife of the President of the United States. She was visiting war plants in the boondocks to raise **morale**.

(*DD* 10) Eleanor Roosevelt, with her dreams of a better world than this one, was well on her way to some other small city by then—to raise **morale**. So she never got to hear me shoot.

(*Gal* 1:22) He guessed right, at any rate, as to what was going to happen to the **morale** of the people of Ecuador within the next hour or so, when he said to Bobby King on the telephone: "Everybody down there is just going to fall apart when they find out that Mrs. Onassis isn't coming after all."

(*Gal* 1:26) One thing which made the Air Force such a high **morale** unit was that its equipment, bought on credit and delivered before the bankruptcy, was so up to date.

(*MWC* 7) But I know now that there is not a chance in hell of America becoming humane and reasonable. Because power corrupts us, and absolute power corrupts us absolutely. Human beings are chimpanzees who get crazy drunk on power. By saying that our leaders are power-drunk chimpanzees, am I in danger of wrecking the **morale** of our

soldiers fighting and dying in the Middle East? Their **morale**, like so many lifeless bodies, is already shot to pieces. They are being treated, as I never was, like toys a rich kid got for Christmas. *See also:* BAG The Package.

"More Stately Mansions" (1951) (*see* **Grace and George McClellan**).

Morgan, Eunice Eliot (*see* **Eunice Eliot Morgan Rosewater**).

Morissey, Bucky. *The son of Midland City Police Chief Francis X. Morissey. The father and son are part of the infamous 1916 hunting party during which August Gunther's head is accidentally blown off by a point-blank shotgun blast from Chief Morissey. Aside from the victim, their hunting companions included Otto Waltz and John Fortune.*

Bucky was often around loose gun play. He and Felix Waltz used to sneak weapons out of Otto's gun room and shoot crows perched on headstones in Calvary Cemetery, and had cut off telephone service to several farms by shooting insulators along the Shepherdstown Turnpike, and had blasted God-only-knows how many mailboxes all over the county, and had actually loosed a couple of rounds at a herd of sheep out near Sacred Miracle Cave (*DD* 9). *Felix once saved his friends by pulling a loaded Colt 45 from his jacket when threatened by a gang of boys.*

Morissey, Francis X. *In* Deadeye Dick, *this Midland City police chief accidentally blows off the head of hunting companion August Gunther in 1916. The other hunters, Otto Waltz, John Fortune, and Bucky Morissey (the chief's son), agreed it didn't pay to ruin Morissey's life because of the accident, so they let Gunther's body drift down Sugar Creek.*

Years later it is Chief Morissey who goes to the Waltz home with news about the death of Eloise Metzger. Morissey knew who used the kind of ammunition that killed her, and he tries to give Otto an opportunity to excuse any knowledge about the incident, but Waltz loudly claims the blame for Rudy's indiscretion. Much to Morissey's consternation, he cannot protect his friend from the harsh treatment handed out by the other officers.

Mother Night (1961) (*see also* **Howard Campbell, cuckoo-clock in Hell,** *and* ***Faust***). (MN Introduction) This is the only story of mine whose moral I know. I don't think it's a marvelous moral; I simply happen to know what it is: We are what we pretend to be, so we must be careful about what we pretend to be. . . .

If I'd been born in Germany, I suppose I would have *been* a Nazi, bopping Jews and gypsies and Poles around, leaving boots sticking out of snowbanks, warming myself with my secretly virtuous insides. So it goes.

Vonnegut's introduction to Mother Night *alludes to the timeless dynamic tension pitting appearance versus reality. Musing about life as a German born and bred parallel to his own time frame as a German American forces the issue of identity to the fore. His fantasizing is in recognition of the fact that one's place and significance within a given moment of existence is simultaneously defined by outsiders considering the facades we present and by ourselves contemplating the various mitigating factors that prompt our actions. An obvious dilemma arises when the spectators of our lives disagree with our own perceptions about the motives and actions we use to define us. As difficult as life may be with those critical of our actions, it is all the more contentious when we can't coalesce our own motives and deeds with our preconceived notions of identity. Vonnegut's real concern is with his hyphenated sense of self and, as a result,* Mother Night *is a study of the stateless schizophrenic Howard Campbell, trapped by the peculiarities of heredity and environment that mitigate any attempt to produce a satisfying self-image. Vonnegut's exploration of hyphenated lineage is more concerned with circumstances contributing to the establishment of identity than it is with coalescing one's multiplicity into a satisfying whole.*

Mothers' Auxiliary of the Paul Revere Association of Militant Gentiles. *This civic association gives the racist Rev. Dr. Lionel J. D. Jones a star sapphire ring in 1940, in* Mother Night.

Mott, Dr. Stewart Rawlings (*affectionately known as* **"Flocka Butt"**). *The Texas physician relocates to Vermont to care for Eliza and Wilbur Swain. The twins hold genuine affection for Mott to the ex-* tent *that Wilbur is excited about the prospect of seeing him in the afterlife along with Eliza. Mott is summarily discharged by the twins' parents when Wilbur and Eliza reveal their true intelligence. Mott's last words to Wilbur are contained in a birthday greeting after he learned of his patients' advanced standing,* "'If you can do no good, at least do no harm.' Hippocrates" (*Slap* 28).

Mott's grandson becomes the King of Michigan

Mott, Stewart Oriole-2. *The King of Michigan and archenemy of the Duke of Oklahoma in* Deadeye Dick. *President Wilbur Swain signs away all the territory governed by the 1803 Louisiana Purchase and turns it over to Mott, but the largest part of the land transaction is already in the hands of the Duke of Oklahoma.*

The King of Michigan is also the grandson of Dr. Stewart Rawlings Mott, the physician who takes care of the Swain twins at their Vermont estate until they revealed their true intelligence.

"Mouth Crazy" (*see* **"Pan-Galactic Straw-boss"**).

Mozart, Wolfgang Amadeus. *Mozart is mentioned in nine Vonnegut works:* Happy Birthday, Wanda June; Breakfast of Champions; Wampeters, Foma & Granfalloons; Slapstick; Palm Sunday; Hocus Pocus; Timequake; *and* A Man Without a Country. *Mozart is known to play shuffleboard in heaven along with Hitler and Einstein in* Wanda June. *In* Breakfast of Champions*, busts of Mozart and Shakespeare still reside in the high niches of the Bannister, at one time Midland City's leading movie house. Vonnegut quotes from Hesse's* Steppenwolf *in his essay "Why They Read Hesse," pointing out that the two leading characters in the text are Goethe and Mozart—both favorites of his father.*

Dr. Cordelia Swain Cordiner is the enraged psychometric expert in Slapstick *who compares her talents with those of Mozart and Einstein. (Slap 16)* ". . . let me say that asking a person of my calibre to come all this distance into the wilderness to personally administer tests to only two children is like asking **Mozart** to tune a piano. It is like asking Albert Einstein to balance a checkbook. Am I getting through to you, 'Mistress Eliza and Master Wilbur,' as I believe you are called?"

Vonnegut heaps more praise on Mozart when Eugene Debs Hartke recounts the plot of "The Protocols of the Elders of Tralfamadore." (HP 26) If the author was right that the whole point of life on Earth was to make germs shape up so that they would be ready to ship out when the time came, then even the greatest human being in history, Shakespeare or **Mozart** or Lincoln or Voltaire or whoever, was nothing more than a Petri dish in the truly Grand Scheme of Things.

(TQ 38) "Of native talent itself I say in speeches: 'If you go to a big city, and a university is a big city, you are bound to run into **Wolfgang Amadeus Mozart**. Stay home, stay home.'"

To put it another way: No matter what a young person thinks he or she is really hot stuff at doing, he or she is sooner or later going to run into somebody in the same field who will cut him or her a new asshole, so to speak.

(TQ 43) I was pleased to reply with an epistle which was frankly vengeful, since he and Father had screwed me out of a liberal arts college education: "Dear Brother: This is almost like telling you about the birds and the bees," I began. "There are many good people who are beneficially stimulated by some, but not all, manmade arrangements of colors and shapes on flat surfaces, essentially nonsense. You yourself are gratified by some music, arrangements of noises, and again essentially nonsense. If I were to kick a bucket down the cellar stairs, and then say to you that the racket I had made was philosophically on a par with *The Magic Flute*, this would not be the beginning of a long and upsetting debate. An utterly satisfactory and complete response on your part would be, 'I like what **Mozart** did, and I hate what the bucket did.'

"Contemplating a purported work of art is a social activity. Either you have a rewarding time, or you don't. You don't have to say why afterward. You don't have to say anything.

"You are a justly revered experimentalist, dear Brother. If you really want to know whether your pictures are, as you say, 'art or not,' you must display them in a public place somewhere, and see if strangers like to look at them. That is the way the game is played. Let me know what happens."

(MWC 7) Back to music. It makes practically everybody fonder of life than he or she would be without it. Even military bands, although I am a pacifist, always cheer me up. And I really like Strauss and **Mozart** and all that, but the priceless gift that African Americans gave the whole world when they were still in slavery was a gift so great that it is now almost the only reason many foreigners still like us at least a little bit. That specific remedy for the worldwide epidemic of depression is a gift called the blues. All pop music today—jazz, swing, bebop, Elvis Presley, the Beatles, the Stones, rock-and-roll, hip-hop, and on and on—is derived from the blues.

Muir, Edward. *An American poet, teacher, and advertising man whose travels, occupations, and personal fate so mirrored Vonnegut's that he proclaims* **Ed Muir** *is surely a member of my karass (TQ 11). Though they did not meet until living on Cape Cod, they previously had simultaneous stops at the University of Chicago and Schenectady, New York. Muir recruited the Vonneguts to lead a Great Books group on Cape Cod. They later divorced at around the same time and found themselves living in New York City.*

Vonnegut recalls sending Muir a letter complaining about his writer's block after praising Reader's Block *by David Markson, a former student of Muir's at Union College in Schenectady. Muir returns Vonnegut's letter reformatted as a poem. Vonnegut reproduces it in italics. (TQ 11)*

And no thanks to Fate.
When we're gone, there won't be anybody
Sufficiently excited by ink on paper
To realize how good it is.

I have this ailment not unlike
Ambulatory pneumonia, which might be
   called
Ambulatory writer's block.

I cover paper with words every day,
But the stories never go anywhere
I find worth going.

Slaughterhouse-Five *has been turned*
Into an opera by a young German,

*And will have its premiere in Munich this
    June.
I'm not going there either.
Not interested.*

*I am fond of Occam's Razor,
Or the Law of Parsimony, which suggests
That the simplest explanation of a phenome-
    non
Is usually the most trustworthy.*

*And I now believe, with David's help,
That writer's block is finding out
How lives of loved ones really ended
Instead of the way we hoped they would end
With the help of our body English.
Fiction is body English.*

Müller, Gerhard. *The Dresden taxi driver who befriends Vonnegut and Bernard V. O'Hare on their
postwar trip to East Germany and the slaughterhouse in which they took refuge. Müller was a German POW held by the Americans. His mother was
killed in the Dresden firebombing. He sent O'Hare a
Christmas card with a sentiment that apparently
made a deep impression on Vonnegut.* (SL5 1) "I
wish you and your family also as to your friend
Merry Christmas and a happy New Year and I hope
that we'll meet again in a world of peace and freedom in the taxi cab if the accident will."

I like that very much: "If the accident will."

Vonnegut dedicates Slaughterhouse-Five *to
Mary O'Hare and Gerhard Müller. Mary was the
one who reminded Vonnegut that he and his war
buddies were mere children in the war: hence, the
subtitle, "The Children's Crusade."*

Muller, Harve and Bea (*see* **Grand Triumvirate**).

Murphy, Hal. *In the short story "Custom-Made
Bride," collected in* Bagombo Snuff Box *(1999),
Murphy is the lawyer of the artist and designer Otto
Krummbein. Krummbein is in danger of going to jail
for failing to pay income taxes. At Murphy's urging,
Krummbein agrees to meet with his friend, an unnamed financial adviser, who is the narrator of the
story. Hal tells the narrator,* "You take care of them
while I try to keep him out of prison. I've told him

all about you, and he says for you to come out to his
house right away."

Murra, George and John. *George Murra is the
fifth husband of Gloria Hilton in the 1962 short
story "Go Back to Your Precious Wife and Son," reprinted in* Welcome to the Monkey House *(1968).
He leaves his wife and son John after meeting Hilton
in preparation for writing a screenplay for her. After
the couple moves to New Hampshire to be closer to
his son's private high school, Hilton becomes disenchanted with Murra, who has failed to write anything since their marriage. She leaves Murra and he
befriends the bathtub enclosure man, the story's narrator.*

*John is aloof and furious with his father. George
is able to win back John's respect only when he follows the advice of his bathtub man and kicks the boy
in the ass. They call Murra's first wife back in Los
Angeles and plan to reunite.*

Murray, Albert. *In* A Man Without a Country,
*Vonnegut cites noted musicologist Albert Murray as
a bridge to understanding the depth of American
cultural empowerment engendered in our only original musical form, jazz. Murray understands that the
unlikeliness of its beginnings becomes its universal
appeal. It strips bare what some would believe to be
strange, anomalous behavior offered as a reversal of
truth.*

*Vonnegut calls upon Murray's message to explain
what he maintains is the reversal of George Bush's
sense of truth. For Vonnegut, Murray's musicology offers a better understanding of the human condition
than is held by the president.* (MWC 7) The wonderful writer **Albert Murray**, who is a jazz historian and
a friend of mine among other things, told me that
during the era of slavery in this country—an atrocity
from which we can never fully recover—the suicide
rate per capita among slave owners was much
higher than the suicide rate among slaves.

Murray says he thinks this was because slaves
had a way of dealing with depression, which their
white owners did not: They could shoo away Old
Man Suicide by playing and singing the Blues. He
says something else which also sounds right to me.
He says the blues can't drive depression clear out of
a house, but can drive it into the corners of any

room where it's being played. So please remember that.

Foreigners love us for our jazz. And they don't hate us for our purported liberty and justice for all. They hate us now for our arrogance.

Musa Dagh. *In a fit of rage about succeeding generations' ignorance of history, Rabo Karabekian's father apostrophizes to the cherished memory of Armenian sacrifice and suffering,* "**Musa Dagh***!" he might say.* This was the name of a place in Turkey where a small band of Armenian civilians fought Turkish militiamen to a standstill for forty days and forty nights before being exterminated—about the time my parents, with me in my mother's belly, arrived safe and sound in San Ignacio (*Blue* 2).

Mushari, Norman. *After graduating first in his class from Cornell Law School, this Lebanese American, son of a Brooklyn rug merchant, is hired by McAllister, Robjent, Reed and McGee, the firm representing the Rosewater Foundation. His hiring is with the express purpose of helping the senior partner, Thurmond McAllister, regain his viciousness. Mushari is viewed as so conniving that other members in the firm whistle "Pop Goes the Weasel" whenever he passes by.*

Mushari's cutthroat demeanor goes back to his boyhood, papering his bedroom walls with pictures of Senator Joe McCarthy and Roy Cohn. As an adult, he took to heart Professor Leonard Leech's words: In every big transaction . . . there is a magic moment during which a man has surrendered a treasure, and during which the man who is due to receive it has not yet done so. An alert lawyer will make that moment his own, possessing the treasure for a magic microsecond, taking a little of it, passing it on. If the man who is to receive the treasure is unused to wealth, has an inferiority complex and shapeless feelings of guilt, as most people do, the lawyer can often take as much as half the bundle, and still receive the recipient's blubbering thanks (GBR 1).

Consequently, Mushari spends all his time trying to find out as much information as possible about Eliot Rosewater's oddities in order to establish legal grounds for shifting control of the Rosewater Foundation to Fred Rosewater of Pisquontuit, Rhode Island.

Mushari, Norman, Jr. *In* Slapstick, *once Wilbur and Eliza reveal their true intelligence to their parents and physician, the twins are separated because it is felt only Wilbur has an opportunity for education and an independent life. While Wilbur attends school in Europe, Eliza is institutionalized. She is eventually released and hires Norman Mushari, Jr., to represent her in two suits: one against her mother to regain her inheritance and another suit against the institution. (Her father had previously died in an automobile accident.)*

Musket Mountain. *The high hill on the western edge of Tarkington College's campus, at the foot of which is the local cemetery, in* Hocus Pocus.

The Musketeer. *The Tarkington College alumni magazine first appearing in 1910, named for Musket Mountain at the edge of campus, in* Hocus Pocus.

Mussolini, Benito. (PP XXIX) "Childish—like Hitler's Brown Shirts, like **Mussolini**'s Black Shirts. Childish like any uniform," said Lasher. "We (*the Ghost Shirt Society*) don't deny it's childish. At the same time, we admit that we've got to be a little childish, anyway, to get the big following we need." (CC 40) In his selfish days he (*Julian Castle*) had been as familiar to tabloid readers as Tommy Manville, Adolf Hitler, **Benito Mussolini**, and Barbara Hutton. His fame had rested on lechery, alcoholism, reckless driving, and draft evasion. He had had a dazzling talent for spending millions without increasing mankind's stores of anything but chagrin.

Mussolini is Dan Gregory's hero. Mussolini's minister of culture, Count Portomaggiore, is also head of the British spy apparatus in Italy all through the war and eventually marries Gregory's lover, Marilee Kemp. (Blue 7) The editor (*of the* Luma County Clarion) asked me (*Rabo Karabekian*) if I could draw a picture of the Italian dictator **Benito Mussolini**, Dan Gregory's hero of heroes, incidentally, and I did so in two or three minutes maybe, without having to refer to a photograph.

Then he had me draw a beautiful female angel, and I did that.

Then he had me draw a picture of **Mussolini** pouring a quart of something into the mouth of the angel. He had me label the bottle CASTOR OIL and the angel WORLD PEACE. **Mussolini** liked to punish people by making them drink a quart of castor oil. That sounded like a comical way to teach somebody a lesson, but it wasn't. The victims often vomited and shit themselves to death. Those who survived were all torn up inside.

(*Blue* 8) **Mussolini** had thanked him (*Dan Gregory*) for a portrait of himself which Gregory had painted as a gift. **Mussolini** was depicted as a general of Alpine troops on a mountaintop at sunrise, and you can bet that every bit of leather and piping and braid and brass and pleating, and all the decorations, were exactly as they should be. Nobody could paint uniforms like Dan Gregory.

(*Blue* 10) Gregory was giving a dinner party in the dining room right below me for, among others, Al Jolson and the comedian W. C. Fields, and the author whose stories Gregory had illustrated countless times, Booth Tarkington. I would never meet any of them because they would never come back to the house again—after a bitter argument with Gregory about **Benito Mussolini**.

(*Blue* 13) Dan Gregory's mansion became three separate brownstones again soon after he and Marilee and Fred Jones left for Italy to take part in **Mussolini**'s great social experiment. Although he and Fred were well into their fifties by then, they would ask for and receive permission from **Mussolini** himself to don Italian infantry officers' uniforms, but without any badges of rank or unit, and to make paintings of the Italian Army in action.

Karabekian is forced to listen to Dan Gregory's invectives against modern art, and Gregory goes on to extend his authority as though he and Mussolini were in close agreement on the subject. (*Blue* 17) "You know the first two things **Mussolini** would do if he took over this country?

". . . He would burn down the Museum of Modern Art and outlaw the word *democracy*. After that he would make up a word for what we really are, make us face up to what we really are and always have been, and then strive for efficiency. Do your job right or drink castor oil!"

"My work is done" (*see* **George Eastman**).

myth, mythological, mythology. (WFG Hello, Star Vega) The saucer **myths** represent a neat com-

promise between the need to believe in a traditional paternal God and the contemporary pressures to accept the pronouncements of science. . . . *Vonnegut quotes Carl Sagan.*

(WFG Address to P.E.N. Conference in Stockholm, 1973) Our influence (*that of writers*) is slow and subtle, and is mainly felt by the young. They are hungry for **myths** which resonate with the mysteries of their own times.

We give them those **myths**.

We will become influential when those who have listened to our **myths** have become influential. Those who rule us now are living in accordance with **myths** created for them by writers when they were young. It is perfectly clear that our rulers do not question those **myths** for even a minute during busy day after busy day. Let us pray that those terribly influential writers who created those our leaders' were humane.

(*PS* The People One Knows) The uneasiness which many people will feel about liking *Something Happened* has roots which are deep. It is no casual thing to swallow a book by Joseph Heller, for he is, whether he intends to be or not, a maker of **myths**. (One way to do this, surely, is to be the final and most brilliant teller of an oft-told tale.) *Catch-22* is now the dominant **myth** about Americans in the war against fascism. *Something Happened*, if swallowed, could become the dominant **myth** about the middle-class veterans who came home from that war to become heads of nuclear families. The proposed **myth** has it that those families were pathetically vulnerable and suffocating. It says that the heads of them commonly took jobs which were vaguely dishonorable or at least stultifying, in order to make as much money as they could for their little families, and they used that money in futile attempts to buy safety and happiness. The proposed **myth** says that they lost their dignity and their will to live in the process.

It says they are hideously tired now.

(*PS* The People One Knows) To accept a new **myth** about ourselves is to simplify our memories—and to place our stamp of approval on what might become an epitaph for our era in the shorthand of history. This, in my opinion, is why critics often condemn our most significant books and poems and plays when they first appear, while praising fee-

bler creations. The birth of a new **myth** fills them with primitive dread, for **myths** are so effective.
(*PS* Mark Twain) "This is a miracle. There is a name for such miracles, which is **myths**.

"Imagine, if you will, the opinion we would now hold of ourselves and the opinions others would hold of us, if it were not for the **myths** about us created by Mark Twain. You can then begin to calculate our debt to this one man."
(*PS* The Sexual Revolution) But then I said to myself, Wait a minute—those steps at the beginning look like the creation **myth** of virtually every society on earth. And then I saw that the stroke of midnight looked exactly like the unique creation **myth** in the Old Testament. And then I saw that the rise to bliss at the end was identical with the expectation of redemption as expressed in primitive Christianity.

The tales were identical. *Vonnegut notes the structural parallels between* Cinderella *and* Genesis.
(*DD* 7) My mind had been trained by heirloom books of fairy tales, and by the **myths** and legends which animated my father's conversation, to think that way. It was second nature for me, and for Felix, too, and for no other children in Midland City, I am sure, to see candle flames as fireflies—and to invent a King of the Early Evening.
(*HP* 26) But down deep the story (*"The Protocols of the Elders of Tralfamadore"*) was beginning to work like a buffered analgesic. What a relief it was, somehow, to have somebody else confirm what I had come to suspect toward the end of the Vietnam War, and particularly after I saw the head of a human being pillowed in the spilled guts of a water buffalo on the edge of a Cambodian village, that Humanity is going somewhere really nice was a **myth** for children under 6 years old, like the Tooth Fairy and the Easter Bunny and Santa Claus.
(*FWD* XIII) Every cockamamie artificial extended family of FSD sufferers resembles Redfield's Folk Society to this extent: it has a **myth** at its core. The Manson family pretended to believe (the same thing as believing) that its murders would be blamed on blacks. Los Angeles would then be purified somehow by a race war. The **myth** at the core of the political family which calls itself "Neo-Conservatives" isn't that explicit, but I know what it is, even if most of them can't put it into words. This is it: They are British aristocrats, graduates of Oxford or Cambridge, living in the world as it was one hundred years ago.

(*TQ* 49) Kilgore Trout, the ornithologist's son, wrote in *My Ten Years on Automatic Pilot:* "The Fiduciary is a **mythological** bird. It has never existed in Nature, never could, never will."

Trout is the only person who ever said a fiduciary was any sort of bird. The noun (from the Latin *fiducia,* confidence, trust) in fact identifies a sort of Homo sapiens who will conserve the property, and nowadays especially paper or computer representations of wealth, belonging to other people, including the treasuries of their governments.

He or she or it cannot exist, thanks to the brain and the ding-dong, et cetera. So we have in this summer of 1996, rerun or not, and as always, faithless custodians of capital making themselves multimillionaires and multibillionaires, while playing beanbag with money better spent on creating meaningful jobs and training people to fill them, and raising our young and retiring our old in surroundings of respect and safety.

For Christ's sake, let's help more of our frightened people get through this thing, whatever it is.
(*TQ* 49) Yes, and any dream of taking better care of our people might as well be a transvestite hermaphrodite without some scheme for giving us all the support and companionship of extended families, within which sharing and compassion are more plausible than in an enormous nation, and a Fiduciary may not be as **mythical** as the Roc and the Phoenix after all.
(*TQ* 51) Prometheus in Greek **mythology** makes the first human beings from mud. He steals fire from Heaven and gives it to them so they can be warm and cook, and not, one would hope, so we could incinerate all the little yellow bastards in Hiroshima and Nagasaki, which are in Japan.
(*TQ* 53) According to Greek **mythology**, Pandora was the first woman. She was made by the gods who were angry with Prometheus for making a man out of mud and then stealing fire from them. Making a woman was their revenge. They gave Pandora a box. Prometheus begged her not to open it. She opened it. Every evil to which human flesh is heir came out of it.

The last thing to come out of the box was hope. It flew away.

I didn't make that depressing story up. Neither did Kilgore Trout. Ancient Greeks did.

(*MWC* 4) What was the beginning of this end? Some might say Adam and Eve and the apple of knowledge, a clear case of entrapment. I say it was Prometheus, a Titan, a son of gods, who in Greek **myth** stole fire from Zeus and gave it to human beings. The gods were so mad they chained him naked to a rock with his back exposed, and had eagles eat his liver. "Spare the rod and spoil the child."

(*MWC* 12) There are old poops who will say that you do not become a grown-up until you have somehow survived, as they have, some famous calamity— the Great Depression, the Second World War, Vietnam, whatever. Storytellers are responsible for this destructive, not to say suicidal, **myth**. Again and again in stories, after some terrible mess, the character is able to say at last, "Today I am a woman. Today I am a man. The end."

When I got home from the Second World War, my Uncle Dan clapped me on the back, and he said, "You're a man now." So I killed him. Not really, but I certainly felt like doing it.

Dan, that was my bad uncle, who said a male can't be a man unless he'd gone to war.

See also: PP VI; *SL5* 2; *WFG* Address at Rededication of Wheaton College Library, 1973; *Slap* 39; *PS* The Sexual Revolution; *JB* 14; *DD* 6; 20; *HP* 25; *FWD* XVII.

Nash, Harry. *The bland, introverted clerk at Miller's Hardware Store who makes an amazing transformation into each character he plays for the North Crawford Mask and Wig Club in the short story "Who Am I This Time?" (reprinted in* Welcome to the Monkey House). *Harry was an orphan, left on the steps of the Unitarian Church when only a baby. Helene Shaw, his co-star in the club's production of* A Streetcar Named Desire, *finally succeeds in developing a relationship with him by giving him new scripts to read with her. She accepts that the only passion she will get from him will be through his portrayal of literary characters.*

Nation, J. Edgar. *The Grand Rapids pharmacist and inventor of the ethical birth control pill (which completely numbs any sexual urges) in the short story "Welcome to the Monkey House," in* Welcome to the Monkey House *(1968). According to the annual Easter television play about him, he and his eleven children were visiting the zoo when he became disturbed by the "immoral" acts they witnessed in the monkey house.* "He didn't have the slightest idea his pills would be taken by human beings someday. . . . His dream was to introduce morality into the monkey house at the Grand Rapids Zoo."

Foxy Grandpa recounts the story to Nancy, one of the hostesses in the Ethical Suicide Parlor. He turns out to be Billy the Poet, the outlaw specializing in kidnapping suicide parlor hostesses, depriving them of ethical birth control pills, and having sex with them once their minds and bodies are no longer numbed by the pills.

Nation of Two (*see **Das Reich der Zwei***).

National Council of Arts and Letters. *In the controlling technocracy of* Player Piano, *even culture is controlled by computer algorithms. The National Council of Arts and Letters has theorized there are only twelve types of readers, so as a matter of economics they establish book clubs for each. Plots are also limited in number, and books are solicited on very strictly contrived terms. The same is true for fine art, as well.* (PP XXIV) "Well, a fully automatic setup like that makes culture very cheap. Book costs [sic] less than seven packs of chewing gum. And there are picture clubs, too—pictures for your walls at amazingly cheap prices. Matter of fact, culture's so cheap, a man figured he could insulate his house cheaper with books and prints than he could with rockwool. Don't think it's true, but it's a cute story with a good point."

"And painters are well supported under this club system?" asked Khashdrahr.

"Supported—I guess!" said Halyard. "It's the Golden Age of Art, with millions of dollars a year poured into reproductions of Rembrandts, Whistlers, Goyas, Renoirs, El Grecos, Dégas' [sic], da Vincis, Michelangelos. . . ."

"These club members, they get just any book, any picture?" asked Khashdrahr.

"I should say not! A lot of research goes into what's run off, believe me. Surveys of public reading tastes, readability and appeal tests on books being considered. Heavens, running off an unpopular book would put a club out of business like that!" He snapped his fingers ominously. "The way they keep culture so cheap is by knowing in advance what and how much of it people want. They get it right, right down to the color of the jacket. Gutenberg would be amazed."

National Steel Foundry. *In the short story "Any Reasonable Offer," first appearing in* Collier's *magazine (January 1952) and later collected in* Bagombo Snuff Box *(1999), National Steel Foundry is the employer of Bradley Peckham, a draftsman who fraudulently plays the part of Colonel Peckham, passing himself off as the current chief of the company. It is in this manner that he and his wife successfully vacation at estates on the market for sale, appearing as a wealthy couple needing to get the feel of these properties for a few days before eventually backing away from the deals and returning to their workaday lives.*

National Union of Belgium Opticians. *Billy Pilgrim reads an article in* The Review of Optometry *in which Jean Thiriart, Secretary of the National Union of Belgium Opticians, presses for the formation of a "European Optometry Society." Billy fails to be moved by Thiriart's appeal, but at just that moment the noon fire siren shrieks causing Billy to travel back in time to the war.* (SL5 3) Billy closed his eyes. When he opened them, he was back in World War Two again. His head was on the wounded rabbi's shoulder. A German was kicking his feet, telling him to wake up, that it was time to move on.

"Nature Cruise of the Century." *The brainstorm of New York businessman Bobby King, the cruise is intended to be a two week cruise to the Galápagos Islands aboard the* Bahía de Darwin, *leaving port from Ecuador on Friday, November 28, 1986. Instead, the ship becomes the link between humanity as it presently exists and the sea-lion-like creatures of humanity's future state.*

Necker, Anne Louise Germaine. *According to Malachi Constant's family history,* The family could trace its line back through an illegitimacy to Benjamin Constant, who was a tribune under Napoleon from 1799 to 1801, and a lover of **Anne Louise Germaine Necker**, Baronne de Stael-Holstein, wife of the then Swedish ambassador to France (ST 3).

neuter. *Aside from a single reference to the spayed Kazakh, Selena MacIntosh's dog, Vonnegut uses this term exclusively to describe those who willfully live without sex and only minimally participate in life's events.* (DD Preface) The **neutered** pharmacist who tells the tale is my declining sexuality.
(DD 19) People talk a lot about all the homosexuals there are to see in Greenwich Village, but it was all the **neuters** that caught my eye that day. These were my people—as used as I was to wanting love from nowhere, as certain as I was that almost anything desirable was likely to be booby-trapped.

I had a fairly funny idea. Someday all we **neuters** would come out of our closets and form a parade. I even decided what banner our front rank should carry, as wide as Fifth Avenue. A single

word would be printed on it in letters four feet high:

EGREGIOUS

(DD 19) RUDY: It's okay. I don't have any more feelings than a rubber ball. You said how nobody sees me, how I never can get waited on . . . ?
GENEVIEVE: You heard that, too.
RUDY: That's because I'm a **neuter**. I'm no sex. I'm out of the sex game entirely. Nobody knows how many **neuters** there are, because they're invisible to most people. I'll tell you something, though: There are millions in this town. They should have a parade sometime, with big signs saying, tried sex once, thought it was stupid, no sex for ten years, feel wonderful, for once in your life, think about something besides sex.
(DD 19) RUDY: **Neuters** don't love anybody. They don't hate anybody either. . . . **Neuters** make very good servants. They're not your great seekers of respect, and they usually cook pretty well.
(DD 22) To have been a perfectly uninvolved person, a perfect **neuter**, I *(Rudy Waltz)* should never have written a play.

To have been a perfect **neuter**, I shouldn't have bought a new Mercedes, either. That's correct: Ten years after Father died, I had saved so much money, working night after night, and living so modestly out in Avondale, that I bought a white, four-door Mercedes 280, and still had plenty of money left over.
(MWC 11) And about the novel I can never finish, *If God Were Alive Today*, the hero, the stand-up comedian on Doomsday, not only does he denounce our addiction to fossil fuels and the pushers in the White House, because of overpopulation he is also against sexual intercourse. Gil Berman tells his audiences:

I have become a flaming **neuter**. I am as celibate as at least fifty percent of the heterosexual Roman Catholic clergy. And celibacy is no root canal. It's so cheap and convenient. Talk about safe sex! You don't have to do anything afterwards, because there is no afterward.

And when my tantrum, which is what I call my TV set, flashes boobs and smiles in my face, and says everybody but me is going to get laid tonight, and this is a national emergency, so I've got to rush out and buy a car or pills, or a folding gymnasium that I can hide under my bed, I laugh like a hyena. I know and you know that millions and millions of good Americans, present company not excepted, are not going to get laid tonight.

And we flaming **neuters** vote! I look forward to a day when the President of the United States, no less, who probably isn't going to get laid tonight either, decrees a **National Neuter Pride Day**. Out of our closets we'll come by the millions. Shoulders squared, chins held high, we'll go marching up Main Streets all over this boob-crazed democracy of ours, laughing like hyenas.

What about God? If He were alive today? Gil Berman says, "God would have to be an atheist, because the excrement has hit the air-conditioning big time, big time."
See also: DD 19; 20; 23; *Gal* 2:5.

"New Dictionary" (1967). *Vonnegut's short essay reprinted in* Welcome to the Monkey House *(1968) praising the new* Random House Dictionary.

New York State Maximum Security Adult Correctional Institution at Athena. *Sitting across the lake from Scipio, New York, the home of Tarkington College, this prison houses Eugene Debs Hartke while he writes his memoirs. Once a teacher at Tarkington and later at the prison, Hartke is imprisoned after a massive and bloody jailbreak, though he did not incite the insurrection.*
(*HP* 3) When I came to work at Tarkington, there were only 300 students, a number that hadn't changed for 50 years. But the rustic work-camp across the lake had become a brutal fortress of iron and masonry on a naked hilltop, the **New York State Maximum Security Adult Correctional Institution at Athena**, keeping 5,000 of the state's worst criminals under lock and key.

This is also the prison where the savior of Kilgore Trout's discarded manuscripts, Dudley Prince, serves an unjust sentence. (*TQ* 16) The timequake was going to zap him back into a solitary confinement cell, into *the hole*, within the walls and towers of the **New York State Maximum Security Adult Correc-**

tional Facility at Athena, sixty miles south of his hometown of Rochester, where he used to own a little video rental store. To be sure, the timequake had made him ten years younger, but that was no break in his case. It meant he was again serving two consecutive life sentences, without hope of parole, for the rape and murder of a ten-year-old girl of Chinese-American and Italian-American parentage, Kimberly Wang, in a Rochester crack house, of which he was entirely innocent! (*See also: TQ* 37.)

Newcomb, Ed. *In the short story "Poor Little Rich Town," collected in* Bagombo Snuff Box *(1999), Newcomb has retired from the volunteer fire department after serving as its secretary for twenty years. He is also the owner of one of the many mansions in Spruce Falls, having inherited it from his father, who was the only bidder for the property during a bank foreclosure. With plans for Federal Apparatus to move its corporate headquarters to Ilium, Spruce Falls property owners are excited that there may finally be some real estate transactions and an injection of much needed cash to the village. Newcomb is buoyed by the real estate agent's optimism.* The Ilium real estate man, who had put stars in every eye except Beaton's, had assured **Newcomb** that his twenty-six-room Georgian colonial, with a little paper and paint, would look like a steal to a corporation executive at fifty-thousand dollars.

It is Newcomb who tries to soften Newell Cady's trauma over losing a little time each day as he goes slightly out of his way to pick up his mail, a complaint he tactlessly makes while standing in Mrs. Dickie's post office. "Good excuse to get out and pass the time of day with people," said **Newcomb**.

Newcomb is representative of how the townspeople feel concerning their warmth and hope for Newell Cady though they were voting him out of the fire department. No one wishes Cady ill; they just want some understanding about their comfort level with their current way of life. "Make sure he understands that we all like him," said **Ed Newcomb**, "and tell him we're proud an important man like him would want to live here."

Newcomb, John L. *In the short story "The Big Space Fuck," reprinted in the "Obscenity" chapter of* Palm Sunday, *Newcomb is Wanda June's evidence* to her parents that they ruined her prospects in life by their degenerate and uncaring actions. Newcomb rose in life to command a South Dakota security force at a government arsenal stockpiling cholera and bubonic plague. Dwayne Hoobler, Wanda June's father, allegedly chased away the potential suitor by answering the door shirtless, drinking beer, and armed with a holstered pistol.

Newport, Rhode Island. *Newport is an important location in* The Sirens of Titan, Cat's Cradle, God Bless You, Mr. Rosewater, Slaughterhouse-Five, *and the short story "Any Reasonable Offer," collected in* Bagombo Snuff Box (1999).

Newport is the site of the Rumfoord estate in The Sirens of Titan. *(TQ 3)* The Rumfoord mansion was marble, an extended reproduction of the banqueting hall of Whitehall Palace in London. The mansion, like most of the really grand ones in **Newport**, was a collateral relative of post offices and Federal court buildings throughout the land.

The Rumfoord mansion was an hilariously impressive expression of the concept: People of substance. It was surely one of the greatest essays on density since the Great Pyramid of Khufu. In a way it was a better essay on permanence than the Great Pyramid, since the Great Pyramid tapered to nothingness as it approached heaven. Nothing about the Rumfoord mansion diminished as it approached heaven. Turned upside down, it would have looked exactly the same.

Winston Niles Rumfoord commemorates his Newport childhood by naming a month after it in the Martian calendar. (TQ 35) The Martian year was divided into twenty-one months, twelve with thirty days, and nine with thirty-one. These months were named January, February, March, April, May, June, July, August, September, October, November, December, Winston, Niles, Rumfoord, Kazak, **Newport**, Chrono, Synclastic, Infundibulum, and Salo.

Mnemonically:

Thirty days have Salo, Niles, June, and September,

Winston, Chrono, Kazak, and November,

April, Rumfoord, **Newport**, and Infundibulum.

All the rest, baby mine, have thirty-one.

The month of Salo was named after a creature

Winston Niles Rumfoord knew on Titan. Titan, of course, is an extremely pleasant moon of Saturn.

Vonnegut uses Newport to characterize an entire class of out-of-touch rich people when offering this in Cat's Cradle. *(CC 3)* Nowhere does Bokonon warn against a person's trying to discover the limits of his *karass* and the nature of the work God Almighty has had it do. Bokonon simply observes that such investigations are bound to be incomplete.

In the autobiographical section of *The Books of Bokonon* he writes a parable on the folly of pretending to discover, to understand:

I once knew an Episcopalian lady in **Newport, Rhode Island**, who asked me to design and build a doghouse for her Great Dane. The lady claimed to understand God and His Ways of Working perfectly. She could not understand why anyone should be puzzled about what had been or about what was going to be.

And yet, when I showed her a blueprint of the doghouse I proposed to build, she said to me, "I'm sorry, but I never could read one of those things."

"Give it to your husband or your minister to pass on to God," I said, "and, when God finds a minute, I'm sure he'll explain this doghouse of mine in a way that even you can understand."

She fired me. I shall never forget her. She believed that God liked people in sailboats much better than He liked people in motorboats. She could not bear to look at a worm. When she saw a worm, she screamed.

She was a fool, and so am I, and so is anyone who thinks he sees what God is Doing, [writes Bokonon].

Newport is also the location where Lionel Boyd Johnson (later known as Bokonon) blows ashore in a storm. He becomes a gardener and carpenter on the Rumfoord estate.

In God Bless You, Mr. Rosewater, *attorney Norman Mushari pays a quarter to tour the Rumfoord estate while waiting to solicit Fred Rosewater for his representation.*

In Slaughterhouse-Five, *Billy Pilgrim has a midnight passing of boats on his honeymoon that connect Newport with Pilgrim's eventual roommate in the hospital after the plane crash.* (TQ 39) A great motor yacht named the Scheherezade now slid past the marriage bed. The song its engines sang was a very low organ note. All her lights were on.

Two beautiful people, a young man and a young woman in evening clothes, were at the rail in the stern, loving each other and their dreams and the lake. They were honeymooning, too. They were Lance Rumford, of **Newport**, **Rhode Island**, and his bride, the former Cynthia Landry, who had been a childhood sweetheart of John F. Kennedy in Hyannis Port, Massachusetts.

There was a slight coincidence here. Billy Pilgrim would later share a hospital room with Rumfoord's uncle, Professor Bertram Copeland Rumfoord of Harvard, official Historian of the United States Air Force.

In the short story "Any Reasonable Offer," Newport is a target for Bradley Peckham who fraudulently poses as Colonel Bradley Peckham, a well-off retired military man who cons real estate agents and owners into letting him "try on" an estate for a few days to see if he wants to make a purchase offer. He and his wife, Pam, make a habit of vacationing at different Newport estates with this subterfuge.

Newt and Catharine. *In the short story "Long Walk to Forever," in* Welcome to the Monkey House *(1968), Catharine is startled by the sudden appearance of Newt, a close but platonic friend since childhood. Newt went AWOL from Fort Bragg to confess his love for her before her planned marriage to Henry Stewart Chasens. Newt's mother tells him about Catharine's approaching wedding. Newt and Catharine take a long walk and nap in the woods, and when it comes time for Newt to leave, Catharine's resolve to wed yields to the long-suppressed love she holds for Newt.*

Newton, Sir Isaac (*see* **God Bless You, Dr. Kevorkian**).

"Next Door" (1955) (*see* **Paul Leonard** and **Lemuel K. Harger**).

Niagara Falls. *In* Hocus Pocus, *the location of the New York State prison for American Indians. Vonnegut notes the Indians call the falls "Thunder Beaver."*

Nicholson, Robert. *Vonnegut's short essay "Where I Live," the first piece in the collection of stories entitled* Welcome to the Monkey House *(1968), describes the people and culture of Barnstable, Massachusetts. Among the many characters is Episcopalian minister Robert Nicholson. By way of describing the insularity of his neighbors, Vonnegut relates that* At a village cocktail party one time—and the villagers do drink a lot—**Father Nicholson** was talking to a Roman Catholic and a Jew, trying to find a word to describe the underlying spiritual unity of Barnstable. He found one. "We're Druids," he said.

In Wampeters, Foma & Granfalloons, *Vonnegut uses Father Nicholson to describe the inability of clerics to create more comforting lies for people.* (WFG Playboy Interview) VONNEGUT: And we do have the freedom to make up comforting lies. But we don't do enough of it. One of my favorite ministers was a guy named **Bob Nicholson**. He looked like Joseph Cotten, and he was a bachelor Episcopalian priest up on Cape Cod. Every time one of his parishioners died, he went all to pieces. He was outraged by death. So it was up to his congregation and the relatives of the deceased to patch him up, get him pumped up on Christianity sufficiently to get through the funeral service. I liked that very much: Nothing he was going to say in the standard Episcopalian funeral oration was going to satisfy *him*. He needed better lies.
PLAYBOY: Did you come up with any?
VONNEGUT: I tried. Everybody did. It was a very creative situation, with a minister of God falling apart like that.

Nightmare Ages. *The time frame for* The Sirens of Titan *is set by recalling:* The following is a true story from the **Nightmare Ages**, falling roughly, give or take a few years, between the Second World War and the Third Great Depression (ST 1).

Nim-nim (*see also* **"The Sisters B-36"**). (TQ 5) A *nim-nim was a banana-like fruit on Booboo.*

"The No-Talent Kid." *First published in the October 1952 edition of* The Saturday Evening Post *and later reprinted in the collection* Bagombo Snuff Box, *the story focuses on the vanity and pride of both Lin-*

coln High School Band Director George Helmholtz and his student Walter Plummer, the last of the clarinetists in the school's C Band, its lowest performing group. The band earned ten consecutive state titles until the previous year when it was beaten out by a band sporting a bass drum whose diameter was seven feet.

Helmholtz is eager to find his own bass drum of equal or larger size in order to refocus the ignorant judges who know little about music but apparently appreciate spectacle. Helmholtz sets his sights on acquiring the oversized drum being sold in the Knights of Kandahar liquidation sale. Their accounts are left in ruins by their embezzling treasurer, an otherwise respected citizen.

Young clarinetist Plummer, who constantly feels singled out for ridicule by Helmholtz each time he challenges better musicians, sets upon another course to earn his coveted band sweater with varsity letter. He, too, learns of the Knights of Kandahar liquidation sale and successfully beats out Helmholtz. Plummer decides to bring the drum to school, convinced that Helmholtz will have to let him play the drum with the elite A Band, but Helmholtz still believes that letting Plummer play any instrument with his competition team would mean certain defeat.

Just as Plummer is about to take his new drum home, Helmholtz strikes a bargain with the young schemer. He tells Plummer the drum will need a full-time band member to haul the cart that will be necessary to make it mobile. He agrees to let Plummer be the one responsible for hauling the drum cart in exchange for awarding him a band sweater with varsity letter. Helmholtz is free to pick his own drummer, and upon Plummer's graduation, the drum belongs to the band.

Nocturnal Goatsucker. The name given to the whippoorwill by Eliza and Wilbur Swain in Slapstick. Later, in a frenzy of creativity, they write a manual on childrearing and call it The Cry of the Nocturnal Goatsucker pseudonymously penned by "Betty and Bobby Brown."

Nolte, Nick. The American actor played Howard W. Campbell, Jr., in the film version of Mother Night and is in attendance at the Timequake clambake with fellow actor Kevin McCarthy. (TQ 62) Also in the flesh at the clambake were five men half my age who made me want to keep on going in my sunset years because of their interest in my work. They weren't there to see me. They wanted at long last to meet Kilgore Trout. They were Robert Weide, who in this summer of 1996 is making a movie in Montreal of Mother Night, and Marc Leeds, who wrote and had published a witty encyclopedia of my life and work, and Asa Pieratt and Jerome Klinkowitz, who have kept my bibliography up-to-date and written essays about me as well, and Joe Petro III, numbered like a World War, who taught me how to silk-screen.

My closest business associate, Don Farber, lawyer and agent, was there with his dear wife, Anne. My closest social pal, Sidney Offit, was there. The critic John Leonard was there, and the academicians Peter Reed and Loree Rackstraw, and the photographer Cliff McCarthy, and other kind strangers too numerous to mention.

The professional actors Kevin McCarthy and **Nick Nolte** were there.

My children and grandchildren weren't there. That was OK, perfectly understandable. It wasn't my birthday, and I wasn't a guest of honor. The heroes that evening were Frank Smith and Kilgore Trout. My kids and my kids' kids had other fish to fry. Perhaps I should say my kids and my kids' kids had other lobsters and clams and oysters and potatoes and corn on the cob to steam in seaweed.

Whatever!

Get it right! Remember Uncle Carl Barus, and get it right!

non-epiphany (see **Terry Kitchen**).

Norman Rockwell Hall. In Hocus Pocus, the one building on the Tarkington College campus not named after a donor family; it was the Moellenkamps who funded it. The building houses the sculpture studio of Artist in Residence Pamela Ford Hall. When Eugene Debs Hartke takes temporary command of the prison encampment established at Tarkington, he installs machine gun nests in its windows and doorways.

North Crawford, New Hampshire. *The setting for the short story "Lovers Anonymous."*

North Crawford Manor. *In the short story "Lovers Anonymous," collected in* Bagombo Snuff Box (1999), *this is the wedding site for Sheila Hinckley and Herb White. During the wedding a group of young men gather in the bar and laughingly gripe about their missed opportunity to woo Sheila. They all thought she was off the market since she had such intellectual promise and the apparent confidence to strive for a demanding profession. This is when they unofficially dub their group "Lovers Anonymous,"* forgoing Hay Boyden's sarcastic suggestion of Brotherhood of People Who Were Too Dumb to Realize That Sheila Hinckley Might Actually Want to Be a Housewife.

North Crawford Mask and Wig Club. *The community theater group in the short story "Who Am I This Time?" (in the 1968 collection* Welcome to the Monkey House) *that brings together the unlikely but highly talented couple Helene Shaw and Harry Nash.*

Noth, Eva. *Howard Campbell's mother-in-law. She witnesses Campbell executing the family's dachshund at the request of his father-in-law. (MN 19)* Like Resi's dog, **Eva Noth** had fattened dropsically on wartime food. The poor woman, made into sausage by unkind time, stood at attention, seemed to think that the execution of the dog was a ceremony of some nobility.

Noth, Helga. *In* Mother Night, *the German actress and wife of Howard Campbell, Jr., also the daughter of Berlin's chief of police and older sister of Resi. Campbell wrote some of his best plays as vehicles for Helga's talents. They were an apolitical couple as far as world events were concerned. Together they formed "Das Reich der Zwei" (The Nation of Two), as described by Campbell. Campbell wrote* Memoirs of a Monogamous Casanova *to honor the eroticism and passion they shared for each other. Campbell often remarked that Helga's great gift to him was her uncritical love, never questioning his very public deeds at the Ministry of Propaganda. Helga lost her life in the Crimea when the Russians broke through the*

German lines. *Unknown to Campbell until long after the war, he relayed the news of her loss to the Americans during one of his encrypted radio broadcasts.*

Noth, Resi. *The younger sister of Helga in* Mother Night. *During the war she is taken prisoner by advancing Soviet forces and long after the war is put to work as an agent helping George Kraft (the Soviet sleeper-spy Iona Potapov) maneuver Howard Campbell out of the United States. In order to do so, she is sent to New York posing as her long-lost sister. Resi convinces Howard she is Helga. He begins to trust her. It is left to Campbell's Blue Fairy Godmother, Frank Wirtanen, to tell Howard the truth. When the FBI breaks into Dr. Jones's basement to arrest the plotters, Resi decides to take cyanide rather than face deportation.*

An interesting minor development in the story occurs when Campbell stops by the Noth household and is asked to kill Resi's dog before they evacuate. The date is February 12, 1945, a day before the Dresden firebombing. In Slaughterhouse-Five, *Campbell spends the night of the firebombing with Billy Pilgrim in the underground meat locker.*

Noth, Werner. *The chief of police of Berlin and Howard Campbell's reluctant father-in-law. Noth hates Campbell for marrying Helga because he wanted a German soldier for a son-in-law. Despite his hatred and suspicion that Campbell really was an American spy, Noth tells him why he no longer cared about what the truth might be, highlighting the eternal dilemma faced by Campbell. (MN 18)* "And do you know why I don't care now if you were a spy or not?" he said. "You could tell me now that you were a spy, and we would go on talking calmly, just as we're talking now. I would let you wander off to wherever spies go when a war is over. You know why?" he said.

"No," I said.

"Because you could never have served the enemy as well as you served us," he said. "I realized that almost all the ideas that I hold now, that make me unashamed of anything I may have felt or done as a Nazi, came not from Hitler, not from Goebbels, not from Himmler—but from you." He took my hand. "You alone kept me from concluding that

Germany had gone insane." *Noth is hanged shortly after Campbell leaves their home.*

nothinghead (*see also* **somethinghead**). *In the short story "Welcome to the Monkey House," in* Welcome to the Monkey House (1968), *those renegades who refuse to take ethical birth control pills are called "nothingheads." The most famous nothinghead is Billy the Poet, also known as Foxy Grandpa. He specializes in kidnapping virgin hostesses from the Ethical Suicide Parlors, depriving them of their ethical birth control pills, deflowering them, and leaving them with normal birth control pills. A* **nothinghead** was a person who refused to take his ethical birth-control pills three times a day. The penalty for that was $10,000 and ten years in jail.

"I don't need to remind you girls," the sheriff went on, "that a **nothinghead** is very sensitive from the waist down. If Billy the Poet somehow slips in here and starts making trouble, one good kick in the right place will do wonders."

It wasn't just Billy the Poet who was attracted to Hostesses in Ethical Suicide Parlors. All **nothingheads** were. Bombed out of their skulls with the sex madness that came from taking nothing, they thought the white lips and big eyes and body stocking and boots of a Hostess spelled sex, sex, sex.

But Nancy dreamed that millions of insects were swarming about her from the waist down. They didn't sting. They fanned her. Nancy was a **nothinghead.** *Nancy was one of the kidnapped hostesses deprived of her ethical birth control pills, now becoming aware of her sexuality.*

Now It Can Be Told. *Kilgore Trout's novel containing the revelation that all human activity up to that point in time was merely preparation for monitoring the reactions of the reader, that the only purpose in life was to respond to what the creator had set before you.* (BC 22, 23) "Dear Sir, poor sir, brave sir. . . .

You are an experiment by the Creator of the Universe. You are the only creature in the entire universe who has free will. You are the only one who has to figure out what to do next—and *why.* Everybody else is a robot, a machine. . . .

"The Creator of the Universe had them invent hundreds of religions, so you would have plenty to choose among. He had them kill each other by the millions, for this purpose only: that you be amazed. They have committed every possible atrocity and every possible kindness unfeelingly, automatically, inevitably, to get a reaction from Y-O-U." *Dwayne Hoover takes this message to heart and goes on a violent rampage.*

Trout had previously purchased copies of Plague on Wheels *and* Now It Can Be Told *to take on his trip to Midland City. Both were the property of pornographic publishers who used the text as filler for their photographs.* (BC 5) The jackets of *Plague on Wheels* and **Now It Can Be Told** both promised plenty of wide-open beavers inside. The picture on the cover of **Now It Can Be Told**, which was the book which would turn Dwayne Hoover into a homicidal maniac, showed a college professor being undressed by a group of naked sorority girls. (BC 24) The two physicians on the disaster vehicle named Martha were Cyprian Ukwende, of Nigeria, and Khashdrahr Miasma, from the infant nation of Bangladesh. Both were parts of the world which were famous from time to time for having the food run out. Both places were specifically mentioned, in fact, in **Now It Can Be Told**, by Kilgore Trout. Dwayne Hoover read in that book that robots all over the world were constantly running out of fuel and dropping dead, while waiting around to test the only free-willed creature in the Universe, on the off-chance that he should appear.

"Now It's the Women's Turn" (*see* **"Windsor Blue Number Seventeen"**).

Offit, Sidney. *Vonnegut's* closest social pal *and a guest at the* Timequake *clambake (TQ 62), Offit wrote the foreword to* Look at the Birdie, *Vonnegut's posthumous 2009 collection of previously unpublished short fiction.*

Oger, Anna Maria. *(PS Roots) They (Vonnegut's great-grandparents) were preceded (to the United States) only by four of his sixteen great-great-grandparents, who were Jacob Schramm and his wife, Julia Junghans; and Johann Blank and his wife,* **Anna Maria Oger***.*

Oglethorpe, James E. *According to Merrihue Rosewater's account of the family, John Rosewater II was placed in debtors' prison in 1731 but was freed in 1732 by* **James E. Oglethorpe***, who paid his debts on the condition that John accompany* **Oglethorpe** *on an expedition to Georgia. John was to serve as chief horticulturalist for the expedition, which planned to plant mulberry trees and raise silk. John Rosewater would also become the chief architect, laying out what was to become the city of Savannah (GBR 11).*

O'Hare, Bernard B. *Inexplicably, Vonnegut approximates the name of his much-respected and valued war buddy to name the lieutenant who captures the double agent Howard W. Campbell, Jr. O'Hare and Campbell appear on the cover of* Life *magazine. That capture remains the highlight of O'Hare's existence. Upon returning from the war, O'Hare married and fathered a number of children, all the while moving from one failed business to another. When George Kraft / Iona Potapov informs O'Hare of Campbell's presence in New York, he travels to New York to destroy him. However, O'Hare first tells all the major newspapers and magazines that the escaped war criminal is still alive and in the United States.*

O'Hare arrives at Campbell's Greenwich Village apartment, gets drunk while waiting for Campbell's return, and his animosity for his old nemesis becomes

a religious quest. (MN 43) **O'Hare** had a far more exciting view of what we were to each other. When drunk, at any rate, he thought of himself as St. George and of me as the dragon.

This meeting produces one of the clearest sentiments in the text by either Campbell or Vonnegut. (MN 43) "You're pure evil," he said. "You're absolutely pure evil. . . . For all the good there is in you, you might as well be the Devil." *Campbell breaks O'Hare's arm, throws him out of the apartment, and chastises him. (MN 43)* "I'm not your destiny, or the Devil, either!" I said. "Look at you! Came to kill evil with your bare hands, and now away you go with no more glory than a man sideswiped by a Greyhound bus! And that's all the glory you deserve!" I said. "That's all that any man at war with pure evil deserves.

"There are plenty of good reasons for fighting," I said, "but no good reason ever to hate without reservation, to imagine that God Almighty Himself hates with you, too. Where's evil? It's that large part of every man that wants to hate without limit, that wants to hate with God on its side. It's that part of every man that finds all kinds of ugliness so attractive.

"It's that part of an imbecile," I said, "that punishes and vilifies and makes war gladly."

O'Hare, Bernard V. *Vonnegut's best friend from World War II, O'Hare was a fellow battalion scout and captured along with Vonnegut at the Battle of the Bulge before being sent together to prison camp in Dresden. They experienced the bombing of Dresden together in the slaughterhouse meatlocker. In 1964, Vonnegut went to visit O'Hare in preparation for writing* Slaughterhouse-Five. *At the time, O'Hare was a district attorney in Pennsylvania. Vonnegut and O'Hare visited Dresden after the war while it was part of East Germany. Vonnegut recounts that when he asked his friend what the bombing of Dresden meant to him, O'Hare replied that he no longer believed what his government said. O'Hare and his wife, Mary, appear in the first chapter of*

Slaughterhouse-Five, *as Vonnegut chronicles his search for materials and meaning of the event.*

In Timequake, *Vonnegut professes his love for O'Hare, his surviving companion from the Battle of the Bulge and through the massacre of Dresden, from the chaos of battlefield to political chaos. It is also obvious each shared great skepticism about any deity or religious rituals.* (TQ 21) My great war buddy **Bernard V. O'Hare**, now dead, lost his faith as a Roman Catholic during World War Two. I didn't like that. I thought that was too much to lose. . . . I knew **Bernie** had lost something important and honorable.

Again, I did not like that, did not like it because I liked him so much.

(TQ 35) My particular war buddy **Bernard V. O'Hare** and I talked to some of them *(German soldiers).* **O'Hare**, having become a lawyer for both the prosecution and the defense in later life, is up in Heaven now. Back then, though, we could both hear the Germans saying that America would now have to do what they had been doing, which was to fight the godless Communists. *(Vonnegut is referring to the moment in the Dresden countryside when they all—captives and prison guards alike—sought refuge during the Russian campaign toward Berlin at the close of the war in Germany. This is also the same scene captured in Rabo Karabekian's 64-foot-long triptych in* Bluebeard, *"Now It's the Women's Turn.")*

In Timequake, *Arthur Garvey Ulm, the pornographic novelist of* God Bless You, Mr. Rosewater, *is now a poet and employee of the American Academy of Arts and Letters. More importantly, he represents the spirit of Vonnegut's deceased war buddy and one time Pennsylvania prosecutor, Bernard V. O'Hare at the climactic clambake.* (TQ 62) Only the dead had doppelgängers at that party back in 2001. Arthur Garvey Ulm, poet and Resident Secretary of Xanadu, an employee of the American Academy of Arts and Letters, was short and had a big nose, like my war buddy **Bernard V. O'Hare**.

O'Hare, Captain Bernard. *In* Slapstick, *Captain O'Hare is the sixty-year-old helicopter pilot who remains stationed in the underground silo in Rock Creek Park with the presidential helicopter. He stays there throughout the gravitational shake-up and the*

renaming of all American citizens. Captain O'Hare flies President Wilbur Swain to Indianapolis for a reunion of Daffodils, then Urbana, Illinois, for an electronic reunion with the dead Eliza via the Hooligan, and lastly to the Swain's childhood home in Vermont. Swain renames O'Hare with the middle name Eagle-1 and later dubs him a Daffodil, making them cousins. Captain O'Hare eventually delivers Wilbur to the observation deck of the Empire State Building, where he lives out the remainder of his life.

O'Hare, Bernie, Wanda, and Willy. *The short story "A Present for Big Saint Nick," collected in* Bagombo Snuff Box (1999), *opens with the O'Hare family shopping in a jewelry store for the most tacky gift they can find for Bernie's employer, the mobster Big Nick of Chicago. Bernie has been under contract to Nick as a middleweight boxer (known as the Shenandoah Blaster), but after he loses sight in one eye, Big Nick keeps him well employed as one of his bodyguards.*

The opening scene in the store has the bruising tough guy taking extra care to calm four-year-old Willy. Like the other children about to attend Big Nick's annual Christmas party, Willy is terrified by all things Santa—even small plastic figurines such as the one Bernie stomps on in the store to alleviate Willy's dread. Small wonder, since Big Nick uses the annual party to dress as Santa, verbally abuse his employees, and hand out gifts to their children to calm their nerves while asking about their parents' private discussions that may reveal their disloyalty or displeasure with Nick. As Mrs. Pullman boldly says of the children's otherwise inexplicable fear of Santa, "Our Santa Claus is a dirty, vulgar, prying, foulmouthed, ill-smelling fake."

Wanda O'Hare shares the same universal dread and frank understanding of their mobster overlord. She participates in the sham as do the other parents, prepping her child to lie before speaking to Santa. However, as with all parents, she does not realize that what Willy hears will manifest itself in telling ways that do not involve answering direct questions. So when Nick (dressed as Santa) gives a long preamble to Willy before handing him the gift of a boat, Willy probably does not fully understand his father's suffering as overheard, capable of only mimicking disconnected bits of information. Instead he looks for a rag to wipe down the brand new gift. "**Willy O'Hare**!" thundered Santa Claus. "Tell Santy the trut', and ya get a swell boat. What's your old man and old lady say about Big Nick?"

"They say they owe him a lot," said **Willy** dutifully.

Santa Claus guffawed. "I guess they do, boy! **Willy**, you know where your old man'd be if it wasn't for Big Nick? He'd be dancin' aroun' in little circles, talking to hisself, wit'out nuttin' to his name but a flock of canaries in his head. Here, kid, here's your boat, an' Merry Christmas."

"Merry Christmas to you," said **Willy** politely. "Please, could I have a rag?"

"A rag?" said Santa.

"Please," said **Willy**. "I wanna wipe off the boat."

"**Willy**!" said **Bernie** and **Wanda** together.

"Wait a minute, wait a minute," said Santa. "Let the kid talk. Why you wanna wipe it off, **Willy**?"

"I want to wipe off the blood and dirt," said **Willy**.

"Blood!" said Santa. "Dirt!"

"**Willy**!" cried **Bernie**.

"Mama says everything we get from Santa's got blood on it," said **Willy**. He pointed at Mrs. Pullman. "And that lady says he's dirty."

"No I didn't, no I didn't," said Mrs. Pullman.

What follows is a series of answers from the children revealing their parents' true feelings though they obviously do so unintentionally. When Nick raises his hand to strike Willy, Bernie quickly grabs Nick's wrists and pleads, "Please," he said, "the kid don't mean nothing." *Nick warns Bernie that defying him is the same as committing suicide, yet when offered the opportunity to apologize to Nick, Bernie says he is sorry just before landing a punch that squarely smashes Nick's cigar before bloodying his face. Furiously embarrassed, Nick declares that everyone laughing is dead, yet the children take the slapstick moment to shout verbal taunts and laughter at their tormentor.*

Just when Bernie tells his wife that he is undoubtedly a dead man, Nick returns to the room with an armload of wrapped presents for himself, many from celebrities. He reaches into the pile for one that came all the way from Italy. Pulling on the red ribbon to *open the box detonates a small bomb, but it is big enough to blow off Nick's head. In the confusion after the blast, when the police arrive to handle the body and take statements, Willy shows his parents the gift card from the package-bomb. It read,* "Merry Christmas to the greatest guy in the world." *It was signed* "The Family."

O'Hare, Mary. *Trained as a nurse, Mary is the wife of Bernard V. O'Hare, Vonnegut's war buddy and fellow witness to the Dresden firebombing. Vonnegut dedicates* Slaughterhouse-Five *to Mary O'Hare and the Dresden cabdriver Gerhard Müller. Vonnegut had gone to the O'Hare house to meet with Bernard and jog his memory about experiences of the war in preparation for writing the text. Mrs. O'Hare gives Vonnegut a chilly reception, thinking he plans to glorify their exploits. She breaks in on the men's reminiscence and proclaims,* "You were just babies in the war—like the ones upstairs!"

I nodded that this was true. We *had* been foolish virgins in the war, right at the end of childhood.

"But you're not going to write it that way, are you." This wasn't a question. It was an accusation.

"I—I don't know," I said.

"Well, *I* know," she said. "You'll pretend you were men instead of babies, and you'll be played in the movies by Frank Sinatra and John Wayne or some of those other glamorous, war-loving, dirty old men. And war will look just wonderful, so we'll have a lot more of them. And they'll be fought by babies like the babies upstairs."

So then I understood. It was war that made her so angry. She didn't want her babies or anybody else's babies killed in wars. And she thought wars were partly encouraged by books and movies.

So I held up my right hand and I made her a promise: "**Mary**," I said, "I don't think this book of mine is ever going to be finished. I must have written five thousand pages by now, and thrown them all away. If I ever do finish it, though, I give you my word of honor: there won't be a part for Frank Sinatra or John Wayne.

"I tell you what," I said, "I'll call it 'The Children's Crusade.'" She was my friend after that (SL5 1).

O'Hare Paint and Varnish Company. *In* Breakfast of Champions, *the Hellertown, Pennsylvania, manu-*

facturers of Hawaiian Avocado, the paint used by Rabo Karabekian for "The Temptation of Saint Anthony," the $50,000 painting purchased for the opening of the Mildred Barry Memorial Center for the Arts. Against the painted background, Karabekian placed a single vertical stripe of orange reflecting tape.

Ohio Adult Correctional Institution. *Dwayne Hoobler is a guard at the institution in the short story "The Big Space Fuck," reprinted in* Palm Sunday *in the chapter entitled "Obscenity."*

Ohio Valley Ornamental Concrete Company. *In* Deadeye Dick, *the company purchases radioactive cement from the Nuclear Regulatory Commission and then resells it to the Maritimo Brothers Construction Company, which uses it to construct, among other things, the fireplace in the Avondale home of Rudy Waltz and his mother. The Waltz brothers find it necessary to sue the Maritimos, the NRC, and the Ohio Valley Ornamental Concrete Company for the wrongful death of their mother.*

Ojumwa. *Indicative of Vonnegut's abiding interest in the beginnings of things and the otherwise ironic connections they precipitate, Vonnegut's inclusion of Ojumwa in* Breakfast of Champions *is one such instance. Ojumwa is the African ancestor of Eddie Key, the Midland City ambulance driver who helps remove the wounded from the streets of Midland City after Dwayne Hoover's violent outburst. Ojumwa was captured by the Indaro ancestors of Dr. Cyprian Ukwende, and sold to British slave traders for a musket. Ukwende is one of the Midland City physicians treating those wounded by Hoover.*

oligomenorrhea. *Paul Proteus sarcastically informs his wife, Anita, exactly what it was about her that drew him to marry her. (PP XVIII) She (Anita) blew her nose. "I must have had something these people don't, or you wouldn't have married me."*

"Oligomenorrhea," *he said.*

She blinked. "What's that?"

"Oligomenorrhea—*that's what you had that these others don't. Means delayed menstrual period."*

Olly-olly-ox-in-free. *The "all clear" signal called out at the end of hide-and-seek when it is safe for all*

players to show themselves. Howard Campbell longs to hear the words that will never be called for him, and Dwayne Hoover deceitfully uses them during his violent rampage to draw out Wayne Hoobler. (MN 6) There was one pleasant thing about my ratty attic: the back window of it overlooked a little private park, a little Eden formed by joined back yards. That park, that Eden, was walled off from the streets by houses on all sides.

It was big enough for children to play hide-and-seek in.

I often heard a cry from that little Eden, a child's cry that never failed to make me stop and listen. It was the sweetly mournful cry that meant a game of hide-and-seek was over, that those still hiding were to come out of hiding, that it was time to go home.

The cry was this: "Olly-olly-ox-in-free."

And I, hiding from many people who might want to hurt or kill me, often longed for someone to give that cry for me, to end my endless game of hide-and-seek with a sweet and mournful—"Olly-olly-ox-in-free."

(MN 10) I can't say I wasn't warned. The man who recruited me that spring day in the Tiergarten so long ago now—that man told my fortune pretty well. "To do your job right," my Blue Fairy Godmother told me, "you'll have to commit high treason, have to serve the enemy well. You won't ever be forgiven for that, because there isn't any legal device by which you can be forgiven.

"The most that will be done for you," he said, "is that your neck will be saved. But there will be no magic time when you will be cleared, when America will call you out of hiding with a cheerful: Olly-olly-ox-in-free."

(MN 43) I looked out through the back windows by the stove, looked down into the foreshortened enchantment of the little private park below, the little Eden formed of joined back yards. No one was playing in it now.

There was no one in it to cry, as I should have liked someone to cry:

"Olly-olly-ox-in-freeeeeee."

There was a stir, a rustle in the shadows of my attic. I imagined it to be the rustle of a rat. I was wrong.

It was the rustle of Bernard B. O'Hare, the man who had captured me so long ago. It was the stir of my own personal Fury, the man who perceived his noblest aspect in his loathing and hounding of me. (BC 23) Dwayne went on calling for Niggers to come talk to him. He smiled. He thought that the Creator of the Universe had programmed them all to hide, as a joke.

Dwayne glanced around craftily. Then he called out a signal he had used as a child to indicate that a game of hide-and-seek was over, that it was time for children in hiding to go home. Here is what he called, and the sun was down when he called it: "Ollyolly-ox-in-freeeeeeeeeeeeeeeeeeeeeeeeeeeeeee."

O'Looney, Francis X. *In* Jailbird, *the Morristown, New Jersey, deputy sheriff who, through a series of odd events, becomes the downfall of the RAMJAC empire. Two years after Walter Starbuck has Mary Kathleen O'Looney quietly buried in Morristown, the engraver of the crypt's doors is arrested for drunken driving and comments on Deputy O'Looney's unusual name, mentioning he had seen it only once before. O'Looney became intrigued about the identity of the woman in the grave and eventually uncovers the truth that she was Mrs. Jack Graham. This leads to charges against Starbuck, who admits to arranging for her burial and keeping secret her last will and testament.*

As it turns out, the deputy was not related to Mary Kathleen, and his obsession for the mystery lady drives him to lose all interest in his grandchild, his wife, and his job. He is eventually dismissed from the sheriff's office, and his wife seeks divorce from their thirty-two year marriage.

O'Looney, Mary Kathleen. *Mary Kathleen is the daughter of one of the victims of the Wyatt Clock Company fiasco. Workers there used to lick their brushes into a point before applying the radium paint to the clock faces. More importantly, she was one of the four women Walter Starbuck could honestly say he loved.*

Mary Kathleen volunteers as the circulation manager for the Bay State Progressive *while Walter is a student at Harvard and cochairman of the paper. While he learns all about socialism at school, Mary Kathleen reads his textbooks on her own. She comes to believe in the rising tide of unionism breaking upon the country. Walter says that though Mary*

Kathleen is the only one of his loves not to speak another language, it is she who became his interpreter with the American workers. Though Walter is seeing Sarah Wyatt at the same time, it is Alexander Hamilton McCone who essentially breaks up his relationship with Mary Kathleen. When Walter graduates from Harvard, he declines to see her or answer her letters.

Once Walter and Mary Kathleen stop seeing each other, she leaves to join forces with Kenneth Whistler, a union organizer in Kentucky. One night Whistler comes home drunk and abusive, so Mary Kathleen leaves and happens upon the kindly Jack Graham who later marries her. The young mining engineer founded the RAMJAC Corporation, became a recluse, and died in 1952.

Mary Kathleen increases the company's holdings and eventually seeks the same kind of protective measures as Howard Hughes. However, she finds security in posing as a bag lady on the streets of New York. She phones her corporate directives to Arpad Leen and confirms those instructions with fingerprinted letters she sends through the mail. Mary Kathleen escapes the terror of New York's streets by discovering a deep, discarded tunnel beneath Grand Central Station once used to repair steam locomotives.

Mary Kathleen never abandons her love for Walter Starbuck. In her tattered basketball shoes she keeps his love letters and a picture of him alongside Kenneth Whistler. In those shoes is another picture of bales of money from Saudi Arabia earned through the McDonald's Hamburgers Division of RAMJAC. Her last will and testament, also in those shoes, leaves all of RAMJAC's earnings and businesses to the guardianship of the United States to benefit the people of the United States. (This is vaguely reminiscent of Eliot Rosewater's determination to accept the ridiculous paternity suits as a way of redistributing wealth.) Walter discovers the document after Mary Kathleen is sideswiped by a taxi and dies in a bathroom stall in her underground refuge. Walter comments on the miscalculations of Mary Kathleen, in part to justify his concealment of her will. (JB Epilogue) What, in my opinion, was wrong with **Mary Kathleen's** *scheme for a peaceful economic revolution? For one thing, the federal government was wholly unprepared to operate all the businesses of*

RAMJAC on behalf of the people. For another thing: Most of those businesses, rigged only to make profits, were as indifferent to the needs of the people as, say, thunderstorms. **Mary Kathleen** might as well have left one-fifth of the weather to the people. The businesses of RAMJAC, by their very nature, were as unaffected by the joys and tragedies of human beings as the rain that fell on the night that Madeiros and Sacco and Vanzetti died in an electric chair. It would have rained anyway.

The economy is a thoughtless weather system—and nothing more. Some joke on the people, to give them such a thing.

Two years later, when the will is discovered and the government gains control of RAMJAC's assets, Walter comments further about the inability of a bureaucracy to care for such money-making enterprises. (JB Epilogue) And I was suddenly offended and depressed by how silly we were. The news, after all, could hardly have been worse. Foreigners and criminals and other endlessly greedy conglomerates were gobbling up RAMJAC. **Mary Kathleen**'s legacy to the people was being converted to mountains of rapidly deteriorating currency, which were being squandered in turn on a huge new bureaucracy and on legal fees and consultants' fees, and on and on. What was left, it was said by the politicians, would help to pay the interest on the people's national debt, and would buy them more of the highways and public buildings and advanced weaponry they so richly deserved.

Onassis, Jacqueline Bouvier Kennedy (*see also* **Jackie**). *In* Galápagos, *she is considered one of the most admired women on the planet. Originally scheduled to take "The Nature Cruise of the Century" aboard the* Bahía de Darwin, *she—along with all the other luminaries—fail to appear.*

Operation Brainstorm. *The military's plan to test the extent of Professor Barnhouse's dynamo psychic abilities, in the 1950 short story "Report on the Barnhouse Effect," reprinted in* Welcome to the Monkey House *(1968). When Barnhouse realizes the government wants to use him as a weapon of destruction rather than as a threat to force worldwide disarmament, he destroys the armaments, preventing their launch, and escapes to a life on the run. This*

brings on what is known as "The Age of Barnhouse." The dismay occasioned by this flat announcement was offset somewhat by the exciting anticipation of **Operation Brainstorm**. The general was in a holiday mood. "The target ships are on their way to the Caroline Islands at this very moment," he declared ecstatically. "One hundred and twenty of them! At the same time, ten V-2s are being readied for firing in New Mexico, and fifty radio-controlled jet bombers are being equipped for a mock attack on the Aleutians. Just think of it!" Happily he reviewed his orders. "At exactly 1100 hours next Wednesday, I will give you the order to concentrate; and you, professor, will think as hard as you can about sinking the target ships, *destroying* the V-2s before they hit the ground, and knocking down the bombers before they reach the Aleutians! Think you can handle it?"

The professor turned gray and closed his eyes. "As I told you before, my friend, I don't know what I can do." He added bitterly, "As for this **Operation Brainstorm**, I was never consulted about it, and it strikes me as childish and insanely expensive."

"Gentlemen," I read aloud, *"As the first superweapon with a conscience, I am removing myself from your national defense stockpile. Setting a new precedent in the behavior of ordnance, I have humane reasons for going off. A. Barnhouse."*

Ophelia (*see also* **Hamlet**). *Two women in Vonnegut's work are called Ophelia. Eliot Rosewater addresses his wife as "Dear Ophelia" in a letter sent from Elsinore, California. He does so because he sees himself possessing the indecision of Hamlet, and his stay in Elsinore provides an apt literary metaphor for his letter home. When Walter Starbuck in* Jailbird *first sees the emaciated Ruth, he recalls,* She was uninterested in ever trusting anybody with her destiny anymore. Her plan was to roam alone and out-of-doors forever, from nowhere to nowhere in a demented sort of religious ecstasy. "No one ever touches me," she said, "and I never touch anyone. I am like a bird in flight. It is so beautiful. There is only God-and me."

I thought this of her: that she resembled gentle **Ophelia** in *Hamlet*, who became fey and lyrical when life was too cruel to bear. I have a copy of *Hamlet* at hand, and refresh my memory as to the nonsense **Ophelia** sang when she would no longer respond intelligently to those who asked how she was.

This was the song: *How should I your true love know / From another one? / By his cockle hat and staff / And his sandal shoon. / He is dead and gone, lady, / He is dead and gone; / At his head a grass-green turf / At his heels a stone—*

And on and on.

Ruth, one of millions of Europe's **Ophelias** after the Second World War, fainted in my motorcar (*JB* 2).

Starbuck later makes a comparison between two of the most significant women in his life. (*JB* 16) And contrast Mary Kathleen, if you will, with my wife Ruth, the **Ophelia** of the death camps, who believed that even the most intelligent human beings were so stupid that they could only make things worse by speaking their minds. It was thinkers, after all, who had set up the death camps. Setting up a death camp, with its railroad sidings and its around-the-clock crematoria, was not something a moron could do. Neither could a moron explain why a death camp was ultimately humane.

organism. *Vonnegut often describes individual as well as collective activity in terms of his biochemical theories of life.* (*SL5* 3) To the guards who walked up and down outside, each *(railway)* car became a single **organism** which ate and drank and excreted through its ventilators.

(*WFG* Address to P.E.N. Conference in Stockholm, 1973) Most writers I know, all over the world, do the best they can. They must. They have no choice in the matter. All artists are specialized cells in a single, huge **organism**, mankind. Those cells have to behave as they do, just as the cells in our hearts or our fingertips have to behave as they do. . . .

Where do these external signals come from? I think they come from all the other specialized cells in the **organism**. Those other cells contribute to use energy and little bits of information, in order that we may increase the **organism**'s awareness of itself—and dream its dreams.

But if the entire **organism** thinks that what we do is important, why aren't we more influential than we are?

(*WFG Playboy* Interview) VONNEGUT: Writers are specialized cells in the social **organism**. They are evolutionary cells. Mankind is trying to become something else; it's experimenting with new ideas all the time. And writers are a means of introducing new ideas into the society, and also a means of responding symbolically to life. I don't think we're in control of what we do.

(*TQ* 12) Trout said this was the story on why AIDS and new strains of syph and clap and the blueballs were making the rounds like Avon ladies run amok: On September 1st of 1945, immediately after the end of World War Two, representatives of all the chemical elements held a meeting on the planet Tralfamadore. They were there to protest some of their members' having been incorporated into the bodies of big, sloppy, stinky **organisms** as cruel and stupid as human beings.

Elements such as Polonium and Ytterbium, which had never been essential parts of human beings, were nonetheless outraged that *any* chemicals should be so misused.

(*TQ* 12) Sodium said enough was enough, that any further testimony would be coals to Newcastle. It made a motion that all chemicals involved in medical research combine whenever possible to create ever more powerful antibiotics. These in turn would cause disease **organisms** to evolve new strains that were resistant to them.

In no time, Sodium predicted, every human ailment, including acne and jock itch, would be not only incurable but fatal. "All humans will die," said Sodium, according to Trout. "As they were at the birth of the Universe, all elements will be free of sin again."

Iron and Magnesium seconded Sodium's motion. Phosphorus called for a vote. The motion was passed by acclamation.
See also: WJ III; *BC* 19; *Slap* 43; *Gal* 33; *Blue* 19; *FWD* X.

Origami Express. *In 1993, Vonnegut and Kentucky artist Joe Petro III entered their artistic partnership producing various silkscreened images and sculpture. The derivation of its name and logo are explained in his Author's Note to* A Man Without a Country (141–142). *Our partnership's name,* **Origami Express,** *is my tribute to the many-layered* packages Joe makes for prints he sends for me to sign and number. The logo for **Origami**, made by Joe, isn't his picture of a picture I sent him, but of a picture by me that he found in my novel *Breakfast of Champions*. It is of a bomb in air, on its way down, with these words written on its side:

GOODBYE
BLUE
MONDAY

Ortiz, Jesus. *The bartender in the Hotel El Dorado, a twenty-year-old descendent [sic] of proud Inca noblemen. . . . Nature's experiment with admiration for the rich (Gal 1:2).*

Orwell, George. (*WFG* Address to the American Physical Society) *. . . a man I admire almost more than any other man.*

(*HP* 27) *Do I (Eugene Debs Hartke) resent rich people? No. The best or worst I can do is notice them. I agree with the great Socialist writer* **George Orwell**, *who felt that rich people were poor people with money. I would discover this to be the majority opinion in the prison across the lake as well, although nobody over there had ever heard of* **George Orwell**. *Many of the inmates themselves had been poor people with money before they were caught, with the most costly cars and jewelry and watches and clothes. Many, as teenage drug dealers, had no doubt owned bicycles as desirable as the one I found in the weeds in the highlands of Scipio.*
See also: WFG Science Fiction; WFG A Political Disease.

Osterman (*see also* **Farmers of Southwestern Ohio for Nuclear Sanity**). *In* Deadeye Dick, *Osterman is presumed to be the name of the farmer who tells Rudy Waltz and Bernard Ketchum his conspiracy theory about who neutron-bombed Midland City. He is busy handing out leaflets for Farmers of Southwestern Ohio for Nuclear Sanity, asking citizens to write their congressmen.*

Ostrovsky, Erika (*see* **Céline**).

oubliette. *Usually considered a dungeon with a trapdoor in the ceiling, Vonnegut uses the device for the salvation of his characters. In Cat's Cradle, Papa Monzano's lavishly outfitted oubliette is designed to fit perfectly such a shelter's needs. When Papa's frozen body falls into the sea, John/Jonah and Celia Aamons Monzano take shelter in the oubliette until the storms subside.*

Prior to this incident, John/Jonah uses the image of an oubliette to characterize Franklin Hoenikker's escape from becoming President of San Lorenzo. (*CC* 101) And I realized that my agreeing to be boss had freed Frank to do what he wanted to do more than anything else, to do what his father had done: to receive honors and creature comforts while escaping human responsibilities. He was accomplishing this by going down a spiritual **oubliette**.
(*CC* 118) Then he (*Bokonon*) speaks of the rack and the peddiwinkus and the iron maiden and the *veglia* and the **oubliette**.

In any case, there's bound to be much crying,
But the **oubliette** alone will let you think while dying.

And so it was in Mona's and my rock womb. At least we could think.

And one thing I thought was that the creature comforts of the dungeon did nothing to mitigate the basic fact of **oubliation**.
(*CC* 119) "Today I will be a Bulgarian Minister of Education," Bokonon tells us. "Tomorrow I will be Helen of Troy." His meaning is crystal clear:

Each one of us has to be what he or she is.
And, down in the **oubliette**, that was mainly what I thought—with the help of *The Books of Bokonon*.

Bokonon invited me to sing along with him:

We do, doodley do, doodley do, doodley do,
What we must, muddily must, muddily
    must, muddily must;
Muddily do, muddily do, muddily do, mud-
    dily do,
Until we bust, bodily bust, bodily bust,
    bodily bust.

I made up a tune to go with that and I whistled it under my breath as I drove the bicycle that drove the fan that gave us air, good old air.

An oubliette is used as a metaphor within Dr. Brown's description of the mental processes one goes through when suffering from Samaritrophia, as did Sylvia Rosewater. (GBR 4) They rebel at last. They pitch the tyrannous conscience down an **oubliette**, weld shut the manhole cover of that dark dungeon. They can hear the conscience no more. In the sweet silence, the mental processes look about for a new leader, and the leader most prompt to appear whenever the conscience is stilled, Enlightened Self-interest, does appear. Enlightened Self-interest gives them a flag, which they adore on sight. It is essentially the black and white Jolly Roger, with these words written beneath the skull and crossbones, "The hell with you, Jack, I've got mine!"
See also: CC 96; 98; 100; 118; 120; 122; *GBR* 4.

Our Lady of Perpetual Astonishment. *The following is the text illustration for chapter three of* A Man Without a Country.

> I DON'T KNOW
> ABOUT YOU,
> BUT I PRACTICE
> A DISORGANIZED
> RELIGION.
> I BELONG TO AN
> UNHOLY DISORDER.
> WE CALL OURSELVES

"OUR LADY OF PERPETUAL ASTONISHMENT."

(*MWC* 3)

Owl's Club (*see* **Grand Triumvirate**).

Owley, Reva. *In the short story "Lovers Anonymous," collected in* Bagombo Snuff Box *(1999),* **Reva Owley,** *the woman who sells cosmetics and runs the library, engages the unnamed narrator in conversation when she sees him investigate the red-covered text returned by Sheila Hinckley White. The text,* Woman, the Wasted Sex, or, The Swindle of Housewifery, *pushes the early 1960s rhetoric found in Betty Friedan's* The Feminine Mystique. *When the narrator declares the text filth, Reva Owley crafts three subtle and targeted insults seamlessly woven into the conversation, all aimed at his intentional ignorance.* "Have you read it?" she asked.

"I've read the table of contents," I said.

"At least you've opened a book," she said. "That's more than any other member of Lovers Anonymous has done in the past ten years."

"I'll have you know I read a great deal," I said.

"I didn't know that much had been written about storm windows." **Reva** is a very smart widow.

"You can sure be a snippy woman, on occasion," I said.

"That comes from reading books about what a mess men have made of the world," she said.

P

Pabu (*see also* **Bokononism**). (CC 85) I learned some things, but they were scarcely helpful. I learned of the Bokononist cosmogony, for instance, wherein *Borasisi*, the sun, held *Pabu*, the moon, in his arms, and hoped that *Pabu* would bear him a fiery child.

But poor *Pabu* gave birth to children that were cold, that did not burn; and *Borasisi* threw them away in disgust. These were the planets, who circled their terrible father at a safe distance. Then poor *Pabu* herself was cast away, and she went to live with her favorite child, which was Earth. Earth was *Pabu*'s favorite because it had people on it; and the people looked up at her and loved her and sympathized.

And what opinion did Bokonon hold of his own cosmogony? "*Foma!* Lies!" he wrote. "A pack of *foma!*"

"The Package." *Originally published in the July 1952 issue of* Collier's *and later collected in* Bagombo Snuff Box *(1999), the story satirizes the views of nouveau riche couple Earl and Maude Fenton. We come upon them having just returned from a trip around the world and entering for the first time their remote-controlled, push-button palatial home. Before they have a chance to unpack or learn how to work most of the buttons that control their living space, they receive two phone calls. The first is from Charley Freeman, one of Earl's wealthy fraternity brothers from his college days. The second is from* Home Beautiful, *a magazine asking to do a photo shoot and story on the couple's newly built, futuristic palace. The extravagant home is wryly nicknamed "the package" by Slotkin, the magazine's photographer, because it has every conceivable luxury controlled in the most scientifically state-of-the-art manner for the consumer market. Most of the story takes place during the photo shoot, traipsing from room to room to luxurious gardens and the barbecue cooking area.*

Earl Fenton worked his way through college by waiting on tables, often sensing derisive looks from his wealthy fraternity brothers though he is unable to give his wife, Maude, a single example of their slights. It was his own sense of financial inferiority that dogged him for years. His financial status changed radically after college, having become a wealthy industrialist. The Fentons' around-the-world trip followed the sale of his manufacturing plant. Their two children, Earl Jr. and Ted, have respectively risen to become a doctor and a lawyer, further confirmation that the Fentons' American Dream will extend to the next generation.

Earl's uneasiness about the surprising call from Charley Freeman is fed by Maude's suspicions. She is the one who notices Charley's worn suit and shoes and assumes he wants to ask Charley for money. Though Earl originally asks Charley to stay at the house, Maude provides Earl with an excuse to get Charley out after dinner. She tells Earl to say that her sister Angela and brother-in-law Arthur are coming to visit and they will not have enough room for everyone. Charley takes the gentleman's way out and leaves in a taxi to a hotel.

It is only once Charley leaves that the Fentons are told by Lou Converse, their home contractor who is there for the photo shoot, about Charley's story since graduating college. Converse learned Freeman's history both from a newspaper story carried in the local paper that day and his conversation with Freeman while all the photos were being taken and the Fentons were changing clothes. Freeman became a doctor in 1916 and had been living in China for the past thirty years, where he used all his family's money to build a hospital for the poor. It was the Chinese Communists who eventually took over the hospital and jailed Dr. Charley Freeman before deporting him. The Fentons had been too busy during their combined photo shoot and hosting of Charley Freeman to have had any significant conversation about his life. Freeman was too much the gentleman to simply tell his story; instead, he listened intently as the Fentons emphasized to the unnamed magazine writer and photographer how hard they had worked to earn all they had.

Entranced by Lou Converse's telling of Freeman's compelling story and his own conspicuous shame, Earl is left numb after his fraternity brother taxis away, searching the remote-control panel for the button that will reset the day, allowing him a second chance to spend meaningful time with his humanitarian friend instead of gushing about the material wonders of his new home. "Maude and I'd like to start today all over again," said Earl. "Show us which button to push, Lou."

Padwee, Dr. Howard. *The veterinarian who diagnoses the false pregnancy of Walter Starbuck's Lhasa apso. The dog cares for a rubber ice-cream cone as though it were her puppy. Starbuck takes this opportunity to reach for some greater insight as he prepares to return to prison. (JB Epilogue)* I observe how profoundly serious Nature has made her about a rubber ice-cream cone—brown rubber cone, pink rubber ice cream. I have to wonder what equally ridiculous commitments to bits of trash I myself have made. Not that it matters at all. We are here for no purpose, unless we can invent one. Of that I am sure. The human condition in an exploding universe would not have been altered one iota if, rather than live as I have, I had done nothing but carry a rubber ice-cream cone from closet to closet for sixty years.

Pahlavi Pavilion. *The student recreation center at Tarkington College in* Hocus Pocus. *In order to construct the building in 1995, the graves of Hermann and Sophia Shultz are moved to Musket Mountain. Aside from displacing graves, the facility's bowling alley, pool hall, and ice-cream parlor forces local Scipio businesses to close.*

One night Pamela Ford Hall gets Eugene Debs Hartke drunk on blackberry brandy and he goes to the Pahlavi Pavilion where he gathers an audience of students and tells them of the atrocities committed during the Vietnam War. Kimberley Wilder records the event on tape, and her father uses it as part of the Board of Trustees' case to fire Hartke—who is charged with "teaching pessimism."

After the prison break in Athena, Hartke serves as temporary warden on the Tarkington campus and orders machine gun placements in the windows and doorways of the recreation center.

Palace of the League of Nations. *The Tralfamadorians use their Universal Will to Become to send messages concerning the status of the replacement part for Salo's spaceship. The messages are conveyed in great architectural monuments on Earth that could be monitored by Salo. (ST 12)* The meaning of the **Palace of the League of Nations** in Geneva, Switzerland, is: "*Pack up your things and be ready to leave on short notice*" [italics in original].

Palladio. *In* Timequake, *this is one of two computer programs remarkable for the their ability to have anyone practice art and science without either talent or significant education, thereby diminishing the achievements of both Pepper bothers, Zoltan and Frank. Zoltan is overwhelmed by the musical composition developed by "a tone-deaf kid next door" utilizing the program Wolfgang. By comparison, Palladio is a do-it-yourself computerized architecture program that proves to be the undoing of architect Frank Pepper. After trying out the program's capabilities by challenging it to come up with a "three-story parking garage in the manner of Thomas Jefferson," he kills himself. Due to the rerun scenario at the core of* Timequake, *Frank Pepper kills himself twice over this program (TQ 10).*

Vonnegut's detailed description of the menu-driven system and programming capabilities of Palladio clearly indicates he had some detailed knowledge and familiarity with technology despite his fabled stance as a neo-Luddite on such matters.

Palm Sunday (1981). *The second of Vonnegut's collections of essays. It is also the title of a sermon he delivered at St. Clement's Episcopal Church in Manhattan, included in the chapter entitled "In the Capital of the World." It is mostly about the Sermon on the Mount, a text of great significance in* Jailbird.

Pan-Galactic Humbug (subtitled Three Billion Dupes). *Written by Winston Niles Rumfoord's chief detractor, Dr. Maurice Rosenau, in* The Sirens of Titan, *the text asserts that despite all of Rumfoord's shortcomings and braggadocio, he never intimated he was God or an agent of God.*

The Pan-Galactic Memory Bank. *(BC 24)* I *(Vonnegut) could go on and on with the intimate details about the various lives of people on the super-ambulance, but what good is more information?

I agree with Kilgore Trout about realistic novels and their accumulations of nit-picking details. In Trout's novel, *The Pan-Galactic Memory Bank*, the hero is on a space ship two hundred miles long and sixty-two miles in diameter. He gets a realistic novel out of the branch library in his neighborhood. He reads about sixty pages of it, and then he takes it back.

The librarian asks him why he doesn't like it, and he says to her, "I already know about human beings."

And so on.

Pan-Galactic Space Service. *Army of Mars recruiters George Helmholtz and Roberta Wiley are members of the Pan-Galactic Space Service in* The Sirens of Titan.

"Pan-Galactic Straw-boss." *In* Breakfast of Champions, *one of Kilgore Trout's short stories that finds its way into publication in a pornographic magazine. Its title is changed to "Mouth Crazy" and it is illustrated with pictures of naked women. No information is provided about the narrative.*

Pan-Galactic Three-Day Pass. *In* God Bless You, Mr. Rosewater, *Eliot purchases this Kilgore Trout novel for his bus trip to Indianapolis and a reunion with his wife, Sylvia. The story is about Sergeant Raymond Boyle, an English teacher attached to an intergalactic crew of explorers. Boyle receives an emergency three-day pass because the Milky Way died. Thrown into a catatonic trance, Eliot looks up and hallucinates a vision of Indianapolis consumed by firestorm. Eliot's only recollection is of another book held so secretly in his bedroom in Rosewater County,* The Bombing of Germany *by Hans Rumpf. (GBR 14) Eliot, rising from his seat in the bus, beheld the firestorm of Indianapolis. He was awed by the majesty of the column of fire, which was at least eight miles in diameter and fifty miles high. The boundaries of the column seemed absolutely sharp and unwavering, as though made of glass. Within the boundaries, helixes of dull red embers turned in stately harmony about an inner core of white. The white seemed holy.*

At this point in the narrative there is a one-year gap during which time Eliot is cared for in Dr. Brown's Indianapolis sanitarium.

Parachute Ski Marines. *One of the military units on Mars preparing to invade Earth in* The Sirens of Titan. *Winston Niles Rumfoord wears their uniform when materializing on Mars for strategy meetings.*

Parker, Theodore. *The Harvard-educated minister and regular member of Boston's Transcendental Club, Parker is quoted as a reference in the text that changes Sheila Hinckley White's outlook on life, the focus of the short story "Lovers Anonymous," collected in* Bagombo Snuff Box *(1999): The domestic function of woman does not exhaust her powers. To make one half the human race consume its energies in the functions of housekeeper, wife and mother is a monstrous waste of the most precious material God ever made. Eight months earlier than Vonnegut's story appears, Betty Friedan used the same reference in* The Feminine Mystique, *and Parker is further cited by Presidents Lincoln and Obama as well as Dr. King.*

Parrot, Wilfred. *The manager of the Pawtucket, Rhode Island, orphanage founded by Castor Buntline in 1878, in* God Bless You, Mr. Rosewater. *The sixty-year old Parrot fought in the Abraham Lincoln Brigade and wrote for the radio series "Beyond the Blue Horizon" in the mid-1930s. The Buntlines regularly take in one of the female orphans to train as domestic servants. Selena Deal is one such girl, and she confides in her weekly letters to "Daddy Parrot" that she doesn't understand the Buntlines.*

Patton, Jack. *The West Point classmate, close friend, and eventual brother-in-law of Eugene Debs Hartke in* Hocus Pocus. *Remembered for his often repeated phrase "I had to laugh like hell," Patton never takes anything too seriously, and Hartke compares him to prison-break leader Alton Darwin. Patton introduces Hartke to his mother Mildred and his sister Margaret when they visit West Point for graduation. Jack was last in his class. As a lieutenant colonel in the Combat Engineers in Vietnam, Patton is killed by a fifteen-year-old sniper. While in high school, Patton built an electric chair for rats, but he never used it.*

It was Patton who sent Hartke a copy of Black Garterbelt *magazine containing the short story "The Protocols of the Elders of Tralfamadore." Hartke doesn't read it until around the same time the prisoners at Athena were learning how to read using the anti-Semitic forgery* The Protocols of the Elders of Zion.

Patton, Margaret and Mildred. *Respectively, the wife and mother-in-law of Eugene Debs Hartke in* Hocus Pocus. *Margaret is the sister of Jack Patton, Hartke's best friend at West Point. She and Hartke meet at his West Point graduation. Both Margaret and Mildred suffer from hereditary insanity that does not set in until middle age. This is unknown to Hartke when they marry and have children, but their children hated them for bringing them into the world so genetically fated. Hartke learns of the family's medical history while standing at the urinal in a Boston Chinese restaurant and speaking with a man who was a hometown acquaintance of the Pattons back in Peru, Indiana.*

After Hartke is incarcerated, Margaret and Mildred are taken to the "Laughing Academy" in Batavia, New York, in the same steel boxes that brought convicts to the prison. (HP 1) The biggest booby trap Fate set for me, though, was a pretty and personable young woman named **Margaret Patton**, who allowed me to woo and marry her soon after my graduation from West Point, and then had 2 children by me without telling me that there was a powerful strain of insanity on her mother's side of the family.

Paul. *In "The Powder-Blue Dragon," Paul is Marion's fiancé and another character who holds Kiah Higgins in low esteem as is evident when he looks around the tony lounge (there are now only four people in there) and fails to believe anyone present could be the owner or driver of the 130-mph Marittima-Frascati parked outside. Despite a brief, dismissive conversation with Kiah, Paul never asks his name and derogatorily recalls the name of the car as Vanilla Frappé. Paul owns a Hampton, once the object of Kiah's own desires before setting his sights on the Marittima-Frascati. He taunts Kiah with the possibility of a race to show whose car is best. Kiah declines, knowing that the car must be properly bro-*

ken in as instructed by Bill Daggett, his car dealer and employer. Kiah follows the pair in his car and flips them the bird when passing them before deciding to blow the engine. (Though nothing in the story helps settle a date for the setting, the British Hampton went through a series of corporate ownerships before ceasing production in 1933. No record of an actual Marittima-Frascati sports car has yet been found.)

Peach, Delbert. *The town drunk in Rosewater, Indiana, who fears Eliot will leave for Indianapolis and never return. As a going-away gift to Eliot, Peach tells him that only ten minutes ago he swore off liquor. Eliot tells Peach not to worry, that his fate is to remain in Rosewater, that even if he tried to leave forces of biblical proportion would bring him back.* (GBR 12) "**Mr. Peach**—" and Eliot rubbed his eyes, "if I were to somehow wind up in New York, and start living the highest of all possible lives again, you know what would happen to me? The minute I got near any navigable body of water, a bolt of lightning would knock me into the water, a whale would swallow me up, and the whale would swim down to the Gulf of Mexico and up the Mississippi, up the Ohio, up the Wabash, up the White, up Lost River, up Rosewater Creek. And that whale would jump from the creek into the Rosewater Inter-State Ship Canal, and it would swim down the canal to this city, and spit me out in the Parthenon. And there I'd be."

Peach, Miss. *The school nurse in the short story "The Boy Who Hated Girls," collected in* Bagombo Snuff Box (1999), *tells George Helmholtz the unadorned truth about the mischief he provokes by becoming so deeply and personally involved in the lives of some of his promising but troubled students. At the moment when Assistant Principal Stewart Haley tells Helmholtz that his unrestrained spending spree on band equipment has got to be stopped, Miss Peach chimes in with her diagnosis of a more deeply troubling problem that the band director fails to recognize.* "That isn't the only kind of spree that's got to be stopped," said **Miss Peach** darkly.

"What do you mean by that?" said Helmholtz.

"I mean," said **Miss Peach**, "all this playing fast and loose with kids' emotions." She frowned.

"George, I've been watching you for years—watching you use every emotional trick in the books to make your kids march and play."

"I try to be friends," said Helmholtz, untroubled.

"You try to be a lot more than that," said **Miss Peach**. "Whatever a kid needs, you're it. Father, mother, sister, brother, God, slave, or dog—you're it. No wonder we've got the best band in the world. The only wonder is that what's happened with Bert hasn't happened a thousand times."

"What's eating Bert?" said Helmholtz.

"You won him," said **Miss Peach**. "That's what. Lock, stock, and barrel—he's yours, all yours."

"Sure he likes me," said Helmholtz. "Hope he does, anyway."

"He likes you like a son likes a father," said **Miss Peach**.

"There's a casual thing for you."

Helmholtz couldn't imagine what the argument was about. Everything **Miss Peach** had said was obvious. "That's only natural, isn't it?" he said. "Bert doesn't have a father, so he's going to look around for one, naturally, until he finds some girl who'll take him over and—"

"Will you please open your eyes, and see what you've done to Bert's life?" said **Miss Peach**. "Look what he did to get your attention, after you stuck him in the Ten Square Band, then sent him off to Mr. Fink and forgot all about him. He was willing to have the whole world laugh at him, just to get you to look at him again."

Peale, Delmar. *In* Jailbird, *the only salesman of the American Harp Company located on the top floor of the Chrysler Building. He and his secretary, eighty-seven-year-old Doris Kramm, are featured in* People *magazine as the oldest boss and secretary team known to man. Peale has Walter Starbuck arrested when he appears in the showroom with stolen clarinet parts as listed on a police circular. When RAM-JAC takes over American Harp and Starbuck becomes the CEO, Delmar Peale makes a present of the police circular to Walter.*

pearls before swine. *Vonnegut uses this biblical phrase as the subtitle for* God Bless You, Mr. Rosewater. *The text is from Matthew 7:6, which reads,* "Give not that which is holy unto the dogs, neither cast ye your **pearls before swine**, lest they trample them under their feet, and turn again and rend you."

Peck, Jerry and Muriel. *The owners of the Mohiga Ice Cream Emporium in Scipio, New York, in* Hocus Pocus. *Though both have degrees in English literature from Swarthmore College, neither becomes a teacher until Muriel fills the vacated position at Tarkington created by Eugene Debs Hartke's dismissal. Jerry is a direct descendant of John Peck, the first President of the Mohiga Valley Free Institute, but is raised in San Diego.*

When the couple first marry, Jerry works for an ice-cream company in his hometown, but he loses his job when Zaire's President Mobutu purchases the company. They decide to return to the home of the family's eastern roots, Scipio, New York. They purchase a store on Clinton Street and Jerry goes to work stripping all the paint and renovating the building for their new enterprise, the Mohiga Ice Cream Emporium. He fails to read the cautionary warnings on the cans of paint stripper, and by the time they open for business, Jerry is wheelchair bound and breathing with the assistance of an oxygen tank. Jerry's disabilities from the renovation eventually kill him.

Six months after the ice-cream parlor opens, the designers of the new Pahlavi Pavilion recreation center take photographs of its interior and incorporate a similar facility into their building. This is yet another business destroyed by the Pahlavi Pavilion. Muriel goes to work as a bartender at the Black Cat Café. She and Hartke eventually become lovers. Muriel is killed in the prison uprising when the escapees came across the frozen lake. She is buried with the others in the shadow of Musket Mountain.

Peck, John. *The twenty-six-year-old school teacher from Athena, New York, brought to nearby Scipio to become the first president of the Mohiga Valley Free Institute, in* Hocus Pocus. *Though a cousin of the founding Tarkington family, his branch of the family did not suffer the dyslexia so common to the others. Elias Tarkington moves John Peck and his family into his own home, which also serves as the school's first building, and moves his own collection of perpetual motion machines to the attic. Eugene Debs Hartke finds the collection in 1978.*

Peckham, Bradley (*also known as* **Colonel Peckham**) **and Pam.** *In the short story "Any Reasonable Offer," first appearing in* Collier's *magazine (January 1952) and later collected in* Bagombo Snuff Box *(1999), Bradley Peckham is a draftsman by vocation, a vacationing fraud by avocation. He works for National Steel Foundry and is answerable to the frighteningly named Ralph L. Thriller.*

Peckham and his wife, Pam, take their vacations at posh private estates on the real estate market. Masquerading as Colonel Peckham and wife, the two often coyly and falsely let real estate agents and estate owners believe they are interested in purchasing property. As people of apparent means, estate owners are charmed by the pair and often invite the prospective buyers use the estate's pool, stables—to get the newness out—etc. The unnamed narrator—a real estate agent who fell victim to and now feels educated by Peckham's scam—becomes schooled in their ways through their use of Mrs. Hellbruner's and later Mr. Hurty's properties. The narrator first introduces the couple to the owners. By the end of the story, he decides to stop working as hard as he does, something we learn as we see him falsely enjoying the amenities of the Van Tuyl estate in Newport, Rhode Island.

An example of the draftsman's coy and vaguely misleading frauds is the implication that Colonel Peckham is only temporarily in charge of straightening out what must be the crookedest lines (of management) at National Steel. The man in charge of National Steel must be a serious buyer of exclusive homes and a worthy buyer to have on premises. The narrator snuffs out the fraud when hearing Peckham's voice as he nears the telephone, a call initiated by the narrator to follow up on Colonel Peckham.

Pefko, Captain Julian. *The officer in charge of visitation to the neutron-bombed Midland City, in* Deadeye Dick. *Pefko agrees to let Hippolyte Paul De Mille and the Waltz brothers visit Calvary Cemetery, where De Mille raises the spirit of the aviator Will Fairchild.*

Pefko, Francine. *There are two appearances of Francine Pefko, though they bear little resemblance to each other. Her first appearance occurs during a tour of the Ilium Research Laboratory by Dr. Breed*

for the visiting narrator of Cat's Cradle. *Miss Pefko is the secretary of Dr. Nilsak Horvath, and she is invited by Dr. Breed to accompany them on their way to Dr. Hoenikker's laboratory.* (CC 15) **Miss Pefko** *was twenty, vacantly pretty, and healthy—a dull normal. Despite working at the lab for nearly a year, Miss Pefko seems terminally baffled by all she types. She is embarrassed by her ignorance, but even more flustered by her superiors.* (CC 15) "You scientists *think* too much," blurted **Miss Pefko**. She laughed idiotically. Dr. Breed's friendliness had blown every fuse in her nervous system. She was no longer responsible. "You *all* think too much."

The vacant Miss Pefko is reinvented for Breakfast of Champions, *becoming the managing secretary at Dwayne Hoover's Exit Eleven Pontiac Village as well as his mistress. Widowed when her husband, Robert Pefko, dies in Vietnam, this is only shortly after Dwayne's wife kills herself by drinking Drano. By the time Dwayne starts to develop a severe case of paranoia, he mistakes Francine's suggestion of starting a new Kentucky Fried Chicken store as her way of looking for repayment for all the sex they had. In reality, she thinks it would simply be a wise investment since the visitors at the Shepherdstown Correctional Facility need a place to eat. Her thinking is innocently pure toward Dwayne and the product of racial stereotyping since she felt fried chicken would be the best product for the black visitors going to the prison.*

Later, when Dwayne begins his violent rampage, Francine is one of his first targets. He drags her from the Pontiac showroom so he could beat her in the parking lot for all to see. (BC 24) Dwayne had already broken her jaw and three ribs in the office. When he trundled her outside, there was a fair-size crowd which had drifted out of the cocktail lounge and the kitchen of the new Holiday Inn. "Best fucking machine in the State," he told the crowd. "Wind her up, and she'll fuck you and say she loves you, and she won't shut up till you give her a Colonel Sanders Kentucky Fried Chicken franchise." *She is saved by Kilgore Trout, who pays for his chivalry by having his ring finger bitten off by Dwayne.*

Pefko, George. *In the short story "The Cruise of the Jolly Roger," this fallen World War II buddy of Major Nathan Durant becomes his focus on his way* *back to New London to sell his cabin cruiser. Pefko was part of a large transient family that briefly lived in a summer rental belonging to Paul Eldredge (staying through the winter) and from where Pefko enlisted. It is when young Tom, standing by Pefko's plaque in the square commemorating his sacrifice, speaks about the meaning of Memorial Day that Durant finally feels that their service is appreciated by the next generation.*

Pefko, Robert. *The husband of Francine Pefko in* Breakfast of Champions. *A West Point graduate and career military officer, he earns a master's degree in anthropology from the University of Pennsylvania and returns to West Point to teach social science. He is sent to Midland City to supervise the construction of military booby traps. From there, he is deployed to Vietnam, where he dies around the same time Celia Hoover commits suicide.*

Pelk, Kennard. *In the short story "Lovers Anonymous," collected in* Bagombo Snuff Box *(1999), Pelk is the North Crawford police chief and a member of the group whose eponymous name comes from their shared longing for Sheila Hinckley. Pelk helps spread the rumor that Herb and Sheila are having marital difficulties because he misinterprets the one glowing candle in the ell of their home.* "I mean, that old house has fifteen rooms, not counting the ell," said **Kennard**, "and a family of four—five, if you count the dog. And I couldn't understand how anybody, especially at that time of night, would want to go out to the ell. I thought maybe it was a burglar. . . .

"Anyway, it was my duty to investigate. . . .

"So I snook up to a window and looked in. And there was Herb on a mattress on the floor. He had a bottle of liquor and a glass next to him, and he had a candle stuck in another bottle, and he was reading a magazine by candlelight." *Herb has the chance to rebuke his old friend for invading his privacy at home, but Pelk later tells the story to the unnamed narrator without the benefit of knowing the truth about the living arrangements between Sheila and Herb.*

Pellegrino, Peter (*see* **God Bless You, Dr. Kevorkian**).

Pembroke, Abraham Lincoln I, III, and IV. *In* Timequake, *though bearing the surname of Julia Pembroke's husband, Elias, a naval architect who serves as Lincoln's assistant secretary of the Navy, the ironically named Abraham Lincoln Pembroke is Julia's bastard lovechild sired during her drugged tryst with paramour and correspondent John Wilkes Booth, the soon-to-be presidential assassin. Vonnegut fixes Abraham's conception precisely two years to the evening before Booth commits the deed. Young Abraham is born in Pembroke, Rhode Island, the town named in honor of one of her husband's ancestors and where Julia goes to deliver the child.*

Abraham Lincoln Pembroke III is the father of Frank Smith, his illegitimate son by the unmarried African-American housemaid, Rosemary Smith. He paid her handsomely for her silence. We was gone when his child Frank Smith was born (*TQ* 60). (*TQ* 60) And **Abraham Lincoln Pembroke**, ignorant of whose son he actually was, in 1889 founded Indian Head Mills, which became the largest textile mill in New England until 1947, when **Abraham Lincoln Pembroke III** locked out his striking employees and moved the company to North Carolina. **Abraham Lincoln Pembroke IV** subsequently sold it to an international conglomerate, which moved it to Indonesia, and he died of drink.

Not an actor in the bunch. Not a murderer in the bunch. No pixie ears.

Pembroke, Elias and Julia (*see also* **Abraham Lincoln Pembroke** *and* **Pembroke Mask and Wig Club**). *Elias and Julia are two thirds of a love triangle described in* Timequake. *One side of the sordid affair is memorialized by Julia's creation of the Pembroke Mask and Wig Club, a community theater.*

(*TQ* 59) **Elias Pembroke**, a fictitious Rhode Island naval architect who was Abraham Lincoln's Assistant Secretary of the Navy during our Civil War, was a character in *Timequake One*. I said he made significant contributions to the design of the power train of the ironclad warship *Monitor*, but was neglectful of his wife, **Julia**, who fell in love with a dashing young actor and rakehell named John Wilkes Booth.

Julia wrote love letters to Booth. A tryst was arranged for April 14th, 1863, two years before Booth shot Lincoln from behind with a derringer. She went to New York City from Washington with a chaperone, the alcoholic wife of an admiral, ostensibly to shop, and to escape the tensions in the besieged capital. They checked into the hotel where Booth was staying, and attended his performance that night, as Marc Antony in *Julius Caesar*, by William Shakespeare.

As Marc Antony, Booth would speak lines horrifyingly prophetic in his case: "The evil that men do lives after them."

* * *

. . . .

John Wilkes gallantly kissed the hand of **Julia**, as though they had just met, and simultaneously slipped her a packet of chloral hydrate crystals, which would be the active ingredient in a Mickey Finn for the chaperone.

Julia had been given to believe by Booth that all she would receive from him when she came to his hotel room would be a single glass of champagne, and a single kiss she would cherish for the rest of her life after the war, back in Rhode Island, a life that would otherwise be humdrum. *Madame Bovary!*

Little did **Julia** suspect that Booth would mousetrap her champagne, just as *she* had mousetrapped her chaperone's beddy-bye slug of wartime white lightning, with chloral hydrate.

Ting-a-ling!

Booth knocked her up! She had never had a kid before. Something was wrong with her husband's ding-dong. She was thirty-one! The actor was twenty-four!

Incredible?

* * *

Her husband, was delighted. She's pregnant? There was nothing wrong with Assistant Secretary of the Navy **Elias Pembroke**'s ding-dong after all! Anchors aweigh!

Pembroke Mask and Wig Club. *Created by Julia Pembroke upon turning fifty in 1882 to secretly commemorate her love affair with John Wilkes Booth, Lincoln's assassin and father of her only child, Abraham Lincoln Pembroke. (TQ 60) Julia shared her*

secret with no one. Did she have regrets? Of course she did, but not about love. When she turned fifty, in 1882, she founded as a memorial for her only love affair, however brief and star-crossed, without saying that's what it was, an amateur acting group, the **Pembroke Mask and Wig Club**.

Kilgore Trout has the opportunity of creating the final sound effect to a matinee performance of the Pembroke Mask and Wig Club's performance of Abe Lincoln in Illinois. *Later that evening is the* Timequake *clambake. (TQ 60)* The only sound effect Trout had to create backstage was in the last moments of the last scene of the last act of the play, of what Trout himself called "a manmade timequake." He was equipped with an antique steam whistle from the heyday of Indian Head Mills. A plumber, who was a club member and looked a lot like my brother, put the gaily mournful whistle atop a tank of compressed air, with a valve in between. That is what Trout was, too, in all he wrote: *gaily mournful.*

Pena, Harry (*also* **Manny and Kenny**). *The chief of the Pisquontuit Volunteer Fire Department, son of a trap fisherman, and former insurance salesman in* God Bless You, Mr. Rosewater. *Having already fallen victim to chemical exposure from a carpet cleaner, Harry is forced to work outdoors. He returns to the sea to make his living as his father did. (GBR 9)* **Harry** was middle-aged and bandy-legged, but he had a head and shoulders Michelangelo might have given to Moses or God.

He and his sons Manny and Kenny do their fish-trapping from their boat, the Mary, *in Pisquontuit Bay, within viewing distance of the patrons at The Weir, the restaurant belonging to Bunny Weeks. Bunny uses the opportunity to inform various guests about the labors of the Penas, using them as part of the restaurant's ambience. (GBR 10)* **Harry Pena** and his boys knew about the salad and the cocktail and the opera glasses, though they had never visited *The Weir.* Sometimes they would respond to their involuntary involvement with the restaurant by urinating off the boat. They called this ". . . *making cream of leek soup for Bunny Weeks*" [*italics in original*].

Bunny Weeks is disgusted with the romanticism attached to the Penas by some of his patrons, particularly Caroline Rosewater. He uses information known to him as one of the local bank's directors to inform her that their romanticism is groundless. (GBR 10) "Real people don't make their livings that way any more. Those three romantics out there make as much sense as Marie Antoinette and her milkmaids. When the bankruptcy proceedings begin—in a week, a month, a year—they'll find out that their only economic value was as animated wallpaper for my restaurant here." Bunny, to his credit, was not happy about this. "That's all over, men working with their hands and backs. They are not needed."

"Men like **Harry** will always win, won't they?" said Caroline.

"They're losing everywhere." Bunny let go of Amanita.

Penfield, Frederic Courtland. (*DD* Preface) This is fiction, not history, so it should not be used as a reference book. I say, for example, that the United States Ambassador to Austria-Hungary at the outbreak of the First World War was Henry Clowes, of Ohio. The actual ambassador at that time was **Frederic Courtland Penfield** of Connecticut.

Pennsylvania Dutchmen. *In the short story "Der Arme Dolmetscher," collected in* Bagombo Snuff Box (1999), *the unnamed narrator meets these three GIs when he hops a ride on a farm truck headed in the direction of the Belgian burgomaster's house, not far from the German defensive position known as the Siegfried Line. The* three disgruntled **Pennsylvania Dutchmen** had applied for interpreters' jobs months earlier. When I made it clear that I was no competition for them, and that I hoped to be liquidated within twenty-four hours, they warmed up enough for me to furnish the interesting information that I was a *Dolmetscher*. They also decoded "Die Lorelei" at my request. This gave me command of about forty words (par for a two-year-old), but no combination of them would get me so much as a glass of cold water.

Additionally, the Pennsylvanians give the narrator a pamphlet purporting to make German easy for the man in the foxhole.

"Some of the first pages are missing," the donor explained as I jumped from the truck before the burgomaster's stone farmhouse. "Used 'em for ciga-rette papers," he said. *Those first few pages had all the translations for polite and brief conversation. The remaining pages had to do with actual interrogatories to be used on captured soldiers, such as* Where are your tank columns?

The Dutchmen later appear in the narrator's twilight fantasy as he lay in bed at the burgomaster's home. The narrator's fantasy opens as a prelude to a sexual tryst between himself and the burgomaster's daughter with all their conversation coming from the little bit of Heine's poem ("Die Lorelei") that the Dutchmen translated for him during the truck ride to the burgomaster's home. Their actual appearance in the fantasy occurs when the narrator turns the tables on the burgomaster and his daughter, getting them to surrender and explain in German that they were spies dropped by parachute behind the American lines.

Pennwalt Biphetamine. *This is the narcotic of choice for Celia Hoover (née Hildreth) in* Deadeye Dick. *When she comes into Rudy Waltz's pharmacy, he mentally constructs a short play of her demanding the drug. When Rudy turns her down, she has a fit and wrecks the pharmacy's counter displays.*

Pepper, Frank. *An architect and older brother of the wheelchair-bound Zoltan Pepper in* Timequake, *Frank would blow his brains out while his wife and three kids watched (10). Another of Vonnegut's characters used to illustrate how people define and value themselves by their work, Frank Pepper's despair sets in shortly after testing Palladio, a computerized architecture program capable of delivering all the artistry and technical knowledge he honed for years. Palladio is so user-friendly and technically complete that a poorly performing sixteen-year-old high school student could turn out accomplished architectural plans. He quickly loses his self-respect after sampling Palladio in an electronics store, hurries home, and commits suicide. Due to the nature of the timequake, Frank Pepper actually commits suicide twice.*

Pepper, Monica and Zoltan. *In Vonnegut's references to his failed* Timequake One *manuscript, Monica Pepper appears as the forty-year-old executive secretary of the American Academy of Arts and*

Letters. She is the same age as her husband, Zoltan (younger brother of Frank Pepper), who twice endures becoming a paraplegic bound to a wheelchair as the result of a freak accident involving his wife. They live in the Turtle Bay section of Manhattan, as did Vonnegut for more than thirty-five years. Monica presents a twisted metafictional element to the text with strangely incestuous implications for Vonnegut. (TQ 9) **Mrs. Pepper**, wife of the wheelchair-ridden composer **Zoltan Pepper**, bore a striking resemblance to my late sister Allie, who hated life so much. Allie died of cancer of the everything way back in 1958, when I was thirty-six and she was forty-one, hounded by bill collectors to the very end. Both women were pretty blondes, which was OK. But they were six-foot-two! Both women were permanently acculturated in adolescence, since nowhere on Earth, save among the Watusis, did it make any sense for a woman to be that tall.

Both women were unlucky. Allie married a nice guy who lost all their money and then some in dumb businesses. **Monica Pepper** was the reason her husband **Zoltan** was paralyzed from the waist down. Two years earlier, she had accidentally landed on top of him in a swimming pool out in Aspen, Colorado. At least Allie had to die so deep in debt, and with four sons to raise, only once. After the timequake struck, **Monica Pepper** would have to swan-dive on top of her husband a second time.

When the Academy's security guard, Dudley Prince, retrieves Kilgore trout's manuscript for "The Sisters B-36" from the trash can outside the institution and delivers the text to Monica, she discounts it as "ridiculous," but Zoltan is reminded of a humiliating experience from his youth. Back in high school, Zoltan had plagiarized one of Trout's stories and was caught by his teacher, Mrs. Wilkerson.

At the moment the timequake hits in 2001, Zoltan is about to ring the doorbell outside the Academy while Monica is inside working on the budget for the Xanadu writers' retreat. His demise is imminent. She lives on in the text as Vonnegut's wife as late as 2010. (TQ 22) When the rerun was over, though, and free will kicked in again, everybody and everything were exactly where they had been when the timequake struck. So **Zoltan** was paraplegic again in a wheelchair, ringing the doorbell again. He didn't realize that it was all of a sudden up to him to decide what his finger was going to do next. His finger, for want of instructions from him or anything else, went on ringing and ringing the doorbell.

That's what it was doing when **Zoltan** was smacked by a runaway fire truck. The driver of the truck hadn't realized yet that it was up to him to steer the thing.

As Trout wrote in *My Ten Years on Automatic Pilot*: "It was free will that did all the damage. The timequake and its aftershocks didn't map as much as a single strand in a spider's web, unless some other force had snapped that strand the first time through."

As a result of his accident with Monica, Zoltan is both confined to a wheelchair and impotent. Whereas Frank Pepper suffers the indignity of learning that the computer program Palladio could summon all the creative talent of an accomplished architect and thereby make his own occupation so banal that he commits suicide, Zoltan is asked to assess the musical stylings of his neighbor's tone-deaf son who creates music with the computer program Wolfgang. Both Frank and Zoltan are creatively and occupationally undone by computer programs, an ironic twist for Zoltan who was a teenaged plagiarist—but that had fatal consequences for Frank who could not handle the humiliation. This familiar and recurring theme in Vonnegut's work is particularly reminiscent of Player Piano *and* God Bless You, Mr. Rosewater. *See also: TQ 25; 60.*

perpetual-motion machine. (JB 19) And I am now compelled to wonder if wisdom has ever existed or can ever exist. Might wisdom be as impossible in this particular universe as a **perpetual-motion machine**? *This is Vonnegut's thinking after noting the social luminaries who telegrammed their support for Sacco and Vanzetti. Judge Thayer did not believe in the evidentiary guilt offered to support the charges for which he would sentence them to death—it was their politics he despised.*

Perpetual motion machines are the intellectual curiosity riveting the attention of Elias Tarkington, founder of the college bearing his name. (HP 3) He was not well educated, and was more a mechanic than a scientist, and so spent his last 3 years trying to invent what anyone familiar with Newton's Laws would have known was an impossibility, a **perpetual-motion machine**. He had no fewer than 27 contraptions built, which he foolishly expected to go on running, after he had given them an initial spin or whack, until Judgment Day.

(HP 3) Still another **perpetual-motion machine** envisioned by Elias Tarkington was what his Last Will and Testament called "The Mohiga Valley Free Institute." Upon his death, this new school would take possession of his 3,000-hectare estate above Scipio, plus half the shares in the wagon company, the carpet company, and the brewery. The other half was already owned by his sisters far away. On his deathbed he predicted that Scipio would 1 day be a great metropolis and that its wealth would transform his little college into a university to rival Harvard and Oxford and Heidelberg.

Once Tarkington passes away, the machines are moved to the attic to make room for classrooms and a library. There they remain until Eugene Debs Hartke finds them in 1978 when searching for the entrance to the bell tower. (HP 3) Yes, and we took the 10 machines we agreed were the most beguiling, and we put them on permanent exhibit in the foyer of this library underneath a sign whose words can surely be applied to this whole ruined planet nowadays:

THE COMPLICATED FUTILITY OF
IGNORANCE

The display and the sign become evidence against Hartke when the Board of Trustees seeks to fire him for, among other things, "teaching pessimism."
See also: HP 3; 8; 15.

Peterson, Captain, and his mother, Joy. *In* Timequake, *the pilot of Joy's Pride and his mother in the Kilgore Trout short story "No Laughing Matter." At the close of World War II, after the U.S. dropped atomic bombs first on Hiroshima and then Nagasaki, Captain Peterson is scheduled to drop the third atomic bomb on Yokohama. He names his bomber in honor of his mother, an obstetrics nurse in Corpus Christi, Texas. After taking off from the island of Banalulu with the "purple motherfucker"* atomic bomb strapped to the plane's belly, Captain Peterson has second thoughts. (TQ 3) *As the plane neared its target, the pilot mused out loud on the intercom that his mother, the obstetrics nurse, would be a celebrity back home after they did what they were about to do. The bomber Enola Gay, and the woman in whose honor it was named, had become as famous as movie stars after it dropped its load on Hiroshima. Yokohama was twice as populous as Hiroshima and Nagasaki combined.*

The more the pilot thought about it, though, the surer he was that his sweet widowed mother could never tell reporters she was happy that her son's airplane had killed a world's record number of civilians all at once. Captain Peterson refuses to continue the bombing run and returns to Banalulu to face a court-martial for his actions.

Petro, Joe III. *Vonnegut's close friend and artistic collaborator from 1993 until his own passing in 2007. Vonnegut is positively effusive in print when speaking about Petro. When describing the attendees at the* Timequake *clambake, Vonnegut notes Petro as one of the* five men half my age who made me want to keep on going in my sunset years because of their interest in my work. They weren't there to see me. They wanted at long last to meet Kilgore Trout. They were Robert Weide, who in this summer of 1996 is making a movie in Montreal of *Mother Night*, and Marc Leeds, who wrote and had published a witty encyclopedia of my life and work, and Asa Pieratt and Jerome Klinkowitz, who have kept my bibliography up-to-date and written essays about me as well, and **Joe Petro III**, numbered like a World War, who taught me how to silk-screen (TQ 62). *Earlier in* Timequake *(44), Vonnegut details his working process with Petro.*

Vonnegut's most heartfelt homage to Petro is found in his Author's Note to A Man Without a Country: The full-page, hand-lettered statements scattered throughout this book, "samplers suitable for framing" if you like, are pictures of products of Origami Express, a business partnership between myself and **Joe Petro III**, with headquarters in **Joe**'s painting and silk-screening studio in Lexington, Kentucky. I paint or draw pictures, and **Joe** makes prints of some of them, one by one, color by color, by means of the time-consuming, archaic silk screen process, practiced by almost nobody else any more: squeegeeing inks through cloths and onto paper. This process is so painstaking and tactile, almost balletic, that each print **Joe** makes is a painting in its own right.

Our partnership's name, Origami Express, is my tribute to the many-layered packages **Joe** makes for prints he sends for me to sign and number. The logo for Origami, made by **Joe**, isn't his picture of a picture I sent him, but of a picture by me that he found in my novel *Breakfast of Champions*. It is of a bomb in air, on its way down, with these words written on its side:

GOODBYE
BLUE
MONDAY

I have to have been one of the luckiest persons alive, since I have survived for four score and two years now. I can't begin to count all the times I should have been dead or wished I were. But one of the best things that ever happened to me, a one-in-a-billion opportunity to enjoy myself in perfect innocence, was my meeting **Joe**.

Here's the thing: Back in 1993, almost eleven years ago now, I was scheduled to lecture on November 1 at Midway College, a women's school on the edge of Lexington. Well in advance of my appearance, a Kentucky artist, **Joe Petro III**, son of the Kentucky artist Joe Petro II, asked me to do a black-and-white self-portrait, which he could then use in silk-screen posters to be used by the school. So I did and he did. **Joe** was only thirty-seven back then, and I was a mere spring chicken of only seventy-one, not even twice his age.

When I got down there to speak, and was so happy about the posters, I learned from **Joe** himself that he painted romantic but scientifically precise pictures of wildlife, from which he made silk screen images. He had majored in zoology at the University of Tennessee. Yes, and some of his pictures were so appealing and informative that they had been used as propaganda by Greenpeace, an organization trying, with scant success so far, to prevent the murder of species, even our own, by the way we live now. And **Joe**, having shown me the poster and

his own work and his studio, said to me in effect, "Why don't we keep on going?"

And so we have, and it seems quite possible in retrospect that **Joe Petro III** saved my life. I will not explain. I will let it go at that.

We have since collaborated on more than two hundred different images, with **Joe** making editions, signed and numbered by me, of ten or more of each of them. The "samplers" in this book are not at all representative of our total oeuvre, but are simply very recent jeux d'esprit. Most of our stuff has been my knockoffs of Paul Klee and Marcel Duchamp and so on.

And since we first met, **Joe** has beguiled others into sending him pictures for him to do with what he so much loves to do. Among them are the comedian Jonathan Winters, an art student long ago, and the English artist Ralph Steadman, whose accomplishments include the appropriately harrowing illustrations for Hunter Thompson's *Fear and Loathing* books. And Steadman and I have come to know and like each other on account of **Joe**.

Yes, and last July (2004) there was an exhibition of **Joe**'s and my stuff, arranged by **Joe**, at the Indianapolis Art Center in the town of my birth. But there was also a painting by my architect and painter grandfather Bernard Vonnegut, and two by my architect and painter father Kurt Vonnegut, and six apiece by my daughter Edith and my son the doctor Mark.

Ralph Steadman heard about this family show from **Joe** and sent me a note of congratulation. I wrote him back as follows: "**Joe Petro III** staged a reunion of four generations of my family in Indianapolis, and he has made you and me feel like first cousins. Is it possible that he is God? We could do worse."

Only kidding, of course.

Peterson, Mrs. Lyman R. *One of the many citizens who answer the call to arms provoked by the invasion from Mars.* (ST 7) At the Battle of Boca Raton, in Florida, U.S.A., for instance, **Mrs. Lyman R. Peterson** shot four members of the Martian Assault Infantry with her son's .22 caliber rifle. She picked them off as they came out of their space ship, which had landed in her back yard. She was awarded the Congressional Medal of Honor posthumously.

Phi Beta Kappa. *A large number of Vonnegut's characters earned membership in this national academic honor society including: the ugly wife of a handsome dullard, both members of Reverend Redwine's Church of God the Utterly Indifferent in Newport, Rhode Island, as well as Winston Niles Rumfoord (Sirens); Caroline Rosewater and Bunny Weeks (Rosewater); Wilbur Swain (Slapstick); Israel Edel (Jailbird); and Jason Wilder (Hocus Pocus). In Jailbird, Walter Starbuck mentions that many of his fellow inmates during the Watergate era were members.*

In reality, his sister Alice was a Phi Beta Kappa from Swarthmore, and had been the outstanding writer there! (TQ 25; *see also* 32, 58). *Fleon Sunoco's theories about alien intelligence on earth includes his interest in the brains of Mensa and Phi Beta Kappa members* (TQ 27).
(*BAG* The Package) "Freeman, Charley Freeman. A name from the past, Maude. I couldn't believe it at first. Charley was a fraternity brother and just about the biggest man in the whole class of 1910. Track star, president of the fraternity, editor of the paper, **Phi Beta Kappa.**"

Phoebe. *In* The Sirens of Titan, *Phoebe is the only city established on Mars by Winston Niles Rumfoord and is powered by Salo's UWTB (Universal Will to Become). At its height, Phoebe is home to eighty-seven thousand people who work mainly in munitions factories. It is also the location of the Schliemann Breathing School and the only grade school on Mars. Phoebe is destroyed when thermonuclear bombs are launched at Mars as part of a counterstrike to the invasion fleet.*

Phoebe is also the name of a moon of Titan. When Chrono, the son of Malachi Constant and Beatrice Rumfoord, joins the Titanic Bluebirds, he is frequently heard crying out to Phoebe as it passes in the night sky.

Piatigorsky, Dr. Albert Aquamarine-1. *In* Slapstick, *President Wilbur Swain's science adviser, who succumbs to the Albanian flu, expiring in the arms of his president in the Oval Office.*

Piatigorsky, Gregor. *In* Deadeye Dick, *the renowned cellist is among the many illustrious people brought to perform at the Midland City YMCA and later tour Otto Waltz's in-home art studio.*

Pieratt, Asa. *The very forward-thinking University of Delaware librarian who partnered with Jerome Klinkowitz to produce the first bibliography of works by and about Vonnegut in 1974. A second edition appeared in 1987 with a third contributor, Julie Huffman-Klinkowitz.*

Pieratt and Vonnegut enjoyed a long friendship, and the librarian is one of the select few in attendance at the climactic Timequake *clambake.*

Pilgrim, Barbara and Robert. *The children of Billy and Valencia Pilgrim.* (SL5 2) In time, his daughter **Barbara** married another optometrist, and Billy set him up in business. Billy's son **Robert** had a lot of trouble in high school, but then he joined the famous Green Berets. He straightened out, became a fine young man, and he fought in Vietnam.
(SL5 2) Some night owls in Ilium heard Billy on the radio, and one of them called Billy's daughter **Barbara. Barbara** was upset. She and her husband went down to New York and brought Billy home. Billy insisted mildly that everything he had said on the radio was true. He said he had been kidnapped by the Tralfamadorians on the night of his daughter's wedding. He hadn't been missed, he said, because the Tralfamadorians had taken him through a time warp, so that he could be on Tralfamadore for years, and still be away from Earth for only a microsecond.
(SL5 2) The orchestration of the moment was this: **Barbara** was only twenty-one years old, but she thought her father was senile, even though he was only forty-six—senile because of damage to his brain in the airplane crash. She also thought that she was head of the family, since she had had to manage her mother's funeral, since she had to get a housekeeper for Billy, and all that. Also, **Barbara** and her husband were having to look after Billy's business interests, which were considerable, since Billy didn't seem to give a damn for business any more. All this responsibility at such an early age made her a bitchy flibbertigibbet. And Billy, meanwhile, was trying to hang onto his dignity, to persuade **Barbara** and everybody else that he was far

from senile, that, on the contrary, he was devoting himself to a calling much higher than mere business.

(SL5 5) Now *(while time tripping)* he was in bed with Valencia in a delightful studio apartment which was built on the end of a wharf on Cape Ann, Massachusetts. Across the water were the lights of Gloucester. Billy was on top of Valencia, making love to her. One result of this act would be the birth of **Robert Pilgrim**, who would become a problem in high school, but who would then straighten out as a member of the famous Green Berets.

(SL5 9) Billy Pilgrim opened his eyes in the hospital in Vermont *(after his plane crashed on the mountain)*, did not know where he was. Watching him was his son **Robert**. **Robert** was wearing the uniform of the famous Green Berets. **Robert**'s hair was short, was wheat-colored bristles. **Robert** was clean and neat. He was decorated with a Purple Heart and a Silver Star and a Bronze Star with two clusters.

This was a boy who had flunked out of high school, who had been an alcoholic at sixteen, who had run with a rotten bunch of kids, who had been arrested for tipping over hundreds of tombstones in a Catholic cemetery one time. He was all straightened out now. His posture was wonderful and his shoes were shined and his trousers were pressed, and he was a leader of men.

Pilgrim, Billy (also **Joe Crone**). *Drawing on Vonnegut's wartime experiences, Billy Pilgrim, the protagonist of* Slaughterhouse-Five, *is unstuck in time and space as he travels across the many significant moments of his life including those on the planet Tralfamadore and when taking refuge from the firebombing of Dresden. He first gains an awareness of his space travels fifteen years after his slaughterhouse reprieve from Allied bombing. This occurs the evening following his daughter's wedding. Paul Lazzaro, who swore revenge for the death of Roland Weary, assassinates Billy thirty-one years after the bombing of Dresden, February 13, 1976. Billy is aware of his death yet continues to live through his unique experience with Tralfamadorian time tripping.*

Billy feels compelled to tell the world of Tralfamadore after surviving the Vermont plane crash that took the lives of all the other convention-bound op-

tometrists on board. Billy is an optometrist, trained by his father-in-law and from whom he inherits the school after the Sugarbush Mountain plane crash.

Billy receives an emergency furlough from the army to return to Ilium after his father is accidentally shot dead while hunting with a friend. Upon returning to service, Billy is assigned as a chaplain's assistant and soon after is captured behind enemy lines at the Battle of the Bulge. His mother resides in an old people's home called Pine Knoll on the edge of Ilium. (SL5 2) **Billy** was preposterous—six feet and three inches tall, with a chest and shoulders like a box of kitchen matches.

(SL5 5) **Billy Pilgrim** says that the Universe does not look like a lot of bright little dots to the creatures from Tralfamadore. The creatures can see where each star has been and where it is going, so that the heavens are filled with rarefied, luminous spaghetti. And Tralfamadorians don't see human beings as two-legged creatures, either. They see them as great millepedes—"with babies' legs at one end and old people's legs at the other," says **Billy Pilgrim**.

(SL5 6) "It is time for you to go home to your wives and children, and it is time for me to be dead for a little while—and then live again." At that moment, **Billy**'s high forehead is in the cross hairs of a high-powered laser gun. It is aimed at him from the darkened press box. In the next moment, **Billy Pilgrim** is dead. So it goes.

(SL5 10) On Tralfamadore, says **Billy Pilgrim**, there isn't much interest in Jesus Christ. The Earthling figure who is most engaging to the Tralfamadorian mind, he says, is Charles Darwin—who taught that those who die are meant to die, that corpses are improvements. So it goes. *Vonnegut writes these lines two nights after Robert Kennedy's assassination, only two months after the murder of Martin Luther King, Jr.*

In Fates Worse Than Death, *Vonnegut for the first time reveals his true life model for Billy Pilgrim.* (FWD XI) The fellow ex-Dresden PW at my National Air and Space Museum lecture was Tom Jones, who had paired off (as ordered) in his 106th Division platoon with **Joe Crone**, the model for **Billy Pilgrim**, the leading character in *Slaughterhouse-Five.* Jones said, in a letter I got only yesterday, "I remember **Crone** in Camp Atterbury. When we went on a forced march I had to walk behind him and pick up all the utensils falling out of his backpack. He could never do it right.

"I bunked with him when he died. One morning he woke up and his head was swollen like a watermelon and I talked him into going on sick call. By midday word came back that he had died. You remember we slept two in a bunk so I had to shake **Crone** several times a night and say, 'Let's turn over.' I recall how in the early morning hours the slop cans at the end of the barracks overflowed. Everyone had the shits, and it flowed down the barracks under everyone's bunk. The Germans never would give us more cans."

Joe Crone is buried somewhere in Dresden wearing a white paper suit.

He let himself starve to death before the firestorm. In *Slaughterhouse-Five* I have him return home to become a fabulously well-to-do optometrist. (Jones and **Crone** were stockpiled college kids like O'Hare and me. We all read a lot at Camp Atterbury.)

Jones, there in Washington, D.C., turned out to have been quite a packrat when it came to wartime memorabilia. He had a copy of a letter given to us by the Germans which urged us to join their army (and get plenty to eat) and go fight for civilization on the Russian Front. (Rumor was that five Americans somewhere else had accepted the offer. If those five didn't exist we would still have had to invent them.) Tom Jones had photographs of several of us, including O'Hare (but not **Joe Crone**, not **Billy Pilgrim**), taken right after the war ended.

Pilgrim, Valencia Merble. *In* Slaughterhouse-Five, *the daughter of Lionel Merble, owner of the Ilium School of Optometry, and Billy Pilgrim's wife. Valencia has severe weight problems due, in part, to her voracious appetite for candy bars. When Valencia visits Billy in the hospital after his first breakdown, Billy realizes that his desire to marry someone so undesirable is a symptom of his illness. However, with the exception of one sexual affair during a drunken episode at a holiday party, Billy treats her well and lovingly. For her part, Valencia is as devoted to Billy as she is to eating, forever promising Billy she will lose weight. When Billy's charter flight crashes on Sugarbush Mountain, Valencia takes her* Cadillac El Dorado Coupe de Ville *and recklessly tries to make her way to Vermont to be with Billy. Though suffering an accident that detaches the exhaust system, Valencia manages to drive to the emergency room of the hospital where she dies from carbon monoxide poisoning.*

Contrasting Billy's most memorable trait, **Valencia** *wasn't a time-traveler, but she did have a lively imagination. While Billy was making love to her, she imagined that she was a famous woman in history. She was being Queen Elizabeth the First of England, and Billy was supposedly Christopher Columbus (SL5 5).*

Pine Knoll. *The Ilium nursing home where Billy Pilgrim is forced to house his mother in 1965, in* Slaughterhouse-Five. *He places her there because she isn't expected to recover from pneumonia, though she lingers for years after that.*

Pinsky, Robert. *Vonnegut recalls listening to the 1997 United States Poet Laureate,* I heard the poet **Robert Pinsky** give a reading this summer, in which he apologized didactically for having had a much nicer life than normal. I should do that, too *(TQ 4). Feeling much the same about his own upbringing as Pinsky, Vonnegut then goes on to praise his Indianapolis roots.*

Pipe City Golf and Country Club. *The country club is the location of all the activity in the short story "Find Me a Dream." Arvin Borders, the manager of the Creon Works of the General Forge and Foundry Company (the largest producers of pipe in the world) can't locate his new fiancée, Hildy Matthews, a New York actress and widowed mother of two, formerly married to a revered jazzman. She spends the evening out on the golf course speaking mostly with the clarinetist and bandleader Andy Middleton.*

Pisquontuit (*also* **Chief Pisquontuit;** *see also* **Buntline**). *The Rhode Island hometown of Fred Rosewater who, at the urging of Norman Mushari, becomes locked in a legal struggle with Eliot Rosewater for control of the family foundation. (GBR 8) About* **Pisquontuit**: *It was pronounced "Pawn-it" by those who loved it, and "Piss-on-it" by those who* didn't. There had once been an Indian chief named **Pisquontuit**.

Pisquontuit wore an apron, lived, as did his people, on clams, raspberries, and rose hips. Agriculture was news to **Chief Pisquontuit**. So, for that matter, were wampum, feather ornaments, and the bow and arrow.

Alcohol was the best news of all. **Pisquontuit** drank himself to death in 1638.

Four thousand moons later, the village that made his name immortal was populated by two hundred very wealthy families and by a thousand ordinary families whose breadwinners served, in one way and another, the rich.

The lives led there were nearly all paltry, lacking in subtlety, wisdom, wit or invention—were precisely as pointless and unhappy as lives led in Rosewater, Indiana. Inherited millions did not help. Nor did the arts and sciences.

Pisquontuit is paired with Rosewater County, Indiana, enabling Kilgore Trout to point out that man's ability to live a purposefully employed life is the greater determinant in assessing the social condition of our communities than is one's financial standing. (GBR 14) "Well—" and Trout rubbed his hands, watched the rubbing, "what you *(Eliot)* did in Rosewater County was far from insane. It was quite possibly the most important social experiment of our time, for it dealt on a very small scale with a problem whose queasy horrors will eventually be made world-wide by the sophistication of machines. The problem is this: How to love people who have no use?

"In time, almost all men and women will become worthless as producers of goods, food, services, and more machines, as sources of practical ideas in the areas of economics, engineering, and probably medicine, too. So—if we can't find reasons and methods for treasuring human beings because they are *human beings*, then we might as well, as has so often been suggested, rub them out."

"Americans have long been taught to hate all people who will not or cannot work, to hate even themselves for that. We can thank the vanished frontier for that piece of common-sense cruelty. The time is coming, if it isn't here now, when it will no longer be common sense. It will simply be cruel."

"A poor man with gumption can still elevate himself out of the mire," said the Senator, "and that will continue to be true a thousand years from now."

"Maybe, maybe," Trout answered gently. "He may even have so much gumption that his descendents [*sic*] will live in a Utopia like **Pisquontuit**, where, I'm sure, the soul-rot and silliness and torpor and insensitivity are exactly as horrible as anything epidemic in Rosewater County. Poverty is a relatively mild disease for even a very flimsy American soul, but uselessness will kill strong and weak souls alike, and kill every time.

"We must find a cure."
See also: GBR 4; 8; 9; 10; 11; 12.

Plague on Wheels. *Kilgore Trout's most popular novel—originally published with pornographic pictures—opens on the planet Lingo-Three, whose inhabitants resembled American automobiles. They had wheels. They were powered by internal combustion engines. They ate fossil fuels. They weren't manufactured, though. They reproduced. They laid eggs containing baby automobiles, and the babies matured in pools of oil drained from adult crankcases* (BC 2).

Homosexual space travelers from the planet Zeltoldimar, all one inch high and led by Kago, could not fulfill the wishes of the dying automobile civilization to take one of its 48-pound eggs to another planet to continue their race. The Zeltoldimarian spacecraft is no bigger than a shoe box. Lingo-Three is running out of fossil fuels and has very nearly depleted its oxygen supply by the time Kago arrives. He promises to tell others in the universe how wonderful the automobile creatures had been. . . . "You will be gone, but not forgotten" (BC 2).

(BC 2) At the time he met Dwayne Hoover, Trout's most widely-distributed book was **Plague on Wheels**. The publisher didn't change the title, but he obliterated most of it and all of Trout's name with a lurid banner which made this promise: WIDE-OPEN BEAVERS INSIDE!

(BC 2) There had been a time when a copy of Trout's most popular book to date, **Plague on Wheels**, had brought as much as twelve dollars, because of the illustrations. It was now being offered for a dollar, and people who paid even that much did so not because of the pictures. They paid for the words.

(BC 3) Within a century of little Kago's arrival on Earth, according to Trout's novel, every form of life on that one peaceful and moist and nourishing blue-green ball was dying or dead. Everywhere were the shells of the great beetles which men had made and worshipped. They were automobiles. They had killed everything.

Little Kago himself died long before the planet did. He was attempting to lecture on the evils of the automobile. But he was so tiny that nobody paid any attention to him. He lay down to rest for a moment, and a drunk automobile worker mistook him for a kitchen match. He killed Kago by trying to strike him repeatedly on the underside of the bar.

(BC 3) The fan letter (*written by Eliot Rosewater*) reached him in his basement in Cohoes. It was hand-written, and Trout concluded that the writer might be fourteen years old or so. The letter said that *Plague on Wheels* was the greatest novel in the English language, and that Trout should be President of the United States.

(BC 5) Trout had come down from Cohoes late that afternoon. He had since visited many pornography shops and a shirt store. He had bought two of his own books, *Plague on Wheels* and *Now It Can Be Told*, a magazine containing a short story of his, and a tuxedo shirt. The name of the magazine was *Black Garterbelt*. . . .

The jackets of *Plague on Wheels* and *Now It Can Be Told* both promised plenty of wide-open beavers inside.

Planck, Alfred (*also known as* **President Jonathan Lynn**). *Alfred Planck, a high school dropout and onetime television personality, is the president of the United States in* Player Piano. (PP XI) The electric car pulled up to the platform, and **President Jonathan Lynn**, born **Alfred Planck**, stood and showed his white teeth and frank gray eyes, squared his broad shoulders, and ran his strong, tanned hands through his curly hair. The television cameras dollied and panned about him like curious, friendly dinosaurs, sniffing and peering. **Lynn** was boyish, tall, beautiful, and disarming, and, Halyard thought bitterly, he had gone directly from a three-hour television program to the White House.

"The Planet Gobblers." *Though this Kilgore Trout story appears nowhere in Vonnegut's fiction, it does appear in his nonfiction. As part of a longer illustration on his religious views, Vonnegut includes his address to the 1974 graduating classes of Hobart and William Smith Colleges.* (PS Religion) "Kilgore Trout wrote a science-fiction story called 'The Planet Gobblers' one time. It was about us, and we were the terrors of the universe. We were sort of interplanetary termites. We would arrive on a planet, gobble it up, and die. But before we died, we always sent out spaceships to start tiny colonies elsewhere. We were a disease, since it was not necessary to inhabit planets with such horrifying destructiveness. It is easy to take good care of a planet.

"Our grandchildren will surely think of us as the **Planet Gobblers**.

"Poorer nations than America think of America as a **Planet Gobbler** right now. But that is going to change. There is welling up within us a willingness to say 'No, thank you' to our factories. We were once maniacs for possessions, imagining that they would somehow moderate or somehow compensate us for our loneliness.

"The experiment has been tried in this most affluent nation in all of human history. Possessions help a little, but not as much as advertisers said they were supposed to, and we are now aware of how permanently the manufacture of some of those products hurts the planet.

"So there is a willingness to do without them.

"There is a willingness to do whatever we need to do in order to have life on the planet go on for a long, long time. I didn't used to think that. And that willingness has to be a religious enthusiasm, since it celebrates life, since it calls for meaningful sacrifices.

"This is bad news for business, as we know it now. It should be thrilling news for persons who love to teach and lead. And thank God we have solid information in the place of superstition! Thank God we are beginning to dream of human communities which are designed to harmonize with what human beings really need and are.

"And now you have just heard an atheist thank God not once, but twice.

"And listen to this:

"God bless the class of 1974."

Player Piano (1952) (*see also* **Paul Proteus, Ghost Shirt Society, Norbert Wiener**). *Player Piano is Vonnegut's vision of how America will be restructured once the value of technocrats and the ramifications of the third industrial revolution take effect. This latter concept is extrapolated from Norbert Wiener's* The Human Use of Human Beings *(which Vonnegut read while witnessing the technological advances made by General Electric in Schenectady, and cited by Paul Proteus in discussion with Katharine Finch, his secretary). Wiener characterizes the first industrial revolution as devaluing manual labor, and the second (describing the long-term effects of computers) as devaluing routine mental work. But the third industrial revolution, as envisioned by Vonnegut and illustrated by EPICAC, would devalue human thinking. Though Wiener fears massive unemployment in the semiskilled and skilled work sectors due to robotics, Vonnegut sees the advancement of unchecked technologies producing a society in which only some Ph.D.s would be employed as anything more than soldiers or road workers: the Reeks and Wrecks. The know-how and ability to produce would outrun our understanding of the purpose and effects of human labor. The ensuing plot, which Vonnegut admits was a rip-off of Eugene Zamiatin's* We *and George Orwell's* 1984, *places Paul Proteus in the middle of two conspiracies. The ruling technocracy seeks to infiltrate the rebellious Ghost Shirt Society by making it seem as though Paul was thrown out of the hierarchy. At the same time, the Ghost Shirt Society kidnaps Paul and releases a declaration in his name for purposeful human labor (written by Professor Ludwig von Neumann).*

Plummer, Walter. *Plummer is the character referred to in the title of the story "The No-Talent Kid," first published in the October 1952 edition of* The Saturday Evening Post *and later reprinted in the 1999 collection* Bagombo Snuff Box. *The story focuses on the vanity and pride of both Lincoln High School band director George Helmholtz and his student Walter Plummer (who is also his newspaper delivery boy), the last of the clarinetists in the school's C Band, its lowest-performing group. Helmholtz tries at various times to gently discourage Plummer's persistence, but even Helmholtz realizes he is bat-*

tling both the teenager's misguided efforts as well as his stubbornly romantic notions about attaining a prized status symbol (especially alluring since the marching band already had ten consecutive state championships). Mr. Helmholtz had tried to tell **Plummer** how misplaced his ambitions were, to recommend other fields for his great lungs and enthusiasm, where pitch would be unimportant. But **Plummer** was in love, not with music, but with the letter sweaters. Being as tone-deaf as boiled cabbage, he could detect nothing in his own playing about which to be discouraged.

Plummer romantically believes in the power of his instrument to help him overcome his adversaries. **Plummer** stroked the satin-black barrel of the instrument as though it were King Arthur's sword, giving magical powers to whoever possessed it. "It's as good as Flammer's," said **Plummer**. "Better, even." There was a warning in his voice, telling Mr. Helmholtz that the days of discrimination were over, that nobody in his right mind would dare to hold back a man with an instrument like this.

Plummer loses in his audacious challenge to Flammer, the A Band's first seat clarinetist and perhaps the best musician in the school. Still, Plummer's perception of failure is immature, believing his continuing disappointment along with the recent second place finish of the band was "Because they stopped running the band on the merit system."

Plummer finally resorts to a winning strategy by dangling something in front of Helmholtz that is simply irresistible—the bass drum from the Knights of Kandahar marching band (due to its need to liquidate assets in the face of financial ruin at the hands of an embezzling treasurer), a drum so large it needed a special cart pulled by a band member during performance, the key ingredient Helmholtz believes he needs to focus attention on his band's otherwise superior performance skills. Helmholtz tells Plummer in absolutely clear terms that he will never get to be the percussionist to play the drum. Just as Plummer is about to walk away in disappointment and taking his drum with him, Helmholtz figures out how to satisfy his own desire for his prized missing piece as well as Plummer's venal and shallow desires. "If the school gets that drum, whoever's pulling it will be as crucial and valued a member of* the A Band as the first-chair clarinet. What if it capsized?"

"He'd win a band letter if it didn't capsize?" said **Plummer**.

And Mr. Helmholtz said this: "I don't see why not."

Poe, Edgar Allan (1809–1849). *When Captain Adolf von Kleist cries out "October!" Mandarax takes it as a command for citing a literary reference and complies with this from Poe.* (Gal 2:7) The skies they were ashen and sober; / The leaves they were crispèd and sere— / The leaves they were withering and sere; / It was night in the lonesome October / Of my most immemorial year.

Polk, Dalton. *The legendary Scipio physician in* Hocus Pocus *who also serves as the first teacher of both biology and Shakespeare upon establishment of the Mohiga Valley Free Institute.*

Pomerantz, Floyd. *One of Rabo Karabekian's East Hampton neighbors, in* Bluebeard. *Though only forty-three, he is given $11 million as severance pay to resign from his presidency of a television network. He asks Rabo if there is still enough time for him to become a painter.*

Pond, Dr. *The manager of the Ilium real estate office in* Player Piano *who tries to talk Paul Proteus out of purchasing the Gottwald farm. He is very proud of his seven years at the Cornell Graduate School of Realty and his 896-page dissertation. Pond is keenly aware of the significance attached to one's real estate and the part it plays in the highly stratified social structure of the text.* (PP XV) "For example, while the *Manual* doesn't tell me to do it, I make very sure that every man gets a house suited to his station on the ladder of life. The way a man lives can destroy or increase the stature of his job—can increase or decrease the stability and prestige of the entire system."

Pontius Pilate Athletic Club. *The ghost of Major Siegfried von Konigswald mentions that* It was almost worth the trip *(to heaven)* to find out that Jesus Christ in Heaven was just another guy, playing shuffleboard. I like his sense of humor, though—

you know? He's got a blue-and-gold warm-up jacket he wears. You know what it says on the back? "**Pontius Pilate Athletic Club.**" Most people don't get it. Most people think there really is a **Pontius Pilate Athletic Club** (WJ II:2).

Ponzi scheme (*see* **di Sanza**).

Poo-tee-weet (*also* **Poo-tee-phweet**). *The dispassionate cry of birds flying above various Vonnegut characters who either experience or imagine great atrocities. John/Jonah lived through the frozen death of the world that results from ice-nine.* (CC 116) I dreamed for a moment of dropping to the platform, of springing up from it in a breath-taking swan dive, of folding my arms, of knifing downward into a blood-warm eternity with never a splash.

I was recalled from this dream by the cry of a darting bird above me.

It seemed to be asking me what had happened. "**Poo-tee-phweet?**" it asked.

We all looked up at the bird, and then at one another.

Eliot Rosewater accidentally kills three volunteer firemen during the war in Germany, but when he reads Kilgore Trout's Pan-Galactic Three-Day Pass *(about the death of the Milky Way) he looks up from the book and imagines seeing Indianapolis consumed by firestorm. He falls into a catatonic trance at which point there is a one-year gap in the narrative while he is treated at Dr. Brown's Indianapolis sanitarium.* (GBR 14) Everything went black for Eliot, as black as what lay beyond the ultimate rim of the universe. And then he awoke to find himself sitting on the flat rim of a dry fountain. He was dappled by sunlight filtering down through a sycamore tree. A bird was singing in the sycamore tree. "*Poo-tee-weet?*" it sang. "*Poo-tee-weet. Weet, weet, weet.*" Eliot was within a high garden wall, and the garden was familiar. He had spoken to Sylvia many times in just this place. It was the garden of Dr. Brown's private mental hospital in Indianapolis, to which he had brought her so many years before. These words were cut into the fountain rim:

"Pretend to be good always, and even God will be fooled. . . ."

"*Poo-tee-weet?*"

Eliot looked up at the bird and all the green

leaves, understood that this garden in downtown Indianapolis could not have survived the fire he saw. So there had been no fire. He accepted this peacefully.

(GBR 14) *"Poo-tee-weet?"*

Eliot looked up into the tree, and the memory of all that had happened in the blackness came crashing back—the fight with the bus driver, the straitjacket, the shock treatments, the suicide attempts, all the tennis, all the strategy meetings about the sanity hearing. And with that mighty inward crash of memories came the idea he had had for settling everything instantly, beautifully, and fairly. *Eliot then decides to accept as valid the fifty-seven false paternity suits against him. Yes, he is going to settle with the plaintiffs and make a lump sum payment to his cousin Fred Rosewater. Fred is suing Eliot for control of the Rosewater Foundation—an action provoked by Norman Mushari's greed.*

Perhaps the most memorable use of the phrase comes in Slaughterhouse-Five. *Vonnegut explains his use of the term to his publisher Seymour Lawrence in this, his Dresden book.* (SL5 1) It is so short and jumbled and jangled, Sam, because there is nothing intelligent to say about a massacre. Everybody is supposed to be dead, to never say anything or want anything ever again. Everything is supposed to be very quiet after a massacre, and it always is, except for the birds.

And what do the birds say? All there is to say about a massacre, things like *"Poo-tee-weet?"*

(SL5 1) I've finished my war book now. The next one I write is going to be fun. This one is a failure, and had to be, since it was written by a pillar of salt. It begins like this:

Listen:

Billy Pilgrim has come unstuck in time. It ends like this:

Poo-tee-weet?

(SL5 5) Night came to the garden of the giraffes, and Billy Pilgrim slept without dreaming for a while, and then he traveled in time. He woke up with his head under a blanket in a ward for nonviolent mental patients in a veterans' hospital near Lake Placid, New York. It was springtime in 1948, three years after the end of the war.

Billy uncovered his head. The windows of the ward were open. Birds were twittering outside.

"Poo-tee-weet?" one asked him. The sun was high. There were twenty-nine other patients assigned to the ward, but they were all outdoors now, enjoying the day. They were free to come and go as they pleased, to go home, even, if they liked—and so was Billy Pilgrim. They had come here voluntarily, alarmed by the outside world.

(SL5 10) And somewhere in there was springtime. The corpse mines were closed down. The soldiers all left to fight the Russians. In the suburbs, the women and children dug rifle pits. Billy and the rest of his group were locked up in the stable in the suburbs. And then, one morning, they got up to discover that the door was unlocked. World War Two in Europe was over.

Billy and the rest wandered out onto the shady street. The trees were leafing out. There was nothing going on out there, no traffic of any kind. There was only one vehicle, an abandoned wagon drawn by two horses. The wagon was green and coffin-shaped.

Birds were talking.

One bird said to Billy Pilgrim, *"Poo-tee-weet?"* *See also: GBR 14.*

pool-pah. (CC 110) "Sometimes the *pool-pah*," Bokonon tells us, "exceeds the power of humans to comment." *Bokonon translates pool-pah at one point in* The Books of Bokonon *as "shit storm" and at another point as "wrath of God."*

"Poor Little Rich Town." *This short story first appeared in* Collier's *magazine in October 1952 and was reprinted in the 1999 collection* Bagombo Snuff Box. *Published on the heels of* Player Piano *(1951), this is a tale of people choosing the liberty of their inefficiency and old-world ways. Chief among their careful calculations is consideration of what it takes to construct a caring community.*

Unlike Player Piano, *which ends in a failed armed insurrection in Ilium, New York, this tale peacefully resolves in nearby Spruce Falls. Its resolution is reached through the passive withholding of valued real estate assets. The quality of life for those in the town's many small mansions is in danger of being lost. The aging heirs of this once rich and now indebted community are in danger of losing its human appeal if Newell Cady approves the commu-*

nity for housing upper-level employees of the Federal Apparatus Corporation should they be relocated to the area. Cady is a newly minted vice president brought in as an efficiency expert.

The company is looking to relocate from its present headquarters. Since the company plans to develop a manufacturing plant in nearby Ilium, Spruce Falls seems like a good place to entice its executives for the relocation.

Newell Cady at first charms the longtime residents, including Fire Chief Atkins, Hal Brayton, and Mrs. Dickie. Atkins has his volunteer department ingratiate themselves by voting Cady a full member of the department and head judge at the annual Hobby Show. Atkins eventually opposes Cady when the latter lays out the economic inefficiency and illogical proposal to purchase a new fire engine (with a twenty-year note) when the old one works perfectly well.

In a most tactless manner, Cady tries coaxing Mrs. Dickie into shifting boxes and hand motions to achieve a faster, more efficient pattern for sorting mail, but she eventually tires of the pattern and is later—unconsciously—targeted for unemployment when Cady loudly suggests switching to rural free delivery to save time and improve convenience.

Brayton redesigns his general store when prompted by Cady, but he, too, reverts to the old, inefficient layout.

Cady always points out the inefficiency and illogical reasoning of the brain trust in Spruce Falls; he does so thoughtlessly, without considering the social behavior of the townspeople. Though the economic base of the community is surely in dire straits, the people had built a protective legacy predicated on a caring community. When Cady changes the rules for the Hobby Show (one based on equal awards for each entrant's unique categorization), opting instead for a single winner, the townspeople are shamed, and even the winner leaves behind her ribbon when she picks up her entry.

It is left to town elder Upton Beaton to explain to the crestfallen real estate agent that they hold no animosity toward Cady or his schemes for industrial progressiveness in town but that the people are not so quick to change their ways. At this point, the town realizes that through a technicality it has to withdraw Cady's fire department membership. More poi-

gnantly, Beaton is watching Brayton's store so he could meet with the fire truck salesman. "We've decided to wait and see how Mr. Cady adapts himself, before we put anything else on the market. He's having a tough time, but he's got a good heart, I think, and we're all rooting for him."

This story develops the themes of the previously published Player Piano and is an early manifestation of Vonnegut's focus on extended families and folk societies.

Pops. In Vonnegut's updated musical version of Dr. Jekyll and Mr. Hyde, Pops is the doddering campus cop. (PS Jekyll and Hyde Revisited) "I was on my way to being a star of stage, screen, and radio. But then my dog was run over, and I entered a period of deep depression from which I never recovered. Nobody starts out to be a campus cop."

Port Zion. In Timequake, the location of Xanadu, the Rhode Island seaside resort that serves as the site of the writers' retreat where Vonnegut plans to share his fictional alter ego, Kilgore Trout, with a select group of people at a clambake on the beach.

Portomaggiore, Count Bruno. In Bluebeard, Mussolini's minister of culture and head of British Intelligence in Italy during the war. The Oxford-educated Count Bruno, one of Italy's largest landowners, marries Marilee Kemp because Mussolini orders it (to suppress rumors of his homosexuality). He is eventually executed by firing squad by Italian authorities for being a pedophile.

Post-Timequake Apathy (also **PTA**). This is the term coined by Kilgore Trout when the ten-year timequake catches up to its own cataclysmic event on February 13, 2001, and time once again begins its linear march forward. (TQ 29) Trout was surely among the first people in the whole wide world, and not just way-the-hell-and-gone up on West 155th Street, to realize that free will had kicked in. This was very interesting to him, as it certainly wasn't to many others. Most other people, after the relentless reprise of their mistakes and bad luck and hollow victories during the past ten years, had, in Trout's words, "stopped giving a shit what was going on, or what was liable to happen next." This syndrome would eventually be given a name: ***Post-Timequake Apathy***, or ***PTA***.

People in Europe and Africa and Asia were in darkness when free will kicked in. Most of them were in bed or sitting down somewhere. Not nearly as many of them fell down in their hemisphere as fell down in ours, where a clear majority was wide awake.

A person walking in either hemisphere was commonly off balance, leaning in the direction he or she was going, and with most of his or her weight unevenly distributed between his or her feet. When free will kicked in, he or she of course fell down, and stayed down, even in the middle of a street with onrushing traffic, because of **Post-Timequake Apathy**.

You can imagine what the bottoms of staircases and escalators, in the Western Hemisphere in particular, looked like after free will kicked in. *See also: TQ* 31; 32; 50; 51; 54; 56.

Potapov, Ilya. *A famous rocket scientist and eldest son of George Kraft / Iona Potapov in* Mother Night.

Potapov, Iona (*see* **George Kraft**).

Potapov, Tanya. *In* Mother Night, *the wife of Soviet spy George Kraft / Iona Potapov dutifully waits for him in Borisoglebsk. Separated by occupation for more than twenty-five years, she raises their nine children and would never again see her husband due to his imprisonment.*

Potter, David. *In the 1955 short story "Deer in the Works" (reprinted in the 1968 collection* Welcome to the Monkey House), *Potter is the new publicity man hired by the Ilium Works of the Federal Apparatus Corporation sent to cover the story of a deer that somehow entered the grounds of the plant. When unexpectedly close at hand, Potter helps the deer escape through the fence, much to the chagrin of his superiors.*

"The Powder-Blue Dragon" (*see also* **Higgins, Kiah**). *First published in the November 1954 issue of* Cosmopolitan *magazine and later reprinted in the 1999 compilation* Bagombo Snuff Box, *this story focuses on the displacement and anonymity of Kiah Higgins, orphaned at the age of sixteen when his parents were killed in a head-on car crash outside the Howard Johnson's motel where his mother worked as a chambermaid.*

Now presumably in his early twenties, one of Kiah's jobs has him working for the sports car dealer Bill Daggett. The setting is an unnamed New England summer vacation retreat, which at one time was an active whaling port. Now it is hopping with rich people and tourists during the summer, the few permanent residents being the people who serve them, such as Kiah. Even Daggett's dealership remains open only six months out of the year. But even Kiah lives the life of a nameless vagabond. Rather than rent an apartment with some measure of permanence, Kiah lives in a boardinghouse. Vonnegut suggests that the various jobs he holds are off the books for cash. Aside from working for Daggett's dealership, he pumps gas in the evenings at Ed's service station and waits tables during the weekends at the Quarterdeck.

Though Kiah lives recessed from the wealthy vacationers, he does have a goal. He is saving money to buy his one obsession, the 130-mph Italian-made Marittima-Frascati sports car, the powder-blue dragon of the story's title. It just so happens that Daggett has one in his New York City showroom. When asked by the town's pharmacist, a septuagenarian who watched Kiah grow up, why he wants such an exotic and extravagant car, Kiah responds with one word: class. Without saying so directly, he hopes to appeal to the transient class of wealthy visitors who visit the town.

Kiah saves enough money to write a check for the full amount of the car, $5,651, much to the surprise of Bill Daggett, who calls a banker named George in the next town to find out if the check is good. It was only the second check Kiah had written. The first was for $5 earlier in the day just to see if his credit was good. The moment also serves to emphasize Kiah's sense of anonymity. Though he writes that first check to cash at the drugstore where he is well known, Kiah takes pains to point out to the pharmacist that his name is printed on the check.

One week later, when Kiah takes delivery of his new sports car, Daggett provides explicit instructions about the critical schedule for breaking in the car's transmission before being tempted to see how fast the car can go. Kiah heads for the turnpike, where he winds up playing cat and mouse with a blonde in a convertible Cadillac. After miles of passing and being passed, Kiah follows Marion off the turnpike and into an empty lounge, save for the bartender. Marion is full of confidence, and with time to kill while waiting for Paul, her fiancé, she and Kiah make brief small talk.

At first she does not recognize Kiah nor associate him with the sports car she was just playing with on the highway, another moment in the story emphasizing his anonymity. The bartender is also incredulous about Kiah's story of the car or that he is its owner. When Paul finally arrives and is filled in by the others about their unidentified acquaintance in the bar, he is also hard to convince and further throws it up to Kiah that he drives a British Hampton, a car he is convinced is faster than Kiah's Vanilla Frappé—or *whatever it is named. Kiah would have taken up Paul on his challenge to race except that he remembers Daggett's instructions. His backing down only convinces Paul that Kiah's story is doubtful on all counts.*

Paul and Marion leave the lounge and head down the turnpike. Kiah, quietly seething, follows them in his car and flips them the bird as he passes them, though they are too busy to notice as they exit the road. Kiah continues down the road, realizing Paul will not now race him and inexplicably has a complete change of mind. "He's got no guts, baby," said Kiah. "Let's show the world what guts are." He pressed the accelerator to the floor. As blurs loomed before him and vanished, he kept it there.

The engine was shrieking in agony now, and Kiah said in a matter-of-fact-tone, "Explode, explode."

But the engine didn't explode or catch fire. Its precious jewels simply merged with one another, and the engine ceased to be an engine. Nor was the clutch a clutch anymore. That allowed the car to roll onto the breakdown lane of the highway, powered by nothing but the last bit of momentum it would ever have on its own. . . .

Kiah left the car where it died. He thumbed a ride back to the village, without having to give his lift a story of any kind. He returned to Daggett's showroom and acted as though he was there to work. . . .

"I gave you the whole day off," said Daggett.

"I know," said Kiah.

"So where's the car?"

"I killed it."

"You what?"

"I got it up to one forty-four, when they said it could only do one thirty-five."

"You're joking."

"Wait'll you see," said Kiah. "That's one dead sports vehicle. You'll have to send the tow truck."

"My God, boy, why would you do such a thing?"

"Call me Kiah."

"Kiah," echoed Daggett, convinced he was dealing with a lunatic.

"Who knows why anybody does anything?" said Kiah. "I don't know why I killed it. All I know is I'm glad it's dead."

In killing the Marittima-Frascati, Kiah asserts his identity, forever to be known in the old whaling village as the man who killed his prized possession on his first day of ownership.

Powers, Dr. *The obstetrician for both the Knechtmann and Sousa families in the 1954 short story* "Adam," *reprinted in* Welcome to the Monkey House (1968). *Dr. Powers breaks the news to Mr. Knechtmann that his wife's malnutrition during the war makes it unlikely that she will have any more children after Adam. Still, the Knechtmanns are overjoyed at the prospect of another generation, since they both survived Nazi death camps.*

Prairie Military Academy (*see also* **Culver Military Academy**). *The military academy in* Cat's Cradle *where Bunny Hoover is sent when he is only ten years old. Bunny is unanimously elected cadet colonel, the highest student rank, in his senior year. The circumstances leading to Bunny's removal there and Vonnegut's opinion of such institutions are included in the following description.* (BC 17) Listen: Bunny was sent away to military school, an institution devoted to homicide and absolutely humorless obedience, when he was only ten years old. Here is why: He told Dwayne that he wished he were a woman instead of a man, because what men did was so often cruel and ugly.

Listen: Bunny Hoover went to **Prairie Military Academy** for eight years of uninterrupted sports, buggery and fascism. Buggery consisted of sticking one's penis in somebody else's asshole or mouth, or having it done to one by somebody else. Fascism was a fairly popular political philosophy which made sacred whatever nation and race the philosopher happened to belong to. It called for an autocratic, centralized government, headed up by a dictator. The dictator had to be obeyed, no matter what he told somebody to do.

prakhouls. (*PP* XXIV) En route by air from Miami Beach to Ithaca, home of Cornell University, the Shah of Bratpuhr caught a nasty cold. When seven *prakhouls* (that quantity of fluid that can be contained in the skin of an adult male Bratpuhrian marmot) of *Sumklish* improved the Shah's spirits but did nothing for his respiratory system, it was decided that the plane should land in Harrisburg, Pennsylvania, in order that the Shah might rest and try the magic of American medicine.

Pratt, Mary. *Eugene Debs Hartke's high school English teacher, who demanded the class learn Hamlet's "To be, or not to be" soliloquy, in* Hocus Pocus. *He recalls her memory when resigning under the coercion of Tarkington's Board of Trustees, but before leaving he recites the speech. Hartke feels it would provide a suitable shock to the trustees, who fear the idea of another Vietnam veteran faculty member's committing suicide at the school. The first to do so was the late president, Sam Wakefield.*

Prince of Candlesticks. *The stillborn child of twelve-year-old Melody Oriole-2 von Peterswald (Wilbur Swain's daughter) who had been raped on her way to New York. Wilbur calls the unnamed child the "Prince of Candlesticks" because he was known as the "King of Candlesticks." Wilbur refers to the child to convey the significance he attaches to his memoirs.* (*Slap* 13) Yes, and if archaeologists of the future find this book of mine, they will be spared the fruitless labor of digging through the pyramid in search of its

meaning. There are no secret treasure rooms in there, no chambers of any kind.

Its meaning, which is minuscule in any event, lies beneath the manhole cover over which the pyramid is constructed. It is the body of a stillborn male.

Prince, Dudley. *A central figure in* Timequake's *narrative and one of the attendees at the clambake, Prince is the African American day shift supervisor of the three guards on duty at the American Academy of Arts and Letters. It is Prince who spies the androgynously garbed and babbling Kilgore Trout outside the Academy as he tosses four manuscripts (not all at once) into the garbage bin, among them "The Sisters B-36," "Bunker Bingo Party," and "Golden Wedding." Prince retrieves the abandoned pages and brings them to Monica Pepper, his boss at the Academy. Dressed like a bag lady, Trout had been living and writing next door to the Academy in the homeless shelter that once served as the Museum of the American Indian.*

Prior to life as a security guard, Prince had been falsely convicted as the rapist and murderer of ten-year-old Italian American Kimberly Wang in his native Rochester, New York. When he is eventually freed from his two life sentences when exculpatory DNA evidence is found in the vault of an unscrupulous district attorney, Prince has already earned a GED and dedicates his life to Jesus.

The timequake transports Prince back in time to solitary confinement in the New York State Maximum Security Adult Correctional Facility at Athena. The nature of the timequake is such that he is aware of his eventual freedom but is nonetheless fated to repeat his incarceration until once again exonerated by the DNA evidence. Vonnegut compares Prince's fate and awareness with his sister's. (TQ 16) Because of what the timequake had done to **Prince**, he had become as contemptuous of the idea of a wise and just God as my sister Allie had been. Allie opined one time, not just about her life but everybody's life, "If there is a God, He sure hates people. That's all I can say."

So great and fearful is Prince's memory of his incarceration that when free will kicks in again, it serves as an ironic element in saving his life. (TQ 31)

You want to talk about luck? When the timequake struck, Monica Pepper's paraplegic husband was ringing the doorbell. **Dudley Prince** was about to go to the steel front door. Before he could take a step in that direction, though, a smoke alarm went off in the picture gallery behind him. He froze. Which way to go?

So when free will kicked in, he was on the horns of the same dilemma. The smoke alarm behind him had saved his life!

It is left to Trout to rouse Prince from his catatonia. (TQ 37) The old science fiction writer wanted to galvanize the armed and uniformed **Dudley Prince** into action, he later confessed, so that he himself wouldn't have to do anything more. "Free will! Free will! Fire! Fire!" he shouted at **Prince**.

Prince did not move a muscle. He batted his eyes, but those were reflexes, and not free will, like me and the chicken noodle soup. One thing **Prince** was thinking, by his own account, was that if he moved a muscle, he might find himself in the New York State Maximum Security Adult Correctional Facility at Athena back in 1991 again.

Understandable!

(TQ 50) **Prince** spoke groggily at first. He didn't pledge allegiance, but indicated instead that he was trying to understand everything Trout had said to him so far. He said, "You told me I had something."

"You were sick, but now you're well, and there's work to do," said Trout.

"Before that," said **Prince**. "You said I had something."

"Forget it," said Trout. "I was all excited. I wasn't making sense."

"I still want to know what you said I had," said **Prince**.

"I said you had free will," said Trout.

"Free will, free will, free will," echoed **Prince** with wry wonderment. "I always wondered what it was I had. Now I got a name for it."

"Please forget what I said," said Trout. "There are lives to save!"

"You know what you can do with free will?" said **Prince**.

"No," said Trout.

"You can stuff it up your ass," said **Prince**.

Vonnegut uses the occasion of free will's resump-tion on February 13, 2001, that moment when Trout rouses Prince from his trance, to juxtapose larger points about man's attempt to command life through science and man's insistence on acting humanely. (TQ 51) When I liken Trout there in the entrance hall of the American Academy of Arts and Letters, awakening **Dudley Prince** from PTA, to Dr. Frankenstein, I am alluding of course to the antihero of the novel *Frankenstein—or, The Modern Prometheus*, by Mary Wollstonecraft Shelley, second wife of the English poet Percy Bysshe Shelley. In that book, the scientist Frankenstein puts a bunch of body parts from different corpses together in the shape of a man.

Frankenstein jazzes them with electricity. The results in the book are exact opposites of those since achieved in real-life American state penitentiaries with real-life electric chairs. Most people think Frankenstein is the monster. He isn't. Frankenstein is the scientist.

Prometheus in Greek mythology makes the first human beings from mud. He steals fire from Heaven and gives it to them so they can be warm and cook, and not, one would hope, so we could incinerate all the little yellow bastards in Hiroshima and Nagasaki, which are in Japan.

In chapter 2 of this wonderful book of mine, I mention a commemoration in the chapel of the University of Chicago of the fiftieth anniversary of the atom-bombing of Hiroshima. I said at the time that I had to respect the opinion of my friend William Styron that the Hiroshima bomb saved his life. Styron was then a United States Marine, training for an invasion of the Japanese home islands, when that bomb was dropped.

I had to add, though, that I knew a single word that proved our democratic government was capable of committing obscene, gleefully rabid and racist, yahooistic murders of unarmed men, women, and children, murders wholly devoid of military common sense. I said the word. It was a foreign word. That word was Nagasaki.

Whatever! That, too, was a long, long time ago, and ten years longer ago than that, if you want to count the rerun. What I find worth exclaiming about right now is the continuing applicability to the human condition, years after free will has ceased to be a novelty, of what jazzed **Dudley Prince** back to life, of what is now known generally as Kilgore's Creed: "You were sick, but now you're well again, and there's work to do. . . ."

On the afternoon of February 13th, 2001, alone, and then during the next two weeks or so, Kilgore's Creed did as much to save life on Earth as Einstein's E equals mc squared had done to end it two generations earlier.

Trout had **Dudley Prince** say the magic words to the other two armed guards on the day shift at the Academy. They went into the former Museum of the American Indian, and said them to the catatonic bums in there. A goodly number of the aroused sacred cattle, maybe a third of them, became anti-PTA evangelists in turn. Armed with nothing more than Kilgore's Creed, these ragged veterans of unemployability fanned out through the neighborhood to convert more living statues to lives of usefulness, to helping the injured, or at least getting them the hell indoors somewhere before they froze to death.

Prince arrives at the clambake in the company of Monica Pepper and Jerry Rivers.
See also: *TQ* 15–16; 18–20; 24, 31; 46; 51; 53–54.

Prince, Joe. *In* Player Piano, *Edgar Rice Burroughs Hagstrohm invokes the name of bowling buddy Joe Prince to avoid staying home with his wife so he could rendezvous with Marion Frascati. His children play along though they know what he is doing, and even Edgar's wife Wanda knows and approves of his relationship with Marion.*

Prince Richard of Croatia-Slavonia. *The owner of a Madison Avenue antique shop who hires homosexual prostitute James Wait for a sexual encounter, in* Galápagos. *The Prince wants to masturbate while Wait strangles him with a silken sash. Wait is supposed to count to twenty after the Prince ejaculates and loses consciousness, but Wait decides to count to three hundred—killing the shop owner.*

Princess Charlotte. *The daughter of a Staten Island roofer who marries* "Prince Richard of Croatia-Slavonia, a direct descendant of James the First of England and Emperor Frederick the Third of Germany and Emperor Franz Joseph of Austria and King Louis the Fifteenth of France" (*Gal* 1:29). *After his death, facilitated by James Wait, she becomes the designer of neckties bearing his family's crest.*

Project Cyclops. *In the short story* "Thanasphere," *this is the military's Cold War effort to have a weather spotter aloft in a manned capsule in geosynchronous orbit around earth in case tensions result in the firing of nuclear weapons. Lieutenant Major Rice is the astronaut sent into space. The mission's ground commander is Lieutenant General Franklin Dane and scientist Dr. Bernard Groszinger. It is this mission that reveals the existence of a congregation of lost souls in what Groszinger terms the Thanasphere.*

Proteus, Anita. *Anita is the wife of Paul Proteus in* Player Piano. *If not for her ambition and cunning during an affair with Paul while employed as his secretary, they might never have married; she had a history of delayed menstruation.* (PP I) As for the Proteus genes' chances of being passed down to yet another generation, there were practically none. Paul's wife, **Anita**, his secretary during the war, was barren. Ironically as anyone would please, he had married her after she had declared that she was certainly pregnant, following an abandoned office celebration of victory. *Their marriage thrives but there is no lasting joy. As it turns out, Anita is barren and this causes a long-felt depression for her and Paul.*

Though fiercely loyal and protective of Paul, his lack of ambition always disappoints her. Their marriage has fallen into clearly defined roles and their verbal patter becomes as predictably mechanical as the Ilium Works ("I love you, Paul." "And I love you, Anita.") *Anita is also fiercely jealous of Dr. Katharine Finch, the woman who succeeds her as Paul's secretary.* (PP I) **Anita** had the mechanics of marriage down pat, even to the subtlest conventions. If her approach was disturbingly rational, systematic, she was thorough enough to turn out a creditable counterfeit of warmth. Paul could only suspect that her feelings were shallow—and perhaps that suspicion was part of what he was beginning to think of as his sickness.

(PP IV) The expression "armed to the teeth" occurred to Paul as he looked at her over his glass. With an austere dark gown that left her tanned shoulders and throat bare, a single bit of jewelry on her finger, and very light make-up, **Anita** had successfully combined the weapons of sex, taste, and an aura of masculine competence.

(*PP* XIII) **Anita** slept—utterly satisfied, not so much by Paul as by the social orgasm of, after years of the system's love play, being offered Pittsburgh. *Of course it is Paul who is offered the Pittsburgh position, though Anita's efforts to be the perfect corporate manager's wife are widely seen as significantly rounding out Paul's candidacy.*

(*PP* XIII) She made the carnage so vivid that he was obliged for a moment to abandon his own thoughts, to see if there was the slightest truth in what she was saying. He went over the scalps she was counting one by one—men who had competed with him for this job or that—and found that they all had done well for themselves and were quite unbroken either financially or in spirit. But to **Anita** they were dead men, shot squarely between the eyes, and good riddance of bad rubbish.

The competing conspiracies for Paul's allegiance by Kroner and Baer on one side and the Ghost Shirt Society on the other eventually force a break in their marriage. Anita eventually takes up with Paul's nemesis, Dr. Lawson Shepherd.

See also: PP I; VI; X; XVI; XXXII.

Proteus, Dr. Paul. *In* Player Piano, *the son of the late Dr. George Proteus (the first National Industrial, Commercial, Communications, Foodstuffs, and Resources Director), Paul is presented as the heir apparent to direct the overwhelming (and overbearing) industrial technocracy that spawns as a result of the engineering achievements during the war.*

Grooming Paul as his father's successor is an attempt to affirm the rightness of the system the engineers devised and EPICAC sustains. Together with their inventions, George and Paul Proteus form the new trinity: the father, the son, and the ghost in the machine. George is father of technocracy's first regime; Paul is the son of EPICAC's first guardian and himself the creator and overseer of lifeless machines that contain the working essence of once productive human spirits.

But Paul avoids becoming a messiah uniting all

to an abiding faith in technocracy. For all Paul's intellectual achievements and rapid advancement in the ruling technocracy (nepotism notwithstanding), his conflict lies in a growing awareness that the system designed to relieve man from physical and mental labor also strips people of their dignity. Developing this awareness is as much the result of his own sheltered experiences becoming juxtaposed with the Homesteaders and the misgivings of Finnerty and Lasher, as it is the result of diabolical scheming on the part of Kroner and Gelhorne.

Paul stands at the center of the scheme developed by the technocrats, a scheme requiring Paul's public resignation so that he could infiltrate the upstart Ghost Shirt Society. At the same time, those in the Ghost Shirt movement seek to use Paul's name regardless of his true allegiance. Neither side is particularly interested in his true convictions.

Proteus's decision to claim leadership of the Ghost Shirt Society enables him to climb atop Vonnegut's soapbox (more rightly, the witness stand in his treason trial). Citing the obvious polarities of life in the technocratic age, Paul reasons that not Every new piece of scientific knowledge is a good thing for humanity, *and that* The main business of humanity is to do a good job of being human beings . . . not to serve as appendages to machines, institutions, and systems (*PP* XXXII).

Proteus, George. *The fabled father of Paul Proteus and the nation's first National Industrial, Commercial, Communications, Foodstuffs, and Resources Director. Though Dr. Francis Gelhorne succeeds George Proteus, it is believed Paul would eventually fill his father's post. For his part, however, Paul sees one significant difference between himself and his father.* (*PP* VI) When Paul thought about his effortless rise in the hierarchy, he sometimes, as now, felt sheepish, like a charlatan. He could handle his assignments all right, but he didn't have what his father had, what Kroner had, what Shepherd had, what so many had: the sense of spiritual importance in what they were doing; the ability to be moved emotionally, almost like a lover, by the great omnipresent and omniscient spook, the corporate personality. In short, Paul missed what made his father aggressive and great: the capacity to really give a damn.

Proteus Park. *Located in Chicago and managed by Dr. Ned Dodge, this is* a postwar development of three thousand dream houses for three thousand families with presumably identical dreams *(PP XVII). It is there the Shah of Bratpuhr is given a guided tour of the home of Edgar and Wanda Hagstrohm. All these prefabricated homes are filled with dozens of electrical appliances intended to instantly perform menial household chores.*

"The Protocols of the Elders of Tralfamadore."

The unsigned science fiction short story appearing in the Black Garterbelt *porn magazine given to Eugene Debs Hartke by his military buddy and brother-in-law, Jack Patton. The story is similar to the one in Vonnegut's* The Sirens of Titan *(Kilgore Trout's novel* Now It Can Be Told) *in that it displaces traditional Western and patriarchal monotheistic beliefs in a God that expects his creation to act in accordance with His given laws, replacing that comforting myth with a no-fault explanation of outside interference. By the time Hartke has an opportunity and the inclination to read the story, he welcomes the harmless untruths it has to offer. (HP 26)* I did not realize at the time how much that story affected me. Reading it was simply a way of putting off for just a little while my looking for another job and another place to live at the age of 51, with 2 lunatics in tow. But down deep the story was beginning to work like a buffered analgesic. What a relief it was, somehow, to have somebody else confirm what I had come to suspect toward the end of the Vietnam War, and particularly after I saw the head of a human being pillowed in the spilled guts of a water buffalo on the edge of a Cambodian village, that Humanity is going somewhere really nice was a myth for children under 6 years old, like the Tooth Fairy and the Easter Bunny and Santa Claus.

The Elders of Tralfamadore are no more than germs that seek to spread themselves throughout the universe. Though their own physiology enables them to easily attach themselves to other life forms, humans are particularly attractive because of their "extra-large brains." (HP 25) So the Elders focused in on them, and wondered if people's brains might not invent survival tests for germs which were truly horrible.

They saw in us a potential for chemical evils on a cosmic scale. Nor did we disappoint them.

The short story points out the critical difference between the humanoids on Tralfamadore, which the germs decided not to infect, and the humanoids on Earth. The Tralfamadorians fail to take anything seriously while Earthlings are deadly serious about any scheme which displaces them from the center of attention. (HP 26) The Elders, incidentally, had given up on influencing the humanoids of Tralfamadore, who were right below where they were meeting. The Tralfamadorians had senses of humor and so knew themselves for the severely limited lunkers, not to say crazy lunkers, they really were. They were immune to the kilovolts of pride the Elders jazzed their brains with. They laughed right away when the idea popped up in their heads that they were the glory of the Universe, and that they were supposed to colonize other planets with their incomparable magnificence. They knew exactly how clumsy and dumb they were, even though they could talk and some of them could read and write and do math. One author wrote a series of side-splitting satires about Tralfamadorians arriving on other planets with the intention of spreading enlightenment.

But the people here on Earth, being humorless, found the same idea quite acceptable.

It appeared to the Elders that the people here would believe anything about themselves, no matter how preposterous, as long as it was flattering. To make sure of this, they performed an experiment. They put the idea into Earthlings' heads that the whole Universe had been created by one big male animal who looked just like them. He sat on a throne with a lot of less fancy thrones all around him. When people died they got to sit on those other thrones forever because they were such close relatives of the Creator.

The people down here just ate that up!

The complete synopsis of "The Protocols of the Elders of Tralfamadore" appears toward the end of chapter 25 and more fully in chapter 26 of Hocus Pocus.

The Protocols of the Elders of Zion *(see also* **Henry Ford***). In the introduction to* Mother Night,

Vonnegut recalls being handed a copy of the fraudulent anti-Semitic tract back in the 1930s.

In *Hocus Pocus, the book is broadly distributed among the convicts in Athena by the Black Brothers of Islam. They received copies from a publisher in Libya. It becomes the de facto textbook for Hartke's prison literacy campaign though he denounces the text's philosophy. Hartke notes that the text's title was later appropriated for a science fiction story entitled "The Protocols of the Elders of Tralfamadore," which appeared in the issue of* Black Garterbelt *magazine bestowed upon him by his military buddy and brother-in-law, Jack Patton. (HP 33)* **The Protocols of the Elders of Zion** was an anti-Semitic work first published in Russia about 100 years ago. It purported to be the minutes of a secret meeting of Jews from many countries who planned to cooperate internationally so as to cause wars and revolutions and financial busts and so on, which would leave them owning everything. Its title was parodied by the author of the story in *Black Garterbelt,* and its paranoia, too.

The great American inventor and industrialist Henry Ford thought it was a genuine document. He had it published in this country back when my father was a boy.

Pruitt, Major General Earl. *In* Player Piano, *Pruitt is the division commander of Pfc. Elmo Hacketts's Army unit and is on hand to greet the visiting Shah of Bratpuhr.*

Pullman, Mr. and Mrs., and son Richard. *In the short story "A Present for Big Saint Nick," collected in* Bagombo Snuff Box *(1999), Mr. Pullman is another of mobster Big Nick's white-collar employees who prospers by their relationship. Nick, dressed as Santa, derisively tells young Richard to be grateful for the $124.50 train set (wholesale!) he is receiving, since he would never get such a gift from his father.* Lemme tell you, kid, he'd still be chasin' ambulances an' missin' payments on his briefcase if it wasn't for me. An' don't nobody forget it. *When prompted by Nick to tell the truth about what his parents say about him at home, Richard does well to repeat his rehearsed answer that his parents love Big Nick.*

The truth, of course, is that the Pullmans disliked Nick, his business, and his crass use of employees' children to find out what is said about him in the privacy of their homes. There is no denying that the Pullmans and the others were grateful for the good livings they made with Nick, but his annual Christmas party scared the children so much that they carried their fear of Santa with them throughout the year. Young Richard shows the signs of his neurosis when we first see him with his family as they enter the jewelry store looking for the most crass gift they can find to give the tasteless Nick. A tall, urbane gentleman with a small mustache came up to the adjoining counter, trailed by a wife in mink and a son. The son was Willy's age, and was snuffling and peering apprehensively over his shoulder at the front door. *Like Willy, the young son of Nick's bodyguard Bernie O'Hare, Richard is apprehensive of all things Santa, a palpable fear at Christmastime with Santas represented in some way in nearly every store.* "It's psychosomatic," said **Mrs. Pullman** "He snuffles every time he sees a Santa Claus. You can't bring a child downtown at Christmastime and not have him see a Santa Claus somewhere. One came out of the cafeteria next door just a minute ago. Scared poor **Richard** half to death."

Pullman is torn between correcting his son's Santa-anxiety and his understanding of the life he enjoys due to working for a mobster. His wife is as emotionally distraught as her son, but her husband is quick to point out they must put up with the situation since they are prospering. "I won't have a snuffling son," said **Pullman.** "**Richard**! Stiff upper lip! Santa Claus is your friend, my friend, everybody's friend."

"I wish he'd stay at the North Pole," said **Richard.**

"And freeze his nose off," said Willy.

"And get ate up by a polar bear," said **Richard.**

"Eaten up by a polar bear," **Mrs. Pullman** corrected.

"Are you encouraging the boy to hate Santa Claus?" said **Mr. Pullman.**

"Why pretend?" said **Mrs. Pullman.** "*Our* Santa Claus *is* a dirty, vulgar, prying, foulmouthed, ill-smelling fake."

The clerk's eyes rolled.

"Sometimes, dear," said **Pullman**, "I wonder if you remember what we were like before we met that jolly elf. Quite broke."

"Give me integrity or give me death," said **Mrs. Pullman**.

"Shame comes along with the money," said **Pullman**. "It's a package deal. And we're in this thing together."

Pullman agrees with the sarcasm expressed by Wanda O'Hare, coincidentally shopping with them looking for Nick's presents, that everybody loves Big Nick, Or they wind up in Lake Michigan with cement overshoes.

Pulsifer, Borders M., General of the Armies. (*ST* 5) The nominal commander of the entire (*Martian*) Army, **General of the Armies Borders M. Pulsifer**, was in fact controlled at all times by his orderly, Corporal Bert Wright. Corporal Wright, the perfect orderly, carried aspirin for the General's almost chronic headaches . . . *due to the mind-riveting sounds running through the general's skull by Wright's electronic transmitter.*

punctual (experiencing time in a **punctual manner**). (*ST* 1) Constant smiled at that—the warning to be **punctual**. To be **punctual** meant to exist as a point, meant that as well as to arrive somewhere on time. Constant existed as a point—could not imagine what it would be like to exist in any other way. That was one of the things he was going to find out—what it was like to exist in any other way. Mrs. Rumfoord's husband existed in another way.

When Malachi Constant asks Winston Niles Rumfoord if he can see into the future, Rumfoord responds, "In a **punctual** way of speaking—yes. . . . When I ran my space ship into the chrono-synclastic infundibulum, it came to me in a flash that everything that ever has been always will be, and everything that ever will be always has been" (*ST* 1).

Rumfoord draws this comparison between his own chrono-synclastic infundibulated existence and those who experience time in a linear fashion. (*ST* 2) "Look," said Rumfoord, "life for a **punctual** person is like a roller coaster." He turned to shiver his hands in her face. "All kinds of things are going to

happen to you! Sure," he said, "I can see the whole roller coaster you're on. And sure—I could give you a piece of paper that would tell you about every dip and turn, warn you about every bogeyman that was going to pop out at you in the tunnels. But that wouldn't help you any."

Purdy and McCloud. *Two aging Cornell football linemen (thirty-seven and thirty-six years old, respectively) who worry that the economic realities of maintaining the Ivy League championship might cost them their jobs, in* Player Piano.

purity. (*WFG* Preface) Mr. Nixon himself is a minor character in this book. He is the first President to hate the American people and all they stand for. He believes so vibrantly in his own **purity**, although he has committed crimes which are hideous, that I am bound to conclude that someone told him when he was very young that all serious crime was sexual, that no one could be a criminal who did not commit adultery or masturbate. (*WFG* Address at Rededication of Wheaton College Library, 1973) And one idea that was put into our heads (*as a result of the revealed atrocities committed by the Nazis*) was that our enemies were so awful, so evil, that we, by contrast, must be remarkably **pure**. That illusion of **purity**, to which we were entitled in a way, has become our curse today. *See also: ST* 10; 12; *MN* 25; *WFG* The Mysterious Madame Blavatsky; *BAG* The Package.

Putty Puss. *Vonnegut recalls this failed invention of James Adams, Vonnegut's brother-in-law, who tragically died in a commuter train accident two days before his wife, Vonnegut's sister, Alice, died of cancer. Vonnegut mentions the episode as a way of undercutting the hopes of his parents' generation in Indianapolis (and elsewhere) who, during the Great Depression, scrimped to maintain the class prospects of their children by sending their daughters to private schools such as Tudor Hall in order to become marriage material for America's upper class.* (*TQ* 6) Jim had plunged them deep in debt by manufacturing a toy of his own invention. It was a corked rubber balloon with a blob of permanently malleable clay inside. It was clay with a skin!

The face of a clown was printed on the balloon.

You could make it open its mouth wide with your fingers, or make its nose protrude or its eyes sink in. Jim called it **Putty Puss**. **Putty Puss** never became popular. Moreover, **Putty Puss** amassed enormous debts for its manufacture and advertising.

Allie and Jim, Indianapolis people in New Jersey, had four boys and no girls. One of the boys was a mewling infant, and none of these people had asked to be born in the first place.

Queen Margaret. *Queen Margaret of the planet Shaltoon is one of the main characters in Kilgore Trout's* Venus on the Half-shell, *in* God Bless You, Mr. Rosewater. *On the back flap of the novel she is characterized as the seductress of the story's hero, the Space Wanderer. There is no reason to believe this reference has any relation to Malachi Constant in* The Sirens of Titan. *Fred Rosewater reads the back cover.* (GBR 9) Fred, thinking Lila wasn't paying any attention to him, now put down *Better Homes and Gardens*, picked up what looked like one hell of a sexy paperback novel, *Venus on the Half-shell*, by Kilgore Trout. On the back cover was an abridgment of a red-hot scene inside. It went like this:

Queen Margaret of the planet Shaltoon let her gown fall to the floor. She was wearing nothing underneath. Her high, firm, uncowled bosom was proud and rosy. Her hips and thighs were like an inviting lyre of pure alabaster. They shone so whitely they might have had a light inside. "Your travels are over, Space Wanderer," she whispered, her voice husky with lust. "Seek no more, for you have found. The answer is in my arms."

"It's a glorious answer, **Queen Margaret**, God knows," the Space Wanderer replied. His palms were perspiring profusely. "I am going to accept it gratefully. But I have to tell you, if I'm going to be perfectly honest with you, that I will have to be on my way again tomorrow."

"But you have found your answer, you have found your answer," she cried, and she forced his head between her fragrant young breasts.

He said something that she did not hear. She thrust him out at arm's length. "What was that you said?"

"I said, **Queen Margaret**, that what you offer is an awfully good answer. It just doesn't happen to be the one I'm primarily looking for."

Queen of the Meadows. *Symbolic of the strict hierarchy imposed by the ruling technocracy in* Player Piano, *the* **Queen of the Meadows** *is the ferry that takes the top one hundred men (by classification number) from the mainland to the island that is the Meadows for their annual retreat. Those with numbers from one hundred one to two hundred fifty board the* Meadow Lark; *the remainder board the* Spirit of the Meadows.

Quezeda, Domingo. *The twisted old man who answers a call to serve as interpreter for the orphanage housing the Kanka-bono girls.* (Gal 1:28) An old drunk and petty thief appeared, a purebred white man who, amazingly, was a grandfather of the lightest of the girls. When a youngster, he had gone prospecting for valuable minerals in the rain forest, and had lived with the Kanka-bonos for three years. . . . He was from excellent stock. His father had been head of the Philosophy Department of the Central University of Quito. If they were so inclined, then, people today might claim to be descended from a long line of aristocratic Spanish intellectuals.

Quezeda taught the Kanka-bono girls to be thieves and introduced them to the world of prostitution. (Gal 1:28) He would do this in order to feed his big brain's thirst for self-esteem and alcohol. He was at last going to be a man of wealth and importance. . . . During their bad old days in Guayaquil, old **Quezeda** offered his stinking body for their experimentation as he taught them, as little as they were, the fundamental skills and attitudes of prostitutes.

Quinn, Bert. *Quinn purchases a restaurant from George M. Helmholtz, the head of the music department at Lincoln High School, ten years before the opening of the 1955 short story "The Kid Nobody Could Handle" (reprinted in the 1968 collection* Welcome to the Monkey House). *Quinn and Helmholtz have differing visions and values. The former looks only at monetary gain, the latter looks to music for self-fulfillment. Quinn gives up on his juvenile delinquent step-nephew Jim Donnini, while Helmholtz reforms the boy by enticing him with John Philip Sousa's trumpet.*

R

Rackstraw, Loree. *An emeritus professor of English at Northern Iowa University, Rackstraw had been Vonnegut's student at the Iowa Writers Workshop and they remained close friends for the rest of his life. She is one of the attendees at the Timequake clambake (62). In 2009 she published a personal memoir of her love affair with Vonnegut entitled,* Love as always, Kurt: Vonnegut as I Knew Him.

Ralph. *In "The Powder-Blue Dragon," Ralph is the bartender at the tony cocktail lounge and known by his first name by Paul, the fiancé of the beautiful Marion. Kiah Higgins drives his Marittima-Frascati to the lounge in a failed attempt to attract Marion's notice, whom he saw driving her Cadillac while out for his first spin in his sports car. In yet another instance emphasizing Kiah's low if not invisible status, even Ralph is unconvinced that Kiah owns the exotic car, believing it is more likely he is the car's mechanic.*

The RAMJAC Corporation. *In* Jailbird, *RAMJAC was once a small company but is transformed by multimillionaire mining engineer Jack Graham, who developed it into a multinational corporation. After Graham's death in 1952, his wife, Mary Kathleen O'Looney, takes control. She hires Arpad Leen to serve as president and chairman of the board. His only orders are to acquire as many properties as possible, and at its height, RAMJAC controlled nineteen percent of everything in the country. Mary Kathleen's last will and testament left RAMJAC to the American people, but the government saw its liquidation as the answer to its short-term economic woes rather than managing the enterprise and realizing a steady income.*

The copyright for Deadeye Dick, *Vonnegut's succeeding novel, is held by the RAMJAC Corporation.*

Rauch, John G. *The husband of Gertrude Schnull Rauch, a first cousin to Kurt Vonnegut, Sr., and the author of "An Account of the Ancestry of Kurt Vonnegut, Jr., by an Ancient Friend of His Family," reprinted in the "Roots" chapter of* Palm Sunday. *It is a most informative piece about the family's history and the influences at work on Vonnegut. Uncle John (1890–1976), as he was known to the family, gave the manuscript to Vonnegut as a gift.* (PS Roots) He was a Harvard graduate and a distinguished Indianapolis lawyer. Toward the end of his life, he made himself an historian, a *griot,* of his wife's family—in part my family, too, although he was not related to it by blood, but only by marriage.

It was painstakingly researched and better written, by **Uncle John** himself, than much of my own stuff, sad to say. That manuscript is the most extravagant gift I ever expect to receive—and it came from a man who had never spoken favorably of my work in my presence, other than to say that he was "surprised by my convincing tone of authority," and that he was sure I would make a great deal of money.

Uncle John Rauch has a doppelgänger representing him at the Timequake clambake. (TQ 62) Among other departed souls whom I would not summon back to life, if I had had the power to do so, but who were represented by doppelgängers . . . my uncle **John Rauch,** husband to another of Father's first cousins. **Uncle John** provided me with a history of my family in America, which I printed in *Palm Sunday.*

Raven. *The British destroyer that captures the Nazi submarine U-99 in* Cat's Cradle. *The sub previously captured Bokonon and sunk his schooner, the* Lady's Slipper.

Ray, James Earl (see **God Bless You, Dr. Kevorkian**).

real estate agent (*otherwise known as the unnamed narrator). In the short story "Any Reasonable Offer," first appearing in* Collier's *magazine (January 1952) and later collected in* Bagombo Snuff Box *(1999), the unnamed narrator is telling shop tales about how his industry has insufferable clients, buy-*

ers and sellers, who screw him out of commissions behind his back. But his centerpiece is the tale of Colonel and Mrs. Peckham, vacationing frauds in their spare time when Bradley Peckham is not busy with his drafting position at National Steel Foundry. Once the agent learns of the Peckhams' fraud, rather than turn in the pair, he explains how he is no longer going to be subject to the staid blue-collar life he once led. He is busy telling his tale while enjoying his own fraudulent vacation at the Van Tuyl estate.

real estate man. *In the short story* "Poor Little Rich Town," *collected in* Bagombo Snuff Box *(1999), the unnamed real estate agent stood in Hal Brayton's grocery store, looking at the deserted street and fiddling with his fountain pen. It is left to Upton Beaton to explain that the town is not interested in selling any of their real estate and that the tables have turned for the little man. Upton is merely presiding over Brayton's while Hal attends a meeting with the fire engine salesman (an unwise investment, according to efficiency expert Newell Cady, Spruce Falls's newest resident, sent by the Federal Apparatus Corporation, and proof incarnate that the townspeople preferred their flawed but personal way of life).* "Red-hot prospects are going to start coming through here in a week, and everybody goes out joy-riding," said the **real estate man** bitterly. He opened the soft drink cooler and let the lid fall shut again. "What's the matter—this thing broken? Everything's warm."

"No, Brayton just hasn't gotten around to plugging it in since he moved things back the way they used to be."

"You said he's the one who doesn't want to sell his place?"

"One of the ones," said Beaton.

"Who else?"

"Everybody else."

"Go on!"

"Really," said Beaton. "We've decided to wait and see how Mr. Cady adapts himself, before we put anything else on the market. He's having a tough time, but he's got a good heart, I think, and we're all rooting for him."

reborn. (MN 13) When (*the Reverend Dr. Lionel J. D.*) Jones' wife died, Jones felt the need to be **re-**born. He was **reborn** a thing he had been latently all along. Jones became the sort of racial agitator who is spoken of as having crawled out from under a rock. Jones crawled out from under his rock in 1928. He sold his funeral home for eighty-four thousand dollars, and he founded *The White Christian Minuteman.*

(GBR 7) Heaven is the bore of bores, Eliot's novel went on, so most wraiths queue up to be **reborn**—and they live and love and fail and die, and they queue up to be **reborn** again. They take pot luck. . . . They don't gibber and squeak to be one race or another, one sex or another, one nationality or another, one class or another. What they want and what they get are three dimensions—and comprehensible little packets of time—and enclosures making possible the crucial distinction between inside and outside.

. . . Uncomfortable as it is here, however, there are a few of us who do not care to be **reborn**. . . .

"Who are these people?" I ask myself. "What is this unimaginably horrible thing that has happened to them?" And I realize that, in order to get proper answers, I am going to have to cease to be dead. I am going to have to let myself be **reborn**. *These excerpts are from the novel Eliot Rosewater writes at the back of his* Domesday Book.

(*MH* Welcome to the Monkey House) "There is nothing like an Easter morning to make a man feel clean and **reborn** and at one with God's intentions."

(WJ I:2) WOODLY: Maybe God has let everybody who ever lived be **reborn**—so he or she can see how it ends. Even Pithecanthropus erectus and Australopithecus and Sinanthropus pekensis and the Neanderthalers are back on Earth—to see how it ends. They're all on Times Square—making change for peepshows. Or recruiting Marines.

(BC 19) And my own pre-earthquake condition must be taken into consideration, too, since I was the one who was being **reborn**. Nobody else in the cocktail lounge was **reborn**, as far as I know. The rest got their minds changed, some of them, about the value of modern art. *This is at the point when Vonnegut enters the text and comments in his own voice.*

(*Slap* 6) Thus did we (*Wilbur and Eliza Swain*) give birth to a single genius, which died as quickly as we were parted, which was **reborn** the moment we got together again.

(*Blue* 8) Only after the war did Marilee, **reborn** as the Contessa Portomaggiore, tell me that I was the reason she had been pushed down the stairs back in 1932.

See also: PP IX; *CC* 49; *WFG* A Political Disease; *PS* The Sexual Revolution.

Reconstruction and Reclamation Corps (*also known as the* **Reeks and Wrecks**). *As explained by Dr. Ewing J. Halyard, the designated host for the visiting Shah of Bratpuhr,* "any man who cannot support himself by doing a job better than a machine is employed by the government, either in the Army or the **Reconstruction and Reclamation Corps**" (*PP* XX). *More explicitly, the "Reeks and Wrecks" perform menial labor, mostly road repair.*

Redfield, Colonel George. *In* Jailbird, *the Sandusky lumber mill owner and son-in-law of the Ohio governor, commissioned to lead the National Guard troops during the strike at the Cuyahoga Bridge and Iron Company. Though lacking any military experience, he dresses as a cavalryman and stands with his troops when ordering them to advance against the strikers. After the shooting breaks out, Redfield is found crazed and naked in a side street.*

Redfield, Dr. Robert. *Vonnegut's faculty adviser in the Department of Anthropology at the University of Chicago. Vonnegut recalls that* While he (Redfield) lived, he had in his head a lovely dream which he called "The Folk Society." He published this dream in *The American Journal of Sociology*, Volume 52, 1947, pages 293 through 308. *He goes on to quote Redfield at great length to fully illustrate his sense of "folk society"* (*WFG* Address to the National Institute of Arts and Letters, 1971).

At *another point, Vonnegut summarizes Redfield when commemorating the two hundredth anniversary of the birth of William Ellery Channing.* (*PS* Religion) "Channing grew up in what the late anthropologist **Robert Redfield** called a folk society, a relatively isolated community of like-thinking friends and relatives, a stable extended family of considerable size. **Redfield** said that we were all descended from persons who lived in such societies, and that we were likely to hanker to live in one ourselves from time to time. A folk society, in his imagination and in our imaginations, too, is an ideal scheme within which people can take really good care of one another, can share fairly, and can distribute honors to one and all."

(*FWD* XIII) When I studied anthropology long ago at the University of Chicago, my most famous professor was **Dr. Robert Redfield**. The idea that all societies evolved through similar, predictable stages on their way to higher (Victorian) civilization, from polytheism to monotheism, for instance, or from the tom-tom to the symphony orchestra, had by then been ridiculed into obscurity. It was generally agreed that there was no such ladder as cultural evolution. But Dr. **Redfield** said in effect, "Wait just a minute." He said that he could describe to every fair-minded person's satisfaction one (and only one) stage every society had passed through or would pass through. He called this inevitable stage and his essay on it "The Folk Society."

(*FWD* XIII) Dr. **Redfield** gave a public lecture on the Folk Society in the springtime each year. It was popular, I think, because so many of us took it as scientific advice about how to find deep and enduring contentment: join or create a Folk Society. (This was back in the 1940s, remember, long before the communes and flower children and shared music and ideals of my children's generation.) Dr. **Redfield** denounced sentimentality about life in Folk Societies, saying they were hell for anyone with a lively imagination or an insatiable curiosity or a need to experiment and invent—or with an irrepressible sense of the ridiculous. But I still find myself daydreaming of an isolated little gang of likeminded people in a temperate climate, in a clearing in a woodland near a lake. . . .

(*FWD* XIII) If I am ever going to find a Folk Society for myself (and time is growing short), it will not be on Manhattan. The members of such a society, Dr. **Redfield** taught me, must feel that a particular piece of land gave birth to them, and has been and always will be theirs. As I say, nobody can really own anything in Skyscraper National Park.

I have said in speeches that Dr. **Redfield**, by describing a Folk Society, deserved to be honored alongside the identifiers of vitamins and minerals essential to our good health and cheerfulness.

(*FWD XIII*) I visited the Anthropology Department of the University of Chicago a few months ago. Dr. Sol Tax was the only faculty member from my time who was still teaching there. I asked him if he knew what had become of my own classmates (including Lisa Redfield, **Dr**. **Redfield**'s daughter). Many of them, Lisa, too, he said, were practicing what he called "urban anthropology," which sounded an awful lot like sociology to me. (We used to look down on the sociologists. I couldn't imagine why and can't imagine why.) If I had stayed with anthropology as a career, I would now be doing, probably, what I am doing, which is writing about the acculturated primitive people (like myself) in Skyscraper National Park.

Redwine, the Reverend C. Horner. *The forty-nine-year-old minister of the Barnstable First Church of God the Utterly Indifferent, also known as the Church of the Weary Space Wanderer, in* The Sirens of Titan. *He is the first to come upon the naked Malachi Constant (the Space Wanderer) emerging from his spaceship.*

Reed, Peter. *Emeritus professor of English at the University of Minnesota, Reed wrote the first book-length critical work about Vonnegut. They later became friends and shared years of correspondence and conversation. Reed is in attendance at the* Time-quake *clambake (TQ 62).*

It was Reed's idea to collect Vonnegut's magazine stories that would later appear in Bagombo Snuff Box, *which also includes his preface. As Vonnegut notes in his introduction to that text,* My longtime friend and critic **Professor Peter Reed**, of the English Department at the University of Minnesota, made it his business to find these stories from my distant past. Otherwise, they might never have seen the light of day again. I myself hadn't saved one scrap of paper from that part of my life. I didn't think I would amount to a hill of beans. All I wanted to do was support a family.

Peter's quest was that of a scholar. I nevertheless asked him to go an extra mile for me, by providing an informal preface to what is in fact his rather than my collection.

God bless you, **Dr**. **Reed**, I think. (*BAG* Introduction)

Reinbeck Abrasives Company. *In the short story "A Night for Love," the family company is under the third-generation ownership of Louis C. Reinbeck.*

Reinbeck, Charlie (**Louis C. Reinbeck, Jr.**). *The defiant namesake of Louis C. Reinbeck and overly protected mama's boy of Natalie in the short story "A Night for Love," first appearing in* The Saturday Evening Post *in November 1957 and later collected in* Bagombo Snuff Box (1999). *The young heir to the Reinbeck Abrasives Company worries his parents with his unknown activities, particularly his mother's jealous desire to protect him from making a marital mismatch.*

While his parents worry themselves in the middle of a full-moon night with Charlie's unexplained absence in the company of an unknown girl, Natalie's own focal point is her jealousy about her husband's long-ago two dates with the beauty queen Milly O'Shea. Her current husband is now a security guard at their plant.

While Natalie protests to her husband that he might have been more happy had he married Milly O'Shea, that she is aware of her coldness and jealousy, that the cycles of the moon have been too influential in her life, her son Charlie is eloping with Milly's daughter, Nancy Whitman. Nancy and Charlie had put their own interpretation on the moonlight. They'd decided that Cinderella and Prince Charming had as good a chance as anybody for really living happily ever after. So they'd married.

Reinbeck, Louis C. *In the short story "A Night for Love," collected in* Bagombo Snuff Box (1999), *Reinbeck is the very wealthy third-generation owner-operator of Reinbeck Abrasives Company, the husband of Natalie and father of Louis C. (Charlie) Jr. He first appears drinking alone on his golf course some time after having thrown a large party at his adjoining home. He is full of unspoken regret about his relationship with his wife, Natalie, as well as with his son who has essentially stopped checking-in with him and sharing confidential moments.*

Along with his personal frustrations, Reinbeck carries with him the regret of an artisan who had to give up his dreams for more practical realities. Along with the house and the Reinbeck Abrasives Com-

pany, **Louis** had inherited from his father and grandfather a deep and satisfying sense of having been corrupted by commerce. And like them, **Louis** thought of himself as a sensitive maker of porcelain, not grinding wheels, born in the wrong place at the wrong time. *(He has a sensibility similar to that of Franklin Waggoner in "This Son of Mine.")*

When Natalie joins him out on the golf course as he looks into the night, she senses Louis's many disappointments, and as her jealousy over long-ago girlfriends morphs into pity for her husband, Natalie's own insecurities are also revealed. She sat up, ransacked her mind for the right word. "All this horrible, empty, aching, nagging regret." She lay back down.

"About Milly?" said **Louis**.

"About Milly, about me, about the abrasives company, about all the things you wanted and didn't get, about all the things you got that you didn't want. Milly and me—that's as good a way of saying it as anything. That pretty well says it all."

But Louis realizes that his fond remembrance for Milly had as much to do with the beauty of the full moon when they dated as with anything else. It is then that he realizes his own sensibilities for the beauty of that night led him astray, so he closes that episode of his life by sharing his understanding with Natalie, assuring her that she is his only and enduring love.

Reinbeck, Natalie. *In the short story "A Night for Love," collected in* Bagombo Snuff Box *(1999), Natalie, a native Bostonian, is married to Louis C. Reinbeck. Natalie's jealousy peaks when their son Charlie stays out all night with Nancy Whitman, the daughter of Milly and Turley, a security guard at Reinbeck Abrasives Company. Milly had been a beauty queen as a young lady, and Natalie never got over that fact and her secret suspicion that her husband was sorry not to have married her years earlier—a weak idea at best since the two had only two dates. Similarly, Milly's husband spends the night jealous of her past and those two dates with Reinbeck.*

Natalie is a manipulative woman, insecure in her position and forever flummoxing Louis with her insecurities. **Natalie** *was a cool, spare Boston girl. Her role was to misunderstand Louis. She did it beauti-*

fully, taking apart his reflective moods like a master mechanic.

When Natalie and Louis stand on their golf course late at night, wondering where young Charlie is, she verbally jabs Louis with his stature as coming from one of the desired and monied families in town. She baits him with the question about what it's like to come from one of the wealthiest, most sought after families in town, a question she poses with self-deprecation intended to provoke guilt and pity within Louis. "What's what like?" said Louis.

"Being a young male Reinbeck—all hot-blooded and full of dreams, swooping down off the hill, grabbing a pretty little town girl and spiriting her into the moonlight." She laughed, teasing. "It must be kind of godlike."

"It isn't," said Louis.

"It isn't godlike?"

"Godlike? I never felt more human in all my life!" Louis threw his empty glass in the direction of the golf course. He wished he'd been strong enough to throw the glass straight to the spot where Milly had kissed him good-bye.

"Then let's hope Charlie marries this hot little girl from town," said **Natalie**. "Let's have no more cold, inhuman Reinbeck wives like me." She stood. "Face it, you would have been a thousand times happier if you'd married your Milly O'Shea."

She went to bed.

religion, religious. *Religion is a frequent concern for Vonnegut. He often mentions his family's legacy of German freethinking, and his first marriage began to unravel when his wife became a born-again Christian.*

Religion is a major plot device in Player Piano, The Sirens of Titan, *and* Cat's Cradle. *(PP XI) And Halyard suddenly realized that, just as **religion** and government had been split into disparate entities centuries before, now, thanks to the machines, politics and government lived side by side, but touched almost nowhere.*

(PP XXIX) "Toward the end of the nineteenth century," said Lasher, "a new **religious** movement *(the Ghost Shirt Society)* swept the Indians in this country, Doctor. . . .

"With the game and land and ability to defend themselves gone," said Lasher, "the Indians found out that all the things they used to take pride in doing . . . were going or gone. . . . Great **religious** leaders could no longer show that the old **religious** beliefs were the way to victory and plenty. . . .

"And the Ghost Dance **religion**," said Lasher, "was that last, desperate defense of the old values. . . ."

(*ST* 3) The Magnum Opus Building was a slender, prismatic, twelve-sided shaft, faced on all twelve sides with blue-green glass that shaded to rose at the base. The twelve sides were said by the architect to represent the twelve great **religions** of the world. So far, no one had asked the architect to name them.

(*ST* 7) As he says in his *Pocket History of Mars:* "Any man who would change the World in a significant way must have showmanship, a genial willingness to shed other people's blood, and a plausible new **religion** to introduce during the brief period of repentance and horror that usually follows bloodshed. . . ."

(*ST* 7) "To that end, devoutly to be wished," said Rumfoord, "I bring you word of a new **religion** that can be received enthusiastically in every corner of every Earthling heart. . . .

"The name of the new **religion**," said Rumfoord, "is The Church of God the Utterly Indifferent. . . .

"The two chief teachings of this **religion** are these," said Rumfoord:

"Puny man can do nothing at all to help or please God Almighty, and Luck is not the hand of God.

"Why should you believe in this **religion**, rather than any others?" said Rumfoord. "You should believe in it because I, as head of this **religion**, can work miracles, and the head of no other **religion** can. What miracles can I work? I can work the miracle of predicting, with absolute accuracy, the things that the future will bring."

(*ST* 11) "You have had the singular accident, Mr. Constant," he said sympathetically, "of becoming a central symbol of wrong-headedness for a perfectly enormous **religious** sect. . . ."

(*ST* 12) "Didn't I give you half my UWTB?" said Salo. ". . . Didn't I spend day after day helping you to design the new **religion**?"

(*ST* Epilogue) He (*Malachi*) respected what his son (*Chrono*) was trying to do with **religion**.

(*CC* 4) Anyone unable to understand how a useful **religion** can be founded on lies will not understand this book either.

(*CC* 78) "When Bokonon and McCabe took over this miserable country years ago," said Julian Castle, "they threw out the priests. And then Bokonon, cynically and playfully, invented a new **religion**."

(*CC* 78) "Well, when it became evident that no governmental or economic reform was going to make the people much less miserable, the **religion** became the one real instrument of hope. . . ."

He asked McCabe to outlaw him and his **religion**, too, in order to give the **religious** life of the people more zest, more tang. . . .

Castle quoted this poem, which does not appear in The Books of Bokonon: So I said good-bye to government, / And I gave my reason: / That a really good **religion** / Is a form of treason.

(*CC* 98) "I agree with one Bokononist idea. I agree that all **religions**, including Bokononism, are nothing but lies."

(*CC* 125) "As far as I know, Bokononism is the only **religion** that has any commentary on midgets."

(*GBR* 7) Mushari was gratified to hear the anxiety in her voice (*Sylvia's*). It meant to him that Eliot's lunacy was not stabilized, but was about to make the great leap forward into **religion**. . . .

"I told her," said Eliot, and Mushari's mind, which was equipped with ratchets, declined to accept this evidence, "that I wasn't a **religious** person by any stretch of the imagination. I told her nothing I did would count in Heaven, but she insisted just the same." *Eliot tells Sylvia that he reluctantly agreed to baptize Mary Moody's twins.*

(*SL5* 2) His (*Billy Pilgrim's*) father had no **religion**. *However, Billy had a large crucifix on his bedroom wall and became a chaplain's assistant in the military.*

(*MH* The Manned Missiles) The more we think about it, the more we're sure it was meant to be. I never got it straight in my mind about **religion** in Russia. You don't mention it. Anyway, we are **religious**, and we think God singled out Bud and your boy, too, to die in a special way for a special reason.

(*WFG* Brief Encounters on the Inland Waterway) "Thinking the guy up ahead knows what he's doing is the most dangerous **religion** there is," he said.

(*WFG* Address to Graduating Class at Bennington

College, 1970) A great swindle of our time is the assumption that science has made **religion** obsolete. All science has damaged is the story of Adam and Eve and the story of Jonah and the Whale. Everything else holds up pretty well, particularly the lessons about fairness and gentleness. People who find those lessons irrelevant in the twentieth century are simply using science as an excuse for greed and harshness.

(WFG In a Manner That Must Shame God Himself) "Losers have thousands of **religions**, often of the *bleeding heart* variety," I would go on. "The single **religion** of the Winners is a harsh interpretation of Darwinism, which argues that it is the will of the universe that only the fittest should survive."

(WFG In a Manner That Must Shame God Himself) One of the things the Indians had come to beg from President Nixon, who never begged anything from anybody, was that their **religions** be recognized as respectable **religions** under law.

(WFG In a Manner That Must Shame God Himself) It was perhaps unkind of me to associate Dr. Kissinger with evil. That is no casual thing to do in a country as deeply **religious** as ours is.

(WFG Address at Rededication of Wheaton College Library, 1973) Our minds aren't crippled anymore by good taste. And I can see now all the other more sinister taboos which mingled with sexuality and excretion, such as **religious** hypocrisy and ill-gotten wealth. If we are to discuss truthfully what America is and what it can become, our discussion must be in absolutely rotten taste, or we won't be discussing it at all.

(WFG *Playboy* Interview) PLAYBOY: What's your **religious** background?

VONNEGUT: My ancestors, who came to the United States a little before the Civil War, were atheists. So I'm not rebelling against organized **religion**. I never had any. I learned my outrageous opinions about organized **religion** at my mother's knee. My family has always had those. They came here absolutely crazy about the United States Constitution and about the possibility of prosperity and the brotherhood of man here. They were willing to work very hard, and they were atheists.

PLAYBOY: Do you think organized **religion** can make anybody happier?

VONNEGUT: Oh, of course. Lots of comforting lies are told in church—not enough, but some. I wish preachers would lie more convincingly about how honest and brotherly we should be. I've never heard a sermon on the subject of gentleness or restraint; I've never heard a minister say it was wrong to kill. No preacher ever speaks out against cheating in business. There are fifty-two Sundays in a year, and somehow none of the subjects comes up.

PLAYBOY: Is there any **religion** you consider superior to any other?

VONNEGUT: Alcoholics Anonymous. Alcoholics Anonymous gives you an extended family that's very close to a brotherhood, because everybody has endured the same catastrophe.

(WFG *Playboy* Interview) I'm grateful that I learned from them (*Vonnegut's parents*) that organized **religion** is anti-Christian and that racial prejudices are stupid and cruel. I'm grateful, too, that they were good at making jokes.

(*Slap* Prologue) Since Alice had never received any **religious** instruction, and since she had led a blameless life, she never thought of her awful luck as being anything but accidents in a very busy place.

(*Slap* Prologue) The old man (*Wilbur Swain*) is writing his autobiography. He begins it with words which my late Uncle Alex told me one time should be used by **religious** skeptics as a prelude to their nightly prayers.

These are the words: "To whom it may concern."

(JB 4) I do not mean to sketch this blubbering leviathan (*Emil Larkin*) as a **religious** hypocrite, nor am I entitled to. He had so opened himself to the consolations of **religion** that he had become an imbecile.

(PS The First Amendment) What you may not know about our own culture is that writers . . . are routinely attacked by fellow citizens as being pornographers or corrupters of children and celebrators of violence and persons of no talent and so on. In my own case, such charges are brought against my works in court several times a year, usually by parents who, for **religious** or political reasons, do not want their children to read what I have to say.

(PS When I Lost My Innocence) An enthusiasm for technological cures for almost all forms of human discontent was the only **religion** of my family during the Great Depression, when I first got to know that family well. It was **religion** enough for me, and one branch of the family owned the largest hardware store in Indianapolis, Indiana.

(*PS* When I Lost My Innocence) But I learned how vile that **religion** of mine could be when the atomic bomb was dropped on Hiroshima.

(*PS* When I Lost My Innocence) But the bombing of Hiroshima compelled me to see that a trust in technology, like all the other great **religions** of the world, had to do with the human soul.

(*PS* Self-Interview) INTERVIEWER: Did the study of anthropology later color your writings?

VONNEGUT: It confirmed my atheism, which was the faith of my fathers anyway. **Religions** were exhibited and studied as the Rube Goldberg inventions I'd always thought they were. We weren't allowed to find one culture superior to any other. We caught hell if we mentioned races much. It was highly idealistic.

INTERVIEWER: Almost a **religion**?

VONNEGUT: Exactly. And the only one for me. So far.

(*PS* Self-Interview) VONNEGUT: It's my **religion** the censors hate. They find me disrespectful toward their idea of God Almighty. They think it's the proper business of government to protect the reputation of God.

(*PS* Mark Twain) "We **religious** skeptics would like to swagger some in heaven, saying to others who spent a lot of time quaking in churches down here, 'I was never worried about pleasing or angering God—never took Him into my calculations at all.'

"**Religious** skeptics often become very bitter toward the end, as did Mark Twain. I do not propose to guess now as to why he became so bitter. I know why I will become bitter. I will finally realize that I have had it right all along: that I will not see God, that there is no heaven or Judgment Day."

(*PS* Religion) "We cannot believe that this Being formed a human being from clay and breathed into it an Immortal Soul, and then allowed this human being to procreate millions, and then delivered them all into unspeakable misery, wretchedness and pain for all eternity. Nor can we believe that the descendents [*sic*] of one or two human beings will inevitably become sinners; nor do we believe that through the criminal executions of an Inno-

cent One may we be redeemed." (*From Clemens Vonnegut's funeral oration.*)

SUCH is my ancestral **religion**.

(*PS* Religion) "Our politicians like to say that we have **religion** and the Communist countries don't. I think it is just the other way around. Those countries have a religion called Communism, and the Free World is where sustaining **religions** are in very short supply."

(*PS* Religion) "I suggest that we need a new **religion**. If suggesting that we need a new **religion** is sacrilege, then the emperor Constantine was guilty of sacrilege, and the emperor Nero was an admirably pious man. And I want to point out that it is impossible to discard an old **religion** entirely. The **religion** of Nero survives today, determining as it does the dates and even moods of so many of our so-called Christian holidays. . . .

"What makes me think we need a new **religion**? That's easy. An effective **religion** allows people to imagine from moment to moment what is going on and how they should behave. Christianity used to be like that. Our country is now jammed with human beings who say out loud that life is chaos to them, and that it doesn't seem to matter what anybody does next. This is worse than being seasick."

(*PS* Religion) "We know too much for old-time **religion**; and in a way, that knowledge is killing us."

(*PS* Religion) "If I have offended anyone here by talking of the need of a new **religion**, I apologize. I am willing to drop the word **religion**, and substitute for it these three words: heartfelt moral code."

(*PS* Religion) "There is a willingness to do whatever we need to do in order to have life on the planet go on for a long, long time. I didn't used to think that. And that willingness has to be a **religious** enthusiasm, since it celebrates life, since it calls for meaningful sacrifices."

(*PS* Religion) "The faith of my ancestors, going back at least four generations, has been the most corrosive sort of agnosticism—or worse. When I was a child, all my relatives, male and female, agreed with H. L. Mencken when he said that he thought **religious** people were comical. Mencken said that he had been widely misunderstood as hating **religious** people. He did not hate them, he said. He merely found them comical. . . .

"Any time I see a person fleeing from reason and

into **religion**, I think to myself, There goes a person who simply cannot stand being so goddamned lonely anymore."

(*PS* Religion) "I have spoken of the long tradition of **religious** skepticism in my family. One of my two daughters has recently turned her back on all that. Living alone and far from home, she has memorized an arbitrary Christian creed, Trinitarianism, by chance. She now has her human dignity regularly confirmed by the friendly nods of a congregation. I am glad that she is not so lonely anymore. This is more than all right with me."

(*Blue* 2) Armenians, incidentally, were the first people to make Christianity their national **religion**. (*HP* 11) The origin of this most poisonous misunderstanding was in my account in Chapel of riding around with Grandfather (*Wills*) in his car one Sunday morning in Midland City, Ohio, when I was a little boy. He, not I, was mocking all organized **religions**.

When we passed a Catholic church, I recalled, he said, "You think your dad's a good chemist? They're turning soda crackers into meat in there. Can your dad do that?"

(*FWD* VII) So the Reverend was not a hypocrite. He was perfectly willing to say in so many words that there was nothing sacred about the First Amendment, and that many images and ideas other than pornography should be taken out of circulation by the police, and that the official **religion** of the whole country should be his sort of Christianity. He was sincere in believing that my *Slaughterhouse-Five* might somehow cause a person to wind up in a furnace for all eternity (see the mass promulgated by Pope St. Pius V), which would be even worse (if you consider its duration) than being raped, murdered, and then mutilated by a man maddened by dirty pictures.

(*FWD* XVI) My late war buddy O'Hare was born a Roman Catholic in Pennsylvania but came home from the war a **religious** skeptic. Bishop Moore, as I've said, went to war a **religious** skeptic and came out of it a profoundly convinced Trinitarian. He told me he had a vision during the fighting on Guadalcanal. He went on from his vision (although he was born rich and had a rich Anglo-Saxon's education and tastes and friends) to minister to the poor in parishes where the prosperous had fled to the

suburbs, to speak loathingly of social Darwinists (Neo-Cons, the FBI, the CIA, humorless, anal-retentive Republicans, and so on). . . .

My second wife is another Episcopalian, and like my first one thinks that I have no **religion** and am a spiritual cripple on that account. When Jill's and my daughter Lily was baptized by the Bishop of New York in the biggest Gothic church in the world (in a neighborhood so poor that the Bishop couldn't get cable service for his TV), I did not attend.

(*FWD* XVI) "I listen to the ethical pronouncements of the leaders of the so-called **religious** revival going on in this country, including those of our President, and am able to distill only two firm commandments from them. The first commandment is this: 'Stop thinking.' The second commandment is this: 'Obey.' Only a person who has given up on the power of reason to improve life here on Earth, or a soldier in Basic Training could accept either commandment gladly: 'Stop thinking' and 'Obey.'

"I was an Infantry Private during World War II and fought against the Germans in Europe. My **religion** as well as my blood type was stamped into my dogtags. The Army decided my **religion** was P, for 'Protestant.' There is no room on dogtags for footnotes and a bibliography. In retrospect, I think they should have put S on my dogtags, for 'Saracen,' since we were fighting Christians who were on some sort of utterly insane Crusade. They had crosses on their flags and uniforms and all over their killing machines, just like the soldiers of the first Christian Emperor Constantine. And they lost, of course, which has to be acknowledged as quite a setback for Christianity.

(*FWD* XVI) "When I say that the Unitarian Universalists, the people who know pure baloney when they hear it, are something like the early Christians in the catacombs, am I suggesting that contempt for baloney will someday be as widespread as Christianity is today? Well the example of Christianity is not encouraging, actually, since it was nothing but a poor people's **religion**, a servant's **religion**, a slave's **religion**, a woman's **religion**, a child's **religion**, and would have remained such if it hadn't stopped taking the Sermon on the Mount seriously and joined forces with the vain and rich and violent. I can't imagine that you would want to do that, to give up everything you believe in order to play a bigger part in world history.

(*FWD* XVI) "And stay clear of the Ten Commandments, as do the television evangelists. Those things are booby-trapped, because right in the middle of them is one commandment which would, if taken seriously, cripple modern **religion** as show business. It is this commandment: 'Thou shalt not kill.'"

(*HP* 24) Freethinkers . . . believed . . . that science had proved all organized **religions** to be baloney, that God was unknowable, and that the greatest use a person could make of his or her lifetime was to improve the quality of life for all in his or her community.

(*FWD* My Reply to a Letter from the Dean of the Chapel at Transylvania University About a Speech I Gave There) I am a fourth generation German American **religious** skeptic ("Freethinker"). Like my essentially puritanical forebears, I believe that God has so far been unknowable and hence unservable, hence the highest service one can perform is to his or her community, whose needs are quite evident. I believe that virtuous behavior is trivialized by carrot-and-stick schemes, such as promises of highly improbable rewards or punishments in an improbable afterlife. (The punishment for counterfeiting in Henry VIII's reign, incidentally, was being boiled alive in public.) The Bible is a useful starting point for discussions with crowds of American strangers, since so many of us know at least a little something about it. It has the added virtue of having for contributors at least two geniuses Moses and Christ.

(*TQ* 7) He asked what relatives of mine had been wounded in wars. As far as I knew, only one. That was my great-grandfather Peter Lieber, an immigrant who became a brewer in Indianapolis after being wounded in one leg during our Civil War. He was a Freethinker, which is to say a skeptic about conventional **religious** beliefs, as had been Voltaire and Thomas Jefferson and Benjamin Franklin and so on. And as would be Kilgore Trout and I.

I told Trout that Peter Lieber's Anglo-American company commander gave his men, all Freethinkers from Germany, Christian **religious** tracts for

inspiration. Trout responded by giving his own revision of the Book of Genesis.

(*TQ* 8) The late British philosopher Bertrand Russell said he lost friends to one of three addictions: alcohol or **religion** or chess.

(*TQ* 16) Then again, I have never made a serious study of the different **religions**, and so am unqualified to comment. About all I know for certain is that devout Muslims do not believe in Santa Claus. . . .

On the first of the two Christmas Eves, 2000, the still **religious** African-American armed guard Dudley Prince thought Trout's "The Sisters B-36" just might be a message for the Academy from God Himself. What happened to the planet Booboo, after all, wasn't a whole lot different from what seemed to be happening to his own planet, and especially to his employers, what was left of the American Academy of Arts and Letters, way-the-hell-and-gone up on West 155th Street, two doors west of Broadway.

(*TQ* 21) Are we enemies of members of organized **religions**? No. My great war buddy Bernard V. O'Hare, now dead, lost his faith as a Roman Catholic during World War Two. I didn't like that. I thought that was too much to lose.

(*TQ* 21) The German philosopher Friedrich Wilhelm Nietzsche, who had syphilis, said that only a person of deep faith could afford the luxury of **religious** skepticism. Humanists, by and large educated, comfortably middle-class persons with rewarding lives like mine, find rapture enough in secular knowledge and hope. Most people can't.

Voltaire, French author of *Candide,* and therefore the Humanists' Abraham, concealed his contempt for the hierarchy of the Roman Catholic Church from his less educated, simpler-minded, and more frightened employees, because he knew what a stabilizer their **religion** was for them.

(*TQ* 31) I like to think they did this not because they were foolish, but to remind him of how comforting and encouraging the make-believe of **religion** can be for common folk. *This is Vonnegut commenting on the religious time-out given to Newton by his church superiors.*

(*TQ* 35) Back then, though, we *(Bernard O'Hare and Vonnegut)* could both hear the Germans saying that America would now have to do what they had been doing, which was to fight the godless Communists.

We replied that we didn't think so. We expected the USSR to try to become more like the USA, with freedom of speech and **religion**, and fair trials and honestly elected officials, and so on. We, in turn, would try to do what they claimed to be doing, which was to distribute goods and services and opportunities more fairly: "From each according to his abilities, to each according to his needs." That sort of thing.

Occam's Razor.

(*TQ* 43) Any work of art is half of a conversation between two human beings, and it helps a lot to know who is talking at you. Does he or she have a reputation for seriousness, for **religiosity**, for suffering, for concupiscence, for rebellion, for sincerity, for jokes?

(*BAG* Hal Irwin's Magic Lamp) Mary didn't mind that. That girl was as wholesome as a peach and a glass of milk. Being poor gave her room to swing her **religion** around. When the end of the month came, and they'd eaten pretty well, and she hadn't asked Hal for an extra dime, she felt like a little white lamb.

(*BAG* Coda to My Career) What geography can give all Middle Westerners, along with the fresh water and topsoil, if they let it, is awe for a fertile continent stretching forever in all directions.

Makes you **religious**. Takes your breath away.

(*GBK* Introduction) About belief or lack of belief in an afterlife: Some of you may know I am neither Christian nor Jewish nor Buddhist, nor a conventionally **religious** person of any sort. I am a humanist, which means, in part, that I have tried to behave decently without any expectation of rewards or punishments after I'm dead. My German-American ancestors, the earliest of whom settled in our Middle West about the time of our Civil War, called themselves "Freethinkers," which is the same sort of thing. My great grandfather Clemens Vonnegut wrote, for example, "If what Jesus said was good, what can it matter whether he was God or not?"

I myself have written, "If it weren't for the message of mercy and pity in Jesus' Sermon on the Mount, I wouldn't want to be a human being. I would just as soon be a rattlesnake."

(*GBK* Introduction) Whereas formal **religions**

surely comfort many members of the WNYC staff, that staff's collective effect on its community is humanism—an ideal so Earthbound and unmajestic that I never capitalize it. As I have used it here, "humanist" is nothing more supernatural than a handy synonym for "good citizenship and common decency."

(*MWC* 2) About Stalin's shuttered churches, and those in China today: Such suppression of **religion** was supposedly justified by Karl Marx's statement that "**religion** is the opium of the people." Marx said that back in 1844, when opium and opium derivatives were the only effective painkillers anyone could take. Marx himself had taken them. He was grateful for the temporary relief they had given him. He was simply noticing, and surely not condemning, the fact that **religion** could also be comforting to those in economic or social distress. It was a casual truism, not a dictum.

The following is a Vonnegut illustration from his text. (*MWC* 3)

> I DON'T KNOW
> ABOUT YOU,
> BUT I PRACTICE
> A DISORGANIZED
> **RELIGION**.
> I BELONG TO AN
> UNHOLY DISORDER.
> WE CALL OURSELVES
> "OUR LADY OF PERPETUAL
> ASTONISHMENT."

(*MWC* 7) No matter how corrupt, greedy, and heartless our government, our corporations, our media, and our **religious** and charitable institutions may become, the music will still be wonderful.

If I should ever die, God forbid, let this be my epitaph:

> THE ONLY PROOF HE NEEDED
> FOR THE EXISTENCE OF GOD
> WAS MUSIC

(*MWC* 8) In case you haven't noticed, as the result of a shamelessly rigged election in Florida, in which thousands of African Americans were arbitrarily disenfranchised, we now present ourselves to the rest of the world as proud, grinning, jut-jawed, pitiless war-lovers with appallingly powerful weaponry—who stand unopposed.

In case you haven't noticed, we are now as feared and hated all over the world as the Nazis once were.

And with good reason.

In case you haven't noticed, our unelected leaders have dehumanized millions and millions of human beings simply because of their **religion** and race. We wound 'em and kill 'em and torture 'em and imprison 'em all we want.

Piece of cake.

In case you haven't noticed, we also dehumanized our own soldiers, not because of their **religion** or race, but because of their low social class.

Send 'em anywhere. Make 'em do anything.

Piece of cake.

The O'Reilly Factor.

So I am a man without a country, except for the librarians and a Chicago paper called *In These Times*.

Before we attacked Iraq, the majestic *New York Times* guaranteed that there were weapons of mass destruction there.

(MWC 10) A man from Little Deer Isle, Maine, wrote me and asked:

> What genuinely motivates al-Qaeda to kill and self-destruct? The president says, "They hate our freedoms"—our freedom of **religion**, our freedom of speech, our freedom to vote and assemble and disagree with each other, which surely is not what has been learned from the captives being held in Guantanamo, or what he is told in his briefings. Why do the communications industry and our elected politicians allow Bush to get away with such nonsense? And how can there ever be peace, and even trust in our leaders, if the American people aren't told the truth?

Well, one wishes that those who took over our federal government, and hence the world, by means of a Mickey Mouse coup d'état, who disconnected all the burglar alarms prescribed by the Constitution, which is to say the House and Senate, and the Supreme Court, and We, the People, were truly Christian. But as William Shakespeare told us long ago, "The devil can cite Scripture for his purpose."

See also: *PP* XI; *ST* 1; 6–8; 10–11; *MN* 11; *CC* 48; 58; 81; 88; 93; 96; *GBR* 7; 9; *BC* 2; 23; *MH* Harrison Bergeron; *MH* Miss Temptation; *WFG* Yes, We Have No Nirvanas; *WFG* Why They Read Hesse; *WFG* The Mysterious Madame Blavatsky; *WFG* In a Manner That Must Shame God Himself; *WFG* Address at Rededication of Wheaton College Library, 1973; *Slap* Prologue; *Slap* 38; *JB* 2–4; 7–8; 12; 20; *PS* The First Amendment; *PS* Roots; *PS* Self-Interview; *PS* Religion; *PS* Children; *DD* 9; *Gal* 1:10; 1:20; 1:28; *Blue* 3–4; 7; *HP* 1; 3; 15; 24; *FWD* III; VI–VII; XV–XVII; From "The Bomber's Baedeker" (*Guide to the Economic Importance of German Towns and Cities, 1944*).

Remenzel, Dr., Sylvia, and Eli. *In the short story "The Lie," reprinted in* Welcome to the Monkey House (1968), *Dr. Remenzel, his wife, Sylvia, and their thirteen-year-old son, Eli, travel to Whitehill School for Boys, a private preparatory school in North Marston, Massachusetts. The lie concerns Eli's deception about his failure to pass the entrance examinations for the elite boarding school. When the rejection letter arrives, he snatches it from the mail.*

Dr. Remenzel, a member of the class of 1939, is also a member of the school's Board of Overseers. Since the eighteenth century, generations of Remenzels have attended Whitehill. While traveling in their chauffeured limousine to campus, Dr. Remenzel reviews plans for the latest family donation, the Eli Remenzel Memorial Dormitory, named in honor of his great-great-grandfather. Dr. Remenzel was a massive, dignified man, a physician, a healer for healing's sake, since he had been born as rich as the Shah of Iran. Despite his dignity, when Dr. Remenzel learns of his son's deceit, he focuses on getting the other Board members to overrule the entrance exam requirements for his son. When young Eli learns of his father's humiliating act of asking for a special favor, he senses how he has shamed his father. Rather than being upset by his son's own lie, Dr. Remenzel leaves the campus in disgrace for his own behavior.

Old Eli funded the school's Scholarship Fund in

1799 by donating forty acres in Boston. The Scholarship Fund enabled boys to attend who were academically gifted but from economically disadvantaged families. Among the many Remenzel gifts were the Sanford Remenzel Bird Sanctuary and the George MacLellan Remenzel Skating Rink.

"Report on the Barnhouse Effect" (1950) (*see* **Professor Arthur Barnhouse** *and* **dynamo-psychism**).

Rettig, John (1858–1932). *The Cincinnati native was one of the expatriate artists working in Europe prior to World War I. In Deadeye Dick, Otto Waltz purchases Rettig's "Crucifixion in Rome," around 1913 while touring Volendam, Holland (though the painting is signed and dated 1888).*

The Waltzes are forced to sell it along with most of their other treasures when George Metzger sues them for his wife's wrongful death. Representatives from the Cincinnati Art Museum make their way to Midland City just to purchase the painting by their native son. (DD 21) "Crucifixion in Rome" is indeed set in Rome, which I have never seen. I know enough, though, to recognize that it is chock-a-block with architectural anachronisms. The Colosseum, for example, is in perfect repair, but there is also the spire of a Christian church, and some architectural details and monuments which appear to be more recent, even, than the Renaissance, maybe even nineteenth century. There are sixty-eight tiny but distinct human figures taking part in some sort of celebration amid all this architecture and sculpture. Felix and I counted them one time, when we were young. Hundreds more are implied by impressionistic smears and dots. Banners fly. Walls are festooned with ropes of leaves. What fun.

Only if you look closely at the painting will you realize that two of the sixty-eight figures are not having such a good time. They are in the lower left-hand corner, and are harmonious with the rest of the composition, but they have in fact just been hung from crosses.

The picture is a comment, I suppose, but certainly a bland one, on man's festive inhumanity to men—even into what to **John Rettig** were modern times.

Reyes, Colonel Guillermo. *The Peruvian pilot in* Galápagos *who fires the first shot in the war between Peru and Ecuador, blowing up the radar dish atop the control tower at Guayaquil International Airport.*

Rice, Ella and Irwin. *In the short story "Hal Irwin's Magic Lamp," collected in* Bagombo Snuff Box *(1999), the title character hires Ella to play the jinni in his elaborate scheme (albeit a little too close to mimicking a minstrel show) to reveal to his wife the much improved life they are about to lead due to his success at shorting stocks.*

Ella is otherwise employed as a domestic by an unnamed friend of Hal's. Pure-hearted Mary Irwin lets the obviously pregnant Ella into her home and rather than treating her as an employee (the cook Hal promised to provide), she engages her in deep conversation and eventually becomes a motherly figure to Ella, sadly and ironically so. **Ella** wasn't married. The father of her child had beaten her up when he found out she was pregnant, and then taken off for parts unknown. She had aches and pains in many places, and no relatives, and didn't know how much longer she could do housework. She repeated what she had told Hal, that her pregnancy still had six weeks to go, she thought. Mary said she wished she could have a baby, but couldn't. That didn't help.

Ella is so grateful for all the kindness bestowed on her that she christens her son Irwin Rice. However, after Hal loses everything in the Wall Street crash of 1929 and throws himself out his seventh-floor office window, Mary and Ella are left penniless and homeless. In a rather touching goodbye without any words passing between them, Vonnegut has the two ladies take refuge with the only remaining family or charitable souls they could find. Mary had another house to go to which was her widowed father's farm outside the town of Crawfordsville. The only place **Ella Rice** could think of to go with her baby was the black church where the baby had been baptized. Mary went there with them. A lot of mothers with babies or children, and old people, and cripples, and even perfectly healthy young people were sleeping there. There was food. Mary didn't ask where it came from. That was the last Mary would see of **Ella** and **Irwin Rice**. **Ella** was eating, and then she would nurse the baby.

Rice, Major Allen. *The veteran flyer specifically chosen to face the rigorous demands of Project Cyclops because of his skill and personal situation.* (BAG Thanasphere) Psychiatrists had picked **Major Rice** from a hundred volunteers, and predicted that he would function as perfectly as the rocket motors, the metal hull, and the electronic controls. His specifications: Husky, twenty-nine years of age, fifty-five missions over Europe during the Second World War without a sign of fatigue, a childless widower, melancholy and solitary, a career soldier, a demon for work.

The **Major**'s mission? Simple: To report weather conditions over enemy territory, and to observe the accuracy of guided atomic missiles in the event of war.

The major eventually hears the voices of the disembodied spirits congregating beyond the stratosphere. His ground controllers, Dr. Groszinger and Lieutenant General Dane, first believe he is losing his mind. He is later proven correct about the voices and has further contact with his own lost wife, Margaret. Speculation ensues about whether or not Rice will safely land his rocket ship when his mission is brought to an end. In fact, his ship crashes into the ocean and no survivors are found, according to the crew of the British luxury liner Capricorn, *sailing 280 miles from New York City and heading for Liverpool.*

"A Rift Between Friends in the War of Ideas." *One of the many publications sent to Stewart Buntline by attorney Reed McAllister, who had forever feared his client might relapse into the socialist thinking he demonstrated when just a teenager. The pamphlet* was supposedly a letter from a conservative to close friends who were socialists without knowing it. Because he did not need to, Stewart had not read what the pamphlet had to say about the recipients of social security and other forms of welfare (GBR 10).

Riley, James Whitcomb (*also* **the Hoosier Poet**). *"The Hoosier Poet" is frequently mentioned as part of Vonnegut's litany of notable Indianans.*

Vonnegut mentions that his mother knew Riley (JB *Prologue), and that his first mother-in-law, Riah Fagan Cox, his sister, and his parents are all buried in the same cemetery as Riley, Crown Hill Cemetery in Indianapolis. When Vonnegut's family lost much of its wealth during the Great Depression, he was sent to Public School 43, "the James Whitcomb Riley School"* (PS 2). *Hoosier Ambassador and Mrs. Minton in* Cat's Cradle *are proud to claim Riley as well.*

Despite Riley's alcoholism, he was a much sought after public speaker who read from his voluminous catalogue of principally children's poetry full of high sentiments and humor. As Vonnegut notes, **James Whitcomb Riley**, *"the Hoosier Poet," was the highest-paid American writer of his time, 1849 to 1916, because he recited his poetry for money in theaters and lecture halls. That was how delighted by poetry ordinary Americans used to be. Can you imagine?* (ARM Clowe's Hall)

Riley's two most famous poems include "Little Orphant Annie" and "The Raggedy Man." The former was originally named "The Elf Child," but he intended to change the title to "Little Orphant Allie" for a subsequent printing. His inspiration for the poem was Mary Alice "Allie" Smith, a twelve-year-old Civil War orphan from Greenfield, Indiana, who was taken in by the Rileys. However, the printer erred, and Riley was left with "Little Orphant Annie."

The odd spelling of "orphaned" may be attributable to the fact that Riley was twenty when he finally finished the eighth grade, or it may reflect a regional dialect familiar from Vonnegut's youth. Though this may have indicated real literacy problems for one becoming a writer, his ear for the language spoken in Indiana is meticulously transcribed within his work. Writing in the vernacular of his home state endeared him to the people because they heard their own voices in his work. "Little Orphant Annie" inspired the character we know today as Little Orphan Annie. The character famously appears in all media formats from cartoons, radio, and television to movies.

Riley's poem "The Raggedy Man" eventually morphed into Raggedy Ann, the iconic doll still with us today, the creation of the Indiana artist Johnny Gruelle. So beloved by Indiana is Riley for his representation of their voice and concerns, which he helped spread across the country, that the children's poet was honored with the naming of the James Whitcomb Riley Hospital for Children.

Riley is also the namesake of Indianapolis Public School 43, the James Whitcomb Riley School. When Vonnegut's family lost so much of their wealth in the Great Depression, young Kurt was taken out of private school and became the first in his family to attend public school, specifically Public School 43. In Vonnegut's work, Riley is chiefly mentioned for either the public school named in his honor or for the fact that his grave rests at the highest part of Crown Point Cemetery, famous for its most infamous occupant, the gangster John Dillinger. (JB 1) Dillinger was the Robin Hood of my early youth. He is buried near my parents—and near my sister Alice, who admired him even more than I did—in Crown Hill Cemetery in Indianapolis. Also in there, on the top of Crown Hill, the highest point in the city, is **James Whitcomb Riley, "The Hoosier Poet."** When my mother was little, she knew **Riley** well.

Vonnegut's parents have their wedding reception in a facility named for the Hoosier Poet as recalled by John Rauch in his history of the family. (PS Roots) "In 1913 the Claypool Hotel, situated on the northwest corner of Washington Street and Illinois Street in the very heart of the city of Indianapolis, was one of the finest hostelries in the Midwest. . . . The mezzanine story had a huge ballroom about 125 feet by 80 feet. This later was named the **Riley** Room after the Hoosier poet—**James Whitcomb Riley**. On the Illinois Street side of the mezzanine floor were a series of private dining rooms decorated in red and gold in Louis XV rococo. The proprietor of this garish caravansary was Henry Lawrence. He and Albert Lieber were buddies. And so Albert decided to throw the wedding celebration party for Edith and Kurt in the Claypool. Henry Lawrence decided to give his all—and did so."

Laid to rest among the local luminaries in Crown Hill Cemetery is Vonnegut's first mother-in-law. His description of her in Palm Sunday *locates her last repose and expresses profound affection for a woman who earned her place in that hallowed ground.* (PS Obscenity) Riah Fagan Cox was a gallant and pretty little woman from Columbia City, Indiana, which is in the northeast corner of the state, about halfway between Fort Wayne and Winona Lake. She was born into a so-called "good family," but her father was an alcoholic. He could not hold a job.

So, although little more than a child, Riah set out to rescue herself and her brother and eventually their descendants from want and obscurity. She sent herself to the University of Wisconsin, and took a master's degree in the classics. Her thesis was a high school textbook on the Latin and Greek roots of common words in English. It was adopted by many school systems all over the country, and earned enough money to enable Riah to put her brother through medical school. He set up practice in Hollywood, and became the beloved obstetrician of many famous movie stars.

She married a lawyer in Indianapolis who did not make much money. She took jobs teaching Latin and Greek and English, and became the Indianapolis representative for touring lecturers and musicians. She also sold silly, witty short stories to magazines from time to time. Thus was she able to send her son and daughter to the best private schools, even during the Great Depression. Her daughter became a Phi Beta Kappa at Swarthmore.

She died three years ago, and is buried in Crown Hill Cemetery in Indianapolis, somewhere between John Dillinger, the bank robber, and **James Whitcomb Riley, the "Hoosier Poet."** I liked her a lot. She was a good friend of mine. She was my first mother-in-law.

Referencing Crown Hill Cemetery compels Vonnegut to navigate the terrain by orienting readers away from thinking this is some out of the way place, lost among countless countryside cemeteries with little reason to care for its history. Whenever a family member or friend is referred to in terms of their final resting place, Vonnegut points to the two stars of the neighborhood. (TQ 10) Allie died in New Jersey. She and her husband, Jim, also a native Hoosier, are buried whole in Crown Hill Cemetery in Indianapolis. So is **James Whitcomb Riley, the Hoosier Poet**, a never-married lush. So is John Dillinger, the beloved bank robber of the 1930s. So are our parents, Kurt and Edith, and Father's kid brother Alex Vonnegut, the Harvard-educated life insurance salesman who said, whenever life was good, "If this isn't nice, what is?" So are two previous generations of our parents' forebears: a brewer, an architect, merchants and musicians, and their wives, of course.

Full house!

When contemplating his brother Bernie's eventual resting place, the stream of Indiana pride flows but the resting place good enough for all other Hoosiers mentioned by Vonnegut is not quite as grand as his brother's accomplishments deserve. Crown Hill, despite its notable occupants and its geographical focal point marking the grave of James Whitcomb Riley, the Hoosier Poet noted for writing in his midwestern vernacular, is simply too local, too pedestrian for his brother's status as a man with more worldly accomplishments. (TQ 9) Bernie still feels fine.

It is much too early to talk about, but when he dies, God forbid, I don't think his ashes should be put in Crown Hill Cemetery with **James Whitcomb Riley** and John Dillinger, who belonged only to Indiana. Bernie belongs to the World.

Bernie's ashes should be scattered over the dome of a towering thunderhead.

When considering the modest place Riley holds in the world of literature, Vonnegut uses him in a sort of sublime-to-the-ridiculous analogy about the relative and real importance of careers in arts versus the sciences. (BAG Coda to My Career) Participation in an art is not simply one of many possible ways to make a living, an obsolescent trade as we approach the year 2000. Participation in an art, at bottom, has nothing to do with earning money. Participation in an art, although unrewarded by wealth or fame, and as the Middle West has encouraged so many of its young to discover for themselves so far, is a way to make one's soul grow.

No artist from anywhere, however, not even Shakespeare, not even Beethoven, not even **James Whitcomb Riley**, has changed the course of so many lives all over the planet as have four hayseeds in Ohio, two in Dayton and two in Akron. How I wish Dayton and Akron were in Indiana! Ohio could have Kokomo and Gary.

Orville and Wilbur Wright were in Dayton in 1903 when they invented the airplane.
See also: CC 42; PS Roots; FWD X; BAG Coda to My Career; MWC 7; ARM Clowe's Hall.

Ritter, Pamela and Harvey. In the short story "Thanasphere," collected in Bagombo Snuff Box (1999), Pamela is the departed wife whose final wishes include having her husband marry again for the sake of the children. Her wishes are made known to Major Rice in his space capsule out among other lost souls in the area soon to be known as the Thanasphere. She did not die under mysterious conditions or criminal conditions. Harvey is a GE engineer and a widower with two children, as reported by R. B. Failey, chief of police in Scotia, New York.

Rivera, Jerry Cha-cha. The first husband of Walter Starbuck, Jr.'s, wife, herself a black nightclub singer. Together they had two children, later adopted by Starbuck, who had since changed his name to Stankiewicz. (JB 2) The former nightclub comedian of Puerto Rican extraction named **Jerry Cha-cha Rivera** . . . was shot as an innocent bystander during the robbery of a RAMJAC carwash in Hollywood.

Rivera, Wanda Chipmunk-5. The intoxicated slave who, at the close of Slapstick, kicks over the Dresden candlestick brought by Melody to her grandfather, Wilbur Swain, also known as the King of Candlesticks. The event occurs on his final birthday. (Slap Epilogue) Melody's candlestick depicted a nobleman's flirtation with a shepherdess at the foot of a treetrunk enlaced in flowering vines.

Rivers, Jerry (see also **Kilgore's Creed**). There are two distinct uses of this name. The first is the Mickey Rooney look-alike boyfriend of Sally Cathcart. He is the student body president of Sweetbread College, in the play The Chemistry Professor reprinted in Palm Sunday. He suggests holding a Broadway musical to raise funds for the bankrupt college. He is the stepson of Fred Leghorn, though he is getting a divorce from Jerry's mother.

The second use of this character's name has no apparent connection to Vonnegut's first use of the character, but this Rivers is also optimistic and tries to deliver Kilgore's Creed to the greatest possible audience. In Timequake, chauffeur Jerry Rivers delivers Zoltan Pepper in his armored limousine to the American Academy of Arts and Letters moments before the timequake ends. Free will kicks in just as Rivers assists Zoltan Pepper in his wheelchair at the front door of the academy. Pepper waits for Rivers as he moves the limo down the street, some fifty yards from the Hudson River.

Moving the limo from the curb outside the Academy meant that Pepper would be killed by the careening firetruck the moment linear time resumes. Moving the limo also meant that Kilgore Trout and Dudley Prince would finally meet when the wall between the Academy and the Museum of the American Indian would be smashed through by the firetruck. In the wake of free will's resumption, It was **Jerry Rivers**, the chauffeur of the Peppers' stretch limousine, however, who steered his dreamboat around wrecked vehicles and their victims, often driving on sidewalks, to reach the studios of the Columbia Broadcasting System down on West 52nd Street. **Rivers** awakened the staff there with, "You were sick, but now you're well again, and there's work to do." And then he got them to broadcast that same message on both radio and TV from coast to coast.

In order to get them to do that, though, he had to tell them a lie. He said everybody was recovering from a nerve gas attack by persons unknown. So the first version of Kilgore's Creed to reach millions in the nation, and then billions in the world, was this: "This is a CBS exclusive! There has been a nerve gas attack by persons unknown. You were sick, but now you're well again, and there's work to do. Make sure all children and senior citizens are safe indoors"*(TQ 53). On March 1, 2001, a few weeks after the resumption of the timeline, Rivers chauffeurs Monica Pepper and Dudley Prince to the clambake. See also: TQ 208.*

Robbins, Eldon. *The ex-con who served time at the Shepherdstown Adult Correctional Institution and is now a dishwasher at the Midland City Holiday Inn. He finds Wayne Hoobler scavenging around the garbage cans and brings him into the kitchen for a steak dinner. Robbins is wearing a "Support the Arts" button and gives one to Wayne with the warning,* "Wear this at all times . . . and no harm can come to you" *(BC 19).*

Robert, Henry Martyn (also ***Robert's Rules of Order***). *In* Slapstick, *when Wilbur Swain attends an extended-family meeting, he applauds the efforts of Henry Martyn Robert (1837–1923), the West Point graduate and Civil War general who authored* Robert's Rules of Order *(1876). General Robert also*

designed the defenses around Washington, D.C., during the Civil War. Swain views Robert's Rules as one of the four great inventions by Americans, the other three being the Bill of Rights, Alcoholics Anonymous, and the concept of artificially extended families that he developed with his twin sister, Eliza.

The Robo-Magic Corporation. *In* Breakfast of Champions, *Fred T. Barry's company started advertising his new fully automatic washing machines in 1933 under the motto "Goodbye Blue Monday"— also the subtitle of the novel. Full production of the machines did not begin until 1934.*

During World War II, the company stopped producing washing machines and became the Midland City Ordnance Company. The main mechanism of the washer became the central component in the "BLINC System" (Blast Interval Normalization Computer), a bomb release mechanism for heavy bombers. The company's emblem was a Greek goddess reclining on an ornate chaise lounge and holding a pennant with the company's motto.

In Hocus Pocus, *Eugene Debs Hartke's father is sent to Robo-Magic by Du Pont to determine how to use plastics technology to lighten military products. Mr. Hartke became the Vice-President in Charge of Research and Development for Barrytron, Ltd., the successor to Robo-Magic.*

The corporate genealogy of Fred T. Barry is as follows: In Breakfast of Champions, *Robo-Magic Corporation of America later became the Midland City Ordnance Company and then Barrytron, Limited. In* Hocus Pocus, *Barrytron, Limited is eventually purchased by E. I. Du Pont de Nemours & Company.*

Rockefeller, Alice (see **Alexander Hamilton McCone**).

Rockefeller, Geraldine Ames (see **Geraldine Ames Rockefeller Rosewater**).

Rockmell, Dr. Eli W. *The pseudonym used by Wilbur Swain to publish the childrearing manual he wrote with his sister Eliza. The pseudonym is "a garbling" of their two names: Wilbur Rockefeller Swain and Eliza Mellon Swain. They wrote the manuscript of* The Cry of the Nocturnal Goatsucker *by Betty* *and Bobby Brown, during one of their heads-together telepathic frenzies. When published under the Rockmell pseudonym, the publisher retitles it* So You Went and Had a Baby.

Roethke, Theodore. *Vonnegut mentions taking two books to read on the flight back to Dresden. One is Erika Ostrovsky's* Céline and His Vision, *and the other is Roethke's* Words for the Wind, *from which he quotes, "I wake to sleep, and take my waking slow. / I feel my fate in what I cannot fear. / I learn by going where I have to go" (SL5 1).*

Roosevelt, Claudia. *In* Hocus Pocus, *Lowell Chung's girlfriend, an equestrian star, from whom he borrows a horse in order to teach Eugene Debs Hartke how to ride. Claudia is a mathematical whiz who lacks personality.*

Roosevelt, Eleanor. *In* Deadeye Dick, *Mrs. Roosevelt goes on a morale-boosting visit to the Green Diamond Plow facility, a Midland City tank manufacturer during World War II. The first lady is given the usual tour and luncheon at Otto Waltz's home studio provided for all visiting dignitaries to the city. Mrs. Roosevelt's visit is brief and sandwiched between historic moments for the town. She arrives the morning Felix is scheduled to depart for military service and leaves hours before Rudy's fateful shot kills the pregnant Eloise Metzger.*

Roseberry, Dr. Harold. *In* Player Piano, *the Cornell football coach who relishes the opportunity to ruin the life of Cornell alumnus Dr. Ewing J. Halyard. Halyard somehow graduated without completing the physical education requirement. Five years before the opening of the text, Halyard wrote a scathing letter to Cornell's president complaining about the behavior of the football team when on a road trip. Roseberry took the letter from his files in preparation for meeting Halyard.*

Rosenau, Dr. Maurice. *There are two Dr. Rosenaus in Vonnegut's early novels. In* Player Piano, *Dr. Rosenau is a lubrication engineer at the Ilium Works. In* The Sirens of Titan, *Dr. Maurice Rosenau is one of Winston Niles Rumford's great detractors*

and has written Pan-Galactic Humbug *(subtitled* Three Billion Dupes) *to establish his position.*

Rosenfeld, Franklin Delano. *This is how Howard Campbell refers to President Roosevelt during his pro-Nazi, anti-Semitic broadcasts in* Mother Night. *Roosevelt was one of the three individuals who knew Campbell's true mission as an American agent.*

Rosenquist, Per Olaf. *In* Galápagos, *the Swedish shipyard foreman who dies of a defective heart, prompting Hjalmar Arvid Boström to recite a bit of black humor which becomes Leon Trout's refrain when recording the deaths of various characters.* (Gal 2:6) *Oh, well—he wasn't going to write Beethoven's Ninth Symphony anyway.*

Rosewater, Abraham. *The grandfather of Fred Rosewater, son of Faith Merrihue and General George Rosewater who became a Congregationalist minister.* **Abraham** went as a missionary to the Congo, where he met and married Lavinia Waters, the daughter of another missionary, an Illinois Baptist.

In the jungle, **Abraham** begat Merrihue. Lavinia died at Merrihue's birth. Little Merrihue was nursed on the milk of a Bantu.

And **Abraham** and little Merrihue returned to Rhode Island. **Abraham** accepted the call to the Congregationalist pulpit in the little fishing village of Pisquontuit (GBR 7).

Rosewater, Caroline. *The wife of Fred Rosewater and mother of Franklin, the Rhode Island cousins of Eliot Rosewater. Her best friend is Amanita Buntline who treats her like her own poorer relation. Her existence is one of bland futility.* (GBR 9) She was a pretty, pinched, skinny, lost little woman, all dolled-up in well-made clothes cast off by her wealthy, Lesbian friend, Amanita Buntline. **Caroline Rosewater** clinked and flashed with accessories. Their purpose was to make the second-hand clothing distinctly her own. . . .

When she spoke to Fred, with Harry Pena watching, she behaved like a woman who was keeping her dignity while being frog-walked. With the avid help of Amanita, she pitied herself for being married to a man who was so poor and dull. That she was exactly as poor and dull as Fred was a possibility she was constitutionally unable to entertain. For one thing, she was a Phi Beta Kappa, having won her key as a philosophy major at Dillon University, in Dodge City, Kansas. That was where she and Fred had met, in Dodge City, in a U.S.O. Fred had been stationed at Fort Riley during the Korean War. She married Fred because she thought everybody who lived in Pisquontuit and had been to Princeton was rich.

She was humiliated to discover that it was not true. She honestly believed that she was an intellectual, but she knew almost nothing, and every problem she ever considered could be solved by just one thing: money, and lots of it. She was a frightful housekeeper. She cried when she did housework, because she was convinced that she was cut out for better things.

As for the Lesbian business, it wasn't particularly deep on **Caroline**'s part. She was simply a female chameleon trying to get ahead in the world.

Rosewater, Eliot. *The enigmatic alcoholic and obese title character who prods science fiction writers out of their disrepute by urging their continued efforts to consider the really great challenges in life, including economic challenges. While on a drunken binge in 1953, Eliot crashes a science fiction writers conference in Milford, Pennsylvania, and extemporaneously admonishes the crowd.* (GBR 2) "I love you sons of bitches," **Eliot** said in Milford. "You're all I read any more. You're the only ones who'll talk about the *really* terrific changes going on, the only ones crazy enough to know that life is a space voyage, and not a short one, either, but one that'll last for billions of years. You're the only ones with guts enough to *really* care about the future, who *really* notice what machines do to us, what wars do to us, what cities do to us, what big, simple ideas do to us, what tremendous misunderstandings, mistakes, accidents and catastrophes do to us. You're the only ones zany enough to agonize over time and distances without limit, over mysteries that will never die. . . .

"I leave it to you, friends and neighbors, and especially to the immortal Kilgore Trout: think about the silly ways money gets passed around now, and then think up better ways."

Eliot becomes the target of Norman Mushari, the venal young lawyer already aware of the silly ways money gets passed around. Mushari seeks to have Eliot declared insane and have the courts declare Fred Rosewater president of the Rosewater Foundation. The legal fees for such a transaction drive Mushari's dreams.

As President of the Rosewater Foundation, Eliot spends $14 million from 1947 to 1953 on numerous public service projects and fine art donations, but he feels detached from the lives of ordinary people. This is due to a number of factors. His parents insulated themselves from the rest of society by traveling only in the rarefied circles of the wealthy and politically influential on the East Coast, despite the fact their ancestral hometown was the poverty-stricken area known as Rosewater County, Indiana. The family returned there each year to keep their legal residency, a political necessity for Senator Lister Ames Rosewater. During those brief visits, Eliot serves as the mascot of the volunteer fire department, sparking a lifelong love for those who selflessly and without reward care for their neighbors.

When only nineteen, Eliot unintentionally commits matricide. While sailing with his mother in Cotuit Harbor, he swings the boom around and knocks his mother overboard.

Eliot makes another tragic error while serving as a captain in the U.S. Army a few years later. While leading his troops on a raid of a Bavarian clarinet factory supposedly infested with SS troops, Eliot tosses a grenade through a window and leads his men into the smoke-filled structure. (GBR 6) He took a step forward, stumbled over one body, fell on another. They were Germans who had been killed by his grenade. He stood up, found himself face-to-face with a helmeted German in a gas mask.

Eliot, like the good soldier he was, jammed his knee into the man's groin, drove his bayonet into his throat, withdrew the bayonet, smashed the man's jaw with his rifle butt.

And then **Eliot** heard an American sergeant yelling somewhere off to his left. The visibility was apparently a lot better over there, for the sergeant was yelling, "Cease fire! Hold your fire, you guys. Jesus Christ—these aren't soldiers. They're firemen!"

It was true: **Eliot** had killed three unarmed fire-men. They were ordinary villagers, engaged in the brave and uncontroversial business of trying to keep a building from combining with oxygen.

When the medics got the masks off the three **Eliot** had killed, they proved to be two old men and a boy. The boy was the one **Eliot** had bayoneted. He didn't look more than fourteen.

Eliot seemed reasonably well for about ten min-utes after that. And then he calmly lay down in front of a moving truck.

The driver of the truck stops in time, but Eliot suf-fers his first catatonic episode. Through innocent ac-tions, Eliot had killed four people with whom he shared a deep spiritual bond.

His marriage to Sylvia suffers due to bouts with alcohol and depression over not doing enough for the poor. She eventually suffers a breakdown as a re-sult of Samaritrophia, a "hysterical indifference to the troubles of those less fortunate than oneself" *(GBR 4). Eliot's final breakdown in New York comes while attending a performance of* Aïda. *He stands up and yells at the singers to stop singing because it would surely cause them to die sooner in the airtight chamber.*

Eliot leaves the theater and takes off on an alco-holic cross-country trek, moving from one volunteer fire department to the next. Writing from the El-sinore, California, volunteer fire department, Eliot feels he found an apt literary analogy for himself— Hamlet. *(GBR 3)* Maybe I flatter myself when I think that I have things in common with Hamlet, that I have an important mission, that I'm tempo-rarily mixed up about how it should be done. Ham-let had one big edge on me. His father's ghost told him exactly what he had to do, while I am operat-ing without instructions. But from somewhere something is trying to tell me where to go, what to do there, and why to do it. Don't worry, I don't hear voices. But there is this feeling that I have a destiny far away from the shallow and preposterous posing that is our life in New York. And I roam.

And I roam.

Eliot eventually finds himself in Rosewater, Indi-ana, where he sets up new Foundation offices above the volunteer fire department. There he dispenses money in accordance with the citizens' needs, pro-vided they ask, and records his charitable transac-tions in his Domesday Book. *At the back of the ledger is his novel-in-progress about resurrection. Eliot becomes a spiritual solace to the community, exemplified by his being asked to perform the bap-tism for Mary Moody's twins.*

All the while, however, his guilt over driving Syl-via from his life and the legal pursuits of Norman Mushari keep closing upon him. Senator Rosewa-ter's scheme to ward off Mushari includes Eliot trav-eling to Indianapolis for a reconciliation meeting with Sylvia. Eliot reads Kilgore Trout's Pan-Galactic Three-Day Pass *while on the bus, and as he reaches the outskirts of Indianapolis (Vonnegut's hometown) Eliot looks up and imagines the city consumed by firestorm.*

This episode is followed by a one-year gap in the narrative, during which time Mushari has pressed ahead with the court challenge. Dressed in tennis whites, Eliot snaps out of his trance on the tennis courts of Dr. Brown's sanitarium while surrounded by the doctor, Senator Rosewater, and Kilgore Trout. It is left to Trout to explain the sanity of Eliot's life and times in Rosewater County. (GBR 14) "It seems to me," said Trout, "that the main lesson **Eliot** learned is that people can use all the uncritical love they can get."

"This is *news?*" the Senator raucously inquired.

"It's news that a man was able to *give* that kind of love over a long period of time. If one man can do it, perhaps others can do it, too. It means that our hatred of useless human beings and the cruelties we inflict upon them for their own good need not be parts of human nature. Thanks to the example of **Eliot Rosewater**, millions upon millions of peo-ple may learn to love and help whomever they see."

Trout glanced from face to face before speaking his last word on the subject. The last word was: "Joy."

Eliot settles with Fred Rosewater for $100,000, cutting Mushari out of his contingency fee, and de-clares all fifty-seven participants in Mushari's false paternity suits to be his offspring. Though a lie, it eliminates Mushari from profit. Moreover, it is per-haps Eliot's single greatest experiment with redistrib-uting wealth, the very subject he asked the science fiction writers to consider.

Eliot Rosewater also appears in Slaughterhouse-Five. *He shares a Lake Placid Veterans Hospital* room with Billy Pilgrim, who suffers a mental break-down while attending the Ilium School of Optometry. Rosewater was there for alcoholism treatment. Eliot coaxes Billy back from his silence by talking about the science fiction stories of Kilgore Trout. Rosewater has a tremendous stack of Trout's books beneath his bed and lets Billy read all he wants. Billy eventually becomes an enormous fan of Trout's, as well.

Rosewater, Eunice Eliot Morgan. The wife of Senator Lister Ames Rosewater and mother of Eliot. The following information is from a letter Eliot writes to be opened after his death. (GBR 1) As a curious footnote to history, **Eunice** became Woman's Chess Champion of the United States in 1927, and again in 1933.

Eunice also wrote an historical novel about a female gladiator, *Ramba of Macedon*, which was a best-seller in 1936. **Eunice** died in 1937, in a sailing accident in Cotuit, Massachusetts. She was a wise and amusing person, with very sincere anxieties about the condition of the poor. She was my mother.

A *later description of Eunice's death concludes:* The statement that Eliot had killed his beloved mother was, in a crude way, true. When he was nineteen, he took his mother for a sail in Cotuit Harbor. He jibed. The slashing boom knocked his mother overboard. **Eunice Morgan Rosewater** sank like a stone (GBR 2).

Rosewater, Franklin. The young son of Fred and Caroline Rosewater in God Bless You, Mr. Rosewater. He purchases a pornographic photograph from Lila Buntline and prevents his father from committing suicide by calling down the basement stairs that Norman Mushari wants to speak with him. Mushari sees Franklin as his opportunity for a chance at forcing a change in stewardship of the Rosewater Foundation and collecting heavy fees for his services.

Rosewater, Fred. The Rhode Island cousin of Eliot Rosewater who is manipulated by Norman Mushari in an attempt to transfer control of the Rosewater Foundation. Though Fred is a Princeton graduate, he makes a meager living selling insurance policies to the working class of Pisquontuit. Despondent over

his poor lot in life, Fred frequently contemplates suicide. He comes within a moment of hanging himself in his basement when Norman Mushari comes knocking at his door.

Fred had been reading the history of his ancestors as chronicled by his father, Merrihue Rosewater. He is elated to find out about their illustrious beginnings in England but crestfallen to find the rest of the history had been eaten by worms.

Fred likes to think that his purpose in life as an insurance salesman is to make sure the survivors of the insured have secure financial futures. His customers understand the underlying irony of the situation. (GBR 8) The workmen had an uneasy respect for **Fred**. They tried to be cynical about what he sold, but they knew in their hearts that he was offering the only get-rich-quick scheme that was open to them: to insure themselves and die soon. And it was **Fred**'s gloomy secret that without such people, tantalized by such a proposition, he would not have a dime.

Fred often thinks about the value of his own death: $42,000. Both Fred and Eliot enjoy the moment when others turn to them and say, "God bless you, Mr. Rosewater." Fred hears it from the survivors who benefit from his policies, and Eliot hears it from the people in Rosewater County who enjoy his charity.

Fred is the son of a suicide. His father shot himself in the head. His wife Caroline maintains an odd friendship with the lesbian Amanita Buntline. Though the ladies don't have a sexual relationship, Caroline wears Amanita's secondhand clothes. Fred and Caroline met when he was stationed at Fort Riley during the Korean War and she was a student at Dillon University. She married him thinking people from Pisquontuit were all rich. Their son Franklin buys pornographic pictures from Lila Buntline.

In order for Eliot to prevent Norman Mushari from succeeding in his plans to transfer control of the foundation to Fred, he gives Fred a check for $1 million, thus preventing Mushari from profiting. Fred never was an active participant in the scheme to uproot the foundation.

Rosewater, George. The younger brother of Noah, George trustingly signs away his share of the family business while going off to serve the Union during *the Civil War, fully expecting Noah to return his half upon safely returning from the war. He raises a company of riflemen from Rosewater County and joins forces with the Black Hat Brigade. He suffers a number of crippling wounds but in all respects was an exemplary and brave soldier.* (GBR 8) By the time of Antietam, **George Rosewater** had become a Lieutenant Colonel, and had, curiously, lost the little fingers from both hands. At Antietam, he had his horse shot out from under him, advanced on foot, grabbed the regimental colors from a dying boy, found himself holding only a shattered staff when [a] Confederate cannister carried the colors away. He pressed on, killed a man with the staff. At the moment he was doing the killing, one of his own men fired off a musket that still had its ramrod jammed down the bore. The explosion blinded **Colonel Rosewater** for life.

He returns home a blind brevet brigadier general without any rights in the family business. Noah is constantly busy in Washington. George refuses to take any legal action to reclaim his share of their enterprise. He chooses instead to make formal calls on all the families who trusted their sons to his rifle company, and then he goes to his brother's new mansion and One morning the workmen found the brigadier's uniform nailed to the front door as though it were an animal skin nailed to a barn door to dry (GBR 8).

He travels to Providence, Rhode Island, seeking work at the Buntline Broom factory, which had a reputation for employing disabled Civil War veterans. Castor Buntline hires General Rosewater and names the whiskbrooms after him. (GBR 8) A "**General Rosewater**" was a *whiskbroom*.

Fourteen-year-old Faith Merrihue is assigned to the general as "his eyes and messenger." They later marry and have Abraham, who eventually takes a pulpit position in Pisquontuit, Rhode Island. General Rosewater is the great-grandfather of insurance salesman Fred Rosewater.

Rosewater, Geraldine Ames Rockefeller. *The wife of Samuel Rosewater and mother of Lister Ames Rosewater, in* God Bless You, Mr. Rosewater.

Rosewater, Merrihue. *Born in the Congo to missionaries Abraham Rosewater and Lavinia Waters,*

Merrihue becomes a real estate agent in Pisquontuit, Rhode Island. (GBR 8) **Merrihue**, the Parson's son, became a realtor, divided his father's land into lots. He married Cynthia Niles Rumford, a minor heiress, invested much of her money in pavement and streetlights and sewers. He made a fortune, lost it, and his wife's fortune, too, in the crash of 1929.

He blew his brains out.

But, before he did that, he wrote a family history and he begat poor Fred, the insurance man. *The title of Merrihue's family chronicle is* A History of the Rosewaters of Rhode Island. *Fred's discovery of the family history leads him to decide not to commit suicide.*

Rosewater, Noah. *Together with his brother George, Noah inherits six hundred fertile acres of Indiana farmland and a saw factory. When the Civil War starts, George raises a rifle company while Noah buys his way out by hiring Fletcher Moon to take his place. Noah persuades George to give him control of the company while he was off at the war. By marrying the notoriously ugly Cleota Herrick (she possessed $400,000), he expanded the factory and bought more farms, all in Rosewater County. He* became the largest individual hog farmer in the North. And, in order not to be victimized by meat packers, he bought controlling interest in an Indianapolis slaughterhouse. In order not to be victimized by steel suppliers, he bought controlling interest in a steel company in Pittsburgh. In order not to be victimized by coal suppliers, he bought controlling interest in several mines. In order not to be victimized by money lenders, he founded a bank (GBR 1).

When his brother returns from the war—a penniless, disabled, blind general—Noah's representatives explain to George he no longer has a share in the family enterprise. Noah is in Washington at the time, which became the center of the family business.

Noah's son Samuel became powerful in Republican Party politics, and his grandson is Senator Lister Ames Rosewater. Great-grandson Eliot becomes the undoing of the great family fortune.

Rosewater, Samuel. *The son of Noah Rosewater, husband of Geraldine Ames Rockefeller, and father of Lister Ames Rosewater. He advances the family's* standing in Republican Party politics and expands the family's influence and wealth by purchasing newspapers. (GBR 1) And **Samuel** bought newspapers, and preachers, too. He gave them this simple lesson to teach, and they taught it well: *Anybody who thought that the United States of America was supposed to be a Utopia was a piggy, lazy, God-damned fool [italics in original].* **Samuel** thundered that no American factory hand was worth more than eighty cents a day. And yet he could be thankful for the opportunity to pay a hundred thousand dollars or more for a painting by an Italian three centuries dead. And he capped this insult by giving paintings to museums for the spiritual elevation of the poor. The museums were closed on Sundays.

Samuel constructs the Samuel Rosewater Veterans' Memorial Park, honoring the memory of local veterans.

Rosewater, Senator Lister Ames. *The father of Eliot, U.S. Senator Rosewater presides over the fourteenth largest family fortune in the United States and creates the Rosewater Foundation in order that tax-collectors and other predators not named Rosewater might be prevented from getting their hands on it (GBR 1). Distraught over his son's alcoholism, obesity, childless marriage, and return to Rosewater County, his attempts to reconcile Eliot's marriage to Sylvia go for naught. He is left to call on Kilgore Trout at Eliot's request prior to the sanity hearing that threatens to strip Eliot of the foundation presidency.*

Senator Rosewater's legislative masterpiece is called the Rosewater Law. (GBR 6) It made the publication or possession of obscene materials a Federal offense, carrying penalties up to fifty thousand dollars and ten years in prison, without hope of parole. It was a masterpiece because it actually defined obscenity.

Obscenity, *it said*, is any picture or phonograph record or any written matter calling attention to reproductive organs, bodily discharges, or bodily hair.

Eliot's ministrations to the poor prompt the Senator's fears that his son has become a Communist. Except for a brief stay each election cycle, Senator Rosewater has long since divorced himself from the impoverished county that bears his name.

Rosewater, Sylvia. *Eliot Rosewater's faithful wife, who is eventually diagnosed by Dr. Ed Brown as the first sufferer from Samaritrophia, which he said meant, "hysterical indifference to the troubles of those less fortunate than oneself" (GBR 4).*

(GBR 3) This was a pale and delicate girl, cultivated, wispy. She played the harpsichord, spoke six languages enchantingly. As a child and young woman, she had met many of the greatest men of her time in her parents' home—Picasso, Schweitzer, Hemingway, Toscanini, Churchill, de Gaulle. She had never seen Rosewater County, had no idea what a night-crawler was, did not know that land anywhere could be so deathly flat, that people anywhere could be so deathly dull.

Dr. Brown's treatment made her an uncaring disconnected, almost disembodied individual. As Brown writes, I had blocked the underground rivers that connected her to the Atlantic, Pacific, and Indian Oceans, and made her content with being a splash pool three feet across, four inches deep, chlorinated, and painted blue (GBR 1).

Sylvia resists Senator Rosewater's attempts to have her reconcile with Eliot in the hopes of producing an heir to continue the family legacy. (GBR 5) This was, of course, a medical decision, and a wise one, too. Her second breakdown and recovery had not turned her back into the old **Sylvia** of the early Rosewater County days. It had given her a distinctly new personality, the third since her marriage to Eliot. The core of this third personality was a feeling of worthlessness, of shame at being revolted by the poor and by Eliot's personal hygiene, and a suicidal wish to ignore her revulsions, to get back to Rosewater, to very soon die in a good cause.

So it was with self-conscious, medically-prescribed, superficial opposition to total sacrifice that she said again, "No."

The Rosewater County Clarion Call. *Eliot read back issues of this local newspaper and learned of the imprisoned Noyes Finnerty, star center on the 1933 undefeated basketball team from Noah Rosewater Memorial High School. (GBR 13)* In 1934, Noyes strangled his sixteen-year-old wife for notorious infidelity, went to prison for life. Now he was paroled, thanks to Eliot. He was fifty-one. Eliot found out about his being in prison by accident,

while leafing through old copies of *The Rosewater County Clarion Call*, made it his business to get him paroled.

Rosewater Creek, Rosewater Inter-State Ship Canal. *Part of the circuitous route which Eliot Rosewater is convinced would form no more than a thoroughfare returning him to Rosewater County should he ever try to leave.* (GBR 12) "Mr. Peach . . . if I were to somehow wind up in New York, and start living the highest of all possible lives again, you know what would happen to me? The minute I got near any navigable body of water, a bolt of lightning would knock me into the water, a whale would swallow me up, and the whale would swim down to the Gulf of Mexico and up the Mississippi, up the Ohio, up the Wabash, up the White, up Lost River, up **Rosewater Creek**. And that whale would jump from the creek into the **Rosewater Inter-State Ship Canal**, and it would swim down the canal to this city, and spit me out in the Parthenon. And there I'd be."

The Rosewater Foundation (*also* **The Rosewater Corporation**). *The first line of* God Bless You, Mr. Rosewater *defines the centrality of these two entities to the plot:* A sum of money is a leading character in this tale about people, just as a sum of honey might properly be a leading character in a tale about bees (GBR 1).

The Rosewaters possessed "the fourteenth largest family fortune in America," *so in 1947 Senator Lister Ames Rosewater had the family's law firm McAllister, Robjent, Reed and McGee create a foundation in order that tax-collectors and other predators not named Rosewater might be prevented from getting their hands on it. And the baroque masterpiece of legal folderol that was the charter of the* **Rosewater Foundation** *declared, in effect, that the presidency of the* **Foundation** *was to be inherited in the same manner as the British Crown. It was to be handed down throughout all eternity to the closest and oldest 15 heirs of the* **Foundation**'s *creator, Senator Lister Ames Rosewater of Indiana.*

Siblings of the President were to become officers of the **Foundation** upon reaching the age of twenty-one. All officers were officers for life, unless proved legally insane. They were free to compensate themselves for their services as lavishly as they pleased, but only from the **Foundation**'s income.

As required by law, the charter prohibited the Senator's heirs having anything to do with the management of the **Foundation**'s capital. Caring for the capital became the responsibility of a corporation that was born simultaneously with the **Foundation**. It was called, straightforwardly enough, **The Rosewater Corporation**. Like almost all corporations, it was dedicated to prudence and profit, to balance sheets. Its employees were very well paid. They were cunning and happy and energetic on that account. Their main enterprise was the churning of stocks and bonds of other corporations. A minor activity was the management of a saw factory, a bowling alley, a motel, a bank, a brewery, extensive farms in Rosewater County, Indiana, and some coal mines in northern Kentucky (GBR 1).

The foundation's money became the focus of attention for Norman Mushari, a young attorney at McAllister, Robjent, Reed and McGee. In 1965 he focused on the insanity clause of the foundation's charter to wrest control away from Eliot in favor of Fred Rosewater.

Eliot became the foundation's first president in 1947. Though there weren't any limitations on how the foundation's money could be used, he rented offices in the Empire State Building and proclaimed them the headquarters for all the beautiful, compassionate and scientific things he hoped to do (GBR 2). *The Rosewater Foundation spent $14 million in its first six years by supporting a Detroit birth control clinic, supporting research in cancer, mental illness, race prejudice and police brutality, and purchasing acclaimed artworks.*

After Eliot moves to the family's ancestral home in Rosewater, Indiana, he sets up a new foundation office in an attic atop both a luncheonette and a liquor store, across the street from the new volunteer firehouse built with foundation support. The foundation makes an anonymous gift to the fire department of the loudest alarm in the Western Hemisphere. It was driven by a seven-hundred-horsepower Messerschmitt engine that had a thirty-horsepower electric starter. It had been the main air-raid siren of Berlin during the Second World War. **The Rosewater Foundation** had bought it from the West German government and presented it to the town anonymously (GBR 7).

Eliot keeps a ledger he calls his Domesday Book, *listing all the charitable deeds done on the foundation's behalf while in Rosewater County. All the entries are kept in code.*

Eliot's way of avoiding the upheaval wrought by Mushari's legal maneuvering is to offer Fred Rosewater an out-of-court settlement and accept responsibility for the fifty-seven paternity suits lodged against him by his neighbors, all of whom were duped by Mushari.

Rosewater Golden Lager Ambrosia Beer. (GBR 4) A Utopian community in the southwest corner of the *(Rosewater)* county, New Ambrosia, invested everything it had in the *(Rosewater Inter-State Ship)* canal, and lost. They were Germans, communists and atheists who practiced group marriage, absolute truthfulness, absolute cleanliness, and absolute love. They were now scattered to the winds, like the worthless papers that represented their equity in the canal. No one was sorry to see them go. Their one contribution to the county that was still viable in Eliot's time was their brewery, which had become the home of **Rosewater Golden Lager Ambrosia Beer**. On the label of each can of beer was a picture of the heaven on earth the New Ambrosians had meant to build. The dream city had spires. The spires had lightning-rods. The sky was filled with cherubim. (GBR 4). *Along with Southern Comfort, the alcoholic Eliot drank Rosewater Golden Lager.*

Roswell Moose and Elks. *In* Player Piano, *these two civic organizations are teamed together to sabotage EPICAC in support of the Ghost Shirt rebellion. They fail, and the implication is that they blew themselves up when trying to pour nitroglycerin into Coke bottles which they intended to place in soda machines in Carlsbad Caverns, EPICAC's home.*

Rothko, Mark (1903–1970). *The Abstract Expressionist painter mentioned by Rabo Karabekian as a drinking buddy, but Rabo more frequently alludes to Rothko's horribly messy suicide.* (Blue 18) Yes, and **Mark Rothko**, with enough sleeping pills in his medicine cabinet to kill an elephant, slashed himself to death with a knife in 1970.

In Hocus Pocus, *one of Rothko's paintings is sold*

to the Getty Museum for $37,000,000. Perhaps this is another of the text's signs of America's pending economic collapse. This is in stark contrast with Karabekian's sale of a Rothko for $1,500,000 in Bluebeard.

Rowley, Jonah K. *The alias used by Malachi Constant during his getaway from the Rumfoord mansion after attending the materialization of Winston Niles Rumfoord and Kazak, in* The Sirens of Titan.

Rowley, Mrs. Theodore. *In the Editor's Note to* Mother Night, *Vonnegut mentions that he hired Mrs. Theodore Rowley, of Cotuit, Massachusetts, a linguist and poetess, to restore three Howard Campbell poems offered in Chapter Twenty-two. Campbell's memoirs are nearly illegible due to his many revisions, so it is left to Mrs. Rowley to make them whole and poetic.*

Rumfoord (*aside from all the* **Rumfoords** *listed below, see also* **Karl Barus**).

Rumfoord, Beatrice. *The wife of Winston Niles Rumfoord, space mate of Malachi Constant (Unk), mother of Chrono, and an instructress at the Schliemann Breathing School on Mars. She is enraged that her husband, who has knowledge of the future, refuses to help her fend off financial ruin or Malachi Constant.*

Bea is sexually assaulted by Malachi on their way to Mars, and the result is the birth of Chrono, the German batball star and deliverer of the spare part to Salo the Tralfamadorian voyager. When Beatrice Rumfoord is on Mars, the spelling of her name is "Bee." All other times she is either "Beatrice" or "Bea." (ST 6) **Bee** . . . had a strong face—high cheek-boned and haughty. She looked strikingly like an Indian brave. But whoever said so was under an obligation to add quickly that she was, all the same, quite beautiful.

(ST 6) **Bee** daydreamed. She daydreamed of a little girl in a starched white dress and white gloves and white shoes, and with a white pony all her own. **Bee** envied that little girl who had kept so clean. *Bee's daydream is actually a remembrance of the painting* **Beatrice Rumfoord as a Young Girl** *that hung in the Rumfoord mansion.*

When she and Chrono crash-land in the Gumbo region of the Amazon rain forest, they are held captive and later initiated into the tribe. (ST 10) During the initiation, mother and son had been staked at the ends of tethers in the middle of the village, with Chrono representing the Sun and **Bee** representing the Moon, as the Sun and the Moon were understood by the Gumbo people.

As a result of their experiences, **Bee** and Chrono were closer than most mothers and sons.

Beatrice and Chrono sell Malachi dolls outside the Rumford estate after their capture in the Martian invasion of Earth. Before Malachi, Chrono, and Beatrice are exiled to Titan, Winston Niles Rumfoord explains to the crowd in Newport why she must be sent packing. Included in his diatribe against her is the veiled message that she had cuckolded Rumfoord while on her trip to Mars. (ST 11) "The excesses of **Beatrice** were excesses of reluctance," said Rumfoord. "As a younger woman, she felt so exquisitely bred as to do nothing and to allow nothing to be done to her, for fear of contamination. Life, for **Beatrice** as a younger woman, was too full of germs and vulgarity to be anything but intolerable.

"We of the Church of God the Utterly Indifferent damn her as roundly for refusing to risk her imagined purity in living as we damn Malachi Constant for wallowing in filth.

"It was implicit in **Beatrice**'s every attitude that she was intellectually, morally, and physically what God intended human beings to be when perfected, and that the rest of humanity needed another ten thousand years in which to catch up. Again we have a case of an ordinary and uncreative person's tickling God Almighty pink. The proposition that God Almighty admired **Beatrice** for her touch-me-not breeding is at least as questionable as the proposition that God Almighty wanted Malachi Constant to be rich. . . ."

In their old age on Titan, Malachi comes to love Beatrice. And though age and circumstances aren't very kind, Bea's strength and bearing remained. She spent her time on Titan writing a refutation of Winston's Tralfamadorian grand scheme. (ST Epilogue) **Beatrice Rumfoord** was a springy, one-eyed, gold-toothed, brown old lady—as lean and tough as a

chair slat. But the class of the damaged and roughly-used old lady showed through.

To anyone with a sense of poetry, mortality, and wonder, Malachi Constant's proud, high-cheekboned mate was as handsome as a human being could be.

She was probably a little crazy. On a moon with only two other people on it, she was writing a book called *The True Purpose of Life in the Solar System.* It was a refutation of Rumfoord's notion that the purpose of human life in the Solar System was to get a grounded messenger from Tralfamadore on his way again.

Beatrice began the book after her son left her to join the bluebirds. The manuscript so far, written in longhand, occupied thirty-eight cubic feet inside the Taj Mahal.

Every time Constant visited her, she read aloud her latest additions to the manuscript.

Rumfoord, Bertram Copeland. *The uncle of Lance Rumfoord of Newport, Rhode Island, Bertram is a seventy-year-old Harvard professor and the official historian of the United States Air Force. Rumfoord breaks his leg in a skiing accident and shares a hospital room with Billy Pilgrim in Vermont after his plane crash. Rumfoord's twenty-three-year-old wife, Lily, brings him research materials for his latest book, a one-volume history of the United States Army Air Corps in World War Two. Rumfoord comments on Billy, and Vonnegut supplies a short description of the professor in the following passage.* (SL5 9) "He *(Billy)* bores the *hell* out of *me!*" **Rumfoord** replied boomingly. "All he does in his sleep is quit and surrender and apologize and ask to be left alone." **Rumfoord** was a retired brigadier general in the Air Force Reserve, the official Air Force Historian, a full professor, the author of twenty-six books, a multimillionaire since birth, and one of the great competitive sailors of all time. His most popular book was about sex and strenuous athletics for men over sixty-five. Now he quoted Theodore Roosevelt, whom he resembled a lot: "'I could carve a better man out of a banana.'"

Lily brings Rumfoord the book entitled The Destruction of Dresden, *because he needed to cover the event in his text.* (SL5 9) **Rumfoord** had a problem about Dresden. His one-volume history of the Army Air Force in World War Two was supposed to be a readable condensation of the twenty-seven-volume *Official History of the Army Air Force in World War Two*. The thing was, though, there was almost nothing in the twenty-seven volumes about the Dresden raid, even though it had been such a howling success. . . .

"Americans have finally heard about Dresden," said **Rumfoord**, twenty-three years after the raid. "A lot of them know now how much worse it was than Hiroshima. So I've got to put something about it in my book. From the official Air Force standpoint, it'll all be new."

"Why would they keep it a secret so long?" said Lily.

"For fear that a lot of bleeding hearts," said **Rumfoord**, "might not think it was such a wonderful thing to do."

Rumfoord and Billy eventually talk about Dresden and agree the destruction of Dresden had to be. Rumfoord looks at it from a military standpoint; Billy sees it from the Tralfamadorian perspective.

Rumfoord, Commodore William Howard Taft and Clarice.

In "The Hyannis Port Story," *reprinted in* Welcome to the Monkey House (1968), *the 1946 commodore of the Hyannis Port Yacht Club and his wife meet the unnamed narrator and storm window salesman while attending a lecture given by their teenage son at the North Crawford (New Hampshire) Lions Club. After the commodore gets into an argument with Hay Boyden, who throws some disrespectful remarks toward the youthful speaker, he engages the narrator in conversation because he and Boyden had also argued—about a bathtub enclosure, not politics. However, the commodore thought the salesman was defending conservative causes against Boyden and orders windows for his entire Hyannis Port home.*

The commodore hadn't been employed since 1946 and had made a full-time career of raging about whoever was President of the United States, including Eisenhower.

Especially Eisenhower.

The commodore is completely knocked off balance when his son Robert becomes engaged to Sheila Kennedy, President Kennedy's fourth cousin, who is visiting from Ireland. He is so shaken that he begins to believe he is nothing but an unproductive rich old man content to let his investments have a life of their own. That night he decides to let the Goldwater poster portrait go without the floodlights. President Kennedy asks that he turn the lights on so Khrushchev's visiting son-in-law could enjoy the view.

The **Commodore** was a short man with very shaggy eyebrows, and pale blue eyes. He looked like a gruff, friendly teddybear, and so did his son. I found out later, from a Secret Service man, that the Kennedys sometimes called the **Rumfoords** *"the Pooh people,"* on account of they were so much like the bear in the children's book *Winnie the Pooh*.

The **Commodore**'s wife wasn't a Pooh person, though. She was thin and quick, and maybe two inches taller than the **Commodore**. Bears have a way of looking as though they're pretty much satisfied with everything. The **Commodore**'s lady didn't have that look. I could tell she was jumpy about a lot of things.

Rumfoord, Cynthia Niles.

The wife of real estate agent Merrihue Rosewater and mother of Fred, the insurance salesman. (GBR 8) He married **Cynthia Niles Rumfoord**, a minor heiress, invested much of her money in pavement and streetlights and sewers. He made a fortune, lost it, and his wife's fortune, too, in the crash of 1929.

Rumfoord, Lance.

In God Bless You, Mr. Rosewater, *Lance is the six-foot-eight-inch Rumfoord heir who shabbily treats Norman Mushari on the one day out of the year the public is invited to tour the Rumfoord estate.* (GBR 11) As Mushari was leaving the estate, **Lance Rumfoord** came loping after him. Predatorily genial, he towered over little Mushari, explained that his mother considered herself a great judge of character, and had made the guess that Mushari had once served in the United States Infantry.

"No."

"Really? She so seldom misses. She said specifically that you had been a sniper."

"No."

Lance shrugged. "If not in this life, in some

other one, then." And he sneered and whinnied again.

In Slaughterhouse-Five, *Lance is momentarily seen honeymooning with new bride Cynthia Landry on the yacht* Scheherezade. *His uncle is Professor Bertram Copeland Rumfoord, the Air Force historian writing about Dresden and who later shares a hospital room with Billy Pilgrim.*

Rumfoord, Lily. *The twenty-three-year-old fifth wife of Bertram Copeland Rumfoord, in* Slaughterhouse-Five. *She was a high school dropout and go-go dancer when they met. Lily dutifully brings Rumfoord's research materials to the hospital so he could continue writing his history of the United States Army Air Corps in World War II.*

Rumfoord, Remington, IV. *Though only briefly mentioned, Remington Rumfoord, IV, enables Lionel Boyd Johnson (later to become Bokonon) to travel the world and gain exposure to other cultures and insights.* (CC 49) When the war ended, the young rakehell of the Rumfoord family, **Remington Rumfoord, IV**, proposed to sail his steam yacht, the *Scheherazade*, around the world, visiting Spain, France, Italy, Greece, Egypt, India, China, and Japan. He invited Johnson to accompany him as first mate, and Johnson agreed.

Johnson saw many wonders of the world on the voyage.

The *Scheherazade* was rammed in a fog in Bombay harbor, and only Johnson survived. He stayed in India for two years, becoming a follower of Mohandas K. Gandhi. He was arrested for leading groups that protested British rule by lying down on railroad tracks. When his jail term was over, he was shipped at Crown expense to his home in Tobago.

Rumfoord, Robert Taft. *The son of Clarice and Commodore William Howard Taft Rumfoord, an ardent Goldwater Republican and neighbor of the Kennedys in the short story "The Hyannis Port Story," reprinted in* Welcome to the Monkey House *(1968). He is the national president of a conservative student organization and is first encountered by the story's narrator while he is guest lecturing at the North Crawford Lions Club in New Hampshire. He becomes the fulcrum for his father's softening when*

the Secret Service unveils the relationship between young Robert and Sheila Kennedy, President Kennedy's fourth cousin, who is visiting from Ireland.

Rumfoord, Winston Niles. *The Newport millionaire in* The Sirens of Titan *whose style and gallantry make him a perfect tool for the Tralfamadorian scheme to get a spare part to their inter-galactic messenger, Salo.* (ST 1) When **Rumfoord** became the first person to own a private space ship, paying fifty-eight million dollars out of his own pocket for it—that was style.

When the governments of the earth suspended all space exploration because of the chrono-synclastic infundibula, and **Rumfoord** announced that he was going to Mars—that was style.

When **Rumfoord** announced that he was taking a perfectly tremendous dog along, as though a space ship were nothing more than a sophisticated sports car, as though a trip to Mars were little more than a spin down the Connecticut Turnpike—that was style.

When it was unknown what would happen if a space ship went into a chrono-synclastic infundibulum, and **Rumfoord** steered a course straight for the middle of one—that was gallantry indeed.

Rumfoord and Kazak existed as wave phenomena—apparently pulsing in a distorted spiral with its origin in the Sun and its terminal in Betelgeuse (ST 1). *Every fifty-nine days their spiral intersects with Earth. At the same time, they are permanently materialized on Titan. Rumfoord's materializations end the same as the Cheshire Cat's, with only his grin remaining.*

The Tralfamadorians use Rumfoord in an elaborate scheme taking thousands of years to complete. Parts of the scheme include: telling his wife, Beatrice, and Malachi Constant a bit about their space traveling futures; using his tremendous wealth to finance the Pan-Galactic Space Service (the Army of Mars) in preparation for their foretold failure in the invasion of Earth; establishing the worldwide Church of God the Utterly Indifferent; excommunicating Beatrice, Malachi, and Chrono to Titan, an act which finally ends Salo's long wait for a spare part.

For all the knowledge Rumfoord possesses about the Tralfamadorian scheme, more than anything else he wishes to know what message Salo carries on his journey to the far side of the galaxy. Despite badgering Salo into opening the sealed wafer containing the message, Salo's acquiescence comes too late. (ST 12) An explosion on the Sun had separated man and dog. A Universe schemed in mercy would have kept man and dog together.

The Universe inhabited by **Winston Niles Rumfoord** and his dog was not schemed in mercy. Kazak had been sent ahead of his master on the great mission to nowhere and nothing. *Shortly after, unaccompanied by his faithful companion, Winston Niles Rumfoord goes spiraling right out of the Solar System.*

Rumfoord mansion. (*ST 1*) The **Rumfoord mansion** was marble, an extended reproduction of the banqueting hall of Whitehall Palace in London. The mansion, like most of the really grand ones in Newport, was a collateral relative of post offices and Federal court buildings throughout the land.

The **Rumfoord mansion** was an hilariously impressive expression of the concept: People of substance. It was surely one of the greatest essays on density since the Great Pyramid of Khufu. In a way it was a better essay on permanence than the Great Pyramid, since the Great Pyramid tapered to nothingness as it approached heaven. Nothing about the **Rumfoord mansion** diminished as it approached heaven. Turned upside down, it would have looked exactly the same.

The density and permanence of the mansion were, of course, at ironic variance with the fact that the quondam master of the house, except for one hour in every fifty-nine days, was no more substantial than a moonbeam.

Rumpf, Hans (*see The Bombing of Germany*).

"Runaways." *Initially published in the April 1961 issue of* The Saturday Evening Post *and later appearing in the 1999 collection* Bagombo Snuff Box, *"Runaways" is the story of the lovestruck sixteen-year-olds Annie Southard (daughter of the Indiana governor) and Rice Brentner (son of a school system supply clerk earning $89.62 per week).*

Though social class is a concern within the story (most pointedly addressed by the Southards), the focus is certainly on the self-involved, attention-starved, misunderstood nature of the teens, eternal themes recurrent in every generation. Their teenaged hearts throb with rock 'n' roll lyrics of desperate love and lovers, an audible mirror of the frustrations inherent in being a teenager, inherent in feeling the victim between adolescence and adulthood.

Despite thinking their love for each other helps overcome their individual problems within their families, it is only when they are headed back to Indiana after their second highly publicized attempt to run away that Annie enunciates a sad epiphany: not too young to be in love. Just too young for just about everything else there is that goes with love.

The story ends with Annie kissing Rice good-bye, and as he drives off in his Ford, the radio accompanies him with a song that fits the moment for lovers too young. (Throughout the story, rock 'n' roll lyrics from the radio deliver the equivalent of a Greek chorus commenting upon the tragic view of life held by the two protagonists.)

*Now's the time for sweet good-bye
To what could never be,
To promises we ne'er could keep,
To a magic you and me.
If we should try to prove our love,
Our love would be in danger.
Let's put our love beyond all harm.
Good-bye—sweet, gentle stranger.*

Each teen's conversation with their parents is a typical exercise in speaking past each other, but more telling are the young lovers' conversations with each other. They also speak past each other. It is when they see another young couple also caught in traffic that reality begins to dawn. Annie and Rice got into a traffic jam in Indianapolis and were locked for stoplight after stoplight next to a car in which a baby was howling. The parents of the child were very young. The wife was scolding her husband, and the husband looked ready to uproot the steering wheel and brain her with it.

As for the parents who alternate between outrage and despair over their teenagers' wild desires, they get their young runaways to come home for good once they grant permission for the two to be wed, a move full of guile and risk. Of course, this news comes to them from an Ohio policeman conveying the message from Governor Southard.

Ryan, Mildred. *The ghost of Harold Ryan's third wife, Mildred claims Harold drove her and his previous two wives to drink because of his habit of premature ejaculation. She exposes the truth behind Ryan's mystique.* (WJ II:2) **MILDRED** No grown woman is a fan of premature ejaculation. Harold would come home trumpeting and roaring. He would kick the furniture with his boots, spit into comers and the fireplace. He would make me presents of stuffed fish and helmets with holes in them. He would tell me that he had now earned the reward that only a woman could give him, and he'd tear off my clothes. He would carry me into the bedroom, telling me to scream and kick my feet. That was very important to him. I did it. I tried to be a good wife. He told me to imagine a herd of stampeding water buffalo. I couldn't do that, but I pretended I did. It was all over—ten seconds after he'd said the word "buffalo." Then he'd zip up his pants, and go outside, and tell true war stories to the little kids. Any little kids.

Ryan, Penelope, Harold, and Paul. *In* Happy Birthday, Wanda June, *Penelope is the fourth wife of Harold Ryan. Penelope thought she lost her husband eight years earlier when he went on Safari and never returned. Since then, she had him declared legally dead and was being courted by effeminate physician Dr. Norbert Woodly and vacuum cleaner salesman Herb Shuttle. Penelope was a carhop when she met Harold, but in his absence she attended college. By the time Harold returns, Penelope can no longer accept Harold's Hemingway lifestyle.*

Harold was a fearless soldier and voracious hunter. He and his sidekick, Colonel Looseleaf Harper, crashed their aircraft while on a hunting trip. The ghost of Mildred Ryan, Harold's third wife, exposes Harold's false macho facade.

Paul is the Ryans' twelve-year-old son. Though without his father since the age of four, Paul idolized him in his absence. Once Harold reappears, Paul rejects his coarse ways, as well.

S

Sacco and Vanzetti (*also* **Dante and Inez Sacco**). *Despite the confession of Celestino Madeiros, Sacco and Vanzetti are falsely convicted of murder and later electrocuted in 1927. Much of the preface to* Jailbird *concerns their case. They are also alluded to in* Palm Sunday *and* A Man Without a Country. *In all cases they are held up as symbols of America's inability to deal equitably with immigrants and those with different social theories.*

The epigraph to Jailbird, *appearing after Vonnegut's preface and before the actual novel, includes the following material from Sacco's last letter to his thirteen-year-old son, Dante.* Help the weak ones that cry for help, help the prosecuted and the victim, because they are your better friends; they are the comrades that fight and fall as your father and **Bartolo** fought and fell yesterday for the conquest of the joy of freedom for all the poor workers. In this struggle of life you will find more love and you will be loved. —**NICOLA SACCO** (1891–1927)

"Bartolo" was Bartolomeo Vanzetti (1888–1927), who was executed after Sacco in the same electric chair. He was followed by history's forgotten man, Celestino Madeiros (1894–1927), who confessed to the crime for which Sacco and Vanzetti had been convicted, even while his own conviction for another murder was being appealed.

(JB 18) When I was a young man, I expected the story of **Sacco and Vanzetti** to be retold as often and as movingly, to be as irresistible, as the story of Jesus Christ some day. Weren't modern people, if they were to marvel creatively at their own lifetimes, I thought, entitled to a Passion like **Sacco and Vanzetti**'s, which ended in an electric chair?

As for the last days of **Sacco and Vanzetti** as a modern Passion: As on Golgotha, three lower-class men were executed at the same time by a state. This time, though, not just one of the three was innocent. This time two of the three were innocent. (JB 19) "Never in our full life," said **Vanzetti**, "could we hope to do such work for tolerance, for justice, for man's understanding of man, as now we do by accident."

(JB 20) **Sacco and Vanzetti** never lost their dignity—never cracked up. Walter F. Starbuck finally did.

(MWC 2) I never met Carl Sandburg or Eugene Victor Debs, and I wish I had. I would have been tongue-tied in the presence of such national treasures.

I did get to know one socialist of their generation—Powers Hapgood of Indianapolis. He was a typical Hoosier idealist. Socialism is idealistic. Hapgood, like Debs, was a middle-class person who thought there could be more economic justice in this country. He wanted a better country, that's all.

After graduating from Harvard, he went to work as a coal miner, urging his working-class brothers to organize in order to get better pay and safer working conditions. He also led protesters at the execution of the anarchists **Nicola Sacco and Bartolomeo Vanzetti** in Massachusetts in 1927.

Sacred Miracle Cave. *Located on the outskirts of Midland City and mentioned in* Breakfast of Champions *and* Deadeye Dick, *the cave is part of Bluebird Farm, originally owned by the former slave Josephus Hoobler. Dwayne's stepfather gained ownership of Bluebird Farm as part of a claims settlement for an auto accident. The owner of the land had bought the mortgage from Midland County Merchants Bank after Josephus Hoobler's descendants failed to meet the payments.*

The cave was discovered in 1937 by Dwayne Hoover after an earthquake. Dwayne and his stepfather opened up the small crack in the earth with crowbars and dynamite. Dwayne owned Sacred Miracle Cave in partnership with his younger stepbrothers Lyle and Kyle Hoover.

The cave became polluted with plastic molecules flowing in from Sugar Creek, which ran through Midland City and beneath the cave. Barrytron Ltd. hired the Maritimo Brothers Construction Company to build a system which would get rid of the waste, but instead they built a simple pipeline emp-

tying into Sugar Creek. Lyle and Kyle become concerned that the many natural and man-made attractions in the cave were now threatened. Among the many sites in danger were the Cathedral of Whispers, Moby Dick, the Pipe Organ of the Gods, and the slaves.

St. Andres. (*PS* Dedication) For my cousins the **de St. Andres** everywhere. Who has the castle now? (*PS* Introduction) I have dedicated this book to the **de St. Andres**. I am a **de St. Andre**, since that was the maiden name of a maternal great-grandmother of mine. My mother believed that this meant that she was descended from nobles of some kind. (*PS* 2) *From John Rauch's history of the Vonneguts in America:* "All of Kurt Vonnegut, Jr.'s eight great-grandparents were part of the vast migration of Germans to the Midwest in the half century from 1820 to 1870. They were: Clemens Vonnegut, Sr., and his wife, Katarina Blank; Henry Schnull and his wife, Matilde Schramm; Peter Lieber and his wife, **Sophia [de] St. Andre**; Karl Barus and his wife, Alice Mollman."
See also: PS Roots.

St. Augustine. (*CC* 48) Young Lionel Boyd Johnson was educated in Episcopal schools, did well as a student, and was more interested in ritual than most. As a youth, for all his interest in the outward trappings of organized religion, he seems to have been a carouser, for he invites us to sing along with him in his "Fourteenth Calypso": When I was young, / I was so gay and mean, / And I drank and chased the girls / Just like young **St. Augustine**. / **Saint Augustine**, / He got to be a saint. / So, if I get to be one, also, / Please, Mama, don't you faint.

Saint Elmo's Fire. *Both Winston Niles Rumfoord and his dog Kazak arrive and depart their chronosynclastic infundibulated rounds in a shower of Saint Elmo's fire, a luminous electrical discharge, and any creature afflicted by it is subject to discomfort no worse than the discomfort of being tickled by a feather. All the same, the creature appears to be on fire, and can be forgiven for being dismayed* (*ST* 12).

In Slaughterhouse-Five, *Ever since Billy had been thrown into shrubbery for the sake of a pic-*ture, he had been seeing **Saint Elmo's fire**, a sort of electronic radiance around the heads of his companions and captors. It was in the treetops and on the rooftops of Luxembourg, too. It was beautiful (*SL5* 3).

The photograph was staged by Billy Pilgrim's captors as part of their own propaganda effort, and, as was the case in Sirens, relates to time travel. (*SL5* 3). Billy's smile as he came out of the shrubbery was at least as peculiar as Mona Lisa's, for he was simultaneously on foot in Germany in 1944 and riding his Cadillac in 1967. Germany dropped away, and 1967 became bright and clear, free of interference from any other time. Billy was on his way to a Lions Club luncheon meeting.

Saint Elmo's fire presages the coming of "*the blue tunnel into the Afterlife*" *for the spirit of Leon Trout in* Galápagos. *He saw it on four distinct occasions. One incident occurred when Mary Hepburn was up in the crow's nest searching for land, but as Leon narrates,* I had seen it three times before: at the moment of my decapitation, and then at the cemetery in Malmö, when Swedish clay was thumping wetly on the lid of my coffin and Hjallar Arvid Boström, who certainly was never going to write Beethoven's Ninth Symphony, said of me, "Oh, well—he wasn't going to write Beethoven's Ninth Symphony anyway." Its third appearance was when I myself was up in the crow's nest—during a storm in the North Atlantic, in the sleet and spray, holding my severed head on high as though it were a basketball.

The question the blue tunnel implies by appearing is one only I can answer: Have I at last exhausted my curiosity as to what life is all about? If so, I need only step inside what I liken to a vacuum cleaner. If there is indeed suction within the blue tunnel, which is filled with a light much like that cast off by the electric stoves and ovens of the *Bahía de Darwin*, it does not seem to trouble my late father, the science fiction writer Kilgore Trout, who can stand right in the nozzle and chat with me (*Gal* 2:7).

Saint Elmo's Remedy. *The foundation of the Waltz family wealth as described by Rudy.* (*DD* 1) My father was Otto Waltz, whose peephole opened in 1892, and he was told, among other things, that he was the heir to a fortune earned principally by a quack medicine known as "**Saint Elmo's Remedy**."

It was grain alcohol dyed purple, flavored with cloves and sarsaparilla root, and laced with opium and cocaine. As the joke goes: It was absolutely harmless unless discontinued.

St. Francis of Assisi. (ST 12) Constant leaned against a statue of **St. Francis of Assisi. St. Francis** was trying to befriend two hostile and terrifyingly huge birds, apparently bald eagles. Constant was unable to identify the birds properly as Titanic bluebirds, since he hadn't seen a Titanic bluebird yet. He had arrived on Titan only an hour before.

St. George and the dragon. *The literary metaphor Howard Campbell uses to describe the imaginary confrontation between pure good and pure evil that consumes the thoughts of former Lt. Bernard B. O'Hare in his quest to get Campbell in New York.* (MN 32) He wasn't my nemesis. . . . To me, O'Hare was simply one more gatherer of wind-blown trash in the tracks of war.

O'Hare had a far more exciting view of what we were to each other.

When drunk, at any rate, he thought of himself as **St. George** and of me as **the dragon.**

Vonnegut uses this hollow image in "The First Amendment" to describe those who ban books in public schools. (PS The First Amendment) A school board has denounced some books again—out in Levittown this time. One of the books was mine. I hear about un-American nonsense like this twice a year or so. One time out in North Dakota, the books were actually burned in a furnace. I had a laugh. It was such an ignorant, dumb, superstitious thing to do.

It was so cowardly, to—to make a great show of attacking artifacts. It was like **St. George** attacking bedspreads and cuckoo clocks.

Yes, and **St. Georges** like that seem to get elected or appointed to school committees all the time. They are actually proud of their illiteracy. They imagine that they are somehow celebrating the bicentennial when they boast, as some did in Levittown, that they hadn't actually read the books they banned.

Such lunks are often the backbone of volunteer fire departments and the United States Infantry and cake sales and so on, and they have been thanked often enough for that. But they have no business supervising the educations of children in a free society. They are just too bloody stupid.

Salo. *The mechanical messenger from the planet Tralfamadore located in a universe known as the Small Magellanic Cloud. Salo is eleven million years old.* (ST 12) In the Earthling year 483,441 B.C., he was chosen by popular telepathic enthusiasm as the most handsome, healthy, clean-minded specimen of his people. The occasion was the hundred-millionth anniversary of the government of his home planet in the Small Magellanic Cloud. The name of his home planet was Tralfamadore, which old **Salo** once translated for Rumfoord as meaning both *all of us* and the *number* 541. . . .

In the Earthling year 203,117 B.C., **Salo** was forced down in the Solar System by mechanical difficulties. He was forced down by a complete disintegration of a small part in his ship's power plant, a part about the size of an Earthling beer-can opener.

The disintegrated part is eventually duplicated through a series of lengthy Tralfamadorian schemes affecting all of Earth's history, resulting in the strip of chrome cherished by Chrono.

Salsedo, Andrea. (JB 18) A printer named **Andrea Salsedo,** who was a friend of Vanzetti's, was also on the list *(a secret list compiled by the Department of Justice to monitor the political activities of foreigners).* He was arrested in New York City by federal agents on unspecified charges, and held incommunicado for eight weeks. On May third of Nineteen-hundred and Twenty, **Salsedo** fell or jumped or was pushed out of the fourteenth-story window of an office maintained by the Department of Justice.

Sacco and Vanzetti organized a meeting that was to demand an investigation of the arrest and death of **Salsedo.** It was scheduled for May ninth in Brockton, Massachusetts, Mary Kathleen O'Looney's home town.

Sam. *A student at Sweetbread College despondent over the institution's bankruptcy, in the play* The Chemistry Professor.

Samaritrophia. *The term coined by Dr. Ed Brown, the Indianapolis psychiatrist who diagnoses Sylvia*

Rosewater's malady that he describes as a "hysterical indifference to the troubles of those less fortunate than oneself."

. . . **Samaritrophia** . . . is the suppression of an overactive conscience by the rest of the mind. "You must all take instructions from me!" the conscience shrieks, in effect, to all the other mental processes. The other processes try it for a while, note that the conscience is unappeased, that it continues to shriek, and they note, too, that the outside world has not been even microscopically improved by the unselfish acts the conscience has demanded.

They rebel at last. They pitch the tyrannous conscience down an oubliette, weld shut the manhole cover of that dark dungeon. They can hear the conscience no more. In the sweet silence, the mental processes look about for a new leader, and the leader most prompt to appear whenever the conscience is stilled, Enlightened Self-interest, does appear. Enlightened Self-interest gives them a flag, which they adore on sight. It is essentially the black and white Jolly Roger, with these words written beneath the skull and crossbones, "The hell with you, Jack, I've got mine!" (*GBR* 4).

Samoza Hall. *The Tarkington College administration building that houses the meeting room of the Board of Trustees, in* Hocus Pocus. *It is in the boardroom that Eugene Debs Hartke loses his faculty position, and later, escaped prisoner Alton Darwin declares himself president of a new country.*

Lyle Hooper, owner of the Black Cat Café, is executed in front of the building.

After Hartke assumes the temporary position as warden in control of Tarkington, he uses Samoza Hall as a makeshift prison wall, outfitting its doors and windows with machine gunners guarding convicts housed in tents on the campus quad.

Sams, Howard W. *In* The Sirens of Titan, *Sams is the author of* Winston Niles Rumfoord, Benjamin Franklin, and Leonardo da Vinci, *which documents that German batball was Rumfoord's only exposure to team sports as a child.*

San Lorenzo Cathedral. *After a British slave ship is overtaken by African slaves and they land on San Lorenzo, formerly claimed by the Spanish, their new*

emperor Tum-Bumwa erected the **San Lorenzo Cathedral** *and the fantastic fortifications on the north shore of the island, fortifications within which the private residence of the so-called President of the Republic now stands (CC 57). It is from those fortifications that the Ambassador and Mrs. Minton plunge to their deaths and Papa Monzano's ice-nine-contaminated body also plunges into the sea. It also contains the oubliette in which John/Jonah and Mona Aamons take refuge from the storms that swirl as a result of the oceans icing over.*

Sandler, Bea (**Bea Sandler's** *The African Cookbook*). (*DD* Preface) There are several recipes in this book, which are intended as musical interludes for the salivary glands. They have been inspired by *James Beard's American Cookery,* Marcella Hazan's *The Classic Italian Cook Book,* and **Bea Sandler's** *The African Cookbook.* I have tinkered with the originals, however—so no one should use this novel for a cookbook.

Sandra. *In* Cat's Cradle, *the former high school classmate of Franklin Hoenikker, now working as a prostitute in the Cape Cod Room of the Del Prado Hotel in Ilium, New York. Sandra chaired the school's Class Colors Committee and was in position to know much about the student body. She and the text's narrator wind up spending the night together prior to his tour of the Ilium Research Laboratory. Before they leave the bar, however, Sandra tells him some little known facts and rumors: that Franklin was derisively called Secret Agent X-9 because he always seemed involved in some clandestine activity outside of school, and that it was generally assumed that Dr. Asa Breed enjoyed a long-term affair with Emily Hoenikker and fathered her three children.*

Interestingly, Sandra's high school Colors Committee chose orange and black for their prom's colors, the same colors used to decorate the anniversary party on the lawn of Billy Pilgrim's home—the same colors which cause Billy to time travel back to the prisoner-of-war train he rode in World War II (in Slaughterhouse-Five*).*

Sandy. *The sheep dog that Vonnegut adopts along with three children from his sister and brother-in-law after they passed away in 1958. Vonnegut becomes* *deeply enamored of Sandy and once recalled to a group of scientists,* You have called me a humanist, and I have looked into humanism some, and I have found that a humanist is person who is tremendously interested in human beings. My dog is a humanist. His name is **Sandy**. He is a sheep dog. I know that **Sandy** is a dud name for a sheep dog, but there it is (WFG Address to the American Physical Society).

Santa Cruz. *The home of the Darwin Research Station from which guides, trained by resident scientists, were to conduct tours of the Galápagos Islands for "the Nature Cruise of the Century," in* Galápagos.

sarooned *(see also* **Bokononism***).* (CC 90) All things conspired to form one cosmic *vin-dit,* one mighty shove into Bokononism, into the belief that God was running my life and that He had work for me to do.

And, inwardly, I *sarooned,* which is to say that I acquiesced to the seeming demands of my *vin-dit.* Inwardly, I agreed to become the next President of San Lorenzo.

Sateen Dura-Luxe. *The miracle paint advertised to "outlive the smile on the 'Mona Lisa'" and which Rabo Karabekian used in the early 1960s. Karabekian's* most famous painting, which no longer exists, and which was sixty-four feet long and eight feet high, and used to grace the entrance lobby of the GEFFCo headquarters on Park Avenue, was called simply "Windsor Blue Number Seventeen." Windsor Blue was a shade of **Sateen Dura-Luxe,** straight from the can (*Blue* 4).

The great tragedy of any artist using the miracle paint was that after a period of time the paint would peel off the canvas in huge sheets. The canvas used for Karabekian's "Windsor Blue Number Seventeen" was wiped clean by the degrading paint and became the base for his eventual masterpiece, "Now It's the Women's Turn."

Karabekian still had sixty-three gallons in his basement. Because it was found to degrade into a deadly poison, he would have had to ship the paints to a special repository near Pitchfork, Wyoming.

Karabekian makes a comparison between Sateen Dura-Luxe's ability to self-destruct (and thereby eradicate cultural artifacts of a given epoch) with Christian fundamentalism of another era. While visiting Marilee Kemp's home in Florence, Italy, Rabo notices that large rectangular white spaces at the base of the clerestory once held murals. (*Blue* 27) The murals were destroyed by the insistence of the Dominican monk Girolamo Savonarola, who wished to dispel every trace of paganism, which he felt had poisoned the city during the reign of the Medicis.

The murals were the work of Giovanni Vitelli, about whom almost nothing else is known, except that he was said to have been born in Pisa. One may assume that he was the Rabo Karabekian of his time, and that Christian fundamentalism was his **Sateen Dura-Luxe.**

Savonarola, Girolamo. *Rabo Karabekian learned that the clerestory in the palazzo of Innocenzo "the Invisible" de Medici, later owned by the Countess Portomaggiore (the former Marilee Kemp) was scraped bare of frescoes depicting lightly clad pagan gods and goddesses. The Medicis were exiled from Florence in 1494, and in their absence,* The murals were destroyed by the insistence of the Dominican monk **Girolamo Savonarola,** who wished to dispel every trace of paganism, which he felt had poisoned the city during the reign of the Medicis (*Blue* 27).

Karabekian goes on to rejoice: **Girolamo Savonarola,** incidentally, was hanged and burned in the piazza in front of what had been the Palazzo of Innocenzo "the Invisible" de Medici in 1494.

I sure love history. I don't know why Celeste and her friends aren't more interested (*Blue* 27).

In 1981 Vonnegut used Savonarola to illustrate his frustration with would-be censors. (PS The First Amendment) Whenever ideas are squashed in this country, literate lovers of the American experiment write careful and intricate explanations of why all ideas must be allowed to live. It is time for them to realize that they are attempting to explain America at its bravest and most optimistic to orangutans.

From now on, I intend to limit my discourse with dim-witted **Savonarolas** to this advice: "Have somebody read the First Amendment to the United States Constitution out loud to you, you God damned fool!"

Saw City Kandy Kitchen. *The candy store that doubles as the Greyhound Bus depot, in* God Bless You, Mr. Rosewater.

Sawyer, Doris. *The theatrical director for the North Crawford Mask and Wig Club in the short story* "Who Am I This Time?" (*in* Welcome to the Monkey House). *She assists the narrator in casting their new production of* A Streetcar Named Desire, *and she plays a key role in bringing out the acting talents of Helene Shaw and Harry Nash.*

Schadenfreude, Dr. *The title character of a Kilgore Trout short story rescued from the trash bin outside the front door of the American Academy of Arts and Letters by their security guard Dudley Prince. Schadenfreude, of course, is the psychiatric term for deriving joy from the misfortunes of others.* (TQ 17) It was set in the office of a psychiatrist in St. Paul, Minnesota.

The name of the shrink was the name of the story, too, which was "**Dr. Schadenfreude**." This doctor had his patients lie on a couch and talk, all right, but they could ramble on only about dumb or crazy things that had happened to total strangers in supermarket tabloids or on TV talk shows.

If a patient accidentally said "I" or "me" or "my" or "myself" or "mine," **Dr. Schadenfreude** went ape.

He leapt out of his overstuffed leather chair. He stamped his feet. He flapped his arms. He put his livid face directly over the patient. He snarled and barked things like this: "When will you ever learn that nobody cares anything about you, you, you, you boring, insignificant piece of poop? Your whole problem is you think you *matter*! Get over that, or sashay your stuckup butt the hell out of here!" (*See also:* TQ 18–19.)

Scharff, Hattie. *In* Mother Night, *the widowed owner of Pittsburgh's Scharff Brothers Funeral Home who hires Lionel J. D. Jones as an apprentice embalmer. Three years later the twenty-four-year-old Jones, by that time the manager of the firm, marries Mrs. Scharff, then fifty-eight. She passes away in 1928. Their marriage was good and satisfying enough for Jones to avoid any anti-Semitic activities. After his wife's death, Jones sold the funeral home for* $84,000 *and used the proceeds to begin publishing* The White Christian Minuteman.

Schildknecht, Heinz. *The best wartime friend of* Mother Night's *Howard Campbell. As with almost every other significant character in the text, Heinz had two personas. While working for the German Ministry for Popular Enlightenment and Propaganda as an expert at propagandizing Australians and New Zealanders, he was simultaneously working as a Jewish member of the anti-Nazi underground. He remained an Israeli agent long after the war, posing as chief groundskeeper for Baron Ulrich Werther von Schwefelbad, a former Nazi residing in Ireland. The Haifa Institute for the Documentation of War Criminals informs Campbell that Heinz verified the death of Hitler after wandering into his bunker while his gasoline soaked body was still recognizable.*

Campbell and Schildknecht forge their friendship by becoming a championship doubles team in ping-pong at the Ministry. Heinz's wife is killed in an air raid, and the two friends become roommates and drinking buddies. Nevertheless, Heinz eagerly travels to Jerusalem prepared to testify against Campbell at his war crimes trial.

schizophrenia. (MN 11) It was typical of his **schizophrenia** as a spy that he would use an institution he so admired for purposes of espionage. *Campbell comments on George Kraft's use of Alcoholics Anonymous as part of his espionage cover.*

It was typical of his **schizophrenia** as a spy that he should also be a true friend of mine, and that he should eventually think of a way to use me cruelly in advancing the Russian cause.
(MN 18) When I call this unit a Nazi daydream, incidentally, I am suffering an attack of **schizophrenia**—because the idea of the Free American Corps began with me. I suggested its creation, designed its uniforms and insignia, wrote its creed.
(MN 31) I've always been able to live with what I did. How? Through that simple and widespread boon to modern mankind—**schizophrenia**.
(MN 39) Kraft thought his situation over, and **schizophrenia** rescued him neatly. "None of this really concerns me," he said, and his urbanity returned.

(*CC* 42) Such music from such a woman (*Angela Hoenikker*) could only be a case of **schizophrenia** or demonic possession.

(*GBR* 4) She was not a **schizophrenic**, but, whenever her husband visited her, which he did three times a week, she manifested all of the sick cutenesses of paranoia.

(*GBR* 9) Fred's gory shins were victims of his wife's interior decorating scheme, which called for an almost **schizophrenic** use of little tables, dozens of them all through the house. . . . And Caroline was forever rearranging the tables, as though for this kind of party one day and another the next. So poor Fred was forever barking his shins on the tables. (*SL5* Title Page)

> THIS IS A NOVEL
> SOMEWHAT IN THE TELEGRAPHIC
>   **SCHIZOPHRENIC**
> MANNER OF TALES
> OF THE PLANET TRALFAMADORE,
> WHERE THE FLYING SAUCERS
> COME FROM.
> PEACE.

(*BC* 4) As it happened, Vernon was having trouble at home. His wife, Mary, was a **schizophrenic**, so Vernon hadn't noticed whether Dwayne had changed or not. Vernon's wife believed that Vernon was trying to turn her brains into plutonium.

(*BC* 18) There in the cocktail lounge, peering out through my leaks at a world of my own invention, I mouthed this word: *schizophrenia*.

(*PS* The People One Knows) ARE many novelists **schizophrenic**—at least marginally so? . . . if writers themselves aren't lunatics, perhaps a lot of their ancestors were.

(*PS* Religion) "They are told to have faith. Faith in what? Faith in faith, as nearly as I can tell. That is as detailed as many contemporary preachers care to be, except when amazing audiences of cavemen. How can a preacher tell us about men and women who heard voices without raising questions about **schizophrenia**, a disease which we know is common in all places and all times."

(*PS* Children) "Mark has taught me never to romanticize mental illness, never to imagine a brilliant and beguiling **schizophrenic** who makes more sense about life than his or her doctor or even the president of Harvard University. . . ."

(*PS* Children) Mark says that **schizophrenia** is as ghastly and debilitating as smallpox or rabies or any other unspeakable disease you care to name. Society cannot be blamed, and neither, thank God, can the friends and relatives of the patient. **Schizophrenia** is an internal chemical catastrophe. It is a case of monstrously bad genetic luck, bad luck of a sort encountered in absolutely every sort of society—including the Australian aborigines and the middle class of Vienna, Austria, before the Second World War.

"Plenty of other writers at this very moment are writing a story about an admirable, perhaps even a divine **schizophrenic**. . . . Why? Because the story is wildly applauded every time it is told. It blames the culture and the economy and the society and everything but the disease itself for making the patient unwell. Mark says that is wrong."

(*DD* 24) "The most severe manifestation of chronic intoxication is psychosis, often indistinguishable from **schizophrenia**."

(*Gal* 1:27) He (*Private Geraldo Delgado*) was only eighteen years old, and was a paranoid **schizophrenic**. He should never have been issued live ammunition.

(*FWD* II) "He was diagnosed, when I took him to a private laughing academy in British Columbia, where he had founded a commune, as **schizophrenic**. He sure looked **schizophrenic** to me, too. I never saw depressed people act anything like that. We mope. We sleep. I have to say that anybody who did what Mark did shortly after he was admitted, which was to jump up and get the light bulb in the ceiling of his padded cell, was anything but depressed.

"Anyway Mark recovered sufficiently to write his book and graduate from Harvard Medical School. He is now a pediatrician in Boston, with a wife and two fine sons, and two fine automobiles. And then, not very long ago, most members of your profession decided that he and some others who had written books about recovering from **schizophrenia** had been misdiagnosed. No matter how jazzed up they appeared to be when sick, they were in fact depressives. Maybe so.

"Mark's first response to news of this rediagnosis

was to say, 'What a wonderful diagnostic tool. We now know if a patient gets well, he or she definitely did not have **schizophrenia.**'"

Toward the close of Fates Worse Than Death, *Vonnegut includes a section entitled "What My Son Mark Wanted Me to Tell the Psychiatrists in Philadelphia, Which Was Also the Afterword to a New Edition of His Book* The Eden Express." (*FWD* What My Son Mark Wanted Me to Tell the Psychiatrists in Philadelphia, Which Was Also the Afterword to a New Edition of His Book *The Eden Express*) The clinical definition of **schizophrenia** has been changed. Under the old definitions there was considerable ambiguity about what to call people like me. Under the new definitions I would be classified as manic depressive rather than **schizophrenic**. I wasn't sick for very long and I didn't follow a downhill course, so I did not fit what has now become a definition of someone who is **schizophrenic**. While it's tempting to dismiss this as an insignificant change in labels and be more than a little irritated that they went and changed the rules after I went and built a book around the old definitions, I have to admit that this too is probably a positive change. It should mean that fewer people with acute breakdowns will be written off as hopeless. . . .

There are probably a dozen or so separate diseases responsible for what we now call **schizophrenia** and manic depression. Until the definitive work is done, many things are plausible and almost anything is possible. This lack of certainty makes mental illness wonderful ground for intellectual speculation and absolute hell for patients and their families.

At the time I wrote my book I felt that the large doses of vitamins with which I was treated, along with more conventional therapies, had a great deal to do with my recovery. It was my hope that many people diagnosed as **schizophrenic** would get better if only their doctors would become more open minded and treat them with vitamins.

Vonnegut translates his tape recording of Kilgore Trout because of problems with his dental plate. He asks his fictional alter ego about his feelings concerning events in Kosovo, Serbia. Trout's answer: (GBK Kilgore Trout) The homicidal paranoia and **schizophrenia** of ethnic cleansing does its worst quickly

now, almost instantly, like a tidal wave or volcano or earthquake—in Rwanda and now Kosovo, and who knows where else? The disease used to take years. One thinks of the Europeans killing off the Aborigines in the Western Hemisphere, and in Australia and Tasmania, and the Turks' elimination of Armenians from their midst—of course the Holocaust, which ground on and on from 1933 to 1945. The Tasmanian genocide, incidentally, is the only one of which I've heard which was one-hundred-percent successful. Nobody on the face of the Earth has a native Tasmanian as a forebear!

Schlesinger, Arthur, Jr. (*MH* The Hyannis Port Story) The next thing I knew, I was in Hyannis, going past the Presidential Motor Inn, the First Family Waffle Shop. . . . It was late in the afternoon, and I'd missed lunch, so I decided to have a waffle. All the different kinds of waffles were named after Kennedys and their friends and relatives. A waffle with strawberries and cream was a *Jackie*. A waffle with a scoop of ice cream was a *Caroline*. They even had a waffle named *Arthur Schlesinger, Jr.*

(*FWD* XX) I said to the historian **Arthur Schlesinger, Jr.**, one time, "If you had to say that the world was divided into only two kinds of people, not counting the sexes, what would they be?" It took him maybe ten seconds before replying, "Roundheads and Cavaliers." (I thought that was a swell answer. I am a Roundhead. Xanthippe *[Vonnegut's nickname for his second wife, Jill Krementz]* is a Cavalier.) I said to the graphic artist Saul Steinberg one time, "There are some novelists I can hardly talk to. It is as though we were in two very unlike professions, like podiatry and deep sea diving, say. What do you think is going on?" He replied, "It is very simple. There are two types of artists, neither superior to the other. One responds to life itself. The other responds to the history of his or her art so far." (Jill and I are both artists of the first sort, which could be why we got married. We are both barbarians, too ignorant to respond to the histories of our arts so far.)

Schliemann Breathing School for Recruits. *Beatrice Rumfoord is one of six instructors at the school located in Phoebe, Mars's only city.* (ST 6) **Schliemann breathing,** of course, is a technique that enables human beings to survive in a vacuum or in an inhospitable atmosphere without the use of helmets or other cumbersome respiratory gear.

It consists, essentially, of taking a pill rich in oxygen. The bloodstream takes on this oxygen through the wall of the small intestine rather than through the lungs. On Mars, the pills were known officially as Combat Respiratory Rations, in popular parlance as goofballs.

Martian attempts to erase Beatrice's memories and sentimental inclinations fail and the result is a sonnet about Schliemann breathing, considered seditious by her superiors. For this, she is sent back to the hospital. (ST 6) Break every link with air and mist, / Seal every open vent; / Make throat as tight as miser's fist, / Keep life within you pent. / Breathe out, breathe in, no more, no more, / For breathing's for the meek; / And when in deathly space we soar, / Be careful not to speak. / If you with grief or joy are rapt, / Just signal with a tear; / To soul and heart within you trapped / Add speech and atmosphere. / Every man's an island as in / lifeless space we roam / Yes, every man's an island: / island fortress, island home.

Schneider, Kurt. *In* The Sirens of Titan, *the alcoholic manager of a failed travel agency in Bremen, Germany, who is recruited for the Army of Mars, captured during the invasion of Earth, and later sells trinkets outside the Rumfoord estate in Newport, Rhode Island. His booth is near that of Beatrice Rumfoord's.*

Schramm's Drugstore. *The Midland City establishment where Rudy Waltz works as the all-night pharmacist six days a week. He got the job right out of pharmacy school after his predecessor, Malcolm Hyatt, was killed by a thief.*

Because so little business is transacted in the middle of the night, Rudy spends much of his time writing "Katmandu," his play about farmer John Fortune. Despite the solitude of the graveyard shift, it brings one unsettling aspect of the all-night job at **Schramm's,** one I hadn't anticipated . . . the telephone there. Hardly a night passed that some young person, feeling wonderfully daring and witty, no doubt, would telephone to ask me if I was Deadeye Dick.

I always was. I always will be (DD 18).

Though the Schramm family in Midland City once owned the store, they had long since sold the business and left the area. The pharmacy now belonged to Mr. Horton of Cincinnati.

Schwartz, Harold D. (*also known as* **Gramps**). *The patriarch of the Schwartz family living in Alden Village in the 1953 short story "Tomorrow and Tomorrow and Tomorrow," reprinted in* Welcome to the Monkey House (1968). *Gramps was seventy years old before the invention of the anti-aging compound "anti-gerasone." Consequently, he is now a wrinkled but quite healthy 172. Anti-gerasone has extended the span of life so greatly that it has precipitated a crushing housing shortage. The Schwartzes' living conditions are so crowded that great-grandchildren old enough to have children of their own can't afford to because of the lack of space. Space allocation is accorded by age, so Gramps is free to impose himself in any room of the house.*

Gramps is well aware that members of the family want to dilute his anti-gerasone to kill him off and get him out of the apartment. One night he leaves a suicide note and disappears. In the note he leaves all his possessions to be divided equally among the entire family. Some assume age should continue to rule the division of space. Others disagree and a huge family brawl ensues. All the Schwartzes are hauled off to jail and face a year's imprisonment. Jail seems nice because everyone has their own bed and sink. They want to stay.

Gramps sees the television coverage of the brawl while sitting in the Alden Village Green, a local bar. He sends away for a new anti-gerasone formula that promises to remove the wrinkles from those over 150, and returns to the apartment—its only inhabitant.

Schwartz, Louis J. and Emerald. *Two of the besieged family members forced to endure the cramped living conditions of their extended family due to the life-prolonging drug anti-gerasone, in the 1953 short story "Tomorrow and Tomorrow and Tomorrow," reprinted in* Welcome to the Monkey House (1968). *Louis is one hundred twelve years old and Emerald is ninety-three. Despite being disinherited by greatgrandpa Harold D. Schwartz, Lou refills the patriarch's anti-gerasone prescription to full strength after* *witnessing Mortimer Schwartz dilute the solution. Louis fears the prospect of a chaotic family power struggle should the old man die.*

Schwartz, Mortimer. *The great-grandnephew of Harold D. Schwartz in the 1953 short story "Tomorrow and Tomorrow and Tomorrow," reprinted in* Welcome to the Monkey House *(1968). Mortimer and his new wife move into the extended family's cramped dwelling, and he dilutes Harold's antigerasone in the hope of eventually freeing up some living space. Louis Schwartz witnesses the event and, fearing a family power struggle, restores the drug to full strength.*

Schweitzer, Albert. *The legendary medical missionary and theologian who founded a hospital in French Equatorial Africa in 1913. Vonnegut invokes his spirit a number of times throughout his work.* Cat's Cradle's *John/Jonah travels to San Lorenzo intending to write a magazine story about Julian Castle, the American sugar millionaire who follows Schweitzer's example by opening a free hospital in the island's jungle. Castle, however, sneeringly tells the narrator Schweitzer was not his hero.*

In God Bless You, Mr. Rosewater, *Sylvia Rosewater meets Schweitzer along with Picasso, Hemingway, Toscanini, Churchill, and de Gaulle as a parade of the world's notable figures were frequent guests in her parents' home.*

In Breakfast of Champions, *when Dwayne Hoover goes into a violent rage, the ambulance called to aid his victims was the Martha Simmons Memorial Mobile Disaster Unit, named in honor of the wife of Newbolt Simmons, a County Commissioner of Public Safety. She had died of rabies contracted from a sick bat she found clinging to her floor-to-ceiling livingroom draperies one morning. She had just been reading a biography of* **Albert Schweitzer,** *who believed that human beings should treat simpler animals lovingly (BC 24).*

Young Kimberly in "The Chemistry Professor" (reprinted in Palm Sunday's *"Jekyll and Hyde Revisited") declares she is a follower of Dr. Schweitzer.*

Vonnegut's most recent reference sarcastically ties in the humanitarian with our continued military insouciance. (FWD 10) *"***Albert Schweitzer,*** a physi-*cian as well as a musician and a philosopher, hoped to teach us reverence for life. He felt that we should not kill even the tiniest, most contemptible organism if we could possibly avoid doing that. On the face of it, this ideal is preposterous, since so many diseases are caused by germs.* **Dr. Schweitzer** *himself must have killed germs by the billions. Either that, or most of his patients died.*

"If I were to speak tonight of the agony experienced by individual germs in the bodies of patients dosed by **Dr. Schweitzer,** *the men in white coats would be entitled to cart me off to St. Elizabeth's. And our frame of mind now, not just in this country but in many, many others, including, no doubt, Libya, is such that civilians attacked from the air are as unworthy of being discussed as individual germs."*

science fiction, science-fiction. *Infamy and adulation—in not so equal measures—will forever be Vonnegut's dual legacy as a result of his forays into the genre.* (WFG Science Fiction) Years ago I was working in Schenectady for General Electric, completely surrounded by machines and ideas for machines, so I wrote a novel about people and machines, and machines frequently got the best of it, as machines will. (It was called *Player Piano,* and it was brought out again in both hard cover and paperback.) And I learned from the reviewers that I was a **science-fiction** writer.

I supposed that I was writing a novel about life, about things I could not avoid seeing and hearing in Schenectady, a very real town, awkwardly set in the gruesome now. I have been a soreheaded occupant of a file drawer labeled "**science fiction**" ever since, and I would like out, particularly since so many serious critics regularly mistake the drawer for a urinal.

To be sure, one of Vonnegut's most famous creations is the science fiction writer Kilgore Trout, who plays a significant role in God Bless You, Mr. Rosewater, Slaughterhouse-Five, *and* Breakfast of Champions, *all novels from his perceived creative pinnacle. Moreover,* Galápagos *is told by the spirit of the decapitated Leon Trout—Kilgore's son;* Jailbird's *Dr. Bob Fender uses Trout's name as one of his pen names; and* Hocus Pocus *contains a wealth of* references to the science fiction author Arthur C. Clarke (highly esteemed by Vonnegut). There are a number of science fiction tropes throughout his short stories, and the topic is a main concern in his anthologized interviews.

Timequake *focuses on two major events: the ending of the ten-year rerun period and the culminating clambake bringing together Vonnegut and Trout with a select number of people close to Vonnegut who want to meet his alter ego.*

Vonnegut uses science fiction as an extension of his personal experience but also as a means for social commentary. (WFG Playboy Interview) PLAYBOY: What attracted you to using the (science fiction) form yourself?
VONNEGUT: I was working for General Electric at the time, right after World War Two, and I saw a milling machine for cutting the rotors on jet engines, gas turbines. . . . This was in 1949 and the guys who were working on it were foreseeing all sorts of machines being run by little boxes and punched cards. *Player Piano* was my response to the implications of having everything run by little boxes. The idea of doing that, you know, made sense, perfect sense. To have a little clicking box make all the decisions wasn't a vicious thing to do. But it was too bad for the human beings who got their dignity from their jobs.
PLAYBOY: So **science fiction** seemed like the best way to write about your thoughts on the subject?
VONNEGUT: There was no avoiding it, since the General Electric Company was **science fiction**.

The short version of how Vonnegut invented ice-nine, arguably one of his most memorable creations appears in Palm Sunday. *(PS Self-Interview)* VONNEGUT: Anyway—(H. G.) Wells came to Schenectady, and Langmuir was told to be his host. Langmuir thought he might entertain Wells with an idea for a **science-fiction** story—about a form of ice that was stable at room temperature. Wells was uninterested, or at least never used the idea. And then Wells died, and then, finally, Langmuir died. I thought to myself: "Finders, keepers—the idea is mine."

Eliot Rosewater introduces readers (fictional and real) to Kilgore Trout in God Bless You, Mr. Rosewater, Slaughterhouse-Five, *and* Breakfast of Champi-

ons. *In the first case, Eliot crashes a convention of science fiction writers and speaks warmly of the prolific Trout. He exhorts the crowd to use their talents to construct a book in which money is the key science fiction device—the very key to Vonnegut's novel. (GBR 1)* And it occurred to him that a really good **science-fiction** book had never been written about money. "Just think of the wild ways money is passed around on Earth!" he said.

In Slaughterhouse-Five, *Eliot Rosewater shares a hospital room with Billy Pilgrim and introduces him to the scores of Trout books beneath his bed. In an interesting connection between Vonnegut's own creation and one of his all time favorite writers, Rosewater said an interesting thing to Billy one time about a book that wasn't* **science fiction**. He said that everything there was to know about life was in *The Brothers Karamazov*, by Feodor Dostoevsky. "But that isn't enough any more," said Rosewater (SL5 5).

Rosewater is also responsible for bringing Trout to the Midland City Arts Festival in Breakfast of Champions.
(MH Preface) I used to be a public relations man for General Electric, and then I became a freelance writer of so-called "slick fiction," a lot of it **science fiction**. . . .

I asked him what the very lowest grade of fiction was, and he told me, "**science fiction**." I asked where he was bound in such a rush, and learned that he had to catch a Fan-Jet. He was to speak at a meeting of the Modern Language Association in Honolulu the next morning. Honolulu was three thousand miles away.

Vonnegut alludes to an unnamed college professor identified by Jerome Klinkowitz as Robert Scholes of Brown University. (WFG Science Fiction) English majors are encouraged, I know, to hate chemistry and physics, and to be proud because they are not dull and creepy and humorless and war-oriented like the engineers across the quad. And our most impressive critics have commonly been such English majors. . . . So it is natural for them to despise **science fiction**.
(WFG Excelsior! We're Going to the Moon! Excelsior!) Good **science-fiction** writers of the present are not necessarily as eager as Arthur C. Clarke to

found kindergartens on Jupiter, to leave the poor Maine ape and his clam rake far behind. Isaac Asimov, who is a great man, perceives three stages so far in the development of American **science fiction**, says we are in stage three now:

1. Adventure dominant.
2. Technology dominant.
3. Sociology dominant.

(WFG *Playboy* Interview) PLAYBOY: *Slaughterhouse-Five* is mainly about the Dresden fire bombing, which you went through during World War Two. What made you decide to write it in a **science-fiction** mode?
VONNEGUT: These things are intuitive. There's never any strategy meeting about what you're going to do; you just come to work every day. And the **science-fiction** passages in *Slaughterhouse-Five* are just like the clowns in Shakespeare. When Shakespeare figured the audience had had enough of the heavy stuff, he'd let up a little, bring on a clown or a foolish innkeeper or something like that, before he'd become serious again. And trips to other planets, **science fiction** of an obviously kidding sort, is equivalent to bringing on the clowns every so often to lighten things up.
(WFG *Playboy* Interview) VONNEGUT: His opponent *(George McGovern's 1972 foe—President Richard Nixon)* had too powerful an issue: the terror and guilt and hatred white people feel for the descendants of victims of an unbelievable crime we committed not long ago—human slavery. How's that for **science fiction**? There was this modern country with a wonderful Constitution, and it kidnapped human beings and used them as machines. It stopped it after a while, but by then it had millions of descendants of those kidnapped people all over the country. What if they turned out to be so human that they wanted revenge of some kind? McGovern's opinion was that they should be treated like anybody else. It was the opinion of the white electorate that this was a dangerous thing to do.
(Gal 1:15) So I *(Leon Trout)* have to say that human brains back then had become such copious and irresponsible generators of suggestions as to what might be done with life, that they made acting for

the benefit of future generations seem one of many arbitrary games which might be played by narrow enthusiasts—like poker or polo or the bond market, or the writing of **science-fiction** novels.
(PS Funnier on Paper Than Most People) "Perhaps you have read the novel *Childhood's End* by Arthur C. Clarke, one of the few masterpieces in the field of **science fiction**. All of the others were written by me. In Clarke's novel, mankind suddenly undergoes a spectacular evolutionary change. The children become very different from the parents, less physical, more spiritual—and one day they form up into a sort of column of light which spirals out into the universe, its mission unknown."
(HP 23) I *(Eugene Debs Hartke)* read a lot of **science fiction** when I was in the Army, including Arthur C. Clarke's *Childhood's End*, which I thought was a masterpiece. He was best known for the movie *2001*, the very year in which I am writing and coughing now.
(TQ Prologue) Only when people got back to when the timequake hit did they stop being robots of their pasts. As the old **science fiction** writer Kilgore Trout said, "Only when free will kicked in again could they stop running obstacle courses of their own construction."
(TQ Prologue) Yes, and I myself was a character in *Timequake One*, making a cameo appearance at a clambake on the beach at the writers' retreat Xanadu in the summer of 2001, six months after the end of the rerun, six months after free will kicked in again.

I was there with several fictitious persons from, the book, including Kilgore Trout. I was privileged to hear the old, long-out-of-print **science fiction** writer describe for us, and then demonstrate, the special place of Earthlings in the cosmic scheme of things.
(TQ 1) That there are such devices as firearms, as easy to operate as cigarette lighters and as cheap as toasters, capable at anybody's whim of killing Father or Fats or Abraham Lincoln or John Lennon or Martin Luther King, Jr., or a woman pushing a baby carriage, should be proof enough for anybody that, to quote the old **science fiction** writer Kilgore Trout, "being alive is a crock of shit."
(TQ 16) When Trout heard about how seriously Prince had taken "The Sisters B-36" on the first

Christmas Eve, 2000, about how Prince believed a bag lady had put on such a show while throwing the yellow manuscript pages away to ensure that Prince would wonder what they were and retrieve them, the old **science fiction** writer commented: "Perfectly understandable, Dudley. For anybody who could believe in God, as you once did, it would be a piece of cake to believe in the planet Booboo."

(*TQ* 17) Here's the explanation of Zoltan Pepper's reaction: When Zoltan was a high school sophomore in Fort Lauderdale, Florida, he copied a story from one of his father's collection of old **science fiction** magazines. He submitted it to his English teacher, Mrs. Florence Wilkerson, as his own creation. It was one of the last stories Kilgore Trout would ever submit to a publisher. By the time Zoltan was a sophomore, Trout was a bum. . . .

Mrs. Wilkerson suspected plagiarism. Zoltan confessed, thinking it was a funny rather than a serious thing he'd done. To him, plagiarism was what Trout would have called a mopery, "indecent exposure in the presence of a blind person of the same sex."

(*TQ* 18) "If I'd wasted my time creating characters," Trout said, "I would never have gotten around to calling attention to things that really matter: irresistible forces in nature, and cruel inventions, and cockamamie ideals and governments and economies that make heroes and heroines alike feel like something the cat drug in."

Trout might have said, and it can be said of me as well, that he created caricatures rather than characters. His animus against so-called mainstream literature, moreover, wasn't peculiar to him. It was generic among writers of **science fiction**.

(*TQ* 37) The old **science fiction** writer wanted to galvanize the armed and uniformed Dudley Prince into action, he later confessed, so that he himself wouldn't have to do anything more. "Free will! Free will! Fire! Fire!" he shouted at Prince.

Trout waxes poetically, philosophically, about the close link between science fiction and altering perceptions. In the following quote, Trout demonstrates how one person's vision of two stars in the night sky brings into question the nature of one's aware- *ness—an example brought to light by the insight of a science speculator whose simultaneous interests broadly reach from the cosmological to the psychological.* (*TQ* 63) At ten o'clock, the old, long-out-of-print **science fiction** writer announced it was his bedtime. There was one last thing he wanted to say to us, to his family. Like a magician seeking a volunteer from the audience, he asked someone to stand beside him and do what he said. I held up my hand. "Me, please, me," I said. . . .

"Even if you'd taken an hour," he said, "something would have passed between where those two heavenly bodies used to be, at, conservatively speaking, a million times the speed of light."

"What was it?" I said.

"Your awareness," he said. "That is a new quality in the Universe, which exists only because there are human beings. Physicists must from now on, when pondering the secrets of the Cosmos, factor in not only energy and matter and time, but something very new and beautiful, which is human awareness."

Trout paused, ensuring with the ball of his left thumb that his upper dental plate would not slip when he said his last words to us that enchanted evening.

All was well with his teeth. This was his finale: "I have thought of a better word than awareness," he said. "Let us call it soul." He paused.

"Ting-a-ling?" he said.

(*MWC* 2) I became a so-called **science fiction** writer when someone decreed that I was a **science fiction** writer. I did not want to be classified as one, so I wondered in what way I'd offended that I would not get credit for being a serious writer. I decided that it was because I wrote about technology, and most fine American writers know nothing about technology. I got classified as a **science fiction** writer simply because I wrote about Schenectady, New York. My first book, *Player Piano*, was about Schenectady. There are huge factories in Schenectady and nothing else. I and my associates were engineers, physicists, chemists, and mathematicians. And when I wrote about the General Electric Company and Schenectady, it seemed a fantasy of the future to critics who had never seen the place.

I think that novels that leave out technology misrepresent life as badly as Victorians misrepresented life by leaving out sex.

(*MWC* 8) I am, incidentally, Honorary President of the American Humanist Association, having succeeded the late, great **science fiction** writer Isaac Asimov in that totally functionless capacity. We had a memorial service for Isaac a few years back, and I spoke and said at one point, "Isaac is up in heaven now." It was the funniest thing I could have said to an audience of humanists. I rolled them in the aisles. It was several minutes before order could be restored. And if I should ever die, God forbid, I hope you will say, "Kurt is up in heaven now." That's my favorite joke.

How do humanists feel about Jesus? I say of Jesus, as all humanists do, "If what he said is good, and so much of it is absolutely beautiful, what does it matter if he was God or not?"

(*MWC* 9) The title of Michael Moore's *Fahrenheit 9/11* is a parody of the title of Ray Bradbury's great **science-fiction** novel *Fahrenheit 451*. Four hundred and fifty-one degrees Fahrenheit is the combustion point, incidentally, of paper, of which books are composed. The hero of Bradbury's novel is a municipal worker whose job is burning books.

While on the subject of burning books, I want to congratulate librarians, not famous for their physical strength, their powerful political connections or great wealth, who, all over this country, have staunchly resisted anti-democratic bullies who have tried to remove certain books from their shelves, and destroyed records rather than have to reveal to thought police the names of persons who have checked out those titles.

(*MWC* 11) That night I got a call from my friend, the out-of-print-**science-fiction** writer Kilgore Trout. He asked me, "Did you watch the State of the Union address?"

"Yes, and it certainly helped to remember what the great British socialist playwright George Bernard Shaw said about this planet."

"Which was?"

"He said, 'I don't know if there are men on the moon, but if there are, they must be using the earth as their lunatic asylum.' And he wasn't talking about the germs or the elephants. He meant we the people."

(*GBK* Mary Wollstonecraft Shelley) I spoke in Heaven today to Mary Wollstonecraft Shelley, author, again before she was twenty, of the most prescient and influential **science fiction** novel of all times: *Frankenstein: Or the Modern Prometheus.* That was in 1818, a full century before the end of the First World War—with its Frankensteinian inventions of posion gas, tanks and airplanes, flame throwers and land mines, and barbed-wire entanglements everywhere.

I hoped to get Mary Shelley's opinions of the atomic bombs we dropped on the unarmed men, women, and children of Hiroshima and Nagasaki—and promise to try again. This time, though, she would only rhapsodize about her parents, who were, of course, William and Mary Wollstonecraft Godwin, and about her husband, Percy Bysshe Shelley, and his friends and hers, John Keats and Lord Byron.

I said many ignorant people nowadays thought "Frankenstein" was the name of the monster, and not of the scientist who created him.

She said, "That's not so ignorant after all. There are two monsters in my story, not one. And one of them, the scientist, is indeed named Frankenstein."

This is Kurt Vonnegut in Huntsville, Texas, signing off.

(*GBK* Kilgore Trout) I have interviewed a person who is still alive.

He is **science-fiction** writer Kilgore Trout. I asked him how he felt about what happened in Kosovo, Serbia. I tape-recorded his reply, but his upper plate came unstuck again and again. For the sake of clarity, I repeat in my own voice what he said.

And I quote:

NATO should have resisted the nearly irresistible temptation to be entertainers on television, to compete with movies by blowing up bridges and police stations and factories and so on. The infrastructure of the Serb tyranny should have been left unharmed in order to support justice and sanity, should they return. All cities and even little towns are world assets. For NATO to make one unliveable is to cut off its nose to spite its face, so to speak.

Show business!

The homicidal paranoia and schizophrenia of ethnic cleansing does its worst quickly now, almost instantly, like a tidal wave or volcano or earth-quake—in Rwanda and now Kosovo, and who knows where else? The disease used to take years. One thinks of the Europeans killing off the Aborigines in the Western Hemisphere, and in Australia and Tasmania, and the Turks' elimination of Armenians from their midst—of course the Holocaust, which ground on and on from 1933 to 1945. The Tasmanian genocide, incidentally, is the only one of which I've heard which was one-hundred-percent successful. Nobody on the face of the Earth has a native Tasmanian as a forebear!

See also: GBR 1; *SL5* 5; 8; *BC* 1; 12; 14; 20; 21; *MH* Tomorrow and Tomorrow and Tomorrow; *WFG* Preface; *WFG* Science Fiction; *WFG* Address to the American Physical Society; *WFG* Thinking Unthinkable, Speaking Unspeakable; *WFG Playboy* Interview; *JB* 4; 5; 6; 7; 16; Epilogue; *PS* Religion; *Gal* 1:14; 1:33; 2:1; 2:4; 2:7; *HP* 16; 23; 35; 40; *TQ* 4; 7; 19; 28; *BAG* Preface by Peter Reed; *BAG* The Package; *GBK* Isaac Asimov.

Scilly Islands. *Merrihue Rosewater writes in his* A History of the Rosewaters of Rhode Island, The Old World home of the Rosewaters was and is in the **Scilly Islands,** *off Cornwall. The founder of the family there, whose name was John, arrived on St. Mary Island in 1645, with the party accompanying the fifteen-year-old Prince Charles, later to become Charles the Second, who was fleeing the Puritan Revolution. . . . John Graham, rechristened John Rosewater in the* **Scilly Islands,** *apparently found the mild climate and the new name congenial, for he remained there for the rest of his life, fathering seven sons and six daughters (GBR 11).*

Scipio. *The fictional town in the Finger Lakes region of New York, ancestral home of the Tarkington family, founders of the Mohiga Wagon Company and the Mohiga Valley Free Institute, which later becomes Tarkington College, in* Hocus Pocus.

Scrotum (*see also* **The Wrinkled Old Family Retainer**). (*TQ* 46) *The eponymous wrinkled old family retainer, crying his rheumy eyes out behind a potted palm* during the marriage ceremony of Flagrante Delicto to Mirabile Dictu.

Seitz, Al and Sue. (*DD* Preface) I found one such bill (*a faded and shrunken American dollar*) in my wallet when I got home from Haiti a couple of years ago, and I mailed it back to **Al** and **Sue Seitz,** the owners and host and hostess of the Oloffson, asking them to release it into its natural environment. It could never have survived a day in New York City. *Rudy Waltz and his brother eventually purchase the hotel from Al and Sue.*

Seren, Leo. *Having just earned his doctorate in physics from the University of Chicago, Seren was asked to work on the Manhattan Project in 1942, a project famously conducted beneath the university's football stadium and that later led to the production of the atom bomb. According to his obituary, Seren was present when the first nuclear reactor achieved critical mass on December 2, 1942. He later worked on nuclear projects until, in 1960, he deemed it impossible to safely dispose of radioactive waste.*

Vonnegut brings him into Timequake *as a way of punctuating one of his core beliefs—that humanity's greatest science minds often work without a conscience or foresight. Seren is one of those scientists Vonnegut came to admire.*

(*TQ* 2) Fifty-three years later, on August 6th, 1995, there was a gathering in the chapel of my university to commemorate the fiftieth anniversary of the detonation of the first atomic bomb, over the city of Hiroshima, Japan. I was there.

One of the speakers was the physicist **Leo Seren**. He had participated in the successful experiment under the lifeless sports facility so long ago. Get this: He apologized for having done that!

Somebody should have told him that being a physicist, on a planet where the smartest animals hate being alive so much, means never having to say you're sorry.

sergeant (*also* **radio operator**). *In the short story "Thanasphere," collected in* Bagombo Snuff Box (1999), *the unnamed ground-based radio operator for Project Cyclops points out the obvious interest people would take in the knowledge that the souls of the departed occupy an outer ring of Earth and are capable of speaking their minds. Lieutenant General Dane insists he participate in keeping the infor-*

mation secret since no one is to know that America even has a man in space, that it could precipitate a war. "Don't you see, sir?" said the **radio operator**. "Don't you see? It's an omen. When people find out about all the spirits out there they'll forget about war. They won't want to think about anything but the spirits."

Sermon on the Mount. *Among the many references Vonnegut makes to the Sermon on the Mount, perhaps the most insightful one for his readers comes from Bernard V. O'Hare's letter commemorating his sixtieth birthday. O'Hare is, of course, Vonnegut's war buddy and fellow survivor of the Dresden firebombing. He and Vonnegut returned to Dresden during the writing of* Slaughterhouse-Five. *(FWD* What Bernard V. O'Hare Said About Our Friendship on My Sixtieth Birthday*) In some reviews Kurt has been characterized as a black humorist. Those reviewers wouldn't know black humor from Good Friday. They don't know that what they read is only his reaction to the sight of the world gone mad and rushing headlong toward Dresden to the hundredth power.*

And they miss his message, in which he pleads that world governments found their rule on something more akin to the **Sermon on the Mount** than the preachings of those who lead the world to Armageddon.

There is certainly nothing wrong with a man like that. And if such thinking constitutes black humor, it's too bad there is not an epidemic of it.

I am glad Kurt and I did not die.

And I would go back to Dresden with him again. Happy Birthday, Kurt.

God Bless You, Mr. Rosewater *is Vonnegut's novel about money, the poor, and man's responsibility for both. This passage recalls a time twenty years earlier when Stewart Buntline's youth and compassion are hammered into a lifelong conservatism by his lawyer and financial adviser, Mr. McAllister.* (GBR 10) "Every year at least one young man whose affairs we manage comes into our office, wants to give his money away. He has completed his first year at some great university. It has been an eventful year! He has learned of unbelievable suffering around the world. He has learned of the

great crimes that are at the roots of so many family fortunes. He has had his Christian nose rubbed, often for the very first time, in the **Sermon on the Mount**.

"He is confused, tearful, angry! He demands to know, in hollow tones, how much money he is worth. We tell him. He goes haggard with shame, even if his fortune is based on something as honest and useful as Scotch Tape, aspirin, rugged pants for the working man, or, as in your case, brooms. You have, if I'm not mistaken, just completed one year at Harvard?"

"Yes."

"It's a great institution, but, when I see the effect it has on certain young people, I ask myself, 'How dare a university teach compassion without teaching history, too?' History tells us this, my dear young Mr. Buntline, if it tells us nothing else: Giving away a fortune is a futile and destructive thing. It makes whiners of the poor, without making them rich or even comfortable. And the donor and his descendents [*sic*] become undistinguished members of the whining poor."

Jailbird's *Kenneth Whistler is based on the real union organizer Powers Hapgood. Walter Starbuck's reply to Richard Nixon during hearings of the House Un-American Activities Committee is the same as Mr. McAllister's in* God Bless You, Mr. Rosewater. *(JB Prologue) Moon Claycomb's father, according to Powers Hapgood, asked him this final question just before lunch:* "Mr. Hapgood," he said, "why would a man from such a distinguished family and with such a fine education choose to live as you do?"

"Why?" said Hapgood, according to Hapgood. "Because of the **Sermon on the Mount**, sir."

And Moon Claycomb's father said this: "Court is adjourned until two P.M."

What, exactly, was the **Sermon on the Mount**?

It was the prediction by Jesus Christ that the poor in spirit would receive the Kingdom of Heaven; that all who mourned would be comforted; that the meek would inherit the Earth; that those who hungered for righteousness would find it; that the merciful would be treated mercifully; that the pure in heart would see God; that the peacemakers would be called the sons of God; that those who were persecuted for righteousness' sake would also receive the Kingdom of Heaven; and on and on.

(*JB* Epilogue) Congressman Nixon had asked me why, as the son of immigrants who had been treated so well by Americans, as a man who had been treated like a son and been sent to Harvard by an American capitalist, I had been so ungrateful to the American economic system.

The answer I gave him was not original. Nothing about me has ever been original. I repeated what my onetime hero, Kenneth Whistler, had said in reply to the same general sort of question long, long ago. Whistler had been a witness at a trial of strikers accused of violence. The judge had become curious about him, had asked him why such a well-educated man from such a good family would so immerse himself in the working class.

My stolen answer to Nixon was this: "Why? **The Sermon on the Mount**, sir."

(*PS* In the Capital of the World) "I am enchanted by the **Sermon on the Mount**. Being merciful, it seems to me, is the only good idea we have received so far. Perhaps we will get another idea that good by and by—and then we will have two good ideas. What might that second good idea be? I don't know. How could I know? I will make a wild guess that it will come from music somehow. I have often wondered what music is and why we love it so. It may be that music is that second good idea's being born."

(*PS* In the Capital of the World) "There are two sisters of Lazarus there—Martha and Mary. They, at least, are sympathetic and imaginatively helpful. Mary begins to massage and perfume the feet of Jesus Christ with an ointment made from the spikenard plant. Jesus has the bones of a man and is clothed in the flesh of a man—so it must feel awfully nice, what Mary is doing to his feet. Would it be heretical of us to suppose that Jesus closes his eyes?

"This is too much for that envious hypocrite Judas, who says, trying to be more Catholic than the Pope: 'Hey—this is very un-Christian. Instead of wasting that stuff on your feet, we should have sold it and given the money to the poor people.'

"To which Jesus replies in Aramaic: 'Judas, don't worry about it. There will still be plenty of poor people left long after I'm gone.'

"This is about what Mark Twain or Abraham Lincoln would have said under similar circumstances.

"If Jesus did in fact say that, it is a divine black joke, well suited to the occasion. It says everything about hypocrisy and nothing about the poor. It is a Christian joke, which allows Jesus to remain civil to Judas, but to chide him about his hypocrisy all the same.

"'Judas, don't worry about it. There will still be plenty of poor people left long after I'm gone.'

"Shall I regarble it for you? 'The poor you always have with you, but you do not always have me.'

"My own translation does no violence to the words in the Bible. I have changed their order some, not merely to make them into the joke the situation calls for, but to harmonize them, too, with the **Sermon on the Mount**. **The Sermon on the Mount** suggests a mercifulness that can never waver or fade."

Eugene Debs Hartke must respond to Kimberly Wilder's clandestinely collected tapes gathered as evidence for her father's denunciation of Hartke at the meeting of Tarkington's Board of Trustees. (*HP* 11) She asked me about my own lecture in Chapel only a month earlier. She hadn't attended and so hadn't taped it. She was seeking confirmation of things other people had said I said. My lecture had been humorous recollections of my maternal grandfather, Benjamin Wills, the old-time Socialist.

She accused me of saying that all rich people were drunks and lunatics.

This was a garbling of Grandfather's saying that Capitalism was what the people with all our money, drunk or sober, sane or insane, decided to do today. So I straightened that out, and explained that the opinion was my grandfather's, not my own.

"I heard your speech was worse than Mr. Slazinger's," she said.

"I certainly hope not," I said. "I was trying to show how outdated my grandfather's opinions were. I wanted people to laugh. They did."

"I heard you said Jesus Christ was un-American," she said, her tape recorder running all the time.

So I unscrambled that one for her. The original had been another of Grandfather's sayings. He repeated Karl Marx's prescription for an ideal society, "From each according to his abilities, to each according to his needs." And then he asked me, meaning it to be a wry joke, "What could be more unAmerican, Gene, than sounding like the **Sermon on the Mount**?"

(*FWD* VII) The Attorney General's Commission on Pornography, a traveling show about dirty books and pictures put on the road during the administration of Ronald Reagan, was something else again. At least a couple of the panel members would later be revealed as having been in the muck of financial or sexual atrocities. There was a clan feeling, to be sure, but the family property in this case was the White House, and an amiable, sleepy, absent-minded old movie actor was its totem pole. And the crazy quilt of ideas all its members had to profess put the Council of Trent to shame for meanspirited, objectively batty fantasias: that it was good that civilians could buy assault rifles; that the contras in Nicaragua were a lot like Thomas Jefferson and James Madison; that Palestinians were to be called "terrorists" at every opportunity; that the contents of wombs were Government property; that the American Civil Liberties Union was a subversive organization; that anything that sounded like the **Sermon on the Mount** was socialist or communist, and therefore anti-American; that people with AIDS, except for those who got it from mousetrapped blood transfusions, had asked for it; that a billion-dollar airplane was well worth the price; and on and on.

(*FWD* XIV) British imperialism was armed robbery. The British class system (which seems so right to the Neo-Cons) was and still is unarmed robbery. (Just because the Soviet Union, which used to brag about being such a friend of the common people, has collapsed, that doesn't mean the **Sermon on the Mount** must now be considered balderdash.)

(*FWD* XVI) "When I say that the Unitarian Universalists, the people who know pure baloney when they hear it, are something like the early Christians in the catacombs, am I suggesting that contempt for baloney will someday be as widespread as Christianity is today? Well the example of Christianity is not encouraging, actually, since it was nothing but a poor people's religion, a servant's religion, a slave's religion, a woman's religion, a child's religion, and would have remained such if it hadn't stopped taking the **Sermon on the Mount** seriously and joined forces with the vain and rich and violent. I can't imagine that you would want to do that, to give up everything you believe in order to play a bigger part in world history."

(*TQ* 1) Jesus said how awful life was, in the **Sermon on the Mount**: "Blessed are they that mourn," and "Blessed are the meek," and "Blessed are they which do hunger and thirst after righteousness."

Henry David Thoreau said most famously, "The mass of men lead lives of quiet desperation."

(*TQ* 9) I still quote Eugene Debs (1855–1926), late of Terre Haute, Indiana, five times the Socialist Party's candidate for President, in every speech:

"While there is a lower class I am in it, while there is a criminal element I am of it; while there is a soul in prison, I am not free." In recent years, I've found it prudent to say before quoting Debs that he is to be taken seriously. Otherwise many in the audience will start to laugh. They are being nice, not mean, knowing I like to be funny. But it is also a sign of these times that such a moving echo of the **Sermon on the Mount** can be perceived as outdated, wholly discredited horsecrap.

Which it is not.

In the introduction to God Bless You, Dr. Kevorkian, *Vonnegut declares*, I myself have written, "If it weren't for the message of mercy and pity in Jesus' **Sermon on the Mount**, I wouldn't want to be a human being. I would just as soon be a rattlesnake."

In episode 7 of God Bless You, Dr. Kevorkian, *Vonnegut enjoys a brief visit with his hero, Eugene Victor Debs (whose name is the title of the episode) in the blue tunnel to the afterlife*. I thanked him for words of his, which I quote again and again in lectures: "As long as there is a lower class, I am in it. As long as there is a criminal element, I am of it. As long as there is a soul in prison, I am not free"

He asked me how those words were received here on Earth in America nowadays. I said they were ridiculed. "People snicker and snort," I said. He asked what our fastest growing industry was. "The building of prisons," I said.

"What a shame," he said. And then he asked me how the **Sermon on the Mount** was going over these days. And then he spread his wings and flew away.

In Man Without a Country, *Vonnegut speaks of another of his heroes, the labor leader Powers Hapgood, also in reference to the Sermon on the Mount.* (MWC 1) Hapgood's family owned a successful cannery in Indianapolis, and when Powers Hapgood inherited it, he turned it over to the employees, who ruined it.

We met in Indianapolis after the end of the Second World War. He had become an official in the CIO. There had been some sort of dust-up on a picket line, and he was testifying about it in court, and the judge stops everything and asks him, "Mr. Hapgood, here you are, you're a graduate of Harvard. Why would anyone with your advantages choose to live as you have?" Hapgood answered the judge: "Why, because of the **Sermon on the Mount**, sir."

And again; Hooray for our team (MWC 2) How do humanists feel about Jesus? I say of Jesus, as all humanists do, "If what he said is good, and so much of it is absolutely beautiful, what does it matter if he was God or not?"

But if Christ hadn't delivered the **Sermon on the Mount**, with its message of mercy and pity, I wouldn't want to be a human being.

I'd just as soon be a rattlesnake.

Vonnegut returns to linking Eugene V. Debs and the Sermon on the Mount in A Man Without a Country *when he simply can not withhold his sarcasm about the administration of President Bush in the chapter entitled "Do Unto Others."* (MWC 2) Doesn't anything socialistic make you want to throw up? Like great public schools, or health insurance for all?

When you get out of bed each morning, with the roosters crowing, wouldn't you like to say. "As long as there is a lower class, I am in it. As long as there is a criminal element, I am of it. As long as there is a soul in prison, I am not free."

How about Jesus' **Sermon on the Mount**, the Beatitudes?

Blessed are the meek, for they shall inherit the Earth.

Blessed are the merciful, for they shall obtain mercy.

Blessed are the peacemakers, for they shall be called the children of God.

And so on.

Not exactly planks in a Republican platform. Not exactly George W. Bush, Dick Cheney, or Donald Rumsfeld stuff.

For some reason, the most vocal Christians among us never mention the Beatitudes. But, often with tears in their eyes, they demand that the Ten Commandments be posted in public buildings. And of course that's Moses, not Jesus. I haven't heard one of them demand that the **Sermon on the Mount**, the Beatitudes, be posted anywhere.

"Blessed are the merciful" in a courtroom? "Blessed are the peacemakers" in the Pentagon? Give me a break!

Sevier County, Tennessee. *Homes and windows are rattled in Sevier County, Tennessee on July 26 when the government launches Project Cyclops from the nearby state forest in Elkmont. The launch supports the mission of Project Cyclops in the 1950 short story "Thanasphere," collected in* Bagombo Snuff Box *(1999). The top-secret project lifts Major Allen Rice into orbit to act as a weather spotter for potential aerial attacks on various Cold War countries.*

shaft. (PP I) The rafters still bore the marks of what Edison had done with the lonely brick barn: bolt holes showed where overhead **shafts** had once carried power to a forest of belts, and the woodblock floor was black with the oil and scarred by the feet of the crude machines the belts had spun.

(PP I) Now, by switching in lathes on a master panel and feeding them signals from the tape, Paul could make the essence of Rudy Hertz produce one, ten, a hundred, or a thousand of the **shafts**.

(ST 1) The fountain itself was marvelously creative . . . a cone described by many stone bowls of decreasing diameters. The bowls were collars on a cylindrical **shaft** forty feet high. *This is the fountain outside the Rumfoord estate.*

(ST 3) The Magnum Opus Building was a slender, prismatic, twelve-sided **shaft**, faced on all twelve sides with blue-green glass that shaded to rose at the base. The twelve sides were said by the architect to represent the twelve great religions of the world. So far, no one had asked the architect to name them. (ST 12) The wafer itself was contained in a gold mesh reticule which was hung on a stainless steel band clamped to the **shaft** that might be called Salo's neck. *The reticule around the Tralfamadorian messenger's neck held the one word message, "Greetings."*

(CC 33) I asked Marvin Breed if he'd known Emily Hoenikker, the wife of Felix; the mother of Angela, Frank, and Newt; the woman under that monstrous **shaft**. *The shaft is an enormous obelisk.*

(SL5 2) Their suction cups were on the ground, and their **shafts**, which were extremely flexible, usually pointed to the sky. At the top of each **shaft** was a little hand with a green eye in its palm. *Part of Billy's description of the Tralfamadorians.*

(PS Obscenity) Codpieces were very much in fashion, and many men were wearing codpieces in the shape of rocket ships, in honor of the Big Space Fuck. These customarily had the letters "U.S.A." embroidered on the **shaft**. Senator Snopes' **shaft**, however, bore the Stars and Bars of the Confederacy. *From Vonnegut's short story "The Big Space Fuck."*

(DD 4) *Rudy describes his parents' weather vane:* Its arrow alone was twelve feet long, and one hollow copper horseman chased another one down that awesome **shaft**. The one in back was an Austrian with a lance. The one in front, fleeing for his life, was a Turk with a scimitar.

(DD 5) And as soon as those relatives of mine got home, according to the paper, Father flew his favorite gift from Hitler from the horizontal **shaft** of the weather vane. It was a Nazi flag as big as a bedsheet.

(TQ 37) He was seeking shelter from the growing din on Broadway, half a block away, and from the sounds of really serious explosions from other parts of the city. A mile and a half to the south, near Grant's Tomb, a massive Department of Sanitation truck, for want of sincere steering, plowed through the lobby of a condominium and into the apartment of the building superintendent. It knocked over his gas range. The ruptured pipe of that major appliance filled the stairwell and elevator **shaft** of

the six-story structure with methane laced with skunk smell. Most of the tenants were on Social Security.

And then KA-BOOM!

"An accident waiting to happen," as Kilgore Trout would say at Xanadu.

See also: PP I; XII; ST 3; 6; 11; CC 29; 33; 100; 117; Slap 79; JB 88; HP 65; TQ 123; 128.

Shah of Bratpuhr. *The spiritual leader of six million members of the Kolhouri sect is a visiting head of state in* Player Piano. *He travels across the United States and is eventually trapped within his limousine during the Ghost Shirt uprising in Ilium. He sees EPICAC as a false god and the Reeks and Wrecks as slaves.*

He is mentioned again in Hocus Pocus. *Eugene Debs Hartke's long-lost son, Rob Roy, is raised by Lowell Fenstermaker, the owner of a Dubuque meatpacking business. Fenstermaker is bought out by the Shah of Bratpuhr, and now Rob Roy Fenstermaker is "fabulously well-to-do."*

Shakely, Norton. *In the short story "The Boy Who Hated Girls," collected in* Bagombo Snuff Box *(1999), Norton Shakely is the next in a long line of promising but vulnerable young student musicians taken in by band director George Helmholtz for private lessons and the kind of paternal surrogacy that proves affirming for some and completely disorienting for others.*

The latter is the case for Bert Higgens, the student preceding Norton, who feels utterly abandoned when Helmholtz promotes him to the Ten Square Band after two years of private trumpet lessons and bonding events. Though Helmholtz views his mentoring as innocent and caring, Bert feels the sting of his father's abandonment all over again when he is passed to Larry Fink for training beyond Helmholtz's ability.

Shakely may be facing the same disruption borne from Helmholtz's best intentions, as is true of Bert and a long string of band alumni. Helmholtz tells Bert why he can't take him back for lessons. "**Norton Shakely**," *said Helmholtz.* "Little fellow—kind of green around the gills. He's just like you were when you started out. No faith in himself. Doesn't think he'll ever make the Ten Square Band, but he will, he will."

Shakespeare, William (*see also* **God Bless You, Dr. Kevorkian**). (GBR 2) Norman Mushari learned that, on the night of *Aïda*, Eliot disappeared again, jumped out of his homeward-bound cab at Forty-second Street and Fifth Avenue.

Ten days later, Sylvia got this letter, which was written on the stationery of the Elsinore Volunteer Fire Department, Elsinore, California. The name of the place set him off on a new line of speculation about himself, to the effect that he was a lot like **Shakespeare**'s Hamlet.

Dear Ophelia—

Elsinore isn't quite what I expected, or maybe there's more than one, and I've come to the wrong one. The high school football players here call themselves "The Fighting Danes." In the surrounding towns they're known as "The Melancholy Danes." In the past three years they have won one game, tied two, and lost twenty-four. That's what happens, I guess, when Hamlet goes in as quarterback.

(BC 20) The novel in question, incidentally, was *The Smart Bunny*. The leading character was a rabbit who lived like all the other wild rabbits, but who was as intelligent as Albert Einstein or **William Shakespeare**. It was a female rabbit. She was the only female leading character in any novel or story by Kilgore Trout.

(WFG Address to Graduating Class at Bennington College, 1970) I should like to give a motto to your class, a motto to your entire generation. It comes from my favorite **Shakespearean** play, which is *King Henry VI, Part Three*. In the first scene of Act Two, you will remember, Edward, Earl of March, who will later become King Edward IV, enters with Richard, who will later become Duke of Gloucester. They are the Duke of York's sons. They arrive at the head of their troops on a plain near Mortimer's Cross in Herefordshire and immediately receive news that their father has had his head cut off. Richard says this, among other things, and this is the motto I give you: "To weep is to make less the depth of grief."

Again: "To weep is to make less the depth of grief."

It is from this same play, which has been such a comfort to me, that we find the line, "The smallest worm will turn being trodden on." I don't have to tell you that the line is spoken by Lord Clifford in Scene One of Act Two. This is meant to be optimistic, I think, but I have to tell you that a worm can be stepped on in such a way that it can't possibly turn after you remove your foot.

(WFG *Playboy* Interview) PLAYBOY: *Slaughterhouse-Five* is mainly about the Dresden fire bombing, which you went through during World War Two. What made you decide to write it in a science-fiction mode?

VONNEGUT: These things are intuitive. There's never any strategy meeting about what you're going to do; you just come to work every day. And the science-fiction passages in *Slaughterhouse-Five* are just like the clowns in **Shakespeare**. When **Shakespeare** figured the audience had had enough of the heavy stuff, he'd let up a little, bring on a clown or a foolish innkeeper or something like that, before he'd become serious again. And trips to other planets, science fiction of an obviously kidding sort, is equivalent to bringing on the clowns every so often to lighten things up.

(*Slap* 16) The People's Republic of China was at that very moment secretly creating literally millions upon millions of geniuses—by teaching pairs or small groups of congenial, telepathically compatible specialists to think as single minds. And those patchwork minds were the equals of Sir Isaac Newton's or **William Shakespeare**'s, say.

(*Slap* 27) It seemed possible to me that she might shoot me from there, or hit me with a bag of excrement. She had traveled all the way from Peru to deliver one-half of a **Shakespearean** sonnet.

"Listen!" she said. "Listen!" she said. And then she said, "Listen!" again.

The flare was meanwhile dying nearby—its parachute snagged in a treetop.

Here is what Eliza said to me, and to the neighborhood:

"O! how thy worth with manners may I sing,
"When thou art all the better part of me?
"What can mine own praise to mine own
        self bring?
"And what is't but mine own when I praise
        thee?

"Even for this let us divided live,
"And our dear love lose name of single one,

"That by this separation I may give

"That due to thee, which thou deserv'st
    alone."

(*PS* Triage) As for your use of language: Remember that two great masters of our language, **William Shakespeare** and James Joyce, wrote sentences which were almost childlike when their subjects were most profound. "To be or not to be?" asks **Shakespeare**'s Hamlet. The longest word is three letters long. Joyce, when he was frisky, could put together a sentence as intricate and glittering as a necklace for Cleopatra, but my favorite sentence in his short story "Eveline" is this one: "She was tired." At that point in the story, no other words could break the heart of a reader as those words do.

(*PS* The People One Knows) I admire anybody who finishes a work of art, no matter how awful it may be. A drama critic from a news magazine, speaking to me on the opening night of a play of mine, said that he liked to remind himself from time to time that **Shakespeare** was standing right behind him, so that he had to be very responsible and wise whenever he expressed an opinion about a play.

I told him that he had it exactly ass backwards— that **Shakespeare** was standing behind me and every other playwright who was foolhardy enough to face an opening night, no matter how bad our plays might be.

(*Slap* Epilogue) "When I thought I was going to talk about reference points, I had in mind the fixtures in a simpler and more stable civilization than what we have today. Examples: **Shakespeare**'s *Hamlet*, Beethoven's Fifth Symphony, Leonardo's Mona Lisa, Lincoln's Gettysburg Address, Mark Twain's *Huckleberry Finn*—the Great Wall of China, the Leaning Tower of Pisa, the Sphinx. These few works of art used to be enormous monuments in the minds of public school graduates in every corner of this country. They have now been drowned in our minds, like Atlantis, if you will, by the latest sensations on television and radio, and in our motion picture palaces and *People* magazine. . . ."

(*PS* The Sexual Revolution) The grades I hand out to myself do not place me in literary history. I am comparing myself with myself. Thus can I give myself an A-plus for *Cat's Cradle*, while knowing that there was a writer named **William Shakespeare**.

(*DD* Epilogue) And I, Rudy Waltz, the **William Shakespeare** of Midland City, the only serious dramatist ever to live and work there, will now make my own gift to the future, which is a legend. I have invented an explanation of why Will Fairchild's ghost is likely to be seen roaming almost anywhere in town—in the empty arts center, in the lobby of the bank, out among the little shitboxes of Avondale, out among the luxurious homes of Fairchild Heights, in the vacant lot where the public library stood for so many years. . . .

Will Fairchild is looking for his parachute.

(*Gal* 1:37) If there were a monument out here in the islands, though, celebrating a key event in the past, that would be a good one: the moment of mating, right before the explosion, between that rocket and that radar dish.

Into the lava plinth beneath it these words might be incised, expressing the sentiments of all who had had a hand in the design and manufacture and sale and purchase and launch of the rocket, and of all to whom high explosives were a branch of the entertainment industry:

> . . . 'Tis a consummation
> Devoutly to be wish'd.
>   **—WILLIAM SHAKESPEARE**
>   (1564–1616)

(*Gal* 2:12) As for what was wrong with the *Captain, Mandarax made the educated guess that he had Alzheimer's disease. The old poop couldn't look after himself anymore, and hardly knew where he was. He would have starved to death if Akiko hadn't brought him food every day and, one way or another, made sure he swallowed at least some of it. He was eighty-six.

Quoth *Mandarax:

> *Last scene of all,*
> *That ends this strange eventful history,*
> *Is second childishness and mere oblivion,*
> *Sans teeth, sans eyes, sans taste, sans every-*
>   *thing.*
>   **—WILLIAM SHAKESPEARE**
>   (1564–1616)

(*Gal* 2:14) The *Captain had a lapse of memory, and so did not know what to make of the bloody water. He didn't even know what part of the world he was in. The most alarming thing to him was that he was being attacked by birds. These were harmless vampire finches going after his bedsores, some of the commonest birds on the island. But to him they were new and terrifying.

He slapped at them, and cried out for help. More and more finches kept coming, and he was so convinced that they meant to kill him that he jumped into the water, where he was eaten by a hammerhead shark. This animal had its eyes on the ends of stalks, a design perfected by the Law of Natural Selection many, many millions of years ago. It was a flawless part in the clockwork of the universe. There was no defect in it which might yet be modified. One thing it surely did not need was a bigger brain.

What was it going to do with a bigger brain? Compose Beethoven's Ninth Symphony?

Or perhaps write these lines:

All the world's a stage,
And all the men and women merely players.
They have their exits and their entrances;
And one man in his time plays many
     parts . . . ?

—WILLIAM SHAKESPEARE
(1564–1616)

(*HP* 16) What I had done to Fred was catch him stealing a Tarkington beer mug from the college bookstore. What Fred Stone did was beyond mere stealing. He took the beer mug off the shelf, drank make-believe toasts to me and the cashier, who were the only other people there, and then walked out.

I had just come from a faculty meeting where the campus theft problem had been discussed for the umpteenth time. . . .

So I followed Fred Stone out to the Quadrangle. He was headed for his Kawasaki motorcycle in the student parking lot. I came up behind him and said quietly, with all possible politeness, "I think you should put that beer mug back where you got it, Fred. Either that or pay for it."

"Oh, yeah?" he said. "Is that what you think?"

Then he smashed the mug to smithereens on the rim of the Vonnegut Memorial Fountain. "If that's what you think," he said, "then you're the one who should put it back."

I reported the incident to Tex Johnson, who told me to forget it.

But I was mad. So I wrote a letter about it to the boy's father, but never got an answer until the Board meeting.

"I can never forgive you for accusing my son of theft," the father said. He quoted **Shakespeare** on behalf of Fred. I was supposed to imagine Fred's saying it to me.

"'Who steals my purse steals trash; 'tis something, nothing,'" he said. "''Twas mine, 'tis his, and has been slave to thousands,'" he went on, "'but he that filches from me my good name robs me of that which not enriches him and makes me poor indeed.'"

"If I was wrong, sir, I apologize," I said.

"Too late," he said.
(*HP* 18) CHAPTER 18

SHAKESPEARE.

I think **William Shakespeare** was the wisest human being I ever heard of. To be perfectly frank, though, that's not saying much. We are impossibly conceited animals, and actually dumb as heck. Ask any teacher. You don't even have to ask a teacher. Ask anybody. Dogs and cats are smarter than we are.
(*HP* 18) Now the Chairman of the Board, Robert Moellenkamp, spoke up. He was illiterate, but legendary among Tarkingtonians, and no doubt back home, too, for his phenomenal memory. Like the father of the founder of the college, his ancestor, he could learn by heart anything that was read out loud to him 3 times or so. I knew several convicts at Athena, also illiterate, who could do that, too.

He wanted to quote **Shakespeare** now. "I want it on the record," he said, "that this has been an extremely painful episode for me as well." And then he delivered this speech from **Shakespeare**'s *Romeo and Juliet*, in which the dying Mercutio, Romeo's gallant and witty best friend, describes the wound he received in a duel:

"No, 'tis not so deep as a well, nor so wide as a church door; but 'tis enough, 'twill serve: ask for me tomorrow, and you shall find me a grave man. I am peppered, I warrant, for this world. A plague on both your houses!"

The two houses, of course, were the Montagues and the Capulets, the feuding families of Romeo and Juliet, whose nitwit hatred would indirectly cause Mercutio's departure for Paradise.

I have lifted this speech from *Bartlett's Familiar Quotations*. If more people would acknowledge that they got their pearls of wisdom from that book instead of the original, it might clear the air.

If there really had been a Mercutio, and if there really were a Paradise, Mercutio might be hanging out with teenage Vietnam draftee casualties now, talking about what it felt like to die for other people's vanity and foolishness.
(HP 20) "I *(Jason Wilder)* venture to say that even Mr. Hartke now agrees that this Board cannot conceive of any alternative to accepting his resignation. Am I right, Mr. Hartke?"

I got to my feet. "This is the second worst day of my life," I said. "The first was the day we got kicked out of Vietnam. **Shakespeare** has been quoted twice so far. It so happens that I can quote him, too. I have always been bad at memorizing, but I had an English teacher in high school who insisted that everyone in her class know his most famous lines by heart. I never expected to speak them as being meaningful to me in real life, but now's the time. Here goes:

"'To be, or not to be: that is the question: Whether 'tis nobler in the mind to suffer the slings and arrows of outrageous fortune, or to take arms against a sea of troubles, and by opposing end them?'

"'To die: to sleep; no more; and by a sleep to say we end the heartache and the thousand natural shocks that flesh is heir to, 'tis a consummation devoutly to be wished.'

"'To die, to sleep; to sleep: perchance to dream: ay, there's the rub; for in that sleep of death what dreams may come when we have shuffled off this mortal coil, must give us pause.'"

There was more to that speech, of course, but that was all the teacher, whose name was Mary Pratt, required us to memorize. Why overdo? It was cer-

tainly enough for the occasion, raising as it did the specter of having yet another Vietnam veteran on the faculty killing himself on school property.

The following concerns the fictitious "Protocols of the Elders of Tralfamadore": (HP 26) There was a lot more to the story than that. The author taught me a new term, which was "Finale Rack." This was apparently from the vocabulary of pyrotechnicians, specialists in loud and bright but otherwise harmless nighttime explosions for climaxes of patriotic holidays. A Finale Rack was a piece of milled lumber maybe 3 meters long and 20 centimeters wide and 5 centimeters thick, with all sorts of mortars and rocket launchers nailed to it, linked in series by a single fuse.

When it seemed that a fireworks show was over, that was when the Master Pyrotechnician lit the fuse of the Finale Rack.

That is how the author characterized World War II and the few years that followed it. He called it "the Finale Rack of socalled Human Progress."

If the author was right that the whole point of life on Earth was to make germs shape up so that they would be ready to ship out when the time came, then even the greatest human being in history, **Shakespeare** or Mozart or Lincoln or Voltaire or whoever, was nothing more than a Petri dish in the truly Grand Scheme of Things.

In the story, the Elders of Tralfamadore were indifferent, to say the least, to all the suffering going on. When 6,000 rebellious slaves were crucified on either side of the Appian Way back in good old 71 B.C., the elders would have been delighted if a crucified person had spit into the face of a centurion, giving him pneumonia or TB.

As part of a more rambling discussion about the creative process, the limitations on our time, and our solid knowledge of archetypes and motifs that make anticipating plots (both fictional and within one's life) that much easier to accept as having a next, expected, act. It can allow one to accept the inevitability of the next predictable stage in the narrative, knowing that life has proven to be a rehash of old plots, familiar schema. (FWD III) "And I will argue that interruptions are commonly beneficial, once a work of art is well begun. I myself, when reading a novel or watching a play or a film, with many chapters or scenes still to come, hear my brain saying a variation on my sister's 'Got it, got it, got it,' which is, 'End it, end it, end it. For the love of God, please end it now.' Yes, and after I have written only about two-thirds of a novel or play of my own, I suddenly feel silly and relieved, as though I were running before the wind in a little sailboat, and headed home.

"I have done all I hoped to do, and more, if I've been really lucky, than when I put to sea.

"That confession will seem as damning and barbarous to humorless persons as my sister's fantasy of whizzing through the Louvre on roller skates. At least it has the virtue of truthfulness. And I beg them to forget my own jerry-built creations, and to consider instead the tragedy of *Hamlet*, by **William Shakespeare**, act 3, scene 4—with two more acts, nine more scenes, to go. Hamlet has just killed the innocent, faithful, tiresome old man Polonius, having mistaken him for his mother's new husband. He discovers who it is that he has murdered, and declares with emotions which are mixed, to say the least: 'Thou wretched, rash, intruding fool, farewell!'

"Got it, got it, got it. All freeze. Bring in a person from Porlock. Lower the curtain. The play is done."

(*FWD XI*) So when the American ad agency for Volkswagen asked me (along with several other fogbound futurologists) to compose a letter to Earthlings a century from now which would be used in a series of institutional ads in *Time* (no friends of mine), I wrote as follows:

"Ladies & Gentlemen of A.D. 2088:

"It has been suggested that you might welcome words of wisdom from the past, and that several of us in the twentieth century should send you some. Do you know this advice from Polonius in **Shakespeare**'s *Hamlet*: 'This above all: to thine own self be true'? Or what about these instructions from St. John the Divine: 'Fear God, and give glory to Him; for the hour of His judgment has come'? The best advice from my own era for you or for just about anybody anytime, I guess, is a prayer first used by alcoholics who hoped to never take a drink again: 'God grant me the serenity to accept the things I cannot change, courage to change the things I can, and wisdom to know the difference.'

(*FWD XX*) **Shakespeare**'s Hamlet, when he sorts through the possible consequences of his doing

himself in with a bare bodkin (sleeping pills and automobile exhaust and .357 Magnums were then unavailable), does not ponder the grief and confusion he might cause many who would still be alive. He was, after all, not only a close friend of Horatio and beloved by darling Ophelia, but the future King of Denmark. (The more recent abdication of Edward VIII from the Throne of England for the love of a gimlet-eyed divorcée from Baltimore comes to mind. My fellow novelist Sidney Zion said in mixed company at supper recently, anent Edward VIII, that blowjobs accounted for the history of the world so far. Some people are so frank nowadays!)

(*FWD XX*) Most people my age and of my social class, no matter what job they held, are retired now. So it seems redundant (even silly) for critics to say, as so many do, that I am not the promising writer I used to be. If they think I am a disappointment, they should see what the passage of time has done to Mozart, **Shakespeare**, and Hemingway.

The older my father was (and he died at seventy-two), the more absentminded he became. People forgave him for that, and I think people should forgive me, too. (I never meant anybody any harm, and neither did he.)

(*TQ 10*) I told Kilgore Trout at the clambake in 2001 about how my brother and sister had made Father ashamed of hunting and fishing. He quoted **Shakespeare**: "How sharper than a serpent's tooth it is to have a thankless child!"

Trout was self-educated, never having finished high school. I was mildly surprised, then, that he could quote **Shakespeare**. I asked if he had committed a lot of that remarkable author's words to memory. He said, "Yes, dear colleague, including a single sentence which describes life as lived by human beings so completely that no writer after him need ever have written another word."

"Which sentence was that, Mr. Trout?" I asked.

And he said, "'All the world's a stage, and all the men and women merely players.'"

(*TQ 33*) My father often misquoted **Shakespeare**, but I never saw him read a book.

Yes, and I am here to suggest that the greatest writer in the English language so far was Lancelot Andrewes (1555–1626), and not the Bard of Avon

(1564–1616). Poetry was certainly in the air back then. Try this:

> The Lord is my shepherd; I shall not want.
> He maketh me to lie down in green pastures:
> he leadeth me beside the still waters.
> He restoreth my soul: he leadeth me in the paths of
> righteousness for his name's sake.
> Yea, though I walk through the valley of the shadow
> of death, I will fear no evil: for thou art with
> me; thy rod and thy staff they comfort me.
> Thou preparest a table before me in the presence of
> mine enemies: thou anointest my head with oil; my cup runneth over.
> Surely goodness and mercy shall follow me all the
> days of my life: and I will dwell in the
> house of the Lord for ever.

Lancelot Andrewes was the chief translator and paraphraser among the scholars who gave us the King James Bible.

(*TQ* 59) Julia (*Pembroke*) wrote love letters to Booth. A tryst was arranged for April 14th, 1863, two years before Booth shot Lincoln from behind with a derringer. She went to New York City from Washington with a chaperone, the alcoholic wife of an admiral, ostensibly to shop, and to escape the tensions in the besieged capital. They checked into the hotel where Booth was staying, and attended his performance that night, as Marc Antony in Julius Caesar, by **William Shakespeare**.

As Marc Antony, Booth would speak lines horrifyingly prophetic in his case: "The evil that men do lives after them."

(*BAG* Coda to My Career) No artist from anywhere, however, not even **Shakespeare**, not even Beethoven, not even James Whitcomb Riley, has changed the course of so many lives all over the planet as have four hayseeds in Ohio, two in Dayton and two in Akron. How I wish Dayton and Akron were in Indiana! Ohio could have Kokomo and Gary.

Orville and Wilbur Wright were in Dayton in 1903 when they invented the airplane.

Dr. Robert Holbrook Smith and William Griffith Wilson were in Akron in 1935 when they devised the Twelve Steps to sobriety of Alcoholics Anonymous. By comparison with Smith and Wilson, Sigmund Freud was a piker when it came to healing dysfunctional minds and lives.

(*GBK* Isaac Newton) My job is to interview dead people for WNYC, but the late Sir Isaac Newton interviewed me instead. He got to make only a single one-way trip down the tunnel. He wants to know what it seems to be made of, fabric or metal or wood or what. I tell him that it's made of whatever dreams are made of, which leaves him monumentally unsatisfied.

Saint Peter quoted **Shakespeare** to him: There are more things in Heaven and Earth, Horatio, than are dreamt of in your philosophy.

(*GBK* William Shakespeare) during my most recent controlled near-death experience, I got to interview **William Shakespeare**. We did not hit it off. He said the dialect I spoke was the ugliest English he had ever heard, "fit to split the ears of groundlings." He asked if it had a name, and I said, "Indianapolis."

(*GBK* William Shakespeare) I asked him if he had love affairs with men as well as women, knowing how eager my WNYC audience was to have this matter settled. His answer, however, celebrated affection between animals of any sort:

"We were as twinn'd lambs that did frisk in the sun, and bleat the one at the other: what we chang'd was innocence for innocence." By changed he meant exchanged: "What we exchanged was innocence for innocence." That has to be the softest core pornography I ever heard.

And he was through with me. In effect, he told your reporter to go screw himself. "Get thee to a nunnery!" he said, and off he went.

I felt like such a fool as I made my way back to the blue tunnel. An enchanting answer to any question I might have asked the greatest writer who ever lived could be found in *Bartlett's Familiar Quotations*. The beaut about exchanging innocence for innocence was from *The Winter's Tale*.

I at least remembered to ask Saint Peter if **Shakespeare** had written **Shakespeare**. He told me that nobody arriving in Heaven, and there was no Hell, had claimed authorship for any of it. Saint Peter added, "Nobody, that is, who was willing to submit to my lie-detector test."

This is your tongue-tied, humiliated, self-loathing, semi-literate Hoosier hack Kurt Vonnegut, signing off with this question for today: "To be or not to be?"

(MWC 3) But he *(Hamlet)* says okay, I got a way to check this out. I'll hire actors to act out the way the ghost said my father was murdered by my uncle, and I'll put on this show and see what my uncle makes of it. So he puts on this show. And it's not like Perry Mason. His uncle doesn't go crazy and say, "I—I—You got me, you got me, I did it, I did it." It flops. Neither good news nor bad news. After this flop Hamlet ends up talking with his mother when the drapes move, so he thinks his uncle is back there and he says, "All right, I am so sick of being so damn indecisive," and he sticks his rapier through the drapery. Well, who falls out? This windbag, Polonius. This Rush Limbaugh. And **Shakespeare** regards him as a fool and quite disposable.

You know, dumb parents think that the advice that Polonius gave to his kids when they were going away was what parents should always tell their kids, and it's the dumbest possible advice, and **Shakespeare** even thought it was hilarious.

"Neither a borrower nor a lender be." But what else is life but endless lending and borrowing, give and take?

"This above all, to thine own self be true." Be an egomaniac!

Neither good news nor bad news. Hamlet didn't get arrested. He's prince. He can kill anybody he wants. So he goes along, and finally he gets in a duel, and he's killed. Well, did he go to heaven or did he go to hell? Quite a difference. Cinderella or Kafka's cockroach? I don't think **Shakespeare** believed in a heaven or hell any more than I do. And so we don't know whether it's good news or bad news.

I have just demonstrated to you that **Shakespeare** was as poor a storyteller as any Arapaho.

But there's a reason we recognize *Hamlet* as a masterpiece: it's that **Shakespeare** told us the truth, and people so rarely tell us the truth in this rise and fall here [indicates blackboard]. The truth is, we know so little about life, we don't really know what the good news is and what the bad news is.

And if I die—God forbid—I would like to go to heaven to ask somebody in charge up there, "Hey, what was the good news and what was the bad news?"

(MWC 10) Well, one wishes that those who took over our federal government, and hence the world, by means of a Mickey Mouse coup d'état, who disconnected all the burglar alarms prescribed by the Constitution, which is to say the House and Senate, and the Supreme Court, and We, the People, were truly Christian. But as **William Shakespeare** told us long ago, "The devil can cite Scripture for his purpose."

(MWC 11) Might not it be possible, then, that the Second World War was a cause of the first one? Otherwise, the first one remains inexplicable nonsense of the most gruesome kind. Or try this: Is it possible that seemingly incredible geniuses like Bach and **Shakespeare** and Einstein were not in fact superhuman, but simply plagiarists, copying great stuff from the future?

See also: BC 17; DD 6; Cal 2:14; *Blue* 2; 4; 7; HP 2; 3; 39; *BAG* Ambitious Sophomore; *GBK* William Shakespeare; *GBK* Isaac Asimov; *MWC* 11.

Shaltoon. *In* God Bless You, Mr. Rosewater, *the home planet of Queen Margaret in Kilgore Trout's sexy science fiction novel* Venus on the Half-shell *(not to be confused with the novel of the same name authored by the real-life science fiction writer Philip Jose Farmer).*

Shapiro, Dr. Ben. *The Harvard classmate of Walter F. Starbuck who becomes a physician and a lieutenant colonel in the Army Medical Corps. He is the commander of the "twenty-bed hospital in the Kaiserburg, the imperial castle," when Starbuck brings the emaciated war refugee Ruth to him for care. Shapiro eventually serves as Walter's best man when he weds Ruth and later, as a full colonel, delivers their child by cesarean section in Wiesbaden. Unfortunately, Shapiro falls victim to McCarthyism.* (JB 3) In a few years Senator Joseph R. McCarthy would find that promotion to have been sinister, since it was well known that **Shapiro** had been a communist before the war. "Who promoted **Shapiro** to Wiesbaden?" he would want to know.

Starbuck later finds out the unhappy though

honored end to his friend's life. (JB 4) He had gone to Israel long ago and gotten himself killed in the Six Day War. I had heard that there was a primary school named in his honor in Tel Aviv.

Shaw, George Bernard. *In* A Man Without a Country, *Vonnegut cites Shaw to make a biting comment about President George W. Bush on the evening of the 2004 State of the Union address. He does so in a metafictional moment recalling his conversation with his alter ego, Kilgore Trout.* (MWC 11) That night I got a call from my friend, the out-of-print-science-fiction writer Kilgore Trout. He asked me, "Did you watch the State of the Union address?"

"Yes, and it certainly helped to remember what the great British socialist playwright **George Bernard Shaw** said about this planet."

"Which was?"

"He said, 'I don't know if there are men on the moon, but if there are, they must be using the earth as their lunatic asylum.' And he wasn't talking about the germs or the elephants. He meant we the people. . . ."

Shaw, Helene. *In the short story "Who Am I This Time?" (in* Welcome to the Monkey House), *Helene is the beautiful but uninspired newcomer to the North Crawford Mask and Wig Club who is teamed with the mercurial Harry Nash in a new production of* A Streetcar Named Desire. *Helene is transferred to North Crawford by the phone company so that she may train the local branch in how to work the automatic billing machine. She decides to accept a friendly invitation to the club's auditions as a way of meeting new people. Though her first reading is poor, once she reads opposite Harry, the two make the roles come alive. By the end of the story, Helene realizes that the only way to maintain a relationship with Harry is to offer him various roles to rehearse. Together, they privately share a rich and romantic life moving from one play to the next, always fully becoming the characters they read.*

Shaw, Marilyn. *One of the many women fondly remembered by Eugene Debs Hartke. Both are veterans of Vietnam and recruited by Sam Wakefield to* teach at Tarkington College. While serving as a nurse in the war, Marilyn's husband divorces her for another woman. After the war she gives up nursing and studies computer science at New York University, which is where Wakefield finds her. She agrees to teach provided Scipio has a chapter of Alcoholics Anonymous.

At Tarkington she becomes a tenured Full Professor and Chair of the Department of Life Sciences. When Wakefield commits suicide, she goes on a week-long drinking binge at the Black Cat Café. Killed by a stray bullet when the escaped convicts take over Scipio, Marilyn is buried at the foot of Musket Mountain. Eugene recalls, I never considered making a pass at **Marilyn**, although she was reasonably attractive and unattached. I don't know why that is. There may have been some sort of incest taboo operating, as though we were brother and sister, since we had both been in Vietnam. . . .

Remembering her now, I wonder if I wasn't in love with her, even though we avoided talking to each other as much as possible.

Maybe I should put her on a very short list indeed: all the women I loved (*HP* 12).

Shazzbutter (*see **How You Doin'?***).

Shelley, Mary Wollstonecraft (*see also **God Bless You, Dr. Kevorkian***). (FWD XII) Which brings us to the differences between men and women. Feminists have won a few modest successes in the United States during the past two decades, so it has become almost obligatory to say that the differences between the two sexes have been exaggerated. But this much is clear to me: Generally speaking, women don't like immoral technology nearly as much as men do. This could be the result of some hormone deficiency. Whatever the reason, women, often taking their children with them, tend to outnumber men in demonstrations against schemes and devices which can kill people. In fact, the most effective doubter of the benefits of unbridled technological advancement so far was a woman, **Mary Wollstonecraft Shelley**, who died 134 years ago. She, of course, created the idea of the Monster of Frankenstein.

(TQ 51) When I liken Trout there in the entrance

hall of the American Academy of Arts and Letters, awakening Dudley Prince from PTA, to Dr. Frankenstein, I am alluding of course to the antihero of the novel *Frankenstein—or, The Modern Prometheus*, by **Mary Wollstonecraft Shelley**, second wife of the English poet Percy Bysshe Shelley. In that book, the scientist Frankenstein puts a bunch of body parts from different corpses together in the shape of a man.

Frankenstein jazzes them with electricity. The results in the book are exact opposites of those since achieved in real-life American state penitentiaries with real-life electric chairs. Most people think Frankenstein is the monster. He isn't. Frankenstein is the scientist.

(*GBK* Mary Wollstonecraft Shelley) I spoke in Heaven today to **Mary Wollstonecraft Shelley**, author, again before she was twenty, of the most prescient and influential science fiction novel of all times: *Frankenstein: Or the Modern Prometheus*. That was in 1818, a full century before the end of the First World War—with its Frankensteinian inventions of posion gas, tanks and airplanes, flame throwers and land mines, and barbed wire entanglements everywhere.

I hoped to get **Mary Shelley**'s opinions of the atomic bombs we dropped on the unarmed men, women, and children of Hiroshima and Nagasaki—and promise to try again. This time, though, she would only rhapsodize about her parents, who were, of course, William and Mary Wollstonecraft Godwin, and about her husband, Percy Bysshe Shelley, and his friends and hers, John Keats and Lord Byron.

I said many ignorant people nowadays thought "Frankenstein" was the name of the monster, and not of the scientist who created him.

She said, "That's not so ignorant after all. There are two monsters in my story, not one. And one of them, the scientist, is indeed named Frankenstein."

This is Kurt Vonnegut in Huntsville, Texas, signing off.

Shepherd, Lawson. *Second-in-command at the Ilium Works under the direction of Paul Proteus, Shepherd is in charge of buildings 53 through 71. Proteus, Lawson, and Ed Finnerty graduate college*

together and join in the project that records the movements of lathe operator Rudy Hertz as part of the movement toward mechanizing repetitive manual labor.

While Finnerty is elevated to the national board level and Proteus becomes the Ilium chief, Shepherd feels slighted by being passed over. Unlike his friends who cared little for the competitiveness of the system, When **Shepherd** had first arrived in Ilium, he had announced to his fellow new arrivals, Paul and Finnerty, that he intended to compete with them. Baldly, ridiculously, he talked of competitiveness and rehashed with anyone who would listen various crises where there had been a showdown between his abilities and those of someone else, crises that the other participants had looked upon as being routine, unremarkable, and generally formless. But, to **Shepherd**, life seemed to be laid out like a golf course, with a series of beginnings, hazards, and ends, and with a definite summing up—for comparison with others' scores—after each hole. He was variously grim or elated over triumphs or failures no one else seemed to notice, but always stoical about the laws that governed the game. He asked no quarter, gave no quarter, and made very little difference to Paul, Finnerty, or any of his other associates. He was a fine engineer, dull company, and doggedly master of his fate and *not* his brother's keeper (*PP* V).

Shepherd achieves a measure of notice when named captain of the Green Team at the Meadows executive retreat. However, his team goes down to humiliating defeat because he tries to win all the events by himself.

When Paul's marriage to Anita breaks down (as a result of the ruling technocracy's plot to infiltrate the Ghost Shirt Society), Anita and Shepherd pair off. Though she previously found Shepherd contemptuous for his public and often hostile competitiveness, it is his desire for upward mobility that she finds sorely lacking in Paul. Despite remaining in love with Paul, she plans to divorce him and marry Shepherd.

Shortridge High School (*also **Shortridge Echo***). *Vonnegut is very proud of his Indianapolis alma mater and appreciative of the opportunity to write* and edit for his high school's daily newspaper. Vonnegut befriends Dan Wakefield, roughly ten years apart in school, in part because of their connection to their high school paper. (WFG Playboy Interview) PLAYBOY: How did you happen to begin writing?

VONNEGUT: The high school I went to had a daily paper, and has had since about 1900. They had a printing course for the people who weren't going on to college, and they realized, "My goodness, we've got the linotypes—we could easily get out a paper." So they started getting out a paper every day, called the **Shortridge Echo**. It was so old my parents had worked on it. And so, rather than writing for a teacher, which is what most people do, writing for an audience of one—for Miss Green or Mr. Watson—I started out writing for a large audience. And if I did a lousy job, I caught a lot of shit in twenty-four hours. It just turned out that I could write better than a lot of other people. Each person has something he can do easily and can't imagine why everybody else is having so much trouble doing it. In my case, it was writing. In my brother's case, it was mathematics and physics. In my sister's case, it was drawing and sculpting.

(TQ 62) Among other departed souls whom I would not summon back to life, if I had had the power to do so, but who were represented by doppelgängers: nine of my teachers at **Shortridge High School**, and Phoebe Hurty, who hired me in high school to write ad copy about teenage clothing for Blocks' Department Store, and my first wife Jane, and my mother, and my uncle John Rauch, husband to another of Father's first cousins.

According to John Rauch, whose passage in Palm Sunday provides extensive details about the Vonneguts' school history, Kurt Vonnegut, Sr., attended Shortridge for one year before being sent to finish school in Germany, and Kurt Jr.'s mother graduated from Shortridge.

See also: WFG Oversexed in Indianapolis; WFG Playboy Interview; PS Roots; PS When I Lost My Innocence; PS Self-Interview; PS Obscenity; FWD IX; X; XVII; TQ 25; 39; 41; 55; BAG Preface; BAG Introduction; MWC 2; ARM Clowe's Hall.

Shoup, Martin. Rabo Karabekian recounts that after being rejected as an art student by Nelson Bau-

erbeck because his art had "no internal message," he sought expression through writing. However, Bauerbeck's perceptions about Rabo's painting were echoed by Shoup's critique of his writing. (Blue 23) So I signed up for a course in creative writing instead—taught three nights a week at City College by a fairly famous short-story writer named **Martin Shoup**. His stories were about black people, although he himself was white. Dan Gregory had illustrated at least a couple of them—with the customary delight and sympathy he felt for people he believed to be orangutans.

Shoup said about my writing that I wasn't going to get very far until I became more enthusiastic about describing the looks of things—and particularly people's faces. He knew I could draw, so he found it odd that I wouldn't want to go on and on about the looks of things.

Shoup, Mary Alice. In Mother Night, the sixty-eight-year-old widowed owner of The Little Rock School of Embalming advertises for a new president and winds up hiring and marrying Lionel J. D. Jones.

Shoup, Naomi. The high school English teacher who encourages Rudy Waltz in his writing after reading his essay on this assigned subject: "The Midland City Person I Most Admire." My hero was John Fortune, who died in Katmandu when I was only six years old. She turned my ears crimson by saying that it was the finest piece of writing by a student that she had seen in forty years of teaching. She began to weep (DD 16).

Rudy hangs on to Miss Shoup's encouraging words, eventually producing the play Katmandu, which sparks horrendous reviews. Rudy had drawn a brief sketch contrasting his play's critical reception with its initial encouraging influence by citing How pathetic they would have found it, if only they had known, that I had been told that I should become a writer, that I had the divine spark, by a high school English teacher who had never been anywhere, either, who had never seen anything important, either, who had no sex life, either. And what a perfect name she had for a role like that: **Naomi Shoup** (DD 16).

Rudy's father worried about the gifts Miss Shoup

believed he possessed because he felt that once such a pronouncement is made the receiver has no choice but to follow that calling until it leads to ruin. Mr. Waltz decries that "She is obviously a siren. . . . A siren is half woman, half bird . . . you know they lure sailors with their sweet songs to shipwrecks on rocks" (DD 16).

Shriver, Sargent. *The 1972 vice presidential candidate of the Democratic Party. In a passage indicating Vonnegut's emerging sense of extended families, which becomes a central concern for President Wilbur Swain in his 1976 novel* Slapstick, *he recalls an incident that gave early shape to this idea.* (PS 11) "I know **Sargent Shriver** slightly. When he was campaigning for vice-president, he asked me if I had any ideas. You remember that there was plenty of money around, but as far as ideas went, both parties were in a state of destitution. So I told him, and I am afraid he didn't listen, that the number one American killer wasn't cardiovascular disease, but loneliness. I told him that he and McGovern could swamp the Republicans if they would promise to cure that disease. I even gave him a slogan to put on buttons and bumpers and flags and billboards: Lonesome No More!

"The rest is history."

Vonnegut also recounts this episode in the "Playboy Interview" reprinted in Wampeters, Foma & Granfalloons. *"Lonesome No More!" became the battle cry of Swain's presidency and serves as Slapstick's subtitle.*

Shultz, Hermann and Sophia. *In* Hocus Pocus, *Elias Tarkington brings brewmaster Hermann Shultz and his wife from Leipzig, Germany, to Scipio to run his new brewery. Hermann becomes a teacher of botany, German, and the flute when Tarkington opens the Mohiga Valley Free Institute. The couple die during a diphtheria epidemic in 1893, and at their request are buried on campus. In 1987 their bodies are moved to the cemetery at the foot of Musket Mountain to make way for the Pahlavi Pavilion recreation center. They share a common gravestone with the single-word inscription: freethinkers.*

Shuttle, Herb. *The vacuum cleaner salesman and suitor of Penelope Ryan in* Happy Birthday, Wanda June. *Though supremely confident in his own sales abilities, he fawns over the returning Harold Ryan. It would appear that Herb is more pleased with dating the wife of the enigmatic Harold Ryan than Penelope herself.*

Sidi Barrani. *The Egyptian site where the artist and Nazi sympathizer Dan Gregory meets his fate.* (Blue 13) They (Dan Gregory and Fred Jones) would be killed almost exactly one year before the United States joined the war—against Italy, by the way, and against Germany and Japan and some others. They were killed around December seventh of 1940 at **Sidi Barrani**, Egypt, where only thirty thousand British overwhelmed eighty thousand Italians, I learn from the *Encyclopaedia Britannica*, capturing forty thousand Italians and four hundred guns.

Siebolt, Dr. *In the short story "Runaways," collected in* Bagombo Snuff Box (1999), *the unseen Dr. Siebolt is the only adult trusted by troubled teen Annie Southard.* "**Dr. Siebolt** is the only person who ever tried to understand me as a human being," said Annie. **Dr. Siebolt** was the governor's family physician.

Later in the story Annie declares that next to Dr. Siebolt, Rice is the closest person to her. Of course, this comes after she and Rice take turns venting their familiar teenage woes, never stopping to comment on the other or even offering comfort. "We sure are lucky we found each other," said Rice.

"What?" said Annie.

"I said, 'We sure are lucky we found each other,'" said Rice.

Annie took his hand. "Oh yes, oh yes, oh yes," she said fervently.

"When we first met out there on the golf course, I almost died because I knew how right we were for each other. Next to **Dr. Siebolt**, you're the first person I ever really felt close to."

"Dr. who?" said Rice.

Simmons, Newbolt and Martha. *Mrs. Simmons is remembered by having the Martha Simmons Memorial Mobile Disaster Unit named in her honor. The wife of Newbolt Simmons, a County Commissioner of Public Safety, Martha dies of rabies con-*

tracted from a bat she finds clinging to her drapes. (*BC* 24) She had just been reading a biography of Albert Schweitzer, who believed that human beings should treat simpler animals lovingly. The bat nipped her ever so slightly as she wrapped it in *Kleenex,* a face tissue. She carried it out onto her patio, where she laid it gently on a form of artificial grass known as *Astro-turf.*

The mobile disaster unit is a converted transcontinental bus complete with an operating room and space for thirty-six patients. It is called into action when Dwayne Hoover goes on a violent rampage near the end of the text.

Simpkins, Darlene. *The International Committee for the Identification and Rehabilitation of Martians has difficulty determining Beatrice Rumfoord's true identity. They thought she was either Florence White or* **Darlene Simpkins**, *a plain and friendless girl who had last been seen accepting a ride with a swarthy stranger in Brownsville, Texas* (ST 10).

sin-wat. *In Cat's Cradle, the Bokononist term for someone who wants all of somebody's love for themselves, unwilling to share that individual with others—a monogamist.*

sinookas. *In Bokononist terms, "the tendrils of one's life."* (*CC* 4) *Dr. Hoenikker himself was no doubt a member of my karass, though he was dead before my sinookas, the tendrils of my life, began to tangle with those of his children.*

The first of his heirs to be touched by my sinookas was Newton Hoenikker, the youngest of his three children, the younger of his two sons.

The Sirens of Titan (1959) (*see also* **Malachi Constant, Winston Niles Rumfoord, Tralfamadore, chrono-synclastic infundibulum, structured moment, Salo, Universal Will to Become**). *The premise of the novel is that all of human history has been one great Rube Goldberg invention designed by the Tralfamadorians for the singular purpose of getting a spare part to their stranded messenger, Salo. Any attempt to impose meaning on the apparent linearity of "history" is futile.*

The text comes to us from long ago yet far beyond

the "punctual" time of Rumfoord and Malachi Constant (because the universe is described by the chrono-synclastic infundibulum: all is-as-it-was-and-is-supposed-to-become). Sirens recounts man's plight before having learned the true state of cosmic affairs (Tralfamadorian intervention). The narration opens as a book of revelation promising to detail the shallow concerns which had riveted man's attention up to the close of the Nightmare Ages, falling roughly, give or take a few years, between the Second World War and the Third Great Depression (ST 1).

Perhaps the most distinguishing narrative feature of Sirens *is the chrono-synclastic infundibulum.* (ST 1) "These places are where all different kinds of truths fit together as nicely as the parts in your daddy's solar watch." *All truths are correct at the intersection of the chrono-synclastic infundibulum, and all truths combine into the greater order of the universe as they always have and always will. The sum of these truths is not a greater, all-encompassing, meaningful truth but rather a greater sense of the cosmic composition.*

Aside from absorbing the polarities of various truths, the more prominent feature of the chrono-synclastic infundibulum is its explanation that time is a continuum, that those riding its electronic waves can see a fully formed future as well as past. Vonnegut's Ancient Mariner, Winston Niles Rumfoord, declares "it's a thankless job telling people it's a hard, hard Universe they're in. . . . When I ran my space ship into the chrono-synclastic infundibulum, it came to me in a flash that everything that ever has been always will be, and everything that ever will be always has been" (ST 1).

Having been caught within the great whirlwind of World War II and the more particular flashpoint that was Dresden (while his genetic ancestors fought for their truths against the truths of his more recent homeland), Vonnegut's career-long obligation has been to tell others how cruel our tensions sometimes appear. Fated to an eternity of conflict without any particular truth above the rest, the chrono-synclastic infundibulum describes a physical trap. Though man tends to believe he is on a linear track toward perfection, Vonnegut's wrinkle in space-time prompts the rhetorical question, "What makes you think you're going anywhere?" (ST 1).

The chrono-synclastic infundibulum denies man's

inherent yearning to attach meaning to each succeeding moment in time. (ST 1) "Things fly this way and that, my boy," *Rumfoord tells Malachi,* "with or without messages." *The eternal strife of dynamic tensions (in which man finds himself groping to understand the meaning of his particular moment in time) is merely a part of the redundant waves of history. Moving from one instance to the next, from the uncertain designs of others to our own self-interested prodding, man's focus is too narrowly obsessed with his finitude. Rumfoord (Vonnegut), our Ancient Mariner, is here to dispel such existential myopia,* "It's chaos, and no mistake, for the Universe is just being born. It's the great becoming that makes the light and the heat and the motion, and hangs you from hither to yon" (ST 1).

The tale that follows is supposed to reveal how man came to understand the fifty-three portals to the soul. Instead, the main focus is "the great becoming" of man's understanding. Malachi's story reveals why such a Copernican shift in man's thinking became necessary—why even the Tralfamadorians weren't the center of the universe. Whether machines of flesh or steel, all are caught on the roller coaster known as the chrono-synclastic infundibulum.

Malachi's exit from the Rumfoord mansion after witnessing Winston's materialization and hearing his explanation of the past that is Malachi's future, establishes the pre-Copernican state of thinking before Salo's eventual return of the aged Malachi to his native Earth. (ST 1) In crossing the bright zodiac on the foyer floor, he sensed that the spiral staircase now swept down rather than up. Constant became the bottommost point in a whirlpool of fate. As he walked out the door, he was delightfully aware of pulling the aplomb of the Rumfoord mansion right out with him.

As a metaphor for the narrative, the spiral staircase is the chrono-synclastic infundibulum, and Malachi imagines his centrality at either end. As he senses it, his destiny as the end point of some larger fate has already begun (or, in the chrono-synclastic infundibulated sense of things, already finished) in that he arrived at the mansion disguised as Jonah K. Rowley. This Jonah portends not the destruction of another Nineveh, but the destruction of man's inflated sense of self across all time. Insisting on the validity of man's contrived meanings for his existence

is as false as personifying a physical structure, the mansion, with "aplomb."

The three sirens of Titan are sculptures made by the Tralfamadorian messenger Salo and inspired by his observations of man's development on Earth. Of the millions of Titanic peat statues created by Salo, these alone are painted to look like real people. (ST 12) It had been necessary to paint them in order to give them importance in the sumptuous, oriental scheme of things in Rumfoord's palace. *Rumfoord's palace is a re-creation of the Taj Mahal.*

Enticing Malachi Constant with the idea of space travel requires Rumfoord showing him a picture of the statues, passing them off as the way all women looked on Titan. Malachi steals the photograph and eventually uses them for MoonMist Cigarette ads. (ST 2) *Pleasure in Depth!* said the headline on the ad. The picture that went with it was the picture of the three **sirens of Titan.** There they were—the white girl, the golden girl, and the brown girl.

The fingers of the golden girl were fortuitously spread as they rested on her left breast, permitting an artist to paint in a MoonMist Cigarette between two of them. The smoke from her cigarette passed beneath the nostrils of the brown and white girls, and their space-annihilating concupiscence seemed centered on mentholated smoke alone.

On Titan, the three statues are in the middle of the rectangular pool at Rumfoord's Taj Mahal, which he calls Dun Roamin. They are covered with bacterial growth ever since Malachi had taken over caring for the house and pool. (ST Epilogue) Constant knew of the significance of the three sirens in his life. He had read about it—both in the *Pocket History of Mars* and *The Winston Niles Rumfoord Authorized Revised Bible.* The three great beauties didn't mean so much to him now, really, except to remind him that sex had once bothered him.

For a more complete telling of this vast novel, refer to the entries for **Malachi Constant, Winston Niles Rumfoord, Tralfamadore, chrono-synclastic infundibulum, structured moment, Salo,** *and* **Universal Will to Become.**

"The Sisters B-36." *This is a Kilgore Trout short story, or at least one that Vonnegut credits to his alter ego.* (TQ 5) All I do with short story ideas now is rough them out, credit them to Kilgore Trout, and put them in a novel. Here's the start of another one hacked from the carcass of *Timequake One*, and entitled "**The Sisters B-36.**" *The story is a parable, equating life on Earth with the fictional planet Booboo, a matriarchal planet in the Crab Nebula. Though all three sisters are beautiful, only two are popular: the artist and short story writer. The third sister, Nim-nim, has a deep and dark interest in science.*

Boobooling society passes on its values through good and attentive parenting, interesting conversation, literature, and art. However, Nim-nim becomes the agent for a technological shift in society, similar to the computer age on Earth, and Vonnegut sees this as the precursor for a loss of a literate and caring culture.

(*TQ* 5) Thus were the brains of most, but not quite all, Booboolings made to grow circuits, microchips, if you like, which on Earth would be called imaginations. Yes, and it was precisely because a vast majority of Booboolings had imaginations that two of the B-36 sisters, the short story writer and the painter, were so beloved.

The bad sister had an imagination, all right, but not in the field of art appreciation. She wouldn't read books or go to art galleries. She spent every spare minute when she was little in the garden of a lunatic asylum next door. The psychos in the garden were believed to be harmless, so her keeping them company was regarded as a laudably compassionate activity. But the nuts taught her thermodynamics and calculus and so on.

When the bad sister was a young woman, she and the nuts worked up designs for television cameras and transmitters and receivers. Then she got money from her very rich mom to manufacture and market these satanic devices, which made imaginations redundant. They were instantly popular because the shows were so attractive and no thinking was involved. . . .

Young Booboolings didn't see any point in developing imaginations anymore, since all they had to do was turn on a switch and see all kinds of jazzy shit. They would look at a printed page or a painting and wonder how anybody could have gotten his or her rocks off looking at things that simple and dead. . . .

And TV wasn't the half of it! She was as unpopular as ever because she was as boring as ever, so she invented automobiles and computers and barbed wire and flamethrowers and land mines and machine guns and so on. That's how pissed off she was.

New generations of Booboolings grew up without imaginations. Their appetites for diversions from boredom were perfectly satisfied by all the crap Nim-nim was selling them. Why not? What the heck.

Without imaginations, though, they couldn't do what their ancestors had done, which was read interesting, heartwarming stories in the faces of one another. So, according to Kilgore Trout, "Booboolings became among the most merciless creatures in the local family of galaxies."

Skag, Delmore. *The lead character in an unnamed Kilgore Trout novel, Skag is* a bachelor in a neighborhood where everybody else had enormous families. And **Skag** was a scientist, and he found a way to reproduce himself in chicken soup. He would shave living cells from the palm of his right hand, mix them with the soup, and expose the soup to cosmic rays. The cells turned into babies which looked exactly like **Delmore Skag**.

Pretty soon, **Delmore** was having several babies a day, and inviting his neighbors to share his pride and happiness. He had mass baptisms of as many as a hundred babies at a time. He became famous as a family man.

And so on.

Skag hoped to force his country into making laws against excessively large families, but the legislatures and the courts declined to meet the problem head-on. They passed stern laws instead against the possession by unmarried persons of chicken soup (*BC* 2).

Skinner, Cornelia Otis. *In real life, Cornelia Otis Skinner (1899–1979) was an actress and screenwriter. In* Deadeye Dick, *Skinner is noted as a famous monologist and one of the many celebrities brought to the Midland City YMCA for a performance and given the routine tour of the Waltz home because of Otto's well-outfitted art studio.*

Skylark. *The British ship that transports Ojumwa to Charleston, South Carolina, in* Breakfast of Champions. *Ojumwa is the ancestor of ambulance driver Eddie Key. Ojumwa is captured and sold into slavery by Dr. Cyprian Ukwende's Indaro ancestors.*

Skyscraper National Park. *Wilbur Swain's nickname for Manhattan, in* Slapstick.

Slapstick (1976) (*see also* **Wilbur Swain** *and* **extended family**). *As is the case with* Slaughterhouse-Five, Slapstick *is also conceived while Vonnegut contemplates the dead. In this case, while flying to Indianapolis to bury their Uncle Alex, Vonnegut and his brother Bernard sit with an open seat between them.*

Uncle Alex was typical of the Vonneguts who remained in Indianapolis in that he had more than a little trouble accepting Kurt's literature. The empty airline seat reminds Vonnegut of his sister, and in light of the rest of the family's displeasure with his lifestyle (particularly his getting divorced), Alice appears to have been Kurt's creative focal point. (Slap Prologue) For my own part, though: It would have been catastrophic if I had forgotten my sister at once. I had never told her so, but she was the person I had always written for. She was the secret of whatever artistic unity I had ever achieved. She was the secret of my technique. Any creation which has any wholeness and harmoniousness, I suspect, was made by an artist or inventor with an audience of one in mind.

More than simply writing with Alice in mind, Vonnegut employs her spirit to complement his own by creating the freakish fraternal twins Eliza and Wilbur Swain, whose intellectual synergism soars beyond the genius level when they literally place their heads together.

Since so many of Vonnegut's novels concern schemes for restructuring communal relationships, it isn't surprising that Slapstick, conceived in the midst of a lost familial spirituality, has as its centerpiece the creation of artificially extended families, a theory developed by the joint efforts of Eliza and Wilbur Swain. In actuality, Vonnegut witnessed a highly prized form of the extended family in January 1970, the final days of the Biafran independence

campaign. In the 1950s, Kurt and Jane Cox Vonnegut adopted (unofficially) three of Alice's children after her death. Two days before Alice succumbed to cancer, her husband had died in a commuter train accident.

Despite the fact that in the novel the Chinese ruin the planet's stable gravity by experimenting with the Swains' scientific treatises, Wilbur is proud of what he and Eliza accomplish by restructuring human relationships. As president, Wilbur successfully institutes their scheme for artificially extended families. In response to the "grotesque situational poetry," reminiscent of slapstick films, Wilbur Swain did his best with every test. Moreover, he reaffirms Vonnegut's denial of suicide as a logical extension of problem solving, as did the finale of Breakfast of Champions.

As autobiography, Vonnegut concludes for himself that "bargaining in good faith with destiny" is the supreme achievement of one's striving. It was Alice Vonnegut who labeled as "slapstick" the bizarre events that would orphan her children within a forty-eight hour period. The only thing to do was precisely what Kurt Vonnegut did: adapt as best he could.

Slaughterhouse-Five (1969) (*subtitled* THE CHILDREN'S CRUSADE—A DUTY-DANCE WITH DEATH) (*see also* **Billy Pilgrim, Tralfamadore, structured moment, Dresden, Yon Yonson**). *The title of the text refers to the location of Vonnegut's barracks while he was a POW in Dresden.*

Slaughterhouse-Five is born from death. In some sense, Vonnegut's life as a novelist was conceived in the death of Dresden. Just as the life of the biblical Adam is described in sensory terms, "And the Lord God formed man of the dust of the ground, and breathed into his nostrils the breath of life; and man became a living soul," Vonnegut, too, inhales the very truth of his experience; the very air he breathes and the soot lining the lungs of his twenty-two-year-old German American frame become part of the breath of his life. (SL5 10) There were hundreds of corpse mines operating by and by. They didn't smell bad at first, were wax museums. But then the bodies rotted and liquefied, and the stink was like roses and mustard gas.

To paraphrase the fictive Rudy Waltz, Vonnegut had caught life; he had come down with life. To "have come down with life," much as one would describe the onset of a disease, is precisely the effect the corpse mines had on Vonnegut. (SL5 1) I have this disease late at night sometimes, involving alcohol and the telephone. I get drunk, and I drive my wife away with a breath like mustard gas and roses. And then, speaking gravely and elegantly into the telephone, I ask the telephone operators to connect me with this friend or that one, from whom I have not heard in years.

Having risen from the meat-locker sepulchre inhaling the death stench of Dresden, Vonnegut continually struggles with the disease of life, not so much pondering the meaning of life as much as tracing the inertial forces that describe life. And so, breathing mustard gas and roses, attempting to look back with compassion and love for the innocents, Vonnegut calls war buddy Bernard O'Hare to aid his own failing memory.

At the time, Vonnegut is concerned with finding meaning in the moment that was Dresden, and he thinks the final illustration should concentrate on the ironic death of Edgar Derby. Though Vonnegut considers Derby's death as a properly ironic closing for the novel, he is not the powerfully tragic figure to reinforce some grand statement about the meaninglessness of war. He is lost within the uncountable carnage reviewed by Vonnegut when considering the Crusades, World War II (both military and civilian casualties), Dresden, Bobby Kennedy, Martin Luther King, Jr., and Vietnam.

As Billy Pilgrim comes to understand life according to the Tralfamadorian fourth-dimensional perspective, Vonnegut's narrative is a world defined by the recurrence of experience. The inevitable failure of the Ghost Shirt rebellion in Player Piano, the predetermined history of humanity in The Sirens of Titan, the netherworld existence of Howard Campbell, Eliot Rosewater's vision of Indianapolis in a firestorm (Vonnegut's hometown), and Cat's Cradle's time-looped fatalism all have their roots in Billy Pilgrim's Slaughterhouse experience. Billy Pilgrim is caught within Vonnegut's structured moment—Dresden, but Billy's predecessors have their roots in the defining moment of Pilgrim/Vonnegut.

For a more complete picture of the totality of Slaughterhouse-Five, see the entries for **Billy Pilgrim**, **Tralfamadore**, **structured moment**, **Dresden**, and **Yon Yonson**.

Slazinger, Paul. The Harvard-educated novelist Paul Slazinger appears in both Bluebeard and Hocus Pocus with greatly varying fortunes. He first appears as the ever-present sidekick of the one-eyed Rabo Karabekian. Though Slazinger officially resides in the house next to Karabekian's, he spends nearly all his waking hours at his friend's larger house. Paul is a novelist with eleven books to his credit, though he hadn't written anything in ages. According to Rabo, every three years or so Paul suffered a mental breakdown. On Okinawa in World War II, Slazinger won a Silver Star for throwing himself on a grenade to save his friends. The grenade failed to explode but he was badly injured. Rabo recalls he had a scar extending from his sternum to his crotch and had only one nipple. Paul's wit once prompted him to ask Rabo the riddle, "What has three eyes, three nipples and two assholes?"

"I give up," I said.

And he said, "**Paul Slazinger** and Rabo Karabekian" (Blue 15).

Slazinger the war hero is descended from a Hessian soldier serving as a mercenary under the leadership of British General John Burgoyne during the Revolutionary War. The mercenary was captured at the second Battle of Freeman's Farm by forces commanded by General Benedict Arnold.

Slazinger is briefly married to the actress Barbira Mencken. Years later while living next door to Rabo, Paul travels to Poland as part of a delegation from PEN to observe the plight of writers living under Communist rule. On his return, he begins suffering a slow mental decline. One evening the local volunteer fire department is called to his home because he was hysterical. He persuades them to take him to Karabekian's house. Later, Paul commits himself to the psychiatric ward at the Veterans Administration hospital in Riverhead, Long Island.

In Hocus Pocus, Slazinger is an out-of-print novelist who takes a last-minute offer to become Tarkington College's 1990–91 Writer in Residence. He spends some of his time playing pool with fellow Silver Star winner Eugene Debs Hartke. In December 1990, Paul receives a Genius Grant from the

MacArthur Foundation, $50,000 a year for five years. During a speech at the school's chapel just before Christmas break, Slazinger predicted . . . that human slavery would come back, that it had in fact never gone away. He said that so many people wanted to come here because it was so easy to rob the poor people, who got absolutely no protection from the Government. He talked about bridges falling down and water mains breaking because of no maintenance. He talked about oil spills and radioactive waste and poisoned aquifers and looted banks and liquidated corporations. "And nobody ever gets punished for anything," he said. "Being an American means never having to say you're sorry" (*HP* 11).

When Hartke later recalls these sentiments, Kimberley Wilder is nearby to tape-record his comments for future use during his dismissal hearing. After receiving notice about the Genius Grant, Slazinger leaves for the Florida Keys. There he is eventually joined by Tarkington's Artist in Residence, Pamela Ford Hall, with whom he enjoys a secret affair while on campus. They plan to wed, but the relationship falls apart. Hartke assumes it was probably due to a combination of her alcoholism and his general attitude.

Slezak, Premier. *The Soviet leader who calls Professor Barnhouse's terrifying displays of power a bourgeois plot to shackle the true democracies of the world (MH Report on the Barnhouse Effect).*

Slotkin. *In the 1952* Collier's *short story appearance of "The Package" (reprinted in* Bagombo Snuff Box, *1999), Slotkin is the talkative European photographer accompanied by an unnamed woman reporter sent by* Home Beautiful *magazine to the palatial state-of-the-art estate of Earl and Maude Fenton. It is Slotkin who nicknames the home "the Package," and he is supported in his narrative insight by his companion.* The photographer, who introduced himself simply as **Slotkin**, took command of the household, and as he was to do for the whole of his stay, he quashed all talk and activities not related to getting the magazine pictures taken. "Zo," said **Slotkin**, "und de gimmick is de pagatch, eh?"

"Baggage?" said Earl.

"Package," said the writer. "See, the angle on the story is that you come home from a world cruise to a complete package for living—everything anybody could possibly want for a full life."

Small Magellanic Cloud. *The galaxy containing the planet Tralfamadore, in* The Sirens of Titan.

The Smart Bunny. *Hotel clerk Milo Maritimo is reading this Kilgore Trout novel when the author checks in for the Midland City Arts Festival. There is a thematic connection between Trout's story and Karabekian's paintings of wavering bands of light representing one's essential core of awareness. The Farrows have no awareness of the bunny's consciousness and those in Midland City can't fathom the meaning of Karabekian's work. The bunny also suffers from the same mental isolation as Dwayne Hoover in that both feel an exaggerated sense of self brought on by bad chemicals.* (BC 20) The novel in question, incidentally, was **The Smart Bunny.** The leading character was a **rabbit** who lived like all the other wild **rabbits**, but who was as intelligent as Albert Einstein or William Shakespeare. It was a **female rabbit**. She was the only female leading character in any novel or story by Kilgore Trout.

She led a **normal female rabbit's life**, despite her ballooning intellect.

She concluded that her mind was useless, that it was a sort of tumor, that it had no usefulness within the rabbit scheme of things.

So she went hippity-hop, hippity-hop toward the city, to have the tumor removed. But a hunter named Dudley Farrow shot and killed her before she got there. Farrow skinned her and took out her guts, but then he and his wife Grace decided that they had better not eat her because of her unusually large head. They thought what she had thought when she was alive—that she must be diseased.

And so on.

Smiley (*see* **Greathouse and Smiley**).

Smiley, Letitia. *Named Tarkington College's 1922 Lilac Queen, Letitia disappears the night after winning the Women's Barefoot Race from the bell tower to the president's house and back again, in* Hocus Pocus. *When the graves of Hermann and Sophia*

Shultz are moved to make room for the Pahlavi Pavilion, an unexpected skull is unearthed. Eugene Debs Hartke presumes it belongs to Letitia Smiley, and he conducts his own investigation, which leads him to presume her killer was Tarkington College Provost Kensington Barber. Hartke believes Barber made her pregnant.

Smith, Frank (*see also* **John Wilkes Booth; Abraham Lincoln Pembroke; Elias and Julia Pembroke;** *and the* **Pembroke Mask and Wig Club**). *The third-generation descendant of a love tryst between the soon-to-be presidential assassin John Wilkes Booth and Julia Pembroke, the wife of Lincoln's assistant secretary of the Navy during the Civil War. Smith has the pointed ears of his infamous great-grandfather.* (TQ 60) **Frank Smith** has pointed ears! **Frank Smith** has to be one of the greatest actors in the history of amateur theatricals! He is half black, half white, and only five feet, ten inches tall. But in the summer of 2001 he gave a stunningly convincing matinee performance in the title role in the Pembroke Mask and Wig Club's production of *Abe Lincoln in Illinois*, by Robert E. Sherwood, with Kilgore Trout doing the sound effects! *The clambake at the close of* Timequake *is both a party for Kilgore Trout and a cast party for Frank Smith and his fellow actors.*

Smith, Rosemary (*see also* **John Wilkes Booth; Abraham Lincoln Pembroke; Elias and Julia Pembroke;** *and the* **Pembroke Mask and Wig Club**). (TQ 60) Before Abraham Lincoln Pembroke III departed the town of Pembroke for North Carolina, he knocked up an unmarried African-American housemaid, **Rosemary Smith**. He paid her handsomely for her silence. He was gone when his child Frank Smith was born.

Rosemary had passed away by the time of the Timequake *clambake, but Vonnegut includes her via a doppelgänger, which is understandable considering how lovingly he refers to her.* (TQ 62) Another look-alike there was **Rosemary Smith**, Mask and Wig's costume mistress, and mother of Frank Smith, its superstar. She resembled Ida Young, grandchild of slaves, who worked for us in Indianapolis when I was little. Ida Young, in combina-

tion with my uncle Alex, had as much to do with my upbringing as my parents did.

Snopes, Senator Flem. *The Mississippi senator and chairman of the Senate Space Committee who manages to locate the biggest jizzum-freezing plant in his "li'l ol' home town," which was Mayhew (PS Obscenity). He wore a codpiece embroidered with the Confederate Stars and Bars. Snopes makes a campaign pledge to change the national symbol from the eagle to the lamprey, since eagles were long since extinct and therefore symbolized degradation rather than survival, let alone supremacy.*

Solomon, Syd. *Vonnegut once wrote an essay for inclusion in an exhibition catalogue for friend, summer neighbor, and professional painter Syd Solomon. In preparing the essay for Solomon's retrospective, Vonnegut asks him what he was trying to do with paint when working, and Solomon answers that he had no idea. This episode is recounted in the essay "Playmates," reprinted in* Palm Sunday.

Rabo Karabekian tries to answer Circe Berman's question about telling good pictures from bad by invoking Syd Solomon. (*Blue* 19) "How can you tell a good painting from a bad one?" he said. This is the son of a Hungarian horse trainer. He has a magnificent handlebar mustache.

"All you have to do, my dear," he said, "is look at a million paintings, and then you can never be mistaken."

It's true! It's true!

In the closing Author's Note to A Man Without a Country, *Vonnegut speaks of trying to elicit a response from Solomon concerning his work with Joe Petro III under the name Origami Express. Both Solomon and Vonnegut's daughter Edith express themselves in a similar manner that harkens back to an image in* God Bless You, Mr. Rosewater: Are Origami's pictures any good? Well, I asked the now regrettably dead painter **Syd Solomon**, a most agreeable neighbor on Long Island for many summertimes, how to tell a good picture from a bad one. He gave me the most satisfactory answer I ever expect to hear. He said, "Look at a million pictures, and you can never be mistaken."

I passed this on to my daughter Edith, a professional painter, and she too thought it was pretty good. She said she "could rollerskate through the Louvre, saying, 'Yes, no, no, yes, no, yes,' and so on."

Okay?

Solzhenitsyn, Aleksandr (1918–2008). *(JB 8)* Cleveland Lawes was reading *The Gulag Archipelago* now, an account of the prison system in the Soviet Union by another former prisoner, **Aleksandr Solzhenitsyn.**

somethinghead *(see also* **nothinghead***). Those who continue to follow the government dictate and take their ethical birth control pills, effectively numbing all sexual urges and sensations below the waist.* (MH Welcome to the Monkey House) The sheaf proved to be photocopies of poems Billy had sent to Hostesses in other places. Nancy read the top one. It made much of a peculiar side effect of ethical birth-control pills: They not only made people numb—they also made people piss blue. The poem was called *What the* **Somethinghead** *Said to the Suicide Hostess,* and it went like this:

> I did not sow, I did not spin,
> And thanks to pills I did not sin.
> I loved the crowds, the stink, the noise.
> And when I peed, I peed turquoise.
>
> I ate beneath a roof of orange;
> Swung with progress like a door hinge.
> 'Neath purple roof I've come today
> To piss my azure life away.
> Virgin hostess, death's recruiter,
> Life is cute, but you are cuter.
> Mourn my pecker, purple daughter—
> All it passed was sky-blue water.

Son of God *(see* **Christ***).*

The Son of Jimmy Valentine. *At the suggestion of Darlene Trout, Kilgore's second wife, he once wrote a short novel about the importance of the clitoris in love-making. . . .* She told him that the hero should understand women so well that he could seduce anyone he wanted. So Trout wrote **The Son of Jimmy Valentine.** . . .

Kilgore Trout invented a son for **Jimmy Valentine,** named Ralston Valentine. Ralston Valentine also sandpapered his fingertips. But he wasn't a safe-cracker. Ralston was so good at touching women the way they wanted to be touched, that tens of thousands of them became his willing slaves. They abandoned their husbands or lovers for him, in Trout's story, and Ralston Valentine became President of the United States, thanks to the votes of women (BC 15).

Sonderkommando. *Former concentration camp inmate Andor Gutman explains to Howard Campbell the nature of the unique group he joined while held captive.* (MN 2) **Sonderkommando** means special detail. At Auschwitz it meant a very special detail indeed—one composed of prisoners whose duties were to shepherd condemned persons into gas chambers, and then to lug their bodies out. When the job was done, the members of the **Sonderkommando** were themselves killed. The first duty of their successors was to dispose of their remains.

Later, when Howard Campbell seeks out the Epstein family so that he may surrender to them, Mrs. Epstein understands his apparent catatonia. (MN 44) What she crooned was this, a command she had heard over the loudspeakers of Auschwitz—had heard many times a day for years.

"*Leichentrager zu Wache,*" she crooned. A beautiful language, isn't it? Translation?

"Corpse-carriers to the guardhouse." That's what that old woman crooned to me.

Sony. *The Japanese electronics firm is mentioned three times in Vonnegut's work. In* Bluebeard, *Marilee Kemp, then the Countess Portomaggiore, becomes Europe's largest Sony distributor after World War II. In* Hocus Pocus, *Hiroshi Matsumoto, the warden of the New York State Maximum Security Adult Correctional Facility at Athena, is a lifelong employee of Sony. The Japanese firm contracts with New York to manage its penal system. A previous reference in the text indicates Sony had purchased a Lexington, Kentucky, hospital and that Matsumoto managed that facility before moving to Athena.*

In the introduction to Bagombo Snuff Box, *Von-*

negut uses the iconic brand to illustrate the foresight of fellow science fiction writer Ray Bradbury. In any case, Ray was sure as heck prescient. Just as people with dysfunctional kidneys are getting perfect ones from hospitals nowadays, Americans with dysfunctional social lives, like the woman in Ray's book, are getting perfect friends and relatives from their TV sets. And around the clock!

Ray missed the boat about how many screens would be required for a successful people-transplant. One lousy little **Sony** can do the job, night and day. All it takes besides that is actors and actresses, telling the news, selling stuff, in soap operas or whatever, who treat whoever is watching, even if nobody is watching, like family.

The Soul Merchants. *The name of Eugene Debs Hartke's high school rock band.* (HP 1) What I would really like to have been, given a perfect world, is a jazz pianist. I mean jazz. I don't mean rock and roll. I mean the never-the-same way-twice music the American black people gave the world. I played piano in my own all-white band in my all-white high school in Midland City, Ohio. We called ourselves "**The Soul Merchants.**"

How good were we? We had to play white people's popular music, or nobody would have hired us. But every so often we would cut loose with jazz anyway. Nobody else seemed to notice the difference, but we sure did. We fell in love with ourselves. We were in ecstasy.

(HP 4) When Du Pont took over Barrytron, the double fence, the Dobermans, my father and all, I was a high school senior, all set to go to the University of Michigan to learn how to be a journalist, to serve John Q. Public's right to know. Two members of my 6-piece band, **The Soul Merchants**, the clarinet and the string bass, were also going to Michigan.

We were going to stick together and go on making music at Ann Arbor.

Who knows? We might have become so popular that we went on world tours and made great fortunes, and been superstars at peace rallies and love-ins when the Vietnam War came along.

(HP 4) During my last 2 years in high school, I don't think my parents even suspected that I was half in the bag a lot of the time. All they ever com-

plained about was the music, when I played the radio or the phonograph or when **The Soul Merchants** rehearsed in our basement, which Mom and Dad said was jungle music, and much too loud.

(HP 4) "You let those 4 years slip by without doing anything but making jungle music," he said.

It occurs to me now, a mere 43 years later, that I might have said to him that at least I managed my sex life better than he had managed his. I was getting laid all the time, thanks to jungle music, and so were the other **Soul Merchants**. Certain sorts of not just girls but full-grown women, too, found us glamorous free spirits up on the bandstand, imitating black people and smoking marijuana, and loving ourselves when we made music, and laughing about God knows what just about anytime.

Sousa, Mr. *The father of seven girls in the 1954 short story "Adam," reprinted in* Welcome to the Monkey House *(1968). He envies his waiting-room companion Mr. Knechtmann, whose wife gives birth to a boy, their first and probably only child. Mrs. Knechtmann's malnutrition during the war makes it unlikely she will be capable of bearing more children.*

Southard, Annie. *In the short story "Runaways," collected in* Bagombo Snuff Box *(1999), Annie is the daughter of distraught Indiana governor Jesse K. Southard and his equally troubled wife, Mary. Their distress is caused by Annie's having run away with her boyfriend, Rice Brentner. The teens' first venture results in their apprehension in Chicago.*

Annie and Rice are mutually alienated from the concerns of their parents, perhaps no more so than any pair of teenagers before or since. Though bonded by similar complaints, their conversations are more rightly parallel monologues without much information seeping into the other's consciousness. By the time they come up for air and look at each other again, nothing more satisfying has occurred than each other's belief that by venting their frustrations with the other, they must be deeply in love. Vonnegut comments on the mechanics of their relationship. The fact was that Rice had told her about a dozen times why he was named Rice, but she never really listened to him. For that matter, Rice never really listened to her, either. Both would have been bored stiff if they had listened, but they spared themselves that.

So their conversations were marvels of irrelevance. There were only two subjects in common—self-pity and something called love.

Annie's alienation from her parents is only one part of her portrait as a teenager with commonly heard complaints about her elders. After being detained with Rice in Chicago, the two let loose with the diatribe of youth, attacking everything from parenting to politics. In Chicago she and the boy had lectured reporters and police on love, hypocrisy, persecution of teenagers, the insensitivity of parents, and even rockets, Russia, and the hydrogen bomb.

Annie is also deeply offended by her parents' acute class consciousness. The fact that Rice's father makes $89.63 per week and the family lives in a minuscule 1926 bungalow in the poorer section of town contributes to the Southards' despondency.

Among adults, only the Southards' family physician, Dr. Siebolt, enjoys Annie's trust. She believes he understands her, and the only other person about whom she feels this way is Rice.

After the runaways make a second break, this time toward Cleveland, their parents hit upon the idea that since their children are nearly adults, let them know that they will be supportive of their decision when they return to Indianapolis. This unexpectedly agreeable attitude is enough to make Annie and Rice rethink matters. Their decision is made easier by seeing another very young couple in the car next to theirs engaged in a heated argument while their young child wails in the backseat.

It is left to Annie to comment on the plight of all teenagers. "You know what?" said **Annie**.

"What?" said Rice.

"We're too young," said **Annie**.

"Not too young to be in love," said Rice.

"No," said **Annie**, "not too young to be in love. Just too young for about everything else there is that goes with love." She kissed him. "Good-bye, Rice. I love you."

Southard, Governor Jesse K. and Mary. *In the short story* "Runaways," *collected in* Bagombo Snuff Box (1999), *these are the parents of sixteen-year-old*

Annie. The Indiana governor is outraged at his daughter's first, highly publicized attempt to run away with her boyfriend, Rice Brentner (to Chicago). He blows up at the media's speculations and defends his daughter's honor by insisting Rice never laid a hand on her because she wanted none of it. Mrs. Southard is similarly outraged, but more because of the vast difference in class standing between the Southards and the Brentners.

After the teens' second attempt to run away, this time to Cleveland, the Brentners are invited to the governor's mansion to discuss how to stop their children's penchant for fleeing. After a particularly sharp exchange with Mrs. Brentner in which she defends both her son and their attempt to parent him, it is finally decided to tell the children they have their parents' full support, whatever their decision. Once the message from Governor Southard is relayed to the young couple by the Ohio policeman who detains them, they decide that perhaps they are, after all, too young to make such life-changing decisions. They return to their waiting parents in Indianapolis.

"Souvenir." *This short frame tale recalls the tragic events of Eddie (a farmer) and Buzzer. The American POWs are held in the Sudetenland and enjoyably stumble through their first day of freedom upon realizing their war is over, their prison gates unlocked and unguarded. First published in the December 1952 issue of* Argosy *magazine and later reprinted in the 1999 collection* Bagombo Snuff Box, *"Souvenir" wraps around the opening scene as Eddie tries to pawn a marvelously jeweled and inscribed pocket watch that he smuggled stateside once repatriated. Though the pocket watch owner is later revealed to the reader, Eddie never learns about his brush with one of Hitler's favorite officers. Instead, Eddie's first appearance is somewhat pathetic but is more charitable than the description of the venally porcine pawnbroker Joe Bane.*

Only a few short years since the war's end, Eddie the POW veteran turns to pawnbroker Joe Bane to sell his singular piece of wartime booty so that he may care for his family. Eddie has his heart set on getting $500 for the watch, but Joe Bane's personal pastime is getting the best bargain possible, even if that means rigging the situation in his favor. The diamonds and ruby set into the four main positions on the watch certainly entice Bane who recognizes the stones alone are worth four times the asking price for the watch, but he offers Eddie $100 saying that the unique piece may be sitting in his shop for a very long time before the right buyer appears. Bane opens the watch's casing to reveal an inscription in German. He takes a pencil rubbing of the phrasing and sends an unnamed shoeshine boy down the street to a German restaurant for translation. While the pawnbroker and rube farmer wait to hear back about the translation, Eddie begins to tell his tragicomic story.

After exiting the unlocked gates of their prison, Eddie and Buzzer come across some freed Canadian POWs who have already found bottles of brandy. Eddie and Buzzer join them, getting sufficiently drunk on very little alcohol since their bodies had so little nourishment or resistance.

As they wander around the town amidst the bustle of people trying to leave before the arrival of a Russian armored division, they come across a young blond German apparently in the service of a much older and well-dressed man sitting in the back of their stalled vehicle. They are desperate to make it across to the American lines rather than fall prey to the advancing Russian tanks.

At first they try to persuade Eddie and Buzzer to sell them their uniforms in exchange for the elder's unique, jewel-encrusted pocket watch. When that doesn't work, the younger German shoots Buzzer in the head but fails to shoot the escaping Eddie. The young German leaves Buzzer stripped to his GI underwear and puts on the uniform for himself. He speaks enough English that he hopes to at least make it to the American lines where he could more safely surrender. However, when the elderly German realizes there will be no uniform for him and that he speaks no English, he commits suicide by shooting himself in the head. His watch, still out after attempting to bribe the two Americans, falls to the ground.

Eddie watches the macabre scene play out, his dead friend stripped of clothing and dog tags; the young German putting on the American uniform and escaping; and the elderly German killing himself and the watch laying in plain view. Eddie takes the watch and eventually makes his way back home with it.

Retelling the tale makes Eddie cling even harder to the watch, his one lasting memory of losing his fellow POW. He takes the watch off Joe Bane's counter and leaves, deciding that not even for $500 can he sell it. Moments later the shoeshine boy returns with the translation from the German restaurateur, To General Heinz Guderian, Chief of the Army General Staff, who cannot rest until the last enemy soldier is driven from the sacred soil of the Third German Reich. ADOLF HITLER.

It should be noted that while Guderian (1888–1954) was an important military leader and innovator of armored warfare, he did not commit suicide. Also, this story is perhaps the first known instance in which Vonnegut looks at those days immediately following liberation from a POW camp. The other two notable examples appear in Slaughterhouse-Five and Bluebeard.

space and time (see **time and space**).

space-time continuum. (TQ 28) When free will kicked in after a ten-year hiatus, Trout made the transition from déjà vu to unlimited opportunities almost seamlessly. The rerun brought him back to the point in the **space-time continuum** when he was again beginning his story about the British soldier whose head was where his ding-dong should have been and whose ding-dong was where his head should have been.

Without warning and silently, the rerun stopped.

Space Wanderer (see **Malachi Constant** and **Queen Margaret**).

Sparks, Jon. In Breakfast of Champions, Vonnegut writes that he was wearing a commemorative bracelet inscribed with the name of Warrant Officer First Class Jon Sparks. He goes on to mention that he left the bracelet so Wayne Hoobler could find it. Hoobler believes it belongs to a woman romantically involved with someone named WO1 Jon Sparks, and he can't figure out how to pronounce "WO1."

Sparky. There are two dogs named Sparky in Vonnegut's work. The first is in the short story "Tom Edison's Shaggy Dog," in Welcome to the Monkey House (1968). Sparky reveals the canine secret that *dogs can talk when he solves Edison's search for a light bulb filament by suggesting a piece of carbonized thread. A pack of dogs later kills Sparky for divulging their secret.*

Sparky is also the name of Dwayne Hoover's Labrador retriever in Breakfast of Champions. *Sparky lost his tail in a car accident, so he had no way of telling other dogs how friendly he was. He had to fight all the time. His ears were in tatters. He was lumpy with scars (BC 2). Vonnegut says Sparky is modeled after a dog once owned by his brother Bernard.*

Sparrow, Harold J. (*see also* **Frank Wirtanen**). *In the Editor's Note to* Mother Night, *Vonnegut discloses he altered the names of various people, including that of Howard Campbell's American sponsor. Previously known as the Blue Fairy Godmother and Colonel Frank Wirtanen, Harold J. Sparrow, serial number 0-61134, is the name used in the intelligence officer's letter to Israeli war crimes investigators. Sparrow is prepared to testify on Campbell's behalf about his espionage activities.*

Speer, Albert. *The grand architect of Hitler's Third Reich.* (WFG Torture and Blubber) Agony never made a society quit fighting, as far I know. A society has to be captured or killed—or offer things it values. While Germany was being tortured during the Second World War, with justice, may I add, industrial output and the determination of its people increased. Hitler, according to **Albert Speer**, couldn't even be bothered with marveling at the ruins or comforting the survivors.

spiral (*also* **spiral nebula**). (*ST 1*) Winston Niles Rumfoord had run his private space ship right into the heart of an uncharted chrono-synclastic infundibulum two days out of Mars. Only his dog had been along. Now Winston Niles Rumfoord and his dog Kazak existed as wave phenomena—apparently pulsing in a distorted **spiral** with its origin in the Sun and its terminal in Betelgeuse.

The earth was about to intercept that **spiral**.
(*ST 1*) With a limp right hand, he (*Winston Niles Rumfoord*) made the magical sign for **spiral staircase**. . . .

There was also the empty suit of armor of an armadillo, a stuffed dodo, and the long **spiral tusk** of

a narwhal, playfully labeled by Skip, *Unicorn Horn*. (*ST 1*) She (*Beatrice Rumfoord*) wore a long white dressing gown whose soft folds formed a **counterclockwise spiral** in harmony with the white staircase. The train of the gown cascaded down the top riser, making Beatrice continuous with the architecture of the mansion.
(*ST 1*) It startled her (*Beatrice*) so much that she took a step back from the head of the staircase, separated herself from the rising **spiral**. The small step backward transformed her into what she was—a frightened, lonely woman in a tremendous house. *This action was a result of Malachi Constant's telling Beatrice that he had access to the world's biggest spaceship, the* Whale.
(*ST 1*) In crossing the bright zodiac on the foyer floor, he (*Malachi Constant*) sensed that the **spiral staircase** now swept down rather than up. Constant became the bottommost point in a whirlpool of fate. As he walked out the door, he was delightfully aware of pulling the aplomb of the Rumfoord mansion right out with him.
(*ST 5*) He (*Unk / Malachi Constant*) could have stared happily at the **immaculate spiral** of the rifling for hours, dreaming of the happy land whose round gate he saw at the other end of the bore. The pink under his oily thumbnail at the far end of the barrel made that far end seem a rosy paradise indeed. Some day he was going to crawl down the barrel to that paradise.
(*ST 6*) At the end of the tour, in the packaging department, the manager's ankle became snarled in a **spiral of steel strapping**, a type of strapping that was used for binding shut the packaged flamethrowers. *The school children of Mars were on a tour of the flamethrower factory. In anger, the manager stomps flat the spiral of steel strapping before it is quietly picked up by Chrono, the son of Malachi and Beatrice. This is the spare part for which Salo has been waiting.*
(*ST 12*) Titan describes, as a consequence, a **spiral** around the Sun.

Winston Niles Rumfoord and his dog Kazak were wave phenomena—pulsing in **distorted spirals**, with their origins in the Sun and their terminals in Betelgeuse. Whenever a heavenly body intercepted their **spirals**, Rumfoord and his dog materialized on that body.

For reasons as yet mysterious, the **spirals** of Rumfoord, Kazak, and Titan coincided exactly. (CC 24) Whatever it (*a wampeter*) is, the members of its *karass* revolve about it in the majestic chaos of a **spiral nebula**. (CC 114) So I once again mounted the **spiral staircase** in my tower; once again arrived at the uppermost battlement of my castle; and once more looked out at my guests, my servants, my cliff, and my lukewarm sea. (PS Funnier on Paper Than Most People) "Perhaps you have read the novel *Childhood's End* by Arthur C. Clarke, one of the few masterpieces in the field of science fiction. All of the others were written by me. In Clark's [*sic*] novel, mankind suddenly undergoes a spectacular evolutionary change. The children become very different from the parents, less physical, more spiritual—and one day they form up into a sort of column of light which **spirals** out into the universe, its mission unknown." (Blue 20) Fred Jones told me one time that the smoke trails of falling airplanes and observation balloons were the most beautiful things he ever expected to see. And I now compare his elation over arcs and **spirals** and splotches in the atmosphere with what Jackson Pollock used to feel as he watched what dribbled paint chose to do when it struck a canvas on his studio floor. (Blue 21) Marilee's and my canvas, so to speak, called for more and wetter kisses, and then a groping, goosey, swooning tango up the **spiral staircase** and through the grand dining room. (HP 31) Warden Hiroshi Matsumoto was a survivor of the atom-bombing of Hiroshima, when I was 5 and he was 8. . . . There was a flash and wind. When he straightened up, his city was gone. He was alone on a desert, with little **spirals of dust** dancing here and there. (BAG Custom-Made Bride) She was tall and slender, with a subtly muscled figure sheathed in a zebra-striped leotard. Her hair was bleached silver and touched with blue, and in the white and perfect oval of her face were eyes of glittering green, set off by painted eyebrows, jet black and arched. She wore one earring, a barbaric gold hoop. She was making **spiral** motions with her hand, and I understood at last that I was to climb the **spiral** ramp that wound around the brick cylinder.

(BAG Custom-Made Bride) His studio was inside the brick cylinder, and he led me through a door and down another **spiral** ramp into it. There were no windows. All light was artificial. (BAG This Son of Mine) He (*Franklin Waggoner*) picked up a sharp, bright **spiral** shaving of steel from the floor. "There's a pretty thing," he said. (BAG Runaways) Annie's mother, Mary, came down the **spiral staircase**. She had been listening to the lies from the landing above. "I think you handled that very well," she said to her husband. *See also: ST* 1; 2; 6; 12; *MN* 31; *CC* 101; 105; *Blue* 10; 17.

spire. (GBR 4) On the label of each can of beer (*Rosewater Golden Lager Ambrosia Beer*) was a picture of the heaven on earth the New Ambrosians had meant to build. The dream city had **spires**. The **spires** had lightning-rods. The sky was filled with cherubim. (MH The Lie) The (*Holly House*) inn was on the edge of the Whitehill Sward, glimpsing the school's rooftops and **spires** over the innocent wilderness of the Sanford Remenzel Bird Sanctuary. (DD 21) "Crucifixion in Rome" is indeed set in Rome, which I have never seen. I know enough, though, to recognize that it is chock-a-block with architectural anachronisms. The Colosseum, for example, is in perfect repair, but there is also the **spire** of a Christian church, and some architectural details and monuments which appear to be more recent, even, than the Renaissance, maybe even nineteenth century. (Gal 1:1) But when this story begins, they were still ugly humps and domes and cones and **spires** of lava, brittle and abrasive, whose cracks and pits and bowls and valleys brimmed over not with rich topsoil or sweet water, but with the finest, driest volcanic ash.

Spirit of the Meadows (*see* **Queen of the Meadows**).

Spruce Falls. *Spruce Falls is the focal point of the 1952 short story "Poor Little Rich Town," collected in* Bagombo Snuff Box *(1999). Not quite a place that stood still in time, it does represent a moment when life was simpler, when the focus of life was* more about community rather than running communities along the production-line model of industrial efficiency. As is typical in so much of Vonnegut's writing (and probably the result of his training in anthropology), he carefully describes the Spruce Falls setting by informing the reader of its development over time leading to its vulnerability due to the activities of man.

The town is nine miles west of Ilium, a city that had virtually died when its textile mills moved south after the Second World War, making it the perfect site for relocating the headquarters of the Federal Apparatus Corporation. Newell Cady, the new corporate vice president and efficiency expert, is sent upstate to oversee the construction of the Ilium facility and be the first of their company executives to relocate. He rents with an option to own a mansion in Spruce Falls, one of many available properties in the economically depressed village, thereby becoming a sign of hope for better times by the locals.

Spruce Falls has a history representative of the fleeting winds of fortune, and in this extended quote, the culminating line uttered by Fire Chief Stanley Atkins indicates the next hope for the town. **Spruce Falls** was a cluster of small businesses and a public school and a post office and a police station and a firehouse serving surrounding dairy farms. During the second decade of the century it experienced a real estate boom. Fifteen mansions were built back then, in the belief that the area, because of its warm mineral springs, was becoming a spa for rich invalids and hypochondriacs and horse people, as had Saratoga, not far away.

In 1922, though, it was determined that bathing in the waters of the spring, while fairly harmless, was nonetheless responsible for several cases of a rash that a Manhattan dermatologist, with no respect for upstate real estate values, named "**Spruce Falls** disease."

In no time at all the mansions and their stables were as vacant as the abandoned palaces and temples of Angkor Thom in Cambodia. Banks foreclosed on those mansions that were mortgaged. The rest became property of the town in lieu of unpaid taxes. Nobody arrived from out of town to bid for them at any price, as though **Spruce Falls** disease were leprosy or cholera or bubonic plague.

Nine mansions were eventually bought from the

banks or the town by locals, who could not resist getting so much for so little. They set up housekeeping in maybe six rooms at most, while dry rot and termites and mice and rats and squirrels and kids wrought havoc with the rest of the property.

"If we can make Newell Cady taste the joys of village life," said Fire Chief Stanley Atkins, speaking before an extraordinary meeting of the volunteer firemen on a Saturday afternoon, "he'll use that option to buy, and **Spruce Falls** will become the fashionable place for Federal Apparatus executives to live."

Squibb, John, Will, and Buck. *Respectively, Vonnegut's son-in-law (a builder) and grandchildren by his daughter Edith are briefly mentioned in Timequake (40) as part of Vonnegut's recollection of his first wife, Jane Cox. The Squibbs live in the house on Cape Cod where Jane and Kurt raised their six children.*

Squires, Anthony. *Patrolman Anthony Squires gives Rudy Waltz the nickname "Deadeye Dick" while escorting him home after visiting with his father in the Midland City jail. Rudy's father is jailed because Rudy is too young to be charged with the accidental murder of Mrs. Eloise Metzger.*

Squires, who had two punctured eardrums as a result of being an abused child, is particularly mean to Rudy. He tells Rudy that if he were him, he would consider committing suicide since he would have to face years of anxiety about one of Metzger's relatives coming after him. Rudy completes his account of Squires with the following: (DD 14) **Patrolman Anthony Squires**, incidentally, would many years later become chief of detectives, and then suffer a nervous breakdown. He is dead now. He was working as a part-time bartender at the new Holiday Inn when he had his peephole closed by ye olde neutron bomb.

Squires, Barbara. *Married to Dr. Jerome Mitchell, she is the younger sister of the policeman Anthony Squires, the man who nicknames Rudy Waltz "Deadeye Dick."*

SS Psychiatrist. *(FWD II)* "Like most writers, I have at home the beginnings of many books which would not allow themselves to be written. About twenty years ago, a doctor prescribed Ritalin for me, to see if that wouldn't help me get over such humps. I realized right away that Ritalin was dehydrated concentrate or pure paranoia, and threw it away. But the book I was trying to make work was to be called **SS Psychiatrist**. This was about an MD who had been psychoanalyzed, and he was stationed at Auschwitz. His job was to treat the depression of those members of the staff who did not like what they were doing there. Talk therapy was all he or anybody had to offer back then. This was before the days of—Never mind.

"My point was, and maybe I can make it today without having to finish that book, that workers in the field of mental health at various times in different parts of the world must find themselves asked to make healthy people happier in cultures and societies which have gone insane.

"Let me hasten to say that the situation in our own country is nowhere near that dire. The goal here right now, it seems to me, is to train intelligent, well-educated people to speak stupidly so that they can be more popular.

"Look at Michael Dukakis.

"Look at George Bush."

Stacks, Dr. Herb. *Rudy Waltz's globe-trotting dentist vacations with his family in Katmandu when Midland City is neutron-bombed, in* Deadeye Dick.

stairs, staircase, stairheads, stairway, stairwell. (*ST* 1) "This room," said Rumford. With a limp right hand, he made the magical sign for **spiral staircase**. "It was one of the few things in life I ever really wanted with all my heart when I was a boy—this little room." *Rumfoord's chimneylike room under the spiral staircase sported the sign* "Skip's Museum."
(*ST* 1) "Well—" murmured Malachi Constant, there in the chimneylike room under the **staircase** in Newport, "it looks like the messenger is finally going to be used."
(*ST* 1) She wore a long white dressing gown whose soft folds formed a counter-clockwise spiral in harmony with the white **staircase**. The train of the gown cascaded down the top riser, making Beatrice continuous with the architecture of the mansion.

(*ST* 1) It startled her so much that she took a step back from the head of the **staircase**, separated herself from the rising spiral. The small step backward transformed her into what she was—a frightened, lonely woman in a tremendous house.
(*ST* 1) In crossing the bright zodiac on the foyer floor, he sensed that the **spiral staircase** now swept down rather than up. Constant became the bottommost point in a whirlpool of fate. As he walked out the door, he was delightfully aware of pulling the aplomb of the Rumfoord mansion right out with him.
(*MN* 42) While the column of air enclosed by the **stairs** had carried in the past a melancholy freight of coal dust and cooking smells and the sweat of plumbing, that air was cold and sharp now. Every window in my attic had been broken. All warm gases had been whisked up the stairwell and out my windows, as though up a whistling flue. . . .

The feeling of a stale old building suddenly laid open, an infected atmosphere lanced, made clean, was familiar to me. I had felt it often enough in Berlin. Helga and I were bombed out twice. Both times there was a **staircase** left to climb.

One time we climbed the **stairs** to a roofless and windowless home, a home otherwise magically undisturbed. Another time, we climbed the **stairs** to cold thin air, two floors below where home had been.

Both moments at those splintered **stairheads** under the open sky were exquisite. . . .

I remember one time, when Helga and I went from the head of a splintered **staircase** in the sky down into a shelter deep in the ground, and the big bombs walked all around above.
(*MN* 43) The railing stopped O'Hare, and he gazed down the **stairwell**, down a beckoning helix to the patch of sure death below.

. . . Whether it was my words or humiliation or booze or surgical shock that made O'Hare throw up, I do not know. Throw up he did. He flashed the hash down the **stairwell** from four stories up.
(*MN* 44) I am in jail because I could not bring myself to walk through or leap over another man's vomit. I am referring to the vomit of Bernard B. O'Hare on the foyer floor at the foot of the **stairwell**.
(*CC* 74) Stanley led me to my room; led me around

the heart of the house, down a **staircase** of living stone, a **staircase** sheltered or exposed by steel-framed rectangles at random.

(*GBR* 11) When Caroline had clumped back up the **cellar stairs**, tremulous with disgust, Fred calmly advised himself that the time had come to *really* die. . . .

He was putting the noose over his head, when little Franklin called down the **stairway** that a man wanted to see him. And the man, who was Norman Mushari, came down the **stairs** uninvited, lugging a fat, cross-gartered, slack-jawed briefcase.

(*SL5* 8) The Americans and their guards and Campbell took shelter in an echoing meat locker which was hollowed in living rock under the slaughterhouse. There was an iron **staircase** with iron doors at the top and bottom.

(*SL5* 8) A guard would go to the head of the **stairs** every so often to see what it was like outside, then he would come down and whisper to the other guards. There was a fire-storm out there.

(*BC* Epilogue) And Trout found **stairs**, but they were the wrong **stairs**. They led him not to the lobby and the finance office and the gift shop and all that, but into a matrix of rooms where persons were recovering or failing to recover from injuries of all kinds.

(*MH* Who Am I This Time?) There was heavy clumping on the library **stairs**. It sounded like a deepsea diver coming upstairs in his lead shoes. It was Harry Nash, turning himself into Marlon Brando.

(*MH* Unready to Wear) I took a couple of steps, headed my spirit in another direction, and that beautiful field marshal, medals and all, went crashing down the **staircase** like a grandfather clock.

(*Slap* 3) This was the secret: There was a mansion concealed within the mansion. It could be entered through trap doors and sliding panels. It consisted of **secret staircases** and listening posts with peep-holes, and secret passageways. There were tunnels, too.

(*Slap* 4) Our servants would tell each other now and then that the mansion was haunted. They heard sneezing and cackling in the walls, and the creaking of **stairways** where there were no **stairways,** and the opening and shutting of doors where there were no doors.

(*JB* 4) But then the person began to sing "Swing Low, Sweet Chariot" as he clumped up the **stairway**, and I knew he was Emil Larkin, once President Nixon's hatchet man.

(*JB* 15) I had assumed that we were as deep in the station as anyone could go. How wrong I was! Mary Kathleen opened the iron door on an **iron staircase** going down, down, down. There was a secret world as vast as Carlsbad Caverns below.

(*JB* 15) She led me through a tunnel under Lexington Avenue, and up a **staircase** into the lobby of the Chrysler Building.

(*JB* Epilogue) She carries it up and down the **stairs** of my duplex. She is even secreting milk for it. She is getting shots to make her stop doing that. *Starbuck's Lhasa apso is experiencing a false pregnancy and carries a rubber ice-cream cone toy around the house.*

(*PS* The Sexual Revolution) An American Indian creation myth, in which a god of some sort gives the people the sun and then the moon and then the bow and arrow and then the corn and so on, is essentially a **staircase**, a tale of accumulation. . . .

Almost all creation myths are **staircases** like. . . . Our own creation myth, taken from the Old Testament, is unique, so far as I could discover.

(*DD* 14) The police actually threw him (*Otto Waltz*) down a flight of **stairs**. They didn't just pretend that was what had happened to him. There was a lot of confused racist talk, evidently. Father would later remember lying at the bottom of the **stairs**, with somebody standing over him and asking him, "Hey, Nazi—how does it feel to be a nigger now?"

(*DD* 26) He was heroically honorable and truthful. He (*Otto Waltz*) was thrown down the **staircase**—like so much garbage.

(*Blue* 8) He (*Dan Gregory*) had given her (*Marilee Kemp*) a shove in his studio which sent her backwards and down the **staircase**. She looked dead when she hit the bottom, and two servants happened to be standing there—at the bottom of the **stairs**.

(*Blue* 8) Only after the war did Marilee, reborn as the Contessa Portomaggiore, tell me that I was the reason she had been pushed down the **stairs** back in 1932.

(*Blue* 11) But think of this: there were fifty-two mirrors of every conceivable period and shape, many of them hung in unexpected places at crazy angles, to multiply even the bewildered observer to infinity. There at the top of the **stairs**, with Dan Gregory invisible to me, I myself was everywhere!

(*Blue* 21) Marilee's and my canvas, so to speak, called for more and wetter kisses, and then a groping, goosey, swooning tango up the **spiral staircase** and through the grand dining room.

(*HP* 14) White cotton strips spliced end to end crisscrossed every which way in the front hall and living room. The newel post of the **stairway** was connected to the inside doorknob of the front door, and the doorknob was connected to the living room chandelier, and so on ad infinitum.

(*TQ* 29) You can imagine what the bottoms of **staircases** and escalators, in the Western Hemisphere in particular, looked like after free will kicked in.

(*TQ* 30) One time when Allie was maybe fifteen and I was ten, she heard somebody fall down our basement **stairs**: *Bloompity, bloomp, bloomp.* She thought it was I, so she stood at the top of the **stairs** laughing her fool head off. This would have been 1932, three years into the Great Depression.

But it wasn't I. It was a guy from the gas company, who had come to read the meter. He came clumping out of the basement all bunged up, and absolutely furious.

That's the New World for you!

(*TQ* 30) That the impulse to laugh at healthy people who nonetheless fall down is by no means universal, however, was brought to my attention unpleasantly at a performance of *Swan Lake* by the Royal Ballet in London, England. I was in the audience with my daughter Nanny, who was about sixteen then. She is forty-one now, in the summer of 1996. That must have been twenty-five years ago now!

A ballerina, dancing on her toes, went *deedly-deedly-deedly* into the wings as she was supposed to do. But then there was a sound backstage as though she had put her foot in a bucket and then gone down an **iron stairway** with her foot still in the bucket.

I instantly laughed like hell.

I was the only person to do so.

(*TQ* 31) And the truth about that situation all over the world will never be worse than it was during the first couple of hours after the rerun stopped. Oh sure, there were millions of pedestrians lying on the ground because the weight on their feet had been unevenly distributed when free will kicked in. But most of them were pretty much OK, except for those who had been near the tops of escalators or **stairways**. Most were no worse hurt than the woman Allie and I saw come shooting out of a streetcar headfirst.

(*TQ* 43) I was pleased to reply with an epistle which was frankly vengeful, since he and Father had screwed me out of a liberal arts college education:

"Dear Brother: This is almost like telling you about the birds and the bees," I began. "There are many good people who are beneficially stimulated by some, but not all, manmade arrangements of colors and shapes on flat surfaces, essentially nonsense.

"You yourself are gratified by some music, arrangements of noises, and again essentially nonsense. If I were to kick a bucket down the **cellar stairs**, and then say to you that the racket I had made was philosophically on a par with *The Magic Flute*, this would not be the beginning of a long and upsetting debate. An utterly satisfactory and complete response on your part would be, 'I like what Mozart did, and I hate what the bucket did.'"

(*TQ* 56) I am still on the third floor of our brownstone in the city, and we don't have an elevator. So down the **stairs** I go with my pages, *clumpity, clumpily, clumpity.* I get down to the first floor, where my wife has her office. Her favorite reading when she was Lily's age was stories about Nancy Drew, the girl detective.

Nancy Drew is to Jill what Kilgore Trout is to me, so Jill says, "Where are you going?"

I say, "I am going to buy an envelope."

(*BAG* Runaways) Annie's mother, Mary (*the First Lady of Indiana*), came down the **spiral staircase**. She had been listening to the lies from the landing above. "I think you handled that very well," she said to her husband.

See also: PP IV; XXVI; *ST* 1; 2; 7; 12; *MN* 12; 14; 15; 16; 17; 38; 39; 42; 44; *CC* 93; 101; 105; 114; 117; *GBR* 5; 9; 11; 12; *SL5* 3; *BC* 18; *MH* Who Am I This Time?; *MH* Miss Temptation; *MH* More Stately Mansions; *MH* Report on the Barnhouse

Effect; *MH* Welcome to the Monkey House; *MH* Deer in the Works; *Slap* 17; 38; 40; Epilogue; *JB* 4; 15; 23; *PS* The People One Knows; *PS* Playmates; *PS* Obscenity; *DD* 13; 15; 21; 26; *Blue* 1; 8; 9; 10; 11; 17; 21; 24; 28; *HP* 3; 4; *FWD* IX; XV; *TQ* 44; 47; *BAG* Bagombo Snuff Box; *BAG* A Present for Big Saint Nick; *BAG* A Night for Love.

Stankiewicz, Juan and Geraldo. *The estranged grandchildren of Walter Starbuck. Starbuck's son changed his name back to the original European spelling to distance himself from his father, who he believed behaved disgracefully during the McCarthy era. Starbuck recalls:* In accordance with my wife's will, incidentally, **Juan** and his brother, **Geraldo**, were receiving reparations from West Germany for the confiscation of my wife's father's bookstore in Vienna by the Nazis after the *Anschluss*, Germany's annexation of Austria in Nineteen-hundred and Thirty-eight. My wife's will was an old one, written when Walter was a little boy. The lawyer had advised her to leave the money to her grandchildren so as to avoid one generation of taxes. She was trying to be smart about money (*JB* Epilogue).

Stankiewicz, Stanislaus. *The Russian-Polish chauffeur and bodyguard to the McCone family, in* Jailbird. *He marries Anna Kairys, the McCones' Russian Lithuanian cook, and together they have Walter F. Stankiewicz, who later changes his name to Starbuck.*

Stankiewicz, Walter F. *Walter F. Starbuck, Jr., is so distraught and embarrassed by his father's behavior during the McCarthy era that upon turning twenty-one he changes his name to its original European spelling. Once his mother passes away, he cuts himself off from any further contact with his father.* (*JB* 4) Our son said this to me, before showing his back to me and the open pit and hastening to a waiting taxicab: "I pity you, but I can never love you. As far as I am concerned, you killed this poor woman. I can't think of you anymore as a father or as any sort of relative. I never want to see or hear of you again."

Stankiewicz earns his living as a book reviewer for The New York Times, *eventually a property of the RAMJAC Corporation.*

Stankowitz. *In* Slapstick, *the original Polish name of Dr. Cordelia Swain Cordiner's grandfather. He changes his name to Swain upon arriving in America. Dr. Cordiner insists she is not related to Eliza and Wilbur Swain.*

Stanley. *In* Cat's Cradle, *Franklin Hoenikker's valet on San Lorenzo who grudgingly produces a copy of* The Books of Bokonon *for the narrator to read.*

Starbuck, Ruth. *The Jewish survivor of a concentration camp near Munich who later marries Walter Starbuck and acts in a manner worthy of her biblical namesake. Starbuck meets her as she helps American military police sort out displaced people after the war. Ruth is a master of languages because she made it a point of learning to speak with fellow prisoners.* Ruth's prewar family owned a rare-book store there before the Nazis took it away from them. She was six years younger than I. Her father and mother and two siblings were killed in concentration camps. She herself was hidden by a Christian family, but was discovered and arrested, along with the head of that family, in Nineteen-hundred and Forty-two. So she herself was in a concentration camp near Munich, finally liberated by American troops, for the last two years of the war. She herself would die in her sleep in Nineteen-hundred and Seventy-Four—of congestive heart failure, two weeks before my own arrest. Whither I went, and no matter how clumsily, there did my **Ruth** go—long as she could. If I marveled at this out loud, she would say, "Where else could I be? What else could I do?" (*JB* 2)

Aside from learning a multiplicity of languages, Ruth teaches herself portraiture using lampblack while in Auschwitz. Before the war, when only sixteen, she photographed one hundred beggars in Vienna, all of whom were terribly wounded veterans of World War One (*JB* 2). *She was also an accomplished pianist.*

Ruth tries to draw on her artistic talents to make a living as a wedding photographer when Walter is down on his luck. However, There was always an air of prewar doom about her photographs, which no retoucher could eradicate. It was as though the entire wedding party would wind up in the trenches or the gas chambers by and by (*JB* 2). *She eventually developed a thriving business as an interior decorator.*

On October 15, 1946, *Ruth and Walter are married*. (JB 2) On the day we were married, and probably conceived our only child as well, *Reichsmarschall* Hermann Göring cheated the hangman by swallowing cyanide.

(JB 2) She believed, and was entitled to believe, I must say, that all human beings were evil by nature, whether tormentors or victims, or idle standers-by. They could only create meaningless tragedies, she said, since they weren't nearly intelligent enough to accomplish all the good they meant to do. We were a disease, she said, which had evolved on one tiny cinder in the universe, but could spread and spread.

(JB 16) . . . my wife **Ruth**, the Ophelia of the death camps . . . believed that even the most intelligent human beings were so stupid that they could only make things worse by speaking their minds. It was thinkers, after all, who had set up the death camps. Setting up a death camp, with its railroad sidings and its around-the-clock crematoria, was not something a moron could do. Neither could a moron explain why a death camp was ultimately humane.

Starbuck, Walter (*né* **Stankiewicz**). *The narrator and title character of* Jailbird, *son of a chauffeur and cook, Walter is brought up in the home of Alexander Hamilton McCone, heir to the Cuyahoga Bridge and Iron Company. In exchange for becoming the chess partner and constant companion of the socially withdrawn McCone, Walter is promised a Harvard education. After Harvard he serves in the military as an officer in charge of resettling displaced persons in postwar Europe. This is how he meets Ruth, the multilingual Jewish concentration camp survivor who eventually becomes his wife.*

During the McCarthy Communist witch hunts of the 1950s, Walter is called before a congressional investigative committee and asked by then Congressman Nixon if he knew anyone in government who had been a Communist. Starbuck volunteers the name of Leland Clewes, thereby ruining his friend's career in government.

When Nixon becomes president, Starbuck is appointed the president's special adviser on youth affairs and given an office in the White House third subbasement. Nixon's Watergate cronies use the safe in Starbuck's office to hide illegal campaign contri-

butions —*eventually used as hush money. This leads to Walter's imprisonment as a coconspirator in the Watergate cover-up.*

Upon release from prison, Walter takes a room in the once fashionable Hotel Arapahoe in New York, where he finds stolen clarinet parts in a dresser. When he and Mary Kathleen O'Looney take refuge in the American Harp Company's Chrysler Building offices and he offers the clarinet pieces to Delmar Peale, he finds himself once again in jail (though he is shortly released).

Starbuck is given control of O'Looney's RAMJAC Corporation upon her death. However, because Starbuck withheld her last will and testament in order to fulfill his promise to her, he is forced to return to prison for another five years.

Walter continually notes there were only four women in his life that he loved: his mother, Sarah Wyatt, Ruth, and Mary Kathleen O'Looney. (JB 1) I will describe them all by and by. Let it be said now, though, that all four seemed more virtuous, braver about life, and closer to the secrets of the universe than I could ever be.

(JB 10) Sarah had spent many summers in Europe. I had never been there. She was fluent in French, and she and the owner performed a madrigal in that most melodious of all languages. How would I ever have got through life without women to act as my interpreters? Of the four women I ever loved, only Mary Kathleen O'Looney spoke no language but English. But even Mary Kathleen was my interpreter when I was a Harvard communist, trying to communicate with members of the American working class.

Starr, Harrison. *In the opening pages of* Slaughterhouse-Five, *Vonnegut recounts how his Dresden experience was forever on his mind in an attempt to give it some literary structure. His exchange with movie producer Harrison Starr expresses his own futility about structuring another antiwar novel, much the like the never-ending loop of his Yon Yonson refrain.* (SL5 1) "You know what I say to people when I hear they're writing anti-war books?"

"No. What *do* you say, **Harrison Starr**?"

"I say, 'Why don't you write an *anti-glacier* book instead?'"

What he meant, of course, was that there would

always be wars, that they were as easy to stop as glaciers. I believe that, too.

And, even if wars didn't keep coming like glaciers, there would still be plain old death.

Steadman, Ralph. *In the closing Author's Note to* A Man Without a Country, *Vonnegut's remarks about Ralph Steadman lead into an appreciation of Joe Petro III's suggestion of an artistic collaboration, enabling Kurt to work with other artists and performers, enlarging his own circle of friends and appreciating Joe for serving as its nexus.* And since we first met, Joe has beguiled others into sending him pictures for him to do with what he so much loves to do. Among them are the comedian Jonathan Winters, an art student long ago, and the English artist **Ralph Steadman**, whose accomplishments include the appropriately harrowing illustrations for Hunter Thompson's Fear and Loathing books. And **Steadman** and I have come to know and like each other on account of Joe.

Yes, and last July (2004) there was an exhibition of Joe's and my stuff, arranged by Joe, at the Indianapolis Art Center in the town of my birth. But there was also a painting by my architect and painter grandfather Bernard Vonnegut, and two by my architect and painter father Kurt Vonnegut, and six apiece by my daughter Edith and my son the doctor Mark.

Ralph Steadman heard about this family show from Joe and sent me a note of congratulation. I wrote him back as follows: "Joe Petro III staged a reunion of four generations of my family in Indianapolis, and he has made you and me feel like first cousins. Is it possible that he is God? We could do worse."

Steel, Roy. *The second husband of Dorothy Karabekian in* Bluebeard. *Terry and Henri Karabekian, Rabo's and Dorothy's sons, take Steel's name as their own.*

Steel, Terrence W., Jr. *The private detective hired by Jason Wilder to document the activities of Eugene Debs Hartke in preparation for his dismissal, in* Hocus Pocus. *"Terry" poses as a gardener working at Tarkington College. In order to gain Hartke's confidence, Steel tells him that his wife ran off with their*

three children and her lesbian lover, a junior high school dietitian.

Steinberg, Saul. *With only one reference to friend and artist Saul Steinberg, Vonnegut recalls their conversation that results in a model for appraising creative work. It comes at the end of the fifth and final section of the last chapter of* A Man Without a Country.

Their conversation is a nearly coded philosophical appreciation about the disparate vagaries of artistic intent and the manner by which one responds to art. Steinberg's response addresses the essence of Vonnegut's concerns about what drives him and his potential for a valued literary legacy (despite the lack of a Nobel Prize).

It is noteworthy that the manner of Vonnegut's recall of this incident is structured in a proposition followed by six alternating anaphoric paragraphs. From the writer often criticized for too easily tossing off his stories without much care, Vonnegut closes the text with a linguistic double helix; his final examination of art may be seen as free verse poetry of the sublime.

(MWC 12) Who was the wisest person I ever met in my entire life? It was a man, but of course it needn't have been. It was the graphic artist **Saul Steinberg**, who like everybody else I know, is dead now. I could ask him anything, and six seconds would pass, and then he would give me a perfect answer, gruffly, almost a growl. He was born in Romania, in a house where, according to him, "the geese looked in the windows."

I said, "**Saul**, how should I feel about Picasso?"

Six seconds passed, and then he said, "God put him on Earth to show us what it's like to be *really* rich."

I said, "**Saul**, I am a novelist, and many of my friends are novelists and good ones, but when we talk I keep feeling we are in two very different businesses. What makes me feel that way?"

Six seconds passed, and then he said, "It's very simple. There are two sorts of artists, one not being in the least superior to the other. But one responds to the history of his or her art so far, and the other responds to life itself."

I said, "**Saul**, are you *gifted?*"

Six seconds passed, and then he growled, "No,

but what you respond to in any work of art is the artist's struggle against his or her limitations."

Stern, Damon. *The head of Tarkington's history department and Eugene Debs Hartke's best and most entertaining friend. He* spoke as badly of his own country as Slazinger and I did, and right into the faces of students in the classroom day after day. I used to sit in on his course and laugh and clap. The truth can be very funny in an awful way, especially as it relates to greed and hypocrisy (HP 14).

Damon Stern is the cause for Hartke's dismissal from Tarkington. Hartke frequently repeats some of the more shocking material Stern told his students. Stern told his students Hitler was a Roman Catholic and that it was no coincidence one of the Nazis' highest medals was the Iron Cross. (HP 15) **Damon Stern**, who was always turning up little-known facts of history, told me, incidentally, that the Battle of the Alamo was about slavery. The brave men who died there wanted to secede from Mexico because it was against the law to own slaves in Mexico. They were fighting for the right to own slaves.

Stern dies during the Athena prison break. While his wife, Wanda June, leaves town with their children, he stays behind to warn the people of Scipio. He is killed by an escaped prisoner who was "gut shooting" horses in the Tarkington Stable. Hartke is led to believe Stern asked the convict to spare the horses. Damon Stern is buried in the shadow of Musket Mountain.

Stevenson, Adlai. *Losing Democratic Party candidate for president in 1952 and 1956. (MH The Hyannis Port Story) I* was feeling pretty sorry for myself, because I was just an ordinary citizen, and had to get stuck in lines like that. But then I recognized the man in the limousine up ahead of me. It was **Adlai Stevenson**. He wasn't moving any faster than I was, and his radiator was boiling, too.

Stevenson, Stony. *Though once a British military unit commander, Stony is recruited for a leadership position in the Army of Mars, in* The Sirens of Titan. *In order to conceal his rank, he and the other Martian leaders pose as privates. Stony is a large, gregarious man often amused by the more difficult or* odd characters on Mars. Stony takes an interest in Unk (Malachi Constant) because they had such difficulty erasing his memory. Stony becomes intrigued with Unk's strong desire to understand what was going on despite numerous visits to the hospital to erase his memory and limit his cognitive abilities.

Unk gleans information about Stony through the letter he writes to himself in a serial format. Though Stony first thinks he would be amused by Unk's ramblings, he quickly realizes that his friend's bits of memory call into question all that he remembered as well as the information he was privy to as one of the Martian leaders. Stony and Unk shared all they knew in an effort to understand their predicament. It finally dawns on Stony that the invasion fleet would be doomed if it landed on Earth. It is Stony's suggestion that Unk write down everything he could remember. Together, Stony and Unk decide that Rumfoord and Kazak are the real commanders of the Martian Army. For their efforts, both have their minds wiped clean and Unk is radio-controlled into publicly strangling Stony.

Boaz witnesses Stony's execution but never reveals this knowledge to Unk while they live in the caves of Mercury. Whenever Unk upset Boaz with the truth about the harmoniums, Boaz would warn him, "Don't truth *me, and I won't* truth *you" (ST 9).*

Though Boaz lets Unk enjoy his own harmless untruths, Winston Niles Rumfoord was not so considerate. He reveals the truth about Stony's execution as part of the ceremony banishing the Space Wanderer to Titan.

It is left to Salo to restore Malachi Constant's pleasant memories of Stony. In Malachi's final moments on the snowy outskirts of Indianapolis, he slips into Salo's posthypnotic suggestion reuniting the two comrades. (ST Epilogue) As the snow drifted over Constant, he imagined that the clouds opened up, letting through a sunbeam, a sunbeam all for him.

A golden space ship encrusted with diamonds came skimming down the sunbeam, landed in the untouched snow of the street.

Out stepped a stocky, red-headed man with a big cigar. He was young.

He wore the uniform of the Martian Assault Infantry, Unk's old outfit.

"Hello, Unk," he said. "Get in."

"Get in?" said Constant. "Who are you?"

"**Stony Stevenson**, Unk. You don't recognize me?"

"**Stony**?" said Constant. "That's you, **Stony**?"

"Who else could stand the bloody pace?" said **Stony**. He laughed.

"Get in," he said.

"And go where?" said Constant.

"Paradise," said **Stony**.

"What's Paradise like?" said Constant.

"Everybody's happy there forever," said **Stony**, "or as long as the bloody Universe holds together. Get in, Unk. Beatrice is already there, waiting for you."

"Beatrice?" said Unk, getting into the space ship. **Stony** closed the airlocks, pressed the on button.

"We're—we're going to Paradise now?" said Constant. "I—I'm going to get into Paradise?"

"Don't ask me why, old sport," said **Stony**, "but somebody up there likes you."

Stevie (*see* **Amy and Harry** *and* **Eddie Laird**).

Stewart, Kerfuit and Ella Vonnegut. *Vonnegut notes that his cousin is not represented at the* Timequake *clambake.* (TQ 62) Nobody resembled my aunt **Ella Vonnegut Stewart**, a first cousin of my father's, either. She and her husband, **Kerfuit**, owned a bookstore in Louisville, Kentucky. They did not stock my books because they found my language obscene. So it was back then, when I was starting out.

Years earlier in Palm Sunday, *in the chapter entitled "Embarrassment," Vonnegut notes,* My **Aunt Ella**, who owned **Stewart's** Bookstore in Louisville, Kentucky, would not stock my books. She found them degenerate, and said so (PS Embarrassment).

Stockmayer, Walter H. *The Dartmouth chemistry professor in* Breakfast of Champions *who provides a drawing of the plastic molecule seeping into Sugar Creek running through Midland City. The endlessness of the molecular representation prompts Vonnegut to continue,* And when he sketched a plausible molecule, he indicated points where it would go on and on just as I have indicated them—

with an abbreviation which means sameness without end.

The proper ending for any story about people it seems to me, since life is now a polymer in which the Earth is wrapped so tightly, should be that same abbreviation, which I now write large because I feel like it, which is this one:
ETC.

And it is in order to acknowledge the continuity of this polymer that I begin so many sentences with "And" and "So," and end so many paragraphs with ". . . and so on."

And so on.

"It's all like an ocean!" cried Dostoevski. I say it's all like cellophane (BC 20).

Stone, Sydney and Fred. *Sydney is a member of Tarkington College's Board of Trustees, and Fred is his son and a student at the school, in* Hocus Pocus. *Eugene Debs Hartke witnesses Fred take a mug from the school bookstore in plain view of the cashier. After following Fred out to the quadrangle and confronting him with his deed, Hartke stands by in astonishment while Stone smashes the mug against the Vonnegut Memorial Fountain. Hartke writes a letter to the Board of Trustees and becomes an eternal enemy of Sydney Stone's. Stone refuses to believe Hartke's accusations about Fred's theft.*

Stone is worth more than a billion dollars earned in commissions for selling American properties to foreign interests, a main concern of the text. He engineered the sale of Hartke's father's former employer, E. I. Du Pont de Nemours & Company, to I. G. Farben in Germany.

Stonehenge. *The Tralfamadorians use their Universal Will to Become (UWTB) to send messages concerning the status of the replacement part for Salo's spaceship. The messages are conveyed in great architectural monuments on Earth that could be monitored by Salo.* (ST 12) The reply was written on Earth in huge stones on a plain in what is now England. The ruins of the reply still stand, and are known as **Stonehenge**. The meaning of **Stonehenge** in Tralfamadorian, when viewed from above, is: "*Replacement part being rushed with all possible speed.*"

Stratton, Samuel W. In Jailbird, *the physicist and President of the Massachusetts Institute of Technology who serves on the three-member review board concerning the death sentences of Sacco and Vanzetti.*

Strax, Dr. Philip (see **God Bless You, Dr. Kevorkian**).

structured moment. *The Tralfamadorian concept that explains in the fourth dimension all existence is-as-it-was-and-is-supposed-to-become, that all moments exist simultaneously.* (SL5 2) "The most important thing I learned on Tralfamadore was that when a person dies he only *appears* to die. He is still very much alive in the past, so it is very silly for people to cry at his funeral. All moments, past, present, and future, always have existed, always will exist. The Tralfamadorians can look at all the different moments just the way we can look at a stretch of the Rocky Mountains, for instance. They can see how permanent all the moments are, and they can look at any moment that interests them. It is just an illusion we have here on Earth that one moment follows another one, like beads on a string, and that once a moment is gone it is gone forever."

stuppa (see also **Bokononism**). (CC 89) "Do you know anybody who *might* want the job?" Frank was giving a classic illustration of what Bokonon calls *duffle. Duffle*, in the Bokononist sense, is the destiny of thousands upon thousands of persons when placed in the hands of a *stuppa*. A *stuppa* is a fog-bound child.

Styron, William. (MH New Dictionary) As you rumple through this new dictionary, looking for dirty words and schoolmarmisms tempered by worldliness.... I worry about the biographies and the works of art, since they seem a mixed bag, possibly locked for all eternity in a matrix of type. Norman Mailer is there, for instance, but not **William Styron** or James Jones or Vance Bourjaily or Edward Lewis Wallant.
(PS The First Amendment) Be that as it may, I was sober then and am sober now, and Felix Kuznetsov and I had become friends during the previous summer—at an ecumenical meeting in New York City,

sponsored by the Charles F. Kettering Foundation, of American and Soviet literary persons, about ten to a side. The American delegation was headed by Norman Cousins, and included myself and Edward Albee and Arthur Miller and **William Styron** and John Updike. All of us had been published in the Soviet Union. I am almost entirely in print over there—with the exception of *Mother Night* and *Jailbird*. Few, if any, of the Soviet delegates had had anything published here, and so their work was unknown to us.
(PS The First Amendment) So Albee and **Styron** and Updike and I sent a cable to the Writers' Union, saying that we thought it was wrong to penalize writers for what they wrote, no matter what they wrote. Felix Kuznetsov made an official reply on behalf of the union, giving the sense of a large meeting in which distinguished writer after distinguished writer testified that those who wrote for Metropole weren't really writers, that they were pornographers and other sorts of disturbers of the peace, and so on.
(FWD X) When I was in Tokyo with **William Styron** a few years ago, he said, "Thank God for the atomic bomb. If it weren't for it, I would be dead." When the bomb dropped, he was a Marine in Okinawa, preparing for the invasion of the Japanese home islands. It seems certain to me that many more Americans and Japanese would have died during the invasion than were burned to crisps at Hiroshima.
(FWD XX) Yes, and I, having just finished reading **William Styron**'s short and elliptical account of his recent attack of melancholia, *Darkness Visible* (a suicide attempt may or may not have been involved), am now prepared to say that suicidal persons can be divided into two sorts. **Styron**'s sort blames the wiring and chemistry of his brain, which could easily fit into a salad bowl. My sort blames the Universe. (Why mess around?) I don't offer this insight as yet another joke ("Why is cream more expensive than milk?"). It is my serious belief that those of us who become humorists (suicidal or not) feel free (as most people do not) to speak of life itself as a dirty joke, even though life is all there is or ever can be.
(TQ 42) This very summer, I asked the novelist **William Styron** in a Chinese restaurant how many

people on the whole planet had what we had, which was lives worth living. Between the two of us, we came up with *seventeen percent.*

The next day I took a walk in midtown Manhattan with a longtime friend, a physician who treats every sort of addict at Bellevue Hospital. Many of his patients are homeless and HIV-positive as well. I told him about **Styron**'s and my figure of seventeen percent. He said it sounded about right to him.

(TQ 51) In chapter 2 of this wonderful book of mine, I mention a commemoration in the chapel of the University of Chicago of the fiftieth anniversary of the atom-bombing of Hiroshima. I said at the time that I had to respect the opinion of my friend **William Styron** that the Hiroshima bomb saved his life. **Styron** was then a United States Marine, training for an invasion of the Japanese home islands, when that bomb was dropped.

I had to add, though, that I knew a single word that proved our democratic government was capable of committing obscene, gleefully rabid and racist, yahooistic murders of unarmed men, women, and children, murders wholly devoid of military common sense. I said the word. It was a foreign word. That word was *Nagasaki.*

(TQ 56) A Luddite to the end, as was Kilgore Trout, as was Ned Ludd, the possibly but not certainly fictitious workman who smashed up machinery, supposedly, in Leicestershire, England, at the beginning of the nineteenth century, I persist in pecking away at a manual typewriter. That still leaves me technologically several generations ahead of **William Styron** and Stephen King, who, like Trout, write with pens on yellow legal pads. (*See also:* PS The People One Knows.)

subbasement (*see also* **basement**). (JB 2) I had an office, but no secretary, in the **subbasement** of the Executive Office Building, directly underneath, as it happened, the office where burglaries and other crimes on behalf of President Nixon were planned. I could hear people walking overhead and raising their voices sometimes. On my own level in the **subbasement** my only companions were heating and air-conditioning equipment and a Coca-Cola machine that only I knew about, I think.

(JB 2) At the end of every futile day in the **subbase-**

ment I would go home to the only wife I have ever had, who was Ruth—waiting for me in our little brick bungalow in Chevy Chase, Maryland.

(JB 5) It became necessary to hide it when the contents of all White House safes were to be examined by the Federal Bureau of Investigation and men from the Office of the Special Prosecutor. My obscure office in the **subbasement** was selected as the most promising hiding place. I acquiesced. *An old steamer trunk was used to store illegal campaign contributions totaling $1 million in unmarked and circulated twenty-dollar bills—eventually used as Watergate payoff money.*

Sublime Chamberlain of the Inner Shrine. *The head of the Knights of Kandahar in the short story "The No-Talent Kid," originally published in the October 1952 issue of* The Saturday Evening Post *and later reprinted in the collection* Bagombo Snuff Box.

Due to an embezzling treasurer, the Knights find themselves with one and a half years of unpaid bills. The Sublime Chamberlain insists all their creditors will be paid. Part of his plan to square accounts involves liquidating their band instruments including its incredibly large bass drum, far larger than the seven-foot-diameter bass that helped defeat Lincoln High School in their quest for an eleventh consecutive state title.

Walter Plummer, the worst musician in Lincoln High school's history, manages to acquire the drum before his teacher and band director Helmholtz has a chance. In the end, Helmholtz offers Plummer the position of bass drum cart puller; successfully doing so will earn him his coveted band sweater and varsity letter. Plummer will also pass the drum to the band upon his own graduation that is still years away.

Sugar Creek. *Mentioned as a waste dumping ground in* Happy Birthday, Wanda June, Breakfast of Champions, *and* Deadeye Dick, *Sugar Creek is the waterway running through Midland City and beneath the Mildred Barry Memorial Center for the Arts.*

(BC 11) **Sugar Creek** flooded now and then. Dwayne remembered about that. In a land so flat, flooding was a queerly pretty thing for water to do.

Sugar Creek brimmed over silently, formed a vast mirror in which children might safely play.

The mirror showed the citizens the shape of the valley they lived in, demonstrated that they were hill people who inhabited slopes rising one inch for every mile that separated them from **Sugar Creek**.

When Dwayne Hoover was younger and dumping the family's weekly trash in Sugar Creek, he and his father witnessed the brutal murder of a black man.

Kilgore Trout's Midland City experience begins once he wades across the threshold that is Sugar Creek. Severely polluted with waste from the Barrytron manufacturing plant, when Trout emerges from the creek, his feet were coated at once with a clear plastic substance from the surface of the creek. When, in some surprise, Trout lifted one coated foot from the water, the plastic substance dried in air instantly, sheathed his foot in a thin, skin-tight bootie resembling mother-of-pearl. He repeated the process with his other foot (BC 20).

The Maritimo Brothers Construction Company is hired by Barrytron to build a waste removal system, but instead the gangster-controlled company builds a simple outlet into Sugar Creek.

When Dwayne Hoover goes on a rampage, he bites off Trout's right ring finger and spits it into the creek.

Dr. Cyprian Ukwende is used to seeing children come to the hospital with the mysterious plasticized sheet on their legs after having played in Sugar Creek. He artfully uses a pair of tinsnips to cut away the castlike forms.

In Deadeye Dick, Sugar Creek is also the threshold crossed by Gino and Marco Maritimo when they enter Midland City after being forced from the freight train they had been riding. It is also where the headless body of August Gunther is found after being accidentally killed by Police Chief Morissey. In an attempt to save Morissey from the criminal investigation that would have ruined him, Otto Waltz and the other hunting buddies send Gunther's body down Sugar Creek and it eventually flows out to the Mississippi River and the Gulf of Mexico.

Despite the history of open sewage flowing into the creek, the Waltz's cook, Mary Hoobler, often prepared locally caught catfish and crayfish for the family.

Sugar Creek High School. *The "elite white high school" in Midland City back when Dwayne Hoover attended. By the time* Breakfast of Champions *unfolds, it has become nearly all black. The only bit of learning Dwayne remembers is a poem he was forced to learn as a sophomore.* (BC 18) The Moving Finger writes; and, having writ, / Moves on: nor all your Piety nor Wit / Shall lure it back to cancel half a Line / Nor all your Tears wash out a Word of it.

Sugarbush Mountain, Vermont. *Billy Pilgrim's charter flight from Ilium carrying optometrists on their way to an international convention in Montreal crashes on top of Sugarbush Mountain, in* Slaughterhouse-Five. *Except for Billy, everyone dies.*

suicidal, suicide (*see also* **Ethical Suicide Parlor**). (*PP V*) "And dope addiction, alcoholism, and **suicide** went up proportionately," said Finnerty. *Finnerty alludes to societal ills that mushroom while the promise of "peacetime uses of atomic energy" are receiving all the attention.*
(ST 5) The big attack on Earth would be **suicide** for sure.
(ST 7) Salo generously donated half of his supply of UWTB (*Universal Will to Become*) to the **suicide** of Mars.
(ST 7) He (*Rumfoord*) wished to change the World for the better by means of the great and unforgettable **suicide** of Mars.
(CC 106) "It's what Bokononists always say when they are about to commit **suicide**." *The phrase is "Now I will destroy the whole world."*
(GBR 7) The book (*Eliot's* Domesday Book) was nearly full. . . . What he wrote now was the name of the **suicidal** man who had called him, who had come to see him, who had just departed. . . .

"Sherman Wesley Little," wrote Eliot. "Indy, Su-TDM-LO-V2-3K3-RF $300." Decoded, this meant that Little was from Indianapolis, was a **suicidal** tool-and-die maker who had been laid off, a veteran of the Second World War with a wife and three children, the second child suffering from cerebral palsy.
(GBR 8) Sons of **suicides** seldom do well.
(GBR 9) Since he (*Fred Rosewater*) was the son of a **suicide**, it was hardly surprising that his secret hankerings were embarrassing and small.

(GBR 11) Sons of **suicides** often think of killing themselves at the end of a day, when their blood sugar is low.

(MH Preface) "I am committing **suicide** by cigarette," I replied.

My brand is Pall Mall. The authentic **suicides** ask for Pall Malls. The dilettantes ask for Pell Mells. . . .

The public health authorities never mention the main reason many Americans have for smoking heavily, which is that smoking is a fairly sure, fairly honorable form of **suicide**.

(BC 6) He even forgot that his wife Celia had committed **suicide**, for instance, by eating Drano—a mixture of sodium hydroxide and aluminum flakes, which was meant to clear drains.

(BC 10) "In the long run, *he's* committing **suicide**," said the driver. "Seems like the only kind of job an American can get these days is committing **suicide** in some way."

(BC 17) Listen: Bunny's mother and my mother were different sorts of human beings, but they were both beautiful in exotic ways, and they both boiled over with chaotic talk about love and peace and wars and evil and desperation, of better days coming by and by, of worse days coming by and by. And both our mothers committed **suicide**. Bunny's mother ate Drano. My mother ate sleeping pills, which wasn't nearly as horrible.

(BC Epilogue) His *(Trout's)* voice was my father's voice. I *heard* my father—and I *saw* my mother in the void. My mother stayed far, far away, because she had left me a legacy of **suicide**.

(WFG Preface) I received a note from a twelve-year-old this morning. He had read my latest novel, *Breakfast of Champions*, and he said, "Dear Mr. Vonnegut: Please don't commit **suicide**." God love him. I have told him I am fine.

(WFG Good Missiles, Good Manners, Good Night) Word of honor—if I had been invited into the Laird home *(Melvin Laird, the former secretary of defense)*, I would have smiled and smiled. I would have understood that the defense establishment was only doing what it had to do, no matter how **suicidally**.

(WFG Address to the National Institute of Arts and Letters, 1971) That was a happy day. My father was the widower of a **suicide** when he told me about that happiest day. *The story is about Vonnegut's par-*

ents breaking into the Indianapolis 500-Mile Speedway and running their new Oldsmobile around the track—prior to the First World War.

(WFG *Playboy* Interview) PLAYBOY: Most of the people in *Breakfast* seem jangled and desperate—in situations they can't get out of—and a number of them consider **suicide**.

VONNEGUT: Yes, **suicide** is at the heart of the book. It's also the punctuation mark at the end of many artistic careers.

(WFG *Playboy* Interview) I want to start believing in things that have shapeliness and harmony. *Breakfast of Champions* isn't a threat to commit **suicide**, incidentally. It's my promise that I'm beyond that now. Which is something for me. I used to think of it as a perfectly reasonable way to avoid delivering a lecture, to avoid a deadline, to not pay a bill, to not go to a cocktail party.

(PS Roots) WE have come now to a rascal, Albert Lieber, whose emotional faithlessness to his children, in my humble opinion, contributed substantially to my mother's eventual **suicide**.

(PS When I Lost My Innocence) "We Americans have guided our destinies so clumsily, with all the world watching, that we must now protect ourselves against our own government and our own industries.

"Not to do so would be **suicide**. We have discovered a brand-new method for committing **suicide**—family style, Reverend Jim Jones style, and by the millions. What is the method? To say nothing and do nothing about what some of our businessmen and military men are doing with the most unstable substances and the most persistent poisons to be found anywhere in the universe.

"The people who play with such chemicals are so *dumb!*"

(PS Triage) My mother, who was also a **suicide** and who never saw even the first of her eleven grandchildren, is another one, I gather, who would not like to see her name anywhere. *Vonnegut groups his mother with his thesis adviser at the University of Chicago, who had also committed suicide.*

(PS Religion) Some guesses are more **suicidal** than others. The belief that a true lover of God is immune to the bites of copperheads and rattlesnakes is a case in point.

(PS The Sexual Revolution) As for real death—it

has always been a temptation to me, since my mother solved so many problems with it. The child of a **suicide** will naturally think of death, the big one, as a logical solution to any problem, even one in simple algebra.

(*DD* 12) Celia would commit **suicide** by eating Drano, a drain-clearing compound of lye and zinc chips, in 1970, twelve years ago now. She killed herself in the most horrible way I can think of—a few months before the dedication of the Mildred Barry Memorial Center for the Arts.

(*DD* 24) I would be glad to attempt a detailed analysis of Celia Hoover's character, if I thought her character had much of anything to do with her **suicide** by Drano. As a pharmacist, though, I see no reason not to give full credit to amphetamine.

(*DD* 24) The word was all over town of how in need of support he (*Dwayne Hoover*) was, of how vocally ashamed he was to have been such a bad husband that his wife had committed **suicide**. He had been quoted to me as having made a public announcement in the Tally-ho Room of the new Holiday Inn, the day after Celia killed herself: "I take half the blame, but the other half goes to that son-of-bitching Doctor Jerry Mitchell. Watch out for the pills your doctor tells your wife to take. That's all I've got to say."

(*DD* 26) Some people, of course, find inhabiting an epilogue so uncongenial that they commit **suicide**. Ernest Hemingway comes to mind. Celia Hoover, née Hildreth, comes to mind.

(*Gal* 1:25) The best-run nations commonly had such symbiotic pairings at the top. And when I think about the **suicidal** mistakes nations used to make in olden times, I see that those polities were trying to get along with just an Adolf von Kleist at the top, without an Hernando Cruz.

(*Blue* 6) And if an artist wants to really jack up the prices of his creations, may I suggest this: **suicide**.

(*Blue* 8) "If I had my way," he said, "American geography books would call those European countries by their right names: 'The Syphilis Empire,' 'The Republic of **Suicide**,' 'Dementia Praecox,' which of course borders on beautiful 'Paranoia.'"

(*Blue* 36) The melancholy roll-call of real-life **suicides** among the Abstract Expressionists again: Gorky by hanging in 1948, Pollock and then almost

immediately Kitchen, by drunken driving and then pistol in 1956—and then Rothko with all possible messiness by knife in 1970.

(*HP* 1) During World War II, he (*Hartke's father*) was too valuable as a civilian deep-thinker about chemicals to be put in a soldier suit and turned into a **suicidal**, homicidal imbecile in 13 weeks.

(*HP* 6) Three years after that, Sam Wakefield would commit **suicide**. So there is another loser for you, even though he had been a Major General and then a College President. I think exhaustion got him. I say that not only because he seemed very tired all the time to me, but because his **suicide** note wasn't even original and didn't seem to have that much to do with him personally. It was word for word the same **suicide** note left way back in 1932, when I was a negative 8 years old, by another loser, George Eastman, inventor of the Kodak camera and founder of Eastman Kodak, now defunct, only 75 kilometers north of here.

Both notes said this and nothing more: "My work is done." In Sam Wakefield's case, that completed work, if he didn't want to count the Vietnam War, consisted of 3 new buildings, which probably would have been built anyway, no matter who was Tarkington's President.

(*HP* 12) Afterward, he (*Sam Wakefield*) had hired both of us for Tarkington, and then committed **suicide** for reasons unclear even to himself, judging from the plagiarized note he left on his bedside table.

(*HP* 40) Hiroshi Matsumoto's **suicide** has hit me so hard, I think, because he was innocent of even the littlest misdemeanors.

(*FWD* II) "We were able to keep her insanity a secret, since it became really elaborate only at home and between midnight and dawn. We were able to keep her **suicide** a secret thanks to a compassionate and possibly politically ambitious coroner." *Vonnegut refers to his mother's suicide.*

(*FWD* V) "We were born in the Middle West, we set out to be reporters, our fathers were gun nuts, we felt profoundly indebted to Mark Twain, and we were the children of **suicides**." *Vonnegut draws a parallel between Hemingway and himself.*

(*FWD* V) "I am reminded of the **suicide** of another American genius, George Eastman, inventor of the

Kodak camera and roll film, and founder of the Eastman Kodak Company. He shot himself in 1932. Eastman, who was not ill and was not suffering from grief, said in his **suicide** note what Ernest Hemingway must have felt when he was close to the end: 'My work is done.'"

(FWD XV) And here is a fascinating statistic: They committed **suicide** less often than their masters did. *Vonnegut refers to the low incidence of suicide among American slaves as opposed to their owners.*

(FWD XVI) My own theory is that the little girl, by allowing herself to be adopted by a dark-skinned Muslim absolutely nobody watching American television could love, in effect committed **suicide**. *Vonnegut sarcastically remarks on America's shallow perceptions of the air raid targeting Libya's Muammar Qaddafi, which failed to hit their target but succeeded in killing his adopted infant daughter.*

(FWD I) The great fiction writer Ray Bradbury (who can't drive an automobile) made up a story called "The Kilimanjaro Device," which was about a person who could somehow undo ignominious **suicides** (or maybe ignominious anythings). . . .

It is possible in Ray Bradbury country that my own **suicide** was as successful as Hemingway's, that I am dead, that all I am seeing now is what might have been, if only I hadn't ended it all. This could be a lesson.

(FWD XX) Yes, and I, having just finished reading William Styron's short and elliptical account of his recent attack of melancholia, *Darkness Visible* (a **suicide** attempt may or may not have been involved), am now prepared to say that **suicidal** persons can be divided into two sorts. Styron's sort blames the wiring and chemistry of his brain, which could easily fit into a salad bowl. My sort blames the Universe. (Why mess around?) I don't offer this insight as yet another joke ("Why is cream more expensive than milk?"). It is my serious belief that those of us who become humorists (**suicidal** or not) feel free (as most people do not) to speak of life itself as a dirty joke, even though life is all there is or ever can be.

(TQ 1) My father, Kurt Senior, an Indianapolis architect who had cancer, and whose wife had committed **suicide** some fifteen years earlier, was arrested for running a red light in his hometown. It turned out that he hadn't had a driver's license for twenty years!

You know what he told the arresting officer? "So shoot me," he said.

(TQ 3) I asked him (*Kilgore Trout*) at the clambake in 2001, at the writers' retreat Xanadu, what he'd done during the war, which he called "civilization's second unsuccessful attempt to commit **suicide**." He said without a scintilla of regret, "I made sandwiches of German soldiers between an erupting Earth and an exploding sky, and in a blizzard of razor blades."

(TQ 6) Now I find myself maundering about parts of plays hardly anybody knows or cares about anymore, such as the graveyard scene in *Our Town*, or the poker game in Tennessee Williams's *A Streetcar Named Desire*, or what Willy Loman's wife said after that tragically ordinary, clumsily gallant American committed **suicide** in Arthur Miller's *Death of a Salesman*.

(TQ 9) As though Zoltan weren't sufficiently destabilized emotionally by legs and a ding-dong that didn't work anymore, his older brother Frank, an architect, had committed **suicide** after a nearly identical blow to his self-respect only a month earlier. Yes, and Frank Pepper would eventually be popped out of his grave by the timequake, so he could blow his brains out while his wife and three kids watched a second time. *Frank kills himself when he becomes familiar with and despondent by the computer program Palladio, an architecture program that can design anything with any famous styles as their basis.*

(TQ 14) He went on, there in the suite named in honor of the **suicide** Ernest Hemingway. . . . *Kilgore Trout holds court at the writers' retreat inside his suite. Here he is telling the story that ends up with "Ting-a-ling" as the punchline.*

(TQ 15) When Trout returned to the shelter, though, the armed guard Dudley Prince unbolted the steel front door and, motivated, by boredom and curiosity, retrieved the manuscript. He wanted to know what it was a bag lady, with every reason to commit **suicide**, one would think, had deepsixed so ecstatically.

(TQ 20) Several of the war criminals wear an Iron Cross, awarded only to Germans who have demonstrated battlefield fearlessness so excessive as to be classifiable as psychopathic. Hitler wears one. He won it as a corporal in Western Civilization's first unsuccessful attempt to commit **suicide**.

(*TQ* 26) This hemisphere is no bed of roses. My mother committed **suicide** in this one, and then my brother-in-law went off an open drawbridge in a railroad train.

(*TQ* 41) I don't think I missed the boat when I failed to write a novel about Albert Lieber, and how he was largely responsible for my mother's **suicide** on Mother's Day Eve, 1944. German-Americans in Indianapolis lack universality. They have never been sympathetically, or even villainously, stereotyped in movies or books or plays. I would have had to explain them from scratch.

Lotsa luck!

(*TQ* 42) As I have written elsewhere, this man is a saint. I define a saint as a person who behaves decently in an indecent society.

I asked him why half his patients at Bellevue didn't commit **suicide**. He said the same question had occurred to him. He sometimes asked them, as though it were an unremarkable part of a diagnostic routine, if they had **thoughts of self-destruction**. He said that they were almost without exception surprised and insulted by the question. An idea that sick had never entered their heads!

(*TQ* 62) My wife Jill was among the living, thank goodness, and was there in the flesh, as was Knox Burger, a Cornell classmate of mine. After Western Civilization's second unsuccessful **suicide** attempt, Knox became a fiction editor at *Collier's*, which published five short stories every week. Knox got me a good literary agent, Colonel Kenneth Littauer, the first pilot to strafe a trench during World War One.

Trout opined, in *My Ten Years on Automatic Pilot*, incidentally, that we had better start numbering timequakes the same way we numbered World Wars and Super Bowls.

(*BAG* Thanasphere) Science had given humanity forces enough to destroy the earth, and politics had given humanity a fair assurance that the forces would be used. There could be no cause for awe to top that one. But proof of a spirit world might at least equal it. Maybe that was the shock the world

needed, maybe word from the spirits could change the **suicidal** course of history.

(*BAG* Thanasphere) Groszinger shook his head. "Everybody's listening to that frequency now. We'd all be in a nice mess if you stopped jamming." He didn't want to hear more. He was baffled, miserable. Would Death unmasked drive men to **suicide**, or bring new hope? he was asking himself. Would the living desert their leaders and turn to the dead for guidance? To Caesar . . . Charlemagne . . . Peter the Great . . . Napoleon . . . Bismarck . . . Lincoln . . . Roosevelt? To Jesus Christ? Were the dead wiser than—

(*BAG* Souvenir) But what chance did the old man, who spoke no English, have to pass himself off to his captors as an American? None. It was the blond who was going to do that. And they were both about to be captured. All the old man could do was commit **suicide**.

(*BAG* 2BR02B) "I wish people wouldn't call it the Catbox, and things like that," she said. "It gives people the wrong impression."

"You're absolutely right," said Dr. Hitz. "Forgive me." He corrected himself, gave the municipal gas chambers their official title, a title no one ever used in conversation. "I should have said '**Ethical Suicide Studios**,'" he said.

(*BAG* Coda to My Career) I still write for periodicals from time to time, but never fiction, and only when somebody asks me to. I am not the dynamic self-starter I used to be. An excellent alternative weekly in Indianapolis, NUVO, asked me only a month ago to write an essay for no pay on the subject of what it is like to be a native Middle Westerner. I have replied as follows:

"Breathes there the man, with soul so dead, who never to himself has said, this is my own, my native land!"

This famous celebration of no-brainer patriotism by the Scotsman Sir Walter Scott (1771–1832), when stripped of jingoistic romance, amounts only to this: Human beings come into this world, for their own good, as instinctively territorial as timber wolves or honeybees. Not long ago, human beings who strayed too far from their birthplace and relatives, like all other animals, would be committing **suicide**.

(*GBK* John Brown) Today's controlled near-death

experience was a real honey! I interviewed John Brown—whose body lies a-moulderin' in the grave, but whose truth goes marchin' on. One hundred forty years ago, come October 2, he was hanged for treason against the United States of America. At the head of a force of only eighteen other anti-slavery fanatics, he captured the virtually unguarded Federal Armory at Harper's Ferry, Virginia. His plan? To pass out weapons to slaves, so they could overthrow their masters. **Suicide**.

(*GBK* Mary Wollstonecraft Shelley) Hint number three: This person was married to a celebrity, as famous for the romantic disorder of his life as for his poetry. He inspired the **suicide** of his first wife, for example. As Romantically as you please, he drowned when he was only thirty.

(*MWC* 2) The French-Algerian writer Albert Camus, who won a Nobel Prize for Literature in 1957, wrote, "There is but one truly serious philosophical problem, and that is **suicide**."

(*MWC* 3) Madame Blavatsky, who knew more about the spirit world than anybody else, said you are a fool to take any apparition seriously, because they are often malicious and they are frequently the souls of people who were murdered, were **suicides**, or were terribly cheated in life in one way or another, and they are out for revenge.

(*MWC* 7) The wonderful writer Albert Murray, who is a jazz historian and a friend of mine among other things, told me that during the era of slavery in this country—an atrocity from which we can never fully recover—the **suicide** rate per capita among slave owners was much higher than the **suicide** rate among slaves.

Murray says he thinks this was because slaves had a way of dealing with depression, which their white owners did not: They could shoo away **Old Man Suicide** by playing and singing the Blues. He says something else which also sounds right to me. He says the blues can't drive depression clear out of a house, but can drive it into the corners of any room where it's being played. So please remember that.

(*MWC* 12) There are old poops who will say that you do not become a grown-up until you have somehow survived, as they have, some famous calamity—the Great Depression, the Second World War,

Vietnam, whatever. Storytellers are responsible for this destructive, not to say **suicidal**, myth. Again and again in stories, after some terrible mess, the character is able to say at last, "Today I am a woman. Today I am a man. The end."

When I got home from the Second World War, my Uncle Dan clapped me on the back, and he said, "You're a man now." So I killed him. Not really, but I certainly felt like doing it

See also: *PP* VI; IX; XXIII; *ST* 7; *MN* 11; 32; *CC* 106; 115; *GBR* 5; 7; 8; 14; *SL5* 5; *MH* Unready to Wear; *WJ* I:2; III; *BC* 2; 4; 10; 14; *WFG* There's a Maniac Loose Out There; *WFG* Fortitude; *WFG* Why They Read Hesse; *WFG* Address to Graduating Class at Bennington College, 1970; *WFG* In a Manner That Must Shame God Himself; *Slap* 5; 10; 17; 29; *JB* 9; 20; 23; *PS* Playmates; *PS* Jekyll and Hyde Updated; *PS* In the Capital of the World; *DD* 5; 14; 20; 25; *Gal* 1:6; 1:16; 1:25; 1:38; *Blue* 1; 3; 18; 22; *HP* 9; 10; 11; 14; 15; 16; 22; 29; 38; 40; *TQ* 42; *BAG* A Present for Big Saint Nick; *GBK* Introduction; *MWC* 12.

Suk, Dr. Kim Bum. *Circe Berman gives Rabo Karabekian a copy of Dr. Suk's* Private Art Treasures of Tuscany *and learns the history of Marilee Kemp's Italian palazzo. The text started out as Dr. Suk's doctoral thesis at MIT. Suk explains the reason for the blank rectangular sections in the rotunda that once held frescoes of barely dressed pagan gods and goddesses. The Dominican monk Girolamo Savonarola had ordered the paintings sanded from its surface.*

Karabekian goes on to include that **Kim Bum Suk**, *incidentally, was thrown out of his native South Korea for forming a union of university students which demanded improvements in the curricula (*Blue* 27).*

Sultan of Brunei. *In* Hocus Pocus, *the Sultan purchases Cincinnati's remaining newspaper and leading television station. He later purchases the Bank of Rochester, prompting Eugene Debs Hartke's mother-in-law to withdraw her life savings ($45,000) and bury it in their backyard in Scipio.*

sumklish (*see also* **prakhouls**). *The Bratpuhrian alcoholic drink of choice for the Shah of Bratpuhr.*

During the Shah's tour of the United States, which is woven throughout the plot of Player Piano, his aide, Khashdrahr Miasma, always has a flask at the ready for the seemingly alcoholic monarch.

Sun Moon Star (illustrations by Ivan Chermayeff, text by Kurt Vonnegut, Harper & Row, 1980). A children's book proposed by Frank Platt, a New York publishing consultant, to Vonnegut and Chermayeff. His idea was to present Vonnegut with a series of unexplained graphics designed by the award-winning commercial artist and branding mogul Ivan Chermayeff, and for Vonnegut to supply the story. They worked under the musical metaphor that Chermayeff would present the tune and Vonnegut would compose the lyrics.

The resulting story is a reinterpretation of Christ's birth as told from the point of view of the infant. In this case, however, the Creator of the Universe has Itself born to Mary in the manger with a midwife and Joseph in attendance. Vonnegut eliminates the confusion of the traditional trinity by having the Creator reborn but with only the slight visual perceptions of a newborn. Mary, the midwife, and Joseph are interpreted through the infant's view as the Sun, Moon, and Star of its limited existence.

The premise has the Creator of the Universe return to be born as a male infant, to see—and to do so imperfectly, through two human eyes, each a rubber little camera. The Creator purposely limits His knowledge and input to only what is put before his eyes. Nothing else exists. The Creator learns with His first blink that humans never really have all-knowing darkness, that even with its eyes closed, imaginary suns could still be seen. This is another way of saying that man's mind is always looking to fill its voids with images, symbols, myths.

A Roman Matron wants to see the spectacle of the baby's birth and dangles a crystal necklace before the baby who sees nothing but the wonder of the prismatic shapes and colors defining and passing through the gems.

When the newborn begins to suckle from Mary, she becomes the world to the Creator. Snuggled and warm, the baby sleeps and four dreams ensue: the first three of stars and streams of light, the fourth simply as the color green. Upon waking, the infant envisions the movement of light over Its mother revealing a shining sun, all the while the light falls away from Joseph, making him seem as a fading moon.

Vonnegut intertwines the traditional story of Moses with his new interpretation by having King Herod declare that all firstborn males are to be executed. The Three Wise Men are sent as secret assassins to seek out the new leader of the Jews, but they are awed by the baby, realizing this is more than the new king of the Jews and in fact the Creator of all. Kneeling before the infant in the courtyard by the manger, they pledge to keep the secret without harming the child and leave their presents.

As babies are sometimes inclined to cross their eyes, so too does the Creator with often jumbled views of the Sun, Moon, and Star of its brief life. However, dreams of Its mother eventually uncross the child's eyes forever. The remaining visions are clear and unambiguous. With Its vision corrected to normal sight, the Creator sees all there is on that ordinary day: the sun in Its sky, an ox yoked to a plow, an ass prepared for carrying firewood, and It hears the crow of a rooster, out of sync with the lateness of the sun's rising. And life went on. Vonnegut's final word is Amen.

There is no precursor of miracles to come, myths to divide and define one belief or one person from another. In short, this is a creation tale that ends with the ordinariness of being on this earth. All that there is to be perceived is before the eyes of the beholder.

Sunoco, Dr. Fleon. The central character of Kilgore Trout's short story "Dog's Breakfast" (Sunoco's science journal description for the 3.5-pound size of the human brain). Though Sunoco works at the National Institutes of Health, he is independently wealthy and uses his personal resources to have grave robbers procure the brains of deceased Mensa members as well as the ordinary Lumpenproletariat. (TQ 27) **Dr. Sunoco** believed really smart people had little radio receivers in their heads, and were getting their bright ideas from somewhere else.

As Trout begins recounting the story to Vonnegut in his hotel room at Xanadu, he seems to be channeling some of his own paranoid beliefs about humanity. (TQ 27) "The smarties *had to be getting outside help,"* Trout said to me at Xanadu. While impersonating the mad **Sunoco**, Trout himself seemed convinced that there was a great big computer somewhere, which, by means of radio, had told Pythagoras about right triangles, and Newton about gravity, and Darwin about evolution, and Pasteur about germs, and Einstein about relativity, and on and on.

"That computer, wherever it is, whatever it is, while pretending to help us, may actually be trying to *kill* us dummies with too much to think about," said Kilgore Trout.

Sunoco spends his evenings dissecting the brains, looking for little radios. He doesn't think Mensa members had them inserted surgically. He thinks they were born with them, so the receivers have to be made of meat. **Sunoco** has written in his secret journal: "There is no way an unassisted human brain, which is nothing more than a dog's breakfast, three and a half pounds of blood-soaked sponge, could have written 'Stardust,' let alone Beethoven's Ninth Symphony." The bumps have to have been the reason the smarties were so good at taking IQ tests. An extra piece of tissue that little, and as nothing but tissue, couldn't possibly have been much more help than a pimple. It has to be a radio! And radios like that have to be feeding correct answers to questions, no matter how recondite, to Mensas and Phi Beta Kappas, and to quiz show contestants.

This is a Nobel Prize–type discovery! So, even before he has published, **Fleon Sunoco** goes out and buys himself a suit of tails for Stockholm (*TQ* 27).

Surrasi. *An extinct infidel tribe in Bratpuhr that made mud and straw holy figures considered by some to be false gods. In* Player Piano, *the Shah of Bratpuhr compares Dr. Halyard's faith and wonder in EPICAC with that of the Surrasi.*

Susann, Jacqueline. *In* Slaughterhouse-Five, *the Tralfamadorians had one English-language book on the ship transporting Billy Pilgrim to their home planet. Billy read Jacqueline Susann's* Valley of the Dolls *while en route, and the Tralfamadorians plan on putting it in one of their museums.*

Susanna (*see also* **Norman Fuller**). *The title character of the short story "Miss Temptation," in* Welcome to the Monkey House.

Sutton, Mrs. *Sarah Wyatt's grandmother in* Jailbird. *Though she was not from the side of the family that lost its wealth in the radium dial liability suit, she lost most of her wealth in the 1929 stock market crash. Her husband jumped out the window of his Wall Street office. Mrs. Sutton lives in a cramped two-bedroom apartment just large enough to house the few aged servants she insists on maintaining despite her comparative poverty from former days. Mrs. Sutton dies two weeks after the death of Tillie, her longest living and devoted servant.*

In her younger days, Mrs. Sutton showed horses in competition. When Walter Starbuck admires the many ribbons she won, she wittily points out it was the horses who won the ribbons. By her own admission, she had no way to improve her standard of living since she was old and brought up to rely on the efforts of men.

Sarah was staying with her grandmother when Walter Starbuck came to pick her up for a date. They provide a comforting deception to Mrs. Sutton, leading her to believe Starbuck's father is an art curator employed by industry mogul Mr. McCone.

Swain, Caleb Mellon and Letitia Vanderbilt. *The parents of the dizygotic twins Wilbur and Eliza. Wilbur goes on to relate that* Our parents were two silly and pretty and very young people named **Caleb Mellon Swain** and **Letitia Vanderbilt Swain**, née Rockefeller. They were fabulously well-to-do, and descended from Americans who had all but wrecked the planet with a form of Idiot's Delight—obsessively turning money into power, and then power back into money again, and then money back into power again (*Slap* 2). *Because of the twins' deformities at birth, the Swains are advised to avoid raising the children themselves, so they leave the children with caretakers at their Vermont mansion, visiting infrequently at best.*

Swain, Carter Paley. *The son of Wilbur Swain and his third cousin Rose Aldrich Ford. In describing his son, Wilbur reveals more of himself than he does* *about his child.* (*Slap* 28) I have never been good at loving. We had a child, **Carter Paley Swain**, whom I also failed to love. **Carter** was normal, and completely uninteresting to me. He was somehow like a summer squash on the vine—featureless and watery, and merely growing larger all the time.

After our divorce, he and his mother bought a condominium in the same building with Eliza, down in Machu Picchu, Peru. I never heard from them again even when I became President of the United States.

Swain, Elihu Roosevelt. *The founder of the Swain family fortune whose name at birth is Elihu Witherspoon Swain. Wilbur and Eliza believe he changed his middle name when he went to M.I.T. so that he would* seem *more aristocratic when he enrolled* (*Slap* 3). *This is what gave the twins their idea for assigning new middle names to everyone in order to create artificially extended families.*

He graduates from M.I.T. at the age of eighteen and at twenty-two starts the Department of Civil Engineering at Cornell University. He founds the Swain Bridge Company, which goes on to construct half the railroad bridges in the entire planet (*Slap* 2). *He builds the Swain family mansion on their ancestral land in Vermont and tells no one about all the hidden passageways, though Wilbur and Eliza enjoy them immensely upon discovery.* (*Slap* 3) This was the secret: There was a mansion concealed within the mansion. It could be entered through trap doors and sliding panels. It consisted of secret staircases and listening posts with peepholes, and secret passageways. There were tunnels, too.

It was actually possible for Eliza and me, for example, to vanish into a huge grandfather clock in the ballroom at the top of the northernmost tower, and to emerge almost a kilometer away—through a trap door in the floor of the mausoleum of **Professor Elihu Roosevelt Swain**.

In the midst of one of the twins' creative frenzies, they wrote theoretical papers about squaring circles, a utopian scheme for artificially extended families, a critique of Darwin's Theory of Evolution, and an essay on the nature of gravity (which they found to be unstable) and hid them in Professor Swain's empty funeral urn in his mausoleum. They often played in the mausoleum. The gravity paper becomes significant when one of Eliza's Chinese associates asks Wilbur to retrieve the paper. The ensuing Chinese experiments confirm the twins' theories that gravity is indeed unstable. (*Slap* 4) Yes, and **Professor Swain** died of his fatness in the mansion, at a dinner he gave in honor of Samuel Langhorne Clemens and Thomas Alva Edison.

Swain, Eliza Mellon (*see* **Wilbur Swain**).

Swain, Sophie Rothschild. *In* Slapstick, *when Wilbur Swain is seventy years old and President of the United States, he marries twenty-three-year-old Sophie Rothschild, a descendant of the famous international banking family. Sophie becomes enraged when Wilbur's scheme for extended families places her in the Peanut clan. She divorces Wilbur and takes refuge in Machu Picchu, Peru, where many of her relatives had already moved.*

Swain, Wilbur Rockefeller and Eliza Mellon. *The intellectually brilliant, telepathically gifted, physically grotesque Swain twins. Wilbur and Eliza Swain were christened in a hospital rather than in* a church, and we were not surrounded by relatives and our parents' friends. The thing was: **Eliza** and I were so ugly that our parents were ashamed.

We were monsters, and we were not expected to live very long. We had six fingers on each little hand, and six toes on each little footsie. We had supernumerary nipples as well—two of them apiece.

We were not mongolian idiots, although we had the coarse black hair typical of mongoloids. We were something new. We were *neanderthaloids.*

We had the features of adult, fossil human beings even in infancy—massive brow-ridges, sloping foreheads, and steamshovel jaws (*Slap* 2).

Because of their appearance, they are sent to the family's Vermont estate to be raised by servants. Their parents visit only on the twins' birthday. Wilbur and Eliza learn from an early age that since all the servants treated them so well but imagined them to be idiots, that it was a good thing to be an idiot. So they hid their intelligence, especially the potency of their intellect when they literally touched their heads together and communicated telepathically. Wilbur writes about the depth of thought they put into their decision to hide their intelligence. (Slap 4) Consider:

We were at the center of the lives of those who cared for us. They could be heroically Christian in their own eyes only if **Eliza** and I remained helpless and vile. If we became openly wise and self-reliant, they would become our drab and inferior assistants. If we became capable of going out into the world, they might lose their apartments, their color televisions, their illusions of being sorts of doctors and nurses, and their high-paying jobs.

So, from the very first, and without quite knowing what they were doing, I am sure, they begged us a thousand times a day to go on being helpless and vile.

There was only one small advancement they wished us to make up the ladder of human achievements. They hoped with all their hearts that we would become toilet-trained.

Again: We were glad to comply.

The unique nature of their intelligence is later recorded by Wilbur. (Slap 6) **Eliza** and I used bodily contact only in order to increase the intimacy of our brains.

Thus did we give birth to a single genius, which died as quickly as we were parted, which was reborn the moment we got together again.

We became almost cripplingly specialized as halves of that genius, which was the most important individual in our lives, but which we never named.

When we learned to read and write, for example, it was I who actually did the reading and writing. **Eliza** remained illiterate until the day she died.

But it was **Eliza** who did the great intuitive leaping for us both. It was **Eliza** who guessed that it would be in our best interests to remain speechless, but to become toilet-trained. It was **Eliza** who guessed what books were, and what the little marks on the pages might mean.

It was **Eliza** who sensed that there was something cockeyed about the dimensions of some of the mansion's rooms and corridors. And it was I who did the methodical work of taking actual measurements, and then probing the paneling and parquetry with screwdrivers and kitchen knives, seeking doors to an alternate universe, which we found.

Hi ho.

Yes, I did all the reading. And it seems to me now that there is not a single book published in an Indo-European language before the First World War that I have not read aloud.

But it was **Eliza** who did the memorizing, and who told me what we had to learn next. And it was **Eliza** who could put seemingly unrelated ideas together in order to get a new one. It was **Eliza** who *juxtaposed.*

When the twins are kept from exercising telepathy, they refer to themselves as the very average "Betty and Bobby Brown." Wilbur goes on to Harvard Medical School and becomes a pediatrician (as does Mark Vonnegut). When reuniting later in life, the twins write a childrearing manual they call The Cry of the Nocturnal Goatsucker, *by Betty and Bobby Brown. It eventually becomes an all-time best seller next to the Bible and* The Joy of Cooking. *He and Eliza also wrote papers criticizing Darwin's theory of evolution, the United States Constitution, gravity (musing on the likelihood that gravity could become as changeable as the weather), and extended families. They got the idea of dispensing new middle names from the example set by the founder of the family fortune, Professor Elihu Roosevelt Swain, whose baptismal certificate reads Elihu Witherspoon Swain. (Slap* 3) He had given himself that middle name in order to seem more aristocratic when he enrolled as a student at M.I.T. *(Slap* 32) "An ideal extended family," **Eliza** and I had written so long ago, "should give proportional representation to all sorts of Americans, according to their numbers. The creation of ten thousand such families, say, would provide America with ten thousand parliaments, so to speak, which would discuss sincerely and expertly what only a few hypocrites now discuss with passion, which is the welfare of all mankind." *Wilbur puts into effect their scheme for extended families upon becoming president of the United States. He lives to be just over one hundred years old and is the nation's last president.*

Wilbur's first wife is Rose Aldrich Ford, a third cousin. Together they have a son, Carter Paley Swain. Wilbur loves neither, and after their divorce, Rose and Carter go to live in Machu Picchu, Peru. His second marriage, to Sophie Rothschild, is childless.

Swift, Dr. Tom. *The number one assistant to Dr. Norbert Frankenstein in the play* Fortitude. *He has degrees in engineering and medicine, as does his mentor. When asked if he's tired after a full day managing the medical and psychological status of Sylvia Lovejoy, their bodiless patient, he replies,* It's a good kind of tiredness—as though I'd flown a big jet from New York to Honolulu, or something like that. (*Taking hold of a lever.*) And now we'll bring Mrs. Lovejoy in for a happy landing. (*He pulls the lever gradually and the machinery slows down.*) (WFG Fortitude)

Szombathy, Lazlo and Miklos. *In* Mother Night, *Lazlo is a respected veterinarian in Hungary who* becomes a freedom fighter and eventually kills his brother Miklos, the Second Minister of Education in Hungary.

Despite his successful veterinary practice in Hungary, Lazlo is not permitted to practice in America. He becomes a New York City garbageman and hangs himself with a noose he finds in the garbage outside Howard Campbell's apartment house. The noose is brought by an unnamed man for Campbell to hang himself once his whereabouts are publicized. Resi Noth throws the noose in the trash and Lazlo hangs himself the next day. His suicide note indicates his only regret was that he couldn't convince American physicians that he knew how to cure cancer.

Taft, Edith. *Rabo Karabekian's second wife, formerly married to the Cincinnati sportsman and investment banker Richard Fairbanks, Jr. Rabo and Edith are married for twenty years, living in the Long Island Victorian estate where she had lived with her first husband. They meet after Rabo's first wife passes away and he persuades the Fairbankses to let him rent their potato barn as his apartment and art studio. Edith has no children by either of her husbands.*

Edith loves Rabo so well and so desires to make him feel at home that she has the estate renovated and outfitted with track lighting to accommodate his large collection of Abstract Expressionist paintings. (*Blue* 14) And then she said, "Call Home Sweet Home Moving and Storage," in whose warehouse I had stored my collection for years and years. "Let them tell your glorious paintings as they bring them out into the daylight, 'You are going *home!*'"

Edith loves uncritically, as Rabo fondly remembers. (*Blue* 1) Dear **Edith**, like all great Earth Mothers, was a multitude. Even when there were only the two of us and the servants here, she filled this Victorian ark with love and merriment and hands-on domesticity. As privileged as she had been all her life, she cooked with the cook, gardened with the gardener, did all our food shopping, fed the pets and birds, and made personal friends of wild rabbits and squirrels and raccoons. (*Blue* 32) She was a magical tamer of almost any sort of animal, an overwhelmingly loving and uncritical nurturer of anything and everything that looked half alive. That's what she would do to me when I was living as a hermit in the barn and she needed a new husband: she tamed me with nature poems and good things to eat which she left outside my sliding doors. I'm sure she tamed her first husband, too, and thought of him lovingly and patronizingly as some kind of dumb animal.

Rabo feels as though he died with the suicide of his friend Terry Kitchen, but it is Edith who brings him back to life. Edith dies the same week as another of Rabo's great loves, Marilee Kemp, the Contessa Portomaggiore.

Takaru. *In* Player Piano, *the Shah of Bratpuhr consistently calls Americans "Takaru," meaning "slave" in his native language.*

Tamanrasset. *While traveling by train through upstate New York, Paul Proteus overhears soldiers (those who chose not to join the Reconstruction and Reclamation Corps) playing cards and bemoaning the fate of one of their buddies, Elmo C. Hacketts.* (PP XXVI) "Where's Hacketts going? You know?"

". . . Yeah, Hacketts gets his overseas duty all right. Shipping out for **Tamanrasset** tomorrow morning."

"**Tamanrasset**?"

"The Sahara Desert, you dumb bastard. Don't you know any geography?" He grinned wolfishly. "How about a little blackjack for laughs?"

Paul sighed for Hacketts, born into a spiritual desert, now being shipped to where the earth was sterile, too.

Tappin, Al. *The staff photographer who misses the opportunity to photograph the deer that has wandered onto the grounds of the Works.* (MH Deer in the Works) "Murder! The story will go all over the country, Potter. Talk about human interest. Front page! Of all the times for **Al Tappin** to be out at the Ashtabula Works, taking pictures of a new viscometer they cooked up out there!"

Tarkington, Aaron. (HP 2) The founder of the Mohiga Wagon Company was **Aaron Tarkington**, a brilliant inventor and manufacturer who nevertheless could not read or write. He now would be identified as a blameless inheritor of the genetic defect known as dyslexia. He said of himself that he was like the Emperor Charlemagne, "too busy to learn to read and write." He was not too busy, however, to have his wife read to him for 2 hours every evening. He had an excellent memory, for he delivered weekly lectures to the workmen at the factory that were laced with lengthy quotations from Shakespeare and Homer and the Bible, and on and on.

The gene for dyslexia was inherited by all his children, and though his son Elias never marries or fathers children, the marriage of his three daughters to prominent families in Cleveland, New York, and Wilmington, Delaware, made "the threat of dyslexia pandemic in an emerging ruling class of bankers and industrialists, largely displaced in time by Germans, Koreans, Italians, English, and, of course, Japanese" (*HP* 2).

Tarkington, Elias. *Aaron Tarkington's only son and author of* "a technical account of the construction of the Onondaga Canal, which connected the northern end of Lake Mohiga to the Erie Canal just south of Rochester" (*HP* 2). *Elias never marries or sires any children.*

After inheriting his father's properties, Elias adds a brewery and a steam-driven carpet factory before being shot at Gettysburg when mistaken for Abraham Lincoln. (*HP* 2) **Elias Tarkington** never married. He was severely wounded at the age of 54 while a civilian observer at the Battle of Gettysburg, top hat and all. He was there to see the debuts of 2 of his inventions, a mobile field kitchen and a pneumatic recoil mechanism for heavy artillery. The field kitchen, incidentally, with slight modifications, would later be adopted by the Barnum & Bailey Circus, and then by the German Army during World War I.

He is better remembered as the Tarkington who tried to invent a perpetual motion machine and who founded the Mohiga Valley Free Institute, the forerunner of Tarkington College. Eugene Debs Hartke records that Elias was poorly educated, "more a mechanic than a scientist, and so spent his last three years trying to invent what anyone familiar with Newton's Laws would have known was an impossibility, a perpetual-motion machine. He had no fewer than 27 contraptions built, which he foolishly expected to go on running, after he had given them an initial spin or whack, until Judgment Day.

"I found 19 of those stubborn, mocking machines in the attic of what used to be their inventor's mansion, which in my time was the home of the College President, about a year after I came to

work at Tarkington. I brought them back downstairs and into the 20th Century. Some of my students and I cleaned them up and restored any parts that had deteriorated during the intervening 100 years. At the least they were exquisite jewelry, with garnets and amethysts for bearings, with arms and legs of exotic woods, with tumbling balls of ivory, with chutes and counterweights of silver. It was as though dying **Elias** hoped to overwhelm science with the magic of precious materials" (*HP* 3).

(*HP* 3) I have discovered from reading old newspapers and letters and diaries from back then that the men who built the machines for **Elias Tarkington** knew from the first that they would never work, whatever the reason. Yet what love they lavished on the materials that comprised them! How is this for a definition of high art: "Making the most of the raw materials of futility"?

(*HP* 3) Still another perpetual-motion machine envisioned by **Elias Tarkington** was what his Last Will and Testament called "The Mohiga Valley Free Institute." Upon his death, this new school would take possession of his 3,000-hectare estate above Scipio, plus half the shares in the wagon company, the carpet company, and the brewery. The other half was already owned by his sisters far away. On his deathbed he predicted that Scipio would 1 day be a great metropolis and that its wealth would transform his little college into a university to rival Harvard and Oxford and Heidelberg.

Tarkington, Felicia. *The youngest daughter of Aaron Tarkington and author of* "a novel called *Carpathia,* about a headstrong, high-born young woman in the Mohiga Valley who fell in love with a half-Indian lock-tender on that same canal" (*Onondaga*) (*HP* 2). *She was a carrier of the gene for dyslexia.*

Tarkington College. *Originally established in 1869 by Elias Tarkington's last will and testament as the Mohiga Valley Free Institute, in 1875 the name is changed to Tarkington College to avoid sounding like a home for the impoverished, and in 1999 the name again changes to the Tarkington State Reformatory to reflect its new status as part of the New York State correctional system.*

Eugene Debs Hartke characterizes the genesis of

Tarkington College as another "perpetual-motion machine" envisioned by Elias Tarkington. (HP 3) It was to offer a free college education to persons of either sex, and of any age or race or religion, living within 40 miles of Scipio. Those from farther away would pay a modest fee. In the beginning, it would have only 1 full-time employee, the President. The teachers would be recruited right here in Scipio. They would take a few hours off from work each week, to teach what they knew. The chief engineer at the wagon company, for example, whose name was Andre Lutz, was a native of Liege, Belgium, and had served as an apprentice to a bell founder there. He would teach Chemistry. His French wife would teach French and Watercolor Painting. The brewmaster at the brewery, Hermann Shultz, a native of Leipzig, would teach Botany and German and the flute. The Episcopalian priest, Dr. Alan Clewes, a graduate of Harvard, would teach Latin, Greek, Hebrew, and the Bible. The dying man's physician, Dalton Polk, would teach Biology and Shakespeare, and so on.

And it came to pass.

In 1869 the new college enrolled its first class, 9 students in all, and all from right here in Scipio. Four were of ordinary college age. One was a Union veteran who had lost his legs at Shiloh. One was a former black slave 40 years old. One was a spinster 82 years old.

The college becomes a haven for dyslexics and those with various other learning disabilities preventing their attendance at any other institution of higher education. Many of the students come from extremely wealthy families who show their gratitude by erecting new buildings and purchasing books for the library. Tarkington becomes so well endowed that among small private schools its only rival, in terms of library holdings, is Oberlin College.

Hartke's continuous comparisons between Tarkington College and the prison across the lake are highlighted by the fact that Every year, 30 inmates at Athena died for every student who was awarded an Associate in the Arts and Sciences Degree by **Tarkington** (HP 10).

Tartakover, Ksawery (1887–1956). *While doing research from his Jerusalem cell in* Mother Night, *Howard Campbell learns that his friend and chess*

partner, the Soviet spy George Kraft / Iona Potapov, beat the chess grand master Tartakover in Rotterdam in 1931. Tartakover was also a chess journalist in the 1920s and '30s.

Tcherkassky, Maria Daffodil-H. *The prima ballerina of the Chicago Opera Ballet and a member of Wilbur Swain's artificially extended family, in* Slapstick.

Tedler, Al. *In the short story "Lovers Anonymous," collected in* Bagombo Snuff Box (1999), *the North Crawford carpenter tells fellow members of the titled group that the building renovation plans for the home of Sheila and Herb White call for two separate entrances and two kitchens, removing any common living space. When Tedler sees Sheila, the object of the group's teenaged infatuation that has lasted well into adulthood, he says to his friends,* By golly . . . if I had that to cook for me, I wouldn't be any two-kitchen man.

Ten Square Band (*see* **Lincoln High School**).

Tennyson, Alfred. *Alfred, Lord Tennyson (1809–1892), was appointed England's poet laureate in 1850. In* God Bless You, Mr. Rosewater, *Tennyson is the answer to a question of bathroom graffiti.* (GBR 7) "Where can I get a good lay around here?" asks a bawdy soul, drawing this reply: "Try 'Lay of the Last Minstrel,' by **Alfred, Lord Tennyson**."

Tennyson is also used as an example of Mandarax's ability to recall popular quotations from literature. (Gal 1:13) . . . if you punched out on its back the word Sunset, for example, these lofty sentiments would appear on its screen: Sunset and evening star / And one clear call for me! / And may there be no moaning of the bar, / When I put out to sea. **Alfred, Lord Tennyson**.

"Thanasphere." *The opening short story in the 1999 collection entitled* Bagombo Snuff Box, *originally published in the September 1950 issue of* Collier's. *The title is derived from "thanatos," the personification of death and mortality in Greek mythology. Vonnegut uses it to describe that portion of space beyond earth's stratosphere where the disembodied voices of the dead congregate and are eventu-*

ally heard by America's first astronaut, Major Allen Rice, during a top-secret military space flight named Project Cyclops, overseen by Dr. Bernard Groszinger and Lieutenant General Dane.

Tharp, Naomi. *The woman who lives next door to Kilgore and Leon Trout and who tries to help raise Leon after Mrs. Trout abandons the family. She appears at the mouth of the blue tunnel to the Afterlife trying to coax Leon to the other side.* (Gal 2:7) "It's **Mrs**. Tharp," she called. "You remember me, don't you, Leon? You come in here just like you used to come in through my kitchen door. Be a good boy now. You don't want to be left out there for another million years."

Thayer, Webster. *The trial judge for Sacco and Vanzetti and recalled by Vonnegut for his anti-immigrant bigotry. Prior to the Sacco and Vanzetti murder trial, Thayer tried Vanzetti for robbery. Vonnegut writes:* Was Vanzetti guilty of this lesser crime? Possibly so, but it did not matter much. Who said it did not matter much? The judge who tried the case said it did not matter much. He was **Webster Thayer**, a graduate of Dartmouth College and a descendent [sic] of many fine New England families. He told the jury, "This man, although he may not have actually committed the crime attributed to him, is nevertheless morally culpable, because he is the enemy of our existing institutions" (JB 19).

Because Sacco and Vanzetti are admitted anarchists, Thayer feels conviction on any grounds is justified. Vonnegut cites the source of his information as Labor's Untold Story, *by Richard O. Boyer and Herbert M. Morais. Thayer's unremitting bigotry is publicized on a banner held by Kenneth Whistler outside the funeral parlor handling the executed pair.* (JB 19) On the banner were painted the words that the man who had sentenced Sacco and Vanzetti to death, **Webster Thayer**, had spoken to a friend soon after he passed the sentence: DID YOU SEE WHAT I DID TO THOSE ANARCHIST BASTARDS THE OTHER DAY?

Theatre de Lys. *The Greenwich Village theater where* Happy Birthday, Wanda June *opened on October 7, 1970. Due to an off-Broadway actors' strike,*

the play moved to the Edison Theatre, where it ran for 142 performances, closing on March 14, 1971.

In Deadeye Dick, *Rudy Waltz's* Katmandu *played for one performance at the Theatre de Lys in 1960.*

Theodorides, Mildred Heliwn-20. *Wilbur Swain's vice president, who dies of the Albanian flu, in* Slapstick.

therefore (when represented by the mathematical symbol ∴). *This mathematical symbol precedes each chapter of* Cat's Cradle *in the first editions and a number of printings thereafter. The effect, theoretically, creates a narrative-in-the-round, a plausible Bokononism. In a letter to this editor, Vonnegut confirms that the three-dot symbol was his contribution to the text, and this was repeated at a lunch with Vonnegut in the summer of 1992. Later reprints were made without the symbol, probably because each appearance took its own line and a couple of pages were saved in the process. Some reprints restore the symbol.*

However, there are unattributed stories that credit the typographer with adding the symbol. Mark Vonnegut recently told this editor that those marks were not in the copy he proofed for his dad back home. Frankly, Vonnegut was kind enough with friends and interested scholars that I would not put it past him to have me believe he contributed the three-dot symbol. He knew I developed their appearance into the basis for reading the text in the round, so to speak. Since "therefore" begins each paragraph, it is possible to read the text beginning anywhere and reading around to the front. Kurt liked this idea when I shared it with him. I can definitely imagine his making me happy with my cleverness by taking credit for the marks. He was just that kind.

Thiriart, Jean. *In* Slaughterhouse-Five, *the Secretary of the National Union of Belgium Opticians has an editorial in a 1968 issue of* The Review of Optometry *advocating the establishment of a "European Optometry Society." Thiriart believes the profession is at a crossroads and the professional status of optometrists is in danger of being reduced to "spectacle sellers." Billy Pilgrim reads the editorial between time travel episodes but can't muster any compassion for his colleagues across the sea.*

"This Son of Mine." *This short story first appeared in the August 1956* Saturday Evening Post *and was later reprinted in the 1999 collection* Bagombo Snuff Box. *Vonnegut's focus here is on fathers and sons: the debt that sons instinctively feel they owe their fathers and the manipulations of fathers to shape their offspring to maintain or improve their own legacies beyond the grave.*

Widower Merle Waggoner, creator and sole proprietor of Waggoner Pump, a centrifugal pump factory, receives a $2-million buyout offer from General Forge and Factory located in Vonnegut's ubiquitous Ilium, New York. Waggoner's great desire is to bequeath the factory to Franklin, his only son (named for Benjamin Franklin). Franklin, however, a student at Cornell University and president of the Intrafraternity Council, begins the story by breaking his father's heart with the announcement that he does not want to run the company; he wants to become an actor. Merle threatens to call Guy Ferguson, his contact at General Forge and Foundry, after the weekend to accept their offer, but Franklin persuades his father to hold off on his decision. In the meantime, Merle sets up a shooting outing of fathers and sons for the next day with his very first employee, Rudy Linberg, and his son Karl, also a Waggoner employee.

When Waggoner Pump is in its infancy, Merle offers Rudy a partnership in the company for $2,000. Rudy has the money but thinks the enterprise a bit too shaky for him to make the investment. Instead, he remains an employee for decades, only to watch Merle grow the business as a sole proprietorship. Merle feels free to confide some of his personal thoughts to Rudy, especially as they concern his son Franklin. Rudy listens, but we later learn that his hope through the years is that Franklin will want nothing to do with the company and he would somehow be able to slide his son Karl into management of the company.

Rudy does whatever he can over the years to bring Karl and Merle closer, making sure that his son shows the kind of interest in the company that Franklin rejects. Rudy goes so far as to fabricate a machinist's sheet metal puzzle into a finely crafted cube that closely passes through its center and has Karl fraudulently present it to Merle as a birthday gift from him. It is supposed to be similar to the one Rudy created years before when he learned his craft in Sweden.

The fraud is revealed by Karl to Franklin when the pair of sons walk down to a distant target during their shooting outing with their fathers. In a sense, Karl and Franklin grew up together, their fathers having no one else close to them. Both fathers did all they could to mold their sons into the men they wanted them to become. Karl's admission to Franklin about his father's plan to manipulate Merle is frank and deceptively offered. No sooner does Karl express a measure of exasperation with his father's plans than he tells Franklin he plans to miss the next shot (the boys had good luck shooting all afternoon and this last target was to settle the sharpshooter for the day). Such is not the case, however. Franklin hits the edge of the foil target, while Karl hits the very center. Whether Karl was trying to con Franklin into shooting poorly without the fear of losing is not clear, but it is in keeping with the seemingly innocent deceptions he learned from his father's long years of plotting against Merle.

The story's closing is a silent revelation by Franklin as he and Merle sit in the hunting cabin listening to Rudy and Karl play duets for flute and clarinet. The two machinists are the ones making music while Franklin, the college boy, interprets their music and the day's events signalling the inevitable passing of an era. With the moment to think about, to puzzle him pleasantly, Franklin found that the music wasn't speaking anymore of just Rudy and Karl. It was speaking of all fathers and sons. It was saying what they had all been saying haltingly, sometimes with pain and sometimes with anger and sometimes with cruelty and sometimes with love: that fathers and sons were one.

It was saying, too, that a time for a parting in spirit was near—no matter how close anyone held anyone, no matter what anyone tried.

Thomas Jefferson High School. *When Kilgore Trout takes his fungi-ridden tuxedo from the steamer trunk in preparation for his trip to the Midland City Arts Festival, he recalls attending his senior prom at Dayton, Ohio's Thomas Jefferson High School, in 1924.* (BC 3) *His high school was named after a slave owner who was also one of the world's greatest theoreticians on the subject of human liberty.*

Thriller, Ralph L. *In "Mnemonics," Vonnegut's second published short story, originally appearing in the April 1951 issue of* Collier's *magazine and later reprinted in the 1999 collection* Bagombo Snuff Box, *Thriller is Alfred Moorhead's boss. He is so well pleased by Moorhead's application of mnemonics to business matters that he promotes him.*

"Mnemonics" is another of Vonnegut's stories presenting technology challenges between lovers. Thriller calls upon Alfred Moorhead to remember five disparate items. This corporate order unexpectedly puts Thriller in the position of Cupid.

Momentarily caught without paper to write down Thriller's list as instructed, Moorhead uses the mnemonics techniques taught by the company to remember his task. The mnemonics strategy unexpectedly leads to Moorhead's revealing his feelings for his secretary Ellen, feelings she has shared for three years.

thumbscrew. (*SL5* 2) Weary's father once gave Weary's mother a Spanish **thumbscrew** in working condition—for a kitchen paperweight.
(*WFG* Torture and Blubber) But it is not easy in real life to make a healthy man blubber, no matter how wicked he may be. So good men have invented appliances which make unconstrained weeping easier—the rack, the boot, the iron maiden, the pediwinkis, the electric chair, the cross, the **thumbscrew**. And the **thumbscrew** is alluded to in the published parts of the secret Pentagon history of the Vietnam war.

Tiglath-pileser the Third. *In* Mother Night, *the eighteen-year-old prison guard Arnold Marx tells Howard Campbell about Tiglath-pileser the Third, an Assyrian who in 732 B.C. captured and burned down Hazor. The Canaanite city had been captured seven hundred years earlier by Solomon, who killed its forty thousand inhabitants, burned it down, and rebuilt it for the Jews. Arnold Marx concentrates on the savagery of the Assyrians against the Jews and gives not a thought to Solomon's ruthless deeds. For all his knowledge of archaeology and history, young Arnold is unaware of people such as Paul Joseph Goebbels, Campbell's old boss in Nazi Germany. This prompts Campbell to look again at his life with a longer view of history.* (MN 1) And I felt the dust of the Holy Land creeping in to bury me, sensed how thick a dust-and-rubble blanket I would one day wear. I felt thirty or forty feet of ruined cities above me; beneath me some primitive kitchen middens, a temple or two—and then—

Tiglath-pileser the Third.

Tillie. *In* Jailbird, *Tillie is the long-devoted maid to Mrs. Sutton, Sarah Wyatt's grandmother. She is the last of the servants to pass away, and two weeks later Mrs. Sutton also passes away.*

time and space (*also* **space and time**). (*ST* 9) The explanation of the bizarre emphasis on the music carried by the Martian mother ships is simple: Rumfoord was crazy about good music—a craze, incidentally, that struck him only after he had been spread through **time and space** by the chrono-synclastic infundibulum.
(*ST* 12) Man and dog spent most of their time by the pool, monitoring signals from their other selves through **space and time**.
(*SL5* 4) It was a flying saucer from Tralfamadore, navigating in both **space and time**, therefore seeming to Billy Pilgrim to have come from nowhere all at once. Somewhere a big dog barked.
(*PS* Playmates) "Even more magically, perhaps, we readers can communicate with each other across **space and time** so cheaply. Ink and paper are as cheap as sand or water, almost."
(*PS* Obscenity) There were at least eighty-seven chrono-synclastic infundibulae, time warps, between Earth and the Andromeda Galaxy. If the *Arthur C. Clarke* passed through any one of them, the ship and its load would be multiplied a trillion times, and would appear everywhere throughout **space and time**.
(*Blue* 11) So I was unprepared for the vista on the top floor, which seemed to violate all laws of **time and space** by going on and on and on. *This is part of Rabo's first impression of Dan Gregory's triple-sized brownstone house in New York.*
(*FWD* IV) "Yes, and I ask the reader of this piece, my indispensable collaborator: Isn't your deepest understanding of **time and space** and, for that matter, destiny shaped like mine by your earliest experiences with geography, by the rules you learned about how to get home again? What is it that can make you feel, no matter how mistakenly, that you

are on the right track, that you will soon be safe and sound at home again?

(TQ Prologue) The premise of *Timequake One* was that a timequake, a sudden glitch in the **space-time continuum**, made everybody and everything do exactly what they'd done during a past decade, for good or ill, a second time. It was déjà vu that wouldn't quit for ten long years. You couldn't complain about life's being nothing but old stuff, or ask if just you were going nuts or if everybody was going nuts.

There was absolutely nothing you could say during the rerun, if you hadn't said it the first time through the decade. You couldn't even save your own life or that of a loved one, if you had failed to do that the first time through.

(TQ 37) Trout himself, as I've said, was nevertheless espousing free will when he entered the Academy, and was invoking the Judeo-Christian deity as well: "Wake up! For God's sake, wake up, wake up! Free will! Free will!"

He would say at Xanadu that even if he had been a hero that afternoon and night, his entering the Academy, "pretending," in his words, "to be Paul Revere in the **space-time continuum**," had been "an act of sheer cowardice."

He was seeking shelter from the growing din on Broadway, half a block away, and from the sounds of really serious explosions from other parts of the city.

Timequake One. *Vonnegut's reference to his first and failing effort after struggling for ten years with the novel (eventually named just* Timequake*) comes after mentioning the great fishing dilemma of Hemingway's eponymous old man as well as Brahms's cessation of writing symphonies after the age of fifty-five. To carve away at or pare down one's writing at his bothersome advanced age is Vonnegut's dilemma.* (TQ Prologue) My great big fish, which stunk so, was entitled *Timequake*. Let us think of it as **Timequake One**. And let us think of this one, a stew made from its best parts mixed with thoughts and experiences during the past seven months or so, as *Timequake Two*.

Hokay?

Vonnegut then goes on to present the premise of

the novel—still the premise of his final narrative stew. (TQ Prologue) The premise of **Timequake One** was that a timequake, a sudden glitch in the space-time continuum, made everybody and everything do exactly what they'd done during a past decade, for good or ill, a second time. It was déjà vu that wouldn't quit for ten long years. You couldn't complain about life's being nothing but old stuff, or ask if just you were going nuts or if everybody was going nuts.

There was absolutely nothing you could say during the rerun, if you hadn't said it the first time through the decade. You couldn't even save your own life or that of a loved one, if you had failed to do that the first time through.

I had the timequake zap everybody and everything in an instant from February 13th, 2001, back to February 17th, 1991. Then we all had to get back to 2001 the hard way, minute by minute, hour by hour, year by year, betting on the wrong horse again, marrying the wrong person again, getting the clap again. You name it!

Only when people got back to when the timequake hit did they stop being robots of their pasts. As the old science fiction writer Kilgore Trout said, "Only when free will kicked in again could they stop running obstacle courses of their own construction."

A significant aspect retained in what Vonnegut refers to as his first and burdensome attempt at the novel is its metafictional element, which he combines with the text's denouement. (TQ Prologue) Yes, and I myself was a character in **Timequake One**, making a cameo appearance at a clambake on the beach at the writers' retreat Xanadu in the summer of 2001, six months after the end of the rerun, six months after free will kicked in again.

I was there with several fictitious persons from the book, including Kilgore Trout. I was privileged to hear the old, long-out-of-print science fiction writer describe for us, and then demonstrate, the special place of Earthlings in the cosmic scheme of things.

Vonnegut shifts the nautical focus of his creative efforts from Hemingway's literary fisherman to Melville's opening line of Moby Dick *("Call me Ishmael"). Vonnegut's metafiction begins with* Call me Junior (TQ 1), *a line that also echoes the nautical* references of Cat's Cradle's opening, Call me Jonah (CC 1).

Taken from Timequake One *are Kilgore Trout's stories "No Laughing Matter," "The Sisters B-36," and Trout's tossing of those manuscripts in the wire trash can in front of the American Academy of Arts next door to his homeless shelter in what had been the Native American museum.*

(TQ 8) In **Timequake One**, I envisioned a writers' retreat called Xanadu, where each of the four guest suites was named in honor of an American winner of a Nobel Prize for Literature. The Ernest Hemingway and Eugene O'Neill were on the second floor of the mansion. The Sinclair Lewis was on the third. The John Steinbeck was in the carriage house.

Vonnegut's explanation of the timequake's origins: (TQ 16) Here, for whatever it may be worth, and from **Timequake One**, is Kilgore Trout's explanation of the timequake and its aftershocks, the rerun, excerpted from his unfinished memoir *My Ten Years on Automatic Pilot:*

"The timequake of 2001 was a cosmic charley horse in the sinews of Destiny. At what was in New York City 2:27 p.m. on February 13th of that year, the Universe suffered a crisis in self-confidence. Should it go on expanding indefinitely? What was the point?

"It fibrillated with indecision. Maybe it should have a family reunion back where it all began, and then make a great big BANG again.

"It suddenly shrunk ten years. It zapped me and everybody else back to February 17th, 1991, what was for me 7:51 a.m., and a line outside a blood bank in San Diego, California.

"For reasons best known to itself, though, the Universe canceled the family reunion, for the nonce at least. It resumed expansion. Which faction, if any, cast the deciding votes on whether to expand or shrink, I cannot say. Despite my having lived for eighty-four years, or ninety-four, if you want to count the rerun, many questions about the Universe remain for me unanswered.

Another significant remnant from "Timequake One" is the assassination of Abraham Lincoln and the entire scheme about the bastard descendants of John Wilkes Booth and his brief affair with Julia

Pembroke, the wife of Lincoln's assistant secretary of the Navy.
See also: TQ 3; 8–9; 13; 25; 30; 58; 59.

ting-a-ling. Jailbird's *Dr. Robert Fender (using the name Frank X. Barlow) publishes a story in* Playboy *about the disembodied beings from Vicuna who temporarily inhabit the bodies of earthlings. "Ting-a-ling" is the Vicunian way of saying "hello" and "goodbye" as well as a few other pleasantries. Oddly, in* Jailbird, *those from Vicuna use the phrase as an expanded "shalom" or Hawaiian "aloha." In* Timequake, *the term becomes the sarcastic punchline for a series of irony-filled, almost comic coincidences stemming from the capture of Trout's father after he tries fleeing the police after killing his wife.*

(JB 5) "But there comes a time for every barnacle, at childhood's end, when the rim of its cone secretes a glue that will stick forever to whatever it happens to touch next. So it is no casual thing on Earth to say to a pubescent barnacle or to a homeless soul from Vicuna, 'Sit thee doon, sit thee doon.'"

The judge from Vicuna in the story tells us that the way the people on his native planet said "hello" and "goodbye," and "please" and "thank you," too. It was this: "**ting-a-ling.**"

(JB Epilogue) There was a telegram to me from Dr. Robert Fender, still in prison in Georgia. Mary Kathleen had wanted RAMJAC to make him a vice-president, too, but there was no way to get him out of prison. Treason was just too serious a crime. Clyde Carter had written to him that I was going back to prison myself, and that there was going to be a party for me, and that he should send a telegram.

This was all it said: "**Ting-a-ling.**"

(TQ 14) A bum on a cot next to Trout's at the shelter wished him a Merry Christmas. Trout replied, "**Ting-a-ling! Ting-a-ling!**"

It was only by chance that his reply was appropriate to the holiday, alluding, one might suppose, to the bells of Santa Claus's sleigh on a rooftop. But Trout would have said "**Ting-a-ling**" to anybody who offered him an empty greeting, such as "How's it goin'?" or "Nice day" or whatever, no matter what the season.

Depending on his body language and tone of

voice and social circumstances, he could indeed make it mean "And a merry Christmas to you, too." But it would also mean, like the Hawaiian's aloha, "Hello" or "Good-bye." The old science fiction writer could make it mean "Please" or "Thanks" as well, or "Yes" or "No," or "I couldn't agree with you more," or "If your brains were dynamite, there wouldn't be enough to blow your hat off." (TQ 14) I asked him at Xanadu in the summer of 2001 how "**Ting-a-ling**" had become such a frequent *appoggiatura*, or grace note, in his conversations. He gave me what would later turn out to have been a superficial explanation. "It was something I crowed during the war," he said, "when an artillery barrage I'd called for landed right on target: '**Ting-a-ling! Ting-a-ling!**'"

Later, Trout asks Vonnegut if he wants to know the real story behind the saying. To do so means telling Vonnegut about how Trout's father killed his mother. In running away from the police, he takes refuge in a woman's house with cathedral ceilings and dark beams. With no time to find a hiding place and naked as a result of not having enough time to slip into clothing from the woman's late husband, he tries to hide in the darkened beams. A policeman eventually notices his testicles hanging down. The woman hiding Trout tells the policeman he is seeing dimly lit Chinese temple bells. For the policeman's part, "He gave them a whack with his billy club, but there was no sound. So he hit them again, a lot harder, a whole lot harder. Do you know what the guy on the rafter shrieked?" Trout asked me. I said I didn't. "He shrieked, '**TING-A-LING**, YOU SON OF A BITCH!'" (TQ 14)

Trout uses the phrase as a punchline to the absurdity of his life, and both he and Vonnegut lay claim to it as shortcomings in their own literary art. (TQ 18) "In my entire career as a writer," said Trout in the former Museum of the American Indian, "I created only one living, breathing, three-dimensional character. I did it with my ding-dong in a birth canal. **Ting-a-ling!**" He was referring to his son Leon, the deserter from the United States Marines in time of war, subsequently decapitated in a Swedish shipyard.

"If I'd wasted my time creating characters," Trout said, "I would never have gotten around to

calling attention to things that really matter: irresistible forces in nature, and cruel inventions, and cockamamie ideals and governments and economies that make heroes and heroines alike feel like something the cat drug in."

Trout might have said, and it can be said of me as well, that he created *caricatures* rather than characters. His animus against so-called *mainstream literature*, moreover, wasn't peculiar to him. It was generic among writers of science fiction. (TQ 41) If there had been a significant body of potential book-buyers who might care about rich German-Americans in Indianapolis, it would have been a piece of cake for me to bang out a *roman-fleuve* demonstrating that my grandfather in fact *murdered* my mother, albeit very slowly, by double-crossing her so long ago.

"**Ting-a-ling**, you son of a bitch!"

Working title: *Gone With the Wind.*

(TQ 44) The beer, at my suggestion, was lightly flavored with coffee. What was so great about that? It tasted really good, for one thing, but it was also an homage to my maternal grandfather Albert Lieber, who was a brewer until he was put out of business by Prohibition in 1920. The secret ingredient in the beer that won a Gold Medal for the Indianapolis Brewery at the Paris Exposition of 1889 was coffee!

Ting-a-ling!. . . .

When I went to Cornell University to become a chemist fifty-six years ago, I was made a fraternity brother of a man named John Hickenlooper.

Ting-a-ling?

This was his son! My fraternity brother had died when this son was only seven. I knew more about him than his own son did! I was able to tell this young Denver brewer that his dad, in partnership with another Delta Upsilon brother, John Locke, sold candy and soft drinks and cigarettes out of a big closet at the top of the stairs on the second floor of the fraternity house.

They christened it *Hickenlooper's Lockenbar.* We called it *Lockenlooper's Hickenbar*, and *Barkenhicker's Loopenlock*, and *Lockenbarker's Loopenhick*, and so on.

Happy days! We thought we'd live forever.

Old beer in new bottles. Old jokes in new people. (*TQ* 49) Bernie's reply is the tag line of yet another joke from long ago, like "**Ting-a-ling**, you son of a bitch!" It seems a guy is off to play cards, and a friend tells him the game is crooked. The guy says, "Yeah, I know, but it's the only game in town." (*TQ* 59) Little did Julia suspect that Booth would mousetrap her champagne, just as she had mouse-trapped her chaperone's beddy-bye slug of wartime white lightning, with chloral hydrate.

Ting-a-ling!

Booth knocked her up! She had never had a kid before. Something was wrong with her husband's ding-dong. She was thirty-one! The actor was twenty-four!

Incredible?

Her husband was delighted. She's pregnant? There was nothing wrong with Assistant Secretary of the Navy Elias Pembroke's ding-dong after all! Anchors aweigh!

(*TQ* 63) There on the beach, whatever Trout said produced laughter and applause. He couldn't believe it! He said the pyramids and Stonehenge were built in a time of very feeble gravity, when boulders could be tossed around like sofa pillows, and people loved it. They begged for more. He gave them the line from "Kiss Me Again": "There is no way a beautiful woman can live up to what she looks like for any appreciable length of time. **Ting-a-ling?**" People told him he was as witty as Oscar Wilde!

Understand, the biggest audience this man had had before the clambake was an artillery battery, when he was a forward spotter in Europe during World War Two.

"**Ting-a-ling!** If this isn't nice, what is?" he exclaimed to us all.

I called back to him from the rear of the crowd: "You've been sick, Mr. Trout, but now you're well again, and there's work to do."

(*TQ* 63) "Your awareness," he said. "That is a new quality in the Universe, which exists only because there are human beings. Physicists must from now on, when pondering the secrets of the Cosmos, factor in not only energy and matter and time, but something very new and beautiful, which is human awareness."

Trout paused, ensuring with the ball of his left thumb that his upper dental plate would not slip when he said his last words to us that enchanted evening.

All was well with his teeth. This was his finale: "I have thought of a better word than awareness," he said. "Let us call it soul." He paused.

"**Ting-a-ling?**" he said.

See also: JB 1; *TQ* 15; 22; 63.

Titan. *The largest moon of Saturn serves for 200,000 earthling years as the home of Salo, the Tralfamadorian messenger whose spaceship breaks down on the way to another galaxy. It is also where the chrono-synclastic infundibulated Winston Niles Rumfoord and his dog Kazak are permanently materialized until a sun storm interrupts their wavelike existence and sends them on separate journeys across time and space. It becomes home to Malachi Constant, Beatrice Rumfoord, and their son Chrono. Beatrice dies on Titan in her old age and Chrono joins a flock of Titanic bluebirds, but not before he unknowingly delivers the spare part for Salo's ship. Salo brings Malachi back to Earth, where he freezes to death waiting for a bus on the outskirts of Indianapolis.*

Vonnegut makes life on Titan sound idyllic. (*ST* 12) The atmosphere of **Titan** is like the atmosphere outside the back door of an Earthling bakery on a spring morning. **Titan** has a natural chemical furnace at its core that maintains a uniform air temperature of sixty-seven degrees Fahrenheit.

Titanic bluebird. *Native inhabitants of Saturn's moon Titan, they befriend Chrono, who does his best to live as they do. He wears a cloak made of their feathers, sits on their eggs, shares their food, and speaks their language.*

Tobin, Andrew and Paul. *In "Thanasphere," Andrew is one of the departed souls adrift in the Thanasphere, and he tells Major Rice that his brother Paul had killed him. Upon further checking by General Dane, he learns from F. B. Johnson, the Evansville, Indiana, chief of police, that Andrew died in a hunting accident and Paul now runs the coal business started by his deceased brother. Andrew's is the first voice in space Major Rice hears that prompts him to investigate further using his ground commanders.*

Tom. *In the short story "The Cruise of the* Jolly Roger," *collected in* Bagombo Snuff Box *(1999), this young schoolboy explains the town's Memorial Day festivities when prompted by Annie and his teacher, and in so doing refocuses Major Nathan Durant's vision of the world—so much so that it takes him out of his shell.* "He died fighting so we could be safe and free. And we're thanking him with flowers, because it was a nice thing to do." He looked up at Annie, amazed that she should ask. "Everybody knows that."

. . . "It's true, isn't it," murmured Durant. "It's so damn simple, and so easy to forget." Watching the innocent marchers under the flowers, he was aware of life, the beauty and importance of a village at peace. "Maybe I never knew—never had any way of knowing. This is what war is about, isn't it. This."

Durant laughed. "George, you homeless, horny, wild old rummy," he said to George Pefko Memorial Square, "damned if you didn't turn out to be a saint."

The old spark was back. Major Durant, home from the wars, was somebody.

"I wonder," he said to Annie, "if you'd have lunch with me, and then, maybe, we could go for a ride in my boat."

"Tom Edison's Shaggy Dog" (1953) (*see* **Harold K. Bullard**).

tomb. (*ST* 8) They (*Unk and Boaz*) determined that their **tomb** was deep, tortuous, endless— airless, uninhabited by anything remotely human, and uninhabitable by anything remotely human. (*MN* 5) Werner Noth lived on the outskirts of Berlin, well outside the target area. He lived with his wife and daughter in a walled white house that had the monolithic, earthbound grandeur of a Roman nobleman's **tomb**. (*CC* 29) There was one more thing I wanted to do in Ilium. I wanted to get a photograph of the old man's **tomb**. *John/Jonah refers to the tomb of Dr. Felix Hoenikker.* (*BC* 12) A pyramid was a sort of huge stone **tomb** which Egyptians had built thousands and thousands of years before. The Egyptians didn't build

them anymore. The **tombs** . . . tourists would come from far away to gaze at them. . . . (*WFG* There's a Maniac Loose Out There) I myself have spoken to a few young people about the Provincetown drug scene, have put this question to them: "If the person who committed the Truro murders was high on something when he killed, what drug do you think he swallowed?" I remind them how crude the butcher was, how shallow the graves were, even though it would have been easy to dig deep **tombs** in the woodland floor which was sand.

The answer, invariably: "Speed."
(*WFG* Address to the National Institute of Arts and Letters, 1971) My own son asked me a month ago what the happiest day of my life had been so far. He called down into my grave, so to speak. This speech is full of **tombs**. My son considered me practically dead, since I smoked so many Pall Malls every day. (He's right, too.)
(*WFG* Address to the National Institute of Arts and Letters, 1971) My father and grandfather were good artists. I'm sorry they can't be here today. They deserved your warm company in this cool **tomb**.
(*Slap* Prologue) He (*Kurt's uncle Alex*) uncovered a scandal involving large expenditures for the maintenance of **Grant's Tomb**, which required very little maintenance indeed.
(*Slap* 13) Since the infant was an heir of mine, the pyramid might be called this: "**The Tomb of the Prince of Candlesticks**."
(*Slap* 17) "To the extent he can read and write," said Dr. Cordiner. "He isn't nearly as socially outgoing as his sister. When he is away from her, he becomes as silent as a **tomb**."
(*Gal* 1:17) And there are no **tombs** in the Galápagos Islands. The ocean gets all the bodies to use as it will. But if there were a **tombstone** for Mary Hepburn, no other inscription would do but this one: "Mother Nature Personified."

Vonnegut's following two passages quote a translation of the traditional Latin mass, then follows with his own mass: (*FWD* English Translation) The trumpet's wondrous call sounding abroad / in **tombs** throughout the world / shall drive everybody toward the throne.
(*FWD* Mass Promulgated by Me) Let no trumpet's

wondrous call sounding abroad / in **tombs** throughout the world / drive ashes toward any Throne.

(*TQ* 10) Allie later had her picture taken with Dillinger's big **tombstone** at Crown Hill, not far from the fence on West Thirty-eighth Street. I myself came upon it from time to time, while shooting crows with a .22 semiautomatic rifle our gun-nut father gave me for my birthday.

(*TQ* 23) Albert Hardy would be buried under an Eternal Flame in France, in the **Tomb of the Unknown Soldier**, "normal at last."

(*TQ* 31) My daughter Nanny and I went to Westminster Abbey the day after I became a pariah at the Royal Ballet. She was thunderstruck when she came face to face with the **tomb** of Sir Isaac Newton. At her age, and in that same place, my big brother Bernie, a born scientist who can't draw or paint for sour apples, would have shit an even bigger brick.

There is this rather violent scene in Timequake *when free will kicks in again.* (*TQ* 37) A mile and a half to the south, near **Grant's Tomb**, a massive Department of Sanitation truck, for want of sincere steering, plowed through the lobby of a condominium and into the apartment of the building superintendent. It knocked over his gas range. The ruptured pipe of that major appliance filled the stairwell and elevator shaft of the six-story structure with methane laced with skunk smell. Most of the tenants were on Social Security.

And then KA-BOOM!

"An accident wailing to happen," as Kilgore Trout would say at Xanadu.

(*BAG* Unpaid Consultant) "But the way things are now, you might as well sink your money in **Grant's Tomb**, for all the action you'll get."

"Um," I said. "Well, Celeste, with your tax situation, I don't think you'd want dividends as much as you'd want growth."

(*GBK* Roberta Gorsuch Burke) The simple epitaph Roberta Gorsuch Burke chose for her **tombstone** here on Earth: "A Sailor's Wife."

(*MWC* 11) And I said good-bye to my friend, hung up the phone, sat down and wrote this epitaph: "The good Earth—we could have saved it, but we were too damn cheap and lazy."

(*opposing page has tombstone in caps that reads:*)

LIFE
IS NO WAY
TO
TREAT AN
ANIMAL

"Tomorrow and Tomorrow and Tomorrow" (1953) (*see also* **Schwartz** *and* **anti-gerasone**). *The science fiction short story, reprinted in* Welcome to the Monkey House (1968), *depicting severe family strife and hellishly cramped living quarters as a result of anti-gerasone, a potion that can indefinitely extend life.*

top floor (*also* **top of the northernmost tower**). (*CC* 27) The room that had been the laboratory of Dr. Felix Hoenikker was on the sixth floor, the **top floor** of the building.

(*SL5* 9) The room (*in the Royalton Hotel*) was small and simple, except that it was on the **top floor**, and had French doors which opened onto a terrace as large as the room.

(*Slap* 3) It was actually possible for Eliza and me, for example, to vanish into a huge grandfather clock in the ballroom at the **top of the northernmost tower**, and to emerge almost a kilometer away—through a trap door in the floor of the mausoleum of Professor Elihu Roosevelt Swain.

(*JB* 11) I (*Walter Starbuck*) sat down on the edge of my bed, wide awake at last, and drenched in sweat. I took an inventory of my condition. Yes, I had gotten out of prison only that morning. Yes, I had sat in the smoking section of the airplane, but had felt no wish to smoke. Yes, I was now on the **top floor** of the Hotel Arapahoe.

(*JB* 23) And so it came to pass that she (*Mary Kathleen O'Looney*) was staying on the **top floor** of a RAMJAC hotel in Managua, Nicaragua.

(*PS* Self-Interview) VONNEGUT: And my father painted pictures in a studio he'd set up on the **top floor** of the house.

(*PS* In the Capital of the World) Jill (*Krementz, Vonnegut's second wife*) runs her photographic business out of the bottom floor. I run my writing business out of the **top floor**. We share the two floors in between.

(*DD* 12) But he was led off to cells in the basement

of police headquarters, and I was taken to a much smaller cellblock on the **top floor**, the third floor, which was reserved for women and for children under the age of sixteen.

(*Gal* 1:15) Turning to look at Ortiz, who had just come in with the filet mignons, *MacIntosh was rehearsing in his head the first thing he was going to say to Gottfried von Kleist in Spanish: "Before you tell me the rest of the good news, dear colleague, give me your word of honor that I am gazing at my own ship in the distance, from the **top floor** of my own hotel."

(*Blue* 11) I had supposed that he owned only the townhouse with the oak door and the Gorgon knocker infected with verdigris. So I was unprepared for the vista on the **top floor**, which seemed to violate all laws of time and space by going on and on and on. Down on the lower floors, including the basement, he had joined up to three houses with doors and archways. On the **top floor**, though, he had ripped out the dividing walls entirely, from end to end and side to side, leaving only those six freestanding fireplaces.

(*Blue* 13) I was mostly curious, though, about the **top floor**, which used to be the part of Gregory's studio with the big, leaky skylight.

topmost. (*PP* I) Paul glimpsed the only life visible through a narrow canyon between Buildings 57 and 59, a canyon that opened onto the river and revealed a bank of gray porches in Homestead. On the **topmost** porch an old man rocked in a patch of sunlight.

(*ST* 1) Standing now in the **topmost**, in the smallest of the baroque fountain's bowls, standing with his feet in the ruins of birds' nests, Malachi Constant looked out over the estate, and over a large part of Newport and Narragansett Bay.

(*BC* 24) Trout's right ring finger somehow slipped into Dwayne's mouth, and Dwayne bit off the **topmost joint**.

(*JB* 15) . . . into the lobby of the Chrysler Building . . . we got into the elevator before he could stop us. The doors shut in his angry face as Mary Kathleen punched the button for the **topmost floor**.

(*DD* 9) I slid forward the bolt, which caught the **topmost cartridge** and delivered it into the chamber.

tower, Eiffel Tower, Leaning Tower of Pisa, Tower of Babel, Waldorf Towers (*see also* **belfry, cupola**). (*ST* 1) Two hours after the firing of *The Whale* was called off indefinitely, the Reverend Bobby Denton shouted at his Love Crusade in Wheeling, West Virginia:

"'And the Lord came down to see the city and the **tower**, which the children of men builded. And the Lord said, "Behold, the people is one . . ."'"

Bobby Denton spitted his audience on a bright and loving gaze, and proceeded to roast it whole over the coals of its own iniquity. "Are these not Bible times?" he said. "Have we not builded of steel and pride an abomination far taller than the **Tower of Babel** of old? . . .

"So why should we cry out in surprise and pain now when God says to us what He said to the people who built the **Tower of Babel**: 'No! Get away from there! You aren't going to Heaven or anywhere else with that thing! Scatter, you hear? Quit talking the language of science to each other! Nothing will be restrained from you which you have imagined to do, if you all keep on talking the language of science to each other, and I don't want that! I, your Lord God on High *want* things restrained from you, so you will quit thinking about crazy **towers** and rockets to Heaven, and start thinking about how to be better neighbors and husbands and wives and daughters and sons! Don't look to rockets for salvation—look to your homes and churches!'"

(*CC* 115) And then there was the sound of a rockslide—and one great **tower** of "Papa's" castle, undermined, crashed down to the sea.

The people on the seaward parapet looked in astonishment at the empty socket where the **tower** had stood.

(*GBR* 4) To the west of the Parthenon was the old Rosewater Saw Company, red brick, too, green-roofed, too. The spine of its roof was broken, its windows unglazed. It was a New Ambrosia for barn swallows and bats. Its four **tower clocks** were handless. Its big brass whistle was choked with nests.

To the east of the Parthenon was the County Courthouse, red brick, too, green-roofed, too. Its **tower** was identical with that of the old saw company. Three of its four clocks still had their hands, but they did not run.

(*SL5* 1) He had to show somebody what was in the bag, and he had decided he could trust me. He caught my eye, winked, opened the bag. There was a plaster model of the **Eiffel Tower** in there. It was painted gold. It had a clock in it.

(*SL5* 5) "How the inhabitants of a whole planet can live in peace! As you know, I am from a planet that has been engaged in senseless slaughter since the beginning of time. I myself have seen the bodies of schoolgirls who were boiled alive in a **water tower** by my own countrymen, who were proud of fighting pure evil at the time." *Billy speaks in response to a Tralfamadorian's question about the most valuable thing he has so far learned on Tralfamadore.*

(*BC* 19) Dwayne Hoover, incidentally, wasn't taking any of this in. He was still hypnotized, turned inward. He was thinking about moving fingers writing and moving on, and so forth. He had bats in his **bell tower**. He was off his rocker. He wasn't playing with a full deck of cards.

(*Slap* 3) It was actually possible for Eliza and me, for example, to vanish into a huge grandfather clock in the ballroom at the **top of the northernmost tower**, and to emerge almost a kilometer away—through a trap door in the floor of the mausoleum of Professor Elihu Roosevelt Swain.

(*Slap* Epilogue) As a reward, the Raspberries brought their most precious possessions to Dr. Swain on the floor of the New York Stock Exchange. There was a clock-radio, an alto saxophone, a fully-fitted toiletries kit, a model of the **Eiffel Tower** with a thermometer in it—and on and on.

(*JB* Prologue) It was from the **belfry of that tower** that Alexander and his father and his brother would watch the Cuyahoga Massacre on Christmas morning. Each would have his own binoculars. Each would have his own little revolver, too.

(*JB* 23) Mary Kathleen went to New York City soon after that. She began to watch shopping-bag ladies through field glasses from her suite in the **Waldorf Towers**. *She eventually assumes the persona of a bag lady because she fears for her safety.*

(*PS* Children) "When I thought I was going to talk about reference points, I had in mind the fixtures in a simpler and more stable civilization than what we have today. Examples: Shakespeare's *Hamlet*, Beethoven's Fifth Symphony, Leonardo's Mona

Lisa, Lincoln's Gettysburg Address, Mark Twain's *Huckleberry Finn*—the Great Wall of China, the **Leaning Tower of Pisa**, the Sphinx. These few works of art used to be enormous monuments in the minds of public school graduates in every corner of this country. They have now been drowned in our minds, like Atlantis, if you will, by the latest sensations on television and radio, and in our motion picture palaces and *People* magazine."

(*Gal* 1:19) What those birds did on camera, though, was supremely erotic all the same. Already breast to breast and toe to toe, they made their sinuous necks as erect as flagpoles. They tilted their heads back as far as they would go. They pressed their long throats and the undersides of their jaws together. They formed a **tower**, the two of them—a single structure, pointed on top and resting on four blue feet.

(*Gal* 1:34) Colonel Reyes had already activated the brain of the tremendous self-propelled weapon slung underneath his airplane. That was its first taste of life, but already it was madly in love with the radar dish atop the **control tower** at Guayaquil International Airport, a legitimate military target, since Ecuador kept ten of its own warplanes there.

(*HP* 1) The greatest stroke of luck for me, the biggest chunk of manna from Heaven, was that Tarkington had need of somebody to play the Lutz Carillon, the great family of bells at the **top of the tower** of the college library, where I am writing now.

(*HP* 3) If Henry Moellenkamp hadn't come out of his mother's womb dyslexic, there would never have been a **tower** in which to hang the Lutz Carillon.

(*HP* 9) Tex, meanwhile, was ascending the **tower** of the library here with a rifle and ammunition. He was going clear to the top, to turn the belfry itself into a sniper's nest.

(*HP* 10) He (*Pierre LeGrand*) tried to win friends by making expensive gifts to them, but that didn't work, so he tried to hang himself from a girder of the **water tower** on top of Musket Mountain. I happened to be up there, in the bushes with the wife of the coach of the Tennis Team.

(*HP* 28) At the very end of his life 2 years ago, though, when Lyle Hooper was a prisoner of the escaped convicts up in the **bell tower**, he was addressed by his captors as "Pimp."

(*HP* 35) At dawn the valley was as quiet as ever, and

the red light on **top of the water tower** on the summit of Musket Mountain, as though nothing remarkable had happened over there, winked off and on, off and on.

(*FWD X*) The firebombing of Dresden, which had no military significance, was a work of art. It was a **tower** of smoke and flame to commemorate the rage and heartbreak of so many who had had their lives warped or ruined by the indescribable greed and vanity and cruelty of Germany. The British and Americans who built the **tower** had been raised, like me, and in response to World War I, to be pacifists.

Two more such **towers** would be built by Americans alone in Japan.

When they were built and then blew away, leaving nothing but ashes and cinders, I was on furlough in Indianapolis, my home. And even though I had seen on the ground the effects of a similar total conflagration, I myself regarded those **twin towers** as works of art. Beautiful!

(*TQ 16*) Dudley Prince ... The timequake was going to zap him back into a solitary confinement cell, into the hole, within the walls and **towers** of the New York State Maximum Security Adult Correctional Facility at Athena, sixty miles south of his hometown of Rochester, where he used to own a little video rental store. To be sure, the timequake had made him ten years younger, but that was no break in his case. It meant he was again serving two consecutive life sentences, without hope of parole, for the rape and murder of a ten-year-old girl of Chinese-American and Italian-American parentage, Kimberly Wang, in a Rochester crack house, of which he was entirely innocent!

(*TQ 38*) Bernie's ashes should be scattered over the dome of a **towering** thunderhead.

(*BAG* Thanasphere) At 1:39 p.m., on Friday, July 28th, the British liner *Capricorn*, two hundred eighty miles out of New York City, bound for Liverpool, radioed that an unidentified object had crashed into the sea, sending up a **towering geyser** on the horizon to starboard of the ship. Several passengers were said to have seen something glinting as the thing fell from the sky. Upon reaching the scene of the crash, the *Capricorn* reported finding dead and stunned fish on the surface, and turbulent water, but no wreckage.

(*BAG* Custom-Made Bride) The ramp brought me up to a catwalk outside the glass walls. A **towering**, vigorous man (*Otto Krummbein*) in his early thirties slid back a glass panel and invited me in. He wore lavender nylon coveralls and sandals. He was nervous, and there was tiredness in his deep-set eyes.

(*BAG* 2BR02B) Dr. Hitz became rather severe with Wehling, **towered** over him. "You don't believe in population control, Mr. Wehling?" he said.

"I think it's perfectly keen," said Wehling.

See also: PP IX; XXXIV; ST 3; CC 101; 114; SL5 15; MH Long Walk to Forever; MH The Hyannis Port Story; BC 5; 15; Slap 16; JB Prologue; 1; 8; PS Children; DD 22; Blue 36; HP 3; 8; 9; 11; 16; 20; 24; 25; 28; 32; 34; FWD XII; BAG The Package; BAG A Night for Love.

Toynbee, Arnold. (*MH* New Dictionary) I wonder now what Ernest Hemingway's dictionary looked like, since he got along so well with dinky words that everybody can spell and truly understand. Mr. Hotchner, was it a frazzled wreck? My own is a tossed salad of instant coffee and tobacco crumbs and India paper, and anybody seeing it might fairly conclude that I ransack it hourly for a vocabulary like **Arnold J. Toynbee's**.

By way of discussing Kilgore Trout's calm but firm response (to everyone, but especially to Dudley Prince) once free will kicks in again at the end of the ten-year rerun in Timequake, *Vonnegut recalls his studies as a graduate student in anthropology at the University of Chicago. The point I want to make, though, is that one course I took required me to read and then be ready to discuss A Study of History by the English historian* **Arnold Toynbee,** *who is up in Heaven now. He wrote about challenges and responses, saying that various civilizations persisted or failed depending on whether or not the challenges they faced were just too much for them. He gave examples (TQ 32). One variant of Trout's mantra at the close of the timequake's rerun is* "You were sick, but now you're well, and there's work to do" (*TQ 50*).

Tralfamadore, Tralfamadorian (*see also* **"The Protocols of the Elders of Tralfamadore"**). *The planet in the Small Magellanic Cloud that is a* central feature of both The Sirens of Titan *and* Slaughterhouse-Five. *The nature of life on Tralfamadore, however, is not consistent across the texts. In Sirens, Tralfamadorians are a race of machines. Though living beings had created them, the machines had long since exterminated their creators and reproduced on their own. (ST 12) The legend was this:*

Once upon a time on **Tralfamadore** *there were creatures who weren't anything like machines. They weren't dependable. They weren't efficient. They weren't predictable. They weren't durable. And these poor creatures were obsessed by the idea that everything that existed had to have a purpose, and that some purposes were higher than others.*

These creatures spent most of their time trying to find out what their purpose was. And every time they found out what seemed to be a purpose of themselves, the purpose seemed so low that the creatures were filled with disgust and shame.

And, rather than serve such a low purpose, the creatures would make a machine to serve it. This left the creatures free to serve higher purposes. But whenever they found a higher purpose, the purpose still wasn't high enough.

So machines were made to serve higher purposes, too.

And the machines did everything so expertly that they were finally given the job of finding out what the highest purpose of the creatures could be.

The machines reported in all honesty that the creatures couldn't really be said to have any purpose at all.

The creatures thereupon began slaying each other, because they hated purposeless things above all else.

And they discovered that they weren't even very good at slaying. So they turned that job over to the machines, too. And the machines finished up the job in less time than it takes to say, "**Tralfamadore**."

Their present form of government is "hypnotic anarchy," *which Salo declines to explain (ST 12).*

According to Salo, the word Tralfamadore means "both *all of us* and the *number 541*" *(ST 12). They use the Universal Will to Become to power their vehicles and transmit messages to Salo. It enables them to influence the psychology and efforts of humans on Earth in order to have them unwittingly write messages to Salo. Among their many messages were* Stonehenge, the Great Wall of China, the Palace of the League of Nations, and Moscow's Kremlin. *When Winston Niles Rumfoord discovers that the meaning of life for human beings, and for himself in particular, is to get a spare part to Salo for his intergalactic journey, he dejectedly exclaims:* "**Tralfamadore** . . . reached into the Solar System, picked me up, and used me like a handy-dandy potato peeler!" (ST 12) *Rumfoord never learned that the message Salo carried across the galaxies was the one word* "Greetings."

Undercutting his own creation, Vonnegut has Eliot Rosewater address the science fiction writers' convention in Milford, Connecticut. (GBR 2) And it occurred to him that a really good science fiction book had never been written about money. "Just think of the wild ways money is passed around on Earth!" he said. "You don't have to go to the **Planet Tralfamadore** in Anti-Matter Galaxy 508 G to find weird creatures with unbelievable powers. Look at the powers of an Earthling millionaire! Look at me! I was born naked, just like you, but my God, friends and neighbors, I have thousands of dollars a day to spend! . . . I leave it to you, friends and neighbors, and especially to the immortal Kilgore Trout: think about the silly ways money gets passed around now, and then think up better ways."

Billy Pilgrim explains the nature of time as understood by Tralfamadorians. (SL5 2) "The most important thing I learned on **Tralfamadore** was that when a person dies he only *appears* to die. He is still very much alive in the past, so it is very silly for people to cry at his funeral. All moments, past, present, and future, always have existed, always will exist. The **Tralfamadorians** can look at all the different moments just the way we can look at a stretch of the Rocky Mountains, for instance. They can see how permanent all the moments are, and they can look at any moment that interests them. It is just an illusion we have here on Earth that one moment follows another one, like beads on a string, and that once a moment is gone it is gone forever.

"When a **Tralfamadorian** sees a corpse, all he thinks is that the dead person is in bad condition in that particular moment, but that the same person is just fine in plenty of other moments. Now, when I myself hear that somebody is dead, I simply shrug and say what the **Tralfamadorians** say about dead people, which is 'So it goes.'"

An unnamed Tralfamadorian who acts as Billy's host on board the flying saucer explains (explained / will explain) how they see time. (SL5 4) I am a **Tralfamadorian**, seeing all time as you might see a stretch of the Rocky Mountains. All time is all time. It does not change. It does not lend itself to warnings or explanations. It simply is. Take it moment by moment, and you will find that we are all, as I've said before, bugs in amber.

Billy learns that reading a Tralfamadorian novel requires the same shift in perception. (SL5 5) . . . you're right: each clump of symbols is a brief, urgent message—describing a situation, a scene. We **Tralfamadorians** read them all at once, not one after the other. There isn't any particular relationship between all the messages, except that the author has chosen them carefully, so that, when seen all at once, they produce an image of life that is beautiful and surprising and deep. There is no beginning, no middle, no end, no suspense, no moral, no causes, no effects. What we love in our books are the depths of many marvelous moments seen all at one time.

This unique vision of time and space yields the Tralfamadorian secret about how the universe comes to an end. A Tralfamadorian pilot testing a new and faulty fuel explodes all existence. They are incapable of altering his actions because that is how the moment is structured.

Tralfamadorians in Slaughterhouse-Five *are sentient beings who communicate via telepathy. They use computers and speakers to converse with Billy Pilgrim and Montana Wildhack. In a letter to the* Ilium News Leader, *Billy describes their physiology. (SL5 2)* The letter said that they were two feet high, and green, and shaped like plumber's friends. Their suction cups were on the ground, and their shafts, which were extremely flexible, usually pointed to the sky. At the top of each shaft was a little hand with a green eye in its palm. The creatures were friendly, and they could see in four dimensions. They pitied Earthlings for being able to see only three. They had many wonderful things to teach Earthlings, especially about time. *Billy sees his own role as a cosmic optometrist capable of enabling others to see time through his knowledge of Tralfamadorian philosophy.*

Tralfamadorians recognize five distinct sexes on their planet, all necessary for reproduction. Billy fails to understand this as well as their claim to have identified seven sexes among humans. Similar to the view expressed in Kilgore Trout's novel Now It Can Be Told *in* Breakfast of Champions, *Tralfamadorians see all creatures in the universe as being various sorts of machines. Billy continues:* On **Tralfamadore** . . . there isn't much interest in Jesus Christ. The Earthling figure who is most engaging to the **Tralfamadorian** mind, he says, is Charles Darwin—who taught that those who die are meant to die, that corpses are improvements *(SL5 10).*

Vonnegut whimsically describes how his father preserved a letter informing him of his son's first commercial success as a writer. (FWD I) I am moved to add that Father tried to make good times revisitable (a trick which was easy as pie for the **Tralfamadorians** in my novel *Slaughterhouse-Five*) by gluing cheerful documents to sheets of masonite and protecting them with varnish.

Tralfamadore makes one other appearance, this time as the setting for a meeting of chemicals in Trout's rendition of why so many new diseases with heightened virulence have appeared since the close of WWII. (TQ 12) Trout said this was the story on why AIDS and new strains of syph and clap and the blueballs were making the rounds like Avon ladies run amok: On September 1st of 1945, immediately after the end of World War Two, representatives of all the chemical elements held a meeting on the planet **Tralfamadore**. They were there to protest some of their members' having been incorporated into the bodies of big, sloppy, stinky organisms as cruel and stupid as human beings.

Treasurer of the Knights of Kandahar. *In the 1952 short story "The No-Talent Kid," originally appearing in* The Saturday Evening Post, *this otherwise respectable citizen turns embezzler in his trusted role as the group's treasurer. The group's leader, the Sublime Chamberlain of the Inner Shrine, vows to pay all their creditors though it means liquidating their band instruments.*

Student musician Walter Plummer eventually acquires the civic group's tremendously large bass drum. The drum becomes the envy of band director George M. Helmholtz. Student and teacher strike a bargain: the band will eventually own the instru-

ment upon Plummer's graduation; until then, he will be the cart puller for the behemoth bass drum, getting him out of C Band and eligible for a coveted band sweater and varsity letter.

tri-benzo-Deportamil. *Wilbur Swain endures a thirty-year addiction to the medication developed by the Eli Lilly Company for those who suffer "the socially unacceptable symptoms of Tourette's Disease."* (*Slap* 32) The "Deport" part of the name had reference to good deportment, to socially acceptable behavior.

He starts taking the medication after becoming disoriented due to the Chinese experiments making gravity unstable. Wilbur gives his remaining small supply to David Daffodil-II von Peterswald, a true sufferer of Tourette's and the son of Wilma Pachysandra-17, wife of the inventor of the Hooligan.

*Swain is out of his mind from the severe withdrawal symptoms, necessitating bed restraints in the von Peterswald home for six days. During that time Wilbur gets the widow pregnant and she eventually gives birth to the son who sires Melody Oriole-2 von Peterswald, the granddaughter who comforts Wilbur in his final days in the Empire State Building. It is also in that confused state that Wilma explains to Wilbur that the Chinese . . . had become successful manipulators of the Universe by combining harmonious minds (*Slap* Epilogue). They had succeeded in proving the Swain twins' theories that were taken from the family mausoleum by Wilbur, then a tri-benzo-Deportamil addict, and delivered to Fu Manchu.*

trinity. (PP XXX) "These are radical proposals (*"that men and women be returned to work as controllers of machines, and that the control of people by machines be curtailed"*), extremely difficult to put into effect. But the need for their being put into effect is far greater than all of the difficulties, and infinitely greater than the need for our national holy **trinity**, Efficiency, Economy, and Quality." (BC 19) His *(Saint Anthony's)* biographer was another Egyptian, Saint Athanasius, whose theories on the **Trinity**, the Incarnation, and the divinity of the Holy Spirit, set down three hundred years after the murder of Christ, were considered valid by Catholics even in Dwayne Hoover's time.

(PS Religion) She *(Vonnegut's first wife, Jane Cox Vonnegut)* believes that Jesus was the Son of God, or perhaps God Himself—or however that goes. I have had even more trouble with the **Trinity** than I had with college algebra. I refer those who are curious about it to what is known about the Council of Nicea, which took place in anno Domini 325. It was there that the **Trinity** was hammered into its present shape. Unfortunately, the minutes have been lost. It is known that the emperor Constantine was there, and probably spoke a good deal. He gave us the first Christian army. He may have given us the Holy Ghost as well.
(TQ 34) Jane *(Cox Vonnegut, his first wife)* could believe with all her heart anything that made being alive seem full of white magic. That was her strength. She was raised a Quaker, but stopped going to meetings of Friends after her four happy years at Swarthmore. She became an Episcopalian after marrying Adam, who remained a Jew. She died believing in the **Trinity** and Heaven and Hell and all the rest of it. I'm so glad. Why? Because I loved her.

Trippingham, Mona Lisa. *The security guard at the old GEFFCo Building, now the Matsumoto Building, who telephones Rabo Karabekian with the sad news that his "Windsor Blue Number Seventeen" has shredded and peeled itself from its canvas. She calls to ask if he wants to come retrieve its remains. The irony of the situation lies in the fact that Rabo's choice of paint, Sateen Dura-Luxe, was advertised to "outlive the smile on the 'Mona Lisa'"* (*Blue* 2). *Now, Mona Lisa was calling to tell Rabo to pick up his scraps.*

Trout, Darlene. *Kilgore's wife is mentioned only once.* (BC 15) Kilgore Trout once wrote a short novel about the importance of the clitoris in lovemaking. This was in response to a suggestion by his second wife, **Darlene**, that he could make a fortune with a dirty book. She told him that the hero should understand women so well that he could seduce anyone he wanted. So Trout wrote *The Son of Jimmy Valentine*.

Trout, Dr. Raymond (*see* **Leo Trout**).

Trout, Kilgore (*see also* **Kilgore's Creed** *and* ***God Bless You, Dr. Kevorkian***). *The fabled science fic-*

tion writer *first appears in* God Bless You, Mr. Rosewater *(Trout is Eliot Rosewater's favorite author and is responsible for his nominal recovery at the end of the text). Vonnegut's self-acknowledged alter ego is a central figure in both* Breakfast of Champions *and* Timequake.

(*GBR* 14) "It seems to me," said **Trout**, "that the main lesson Eliot learned is that people can use all the uncritical love they can get."

"This is *news*?" the Senator raucously inquired.

"It's news that a man was able to *give* that kind of love over a long period of time. If one man can do it, perhaps others can do it, too. It means that our hatred of useless human beings and the cruelties we inflict upon them for their own good need not be parts of human nature. Thanks to the example of Eliot Rosewater, millions upon millions of people may learn to love and help whomever they see."

Trout glanced from face to face before speaking his last word on the subject. The last word was: "Joy."

In Breakfast of Champions, *Kilgore Trout is asked to come to the Midland City Arts Festival as one of the honored guests. Eliot Rosewater bargains for Kilgore's invitation in exchange for the loan of an El Greco painting. Trout's novel* Now It Can Be Told *contributes to Dwayne Hoover's mental breakdown. Vonnegut records that Trout dies in 1981 at the age of seventy-four (though Vonnegut creates a new death date for Trout in* Timequake — *see further in this entry below), and the American Academy of Arts and Sciences places a monument over his grave with a quote from his unfinished 209th novel,* WE ARE HEALTHY ONLY TO THE EXTENT THAT OUR IDEAS ARE HUMANE (*BC* 1 *illustration*).

We learn a little about Trout's personal history in Breakfast of Champions. *He was born in Bermuda, the son of Leo Trout, a scientist working for the Royal Ornithological Society responsible for protecting the only remaining nesting grounds of the Bermuda Ern. We also learn that he had three failed marriages, though the only spouse mentioned by name is Darlene. He also has a son named Leo who ran away from home when only fourteen.*

In Galápagos, *Trout's son is named Leon, the narrator of the text. Kilgore comes back from beyond the grave at regular though distant intervals of time, asking his son to step through the blue tunnel into the afterlife.*

In Jailbird, *imprisoned veterinarian and science fiction writer Dr. Bob Fender alternately publishes under the pseudonyms Frank X. Barlow and Kilgore Trout.*

It is in Timequake, *however, where Trout becomes a central character, has repeated interactions with Vonnegut as a character within his own fiction, has a change in death dates and lifespan from previous texts (that ironically came to match Vonnegut's own lifespan), and is lauded by admirers invited by Vonnegut attending the clambake on the Rhode Island shoreline during the writers' retreat at the hotel Xanadu, six months after the resumption of linear time. Vonnegut writes that Trout passes away on Labor Day 2001.*

And it is in Timequake *that Vonnegut reveals this additional information about his alter ego,* "This was a man," I said in *Timequake One,* "an only child, whose father, a college professor in Northampton, Massachusetts, murdered his mother when the man was only twelve years old" (*TQ* 13).

The list below contains all the titled Trout works followed by tales without titles and one tale that probably belongs to Trout, though Vonnegut leaves its authorship unspecified. Separate entries for each titled story are included in this encyclopedia. Untitled stories also have separate entries but are entered under the leading character's name or, when a name is not provided, under the tale's primary topic.

1. 2BR02B (*GBR* 2) *Kilgore Trout's novel (the alphanumeric abbreviation of Hamlet's question, "To be or not to be") as described in* God Bless You, Mr. Rosewater, *is a thematic cross between* Player Piano *and* "Welcome to the Monkey House" *complete with Ethical Suicide Parlors outfitted with pretty hostesses and Barca Loungers (industrial mechanization leading to unemployment and depression combined with severe overpopulation leading to ethical suicide.)* (*GBR* 2) All serious diseases had been conquered. So death was voluntary, and the government, to encourage volunteers for death, set up a purple-roofed Ethical Suicide Parlor at every major intersection, right next to an orange-roofed Howard Johnson's. There were pretty hostesses in the parlor, and Barca-Loungers, and Muzak, and a choice of four-

teen painless ways to die. "2BR02B" *is also the title of a short story in Vonnegut's* Bagombo Snuff Box.

2. *Venus on the Half-shell* (GBR 9)
3. *Oh Say Can You Smell?* (GBR 12)
4. *The First District Court of Thankyou* (GBR 13)
5. *Pan-Galactic Three-Day Pass* (GBR 13)
6. *Maniacs in the Fourth Dimension* (SL5 5)
7. *The Gospel from Outer Space* (SL5 5)
8. *The Gutless Wonder* (SL5 8)
9. *The Big Board* (SL5 9)
10. *untitled Trout novel about a man who builds a time machine and visits Jesus as a young boy learning carpentry from his father and grateful for the work order coming from Roman soldiers for a crucifixion stand* (SL5 9; *see also* **Christ, Jesus**)
11. "Pan Galactic Straw-boss" *became* "Mouth Crazy" (BC 2)
12. untitled story about reproductive scientist Delmore Skag (BC 2)
13. *Plague on Wheels* (BC 2)
14. "The Dancing Fool" (BC 5)
15. *untitled story about the astronaut Don (no last name) who travels to an unnamed planet where pollution has killed all plant and animal life but has strangely spared humanoids* (BC 5)
16. "This Means You" (BC 8)
17. "Hail to the Chief" (BC 10)
18. *The Barring-gaffner of Bagnialto, or This Year's Masterpiece* (BC 14)
19. *The Son of Jimmy Valentine* (BC 15)
20. *How You Doin'?* (BC 15)
21. *untitled* (BC 17) **Kilgore Trout** wrote a story one time about a town which decided to tell derelicts where they were and what was about to happen to them by putting up actual street signs . . . *which read* SKID ROW.
22. *The Smart Bunny* (BC 20)
23. *Now It Can Be Told* (BC 22)
24. *The Pan-Galactic Memory Bank* (BC 24)
25. *untitled* (WFG *Playboy* Interview): *Vonnegut mentions that he is at work on a Kilgore Trout novel about extended families, a central concept in* Slapstick *though not told as a Trout story.*
26. *untitled* (JB 5): *Dr. Fender, who previously published under Trout's name, publishes a story in* Playboy *magazine about disembodied spirits*

from the planet Vicuna. Fender writes this story under the name Frank X. Barlow.

27. "Asleep at the Switch" (JB 20), *published by Dr. Robert Fender under Kilgore Trout's name.*
28. *The Planet Gobblers* (PS Religion)
29. *The Era of Hopeful Monsters* (Gal 1:16)
30. *Though not specifically attributed to Kilgore Trout,* "The Protocols of the Elders of Tralfamadore" *appears in a magazine that published Trout's work in the past* (HP 16).
31. "The Sisters B-36" (TQ 5, 8–9, 15–17)
32. "Kiss Me Again" (TQ 6, 63)
33. *unnamed story plagiarized by Zoltan Pepper while he is a Ft. Lauderdale student of Mrs. Wilkerson. His punishment includes wearing a large placard with the letter* P *written on it* (TQ 17). *He is reminded of the story when his wife Monica hands him* **Trout**'s *discarded story* "The Sisters B-36," *reclaimed from the trash bin by Dudley Prince.*
34. *unnamed story featuring Albert Hardy, who was born with his head between his legs and his penis atop his shoulders* (TQ 22, 23). *Trout is writing this story when he is interrupted by the timequake, so it is ten years before he can finish the story when free will kicks in again.*
35. "Golden Wedding" (TQ 24)
36. "Dog's Breakfast" (TQ 27) (*Trout's first story after timeline resumes in 2001.*)
37. rewritten Book of Genesis story (TQ 7)
38. "No Laughing Matter" (TQ 3, 21)
39. "An American Family Marooned on the Planet Pluto" (TQ 8)
40. *My Ten Years on Automatic Pilot,* also referred to as *MTYOAP* (TQ 13)
41. "Dr. Schadenfreude" (TQ 17, 18, 19)
42. "Empire State" (TQ 31)
43. "Bunker Bingo Party" (TQ 19, 20, 21)
44. *The Wrinkled Old Family Retainer* (TQ 46); *Trout's only play*

Vonnegut writes in the prologue to Timequake, **Trout** doesn't really exist. He has been my alter ego in several of my other novels. But most of what I have chosen to preserve from *Timequake One* has to do with his adventures and opinions. I have salvaged a few of the thousands of stories he wrote between 1931, when he was fourteen, and 2001, when he died at the age of eighty-four. A hobo for much of his life, he died in luxury in the Ernest Hemingway Suite of the writers' retreat Xanadu in the summer resort village of Point Zion, Rhode Island. That's nice to know (*TQ* Prologue). *Kurt Vonnegut died when he himself was eighty-four, in 2007.*

In A Man Without a Country, *Vonnegut melds the politics of the present, Kilgore Trout, and* In These Times *editor and friend Joel Bleifuss in a scathing metafictional attack on George W. Bush moments before the 2004 State of the Union address. In this particular exchange between Vonnegut and his alter ego, it is Vonnegut who rants to his friend, not the other way around.* (MWC 11; *the facing page bears one of Vonnegut's many drawings with the epitaph at the close of this entry.*) On Tuesday, January 20, 2004, I sent Joel Bleifuss, my editor at *In These Times,* this fax:

ON ORANGE ALERT HERE.
ECONOMIC TERRORIST ATTACK
EXPECTED AT 8 PM EST. KV

Worried, he called, asking what was up. I said I would tell him when I had more complete information on the bombs George Bush was set to deliver in his State of the Union address.

That night I got a call from my friend, the out-of-print-science-fiction writer **Kilgore Trout.** He asked me, "Did you watch the State of the Union address?"

"Yes, and it certainly helped to remember what the great British socialist playwright George Bernard Shaw said about this planet."

"Which was?"

"He said, 'I don't know if there are men on the moon, but if there are, they must be using the earth as their lunatic asylum.' And he wasn't talking about the germs or the elephants. He meant we the people."

"Okay."

"You don't think this is the Lunatic Asylum of the Universe?"

"Kurt, I don't think I expressed an opinion one way or the other."

"We are killing this planet as a life-support system with the poisons from all the thermodynamic whoopee we're making with atomic energy and fos-

sil fuels, and everybody knows it, and practically nobody cares. This is how crazy we are. I think the planet's immune system is trying to get rid of us with AIDS and new strains of flu and tuberculosis, and so on. I think the planet should get rid of us. We're really awful animals. I mean, that dumb Barbra Streisand song, 'People who need people are the luckiest people in the world'—she's talking about cannibals. Lots to eat. Yes, the planet is trying to get rid of us, but I think it's too late."

And I said good-bye to my friend, hung up the phone, sat down and wrote this epitaph: "The good Earth—we could have saved it, but we were too damn cheap and lazy."

Trout, Leo and **Dr. Raymond** (*see also* **Leon Trotsky Trout**). *There are citations for two Leo Trouts in* Breakfast of Champions. *The first is Kilgore's father, an American citizen working in Bermuda for the Royal Ornithological Society. He is protecting the remaining nesting ground for the endangered Bermuda Ern. Kilgore is born and brought up on Bermuda, assisting his father in monitoring the habitat.*

The second Leo in Breakfast of Champions *is Kilgore's son, though in* Galápagos, *Kilgore's son is named Leon. The history of the Galápagos Leo is significantly different from that of the one in* Breakfast of Champions. *In* Galápagos, *Leo did not join the Viet Cong, though he did desert.* (BC 12) **Leo** left home forever at the age of fourteen. He lied about his age, and he joined the Marines. He sent a note to his father from boot camp. It said this: "I pity you. You've crawled up your own asshole and died."

That was the last Trout heard from **Leo,** directly or indirectly, until he was visited by two agents from the Federal Bureau of Investigation. **Leo** had deserted from his division in Viet Nam, they said. He had committed high treason. He had joined the Viet Cong.

Here was the F.B.I. evaluation of **Leo**'s situation on the planet at that time: "Your boy's in bad trouble," they said.

In Timequake, *Kilgore's father is named Raymond, and much new material can be found in his brief passages including the scope of his research (which becomes evidence in a race riot in Detroit) and the very key fact that he coldly murdered his wife, a poetess, and that he was the source of Kilgore's "Ting-a-Ling" refrain.*

(*TQ* 14) I asked him at Xanadu in the summer of 2001 how "Ting-a-ling" had become such a frequent appoggiatura, or grace note, in his conversations. He gave me what would later turn out to have been a superficial explanation. "It was something I crowed during the war," he said, "when an artillery barrage I'd called for landed right on target: 'Ting-a-ling! Ting-a-ling!'"

About an hour later, and this was on the afternoon before the clambake, he beckoned me into his suite with a crooked finger. He closed the door behind us. "You really want to know about 'Ting-a-ling'?" he asked me.

I had been satisfied with his first account. Trout was the one who wanted me to hear much more. My innocent question earlier had triggered memories of his ghastly childhood in Northampton. He could exorcise them only by telling what they were.

"My **father** murdered my mother," said Kilgore Trout, "when I was twelve years old."

"Her body was in our basement," said Trout, "but all I knew was that she had disappeared. **Father** swore he had no idea what had become of her. He said, as wife-murderers often do, that maybe she had gone to visit relatives. He killed her that morning, after I left for school.

"He got supper for the two of us that night. **Father** said he would report her as a missing person to the police the next morning, if we hadn't heard from her by then. He said, 'She has been very tired and nervous lately. Have you noticed that?'"

"He was insane," said Trout. "How insane? He came into my bedroom at midnight. He woke me up. He said he had something important to tell me. It was nothing but a dirty joke, but this poor, sick man had come to believe it a parable about the awful blows that life had dealt him. It was about a fugitive who sought shelter from the police in the home of a woman he knew. . . .

He went on, there in the suite named in honor of the suicide Ernest Hemingway: "She was a widow, and he stripped himself naked while she went to fetch some of her husband's clothes. But before he could put them on, the police were hammering on the front door with their billy clubs. So the fugitive hid on top of a rafter. When the woman let in the police, though, his oversize testicles hung down in full view."

Trout paused again. . . .

"One of the cops saw the testicles hanging down from a rafter and asked what they were. She said they were Chinese temple bells. He believed her. He said he'd always wanted to hear Chinese temple bells.

"He gave them a whack with his billy club, but there was no sound. So he hit them again, a lot harder, a whole lot harder. Do you know what the guy on the rafter shrieked?" Trout asked me. I said I didn't. "He shrieked, 'TING-A-LING, YOU SON OF A BITCH!'"

(*TQ* 16) "I have my doubts. I can't help it. That's the way I am. Even if my **father**, the ornithologist **Professor Raymond Trout** of Smith College in Northampton, Massachusetts, hadn't murdered my mother, a housewife and poet, I believe I would have been that way. Then again, I have never made a serious study of the different religions, and so am unqualified to comment. About all I know for certain is that devout Muslims do not believe in Santa Claus."

(*TQ* 48) Kilgore Trout was born in a hospital in Bermuda, near where his **father**, **Raymond**, was gathering material for a follow-up on his doctoral dissertation on the last of the Bermuda Erns. The sole remaining rookery of those great blue birds, the largest of all pelagic raptors, was on Dead Man's Rock, an otherwise uninhabited lava steeple in the center of the notorious Bermuda Triangle. Trout was in fact conceived on Dead Man's Rock during his parents' honeymoon. . . .

But when **Raymond Trout** went there as a doctoral candidate with his bride, he found that the females had taken to bowdlerizing the nurturing process by kicking the eggs off the top of the steeple.

* * *

Thus did **Kilgore Trout's father** providentially become a specialist, thanks to the female Bermuda Erns' initiative, or whatever you want to call it, in evolutionary mechanisms governing fates of species, mechanisms other than the Occam's Razor of Darwin's Natural Selection.

Nothing would do, then, but that the Trout family, when little Kilgore was nine, spend the summer of 1926 camped on the shore of Disappointment Lake in inland Nova Scotia. . . .

So the Trout family spent the summer up there dressed like beekeepers night and day, in gloves, in long-sleeved shirts tied at the wrists, and long pants tied at the ankles, in wide-brimmed hats draped with gauze, to protect their heads and necks, no matter how hellishly hot the weather.

* * *

Father, mother, and son dragged the camping gear and a heavy motion picture camera and tripod to the marshy campsite while harnessed to a travois.

Dr. **Trout** expected to film nothing more than ordinary Dalhousies, indistinguishable from other Dalhousies, but. . . .

Was **Dr. Trout** ever in for a surprise, though! Not only were these birds obscenely fat, and thus easy prey for predators. They were exploding, too! Spores from a tree fungus growing near Dalhousie nests found an opportunity to become a new disease in the intestinal tracts of the overweight birds, thanks to certain chemicals in the bodies of blackflies.

The new life-style of the fungus inside the birds at one point triggered the sudden release of quantities of carbon dioxide so copious that the birds blew up! One Dalhousie, perhaps the last veteran of the Disappointment Lake experiment, would explode a year later in a park in Detroit, Michigan, setting off the second-worst race riot in the Motor City's history.

Trout, Leon Trotsky (*see also* **Leo Trout**). *The only child of Kilgore Trout and narrator of* Galápagos *(and only briefly mentioned in* Timequake*). While a U.S. Marine serving in Vietnam, Leon re-*calls how I felt after I shot a grandmother in Vietnam. She was as toothless and bent over as Mary Hepburn would be at the end of her life. I shot her because she had just killed my best friend and my worst enemy in my platoon with a single hand-grenade.

This episode made me sorry to be alive, made me envy stones (*Gal* 1:23). *Leon is soon hospitalized for nervous exhaustion, and he later learns that* his unit took revenge by killing all fifty-nine villagers. His orders are to keep it a secret.

While enjoying a pass from the hospital, Leon contracts syphilis from a prostitute in Saigon. He fears getting treatment from a military physician because his pay would be docked and the period of treatment would be added to his tour in Vietnam. Instead, he goes to a Swedish physician working at a local medical school. It turns out that the doctor was a great fan of his father's books. Instantly, Leon forms a strong emotional bond with the doctor who persuades Leon to desert to Sweden.

Leon goes to work as a welder in the Malmö ship-yard where the Bahía de Darwin *is under construction.* (*Gal* 1:23) I was painlessly decapitated one day by a falling sheet of steel while working inside the hull of the *Bahía de Darwin*, at which time I refused to set foot in the blue tunnel leading into the Afterlife. *He stays behind because he is curious about how humanity will develop. He haunts the ship and observes humanity from the shores of the Galápagos Islands.*

It falls to Kilgore to convince Leon of the futility of his continued observations. (*Gal* 2:7) "**Leon! Leon! Leon!**" he implored. "The more you learn about people, the more disgusted you'll become. I would have thought that your being sent by the wisest men in your country, supposedly, to fight a nearly endless, thankless, horrifying, and, finally, pointless war, would have given you sufficient insight into the nature of humanity to last you throughout all eternity!

"Need I tell you that these same wonderful animals, of which you apparently still want to learn more and more, are at this very moment proud as Punch to have weapons in place, all set to go at a moment's notice, guaranteed to kill everything?

"Need I tell you that this once beautiful and nourishing planet when viewed from the air now resembles the diseased organs of poor Roy Hepburn when exposed at his autopsy, and that the apparent cancers, growing for the sake of growth alone, and consuming all and poisoning all, are the cities of your beloved human beings?

"Need I tell you that these animals have made such a botch of things that they can no longer imagine decent lives for their own grandchildren, even, and will consider it a miracle if there is anything left to eat or enjoy by the year two thousand, now only fourteen years away?

"Like the people on this accursed ship, my boy, they are led by captains who have no charts or compasses, and who deal from minute to minute with no problem more substantial than how to protect their self-esteem."

Leon Trotsky Trout's full name is revealed only once, in Galápagos (2:12), *when he offers his own sarcastic maxim about Mary Hepburn's secret artificial insemination of the Kanka-bono women with Captain von Kleist's sperm, in reply to a Mandarax offering quoting Robert Frost about boundaries and barriers.* (Gal 2:12)

Quoth Mandarax:

Something there is that doesn't love a wall.
— ROBERT FROST (1874–1963)

To which I add:

Yes, but something there is which adores a mucous membrane.
— **LEON TROTSKY TROUT**
(1946–1,001,986)

Leon Trout is briefly mentioned in Timequake *with no mention of his turning sides in Vietnam.* (TQ 13) I said Trout had been a hobo, throwing away his stories instead of offering them to publications, since the autumn of 1975. I said that was after he received news of the death of his own only child, **Leon**, a deserter from the United States Marine Corps. **Leon**, I said, was accidentally decapitated in a shipyard accident in Sweden, where he had been granted political asylum and was working as a welder.

Trout, Mrs. (*see also* **Raymond Trout**). *In* Timequake, *a poetess, the mother of Kilgore Trout, and her deranged husband's murder victim. Raymond Trout, a professor at Smith College, kills his wife when Kilgore is only twelve years old. Professor Trout stores her in the basement, telling young Kilgore that she probably went to visit relatives. He later wakes his young son to tell him the story of the burglar that ends with the catchphrase "Ting-a-ling."*

Years later, when Kilgore speaks to Vonnegut

about his Timequake One *manuscript in the hours immediately preceding the clambake, he expresses the notion that his doubts about God have little to do with being the son of a murderer who killed his mother.* (TQ 16) "That the rerun lasted ten years, short a mere four days, some are saying now, is proof that there is a God, and that He is on the Decimal System. He has ten fingers and ten toes, just as we do, they say, and uses them when He does arithmetic.

"I have my doubts. I can't help it. That's the way I am. Even if my father, the ornithologist Professor Raymond Trout of Smith College in Northampton, Massachusetts, hadn't murdered my **mother**, a housewife and poet, I believe I would have been that way. Then again, I have never made a serious study of the different religions, and so am unqualified to comment."
See also: TQ 14.

The True Purpose of Life in the Solar System.
Beatrice Rumfoord spends much of her time on Titan writing this text, which was a refutation of Rumfoord's again.

Beatrice began the book after her son left her to join the bluebirds. The manuscript so far, written in longhand, occupied thirty-eight cubic feet inside the Taj Mahal (ST Epilogue).

Tucci, Alfy. *Alfy Tucci is "the master of silent television," a title given him for his ability to watch musicians on television without sound and still discern the song being played, though he admits classical music is his weakest area. He is also one of the cooks at the Meadows executive retreat.* (PP XIX) As Paul's teammates carried him back to his seat, he realized fleetingly, as a fragment of a nightmare, that the cook had been **Alfy**, the master of silent television.

Tudor Hall. *The Indianapolis private school attended by both Jane Marie Cox (later to become Vonnegut's first wife) and his sister Allie during the Great Depression. Vonnegut views sending them to such a school in the midst of the nation's financial ruin as a hopeful vestige of a bygone era.* (TQ 25) But Mother was as full of baloney about Allie's prospects for marrying a rich man, and how important it was for Allie to do so, as Father was about the art she did. During the Great Depression, financial sacrifices were made to send Allie to school with Hoosier heiresses at **Tudor Hall**, School for Girls, or *Two-Door Hell, Dump for Dames*, four blocks south of Shortridge High School, where she could have received what I received, a free and much richer and more democratic and madly heterosexual education.

The parents of my first wife Jane, Harvey and Riah Cox, did the same thing: sent their only daughter to **Tudor Hall**, and bought her rich girls' clothes, and maintained for her sake membership in the Woodstock Golf and Country Club they could ill afford, so she could marry a man whose family had money and power.

When the Great Depression and then World War Two were over, the idea that a man from a rich and powerful Indianapolis family would be allowed to marry a woman whose family didn't have a pot to piss in, as long as she had the manners and tastes of a rich girl, turned out to be as dumb as trying to sell balloons with blobs of moistened clay inside.

Business is business. *Vonnegut's reference to selling "balloons with blobs of moistened clay inside" alludes to the seriously failed commercial venture called Putty Puss, the brainchild of Allie's husband, James Adams.*

Tum-bumwa. *The enslaved African who takes part in the 1786 insurrection aboard a British slave ship and sets it ashore on San Lorenzo. He becomes the island's first emperor.* (CC 57) "The emperor was **Tum-bumwa**, the only person who ever regarded the island as being worth defending. A maniac, **Tum-bumwa** caused to be erected the San Lorenzo Cathedral and the fantastic fortifications on the north shore of the island, fortifications within which the private residence of the so-called President of the Republic now stands."
(CC 95) Its parapets to the north were continuous with the scarp of a monstrous precipice that fell six hundred feet straight down to the lukewarm sea.

It posed the question posed by all such stone piles: how had puny men moved stones so big? And, like all such stone piles, it answered the question itself. Dumb terror had moved those stones so big.

The castle was built according to the wish of **Tum-bumwa**, Emperor of San Lorenzo, a demented man, an escaped slave. **Tum-bumwa** was said to have found its design in a child's picture book.

A gory book it must have been.

The fortification also holds the oubliette in which John/Jonah and Mona Aamons Monzano take refuge when "Papa" Monzano slips into the oceans, causing ice-nine to lock the world's surface moisture.

tunnel (*see also* **blue tunnel**). (PP XVIII) He (*Paul*) led her (*Anita*) to the front door of the low little house through a dark, fragrant **tunnel** roofed and walled by lilacs.
(ST 10) The effect of the closing inside the booths was to turn the line of concessions into a twilit **tunnel**.
(ST 10) The isolation of the concessionaires in the **tunnel** had an extra dimension of spookiness, since the tunnel contained only survivors from Mars.
(ST 10) It was the proud and impudent custom of all concessionaires to stay away from ceremonies — to stay in the twilit **tunnel** of their booths until Rumfoord and his dog had come and gone.
(SL5 5) They (*the British POWs*) could **tunnel** all they pleased. They would inevitably surface within a rectangle of barbed wire, would find themselves greeted listlessly by dying Russians who spoke no English, who had no food or useful information or escape plans of their own.
(BC 10) He (*Rabo Karabekian*) got a ride in a truck. . . . It picked him up at the mouth of the Lincoln **Tunnel**, which was named in honor of a man who had had the courage and imagination to make human slavery against the law in the United States of America.
(BC 15) The man at the controls of the *Galaxie* was a traveling salesman for a device which engulfed the rear ends of trucks at loading docks. It was a telescoping **tunnel** of rubberized canvas.
(WFG Address to Graduating Class at Bennington College, 1970) I saved our marriage many times by exclaiming, "Wait! Wait! I see light at the end of the **tunnel** at last!" And I wish I could bring light to *your* **tunnels** today. My wife begged me to bring you light, but there is no light. Everything is going to become unimaginably worse, and never get better again.

(*Slap* 29) It must have been a horrible sight—the **tunnel** with all the hair and bits of wax inside.

(*JB* 15) She led me through a **tunnel** under Lexington Avenue, and up a staircase into the lobby of the Chrysler Building.

(*JB* 18) He said he had been working as "a robber," taking out supporting pillars of coal from a **tunnel** where the seam had otherwise been exhausted. Something had fallen on him (*Kenneth Whistler*).

(*Gal* 1:29) This, of course, was the **tunnel** into the Afterlife.

(*Gal* 2:8) The decision was made for me by Mary Hepburn, by "Mrs. Flemming," whose joy in the crow's nest held my attention so long that when I looked back at the **tunnel**, the **tunnel** was gone.

(*Blue* 8) Yes, and when the Twentieth Century Limited from Chicago plunged into a **tunnel** under New York City, with its lining of pipes and wires, I was out of the womb and into the birth canal.

(*HP* 6) I had won my Silver Star for finding and personally killing 5 enemy soldiers who were hiding in a **tunnel** underground.

(*HP* 32) During our interview, he used all the antiwar rhetoric he had heard at Harvard in the '60s to denounce his own country's overseas disaster. We were a quagmire. There was no light at the end of the **tunnel** over here, and on and on. *Hartke notes the parallel drawn by Hiroshi Matsumoto between America's intervention in Vietnam with Japan's corporate occupation of America.*

(*HP* 33) But as I've said, there were other veterans there who had heard of me and knew, among other things, that I had pitched a grenade into the mouth of a **tunnel** one time, and killed a woman, her mother, and her baby hiding from helicopter gunships which had strafed her village right before we got there.

(*TQ* 32) The same might be said for individuals who would like to behave heroically, and most strikingly in the case of Kilgore Trout on the afternoon and evening of February 13th, 2001, after free will kicked in. If he had been in the area of Times Square, or near the entrance or exit of a major bridge or **tunnel**, or at an airport, where pilots, as they had learned to do during the rerun, had expected their planes to take off or land safely of their own accord, the challenge would have been too much not only for Trout but for anyone else.

(*GBK* Introduction) My first near-death experience was an accident, a botched anesthesia during a triple bypass. I had listened to several people on TV talk shows who had gone down the **blue tunnel** to the Pearly Gates, and even beyond the Pearly Gates, or so they said, and then come back to life again. But I certainly wouldn't have set out on such a risky expedition on purpose, without first having survived one, and then planned another in cooperation with Dr. Jack Kevorkian and the staff at the state-of-the-art lethal injection execution facility at Huntsville, Texas.

(*GBK* Introduction) There will be no more round trips for me, barring another accident. For the sake of my family, I am trying to reinstate my health and life insurance policies, if possible. But other journalists, and perhaps even tourists, will surely follow the safe two-way path I pioneered. I beg them to be content, as I learned to be, with interviews they are able to conduct on the hundred yards or so of vacant lot between the far end of the **blue tunnel** and the Pearly Gates.

(*GBK* Mary D. Ainsworth) on my near death experience this morning, I found out what becomes of people who die while they're still babies. Finding that out was accidental, since I'd gone down the **blue tunnel** to interview Dr. Mary D. Ainsworth, who died last March 21, age eighty-five, in Charlottesville, Virginia. . . .

Dr. Ainsworth was bubbling over with excitement over how her theories were confirmed in Heaven. Never mind all those honors she'd received from fellow psychologists on Earth. It turns out that there are nurseries and nursery schools and kindergartens in Heaven for people who died when they were babies. Volunteer surrogate mothers, or sometimes the babies' actual mothers, if they're dead, bond like crazy with the little souls. Cuddle, cuddle, cuddle, Kiss, kiss, kiss. Don't cry, little baby. Your mommy loves you. Bet you have to burp. I'll bet that's the trouble. There. Feel better? Time to go sleepy-bye. Goo, goo, goo.

And the babies grow up to be angels. That's where angels come from!

This is Kurt Vonnegut, signing off in the lethal injection facility in Huntsville, Texas. Until the next time, goo goo goo and ta ta.

(*GBK* Salvatore Biagini) this morning, thanks to a

controlled near-death experience, I was lucky enough to meet, at the far end of the **blue tunnel**, a man named Salvatore Biagini. Last July 8th, Mr. Biagini, a retired construction worker, age seventy, suffered a fatal heart attack while rescuing his beloved schnauzer, Teddy, from an assault by an unrestrained pit bull named Chele, in Queens.

(*GBK* Birnum Birnum) after this morning's controlled near-death experience I am almost literally heartbroken that there was no way for me to take a tape recorder down the **blue tunnel** to Heaven and back again. Never before had there been a New Orleans–style brass band, led by the late Louis Armstrong, to greet a new arrival with a rousing rendition of "When the Saints Come Marching In." The recipient of this very rare and merry honor, accorded to only one in ten million newly dead people, I'm told, was an Australian Aborigine, with some white blood, named Birnum Birnum. . . . He was the first of his people to attend law school.

(*GBK* Roberta Gorsuch Burke) If past performance is any indication, they will surely stay married there at the far end of the **blue tunnel** throughout all eternity. She said to me, "Why fool around?" President Clinton told her at her husband's funeral, when she still had a year to live, "You have blessed America with your service and set an example not only for navy wives today, and to come, but for all Americans."

The simple epitaph Roberta Gorsuch Burke chose for her tombstone here on Earth: "A Sailor's Wife."

(*GBK* Clarence Darrow) dr. jack kevorkian [*sic*] has again unstrapped me from what has become my personal gurney, here, in the lethal injection facility at Huntsville, Texas. Jack has now supervised fifteen controlled near-death experiences for me. Hey, Jack, way to go! On this morning's trip down the **blue tunnel** to the pearly gates, Clarence Darrow, the great American defense attorney, dead for sixty years now, came looking for me. He wanted WNYC's listeners to hear his opinion of television cameras in courtrooms. "I welcome them," he said, if you can believe it. This man with the reputation of a giant, comes from a rinky dink little farm town in Ohio.

(*GBK* Eugene Victor Debs) And then, guess what, yesterday afternoon none other than Eugene Victor Debs, organizer and leader of the first successful strike against a major American industry, the railroads, was waiting for me at the far end of the **blue tunnel**. We hadn't met before. This great American died in 1926 at the age of seventy-one when I was only four years old.

(*GBK* Isaac Newton) during my controlled near-death experiences, I've met Sir Isaac Newton, who died back in 1727, as often as I've met Saint Peter. They both hang out at the Heaven end of the **blue tunnel** of the Afterlife. Saint Peter is there because that's his job. Sir Isaac is there because of his insatiable curiosity about what the **blue tunnel** is, how the **blue tunnel works**. . . .

My job is to interview dead people for WNYC, but the late Sir Isaac Newton interviewed me instead. He got to make only a single one-way trip down the **tunnel**. He wants to know what it seems to be made of, fabric or metal or wood or what. I tell him that it's made of whatever dreams are made of, which leaves him monumentally unsatisfied.

(*GBK* William Shakespeare) In effect, he told your reporter to go screw himself. "Get thee to a nunnery!" he said, and off he went.

I felt like such a fool as I made my way back to the **blue tunnel**. An enchanting answer to any question I might have asked the greatest writer who ever lived could be found in Bartlett's Familiar Quotations. The beaut about exchanging innocence for innocence was from *The Winter's Tale*.

(*GBK* Carla Faye Tucker) It is late in the afternoon of February 3, 1998. I have just been unstrapped from a gurney following another controlled near-death experience in this busy execution chamber in Huntsville, Texas.

For the first time in my career, I was actually on the heels of a celebrity as I made my way down the **blue tunnel** to Paradise. She was Carla Faye Tucker, the born again murderer of two strangers with a pick-axe. Carla Faye was completely killed here, by the State of Texas, shortly after lunch time.

Two hours later, on another gurney, I myself was made only three-quarters dead. I caught up with Carla Faye in the **tunnel**, about a hundred fifty yards from the far end, near the Pearly Gates. Since she was dragging her feet, I hastened to assure her that there was no Hell waiting for her, no Hell waiting for anyone.

turkey farm. *Dr. von Peterswald coins this term after accidentally inventing the Hooligan, a device enabling one to speak with the dead. (Slap* Epilogue) The talkers identified themselves as persons in the afterlife. They were backed by a demoralized chorus of persons who complained to each other of tedium and social slights and minor ailments, and so on.

As Dr. von Peterswald said in his secret diary: "It sounded like nothing so much as the other end of a telephone call on a rainy autumn day—to a badly run **turkey farm**."

Hi ho.
See also: Slap 40; 43.

Turner, Jeffrey. *The head of the Jamaican drug cartel whose televised trial lasts eighteen months. Though given twenty-five consecutive life sentences, he is housed in the prison at Athena for only six months before his associates execute the enormously elaborate and high-powered jail break. (HP* 10) Now a well-rehearsed force of his employees, variously estimated as being anything from a platoon to a company, had arrived outside the prison with explosives, a tank, and several halftracks taken from the National Guard Armory about 10 kilometers south of Rochester, across the highway from the Meadowdale Cinema Complex. One of their number, it has since come out, moved to Rochester and joined the National Guard, swearing to defend the Constitution and all that, with the sole purpose of stealing the keys to the Armory.

The Japanese guards were wholly unprepared and unmotivated to resist such a force, especially since the attackers were all dressed in American Army uniforms and waving American flags. So they hid or put their hands up or ran off into the virgin forest. This wasn't their country, and guarding prisoners wasn't a sacred mission or anything like that. It was just a business. *The half-hour precision attack on the prison left the facility's armory and gates wide open. This precipitates the escape of large numbers of prisoners and the subsequent takeover of nearby Scipio and Tarkington College.*

Turtle Bay. *Vonnegut lived in this mid-Manhattan East Side neighborhood after permanently moving* to New York shortly after the theatrical production of Happy Birthday, Wanda June *in 1970.*

Among his fictional characters, the parents of Wilbur and Eliza Swain prefer living in Turtle Bay rather than their Vermont estate with their freakish offspring. At one point Eliza exclaims, "**Turtle Bay**, **Turtle Bay**," she mused. "Did it ever occur to you, dear Brother, that dear Father was not our Father at all?"

"What do you mean?" I said.

"Perhaps Mother stole from the bed and out of the house on a moonlit night," she said, "and mated with a giant sea turtle in **Turtle Bay**."

Hi ho (*Slap* 23).

Dan Gregory's cook meets her fate in the same neighborhood. (Blue 18) I don't know where this fits into my story, and probably it doesn't fit in at all. It is certainly the most trivial footnote imaginable in a history of Abstract Expressionism, but here it is:

The cook who had begrudgingly fed me my first supper in New York City, and who kept asking, "What next, what next?" died two weeks after I got there. That finally became what was going to happen next: she would drop dead in **Turtle Bay Chemists**, a drugstore two blocks away.

But here was the thing: the undertaker discovered that she wasn't just a woman, and she wasn't just a man, either. She was somewhat both. She was a hermaphrodite.

It was outside Vonnegut's Turtle Bay home that he fell and eventually died from his injuries in 2007.

Twain, Mark. *Vonnegut well illustrates his appreciation for Mark Twain in more than fifty references. Arguably the best starting point for understanding Vonnegut's affinity for his literary ancestor is in* Palm Sunday, *words spoken by Vonnegut commemorating the hundredth anniversary of Twain's Hartford home. (PS* Mark Twain) I have meditated with **Mark Twain**'s mind. I began doing it when a child. I do it still. It encouraged me when I was young to believe that there was so much that was amusing and beautiful on this continent that I need not be awed by persons from anywhere else. I should model myself after other Americans. I now have mixed feelings about such advice. It hasn't always been convenient or attractive to comport myself as the purely American person I am.

Twain's brand of religious skepticism dovetails with the freethinking views Vonnegut grew up with as part of his family's tradition. Twain's humor and midwestern voice are common favorites for young Kurt and big brother Bernard. So enamored with Twain is Vonnegut that he declares, I myself have named my only son after **Mark Twain**, another American Saint *(PS Roots).*

Twain—The Essential American Voice

Vonnegut notes the worldwide appeal of Twain's singular American voice in the 1958 short story "The Manned Missiles," reprinted in Welcome to the Monkey House *(1968). In this tale, written and set during the Cold War, Mikail Ivankov dictates a condolence letter to Charles Ashland. Both men have lost their sons to the depths of space, casualties of the race to control space and their own engineering malfunctions. In the midst of his sorrow, Ivankov wishes to console his counterpart with knowledge that both families have much to learn from each other, as do their nations. He notes that his younger son, Alexei, the one translating his letter into English, is open to iconic American voices.* He admires your Jack London and your O. Henry and your **Mark Twain**. Alexei is seventeen. He is going to be a scientist like his brother Stepan.

For Vonnegut, Twain depicts the essential American character as offering the best insights available to immigrants about their new land and neighbors. As he says, "It seems clear to me, as an American writing one hundred years after this house was built, that we would not be known as a nation with a supple, amusing, and often beautiful language of our own, if it were not for the genius of **Mark Twain**. Only a genius could have misrepresented our speech and our wittiness and our common sense and our common decency so handsomely to ourselves and the outside world" *(PS Mark Twain).*

Twain and Presentation of the American Character

Beyond the unique sounds and wit captured by Twain, Vonnegut asserts that Twain's characterization of the American psyche—the myths that most accurately capture the purest insights of the American soul—is the best explanation of our own and others' sense of Americana. (PS Mark Twain) "Imagine, if you will, the opinion we would now hold of ourselves and the opinions others would hold of us, if it were not for the myths about us created by **Mark Twain**. You can then begin to calculate our debt to this one man." One man. Just one man! "I named my firstborn son after him!" I thank you for your attention."

Vonnegut sees parallels in Twain's appreciation of his life's experiences and work, similar to other famous friends and acquaintances in his post–World War II generation of writers. These are sentiments shared by men of great and weighty experiences during two unique periods in our nation's history: the Civil War and World War II. (PS The People One Knows) **Mark Twain** is said to have felt that his existence was all pretty much downhill from his adventures as a Mississippi riverboat pilot. Mr. Heller's two novels, when considered in sequence, might be taken as a similar statement about an entire white, middle-class generation of American males, my generation, Mr. Heller's generation, Herman Wouk's generation, Norman Mailer's generation, Irwin Shaw's generation, Vance Bourjaily's generation, James Jones's generation, and on and on—that for them everything has been downhill since World War II, as absurd and bloody as it often was.

Twain's appreciation for developing characters is seen by Vonnegut as having parallels to Christian scripture but devoid of any overt religious beliefs. The religious skepticism Twain introduces to Vonnegut as a young reader provides a comforting corollary to his family's freethinking beliefs.

"I now quote a previous owner of this house: 'When I find a well-drawn character in fiction or biography, I generally take a warm personal interest in him, for the reason that I have known him before—met him on the river.'

"I submit to you that this is a profoundly Christian statement, an echo of the Beatitudes. It is constructed, as many jokes are, incidentally, with a disarmingly pedestrian beginning and an unexpectedly provoking conclusion.

"I will repeat it, for we are surely here to repeat ourselves. Lovers do almost nothing but repeat themselves.

"'When I find a well-drawn character in fiction or biography, I generally take a warm personal interest in him, for the reason that I have known him before—met him on the river.'

"Three words, in my opinion, make this a holy joke. They are 'warm' and 'personal' and 'river.' The river, of course, is life—and not just to river pilots but even to desert people, to people who have never even seen water in that long and narrow form. **Mark Twain** is saying what Christ said in so many ways: that he could not help loving anyone in the midst of life" (PS Mark Twain).

Twain's Spiritual Commitment

Vonnegut mentions his own spiritual beliefs that have nothing to do with the myths of organized religion. He and Twain agree on the need to do good works and charitable deeds simply because the need is there, not because of the notion that our actions are forever being monitored by an omnipotent and often vengeful God. These were the teachings of his parents and what he found in Twain. Moreover, traditional monotheism commands us to act in accord with God's word or pay the consequences. Vonnegut's (and Twain's) philosophy is that coerced acts of goodness lack sincerity since they are only a buffer to their fears of an eternity with a disappointed deity. As Vonnegut tells the assembled crowd at Mark Twain's Hartford home, "I am of course a skeptic about the divinity of Christ and a scorner of the notion that there is a God who cares how we are or what we do. I was raised this way-in the midst of what provincial easterners imagine to be a Bible Belt. I was confirmed in my skepticism by **Mark Twain** during my formative years, and by some other good people, too. I have since bequeathed this lack of faith and my love for the body of literature which supports it to my children.

"I am moved on this occasion to put into a few words the ideal my parents and Twain and the rest held before me, and which I have now passed on. The ideal, achieved by few, is this: 'Live so that you can say to God on Judgment Day, "I was a very good person, even though I did not believe in you."' The word 'God,' incidentally, is capitalized throughout this speech, as are all pronouns referring to Him.

"We religious skeptics would like to swagger some in heaven, saying to others who spent a lot of time quaking in churches down here, 'I was never worried about pleasing or angering God—never took Him into my calculations at all'" (PS Mark Twain).

This line of thinking provokes a minor epiphany for Vonnegut that stems in part from humanity's selfish motives for pursuing eternal salvation. It touches on the teachings of his childhood—and that includes reading Twain. Disappointed with a world operating with too much faith in myth-makers and the threat of a vengeful god, Vonnegut senses how his contrarian beliefs will play out. (PS Mark Twain) I know why I will become bitter. I will finally realize that I have had it right all along: that I will not see God, that there is no heaven or Judgment Day.

For Vonnegut the religious skeptic, talk of faith and deep examination of biblical stories are never far away and often the focus of a character or an entire work. Though he can't bring himself to believe in a supernatural deity or the stories in support of such a being, his faith in humanity's capacity to rationally approach vexing if not life-threatening problems is ever present. It is through Nietzsche that he sees a new way of appreciating his own brand of faith— and Twain's as well. (FWD XVI) "I myself seem to be coming across really important stuff very late in life. I am sixty-three, but it was only two months ago that I found a quotation from the works of Friedrich Wilhelm Nietzsche, a contemporary of **Mark Twain**, which explains and justifies the spiritual condition of myself, my Indiana ancestors, and my children, and of **Mark Twain** as well, I think. Nietzsche said in effect, and in German of course, that only a person of great faith could afford to be a skeptic.

For both Twain and Vonnegut, the fiction of resurrection implies a return to an often hostile world. As Vonnegut notes, The funniest American of his time, **Mark Twain**, found life for himself and everybody else so stressful when he was in his seventies, like me, that he wrote as follows: "I have never wanted any released friend of mine restored to life since I reached manhood." That is in an essay on the sudden death of his daughter Jean a few days earlier. Among those he wouldn't have resurrected were Jean, and another daughter, Susy, and his beloved wife, and his best friend, Henry Rogers.

Twain didn't live to see World War One, but still he felt that way (*TQ* 1).

Twain as Icon

Vonnegut uses Twain's iconic stature along with that of others to help settle the puzzling psyche of Eliot Rosewater. When examined by Dr. Browne for explanations about Eliot Rosewater's dedication to social justice and schemes for the redistribution of wealth, Eliot recalls dreaming about genuine American legends as well as Thorsten Veblen. "I ask him what he dreams about," the doctor continued, "and he tells me, 'Samuel Gompers, **Mark Twain**, and Alexander Hamilton.' I ask him if his father ever appears in his dreams, and he says, 'No, but Thorsten Veblen often does.' Mrs. Rosewater, I'm defeated. I resign" (*GBR* 2). *Gompers represents the expansionist mentality of a growing America (as well as Vonnegut's own newspaper roots), Twain its moral compass, and Hamilton the advocate for what became the financial structure of the newly established American democracy. Veblen, however, is the check on unbridled American capitalism at the core of the novel's concerns. As Vonnegut says about the doctor's limited imagination that leads to his resignation,* Eliot seemed merely amused by the doctor's dismissal.

Vonnegut uses Twain as another of those hopeful American tinkerers, or at least enlightened industrial thinkers, whose best intentions sometimes go nowhere but not for trying. Their technology lags behind their vision. (*PS* 1) Neither utopia now works much better than the Page typesetting machine, in which **Mark Twain** invested and lost a fortune. That beautiful contraption actually set type just once, when only **Twain** and the inventor were watching. **Twain** called all the other investors to see this miracle, but, by the time they got there, the inventor had taken the machine all apart again. It never ran again. Peace.

In A Man Without a Country, Vonnegut pairs Twain with President Lincoln as part of his continuing pride in hailing from the Midwest. He sees in them the plain-spoken, sensible concerns that put

man at the forefront of earthly existence. He also sees in them the sober reflections of adults who faced the unanticipated twists of war that forever provoke heinous atrocities and countless tragedies. Vonnegut obliquely parallels the essential Twain with himself, observing behaviors that are all too real and all too predictable from one conflict, one era, to the next. In this case, Vonnegut's reflections have to do with President George W. Bush's invasion of Iraq. Vonnegut finds comfort with his midwestern predecessors. As is so often the case for Vonnegut, his desire to reach back in time for the combined wisdom of Twain and Lincoln has to do with the effects of realpolitik when faced with the very inhumane behaviors of countries at war.

Where are **Mark Twain** and Abraham Lincoln now when we need them? They were country boys from Middle America, and both of them made the American people laugh at themselves and appreciate really important, really moral jokes. Imagine what they would have to say today.

One of the most humiliated and heartbroken pieces **Mark Twain** ever wrote was about the slaughter of six hundred Moro men, women, and children by our soldiers during our liberation of the people of the Philippines after the Spanish-American War. Our brave commander was Leonard Wood, who now has a fort named after him. Fort Leonard Wood in Missouri (*MWC* 7).

At a later point in A Man Without a Country, Vonnegut pairs Twain with Einstein as celebrated humanitarians who see no relief or salvation in man's endeavors. The credibility of his respected idols makes it no easier to reluctantly agree with their assessments about the predictability of inhumane acts and eternal fearfulness throughout man's checkered history and promised future. (*MWC* 8) Like my distinct betters Einstein and **Twain**, I now give up on people, too. I am a veteran of the Second World War and I have to say this is not the first time I have surrendered to a pitiless war machine.

My last words? "Life is no way to treat an animal, not even a mouse."

While writing in the midst of America's second war with Iraq, Vonnegut laments the lame series of actions that he believes wrongfully installed George W. Bush as president. In correspondence with an unknown acquaintance, Vonnegut lets fly at the series of mistakes, illogical reasoning, and vaporous myths that should have prevented such incidents and the war itself. In the end, Vonnegut cites Twain's The Mysterious Stranger *almost as a protest against America's holy warriors, the god and guns constituency that is the political bedrock of America's right wing.*

(MWC 10) How can the American public be so stupid? People still believe that Bush was elected, that he cares about us and has some idea of what he is doing. How can we "save" people by killing them and destroying their country? How can we strike first on the belief that we will soon be attacked? No sense, no reason, no moral grounds have gotten through to him. He is nothing but a moron puppet leading us all over the precipice. Why can't people see that the military dictator in the White House has no clothes?

I told him that if he doubted that we are demons in Hell, he should read *The Mysterious Stranger,* which **Mark Twain** wrote in 1898, long before the First World War (1914–1918). In the title story he proves to his own grim satisfaction, and to mine as well, that Satan and not God created the planet earth and "the damned human race." If you doubt that, read your morning paper. Never mind what paper. Never mind what date.

Vonnegut's Parallels with Twain's Humor

Vonnegut sees a parallel in using humor to defuse both his anxieties and his audience's about past associations (valid or not) with what Twain may have faced. (PS Funnier on Paper Than Most People) And it may be that **Mark Twain** drew some of his comic energy from a similar uneasiness. He had served the Confederacy briefly, after all, in the bloodiest war in American history, and later faced paying audiences of, among others, Union veterans and their wives.

Aware that most people are prompted by negative connotations when hearing a German name, Vonnegut resorts to humor as a bridge with his audience. He bares the shame of his ancestral homeland's leg- *acy but quickly points out his honorable service in the American military.*

ONE reason I feel the need to be funnier on paper than most of my colleagues is that I have a German name, which can be counted on to remind almost any sort of American for at least a microsecond of German enemies in two world wars. I myself, a prisoner of war of the Germans, am so reminded for at least that microsecond when I hear a German name. I was on our side, remember? So it is a good idea for me to tell a joke as soon as possible. I have spoken to, and actually liked, several German veterans of the Second World War who live in America now. They, too, become screamingly funny as soon as possible. (PS Funnier on Paper Than Most People)

Understanding Twain's Sense of Story

Among other talents, Vonnegut proves to be an apt literary critic when presenting the structure of storytelling by referencing Twain's A Connecticut Yankee in King Arthur's Court. *Jokesters such as Twain and himself are at a disadvantage if the humor fails to take hold, but the rewards are high since such narratives may be highly efficient in delivering nuanced answers to complex narrative propositions. Between the humor and multi-level appreciation of the human predicament, Vonnegut's prescription for his audience is one that is able to piece together disparate ideas streaming through the narrative veil. He requires a level of critical thinking and reasoning that is too often missing.*

Using humor to present essential questions and answers to complex social problems, Vonnegut notes that Twain and he are particularly equipped to handle a succession of weighty matters without needing to present dry, lengthy, academic explanations of the matters at hand, enabling readers to quickly move from one concern to another, maintaining a high level of entertainment without preaching. However, he is aware that critics are often loath to find spiritual insights from breezy, comedy-filled text (especially while the author is alive). "This is the secret of good storytelling: to lie, but to keep the arithmetic sound. A storyteller, like any other sort of enthusiastic liar, is on an unpredictable adventure. His initial lie, his premise, will suggest many new lies of its own. The storyteller must choose among them, seeking those which are most believable, which keep the arithmetic sound. Thus does a story generate itself" (PS Mark Twain).

While making passing references to Twain's A Tramp Abroad, The Prince and the Pauper, Life on the Mississippi, *and* Huckleberry Finn, *Vonnegut digests the secret of good storytelling through* A Connecticut Yankee in King Arthur's Court. *His more extended illustration of this novel serves to present a science-fiction precursor that is more about human questions than it is science. As he explains,*

(PS Mark Twain) "**Mark Twain** died in 1910, at the age of seventy-five and four years before the start of World War One. I have heard it said that he predicted that war and all the wars after that in *A Connecticut Yankee*. It was not **Twain** who did that. It was his premise.

"How appalled this entertainer must have been to have his innocent joking about technology and superstition lead him inexorably to such a ghastly end. Suddenly and horrifyingly, what had seemed so clear throughout the book was not clear at all— who was good, who was bad, who was wise, who was foolish. I ask you, Who was most crazed by superstition and bloodlust, the men with the swords or the men with the Gatling guns?

"And I suggest to you that the fatal premise of *A Connecticut Yankee* remains a chief premise of Western civilization, and increasingly of world civilization, to wit: the sanest, most likeable persons, employing superior technology, will enforce sanity throughout the world."

As Peter Reed notes in reference to Vonnegut's early short stories, **Twain**'s literary legacy casts a long shadow that easily fits Vonnegut's structures and sensibilities. Vonnegut's humorous stories fit that American tradition of the tall tale epitomized by **Mark Twain**. "Tom Edison's Shaggy Dog," which appears in *Welcome to the Monkey House*, is the classic example of the form. Both "Mnemonics" and "Any Reasonable Offer" in this collection rise to an abrupt joke ending (BAG Preface).

Between the science and humor, the midwestern voice and rationalism, Kurt and big brother Ber-

nard *find much of their own reflection in Twain. Vonnegut recalls flying to Indianapolis to bury their sister Alice when Bernard offers them a moment of comic relief through Twain.* (Slap Prologue) While my brother and I waited for the plane to take off for Indianapolis, he made me a present of a joke by **Mark Twain**—about an opera **Twain** had seen in Italy. **Twain** said that he hadn't heard anything like it " . . . since the orphanage burned down."

We laughed.

Mark Vonnegut Recalls His Father's Connection to Twain

Mark Vonnegut confirms in the introduction to his father's posthumously published collection of previously unpublished short stories, Armageddon in Retrospect, *that writing was a spiritual pursuit for his father, supported by the models of* Jonah, Lincoln, Melville, *and* **Twain**.

(ARM Introduction) "Writing was a spiritual exercise for my father, the only thing he really believed in. He wanted to get things right but never thought that his writing was going to have much effect on the course of things. His models were Jonah, Lincoln, Melville, and **Twain**.

"He rewrote and rewrote and rewrote, muttering whatever he had just written over and over, tilting his head back and forth, gesturing with his hands, changing the pitch and rhythm of the words. Then he would pause, thoughtfully rip the barely written-on sheet of typing paper from the typewriter, crumple it up, throw it away, and start over again. It seemed like an odd way for a grown-up to spend his time, but I was just a child who didn't know much."

Mark Vonnegut uses the Twain and Lincoln pairing in his introduction to Armageddon in Retrospect *to cast his father's lot with the wise perspective of his idols.* "He tried always to be on the side of the angels. He didn't think the war in Iraq was going to happen, right up until it did. It broke his heart not because he gave a damn about Iraq but because he loved America and believed that the land and people of Lincoln and **Twain** would find a way to be right. He believed, like his immigrant forefathers, that America could be a beacon and a paradise" (*ARM* Introduction).

See also: Slap Prologue; *PS* The First Amendment; *PS* Roots; *PS* People; *PS* "Mark Twain"–speech by KV at the one-hundredth anniversary celebration of the completion of Mark Twain's fanciful residence in Hartford, Conn."; *PS* In the Capital of the World; *FWD* V; VII; XVI; XIX–XXI; *TQ* 6; *MWC* 7; 12; *ARM* Introduction (by Mark Vonnegut).

U-99. *This Nazi submarine intercepts Bokonon on his return voyage from England to Tobago. They take him prisoner and sink his schooner, the* Lady's Slipper. *The sub is then captured and sunk by the British destroyer* Raven.

Ubriaco, Frank and Marilyn. *Frank is the fifty-three-year-old owner of the Hotel Royalton Coffee Shop, which in turn is owned by Hospitality Associates, Ltd., a RAMJAC subsidiary, in* Jailbird. *Frank eagerly participates in every aspect of the restaurant's operation, from taking orders to cooking to working the cash register. Despite feeling ugly and dirty, Walter Starbuck is greeted warmly and treated well by Frank and his employees. In recognition of the humane way Walter is treated, Mary Kathleen O'Looney makes Ubriaco an executive vice president of RAMJAC's McDonald's Hamburgers Division.*

Ubriaco is most notable for his misshapen hand. A year before Walter met him, Frank dropped his Accutron Bulova watch into the Fry-o-lator and thoughtlessly stuck his hand in to retrieve it.

Once living the high life as a RAMJAC executive, Frank meets the seventeen-year-old Marilyn at a discotheque and marries her. He plays on Marilyn's intrigue over the single white glove worn over his bad hand by telling her he was burned by a Chinese Communist flamethrower in the Korean War. He eventually tells her the truth.

Frank's one great innovation for McDonald's is to replace the numbers on the cash registers with pictures of food items. This is necessary because of the increasing difficulty of getting new employees smart enough to deal with basic restaurant arithmetic.

Ukwende, Dr. Cyprian. *From the Indaro tribe in Nigeria and equipped with a medical degree from Harvard, Ukwende is an intern at the Midland City County Hospital.* (BC 6) He felt no kinship with . . . any American blacks. He felt kinship only with Indaros. *He is the presiding physician when 108-year-old Mary Young dies, the black woman from Kentucky whose* parents had been slaves in Kentucky.

Ukwende was staying at Dwayne Hoover's Holiday Inn until he could find a suitable apartment. He was one of the physicians on the ambulance responding to the havoc wrought by Dwayne Hoover's violent outburst.

Ukwende's ancestors had kidnapped an ancestor of *(Eddie)* Key's on the West Coast of Africa, a man named Ojumwa. The Indaros sold him for a musket to British slave traders, who took him on a sailing ship named the "Skylark" to Charleston, South Carolina, where he was auctioned off as a self-propelled, self-repairing farm machine (BC 24).

Ulm, Arthur Garvey. *One of the many examples of Eliot Rosewater's altruism gone awry.* (GBR 6) "That poor **Arthur** told Eliot he wanted to be free to tell the truth, regardless of the economic consequences, and Eliot wrote him a tremendous check right then and there." *Eliot's belief in and hopes for an unfettered and truthful arts community come crashing down after giving Ulm the freedom to produce without the perpetual fear of poverty.*

Under the spell of Eliot's beneficence and cryptic quips, Ulm takes the money and is transformed into a novelist whose sense of truth and courage are manifested in an eight-hundred-page pornographic novel. (GBR 6) The name of the book was *Get with Child a Mandrake Root,* a line from a poem by John Donne. The dedication read, "For Eliot Rosewater, my compassionate turquoise." And under that was another quotation from Donne:

A compassionate turquoise which doth tell
By looking pale, the wearer is not well.

A covering letter from **Ulm** explained that the book was going to be published by Palindrome Press in time for Christmas, and was going to be a joint selection, along with *The Cradle of Erotica,* of a major book club.

You have no doubt forgotten me, Compassionate Turquoise, *the letter said in part.* The

Arthur Garvey Ulm you knew was a man well worth forgetting. What a coward he was, and what a fool he was to think he was a poet! And what a long, long time it took him to understand exactly how generous and kind your cruelty was! How much you managed to tell me about what was wrong with me, and what I should do about it, and how few words you used! Here then (fourteen years later) are eight hundred pages of prose by me. They could not have been created by me without you, and I do not mean your money. (Money is shit, which is one of the things I have tried to say in the book.) I mean your insistence that the truth be told about this sick, sick society of ours, and that the words for the telling could be found on the walls of restrooms*: . . .

"Let them shoot me, let them hang me, but I have told the truth. The gnashing of the teeth of the Pharisees, Madison Avenue phonies and Philistines will be music to my ears. With your divine assistance, I have let the Djin of truth about them out of the bottle, and they will never, never, never ever get it back in!"

Eliot began to read avidly the truths **Ulm** expected to get killed for telling:

"CHAPTER ONE"

"I twisted her arm until she opened her legs, and she gave a little scream, half joy, half pain (how do you figure a woman?): as I rammed the old avenger home."

In Timequake, *the pornographic novelist of* God Bless You, Mr. Rosewater *is now a poet and an employee of the American Academy of Arts and Letters. More important, he represents the spirit of Vonnegut's deceased war buddy and onetime Pennsylvania prosecutor Bernard V. O'Hare at the climactic clambake.* (TQ 62) Only the dead had doppelgängers at that party back in 2001. **Arthur Garvey Ulm**, poet

* The reference is to the couplet Eliot earlier recalls, tellingly, as one of his favorite rhymes: "We don't piss in your ashtrays, / So please don't throw cigarettes in our urinals" (GBR 6).

and Resident Secretary of Xanadu, an employee of the American Academy of Arts and Letters, was short and had a big nose, like my war buddy Bernard V. O'Hare.

Ulm, Lowell. *The owner of a local car wash and director of Midland County's civil defense response unit. Rudy Waltz asks Ulm to take radioactivity measurements with his government-issued Geiger counter inside the Waltz's Avondale home. Ulm contacts the federal government with news about the extremely hot mantelpiece.* (DD 27) Mother and I had not yet begun to speculate seriously about what the radioactive mantelpiece might have done to our health, nor had we been encouraged to do so. Nor would we ever be encouraged to do so. **Ulm**, the director of civil defense and car-wash tycoon, had been getting advice on our case over the telephone from somebody at the Nuclear Regulatory Commission in Washington, D.C., to the effect that the most important thing was that nobody panic. In order to prevent panic, the workmen who had torn out our fireplace, wearing protective clothing provided by **Ulm**, had been sworn to secrecy—in the name of patriotism, of national security.

uncritical, uncritically (love, bliss, companionship, respect, nurturer). (ST 5) Unk had no way of judging the quality of the information contained in the letter. He accepted it all hungrily, **uncritically**.

(MN 10) No matter what I was really, no matter what I really meant, **uncritical love** was what I needed—and my Helga was the angel who gave it to me.

No young person on earth is so excellent in all respects as to need no **uncritical love**. Good Lord—as youngsters play their parts in political tragedies with casts of billions, **uncritical love** is the only real treasure they can look for.

(GBR 5) There was a tough element among the Rosewater County poor who, as a matter of pride, stayed away from Eliot and his **uncritical love**, who had the guts to get out of Rosewater County and look for work in Indianapolis or Chicago or Detroit. (GBR 14) "It seems to me," said Trout, "that the main lesson Eliot learned is that people can use all the **uncritical love** they can get."

(*BC* 19) And somebody squealed on him. The Emperor Diocletian had him shot by archers. The picture Mary Alice smiled at with such **uncritical bliss** showed a human being who was so full of arrows that he looked like a porcupine. *The painting described by Vonnegut is an El Greco depicting the death of Saint Sebastian.*

(*WFG* Why They Read Hesse) Again and again, his *(Hesse's)* holy wanderers love wine too much. They do something about it, too. They resolve to keep out of taverns, though they miss the **uncritical companionship** they've had there.

(*Slap* Prologue) When a child, and not watching comedians on film or listening to comedians on the radio, I used to spend a lot of time rolling around on rugs with **uncritically** affectionate dogs we had.

(*PS* Religion) What is human dignity, then? It is the favorable opinion, respectful and **uncritical**, which we hold of those most familiar to us. It has been found that we can hold that same good opinion of strangers, if those who teach us and otherwise lead us tell us to.

(*PS* Religion) "There is this drawback, though: If you give to that sort of a stranger the **uncritical respect** that you give to friends and relatives, you will also want to understand and help him. There is no way to avoid this."

(*Blue* 8) The other fillip was the undertaker's assumption that Father was a Mohammedan. This was exciting to him. It was his biggest adventure in being **uncritically pious** in a madly pluralistic democracy.

(*Blue* 32) She (*Edith Taft Fairbanks, Rabo's second wife*) was a magical tamer of almost any sort of animal, an overwhelmingly loving and **uncritical nurturer** of anything and everything that looked half alive.

(*FWD* II) Our father when I, his youngest child, got to know him was, understandably, desperate for **uncritical friendship** from a member of the reputedly compassionate sex, since our mother (his wife) was going insane. Late at night, and always in the privacy of our home, and never with guests present, she expressed hatred for Father as corrosive as hydrofluoric acid. Hydrofluoric acid can eat its way out of a glass bottle, and then through a tabletop and then through the floor, and then straight to Hell.

(*FWD* XI) Back in the Great Depression, the Royal Astronomers used to say that a United States deprived of that wisdom was nothing but a United States of radio quiz shows and music straight out of the jungles of Darkest Africa. They say now that the same subtraction leaves us a United States of nothing but television quiz shows and rock and roll, which leads, they say, inexorably to dementia. But I find **uncritical respect** for most works by great thinkers of long ago unpleasant, because they almost all accepted as natural and ordinary the belief that females and minority races and the poor were on earth to be uncomplaining, hardworking, respectful, and loyal servants of white males, who did the important thinking and exercised leadership.

(*BAG* Introduction) My own stories may be interesting, nonetheless, as relics from a time, before there was television, when an author might support a family by writing stories that satisfied **uncritical readers** of magazines, and earning thereby enough free time in which to write serious novels. When I became a full-time freelance in 1950, I expected to be doing that for the rest of my life.

underground. (*PP* XXX) There were circles under Katharine's gentle, wondering eyes, and she looked startled when Lasher called on her, as though Lasher, the meeting, the **underground chamber**, had suddenly risen about her in her clean, girlish world. "Oh," she said, and rattled the papers on the table before her.

(*MN* Introduction) There were no particular targets for the bombs. The hope was that they would create a lot of kindling and drive firemen **underground**.

(*MN* 11) He had a wife, all right, but not **underground** in Indianapolis. *George Kraft / Iona Potapov lied to Campbell about his marital status.*

(*MN* 44) That was the undiluted evil in me, the evil that had had its effect on millions, the disgusting creature good people wanted dead and **underground**—

(*MN* 45) Surprise: Heinz is a Jew, a member of the **anti-Nazi underground** during the war, an Israeli agent after the war and up to the present time.

(*CC* 118) During our first day and night **underground**, tornadoes rattled our manhole cover many times an hour.

(*CC* 122) The menage consisted of Frank, little Newt, and the Crosbys. They had survived in a **dungeon** in the palace, one far shallower and more unpleasant than the **oubliette**. They had moved out the moment the winds had abated, while Mona and I had stayed **underground** for another three days.

(*GBR* 2) I had blocked the **underground rivers** that connected her to the Atlantic, Pacific, and Indian Oceans, and made her content with being a splash pool three feet across, four inches deep, chlorinated, and painted blue. *This is part of Dr. Brown's description of his treatment of Sylvia Rosewater.*

(*MH* Unready to Wear) "You're right about how fast things change," said Doctor Remenzel. "You're wrong about the colored people who've eaten here. This used to be a busy part of the **Underground Railroad**."

(*BC* 13) The **underground stream** which passed through the bowels of Sacred Miracle Cave was polluted by some sort of industrial waste which formed bubbles as tough as ping-pong balls.

(*Slap* 41) The truth was, though, that he was perfectly sane. He had been stationed for the past eleven years in the bottom of a secret, **underground silo** in Rock Creek Park. I had never heard of the silo before. *This is Wilbur Swain's recollection of his meeting with Captain Bernard O'Hare.*

(*PS* Self-Interview) VONNEGUT: The Germans got funeral pyres going, burning the bodies to keep them from stinking and from spreading disease. 130,000 corpses were hidden **underground**. It was a terribly elaborate Easter egg hunt.

(*Blue* 4) "I wrote a book about it," she said. "Rather—I wrote about people like you: children of a parent who had survived some sort of mass killing. It's called *The* **Underground**. . . ."

The formidable widow Berman told me the plot of *The* **Underground**, which is this: Three girls, one black, one Jewish and one Japanese, feel drawn together and separate from the rest of their classmates for reasons they can't explain. They form a little club which they call, again for reasons they can't explain, "*The* **Underground**."

(*Blue* 34) They (*the canvases of the triptych "Windsor Blue Number Seventeen"*) were recognized for what they were, with shreds of Sateen DuraLuxe

clinging to them here and there, by an inspector from Matsumoto's insurance company, who was looking for fire hazards deep **underground**.

(*Blue* 35) And I had made a schematic cut through the earth below them, so as to show their cellars, too, just as a museum display might give away the secrets of animals' burrows **underground**. *This is part of Karabekian's description of his* "Now It's the Women's Turn."

(*HP* 6) I had won my Silver Star for finding and personally killing 5 enemy soldiers who were hiding in a **tunnel underground**.

(*FWD* XV) What I should have said from the pulpit was that we weren't *going* to Hell. We were *in* Hell, thanks to technology which was telling us what to do, instead of the other way around. And it wasn't just TV. It was weapons which could actually kill everything half a world away. It was vehicles powered by glurp from **underground** which could make a fat old lady go a mile a minute while picking her nose and listening to the radio. And so on. (In what spiritual detail, I should have asked, did the glurp-powered automobile or Harley-Davidson differ from freebased cocaine? And was there anything we wouldn't do to ensure that the glurp kept on coming?)

(*BAG* Preface by Peter Reed) This collection includes stories that draw on Vonnegut's World War Two experiences. The events on which *Slaughterhouse-Five* was based are by now widely known: how Vonnegut was captured by the Germans at the Battle of the Bulge, was held as a prisoner of war in Dresden, was sheltered in an **underground meat storage room** when that city was incinerated in massive air raids, and after the Nazi defeat wandered briefly in a Germany awash in refugees before he was reunited with American forces. "Der Arme Dolmetscher," "Souvenir," and "The Cruise of the *Jolly Roger*" treat the aftermath of war with a varying mix of humor and poignancy.
See also: PP XXI; *CC* 22; *Blue* 4.

The Underground. *The name of Circe Berman's book, which is thematically centered on survivor's syndrome. Rabo recalls:* The formidable widow Berman told me the plot of *The* **Underground,** which is this: Three girls, one black, one Jewish and one Japanese, feel drawn together and separate from the rest of their classmates for reasons they can't explain. They form a little club which they call, again for reasons they can't explain, "**The Underground.**"

But then it turns out that all three have a parent or grandparent who has survived some man-made catastrophe, and who, without meaning to, passed on to them the idea that the wicked were the living and that the good were dead.

The black is descended from a survivor of the massacre of Ibos in Nigeria. The Japanese is a descendant of a survivor of the atom-bombing of Nagasaki. The Jew is a descendant of a survivor of the Nazi Holocaust (*Blue* 4).

Unger, Craig. *While Vonnegut often decries the lack of informed literacy among the general populace, he foists a spirited defense of books versus tabloids, citing the heroic work of librarians and serious writers to keep the pursuit of knowledge private and expansive. He cites Unger as one of the serious writers helping to maintain an informed populace while staring down the competition from an increasingly useless, irrelevant but loud mass media.* (MWC 9) While on the subject of burning books, I want to congratulate librarians, not famous for their physical strength, their powerful political connections or great wealth, who, all over this country, have staunchly resisted antidemocratic bullies who have tried to remove certain books from their shelves, and destroyed records rather than have to reveal to thought police the names of persons who have checked out those titles.

So the America I loved still exists, if not in the White House, the Supreme Court, the Senate, the House of Representatives, or the media. The America I loved still exists at the front desks of our public libraries.

And still on the subject of books: Our daily news sources, newspapers and TV, are now so craven, so unvigilant on behalf of the American people, so uninformative, that only in books do we learn what's really going on.

I will cite an example: *House of Bush, House of Saud* by **Craig Unger**, published in early 2004, that humiliating, shameful, blood-soaked year.

Unification Church Korean Evangelical Association. *The church owns the Niagara Power and Light Company, which shuts off the electricity to the* prison in Scipio and Tarkington College after the inmates break out (HP 14).

Unitarian, Unitarian Universalist. *Vonnegut often claims to be a Unitarian, though how he distinguishes Unitarianism from agnosticism is unclear—and perhaps irrelevant. His parents were married in Indianapolis's First Unitarian Church. His son Mark was interested in becoming a Unitarian minister when an undergraduate at Swarthmore.*

Vonnegut's first expression of Unitarian uncertainty is meant as a partial explanation of the mercurial Harry Nash. (MH Who Am I This Time?) Somebody said one time that Harry ought to go to a psychiatrist so he could be something important and colorful in real life, too—so he could get married anyway, and maybe get a better job than just clerking in Miller's Hardware Store for fifty dollars a week. But I don't know what a psychiatrist could have turned up about him that the town didn't already know. The trouble with Harry was he'd been left on the doorstep of the **Unitarian Church** when he was a baby, and he never did find out who his parents were.

(WFG Yes, We Have No Nirvanas) A **Unitarian** minister heard that I had been to see Maharishi Mahesh Yogi, guru to The Beatles and Donovan and Mia Farrow, and he asked me, "Is he a fake?" His name is Charley. **Unitarians** don't believe in anything. I am a **Unitarian.**

Walter Starbuck's religious background is somewhat complex, though his son takes a more determined position. (JB 4) I myself was nothing. My father had been secretly baptized a Roman Catholic in Poland, a religion that was suppressed at the time. He grew up to be an agnostic. My mother was baptized a Greek Orthodox in Lithuania, but became a Roman Catholic in Cleveland. Father would never go to church with her. I myself was baptized a Roman Catholic, but aspired to my father's indifference, and quit going to church when I was twelve. When I applied for admission to Harvard, old Mr. McCone, a Baptist, told me to classify myself as a Congregationalist, which I did.

My son is an active **Unitarian**, I hear. His wife told me that she was a Methodist, but that she sang in an Episcopal Church every Sunday for pay. Why not?

(*PS* Religion) I went to a **Unitarian church** for a while, and it might show. The minister said one Easter Sunday that, if we listened closely to the bell on his church, we would hear that it was singing, over and over again, 'No hell, no hell, no hell.' No matter what we did in life, he said, we wouldn't burn throughout eternity in hell. We wouldn't even fry for ten or fifteen minutes. He was just guessing, of course.

(*PS* Religion) In this dream, if it is a dream, it is the two-hundredth anniversary of the birth of William Ellery Channing, a principal founder of **Unitarianism** in the United States. I wish that I had been born into a society like his—small and congenial and prosperous and self-sufficient. The people around here had ancestors in common then. They looked a lot like each other, dressed a lot like each other, enjoyed the same amusements and food. They were generally agreed as to what was good and what was evil—what God was like, who Jesus was.

(*PS* Religion) When Channing began preaching a new sort of sermon in this town, a sort of sermon we now perceive as **Unitarian**, he was urging his parishioners to credit with human dignity as great as their own persons not at all like their friends and relatives. The time to acknowledge the dignity of strangers, even black ones, had come.

(*FWD* XVI) In order not to seem a spiritual quadriplegic to strangers trying to get a fix on me, I sometimes say I am a **Unitarian Universalist** (I breathe). So that denomination claims me as one of its own. It honored me by having me deliver a lecture at a gathering in Rochester, New York, in June 1986. I began (almost exactly as I would begin at the graduation ceremonies at the University of Rhode Island):

"There was a newspaper humorist named Kin Hubbard in my hometown of Indianapolis, where my ancestors were Freethinkers and then **Unitarians** or not much of anything as far as religious labels go. Kin Hubbard attended a graduation ceremony out there in Indiana. He commented afterward on the graduation address to the departing seniors. He said it might be better to spread out the really important stuff over four years instead of saving it all up until the very end."

(*FWD* XVI) "When I say that the **Unitarian Uni-**

versalists, the people who know pure baloney when they hear it, are something like the early Christians in the catacombs, am I suggesting that contempt for baloney will someday be as widespread as Christianity is today? Well the example of Christianity is not encouraging, actually, since it was nothing but a poor people's religion, a servant's religion, a slave's religion, a woman's religion, a child's religion, and would have remained such if it hadn't stopped taking the Sermon on the Mount seriously and joined forces with the vain and rich and violent. I can't imagine that you would want to do that, to give up everything you believe in order to play a bigger part in world history.

See also: *ST* 10; *MN* 13; 38; *PS* Roots; *PS* Playmates; *PS* Religion; *FWD* Preface.

Universal Will to Become (**UWTB**). *The mystical Tralfamadorian source of energy and intergalactic communication.* (*ST* 6) **UWTB** is what makes universes out of nothingness—that makes nothingness insist on becoming somethingness.

UWTB powers Salo's spaceship, and he uses half his supply for Winston Niles Rumfoord's Martian colonization and invasion force.

As a communications medium, UWTB transmits messages and helps bring about behavioral changes in other life forms. (*ST* 12) It is grotesque for anyone as primitive as an Earthling to explain how these swift communications were effected. Suffice it to say, in such primitive company, that the Tralfamadorians were able to make certain impulses from the **Universal Will to Become** echo through the vaulted architecture of the Universe with about three times the speed of light. And they were able to focus and modulate these impulses so as to influence creatures far, far away, and inspire them to serve Tralfamadorian ends.

It was a marvelous way to get things done in places far, far away from Tralfamadore. It was easily the fastest way.

In this manner, all sorts of famous architectural landmarks were used over centuries of Earthling time to transmit messages to Salo. This included the Great Wall of China, the Golden House of the Roman Emperor Nero, the Kremlin, and the Palace of the League of Nations.

University of Vermont. *In the short story "Lovers Anonymous," the promising and beautiful Sheila Hinckley attends the University of Vermont before dropping out as a junior to marry Herb White.*

Unk (*see* **Malachi Constant**).

unnamed bartender. *In the short story "Bagombo Snuff Box" (q v), Eddie Laird stops in for a drink in the town of his military posting during the war and strikes up a conversation with the bartender, telling him a series of romantic lies about his globetrotting life and wondering out loud if it was okay to call up his ex-wife for a visit. The bartender listens patiently and recounts for Eddie many of the changes to the town since his military service. Much of the town had been converted to large chain stores in place of the locally owned establishments Eddie once knew.*

unnamed bartender. *In the short story "Find Me a Dream," the unnamed bartender is first asked by Arvin Borders about the whereabouts of his new fiancée. Later, while serving drinks for the clarinetist and bandleader Andy Middleton (the second drink is for her), the bartender tells Middleton that Borders is looking for Hildy.*

unnamed beautiful woman. *In the short story "The Cruise of the* Jolly Roger," *collected in* Bagombo Snuff Box (1999), *this enigmatic beauty helps reaffirm Major Durant's sense of displacement now that he is retired, an emptiness he has not felt since his homeless days during the Great Depression. Durant fled to Chatham, at the elbow of Cape Cod, and found himself beside a* **beautiful woman** *at the foot of a lighthouse there. Had he been in his old uniform, seeming as he'd liked to seem in the old days, about to leave on a dangerous mission, he and the* **woman** *might have strolled off together. Women had once treated him like a small boy with special permission to eat icing off cakes. But the* **woman** *looked away without interest. He was nobody and nothing. The spark was gone.*

His former swashbuckling spirits returned for an hour or two during a brief blow off the dunes of Cape Cod's east coast, but there was no one aboard to notice. When he reached the sheltered harbor at Provincetown and went ashore, he was a hollow man again, who didn't have to be anywhere at any time, whose life was all behind him.

unnamed blond German escort. *In the short story "Souvenir," collected in* Bagombo Snuff Box (1999), *this out-of-uniform soldier is in the service of General Heinz Guderian as they try to escape advancing Russian tanks and instead head for the American lines to surrender. The pair of fleeing Nazis come upon Eddie and Buzzer, American POWs on the day of their release from captivity. They try negotiating a deal for the Americans' uniforms in exchange for the general's bejeweled pocket watch. At the moment they lead the Americans behind a wall to make the exchange, Soviet tanks begin an assault on the town and the Germans' true plan becomes tragically clear. Eddie and Buzzer and the old man and the* **blond** *found themselves behind the wall where the* **blond** *had said the Americans could swap their uniforms for the watch and civilian clothes. In the uproar, during which anybody could do anything, and nobody cared what anybody else did, the* **blond** *shot Buzzer in the head. He aimed his pistol at Eddie. He fired. He missed.*

That had evidently been the plan all along, to kill Eddie and Buzzer. . . . Everything the **blond** *needed was on Buzzer's body. When Eddie peered over the wall to see if Buzzer was still alive, the* **blond** *was stripping the body. The old man now had the pistol. He put its muzzle in his mouth and blew his brains out.*

The **blond** *walked off with Buzzer's clothes and dog tags.*

unnamed butler. *In the short story "Runaways," the unnamed butler passes Rice Brentner's phone call to Annie Southard into the hands of her mother, who believes it is Bob Counsel calling to check on Annie. Believing it is Bob Counsel allows Mrs. Southard to have hope again for her daughter's future, but its greater purpose is to set up the second attempt for Rice and Annie to run away.*

unnamed clerk. *In the opening of "A Present for Big Saint Nick," the unnamed clerk in the jewelry store helps Bernie O'Hare and Mr. Pullman find the most unimaginably gauche gifts for their employer, the mobster Big Nick. Each customer has their fam-*

ily with them on the way to the Christmas party, so clearly buying a gift for their cruel and tasteless boss is something they have put off until the last possible minute. The clerk is an unassuming bystander to the banter between the two families about their low opinion of Big Nick, and he also witnesses the two families trying to care for their sons suffering Santa-phobia. Nick's tradition of dressing up as Saint Nick for his Christmas party, where he bribes the children with presents in between berating their parents, has resulted in their tremulous fear of even small plastic Santa Claus figurines.

unnamed customer. *In the short story "The Powder-Blue Dragon," collected in* Bagombo Snuff Box (1999), *the customer speaks with car dealer Bill Daggett about purchasing an MG for his unseen son. The young man had been hounding his father about getting a Marittima-Frascati. The $5,651 price tag is way over the line for his father,* an urbane and tweedy gentleman, *but he has no problem writing a check for the car before him.*

Though the customer has difficulty recalling the name of the car that is the subject of his son's great desire, Kiah Higgins has no problem jogging his memory despite having only "Mara-something" as a prompt because it is Kiah's obsession. Further proof of Kiah's intensity about the car is his ability to rattle off the car's cost down to the dollar. Despite his help-fulness, the customer neither thanks Kiah for his as-sistance nor asks his name, leaving the orphaned young man anonymous and unacknowledged, traits very much at the core of his psychological troubles.

unnamed delivery boy (*see* **Mr. Kornblum**).

unnamed drum major. *In the short story "Ambi-tious Sophomore," collected in* Bagombo Snuff Box (1999), *this insolent and sneering high school stu-dent from another school disrespectfully challenges Lincoln High's band director, George M. Helm-holtz, when he sees the opulence of the latter's uni-form by asking,* Is this the Doormen's Convention? *Helmholtz sends the rude young man back to his own band where he finds Leroy Duggan, the bell-shaped star sophomore piccolo player from Lincoln, dressed in a heavily padded custom-fit tunic that transforms his appearance into a larger-than-life, tri-*

angular, heroic silhouette. Duggan is fraternizing with a young female piccoloist from the drum ma-jor's band. The drum major, probably out of frustra-tion over losing to Lincoln in previous years, begins to poke and prod Duggan's uniform with his march-ing baton trying to find where he is beneath all that padding. The verbal provocation quickly turns into a fight. The otherwise shy and retreating Leroy, appar-ently transformed by a newly found confidence and vigor within his new uniform, beats the drum major into submission and is saved only when Helmholtz asserts his authority before Leroy's rage goes any fur-ther. Leroy thoroughly dismantles his foil.

"Ask your boyfriend to take off his jacket so we can all see his rippling muscles," the **drum major** said to Leroy's new girl. He challenged Leroy, "Go on, take it off."

"Make me," said Leroy.

"All righty, all righty," said Helmholtz, stepping between the two.

"You think I can't?" said the drum major.

Leroy swallowed and thought for a long time. "I know you can't," he said at last.

The **drum major** pushed Helmholtz aside and seized Leroy's jacket by its shoulders. Off came the epaulets, then the citation cord, then the sash. But-tons popped off, and Leroy's undershirt showed.

"Now," said the **drum major**, "we'll simply undo this, and—" Leroy exploded. He hit the **drum ma-jor**'s nose, stripped off his buttons, medals, and braid, hit him in the stomach, and went over to get his baton, with the apparent intention of beating him to death with it.

"Leroy! Stop!" cried Helmholtz in anguish. He wrenched the baton from Leroy.

unnamed father of Mary Irwin. *In the short story "Hal Irwin's Magic Lamp," collected in* Bagombo Snuff Box (1999), *Mary returns to her father's leaky farmhouse after her husband commits suicide in the panic following the Wall Street crash of 1929. Once she delivers Ella Rice and her young son Irwin to the black church of his christening, Mary describes to her father what she had seen. His are the final words of the story, quite contrary to the money-hoarding Hal at the beginning of the story, but not before Von-negut sets the scene with an oblique reference to and near biblical cadence.* But her father took her in.

How could he not? She told him about the homeless people in the black church. She asked him what he thought would become of them in such awful times.

"The poor take care of the poor," he said.

unnamed female maid (*see* **Slotkin**). *In Vonnegut's 1952* Collier's *short story "The Package," an unnamed maid waits on constant orders throughout the day by the new homeowners, the newly retired industrialist millionaire Earl Fenton and his wife, Maude.*

unnamed German restaurateur. *In the short story "Souvenir," collected in* Bagombo Snuff Box *(1999), the pawnbroker, Joe Bane, sends a shoeshine boy down the street to a German restaurant to ask the proprietor to translate the pencil rubbing he made from the inside of Eddie's bejeweled watch. Though the reply comes too late for Joe Bane to continue negotiating with Eddie, it reveals just how close was Eddie's brush with greatness (and death) in the war.* Ten minutes later, the **shoeshine boy** returned with a translation of the inscription inside the watch. This was it:

"To General Heinz Guderian, Chief of the Army General Staff, who cannot rest until the last enemy soldier is driven from the sacred soil of the Third German Reich. ADOLF HITLER."

It should be noted that while Guderian (1888–1954) was an important military leader and innovator of armored warfare, in real life he did not commit suicide as suggested by Vonnegut in this short story.

unnamed injured veteran. *In the short story "The Cruise of the* Jolly Roger," *collected in* Bagombo Snuff Box *(1999), the recuperating Major Nathan Durant shares a hospital room with an unnamed injured veteran who has big dreams of owning a boat. Without a military task at hand, Durant is without focus, purpose, or personal desire. Without the creativity to create a future for himself, he latches on to the dreams of his roommate.* In the hospital, the man in the next bed talked constantly of the boat he was going to own when he was whole again. For want of exciting peacetime dreams of his own, for want of a home or family or civilian friends, Durant borrowed his neighbor's dream.

With a deep scar across his cheek, with the lobe of his right ear gone, with a stiff leg, he limped into a boatyard in New London, the port nearest the hospital, and bought a secondhand cabin cruiser. He learned to run it in the harbor there, christened the boat *The Jolly Roger* at the suggestion of some children who haunted the boatyard, and set out arbitrarily for Martha's Vineyard.

unnamed jazzman. *In the short story "Find Me a Dream," collected in* Bagombo Snuff Box *(1999), Hildy Matthews is the widowed mother of two young children, once the wife of the unnamed jazzman, who was widely revered, especially by Andy Middleton, the clarinetist and bandleader of the Creon Pipe-Dreams, though Hildy describes her late husband as* the worst husband a woman could have, *and Arvin Borders previously described him derisively as* A dope fiend, an alcoholic, a wife-beater, and a woman-chaser who was shot dead last year by a jealous husband. . . . "Why anybody would think there was anything wonderful about a man like that I'll never know," he said. And then he gave the name of the man, a man who was probably the greatest jazz musician who had ever lived.

unnamed muralist. *In the short story "2BR02B," collected in* Bagombo Snuff Box *(1999), the unnamed muralist, present for most of the entire encounter, is intimately involved with a number of elements in the story.* The room was being redecorated. It was being redecorated as a memorial to a man who had volunteered to die.

A sardonic old man, about two hundred years old, sat on a stepladder, painting a mural he did not like. Back in the days when people aged visibly, his age would have been guessed at thirty-five or so. Aging had touched him that much before the cure for aging was found.

The mural he was working on depicted a very neat garden. Men and women in white, doctors and nurses, turned the soil, planted seedlings, sprayed bugs, spread fertilizer. Men and women in purple uniforms pulled up weeds, cut down plants that were old and sickly, raked leaves, carried refuse to trash burners.

Never, never, never—not even in medieval Holland or old Japan—had a garden been more formal, been better tended. Every plant had all the loam, light, water, air, and nourishment it could use.

Perched above it all, the muralist comments upon the world's overpopulation based upon the very real and painful scene played out before him. The painter sat on the top of his stepladder, looking down reflectively on the sorry scene. He pondered the mournful puzzle of life demanding to be born and, once born, demanding to be fruitful . . . to multiply and to live as long as possible—to do all that on a very small planet that would have to last forever.

All the answers that the painter could think of were grim. Even grimmer, surely, than a Catbox, a Happy Hooligan, an Easy Go. He thought of war. He thought of plague. He thought of starvation.

He knew that he would never paint again. He let his paintbrush fall to the dropcloths below. And then he decided he had had about enough of the Happy Garden of Life, too, and he came slowly down from the ladder.

He took Wehling's pistol, really intending to shoot himself. But he didn't have the nerve.

And then he saw the telephone booth in a corner of the room. He went to it, dialed the well-remembered number: 2BR02B. "Federal Bureau of Termination," said the warm voice of a hostess.

"How soon could I get an appointment?" he asked, speaking carefully.

"We could probably fit you in late this afternoon, sir," she said. "It might even be earlier, if we get a cancellation."

"All right," said the painter, "fit me in, if you please." And he gave her his name, spelling it out.

"Thank you, sir," said the hostess. "Your city thanks you, your country thanks you, your planet thanks you. But the deepest thanks of all is from future generations."

unnamed narrator. *The short story* "Custom-Made Bride" *is narrated by an unnamed person employed as a personal financial agent for an investment firm. Attorney Hal Murphy asks his unnamed friend to unravel the financial mess of his newest client, the wealthy and intellectually challenging designer Otto Krummbein. During the narrator's recollection of his first evening with Otto and Falloleen Krummbein, he*

is at first taken with the opulent and eclectic nature of the Krummbeins' residence as well as with Falloleen's highly stylized appearance, both of these the result of Otto's compulsion for avant-garde design. By the end of the evening, the adviser gets Otto to abide by his plan to pay his taxes while also serving as the catalyst for the couple's renewed commitment to each other. Falloleen openly supports their new austerity, while Otto insists that the essential and sensible Kitty Cahoun (Falloleen's real name) remains the free spirit of his otherwise custom-made bride.

unnamed narrator. *In the short story* "Der Arme Dolmetscher" (The Army Translator), *collected in* Bagombo Snuff Box (1999), *the foot soldier–narrator becomes the interpreter for his battalion through rather odd circumstances. As he recalls,* I qualified for the position while waiting to move from France into the front lines. While a student, I had learned the first stanza of Heinrich Heine's "Die Lorelei" by rote from a college roommate, and I happened to give those lines a dogged rendition while working within earshot of the battalion commander. *(The poem is a ballad about a siren perched atop the Lorelei rock at one of the narrowest points on the eastern bank of the Rhine.)*

The colonel has his executive officer station the soldier at the home of the nearby Belgian burgomaster. Since the area was only recently seized by the Americans, he wanted to make sure the town's mayor had no part to play in relaying information back to the Germans.

The narrator meets three other GIs (all German-speaking Pennsylvania Dutch who a few months earlier had been denied in their own requests to be interpreters) on a farm truck headed in the direction of the Belgian burgomaster's house, not far from the German defensive position known as the Siegfried Line. They translate the bit of Heine's poem the narrator had been overheard reciting when he was mistakenly assigned to serve as an interpreter. They also give him the remains of a rather torn-up military pamphlet filled with interrogation questions to be used on captured German soldiers.

Once at the burgomaster's home, the narrator's frustration with even basic, polite conversation with his host eventually drives him to his bedroom for some rest. Vexed by his inability to satisfy the de-

mands of his task, he lies in bed and finds himself fantasizing a tryst with the burgomaster's daughter. The two speak only in the phrases the narrator learned from Heine's poem. Once he imagines carrying her to his bed, her father suddenly appears, pointing a Luger at him, and all the language switches to the phrases he read in the military pamphlet. The narrator gets the better of the situation when he reaches under his pillow for his gun. The burgomaster and his daughter surrender just as the narrator imagines the Pennsylvania Dutch GIs reappearing to witness the event—all spoken according to the interrogation questions he was given by the Pennsylvanians. Once the narrator snaps out of his fantasy and realizes how absurd it is to remain in his position, he tidies up his bedroom and slips out of the house to make his way back to battalion headquarters.

The colonel and executive officer are surprised to see der arme dolmetscher so soon. The narrator lies and says the burgomaster spoke only a low class of German but that he spoke only high German, so he returned for reassignment. The colonel tells the narrator to stay put because he will be needed as his personal interpreter very shortly. Their position was surrounded by German tanks and they would undoubtedly have to surrender.

Sure enough, twenty minutes later the German tanks come rolling up to headquarters. When a German tank commander enters the American headquarters, he first takes out his own translation pamphlet before asking in English, "Where are your howitzers?"

unnamed narrator. The short story "Lovers Anonymous," collected in Bagombo Snuff Box (1999), is a first-person narrative told by the North Crawford storm door and window salesman concerning the influence of a red-covered feminist text on the town's much admired and enigmatic heartthrob, Sheila Hinckley White. The narrator is at the center of a group of locals who are shocked when the intellectually promising Sheila leaves the University of Vermont as a junior to marry Herb White. He dubs their small but locally well-known group as Lovers Anonymous, men who pine for what they think they could have had if they had even a remote thought that Sheila would give up her path toward academic

achievement and settle down with one of them. Instead, Sheila's marriage to Herb endures in a most conventional manner with her relishing the role of housewife and mother of twin girls.

After more than ten years of marriage, Sheila reads Woman, the Wasted Sex, or, The Swindle of Housewifery, provoking an abrupt return to a life of the mind filled with school and lofty career aspirations. The narrator is one of a series of tradesmen and craftsmen, all members of Lovers Anonymous, who benefit by the renovations Sheila and Herb make to their home in the wake of reading the text. They are closing off the ell and making two separate living spaces out of their sprawling home. It is not because their relationship has suffered. Quite the contrary, Sheila and Herb are as much in love as ever: she is pursuing her studies; he is more relaxed about his role within the family.

The narrator is present for Sheila's revelation after having read the red-covered text. "I was crying because I was understanding what a bluffer I'd been in school," she said. "I was only pretending to care about the things I was learning, back in those silly old days. Now I do care. That's why I was crying. I've been crying a lot lately, but it's good crying. It's about discovery, it's about grown-up joy."

The narrator also hears for himself Sheila's protests about any rumors that their divided house prevents them from being lovers. As she coyly tells him, Love laughs at locksmiths.

The narrator reads the book and fearlessly gives it to his wife to read, confident she will not have the same aspirations as Sheila after reading the text. He made sure to place her high school report card in the text as a bookmark to remind her of her own very ordinary intellect.

unnamed narrator. In "Unpaid Consultant," collected in Bagombo Snuff Box (1999), the onetime high school beau of Celeste Divine opens the story with a string of jaded observations learned through years of retail sales and the often odd connections with old female friends as the result of their wanting some sort of deal on products. Most married women won't meet an old beau for cocktails, send him a Christmas card, or even look him straight in the eye. But if they happen to need something an old beau sells—anything from an appendectomy to venetian blinds—they'll come bouncing back into his life, all pink and smiling, to get it for wholesale or less.

If a Don Juan were to go into the household appliance business, his former conquests would ruin him inside of a year.

What I sell is good advice on stocks and bonds. I'm a contact man for an investment counseling firm, and the girls I've lost, even by default, never hesitate to bring their investment problems to me.

I am a bachelor, and in return for my services, which after all cost me nothing, they sometimes offer me that jewel beyond price—the home-cooked meal.

In this case, he gets the home-cooked meal and a deep understanding of the lengths one will go to hold on to self-esteem when the financial balance in a marriage radically shifts and is further amplified by fame. He also learns that unlike the old acquaintances who disingenuously cozy up to past friends to make a better deal, there are those (such as Arthur J. Bunting) whose integrity, honor, discretion, and forgiving nature make them admirable confidants and trusted business partners.

Celeste Divine reaches across the years (seventeen, to be exact) to ask the narrator for an honest review of her accounts. Just two years before the opening of the story, Celeste was honing her singing skills while Harry barely got them by on a meager mechanic's salary at Joe's Greasing Palace. That was when she hit it big, landing a television contract for a weekly show paying her $5,000 per episode. When they moved back to their hometown, The nest she'd bought for herself and her mate was an old mansion on the river, as big and ugly as the Schenectady railroad station.

However, Harry feels displaced within the marriage. He went from being the sole breadwinner to a marginal contributor. More than anything else, he wants to remain vital and interesting to Celeste. As he later confides to the narrator about what it was like to move back to town with all her money setting them up in such gaudy splendor, "For eighteen months after Celeste struck it rich and we moved here," said Harry, "I walked the streets, looking for a job suitable for the husband of the famous and beautiful Celeste."

Remembering those dark days, he rubbed his eyes, reached for the catchup. "When I got tired, cold, or wet," he said, "I'd sit in the public library, and study all the different things men could do for a living. Making catchup was one of them." *Harry uses this knowledge to make Celeste believe he has become a wise and valued unpaid consultant to the catchup industry. He rants with ideas for rebuilding the industry if only the shortsighted owners would pay more attention to his ideas. She appreciates the niche he found for himself, not knowing it was all pretense. If she did know, she certainly never let on, either to Harry or the narrator.*

Harry feels compelled to confess his fabricated persona because his charade nearly loses the narrator's largest account of his life. Arthur J. Bunting, the third-generation owner of a catchup factory, becomes highly insulted by Harry's ignorant rants as he walks through a restaurant on his way to join the narrator and his mystery guest for lunch.

Harry saves the potential client for the narrator by calling Bunting the next day to apologize while explaining the truth of his situation. Bunting then calls the narrator to assure him that there is no need to discuss the particulars of Harry's call, and that he is willing to resume their exploration of the investment possibilities for the additional wealth he made from his company's sale.

Though the story opens with the narrator's jaded observations about past acquaintances, it closes with his appreciation for both the sincere and humble love Harry has for Celeste Divine and for the gentlemanly conduct of Arthur J. Bunting, an exemplar of personal integrity and discretion.

unnamed narrator's wife. *In the short story "Lovers Anonymous," the unnamed narrator's wife is the first to spread the rumor to her husband that Herb and Sheila Hinckley White are splitting. He knows otherwise, since he is one of the contractors renovating their fifteen-room house and has already handled an order from Herb for very expensive storm windows. The couple have a good marriage. He trusts her enough to give her the red-covered book to read that turned around Sheila and Herb. However, he guards against her getting similarly liberating thoughts by placing her high school report card into* *the book to be used as a marker and a reminder of her own very average intellect.*

unnamed orderly. *In the short story "2BR02B,"* collected in Bagombo Snuff Box *(1999), the intellectually weak, unnamed orderly is the common man in the room. He has no axe to grind, unlike Edward K. Wehling, Jr., struggling with his own dilemma. However, the orderly serves to help the unnamed muralist find a platform to speak his own mind.* The **orderly** looked in at the mural and the muralist. "Looks so real," he said, "I can practically imagine I'm standing in the middle of it."

"What makes you think you're not in it?" said the painter. He gave a satiric smile. "It's called The Happy Garden of Life, you know."

"That's good of Dr. Hitz," said the orderly.

He was referring to one of the male figures in white, whose head was a portrait of Dr. Benjamin Hitz, the hospital's chief obstetrician. Hitz was a blindingly handsome man.

Despite the orderly's string of questions for the muralist, his final observation about the state of the world's population balance versus a moral natural state is also the true analogy between the painter's sense of identity as recreated through art. Artists, in the end, expect chaos, indeterminacy, open-endedness. "Lot of faces still to fill in," said the **orderly**. He meant that the faces of many of the figures in the mural were blank. All blanks were to be filled with portraits of important people either on the hospital staff or from the Chicago office of the Federal Bureau of Termination.

"Must be nice to be able to make pictures that look like something," said the **orderly**.

The painter's face curdled with scorn. "You think I'm proud of this drab? You think this is my idea of what life really looks like?"

"What's your idea of what life looks like?"

The painter gestured at a foul dropcloth. "There's a good picture of it," he said. "Frame that, and you'll have a picture a damn sight more honest than this one."

The unnamed orderly is also an example of the extent that Ethical Suicide Studios have become part of the modern imagination through popular music. As he sings,

If you don't like my kisses, honey,
Here's what I will do:
I'll go see a girl in purple,
Kiss this sad world toodle-oo
If you don't want my lovin',
Why should I take up all this space?
I'll get off this old planet,
Let some sweet baby have my place.

unnamed policeman. *In the short story "The Cruise of the* Jolly Roger," *collected in* Bagombo Snuff Box *(1999), this New London policeman is sandwiched between the school band in the Memorial Day parade and marching children holding aloft their commemorative lilac bouquets. Vonnegut contrasts the officiousness of his appearance with that of the children behind him, symbolic of an angelic innocence, and then by the stereotypically regional grimness of their teachers.* The bandsmen were in sight now, all eight of them, teenagers, out of step, rounding a corner with confident, proud, sour, and incoherent noise intended to be music.

Before them rode the **town policeman**, fat with leisure, authority, leather, bullets, pistol, handcuffs, club, and a badge. He was splendidly oblivious to the smoking, backfiring motorcycle beneath him as he swept slowly back and forth before the parade.

Behind the band came a cloud of purple, seeming to float a few feet above the street. It was lilacs carried by children. Along the curb, teachers looking as austere as New England churches called orders to the children.

There are additional unnamed police officers in the short story "Runaways." Several unnamed Illinois and Ohio state troopers and local police intercept Annie Southard and Rice Brentner during their flight from home. The first grouping is responsible for returning them from Chicago. The second group relays the unexpected message to the young lovers that they will be welcomed home and receive all the help they ask for in setting up life with each other. That bit of unexpected news is the undoing of the runaways' rebelliousness.

unnamed postmistress. *In the short story "The Cruise of the* Jolly Roger," *collected in* Bagombo

Snuff Box (1999), *the unnamed New London post-mistress is unable to recall the Pefkos when asked by Major Nathan Durant. Her memory is only slightly jogged when assisted by Annie, a legal secretary from across the street who overhears the conversation while on line in the post office.*

unnamed shoeshine boy. *In the short story "Souvenir," collected in* Bagombo Snuff Box (1999), *the pawnbroker, Joe Bane, hires the nondescript shoeshine boy to take his pencil rubbing of the German inscription on Eddie's bejeweled pocket watch to a local restaurateur for translation as part of his price-haggling for the piece. In the span of ten minutes, apparently all the time it took for Eddie to relate his tale that included both his acquisition of the watch and the death of his best friend, Buzzer, the shoeshine boy returns with the translation, but too late for Eddie to hear of the true significance of the watch.* Ten minutes later, the **shoeshine boy** returned with a translation of the inscription inside the watch. This was it:

"To General Heinz Guderian, Chief of the Army General Staff, who cannot rest until the last enemy soldier is driven from the sacred soil of the Third German Reich. ADOLF HITLER."

unnamed teacher. *In the short story "The Cruise of the* Jolly Roger," *collected in* Bagombo Snuff Box (1999), *the teacher directs the schoolchildren from one memorial square to the other as they lay lilacs at each plaque along their parade route. The newly retired and wounded veteran Major Nathan Durant responds to their actions with his first sign of real emotion:* "It would make a statue want to cry. But what does it mean?" *At this point the teacher prompts young Tom with the offer of an answer that is above his ability to understand, but the lessons taught in the days leading up to the parade were obviously absorbed in school as Tom then explains.* "Tell them you're paying homage to one of the fallen valiant who selflessly gave his life," prompted a **teacher**.

Tom looked at her blankly, and then back at the flowers. "Don't you know?" said Annie.

"Sure," said Tom at last. "He died fighting so we could be safe and free. And we're thanking him with flowers, because it was a nice thing to do." He

looked up at Annie, amazed that she should ask. "Everybody knows that."

The policeman raced his motorcycle engine. The **teacher** shepherded the children back into line. The parade moved on.

unnamed young man and woman. *In the short story "The Cruise of the* Jolly Roger," *collected in* Bagombo Snuff Box (1999), *the couple shoot first with their camera and ask questions later. As retired major Nathan Durant steps ashore in Provincetown, Cape Cod, the couple accost him for a photo before learning he is not part of the artists' community in town. Disappointed to learn Durant's Army background, they turn their eye toward others near the shore who are more obviously artists.* "Look up, please," commanded a gaudily dressed young man with a camera in his hands and a girl on his arm.

Surprised, Durant did look up, and the camera shutter clicked. "Thank you," said the young man brightly.

"Are you a painter?" asked his girl.

"Painter?" said Durant. "No—retired Army officer."

The couple did a poor job of covering their disappointment.

"Sorry," said Durant, and he felt dull and annoyed.

"Oh!" said the girl. "There's some real painters over there."

un-neurotic courage (*see* **Waltham Kittredge**).

"Unpaid Consultant." *Originally appearing in the April 1955 issue of* Cosmopolitan *magazine and reprinted in the 1999 collection entitled* Bagombo Snuff Box, *this is another touching love story about the lengths some people will go to remain vital, respected, and loved by their mates. Though the story opens with the unnamed narrator's jaded observations about past acquaintances, it closes with his appreciation for both the sincere and humble love Harry has for Celeste Divine and for the gentlemanly conduct of Arthur J. Bunting, an exemplar of personal integrity and discretion.*

The narrator is a financial adviser and onetime high school beau of Celeste Divine. The bulk of the brief tale takes place in the opulent home of Celeste and her husband, Harry (no last name is disclosed). Without having passed a word with him during the intervening seventeen years, she calls the narrator to review their financial life now that she has hit it big in television, earning $5,000 per episode.

The brief backstory between Celeste and the narrator is that though they dated in high school, she was wooed away by Harry and they married one week after graduation. She was a singer back then and pursued a theatrical career while Harry immediately went to work as a mechanic at Joe's Greasing Palace.

Harry remained a mechanic all through their salad days while Celeste worked her way up. Once Celeste hits it big and they move back to their hometown and into their stately new house, Harry feels completely overshadowed and purposeless. "For eighteen months after Celeste struck it rich and we moved here," said Harry, "I walked the streets, looking for a job suitable for the husband of the famous and beautiful Celeste."

Remembering those dark days, he rubbed his eyes, reached for the catchup. "When I got tired, cold, or wet," he said, "I'd sit in the public library, and study all the different things men could do for a living. Making catchup was one of them."

He shook the bottle of catchup over his hamburger, violently. The bottle was almost full, but nothing came out. "There—you see?" he said. "When you shake catchup one way, it behaves like a solid. You shake it another way, and it behaves like a liquid." He shook the bottle gently, and catchup poured over his hamburger. "Know what that's called?"

"No," I said.

"Thixotropy," said Harry. He hit me playfully on the upper arm. "There—you learned something new today."

Harry's playful and revealing confession comes after he nearly spoiled the narrator's opportunity at landing his biggest account. Arthur J. Bunting, a third-generation catchup manufacturer, recently sold the family business and sought out the narrator to help with his increased wealth. The narrator invites Bunting to a lunch and thinks it would be a good idea to also invite Harry and Celeste. Of

course, this was before he learned of Harry's pretensions. Similarly, Harry was unaware of Bunting's attendance at the lunch.

Forever trying to sound important, Harry loudly expostulates his criticism of the catchup industry while being led to their table. Bunting hears Harry's insensitive remarks as the couple approach. Bunting blows up in a fit of pique and storms out. The narrator is crestfallen, but Harry, never meaning to do anything other than remain interesting to Celeste as a man worth more than his meager mechanic's income, promises to call Bunting to apologize.

Though Harry sets things right between Bunting and the narrator so they can go forward with business, he manages to conceal his pretensions from Celeste. After promising Bunting that he will never utter another word about the catchup industry, Harry shifts his unpaid consultant interests to the birdseed industry while secretly working once more as a mechanic—and happily so.

"Unready to Wear" (1953) (see also **Dr. Ellis Konigswasser**). The science fiction short story (reprinted in the 1968 collection Welcome to the Monkey House) about Dr. Ellis Konigwasser's discovery that helps people leave their bodies and be free of the illnesses associated with such a bodily existence. Those who practice Kongiswasser's techniques are called amphibians. The government, however, viewed amphibians as traitors. The charge against us was a capital offense on the books of the enemy—desertion. As far as the enemy was concerned, the amphibians had all turned yellow and run out on their bodies, just when their bodies were needed to do brave and important things for humanity.

Updike, Norman. The droll mortician in Hocus Pocus in charge of moving the graves of Hermann and Sophia Shultz from the nearby Tarkington stables to make room for the new Pahlavi Pavilion. (HP 24) The mortician, who is himself now in a covered trench by the stable, was **Norman Updike**, a descendant of the valley's early Dutch settlers. He went on to tell me with bow-wow cheerfulness back in 1987 that people were generally mistaken about how quickly things rot, turn into good old dirt or fertilizer or dust or whatever. He said scientists had discovered well-preserved meat and vegetables deep in city dumps, thrown away presumably years and years ago. Like Hermann and Sophia Shultz, these theoretically biodegradable works of Nature had failed to rot for want of moisture, which was life itself to worms and fungi and bacteria.

"Even without modern embalming techniques," he said, "ashes to ashes and dust takes much, much longer than most people realize."

Urbana Massacre. *In* Slapstick, *Wilbur Swain's illegitimate son by Wilma Pachysandra-17 von Peterswald is one of the few survivors in this victory by the Duke of Oklahoma. Forced to become a drummer boy in the Duke's army, at fourteen he paired off with a forty-year-old laundress and sired Melody Oriole-2 von Peterswald.*

Utopia. (CC 126) I directed our conversation into the area of **Utopias**, of what might have been, of what should have been, of what might yet be, if the world would thaw.

But Bokonon had been there, too, had written a whole book about **Utopias**, *The Seventh Book*, which he called "Bokonon's Republic." In that book are these ghastly aphorisms:

The hand that stocks the drug stores rules the world.

Let us start our Republic with a chain of drug stores, a chain of grocery stores, a chain of gas chambers, and a national game. After that, we can write our Constitution.

(GBR 1) When the United States of America, which was meant to be a **Utopia** for all, was less than a century old, Noah Rosewater and a few men like him demonstrated the folly of the Founding Fathers in one respect: those sadly recent ancestors had not made it the law of the **Utopia** that the wealth of each citizen should be limited. This oversight was engendered by a weak-kneed sympathy for those who loved expensive things, and by the feeling that the continent was so vast and valuable, and the population so thin and enterprising, that no thief, no matter how fast he stole, could more than mildly inconvenience anyone.

Noah and a few like him perceived that the continent was in fact finite, and that venal officeholders, legislators in particular, could be persuaded

to toss up great hunks of it for grabs, and to toss them in such a way as to have them land where Noah and his kind were standing.

Thus did a handful of rapacious citizens come to control all that was worth controlling in America. Thus was the savage and stupid and entirely inappropriate and unnecessary and humorless American class system created. Honest, industrious, peaceful citizens were classed as bloodsuckers, if they asked to be paid a living wage. And they saw that praise was reserved henceforth for those who devised means of getting paid enormously for committing crimes against which no laws had been passed. Thus the American dream turned belly up, turned green, bobbed to the scummy surface of cupidity unlimited, filled with gas, went bang in the noonday sun.

E pluribus unum is surely an ironic motto to inscribe on the currency of this **Utopia** gone bust, for every grotesquely rich American represents property, privileges, and pleasures that have been denied the many. An even more instructive motto, in the light of history made by the Noah Rosewaters, might be: *Grab much too much, or you'll get nothing at all.*

(GBR 1) And Eliot became a drunkard, a **Utopian dreamer**, a tinhorn saint, an aimless fool.

Begat he not a soul.

(GBR 6) "'Good,' he said again. 'The most exquisite pleasure in the practice of medicine comes from nudging a layman in the direction of terror, then bringing him back to safety again. Eliot certainly has his wires crossed, but the inappropriate thing to which the short circuit has caused him to bring his sexual energies isn't necessarily such a very bad thing.'

"'What is it?' I cried, thinking in spite of myself of Eliot stealing women's underwear, of Eliot snipping off locks of hair on subways, of Eliot as a Peeping Tom." The Senator from Indiana shuddered. "'Tell me, Doctor—tell me the worst. Eliot is bringing his sexual energies to what?'

"'To **Utopia**,' he said."

Frustration made Norman Mushari sneeze.

(WFG Preface) Mr. Nixon himself is a minor character in this book. He is the first President to hate the American people and all they stand for. He believes so vibrantly in his own purity, although he has committed crimes which are hideous, that I am bound to conclude that someone told him when he was very young that all serious crime was sexual, that no one could be a criminal who did not commit adultery or masturbate.

He is a useful man in that he has shown us that our Constitution is a defective document, which makes a childlike assumption that we would never elect a President who disliked us so. So we must amend the Constitution in order that we can more easily eject such a person from office and even put him in jail.

That is my chief **Utopian scheme** for the moment.

(WFG *Playboy* Interview) VONNEGUT: It's a sunny little dream I have of a happier mankind. I couldn't survive my own pessimism if I didn't have some kind of sunny little dream. That's mine, and don't tell me I'm wrong: Human beings will be happier—not when they cure cancer or get to Mars or eliminate racial prejudice or flush Lake Erie but when they find ways to inhabit primitive communities again. That's my **utopia**. That's what I want for me.

(PS The First Amendment) And all that argle-barging that goes on between educated persons in the United States and the Soviet Union is so touching and comical, really, as long as it does not lead to war. It draws its energy, in my opinion, from a desperate wish on both sides that each other's **utopias** should work much better than they do. We want to tinker with theirs, to make it work much better than it does—so that people there, for example, can say whatever they please without fear of punishment. They want to tinker with ours, so that everybody here who wants a job can have one, and so that we don't have to tolerate the sales of fist-fucking films and snuff films and so on.

Neither **utopia** now works much better than the Page typesetting machine, in which Mark Twain invested and lost a fortune. That beautiful contraption actually set type just once, when only Twain and the inventor were watching.

See also: PP IV; CC 58; GBR 1; 4; 10; 210; WFG Address to Graduating Class at Bennington College, 1970; *Slap* 19; 32; JB Prologue, HP 19, 36, BAG Lovers Anonymous.

Valentine, Ralston (see **The Son of Jimmy Valentine**).

Valley of the Dolls (see **Jacqueline Susann**).

Van Arsdale, Herbert. (*HP* 24) The president of Tarkington at that time, who was **Herbert Van Arsdale**, no relation to Whitey VanArsdale, the dishonest mechanic, ascribed the Provost's (*Kensington Barber's*) crackup to exhaustion brought on by his tireless efforts to solve the mystery of the disappearance of the golden-haired Lilac Queen.

van Curler, Dr. Ormand. *The manager of Ilium County's farming establishment in* Player Piano. *What was once a series of family farms throughout the Iroquois Valley is now a single farming entity managed with one hundred workers and machines. So vast is Dr. van Curler's responsibility that he declines to take over the mere two hundred acres of the Gottwald estate.* (*PP* XV) As though to point up the anachronism of Mr. Haycox and the Gottwald place for Paul, one of **Doctor Ormand van Curler's** men, riding on a tractor, appeared on the other side of the windbreak, snappy in spotless white coveralls, a red baseball cap, cool sandals which almost never touched the ground, and white gloves which, like Paul's hands, rarely touched anything but steering wheels, levers, and switches.

Van Gogh, Vincent. *In* Timequake, *Kilgore Trout uses the name of the famed painter when checking in to the homeless shelter that was once the Museum of the American Indian. In a truly metafictional moment, Vonnegut's alter ego explains to his creator why he uses Van Gogh's name, echoing Vonnegut's famous midwestern deadpan about his own occupation.* (*TQ* 27) Trout said he hadn't minded writing "Dog's Breakfast" again, or the three hundred or more stories he redid and threw away before free will kicked in again. "Write or rewrite, it's all the same to me," he said. "At the age of four score and four, I am as amazed and entertained as I was when I was only fourteen, and discovered that if I put the tip of a pen on paper, it would write a story of its own accord.

"Wonder why I tell people that my name is **Vincent van Gogh**?" he asked. And I had better explain that the real **Vincent van Gogh** was a Dutchman who painted in the south of France, whose pictures are now numbered among the world's most precious treasures, but who in his own lifetime sold only two of them. "It isn't only because he, like me, took no pride in his appearance and disgusted women, although that surely has to be factored in," said Trout.

"The main thing about **van Gogh** and me," said Trout, "is that he painted pictures that astonished him with their importance, even though nobody else thought they were worth a damn, and I write stories that astonish me, even though nobody else thinks they're worth a damn.

"How lucky can you get?" (*See also: TQ* 15.)

Trout's sentiments are in keeping with Vonnegut's earlier thoughts about making art right down to using van Gogh as his exemplar. (*FWD* III) "And professional picture painters, who are what a lot of this made-up story is about, are people who continue to play children's games with goo, and dirt, with chalks and powdered minerals mixed with oil and dead embers and so on, dabbing, smearing, scrawling, scraping, and so on, for all their natural lives. When they were children, though, there was just they and the Universe, with only the Universe dealing in rewards and punishments, as a dominant playmate will. When picture painters become adults, and particularly if other people depend on them for food and shelter and clothing and all that, not forgetting heat in the wintertime, they are likely to allow a third player, with dismaying powers to hold up to ridicule or reward grotesquely or generally behave like a lunatic, to join the game. It is that part of society which does not paint well, usually, but which knows what it likes with a vengeance. That third player is sometimes personified by an actual dictator, such as Hitler or Stalin or Mussolini, or simply by a critic or curator or collector or dealer or creditor, or in-laws.

"In any case, since the game goes well only when played by two, the painter and the Great Big Everything, three's a crowd.

"**Vincent van Gogh** excluded that third player by having no dependents, by selling no paintings save for a few to his loving brother, Theo, and by conversing as little as possible. Most painters are not that lucky, if you want to call that much solitude luck."

Van Tuyl estate. *In the short story "Any Reasonable Offer," first appearing in* Collier's *magazine (January 1952) and later collected in* Bagombo Snuff Box *(1999), the Van Tuyl estate in Newport marks a turning point in the life of the unnamed narrator. After learning the fraudulent ways of the Peckhams who wrangle luxurious outings on estates up for sale, the narrator closes his tale of middle-class deception to try on the life of the opulently rich. He is enjoying his time at the Van Tuyl estate as would the Peckhams, and it appears to have all the luxuries they once enjoyed and even more. As he recalls, the estate* has almost everything: private beach and swimming pool, polo field, two grass tennis courts, nine-hole golf course, stables, paddocks, French chef, at least three exceptionally attractive Irish parlor maids, English butler, cellar full of vintage stuff—

The labyrinth is an interesting feature, too. I get lost in it almost every day. Then the real estate agent comes looking for me, and he gets lost just as I find my way out. Believe me, the property is worth every penny of the asking price. I'm not going to haggle about it, not for a minute. When the time comes, I'll either take it or leave it.

But I've got to live with the place a little longer—to get the newness out—before I tell the agent what I'm going to do. Meanwhile, I'm having a wonderful time. Wish you were here.

VanArsdale, Whitey. *In* Hocus Pocus, *Whitey is the unscrupulous auto mechanic who tries to sell everyone a new transmission. During the prison break, he and Lyle Hooper ambush and kill three escaped convicts carrying a white flag on their way to negoti-*ate with the legal authorities. Ten minutes later, Whitey is shot dead by another escapee and Hooper is taken prisoner.

Vanzetti, Bartolomeo (*see* **Sacco and Vanzetti**).

Veblen, Thorstein. *Eliot Rosewater doesn't recall dreaming of his father, but he frequently dreams of Veblen. Vonnegut also recalls his first exposure to the famous economist.* (PS Roots) But Father's younger brother, Uncle Alex, a Harvard graduate and life insurance salesman, was responsive and amusing and generous with me, was my ideal grown-up friend.

He was also then a socialist, and among the books he gave me, when I was a high school sophomore, was **Thorstein Veblen**'s *Theory of the Leisure Class.* I understood it perfectly and loved it, since it made low comedy of the empty graces and aggressively useless possessions which my parents, and especially my mother, meant to regain someday.

Venus on the Half-shell (*see also* **Queen Margaret**). *A Kilgore Trout novel lightly skimmed by Fred Rosewater in* God Bless You, Mr. Rosewater. *On the back cover of the novel,* There was a photograph of Trout. He was an old man with a full black beard. He looked like a frightened, aging Jesus, whose sentence to crucifixion had been commuted to imprisonment for life (GBR 9).

Science fiction writer Philip Jose Farmer appropriated both the name Kilgore Trout and the title Venus on the Half-shell *for his own book. Vonnegut wasn't happy about the event, but he declined to sue over the issue.*

Vicuna. *A fictitious planet in a science fiction short story by Frank X. Barlow published in* Playboy. *Walter Starbuck recalls* (JB 5): they ran out of time on **Vicuna**, he says. The tragedy of the planet was that its scientists found ways to extract time from topsoil and the oceans and the atmosphere—to heat their homes and power their speedboats and fertilize their crops with it; to eat it; to make clothes out of it; and so on. They served time at every meal, fed it to household pets, just to demonstrate how rich and clever they were. They allowed great gobbets of it to putrefy to oblivion in their overflowing garbage cans.

"On **Vicuna**," says the judge, "we lived as though there were no tomorrow."

The Vicunians are forced to take their souls and leave their bodies behind as they search the galaxy for compatible bodies to inhabit. The judge's soul hovers over the Finletter Air Force Base and imagines the compound houses philosophers in a meditation center. (JB 6) The judge in Dr. Bob Fender's story tries to guess which of the philosophers in the meditation center is the wisest and most contented. He decides that it is a little old man sitting on a cot in a second-story dormitory.

Every so often that little old man is so delighted with his thoughts, evidently, that he claps three times.

So the judge flies into the ear of that little old man and immediately sticks to him forever, sticks to him, according to the story ". . . as tightly as Formica to an epoxy-coated countertop." And what does he hear in that little old man's head but this: *Sally in the garden, / Sifting cinders, / Lifted up her leg / And farted like a man. . . . That philosopher, of course, is Walter Starbuck [italics in the original].*

Villavicencio, Carlos Daffodil-11. *The dishwasher embraced as a brother by Wilbur Swain because they share the same extended family name designation. Carlos becomes a devoted "Sancho Panza" to Wilbur* (Slap 40). *Transported by helicopter pilot Captain Bernard O'Hare, Wilbur decides to leave Carlos in Indianapolis where he would be cared for in his later years by the large population of Daffodils living there who had already greeted their arrival with parades and feasts.*

vin-dit (*see also* **Bokononism**). (CC 34) It was in the tombstone salesroom that I had my first *vin-dit*, a Bokononist word meaning a sudden, very personal shove in the direction of Bokononism, in the direction of believing that God Almighty knew all about me, after all, that God Almighty had some pretty elaborate plans for me.

(CC 90) All things conspired to form one cosmic *vin-dit*, one mighty shove into Bokononism, into the belief that God was running my life and that He had work for me to do.

And, inwardly, I *sarooned*, which is to say that I acquiesced to the seeming demands of my *vin-dit*.

Inwardly, I agreed to become the next President of San Lorenzo.

virtue. (PP I) On his office wall, Paul had a picture of the shop as it had been in the beginning. . . . In each face was a defiant promise of physical strength, and at the same time, there was the attitude of a secret order, above and apart from society by **virtue** of participating in important and moving rites the laity could only guess about—and guess wrong.

(PP XXX) "And then we get back to basic values, basic **virtues**!" said Finnerty. "Men doing men's work, women doing women's work. People doing people's thinking."

(PP XXX) "That there must be **virtue** in imperfection, for Man is imperfect, and Man is a creation of God.

"That there must be **virtue** in frailty, for Man is frail, and Man is a creation of God.

"That there must be **virtue** in inefficiency, for Man is inefficient, and Man is a creation of God.

"That there must be **virtue** in brilliance followed by stupidity, for Man is alternately brilliant and stupid, and Man is a creation of God." *Excerpted from the Ghost Shirt Society declaration letter written by Professor Ludwig von Neumann and signed by Paul Proteus.*

(ST 1) Constant found his memory stuffed with rumpled, overexposed snapshots of all the women he had had, with preposterous credentials testifying to his ownership of even more preposterous enterprises, with testimonials that attributed to him **virtues** and strengths that only three billion dollars could have.

(MN 23) "**Virtues** and vices, pleasures and pains cross boundaries at will." *Howard Campbell protests when, on their very first meeting, Colonel Frank Wirtanen assumes he hates America.*

(SL5 1) History in her solemn page informs us that the crusaders were but ignorant and savage men, that their motives were those of bigotry unmitigated, and that their pathway was one of blood and tears. Romance, on the other hand, dilates upon their piety and heroism, and portrays, in her most glowing and impassioned hues, their **virtue** and magnanimity, the imperishable honor they acquired for themselves, and the great services they rendered to Christianity. *Vonnegut quotes from Charles Mac-*

kay's Extraordinary Popular Delusions and the Madness of Crowds, *read aloud by Bernard O'Hare while Vonnegut visits and hopes to refresh his memory in preparation for writing* Slaughterhouse-Five.

(SL5 2) He *(Roland Weary)* dilated upon the piety and heroism of "The Three Musketeers," portrayed, in the most glowing and impassioned hues, their **virtue** and magnanimity, the imperishable honor they acquired for themselves, and the great services they rendered to Christianity. *The Three Musketeers in this case are Roland Weary and two unnamed battalion scouts.*

(BC 15) A booby trap was an easily hidden explosive device, which blew up when it was accidentally twiddled in some way. One of the **virtues** of the new type of booby trap was that it could not be smelled by dogs.

(WFG Yes, We Have No Nirvanas) This new religion (which-is-not-a-religion-but-a-technique) *(transcendental meditation)* offers tremendous pleasure, opposes no existing institutions or attitudes, demands no sacrifices or outward demonstrations of **virtue**, and is risk free.

(WFG Thinking Unthinkable, Speaking Unspeakable) The prohibition of the sale of alcoholic beverages in this country was called "The Noble Experiment," among other things. . . . The war in Vietnam might aptly be called "Noble Experiment II," since it is a similarly narrow-minded adventure in **virtue**.

(JB Prologue) The architect had also been matter-of-fact about the **virtues** of the factory as a fort. Any mob meaning to storm the front gate would first have to cross all that open ground.

(PS When I Lost My Innocence) "I pity you *Sun* people of today for not having truly great leaders to write about—Roosevelt and Churchill and Chiang Kai-shek and Stalin on the side of **virtue**, and Hitler and Mussolini and Emperor Hirohito on the side of sin." *On May 3, 1980, Vonnegut addressed those attending the 100th anniversary celebration of* The Cornell Daily Sun.

(PS Religion) "We also wish Knowledge, Goodness, Sympathy, Mercy, Wisdom, Justice, and Truthfulness. We also strive for and venerate all of those attributes from which the fantasy of man has created a God. We also strive for the **virtues** of Temperance, Industriousness, Friendship, and Peace.

We believe in pure ideas based on Truth and Justice." *From Clemens Vonnegut's self-eulogy.*

(PS Children) Can I say now, with all my heart, what he *(Clemens Vonnegut)* said in his little book in 1900: "We believe in **virtue**, in perfectibility, in progress, in stability of the laws of nature, in the necessity of improving the social conditions and relations, which should be in harmony with that benevolence which conditions the coherence of men"? *Vonnegut's answer—No.*

(PS Jekyll and Hyde Updated) *(The following is stage direction, italicized in the original text.) Dr. Jekyll played by JERRY comes out of his house, the image of civic decency, and is recognized and adored by all. . . . While biding his time, he performs acts of* **civic virtue** *which are noted and admired by one and all. He picks up a piece of trash dropped by somebody else, puts it in a waste barrel, gives money to a beggar, politely declines an invitation from SALLY the whore, giving her a gentle lecture, and so on.*

(DD 6) On his deathbed at the County Hospital, when Father was listing all his **virtues** and vices, he said that at least he had been wonderful with children, that they had all found him a lot of fun. "I understand them," he said.

(DD 17) I made no reply and he went on: "You and I and your mother and your brother are descended from solid, stolid, thick-skulled, unimaginative, unmusical, ungraceful German stock whose sole **virtue** is that it can never leave off working."

(HP 9) And of course, this enriched their dreams of escaping, but what were those but what we could call in any other context the **virtue** hope?

(HP 18) I said that the doubts I might have raised in the students' minds about the **virtues** of the Free Enterprise System, when telling them what my grandfather believed, could in the long run only strengthen their enthusiasm for that system. . . . "People are never stronger," I said, "than when they have thought up their own arguments for believing what they believe. They stand on their own 2 feet that way."

(FWD Preface) Q: What do you consider the most overrated **virtue**?
A: Teeth.

(FWD III) "That confession will seem as damning and barbarous to humorless persons as my sister's fantasy of whizzing through the Louvre on roller skates. At least it has the **virtue** of truthfulness." *Vonnegut refers to the ultimately predictable—if not clichéd—construction of most artistic creations. His confession is that he sees the endpoint of the work long before the machinery has worked itself out, and he longs for its completion.*

(FWD XI) "So what is going on over there is really a touching thing for us to watch and hear about, an honest effort to give the common people of a powerful nation more liberty than they or their ancestors have ever known. If the experiment goes on for any length of time—and just a few people could shut it down instantly—we can expect to see it dawn on the citizens of the Soviets that liberty, like **virtue**, is its own reward, which can be a disappointment. There as here and, in fact, almost everywhere on the planet, the great mass of human beings yearns for rewards that are more substantial.

(FWD XXI) Before World War I, the Freethinkers had cheerful congregations, and picnics, too, in many parts of this country. If not God, what was there for them to serve during their short stay on Earth? Only one thing was left to serve under such circumstances, which was their community. Why should they behave well (which they did), quite certain as they were that neither Heaven nor Hell awaited them? **Virtue** was its own reward.

(FWD My Reply to a Letter from the Dean of the Chapel at Transylvania University About a Speech I Gave There) The Bible is a useful starting point for discussions with crowds of American strangers, since so many of us know at least a little something about it. It has the added **virtue** of having for contributors at least two geniuses—Moses and Christ.

(TQ Prologue) Sir Galahad, the purest in heart and mind, familiarizes himself with this new **virtue-compelling appliance** (*a Thompson submachine gun*). While doing so, he puts a slug through the Holy Grail and makes a Swiss cheese of Queen Guinevere.

(TQ 63) I replied that what made being alive almost worthwhile for me was the saints I met, people behaving unselfishly and capably. They turned up in the most unexpected places. Perhaps you, dear reader, are or can become a saint for her sweet child to meet. I believe in original sin. I also believe in original **virtue**. Look around! *This is Vonnegut's partial reply to a letter from a depressed, pregnant woman fearful of bringing a new life into a troubled world.*

(BAG Preface by Peter Reed) Several stories rely on a convenient narrator, someone like a storm window salesman or a financial advisor, with access to many different social settings. Such a person can enter the homes of rich celebrities, as happens in "Custom-Made Bride" and "Unpaid Consultant," and deliver matter-of-fact observations. These narrators lend the immediacy of an intimate voice, a presence who, by **virtue** of being there, authenticates the account. Often theirs is the perspective of sound common sense that keeps the bizarre grounded in the everyday, and their wry commentary or ironic tone is a source of humor.

Vitelli, Giovanni. *The artist whose frescoes of scantily dressed gods and goddesses once adorned the walls of the de Medici palazzo in Italy, later owned by Marilee Kemp. After Rabo reads about the Dominican monk Girolamo Savonarola and his successful efforts to scrape the paintings from the walls, he jibes,* One may assume that he was the Rabo Karabekian of his time, and that Christian fundamentalism was his Sateen Dura-Luxe (*Blue* 27).

Voce, Sotto. *In Italian the phrase means to lower one's voice to gain emphasis. Kilgore Trout's play* The Wrinkled Old Family Retainer *has a character named Sotto Voce who exchanges sardonic quips with another guest.* (TQ 46) **Sotto Voce**, a male guest standing at the fringe of the ceremony, says out of the corner of his mouth to a guy standing next to him, "I don't bother with all this. I simply find a woman who hates me, and I give her a house."

And the other guy says, as the groom is kissing the bride, "All women are psychotic. All men are jerks."

Voltaire. (PS Roots) "Clemens had a far better formal education than ninety-eight percent or more of the German or other immigrants. He had completed his 'Abitur' at the Hochschule in Hannover; which meant that he had the equivalent at that time of an American college education and was qualified to attend one of the Universities as a candidate for a Ph.D. degree. He had an acquaintance with Latin and Greek, and spoke French fluently in addition to his native German. He had read widely in History and Philosophy; had acquired a fine vocabulary; and was able to write with clarity. Although raised and instructed in the Roman Catholic Church, he rejected formalized religion and disliked clergymen. He greatly admired **Voltaire**, and shared many of the latter's philosophical views. . . ."

(*DD* 9) I had to chop the heads off two chickens for supper that night. This was another privilege which had been accorded Felix, who used to make me watch him.

The place of execution was the stump of the walnut tree, under which Father and old August Gunther had been lunching when the Maritimo brothers arrived in Midland City so long ago. There was a marble bust on a pedestal, which also had to watch. It was another piece of loot from the von Furstenberg estate in Austria. It was a bust of **Voltaire**.

(*DD* 15) At the end of her life, she (*Emma Waltz*) would become combative and caustically witty, a sort of hicktown **Voltaire**, cynical and sceptical and so on. An autopsy would reveal several small tumours in her head, which doctors felt almost certainly accounted for this change in personality.

(*HP* 26) If the author was right that the whole point of life on Earth was to make germs shape up so that they would be ready to ship out when the time came, then even the greatest human being in history, Shakespeare or Mozart or Lincoln or **Voltaire** or whoever, was nothing more than a Petri dish in the truly Grand Scheme of Things.

(*FWD* XX) If Hamlet hoped to be remembered after he slammed the big door (or after somebody slammed it for him), I am sure he would have said so. Mark Twain (who wrote as though he would have liked to be remembered) said his reputation might outlive his body for at least a little while because he had moralized. (And indeed, his reputation has outlived his body.) I am sure he would have moralized in any case, but he had noticed that (for whatever reason) ancient writings which were still interesting in his day were all moralized. The anthology we call "The Bible" comes to mind. So should *Lysistrata* by Aristophanes (ca. 448–380 B.C.) and the Second Inaugural Address of Abraham Lincoln (1809–1865) and *Candide* by Vol-

taire (1694–1778) and *Heart of Darkness* by Joseph Conrad (1857–1924) and *The Theory of the Leisure Class* by Thorstein Veblen (1857–1929) and *Spoon River Anthology* by Edgar Lee Masters (1869–1950) and *Gulliver's Travels* by Jonathan Swift (1667–1745) and *Modern Times* by Charlie Chaplin (1889–1977) and on and on. So good advice to a young writer who wishes to circumvent mortality might be: "Moralize." I would add this caveat: "Be sure to sound reader-friendly and not all that serious when doing it." *Don Quixote* by Miguel de Cervantes (1547–1616) comes to mind. The sermons of Cotton Mather (1663–1728) do not.

(*TQ* 7) He asked what relatives of mine had been wounded in wars. As far as I knew, only one. That was my great-grandfather Peter Lieber, an immigrant who became a brewer in Indianapolis after being wounded in one leg during our Civil War. He was a Freethinker, which is to say a skeptic about conventional religious beliefs, as had been **Voltaire** and Thomas Jefferson and Benjamin Franklin and so on. And as would be Kilgore Trout and I.

(*TQ* 21) I couldn't recommend Humanism for such a person. I wouldn't do so for the great majority of the planet's population.

The German philosopher Friedrich Wilhelm Nietzsche, who had syphilis, said that only a person of deep faith could afford the luxury of religious skepticism. Humanists, by and large educated, comfortably middle-class persons with rewarding lives like mine, find rapture enough in secular knowledge and hope. Most people can't.

Voltaire, French author of *Candide*, and therefore the Humanists' Abraham, concealed his contempt for the hierarchy of the Roman Catholic Church from his less educated, simpler-minded, and more frightened employees, because he knew what a stabilizer their religion was for them.

(*TQ* 35) If bashers are unwilling to settle for the basher **Voltaire**'s "*Il faut cultiver notre jardin*" (*we must cultivate our garden*) that leaves the politics of human rights, which I am prepared to discuss. I begin with a couple of true stories from the end of Trout's and my war in Europe.

Early in A Man Without a Country, *Vonnegut defends his use of humor when writing about topics that many would consider inappropriate, distasteful, or disrespectful by referencing Voltaire's* Candide *and the work of Sigmund Freud.* (MWC 1) When I'm being funny, I try not to offend. I don't think much of what I've done has been in really ghastly taste. I don't think I have embarrassed many people, or distressed them. The only shocks I use are an occasional obscene word. Some things aren't funny. I can't imagine a humorous book or skit about Auschwitz, for instance. And it's not possible for me to make a joke about the death of John F. Kennedy or Martin Luther King. Otherwise I can't think of any subject that I would steer away from, that I could do nothing with. Total catastrophes are terribly amusing, as **Voltaire** demonstrated. You know, the Lisbon earthquake is funny.

I saw the destruction of Dresden. I saw the city before and then came out of an air-raid shelter and saw it afterward, and certainly one response was laughter. God knows, that's the soul seeking some relief.

Any subject is subject to laughter, and I suppose there was laughter of a very ghastly kind by victims in Auschwitz.

Humor is an almost physiological response to fear. Freud said that humor is a response to frustration—one of several.

von Braun, Wernher. *The German engineer who headed the Nazi rocket program against England. In* Mother Night, *he is an acquaintance of Howard W. Campbell's and dances with Helga at the birthday party of General Walter Dornberger. Campbell tells Kraft/Potapov he ran into von Braun while walking on Fifty-Second Street in Manhattan.*

von Furstenberg, Rudolf. *The Salzburg, Austria, friend of the Waltz family who was killed in World War I. Rudy Waltz is named for him. When Rudy's parents went to visit the remaining members of old Rudolf's family, they found only his mother and youngest brother. Impoverished by the war, they were selling their entire estate.* (DD 4) And Mother and Father bought a lot of the **von Furstenbergs'** furniture and linens and crystal, and some battle-axes and swords, chain maces, and helmets and shields.

My brother and I were both conceived in a **von Furstenberg** bed, with a coat of arms on the head-

board, and with "The Minorite Church of Vienna," by Adolf Hitler, on the wall. . . .

Father and Mother also bought the enormous weather vane from the gatehouse of the **von Furstenberg** estate, and put it atop their cupola back home, making the studio taller than anything in the county, except for the dome of the county courthouse, a few silos, the Fortunes' dairy barn, and the Midland County National Bank.

That weather vane was instantly the most famous work of art in Midland City. Its only competition was a statue of a Union soldier on foot in Fairchild Park. Its arrow alone was twelve feet long, and one hollow copper horseman chased another one down that awesome shaft. The one in back was an Austrian with a lance. The one in front, fleeing for his life, was a Turk with a scimitar.

This engine, swinging now toward Detroit, now toward Louisville, and so on, commemorated the lifting of the Turkish siege of Vienna in 1683.

They also purchased a marble bust of Voltaire, which the Waltz's placed out in the yard where the family slaughtered chickens.

von Killinger, Baron Manfred Freihert. *In 1939, as the German Consul General of San Francisco, the Baron bestows upon Dr. Lionel Jones the gift of a diamond swastika on an onyx field* (MN 14).

von Kleigstadt, Dr. Ormand (*see also* **"EPICAC"**). *The Wyandotte College professor who creates EPICAC in the 1950 short story of that name, reprinted in* Welcome to the Monkey House (1968).

Hell it's about time somebody told about my friend EPICAC. After all, he cost the taxpayers $776,434,927.54. They have a right to know about him, picking up a check like that. EPICAC got a big send-off in the papers when **Dr. Ormand von Kleigstadt** designed him for the Government people. Since then, there hasn't been a peep about him—not a peep. It isn't any military secret about what happened to EPICAC, although the Brass has been acting as though it were. The story is embarrassing, that's all. After all that money, EPICAC didn't work out the way he was supposed to.

EPICAC covered about an acre on the fourth floor of the physics building at Wyandotte College.

Ignoring his spiritual side for a minute, he was seven tons of electronic tubes, wires, and switches, housed in a bank of steel cabinets and plugged into a 110-volt A.C. line just like a toaster or a vacuum cleaner.

Von Kleigstadt and the Brass wanted him to be a super computing machine that (who) could plot the course of a rocket from anywhere on earth to the second button from the bottom on Joe Stalin's overcoat, if necessary. Or, with his controls set right, he could figure out supply problems for an amphibious landing of a Marine division, right down to the last cigar and hand grenade. He did, in fact.

Any ordinance or supply officer above field grade will tell you that the mathematics of modern war is far beyond the fumbling minds of mere human beings. The bigger the war, the bigger the computing machines needed. EPICAC was, as far as anyone in this country knows, the biggest computer in the world. Too big, in fact, for even **Von Kleigstadt** to understand much about.

I had hoped to sleep late the next morning, but an urgent telephone call roused me before eight. It was **Dr. von Kleigstadt**, EPICAC's designer, who gave me the terrible news. He was on the verge of tears. "Ruined! Ausgespielt! Shot! Kaput! Buggered!" he said in a choked voice. He hung up.

When I arrived at EPICAC's room the air was thick with the oily stench of burned insulation. The ceiling over EPICAC was blackened with smoke, and my ankles were tangled in coils of paper ribbon that covered the floor. There wasn't enough left of the poor devil to add two and two. A junkman would have been out of his head to offer more than fifty dollars for the cadaver.

Dr. von Kleigstadt was prowling through the wreckage, weeping unashamedly, followed by three angry-looking Major Generals and a platoon of Brigadiers, Colonels, and Majors.

I reeled up the tangled yards of paper ribbon from the floor, draped them in coils about my arms and neck, and departed for home. **Dr. von Kleigstadt** shouted that I was fired for having left EPICAC on all night. I ignored him, too overcome with emotion for small talk.

I loved and won—EPICAC loved and lost, but he bore me no grudge. I shall always remember him as a sportsman and a gentleman. Before he departed this vale of tears, he did all he could to make our marriage a happy one. EPICAC gave me anniversary poems for Pat—enough for the next 500 years. *De mortuis nil nisi bonum*—Say nothing but good of the dead.

von Kleist, Adolf. *Deemed incompetent by* Galápagos's *narrator, Leon Trout, Adolf von Kleist unwittingly becomes the sire of the human race after Mary Hepburn steals his sperm. He fears having children of his own because his father had Huntington's chorea, yet his offspring are free of the disease and begin man's return to the sea as something resembling sea lions.* (Gal 1:11) **Adolf von Kleist**, the Captain of the *Bahía de Darwin*, would in fact become the ancestor of every human being on the face of the earth today.

(Gal 1:21) The Captain of the *Bahía de Darwin*, **Adolf von Kleist**, was a graduate of the United States Naval Academy at Annapolis.

(Gal 1:22) **Adolf von Kleist** . . . was regularly bailed out by his parents from gambling debts and charges of drunken driving and assault and resisting arrest and vandalism and so on until he was twenty-six—when his father came down with Huntington's chorea and murdered his mother. Only then did he begin to assume responsibility for mistakes he made.

von Kleist, Gottfried and Wilhelm. *The uncles of Adolf and Siegfried von Kleist, in* Galápagos. *Gottfried is chairman of Ecuador's largest bank and co-owner with older brother Wilhelm of the* Bahía de Darwin *and the Hotel El Dorado.*

von Kleist, Sebastian. *The highly successful Ecuadorian sculptor and architect, father of Adolf and Siegfried, is also afflicted with Huntington's chorea.* (Gal 1:16) It *(the disease)* usually lay in ambush, and undetectable by any known test, until the wretch who had inherited it was well into his or her adult years. The father of the brothers, for example, led an unclouded and productive life until he was fifty-four—at which time he began to dance involuntarily, and to see things which weren't there. And then he killed his wife, a fact which was hushed up.

The murder was reported to the police, and so treated by them, as a household accident.

von Kleist, Siegfried. *The manager of the Hotel El Dorado and the younger brother of Captain Adolf von Kleist. Both he and his brother fear carrying the gene for Huntington's chorea, so neither ever marries or reproduces. Siegfried was generally an idler, having inherited considerable money, but had been shamed by his uncles into, so to speak, "pulling his own weight" in this particular family enterprise* (Gal 1:11).

On the afternoon of November 27, 1986, the same day Peru declares war on Ecuador, Siegfried comes down with the same frightful symptoms of the disease his father suffered. After watching Zenji Hiroguchi and Andrew MacIntosh get shot to death and listening to the beginning of the air attack, Siegfried bravely takes a bus and gathers together the few travelers who booked passage on "the Nature Cruise of the Century" and makes his way down to the docks. He and his drunken brother manage to get them on board the Bahía de Darwin.

The prospects of the disease so horrify Siegfried that he plans on committing suicide by ramming the bus into a downtown building. However, a Peruvian pilot explodes a rocket in a nearby estuary, causing a surging six-meter wave that washes the bus off the dock, simultaneously snapping the ship's mooring line. All in the same moment Siegfried is killed and his brother set free in the harbor to become the unwitting father of humanity's next step along the evolutionary chain.

von Koenigswald, Dr. Schlichter. *The fourteen-year veteran of the Nazi SS and former Auschwitz camp physician who becomes "Papa" Monzano's personal physician as well as an attending physician at Julian Castle's House of Hope and Mercy in the Jungle. Jokingly considered penance, Castle says, If he keeps going at his present rate, working night and day, the number of people he's saved will equal the number of people he let die—in the year 3010* (CC 83).

When "Papa" lay dying in the castle, it is von Koenigswald who climbs in his bed (Bokonon's boat, the Lady's Slipper) *and delivers the Bokononist last rites. After "Papa" swallows the bit of ice-nine hang-ing in the cylinder around his neck, von Koenigswald becomes the second person to die from Dr. Hoenikker's creation. He touches the dusty whiteness on Monzano's stone cold lips, goes to the wash basin and unwittingly turns the water into a solid sphere of ice. Out of curiosity, he touches his tongue to the orb and solidifies in the way only ice-nine could effect.*

von Konigswald, Major Siegfried. *The Nazi SS officer known as the Beast of Yugoslavia, killed in hand-to-hand combat with Harold Ryan. Unabashedly, he recalls,* They used to call me "The Beast of Yugoslavia," on account of all the people I had tortured and shot—and hanged. We'd bop 'em on the head. We'd hook 'em up to the electricity. We'd stick 'em with hypodermic syringes full of all kinds of stuff. One time we killed a guy with orange juice. There was a train wreck, and two of the freight cars were loaded with oranges, so we had oceans of orange juice. It was a joke—how much orange juice we had. And we were interrogating a guy one day, and he wouldn't talk, and the next thing I know—somebody's filling up this big syringe with orange juice.

There was a guerrilla war going on. You couldn't tell who was a guerrilla and who wasn't. Even if you got one, it was still a civilian you got. Telling Americans what a guerrilla war is like—that's coals to Newcastle. How do you like that for idiomatic English? "Coals to Newcastle". . . .

I'm up in Heaven now, like that little Wanda June kid. I wasn't hit by no ice-cream truck. Harold Ryan killed me with his bare hands. He was good. My eyes popped out. My tongue stuck out like a red banana. I shit in my pants. It was a mess (WJ I:7).

von Neumann, Ludwig. *The former political science professor at Union College in Schenectady, New York, who becomes the chief public information officer for the Ghost Shirt Society's rebellion. Displaced by the decision to tear down the university's Social Sciences Building and replace it with a Heat and Power Laboratory, Professor von Neumann's academic life lay in shambles. Both he and Paul Proteus are members of the Ilium Historical Society before that is torn down to make way for the Ilium Atomic Reactor.*

Professor von Neumann forges Paul's name on

the Ghost Shirt press release outlining their philosophy and demands. The letter asserts that technology is, indeed, an overall benefit to humanity; however, when society abdicates self-governance in favor of designs determined by inanimate entities, the result goes against natural law. (PP XXX) "Again, let me say we are all in this together, but the rest of us, for what we perceive as good, plain reasons, have changed our minds about the divine right of machines, efficiency, and organization, just as men of another age changed their minds about the divine right of kings, and about the divine rights of many other things.

"During the past three wars, the right of technology to increase in power and scope was unquestionably, in point of national survival, almost a divine right. Americans owe their lives to superior machines, techniques, organization, and managers and engineers. For these means of surviving the wars, the Ghost Shirt Society and I thank God. But we cannot win good lives for ourselves in peacetime by the same methods we used to win battles in wartime. The problems of peace are altogether more subtle.

"I deny that there is any natural or divine law requiring that machines, efficiency, and organization should forever increase in scope, power, and complexity, in peace as in war. I see the growth of these now, rather, as the result of a dangerous lack of law.

"The time has come to stop the lawlessness in that part of our culture which is your special responsibility. . . .

"I propose that men and women be returned to work as controllers of machines, and that the control of people by machines be curtailed. I propose, further, that the effects of changes in technology and organization on life patterns be taken into careful consideration, and that the changes be withheld or introduced on the basis of this consideration.

"These are radical proposals, extremely difficult to put into effect. But the need for their being put into effect is far greater than all of the difficulties, and infinitely greater than the need for our national holy trinity, Efficiency, Economy, and Quality.

"Men, by their nature, seemingly, cannot be happy unless engaged in enterprises that make them feel useful. They must, therefore, be returned to participation in such enterprises.

"I hold, and the members of the Ghost Shirt Society hold:

"That there must be virtue in imperfection, for Man is imperfect, and Man is a creation of God.

"That there must be virtue in frailty, for Man is frail, and Man is a creation of God.

"That there must be virtue in inefficiency, for Man is inefficient, and Man is a creation of God.

"That there must be virtue in brilliance followed by stupidity, for Man is alternately brilliant and stupid, and Man is a creation of God.

"You perhaps disagree with the antique and vain notion of Man's being a creation of God.

"But I find it a far more defensible belief than the one implicit in intemperate faith in lawless technological progress—namely, that man is on earth to create more durable and efficient images of himself, and, hence, to eliminate any justification at all for his own continued existence."

The professor and the other leaders of the rebellion are more understanding about the benign benefits of technology than is the great mass of rebels. He pays for this understanding by getting struck in the head by a rioter wielding the Sacred Mace of the Order of the Aurora Borealis while trying to prevent the destruction of a radio tower. Paul thinks of von Neumann as the consummate academician. (PP XXXV) *He had been less interested in achieving a premeditated end than in seeing what would happen with given beginnings.*

As the Ghost Shirt leadership looks out over the ruins of Ilium and prepares to surrender, von Neumann concludes, "This isn't the end, you know. . . . Nothing ever is, nothing ever will be—not even Judgment Day" *(PP XXXV).*

von Peterswald, David Daffodil-H. *The Tourette's stricken, fifteen-year-old son of Wilma Pachysandra-17 von Peterswald and the brother of Wilbur Swain—related through the government-sponsored extended family program.*

von Peterswald, Dr. Felix Bauxite-13. *The husband of Wilma von Peterswald, Felix invents "the Hooligan," enabling people to talk with the dead (named after the janitor who first discovered the device's unique feature and whose lunch pail served as the antennae). Wilbur uses the device to speak with* *his sister Eliza. (Slap 40)* "It was the Chinese who told me about the astonishing discovery my husband, **Dr. Felix Bauxite-13 von Peterswald**, made just before he died. My son, who is incidentally a Daffodil-II, like yourself, and I have kept this discovery a secret ever since, because the light it throws on the situation of human beings in the Universe is very demoralizing, to say the least. It has to do with the true nature of what awaits us all after death. What awaits us, Dr. Swain, is tedious in the extreme."

(Slap Epilogue) The talkers identified themselves as persons in the afterlife. They were backed by a demoralized chorus of persons who complained to each other of tedium and social slights and minor ailments, and so on.

As **Dr. von Peterswald** said in his secret diary: "It sounded like nothing so much as the other end of a telephone call on a rainy autumn day—to a badly run turkey farm."

von Peterswald, Melody Oriole-2.

The sixteen-year-old granddaughter of Wilbur Swain and Wilma Pachysandra-17 von Peterswald. Melody comes to live with Wilbur when she is only twelve. She has already been impregnated by the King of Michigan, who kept her in his harem. Shortly after making her way to her grandfather, Melody gives birth to a still-born son, which Wilbur cryptically cites as symbolic of his memoir's meaning. (Slap 13) Yes, and if archaeologists of the future find this book of mine, they will be spared the fruitless labor of digging through the pyramid in search of its meaning. There are no secret treasure rooms in there, no chambers of any kind.

Its meaning, which is minuscule in any event, lies beneath the manhole cover over which the pyramid is constructed. It is the body of a stillborn male. . . . The pyramid itself is entirely the idea of **Melody** and Isadore, who became her lover later on. It is a monument to a life that was never lived—to a person who was never named.

Melody is the daughter of Swain's illegitimate son by the widowed Mrs. von Peterswald. Her father survives the Urbana Massacre and becomes a drummer in the victorious army of the Duke of Oklahoma. At fourteen, the (unnamed) son and a forty-year-old

laundress working for the army give birth to Melody. Melody's middle name is intended to guard against future confrontations with the King of Michigan, the Duke of Oklahoma's arch-rival. Nevertheless, she is orphaned at age six after the Battle of Iowa City, and placed in the King of Michigan's harem composed of children with the same middle name as his.

Melody steals a Dresden candlestick from the king and escapes one night to search for her grandfather, whom her father often told her was also a king.

As Wilbur begins to write his memoirs, Melody is pregnant again. The father is Isadore Raspberry-19 Cohen, and he also lives with Swain.

Vonnegut's prologue to Slapstick, *in which he explains the special relationship he shared with his sister, Alice, closes with his musings about the true identities of both Wilbur and Melody. (Slap Prologue)* He *(Wilbur)* lives there *(Manhattan)* with his illiterate, rickety, pregnant little granddaughter, **Melody**. Who is he really? I guess he is myself—experimenting with being old.

Who is **Melody**? I thought for a while that she was all that remained of my memory of my sister. I now believe that she is what I feel to be, when I experiment with old age, all that is left of my optimistic imagination, of my creativeness.

von Peterswald, Wilma Pachysandra-17.

The Urbana, Illinois, wife of Dr. von Peterswald, inventor of "the Hooligan," a device that enables one to speak with the dead. After her husband dies, she earns a living for herself and David, her Tourette's-stricken son, by giving piano lessons. (Most members of the Pachysandra extended family are musical.)

Mrs. von Peterswald writes to Wilbur Swain on behalf of his twin sister, Eliza, asking him to visit and speak with her through "the Hooligan." After Wilbur donates part of his large supply of tri-benzo-Deportamil to help control David's affliction, Wilbur goes into a six-day fit of withdrawal during which he has sex with Wilma. The result is a son who eventually sires Melody Oriole-2 von Peterswald. (Slap Epilogue) Yes, and somewhere in there the widow passed on to him *(Wilbur)* what she had learned from the Chinese—that they had become successful manipulators of the Universe by combining harmonious minds.

von Schwefelbad, Baron Ulrich Werther. *While imprisoned in Jerusalem, Howard Campbell receives news that his best friend in Germany, Heinz Schildknecht, is employed in Ireland by the former German aristocrat. In fact, Heinz was a double-agent during the war and never left the intelligence game.* (MN 21) The Institute delights me with the news that Heinz is now in Ireland, is chief grounds-keeper for **Baron Ulrich Werther von Schwefelbad. Von Schwefelbad** bought a big estate in Ireland after the war.

von Strelitz, Arthur. *In* Jailbird, *the Harvard associate professor of anthropology who befriends Walter Starbuck and Mary Kathleen O'Looney, allowing them to use his house on Brattle Street to make love. His academic specialty includes the headhunters of the Solomon Islands.*

Born into an aristocratic Prussian family, von Strelitz was lecturing at Harvard in 1933 when Hitler took power in Germany. He never returned home. His father died of pneumonia during the Siege of Leningrad while commanding a corps of SS troops. Arthur von Strelitz eventually disappears while serving as an American spy on the Japanese-occupied Solomon Islands.

Vonnegut, (Uncle) Alex. *If the Harvard-educated, lifelong bachelor, insurance salesman, and alcoholic Alex Vonnegut were a fictional character, he might come off as mystic or private holy man remembered only for his insistence on consciously appreciating goodness when it made its rare appearance. His frequently offered advice to make mental notes of the good times is often quoted by his appreciative nephew:* If this isn't nice, what is? *(TQ 4) From Vonnegut's dedication in* The Sirens of Titan *(1951) through* A Man Without a Country *(2005), Uncle Alex is slowly revealed, reimagined, and always repurposed for the family's freethinking legacy that is part of the core of every Vonnegut novel.*

A Man Without a Country *contains Vonnegut's final presentation of his beloved uncle, accomplished by comparing him to his uncle Dan, whose thoughts of manhood are cast in the most barbaric of contexts. For Uncle Dan, manhood is earned by seeing and contributing to the deaths of others while at war, something he learned as an army lifer, vet-*eran of two world wars, an infantry colonel in both world wars. Sharing this mindset with the young Kurt Vonnegut only months removed from the Battle of the Bulge and the firebombing of Dresden leads the young war vet to completely disdain the apparent ignorance and lack of humanity exhibited by Uncle Dan.

Vonnegut counters this memory of Dan's ignorance and callousness with his superlative appreciation for Uncle Alex. He commends his uncle's advice to his readers, a completely heartfelt appeal. (MWC 12) When I got home from the Second World War, my Uncle Dan clapped me on the back, and he said, "You're a man now." So I killed him. Not really, but I certainly felt like doing it.

Dan, that was my bad uncle, who said a male can't be a man unless he'd gone to war.

But I had a good uncle, my late **Uncle Alex.** He was my father's kid brother, a childless graduate of Harvard who was an honest life-insurance salesman in Indianapolis. He was well-read and wise. And his principal complaint about other human beings was that they so seldom noticed it when they were happy. So when we were drinking lemonade under an apple tree in the summer, say, and talking lazily about this and that, almost buzzing like honeybees, **Uncle Alex** would suddenly interrupt the agreeable blather to exclaim, "If this isn't nice, I don't know what is."

So I do the same now, and so do my kids and grandkids. And I urge you to please notice when you are happy, and exclaim or murmur or think at some point, "If this isn't nice, I don't know what is."

Despite Vonnegut's fondness and spiritual indebtedness to his Uncle Alex, there was no doppelgänger for him at the Timequake *clambake, as there was none for other members of the family who did not appreciate his writing.* (TQ 62) Nobody was a near double for **Uncle Alex.** He did not like my writing. I dedicated *The Sirens of Titan* to him, and **Uncle Alex** said, "I suppose the young people will like it." Nobody resembled my aunt Ella Vonnegut Stewart, a first cousin of my father's, either. She and her husband, Kerfuit, owned a bookstore in Louisville, Kentucky. They did not stock my books because they found my language obscene. So it was back then, when I was starting out.

(*GBK* Introduction) What **Uncle Alex** found particularly objectionable about human beings in general was that they so seldom noticed it when they were happy.

(*ST* Dedication) FOR **ALEX VONNEGUT**, SPECIAL AGENT, WITH LOVE

(*WFG* Reflections on My Own Death) **My Uncle Alex** has just calculated in a letter to me that he is a thousand months old, and he told me another time that dying is like a candle's going out. Combustion stops. **Uncle Alex** is right.

(*Slap* Prologue) We went back (*to Indianapolis*) last July for the funeral of our **Uncle Alex Vonnegut**, the younger brother of our late father—almost the last of our old-style relatives, of the native American patriots who did not fear God, and who had souls that were European.

(*Slap* Prologue) At any rate, if **Uncle Alex**, the atheist, found himself standing before Saint Peter and the Pearly Gates after he died, I am certain he introduced himself as follows: "My name is **Alex Vonnegut**. I'm an alcoholic." Good for him.

(*Slap* Prologue) There was an empty seat between us, which was spooky poetry. It could have been a seat for our sister Alice, whose age was halfway between mine and Bernard's. She wasn't in that seat and on her way to her beloved **Uncle Alex**'s funeral, for she had died among strangers in New Jersey, of cancer—at the age of forty-one.

(*Slap* Prologue) She (*Kurt's sister, Alice*) died at about the same time of day that **Uncle Alex** died—an hour or two after the sun went down.

(*Slap* Prologue) Be that as it may, she (*Alice*) had vanished entirely as my audience by the time **Uncle Alex** died.

(*Slap* Prologue) "People from our great-grandfathers' generation would mingle with our own, when we were young—" I said, "and all the generations in between. Arrivals and departures would be announced. **Uncle Alex** would leave for his job as a spy in Baltimore. You would come home from your freshman year at M.I.T."

(*Slap* Prologue) The old man is writing his autobiography. He begins it with words which my late **Uncle Alex** told me one time should be used by religious skeptics as a prelude to their nightly prayers.

These are the words: "To whom it may concern." *Vonnegut sets up the opening of* Slapstick, *the autobiography of Wilbur Swain, as the "old man" referred to here.*

(*JB* Prologue) I had lunch with him (*Powers Hapgood*) and Father and my **Uncle Alex**, my father's younger brother, in Stegemeier's Restaurant in downtown Indianapolis after I came home from the European part of World War Two. That was in July of 1945. The first atomic bomb had not yet been dropped on Japan. That would happen in about a month. Imagine that.

Powers Hapgood is fictionalized as Kenneth Whistler in Jailbird.

It was **Uncle Alex** who had arranged the lunch. He and Powers Hapgood had been at Harvard together. . . .

Uncle Alex was so conservative politically that I do not think he would have eaten lunch with Hapgood gladly if Hapgood had not been a fellow Harvard man. Hapgood was then a labor union officer, a vice-president of the local CIO. His wife Mary had been the Socialist Party's candidate for vice-president of the United States again and again.

(*JB* Prologue) The meeting with Hapgood came about because I had told **Uncle Alex** that I might try to get a job with a labor union after the Army let me go. . . .

Uncle Alex must have thought something like this: "God help us.

"Against stupidity even the gods contend in vain. Well—at least there is a Harvard man with whom he can discuss this ridiculous dream."

So **Uncle Alex** and I sat down at a front table in Stegemeier's and ordered beers and waited for Father and Hapgood to arrive.

(*JB* Prologue) **Uncle Alex**, by the way, could do nothing with his hands. Neither could my mother. She could not even cook a breakfast or sew on a button.

(*JB* Prologue) So we ordered more beers. **Uncle Alex** would later become a cofounder of the Indianapolis chapter of Alcoholics Anonymous, although his wife would say often and pointedly that he himself had never been an alcoholic. He began to talk now about The Columbia Conserve Company, a cannery that Powers Hapgood's father, William, also a Harvard man, had founded in Indianapolis in 1903. It was a famous experiment in industrial democracy, but I had never heard of it before. There was a lot that I had never heard of before.

(*JB* Prologue) "It went bust," said **Uncle Alex**, with a certain grim, Darwinian satisfaction. . . . It did not go completely bust for a while. In fact it still existed when **Uncle Alex** and Father and Powers Hapgood and I had lunch.

(*JB* Prologue) Now Powers Hapgood came into the restaurant, an ordinary-looking Middle Western Anglo-Saxon in a cheap business suit. He wore a union badge in his lapel. He was cheerful. He knew my father slightly. He knew **Uncle Alex** quite well. . . .

He was a talker, with far more wonderful stories than Father or **Uncle Alex** had ever told. He was thrown into a lunatic asylum after he led the pickets at the execution of Sacco and Vanzetti.

(*PS* Roots) But Father's younger brother, **Uncle Alex**, a Harvard graduate and life insurance salesman, was responsive and amusing and generous with me, was my ideal grown-up friend.

(*PS* Embarrassment) I would describe the hum that is with me all the time as *embarrassment*. I have somehow disgraced myself.

My Indianapolis relatives may actually feel that I have done so. They are not enthusiastic about my work. I have already described my Uncle John's distaste for it. As for my **Uncle Alex**: I dedicated *The Sirens of Titan* to him, and he said he could not read it. He supposed that beatniks would think it was wonderful.

(*PS* Embarrassment) In Indianapolis his aunts, cousins and old friends call him Kay, and their memories of him are fond and lively. His Aunt, Irma Vonnegut Lindener, says warmly, "He's a dear, awfully nice," and her eyes light up with affection as she recounts thoughtful things he has done for the family over the years. He shared an enviable rapport with his uncle, **Alex Vonnegut** . . . though they were worlds apart in their convictions. *(This is an excerpt from an article about Vonnegut in the October 1976 issue of* Indianapolis Magazine.*)*

(*FWD* I) It was a tradition in the Indianapolis branch of our once large and cohesive family that we should go east to college but then come back to Indianapolis. My **Uncle Alex** went to Harvard, and his first assignment was to write an essay about why

he had chosen to study there. His opening sentence, he told me, was, "I came to Harvard because my big brother is at MIT."

(*FWD* II) "Dr. Bruetsch couldn't have helped my mother, and he was the greatest expert on insanity in the whole State of Indiana. Maybe he knew she was crazy. Maybe he didn't. If he did know she was crazy after midnight, and he was very fond of her, he must have felt as helpless as my father. There was not then an Indianapolis chapter of Alcoholics Anonymous, which might have helped. One would be founded by my father's only brother, **Alex**, who was an alcoholic, in 1955 or so.

"There—I've told you another family secret, haven't I? About **Uncle Alex**?"

(*FWD* III) "And I think yet again about my father, who struggled to become a painter after he was forced into early and unwelcome retirement by the Great Depression. . . . I remember a portrait he did of his only brother, **Alex**, who was an insurance salesman, which he called Special Agent. When he roughed it in, his hand and eye conspired with a few bold strokes to capture several important truths about **Alex**, including a hint of disappointment. **Uncle Alex** was a proud graduate of Harvard, who would rather have been a scholar of literature than an insurance man.

"When Father finished the portrait, made sure of every square inch of masonite had its share of paint, **Uncle Alex** had disappeared entirely. We had a drunk and lustful Queen Victoria instead."

(*TQ* 4) "My **uncle Alex Vonnegut**, a Harvard-educated life insurance salesman who lived at 5033 North Pennsylvania Street, taught me something very important. He said that when things were really going well we should be sure to *notice* it.

"He was talking about simple occasions, not great victories: maybe drinking lemonade on a hot afternoon in the shade, or smelling the aroma of a nearby bakery, or fishing and not caring if we catch anything or not, or hearing somebody all alone playing a piano really well in the house next door.

"**Uncle Alex** urged me to say this out loud during such epiphanies: 'If this isn't nice, what is?'"

(*TQ* 36) In the waning summer of 1996, I ask myself if there were ideas I once held that I should now repudiate. I consider the example set by my father's only brother, **Uncle Alex**, the childless,

Harvard-educated Indianapolis insurance salesman. He had me reading high-level socialist writers
like Shaw and Norman Thomas and Eugene Debs
and John Dos Passos when I was a teenager, along
with making model airplanes and jerking off. After
World War Two, **Uncle Alex** became as politically
conservative as the Archangel Gabriel.

See also: FWD II; V; TQ 47; 63, Epilogue; GBK
Introduction; MWC 12.

Vonnegut, Alice. *Alice Vonnegut (Kurt's sister) and
her husband, James Carmalt Adams, died within
forty-eight hours of each other. He died first, in a
commuter train accident, and Alice saw the notice in
the* New York Daily News. *She was dying of cancer
and in the hospital at the time. Kurt and Jane Cox
Vonnegut adopted (informally) their three oldest
children.*

Alice Vonnegut is such a central inspiration for
Timequake *that it may justifiably be termed his
homage to her, perhaps even more so than* Slapstick.
*She is the physical model for the fictional Monica
Pepper, the chief administrator of the Academy of
Arts and Letters who must also bear the loss of her
husband—twice. It is also his sister's derisive sense of
humor, chiefly about art and religion, that Vonnegut
returns to again and again. Vonnegut often said that
a writer needed to write with an audience of one in
mind, and he always maintained his audience was
his big sister Alice.*

(MH Preface) My only sister, five years older than
I, died when she was forty. She was over six feet tall,
too, by an angstrom unit or so. She was heavenly to
look at, and graceful, both in and out of water. She
was a sculptress. She was christened "**Alice,**" but
she used to deny that she was really an **Alice**. I
agreed. Everybody agreed. Sometime in a dream
maybe I will find out what her real name was.

Her dying words were, "No pain." Those are
good dying words. It was cancer that killed her.

And I realize now that the two main themes of
my novels were stated by my siblings: "Here I am
cleaning shit off of practically everything" and "No
pain." The contents of this book are samples of
work I sold in order to finance the writing of the
novels. Here one finds the fruits of Free Enterprise.
(*Slap* Prologue) There was an empty seat between
us, which was spooky poetry. It could have been a

seat for our sister **Alice**, whose age was halfway between mine and Bernard's. She wasn't in that seat
and on her way to her beloved Uncle Alex's funeral,
for she had died among strangers in New Jersey, of
cancer—at the age of forty-one.

"Soap opera!" she said to my brother and me
one time, when discussing her own impending
death. She would be leaving four young boys behind, without any mother.

"Slapstick," she said.

Hi ho.

(*Slap* Prologue) Since **Alice** had never received
any religious instruction, and since she had led a
blameless life, she never thought of her awful luck
as being anything but accidents in a very busy
place.

Good for her.

(FWD II) In the household of my childhood and
youth, my sister **Alice**, dead for many years now
(and missed like heck by me), was the maiden and
our father was the elusive and spookily enchanted
unicorn. My only other sibling, my own big brother
who went to MIT, Bernard, and I could never catch
him. To him we weren't all that interesting. As far
as the two of us are concerned, this is not a remotely
tragic tale. We were tough. We could take it. We
had other fans.

(FWD III) But to get back to the thing between my
father and my sister, the unicorn and the maiden:
Father, no more a Freudian than Lewis Carroll,
made **Alice** his principal source of encouragement
and sympathy. He made the most of an enthusiasm
they had in common, which was for the visual arts.
Alice was just a girl, remember, and aside from the
embarrassment of having a unicorn lay its head in
her lap, so to speak, she was traumatized mainly by
having every piece of sculpture or picture she made
celebrated by Father as though it were Michelangelo's Pieta or the ceiling of the Sistine Chapel. In
later life (which was going to last only until she was
forty-one) this made her a lazy artist. (I have often
quoted her elsewhere as saying, "Just because people have talent, that doesn't mean they have to do
something with it.")

"My only sister, **Alice,**" I wrote, again in *Architectural Digest,* "possessed considerable gifts as a
painter and sculptor, with which she did next to
nothing. **Alice,** who was six feet tall and a platinum

blonde, asserted one time that she could roller-skate through a great museum like the Louvre, which she had never seen and which she wasn't all that eager to see, and which she in fact would never see, and fully appreciate every painting she passed. She said that she would be hearing these words in her head above the whir and clack of her wheels on the terrazzo: 'Got it, got it, got it.'"

(*FWD* IV) "We went out in an old, leaky rowboat, which all my life I had called 'The Beralikur,' a mixture of my first name with those of my siblings, Bernard and **Alice**. But that name was not painted on the boat, which would have been redundant. Everybody who was anybody at Maxincuckee already knew that the name of that leaky boat was the Beralikur."

(*FWD* VI) (Speaking of composers: My sister **Alice** asked our father when she was about ten years old if he and Mother used to dance to Beethoven.)

(*FWD* X) One nice thing: Camp Atterbury was so close to Indianapolis that I was able to sleep in my own bedroom and use the family car on weekends. But Mother died on one of those. My sister **Alice** gave birth to Mother's first grandchild (whom I would adopt along with his two brothers when he was fourteen) maybe six weekends after that, about the time of the D-Day landings in France.

(*FWD* XIX) Not only would I have written that if I hadn't died, but I would have rejoiced in the birth of three more grandchildren. I already had three. My mother never saw any of her one dozen grandchildren, although my sister **Alice** was pregnant with her first one, Jim, when **Alice** and I found Mother dead. (No prospect of good news, obviously, could rescue Mother. She felt as awful as anybody does nowadays in Mozambique, where there is no end to murdering but almost no suicide.)

(*TQ* 1) It appears to me that the most highly evolved Earthling creatures find being alive embarrassing or much worse. Never mind cases of extreme discomfort, such as idealists being crucified. Two important women in my life, my mother and my only sister, **Alice**, or **Allie**, in Heaven now, hated life and said so. **Allie** would cry out, "I give up! I give up!"

(*TQ* 9) Mrs. Pepper, wife of the wheelchair-ridden composer Zoltan Pepper, bore a striking resemblance to my late sister **Allie**, who hated life so much. **Allie** died of cancer of the everything way back in 1958, when I was thirty-six and she was forty-one, hounded by bill collectors to the very end. Both women were pretty blondes, which was OK. But they were six-foot-two! Both women were permanently acculturated in adolescence, since nowhere on Earth, save among the Watusis, did it make any sense for a woman to be that tall.

Both women were unlucky. **Allie** married a nice guy who lost all their money and then some in dumb businesses. Monica Pepper was the reason her husband Zoltan was paralyzed from the waist down. Two years earlier, she had accidentally landed on top of him in a swimming pool out in Aspen, Colorado. At least **Allie** had to die so deep in debt, and with four sons to raise, only once. After the timequake struck, Monica Pepper would have to swan-dive on top of her husband a second time.

(*TQ* 16) Trout got to know Prince, just as he got to know Monica Pepper and me, after the rerun ended and free will had kicked in again. Because of what the timequake had done to Prince, he had become as contemptuous of the idea of a wise and just God as my sister **Allie** had been. **Allie** opined one time, not just about her life but everybody's life, "If there is a God, He sure hates people. That's all I can say."

(*TQ* 23) I was reminded of Steve Adams, one of my sister **Allie**'s three sons my first wife Jane and I adopted after **Allie**'s unlucky husband Jim died in a railroad train that went off an open drawbridge in New Jersey, and then, two days later, **Allie** died of cancer of the everything.

(*TQ* 25) Boys and girls of our family often come into this world, as did **Allie**, with natural gifts for drawing and painting and sculpting and so on. Jane's and my two daughters, Edith and Nanette, are middle-aged professional artists who have shows and sell pictures. So does our son the doctor Mark. So do I. **Allie** could have done that, too, if she had been willing to work hard and hustle some. But as I have reported elsewhere, she said, "Just because you're talented, that doesn't mean you have to do something with it."

I say in my novel *Bluebeard*, "Beware of gods bearing gifts." I think I had **Allie** in mind when I wrote that, and **Allie** in mind again when, in *Timequake One*, I had Monica Pepper spray-paint

"FUCK ART!" in orange and purple across the steel front door of the Academy. **Allie** didn't know there was such an institution as the Academy, I'm almost sure, but she would have been happy to see those words emblazoned anywhere.

(*TQ* 30) Yes, and all the people falling down in *Timequake One*, and now in this book, are like "FUCK ART!" spray-painted across the steel front door of the Academy. They are homage to my sister **Allie**. They are **Allie**'s kind of porno: people deprived of dignified postures by gravity instead of sex.

(*TQ* 34) My first wife Jane and my sister **Allie** had mothers who went nuts from time to time. Jane and **Allie** were graduates of Tudor Hall and had once been two of the prettiest, merriest girls at the Woodstock Golf and Country Club. All male writers, incidentally, no matter how broke or otherwise objectionable, have pretty wives. Somebody should look into this.

Jane and **Allie** missed the timequake, thank goodness. My guess is that Jane would have found some goodness in the rerun. **Allie** would not have. Jane was life-loving and optimistic, a scrapper against carcinoma to the very end. **Allie**'s last words expressed relief, and nothing more. They were, as I've recorded elsewhere, "No pain, no pain." I didn't hear her say it, and neither did our big brother Bernie. A male hospital attendant, with a foreign accent, relayed those words to us via telephone.

(*BAG* Thanasphere) **Allie** is up in Heaven now, with my first wife Jane and Sam Lawrence and Flannery O'Connor and Dr. Bergler, but I still write to please her. **Allie** was funny in real life. That gives me permission to be funny, too. **Allie** and I were very close.

(*ARM* 28) You know what my sister Allie used to say? She used to say, "Your parents ruin the first half of your life, and your kids ruin the second half."

See also: *TQ* 10; 15; 25; 29–31; 35; 39; 41; 60; Epilogue; *BAG* Thanasphere.

Vonnegut, Bernard. *There are two Bernard Vonneguts, Kurt's paternal grandfather and his older brother. His grandfather was artistic from an early age, and when he grew older he didn't want to work in the family hardware business. He eventually became an architect in New York City and later returned to Indianapolis at the insistence of his parents. He married Nanette Schnull, a sociable woman uninterested in the arts. Their three children were Kurt, Irma, and Alex.*

(*PS* Roots) "Old Clemens, as he advanced into his seventies, turned over management of his business to the competent hands of his three sons: Clemens, Jr., Franklin, and George. His son **Bernard** had a brief connection with the Company but disliked what he called 'the trade in nails' and confined his attention to his profession of architecture and to his avocations in the arts."

(*PS* Roots) And Clemens Vonnegut, the Free Thinker and founder of the Vonnegut Hardware Company, and his wife Katarina begat **Bernard Vonnegut**, who, Uncle John says, "was from earliest youth artistic. He could draw and paint with skill. **Bernard** was extremely modest and retiring. He had no intimates, and took but little part in social activities. He was never a happy, extroverted personality, but was inclined to be reticent, shy, and somewhat contemptuous of his environment." He was my father's father.

(*PS* Roots) AS has already been said, my father's mother Nanette was cheerful and sociable, and uninterested in the fine arts save for music—and my father's father **Bernard** was a freak in the family for being able to draw and paint so well at an early age. He was also unsociable, and evidently unhappy in Indianapolis most of the time.

(*PS* Roots) Uncle John said to me in conversation one time that my grandfather **Bernard** was probably relieved to die young—"to be well out of it." He died of intestinal cancer at fifty-three, five years younger than I am now. That was in 1908, so he did not see any of his grandchildren. He did not even see his children married.

(*TQ* 47) Listen: A Harvard education for my Uncle Alex wasn't the trophy of a micromanaged Darwinian victory over others that it is today. His father, the architect **Bernard Vonnegut**, sent him there in order that he might become *civilized*, which he did indeed become, although fabulously henpecked, and nothing more than a life insurance salesman.

(*ARM* 17) His father, my grandfather the architect **Bernard Vonnegut**, designed, among other things, The Athenæum, which before the First World War was called "Das Deutsche Haus." I can't imagine why they would have changed the name to "The Athenæum," unless it was to kiss the ass of a bunch of Greek-Americans.

See also: PS Roots; FWD V; MWC Author's Note; ARM Clowe's Hall.

Bernard Vonnegut's son Kurt sired Bernard (named for the grandfather), Alice, and Kurt, Jr. This younger Bernard was a chemistry professor at the State University of New York at Albany. He helped invent the method for seeding rain clouds. He received his undergraduate and doctoral degrees from the Massachusetts Institute of Technology. (WFG Address to the American Physical Society) He was notorious in Schenectady for having a horrendously messy laboratory. There was a safety officer in the laboratory who called on him regularly, begging him to clean up the death traps all around the room. One day my brother said to him, "If you think this is a mess, you should see what it's like up here." And my brother pointed to his own head. I loved him for that. We love each other very much, even though I am a humanist and he is physicist. (WFG Excelsior! We're Going to the Moon! Excelsior!) My brother **Bernard** saw a spaceship go up one time from Cape Kennedy, and he told me: "You know, if you're right there, the whole thing almost seems worth it." It was almost a billion-dollar thrill, he said—the noise in particular. (WFG Address to Graduating Class at Bennington College, 1970) My brother **Bernard**, who was nine years older, was on his way to becoming an important scientist. He would later discover that silver iodide particles could precipitate certain kinds of clouds as snow or rain. He made me very enthusiastic about science for a while. I thought scientists were going to find out exactly how everything worked, and then make it work better. I fully expected that by the time I was twenty-one, some scientist, maybe my brother, would have taken a color photograph of God Almighty—and sold it to *Popular Mechanics* magazine.

Scientific truth was going to make us so happy and comfortable. (*Slap* Prologue) My longest experience with common decency, surely, has been with my older brother, my only brother, **Bernard**, who is an atmospheric scientist in the State University of New York at Albany.

He is a widower, raising two young sons all by himself. He does it well. He has three grown-up sons besides.

We were given very different sorts of minds at birth. **Bernard** could never be a writer. I could never be a scientist. And, since we make our livings with our minds, we tend to think of them as gadgets separate from our awarenesses, from our central selves.

We have hugged each other maybe three or four times at birthdays, very likely, and clumsily. We have never hugged in moments of grief.

The minds we have been given enjoy the same sorts of jokes, at any rate—Mark Twain stuff, Laurel and Hardy stuff.

They are equally disorderly, too.

Here is an anecdote about my brother, which, with minor variations, could be told truthfully about me:

Bernard worked for the General Electric Research Laboratory in Schenectady, New York, for a while, where he discovered that silver iodide could precipitate certain sorts of clouds as snow or rain. His laboratory was a sensational mess, however, where a clumsy stranger could die in a thousand different ways, depending on where he stumbled.

The company had a safety officer who nearly swooned when he saw this jungle of deadfalls and snares and hair-trigger booby traps. He bawled out my brother.

My brother said this to him, tapping his own forehead with his fingertips: "If you think this laboratory is bad, you should see what it's like in here."

And so on.

But, because of the sorts of minds we were given at birth, and in spite of their disorderliness, **Bernard** and I belong to artificial extended families which allow us to claim relatives all over the world.

He is a brother to scientists everywhere. I am a brother to writers everywhere.

This is amusing and comforting to both of us. It is nice.

It is lucky, too, for human beings need all the relatives they can get—as possible donors or receivers not necessarily of love, but of common decency. (*FWD "On Literature"*) Scientists like my big brother **Bernard**, who is engaged in pure research, also have eyes which are childlike with astonishment and fascination. **Bernard** and I have such eyes in common. His wonderment, however, is reserved for the lusty strength and skill of whatever created the Universe. As I write this, I am confident that **Bernard**, although he is one hundred miles away and I haven't talked to him on the telephone for three days, is thinking about thunderstorms. He in turn can be confident that I am usually thinking about human wickedness.

(*FWD* XX) My big brother **Bernard** says that the Christmas season makes him feel as though somebody were beating him in the face with a bladder.

(*TQ* 49) I asked my big brother **Bernie** in the American Museum of Natural History in New York, and this was long before the period of the rerun, whether he believed in Darwin's theory of evolution. He said he did, and I asked how come, and he said, "Because it's the only game in town."

Bernie's reply is the tag line of yet another joke from long ago, like "Ting-a-ling, you son of a bitch!" It seems a guy is off to play cards, and a friend tells him the game is crooked. The guy says, "Yeah, I know, but it's the only game in town."

(*TQ* 38) More news of this day in August, halfway through the rerun, as yet another autumn draws near:

My big brother **Bernie**, the born scientist who may know more about the electrification of thunderstorms than anyone, has an invariably fatal cancer, too far advanced to be daunted by the Three Horsemen of the Oncologic Apocalypse, Surgery, Chemotherapy, and Radiation.

Bernie still feels fine.

It is much too early to talk about, but when he dies, God forbid, I don't think his ashes should be put in Crown Hill Cemetery with James Whitcomb Riley and John Dillinger, who belonged only to Indiana. Bernie belongs to the World.

Bernie's ashes should be scattered over the dome of a towering thunderhead.

(*TQ* 43) And just get a load of this: My big brother **Bernie**, who can't draw for sour apples, and who at his most objectionable used to say he didn't like paintings because they didn't do anything, just hung there year after year, has this summer become an artist!

I shit you not! This Ph.D. physical chemist from MIT is now the poor man's Jackson Pollock! He squoozles glurp of various colors and consistencies between two flat sheets of impermeable materials, such as windowpanes or bathroom tiles. He pulls them apart, *et voilà!*

(*TQ* 53) The monster in *Frankenstein*—or, *The Modern Prometheus* turns mean because he finds it so humiliating to be alive and yet so ugly, so unpopular. He kills Frankenstein, who, again, is the scientist and not the monster. And let me hasten to say that my big brother **Bernie** never has been a Frankenstein-style scientist, never has worked nor would have worked on purposely destructive devices of any sort. He hasn't been a Pandora, either, turning loose new poisons or new diseases or whatever.

(*TQ* Epilogue) My big and only brother **Bernard**, a widower for twenty-five years, died after prolonged bouts with cancers, without excruciating pain, on the morning of April 25th, 1997, at the age of eighty-two, now four days ago. He was a Senior Research Scientist Emeritus, in the Atmospheric Sciences Research Center of the State University of New York at Albany, and the father of five fine sons.

I was seventy-four. Our sister Alice would have been seventy-nine. At the time of her humbling death at the age of forty-one, I said, "What a wonderful old lady Allie would have been." No such luck.

See also: Slap Prologue; *PS* Religion; *PS* Children; *DD* Preface; *FWD* II; V; XII; XX; *TQ* 25; 34; 39; 55; Epilogue.

Vonnegut, Carl Hiroaki and Emiko Alice. *Kurt Vonnegut's grand-nephew and grand-niece, the children of Peter Vonnegut and Mishi Minatoya,* my brother's only grandchildren. They, too, are, among other things, de St. Andres. Strange and nice (*PS* Children).

Vonnegut, Clemens. *Vonnegut's great-grandfather, who wrote the text* Instruction in Morals, *from which Vonnegut takes the following quotation for his epigraph to* Palm Sunday: "Whoever entertains liberal views and chooses a consort that is captured by superstition risks his liberty and his happiness."

Born in Munster, Westphalia, in 1824, Clemens Vonnegut came to the United States in 1848, settling in Indianapolis in 1850. His father had been a tax collector for the Duke of Westphalia. In Indianapolis he met another German immigrant named Vollmer who had been settled here a few years and was already established in business for himself in a small way as a retail merchant in hardware and sundry merchandise. The two became friends, and Vollmer invited **Vonnegut** *to join him in this enterprise. The firm then became known as Vollmer &* **Vonnegut.** *After a short association Vollmer decided to make a journey out West to explore the new country and visit the gold fields recently discovered in California. He was never heard from again, and presumably lost his life in the "Wild West" (PS Roots). Vollmer & Vonnegut became the Vonnegut Hardware Company, a family business that thrived into the twentieth century. In 1852 Clemens married Katarina Blank.*

(PS Roots) "Many tales were told of **Clemens Vonnegut.** When he was elected to the Board of School Commissioners, he found that the local banks did not pay interest on the somewhat large deposits which the Board carried to finance its operations. He demanded that the banks pay interest on the Board's deposits. This was then considered to be an offensive innovation in the customary and comfortable practice which until then had prevailed. The banker John P. Frenzel then called upon **Clemens** at his office and loudly upbraided him. **Clemens** pretended to be hard of hearing, and capped his ears. Frenzel shouted louder. Still **Clemens** pretended not to hear. Frenzel raised his voice and interjected profanity, but to no avail. **Clemens** would not 'hear' him. Finally Frenzel stormed out—still not heard. But thenceforth the banks paid interest and have continued to do so to this day."

Clemens Vonnegut's significance stems in part from the fact that he was a self-professed freethinker, though raised Roman Catholic. Vonnegut says Clemens was what he only aspired to be, "a cultivated eccentric." He also calls him "a skeptic, one who rejects faith in the unknowable," something Vonnegut wishes to ascribe to himself as well.

More significantly, Vonnegut and his great-grandfather seemingly shared more than a similarity of views upon such weighty matters as religion; they share a manner of expression that is wholly original for each. In 1874 Clemens planned his own funeral, including his eulogy. In 1981, while Vonnegut was preparing Palm Sunday, *his brother Bernard sent him a copy of Clemens's* Instruction on Morals *as well as some of his "comments on life and death." The similarity of expression is so close, some scholars thought Kurt Vonnegut wrote them.* (PS Religion) "Friends or Opponents: To all of you who stand here to deliver my body to the earth:

"To you, my next of kin:

"Do not mourn! I have now arrived at the end of the course of life, as you will eventually arrive at yours. I am at rest and nothing will ever disturb my deep slumber.

"I am disturbed by no worries, no grief, no fears, no wishes, no passions, no pains, no reproaches from others. All is infinitely well with me.

"I departed from life with loving, affectionate feelings for all mankind; and I admonish you: Be aware of this truth that the people on this earth could be joyous, if only they would live rationally and if they would contribute mutually to each other's welfare.

"This world is not a vale of sorrows if you will recognize discriminatingly what is truly excellent in it; and if you will avail yourself of it for mutual happiness and well-being. Therefore, let us explain as often as possible, and particularly at the departure from life, that we base our faith on firm foundations, on Truth for putting into action our ideas which do not depend on fables and ideas which Science has long ago proven to be false.

"We also wish Knowledge, Goodness, Sympathy, Mercy, Wisdom, Justice, and Truthfulness. We also strive for and venerate all of those attributes from which the fantasy of man has created a God. We also strive for the virtues of Temperance, Industriousness, Friendship, and Peace. We believe in pure ideas based on Truth and Justice.

"Therefore, however, we do not believe, cannot believe, that a Thinking Being existed for millions and millions of years, and eventually and finally out of nothing—through a Word—created this world, or rather this earth with its Firmament, its Sun and Moon and the Stars.

"We cannot believe that this Being formed a human being from clay and breathed into it an Immortal Soul, and then allowed this human being to procreate millions, and then delivered them all into unspeakable misery, wretchedness and pain for all eternity. Nor can we believe that the descendents [*sic*] of one or two human beings will inevitably become sinners; nor do we believe that through the criminal executions of an Innocent One may we be redeemed."

(*PS* Children) "Truth," he (*Clemens Vonnegut*) says, "must always be recognized as the paramount requisite of human society." As I myself said in another place, I began to have my doubts about truth after it was dropped on Hiroshima.

Clemens Vonnegut wrote of powerful and rich families founded by criminals. He despised them. He himself founded a dynasty based on hard work, prudence, and honest dealing.

(*GBK* Introduction) About belief or lack of belief in an afterlife: Some of you may know I am neither Christian nor Jewish nor Buddhist, nor a conventionally religious person of any sort. I am a humanist, which means, in part, that I have tried to behave decently without any expectation of rewards or punishments after I'm dead. My German-American ancestors, the earliest of whom settled in our Middle West about the time of our Civil War, called themselves "Freethinkers," which is the same sort of thing. My great grandfather **Clemens Vonnegut** wrote, for example, "If what Jesus said was good, what can it matter whether he was God or not?"

Vonnegut, Dan (Uncle). *Contrasting with Vonnegut's favorite uncle, Alex, Dan is so irksome that he appears only twice in his nephew's texts and in precisely the same way each time. Dan is a retired colonel who served in both world wars. He is also referred to this way in various unpublished graduation speeches and interviews.* (*TQ* 20) When I got home from my war, my **uncle Dan** clapped me on the back, and he bellowed, "You're a *man* now!"

I damn near killed my first German.

(*MWC* 12) When I got home from the Second World War, my **Uncle Dan** clapped me on the back, and he said, "You're a man now." So I killed him. Not really, but I certainly felt like doing it.

Dan, that was my bad uncle, who said a male can't be a man unless he'd gone to war.

Vonnegut, Edith. *Vonnegut named his daughter in honor of his mother. Young Edith became an artist and writer, having provided illustrations for various Franklin Library editions of her father's novels. Nicknamed "Edie Bucket," she was briefly married to television reporter Geraldo Rivera and later married John Squibb. They live in Barnstable, Massachusetts, on the property once owned by her parents.*

In the Author's Note to A Man Without a Country, *Vonnegut twice mentions Edith in reference to their shared interest in making art.* Yes, and last July (2004) there was an exhibition of Joe's and my stuff, arranged by Joe, at the Indianapolis Art Center in the town of my birth. But there was also a painting by my architect and painter grandfather Bernard Vonnegut, and two by my architect and painter father Kurt Vonnegut, and six apiece by my daughter **Edith** and my son the doctor Mark.

Shortly after in the text, Vonnegut recalls his conversation with Syd Solomon and Edith's response to Solomon's learnedness: I asked the now regrettably dead painter Syd Solomon, a most agreeable neighbor on Long Island for many summertimes, how to tell a good picture from a bad one. He gave me the most satisfactory answer I ever expect to hear. He said, "Look at a million pictures, and you can never be mistaken."

I passed this on to mystic daughter **Edith**, a professional painter, and she too thought it was pretty good. She said she "could rollerskate through the Louvre, saying, 'Yes, no, no, yes, no, yes,' and so on."

Vonnegut notes with appreciation both Edith's artistic talent and her good sense in marrying John Squibb, getting past her marriage to the tabloid videojournalist Geraldo Rivera. (FWD XIV) I tried to deal some with the Neo-Cons' wrong-centuryism and wrong-countryism in a novel I finished four months ago, *Hocus Pocus*. The Franklin Library is (at this writing) preparing a deluxe edition of *Hocus Pocus* (with an illustration by my daughter **Edith**, the former Mrs. Geraldo Rivera, now married to a really great guy) for which I have provided a special preface.

In Timequake, *Vonnegut reveals that Edith's nickname is Edie Bucket* (8) *and that she lives in the family house in Barnstable, Cape Cod, with her husband and their two sons, Will and Buck* (40).

See also: WFG Preface; WFG There's a Maniac Loose Out There; *PS* Embarrassment; *PS* Children; *FWD* III; *TQ* 25, 37.

Vonnegut, Edith Lieber. *Vonnegut's mother, who committed suicide in the early morning hours of Mother's Day 1944. This is the same date Vonnegut gives to the death of the pregnant Eloise Metzger when Rudy Waltz fires an errant shot from the upstairs gun room of their Midland City home, in* Deadeye Dick. *(In Vonnegut's public lectures he has stated that Rudy did no more than he had done as a young boy in Indianapolis.)*

Though Vonnegut often refers to his mother's clinical depression after the family's fortune was greatly diminished by the Great Depression, it is his uncle John Rauch who left the most detailed record of his mother. This can be found in the section of Palm Sunday *entitled "Roots."*

(PS Roots) "**Edith** was a very beautiful woman, tall and statuesque. Kurt always admired her beauty and was very proud of her. They fell in love, became engaged, and were married on November 22, 1913. They remained a devoted couple until the day of **Edith**'s death thirty-one years later. The marriage was approved by both families; but the Schnull-Vonnegut clan was slightly condescending. In the pecking order in the social hierarchy of the community, and particularly in the German group it was generally understood that the Schnull-Vonnegut clan ranked ahead of the Lieber-Barus clan.

"**Edith** was a rather tall woman, about five feet eight inches, with a fine graceful figure. She was auburn-haired, not quite red, with a very fair, clear skin, finely modeled features, and blue-green eyes. She was stately and dignified in bearing. She had a lively sense of humor and laughed easily. Her adolescent years had been difficult with her odious stepmother, but she was strong enough in spirit and courage to endure her ordeal, although the scars were there.

"Prior to her engagement and marriage to Kurt, **Edith** had been engaged to other men but had each time broken her engagement."

(PS Roots) "They continued to invade their diminishing capital. But Kurt had two $1,000 corporate bonds which he had inherited from his mother. **Edith**, true to her delusions to grandeur, said: 'Let's take one more trip abroad.' So they sold the two bonds, went to Paris for three weeks and returned broke. But it was a rare example of esprit—what the French call *panache*. It was going out with flair—all banners flying.

"Meanwhile came the Second World War in December 1941 and once again America was arrayed against Germany. Bernard at twenty-four escaped the draft, but Kurt, Jr., at nineteen was caught. He was enlisted in the army as a private and sent to training camp. This came as a great shock with acute distress to **Edith**. With her other financial problems the prospect of losing her son in the impending holocaust made her cup of troubles overflow. She became despondent and morose. Wanting money desperately, she attempted to write short stories which she could sell, but it was a futile, hopeless venture; a tragic disillusion. She simply could not see daylight. Kurt, Jr., got leave from his regiment to come home and spend Mother's Day in May 1944 with his family. During the night before, **Edith** died in her sleep in her fifty-sixth year on May 14, 1944. Her death was attributed to an overdose of sleeping tablets taken possibly by mistake. Her gross estate was inventoried in probate at $10,815.50. It was all that was left as her share of her grandfather's fortune and of her father's residue.

"She missed by a matter of two months the birth of her first grandchild, the son of her daughter Alice. She would miss seeing twelve grandchildren in all. She missed by seven months the capture of her son K by the Germans in the Battle of the Bulge, and his imprisonment in Dresden until the end of the war."

(PS Self-Interview) INTERVIEWER: Which member of your family had the most influence on you as a writer?

VONNEGUT: My mother, I guess. **Edith Lieber Vonnegut**. After our family lost almost all of its money in the Great Depression, my mother thought she might make a new fortune by writing for the slick magazines. She took short story courses at night. She studied magazines the way gamblers study racing forms.

(TQ 10) Allie died in New Jersey. She and her husband, Jim, also a native Hoosier, are buried whole in Crown Hill Cemetery in Indianapolis. So is James Whitcomb Riley, the Hoosier Poet, a never-married lush. So is John Dillinger, the beloved bank robber of the 1930s. So are our parents, Kurt and **Edith**, and Father's kid brother Alex Vonnegut, the Harvard-educated life insurance salesman who said, whenever life was good, "If this isn't nice, what is?" So are two previous generations of our parents' forebears: a brewer, an architect, merchants and musicians, and their wives, of course.

Full house!

See also: PS Roots; TQ 8; 10.

Vonnegut, Emma. *(TQ* 3) Trout's story *("No Laughing Matter")* reminds me of the time my late great-aunt **Emma Vonnegut** said she hated the Chinese. Her late son-in-law Kerfuit Stewart, who used to own Stewart's Book Store in Louisville, Kentucky, admonished her that it was *wicked* to hate that many people all at once.

Vonnegut, Irma. *The sister of Kurt Sr. and Alex Vonnegut,* my aunt **Irma**, said to me one time when I was a grownup, "*All* Vonnegut men are scared to death of women." Her two brothers were sure as heck scared of *her* (TQ 47).

Vonnegut, Jane Cox. *Vonnegut's childhood sweetheart and first wife to whom he was married for twenty-five years until they separated and divorced in 1970. He dedicates* Player Piano *to her with a quote from the Bible,*

For **Jane**—God Bless Her

CONSIDER THE LILIES OF THE
    FIELD, HOW THEY GROW:
THEY TOIL NOT, NEITHER DO THEY
    SPIN;
AND YET I SAY UNTO YOU,
THAT EVEN SOLOMON IN ALL HIS
    GLORY
WAS NOT ARRAYED LIKE ONE OF
    THESE. . . .

MATTHEW 6:28.

About their breakup Vonnegut wrote: We are still good friends, as they say. Like so many couples who are no longer couples these days, we have been through some terrible, unavoidable accident that we are ill-equipped to understand. Like our six children, we only just arrived on this planet and we were doing the best we could. We never saw what hit us. It wasn't another woman, it wasn't another man.

We woke up in ambulances headed for different hospitals, so to speak, and would never get together again. We were alive, yes, but the marriage was dead.

And it was no Lazarus.

It was a good marriage for a long time—and then it wasn't. The shock of having our children no longer need us happened somewhere in there. We were both going to have to find other sorts of seemingly important work to do and other compelling reasons for working and worrying so. But I am beginning to explain, which is a violation of a rule I lay down whenever I teach a class in writing: "All you can do is tell what happened. You will get thrown out of this course if you are arrogant enough to imagine that you can tell me why it happened. You do not know. You cannot know."

So I am embarrassed about the failure of my first marriage (PS Embarrassment).

(PS Religion) Toward the end of our marriage, it was mainly religion in a broad sense that **Jane** and I fought about. She came to devote herself more and more to making alliances with the supernatural in her need to increase her strength and understanding—and happiness and health. This was painful to me. She could not understand and cannot understand why that should have been painful to me, or why it should be any of my business at all.

And it is to suggest to her and to some others why it was painful that I chose for this book's epigraph a quotation from a thin book, *Instruction in Morals*, published in 1900 and written by my Free Thinker great-grandfather Clemens Vonnegut, then seventy-six years old:

"Whoever entertains liberal views and chooses a consort that is captured by superstition risks his liberty and his happiness."

(TQ 8) The late British philosopher Bertrand Russell said he lost friends to one of three addictions:

alcohol or religion or chess. Kilgore Trout was hooked on making idiosyncratic arrangements in horizontal lines, with ink on bleached and flattened wood pulp, of twenty-six phonetic symbols, ten numbers, and about eight punctuation marks. He was a black hole to anyone who might imagine that he or she was a friend of his.

I have been married twice, divorced once. Both my wives, **Jane** and now Jill, have said on occasion that I am much like Trout in that regard.

(*TQ* 25) The parents of my first wife **Jane**, Harvey and Riah Cox, did the same thing: sent their only daughter to Tudor Hall, and bought her rich girls' clothes, and maintained for her sake membership in the Woodstock Golf and Country Club they could ill afford, so she could marry a man whose family had money and power.

(*TQ* 25) The best **Jane** could do, and it was a time of panic for unmarried women, was a guy who came home a PFC, who had been flunking all his courses at Cornell when he went off to war, and who didn't have a clue as to what to do next, now that free will had kicked in again.

Get this: Not only did **Jane** have rich girls' manners and clothes. She was a Phi Beta Kappa from Swarthmore, and had been the outstanding writer there!

(*TQ* 32) The real reason my interest in the study of man as an animal flagged was that my wife **Jane Marie Cox Vonnegut**, who would die as **Jane Marie Cox Yarmolinsky**, gave birth to a baby named Mark. We needed bucks.

Jane herself, a Swarthmore Phi Beta Kappa, had won a full scholarship in the university's Russian Department. When she got pregnant with Mark, she resigned the scholarship. We found the head of the Russian Department in the library, I remember, and my wife told this melancholy refugee from Stalinism that she had to quit because she had become infected with progeny.

Even without a computer, I can never forget what he said to **Jane**: "My dear Mrs. Vonnegut, pregnancy is the beginning, not the end, of life."

(*TQ* 34) My first wife **Jane** and my sister Allie had mothers who went nuts from time to time. **Jane** and Allie were graduates of Tudor Hall and had once been two of the prettiest, merriest girls at the Woodstock Golf and Country Club.

Jane and Allie missed the timequake, thank goodness. My guess is that **Jane** would have found some goodness in the rerun. Allie would not have. **Jane** was life-loving and optimistic, a scrapper against carcinoma to the very end. Allie's last words expressed relief, and nothing more. They were, as I've recorded elsewhere, "No pain, no pain." I didn't hear her say it, and neither did our big brother Bernie. A male hospital attendant, with a foreign accent, relayed those words to us via telephone.

I don't know what **Jane**'s last words may have been. I've asked. She was Adam Yarmolinsky's wife by then, not mine. **Jane** evidently slipped away without speaking, not realizing that she wouldn't be coming up for air again. At her funeral, in an Episcopal church in Washington, D.C., Adam said to those gathered that her favorite exclamation was, "I can't wait!"

What **Jane** anticipated with such joy again and again was some event involving one or more of our six children, now all adults with children of their own: a psychiatric nurse, a comedy writer, a pediatrician, a painter, an airline pilot, and a printmaker.

(*TQ* 34) Our last conversation was intimate. **Jane** asked me, as though I knew, what would determine the exact moment of her death. She may have felt like a character in a book by me. In a sense she was. During our twenty-two years of marriage, I had decided where we were going next, to Chicago, to Schenectady, to Cape Cod. It was my work that determined what we did next. She never had a job. Raising six kids was enough for her.

I told her on the telephone that a sunburned, raffish, bored but not unhappy ten-year-old boy, whom we did not know, would be standing on the gravel slope of the boat-launching ramp at the foot of Scudder's Lane. He would gaze out at nothing in particular, birds, boats, or whatever, in the harbor of Barnstable, Cape Cod. . . .

I told **Jane** that this boy, with nothing better to do, would pick up a stone, as boys will. He would arc it over the harbor. When the stone hit the water, she would die.

Jane could believe with all her heart anything that made being alive seem full of white magic. That was her strength. She was raised a Quaker, but stopped going to meetings of Friends after her four happy years at Swarthmore. She became an Episcopalian after marrying Adam, who remained a Jew. She died believing in the Trinity and Heaven and Hell and all the rest of it. I'm so glad. Why? Because I loved her.

(*TQ* 39) The ashes of my Indianapolis wife **Jane Marie Cox** are mixed with the roots of a flowering cherry tree, unmarked, in Barnstable Village, Massachusetts.

(*TQ* 58) **Jane**, my first wife, won her Phi Beta Kappa key at Swarthmore College over the objections of the History Department. She had written, and then argued in oral examinations, that all that could be learned from history was that history itself was absolutely nonsensical, so study something else, like music.

I agreed with her, and so would have Kilgore Trout. But history still hadn't been erased back then.

(*TQ* 62) Colonel Littauer sold a dozen or more of my stories, several to Knox, making it possible for me to quit my job with General Electric and move with **Jane** and our then two kids to Cape Cod as a free-lance writer.

(*BAG* Introduction) Listen: After I came home from World War Two, a brevet corporal twenty-two years old, I didn't want to be a fiction writer. I married my childhood sweetheart **Jane Marie Cox**, also from Indianapolis, up in Heaven now, and enrolled as a graduate student in the Anthropology Department of the University of Chicago. But I didn't want to be an anthropologist, either.

I only hoped to find out more about human beings. I was going to be a journalist!

(*BAG* Introduction) While my future two-term president *(Ronald Reagan)* was burbling out on the rubber-chicken circuit in 1950, I started writing short stories at nights and on weekends. **Jane** and I had two kids by then. I needed more money than GE would pay me. I also wanted, if possible, more self-respect.

(*BAG* Introduction) By 1953, **Jane** and I had three kids. So I taught English in a boarding school there on the Cape. Then I wrote ads for an industrial agency in Boston. I wrote a couple of paperback originals, *The Sirens of Titan* and *Mother Night*. They were never reviewed. I got for each of them what I used to get for a short story.

(*BAG* Introduction) Allie is up in Heaven now, with my first wife **Jane** and Sam Lawrence and Flannery O'Connor and Dr. Bergler, but I still write to please her. Allie was funny in real life. That gives me permission to be funny, too. Allie and I were very close.

(*MWC* 5) I am a German-American, a pure one dating back to when German-Americans were still endogamous, marrying each other. When I asked the Anglo-American **Jane Marie Cox** to marry me in 1945, one of her uncles asked her if she really "wanted to get mixed up with all those Germans." Yes, and even today there is a sort of San Andreas fault line running between German-Americans and Anglos, but fainter all the time.

See also: TQ 11; 20; 23; 25; 35; 39; 62.

Vonnegut, Kurt, Sr. *Kurt Vonnegut's father worked as an architect in Indianapolis, as did his father. There is a fairly lengthy treatment of the family in the "Roots" chapter of* Palm Sunday. *That particular section of the chapter is excerpted from John Rauch's "An Account of the Ancestry of Kurt Vonnegut, Jr., by an Ancient Friend of His Family." Vonnegut's father inspired clarity about his son's stories, clarity that Vonnegut recalls in his preface to* Wanda June. (*WJ* About This Play) Somewhere in there my **father** died, and one of the last things he said to me was that I had never written a story with a villain in it. That was surely one of the troubles with my play—and that remains a major trouble with it to this day. Even after we opened *Happy Birthday, Wanda June*, we experimented shamelessly with endings. We had various people shoot Harold, including children. We had Harold shoot various people, including children. We had Harold do the world the favor of shooting himself.

Nothing satisfied, and I am persuaded that nothing could satisfy, since the author did not have the balls to make Harold or anybody thoroughly vile.

(*MH* Preface) My **father** and paternal grandfather were architects in Indianapolis, Indiana, where I was born. My maternal grandfather owned a brewery there. He won a Gold Medal at the Paris Exposition with his beer, which was Lieber Lager. The secret ingredient was coffee.

(*MH* Preface) My sister smoked too much. My **father** smoked too much. My mother smoked too much. I smoke too much. My brother used to

smoke too much, and then he gave it up, which was a miracle on the order of the loaves and fishes.
(SL5 1) Shortly before my **father** died, he said to me, "You know—you never wrote a story with a villain in it."

I told him that was one of the things I learned in college after the war.
(SL5 10) My **father** died many years ago now—of natural causes. So it goes. He was a sweet man. He was a gun nut, too. He left me his guns. They rust.
(WJ About This Play) My **father** and mother also tended to make me chickenhearted. My **father** was a frail architect and painter. He was also a gun nut, which used to amaze me. It seemed so inharmonious with the rest of him, that he should fondle guns.

He left me some guns.

My two siblings didn't like his gunplay, either. One time, I remember, my brother looked at a quail **Father** had shot, and he said, "My gosh—that's like smashing a fine Swiss watch." My sister used to cry and refuse to eat when **Father** brought home game.

Some homecoming for Odysseus!

This passage from Breakfast of Champions *reveals how Vonnegut pictures his alter ego Kilgore Trout as based on the image of his father.* (BC 3) I do know who invented Kilgore Trout. I did.

I made him snaggle-toothed. I gave him hair, but I turned it white. I wouldn't let him comb it or go to a barber. I made him grow it long and tangled.

I gave him the same legs the Creator of the Universe gave to my **father** when my **father** was a pitiful old man. They were pale white broomsticks. They were hairless. They were embossed fantastically with varicose veins.
(BC 20) While my life was being renewed by the words of Rabo Karabekian, Kilgore Trout found himself standing on the shoulder of the Interstate, gazing across Sugar Creek in its concrete trough at the new Holiday Inn. There were no bridges across the creek. He would have to wade.

So he sat down on a guardrail, removed his shoes and socks, rolled his pantlegs to his knees. His bared shins were rococo with varicose veins and scars. So were the shins of my **father** when he was an old, old man.

Kilgore Trout had my **father's** shins. They were a present from me. I gave him my **father's** feet, too, which were long and narrow and sensitive. They were azure. They were artistic feet.
(BC Epilogue) "Look up, Mr. Trout," I said, and I waited patiently. "Kilgore—?"

The old man looked up, and he had my **father's** wasted face when my **father** was a widower—when my **father** was an old old man.
(BC Epilogue) I somersaulted lazily and pleasantly through the void, which is my hiding place when I dematerialize. Trout's cries to me faded as the distance between us increased.

His voice was my **father's** voice. I heard my **father**—and I saw my mother in the void. My mother stayed far, far away, because she had left me a legacy of suicide.

A small hand mirror floated by. It was a leak with a mother-of-pearl handle and frame. I captured it easily, held it up to my own right eye, which looked like this:

[here, Vonnegut included an illustration of an eye with a tear falling]

Here was what Kilgore Trout cried out to me in my **father's** voice: "Make me young, make me young, make me young!"

ETC.

(WFG Address to the American Physical Society) My **father** said he would help to pay for my college education only if I studied something serious. This was in the late Thirties. *Reader's Digest* magazine was in those days celebrating the wonderful things Germans were doing with chemicals. Chemistry was obviously the coming thing. So was German. So I went to Cornell University, and I studied chemistry and German.
(WFG Why They Read Hesse) I have said that Hesse was about the same age as my **father**. My **father** wasn't a European, but part of his education took place in Strasbourg—before the First World War. And when I got to know him, when Hesse was writing *Steppenwolf*, my **father**, too, was cursing radios and films, was dreaming of Mozart and Goethe, was itching to pot-shot automobiles.

Curiously, Hesse, a man who spoke for my **father**'s generation, is now heard loud and clear by my daughters and sons.

And I say again: What my daughters and sons are responding to in *Steppenwolf* is the homesickness of the author. I do not mock homesickness as a silly affliction that is soon outgrown. I never outgrew it and neither did my **father** and neither did Hesse. I miss my Mommy and **Daddy**, and I always will—because they were so nice to me. Now and then, I would like to be a child again.

(WFG Address to the National Institute of Arts and Letters, 1971) My **father** was the widower of a suicide when he told me about that happiest day.

(WFG Reflections on My Own Death) My mother knocked herself off with sleeping pills, which was painless, too. My **father** thought she had walked out on him. **Father** was right.

(WFG Address at Rededication of Wheaton College Library, 1973) My **father** collected guns. He kept them oiled. He traded them with other gun nuts—those man-killing machines. This was his way of proving to Indianapolis, Indiana, that he wasn't a pansy, even though he was in the arts: He was an architect. I simply left Indianapolis, which is a big improvement on spitting into corners and collecting guns.

(WFG *Playboy* Interview) My **father** and grandfather were both architects—my grandfather was the first licensed architect in Indiana—and he built a home with the idea that it would be inhabited by several generations. Of course, the house is an undertaking parlor or a ukulele institute now. But during his lifetime, my **father** built two dream homes with the idea that further generations would live there. I would like there to be ancestral homes for all Americans somewhere.

(WFG *Playboy* Interview) Part of the trick for people my age, I'm certain, is to crawl out of the envying, life-hating mood of the Great Depression at last. Richard M. Nixon, who has also been unintelligent and unimaginative about happiness, is a child of the Great Depression, too. Maybe we can both crawl out of it in the next four years. I know this much: After I'm gone, I don't want my children to have to say about me what I have to say about my **father**: "He made wonderful jokes, but he was such an unhappy man."

(JB 1) **Father** by then *(near the end of World War II)* had lost all interest in politics and history and economics and such things. He had taken to saying that people talked too much. Sensations meant more to him than ideas—especially the feel of natural materials at his fingertips. When he was dying about twenty years later, he would say that he wished he had been a potter, making mud pies all day long.

To me that was sad—because he was so well-educated. It seemed to me that he was throwing his knowledge and intelligence away, just as a retreating soldier might throw away his rifle and pack.

Other people found it beautiful. He was a much-beloved man in the city, with wonderfully talented hands. He was invariably courteous and innocent. To him all craftsmen were saints, no matter how mean or stupid they might really be. . . .

So I have to say that my **father**, when I got to know him, when I myself was something like an adult, was a good man in full retreat from life.

(JB 1) I tried to write a story about a reunion between my **father** and myself in heaven one time. An early draft of this book in fact began that way. I hoped in the story to become a really good friend of his. But the story turned out perversely, as stories about real people we have known often do. It seemed that in heaven people could be any age they liked, just so long as they had experienced that age on Earth. Thus, John D. Rockefeller, for example, the founder of Standard Oil, could be any age up to ninety-eight. King Tut could be any age up to nineteen, and so on. As author of the story, I was dismayed that my **father** in heaven chose to be only nine years old.

I myself had chosen to be forty-four—respectable, but still quite sexy, too. My dismay with **Father** turned to embarrassment and anger. He was lemur-like as a nine-year-old, all eyes and hands. He had an endless supply of pencils and pads, and was forever tagging after me, drawing pictures of simply everything and insisting that I admire them when they were done. New acquaintances would sometimes ask me who that strange little boy was, and I would have to reply truthfully, since it was impossible to lie in heaven, "It's my **father**."

This passage is from John Rauch's detailed history of the family appearing in Palm Sunday. (PS

Roots) "**Kurt** and Edith's marriage was a happy and congenial one—as marriages go. At first they were reasonably affluent—had servants, governesses for their children, and lived well. But they were both inclined to be extravagant. They traveled and entertained rather lavishly. If they needed money, they sold securities or borrowed. After Prohibition in 1929, Albert was no longer able to help them.

"But they had enough economic fat which, with **Kurt**'s income from his profession, saw them through the twenties. **Kurt**'s mother, Nannie Schnull Vonnegut, died in 1929 and left **Kurt** his share of her then modest fortune derived from her father, Henry Schnull. They soon used this up. **Kurt** had acquired a plot of land on the east side of North Illinois Street at about Forty-fifth Street. Here he designed and built a large and very beautiful brick residence. They sent their older children in the twenties and thirties to private schools; Bernard to Park School, and Alice to Tudor Hall School for girls. Bernard went on to the Massachusetts Institute of Technology where he took his degree of Bachelor of Science and remained to take his Ph.D. degree in Chemistry. . . . Alice married James Adams. But by the time K[urt, Jr.] came along to his adolescence, the family was in financial trouble. He knew only the hard times of the 1930s. He was taken out of private school after the third grade, and sent to Public School No. 43 and then Shortridge High School. He was sent to Cornell University with specific instructions not to waste time or money on 'frivolous' courses, but to give full attention to practical studies, principally physics and chemistry and math.

"His parents were in straitened circumstances. There was practically no building in the Depression years and **Kurt**'s professional income vanished. They began to live on their capital which, to a good bourgeois, is a heresy looked upon with horror and usually followed by disaster."

(PS Self-Interview) VONNEGUT: My **father**, an architect of modest means, married one of the richest girls in town. It was a brewing fortune based on Lieber Lager Beer and then Gold Medal Beer. Lieber Lager became Gold Medal after winning a prize at some Paris exposition.

(PS Self-Interview) INTERVIEWER: If your parents hadn't lost all their money, what would you be doing now?

VONNEGUT: I'd be an Indianapolis architect—like my **father** and grandfather. And very happy, too. I still wish that had happened. One thing, anyway: One of the best young architects out there lives in a house my **father** built for our family the year I was born—1922. My initials, and my sister's initials, and my brother's initials are all written in leaded glass in the three little windows by the front door.

(PS The People One Knows) But during the 1930s they were both going broke. His father owned a furniture store which was bankrupt, and my **father** could find no work as an architect, and my mother and **father** were becoming widely known as deadbeats who would run huge charge accounts and never pay.

(PS Obscenity) But even when I was in grammar school, I suspected that warnings about words that nice people never used were in fact lessons in how to keep our mouths shut not just about our bodies, but about many, many things—perhaps too many things.

When I was in the fourth grade or so, I had this hunch confirmed. My **father** hit me for my bad manners in front of guests. It was the only time either one of my parents ever hit me. I hadn't said "shit" or "piss" or "fart" or "fuck" or anything like that in front of the guests. I had asked them a question in the field of economics. But my father was so offended by my question that I might as well have called the guests "silly shitheads." They really were silly shitheads, by the way.

(FWD I) "When my **father** was sixty-five and I was twenty-seven, I said to him, thinking him a very old man, that it must have been fun for him to be an architect. He replied unexpectedly that it had been no fun at all, since architecture had everything to do with accounting and nothing to do with art. I felt that he had mousetrapped me, since he had encouraged me up until that moment to believe that architecture for him had indeed been a lark."

(FWD I) "**Father** retired alone to Brown County, Indiana, soon after that, to spend the rest of his life as a potter. He built his own potter's wheel. He died down there in the hills in 1957, at the age of seventy-two.

"When I try to remember now what he was like when I was growing up and he had so little satisfying work to do, I see him as Sleeping Beauty, dormant in a brier patch, waiting for a prince. And it is easy to jump from that thought to this one: All architects I have known, in good times or bad, have seemed to be waiting forever for a generous, loving client who will let them become the elated artists they were born to be.

"So my **father**'s life might be seen as a particularly lugubrious fairy tale. He was Sleeping Beauty, and in 1929 not one but several princes, including Bell Telephone, had begun to hack through the briers to wake him up. But then they all got sick for sixteen years. And while they were in the hospital a wicked witch turned Sleeping Beauty into Rip Van Winkle instead.

"When the Depression hit I was taken out of private school and put into public school. So I had a new set of friends to bring home to have a look at whatever my **father** was. These were the ten-year-old children of the yeomanry of Hoosierdom, and it was they who first told me that my **father** was as exotic as a unicorn.

"In an era when men of his class wore dark suits and white shirts and monochromatic neckties, **Father** appeared to have outfitted himself at the Salvation Army. Nothing matched. I understand now, of course, that he had selected the elements of his costume with care, that the colors and textures were juxtaposed so as to be interesting and, finally, beautiful.

"While other fathers were speaking gloomily of coal and iron and grain and lumber and cement and so on, and yes, of Hitler and Mussolini, too, my **father** was urging friends and startled strangers alike to pay attention to some object close at hand, whether natural or man-made, and to celebrate it as a masterpiece. When I took up the clarinet, he declared the instrument, black studded with silver, to be a masterpiece. Never mind whether it could make music or not. He adored chess sets, although he could not play that game worth a nickel. My new friends and I brought him a moth one time, wanting to know what sort of moth it was. He said that he did not know its name, but that we could all agree wholeheartedly on this much: that it was a masterpiece.

"And he was the first planetary citizen my new friends had ever seen, and possibly the last one, too.

He was no more a respecter of politics and national boundaries than (that image again) a unicorn. Beauty could be found or created anywhere on this planet, and that was that."

(*FWD* III) But to get back to the thing between my **father** and my sister, the unicorn and the maiden: **Father**, no more a Freudian than Lewis Carroll, made Alice his principal source of encouragement and sympathy. He made the most of an enthusiasm they had in common, which was for the visual arts. Alice was just a girl, remember, and aside from the embarrassment of having a unicorn lay its head in her lap, so to speak, she was traumatized mainly by having every piece of sculpture or picture she made celebrated by **Father** as though it were Michelangelo's *Pietà* or the ceiling of the Sistine Chapel. In later life (which was going to last only until she was forty-one) this made her a lazy artist. (I have often quoted her elsewhere as saying, "Just because people have talent, that doesn't mean they have to do something with it.")

Vonnegut often uses his own advancing age as proof that artists frequently live and work past their primes, producing inferior art. He often alludes to his father among other artists to prove his point. (*TQ* Prologue) And then I found myself in the winter of 1996 the creator of a novel which did not work, which had no point, which had never wanted to be written in the first place. *Merde!* I had spent nearly a decade on that ungrateful fish, if you will. It wasn't even fit for shark chum.

I had recently turned seventy-three. My mother made it to fifty-two, my **father** to seventy-two. Hemingway almost made it to sixty-two. I had lived too long! What was I to do?

Answer: Fillet the fish. Throw the rest away. . . .

Johannes Brahms quit composing symphonies when he was fifty-five. Enough! My architect **father** was sick and tired of architecture when he was fifty-five. Enough!

(*TQ* 10) I told Kilgore Trout at the clambake in 2001 about how my brother and sister had made **Father** ashamed of hunting and fishing. He quoted Shakespeare: "How sharper than a serpent's tooth it is to have a thankless child!"

(*TQ* 25) Our **father** the architect was so full of ecstatic baloney about any work of art Allie made when she was growing up, as though she were the new Michelangelo, that she was shamed. She wasn't stupid and she wasn't tasteless. **Father**, without meaning to do so rubbed her nose in how limited her gifts were, and so spoiled any modest pleasure that she, not expecting too much, might have found in using them.

Allie may have felt patronized, too, lavishly praised for very little because she was a pretty girl. Only men could become great artists.

(*TQ* 25) But Mother was as full of baloney about Allie's prospects for marrying a rich man, and how important it was for Allie to do so, as **Father** was about the art she did. During the Great Depression, financial sacrifices were made to send Allie to school with Hoosier heiresses at Tudor Hall, School for Girls, or *Two-Door Hell, Dump for Dames*, four blocks south of Shortridge High School, where she could have received what I received, a free and much richer and more democratic and madly heterosexual education.

(*TQ* 40) The hunters agreed that anybody who complained about **Father**'s cooking became the cook. So **Father** prepared worse and worse meals, while the others were having one hell of a good time in the forest. No matter how awful a supper was, though, the hunters pronounced it lip-smacking delicious, clapping **Father** on the back and so on.

After they marched off one morning, **Father** found a pile of fresh moose poop outside. He fried it in motor oil. That night he served it as steaming patties.

(*TQ* 60) The cast party afterward was a clambake on the beach at Xanadu. As in the last scene of 8½, the motion picture by Federico Fellini, *tout le monde* was there, if not in person, then represented by look-alikes. Monica Pepper resembled my sister Allie. The bakemaster, a local man who is paid to stage such parties in the summertime, resembled my late publisher Seymour Lawrence (1926–1993), who rescued me from certain oblivion, from smithereens, by publishing *Slaughterhouse-Five*, and then bringing all my previous books back into print under his umbrella.

Kilgore Trout looked like my **father**.

(*TQ* 63) I got a sappy letter from a woman a while back. She knew I was sappy, too, which is to say a northern Democrat. She was pregnant, and she wanted to know if it was a mistake to bring an innocent little baby into a world this bad.

I replied that what made being alive almost worthwhile for me was the saints I met, people behaving unselfishly and capably. They turned up in the most unexpected places. Perhaps you, dear reader, are or can become a saint for her sweet child to meet. I believe in original sin. I also believe in original virtue. Look around!

Xanthippe thought her husband, Socrates, was a fool. Aunt Raye thought Uncle Alex was a fool. Mother thought **Father** was a fool. My wife thinks I'm a fool.

I'm wild again, beguiled again, a whimpering, simpering child again. Bewitched, bothered, and bewildered am I.

See also: WJ About This Play; BC Preface; 3; WFG Preface; WFG Why They Read Hesse; WFG Address to the National Institute of Arts and Letters, 1971; WFG In a Manner That Must Shame God Himself; *Slap* Prologue; 13; FWD I–IV; VI; VIII; XI–XII; XIV; XIX–XXI; Unpublished Essay by Me, Written After Reading Galleys of an Anthology of First-Rate Poems and Short Prose Pieces by Persons Who Were or Are in Institutions for the Mentally Ill; TQ 1; 10; 26; 33; 36; 39–41; 43; 62; GBK Introduction; MWC 2; 8; 12; Author's Note.

Vonnegut, Lily. *Adopted as an infant by Vonnegut (then sixty years old) and his second wife, the photographer and author Jill Krementz, Lily is, at various times, a reflection of Kurt's parenting; a symbol of the preciousness of youth; and, in* Timequake, *the agent for a living timequake experienced by Vonnegut as the confluence of theater, youth, and a recognition of the brevity of life.*

Vonnegut echoes his father's response to Alice Vonnegut's art in his own response to Lily's. (FWD Preface) Jill and I had our reception at the Regency Hotel, only a block north of the church. (If you have your reception at the Regency, including the cake, they throw in the bridal suite for the night; my grandchildren were stashed there during the ceremony.) That was eleven years ago now, and our understanding then was that I had had enough children (three of my own and three adopted nephews). But after a while we adopted a darling infant (three days old) named **Lily**, who has become my principal companion. (She will be a lazy artist when she grows up, since I celebrate every creation of hers as though it were Michelangelo's *Pietà* or the ceiling of the Sistine Chapel.)

Vonnegut refers to Lily when addressing the National Air and Space Museum concerning the aerial firebombing of Dresden, taking the opportunity to steer the discussion to the recent United States attempt to assassinate Libya's Muammar Qaddafi, an attack that failed due to faulty intelligence but succeeded in killing his infant daughter. (FWD X) There was no press coverage of my wonderful remarks. . . . I was well-known. The National Air and Space Museum was well-known. The firebombing of Dresden was well-known. In combination, you would think, some reporter might have found us interesting. Another American ex-PW who was in Dresden with me and O'Hare showed up unexpectedly, and testified from the audience that all I said was true. And my adopted seven-year-old daughter **Lily** was sitting near him with my wife Jill. I had **Lily** stand up on her seat as an approximation of the sort of germ Muammar Qaddafi's adopted daughter had been before we killed her with the very latest in air-to-ground weapons technology. Some people might argue that my equation was misleading, since Qaddafi's kid was an infant and mine would soon be eight years old.

Lily becomes an emblematic point of comparison for the kind of desensitization that can occur when surrounded by genocide, as he witnesses in Biafra. (FWD 17) I ran into an old friend from Shortridge High School, a great inventor and mechanical engineer named Herb Harrington, while I was writing my dry-eyed piece about Mozambique. I confessed that something had happened to me since Biafra, that Mozambique had impressed me intellectually but not emotionally. I told Herb that I had seen little girls about the age of my own precious **Lily** drifting off to death, having been in the bush too long before reaching a refugee center, but that I felt hardly anything afterward. He said that the same thing had happened to him when he was in the Army during World War II, with a small crew installing radio stations along the coast of China. Wagonloads of Chinese who had starved to death were a common sight, and he soon (in less than a week) no longer noticed them.

In Timequake, *Vonnegut is most taken with Lily's participation in a school production of Thornton Wilder's* Our Town, *reminding him of Uncle Alex's dictate to take note of happy moments.* (TQ 2) The artificial timequake that has moved me most so far this year is an old one. It is *Our Town,* by the late Thornton Wilder, I had already watched it with undiminished satisfaction maybe five or six times. And then this spring my thirteen-year-old daughter, dear **Lily,** was cast as a talking dead person in the graveyard of Grover's Corners in a school production of that innocent, sentimental masterpiece. . . .

I reflected sadly that night, with **Lily** pretending to be a dead grownup, that I would be seventy-eight when she graduated from high school, and eighty-two when she graduated from college, and so on. Talk about remembering the future!

What hit me really hard that night, though, was the character Emily's farewell in the last scene, after the mourners have gone back down the hill to their village, having buried her. She says, "Goodby, good-by, world. Good-by, Grover's Corners . . . Mama and Papa. Good-by to clocks ticking . . . and Mama's sunflowers. And food and coffee. And new-ironed dresses and hot baths . . . and sleeping and waking up. Oh, earth, you're too wonderful for anybody to realize you.

"Do any human beings ever realize life while they live it? — every, every minute?" (TQ 55) My dear thirteen-year-old daughter **Lily,** having become a pretty adolescent, appears to me, as do most American adolescents, to be holding her self-respect together the best she can in a really scary steeplechase.

See also: FWD XI; XVI; XIX; TQ 7; 22; 46; 56.

Vonnegut, Dr. Mark. *Vonnegut's son, known principally for his brief bout with mental illness that he chronicled in* The Eden Express: A Memoir of Insanity. *He eventually became a pediatrician after graduating from the Harvard Medical School. His most recent book is* Just Like Someone Without Mental Illness Only More So: A Memoir *(2011).* (PS Roots) I myself have named my only son after Mark Twain, another American Saint.
(PS Children) "I don't know why you invited me. Perhaps it is because my son **Mark** went insane. He is not the gag writer. That is another son. The one

who went insane is well now. He graduated from Harvard Medical School a year ago, and is an intern in Boston now. He, too, is a magnificent speaker. He loves to ask an audience of workers in the mental health field, 'How many of you have ever taken Thorazine?' Almost no hands go up, and my son the doctor gives a little smile, and he says: 'It won't hurt you. You really ought to try it sometime, just to get an inkling, anyway, of what your patients are going through.'"

Vonnegut illustrates his limited understanding of Mark's illness within Kilgore Trout's short story "The Dancing Fool." (PS Children) "But I am a storyteller, not a cultural anthropologist, no matter what the diploma says. And I am not even the best storyteller in my own family when it comes to the relationship of culture to mental health. My son **Mark** is the best storyteller in that area. He wrote an excellent book about going crazy and recovering. It is called *The Eden Express*. **Mark** remembers everything. His wish is to tell people who are going insane something about the shape of the roller coaster they are on. It helps sometimes to know the shape of a roller coaster. How many of you here have taken Thorazine?

"**Mark** has taught me never to romanticize mental illness, never to imagine a brilliant and beguiling schizophrenic who makes more sense about life than his or her doctor or even the president of Harvard University. **Mark** says that schizophrenia is as ghastly and debilitating as smallpox or rabies or any other unspeakable disease you care to name. Society cannot be blamed, and neither, thank God, can the friends and relatives of the patient. Schizophrenia is an internal chemical catastrophe. It is a case of monstrously bad genetic luck, bad luck of a sort encountered in absolutely every sort of society—including the Australian aborigines and the middle class of Vienna, Austria, before the Second World War.

"Plenty of other writers at this very moment are writing a story about an admirable, perhaps even a divine schizophrenic. Why? Because the story is wildly applauded every time it is told. It blames the culture and the economy and the society and everything but the disease itself for making the patient unwell. **Mark** says that is wrong.

"As his father, though, I am still free to say this, I think: I believe that a culture, a combination of ideas and artifacts, can sometimes make a healthy person behave against his or her best interests, and against the best interests of the society and the planet, too."

In his epigraph to Bluebeard, *Vonnegut quotes his son:* "We are here to help each other get through this thing, whatever it is." —**Dr. Mark Vonnegut, M.D.** (Letter to Author, 1985)

(FWD II) "Anyway—**Mark** recovered sufficiently to write his book and graduate from Harvard Medical School. He is now a pediatrician in Boston, with a wife and two fine sons, and two fine automobiles. And then, not very long ago, most members of your profession decided that he and some others who had written books about recovering from schizophrenia had been misdiagnosed. No matter how jazzed up they appeared to be when sick, they were in fact depressives. Maybe so.

"**Mark**'s first response to news of this rediagnosis was to say, 'What a wonderful diagnostic tool. We now know if a patient gets well, he or she definitely did not have schizophrenia.'"

(FWD XIII) Dr. Redfield gave a public lecture on the Folk Society in the springtime each year. It was popular, I think, because so many of us took it as scientific advice about how to find deep and enduring contentment: join or create a Folk Society. (This was back in 1945, remember, long before the communes and flower children and shared music and ideals of my children's generation.) Dr. Redfield denounced sentimentality about life in Folk Societies. . . . But I still find myself daydreaming of an isolated little gang of likeminded people in a temperate climate, in a clearing in a woodland near a lake (an ideal spot, by the way, for a daydreaming maiden to find herself the captrix of a unicorn). My son **Mark** would help found and bankroll such a commune in British Columbia, and later write about it in *The Eden Express*. (I said in my own *Palm Sunday* that sons try to make their mothers' impractical dreams for themselves come true. Here was a case of a son's making his father's impractical dream come true. It worked OK for a while.)

(FWD XVII) (Our son the doctor, **Mark**, said after her death that he himself would not have submitted to the ghastly treatments which allowed Jane to stay alive with cancer for so long.)

Toward the close of Fates Worse Than Death, *Vonnegut includes the full text of his afterword to a new edition of his son's book. Here Vonnegut expands his personal concerns that his family's tragedy is similar to the medical community's general struggle with treating mental disorders.* (FWD What My Son Mark Wanted Me to Tell the Psychiatrists in Philadelphia, Which Was Also the Afterword to a New Edition of His Book *The Eden Express*) **Mark** inherited a World War II conscience (as did O'Hare's kids, and on and on). So he had to maim if not kill it, if he was to stay out of the Vietnam nightmare, which must have hurt a lot. He, like so many members of his generation, became a man without a country because his Government was behaving in a manner toward the young of its own lower classes, not to mention the Vietnamese, which was not only cruel and hideously wasteful, but as I've said so often before, gruesomely ridiculous.

Mark did not like it here, nor should he have liked it. So although he was no longer subject to military service, or running from anything but a power structure (like the one today) shamelessly rigged in favor of his own race and economic and intellectual class, he went to Canada. All this is in *The Eden Express*. . . .

Mark's only crime against his government, and the only crime committed by Abbie Hoffman and so many others of that generation during the Vietnam War, was a sublimely Jeffersonian form of treason. It was disrespect.
(TQ 4) My son the doctor **Mark Vonnegut**, who wrote a swell book about his going crazy in the 1960s, and then graduated from Harvard Medical School, had an exhibition of his watercolors in Milton, Massachusetts, this summer. A reporter asked him what it had been like to grow up with a famous father.

Mark replied, "When I was growing up, my father was a car salesman who couldn't get a job teaching at Cape Cod Junior College."
(TQ 34) Our son the doctor **Mark** would say after she *(his mother, Jane Cox Vonnegut)* died that he himself would never have submitted to all the medical procedures she acquiesced to in order to stay alive as long as she could, to go on saying, her eyes shining, "I can't wait!"

See also: PS Self-Interview; PS The People One Knows; PS Children; PS The Sexual Revolution; FWD II; III; XVI; XVIII; What My Son Mark Wanted Me to Tell the Psychiatrists in Philadelphia, Which Was Also the Afterword to a New Edition of His Book *The Eden Express*; TQ 20; 25; 32.

Vonnegut Memorial Fountain. *In* Hocus Pocus, *the fountain is outside the Tarkington College campus bookstore. When Eugene Debs Hartke confronts Fred Stone about stealing a mug from the store, Stone smashes it on the rim of the fountain.*

Vonnegut, Nanette. *Vonnegut's youngest daughter by his first wife, the only child he left behind in Cape Cod when he split with Jane and moved to Manhattan in 1971. Nearly all his references to Nanette include mention of her work as an artist or as a nurse.*

In 2012, Nanette served as the editor of We are what we pretend to be: The first and last works of Kurt Vonnegut. *It contains unpublished drafts of "Basic Training," his earliest try at autobiographical fiction penned under the name Mark Harvey. The second work is the unfinished last novel Vonnegut was working on at the time of his passing,* If God Were Alive Today. *Its protagonist is Gil Berman, an environmentalist, lecturer, and self-styled comedian whose main concern is the plight of the planet.*
(PS Children) So what am I, if I believe that, to make of myself as mirrored in my own children, who cheerfully compete in every area, including writing, in which I have ever dabbled while they were watching? I played chess a little, and now all of them can beat me at chess. I painted and drew some, and now Jim Adams and Mark Vonnegut and Edith Vonnegut and **Nanette Vonnegut** can all paint and draw circles around me. Desperately, this old man is going to have a one-man show of his drawings this fall, but they're no damn good. . . .

I find that I want to protect the privacy of my two daughters, and so will talk about them very little. **Nanette** and Edith are both gifted artists. Both have found the life of an artist a lonely one. Edith has determined that loneliness is not too high a price to pay. **Nanette** is becoming a nurse who will make pictures for fun.
(PS Children) What is my favorite among all the

works of art my children have so far produced? It is perhaps a letter written by my youngest daughter **Nanette**. It is so organic! She wrote it to "Mr. X," an irascible customer at a Cape Cod restaurant where she worked as a waitress in the summer of 1978. The customer was so mad about the service he had received one evening, you see, that he had complained in writing to the management. The management posted the letter on the kitchen bulletin board.

(*TQ* 25) Boys and girls of our family often come into this world, as did Allie, with natural gifts for drawing and painting and sculpting and so on. Jane's and my two daughters, Edith and **Nanette**, are middle-aged professional artists who have shows and sell pictures. So does our son the doctor Mark. So do I. Allie could have done that, too, if she had been willing to work hard and hustle some. But as I have reported elsewhere, she said, "Just because you're talented, that doesn't mean you have to do something with it."

See also: PS Children (Nanette's letter); *PS* The Sexual Revolution; *FWD* III.

Vonnegut, Raye. (*TQ* 47) Uncle Alex Vonnegut, who said we should exclaim out loud whenever we were accidentally happy, was considered a fool by his wife, **Aunt Raye**. Uncle Alex was asked to explain in an essay why he had come to Harvard all the way from Indianapolis. By his own gleeful account, he wrote, "Because my big brother is at MIT."

He never had a kid, and never owned a gun. He owned a lot of books, though, and kept buying new ones, and giving me those he thought were particularly well done. It was an ordeal for him to find this book or that one, so he could read some particularly magical passage aloud to me. Here's why: His wife **Aunt Raye**, who was said to be autistic, arranged his library according to the size and color of the volumes, and stairstep style.

(*TQ* 63) Xanthippe thought her husband, Socrates, was a fool. **Aunt Raye** thought Uncle Alex was a fool. Mother thought Father was a fool. My wife thinks I'm a fool.

I'm wild again, beguiled again, a whimpering, simpering child again. Bewitched, bothered, and bewildered am I.

Waggoner, Aunt Margaret. *In the short story "This Son of Mine" (The Saturday Evening Post, August 1956; reprinted in the 1999 collection* Bagombo Snuff Box*), Margaret is Merle's sister and the aunt of his son Franklin. With no other maternal figure in his life, Franklin resolves to visit her after disappointing his father with his desire to make his own way in the world rather than take over the family business, Waggoner Pump. Since Franklin is home for only a brief time before returning to Cornell and his father arranged for an afternoon of shooting the next day, Franklin leaves the factory and visits her that day.*

Aunt Margaret does not appear in the story, but her influence is strong. Franklin returns from his visit with a decidedly different take on his future. At supper, feeling no pain after two stiff cocktails and a whirlwind of mothering at **Aunt Margaret**'s, Franklin told his father that he wanted to take over the factory in due time. He would become the Waggoner in Waggoner Pump when his father was ready to bow out.

Waggoner, Franklin. *In the short story "This Son of Mine," collected in* Bagombo Snuff Box *(1999), Franklin is the twenty-year-old son of widower Merle Waggoner. Though named for Benjamin Franklin, Merle's son shares none of the entrepreneurial zeal of his namesake, much to the chagrin of his father, who has always hoped Franklin would take over the company he built from scratch, Waggoner Pump. Instead, the Cornell undergrad busies himself with being president of the interfraternity council and acting, which his father views as no more than a dilettante's pursuit. He was being asked to match his father's passion for the factory with an equal passion for something else. And* **Franklin** *had no such passion—for the theater or anything else.*

Despite Franklin's never showing much interest in the company, his announcement to his father during a weekend visit home about his plans to pursue a career on the boards so distresses Merle that he threatens to call Guy Ferguson at General Forge and

Foundry to take him up on their offer of a buyout. *Franklin's disclosure to his father makes him appear shallow, a shell of a man buried beneath drab monotones,* He was tall and thin, in cashmere and gray flannel. He was almost goofy with shyness and guilt. He had just told his father that he wanted to be an actor, that he didn't want the factory. And shock at his own words had come so fast that he'd heard himself adding, out of control, the hideously empty phrase, "Thanks just the same." *Father and son call a truce to their disagreement and Merle hastily arranges an afternoon of target shooting with Rudy and Karl Linberg, father and son lathe operators at Waggoner Pump.*

Franklin leaves his father's office to visit the only mother figure in his life, his aunt Margaret Waggoner. She does not appear in the story, but her influence is strong. Franklin returns from his visit with a decidedly different take on his future. At supper, feeling no pain after two stiff cocktails and a whirlwind of mothering at Aunt Margaret's, **Franklin** told his father that he wanted to take over the factory in due time. He would become the **Waggoner** in **Waggoner Pump** when his father was ready to bow out.

Unbeknownst to Merle or Franklin, Rudy Linberg had been aware of Franklin's lack of interest in the company ever since he was a little boy. Having foolishly turned down Merle's offer of a partnership for $2,000 early in the company's life, Rudy remained a loyal employee and silent confidant to Merle, but he groomed his own son to take over the company when the fateful day would come for Franklin to decline his birthright. Rudy goes so far as to fabricate a master craftsman's metal puzzle for Merle's birthday, pretending it is from Karl. It is a copy of one Rudy made for Merle years earlier, and the gesture proves very moving for Merle.

Rudy's lifelong plotting comes to naught, however, when Karl reveals to Franklin the falsity of his father's relationship with Merle. The two are alone, walking down the firing line to adjust their targets, when Rudy's conscience pours out, but it is Franklin who trumps his boyhood friend with news that he did indeed plan to fulfill his father's wish to accept ownership of the company when his father retired.

Once Franklin decides to accede to his father's wishes, he begins to agree with his father's assessment and wonder that the younger generation has no wishes to follow in the traditions of their families' livelihood. To Merle they all seemed full of ennui, and Franklin's new approach to the world matches his father's. Suddenly he didn't want to see his friends the killers of their fathers' dreams. Their young faces were the faces of old men hanging upside down, their expressions grotesque and unintelligible. Hanging upside down, they swung from bar to ballroom to crap game, and back to bar. No one pitied them in that great human belfry, because they were going to be rich, if they weren't already. They didn't have to dream, or even lift a finger.

Franklin went to a movie alone. The movie failed to suggest a way in which he might improve his life. It suggested that he be kind and loving and humble, and **Franklin** was nothing if he wasn't kind and loving and humble.

Having rejected the shallow concerns of his friends, Franklin now views the continuity with family tradition as presaging a necessary break with even old family dynamics. While listening to Rudy and Karl play their closely coordinated duet, With the moment to think about, to puzzle him pleasantly, **Franklin** found that the music wasn't speaking anymore of just Rudy and Karl. It was speaking of all fathers and sons. It was saying what they had all been saying haltingly, sometimes with pain and sometimes with anger and sometimes with cruelty and sometimes with love: that fathers and sons were one.

It was saying, too, that a time for a parting in spirit was near—no matter how close anyone held anyone, no matter what anyone tried.

Waggoner, Merle. In the short story "This Son of Mine," collected in Bagombo Snuff Box (1999), Merle is the founder of Waggoner Pump. He is a 51-year-old widower, having lost his wife shortly after the birth of his only son, Franklin. Merle's greatest desire is for Franklin to take over the company once he is ready to retire, but at twenty, Franklin has not yet found his life's calling or passion. During a week-

end visit home from Cornell, Franklin tells his father that he has no intention of becoming the head of Waggoner Pump, that he is thinking of pursuing an acting career. Enraged at the news, Merle threatens to call Guy Ferguson at General Forge and Foundry to take them up on their buyout offer for $2 million. Cooler heads prevail, Franklin goes to visit his paternal aunt Margaret, and Merle arranges for an afternoon of target shooting with Rudy and Karl Linberg the next day.

Rudy and Merle have this much in common: they both became single parents at around the same time, and Rudy also has plans to keep Waggoner Pump in the family—his family. Having watched Franklin grow up indifferent to the family business, Rudy has groomed Karl to be the son Merle never had, hoping that once Franklin gives up his birthright, Merle would turn to his first and most trusted employee (and his well-trained son) to run the company.

Early in the company's development, Merle offered Rudy a partnership in the company for just a $2,000 investment. Rudy did not think much of the company's prospects and passed on the offer. Ever since, Rudy has had to watch the value of the company grow ever larger, doing nothing more than increasing his covetousness and devious acts to persuade Merle that Karl would be a fit replacement when the time comes.

Franklin dashes Rudy's hopes by returning from his visit to Aunt Margaret having decided to accept his father's offer when he is ready to retire. Though the bonds of both fathers and sons remain strong, one is left wondering what will be the future basis of Rudy's relationship with Karl once it is known that Karl will remain only an employee, not an owner.

Waggoner Pump. In the short story "This Son of Mine," collected in Bagombo Snuff Box (1999), the centrifugal pump company is the family business created by Merle Waggoner, the fifty-one-year-old widowed single parent who is near the end of his rope while waiting for his twenty-year-old son Franklin to agree to take over the company when he retires. General Forge and Foundry of Ilium, New York, has a standing offer of $2 million through Guy Ferguson to buy the company, but Waggoner wants his son to run the company. He is nostalgic for an earlier era when local inventors and entrepreneurs successfully *passed their businesses to succeeding generations. When Franklin finally agrees to take over the company, Merle frames his pride in Franklin as one returning to a valued American tradition, willing to break with the modern era's penchant for selling out to conglomerates.* "You're the only one—do you know that?" choked Merle.

"The only one—I swear!"

"The only one what, sir?" said Franklin.

"The only son who's sticking with what his father or his grandfather or sometimes even his great-grandfather built." Merle shook his head mournfully. "No Hudson in Hudson Saw," he said. "I don't think you can even cut cheese with a Hudson saw these days. No Flemming in Flemming Tool and Die. No Warner in Warner Street. No Hawks, no Hinkley, no Bowman in Hawks, Hinkley, and Bowman."

Merle waved his hand westward. "You wonder who all the people are with the big new houses on the west side? Who can have a house like that, and we never meet them, never even meet anybody who knows them? They're the ones who are taking over instead of the sons. The town's for sale, and they buy. It's their town now—people named Ferguson from places called Ilium."

Waggoner Pump is also the focus of Rudy Linberg's long-term plan to have his son Karl take over the company when Merle realizes Franklin wants nothing to do with it. However, his twenty-year plan, one that warped his relationship with his son and his son's friendship with Franklin, ends the instant Franklin declares his desire to continue the company. Merle's sister, Aunt Margaret, is largely responsible (though unseen in the text) for persuading Franklin to do what is expected.

Wainwright, the Right Reverend William Uranium-8. *In* Slapstick, *the evangelistic Founder of the Church of Jesus Christ the Kidnapped, located at 3972 Ellis Avenue, Chicago, Illinois.*

Wainwright, Tawny. *When Eliot Rosewater goes to the Saw City Kandy Kitchen to catch the Greyhound bus for a planned reunion in Indianapolis with Sylvia, he startles the teenager inside.* (GBR 13) The customer was a fourteen-year-old nymphet, pregnant by her stepfather, which stepfather was in prison now. The *(Rosewater)* Foundation was paying for her medical care. It had also reported the stepfather's crime to the police, had subsequently hired for him the best Indiana lawyer that money could buy.

The girl's name was **Tawny Wainwright**. When she brought her troubles to Eliot, he asked her how her spirits were. "Well," she said, "I guess I don't feel too bad. I guess this is as good a way as any to start out being a movie star."

Wait, James (*also known as* **Willard Flemming**). "Nature's experiment with purposeless greed" (*Gal* 1:16), *Wait has one of the most checkered histories of all Vonnegut's characters. The incestuous issue of a father and daughter in Midland City, Ohio, he is placed in a foster home shortly after birth when his parents flee town. He grows up in five foster homes, often enduring the cruelty of his guardians. In Midland City he studies auto mechanics at a vocational high school. While still in high school, Wait fathers Celia Hoover's only child, George. Wait is mowing the lawn at the home of Dwayne and Celia when she invites James in for iced tea. Dwayne was in Cincinnati on business at the time. Though this scenario is not mentioned in* Breakfast of Champions, *it does not conflict with previous character histories.*

James Wait runs away to New York City after completing only two years of high school. A pimp teaches him to become a homosexual prostitute. He also works as a ballroom dancing instructor, a talent he apparently inherited from his parents. He eventually makes his living, however, as a bigamist using various identities. By the time he is introduced to Mary Hepburn, he is already a millionaire, having swindled seventeen brides and stashed their assets in various accounts across the country. He travels down to Guayaquil to escape his most recent wife, a seventy-year-old widow in Skokie, Illinois, right outside Chicago. Guayaquil sounded to him like the last place she would ever think of looking for him.

This woman was so ugly and stupid, she probably never should have been born. And yet Wait was the second person to have married her (*Gal* 1:3).

Wait decides to make a play for Mary Hepburn after learning she may be a wealthy widow. He introduces himself as Willard Flemming, an engineer

from Moose Jaw, Saskatchewan. Mary becomes convinced of his goodness when she sees him feeding the
Kanka-bono girls at the bar in the Hotel El Dorado.
He and Mary later throw their bodies over the girls
when the glass on their bus shatters during the air
raid. The excitement of the moment taxes his congenitally weak heart and he dies the next day of a
heart attack. (Both his parents died of heart attacks
in their forties.) Before his death, however, Captain
Adolf von Kleist married Mary Hepburn to "Willard
Flemming."

Earlier in the text, while Wait worked as a homosexual prostitute in Manhattan, he had killed Prince
Richard of Croatia-Slavonia. The prince had hired
Wait to strangle him with a silken sash while he mas-
turbated. Wait was supposed to count to twenty after
the prince ejaculated and lost consciousness, but he
decided to count to three hundred.

Wakeby, Stella. A poor though proud old woman
in Rosewater County who fights calling Eliot for any
help from the Foundation. One rainy evening, Stella
comes to her wits end and asks a neighbor to drive
her to a pay phone. Her pride and independence are
characterized by her admission, "Oh, Mr. Rosewater—if you only knew—" And she burst into violent
tears. "We always said we were Senator Rosewater
people and not Eliot Rosewater people!" (GBR 7)
Though she doesn't explain the exact nature of her
problem, just hearing Eliot's voice soothes her. He
easily gets Stella to relax and agree to visit him in
person the next day to help solve her problem.

Wakefield, Andrea. The wife of General Sam Wakefield, the man who recruited Hartke for both West
Point and Tarkington College, she becomes close
friends with Hartke. (HP 22) He (Sam Wakefield)
had a very rich wife, **Andrea**, who would become
Tarkington's Dean of Women after he committed
suicide. **Andrea** died 2 years before the prison break,
and so is not buried with so many others next to the
stable, in the shadow of Musket Mountain when the
Sun goes down.

Andrea Wakefield is a graduate of the Sorbonne
in France. (HP 22) In addition to her duties as
Dean, dealing with unwanted pregnancies and
drug addiction and the like, she also taught French
and Italian and oil painting. She was from a genu-

inely distinguished old Philadelphia family, which
had given civilization a remarkable number of edu-
cators and lawyers and physicians and artists. She
actually may have been what Jason Wilder and several of Tarkington's Trustees believed themselves to
be, obviously the most highly evolved creatures on
the planet.

She was a lot smarter than her husband.

I always meant to ask her how a Quaker came to
marry a professional soldier, but I never did.
(HP 22) Even at her age then, which was about
60, 10 years older than me, **Andrea** was the best
figure skater on the faculty. I think figure skating,
if **Andrea Wakefield** could find the right partner,
was eroticism enough for her. General Wakefield
couldn't skate for sour apples. The best partner
she had on ice at Tarkington, probably, was Bruce
Bergeron. . . .
(HP 22) **Andrea** and I had never been lovers. She
was too contented and old for me.
(HP 22) "I want you to know I think you're a Saint,"
said **Andrea**. Andrea says so because she admires
Hartke's commitment to caring for his ill wife and
mother-in-law.

Wakefield, Sam. The man who recruits Eugene
Debs Hartke for West Point and later hires him to
teach physics at Tarkington College. In both instances Wakefield shows up when Hartke reaches
new lows in his life. In the first instance, Wakefield
was at the Cleveland Science Fair when Hartke and
his father were shamed by the judges who quickly
saw the crystal display was fraudulently submitted
as student work. He stops Eugene with the innocent
introduction, "What's the hurry, son?" Wakefield arranged Eugene's appointment to West Point through
his father.

In the second instance, Wakefield is on the street
outside a Boston Chinese restaurant when Hartke
explodes at another customer who harasses him
about his military uniform. This is immediately after
Hartke's visit to the bathroom where, through casual
conversation with a family friend of his wife's, he
finds out about the hereditary insanity which would
soon strike his wife. Wakefield was there to calm
down Eugene and offer him a teaching post at Tarkington. (HP 20) I ran outside. Everybody and everything was my enemy. I was back in Vietnam!

But a Christ-like figure loomed before me. He was wearing a suit and tie, but he had a long beard, and his eyes were full of love and pity. He seemed to know all about me, and he really did. He was **Sam Wakefield**, who had resigned his commission as a General, and gone over to the Peace Movement, and become President of Tarkington College.

He said to me what he had said to me so long ago in Cleveland, at the Science Fair: "What's the hurry, Son?"

Wakefield was a veteran of World War II, Korea, and Vietnam, where he becomes a major general and awards Hartke a Silver Star for his heroism in enemy tunnels. A year before the war ends, Wakefield resigns his commission to join the peace movement. He becomes president of Tarkington College and commits suicide three years later by shooting himself in the head. Hartke doesn't believe Wakefield was depressed as much as he was exhausted. He believes this because Wakefield "plagiarized" his suicide note. (HP 6) I think exhaustion got him. I say that not only because he seemed very tired all the time to me, but because his suicide note wasn't even original and didn't seem to have that much to do with him personally. It was word for word the same suicide note left way back in 1932, when I was a negative 8 years old, by another loser, George Eastman, inventor of the Kodak camera and founder of Eastman Kodak, now defunct, only 75 kilometers north of here.

Both notes said this and nothing more: "My work is done."

Walker, Shelton. *Walker served as assistant secretary of the Army in President Eisenhower's administration.* (JB 7) He had been in the war and had risen to the rank of major in the Field Artillery and had made the landings in North Africa and then, on D-Day, in France. But he was essentially an Oklahoma businessman. Someone would tell me (*Walter Starbuck*) later that he owned the largest tire distributorship in the state. *Two years after Starbuck testifies before Congress and implicates Leland Clewes in the McCarthy witch hunt against Communists in the government, it falls to Walker to gently fire Starbuck.* (JB 7) I am unable to say even now whether he was being unkind or not when he said to me, rising and extending his hand, "You can now

sell your considerable skills, Mr. Starbuck, for their true value in the open marketplace of the Free Enterprise System. Happy hunting! Good luck!"

Waltz, Barbara. *(DD 15)* Felix's *(Waltz)* fifth wife, **Barbara**, and the first loving wife he had ever had, in my opinion, found the solitude of old George Metzger in Cedar Key intolerable. She was a native of Midland City like the rest of us, and a product of its public schools. She was an X-ray technician. That was how Felix had met her. She had X-rayed his shoulder. She was only twenty-three. She was pregnant by Felix now, and so happy to be pregnant. She was such a true believer in how life could be enriched by children.

Waltz, Charlotte. *The socialite wife of Felix Waltz who, in his opinion, is more interested in being married to the president of the National Broadcasting Company. At the peak of her hurt and fury over their divorce, Charlotte cuts off all the buttons from Felix's clothes and tosses the buttons down the incinerator, in* Deadeye Dick.

Waltz, Donna. *Felix Waltz's first wife and twin sister of Dina—no last name given.* In Deadeye Dick, *Donna and her sister are joyriding in a car when Felix crashes into them. Donna suffers disfiguring scars and later marries Felix.*

Waltz, Emma Wetzel. *The wife of Otto Waltz and mother of Rudy Waltz, in* Deadeye Dick. *She was born in 1901 and died in 1978 of cancer brought about by radiation exposure. She died before the famous neutron-bombing of Midland City. Her exposure was to the radioactive cement used to build the fireplace in her Avondale home. The cement was sold by the Nuclear Regulatory Commission—against its own rules—as surplus from the government's work on the Manhattan Project. She died penniless save for the money brought in by Rudy, having lost their wealth in the wrongful-death lawsuit brought by George Metzger after his wife's death.*

Waltz, Felix. *Rudy Waltz's older brother, Felix frequently fell victim to his father's eccentricities. In 1934, when the Waltzes are invited to Germany by Otto's old friend Adolf Hitler, Otto dresses Felix in a*

Hitler Youth brown shirt uniform (though he was only twelve years old), and the family photo depicting the scene was eventually published in The Midland City Bugle-Observer. Later, Otto so scared Felix's prom date, Celia Hildreth, that she runs from the Waltz house across town to her own home.

Felix was drafted in 1944 while a student at Ohio State University. He was scheduled to leave on the afternoon of Mother's Day 1944, and Felix's family obligations fell to Rudy.* Among his many responsibilities was caring for the small arsenal in the upstairs gun room. Felix handed the key to Rudy, caught the bus for boot camp, and that evening Rudy shot Eloise Metzger from the cupola. Years later, Felix explains to Rudy why their father so readily surrendered. (DD 11) "You know why the old man confessed? . . . It was the first truly consequential adventure life had ever offered him. He was going to make the most of it. At last something was happening to him! He would keep it going as long as he could!"

Felix returned from the war and became general manager of radio station WOR in New York, and later president of NBC. Along the way he collected five wives. He met Donna in a car accident and married her out of sympathy for the horrible facial scars she suffered. Genevieve was the second or third wife (there is an inconsistency in the text); she worked at WOR, and Felix called her "Anyface." She had almost no eyebrows, and very thin lips, so that, if she wanted anything memorable in the way of features, she had to paint them on (DD 18). Charlotte, wife number three or four, got so enraged with him that she cut the buttons off all his clothes. She was upset about his being fired from NBC. Depressed and disheveled, he returned to Midland City (in time for Celia Hildreth Hoover's funeral) addicted to prescription drugs. Felix truly loved Barbara, wife number five. She was a Midland City X-ray technician and was carrying Felix's first child at the close of the text.

Though Rudy took personal care of their parents, Felix regularly contributed large sums of money to support them. After Mrs. Waltz died from radiation exposure, he and Rudy sued the Nuclear Regulatory

Commission, the Maritimo Brothers Construction Co., and the Ohio Valley Ornamental Concrete Co. With the proceeds they bought the Grand Hotel Oloffson in Port au Prince, Haiti, which is where they are when Midland City is neutron-bombed. While visiting Calvary Cemetery after the bombing, Felix declines an offer from the chef and voodoo priest Hippolyte Paul De Mille to raise the spirit of Celia Hoover.

Waltz, Genevieve. *Either the second or third wife of Felix Waltz, depending on which reference is cited from the text (DD 15, 19). Rudy stays with her in their Greenwich Village apartment when he comes to New York for the theater production of* Katmandu. *During his stay, Rudy witnesses his brother's marriage dissolve, and in his mind he writes a comic play about it called* Duplex. *Long after the marriage is over, Felix starts calling her "Anyface." She had almost no eyebrows, and very thin lips, so that, if she wanted anything memorable in the way of features, she had to paint them on (DD 18). She worked for WOR radio in New York when Felix was its general manager.*

Waltz, Otto (1892–1960). *The eccentric father of Rudy and Felix Waltz whose family indulged his slight art talent, but he never learned to apply himself. (DD 1) . . . he was told, among other things, that he was the heir to a fortune earned principally* by a quack medicine known as "Saint Elmo's Remedy." It was grain alcohol dyed purple, flavored with cloves and sarsaparilla root, and laced with opium and cocaine. As the joke goes: It was absolutely harmless unless discontinued.

Placed under the tutelage of August Gunther who does little to advance the knowledge or skill of the aspiring artist; however, he does take him on trips around the Midwest under the guise of visiting art museums. Instead, the two visit whorehouses. Otto is sent to Vienna for treatment of gonorrhea, contracted on his trips with Gunther, and to enroll in the Academy of Fine Arts.

After being rejected by the art school, he meets up with another rejected and despondent artist, Adolf Hitler. Otto purchases Hitler's painting, "The Minorite Church of Vienna," eventually hanging it in his Midland City bedroom. At the time, however,

---

* Mother's Day 1944 is also the date Vonnegut's mother committed suicide. He and his sister Alice found her body in her bedroom.

Otto and Adolf pair off on their daily excursions with Otto paying their way. Their friendship lasts until Hitler declares war on Europe. It also prompts Rudy to surmise: Think of that: My father could have strangled the worst monster of the century, or simply let him starve or freeze to death. But he became his bosom buddy instead.

That is my principal objection to life, I think: It is too easy, when alive, to make perfectly horrible mistakes (DD 1).

Otto leaves Vienna at the start of World War I after foolishly seeking a commission in the Hungarian Life Guard. He likes their uniforms, which include a panther skin. Henry Clowes, the American ambassador to the Austro-Hungarian Empire, chases Otto home, threatening to tell his parents how he had really been spending his days while they thought he was studying art.

Back in Midland City, Otto renews his friendship with August Gunther. While on a hunting trip with Police Chief Morissey, his son Bucky Morissey, John Fortune, and August Gunther, it is Otto's idea to conceal the truth about Gunther's death—his head having been blown off by Chief Morissey's accidental shotgun blast. Otto takes charge and instructs the others to help send Gunther's headless body down Sugar Creek. Later, when Chief Morissey makes an official visit to the Waltz home knowing the bullet that killed Eloise Metzger had to have come from Otto's unique gun collection, Otto refuses Morissey's entreaties to feign knowledge about the incident. Waltz loudly takes the blame for his son's actions resulting in Mrs. Metzger's death.

For all of Otto's eccentricities, including chasing away Celia Hildreth on the night of her prom date with Felix, he becomes a god to the Maritimo brothers. Otto shelters and feeds the illegal immigrants, earning their lifelong respect and loyalty.

Otto dies from the effects of the February 1960 snowstorm that buries Midland City. It comes only days after the February 14 performance of Rudy's Katmandu *at New York City's Theatre de Lys.*

Waltz, Rudy. *The lead character in* Deadeye Dick *receives his nickname for killing the pregnant Eloise Metzger with an errant shot fired from his home's cupola on the evening of Mothers Day 1944. (That is the date on which Edith Vonnegut committed sui-*

cide. Moreover, in a speaking engagement in Iowa, in April 1989, Vonnegut admitted to firing off a shot from his family's home in the same manner.) Rudy is twelve years old at the time. Otto Waltz claims responsibility for his son's action.

Despite the handicap of his legacy, Rudy grows up to become a pharmacist. He is a self-described "neuter," living without any female companionship. His teachers encourage his small writing talent exhibited in a short sketch about his boyhood hero, John Fortune. Years later, while working the graveyard shift at Midland City's Schramm's Pharmacy (after receiving his pharmacy degree from Ohio State University), he turns the essay into the play Katmandu. *He enters and wins a new playwright's contest. His prize is a professional production in New York City.* Katmandu *plays for one night in Greenwich Village's Theatre de Lys (the same theater that staged Vonnegut's* Wanda June). *The timing of the occasion means that Rudy is in New York when Midland City is hit with a record-breaking blizzard. Rudy's father Otto dies from the pneumonia he contracts during the storm.*

Rudy and his mother move into Avondale, a real estate development of the Maritimo Brothers Construction Company. Unknown to the builders, the mantelpiece is built with contaminated concrete left over from the Manhattan Project. Rudy's mother dies from radioactive exposure leaching from the fireplace. Rudy avoids the same fate because he spends his free time in the kitchen.

Rudy and his brother Felix sue the Nuclear Regulatory Commission, the Maritimo Brothers Construction Company, and the Ohio Valley Ornamental Concrete Company for the wrongful death of their mother. They retire to Port au Prince, Haiti, where they purchase the Grand Hotel Oloffson. Their new wealth means the brothers are out of Midland City for a second disaster, the neutron-bombing. When the brothers visit Calvary Cemetery after the bombing, Felix declines an offer from hotel chef and voodoo priest Hippolyte Paul De Mille to raise the spirit of Celia Hoover.

wampeter (*see also* **Bokononism**); ***Wampeters, Foma & Granfalloons*** (1965—*Vonnegut's first collection of essays*). (CC 24) Which brings me to the Bokononist concept of a ***wampeter***.

A *wampeter* is the pivot of a *karass*. No *karass* is without a *wampeter*, Bokonon tells us, just as no wheel is without a hub.

Anything can be a *wampeter*: a tree, a rock, an animal, an idea, a book, a melody, the Holy Grail. Whatever it is, the members of its *karass* revolve about it in the majestic chaos of a spiral nebula. The orbits of the members of a *karass* about their common *wampeter* are spiritual orbits, naturally. It is souls and not bodies that revolve. As Bokonon invites us to sing:

> Around and around and around we spin,
> With feet of lead and wings of tin. . . .

And *wampeters* come and *wampeters* go, Bokonon tells us.

At any given time a *karass* actually has two *wampeters*—one waxing in importance, one waning.
(CC 86) The contents of those jugs, of course, were parts of the legacies from Dr. Felix Hoenikker, were parts of the *wampeter* of my *karass*, were chips of *ice-nine*.
(WFG Preface) DEAR READER: The title of this book is composed of three words from my novel *Cat's Cradle*. A *wampeter* is an object around which the lives of many otherwise unrelated people may revolve. The Holy Grail would be a case in point. *Foma* are harmless untruths, intended to comfort simple souls. An example: "Prosperity is just around the corner." A *granfalloon* is a proud and meaningless association of human beings. Taken together, the words form as good an umbrella as any for this collection of some of the reviews and essays I have written, a few of the speeches I have made. Most of my speeches were never written down.

Wang, Kimberly. *In* Timequake, *Kimberly is the unfortunate victim of rape and murder, and that leads to the unjust imprisonment of Dudley Prince—an experience he would endure twice as a result of the timequake and the shady dealings of the district attorney.* (TQ 16) *It meant he was again serving two consecutive life sentences, without hope of parole, for the rape and murder of a ten-year-old girl of Chinese-American and Italian-American parent-*

age, **Kimberly Wang**, *in a Rochester crack house, of which he was entirely innocent!*

Warmergram, Charley (*also spelled* **Warmergran**). *Aside from being an insurance salesman in Rosewater, Indiana,* "He was one of about seven in the county who had actually done quite well under real free enterprise. Bella of Bella's Beauty Nook was another. Both of them had started with nothing, both were children of brakemen on the Nickel Plate. **Charley** was ten years younger than Eliot. He was six-feet-four, had broad shoulders, no hips, no belly. In addition to being Fire Chief, he was Federal Marshal and Inspector of Weights and Measures. He also owned, jointly with Bella, La Boutique de Paris, which was a nice little haberdashery and notions store in the new shopping center for the well-to-do people in New Ambrosia. Like all real heroes, **Charley** had a fatal flaw. He refused to believe that he had gonorrhea, whereas the truth was that he did" (GBR 13).

Charley is a good friend of Eliot's and drives Sylvia Rosewater to the private mental hospital in Indianapolis when she breaks down with Samaritrophia.

He is also the butt of a local Rosewater joke concerning the air raid siren Eliot brought to town and discharges every day at noon. (GBR 12) *And wits throughout the county poised themselves to tell a tired and untruthful joke about* **Fire Chief Charley Warmergran**, *who had an insurance office next to the firehouse:* "Must have scared **Charley Warmergram** half out of his secretary." (*N.B.: the two spellings of the fire chief's name are interchangeable in Vonnegut's text.*)

He wins the 1962 Young Hoosier Horatio Alger Award from the Indiana Federation of Conservative Young Republican Businessmen's Clubs. Eliot persuades him to return the award when he learns that thirteen of the sixteen previous recipients were either in jail, under indictment, had falsified military records, or had been executed. Charley is genuinely fond of Eliot and enchanted by the memories he had of their battling fires together.

Warren, Dr. *The elderly headmaster of Whitehill School in the 1962 short story "The Lie," reprinted in* Welcome to the Monkey House (1968). *The story centers on the fact that Eli Remenzel, the thirteen-*

year-old son of Sylvia and Dr. Remenzel, tears up Dr. Warren's letter informing the family that Eli wasn't up to the academic standards necessary for admission to Whitehill. The family rides in their limousine to the school only to find out the truth from an embarrassed Dr. Warren.

Washington, Elgin. *After Kilgore Trout is treated at the hospital for the thumb Dwayne Hoover bit off, he meets this Midland City well-to-do black pimp who recently had his leg amputated. Washington is snorting cocaine after being visited by his ladies. He is yet another Vonnegut character living life compulsively as a dedicated machine, as do Trout's characters in* Now It Can Be Told, *the novel that sends Dwayne Hoover over the edge to insanity.* (BC Epilogue) And, in the midst of the uproar, **Elgin Washington** said something wheedlingly to Trout. "Hey man, hey man, hey man," he wheedled. He had his foot amputated earlier in the day by Khashdrahr Miasma, but he had forgotten that. "Hey man, hey man," he coaxed. He wanted nothing particular from Trout. Some part of his mind was idly exercising his skill at making strangers come to him. He was a fisherman for men's souls. "Hey man—" he said. He showed a gold tooth. He winked an eye.

Trout came to the foot of the black man's bed. This wasn't compassion on his part. He was being machinery again. Trout was, like so many Earthlings, a fully automatic boob when a pathological personality like **Elgin Washington** told him what to want, what to do.

Wataru, Watanabe and Beverly June. *The Rumfoord family gardener and his daughter against whom young Winston plays German batball. Rounding out the opposition is* Edward Seward Darlington, *the half-wit stable boy* (ST 6).

Waterman, Earl. *The congressman for the Ashland family of Titusville, Florida, in the 1958 short story "The Manned Missiles," reprinted in* Welcome to the Monkey House (1968). *He learns the truth about the death of their astronaut son but is unable to disclose the information.* **Mr.** **Waterman** came and talked to us personally, and he looked like he had seen God. He said he couldn't tell us what Bud

had done, but it was one of the most heroic things in United States history.

Waters, Lavinia. *In* God Bless You, Mr. Rosewater, *the daughter of an Illinois Baptist missionary, Lavinia marries Abraham Rosewater, travels with him on his mission to the Congo, and dies while giving birth to their son, Merrihue (the maiden name of Rosewater's mother, Faith Merrihue).*

In The Sirens of Titan, *Lavinia Waters is the author of* Too Wild a Dream, *which details the strange history of Noel Constant and Florence Whitehill.*

Watson, Myron S. *In* The Sirens of Titan, *the alcoholic Watson mysteriously disappears from his job as a bathroom attendant at Newark Airport. He is next seen selling trinkets outside the Rumfoord mansion in advance of the materializations. Apparently, he was recruited for the Army of Mars and survived their invasion of Earth.*

Watson Brothers. *In Midland City, Watson Brothers was the name of the funeral parlor for white people who were at least moderately well-to-do* (BC 4). *Dwayne Hoover suggests to Harry LeSabre that if he fails to wear colorful attire for the Hawaiian Week sale at the Pontiac dealership, he should wear his usual funeral director's suit and take a job at Watson Brothers, or perhaps get embalmed.*

Weary, Roland. *In* Slaughterhouse-Five, *the eighteen-year-old antitank gunner from Pittsburgh, Pennsylvania, captured with Billy Pilgrim behind German lines at the Battle of the Bulge. Weary's tank crew fires one shot and misses before a Sherman tank fires and kills the rest of his crew.*

Back home, Weary had been unpopular because he was stupid and fat and mean, and smelled like bacon no matter how much he washed. He was always being ditched in Pittsburgh by people who did not want him with them (SL5 2). *He becomes violent with the few friends he did have. He shares his father's great interest in weaponry and openly brandishes a triple-edged dagger to Billy Pilgrim when the two are captured.*

Upon capture, Weary's new combat boots are taken and exchanged for the wooden clogs of his captor. His feet become infected and he eventually dies on the train to the prison camp. However, before dying, he blames Billy for his death, thinking that it was his timidity in the snow that caused their capture in the first place. It also didn't help that Billy frequently, though accidentally, steps on Weary's bloody feet. Paul Lazzaro, another captured American prisoner on the train, vows to avenge Weary's death, and he does.

One of Roland Weary's prize possessions is a photo of the daguerreotype depicting a woman having intercourse with a pony. A copy of that photo is sold by Lila Buntline to Fred Rosewater, Jr., in God Bless You, Mr. Rosewater.

Weeks, Bunny. In God Bless You, Mr. Rosewater, the flamingly gay owner of The Weir, a restaurant in Pisquontuit, Rhode Island, fawns over the wealthy Amanita Buntline while tolerating her companion, Caroline Rosewater. He is the great-grandson of Captain Hannibal Weeks of New Bedford, the man who killed Moby Dick.

Weeks, Captain Hannibal. The great-grandfather of Bunny Weeks, owner of The Weir, a restaurant in Pisquontuit, Rhode Island. Captain Weeks was from New Bedford and killed the famed Moby Dick. Out at Bunny's restaurant, No less than seven of the irons resting on the rafters overhead were said to have come from the hide of the Great White Whale (GBR 9).

Wehling, Edward K., Jr. In the short story "2BR02B," Wehling is the conflicted, despairing fifty-six-year-old new father of triplets sitting in the waiting room of the Chicago Lying-in Hospital. He has to face the country's stringent population control laws resulting from science's uncanny ability to reinvent the future, in this case extending life expectancy into the hundreds of years. As a result, unforgiving laws require that each birth be accompanied by a volunteer suicide or other suitable removal of an equal number of the living. His maternal grandfather has already agreed to comply with the law by committing natal-balanced ethical suicide so that at least one of the triplets could live. While the conversation in the waiting room revolves around the painting of a mural depicting Dr. Hitz's great achievements and science's ability to make all things possible for a good life, Wehling

closes the story by shooting and killing Dr. Hitz and Leora Duncan (an ethical suicide hostess) before committing suicide—thereby making room for all three of his newborn triplets. His actions move the two-hundred-year-old muralist (unnamed—q.v.) to make an appointment for himself that afternoon with an Ethical Suicide Suite.

Weide, Robert. The Emmy-award-winning documentarian and filmmaker who started a friendship with Vonnegut in the 1980s and has been working on a comprehensive documentary of his idol for more than twenty-five years. Most of his film work documents top-level comedians: W. C. Fields, Straight Up (winner of a Primetime Emmy); Mort Sahl, The Loyal Opposition; Lenny Bruce, Swear to Tell the Truth (Oscar nominee, Emmy winner); and Woody Allen, Woody Allen: A Documentary for the PBS documentary series American Masters. In 2015, Weide successfully raised more than $300K on Kickstarter to complete his Vonnegut film. It is due out in 2016.

In Timequake, Weide is among the five clambake guests invited by Vonnegut to finally meet his alter ego. (TQ 62) They were **Robert Weide**, who in this summer of 1996 is making a movie in Montreal of Mother Night, and Marc Leeds, who wrote and had published a witty encyclopedia of my life and work, and Asa Pieratt and Jerome Klinkowitz, who have kept my bibliography up-to-date and written essays about me as well, and Joe Petro III, numbered like a World War, who taught me how to silk-screen.

The Weir. In God Bless You, Mr. Rosewater, The Weir is Bunny Weeks's restaurant on the outskirts of Pisquontuit, overlooking the favorite fishing bed of Harry Pena and his sons. It contains the world's largest private collection of harpoons and is decorated with the bones of Moby Dick, the great white whale captured by his great-grandfather Captain Hannibal Weeks. Bunny places opera glasses on the tables so customers can watch the Pena men haul in their catch. Amanda Buntline and Caroline Rosewater are frequent guests at The Weir.

Welcome to the Monkey House (1968) (see also **Billy the Poet, ethical birth control,** and **ethical suicide**). This collection of Vonnegut's short stories contains all the same stories as his one previous collection with the exception of "Hal Irwin's Magic Lamp."

The short story is well described in this text's entries for Billy the Poet and ethical birth control. Suffice it to say that Billy the Poet seduces ethical suicide hostesses, kidnaps them, delays the administration of their birth control, rendering them "nothingheads," and often deflowers them after the drug's antisexuality effects have worn off.

Weltschmerz. The German term signifies world-weariness; worn-down spirits; psychologically overwhelmed, calmly buried psyches.

The first time Vonnegut uses this term is in Player Piano. Paul is reminded of the first time he saw the allegory on stage at the Meadows executive retreat. He was with his father. (PP XXI) The play was virtually the same play that had begun every Meadows session, even before the war, when the island had belonged to a steel company. Twenty years ago, Paul's father had brought him up here, and the play's message had been the same: that the common man wasn't nearly as grateful as he should be for what the engineers and managers had given him, and that the radicals were the cause of the ingratitude.

When Paul had first seen the allegory, as a teenager, he'd been moved deeply. He had been struck full force by its sublime clarity and simplicity. It was a story in a nutshell, and the heroic struggle against ingratitude was made so vivid for his young mind that he'd worshipped his father for a little while as a fighter, a latter-day Richard the Lionhearted.

"Well," his father had said after that first play, years ago, "what are you thinking, Paul?"

"I had no idea—no idea that's what was going on."

"That's the story," his father had said sadly. "The whole story. That's the way it is."

"Yessir." Their eyes had met, and an inexpressibly sweet sense of eternal tragedy had passed between them, between their generations—a legacy of **Weltschmerz** as old as humanity.

The next citation of the term occurs in John Rauch's biography of the Vonneguts, reprinted in Palm Sunday. (PS Roots) "After Edith's death Kurt lived almost as a recluse, for some ten years. But his

sister, Irma Vonnegut Lindener, who was then a resident of Hamburg, Germany, paid him protracted visits—sometimes for months at a time. They were very congenial and deeply attached to each other. She understood his vagaries, respected his privacy and fierce independence, and gave him the only sort of companionship which he would tolerate. They resembled each other in many ways and were deeply empathetic. They were both blond and blue-eyed. They both spoke German fluently and shared their attachment to their German traditions of music and literature. Kurt acquired a sort of skeptical and fatalistic contempt for life—what the Germans call **Weltschmerz**."

The third citation is from Vonnegut's essay on the religious traditions of his family. After quoting freethinker Clemens Vonnegut's comments on life and death, Vonnegut continues, Such is my ancestral religion. How it was passed on to me is a mystery. By the time I got to know them, my parents were both so woozy with **Weltschmerz** that they weren't passing anything on—not the German language, not their love for German music, not the family history, nothing. Everything was all over with. They were kaput (PS Religion).

The final citation comes as part of the world-weary description of the local burgomaster in a wartime short story. (BAG Der Arme Dolmetscher). The burgomaster himself, old, thin, and night-shirted, ushered me into the first-floor bedroom that was to be mine. He pantomimed as well as spoke his welcome, and a sprinkling of "Danke schön" was adequate dolmetsching for the time being. I was prepared to throttle further discussion with "Ich weiss nicht, was soll es bedeuten, dass ich so traurig bin." This would have sent him padding off to bed, convinced that he had a fluent, albeit shot-full-of-**Weltschmerz**, Dolmetscher. The stratagem wasn't necessary. He left me alone to consolidate my resources.

The Western Hemisphere University (also **Western Hemisphere University of the Bible**). There are two references to this mail-order diploma mill. The first appears in Mother Night, in which it is the creation of Dr. Lionel J. D. Jones. The second occurs in Cat's Cradle in connection with the enigmatic Dr. Vox Humana.

(*MN* 13) The school he headed was named, straightforwardly enough, The Little Rock School of Embalming. It was losing eight thousand dollars a year. Jones took it out of the high-overhead field of embalming education, sold its real estate, and had it rechartered as **The Western Hemisphere University of the Bible**. The university held no classes, taught nothing, did all its business by mail. Its business was the awarding of doctorates in the field of divinity, framed and under glass, for eighty dollars a throw.

And Jones helped himself to a W.H.U.B. degree, out of open stock, so to speak. When his second wife died, when he brought out *The White Christian Minuteman* again, he appeared on the masthead as, "The Reverend Doctor Lionel J. D. Jones, D.D.S., D.D."

(*CC* 96) He turned out to be an intelligent man. His doctorate, which he invited me to examine, was awarded by the **Western Hemisphere University of the Bible** of Little Rock, Arkansas. He made contact with the University through a classified ad in *Popular Mechanics*, he told me. He said that the motto of the University had become his own, and that it explained the chicken and the butcher knife. The motto of the University was this:

MAKE RELIGION LIVE!

Westlake, Ian. *The Englishman liberated from a German POW camp by advancing Soviet forces who later witnesses the hanging of Werner Noth. He takes photographs and writes a skillful account of the incident, only to be published in the pages of a lurid girlie magazine (a manner reminiscent of Kilgore Trout's publishing history). In the late 1950s, while Howard Campbell waited his turn in a Greenwich Village barber shop, his eye caught the provocative title "Hangwomen for the Hangman of Berlin." Ironically, Westlake's article informed Campbell more about his father-in-law's activities than he ever knew.* (*MN* 20) "Terror and torture were the provinces of other branches of the German police," said **Westlake**. "Werner Noth's own province was what is regarded in every big city as ordinary law and order. The force he directed was the sworn enemy of drunks, thieves, murderers, rapists, looters, confidence men, prostitutes, and other disturbers of the peace, and it did its best to keep the city traffic moving.

"Noth's principal offense," said **Westlake**, "was that he introduced persons suspected of misdemeanors and crimes into a system of courts and penal institutions that was insane. Noth did his best to distinguish between the guilty and the innocent, using the most modern police methods; but those to whom he handed over his prisoners found the distinction of no importance. Merely to be in custody, with or without trial, was a crime. Prisoners of every sort were all to be humiliated, exhausted and killed."

Campbell also learns from Westlake's article that it took nine attempts to hang Werner Noth.

Wetzel, Richard. *In* Deadeye Dick, *the founder and principal stockholder of the Midland County National Bank and father of one child, Emma. Emma Wetzel marries Otto Waltz in her parents' mansion, next door to the Waltz family home. Both families are agnostics, so a local judge performs the ceremony.*

The Whale. *In* The Sirens of Titan, *the three-hundred-foot-high spacecraft with living quarters for five, built by Malachi Constant's Galactic Spacecraft Corporation. Its launch is suspended when scientists discover the chrono-synclastic infundibulum. After Winston Niles Rumfoord tells his wife and Malachi Constant about their future together on Titan, Malachi tries to divest his holdings in Galactic Spacecraft. At the same time, Beatrice uses her wealth to buy into Galactic in order to prevent the launch of the spacecraft. Nevertheless, the president declares a New Age of Space and rechristens the* **Whale** *the* Rumfoord, *and Malachi and Beatrice are soon on a collision course to their future on Mars and, later, Titan.*

Wheeler, Elm. *Professional barber Homer Bigley delivers a monologue to Dr. Ewing J. Halyard about the virtues of military service over civilian life and holds up the life and death of Sergeant Elm Wheeler as proof that there was more opportunity for heroism and greatness in the military than anywhere else. In recalling the war, Bigley tells Halyard, "But you know, terrible as that mess was—not just* **Wheeler,**

but the whole war—it brought out the greatness in the American people. There's something about war that brings out greatness. I hate to say that, but it's true. Of course, maybe that's because you can get great so quick in a war. Just one damn fool thing for a couple of seconds, and you're great. I could be the greatest barber in the world, and maybe I am, but I'd have to prove it with a lifetime of great hair-cutting, and then nobody'd notice. That's just the way peacetime things are, you know?

"But **Elm Wheeler**, you couldn't help but notice him when he went hog-wild after he got a letter from his wife saying she'd had a baby, and he hadn't seen her for two years. Why, he read that and ran up to a machine-gun nest and shot and hand-grenaded everybody in it something awful, then he ran up to another one and mashed up all the people there with his rifle butt, and then, after he'd busted that, he started after a mortar emplacement with a rock in each hand, and they got him with a shell fragment. You could of paid a surgeon a thousand dollars, and he couldn't of done a nicer job. Well, **Elm Wheeler** got the Congressional Medal for that, and they laid it in his coffin with him. Just laid it there. Couldn't hang it around his neck, and if they'd put it on his chest, I expect they'd of had to use solder, he was so full of lead and scrap iron.

"But *he* was great, and nobody'd argue about that, but do you think he could of been great today, in this modem day and age? **Wheeler**? **Elm Wheeler**? You know what he would be today? A Reek and Wreck, that's all. The war made him, and this life would of killed him" (PP XX).

Wheelock, Harley, II and III. *Lieutenant Colonel Harley Wheelock III is the West Point graduate in charge of the 62nd Airborne Division, which vanquishes the marauding prisoners from Athena who overrun Scipio. Though preparing for leave from his post in the South Bronx when the prison break occurs, Wheelock knows Eugene Debs Hartke by his military nickname, "the Preacher." He puts Hartke in charge of the troops he leaves behind, securing for him a commission to become a brigadier general in the National Guard.*

The two military men become quick comrades. Harley II was three years ahead of Hartke at the academy. Harley III shared with Hartke information

about his father's death. (HP 38) He told me his father drowned while trying to rescue a Swedish woman who committed suicide by opening the windows of her Volvo and driving it off a dock and into the Ruhr River at Essen, home, as it happens, of that premier manufacturer of crematoria, A. J. Topf und Sohn.

Small World.

Harley III and his wife are infertile, so they adopt twin orphan girls from Peru, South America.

"Where I Live" (1964). *The opening essay in* Welcome to the Monkey House *describing Vonnegut's family and cultural life while living in West Barnstable, Cape Cod.*

Whistler, Henry Niles. *In* Jailbird, *the Harvard graduate and poet who goes to Cleveland to lend his support to the striking workers at the Cuyahoga Bridge and Iron Company. He writes the letter sent by the workers to Daniel McCone.* (JB Prologue) "We wish only . . . to take one last look at the factory to which we gave the best years of our lives, and to show our faces to all who may care to look upon them, to show them to God Almighty alone, if only He will look, and to ask, as we stand mute and motionless, 'Does any American deserve misery and heartbreak such as we now know?'" *McCone's response was to have the Riot Act read to the strikers just before the ensuing massacre. When it was learned an infant was shot dead in the fracas, Whistler wrote the song "Bonnie Failey," which includes the couplet,* "Damn you, damn you, Dan McCone, / With a soul of pig iron and a heart of stone. . . . " (JB Prologue)

Whistler, Kenneth. *The spellbinding Harvard-educated labor organizer in* Jailbird, *patterned after the real-life organizer Powers Hapgood. Whistler repeats Hapgood's unionization efforts in Kentucky's coalfields and his leadership in protest of the executions of Sacco and Vanzetti. Walter Starbuck and Mary Kathleen O'Looney first hear Whistler speak at a labor rally in Boston for the International Brotherhood of Abrasives and Adhesives Workers. Mary Kathleen becomes so infatuated with Whistler that after Walter graduates from Harvard and no longer communicates with her, she takes off to Kentucky in search of Whistler.*

Mary moves into Whistler's life and has a brief re-lationship. However, Whistler drinks heavily and physically abuses Mary. One night he comes home drunk and dangerous, so Mary flees into the street, where she literally runs into Jack Graham, the young mining engineer and owner of the fledgling RAMJAC Corporation—and he soon becomes her husband.

Whistler dies in a 1911 mining disaster. Mary's infatuation for Whistler the socialist sustains her long after the death of her husband. As she roams the streets of New York City disguised as a bag lady, she keeps a picture of Whistler and Starbuck in her rag-gedy sneakers.

Starbuck is also influenced by Whistler. At his fare-well dinner before returning to prison, his RAMJAC colleagues play a recording of his testimony before a 1949 session of the House Un-American Activities Committee: Congressman Nixon had asked me why, as the son of immigrants who had been treated so well by Americans, as a man who had been treated like a son and been sent to Harvard by an American capitalist, I had been so ungrateful to the American economic system *(JB Epilogue). Starbuck confides that his answer was the same one he heard his one-time hero confess in response to a similar question by a judge presiding over a case of alleged violence by strikers.* My stolen answer to Nixon was this: "Why? The Sermon on the Mount, sir" *(JB Epilogue).*

White, Allison. *In* Bluebeard, *the cook and house-keeper for Rabo Karabekian as well as the mother of Celeste. Though she doesn't care for Karabekian's collection of Abstract Expressionist paintings, she is extremely curious about what kind of painting is locked inside the potato barn. She did, however, ex-press great admiration for a Dan Gregory painting of black and white boys squaring off in an alley.*

White, Celeste. *The fifteen-year-old daughter of Allison, Rabo Karabekian's live-in cook, in* Blue-beard. *She is a devoted fan of the Polly Madison novels, having read the entire collection. Celeste spends her time lounging with her friends around Karabekian's home. She takes birth control pills, much to Rabo's consternation, and constantly disap-points him with her inability to identify historical figures that he considers to be the principal elements of a basic education.*

White, Gloria. *The traveling companion of the bil-lionaire hot air balloonist and motorcyclist Arthur K. Clarke.* (HP 23) He himself was on a motorcycle, and on the saddle behind him, holding on for dear life, her skirt hiked up to her crotch, was **Gloria White**, the 60-year-old lifelong movie star! They wore gold helmets festooned with dollar signs as they motored into Scipio.

White, Herb. *As the unnamed narrator begins the short story "Lovers Anonymous," collected in* Bagombo Snuff Box (1999), **Herb White** *keeps books for the various businesses around our town, and he makes out practically everybody's income tax. Our town is North Crawford, New Hampshire.* **Herb** *never got to college, where he would have done well. He learned about bookkeeping and taxes by mail.* **Herb** *fought in Korea, came home a hero. And he married Sheila Hinckley, a very pretty, intelligent woman practically all the men in my particular age group had hoped to marry. My particular age group is thirty-three, thirty-four, and thirty-five years old, these days.*

Despite initially appearing among the most con-ventional of men during his era, Herb's mystique is in the unexplored backstory to this brief tale of his wife's melding of feminism and independence. In keeping with the influence exerted upon her by read-ing Woman, the Wasted Sex, or, The Swindle of Housewifery, *Herb agrees to make a separate living space for himself out of his huge home's ell. Rather than signifying a break with his wife, this puzzling development in their household (especially as per-ceived by the members of Lovers Anonymous) is a positive sign of Herb's freedom, thanks to Sheila's liberation through feminist literature and a genuine desire to further her storied academic achievement. Herb and Sheila have twin girls who are neither seen nor referred to by name.*

White, Maggie. *The beautiful former dental assis-tant who becomes a homemaker when she marries an Ilium optometrist.* (SL5 8) She was a dull person, but a sensational invitation to make babies. Men looked at her and wanted to fill her up with babies right away.

At Billy and Valencia Pilgrim's eighteenth wed-ding anniversary, the vacuous and gullible Maggie has a terrifying conversation with Kilgore Trout, a specially invited guest. Trout first makes up a story about the funeral of a great French chef over whose body the mourners sprinkled parsley and paprika before closing the casket. Maggie believes Trout when he swears it is no fiction. She fears Trout when he says that everything he experiences is later used in his stories. Her dim-wittedness is used by Vonnegut to make her the butt of Kilgore Trout's playful torment in a bit of burlesque humor. He tells her that God is listening as well, "And on Judgment Day he's going to tell you all the things you said and did. If it turns out they're bad things instead of good things, that's too bad for you, because you'll burn forever and ever. The burning never stops hurting."

Poor **Maggie** turned gray. She believed that, too, and was petrified. Kilgore Trout laughed uproariously. A salmon egg flew out of his mouth and landed in **Maggie**'s cleavage (SL5 8).

White, Sheila Hinckley. *In the short story "Lovers Anonymous,"* collected in Bagombo Snuff Box (1999), *Sheila Hinckley is the deserved focus of attention while attending high school in North Crawford, New Hampshire. However, her desirability is expressed by others through only passing reference to her beauty while concentrating instead on her easy brilliance. Sheila's story stands opposite the boilerplate stories of traditional women's magazines of the day. Instead, hers is the story of feminine awakening to academic and professional aspirations alongside marriage and motherhood.*

As the unnamed narrator recalls slobbering atop the bar of the North Crawford Manor on the evening of Sheila's wedding to Herb White, "Gentlemen, friends, brothers, I'm sure we wish the newlyweds nothing but happiness. But at the same time I have to say that the pain in our hearts will never die. And I propose that we form a permanent brotherhood of eternal sufferers, to aid each other in any way we can, though Lord knows there's very little anybody can do for pain like ours."

The crowd thought that was a fine idea.

. . . **Sheila** had been the smartest girl in high school, and had been going like a house afire at the University of Vermont, too. We'd all assumed there wasn't any point in serious courting until she'd finished college.

And then, right in the middle of her junior year, she'd quit and married Herb.

Sheila and Herb have twin daughters who are neither named nor seen in the text. After more than ten years of marriage, still looking as youthful as when twenty-two, Sheila reads the big red book. Titled Woman, the Wasted Sex, or, The Swindle of Housewifery *(a transparent reference eight months after the publication of Betty Freidan's* The Feminine Mystique*), the text provokes Sheila's teary epiphany about the ease of her past formal schooling, her life since marriage and motherhood, this newly awakened capacity for learning, and the positive consequences it has for her already loving relationship with Herb.* "I was crying because I was understanding what a bluffer I'd been in school," she said. "I was only pretending to care about the things I was learning, back in those silly old days. Now I do care. That's why I was crying. I've been crying a lot lately, but it's good crying. It's about discovery, it's about grown-up joy."

As the unnamed narrator, a storm window salesman and the one who dubbed his group of lovelorn friends Lovers Anonymous, yields to the most personal intrusion, curiously trying to decipher how Sheila's liberation affects their love life, her answer indicates the strength of their intimacy (a cautionary swipe at those who regarded women's liberation as being synonymous with hatred for males). I had to admit it was an interesting adjustment **Sheila** and Herb were making. One thing bothered me, though, and there wasn't any polite way I could ask about it. I wondered if they were going to quit sleeping with each other forever.

Sheila answered the question without my having to ask it.

"Love laughs at locksmiths," she said.

The White Christian Minuteman. ". . . a scabrous, illiterate, anti-Semitic, anti-Negro, anti-Catholic hate sheet published by the Reverend Doctor Lionel J. D. Jones, D.D.S. (MN 12) *Jones founded the paper in 1928 after the death of his first wife, Hattie Sharf (who was fifty-eight when they married; he was twenty-four), bankrolling the venture with the $84,000 he gets for selling his funeral home inheritance. The paper is a tool to vent his latent racism that he managed to keep in check while his wife was* *alive. He suspends publication in 1929 after the stock market crash, though he manages to send free copies of all fourteen issues to everyone in* Who's Who. *He originally uses the paper to publish his theories about racial superiority that had long ago gotten him thrown out of dental school.*

When his second wife dies (Mary Alice Shoup — the sixty-eight-year-old owner of the Little Rock Embalming School), Jones revives the paper. However, the paper increases in size and style because "Jones had been recruited and financed as a propaganda agent for Hitler's then-rising Third German Reich. Jones' news, photographs, cartoons and editorials were coming straight from the Nazi propaganda mills in Erfurt, Germany" (MN 13).

In 1955, after serving fourteen years in prison for a federal conviction of conspiracy to commit seditious acts, Jones again publishes the paper. George Kraft / Iona Potapov (the Soviet sleeper-spy), sends a notice to the newspaper, among many others, chronicling the postwar existence of Howard Campbell — his close friend. This is all part of Kraft's convoluted but failed plot to kidnap Campbell and send him to Moscow for a war crimes trial.

Whitefeet, Elbert. *The president of the bankrupt Sweetbread College in the play* Jekyll and Hyde Revisited. *Whitefeet destroys the financial underpinnings of the college by withdrawing its investments in IBM, Xerox, and Polaroid and reinvesting them in cocoa futures. This sets in motion the students' musical production of* Dr. Jekyll and Mr. Hyde *to raise funds for the college. It also spurs the college's own Dr. Jekyll figure to search for a new discovery to raise funds.*

Whitehall, Major General Daniel. *The highly suggestible commander of the Corps of Engineers combat troops who asks that Private Rabo Karabekian be permitted to paint his portrait prior to his retirement (due to failing kidneys). Whitehall wants Karabekian for the task because he believed that somebody with a foreign-sounding name could do the best job (Blue 25). The general leaves the service before America's involvement in World War II, having joined the military shortly after World War I. (Blue 25) If I had realized that at the time (that this painting "might actually outlive the 'Mona Lisa'") I might have given*

him a puzzling half-smile, whose meaning only I knew for certain: he had become a general, but had missed the two big wars of his lifetime.

Rabo takes the opportunity presented by long hours alone with the general to make small talk about the strategic impact brought about by aerial photography, suggesting it should be the Corps of Engineers, Whitehall's command, to lead the way in camouflage techniques to counteract aerial surveillance. (Blue 25) In what must surely have been the manner of powerless Armenian advisors in Turkish courts, I congratulated him on having ideas he might never have had before. An example: "You must be thinking very hard how important aerial photography is going to be, if war should come." War, of course, had come to practically everybody but the United States by then.

"Yes," he said. . . . And then I added almost absentmindedly as I laid the paint on: "Every branch of the service is claiming camouflage from the air as their specialty, even though it's obviously the business of the Engineers."

At the general's retirement party and portrait unveiling, He lectured on aerial photography, and the clear mission of the Engineers to teach the other branches of the service about camouflage. He said that among the last orders he would ever give was one which called for all enlisted men with what he called "artistic experiences" to be assigned to a new camouflage unit under the command of, now get this: "Master Sergeant Rabo Karabekian. I hope I pronounced his name right" (*Blue* 25).

Whitehall Palace (*see* **Rumfoord mansion**).

Whitehill, Florence. *The chambermaid at the Wilburhampton Hotel who becomes Noel Constant's only visitor during his first two years there. She spent one night out of ten with him for a small, flat fee (ST 3).*

An account of the affair between Noel Constant and Florence Whitehill is included in Lavina Waters's Too Wild a Dream? *(ST 3) Miss Waters' volume, while fuddled as to business details, contains the better account of the chambermaid* **Florence Whitehill**'s *discovery that she was pregnant by Noel Constant, and her discovery that Noel Constant was a multi-multi-millionaire.*

Noel Constant married the chambermaid, gave her a mansion and a checking account with a million dollars in it. He told her to name the child Malachi if it was a boy, and Prudence if it was a girl. He asked her to please keep coming to see him once every ten days in Room 223 of the Wilburhampton Hotel, but not to bring the baby.

white humor (*see* **humor**).

Whitman, Grantland. *In "Thanasphere," the disembodied voice of the Hollywood actor complains loudly enough out in the Thanasphere that astronaut Major Rice hears the story about his nephew Carl tampering with his last will and testament.*

Whitman, Milly (**O'Shea**). *In the short story "A Night for Love," collected in* Bagombo Snuff Box *(1999), Milly is the onetime beauty queen who long ago had two dates with Louis C. Reinbeck, the man who would eventually inherit the source of his family's wealth, Reinbeck Abrasives Company. Today Milly is married to Turley Whitman, a security guard at Reinbeck Abrasives. Milly's brief history with Reinbeck is the source of Turley's jealousy, something that rears its head on the night of the story as he stares up at the full moon and fears for the whereabouts of his daughter Nancy, who, like her mother, is the current local beauty queen. For her part, Milly had long ago made peace with her choices in life. Nancy left hours before to attend a fancy party at the Reinbeck estate.*

Whereas the full moon keeps Turley awake with worry, ruminating on his daughter's safety and his wife's past, Milly is far more composed than her husband and lives without looking back or consuming self-recrimination. **Milly** opened her eyes wide and stared at the moon.

Her attitude was what threw Turley as much as anything. **Milly** refused to worry about what was maybe happening to Nancy out in the moonlight somewhere so late at night. **Milly** would drop off to sleep without even knowing it, then wake up and stare at the moon for a while, and she would think big thoughts without telling Turley what they were, and then drop off to sleep again.

Whitman, Nancy. *In the short story "A Night for Love," collected in* Bagombo Snuff Box *(1999),*

Nancy is the only child of Milly and Turley Whitman. Like her mother before her, Nancy is a local beauty pageant queen. Her late night out causes her father both alarm and jealousy. She is extremely late returning from a party at the home of Natalie and Louis C. Reinbeck, the parents of Charlie and fabulously wealthy owners of Reinbeck Abrasives Company. When Louis C. Reinbeck was a young man, he had two dates with Nancy's mother, Milly O'Shea, a fact that gnaws at Turley as he paces the floor waiting for his daughter's return.

Turley is a private security guard employed by Reinbeck, a fact that only feeds his jealousy. Though Turley believes the moon may have caused unwarranted jealousies, it is the very same moon that drives Nancy to elope with young Charlie Reinbeck.

Whitman, Turley. *In the short story "A Night for Love," collected in* Bagombo Snuff Box *(1999), the breadth of Turley Whitman's moonlight jealousies and paternal terrors are evident from the outset.* Moonlight is all right for young lovers, and women never seem to get tired of it. But when a man gets older he usually thinks moonlight is too thin and cool for comfort. **Turley Whitman** thought so. **Turley** was in his pajamas at his bedroom window, waiting for his daughter Nancy to come home.

He was a huge, kind, handsome man. He looked like a good king, but he was only a company cop in charge of the parking lot at the Reinbeck Abrasives Company. His club, his pistol, his cartridges, and his handcuffs were on a chair by the bed. **Turley** was confused and upset.

Turley's jealousy and terror are tied to insecurities about his wife's past and his daughter's absence well into the night. As a young, local beauty queen, Milly had two dates (also bathed in moonlight) with Louis C. Reinbeck, Turley's eventual employer. He harbors doubt about his wife's remembrance of those dates and the relatively poor station their marriage has tied her to. As for Nancy, she is off on a date with young Reinbeck, Jr. Turley builds his tension into an accusation that his wife still wants to be seen as the beauty queen—this time for young Reinbeck. "If you'll pardon me saying so, you're treating this thing like it was some kind of holiday. You're acting like her being out with that rich young smart-aleck in his three-hundred-horsepower car was one of the greatest things that ever happened."

Milly stood, shocked and hurt. "Holiday?" she whispered.

"Me?"

"Well—you left your hair down, didn't you, just so you'd look nice in case he got a look at you when he finally brought her home?"

Milly bit her lip. "I just thought if there was going to be a row, I didn't want to make it worse by having my hair up in curlers."

Milly's spirited defense of herself eventually breaks Turley's jealousy. She shames him for cavalierly mentioning her name when phoning Reinbeck as a way to make him care a bit more about the situation of his daughter's late date with his son. In the end, Turley is left with his emptiness about his daughter's absence, but he is assured of Milly's love.

"Who Am I This Time?" (1961). *The short story, reprinted in* Welcome to the Monkey House *(1968), about the North Crawford Mask and Wig Club, particularly the mercurial Harry Nash. The otherwise silent and rather vapid hardware clerk perfectly assumes the persona of his stage roles. In order to maintain any sort of relationship with him, his new costar, Helene Shaw, keeps bringing him scripts to rehearse. Under these circumstances, they share a rich and passionate life.*

Wiener, Norbert. *The MIT mathematician whose essays gave Vonnegut a central image and thematic focus for* Player Piano, *Vonnegut's vision of how American society will become restructured once the value of technocrats and the third industrial revolution take effect. This latter concept is extrapolated from Wiener's* The Human Use of Human Beings: Cybernetics and Society *(1950). Wiener characterizes the first industrial revolution as devaluing muscle work, and the second (describing the long-term effects of computerization) as devaluing routine mental work. But the third industrial revolution, as envisioned by Vonnegut and illustrated by EPICAC, would devalue human thinking.*

While Wiener fears massive unemployment in the semiskilled and skilled work sectors due to robotics, Vonnegut sees the advancement of unchecked technologies producing a society in which only some

Ph.D.s would be employed at anything more than soldiers or road workers: the Reeks and Wrecks. The know-how and ability to produce would outrun our understanding of the purpose and effects of production. Paul Proteus outlines these ideas and credits Wiener for his industrial revolution model in a conversation with Katharine Finch, his secretary (PP I).

The entire dilemma of technological "know-how" and the engineers' role in shaping society, as well as the source of Vonnegut's title, are bound within a few sentences from Wiener's seminal 1950 text: Our papers have been making a great deal of American know-how ever since we had the misfortune to discover the atomic bomb. There is one quality more important than *know-how* and we cannot accuse the United States of any undue amount of it. This is *know-what* by which we determine not only how to accomplish our purposes, but what our purposes are to be. I can distinguish between the two by an example. Some years ago, a prominent American engineer bought an expensive player-piano. It became clear after a week or two that this purchase did not correspond to any particular interest in the piano mechanism. For this gentleman, the player-piano was not a means of producing music, but a means of giving some inventor the chance of showing how skillful he was at overcoming certain difficulties in the production of music. This is an estimable attitude in a second-year high school student. How estimable is it in one of those on whom the whole cultural future of the country depends.

Vonnegut praises Wiener because he wrote in Atlantic *that he wasn't going to give any more information to industry or the Government, because they weren't gentle people, because they don't have humane uses for things (WFG* Playboy *Interview).*

Wilbur, Harold Newcomb. *The second-most-decorated veteran in Midland City, next to the child killer Ned Lingamon. Wilbur fought in the Pacific Theater of World War II and earned the Silver Star, the Bronze Star, the Soldier's Medal, the Good Conduct Medal, and a Purple Heart with two oak leaf clusters. Lingamon had all those and a Congressional Medal of Honor as well.*

Wilbur is the bartender in Dwayne Hoover's Holiday Inn. Through Wilbur, Vonnegut illustrates the relationship he has with his literary creations, high-

lighting one of the text's central concerns—free will. (BC 19) The bartender took several anxious looks in my direction. All he could see were the *leaks* over my eyes. I did not worry about his asking me to leave the establishment. I had created him, after all. . . .

And he went on staring at me, even though I wanted to stop him now. Here was the thing about my control over the characters I created: I could only guide their movements approximately, since they were such big animals. There was inertia to overcome. It wasn't as though I was connected to them by steel wires. It was more as though I was connected to them by stale rubberbands.

So I made the green telephone in back of the bar ring. **Harold Newcomb Wilbur** answered it, but he kept his eyes on me. I had to think fast about who was on the other end of the telephone.

Wild Bob. *In* Slaughterhouse-Five, *the commanding officer and sole survivor of the 451st Infantry Regiment who wants to be known as "Wild Bob." He tells everyone "If you're ever in Cody, Wyoming, just ask for Wild Bob!"*

Wild Bob dies in a boxcar on the same train transporting Billy Pilgrim and others to a POW camp. His invitation to Cody becomes a refrain repeated by Billy Pilgrim and Kurt Vonnegut. When in the Vermont hospital after the airplane crash, Billy hears his roommate Bertram Copeland Rumfoord recite the carnage of Dresden and Hiroshima and drones out the colonel's "If you're ever in Cody, Wyoming, just ask for **Wild Bob**!" (SL5 9)

Billy nervously repeats the invitation to himself while being introduced by a radio talk show host. Vonnegut says it later in the text when, after recalling how many people were killed in Dresden, he and Bernard V. O'Hare had survived and prospered (SL5 10).

Wilder, Jason. *A Rhodes Scholar and graduate of either Yale or Princeton (there is an inconsistency in the text) and member of the Tarkington Board of Trustees, it is Wilder who leads the investigation culminating in the firing of Eugene Debs Hartke.*

Aside from hiring a private detective to take surveillance photos, he enlists his learning-disabled daughter Kimberley to tape Hartke's lectures and informal conversations. Wilder is a very high-profile individual, an esteemed conservative newspaper columnist, lecturer, and television talk show host. Hartke reflects on his firing that He saved my life by doing that. If it weren't for him, I would have been on the Scipio side of the lake instead of the Athena side during the prison break (HP 11).

Wilder threatened the other board members that if they did not fire Hartke, he would publicly denounce the college through his various media outlets.

Wilder, Kimberley. *The learning-disabled daughter of Jason Wilder, enlisted by her father to surreptitiously tape the lectures and informal conversations of Eugene Debs Hartke for evidence at his dismissal hearing. For the most part, what she actually tapes is Hartke repeating stories and lectures he heard from other Tarkington faculty, particularly Damon Stern and Paul Slazinger.* (HP 11) She was pitiful because she was a dimwit from a brilliant family and believed that she at last had done something brilliant, too, in getting the goods on a person whose ideas were criminal. I didn't know yet that her Rhodes Scholar father, a Phi Beta Kappa from Princeton, had put her up to this. I thought she had noted her father's conviction, often expressed in his columns and on his TV show, and no doubt at home, that a few teachers who secretly hated their country were making young people lose faith in its future and leadership.

I thought that, just on her own, she had resolved to find such a villain and get him fired, proving that she wasn't so dumb, after all, and that she was really Daddy's little girl.

Wrong.

Wildhack, Montana. *The twenty-year-old porn queen abducted from a Palm Springs poolside and transported to a dome in a Tralfamadorian zoo to be the mate of Billy Pilgrim. She wears a locket around her neck* containing a photograph of her alcoholic mother—a grainy thing, soot and chalk. It could have been anybody. Engraved on the outside of the locket were these words: God grant me the serenity / to accept the things I / cannot change, courage / to change the things / I can, and the wisdom / always to tell the / difference (SL5 9 illustration).

Billy adores Montana. (SL5 5) Billy switched on

a floor lamp. The light from the single source threw the baroque detailing of **Montana**'s body into sharp relief. Billy was reminded of fantastic architecture in Dresden, before it was bombed. *Eventually, she learns to love Billy, and only then does she invite him into her bed. Together they have a baby. Billy often tells her about the firebombing of Dresden, and she never tires of listening.*

Wiley, Roberta (*see also* **George Helmholtz**). *The former algebra teacher teamed with the former high school bandmaster George Helmholtz to work as recruiting agents for the Pan-Galactic Space Service, Rumfoord's Army of Mars. Roberta is really a man dressed as a woman to avoid suspicion about the couple's activities. Wiley's true name is not revealed. They successfully recruit more than fourteen thousand people.* (ST 3) Their usual technique was to dress like civil engineers and offer not-quite-bright men and women nine dollars an hour, tax free, plus food and shelter and transportation, to work on a secret Government project in a remote part of the world for three years. It was a joke between Helmholtz and **Miss Wiley** that they had never specified what government was organizing the project, and that no recruit had ever thought to ask. *They were among the few in the Pan-Galactic Space Service who did not have their minds wiped clean.*

Rumfoord tells Helmholtz and Wiley the precise moment to enter Malachi Constant's Wilburhampton Hotel room to offer him a commission in the service. This occurs the moment he finishes reading his father's letter asking what life is all about. A short while later, Helmholtz and Wiley pose as estate appraisers and kidnap Beatrice Rumfoord.

Wilkerson, Mrs. Florence. *In* Timequake, *when Kilgore Trout's "The Sisters B-36" appears on the desk of Monica Pepper, her husband, Zoltan, is awestruck that twenty-five years after an embarrassing high school incident, Trout's name again becomes prominent in his life. Mrs. Wilkerson was the young Zoltan Pepper's sophomore English teacher in Fort Lauderdale, Florida.* (TQ 17) When Zoltan plagiarized a Trout story and submitted it as his own, **Mrs. Wilkerson** decided to teach Zoltan a lesson. She had him write, "I STOLE PROPERTY FROM KILGORE TROUT," on the blackboard while the class watched. Then, for the next week, she made him wear a shirt cardboard with the letter P on it, hung on his chest from around his neck, whenever he was in her classroom. She could get the piss sued out of her for doing that to a student nowadays. But then was then, and now is now.

The inspiration for what **Mrs. Wilkerson** did to young Zoltan Pepper was of course *The Scarlet Letter* by Nathaniel Hawthorne. In that one, a woman has to wear a big A for *adultery* on her bosom because she let a man not her husband ejaculate in her birth canal. She won't tell what his name is. He's a *preacher!*

Wills, Ben. (HP 32) Unlike my (*Eugene Debs Hartke's*) Socialist grandfather **Ben Wills**, who was a nobody, I have no reforms to propose. I think any form of government, not just Capitalism, is whatever the people who have all our money, drunk or sober, sane or insane, decide to do today.

Wilson, Robert Sterling. *The self-styled "Black Fuehrer of Harlem," imprisoned in 1942 for spying for Japan, Wilson is the seventy-three-year-old chauffeur and butler for the Reverend Dr. Lionel J. D. Jones. Wilson gives Dr. Jones a ring to wear among all his other baubles, an American eagle carved in jade and mounted in silver, a piece of Japanese craftsmanship* (MN 14).

Howard Campbell sees Wilson's joining forces with Jones and August Krapptauer as symptomatic of the "cuckoo-clock in hell," the totalitarian mind. As further evidence of the inexplicable associations made by the totalitarian mind, Campbell offers this bit of conversation with Wilson. (MN 17) "I tell this Reverend gentleman here the same thing every morning, the same thing I tell you now. I give him his hot cereal for breakfast, and then I tell him: 'The colored people are gonna rise up in righteous wrath, and they're gonna take over the world. White folks gonna finally lose!'"

"All right, **Robert**," said Jones patiently.

"The colored people gonna have hydrogen bombs all their own," he said. "They working on it right now. Pretty soon gonna be Japan's turn to drop one. The rest of the colored folks gonna give them the honor of dropping the first one."

"Where they going to drop it?" I said.

"China, most likely," he said.

"On other colored people?" I said.

He looked at me pityingly. "Who ever told you a Chinaman was a colored man?" he said.

"Windsor Blue Number Seventeen." *Windsor Blue was a shade of the ill-fated Sateen Dura-Luxe paint used by Rabo Karabekian in his Abstract Expressionist days. This particular item was an eight-panel, sixty-four-foot painting purchased by GEFFCo and hung in their Park Avenue headquarters as proof it was a company in tune with the latest developments in business and culture.*

Years later Karabekian is asked to retrieve his canvas from GEFFCo's subbasement storage facility where the painting has been shedding its defective paint. (Blue 34) I had the eight panels purged of every trace of faithless Sateen Dura-Luxe, and restretched and reprimed. I had them set up in the barn, dazzling white in their restored virginity, just as they had been before I transmuted them into **"Windsor Blue Number Seventeen."**

I explained to my wife that this eccentric project was an exorcism of an unhappy past, a symbolic repairing of all the damage I had done to myself and others during my brief career as a painter. That was yet another instance, though, of putting into words what could not be put into words: why and how a painting had come to be.

Karabekian uses the freshened canvases to create his masterpiece "Now It's the Women's Turn" (shortened from his first impulse, "I Tried and Failed and Cleaned Up Afterwards, so It's Your Turn Now"). It is the scene Karabekian (Vonnegut) saw when released from his prison camp at the end of the war. Karabekian painted in realistic detail, including more than five thousand individuals he saw in the countryside.

Winkler, Kermit. *In* Jailbird, *Winkler, two years behind Walter Starbuck at Harvard, is secretary of the Treasury when Starbuck's prison sentence ends for his Watergate conviction.*

Winslow, Bernard K. *One of the Martian veterans who survives the invasion and now sells* twittering

mechanical birds *outside the Rumfoord mansion nearby Beatrice Rumfoord's stall. (ST 10)* The International Committee for the Identification and Rehabilitation of Martians had, with the help of fingerprints, identified the bird man as **Bernard K. Winslow**, an itinerant chicken sexer, who had disappeared from the alcoholic ward of a London hospital. . . . "Thanks very much for the information. . . . Now I don't have that lost feeling any more."

Wirtanen, Carly. *The first mate and son of Frank Wirtanen, skipper of the Kennedy yacht* Marlin. *Carly is not seen, but a statue of him with his father are on display at the Kennedy Museum, in the short story "Welcome to the Monkey House."*

Wirtanen, Major Frank. *Called by Howard Campbell his "Blue Fairy Godmother" and later revealed to be Colonel Harold J. Sparrow, Wirtanen recruits Campbell to serve as a spy before the United States enters World War II, in* Mother Night. *Wirtanen releases Campbell from custody after the war and sets him up with money and a new life. He later bails Campbell out of trouble when the FBI plans its raid on Dr. Jones's meeting of the Iron Guard of the White Sons of the American Constitution, but not before Wirtanen discloses the fate of Campbell's manuscripts in the hands of Stepan Bodovskov and the secret transmission of Helga Noth's death.*

At the close of the text, Wirtanen sends Campbell a letter in his Jerusalem jail cell offering to appear at his trial in Israel and testify that Campbell's wartime activities were on behalf of the United States government. It is then he reveals his true name.

In the short story "Brief Encounters on the Inland Waterway," reprinted in Wampeters, Foma & Granfalloons, *Wirtanen is a native of West Barnstable, Cape Cod, skipper of the yacht* Marlin, *for the Kennedy family.*

Witherspoon, Withers. *A staff member at the Swain mansion in Galen, Vermont, serving variously as guard, chauffeur, and handyman. He is the only one of the Witherspoons to travel outside Vermont, and that is only because he served in the military. In keeping with the theme of extended families, Wilbur notes that Witherspoon was of course distantly re-*

lated to Eliza and me, too, since our Vermont ancestors had once been content to dogpaddle endlessly,
so to speak, in the same tiny genetic pool.

But, in the American scheme of things at that
time, they were related to our family as carp were
related to eagles, say—for our family had evolved
into world-travelers and multimillionaires (*Slap* 2).

Wojciehowitz, Doris, Robert, and Joseph. *In*
Galápagos, *Akiko Hiroguchi enjoys hearing the true-
life love stories told by Mary Hepburn, especially the
one depicting Mary's own affair with Robert Wojciehowitz. He chaired the English Department at Ilium
High School before its closing. While Doris lies
dying, she decides to buy her loving husband a Jaguar automobile as a sign of her love. Their son Joseph gets drunk and wrecks the car.*

*After Doris dies, Robert proposes to Mary Hep-
burn. Her rejection so embarrasses Robert that he
climbs a tree and sits there for an hour. Mary coaxes
him down and he vomits all over himself. Doris is
so revered by Akiko that she names her daughter
after her.*

**Woman, the Wasted Sex, or, The Swindle of
Housewifery.** *Appearing in the October 1963 issue
of* Redbook *magazine, later collected in* Bagombo
Snuff Box *(1999), "Lovers Anonymous" features*
Woman, the Wasted Sex, or, The Swindle of
Housewifery, *Vonnegut's fictional reference to Betty
Friedan's* The Feminine Mystique, *published eight
months earlier. As presented by Vonnegut's unnamed
storm window salesman, It was written by the presi-
dent of some women's college. The title of it was*
**Woman, the Wasted Sex, or, The Swindle of
Housewifery.** *. . . divided in these five parts:*

  I. 5,000,000 B.C.–A.D. 1865, The Involuntary
     Slave Sex
 II. 1866–1919, The Slave Sex Given Pedestals
III. 1920–1945, Sham Equality—Flapper to Rosie
     the Riveter
IV. 1946–1963, Volunteer Slave Sex—Diaper
     Bucket to Sputnik
 V. Explosion and Utopia
     *The text is responsible for reawakening the aca-
demic and career aspirations of Sheila Hinckley*

White. *As a consequence of its influence, Sheila and
Herb divide the living space in their sprawling home,
she begins a two-year education plan to get back on
a career path, and both feel that their new feminist
perspective on the world has made each happier in
their relationship.*

*Touchstones in both Freidan's and Vonnegut's
texts call on the words of Theodore Parker, the
nineteenth-century American transcendentalist and
a reform minister in the Unitarian Church.* The domestic function of woman does not exhaust her
powers. To make one half the human race consume its energies in the functions of housekeeper,
wife and mother is a monstrous waste of the most
precious material God ever made.

womb, womblike. (PP VI) Paul (*Proteus*) had the
comforter pulled up over his face and was trying to
get to sleep tightly curled in the dark, muffled
womb he made of his bed each night.
(PP XXVIII) "Do?" said Harrison. "Do? That's just
it, my boy. All of the doors have been closed.
There's nothing to do but to find a **womb** suitable
for an adult, and crawl into it. One without machines would suit me particularly."
(CC 118) And so it was in Mona's (*Aamons*) and
my rock **womb**. At least we could think. And one
thing I thought was that the creature comforts of
the dungeon did nothing to mitigate the basic fact
of oubliation.
(GBR 8) A child in her (*Sylvia Rosewater's*) **womb**
would have an unbreakable claim to control of the
Foundation, whether Eliot was crazy or not.
(Gal 1:13) And when Mandarax was asked to come
up with quotations from world literature which
could be used in a celebration of some event on the
slag heap of Santa Rosalia, the instrument almost
always came up with clunkers. Here were its
thoughts when Akiko (*Hiroguchi*) gave birth. . . . *In
the dark* **womb** *where I began / My mother's life
made me a man. / Through all the months of human
birth / Her beauty fed my common earth. / I cannot
see, nor breathe, nor stir / But through the death of
some of her.*

                 John Masefield (1878–1967)*

* Masefield's poem is one of three poems and one biblical inscription Mandarax provides for the occasion.

(*Gal* 2:2) He (*James Wait*) wasn't having any visions of the future or the past. He was little more than a fibrillating heart, just as Hisako Hiroguchi, wedged between the vibrating toilet and washbasin below, was little more than a fetus and a **womb**.

(*Blue* 8) Yes, and my mind really was as blank as an embryo's as I crossed this great continent on **womblike** Pullman cars. It was as though there had never been a San Ignacio. Yes, and when the Twentieth Century Limited from Chicago plunged into a tunnel under New York City, with its lining of pipes and wires, I was out of the **womb** and into the birth canal.

(*Blue* 8) Circe Berman has just suggested that I was a replacement for the Armenian baby which had been taken from her **womb** in Switzerland.

(*Blue* 13) What a satisfactory form of transportation that proved to be! That Cadillac was better than **womblike**. The Twentieth Century Limited, as I have said, really was **womblike**, in constant motion, with all sorts of unexplained thumps and bangs outside. But the Cadillac was *coffinlike*. Pomerantz and I got to be *dead* in there. The hell with this baby stuff. It was so cozy, two of us in a single, roomy, gangster-style casket. Everybody should be buried with somebody else, just about anybody else, whenever feasible.

(*HP* 3) If Henry Moellenkamp had not come out of his mother's **womb** dyslexic, Tarkington College wouldn't even have been called Tarkington College. . . .

If Henry Moellenkamp hadn't come out of his mother's **womb** dyslexic, and if that mother hadn't been a Tarkington and so known about the little college on Lake Mohiga, this library would never have been built and filled with 800,000 bound volumes.

(*HP* 3) If Henry Moellenkamp hadn't come out of his mother's **womb** dyslexic, there would never have been a tower in which to hang the Lutz Carillon. . . .

If Henry Moellenkamp had not come out of his mother's **womb** dyslexic, these heights above Scipio might have been all darkness on the cold winter night 2 years ago, with Lake Mohiga frozen hard as a parking lot, when 10,000 prisoners at Athena were suddenly set free.

(*HP* 4) REGARDLESS of whether Henry Moel-lenkamp came out of his mother's **womb** dyslexic or not, I was born in Wilmington, Delaware, 18 months before this country joined the fighting in World War II.

(*HP* 39) His stepfather had been very good to him. Rob Roy said that the only thing he didn't like about him (*his stepfather*) was the way he raised calves for veal. The baby animals, scarcely out of the **womb**, were put in cages so cramped that they could hardly move, to make their muscles nice and tender.

(*HP* 40) Add the greatest number of children known to have come from the **womb** of just 1 woman, and there you are, by gosh. *This is one of the steps in Hartke's riddle about how many people he killed in war—equivalent to the number of women he made love to throughout his life.*

(*FWD* VII) The Attorney General's Commission on Pornography, a traveling show about dirty books and pictures put on the road during the administration of Ronald Reagan, was something else again. At least a couple of the panel members would later be revealed as having been in the muck of financial or sexual atrocities. There was a clan feeling, to be sure, but the family property in this case was the White House, and an amiable, sleepy, absent-minded old movie actor was its totem pole. And the crazy quilt of ideas all its members had to profess put the Council of Trent to shame for mean-spirited, objectively batty fantasias: that it was good that civilians could buy assault rifles; that the con-tras in Nicaragua were a lot like Thomas Jefferson and James Madison; that Palestinians were to be called "terrorists" at every opportunity; that the contents of **wombs** were Government property; that the American Civil Liberties Union was a sub-versive organization; that anything that sounded like the Sermon on the Mount was socialist or com-munist, and therefore anti-American; that people with AIDS, except for those who got it from mouse-trapped blood transfusions, had asked for it; that a billion-dollar airplane was well worth the price; and on and on.

Wood, Leonard. *Vonnegut uses Wood as a warning to the historically ignorant. This includes those who politically thrive on historical ignorance and those who forget what they knew as well as those who re-*

mained silent. He uses Wood to cudgel the uninformed military strategists, the worst guessers of their time, in a manner that ties Vonnegut to the midwestern voices heard in Twain and Lincoln, his own literary tradition.

Wood commanded soldiers responsible for the crime of killing six hundred Moro men, women, and children by our soldiers during our liberation of the people of the Philippines after the Spanish-American War (MWC 7).

Vonnegut alludes to the literary tongue-lashing Twain delivers but remains unsourced by Vonnegut. However, he supports its vigor and purist spirit by paraphrasing then congressman Abraham Lincoln's objections in 1848 to President Polk's imperialist war against Mexico. This border dispute about slavery was a war of choice for the United States against a sovereign nation that had not attacked it. Lincoln's charge:

> Trusting to escape scrutiny, by fixing the public gaze upon the exceeding brightness of military glory—that attractive rainbow, that rises in showers of blood—that serpent's eye, that charms to destroy—he plunged into war.

Holy shit! And I thought I was a writer! (MWC 7)

As one midwesterner gazes upon the words of another freethinking midwesterner, Vonnegut cites Lincoln's poetic indictment of the excesses of power, fixing attention on the imperialist, militarist moment of his time, including its inherent qualities of seduction, tragedy, and destruction.

From Twain on Wood to Lincoln on Polk, Vonnegut's voice is firmly in the midwestern tradition when he takes on the imbecility of George W. Bush in the next section.

Woodcock, Sheldon. In Deadeye Dick, Woodcock is chosen to play the part of John Fortune in the New York production of Rudy Waltz's Katmandu. Woodcock is frustrated because Rudy can't articulate Fortune's behavior. The actor points out that Fortune says something about Shangri-La thirty-four times, seventeen times proclaiming that no one dies there. And yet the climax of the play shows John Fortune dying in Shangri-La.

Woodly, Dr. Norbert. The effeminate physician dating Penelope Ryan, in Happy Birthday, Wanda June. Woodly is such a pacifist that despite Penelope's disgust with her husband's Hemingway lifestyle, she comes to view Woodly as too wimpish for her tastes.

The Woodpile. The title of the family newspaper for those whose government-issued middle name is Chipmunk. (Slap 37) . . . the motto of The Woodpile used to be this: "A Good Citizen is a Good Family Woman or a Good Family Man."

Woollcott, Alexander Humphreys. Alexander Humphreys Woollcott (1887–1943) was born into the North American Phalanx commune in Red Bank, New Jersey, and became the New York Times drama critic (1914–1922), moving to the New York World from 1925 to 1928. He hosted The Town Crier radio show from 1929 to 1942 while writing for The New Yorker. He was a member of the Algonquin Round Table and through the 1930s was known as an arbiter of popular literary taste (Benet's Reader's Encyclopedia, third edition). (DD 9) Whenever a famous visitor came to Midland City, he or she was usually brought to Father's studio at one point or another, since there was so little else to see. . . . That was how I got to meet Nicholas Murray Butler, the president of Columbia University, when I was a boy—and Alexander Woollcott, the wit and writer and broadcaster, and Cornelia Otis Skinner, the monologist, and Gregor Piatigorsky, the cellist, and on and on. (DD 12) I have mentioned Alexander Woollcott, the writer and wit and broadcaster and so on, who was a guest at our house one time. He coined that wonderful epithet for writers, "ink-stained wretches."

wrang-wrang. John/Jonah suspects there must be some unseen purpose served by the destructive, nihilistic poet Sherman Krebbs. (CC 36) I have not seen Krebbs since. Nonetheless, I sense that he was my karass. If he was, he served it as a wrang-wrang. A wrang-wrang, according to Bokonon, is a person who steers people away from a line of speculation by reducing that line, with the example of the wrang-wrang's own life, to an absurdity.

Wright, Bert. (ST 5) The nominal commander of the entire Army, General of the Armies Borders M.

Pulsifer, was in fact controlled at all times by his orderly, **Corporal Bert Wright**. **Corporal Wright**, the perfect orderly, carried aspirin for the General's almost chronic headaches.

The Wrinkled Old Family Retainer. (TQ 46) Can you believe it? Kilgore Trout, who never even saw a stage play until he got to Xanadu, not only wrote a play after he got home from our war, which was World War Two, but he copyrighted it! I have just retrieved it from the memory banks of the Library of Congress, and it is entitled ***The Wrinkled Old Family Retainer***.

It is like a birthday present from my computer here in the Sinclair Lewis Suite at Xanadu. Wow! The date yesterday was November 11th, 2010. I have just turned eighty-eight, or ninety-eight, if you want to count the rerun. My wife, Monica Pepper Vonnegut, says eighty-eight is a very lucky number, and so is ninety-eight. She is heavily into numerology.

My darling daughter Lily will turn twenty-eight on December 15th! Who ever thought I would live to see that day?

The Wrinkled Old Family Retainer is about a wedding. The bride is Mirabile Dictu, a virgin. The groom is Flagrante Delicto, a heartless womanizer.

Sotto Voce, a male guest standing at the fringe of the ceremony, says out of the corner of his mouth to a guy standing next to him, "I don't bother with all this. I simply find a woman who hates me, and I give her a house."

And the other guy says, as the groom is kissing the bride, "All women are psychotic. All men are jerks."

The eponymous **wrinkled old family retainer**, crying his rheumy eyes out behind a potted palm, is **Scrotum**.

Wu, Sam. *In* Bluebeard, *Wu serves as cook for Dan Gregory before World War II, and on occasion sits modeling for Gregory when he needs to illustrate Fu Manchu. Later, Wu opens a Chinese laundry in New York City while maintaining a caring and warm relationship with Gregory's apprentice, Rabo Karabekian. Hearing about how lonesome soldiers are stationed overseas, Wu asks Rabo for his address before he is sent to Europe. While stationed in* France, Rabo *acquires a number of valuable paintings that he sends to Wu for safekeeping. After the war, Wu has the collection ready for Rabo's return.*

Wyandotte College. *The institution appears twice in Vonnegut's writings. It is the employer of the dynamo psychic Professor Barnhouse in "Report on the Barnhouse Effect" (q.v.) and the first known home of the computer EPICAC, designed by Dr. Ormand von Kleigstadt of Wyandotte's physics department in the 1950 short story "EPICAC." Both stories are reprinted in* Welcome to the Monkey House *(1968).*

Wyatt, Radford Alden. *Walter Starbuck's roommate at Harvard and the twin brother of Sarah Wyatt. Though he is an heir to the Wyatt Clock Company fortune, the terrible losses the company suffers in the radium dial disaster force him to drop out of Harvard. He goes to work in a tuberculosis sanitarium and, as a consequence, contracts the disease that also keeps him out of the armed forces during World War II. He then works as a welder in a Boston shipyard, and* died of a heart attack in Nineteen-hundred and Sixty-five—*in a cluttered little welding shop he ran singlehanded in the village of Sandwich, on Cape Cod* (JB 10).

Wyatt, Sarah. *One of the four great loves of Walter Starbuck's life, the twin sister of Radford Alden Wyatt (Starbuck's Harvard roommate) and wife of Leland Clewes. Her early relationship with Starbuck is marred by her innocence and naïveté.* (JB 9) This would continue to be the case for the next seven years. **Sarah Wyatt** believed that sex was a sort of pratfall that was easily avoided. To avoid it, she had only to remind a would-be lover of the ridiculousness of what he proposed to do to her. The first time I kissed her, which was in Wellesley the week before, I suddenly found myself being played like a tuba, so to speak. **Sarah** was convulsed by laughter, with her lips still pressed to mine. She tickled me. She pulled out my shirttails, leaving me in humiliating disarray. It was terrible. Nor was her laughter about sexuality girlish and nervous, something a man might be expected to modulate with tenderness and anatomical skill. It was the unbridled heehawing of somebody at a Marx Brothers film.

She and Starbuck develop a great friendship de-

spite their disastrous date at the Hotel Arapahoe. (*JB* 10) I told her brokenly in the taxicab that nothing about the evening had been my own idea, that I was a robot invented and controlled by Alexander Hamilton McCone. I confessed to being half-Polish and half-Lithuanian and nothing but a chauffeur's son who had been ordered to put on the clothing and airs of a gentleman. I said I wasn't going back to Harvard, and that I wasn't even sure I wanted to live anymore.

I was so pitiful, and **Sarah** was so contrite and interested, that we became the closest of friends, as I say, off and on for seven years.

Wyatt Clock Company. *The seemingly ancient Brockton, Massachusetts, firm partly owned by the parents of Sarah and Radford Wyatt. The company, the workers, and the Wyatt family are all victimized by the terrible error in instruction given by the foreman.* (*JB* 9) It went like this: In the nineteen twenties the United States Navy awarded **Wyatt Clock** a contract to produce several thousand standardized ships' clocks that could be easily read in the dark. The dials were to be black. The hands and the numerals were to be hand-painted with white paint containing the radioactive element radium. About half a hundred Brockton women, most of them relatives of regular **Wyatt Clock Company** employees, were hired to paint the hands and numerals. It was a way to make pin money. Several of the women who had young children to look after were allowed to do the work at home.

Now all those women had died or were about to die most horribly with their bones crumbling, with their heads rotting off. The cause was radium poisoning. Every one of them had been told by a foreman, it had since come out in court, that she should keep a fine point on her brush by moistening it and shaping it with her lips from time to time.

Among the victims is Mary Kathleen O'Looney's mother. Sarah Wyatt's father is an inactive partner in the company but still shoulders financial liability for the radium poisoning. Once the largest yacht broker in Massachusetts, they are left penniless by 1931 as a result of the Great Depression and the radium case.

Wysocki, Mary Ann. *One of the unfortunate victims of mass murderer Anthony Costa, included in Vonnegut's essay "There's a Maniac Loose Out There."* (WFG There's a Maniac Loose Out There) Young women in America will continue to look for love and excitement in places that are as dangerous as hell. Salute them for their optimism and their nerve.

Vonnegut is unsettled about the innocence of Costa's victims, recalling that his daughter Edith also spent a summer in Provincetown and had been involved with a man who often said he wanted to kill her. He goes on to say, When Tony was arrested, I called her up in Iowa City, and I said, "Edith—that guy who kept saying he was going to kill you: was his name Tony Costa?"

"No, no," she said. "Tony wouldn't say anything like that. Tony wasn't the one."

Then I told her about Tony Costa's arrest.

X, Muhammad Daffodil-11. *While reading through the Daffodil directory, Wilbur learns he is artificially related to the former light-heavyweight boxing champion of the world, in* Slapstick.

Xanadu Writers' Retreat. *In* Timequake, *this is the writers' retreat funded by the Julius King Bowen Foundation and administered by Monica Pepper and the American Academy of Arts and Letters (26). It is a focal point throughout the book, since its culminating event is the long-awaited clambake on the beach attended by various fictional characters, living individuals, and doppelgängers representing important people from Vonnegut's past—all there to meet and celebrate Vonnegut's literary alter ego, Kilgore Trout. It is also the site of Trout's passing. (TQ 4) A* hobo for much of his life, he died in luxury in the Ernest Hemingway Suite of the **writers' retreat Xanadu** in the summer resort village of Point Zion, Rhode Island. That's nice to know.

The event is held in the summer of 2001, six months after the end of the rerun, six months after free will kicked in again (*TQ 4*). *As Vonnegut describes the purpose of the event,* I was there with several fictitious persons from the book, including Kilgore Trout. I was privileged to hear the old, long-out-of-print science fiction writer describe for us, and then demonstrate, the special place of Earthlings in the cosmic scheme of things (*TQ 4*).

Much of what Trout has to say at Xanadu actually happens during conversations in his room with Vonnegut and not to the larger group later at the clambake. It is there that Trout describes his role as a field artillery officer in World War II, which he called "civilization's second unsuccessful attempt to commit suicide" (*TQ 3*).

(*TQ 8*) Side effects of Satan's booze recipes have played a deleterious part in the lives and deaths of many great American writers. In *Timequake One,* I envisioned a **writers' retreat called Xanadu,** where each of the four guest suites was named in honor of an American winner of a Nobel Prize for Literature. The Ernest Hemingway and Eugene O'Neill

were on the second floor of the mansion. The Sinclair Lewis was on the third. The John Steinbeck was in the carriage house.

Kilgore Trout exclaimed upon arriving at **Xanadu,** two weeks after free will kicked in again, "All four of your ink-on-paper heroes were certifiable alcoholics!"

(TQ 32) He *(Trout)* would say at **Xanadu**: "In real life, as in Grand Opera, arias only make hopeless situations worse."

(TQ 33) Did Kilgore Trout ever write poems? So far as I know, he wrote only one. He did it on the penultimate day of his life. He was fully aware that the Grim Reaper was coming, and coming soon. It is helpful to know that there is a tupelo tree between the mansion and the carriage house at **Xanadu.**

Wrote Trout:

When the tupelo
Goes poop-a-lo,
I'll come back to youp-a-lo.

(TQ 52) "America," wrote Kilgore Trout in MTYOAP, "is the interplay of three hundred million Rube Goldberg contraptions invented only yesterday.

"And you better have an extended family," he added, although he himself had done without one between the time he was discharged from the Army, on September 11th, 1945, and March 1st, 2001, the day he and Monica Pepper and Dudley Prince and Jerry Rivers arrived by armored limousine, with an overloaded trailer wallowing behind, at **Xanadu.**

(TQ 60) The cast party afterward was a clambake on the beach at **Xanadu.** As in the last scene of 8½, the motion picture by Federico Fellini, *tout le monde* was there, if not in person, then represented by look-alikes. Monica Pepper resembled my sister Allie. The bakemaster, a local man who is paid to stage such parties in the summertime, resembled my late publisher Seymour Lawrence (1926–1993), who rescued me from certain oblivion, from *smith-*

ereens, by publishing *Slaughterhouse-Five*, and then bringing all my previous books back into print under his umbrella.

Kilgore Trout looked like my father. (*TQ* 62) Only the dead had doppelgängers at that party back in 2001. Arthur Garvey Ulm, poet and Resident Secretary of **Xanadu**, an employee of the American Academy of Arts and Letters, was short and had a big nose, like my war buddy Bernard V. O'Hare.

See also: TQ 4–11; 13–15. *There is also a single reference in* Fates Worse Than Death *to Coleridge's unfinished poem with the opening couplet "In* **Xanadu** *did Kubla Khan / A stately pleasure-dome decree"* (3).

Ximenez, Eduardo. *The Ecuadorian bush pilot who sees the SOS tramped in the riverbank of the Tiputini River, lands his amphibious plane, and meets with Father Bernard Fitzgerald, the Roman Catholic priest who has been living with the Kanka-bonos for the past fifty years. Fitzgerald persuades Ximenez to take the last remaining six Kanka-bonos (all young girls) to Guayaquil. They eventually wind up on the Galápagos Islands with Mary Hepburn and Captain von Kleist and unwittingly participate in Hepburn's procreation schemes that also involve Akiko Hiroguchi.*

Leon Trout sees a parallel between the efforts of Ximenez and bomber pilot Paul W. Tibbets, the man who dropped the atomic bomb on Hiroshima. (*Gal* 1:28) So **Ximenez** was one aviator who had quite a lot to do with the future of humanity. And another one was an American named Paul W. Tibbets. It was Tibbets who had dropped an atomic bomb on Hisako Hiroguchi's mother during World War Two. People would probably be as furry as they are today, even if Tibbets hadn't dropped the bomb. But they certainly got furrier faster because of him.

Y

Yadin, Yigael (1917–1984). *Arnold Marx and his father are amateur archaeologists working on the ruins of Hazor.* They do so under the direction of **Yigael Yadin**, who was Chief of Staff of the Israeli Army during the war with the Arab States (*MN* 1).

Yamashiro, Hiroshi Raspberry-20. *In* Slapstick, *the patriarch of the Manhattan Roseberry clan who is near death when Wilbur Swain arrives in the city. The Raspberries abduct Wilbur because he is a physician—not because he is the president. Wilbur's abductors give him the antidote to the Green Death, the plague of the city, and bring him to the Financial District, where he is expected to treat Hiroshi Yamashiro. After he cures his patient, the Raspberries bring Wilbur all sorts of prized possessions. Rather than taking all their valuables, Wilbur selects a single brass candlestick. His legend grows, and he becomes known as the King of Candlesticks.*

Yarmolinsky, Adam (1922–2000). *The second husband of Vonnegut's first wife, Jane Marie Cox Vonnegut, a public official who served with distinction in a variety of posts in the administrations of Presidents Kennedy, Johnson, and Carter. A graduate of Harvard College and later Yale Law School, his early criticisms of the Vietnam War were undoubtedly heard by Secretary of Defense Robert McNamara, for whom he served as an aide. He later served as deputy director of President Johnson's task force for the War on Poverty. He served President Carter as counselor to the United States Arms Control and Disarmament Agency in 1977. His latter days were spent at the University of Maryland, first as professor and then as provost.*
(*FWD* 16) My first wife, Jane Marie, née Cox, whom I met in kindergarten, was born a Quaker and (as Mrs. **Adam Yarmolinsky**) died a high Episcopalian.
(*TQ* 34) I don't know what Jane's last words may have been. I've asked. She was **Adam Yarmolinsky**'s wife by then, not mine. Jane evidently slipped away without speaking, not realizing that she

wouldn't be coming up for air again. At her funeral, in an Episcopal church in Washington, D.C., Adam said to those gathered that her favorite exclamation was, "I can't wait!"

What Jane anticipated with such joy again and again was some event involving one or more of our six children, now all adults with children of their own: a psychiatric nurse, a comedy writer, a pediatrician, a painter, an airline pilot, and a printmaker. *See also:* TQ 32.

Yarmolinsky, Jane Cox. *Vonnegut's first wife was also from Indianapolis, and the two knew each other since kindergarten. A graduate of Swarthmore College and member of Phi Beta Kappa, Jane married Kurt in September 1945. Together they had three children and later took in as their own three of the four children newly orphaned after the deaths of Vonnegut's sister Alice and her husband. Vonnegut always speaks lovingly, and sometimes wistfully, of Jane. She wrote* Angels Without Wings, *a book about their parenting experiences on Cape Cod. Jane has an unnamed doppelgänger at the* Timequake *clambake who is apparently worthy of Jane's academic mind while also uttering Jane's legendary eagerness for the next big experience.*
(*Slap* Prologue) From then on, the three oldest were raised by me and my wife, **Jane Cox Vonnegut**, along with our own three children, on Cape Cod. The baby, who lived with us for a while, was adopted by a first cousin of their father, who is now a judge in Birmingham, Alabama.

So be it.

The three oldest kept their dogs.
(*PS* Embarrassment) **Jane Cox Vonnegut** and I, childhood sweethearts in Indianapolis, separated in 1970 after a marriage which by conventional measurement was said to have lasted twenty-five years. We are still good friends, as they say. Like so many couples who are no longer couples these days, we have been through some terrible, unavoidable accident that we are ill equipped to understand. Like our six children, we only just arrived on this planet

and we were doing the best we could. We never saw what hit us. It wasn't another woman, it wasn't another man.

We woke up in ambulances headed for different hospitals, so to speak, and would never get together again. We were alive, yes, but the marriage was dead. And it was no Lazarus.

It was a good marriage for a long time—and then it wasn't. The shock of having our children no longer need us happened somewhere in there. . . .

So I am embarrassed about the failure of my first marriage.

(*PS Funnier on Paper Than Most People*) Toward the end of our marriage, it was mainly religion in a broad sense that **Jane** and I fought about. She came to devote herself more and more to making alliances with the supernatural in her need to increase her strength and understanding—and happiness and health. This was painful to me. She could not understand and cannot understand why that should have been painful to me, or why it should be any of my business at all.

And it is to suggest to her and to some others why it was painful that I chose for this book's epigraph a quotation from a thin book, *Instruction in Morals*, published in 1900 and written by my Free Thinker great grandfather Clemens Vonnegut, then seventy-six years old:

"Whoever entertains liberal views and chooses a consort that is captured by superstition risks his liberty and his happiness."

(*FWD* XVI) My first wife, **Jane Marie**, née **Cox**, whom I met in kindergarten, was born a Quaker and (as Mrs. Adam Yarmolinsky) died a high Episcopalian.

(*FWD* XVI) But **Jane** never went to a Quaker Meeting after we were married, although she always made it a first order of business to find out where the nearest one was whenever we took up residence in a new community. She didn't go to Meetings, I think, because Quaker congregations in the East (and we had become easterners) were so close to being Folk Societies as described by Robert Redfield. They were united by blood ties and inhabited a territory which had been theirs for several generations. And here was what was so daunting to **Jane** or anybody else who might want to join them: They did not welcome strangers, save as well-behaved visitors who would soon have the good manners to go away again. (They were like Israeli youngsters raised on kibbutzim as described in *The Children of the Dream* by Bruno Bettelheim.). . . .

An early expression of **Jane**'s powerful longing for a big likeminded family was a persistent prediction she began to make in her early teens, that she would one day have seven children.

(*FWD* XVI) When **Jane**'s beloved children became grownups and flew the coop one by one, she was again attacked by a terrible loneliness which I (only one person, and a chain-smoker at that) surely couldn't begin to satisfy.

So she went in for Transcendental Meditation (TM) with what seemed to me total abandon. One contemporary of our grown kids, Jody Clarke, went to work for Maharishi Mahesh Yogi as a TM recruiter and instructor. He had meditated for thousands of hours (and would be killed in the crash of an airplane while looking for a good location for a TM ashram in North Carolina). When **Jane** told Jody all the glorious things she saw when she meditated, he was astonished. He said, "My goodness, I never saw anything like that!"

For almost everybody but **Jane**, TM was blank, brightly lit, air-conditioned, keenly alert peacefulness. For her it was like going to the movies. So was Holy Communion, I think, when she became an Episcopalian. (I doubt that the Pope or Bishop Paul Moore, Jr., or the battle-axe who wouldn't let Jill and me get married in The Little Church Around the Corner ever came as close to Christ as **Jane** did with a wafer and wine.) Like her mother, and like her son Mark, too, before he recovered, she was a hallucinator. (Unlike Mark and me, though, she never had to be locked up somewhere.) TM and then Episcopalianism made her visions not only reputable and unfrightening, but holy and fun. (There must be uncounted millions like her, so rapt in churches and concert halls, or on park benches on sunny days with a carousel playing not far away.)

(*TQ* 8) Kilgore Trout was hooked on making idiosyncratic arrangements in horizontal lines, with ink on bleached and flattened wood pulp, of twenty-six phonetic symbols, ten numbers, and about eight punctuation marks. He was a black hole to anyone who might imagine that he or she was a friend of his.

I have been married twice, divorced once. Both my wives, **Jane** and now Jill, have said on occasion that I am much like Trout in that regard.

One of the more telling comments Vonnegut makes about Jane appears in a comparison he creates between her and his beloved sister, Allie. (TQ 34) My first wife **Jane** and my sister Allie had mothers who went nuts from time to time. **Jane** and Allie were graduates of Tudor Hall and had once been two of the prettiest, merriest girls at the Woodstock Golf and Country Club. All male writers, incidentally, no matter how broke or otherwise objectionable, have pretty wives. Somebody should look into this.

Jane and Allie missed the timequake, thank goodness. My guess is that **Jane** would have found some goodness in the rerun. Allie would not have. **Jane** was life-loving and optimistic, a scrapper against carcinoma to the very end. Allie's last words expressed relief, and nothing more. They were, as I've recorded elsewhere, "No pain, no pain." I didn't hear her say it, and neither did our big brother Bernie. A male hospital attendant, with a foreign accent, relayed those words to us via telephone.

(TQ 34) **Jane** could believe with all her heart anything that made being alive seem full of white magic.

That was her strength. She was raised a Quaker, but stopped going to meetings of Friends after her four happy years at Swarthmore. She became an Episcopalian after marrying Adam, who remained a Jew. She died believing in the Trinity and Heaven and Hell and all the rest of it. I'm so glad. Why? Because I loved her.

Concerning Jane's doppelgänger at the clambake, **Jane**'s *unknowing stand-in, a pert young woman who teaches biochemistry at Rhode Island University, over at Kingston, said within my hearing, and apropos of nothing more than that day's theatrical performance and the setting sun: "I can't wait to see what's going to happen next (TQ 62)." "I can't wait" was Jane's favorite expression.*

See also: PS Children; PS Sexual Revolution; FWD IV; VI; XVI; XVII; TQ 11; 20; 23; 25; 32; 35; 39; 58; 62.

Ying, Pi (*see also* **Colonel Bryan Kelly** *and* **Major Barzov**). *The sadistic military commander of a brigade in an unnamed Far East Communist country in the 1953 short story "All the King's Horses," reprinted in* Welcome to the Monkey House (1968). *He challenges Colonel Kelly to a game of chess using Kelly's wife, children, and soldiers as various chess pieces to be killed if captured during the game. Ying's mistress kills him when she realizes he is preparing to kill Kelly's son.*

Yonson, Yon. *In the opening chapter of* Slaughterhouse-Five, *Vonnegut writes about the frequency with which he has returned to Dresden as a literary subject. In some ways he feels spent by the recurring desire to write about the firebombing, and at the same time the desire to write about it defines him. These feelings are expressed in both the limerick and poem he recites.* (SL5 1) There was a young man from Stamboul, / Who soliloquized thus to his tool: / "You took all my wealth / And you ruined my health, / And now you won't *pee*, you old fool."

and,

"My name is **Yon Yonson**, / I work in Wisconsin, / I work in a lumbermill there. / The people I meet when I walk down the street, / They say, "What's your name?" / And I say, / "My name is **Yon Yonson**, / I work in Wisconsin. . . ."

Young, Buck. *In* Player Piano, *Buck Young is the "young buck" Cornell football player coach Doctor Roseberry is trying to lure into playing for the university rather than his Delta Upsilon fraternity. Buck is determined to become an engineer, insisting he plays football just for fun.*

As a commentary on the often perceived sham of intercollegiate athletics, Vonnegut characterizes college football in the days of the ruling technocracy as a business without pretense employing student athletes. Doctor Roseberry is prepared to sell linemen to Harvard so he can have the funds to offer Buck Young a $35,000 contract. Similarly, the linemen see no reason why a well-trained college athlete couldn't play into their forties. Buck Young decides to play ball for Cornell just as Doctor Edmond L.

Harrison of the Ithaca Works appears in The Dutch bar while Roseberry is making his sales pitch.

Harrison is drunk and depressed about the apparent fall from grace of Paul Proteus while at the Meadows executive retreat. Buck Young had been brought up to believe that people do lousy work as compared to machines and can't understand Harrison's disenchantment. Harrison tells him that machines are slaves and "Anybody that competes with slaves becomes a slave" (PP XXVIII).

Young, Ida. *The Vonnegut family cook when Kurt was a young child. He writes lovingly about her, acknowledging a debt accrued during long hours in a warm kitchen.* (WFG Preface) One of the lost pieces of mine which I hope Professors Klinkowitz and Somer will never find has to do with my debt to a black cook my family had when I was a child. Her name was **Ida Young**, and I probably spent more time with her than I spent with anybody—until I got married, of course. She knew the Bible by heart, and she found plenty of comfort and wisdom in there. She knew a lot of American history, too—things she and other black people had seen and marveled at, and remembered and still talked about, in Indiana and Illinois and Ohio—and Kentucky and Tennessee. She would read to me, too, from an anthology of sentimental poetry about love which would not die, about faithful dogs and humble cottages where happiness was, about people growing old, about visits to cemeteries, about babies who died. I remember the name of the book, and wish I had a copy, since it has so much to do with what I am.

The name of the book was *More Heart Throbs*; and it was an easy jump from that to *The Spoon River Anthology*, by Edgar Lee Masters, to *Main Street*, by Sinclair Lewis, to *U.S.A.*, by John Dos Passos, to my thinking now. There is an almost intolerable sentimentality beneath everything I write. British critics complain about it. And Robert Scholes, the American critic, once said I put bitter coatings on sugar pills.

It's too late to change now. At least I am aware of my origins—in a big, brick dreamhouse designed by my architect father, where nobody was home for long periods of time, except for me and **Ida Young**.

Ida Young is the model for Mary Young in Breakfast of Champions, and in Timequake Ida's doppelgänger appears at the climactic clambake. Vonnegut follows that description with an affirmation of her importance during his upbringing. (TQ 62) Another look-alike there was Rosemary Smith, Mask and Wig's costume mistress, and mother of Frank Smith, its superstar. She resembled **Ida Young**, grandchild of slaves, who worked for us in Indianapolis when I was little. **Ida Young**, in combination with my uncle Alex, had as much to do with my upbringing as my parents did.

Young, Mary. *Loosely modeled after Ida Young, the Vonnegut family cook when Kurt was a small boy, Mary Young is 108 years old when she dies of pneumonia at the Midland County Hospital, the oldest citizen in town. Her parents were slaves in Kentucky. Mary worked as a laundress for Dwayne Hoover's family when he was quite young.* (BC 6) She told Bible stories and stories about slavery to little Dwayne. She told him about a public hanging of a white man she had seen in Cincinnati, when she was a little girl.

. . . Here is all she had to say about death: "Oh my, oh my."

Like all Earthlings at the point of death, **Mary Young** sent faint reminders of herself to those who had known her. She released a small cloud of telepathic butterflies, and one of these brushed the cheek of Dwayne Hoover, nine miles away.

Dwayne heard a tired voice from somewhere behind his head, even though no one was back there. It said this to Dwayne: "Oh my, oh my."

Z

zah-mah-ki-bo. *In Bokononist thinking,* "Fate—
inevitable destiny" (CC 82).
(CC 85) Frank's servants brought us gasoline lan-
terns; told us that power failures were common in
San Lorenzo, that there was no cause for alarm. I
found that disquiet was hard for me to set aside,
however, since Frank had spoken of my **zah-mah-
ki-bo.**

He had made me feel as though my own free
will were as irrelevant as the free will of a piggy-wig
arriving at the Chicago stockyards.

Zamiatin, Eugene. *Vonnegut credits the Russian
author Yevgeny Zamyatin's 1920 novel* We *as the
source for novels about regimented totalitarian societies, including his own* Player Piano. (WFG *Playboy* Interview) VONNEGUT: This was in 1949
and the guys working on it (*a computer-operated
milling machine at General Electric*) were foreseeing all sorts of machines being run by little boxes
and punched cards. *Player Piano* was my response
to the implications of having everything run by little boxes. . . .
PLAYBOY: So science fiction seemed like the best
way to write about your thoughts on the subject?
VONNEGUT: There was no avoiding it, since the
General Electric Company *was* science fiction. I
cheerfully ripped off the plot of *Brave New World,*
whose plot had been cheerfully ripped off from **Eugene Zamiatin's** We.

Zappa, Lee Razorclam-13. *The husband of Vera
Chipmunk-5 Zappa. Together they serve as cooks in
the King of Michigan's field kitchens during the battle of Lake Maxinkuckee, in* Slapstick.

Zappa, Vera Chipmunk-5 (*also cited as* **Vera
Chipmunk-17 Zappa**). *After the world is in shambles and Wilbur Swain is living on the first floor of
the Empire State Building, his nearest neighbor is*
Vera Chipmunk-5 Zappa, *a woman who loves life
and is better at it than anyone I ever knew. She is a
strong and warm-hearted and hard-working farmer*

in her early sixties. She is built like a fireplug. She
has slaves whom she treats very well. And she and
the slaves raise cattle and pigs and chickens and
goats and corn and wheat and vegetables and fruits
and grapes along the shores of the East River
(*Slap* 1).

*It is she who supplies the thousand candles even-
tually used in Wilbur's death scene.*

Zeltoldimar (*see also* **Plague on Wheels**). *The
home planet of Kago and his band of homosexual
space travelers who make stops at Lingo-Three and
Earth, in Kilgore Trout's* Plague on Wheels, *which
appears in* Breakfast of Champions. *Kago and his
crew roam the galaxy spreading the tragic story of
Lingo-Three. Their inhabitants are self-producing
automobiles whose own basic needs were killing its
planet. As Vonnegut recalls Trout's text,* The words
in the book, incidentally, were about life on a dying
planet named *Lingo-Three,* whose inhabitants resembled American automobiles. They had wheels.
They were powered by internal combustion engines. They ate fossil fuels. They weren't manufactured, though. They reproduced. They laid eggs
containing baby automobiles, and the babies matured in pools of oil drained from adult crankcases.

Lingo-Three was visited by space travelers, who
learned that the creatures were becoming extinct
for this reason: they had destroyed their planet's resources, including its atmosphere.

The space travelers weren't able to offer much in
the way of material assistance. The automobile
creatures hoped to borrow some oxygen, and to
have the visitors carry at least one of their eggs to
another planet, where it might hatch, where an automobile civilization could begin again. But the
smallest egg they had was/a forty-eight pounder, and
the space travelers themselves were only an inch
high, and their space ship wasn't even as big as an
Earthling shoebox. They were from **Zeltoldimar.**

The spokesman for the Zeltoldimarians was
Kago. Kago said that all he could do was to tell others in the Universe about how wonderful the auto-

mobile creatures had been. Here is what he said to all those rusting junkers who were out of gas: "You will be gone, but not forgotten."

The illustration for the story at this point showed two Chinese girls, seemingly identical twins, seated on a couch with their legs wide open.

So Kago and his brave little Zeltoldimarian crew, which was all homosexual, roamed the Universe, keeping the memory of the automobile creatures alive. They came at last to the planet Earth. In all innocence, Kago told the Earthlings about the automobiles. Kago did not know that human beings could be as easily felled by a single idea as by cholera or the bubonic plague. There was no immunity to cuckoo ideas on Earth.

And here, according to Trout, was the reason human beings could not reject ideas because they were bad: "Ideas on Earth were badges of friendship or enmity. Their content did not matter. Friends agreed with friends, in order to express friendliness. Enemies disagreed with enemies, in order to express enmity.

"The ideas Earthlings held didn't matter for hundreds of thousands of years, since they couldn't do much about them anyway. Ideas might as well be badges as anything.

"They even had a saying about the futility of ideas: 'If wishes were horses, beggars would ride.'

"And then Earthlings discovered tools. Suddenly agreeing with friends could be a form of suicide or worse. But agreements went on, not for the sake of common sense or decency or self-preservation, but for friendliness.

"Earthlings went on being friendly, when they should have been thinking instead. And even when they built computers to do some thinking for them, they designed them not so much for wisdom as for friendliness. So they were doomed. Homicidal beggars could ride."

CHAPTER 3

Within a century of little Kago's arrival on Earth, according to Trout's novel, every form of life on that once peaceful and moist and nourishing bluegreen ball was dying or dead. Everywhere were the shells of the great beetles which men had made and worshiped. They were automobiles. They had killed everything (BC 2–3).

Zerbe, Mr., and daughter Gwen. *In the short story* "A Present for Big Saint Nick," *collected in* Bagombo Snuff Box (1999), *Mr. Zerbe, a short, pudgy man, is the mobster Big Nick's chief accountant. As with the rest of Nick's mostly white-collar office help, the Zerbes are compelled to attend his Christmas party. Nick uses the party to glean, through bribery of the children, any inappropriate personal comments made by their parents about him that were accidentally picked up by their young ears. With a firm grasp on the doll given to her by Santa, Gwen endangers her terrified father when she fails to recognize the cigar-chomping Santa at the party as Nick.* "My **father,**" said **Gwen Zerbe,** breaking the dreadful silence, "says kissing Santa Claus isn't any worse than kissing a dog."

"**Gwen!**" cried her **father.**

"I kiss the dog all the time," said **Gwen,** determined to complete her thought, "and I never get sick."

Zine, Clara. *The* "strikingly beautiful" *woman who works for Monica Pepper at the American Academy of Arts and Letters and is accused by Ms. Pepper of causing the fire alarm to go off at the very moment the timequake hit. (TQ 53)* There was at least one strikingly beautiful woman involved. That was a member of the Academy's office staff. That was **Clara Zine.** Monica Pepper is certain that **Clara Zine** was the one who was smoking the cigar that set off the smoke alarm in the picture gallery. When confronted by Monica, **Clara Zine** swore that in her whole life she had never smoked a cigar, that she hated cigars, and she disappeared.

I have no idea what has become of her.

Clara Zine and Monica were tending the wounded in the former Museum of the American Indian, which Trout had turned into a hospital, when Monica asked **Clara** about the cigar, and then **Clara** departed in a huffmobile.

Zinka. *In Cat's Cradle, the Ukrainian midget working as a dancer with the Borzoi Dance Company. Newt Hoenikker sees her perform in Indianapolis and again while he is attending Cornell. His infatuation with her leads to a whirlwind romance, a quickie marriage, and a honeymoon at the Hoenikker Cape Cod cottage, with the United States grant-*

ing her political asylum. Just as quickly, Zinka returns to the Soviet Union, claiming disgust over American materialism. An American correspondent in Moscow discovers that Zinka was not twenty-three, but forty-two years old. When she left Newt, she took his chip of ice-nine with her and gave it to her government.

Zircon-212 (*see also* **The Big Board**). *Billy Pilgrim reads Eliot Rosewater's copy of Kilgore Trout's The Big Board while he is in the Veterans' Hospital in Ilium. The story takes place on the planet Zircon-212 and partially parallels Billy's Tralfamadorian experience. (SL5 9) It was about an Earthling man and* woman who were kidnapped by extra-terrestrials. They were put on display in a zoo on a planet called **Zircon-212**. *Billy reads the story again in a Times Square bookstore while time-tripping.*

Zog (*see also* **"The Dancing Fool"**). *In Kilgore Trout's "The Dancing Fool," Zog is the diminutive creature from the planet Margo who comes in friendship to Earth, prepared to offer world peace and cures for cancer. He is killed by a golf-club-wielding homeowner who is startled by Zog and his crude speech, which consists of a series of farts and tap-dancing. Zog was trying to tell the man his house was on fire.*

CONCERNING VONNEGUT'S FIRST LETTER HOME AFTER HIS POW LIBERATION

Though the letter is reproduced in Armageddon in Retrospect (published posthumously and without editorial input by Vonnegut), I refer to it here because of its seminal value in tracing Vonnegut's path as a writer from the first moment he had a chance to collect his thoughts about what he had just experienced. I encourage all Vonnegut fans to refer to its full text as reproduced in Armageddon in Retrospect.

Letter from PFC Kurt Vonnegut, Jr., to his family, May 29, 1945

This letter from the twenty-two-year-old Kurt Vonnegut, Jr., to his family after being temporarily settled in a Le Havre POW repatriation camp has become famous for a number or reasons.

This letter is the first contact Vonnegut has with his family after his mother's suicide and his own wartime experiences. Some saw it years before it was put into general circulation, and it became a "did you know" kind of thing among Vonnegut scholars. (Vonnegut sent me a copy of this letter in the late 1990s.)

The letter contains flashes of Vonnegut's later style, showing off a series of epistrophes at the ends of paragraphs to indicate he was left physically unharmed by the chaos around him (But I didn't. . . . But not me.) (ARM 11–12).

Vonnegut's narrative covering the most important six-month period of his young life is told succinctly, with sober observations, occasional mocking of his Nazi captors (derisively referring to their eugenics theories and the myth of the Aryan "superman"), and descriptions of economic dissolution that foreshadow Eliot Rosewater.

Aside from the understatements Vonnegut makes about his division's inability to escape certain capture by multiple Panzer divisions, he is thankful for his own salvation through such a string of barbaric horrors. However, he does not believe the loss of life was worth the military strategy that left his group of scouts to be surrounded and taken prisoner. He bristles at his unit's awarding of a Presidential Citation and a British decoration delivered by Field Marshal Montgomery, instead believing his comrades did not need to be sacrificed to lure out the enemy.

Vonnegut recalls the freezing days he spent in a cattle boxcar on a railroad siding, re-

counting how the Royal Air Force unknowingly killed about 150 prisoners when they strafed the boxcars; how there was frozen cow dung from one end of the boxcar to the other; how he was on two trains for about 330 miles until he and 150 prisoners were sent to work as prisoners in Dresden; and how he got beaten up and fired as an unofficial leader of the prisoners because he mouthed off to his captors. After desperately trying to improve our situation for two months and having been met with bland smiles I told the guards just what I was going to do to them when the Russians came. They beat me up a little. I was fired as group leader (ARM 10).

He goes on to tell of the Dresden firebombing in the most bland manner, one that prompts the question of his dissociative relationship to the events. (ARM 11) He devotes only two sentences to the horror of retrieving German victims and the vilification his fellow POW corpse bearers suffered from the German survivors for their efforts. On about February 14th the Americans came over, followed the R.A.F. their combined labors killed 250,000 people in twenty-four hours and destroyed all of Dresden—possibly the world's most beautiful city. But not me.

After that we were put to work carrying corpses from Air-Raid shelters; women, children, old men; dead from concussion, fire or suffocation. Civilians cursed us and threw rocks as we carried bodies to huge funeral pyres in the city.

Though Vonnegut's numbers later changed when he came to write Slaughterhouse-Five *(at the time he wrote his letter, he was relying on the evidence of David Irving, then a respected historian and not yet a Holocaust denier), Vonnegut saw the city as a bustling waypoint for those escaping the Eastern Front. His sense of Dresden's loss has always been that it was greater than anyone could reliably estimate in human terms, and he was never comfortable with the way people blandly equated leveling Dresden as justifiable payback for what the Nazis had done to Coventry.*

He then recalls how the Russians strafed his prison group set free in an open field, killing another fourteen prisoners by friendly fire (the event rendered in the triptych "Now It's the Women's Turn" by Rabo Karabekian at the close of Bluebeard).

Vonnegut very briefly mentions stealing a wagon and team of horses with seven other released POWs, looting their way back to Dresden, being picked up by friendly Russian troops, and eventually finding their way to the camp in Le Havre. As mundane as it may sound in the context, he closes the letter by calculating how much back pay the Army owes him as well as the length of furlough time he has coming.

Aspects of the letter appear throughout his fiction and in differently detailed ways, but the tone of dissociation in the letter is one that stays with Vonnegut and helps shape the narrative voice of his fiction.

ACKNOWLEDGMENTS

For the production of this present volume, I have many people to thank. First and foremost is Donald Farber, agent and lawyer extraordinaire, a caring soul with the gravelly delivery of a longshoreman. Donald was not only my representative but a friend who graciously shared with me the richness of his stories. Annie, Donald's partner for nearly sixty-nine years, was responsible for putting the soft edges on this man whose legal advice could come across as loving elbow-jabs to the face. Blessed was their union.

There are also friends and colleagues who entered my life during the writing of this text and must be noted. Julia Whitehead, now the executive director of the Kurt Vonnegut Memorial Library in Indianapolis, first contacted me when her project was only a dream. Since then, at her invitation, I have been serving as a charter member of the board for the KVML. The Vonnegut Library is an active contributor to the cultural life of Indianapolis, serves the interests of veterans groups, and is a worldwide nexus for Vonnegut queries.

Professors Rodney Allen, Robert Tally, Susan Farrell, and Gregory Sumner have all provided inspiration and encouragement as I worked on this text. In particular, Rodney, Robert, and Susan were with me in San Francisco a few years ago when we started the Kurt Vonnegut Society.

Friends and supporters of this work are far too numerous to list here, and I certainly would not want to commit any more errors of omission. For all of you who have urged me over the years to write this logical second edition, thank you.

I especially want to thank Kurt's children, Nanette, Edith, and Mark. Mark has been especially gracious to write a foreword to be paired with the one his dad wrote for the first edition of this encyclopedia. They all were most generous in conversation with me at the KVML. It is hard for me to understand growing up with such a looming literary savant in the house, but I appreciate the esprit with which they jump into conversation to straighten out lore from rumor and to do so with the same openness readers expect from their father.

The delivery of this book has a bit of melodrama attached to it since I finished writing the day before going in for what was supposed to be an overnight stay for surgery. Twenty-one days later, three open abdominal surgeries and three bronchoscopies later, the doctors lifted the veil of my morphine-induced coma. I have since endured two abdominal reconstructions and am still on the mend. For their patience and good cheer about this project, I wish to thank all those at Random House who expressed concern for my welfare before discussion of the manuscript.

I want to also apologize to my readers for any overt errors found in the text. Please join me in blaming the morphine. Or the Oxycodone. Or the combination of the two that I know I sometimes confused. I really did try to get everything right because this has been a thirty-year labor of love. A love letter to Kurt, if you will.

This text's very submission required a technology twist that Kurt would certainly have enjoyed. After a twenty-one-day coma, from a bed in the hospital's ICU, I sent Noah Eaker (my editor at Random House) an email containing a shared link to the manuscript stored on Dropbox. The file was a 2,001-page pdf file. Thank goodness for password recovery programs because my mind at the time was scrambled.

A special note is in order for Noah. He inherited this project more than a year after contracts were signed and has proven to be patient and encouraging all at once. I will always be touched by his personal considerations for my failing health when he learned of my hospitalization.

And this is where, as Kurt has so often noted in his own work, a woman rescued me in these closing stages. Caitlin McKenna, branding a name more akin to a widowed pioneer settler in a John Wayne movie and ready to take on all challenges, absolutely saved the day. From the beginning of our association she proved to be the kindly taskmaster I needed to finish. Thoughtful, resourceful, intelligent, and funny, I sincerely hope I get to work with her some more.

A special nod must be made to WordSmith's Mike Scott, without whose software creation the development of this text would have been infinitely more difficult. The utility of such lexical tools must be continuously enhanced and taught as a primary, textual exploratory tool regardless of one's field of endeavor. Understanding the distribution of key words is as important for advanced literary study as is the understanding of spreadsheets or statistics for advanced numeracy.

As grateful as I am for the technology that made possible both editions of this work, I am even more grateful for my family who stood by my bed every day through this ordeal. My eighty-seven-year-old mother, Lila, sat by my bed every day and watched with horror at her son's condition—and is still ministering to my recovery with daily email. I especially want to thank my younger daughter, Whitney, for sitting at my bedside and reading aloud *The Sirens of Titan* while the doctors kept me knocked out. Indeed, someone up there likes me, too. And as for my eldest, Marisa, I still shudder to think of what my trauma could have meant to your pregnancy. I will always be thankful to Saralyn Gold for letting me upset family schedules for years so I may pursue this passion.

Fortunately, I have the happy occasion to mark this book with notice to my new granddaughter, Alice Elizabeth Simmons. Dear Alice, named for the *Wonderland* heroine and my late father-in-law, Allan Gold, I hope you find as much to bemuse, beguile, and clarify the world through the assistance of stories written for young and old, as I have.

One day you will comfortably move between your namesake's ponderous simplicity and the moons of Titan, the airless refuge of Tralfamadore and the Rhode Island clambake where your *Sabba* is invited to meet with Kurt Vonnegut and Kilgore Trout. Thank you, Marisa and Billy, for gifting the world with the love and the promise of another helping hand for humanity.

I must also thank Judy, Jill, and Heather for making my most recent recuperation full of joy and productivity.

I want to also thank my many students who took on the challenge of Kurt's work over the years and for teaching me a thing or two along the way. I especially want to thank Simon Fuchs and Zachary Herbert for their technical assistance.

My final words must be for Kurt. For nearly twenty years you wrote and called, worried that my jobs were not quite right for me, interested in the developments of my growing daughters, helpful and unintrusive with the other books Peter Reed and I edited about you, and very quickly becoming a loving uncle. You did not have to kiss my forehead, but you did. You did not need me to write an encyclopedia about your work, but you let me. You did not have to shower my family with personalized artwork, but you did that, too. For all this, for all your books, for your friendship, for happily occupying nearly all my professional time out of the classroom, thank you. You are sorely missed.

INDEX

Page numbers in **boldface** refer to encyclopedia entries.

2BR02B, "2BR02B," **3–4**, 38, 65, 67, 132, 212, 226, 237, 310, 323, 619–20, 643, 647, 695
27 Bethune Street, New York, N.Y., **4**, 58, 164
3972 Ellis Avenue, Chicago, Ill., **4**, 688
4918 North Meridian Street, Indianapolis, Ind., **4**, 340
5644 North Meridian Street, Indianapolis, Ind., **4**

Aamons, Celia, 7
Aamons, Mona, *see* Monzano, Mona Aamons
Aamons, Nestor, **7**, 109, 131, 442
Aborigines, 271, 277
Abstract Expressionism, 72, 88, 143, 228, 241, 258, 280, 284, 322, 354, 357, 359–61, 367, 401, 529, 592, 601, 628, 699, 706
"Adam," **11**, 368, 574
Adams, Alice, *see* Vonnegut, Alice "Allie"
Adams, James Carmalt, **11**, 169, 252, 341, 482, 502–3, 519, 569, 625, 666, 667, 674, 679, 684
Adams, James Carmalt, Jr., **11**, 187
Adams, Joey, 161
Adams, Kurt, **11**
Adams, Steve, **11–12**, 252, 667
Adams, Tiger, **12**
Adler, Ted, **11**
adolescence, 574–75

Adult Correctional Institute at Shepherdstown, **12**, 316, 319, 356, 400, 423, 438, 478, 521
Adventures of Augie March, The (Bellow) 438
"African Cookbook, The," **538**
Afterlife, afterlife (*see also* blue tunnel; *God Bless You, Dr. Kevorkian*), 5, **12–14**, 25, 53, 55, 69, 120, 197, 206, 248, 254, 285, 295, 301, 325–27, 328, 358, 383, 409, 449, 536, 548, 561, 586–87, 588, 604, 628, 654, 660, 664, 672, 676, 716
Afterlife cavalcade, **268–78**
Agnes and Agnes (Barbara and Martha), **14**
Agnew, Spiro T., **14**
agnosticism, atheism, 12, 20, 38, 52–53, 56, 111–13, 250–51, 267, 269, 326, 341, 446, 511–16, 618, 624, 629, 639, 657, 664, 666, 671–72, 674, 697
   see also Freethinkers, free thinkers
Aïda, **14**, 240, 524, 555
AIDS, 10–11, 15, 29, 127, 470, 552, 617, 708
Aiken, Conrad, **14**
Ainsworth, Mary D., **14**, 70
   Afterlife interview with, 268, 270–71, 626
Ainus, **14–15**, 22
air raids, air-raid shelters, **15**
Ajax, **16**

A. J. Topf und Sohn, **15–16**, 29
Akhbahr, Abdullah, **16**, 67, 119
Al, **16**
Albanian Flu, **16**, 223, 283, 368, 428, 485, 604
Alberti, Leon Battista, **16**, 179, 193
Alcoholics Anonymous, 371, 407, 511, 521, 560, 562, 664–65
alcoholism, 126–27, 166, 192, 256, 269, 277, 285, 364, 476, 486, 488, 519, 524, 527, 541, 543, 571, 590, 663–65
Algonquin Hotel, **16**
Algonquins, **16**
Algren, Nelson, **16–17**
Alice in Wonderland (Carroll) **17**
Allen, Lester, **17**
All in the Family (TV show), 95
All-Night Sam, **17**, 115, 124, 297, 385
"All the King's Horses," **17**, 43, 363, 716
alter ego, Kilgore Trout as Vonnegut's, 567, 582, 591, 619–21, 652, 657, 675, 676, 677, 712, 715–16
"Ambitious Sophomore," **17–18**, 47, 173, 186, 213, 293, 303–4, 355, 370, 391, 642
American Academy of Arts and Letters, **18**, 482, 496–97, 514, 520, 540, 635, 712, 713, 719
American Dream, 238, 312
"American Family Marooned on the Planet Pluto, An," **19**

American Humanist Association, 25, 62, 325, 327, 409, 548

American humor, 333

American Philosopher Kings, The (Kittredge), 368

American values, 490
  as characterized by Twain, 629–32
  foreign viewpoint on, 107
  letters of personal concern about, 414–15
  Vonnegut's repudiation of, 447–448, 452, 488, 515–516, 535, 553, 556, 561, 571, 580, 589, 639, 703, 708–709; *see also Man Without a Country, A*

Amphibious Pioneers Society, Amphibians, 19, 400, 649

Amy and Harry, 18–19

Anderson Trailer, 19

Andrews, Lancelot, 559–60

Angela and Arthur, 19

angels, 70

Annie, 20, 214–15, 648

Annie, Little Orphan, Little Orphant, 518

Anschluss, 20

anthropoids, 20

anthropology, 20–21, 115, 147, 149, 170, 185, 194, 228, 243, 507–8, 663

anthropomorphic, 21, 420

anti-gerasone, 22, 543, 612

anti-Semitism, 28, 67, 96, 117, 128, 133, 139, 164, 244–45, 328, 363, 422, 500–501, 522, 540

"Any Reasonable Offer," 22, 199, 302, 334, 336, 432, 456, 460, 478, 505–6, 653

apocalyptic, 22

Arapahos, 22–23, 295

Archangel Gabriel, 23, 197, 254, 342, 666

Archimedes' screw, 23

Aristotle, 23–24

Armageddon in Retrospect, 309, 721–22

"Arme Dolmetscher, Der" ("The Army Interpreter"), 46, 99, 156, 160, 200–201, 210, 227, 259, 334, 481, 638, 696
  unnamed narrator of, 644–45

Arnold, Benedict, 24

art, artists, 470–71, 483, 585–86, 644, 647, 648, 665, 666–68, 670, 672, 680–82, 684, 691, 706
  cultural value of, 402–3, 453, 456
  see also Abstract Expressionism; Karabekian, Rabo; *specific artists and works*

Arthur, Chester Alan, 24

Arthur C. Clarke, 150, 318, 379, 606

Ashland, Bryant, 24, 25, 346–47, 357, 422

Ashland, Charlene, 24–25

Ashland, Charles, 25, 346

Asimov, Isaac, 25, 53, 62, 131, 267, 325–26, 383, 409, 546, 547
  Afterlife interview with, 270, 277–78

"Asleep at the Switch," 25, 237

asterisks, 102, 417

Astor, Madelaine, 25–26, 159

astronauts, 24–25, 246–47, 370, 498, 637

athletics, 366

Atkins, Carol, 26–27, 395, 406
  see also Ludd, Ned

Atkins, Fire Chief Stanley, 26, 46, 48, 102, 422, 493, 578

Atlas, Charles, 27, 74, 216

atomic bomb, A-bomb, 8–11, 60, 128, 276, 296, 312, 328, 331, 426, 482–483, 548, 563, 588–589, 639, 713
  see also specific uses

atomic energy, 9–10

Attucks, Crispus, 174

Augustus, Caesar, 27–28

Aurelius, Marcus, 28

Auschwitz, 15–16, 28–30, 78, 128, 161, 181, 224–25, 288, 314, 327, 433, 573, 583, 658

Auschwitzer, 30

Auschwitzian, 31

automobiles, 417, 718–19

Averageman, John, 31

Avondale, 31

B-1, 32

B-17, 32

B-36, 32

B-36 Mother, 32

B-52, 32

Babel, Tower of Babel, 32, 392, 613–15

Babylon, Babylonian, 33

Bach, Johann Sebastian, 33–34

bacteria, bacterium, 34, 62, 141, 270

Baer, Dr., 34–35, 110, 241, 262, 373–74, 447, 499

"Bagladies," *see* Pamela Ford Hall

Bagnialto, 35

Bagombo Snuff Box, 36, 383

"Bagombo Snuff Box," 18, 35–36, 377, 422

Bahía de Darwin, 15, 36, 69–70, 170, 180, 190, 194, 243, 306, 328, 457, 468, 536, 623, 659–60

bakemaster, 36

Baku, 36

ballooning, 274

Baltra, 36, 81

Bane, Joe, 36–37, 100, 218, 575–76, 648

Bannister, George Hickman, 37, 104–5

Bannister, Lucy, 37

Bannister, The, 37

Bannister Memorial Fieldhouse, 37, 90, 104, 363

baptism, 37–38

Baptists, 37

barbarity, 298

Barber, Kensington, 38

Barca-Lounger, Barcalounger, 3, 38–39, 65, 225, 619

Barker, Honus, 39

Barkley, Ben, 39

Barlow, Frank X., 39, 163, 237, 608, 619, 620, 653

Barnhouse, Arthur, 34, 39, 107, 184, 469, 571, 710

Barnhouse, First Church of, 39
  see also dynamopsychism

Barnhouse Effect, 39, 80, 99, 108, 117–18, 132–33, 156, 169, 184, 216, 247, 328, 334, 375, 469

Barnstable, Mass., 39–40, 64, 174, 460, 672, 675–76

Barnstable First Church of God the Utterly Indifferent, **39–40,** 508

barracks humor (see humor), 40

Barring-gaffner, 35, 41, **41,** 279, 280

Barry, Fred T., 12, 31, 39, **41,** 42, 51, 195, 355, 429, 437, 521

Barry, Mildred, **41**

Barry, Roland, **41–42,** 245

Barrytron, Ltd., 41, **42,** 201, 295, 321, 338, 356, 437, 521, 535, 574, 589

bartenders, unnamed, **641**

Barus, Alice, *see* Lieber, Alice Barus

Barus, Carl (Karl), **42–43,** 50, 461, 529, 536

Barzov, Major, 17, **43–44,** 363

basements, 15, **44–45,** 153, 255, 624

    see also subbasements

Bassett, Ernest S., **45–46,** 375

Batavia, 38, 46

Batchelor, Meg, 265

Batsford, Ted, 46

Battle Hymn of the Republic, **46**

Batten, Barton, Durstine & Osborn, 46

Battola, Will, **47**

Bauerbeck, Nelson, 47, 564

Bavaria, **47**

Bay State Progressive, 47, **47**

Beagle, HMS, **47**

Beame, Timothy, **47**

Beardon, Miss, **47–48**

Bearse, Alfy, **48**

Beaton, Upton, 46, **48–49,** 86, 102–3, 202–3, 422, 458, 493, 506

beautiful woman, unnamed, **641**

Beelzebub, **49,** 440

Beethoven, Luwig van, **49–50,** 84–85, 205, 260, 520, 536, 556–57, 597, 614

begetting, **50**

beginning, middle . . . and end, **50–51**

Begum, Arjumand Banu, **51**

belfry, **51**

belief, **51–53**

Bella, Bella's Beauty Nook, 44, **53,** 603

Bellevue Hospital, **53**

Bellow, Saul, 438

Belvoir, Fort, **245**

Benjamin Harrison, Fort, **245,** 341, 360

Benning, Fort, **245**

Bennington College, 245, 510–11

Bergeron, Bruce, **53–54,** 317

Bergeron, Ed, 53, **54**

Bergeron, George and Hazel, **54**

Bergeron, Harrison, **54,** 264

Bergler, Edmund, **55**

Berman, Abe, **55**

Berman, Circe, **55,** 71–72, 81, 82, 120, 167, 171, 215, 359, 360, 383, 400, 595, 638, 708

Berman, Gil, **55–56,** 161–62, 416, 684

Berringer, Dave, **56,** 124, 165

Berringer, Fred, **56,** 82, 241

Bert, **56–57,** 124, 477

Beryllium, **57,** 431

Beskudnikov, **57,** 133, 284, 360

Betelgeuse, Betelguese, **57,** 532, 577

Bethlehem, **57**

Bethlehem, Star of, **57**

Bethune, **58**

Biafra, 569, 682

Biagini, Salvatore, **58**

    Afterlife interview with, 70, 268, 271, 626–27

BIBEC, **58**

Bible, 135, 137, 140, 166–67, 257–58, 400, 409, 560, 656, 657, 674

    see also Gospels

Bierce, Ambrose, **58,** 74, 343, 402

Big Board, The, **58–59,** 189

big eye, **59**

Bigley, Homer and Clara, **60,** 697

Big Nick, 5–7, **59–60,** 465, 501–2

"Big Space Fuck, The," **60,** 63, 145, 231, 318, 358, 379, 457, 467, 554

Bijou Theater, **60,** 357

Bikini Atoll, **60**

Bill (parakeet), **60–61,** 302, 328

Billy (Bill) the Poet, **61,** 174, 226, 259, 358, 431, 444, 456, 463, 573, 695

Bingo, 96

biochemistry, 25, **61–62,** 470

biochemistry professor, **62**

biodegradable, **62**

biology, **20–21,** 369–70

Birch (John Birch Society), **62**

birds, **62–65,** 149, 491–92, 557

    see also Bill; canaries; Titanic Bluebird

Birnum, Birnum, **65**

    Afterlife interview with, 70, 268, 271, 627

birth, **65–67**

    see also womb, womblike

birth control pill, 67, 225, 358, 431, 456, 463, 573, 696

Blackbeard, **68,** 79

Black Brothers of Islam, 16, **67**

Black Cat Café, **67,** 150, 164, 319, 477, 538, 562

Black Garterbelt, **67–68,** 187–88, 240, 331, 423, 476, 489, 500–501

    see also Plague on Wheels

black humor, 332–34, 550

Black Panthers, 68, 303, **390–91**

Blake, William, 68, 432

Blank, Katarina, 68, 536, 671

Blankenship, Martin Peale, **68–69,** 431

Bleifuss, Joel, 621

BLINC (Blast Interval Normalization Computer) system, 69, **69,** 78, 80, 521

blivit, **69**

blond German escort, unnamed, 100–101, **642–43**

Bluebeard, **71–72**

Bluebeard, 45, 55, 57, 60, **71–72,** 100, 115, 145, 146, 167, 210, 215, 227, 231, 241, 245, 256, 284, 309, 316, 341, 354, 359, 360–61, 363, 367, 385, 400, 422, 426–27, 432, 440, 465, 491, 493, 529, 570, 573, 576, 585, 667–68, 683, 699, 710, 722

Bluebird Farm, **72**, 318, 364–65, 437, 535

Blue Fairy Godmother, 44, **69**, 105–6, 120, 147, 155, 192, 207, 371, 444, 462, 577, 706

see also Frank Wirtanen

Blue Mill, **69**

blue tubing, **69–71**

blue tunnel, 13, 25, 69–71, 197, 248, 328, 536, 619, 623, **626–27**

Afterlife interviews in, 266–78

Boaz, 37, 44, 46, 63, **72**, 98–99, 114, 132, 166, 297–98, 439, 586, 611

Bob, *see* Wild Bob

Bob & Ray, **72–73**, 161, 332

Boca Raton, Battle of, **46**, 72, 86, 484

Bockman, Fred, **73**, 226, 299

Bockman, Marion, **73**

Bodovskov, Stepan, **73**, 371, 432

Bohn, Arthur, **73–74**

boko-maru, boko-maruing, **74**, 76, 109

Bokonon (Lionel Boyd Johnson), 25, 68, **74–75**, 76, 109–10, 111–12, 138, 193, 214, 216, 244, 268, 278, 331, 344, 361, 377, 428, 442, 459, 471, 492, 505, 510, 532, 536, 650, 660, 709

Bokononism, Bokonoist, 51–52, **75–76**, 84, 89, 90, 105, 109, 111–12, 139, 166, 213, 235, 244, 282, 323, 328, 352–53, 359, 361, 372, 428, 442, 473, 510, 539, 566, 583, 588, 654, 692–93, 718

Bolivar, **76–77**, 115, 313, 336, 428

Bolívar, Simón, 76

Böll, Heinrich, **77**, 120, 133

bombardiers, 32, **78–79**, 132

bombardment, **79**

bombenfest, **79**

bombers, 32, **79–81**, 309, 395, 396, 521

see also fighter planes

Bombing of Germany, The, **81**, 85, 475

bomb-release, **81–82**

bombs, bombing, 30, 42, **77–78**, 85, 103, 111, 134, 157–58, 185, 296, 328, 356, 411, 475

see also specific bombs and bomb attacks

bombsight, **82**, 133, 395

Bonesana, Cesare, Marchese di Beccaria, **82**

Bonner, Elena, 9

Booboo, **82**, 460, 547, 568

see also "The Sisters B-36, The"

booby traps, **82–83**

book-banning, **83**

Boone, Michael (Miklós Gömbos), **83**

Booth, John Wilkes, 67, **83–84**, 123, 138, 479–80, 560, 572, 608, 610

Booth, Junius, and Edwin, **83–84**

Borasisi, **84**, 244, 473

see also Bokononism

Borders, Arvin, **84**, 174, 240–41, 427, 435, 487, 613

Borders, Lance and Leora, **84**

Boris (computer), **84**, 108, 153, 348

Borisoglebsk, **84**

Bormann, Martin, **84**

born again, **84**, 88, 139, 277, 509

Borzoi Dance Company, **84**, 314, 340, 719

Boström, Hjalmar Arvid, **84–85**, 522, 536

Bowen, Julius King, **85**, 334, 712

Boyden, Hay, **85**, 394, 462, 531

Boyer, Richard O., **85**

Boyle, Raymond, **85**, 337

"Boy Who Hated Girls, The," 390, 476, 554

Brackman, Henry, 46, **86**, 168, 199, 245, 256, 431

Bradbury, Ray, 413, 548, 574, 593

Bragg, Fort, **245**, 260

Brainard, *see* Bullard, Brainard Keyes

Bratpuhr, Shah of, 36, 60, 93, 107, 168, 204, 224, 290, 294, 369, 435, 496, 500, 501, 507, **554**, 597, 601

Braun, Eva, 67, **86**, 96, 247, 273, 278, 310

Braxton, Carter, 86

Brayton, Hal, **86**, 102, 493, 506

Breakfast of Champions, 12, 37, 41, 42, 44, 49, 65, 67, 72, **86–89**, 93–94, 95, 99, 104, 121, 130, 147, 158, 192, 201, 208, 218, 220, 225, 231, 245, 255, 263, 296, 301, 302, 311, 316–20, 336, 341, 351, 356, 359–60, 362, 385, 391, 400, 423–25, 432, 435, 437, 440, 449, 466–67, 470, 474, 478–79, 484, 521, 535, 544, 545, 569, 576–77, 587, 589, 590, 591, 617, 619, 677, 688, 717

Midland City events and institutions in, 436

Breed, Asa, **89–90**, 235, 257, 313, 440, 470, 538

Breed, Avram, **90**

Breed, Marvin, **90**, 313, 314, 554

Breedlove, Don, **90**, 94, 363

Brentner, Mr. and Mrs., **90–91**

Brentner, Rice, **91–92**, 171, 533, 565, 574–75, 641, 647

Breslaw, **92**

Brewer, Ansel, **92**

briquet, **92**, 371

Brokenshire, David, **93**, 246

Bromley, Milford S., **93**

Bronk, Mr., **93**

Brown, Betty, **93**, 181, 461, 522, 599

Brown, Bobby, 24, **93**, 181, 461, 522, 599

Brown, Ed, **93**, 341, 475, 491, 524, 527, 537, 638

Brown, John, **93**

Afterlife interview with, 46, 268, 271–72, 594

Brown, Payton, **93–94**

Brown Bomber, *see* Heinz, Karl

Browning, Gloria, 90, **94**

Brown University, 42–43

Brunei, Sultan of, **595**

Buchanon, Irving, **92**

Buchenwald, **94**

Buchwald, Art, 158

Buffalo Works, **94**

bugger, buggery, **94–95**, 320

Bugle-Observer, see Midland City Bugle-Observer

Building 58 Suite, **95**, 103, 219
Bulge, Battle of the, **46**, 96, 201,
210, 384, 464–65, 486, 638,
663, 673, 694
Bullard, Brainard Keyes, **95**
Bullard, Harold K., **95**
Bunker, Archie, **95–96**
"Bunker Bingo Party," 86, **96–97**,
278, 309, 496
Bunting, Arthur J., **97**, 203–4, 646,
648–49
Buntline, Amanita, **97**, 98, 196, 522,
525, 695
Buntline, Castor, **97**, 196, 475, 526
Buntline, Elihu, **98**
Buntline, Lila, **98**, 384, 525, 695
Buntline, Stewart, **98**, 139, 196, 316,
427–28, 518
Bunty, **98**
Burch, Arnold, **98–99**
Burger, Knox, **99**, 169, 334, 391,
594
burgomaster, **99**, 201, 481, 644–45,
696
burgomaster's daughter, **99–100**,
160, 201, 481
Burgoyne, General John, **100**
Burke, Arleigh, 268, 272
Burke, Roberta Gorsuch, 70–71,
100, 153, 272
Afterlife interview with, 268, 272,
612, 627
Burr, Aaron, 294
Bush, George H. W., 63
Bush, George W., 10, 63, 138, 141,
151, 230, 270, 277, 402, 405,
407, 408, 410, 411, 413–16,
446, 451, 553, 562, 580, 621,
631–32, 709
Butler, Nicholas Murray, **100**, 709
butler, unnamed, **641**
Buzzer, **100–101**, 218, 285–86,
575–76, 642–43, 648

Cady, Newell, 27, 46, 48–49, 86,
102–3, 202, 237, 311, 458–59,
492–93, 506, 579
calcimine, **103**
Caldwell Foundation, **103**
Cale, Cathy, 265
Calhoun, Bud, **103–4**, 240, 344

Calhoun, Kitty, *see* "Custom-Made
Bride"; Krummbein, Falloleen
Calvary Cemetery, 37, **104–5**, 232,
364, 435, 448, 691, 692
see also Golgotha
Calvin, Ned, **105**, 264
Calypso, 76, **105**, 216, 536
Campbell, Archibald, **105**
Campbell, Helga, *see* Noth, Helga
Campbell, Howard W., Jr., 4, 15, 22,
28, 30, 37, 44, 50, 58, 66, 68,
69, 73, 92, **105–6**, 111, 117,
120, 123, 124, 138, 154, 155,
164, 173–74, 192, 201, 204,
207, 219, 220, 223, 224–25,
233, 247, 250, 253, 260, 263,
266, 278, 288–89, 297, 301–2,
314, 327–28, 331, 340, 355,
363, 449, 368, 371, 372, 425,
432–33, 444, 461–63, 464, 467,
522, 529, 537, 540, 570, 573,
577, 581, 600, 603, 606, 637,
654, 658, 663, 697, 701, 706
canaries, 63, **106**
Canby, Sarah Horne, **106**, 439
Canterbury Tales (Chaucer), 268
Cape Cod, 12, 39–40, 48, 154, 170,
179, 278, 313, 338, 440, 450,
579, 641, 648, 676, 685, 714,
719
see also Barnstable, Mass.
Capone, Al, 59, **106**, 334, 424
Carlsbad Caverns, **106–7**, 529, 581
Carlyle Hotel, **107**
Caroline, **107–8**
Caroline Islands, **108**
Carpathia, **108**, 602
Carroll, Madeleine, **108**
Carson, Johnny, **108**
Carter, Clyde, 84, **109**, 131, 153,
608
Carter, Jimmy, 714
Carver, George Washington, **108–9**,
128
Casa Mona, **108**, 109
Casey, Dwight, **109**, 169
Castle, Julian, 7, 29, 74, **109**, 312,
428, 442, 452, 544, 660
Castle, Morris N., **109**
Castle, Philip, 68, **109**, 216, 233,
317

Castle Sugar, Incorporated, 74,
109–10
catacombs, **110**
Catharine, 124, 245, **460**
Cathcart, Sally, **110**, 520
Cat's Cradle, 3, 4, 7, 8, 20, 27, 29,
74, 84, 89, 94, 105, **110–14**,
115, 163, 169, 175, 199, 217,
231, 235, 239, 244, 245, 257,
268, 276, 278, 282, 308, 309,
313–14, 322, 323, 338–39, 340,
348, 352, 377, 391, 417, 420,
429, 440, 441, 459, 471, 478,
495, 505, 509, 518, 538, 544,
556, 570, 583, 604, 608, 693,
696, 719
caverns, 106–7
caves, cave-dwellers, **114–15**
see also Sacred Miracle Cave
Caz-ma-cas-ma, 76, **115**
Cedar Tavern, **115**, 241
celibacy, 56, 162, 457–58, 692
Céline, Louis-Ferdinand, 68,
115–17, 216, 323
Céline and His Vision (Ostrovsky),
216, 522
cellars, **120–21**, 295
cells, cell-blocks, 28, 65, **117–20**,
242, 253, 255, 433, 568,
612–13
Channing, William Ellery, 507, 640
chaos, **121–23**
Chaperone, **123**
Chaplin, Charlie, 79, **123–24**, 161
Charity Anne Browning, 56–57, **124**
Charlestown Prison, **124**
Charley, **124**
Charlotte, **124**
Charlotte, Princess, **498**
Chasens, Henry Stewart, **124**, 460
Checker Charley, 56, 82, **124**, 165,
241, 327, 447
chemicals, **124–27**
chemistry, **129–31**, 370
"Chemistry Professor, The," **131**,
187, 366, 520, 537, 544
chemists, **127–29**
Cheney, Dick, 413, 553
Chermayoff, Ivan, 596
Chessman, Caryl, **131**
Chetniks, 7, **131**

Chevy Chase, Md., **131**

Chez Armando, **131–32**

Chicago, University of, 20–21, 68, 113, 147, 170, 227–28, 242, 243, 294, 507–8, 549

Chicago City News Bureau, 20–21

Chicago Lying-in Hospital, 67, **132**, 310, 311, 695

Childhood's End (A. C. Clarke), 546, 578

chimneys, **132–33**

China, Great Wall of, **283**

Christ, Jesus, 13, 104, **133–38**, 139–41, 144, 146, 157, 159, 170, 176–78, 279, 280, 316, 324, 327, 332, 355, 370, 383, 400, 409, 414, 420, 486, 491, 515, 535, 547, 595–96, 618, 620, 656, 672, 715

see also Sermon on the Mount

christening, **138**

Christianity, 110, 122, 130, 136, **142–44**, 222, 227, 270, 280, 310, 323, 392, 403, 408–9, 413, 513, 539, 640

Christians, **138–42**, 178, 193, 270, 273, 277

Christian Scientists, **138**

Chrono, 37, 63, 86, **144**, 165, 172, 237, 256, 259, 287, 302, 358, 485, 510, 529–30, 532, 537, 577, 610

chrono-synclastic infundibula, 32, 106, **144–45**, 166, 194, 293, 368, 392, 566–67, 606, 610

Chrysler Building, **145**, 350, 371, 581, 584, 613, 626

Chung, Lowell, **145–46**, 522

Chung, Mrs., **146**

Churchill, Winston, **146**

Church of God the Utterly Indifferent, 22, 23, **146**, 166, 255, 485, 510, 530, 532

see also Barnstable First Church of God the Utterly Indifferent

Church of Jesus Christ the Kidnapped, 4, **146**, 688

Church of the Weary Space Wanderer, 508

cigarettes, 404–5, 443, 567, 590, 611, 676–77

Cincinnati Bengals, **146**, 231

Cinderella, **147–48**, 179, 294–95, 404, 454, 508

Circe (goddess), 55

civics, civic managers, **148–49**, 374

civil rights, violations of, 414–15

Civil War, Rosewaters in, 525–26

Claessen, **149**

Claggett, Noble, **149**

clans, **149–50**

Clarke, Arthur C., 60, 63, 145, **150–51**, 158–59, 264, 358, 367, 545–46, 578

Clarke, Arthur K., **151**, 699

Claycomb, Judge and Moon, **151**, 296, 550

Cleckley, Hervey, 142, **151–52**

clerk, unnamed, **641–42**

Cleveland Science Fair, **152**, 300

Clewes, Alan, **152**, 261, 396, 603

Clewes, Leland, 44, 84, 108, **152–53**, 237, 263, 295, 348, 689, 710

Clewes, Sarah Wyatt, 44, 152, **152–53**

Clinton, Bill, 70–71, **153**, 272

Clinton Street, **153**

Clough and Higgins, **153**

Clowes, Henry, **153**, 481, 692

Club Cybernetics, 1, **153**

Coates, Arnold, **153**

cocoons, **154**

"Coda to My Career as a Writer for Periodicals," 50, **154–55**, 260, 297, 342–43

Coffin, Tris and Margaret, 53

Coggin's Pond, **155**

Cohen, Abe, **155**

Cohen, Isadore Raspberry-19, **155**, 223, 662

Cohen, Israel, **155**

Cohen Rink, **155**

Cohn, Roy, **155**, 430, 452

Cohn, Roy M., **155**

Cohoes, N.Y., **155**

Cohoes High School, **155**

coils, **156**

college humor, *see* humor

Collier's, 99, 102, **156**, 169, 192

colonel, Colonel, **156–57**

Colson, Charles W., **157**

Columbia Conserve Company, **157**, 664

columns, **157–60**

Combat Respiratory Rations (CRRs; goofballs), **160**

comedians, **160–62**

common decency, **162**

computers, 27, 255, 306, 435, 456, 474, 481, 482

games, *see* Checker Charley; GRIOT

see also Boris; Gokubi; Mandarax

cones, **162–63**, 182

Conestoga, **163**

con games, 410

Conners, Harrison C., **163–64**, 231, 312, 340

Conners, Mrs. Harrison C., *see* Hoenikker, Angela

conspiracy, **164**, 195

conspiratorial, **165**

conspirators, **165**

conspire, **165–66**

Constant, Benjamin, **166**

Constant, Malachi (Unk), 15, 19, 32, 40, 44, 46, 63, 72, 86, 98, 104, 110–11, 114, 132, 144, 157, 165, **166**, 167, 172, 181, 184–85, 233, 259, 297–98, 304, 340, 358, 439, 443, 444, 457, 485, 502, 504, 508, 510, 529–30, 532, 537, 566–67, 577, 580, 586–87, 610, 611, 613, 693, 701, 705

Constant, Noel, 19, 153, **166–67**, 233, 239, 257, 279, 400–401, 444, 694, 701–2

Constant, Sylvanus, **167**

Constitution, U.S., 122, 196, 372, 409, 539, 546, 561, 650–51

Converse, Lou, **167**, 238, 473–74

Cooley, Franklin, **167**

Cooper, Oveta, **167–68**, 366

Corbett, William K., **168**

Cordiner, Cordelia Swain, **168**, 192, 220, 449, 583, 611

corks, corkscrews, **168–69**

Cormody, **169**

Cornell Daily Sun, 159, **169–70**, 334, 655

Cornell University, 68, 81, 92, 128, 129, 131, **168–70**, 199, 215, 234, 294, 306, 314, 353, 366, 389, 452, 496, 502, 522, 597, 679, 716

Corpus Christi, Tex., **170**

Cortes, Hernando, **170**

Cortez, Ricardo, **170**

Corwin, Lance, **170**

Cosby, Janet, **170**

Costa, Antone C. "Tony," 17, **170–71**, 711

Cotuit Harbor, Mass., **171**

Coulomb, Marc, **171**, 385

Coulomb Frères et Cie, 171, 385

Counsel, Bob, **171**, 641

counter-clockwise, **172**

Cowper, William, **172**

Cox, Harvey, **172–73**, 625, 675

Cox, Riah Fagan, **172–73**, 518, 519, 625, 675

Cozier, Jane, 265

Craig, David, **173**, 222

Crane, Harold, 18, **173**

Crawfordsville, Ind., **173**

Creative Playthings, Inc., **173–74**

crematoria, 28–30, 470

Creon, Pa., **174**

Creon Pipe-Dreamers, **174**, 257, 435, 643

Crimea, **174**

Crispus Attucks High School, **174**, 435

critical thinking, 411, 419

Crocker, Harry, **174**

Crocker, Pete, **174**

Crocker, Virginia, **174**, 340

Cro-Magnon, **114–15**

Crone, Edward Reginald, Jr., 175

Crone, Joe, **175**, 486–87

Crosby, Hazel, **175**, 282

Crosby, H. Lowe, **175**, 199, 439, 638

Crown Hill Cemetery, **175**, 341–42, 518–20, 612, 670, 674

crucifix, **176**

crucifixion, crucify, 33, 51, 104, 134, 170, **176–79**, 279, 280, 400, 420, 426

"Crucifixion in Rome," **176–79**, 517, 578

cruciform, **179**, 193, 310

"Cruise of the *Jolly Roger*, The," 20, 46, 138, **179–80**, 210, 214, 222, 334, 423, 478, 611, 638, 641, 643, 647–48

crurifragium, 178

Crusades, 399–400

Cruz, Hernando, **180**, 250, 592

Cry of the Nocturnal Goatsucker, The, **181**, 461, 521–22, 599

cuckold, cockolding, **181**

cuckoo clock in Hell, **181**, 233, 314, 425, 436, 449, 705

Culver Citizen, The, **181**

Culver Military Academy, **181–82**

cupolas, 65, 95, **182–83**

Custer, George Armstrong, 392

"Custom-Made Bride," 131, **183–84**, 186, 334, 375–76, 451, 578, 656

unnamed narrator of, **644**

Cuthrell, William K., **184**

Cuyahoga Bridge and Iron Company, 51, **184**, 225, 231, 284, 348, 351, 430–31, 507, 698

Cuyahoga Massacre, 33, 51, 151, **184**, 231, 348–49, 430, 614

Cyclone Bill, *see* Bill

cylinders, **184–86**

Daffy-nition, The, **187**, 280

Daggett, Bill, **187**, 259, 307, 476, 494–95, 641

dagonite, 50, **187**

Daguerre, Louis J. M., 384

Daily Pancreas, **187**

Dalhousies, 64, 127, 623

"Dancing Fool, The," **187–88**, 423, 683, 720

Dane, Franklin, **188**, 498, 518, 549–50, 604, 610

Dangerfield, Rodney, 161

Darkness Visible (Styron), 588, 593

Darlington, Edward Seward, **188**, 259, 400, 694

Darrow, Clarence, 71, **188**, 272

Afterlife interview with, 268, 272, 324, 627

D'Arthanay, Barbara, 187

Darwin, Alton, 155, **188–89**, 475, 538

Darwin, Charles, 47, 106, 107, **189–91**, 205, 213, 254, 331, 486, 596, 598, 599, 617

Darwinian, Darwinism, Darwinists, 26, **189–91**, 208, 511, 599, 621

Davenport Spot-welding Company, **192**, 443

Davenport Wire and Cable Company, **192**, 443

Davis, Alvin, **192**

Davis, Benjamin, **192**

Davis, Lottie, **192–93**

Day the World Ended, The, 89, **193**, 198, 313, 352, 359, 361

Deadeye Dick, 8, 11, 12, 31, 37, 41, 42, 44, 46, 51, 65, 93, 95, 100, 104, 192, **194–96**, 203, 208, 216, 231–32, 235, 241, 245, 246, 252, 254, 256, 284, 288, 299, 308, 309, 316, 318, 320, 321, 337, 360, 364, 372, 377, 423, 424, 428, 434, 435, 440, 448, 449, 467, 470, 478, 481, 485, 505, 517, 522, 535, 568, 580, 589, 604, 673, 690–92, 697, 709

Midland City events and institutions in, 436–37

Deadeye Dick (Rudy Waltz), 37, **194**, 362

Deal, Borden, **196**, 351, 382

Deal, Selena, **196**

Deal, Selma, **196–97**, 475

Dearborn *Independent*, 244–45

death:

birth and, 66

see also Afterlife, afterlife

Debs, Eugene Victor, 22, 71, 137–38, 154, **197–98**, 205, 260, 273, 291, 296, 299, 310, 341, 342, 343, 413, 434, 535, 666

Afterlife interview with, 268, 272, 552–53, 627

Deerfield Academy, **198–99**

"Deer in the Works," 169, **198**, 207, 214, 338, 339, 351, 494, 601

Deer Park, Long Island, **198**

Delahanty, Dennis, 22, 198, **199**

de la Madrid, Jose Sepulveda, 193

Delany, Ed, **199**

Delbert, **199**

DeLee, Joseph Bolivar, 132
Delgado, Geraldo, **199**, 309, 398, 541
Delicto, Flagrante, **199**, 203, 549, 710
delivery boy, unnamed, *see* Kornblum, Mr.
Del Prado Hotel, **199**, 538
Delta Upsilon, 169, **199–200**
de Medici, Innocenzo, 16, 179, **193**, 539
De Mille, Hippolyte Paul, 37, 104, 115, **193–94**, 195, 232, 364, 435, 478, 691, 692
Democratic Party, 95, 189, 565, 586
Denny, Kyle, **200**
Denton, Bobby, 32–33, **200**, 392, 613
depression, 130, 228, 412, 419, 524, 588, 673
  Vonnegut's experience of, 407, 419
Derby, Edgar, 69, 110, 147, **201**, 265, 341, 570
Derby, Howard, **201**
de St. Andres, *see* St. Andres
de Stael-Holstein, Baronne, **194**, 457
Destouches, Louis-Ferdinand, *see* Céline, Louis-Ferdinand
Destruction of Dresden, The (Irving), 79–80, 218, 344, 530–31
de Sucre, Antonio Jose, **194**
de Wet, Marthinus, **194**, 261
Diary of Anne Frank, The, 247–48, 444
Di Capistrano, Paulo, **201**
Dickie, Mrs., 46, 48, 86, 102, **202–3**, 458, 493
Dictu, Mirabile, 199, **203**, 549, 710
Dillon University, **202**
DiMaggio, Joe, 276
Dina and Donna, **202**, 690
di Sanza, Carlo, **201–2**
disarmament, 39
District Attorney, **203**
Divine, Celeste and Harry, **203–4**, 645–46, 648–49
divorce, 228, 267, 269, 274, 373, 405, 450, 597, 599, 690
  of Vonneguts, 674–75, 714–16

Dobrowitz, Alvin, 173, 204, **204**
Dodge, Ned, **204**, 500
"Dog's Breakfast," **204–5**, 596
Dole, Helen, **205**
Domesday Book, **205–6**, 301, 386, 391, 506, 524, 529, 590
Don, **206**
Donald, **206**
Donna, **202**, **206**, 690, 691
Donne, John, 635
Donner, John, **206**
Donner Party, **206**
Donnini, Jim, **206–7**, 365, 390, 504
Donoso, Teodoro, **207**
Donovan, General, **207**
doppelgängers, 36, 62, 169, 336, 342, 382, 465, 505, 572, 636, 663, 712–13, 716, 717
  see also Timequake clambake
Doris, **207**
Dornberger, Walter, **207**, 658
Dorset, **207**
Dostoevski, Feodor, 168, **207–8**, 545, 587
Dougie, **208**
Downs, Roger, 40, **208**
"D.P.," 187, 302, 361
Dracula, Count, **171–72**
Drano, **208–9**, 591
Dreiser, Theodore, 441
Dresden, 38, 72, 79, 116, 175, 201, 223, 333, 434, 487, 532
  firebombing of, 8–9, 15, 30, 77–78, 80–81, 120, 121, **209–12**, 218, 235–36, 250, 266, 295, 335, 341, 362, 369, 383–84, 422, 462, 464, 486, 530–31, 546, 550, 555, 569–70, 615, 658, 682, 704, 705, 716, 721–22
Dresden, History, Stage and Gallery (Endell), *see* Endell, Mary
Dresden, Vonnegut's experience in, 15, 30, 46, 82, 111, 120, 209–11, 216, 287, 298, 408, 418, 451, 464–65, 486, 522, 550, 566, 584, 658, 663, 716, 721–22
Dresser, Paul, **212**, 441
"Dr. Jekyll and Mr. Hyde" (Stevenson), 131, 149

"Dr. Schadenfraude," **208**
druggist, **212**
drug use, 146, 248, 256, 264, 274, 277, 321, 392, 431, 440, 481, 529, 536, 579, 590, 618, 628, 673, 683, 691
drum major, unnamed, **242**
drupelets, **212**
DSM (Dog Story of the Month), **212**
Duchamp, Marcel, **212–13**, 484
duffle, 76, 588
Duggan, Leroy, 17–18, 17–48, 173, **213**, 293, 304, 355, 370, 642
Duke of Oklahoma, **213**, 449, 650, 662
Dumas, Alexandre, **213**
Duncan, Leora, 4, 132, 212, **213–14**, 226, 237, 310–11, 695
Dunkel, Stan, **214**
Dun Roamin, **213**, 567
duprass, **214**, 268, 439
Durant, Nathan, 20, 138, 179, **214–15**, 423, 478–79, 611, 641, 643, 648
Dürer, Albrecht, **215**
Dutch, **215**
Duty-Dance with Death, A, **215–16**
Duveneck, Frank, **216**, 429
Dynamic Tension, 26, 74, 76, **216**
dynamopsychism, 39, 184, **216–17**
Dyot, **217**
dyslexia, **217**, 602–3

Eagle-l, *see* O'Hare, Captain Bernard
Eaker, Ira C., 79, **218**
Eastman, George, **218**, 592, 690
echolalia (echophrasia), **218**
economic disparity, 278, 291–92, 331–32, 346, 473, 488, 523, 527, 575
Ed (artist), 179, **423**
Eddie (the farmer), 36–37, 100–101, **218**, 285–86, 575–76, 642–43, 648
Edel, Israel, 163, **219**, 485
Edel, Norma, **219**
Eden Express, The (M. Vonnegut), 119, 542, 682–84

Edison, Thomas, 95, **219**, 553, 577, 598

Edison Park, **219**

education, value of, 402–3

Ehrens, Kurt and Heinrich, **219**

Eichmann, Adolf, **220**, 368, 371

Eiffel Tower, **614**

8 1/2 (film), 36

Einstein, Albert, 25, 34, 64, 127, 191, **220–22**, 274, 366, 411, 449, 555, 561, 571, 596

Eldredge, Paul, 180, **222**, 479

El Greco, **222**, 438

Ellen, **222**

Elliott, Ray, see Bob & Ray

Ellison, Ralph, 116

Emmy, **222**

"Empire State," **222–23**, 427

Empire State Building, 146, 155, **223**, 353, 465, 528, 618, 718

Endell, Mary, **223**

enlaced, **223**

Enlightened Self-interest, **223**, 472, 538

enlightenment, **223**

entombed, **223**

environmental destruction, 10–11, 54, 60, 206, 209, 225, 263, 295, 329–31, 359, 391, 399, 402–5, 407, 416, 418, 420, 489, 535–36, 589–90, 594, 621, 684, 718

EPICAC, 8, 36, 94, 106–7, 156, **223–24**, 256, 262, 335, 365, 490, 499, 529, 597, 658–59, 703, 710

Epstein, Abraham, 28–30, **224–25**, 573

mother of, 28–30, **224–25**, 288

Epstein, Esta, 272–73, 573

Epstein, Harold, **225**

Afterlife interview with, 268, 273

equilibrium, **225**

Era of Hopeful Monsters, The, **225**, 331

Erie Coal and Iron, **225**

Ernest Hemingway Suite, 305

ETC, 89

ethical birth control, 61, 65, **225**, 456, 463

ethical suicide, 3–4, 38–39, 132, **225**, 311, 695, 696

Ethical Suicide Parlors, 3, 38–39, 61, 65, 212, 214, 225, **226**, 237, 259, 310, 323, 358, 371, 431, 444, 456, 463, 573, 619, 695

Ethical Suicide Service (E.S.S.), **226**

Ethical Suicide Studio, **226**, 594, 647

ethnic cleansing, 270, 271, 277, 542, 548

see also Holocaust

"Euphio Question, The," 73, 94, **226**, 299

euphoriaphone, 73, **226–27**

Evelyn and Her Magic Violin, **227**

Everett, Norman, **227**

evolution, 10, 188–91, 205, 254–55, 305, 331, 402, 457, 598, 599

cultural, 244, 507

Ewald, Lincoln, **227**

executive officer, **227**

extended families, 20, 143, 158, **227–30**, 392, 398, 405–6, 427, 454, 493, 511, 543, 569, 597, 598, 599, 603, 620, 706, 712

Fabri-Tek (Fabritek), 163, **231**, 340

Failey, Bonnie, **231**, 698

Failey, Dr., **231**

Failey, William H. C. "Skip," 208, **231**

Fairbanks, Charles Warren, **231**

Fairbanks, Richard, Jr., **231**, 360, 601

Fairchild, Will, 37, 104, 193, 196, **231–32**, 254, 377, 435, 478, 556

family values, 342

Fahrenheit 451 (Bradbury), 413, 548

Fahrenheit 9/11 (film) 413, 458

Farber, Don and Anne, **232**, 461

Farewell to Arms, A (Hemingway), 12

Farmer, Philip Jose, 561, 653

Farmers of Southwestern Ohio for Nuclear Sanity, **232–33**, 471

Farrow, Dudley and Grace, **233**, 571

fascism, fascists, **233**

Fates Worse Than Death, 17, 46, 61, 78, 145, 175, 188, 206, 218, 227, 282, 341, 360, 372, 378, 486, 542, 684, 713

father, sons and, **233–35**, 687

Faust (Goethe), **235**, 399, 449

Faust, Naomi, 20, **235**

February 13, 1944, **235–36**

"Febs, The," 236

Fedders, John W., Jr., 145, **236**

Federal Apparatus Corporation, 27, 198, 214, **237**, 242, 311, 339, 351, 422, 458, 493, 506, 579

see also Ilium Works

Federal Bureau of Termination, 65, 226, **237**, 358, 647

Federal Minimum Security Adult Correctional Facility, **237**

Fellini, Federico, 36, 712

female maid, unnamed, **642**

Feminine Mystique, The (Friedan), 393, 472, 475, 707

feminism, 393, 472, 475, 645, 699–700, 707

Fender, Robert, 25, 39, 163, **237**, 347, 544, 608, 619, 620, 654

Fenstermaker, Isabel, 165, **237**

Fenstermaker, Lowell, **237**, 288, 554

Fenstermaker, Rob Roy, **237–38**, 288, 300, 554, 708

Fenton, Earl, Jr., and Ted, Esq., **238**, 259

Fenton, Earl and Maude, 19, 167, **238**, 252, 259, 473, 571, 642

Ferguson, Guy, **239**, 257, 339, 604, 686

Fern, Ransom K., 22, **239**, 264, 400, 443

Fernandina Island, **239**

Fieser, Louis, **239**

fighter planes, 36, 81, **239–40**

Fighting Danes, The, **240**

Finale Rack, **240**

Finch, Katharine, 104, **240**, 498

"Find Me a Dream," 84, 174, **240–41**, 257, 427, 435, 487, 643

Finkelstein, Isadore and Rachel, **241**

Finletter Air Force Base, 39, 201, **237**, 379, 382, 654

Finnerty, Edward Francis, 14, 17, 95, 117, 124, 165, **241**, 250, 252, 306, 317, 373–74, 380, 395, 433, 447, 499, 563, 654
Finnerty, Noyes, **241–42**, 527
firearms, 434–35, 546
Firehouse Harris, *see* Foster Portfolio, The
firemen, unintentional killing of, 523–24
First District Court of Thank You, The, **242**
Fishbein, Mrs., **242**
Fitzgerald, Bernard, **242**, 359, 713
Flammer, 199, **242**, 490
Flammer, Lou, 198, **242–43**
Flemming, Mary, **243**
Flemming, Pearl, **243**, 264
Flemming, Willard (James Wait), 190, **243**, 253, 306, 317, 320, 399, 435–36, 498, 688–89
"Flocka Butt," *see* Mott, Stuart Rawlings
Florio, Lucas, **243**
folk society, 20, 228, **243–44**, 493, 507–8, 683
   see also extended families
folk society deficiency (FSD), 228, **243–44**
foma, 76, **244**, 282, 286, 473
Forbes, Malcolm, 398
Ford, Henry, **244–45**, 501
Ford, Rose Aldrich, **245**, 597, 599
"Fortitude," 3, 124, 201, **245–46**, 248, 264, 391, 599
Fortune, John, 31, 93, 194, 195, **246**, 288, 297, 361, 424, 448, 543, 564, 692, 709
Foster, Alma, **246–47**
Foster, Herbert, 33, **246–47**
Foster, Herbert, Jr., 246
"Foster Portfolio, The," 33, **246–47**
Foust, Warren, **247**
Foxy Grandpa, *see* Billy the Poet
Francis, Dick, **247**
Francis X. Donovan Post, American Legion, Brookline, **247**
Frank, Anne, 117, **247**
Frankenstein, Norbert, 124, 245–46, **248**, 264, 391, 392, 599

Frankenstein, Victor, 10, **248–49**, 269, 276, 497, 548, 563
Frankenstein—or, The Modern Prometheus (Shelley), 249, 275–76, 497, 548, 562–63, 670
Frankenstein monster, 10, **248–49**, 269, 276, 329, 497, 548, 563
Franklin, Benjamin, **249–50**, 341, 389, 446, 514
Frascati, Lou, **250**, 290–91
Frascati, Marion, 63, **250**, 290–91, 496
Free American Corps, 105, **250**, 540
Freeman, Charley, 11, 167, 238, **252**, 473, 483
Freeman, Sally, **252**
Freethinkers, free thinkers, 12, 13, 20, 50, 136, 137, 139, 229, **250–51**, 258, 267, 326, 341, 388–89, 409–10, 420, 445, 514–15, 629, 656, 657, 671, 674
free will, 236, **251–52**, 270, 297, 366, 435, 482, 497, 521, 546, 576, 582, 607, 612, 615, 626, 674
French, Mary Alice, 115, **252–53**
Freud, Sigmund, 332, 560, 658
Friedan, Betty, 393, 472, 475, 700, 707
Friedman, Bruce Jay, 332
Friedmann, Tuvia, **253**, 291
Frost, Robert, 624
fubar, **253**
Fuller, Norman, 208, **253**, 308
funnels, **253**

Gabriel horns, **23**
Galactic Spacecraft Corporation, 32, 443, 693
Galápagos, 8, 12, 50, 63–64, 69, 81, 83, 84, 86, 108, 145, 153, 155, 169, 170, 193, 206, 242, 243, 247, **254**, 256, 279, 305–6, 310, 320, 330, 338, 339, 359, 362, 366, 367, 398–99, 421, 426, 435, 468, 517, 522, 536, 539, 544, 623–24, 659, 707
Galápagos Islands, 36, 47, 163, 180, 190, 239, 248, **254–55**, 285,

308, 330–31, 457, 539, 611, 619, 713
Galen, Vt., **255**
"gallows bird," 64
gallows humor, 332, 335
Garland, Dorothy Daffodil-7, **255**
Garr, Vernon and Mary, **255**
Garth, Bud, Alice, and Ewing, **255**
Garth, Fred, 94, **255**, 431
Garu, Krishna (Krishna Gatu), **255–56**
Gatch, **256**
Gates, Bill, **255**
GCT (General Classification Tests), 255, **256**
GEFFCo, 45, 223, **256**, 305, 316, 339, 426, 539, 618, 706
Gelderman, Carol, 244
Gelhorne, Francis Eldgrin, **256–57**, 262, 340, 373, 499
Gelhorne Enterprises, **256–57**
gender gap, 348, 392–94
General Electric, 112–13, 159, 211, 313, 437, 444, 490, 544, 545, 547, 669, 676, 718
General Forge and Foundry Company, 84, 88, 174, 239, 250, **257**, 313, 322, 338, 339, 352, 369, 487, 604, 686
generation gap, **257**
Genesis, Book of, **257–58**
genesis, Genesis Gang, **257–58**
geodesic dome, **259**
geopolitics, 407–8, 410–11
George (banker), **259**, 307, 494
George (Fenton relative), **259**
George Washington Carver High School, **108**
German batball, 144, 188, 237, 249, **259**, 400, 529, 538, 694
German restaurateur, unnamed, **643**
German tank officer, **259**
Gettysburg, Battle of, **260–61**, 602
Gettysburg Address, **260–61**, 408, 614
Ghost Dance, 261, 381, 433–34, 510
Ghost Shirt Society, 15, 16, 17, 44, 51, 95, 104, 110, 241, 256, **261–63**, 294, 298, 301, 338,

Ghost Shirt Society (*cont'd*): 369, 373, 380–81, 395, 398, 431, 433–34, 452, 490, 499, 509, 529, 563, 570, 654, 660–61

Gibney, Peter, **263**

"Gilgongo," **263**

Gingiva-Tru, 127, **263**, 321, 354

Ginsberg, Allen, **263–64**

Glampers, Diana Moon, 55, 105, **264**, 385, 433

Glinko-X-3, 85, **264**

Globular Cluster M13, **264**

Gloria, **264**

Glossbrenner, Daniel Independence "Uncle Dan," **264–65**

Gluck, Werner, **265–66**

"Go Back to Your Precious Wife and Son," 174, **266**, 308, 451

Goblet, The, **266**

God Bless You, Dr. Kevorkian, 12, 13, 153, 227, **266–78**
Afterlife interviews in, 13, 25, 86, 197, 248, **270–78**, 309, 626–27

God Bless You, Mr. Rosewater, 3, 31, 44, 47, 49, 53, 81, 85, 97–98, 120, 169, 171, 192, 196, 203, 222, 239, 241, 243, 245, 264, 278, 312, 316, 323, 384, 391, 427–28, 430, 459, 465, 475, 477, 480, 482, 504, 525, 526, 531, 540, 544, 545, 550, 552, 561, 572, 603, 635–36, 694–95
see also Rosewater family members

Godwin, Mary Wollstonecraft, 276

Godwin, William, 276, 563

Goebbels, Paul Joseph, 46, 96, **278**, 301–2, 309, 371, 425, 462, 606

Goethe, Wolfgang von, **235**, 257, 399, 449

Gokubi, 119, **279**, 398, 421–22, 426

Golden House of the Roman Emperor Nero, **279**

Golden Rule, 413–14

"Golden Wedding," **279**, 496

Goldwater, Barry, **279**

Golgotha, **279**, 535

Gömbos, Miklós, *see* Boone, Michael

Gomburg, Crowther, **279**, 401

Goober Gossip, The, 187, **279–80**

goofballs, **160**, **280**

Gooz, 41, 279, **280**

Göring, Hermann, 144, **280**

Gorky, Arshile, **280**

Gospel from Outer Space, The, **280**

Gospels, **280**

Gossett, George and Nancy, *see* Grand Triumvirate

Gothic novels, 196

Gottlieb, Adolph, **280–81**

Gottwald's estate, **281**, 301, 491, 652

Goulding, Bob, *see* Bob & Ray

Grace Daffodil-13 (Cousin Grace), **281**

Graham, Jack, **281**, 467, 699

Graham, James and John, Fifth Earl and First Marquis of Montrose, **281–82**

Graham, John, 105, 549

Grand Hotel Oloffson, 193, **281**, 692

Grand Triumvirate, **281–82**, 346

granfalloon, 244, **282**

Grant, Robert, **282**

Grant's Tomb, 612

graphs, of classical stories, 404

Grass, Günter, 229, **282**

Grasso, Elmer Glenville, **282**

great becoming, **282–83**

Greathouse, Virgil, **283**, 357, 382

Greathouse and Smiley, **283**

Green Death, 16, 223, **283**, 346, 714

Green Diamond Plow, **284**, 522

Greenfield Bank and Trust Company, **284**

Green River Cemetery, **284**, 367

Green Team, **287**, 563

Gregory, Dan (Daniel Gregorian), 45, 57, 66, 132, 149, 153, 171, 181, 245, **284–85**, 354, 360, 363–64, 440, 446, 452–53, 564, 565, 581–82, 606, 613, 628, 699, 710

GRIOT, **285**

Groszinger, Bernard, 160, **285**, 329, 498, 518, 594, 604

Gruelle, Johnny, 518

Guayaquil, Ecuador, 180, 187, 190, **285**, 309, 359, 504, 517, 614, 688, 713

Guderian, Heinz "the old man," 106, **285–86**, 576, 642–43, 648

guessers, guessing, **286–87**, 329–30, 410–14, 417

Guggenheim Museum and Foundation, 287

Guido, 287

Gulag Archipelago, The (Solzhenitsyn), 573

Gulliver's Travels (Swift), 31

Gumbo, 144, **287**, 530

Gummer, Harriet, 237–38, **287–88**, 300

Gumps, Andy, 288

Gunther, 288

Gunther, August, 194, 246, **288**, 448, 590, 657, 691–92

Gunther, Grace, 288

Gutless Wonder, The, 288

Gutman, Andor, 28, 92, **288–89**, 370, 573

Hacketts, Elmo C., Jr., **290**, 501, 601

Haggedorn, Elbert, **290**

Hagstrohm, Delores, **290**

Hagstrohm, Edgar, Jr., 204, **290**

Hagstrohm, Edgar Rice Burroughs, 63, 250, **290–91**, 496, 500

Hagstrohm, Wanda, 204, 250, **290**, 496, 500

Haifa Institute for the Documentation of War Criminals, 253, **291**, 540

Haley, Stewart, **293**, 476

"Hal Irwin's Magic Lamp," 4, 38, 45, 138, 154, 173, 281–82, **291–93**, 341, 345, 515, 517, 642, 696

Hall, Cyril, **293**

Hall, Pamela Ford, **293–94**, 296, 461, 474, 571

Hallinan, Terrence, 268

Hallinan, Vincent, 268, 273

Hallinan, Vivian, **294**
Afterlife interview with, 268, 273

Halporn, Amy, **294**

Halyard, Ewing J., 60, 107, 121, 153, 169, 215, **294**, 306, 340, 507, 509, 522, 597, 697–98

Hamilton, Alexander, **294**

Hamlet, *Hamlet*, 3, 148, 167, 179, 240, 260, **294–95**, 404, 469–70, 496, 524, 554, 555, 559–61, 614, 657

Handy, Fred, **295**

Hanfstaengl, Putzi, **295**

Hansels and Gretels, **295**

Hanson, Miss, **295–96**

Hanson Center for the Arts, 293, **295–96**

Hapgood, Powers, 151, 198, 296, 341, 343–44, 403, 535, 550, 553, 664–65, 698

Hapgood brothers, 157, 296

Hapgoods, The, Three Earnest Brothers (Maraccio), 296

Happy Birthday, Wanda June, 8, 103, 145, 221, **296–97**, 298, 309, 358, 361, 364, 429, 449, 534, 565, 589, 604, 628, 676, 692, 709

Hardy, Albert, 46–47, **297**, 612, 620

Hardy, Norvell, 351

Harger, Lemuel K., 17, 115, 124, 168, **297**, 385

Harger, Rose, 17, 124, **297**, 385

Hari, Mata, **297**

harmoniums, 72, 114, 117, **297–98**, 439, 586

Harper, Alice, **298**, 364

Harper, Looseleaf, 8, 296, **298**, 364, 534

Harrell, Charles, **298**

Harrington, Herb, **298**

Harrison, Edmund L. (Edmond), **298**, 716–17

Harrison, Lew, 73, 226, **299**

"Harrison Bergeron," 146, 264, **299**

Harry, *see* Amy and Harry; Divine, Celeste and Harry; Laird, Eddie; "Unpaid Consultant"

Hartke, Eugene, Jr., 299, **300–301**, 436

Hartke, Eugene Debs, 3, 12, 15, 16, 24, 26, 29, 32, 33, 42, 45, 48, 53–54, 57, 67–68, 77–78, 81, 83, 109, 115, 126, 130, 136, 145, 150, 152, 156, 163, 188, 194, 197, 205, 206, 212, 217, 218, 227, 237, 238, 240, 243, 244, 245, 251, 285, 287–88,

293–94, 295, **299–300**, 309, 311, 337, 341, 353, 357, 364, 367, 382, 385, 392, 396, 425–26, 431, 436, 441, 450, 458, 461, 471, 474, 475–76, 477, 496, 500, 521, 522, 538, 546, 551, 554, 558, 562, 570–71, 572, 574, 584, 586, 587, 602–3, 684, 689, 698, 704, 705, 708

Hartke, Melanie, **300–301**

Harvard University, 47, 191, 239, 295, 326, 344, 348, 352, 364, 430, 467, 541, 550, 584, 663, 664, 716

Hatfield, Byron, 57, **301**, 431

Hausmännin, Walpurga, 301

Haycox, Mr., 281, **301**, 652

Hazor, **301**, 714

heartfelt moral code, 445–46

Heath, Durling, **301**

Hederich, Oberdienstleiter Karl, **301**

Heine, Heinrich, 99–100, 156, 200–201, 481

Heinz, Karl (Joe Louis; Brown Bomber), 187, **302**, 361, 636

Heliogabalus, **302**

helix, **302**

Hell, 181, 233, 270, 277, 278, 314, 326, 358, 449, 638

Hellbrunner, Mrs., 22, 45, **302**, 478

Heller, Charlene, 256, **302**

Heller, Joseph, 332

Helmholtz, George M., 17–18, 47, 173, 186, 199, 206–7, 213, 242, 293, **302–4**, 354, 355, 369, 370, 390–91, 461, 475, 476–77, 490–91, 504, 554, 599–600, 617–18, 642, 705

Hemingway, Ernest, 12, 25, 40, 58, 117, 131, 192, 211, 247, **304–5**, 317, 322, 324, 326, 592, 593, 607, 615, 622, 709, 712

Henry IV, Part Three (Shakespeare), 555

Hepburn, Mary, 83, 119, 149, 206, 207, 242, 243, 250, **305–6**, 308, 339, 359, 399, 611, 623, 624, 626, 659, 688–89, 707, 713

Hepburn, Roy, 60, 206, 256, **305–6**, 339

Herald, Randy, **306**

Herpers, Albert, 153, 169, 294, **306**

Herrick, Cleota, **3–6**

Hertz, Rudy, **306**, 553

Hesse, Hermann, 449, 677–78

Hickenlooper, John, Jr. and Sr., 129, 169, 199–200, **306–7**, 392, 609

Higgins, Bert, 554

Higgins, Kiah, 187, 212, 259, **307–8**, 404, 423, 476, 494–95, 505, 641–42

Higgins, Mr. and Mrs., **308**

Hildreth, Celia, *see* Hoover, Celia

Hildreth, Gerald, **308**

Hildreth, Shirley, **308**

Hilton, Gloria, 174, 266, **308**, 451

Hilton, James, 246

Hilyer, Tom, **308**

Hinckley, Sheila, *see* White, Sheila Hinckley

Hinkley, Bearse, 308, **308**

Hiroguchi, Akiko, 50, 207, 254–55, 305, **308–9**, 399, 421–22, 707, 713

Hiroguchi, Hisako, 8, 308, **309**, 399, 421–22, 708, 713

Hiroguchi, Zenji, 50, 199, 279, 308, **309**, 398–99, 421, 426, 660

Hiroshima, bombing of, 8–10, 30, 77, 80, 111, 139, 193, 240, 276, 305, 308, 314, 316, 328, 352, 369, 425, 483, 497, 512, 531, 548, 549, 563, 578, 588–89, 713

Hiscock, Ernest Hubble, 81, **309**, 396

Hitler, Adolf (Adolph), 24, 30, 46, 86, 96–97, 103, 128, 141, 166, 246, 278, 285, 286, 295, **309–10**, 328, 334, 410, 439, 449, 452, 462, 540, 554, 575–76, 577, 594, 648, 655, 658, 663, 680, 690–91

Afterlife interview with, 268–69, 273

Hitz, Benjamin D., 3–4, 212, 213, 226, **310–11**, 594, 615, 647, 695

Hitz, Lowell W., **311**

Hobby Show, 48, 86, 102, 203, 493
  prizewinner, **311**
Hocus Pocus, 3, 8, 12, 22, 42, 45, 46,
  51, 53–54, 58, 67, 68, 146, 152,
  153, 163, 169, 188, 197, 198,
  212, 218, 220, 236, 237, 240,
  243, 244, 245, 285, 287–88,
  295, 299, 309, **311–12**, 331,
  333, 338, 358, 364, 367, 392,
  431, 436, 440–41, 452, 460,
  461, 474, 475–76, 477, 490,
  496, 500–501, 521, 522, 529,
  538, 544–45, 549, 554, 564,
  570, 571, 573, 584, 595, 649,
  653, 672, 684
Hoenikker, Angela, 4, 33, 163–64,
  231, **312–13**, 340, 541
Hoenikker, Celia, **313**, 314
Hoenikker, Emily, **313–14**, 554
Hoenikker, Felix, 4, 89, 90, 113,
  133, 163, 193, 235, 276, 278,
  312, **313**, 314, 316, 338, 339,
  352, 369, 440, 441, 478, 566,
  611, 612, 660
Hoenikker, Franklin, 49, 114–15,
  172, 175, 231, 313, **314**, 348,
  441, 471, 538, 583
Hoenikker, Newton, 4, 84, 169, 175,
  199, 312, 313, **314**, 338, 340,
  566, 719–20
Hoenikker, Rudolph, **314**
Hoess, Rudolf Franz, 28, 181, **314**,
  433
Hoffman, Abbie, 136, **314–16**, 684
Hokkaido, Japan, 14–15, 22
Holdermann, Bill, **316**
Holderness, Marvin Sharpe, **316**
Holiday Inn, 49, 51, 90, 201, **316**,
  317, 320, 321, 356, 391, 423,
  424, 438, 478, 521, 579, 635,
  703
Holocaust, 15, 128, 210, 220,
  247–48, 277, 288–89, 291,
  368–69, 402, 495, 549, 583–84,
  639
  see also Auschwitz
Holy Grail, 266, 355, 361, 656, 693
Homestead, 241, **316**
Home Sweet Home Moving and
  Storage, **316**
Homo sapiens, 316

homosexuality, 61, 87, 97, 231,
  316–18, 319, 354, 363, 404,
  424, 457, 488, 522–23, 525,
  585, 688–89, 695, 718–19
Hoobler, **318**
Hoobler, Cynthia, **318**
Hoobler, Dwayne, 60, 63, 93–94,
  118, 119, 125, 222, 279, **318**,
  320, 358, 379, 438, 457, 467,
  495
Hoobler, Grace, 60, **318**, 358, 379
Hoobler, Josephus, **318**, 319, 437,
  535
Hoobler, Mary, **318–19**, 590
Hoobler, Wanda June, 60, **318**, 358,
  457
Hoobler, Wayne, 118, 201, 222,
  319, 340, 438, 521, 576
Hooligan, Francis Iron-7, **319**
"Hooligan, The," 12, 301, **319**, 465,
  628, 661–62
Hooper, Charlton, 164, **319**
Hooper, Lyle, 16, 67, 164, **319–20**,
  538, 614
Hoosier humor, *see* humor
Hoosier Poet, *see* Riley, James
  Whitcomb
Hoover, Bunny (*né* George), 94,
  208, 231, 233, 316, 317, **320**,
  321, 400, 495–96, 590, 688
Hoover, Celia (Celia Hildreth), 11,
  12, 72, 192–93, 208–9, 252,
  256, 296, 308, 316, **320–21**,
  424, 440, 479, 481, 590–92,
  688, 691
Hoover, Dwayne, 12, 42, 65, 72, 87,
  90, 108, 115, 174, 192, 208,
  218, 231, 252, 255, 311, 316,
  317, 319, 320, **321**, 340, 350,
  362, 363, 365, 385, 400, 435,
  437, 440, 463, 467, 478, 488,
  535, 544, 566, 577, 589–90,
  591–92, 614, 618, 619, 635,
  688, 694, 703, 717
Hoover, Lyle and Kyle, 72, 115,
  321, 535–36, 653
horse racing, 247
Horthy, Lomar, 263, 354
Horthy, Nilsak, **321**
Horton, **321**
Horvath, Nilsak, **322**, 478

Hotchner, A. E., **322**, 615
Hotel Arapahoe, **322**, 348, 584, 612,
  711
Hotel El Dorado, 190, **322**, 470,
  659, 660, 689
House of Bush, House of Saud
  (Unger), 414, 639
House of Hope and Mercy in the
  Jungle, 7, 29, 74, 109, 172,
  322, 442, 660
Hovanessian (Hovanissian), Kevork,
  322
Howard Johnson's, 226, 308, **323**,
  494, 619
How You Doin'?, **322–23**
Hoyle, Fred, 191
Hubbard, Kin, 331, 332, 334, 335,
  640
Huffman-Klinkowitz, Julie, 485
Huie, William Bradford, **323**
Humana, Vox, **323**, 696
humane, **323–24**
humanism, humanists, 20, 25,
  52–53, 62, 137, 251, 267, 268,
  277, **324–27**, 383, 403, 408–13,
  417, 420, 446, 514, 539, 657
  see also Free thinkers,
  freethinkers
humanistic physicist, **327**
humanitarian, humanitarianism, 97,
  167, **327**, 403
humanity, **327–30**
humankind, **330–31**
humanness, **331**
humanoid, **331**
Human Use of Human Beings, The
  (Wiener), 490, 703
humor, 18, 58, 72–73, 85, 103, 123,
  136, 160–62, 204, 276, 306–7,
  309, 314–16, **331–35**, 381–82,
  402, 403, 415, 417–18, 522,
  550, 582, 586, 657–58
  parallels between Vonnegut's and
  Twain's, 632
humorists, 315, **331–35**, 382, 593,
  640
  Weide documentaries on, 695
Hundred Martyrs to Democracy,
  335–36, 442
Hurty, Mr., 22, **336**, 478
Hurty, Phoebe, 158, **335**, 341, 564

Hurty place, **336**

"Hyannis Port Story, The," 85, 107–8, 132, 279, **337**, 348, 531, 532, 542

Hyatt, Malcolm, **337**, 543

hydrogen bomb, H-bomb, **8–11**, 128, 259, 329–30, 407

see also specific uses

Ibos, 229–30, 342

ice-nine, 4, 84, 89–90, 113, 114, 133, 239, 312–14, 327, 335, **338**, 340, 352, 377, 440, 441–42, 444, 538, 545, 660, 719

If God Were Alive Today, **55–56**, 162, 415, 457, 684

I.G. Farben, **338**, 587

Iliad (Homer), 16

Ilium, N.Y., 16, 44, 56, 90, 102, 103, 153, 198, 206, 214, 219, 235, 239, 240, 241, 242, 256, 257, 294, 305, 313, 316, **338–39**, 351, 425, 440, 458, 478, 485, 486, 487, 491, 492, 538, 579, 652, 661, 699, 720

Ilium Gazette, **339**

Ilium Historical Society, 338, **340**

Ilium Merchants National Bank and Trust, 339, **340**

Ilium News Leader, **340**

Ilium School of Optometry, 338, **340**, 433, 525

Ilium Works, 242, 284, 306, 316, 338–39, 374, 494, 498, 522, 563

immigration, 405–6

incantation, **340**

Indianapolis, Ind., 67, 69, 73, 81, 85, 121, 122, 154, 168, 172, 174, 175, 222, 255, 256, 288, 314, **340–44**, 435, 465, 487, 492, 512, 524, 553, 560, 564, 569, 570, 593, 624–25, 671, 676, 714, 717

in flagrante delicto, 199

injured veteran, unnamed, **643**

Innocent Bystander High School, **174**

instructors, **344**

Iowa Writer's Workshop, 16, 505

Iron Guard of the White Sons of the American Constitution, 120, **344**, 355, 363, 372

Iron Maiden, **344**

Irving, David, 8, 218, **344–45**, 722

Irwin, Hal, 45, 138, 281–82, 291–93, **345–46**, 379, 517, 642

Irwin, Mary, 45, 138, 173, 282, 291–93, **345–46**, 517

unnamed father of, **642**

Iscariot, Judas, 135–36, 158

"Island of Death, The," **346**

Ivankov, Aksinia, **346**

Ivankov, Alexei, **346**

Ivankov, Mikhail, 24, 25, **347**

Ivankov, Stepan, 24, 25, **346–47**, 370, 422

Ivanoff, Prokhor, **347**

Izumi, 237, **347**

Jackie, **348**

Jack's Hobby Shop, 314, **348**

Jackson, George Miramar, **348**

Jahan, Shah, 51

Jailbird, 3, 30, 44, 51, 58, 64, 84, 85, 107, 124, 131, 157, 201, 218, 225, 231, 237, 240, 263, 280, 282, 295, 338, 347, **348–51**, 352, 394, 400, 430, 467, 468, 474, 477, 485, 505, 535, 544, 550, 583–84, 588, 606, 619, 663, 698, 706

James, Jesse, **351**

Jarvis, Colin and Ma, **351**

Jason, Ed, **351**

jazz, American cultural value of, 407, 451–52

jazzman, unnamed, **643**

Jefferson, Arthur Stanley, **351–52**

Jefferson Observatory, **352**

Jekyll, Henry, **352**, 385, 438

Jekyll, Hortense, **352**

Jesus, *see* Christ, Jesus

Jesus, Fort, 245

Jewish humor, 332

jingoism, 408–9, 594

Johannsen, Nils, **352**

Johannsen Grinder Company, **352**

John Birch Society (Birch), 62

John/Jonah, 8, 15, 29, 33, 77, 89, 90, 109, 111–13, 114, 175, 193, 199, 223, 276, 278, 312, 335, **352–53**, 372, 439, 470, 538, 544, 611, 625, 709

Johnson, Clarence Daffodil-H, 46, **353**

Johnson, Fred Bates, 342, **353**, 610

Johnson, Henry "Tex," 33, 51, 170, 177, 181, **353**, 397, 557

Johnson, Lionel Boyd, *see* Bokonon

Johnson, Zuzu, 170, 177, **353–54**, 397

Johnstown High School, 303, **354**, 391

Jolson, Al, **354**

Jones, Fred, 245, 284, 302, **354**, 357, 364, 453, 565, 578

Jones, Jim, 228, 244

Jones, Lionel J. D., 120, 133, 139, 165–66, 181, 223, 236, 321, 344, **354–55**, 363, 448, 449, 462, 506, 540, 564, 658, 696–97, 700–701, 705–6

Jones, Tom, 486–87

Jorgenson, Coach, **355**

journalists, journalism, **355–56**

Journey to the End of the Night (Céline), 116

Joyce, James, 556

Joyce, John Wesley, **356**

Afterlife interview with, 269, 273–74

Joyce, Leroy, **356–57**, 400

Joy's Pride, 25, 170, 240, 325, **356**, 482

Judgment Day, **357**

June, Wanda, 17, 60, 135, 296–97, **358**, 586, 660

see also Happy Birthday, Wanda June; Hoobler, Wanda June

Juno, **358**

Kafka, Franz, 148, 295

Kago, **359**, 488–89, 718–19

Kairys, Anna, **359**, 583

Kanka-bonos, Kanka-bono girls, 207, 242, 305, 308–9, 330, **359**, 362, 399, 504, 624, 689, 713

kan-kan, **359**

Karabekian, Dorothy, **359**, 360, 367, 585

Karabekian, Edith Fairbanks, 284, 360, 361, 364, 367, 368, 383, 637

Karabekian, Rabo, 15, 16, 34, 45, 47, 49, 51, 55, 57, 59, 60, 66, 71, 72, 79, 82, 84, 88, 108, 115, 118, 120, 122, 124, 132, 145, 146, 149, 153, 155, 159, 164, 167, 168, 171, 181, 215, 227, 228, 231, 241, 245, 253, 256, 258, 280, 284, 287, 308, 316, 322, 341, 354, 357, **359–60**, 361, 362, 363–64, 367–68, 382, 395, 396, 400, 401, 422, 423, 425, 427, 438, 452, 465, 467, 491, 529, 539, 564, 570, 571, 572, 585, 601, 606, 618, 625, 638, 656, 677, 699, 701, 706, 710, 722

Karabekian, Terry and Henri, **360–61**, 367, 585

karass, 75, 114, 121, 282, 359, **361**, 450, 566

Karlswald, **361**

Karpinski, Big John, Dorene, and Little John, **361**

Kasabian, F. Donald, **361**

Katmandu, 103, 193, 194, 235, 246, 297, 318, **361–62**, 437, 543, 564, 604, 691, 692, 709

Kazak, Kazakh, 57, 144, 145, 192, 358, **362**, 379, 399, 423, 457, 529, 532–33, 536, 577–78, 586, 610

Keane, Frances, **362**
  Afterlife interview with, 269, 274

Keedsler, Beatrice, 51, 164, 231, **362–63**, 400

Keeley (Keely), Patrick, 233, 327, 355, **363**

Keene, Patty, 90, 118, **363**

Kelly, Bryan, 17, **363**, 716

Kelly, Jerry and Paul, **363**

Kelly, Margaret, **363**

Kemp, Marilee (Countess Portomaggiore), 108, 122, 149, 153, 168, 179, 181, 193, 258, 284, 317, 360, **363–64**, 367, 401, 452, 493, 507, 539, 573, 578, 581–82, 601, 656

Kennedy, John F., 144, 161, 195, 232, 242, 272, 334, 337, 379, 402, 460, 531, 532, 714

Kennedy, Joseph P., 334

Kennedy, Robert, 189, 364, **364**, 486, 570

Kennedy, Sheila, 337, 531, 532

Kennedy family, 85, 132, 230, 259, 279, 431, 542

Kent State shootings, 14

Keough, William, 58, 333

Kern, Shirley, **364**

Kestenbaum, Stanley, **364**

Ketchum, Bernard, 195, 232, **364**, 434, 470

Kevorkian, Jack, 266, 626
  see also God Bless You, Dr. Kevorkian

Key, Eddie, 72, **364–65**, 467, 569, 635

Key, Francis Scott, 364–65

"Kid Nobody Could Handle, The," 206–7, 304, **365**, 390, 504

Kilgallen, Pat, 224, **365**

Kilgore's Creed, **365–66**, 498, 520–21

Kilyer, Tom, **366**

Kimberly, **366**

King, Bobby, 145, 194, 207, **366**, 448, 457, 570

King, Martin Luther, Jr., 268, 274–75, 364, 402, 475, 486, 546

King of Candlesticks, 206, 283, **366**, 496, 520, 714

King of Michigan, 662, 718

Kirk, Mary Selwyn, **167–68**, **366**

Kisco, Buddy, **366**

Kissinger, Henry, **367**, 511

"Kiss Me Again," **366–67**, 446

Kitchen, Terry, 14, 16, 55, 66, 79, 115, 280, 284, 302, 308, 354, 361, **367–68**, 383, 601

Kittredge, Waltham, **368**

Klee, Paul, **368**, 484

Kleindienst, Edward Strawberry-4, **368**

Klinkowitz, Jerome, **368**, 384, 461, 485, 545, 695, 717

Klopfer, Arndt, 220, **368**

Knechtmann, Avchen and Heinz, 11, **368–69**, 495, 574

Knechtmann family medley, 11, 368–69

Knights of Kandahar, **369**, 390, 461, 490, 599
  Treasurer of, **617–18**

Knowles, Lyman Enders, 20, **369**

Kolhouri,, **367**

Konigswasser, Ellis, 18, **369–70**, 400, 649

Koradubian, Martin, 133, **370**

Kornblum, Mr., 293, **370**

Koshevoi, Mr., **370**

Kosovo, Serbia, 277, 542, 548–49

Kouyoumdjian, Marktich, *see* Coulomb, Marc

Kovacs, Arpad, **370–71**

Kraft, George (Iona Potapov), 22–23, 73, 84, 105, 120, 123, 164, 247, 266, 340, 355, **371**, 462, 464, 494, 540, 603, 637, 658, 701

Kraft, Mary, **371**

Kramm, Doris, **371**, 477

Krapptauer, August, 120, 181, 225, 344, 355, **372**, 705

Krebbs, Sherman, **372**, 709

Krementz, Jill, 169, 225, 281, 342, **372–73**, 513, 542, 594, 612, 675, 681, 715, 716

Kremlin, **373**

Kroner, Anthony, 34–35, 45, 56, 95, 110, 241, 262, 294, 298, **373–75**, 381, 447, 499

Kroner, Janice, **375**

Kropotnik, Commissar, **375**

Krummbein, Falloleen, 131–32, 183–84, **375–76**, 644

Krummbein, Otto, 131–32, 183–84, 186, **375–76**, 451, 615, 644

Kuznetzov, Felix, 588

Lady's Slipper, 74, **377**, 442, 505, 635, 660

Lafayette Escadrille, 231–32, **377**, 391

Laird, Eddie, 18–19, 35, **377**, 422

Laird, Selma, Arthur, and Dawn, 19, 36, **377**

lambos, **379**

lamprey, **379**

Lancer, **379**

Landry, Cynthia, **379**, 460, 532
Langmuir, Irving, 113, 313, 338, 352, 545
Lapp, Marlin T., **379**
Larkin, Emil, 158, 283, **379**, 511, 581
Lasher, James J., 117, 241, 261–63, **380–81**, 395, 433, 452, 499, 509, 636
"Last Full Measure," **381**
Laurel and Hardy, 79, 123–24, 161, 196, 335, 351–52, **381–82**, 669
Lawes, Cleveland, **382**, 384, 573
Lawes, Eucharist "Ukey," **382**
Lawrence, Seymour "Sam," 36, 325, **382–83**, 668, 676, 681, 712
Lazarus, 55, 135, 325, **383**, 551, 674
Lazzaro, Paul, 69, 120, 147, 201, 259, **383–84**, 486, 695
leaks, **384**
Leaning Tower of Pisa, **614**
Lee, Robert E., 268, 271, 392
Leech, Leonard, **384**, 452
Leeds, Marc, **384**, 437, 461, 483, 695
Leen, Arpad, 58, 349, **384–85**
Le Fèvre, Andre, 158, **384**
Leghorn, Fred, 131, 352, **385**, 520
LeGrand, Pierre, **385**, 614
Leidveld and Moore, **385**
Lembrig, Thor, **384**
Lenin Observatory, **352**, 385
Leonard, Dawn, 264, **385**
Leonard, John, **385**, 461
Leonard, Paul, 297, **385**
LeSabre, Harry and Grace, **385**, 694
lesbianism, *see* homosexuality
Letter from PFC Kurt Vonnegut, Jr., to his family, May 29, 1945, 721–22
Letzinger, Coach, **386**
Levittown, N.Y., 36
libraries, librarians, 413–14
"Lie, The," 39, 63, 308, 366, **386**, 516–17, 693–94
Lieber, Albert, 43, 67, 306, 342, **386–87**, 519, 593, 676, 679
Lieber, Albert, II, **387**
Lieber, Alice Barus, **42–43**, 50, 67, **386–87**, 389, 536

Lieber, Andy, **387**
Lieber, Pete, **387**
Lieber, Peter, 50, 250, 258, 341, 386, **387–89**, 514, 536, 657
Lieber, Rudy, 67, **389**
Liebold, Ernest, 244–45
life, purpose of, 406–8, 412–13
Linberg, Karl, **389–90**, 604, 686–87
Linberg, Rudy, 389, **390**, 604, 686–87
Lincoln, Abraham, 260–61, 278, 310, 406, 408–10, 447, 450, 475, 479–80, 546, 551, 556, 572, 608, 631, 633–34, 657, 709
Lincoln High School, 17, 47, 173, 242, 293, 302–4, 354, 355, 369, 370, **390–91**, 460–61, 504, 642
Lind, Jenny, **391**
Lindener, Irma Vonnegut, *see* Vonnegut, Irma
Lindener, Kurt, 265
Lingamon, Cynthia Anne, **391**
Lingamon, Ned, **391**, 703
Lingo-Three, 359, **391**, 488, 718
literature, 403–4
Littauer, Kenneth, 99, 156, 334, 377, **391**, 594
Little, Elbert, 248, **391**
Little, Sherman Wesley, **391**, 590
Little Bighorn, 263, **392**
"Little Orphant Annie" (Riley), 518
Locke, John, 200, **392**
Lonesome No More, **392**
"Long Walk to Forever," 124, 245, **394**, 460
Look at the Birdie, 464
"Lorelei, Die" (Heine), 99–100, 156, 200, 481, 644
Lou (artist), 179, **423**
Loud family, 445
Louis, Joe, *see* Heinz, Karl
Love as always, Kurt (Rackstraw), 505
Love Crusade, **392**, 613
Lovejoy, Sylvia, 124, 245–46, 248, 264, 391, **392**, 599
"Lovers Anonymous," 47, 85, 196–97, **392–94**, 462, 472, 475, 479, 603, 641, 699–700, 707
unnamed narrator of, **645**, 699

unnamed narrator's wife in, **646–47**
Lowell, A. Lawrence, 282, **394–95**
Lubbock, Luke, **395**
Lucretia A. Mott, **395**
Ludd, Ned, 26–27, **395–96**, 589
Luddites, 241, 261, 338, 373, 406, 474, 589
Luma County Clarion, **396**
Luma County Savings and Loan Association ("El Banco Busto"), **396**
Lutz, Andre, 152, 261, **396**, 603
Lutz Carillon, 49, 217, 261, 300, 309, **396–97**, 440, 614
Lynn, Jonathan, *see* Planck, Alfred
Lyon, Billie, 420n
Lyon, Ollie, 420n, 437

McAllister, Reed, 97–98, 139, 233, 316, **427–28**, 518, 550
McAllister, Robjent, Reed, and McGee, 97–98, 427, **428**, 452, 528
McAllister, Thurmond, 93, **428**, 452
McBundy, Hortense Muskellunge-13, **428**
McCabe, Earl, 27, 74–76, 109, 110, 112, 331, 377, **428**, 442, 510
McCarthy, Cliff, 195, 216, **428–29**, 461
McCarthy, Joseph, McCarthyism, 44, 152, 155, 273, 295, 348–49, **429–30**, 439, 452, 561, 583, 584
McCarthy, Kevin, **429**, 461
McCarty, Eddie, **92**, 430
MacCleary, Lou, **398**
McClellan, Grace and George, **430**
McCloud, **502**
McCone, Alexander Hamilton, 47, 51, 84, 184, 348–49, 359, **430**, 467, 583, 584, 597, 698, 711
McCone, Alice Rockefeller, 430
McCone, Clara, **430**
McCone, Daniel, 51, 184, 351, **430–31**
McCone, John, 51, **430–31**
McCoy, Newton, 57, 301, **431**
McGarvey Family, The, **431**
McGovern, George, 546, 565

Machu Picchu, **398**

MacIntosh, Andrew, 199, 309, **398–99**, 613, 660

MacIntosh, Selena, 309, **399**, 457

MacIntyre, Carlyle F., **399**

Mackay, Charles, **399–400**, 654–55

MacKenzie, Joyce, 188, 249, 259, **400**

Mackintosh, Selena, 362

McLuhan, Nancy, 358, 371, **431**, 573

MacMahon, Bonnie, 122, 356–57, **400**

MacMahon, Ralph, 356–57, **400**

McSwann, Ross L., **431**

Madeiros, Celestino, **400**, 535

Madge, **400**

Madison, Polly, 55, **400**, 699

Magnum Opus, Incorporated, 153, 166–67, 239, 257, 279, **400–401**, 443, 510, 553–54

Mainland, *see* Meadows

Mamigonian, Leo, **401**

Mamigonian, Vartan, **401**

Manchu, Fu, 398, **421**, 427, 618

Mandarax, 50, 58, 82, 119, 149, 199, 213, 279, 309, 398–99, **421–22**, 426, 490, 556, 603, 624, 707

Maniacs in the Fourth Dimension, **422**

"Manned Missiles, The," 24–25, 346–47, 370, **422**, 694

Mansfield, Dave, **422**

Manson, Charles, 135, 143, 228, 244

Man Without a Country, A, 26, 55, 74, 212, 227, 265, 286, 296, 310, 368, 373, 395, 440, 447, 451, 470, 472, 483, 515–16, 535, 553, 562, 572, 585–86, 621, 631, 657, 672

chapter-by-chapter analysis of, **401–21**

man-woman hours, 279, **421**

Maraccio, Michael D., 296

Mare Imbrium, **352**, **423**

Margaret, Queen, **504**, 561

Margo, **423**, 720

Margoles, Sydney, 61, 317

Marion (artist), 179–80, **423**

Marion (Paul's fiancée), 307, **423**, 476, 496, 505

Maritimo, Alan, **423**

Maritimo, Alfred, 316, **423**, 438

Maritimo, Carlo, **423**

Maritimo, Gino, 31, 182, **423–24**, 590

Maritimo, Guillermo "Little Willy," 106, **424**

Maritimo, Julio, **424**

Maritimo, Marco, 31, 182, **423–24**, 590

Maritimo, Milo, 87–88, 106, 317, **424**, 438, 571

Maritimo Brothers Construction Company, 195, 256, 362, 364, 423–24, 467, 535–36, 589, 657, 691, 692

Markson, David, 450

marriage, 272–73, 279, 498, 508–9, 524, 601, 645–46

see also specific couples

Martha, **425**, 435

Martian calendar, 459

Marx, Arnold, 233, 301, **425**, 606

Mary, **425**, 480

Masefield, John, 707

Mashtots, Mesrob, **425**

Mask of Sanity, The (Cleckley), 142, 151–52

Maslansky, Robert, 53

masochism, 196

Masters, Barbara, **425**

Matheson, **425**

Matsumoto, Hiroshi, 8, 15, 29, 62, 77, 305, **425–26**, 573, 578, 592

Matsumoto Corporation, 223, 256, 279, 305, 309, 339, 360, **426–27**, 618, 638

Matthews, Hildy, 84, 240–41, **427**, 435, 487, 643

mausoleums, 15, **427**

Max, **427**

Maxincuckee (Maxinkuckee), Lake, **378–79**, 718

Meadow Lark, see Queen of the Meadows

Meadows, 31, 45, 162, 255, 256, 262, 284, 298, 316, 327, 375, 395, 398, **431**, 447, 563, 624, 717

medical establishment, 412

Mellon, Hortense, 68, **431–32**

Melrose, Mr., **432**

Melville, Herman, 440, 607

Memoirs of a Monogamous Casanova, 73, **432**, 444, 462

Memory Clinic, 344, **432**, 440, 443

Mencken, Barbira, **432**, 570

Mencken, H. L., 512

Mendoza, Jose, **432**

Mengel, Bernard, 28, 314, **432–33**

Mensa, 596

mental illness, 61–62, 93, 125–26, 151–52, 300–301, 320, 340, 341, 436, 476, 491–92, 507, 510, 523, 524, 570, 579, 619, 665, 682–84, 689, 694

see also schizophrenia

Merble, Lionel, 340, **433**, 487

Merganthaler, Corporal, **433**

Merrihue, Faith, **433**, 522, 526, 694

Messiah, 38, 381, **433–34**

Metzger, Eloise, 15, 44, 51, 65, 95, 100, 104, 119, 194, 195, 196, 245, 284, 297, 299, 320, 364, 424, **434**, 435, 448, 522, 579, 673, 690, 691, 692

Metzger, Eugene Debs, 197, 299, **434**

Metzger, George, 95, 196, **434–35**, 690

Metzger, Jane Addams, **434**

Miasma, Khashdrahr, **435**, 463, 694

Microsecond Arbitrage, Inc., 222, 432, **435**

Middle East, conflict in, 407–8, 414, 448, 516, 714

middle-European humor, 332

Middleton, Andy, 84, 174, 240–41, 427, **435**, 487

Midland City, 8, 12, 15, 31, 32, 37, 41, 45, 49, 51, 65, 81, 84, 87–88, 95, 100, 104, 108, 115, 122, 153, 163, 174, 182, 218, 231–33, 241, 246, 284, 288, 308, 316, 318, 320, 362, 364, 391, **435–37**, 448, 454, 467, 479, 517, 543, 568, 587, 589–90, 636, 657, 658, 688, 692, 703, 709

neutron bombing of, 193–95, 232–33, 281, 316, 341, 372,

423, 435, 470, 478, 579–80, 690, 691, 692

Midland City Arts Festival, 49, 60, 67, 188, 220, 263, 296, 302, 359, 362, 424, 435, 438, 545, 571, 605, 619

Midland City Bugle-Observer, 93, 95, 246, 434, 691

Midland City Ordnance Co., 42, 437, 521

Midland County Mask and Wig Club, 347, 362

Midland County Merchants Bank, 437, 535

Midnight Pussycats, 437

Midway College, 437, 483

Midwest, American, 402–3, 518–20, 560

see also Indianapolis, Ind.; Midland City

Mihalich, Jeff, 437–38

Mildred Barry Memorial Center for the Arts, 41, 320–21, 359, 424, 435, 467, 589, 591

Mildred Peasely Bangtree Memorial Theater, 438

military establishment: disillusionment with, 408, 411–12 morale in, 448

Miller, Bill/Don, 316, 319, 423, 438

Miller, Lydia and Verne, 438

Miller, Mary Alice, 155, 222, 319, 400, 424, 438

Miller's Hardware Store, 438, 456, 639

Ministry of Popular Enlightenment and Propaganda, 105, 438

"Minorite Church of Vienna, The," 438–39, 658, 691

Minot, Frank, 439

Minton, Claire, 214, 439, 518, 538

Minton, Horlick, 214, 430, 439, 518, 538

Miss Canal Zone, 439

"Miss Temptation," 208, 253, 308, 439, 597

Mitchell, Allison, 439–40

Mitchell, Jerome, 321, 440, 579, 592

"Mnemonics," 93, 192, 222, 334, 344, 432, 440, 443, 606

Moakely, George Minor, 440

Mobutu, President, 440, 440, 477

Moby Dick, *Moby Dick* (Melville), 352, 440, 607, 695

Moellenkamp, Henry, 54, 212, 217, 396, 440–41, 461, 614, 708

Moellenkamp, Robert W., 54, 222, 435, 441, 461, 557

Mohiga Ice Cream Emporium, see Peck, Jerry and Muriel

Mohiga Valley Free Institute, 217, 396, 440, 441, 477, 484, 491, 549, 564, 565, 602

Mohiga Wagon Company, 163, 312, 396, 441, 549, 601

Moncrief, Earl, 259, 400, 441

Money River, 22

Monzano, Miguel "Papa," 15, 76, 185, 216, 239, 323, 335, 338, 352, 377, 441–42, 471, 538, 660

Monzano, Mona Aamons, 7, 76, 108, 131, 317, 442, 471, 538, 625, 707

Moody, Foxcroft and Melody, 415, 442

Moody, Mary, 38, 433, 442, 510, 524

Moon, Fletcher, 442–43

MoonMist Tobacco, Ltd., 443, 567

Moore, Michael, 413, 548

Moorhead, Alfred, 93, 222, 344, 432, 440, 443, 606

mopery, 443, 547

Morais, Herbert M., 85

morale, morale-builders, 408, 447–48

morality, 408–13, 443–47

"More Stately Mansions," 430, 447

Morgan, Eunice Eliot, see Rosewater, Eunice Eliot Morgan

Morissey, Bucky, 104, 115, 246, 448

Morissey, Francis X., 194, 246, 288, 448, 590, 692

Mother Night, 4, 44, 58, 66, 73, 77, 84, 105, 111, 120, 154, 173, 174, 207, 223, 235, 247, 250, 253, 260, 263, 269, 273, 278, 288–89, 291, 297, 301, 309, 314, 321, 340, 344, 349, 363,

384, 425, 432, 449, 461–62, 483, 494, 500–501, 522, 529, 540, 564, 577, 600, 603, 606, 658, 676, 695, 696, 706

Mothers' Auxiliary of the Paul Revere Association of Militant Gentiles, 449

Mott, Lucretia, 395

Mott, Stewart Oriole-2, 213, 449

Mott, Stewart Rawlings "Flocka Butt," 449

"Mouth Crazy," see "Pan-Galactic Straw-boss"

Mozart, Wolfgang Amadeus, 121, 257, 449–50

Muir, Edward, 114, 450–51

Müller, Gerhard, 451

Muller, Harve and Bea, see Grand Triumvirate

mural, 644, 647

muralist, unnamed, 643–44

Murphy, Hal, 183, 451, 644

Murra, George, 266, 308, 451

Murra, John, 451

Murray, Albert, 407, 451–52, 594–95

Musa Dagh, 452

Muscular Christianity, 143–44, 409

Mushari, Norman, 14, 37–38, 155, 169, 234, 239, 248, 384, 428, 430, 433, 434, 452, 459, 492, 510, 523–25, 528–29, 531, 555, 581, 650

Mushari, Norman, Jr., 452

music, cultural value of, 407–8, 450, 451, 515

Musketeer, The, 396–97, 452

Musket Mountain, 354, 385, 452, 474, 477, 562, 564, 586, 614–15, 689

Muslims, 140, 514, 592

Mussolini, Benito, 284, 354, 364, 396, 452–53, 493, 655, 680

Mycobacterium, 34, 141, 270

"Mysterious Madame Blavatsky, The," 219

Mysterious Stranger, The (Twain), 415, 447, 632

myth, mythology: cultural value of, 453–55 Greek, 454–55, 497 political, 409–13, 454

"My work is done," *see* Eastman, George

Nagasaki, bombing of, 296, 298, 497–98, 548, 563, 589, 639
napalm, 239
narrators, unnamed, 99, 308, 392, 400, 479, **644–46**
narrator's wife, unnamed, **646–47**
Nash, Harry, 438, **456**, 462, 540, 562, 639, 703
Nation, J. Edgar, 65, 225, **456**
National Council of Arts and Letters, **456**
National Steel Foundry, 22, 302, 432, **456**, 478, 506
National Union of Belgium Opticians, **457**, 604
Nation of Two, *see Reich der Zwei, Das*
Native Americans, 261, 339, 378, 381, 392, 460, 488, 510, 581
Natural Selection, 191
"Nature Cruise of the Century," 36, 145, 193, 207, 285, 305, 309, 322, 366, 367, 398–99, 421, **457**, 468, 537, 660
near-death experience, 70
Necker, Anne Louise Germaine, 166, 194, **457**
neo-Luddites, 395, 474
neuters, **457–58**, 692
neutron bomb, **8**, 11, 37, 193–95, 232–33
   see also Midland City, neutron bombing of
Newcomb, Ed, 103, 422, **458–59**
Newcomb, John L., 318, **458**
"New Dictionary," **458**
New Journalism, **355–56**
New Journalists, **356**
Newport, R.I., 22, 98, 132, 259, 379, 384, 427, 441, **459–60**, 478, 485, 530, 532, 533, 543
Newt, **460**
Newton, Isaac, 13, 71, 191, 222, 427, **460**, 555, 596, 602
   Afterlife interview with, 269, 274, 627
New York State Maximum Security Adult Correctional Facility at

Athena, 119, 189, 206, 236, 243, 299, 425, **458**, 474, 476, 477, 496–97, 573, 586, 603, 615
"Next Door," 115, 124, 231, 297, 385
Niagara Falls, **460**
Nicea, Council of, 139
Nicholson, Robert, 142, **460**
"Night for Love, A," **5**, 69, 148, 508, 509, 702
Nightmare Ages, **460**, 566
nihilism, 372
Nim-nim, 42, **460**, 568
Ninth Symphony (Beethoven), **49–50**, 84–85, 205, 260, 536, 556, 557, 596, 614
Nixon, Richard, 502, 511, 546, 550–51, 581, 584, 650, 678, 699
Nobel Prize, Vonnegut's lack of, 417, 419
Nocturnal Goatsucker, 93, **461**
"No Laughing Matter," 79, 482, 674
Nolte, Nick, **461**
non-epiphany, 367–68
Norman Rockwell Hall, **461**
North Crawford, N.H., **462**, 479
North Crawford Manor, **462**
North Crawford Mask and Wig Club, 438, 456, **462**, 540, 562, 703
Norwood, George F., Jr., 327
"No-Talent Kid, The," 199, 242, 303, 354, 369, 390, **460–61**, 490, 599, 627–728
Noth, Eva, **462**
Noth, Helga, 28, 73, 105–6, 123, 174, 371, 432, **462**, 658
Noth, Resi, 28, 92, 106, 120, 123, 138, 174, 225, 371, 432, **462**, 600
Noth, Werner, 28, 105, **462–63**, 697
nothinghead, 61, 174, **463**, 695
Now It Can Be Told, 88, 118, 252, 391, 434, **463**, 489, 500, 617, 619, 694
"Now It's the Women's Turn," 15, 45, 79, 120, 124, 167, 171, 360, 382, 422, 539, 638, 706, 722
   see also "Windsor Blue Number Seventeen"

nuclear weapons, **8–11**, 327
NUVO, 154

Obama, Barack, 475
obelisk, 37
Odyssey (Homer) 296
Offit, Sidney, 232, 305, 461, **464**
Oger, Anna Maria, **464**
Oglethorpe, James E., **464**
O'Hare, Bernard B., 105–6, 225, 247, **464**, 467, 537, 580, 638, 654
O'Hare, Bernard V., 72, 78, 82, 169, 175, 197, 211, 223, 250, 305, 333, 395, 399, 439, 446, 451, **464–65**, 487, 513, 514, 550, 570, 636, 704, 713
O'Hare, Bernie, 5–7, 59, **465–66**, 501, 641
O'Hare, Captain Bernard, **465**
O'Hare, Mary, 211, 223, 451, 464–65, **466**
O'Hare, Wanda, 5–7, **465–66**, 502
O'Hare, Willy, 5–7, 59–60, 78, 82, 133, **465–66**, 501
O'Hare Paint and Varnish Company, **466–67**
Ohio Adult Correctional Institution, **467**
Ohio Valley Ornamental Concrete Company, 195, 364, 424, **467**, 691, 692
Ojumwa, 365, **467**, 635
Old Man and the Sea, The (Hemingway), 304, 607
oligomenorrhea, **457**
Olly-olly-ox-in-free, **467–68**
O'Looney, Francis X., **468**
O'Looney, Mary Kathleen, 15, 20, 44, 47, 95–96, 107, 108, 133, 152, 219, 237, 281, 350, 357, 372, **468–69**, 470, 505, 537, 581, 584, 608, 612, 614, 635, 663, 698–99, 711
Onassis, Jacqueline Bouvier Kennedy, 81, 96, 421, 448, **469**
Operation Brainstorm, 39, 108, 216–17, **469**
Ophelia, **469–70**
orderly, unnamed, **647**
organisms, 118–19, 142, **470**

Origami Express, 421, **470–71**, 483, 572

orphans, 186

Ortiz, Jesus, **471**, 613

Orwell, George, **471**, 490

Osterman, 232–33, **471**

Ostrovsky, Erika, 216, 522
   see also Céline, Louis-Ferdinand

oubliette, 15, 112, **171–72**, 538, 625, 638

Our Lady of Perpetual Astonishment, **472**

Our Town (Wilder), 682

Owley, Reva, **472**

Owl's Club, *see* Grand Triumvirate

Pabu, 84, 244, **473**

"Package, The," 19, 167, 238, 252, 259, **473–74**, 571, 643

Padwee, Howard, 163, **474**

Pahlavi Pavilion, **474**, 477, 565, 572, 648

Palace of the League of Nations, **474**

Palladio, **474**, 481, 482, 593

Palm Sunday, 8, 11, 42, 43, 60, 69, 112, 117, 126, 163, 169, 209, 227, 318, 336, 341, 358, 391, **474**, 505, 628, 671, 676

Pandora, 454–55

Pan-Galactic Humbug, **474**, 522

Pan-Galactic Memory Bank, The, **474**

Pan-Galactic Space Service, **475**, 532, 705

"Pan-Galactic Straw-boss," **475**

Pan-Galactic Three-Day Pass, 81, 85, 264, 340, **475**, 491, 524

Parachute Ski Marines, 79, **475**

Parker, Theodore, 393, **475**, 707

Parrot, Wilfred, 196, **475**

Patton, Jack, 67–68, 83, 188, 300, **475–76**, 501

Patton, Margaret, 83, 300–301, 475, **476**

Patton, Mildred, 300–301, 475, **476**

Paul, 124, 307, 423, **476**, 495, 505

Peach, Delbert, **476**, 528

Peach, Miss, **476–77**

Peale, Delmar, 350, 371, **477**, 584

pearls before swine, **477**

Pearly Gates, 70–71, 120, 266–78

Peck, Jerry, 440, **477**

Peck, John, **477**

Peck, Muriel, 109, 440, **477**

Peckham, Bradley, 22, 302, 336, 432, 456, 460, **478**, 506, 653

Peckham, Pam, 22, 302, 336, 460, **478**, 506, 653

Pefko, Francine, 94, 245, 321, 322, **478**, 479, 648

Pefko, George, 20, 180, 214–15, 222, **478–79**, 611, 648

Pefko, Julian, 104, **478**

Pefko, Robert, 20, 245, 478, **479**

Pelk, Kennard, **479**

Pellegrino, Peter, **479**
   Afterlife interview with, 269, 274

Pembroke, Abraham Lincoln, I, III, and IV, 83–84, 138, **479**, 480, 572

Pembroke, Elias, 83, **479–80**, 610

Pembroke, Julia, 83, 123, 138, **479–80**, 560, 572, 608, 610

Pembroke Mask and Whig Club, **480**, 572

Pena, Harry, 425, **480–81**, 522, 695

Pena, Manny and Kenny, 425, **480–81**, 695

Penfield, Frederic Courtland, **481**

Pennsylvania Dutchmen, **481**

Pennwalt Biphetamine, **481**

Pepper, Frank, 474, **481**, 482, 593

Pepper, Monica, 49, 72, 85, 140, **481–82**, 496–97, 667–68, 681, 710, 712, 719

Pepper, Zoltan, 49, 66, 140, 443, 474, **481–82**, 520–21, 547, 593, 620, 667, 705

perpetual-motion machine, **482**, 602–3

Peterson, Captain and Joy, **483**

Peterson, Mrs. Lyman R., **484**

Petro, Joe, III, 162, 212, 368, 384, 402, 420–21, 437, 461, 470–71, **483–84**, 572, 585, 672, 695

Petro, Joe II, 437, 483

pharmaceutical houses, 258–59

Phi Beta Kappa, **485**

Phoebe, **485**

Piatigorsky, Albert Aquamarine-1, **485**

Piatigorsky, Gregor, **485**, 709

Pieratt, Asa, 368, 384, 461, 483, **485**, 695

Pilgrim, Barbara and Robert, **485–86**

Pilgrim, Billy, 15, 33–34, 38, 44, 46, 58, 62, 69, 80, 87, 107, 111, 117, 121, 132, 134, 147, 166, 170, 175, 176, 182, 201, 218, 235, 236, 251, 257, 259, 265–66, 280, 316, 317, 323, 339, 340, 344, 364, 379, 385–86, 395, 422, 433, 434, 437, 457, 459–60, 462, 485, **486–87**, 492, 510, 525, 538, 530–32, 536, 570, 590, 597, 604, 606, 614, 616–17, 694–95, 699–700, 704–5, 720

Pilgrim, Valencia Merble, 236, 316, 379, 485–86, **487**, 699

Pine Knoll, 486, **487**

Pinsky, Robert, **487**

Pipe City Golf and Country Club, 84, 427, 435, **487**

Pisquontuit, Chief, **487–88**

Pisquontuit, R.I, 98, 120, 196, 278, 452, 480, **487–88**, 522–24, 525, 695

Plague on Wheels, 67, 359, 463, **488–89**, 718–19

Planck, Alfred (Jonathan Lynn), 107, **489**

"Planet Gobblers, The," **489**

Platt, Frank, 595

Player Piano, 3, 15, 31, 36, 38, 44, 51, 60, 63, 92, 94, 107, 110, 124, 129, 153, 169, 198, 199, 212, 215, 219, 223, 240, 241, 242, 250, 254, 256, 261, 278, 280, 290, 294, 301, 306, 316, 334, 335, 338–40, 366, 369, 373, 395, 398, 425, 435, 456, 482, **490**, 491, 492, 493, 496, 498–99, 501, 502, 504, 509, 522, 529, 544, 545, 547, 554, 570, 597, 601, 652, 695, 703, 716, 718

Plummer, Walter, 242, 303, 369, 461, **490–91**, 599–600, 617–18

Poe, Edgar Allan, **490**

policeman, unnamed, **647**

political establishment, disillusionment with, 10, 63, 138, 141, 151, 230, 270, 277, 402, 405, 407–11, 413–16, 446–47, 451, 553, 562, 580, 621, 631–32, 709

Polk, Dalton, **490**, 603

Polk, James, 408, 709

Pollock, Jackson, 367, 578, 592

Pomerantz, Floyd, 171, **490**, 708

Pond, Dr., 169, 301, **490**

Pontius Pilate Athletic Club, 135, 332, **490**

Ponzi scheme, 201–2
    see also di Sanza, Carlo

pool-pah, **492**

"Poor Little Rich Town," 26, 46, 48, 86, 102, 202, 237, 311, 338, 339, 422, 458, **492–93**, 506, 578–79

Poo-tee-weet (Poo-tee-phweet), 9, 62, **491–92**

Pops, **493**

pornography, 67, 97, 143, 149, 187–88, 206, 331, 384, 423, 437, 444, 474, 489, 500, 525, 527, 552, 636, 697, 704, 708

Portomaggiore, Bruno, 317, 364, 401, 452, **493**

Portomaggiore, Countess, *see* Kemp, Marilee

Port Zion, **493**

postmistress, unnamed, **648**

Post-Timequake Apathy (PTA), **493–94**

Potapov, Ilya, 73, **494**

Potapov, Iona, *see* Kraft, George

Potapov, Tanya, **494**

Potter, David, 198, 207, 214, 243, 351, **494**

poverty, 278, 291–92, 331–32, 346

"Powder-Blue Dragon, The," 1, 187, 212, 259, 307–8, 423, 476, **494–95**, 505, 642

Powers, Dr., **495**

POWs, 69, 100, 132, 147, 218, 250, 259, 285, 434, 575–76, 625, 642, 697, 704
    Canadian, **106**, 576
    Vonnegut's experience as, 15, 46, 78, 81, 175, 197, 206, 209–11,

360, 395, 451, 465, 569, 576, 721–22

PPs (psychopathic personalities), 141–42, 151–52, 412, 414

Prairie Military Academy, 94, **495–96**

prakhouls, **496**

Pratt, Mary, **496**, 558

prayer, 59

"Present for Big Saint Nick, A," **5–7**, 59, 78, 465, 501, 641, 719

Prince, Dudley, 18, 96, 119, 130, 140, 203, 236, 249, 279, 305, 365, 458, 482, **496–98**, 520, 521, 540, 547, 593, 615, 693, 712

Prince, Joe, 290, **498**

Prince of Candlesticks, **496**, 611

Project Cyclops, 285, **498**, 518, 549, 553, 604

Prometheus, 249, 454–55, 497

prostitution, 67, 317

Proteus, Anita, 50, 95, 165, 240, 262, 281, 294, 301, 374, 381, 467, **498–99**, 563

Proteus, George, 256, 261, 373, **499**

Proteus, Paul, 15, 16, 35, 44, 50, 51, 56, 95, 103–4, 110, 117, 124, 133, 164, 165, 219, 224, 240, 241, 255, 256–57, 261–63, 281, 284, 290, 294, 298, 301, 306, 327, 338–39, 344, 373–75, 380–81, 431, 433, 467, 490, 491, 498, **499**, 563, 601, 613, 652, 660–61, 703, 707, 717

Proteus Park, 204, **499**

"Protocols of the Elders of Tralfamadore, The," 68, 240, 328, 331, 450, 454, 476, **500**, 501, 558

Protocols of the Elders of Zion, 16, 67, 233, 244, 476, **500–501**

Pruitt, Earl, **501**

psychiatry, 29

psychopathic personalities (PPs), psychopaths, 141–42, 151–52, 412, 414

Pulitzer Prize, 14

Pullman, Mr. and Mrs., 5–6, **501–2**, 641

Pullman, Richard, 59, **501–2**

Pulsifer, Borders M., 84, **502**, 710

Punchlines, 161, 333

Purdy, **502**

purity, **502**

Putty Puss, 11, **502–3**, 625

Qaddafi, Muammar, 593, 682

Queen of the Meadows, **504**

Quezeda, Domingo, 359, **504**

Quinn, Bert, 206–7, 390, **504**

rabbits, 571

racism, 14–15, 22, 41, 108, 139, 164, 174, 178, 243, 263, 271, 275, 287, 318, 344, 345–46, 354–55, 372, 430–31, 449, 506, 511, 515–16, 546, 564, 574, 581, 590, 697, 700–701, 705–6, 717

Rackstraw, Loree, 461, **505**

radiation, 31

radio operator, **549–50**

"Raggedy Man, The" (Riley), 518–19

Ralph, **505**

RAMJAC Corporation, 58, 84, 95–96, 107, 108, 110, 145, 152, 155, 219, 281, 283, 322, 338, 349, 372, 379, 382, 384, 430, 467–68, 477, **505**, 520, 583, 584, 608, 612, 635, 699

Rauch, John G., 42, 43, 169, 336, **505**, 519, 536, 564, 678–79, 695

Raven, **505**

Ray, James Earl, 119–20, **505**
    Afterlife interview with, 269, 274–75

real estate agent, **505–6**

real estate man, **505**

reborn, 206, **506–7**

Reconstruction and Reclamation Corps (Reeks and Wrecks), 104, 224, 261, 281, 290, 316, 490, **507**, 601, 698, 703

Redfield, George, **507**

Redfield, Robert, 20, 185, 227–28, 243, **507–8**, 683

Redwine, C. Horner, 40, 485, **508**

Reed, Peter, 72, 391, 420*n*, 437, 461, **508**, 656

Reeks and Wrecks, *see* Reconstruction and Reclamation Corps
Reich der Zwei, Das (*The Nation of Two*), 105, **192, 456,** 462
Reinbeck, Charlie (Louis C. Reinbeck, Jr.), 5, **508,** 509, 702
Reinbeck, Louis C., 5, 69, **508–9,** 702
Reinbeck, Natalie, 508, **509,** 702
Reinbeck Abrasives Company, 5, **508,** 509, 702
religion, religious, 8, 12, 20, 32–33, 37–38, 52–53, 57, 122, 189–90, 323, 381, 427, 460, 472, 489, **509–16,** 618, 639–40, 672, 674, 676, 696, 697, 715–16
  morale and, 448
  morality and, 445–46
  see also Bokononism, Bokononist; *specific religions*
Remenzel, Dr., 39, 63, 308, **516–17,** 638, 693
Remenzel, Eli, 39, 308, **516–17,** 693
Remenzel, Sylvia, **516–17,** 693
"Report on the Barnhouse Effect," 39, 80, 99, 108, 117–18, 132–33, 156, 169, 184, 216, 247, 328, 334, 469, 571, 710
  see also Barnhouse, Arthur; dynamopsychism
Republican Party, 27, 33, 85, 138, 189–91, 306, 337, 413, 513, 526–27, 532, 553, 565
  National Convention (1972), 52, 258, 327, 356
resurrection, 195–96, 232, 364, 383, 435, 478, 524, 691
Rettig, John, 176–77, **517**
Reyes, Guillermo, 81, **517,** 614
Rice, Allen, 498, **518,** 520, 553, 604, 610, 702
Rice, Ella, 38, 173, 291–93, 345–46, **517–18,** 642
Rice, Irwin, 292, 345–46, **517–18,** 642
Richard, prince of Croatia-Slavonia, **498,** 689
"Rift Between Friends in the War of Ideas," **518**

Riley, James Whitcomb, 50, 154, 172, 175, 341–42, **518–20,** 560, 670, 674
Ritter, Pamela and Harvey, **520**
Rivera, Geraldo, 672
Rivera, Jerry Cha-Cha, 110, **520,** 712
Rivera, Wanda Chipmunk-5, **520**
Rivers, Jerry, 366, 385, **520**
Robbins, Eldon, **521**
Robert, Henry Martyn, **521**
Robert's Rules of Order, **521**
Robo-Magic Corporation, 32, 41, 42, 69, 81–82, 436, 437, **521**
robots, 288, 463
Rockefeller, Alice, *see* McCone, Alice Rockefeller
Rockefeller, Geraldine Ames, *see* Rosewater, Geraldine Ames Rockefeller
Rockmell, Eli W., 93, 181, **521–22**
Roethke, Theodore, **522**
Rome, ancient, 27–28, 176–77, 358, 512, 578
Romeo and Juliet (Shakespeare), 557–58
Roosevelt, Claudia, 188, **522**
Roosevelt, Eleanor, 284, 318, 448, **522**
Roosevelt, Franklin D., 105, 165, 207, 273, 522
Roosevelt, Theodore, 231, 265, 530
Roseberry, Harold, 92, 153, 169, 199, 215, 306, **522,** 717
Rosenau, Maurice, 475, **522**
Rosenfeld, Franklin Delano, 47, **522**
Rosenquist, Per Olaf, 49, **522**
Rosewater, Abraham, 433, **522,** 526, 694
Rosewater, Bertram Copeland, 422
Rosewater, Caroline, 49, 97, 203, 481, 485, **522–23,** 525, 581, 695
Rosewater, Eliot, 14, 15, 22–23, 31, 37–38, 41–42, 47, 50, 53, 242, 243, 264, 278, 280, 294, 296, 301, 302, 306, 340–41, 385, 386, 424, 433, 442, 475, 476, 488, 489, 491–92, 506, 510, 522, **523–25,** 526–29, 545, 555, 415, 570, 588, 590, 615, 619,

635–36, 650, 653, 688, 689, 693, 707
Rosewater, Eunice Eliot Morgan, 50, 171, **525**
Rosewater, Franklin, 522, **525,** 581
Rosewater, Fred, 44, 50, 120–21, 281, 306, 452, 487, 492, 522–23, 524, **525,** 528, 531, 541, 581, 590, 695
Rosewater, George, 50, 433, 442, 522, **525–26**
Rosewater, Geraldine Ames Rockefeller, 33, 50, **526**
Rosewater, John, II, 464
Rosewater, Lister Ames, 27, 50, 442, 523, 525, 526, **527,** 528
Rosewater, Merrihue, 50, 105, 120, 281, 464, 525, **526,** 531, 549, 694
Rosewater, Noah, 33, 306, 340, 442–43, 525, **526,** 650
Rosewater, Samuel, 33, 50, 306, **526 27**
Rosewater, Sylvia, 31, 38, 81, 93, 234, 294, 340, 442, 472, 475, 491, 510, 524, **527,** 537–38, 544, 555, 603, 638, 688, 707
Rosewater Corporation, 31, **528–29**
Rosewater County Clarion Call, The, 241, **527–28**
Rosewater Creek, **528**
Rosewater family history, 105, 281, 306, 464, 549
Rosewater Foundation, 391, 428, 452, 492, 523–25, 527, **528–29,** 688, 689
Rosewater Golden Lager Ambrosia Beer, **529,** 578
Rosewater Inter-State Ship Canal, **528,** 529
Rosewater Saw Company, 227, 613
Roswell Moose and Elks, **529**
Rothko, Mark, 16, 280, **529,** 592
Rowley, Jonah K., **529,** 567
Rowley, Mrs. Theodore, **529**
Rumford, Beatrice "Bee," "Bea," 132, 144, 160, 166, 250, 259, 287, 302, 358, 368, 379, 485, 502, **529–30,** 532, 542–43, 566–67, 577, 580, 587, 610, 624, 697, 705, 706

Rumfoord, Bertram Copeland, 460, **530–31**, 532, 704
Rumfoord, Clarice, **531**, 532
Rumfoord, Cynthia Niles, 526, **531**
Rumfoord, Lance, 379, 460, 530, **531–32**
Rumfoord, Lily, 530, **532**
Rumfoord, Remington, IV, **532**
Rumfoord, Robert Taft, 85, 337, 531, **532**
Rumfoord, William Howard Taft, 85, **531**, 532
Rumfoord, Winston Niles, 22, 57, 110, 114, 132, 145, 146, 154, 166, 181, 188, 213, 218, 245, 249, 259, 282, 297–98, 327, 337, 358, 362, 368, 370, 379, 400, 439, 441, 443, 459, 474–75, 485, 502, 510, 522, 529–30, **532–33**, 536, 537, 538, 566, 577–78, 580, 586, 590, 606, 610, 615, 697, 705
Rumfoord mansion, 17, 22, 49, 86, 157, 188, 199, 255, 279, 302, 358, 379, 459, 529–31, **533**, 543, 553, 567, 577, 580, 694, 706
Rumpf, Hans, *see Bombing of Germany, The*
Rumsfeld, Donald, 413, 553
"Runaways," 90–92, 171, **533–34**, 565, 574–75, 579, 641, 647
Ryan, Harold, 296, 298, 429, **534**, 565, 660
Ryan, Mildred, **534**
Ryan, Paul, **534**
Ryan, Penelope, 296, **534**, 565, 709

Saab Cape Cod, 417
Sacco, Dante and Inez, **535**
Sacco, Nicola, *see* Sacco and Vanzetti
Sacco and Vanzetti, 85, 106, 124, 135, 219, 220, 268, 279, 282, 296, 344, 351, 394–95, 400, 445, 484, **535**, 537, 588, 604, 698
Sacred Miracle Cave, 72, 104, 115, 318, 321, 350, 364, 437, 440, 448, 535, **535–36**, 538

St. Andres, **536**, 670
St. Augustine, **536**
Saint Elmo's fire, **536**
Saint Elmo's Remedy, **536–37**, 691
St. Francis of Assisi, **537**
St. George and the Dragon, 464, **537**
Saint Peter, 267–78, 560
Sakharov, Andrei, 9
Salo, 59, 114, 144, 154, 166, 237, 279, 283, 373, 441, 443, 474, 485, 529, 532–33, **537**, 554, 566–67, 577, 586, 587, 590, 610, 615, 640
Salsedo, Andrea, **537**
Sam, **537**
Samaritrophia, 93, 223, 340, 472, 527, **537–38**
Samoza Hall, **538**
"samplers" (aphorisms), 402, 420
Sams, Howard W., 249, 259, **538**
Sandburg, Carl, 198, 535
Sandler, Bea, **538**
Sandra, **538**
Sandy, **538–39**
San Lorenzo, 15, 26, 68, 74–77, 108, 109, 111, 114, 170, 172, 193, 245, 248, 312, 314, 331, 335–36, 348, 352, 439, 441–42, 471, 538, 544, 625, 654, 718
San Lorenzo Cathedral, **538**
Santa Claus, *see* Big Nick
Santa Cruz, **539**
sarooned, **539**, 654
Saroyan, William, 192
Sartre, Jean-Paul, 278
Satan (Devil), 258–59, 447, 464
Sateen Dura-Luxe, 15, 45, 287, **539**, 618, 638, 656, 706
Savonarola, Girolamo, 83, **539**, 595, 656
Saw City Kandy Kitchen, 123, **540**, 688
Sawyer, Doris, **540**
Schadenfreude, Dr., **540**
Scharff, Hattie, 354, **540**
Schenectady, N.Y., 129, 159
Schildknecht, Heinz, 219, 302, **540**, 663

schizophrenia, 28, 111–12, 194, 199, 250, 255, 309, 350, 449, **540–42**, 683
Schlesinger, Arthur, Jr., **542**
Schliemann breathing, Schliemann Breathing School for Recruits, 160, 529, **542–43**
Schneider, Kurt, 256, **543**
Schnull, Henry, 50, 149, 536
Schnull (Schnuell) family, 50, 149, 265, 386, 668, 673
Schramm's Drugstore, 194, 321, 337, **543**, 692
Schwartz, Harold D. "Gramps," **543**, 544
Schwartz, Louis J. and Emerald, **543–44**
Schwartz, Mortimer, **544**
Schweitzer, Albert, 109, **544**
science, 669–70
  morality and, 444–45, 549
science fiction, 25, 129, 150–51, 275, 321, 403–4, 416, 489, 523, **544–49**, 555, 615
Scilly Islands, 105, 281, **549**
Scipio, N.Y., 189, 206, 217, 243, 261, 312, 319, 358, 426, 435, 440, 441, 458, 474, 477, 484, **549**, 562, 586, 595, 602, 628, 639, 698, 704
Scott, Walter, 343, 594
Scrotum, **549**, 710
Sebastian, Saint, 222, 438
Seitz, Al and Sue, **549**
self-respect, 247
Semmelweis, Ignaz, 117, 330, 412
Seren, Leo, **549**
sergeant, **549–50**
Sermon on the Mount, 136–38, 141, 151, 197–98, 251, 267, 268, 270, 286, 296, 333, 344, 351, 403, 409, 413, 414, 474, 513, 515, **550–53**, 640, 699, 708
Seventy Times Seven, 266
Sevier County, Tenn., **553**
sexist stereotyping, 183–84
"Sexual Revolution, The," 147
shafts, **553–54**
Shakely, Norton, **554**

Shakespeare, William, 22, 34, 50, 71, 220, 240, 260, 274, 295, 326, 404, 447, 449, 491, 516, 520, 546, **555–61**, 571, 657, 680
   Afterlife interview with, 269, 275, 343, 560, 627
Shaltoon, 504, **561**
Shangri-La, 246, 709
Shapiro, Ben, 430, **561–62**
Shaw, George Bernard, 548, **562**, 621
Shaw, Helene, 438, 456, 462, 540, **562**, 703
Shaw, Marilyn, **562**
Shazzbutter, 322–23
Shelley, Mary Wollstonecraft, 10, 68, 191, 248–49, 497, **562–63**
   Afterlife interview with, 269, 275–76, 548, 563, 594
Shelley, Percy Bysshe, 563
Shepherd, Lawson, 95, 106, 241, 284, 306, 374, 381, 499, **563**
shoeshine boy, unnamed, **648**
Shortridge Echo, 169, **563–64**
Shortridge High School, 58, 61, 159, 169, 172, 222, 298, 334, 336, 343, **563–64**, 625, 679
short stories, 305
Shoup, Martin, **564**
Shoup, Mary Alice, 354, **564**, 701
Shoup, Naomi, 246, **564–65**
Shriver, Sargent, 392, **565**
Shroud of Turin, 177
Shultz, Hermann and Sophia, 34, 62, 250, 474, **565**, 572, 603, 649–50
Shuttle, Herb, 296–97, 534, **565**
Sidi Barrani, **565**
Siebolt, Dr., **565**, 575
Siegfried Line, 200, 481
Simmons, Newbolt and Martha, 544, **565–66**
Simpkins, Darlene, **566**
sin, 444, 480, 656
sinookas, 566
sin-wat, 566
Sirens of Titan, The, 17, 40, 44, 46, 52, 72, 86, 89, 109, 110–11, 114, 115, 145, 153, 188, 237,

245, 254, 255, 293, 297, 304, 334, 335, 352, 358, 362, 370, 379, 392, 400, 443, 460, 474, 475, 485, 500, 508, 509, 522, 529, 532, 538, 543, **566–67**, 570, 571, 586, 663, 676, 694, 697
"Sisters B-36, The," 32, 42, 82, 340, 482, 496, 514, 516–47, **567–68**, 705
Skag, Delmore, 38, 118, **568**, 620
Skinner, Cornelia Otis, **568**, 709
Skylark, 365, **569**, 635
Skyscraper National Park, 507–8, **569**
Slapstick, 4, 11, 12, 16, 57, 93, 95, 103, 181, 206, 213, 219, 220, 255, 283, 301, 319, 341, 346, 351, 366, 368, 379, 381, 392, 398, 428, 431, 449, 452, 465, 485, 520, 521, 564, **569**, 583, 598, 604, 650, 662, 688, 712, 714, 718
Slaughterhouse-Five, 8–9, 15, 30, 33, 36, 38, 44, 46, 69, 78, 81, 87, 94, 105, 106, 107, 116, 159, 175, 201, 210–11, 218, 223, 235–36, 254, 257, 259, 280, 287, 309, 316, 325, 334, 338–41, 344–45, 379, 382, 383, 395, 399, 403, 417, 422, 433, 439–40, 451, 459–60, 462, 464, 485, 487, 513, 524–25, 532, 536, 538, 544–46, 550, 555, **569–70**, 576, 584, 590, 596, 604, 616–17, 638, 681, 694–95, 704, 712, 716, 722
slavery, 30, 595
Slazinger, Paul, 432, **570–71**, 586, 704
Sleeping Beauty, 680
Slezak, Premier, **571**
Slotkin, 167, **571**
Slovik, Private, 323
Small Magnetic Cloud, **571**
Smart Bunny, The, 424, 554, **571**
Smiley, *see* Greathouse and Smiley
Smiley, Letitia, 38, 311, **571–72**
Smith, Frank, 342, 461, 479, **572**
Smith, Mary Alice, 518

Smith, Rosemary, 342, **572**, 717
Snopes, Flem, **572**
Snow Rose, The, **266**
Social Darwinism, 190
socialism, 144, 196–98, 272, 296, 310, 341, 342, 343, 403, 413, 414, 518, 551, 666, 699, 705
Solomon, Syd, 421, **572–73**
Solzhenitsyn, Aleksandr, **573**
somethinghead, **573**
Somme, Battle of the, **46–47**, 297
Sonderkommando, 28, 288–89, 314, **573**
Son of God, *see* Christ, Jesus
Son of Jimmy Valentine, The, **573**, 619
sons, fathers and, **233–35**, 687
Sony, **573–74**
Soul Merchants, The, **574**
Sousa, Mr., 11, 495, **574**
Southard, Annie, 91–92, 171, 533, 565, **574–75**, 578, 582, 641, 617
Southard, Jesse K., 574, **575**, 578
Southard, Mary, 171, 574, **575**, 578, 582
"Souvenir," 36, 46, 100, 106, 210, 218, 285, 334, **575–76**, 638, 641, 648
So You Went and Had a Baby, 181, 522
space and time, *see* time and space
space program, 164
space-time continuum, **576**, 607
Space Wanderer, 23, 157, 504, 508
   see also Constant, Malachi; Margaret, Queen
Sparks, Jon, **576**
Sparky (dog), 95, 219, **576–77**
Sparrow, Harold J., 69, 105, 155, 207, **577**, 706
Speer, Albert, 577
spirals, spiral nebula, **577–78**
spires, **578**
Spirit of the Meadows, see Queen of the Meadows
Spruce Falls, 46, 86, 102, 202, 237, 311, 339, 506, **578–79**
   Volunteer Fire Department, 27, 48–49, 458

Squibb, John, **579**, 672
Squibb, Will, and Buck, **579**
Squires, Anthony, 44, 194, 440, **579**
Squires, Barbara, 440, **579**
SS Psychiatrist, 30, **579–80**
Stacks, Herb, **580**
stairs, staircases, **580–83**
Stankiewicz, Juan and Geraldo, 20, 583
Stankiewicz, Stanislaus, 359, **583**
Stankiewicz, Walter F., **583**
  see also Starbuck, Walter
Stankowitz, **583**
Stanley, **583**
Starbuck, Ruth, 20, 63, 131, 215, 280, 469–70, 520, 561, **586–87**
Starbuck, Walter (Walter Stankiewicz), 15, 20, 33, 39, 44, 47, 63, 84, 107, 108, 118, 131, 152–53, 155, 157, 158, 184, 200, 215, 218, 220, 237, 240, 263, 280, 283, 295, 322, 325, 348–50, 359, 367, 382, 384, 394–95, 430, 467, 468, 474, 477, 485, 520, 535, 550, 561, 583, **584**, 597, 612, 635, 639, 653, 663, 689, 698–99, 706, 710–11
Starr, Harrison, **584–85**
Steadman, Ralph, 420, 484, **585**
Steel, Roy, 361, **585**
Steel, Terrence W., Jr., **585**
Steinberg, Saul, 417, 419–20, 542, **585–86**
Steppenwolf (Hesse), 677–78
Stern, Damon, 29, 176, 300, 358, **586**, 704
Stevenson, Adlai, **586**
Stevenson, Stony, 111, **586–87**
Stevie, *see* Amy and Harry; Laird, Eddie
Stewart, Kerfuit and Ella Vonnegut, **587**, 663, 674
Stockmayer, Walter H., 128, **587**
Stone, Fred, 556, **587**, 684
Stone, Sydney, 338, **587**
Stonehenge, **587**
Stratton, Samuel W., 282, **588**
Strax, Philip, **588**
  Afterlife interview with, 269–70, 276, 277

structured moment, 570, **588**
Studge, Philboyd, 99
stuppa, 76, 213, **588**
Styron, William, 9–10, 53, 333, 497, **588–89**, 593
subbasements, 15, 256, 349, **589**
Sublime Chamberlain of the Inner Shrine, **589**
Sugarbush Mountain, Vt., 433, 486–87, **580**
Sugar Creek, 41, 42, 195, 288, 448, 535–36, 587, 589, **589–90**
Sugar Creek High School, **590**
suicide, suicidal, 14, 53, 106, 120–21, 125, 140, 177, 208, 218, 225, 231, 248, 264, 280, 286, 311, 316, 320, 322, 333, 341, 353, 363, 367, 391, 392, 399, 424, 426, 440, 442, 451, 455, 462, 474, 478, 479, 481, 525, 526, 529, 569, 576, 579, 584, 588, **590–95**, 597, 600, 601, 622, 643, 689, 695
  of Edith L. Vonnegut, 14, 65, 121, 125, 126, 195, 208, 265, 342, 418, 435, 591–93, 673, 677, 691*n*, 692, 696
  of Hitler, 97, 103, 278, 309, 334, 540
  see also ethical suicide
Suk, Kim Bum, **595**
sumklish, 496, **591**
Sun Moon Star, **596**
Sunoco, Fleon, 49, 191, 204–5, 485, **596–97**
supernova, 57
Surrasi, 36, **597**
Susann, Jacqueline, **597**
Susanna, 253, 308, **597**
Sutton, Mrs., **597**, 606
Swain, Caleb Mellon and Letitia Vanderbilt, **597**
Swain, Carter Paley, 245, **597**, 599
Swain, Elihu Roosevelt, 169, 255, 357, 427, **598**, 599, 612, 614
Swain, Eliza Mellon, 12, 93, 167–68, 181, 185, 192, 227, 255, 281, 319, 366, 398, 421, 427, 449, 452, 461, 465, 507–8, 521–22, 555, 569, 583,

597, **598–99**, 614, 628, 662, 707
Swain, Sophie Rothschild, **598**, 599
Swain, Wilbur Rockefeller, 12, 15, 24, 46, 57, 93, 135, 138, 155, 167–68, 181, 185, 192, 206, 208, 219, 223, 227, 245, 248, 255, 281, 282, 283, 301, 319, 341, 353, 365, 368, 379, 392, 398, 421, 427, 428, 431, 449, 452, 461, 465, 485, 496, 507–8, 511, 520, 521–22, 565, 569, 583, 597, **598–99**, 603, 618, 628, 638, 650, 654, 661–62, 712, 714, 718
Sweetbread College, 366, 701
Swift, Jonathan, 31, 139–40
Swift, Tom, **600**
Szombathy, Lazlo and Miklos, **600**

Taft, Edith, 231, **601**
Takaru, 93, 107, 601, **601**
Tamanrasset, **601**
Tappin, Al, **601**
Tarkington, Aaron, 108, 217, 441, **601–2**
Tarkington, Elias, 312, 357, 441, 477, 484, 564, 565, **602**, 603
Tarkington, Felicia, 108, **602**
Tarkington College, 25–26, 29, 32, 38, 51, 53–54, 57, 67, 68, 109, 145–46, 151, 156, 169, 177, 205, 217, 218, 220, 227, 236, 238, 243, 261, 293, 296, 299, 300, 309, 311–12, 338, 353, 358, 367, 396, 426, 431, 435, 440, 441, 452, 458, 461, 474, 477, 484, 496, 538, 549, 551, 562, 570, 587, 571–72, 584–85, 592, 602, **602–3**, 628, 639, 652, 684, 689–90, 704, 708
  see also Mohiga Valley Free Institute
Tartakover, Ksawery, 371, **603**
Tarzan, 290
Tcherkassky, Maria Daffodil-H, **603**
teacher, unnamed, **648**
technology, technocracy, 261–62, 395–96, 403, 407, 408, 417,

431, 433, 456, 490, 499, 504, 547, 661, 703

deleterious effects of, 406, 568

Teddy (artist), 179, **423**

Tedler, Al, **603**

telepathy, 168, 192, 599

"Temptation of Saint Anthony, The," 259–60, 467

Tennyson, Alfred, **603**

Ten Square Band, 304, **390–91**, 477, 554, **603**

see also Lincoln High School

"Thanasphere," 188, 285, 329, 334, 353, 498, 520, 549, 553, 594, **603–4**, 610, 668, 702

Tharp, Naomi, **604**

Thayer, Webster, 85, 282, 350, 445, 484, **604**

Theatre de Lys, 103, 246, 361, **604**, 692

Theodorides, Mildred Heliwn-20, **604**

Theory of the Leisure Class (Veblen), 653

therefore (symbol), **604**

Thiriart, Jean, 457, **604**

"This Son of Mine," 51, 169, 234–35, 239, 250, 257, 339, 348, 389–90, 509, 578, **605**, 686–87

Thomas Jefferson High School, **605**

Thompson, Francis J., see Brackman, Henry

Thompson, Hunter, 356, 484, 585

Three Horsemen of the Oncologic Apocalypse, 22, 670

Thriller, Ralph L., 440, 478, **606**

Thurber, James, 333

Tibbets, Paul W., 713

Tiglath-pileser the Third, 301, 350, 425, **606**

Tillie, 597, **606**

time and space, **606–7**, 617

timequake, 235–36, 297, 458, 482, 493–94, 496, 506, 594, 607–8, 668, 675, 716

Timequake, Timequake One, 11, 12, 18, 25, 32, 36, 40, 42, 49–50, 61, 62, 72, 84, 99, 121, 170, 192, 196, 199, 203, 221, 222, 227, 232, 235, 247, 258, 270,

278, 279, 282, 297, 304, 306, 309, 353, 366, 373, 382, 384, 386, 392, 437, 446, 474, 479, 481–82, 493, 496–98, 520, 545, 546, 549, 568, 579, **607–8**, 619, 620–21, 624, 636, 666–68, 672, 681–82, 693, 705, 712, 717

Timequake clambake, 336, 342, 351–52, 366–67, 368, 382–83, 384, 385, 428, 429, 461, 464, 465, 480, 483, 485, 493, 498, 505, 508, 521, 545, 559, 572, 587, 593, 610, 622, 626, 663, 680, 681, 695, 712–13, 716

time-travel, 170, 457, 486, 487, 720

ting-a-ling, 237, 297, **608–10**

Titan, **610**

Titanic bluebird, 63, 144, 485, 530, 537, **610**

Tobin, Andrew, 353, **610**

Tobin, Paul, **610**

Tom, **611**, 648

tombs, **611–12**

"Tom Edison's Shaggy Dog," 95, 219, 334, 576–77

see also Bullard, Harold K.

"Tomorrow and Tomorrow and Tomorrow," 3, 22, 95, 118, 290, 311, 431, 543–44, **612**

top floor (top of the northernmost tower), **612–13**

topmost, **613**

totalitarian mind, **181**, 269, 273, 314, 436, 705

Tourette's Disease, Tourette's Syndrome, 94, 341, 618, 661, 662

Tower of Babel, **32**, 392, **613–15**

towers, **613–15**

Toynbee, Arnold, **615**

Tralfamadore, Tralfamadorian, 33–34, 38, 50–51, 85, 110, 114, 142, 144, 178, 223, 237, 254, 259, 279, 280, 283, 317, 331, 338, 339, 364, 373, 444, 474, 480, 485, 486, 500, 530–32, 537, 541, 554, 566–67, 570, 571, 587, 588, 596, 610, 614, **615–17**, 640, 704, 720

Transcendental Meditation, 715

transvestites, 385

Treasurer of the Knights of Kandahar, **617–18**

tri-benzo-Deportamil, 341, **618**, 662

trinity, **618**

Trippingham, Mona Lisa, **618**

Trout, Darlene, 573, **618**

Trout, Kilgore, 9, 18, 25, 36, 44–46, 48, 55, 57, 60–61, 64, 66–68, 81, 85, 86–89, 93, 94, 96, 99, 108, 118, 122, 127, 130, 134, 137, 139, 140–42, 173, 174, 176, 187–88, 189, 191, 192, 199, 203, 204, 206–8, 220, 222–23, 225, 229, 231, 233, 236, 237, 240, 249–51, 254, 258, 263, 264, 278, 280, 288, 297, 301, 302, 305, 309, 316, 323, 328, 339, 341, 357, 362, 365, 384, 385, 388–89, 398, 416, 420, 423, 424, 438, 443, 454–55, 478, 480, 488, 497–98, 514, 521, 523–25, 536, 562–63, 581, 603, 615, **618–21**, 636, 667, 700

in Afterlife interview, 266, 270, 277, 542, 548, 562

family of, 622–24

maxims of, 427

as messiah, 433–34

Midland City trip of, 589–90, 605, 613, 619, 694

and science fiction, 544–48

at *Timequake* clambake, 351–52, 366–67, 461, 480, 483, 493, 559, 572, 593, 610, 622, 626, 680, 712–13

as Vonnegut's alter ego, 17, 52, 416, 420, 567, 582, 591, 619–21, 652, 657, 675, 676, 677, 712, 715–16

at Xanadu, 554, 596, 607–9, 612, 622

see also Kilgore's Creed

Trout, Kilgore, works of, 3, 11–13, 19, 35, 38–39, 41, 82, 316, 317, 321, 322–23, 325, 329, 331, 340, 356, 359, 366–67, 379, 391, 415, 422, 423, 427, 435, 446–47, 458, 463, 474–75, 482, 488–89, 491, 500, 504, 524,

Trout, Kilgore, works of, (cont'd):
540, 555, 561, 567–68, 571,
573, 589, 594, 596, 617,
619–20, 653, 656, 674, 683,
694, 697, 705, 710, 712,
718–19, 720
see also specific works
Trout, Leo, 36, 619, **621–23**
Trout, Leon Trotsky, 13, 15, 61, 64,
66, 69, 84–85, 86, 122, 155,
180, 187, 199, 224, 254, 328,
421, 522, 536, 544, 546, 603–4,
619, **623–24**, 659, 713
Trout, Mrs., 603, **624**
Trout, Raymond, 64, 191, **622–23**,
624
*True Purpose of Life in the Solar
System, The*, **624**
Tucci, Alfy, **624**
Tucker, Carla (Karla) Faye, 71
Afterlife interview with, 270,
276–77, 627
Tudor Hall, 172–73, **624–25**, 668,
675, 681
Tum-Bumwa, 538, **625**
tunnels, **625–28**
turkey farm, 12, **628**
Turner, Jeffrey, **628**
Turtle Bay, 128, **628–29**
Twain, Mark, 85, 123, 161, 162,
221–22, 249, 260, 294, 333–35,
357, 406, 408–10, 415, 418,
447, 512, 551, 556, 592, 598,
628–34, 651, 669, 682, 709
American character presented by,
629–30
as essential American voice, 629
humor of, 418, 632
iconic stature of, 631
and Kurt Vonnegut Sr., 633
sense of story of, 632–33
spiritual committment of, 630–31
twerps, 402
twins, 11, 12, 24, 36, 38, 72, 167–68,
192, 203, 219, 321, 331, 377,
398, 415, 421, 442, 449, 452,
510, 524, 569, 597, 598–99,
645, 698, 699, 719
Two-Seed-in-the-Spirit
Predestinarian Baptist, 37

U-99, **635**
Ubriaco, Frank and Marilyn, **635**
UFOs, 164
Ukwende, Cyprian, 365, 435, 463,
467, 569, 590, **635**
Ulm, Arthur Garvey, 169, 465,
635–36, 713
Ulm, Lowell, **636**
uncritical, **636–37**
underground, **637–38**
Underground, The, **638**
Unger, Craig, 414, **639**
Unification Church Korean
Evangelical Association, **639**
Unitarian, Unitarian Universalist,
22, 40, 110, 251, 420, 456, 513,
552, **639–40**, 707
Universal Will to Become
(UWTB), 373, 474, 485, 587,
590, **640**
Unk, *see* Constant, Malachi
unnamed characters, **641–48**
un-neurotic courage, **641**
see also Kittredge, Waltham
"Unpaid Consultant," 97, 148, 160,
203, 334, **648–49**, 656
unnamed narrator of, **645–46**,
648–49
"Unready to Wear," 18, 369–70, 400,
649
Updike, Norman, 34, **649–50**
Urbana Massacre, 213, **650**, 662
Utopia, 98, 488, 527, **650–51**

Valentine, Ralston, *see Son of Jimmy
Valentine, The*
Valley of the Dolls (Susann), *see*
Susann, Jacqueline
Van Arsdale, Herbert, **652**
VanArsdale, Whitey, 16, 319, **653**
van Curler, Ormand, **652**
Van Gogh, Vincent, **652–53**
Van Tuyl estate, 22, 478, 506, **653**
Vanzetti, Bartolomeo, *see* Sacco and
Vanzetti
Veblen, Thorsten, 294, **653**
Venus on the Half Shell, 504, 561,
653
Vermont, University of, **671**
Vicuna, 237, 608, **653–54**

Vietnam War, 68, 70, 77, 123, 136,
149, 150, 158, 188, 189, 190,
227, 245, 271, 293–94,
299–300, 311, 315, 361, 364,
372, 391, 392, 403, 426, 455,
474, 475, 478, 500, 562, 570,
574, 606, 623, 655, 684, 690,
714
Villavicencio, Carlos Daffodil-II,
654
vin-dit, 76, 90, 539, **654**
Virgin Mary, 135, 159, 367, 595–96
virtue, **654–56**
Vitelli, Giovanni, **656**
Viverine, 127, **263**, 321, 354
Voce, Sotto, **656**, 710
Voltaire, **656–58**
von Braun, Werner, 207, 444, **658**
von Furstenberg, Rudolf, **658**
von Killinger, Manfred Freihert,
658
von Kleigstadt, Ormand, 94, 224,
658–59, 710
von Kleist, Adolf, 22, 36, 108, 180,
242, 243, 249–50, 254–55,
305–6, 308, 322, 330, 359, 399,
491, 557, 592, 624, **659**, 660,
689, 713
von Kleist, Gottfried and Wilhelm,
322, 613, **659**
von Kleist, Sebastian, **659–60**
von Kleist, Siegfried "Beast of
Yugoslavia," 169, 187, 659, **660**
von Koenigswald, Schlichter, 29, 76,
312, 327, 442, **660**
von Konigswald, Siegfried, 134, 297,
332, 491, **660**
Vonnegut, Alice "Allie," 11, 43, 55,
67, 72, 117, 138, 169, 172, 175,
178, 252, 254, 267, 341, 378,
482, 485, 502–3, 511, 519, 559,
569, 582, 612, 624, 662, 664,
666–68, 670, 673–74, 675,
676–77, 679, 680–81, 684,
691*n*, 714, 716
Vonnegut, Bernard (brother), 43, 50,
67, 68, 121, 129, 130, 148, 161,
162, 175, 191, 221, 227, 249,
265, 278, 288, 338, 344, 378,
484, 520, 569, 577, 612, 615,

664, 666–68, **668–70**, 671, 676–77, 716

Vonnegut, Bernard (grandfather), 420, 585, **668–70**, 672, 676, 678

Vonnegut, Carl Hiroaki and Emiko Alice, **670**

Vonnegut, Clemens, 13, 50, 68, 139, 249, 250–51, 267, 415, 515, 536, 655, 668, **670–72**, 674, 696, 715

Vonnegut, Dan, 265, 418, 455, 595, 663, **672**

Vonnegut, Edith, 11, 67, 72, 170–71, 251, 344, 420, 572–73, 585, 667, **672–73**, 684, 711

Vonnegut, Edith Lieber, 14, 65, 121, 126, 149, 175, 178, 228, 247, 305, 320, 336, 342, 389, 519, 564, 572, 591–93, 667, 672, **673–74**, 679, 696

Vonnegut, Emma, **674**

Vonnegut, Irma, 265, 668, **674**, 696

Vonnegut, Jane Marie Cox, 11, 21, 40, 55, 62, 64, 67, 117, 169, 172, 175, 250–51, 336, 342, 391, 405, 445, 509, 579, 618, 624, 625, 666, 668, **674–76**, 683, 684, 714–16

Vonnegut, Kurt, Sr., 67, 149, 175, 234, 265, 278, 341, 342, 344, 420, 449, 484, 505, 519, 559, 564, 572, 585, 593, 612, 617, 665, 666, 668–69, 673, 674, **676–81**, 696, 713, 717
and Twain, 633

Vonnegut, Lily, 10, 38, 247, 251, 297, 298, 513, 582, **681–82**, 710

Vonnegut, Mark, 11, 21, 61, 67, 119, 126, 137, 198, 228, 315, 324, 344, 353, 407, 414, 420, 541–42, 585, 599, 604, 611, 639, 667, 672, 675, **682–84**, 685, 715

Vonnegut, Nanette "Nanny," 265, 440, 582, 612, 667, **684–85**

Vonnegut, Peter and Mishi, 670

Vonnegut, Raye, 681, **685**

Vonnegut, Richard, 264

Vonnegut, Uncle Alex, 23, 151, 161, 175, 191, 197, 265, 267, 288, 296, 326, 342, 366, 418–19, 519, 569, 572, 611, **663–66**, 668, 672, 681, 682, 685, 717

Vonnegut family heritage, 50, 149, 228, 265, 341–42, 378, 386–89, 402, 405–6, 409, 410, 418–19, 464, 484, 505, 509, 511–14, 518–20, 536, 585, 664, 668–72, 673–74, 676, 696, 698

Vonnegut Memorial Fountain, **684**

von Neumann, Ludwig, 262–63, 357, 490, **660–61**

von Peterswald, David Daffodil-II, 94, 618, **661**, 662

von Peterswald, Felix Bauxite-13, 319, 628, **661–62**

von Peterswald, Melody Oriole-2, 155, 213, 223, 496, 618, 650, **662**

von Peterswald, Wilma Pachysandra-17, 57, 301, 431, 650, 661, **662**

von Sacher-Masoch, Leopold, 196

von Schwefelbad, Ulrich Werther, **663**

von Strelitz, Arthur, 20, **663**

Voyage of the Beagle (Darwin), **47**, 190

Voyager 2, 63, 218

Waggoner, Aunt Margaret, 248, **686**, 688

Waggoner, Franklin, 234, 250, 389–90, 509, 578, 605, **686–87**, 688

Waggoner, Merle, 234, 239, 250, 257, 339, 348, 605, 686, **687**, 688

Waggoner Pump, 239, 257, 339, 348, 389, 605, 686, **687–88**

Wainwright, Tawny, **688**

Wainwright, William Uranium-8, 4, 146, **688**

Wait, James (Willard Flemming), 190, 243, 253, 306, 317, 320, 399, 435–36, 498, **688–89**, 708

Wait, Mary, 36

Wakeby, Stella, **689**

Wakefield, Andrea, 317, **689**

Wakefield, Dan, 564

Wakefield, Sam, 152, 177, 218, 300, 353, 496, 562, 592, **689–90**

Waldorf Astoria, Martians in, 416

Waldorf Towers, **614**

Walker, Shelton, **690**

Wall Street crash (1929), 292, 346, 354, 531, 642

Waltz, Barbara, **690**, 691

Waltz, Charlotte, 690, 691

Waltz, Donna, **690**, 691

Waltz, Emma Wetzel, 195, 657, **690**, 697

Waltz, Felix, 11, 39, 46, 104, 115, 147, 193, 195, 203, 245, 252, 281, 320, 362, 364, 424, 440, 522, 658, **690–91**

Waltz, Genevieve, **691**

Waltz, Otto, 31, 100, 147, 153, 216, 241, 246, 252, 284, 288, 337, 424, 429, 434, 438–39, 448, 485, 517, 522, 536, 568, 579, 581, 590, 690, **691–92**

Waltz, Rudy "Deadeye Dick," 15, 31, 37, 39, 44–45, 51, 65, 82, 93, 95, 100, 103, 104, 159, 182, 183, 193–95, 209, 216, 232, 235, 245, 246, 256, 281, 283, 288, 297, 299, 317–18, 321, 337, 361–62, 364, 424, 428–29, 434, 435, 437, 438–39, 457, 467, 470, 481, 522, 536–37, 543, 549, 556, 564–65, 570, 579, 580, 604, 636, 658, 673, 690, 691, 692, **692**, 709

wampeters, 75, 121, 244, 282, 361, **692–93**

Wampeters, Foma & Granfalloons, 17, 40, 57, 69, 112, 227, 372, 460, **692–93**

Wanda June, *see* June, Wanda

Wang, Kimberly, 458, 615, **693**

Warmergram (Warmergran), Charley, 93, 241, **693**

Warren, Dr., **693–94**

Washington, Elgin, **694**

Wataru, Watanabe and Beverly June, 259, 400, **694**

Waterman, Earl, **694**

Waters, Lavinia, 401, 522, 526, **694**, 701

Watson, Myron S., 256, **694**

Watson Brothers, **694**

Weary, Roland, 142, 344, 383, 384, 486, 606, 655, **694–95**

Weeks, Bunny, 316, 317, 480–81, 485, **695**

Weeks, Hannibal, **695**

Wehling, Edward K., Jr., 3–4, 87, 132, 212, 311, 615, 647, **695**

Weide, Robert, 384, 461, 483, **695**

Weir, The, 316, 480, **695**

Welcome to the Monkey House, **695–96**

"Welcome to the Monkey House," 38, 40, 61, 65, 174, 212, 226, 259, 323, 358, 371, 431, 456, 463, 706

Wells, H. G., 112–13, 128, 129, 220, 313, 338, 352, 545

Weltschmerz, **696**

West Barnstable, Mass., **39–40**, 75, 417, 698, 706

West Barnstable Volunteer Fire Department, **39–40**, 75

Western Hemisphere University, Western Hemisphere University of the Bible, 355, **696–97**

Westlake, Ian, 28, **697**

Wetzel, Richard, **697**

Whale, The (later *Rumfoord*), 32, 577, **697**

Wheeler, Elm, **697–98**

Wheelock, Harley, II and III, **698**

"Where I Live," 460, **698**

Whistler, Henry Niles, 231, **698**

Whistler, Kenneth, 132–33, 296, 341, 352, 467, 550–51, 604, 664, **698–99**

White, Allison, **699**

White, Celeste, **699**

White, Gloria, 151, 367, **699**

White, Herb, 47, 85, 392–93, 462, 479, 603, 645, 646–47, **699**, 700

White, Maggie, **699–700**

White, Sheila Hinckley, 47, 85, 392–93, 462, 472, 475, 479,

603, 645, 646–47, 699, **700**, 707

White Christian Minuteman, The, 92, 139, 164, 263, 354–55, 506, 540, 697, **700–701**

Whitefeet, Elbert, **701**

Whitehall, Daniel, **701**

Whitehall Palace, *see* Rumfoord mansion

Whitehill, Florence, 166, 167, 694, **701–2**

Whitehill School for Boys, 39, 63, 308, 366, 516–17, 693–94

white humor, *see* humor

Whitman, Grantland, **702**

Whitman, Milly O'Shea, 5, 69, 508–9, **702**, 703

Whitman, Nancy, 5, 508, **702**

Whitman, Turley, 5, 509, **702**

"Who Am I This Time?," 438, 456, 462, 540, 562, **703**

Wicks, Frank, 149

Wiener, Norbert, 224, 323, 490, **703**

Wiesel, Elie, 209–10, 229

Wilbur, Harold Newcomb, 391, **703–4**

Wilburhampton Hotel, 23, 304, 400, 701, 705

Wild Bob, **704**

Wilder, Jason, 26, 54, 68, 159, 312, 397, 485, 558, 585, 689, **704**

Wilder, Kimberley, 26, 159, 474, 551, 571, **704**

Wildhack, Montana, 121, 259, 437, 617, **704–5**

Wiley, Roberta, 304, 475, **705**

Wilkerson, Florence, 66, 156, 482, 547, 620, **705**

Wilkinson, Max, 156, 334, 391

Wills, Ben, 250, 341, 513, 551, **705**

Wilson, Charles Thompson Rees, 185–86

Wilson, Robert Sterling, **705–6**

"Windsor Blue Number Seventeen," 15, 45, 167, 171, 223, 256, 316, 360, 427, 539, 618, 638, **706**

Winkler, Kermit, **706**

Winslow, Bernard K., **706**

Winters, Jonathan, 420

Wirtanen, Carly, **706**

Wirtanen, Frank, 40, 44, 69, 105, 124, 266, 432, 444, 462, 577, **706**

Witherspoon, Withers, **706–7**

WNYC, Afterlife interviews aired on, 266–78, 627

Wojciehowitz, Doris, 207, **707**

Wojciehowitz, Joseph, **707**

Wojciehowitz, Robert, 305–6, **707**

Woman, The Wasted Sex, or, The Swindle of Housewifery, 393, 472, 645, 699–700, **707**

womb, womblike, **707–8**

women's movement, 392–94, 395

Wood, Leonard, 408, 631, **708–9**

Woodcock, Sheldon, **709**

Woodly, Norbert, 296–97, 506, 534, **709**

Woodpile, The, **709**

Woollcott, Alexander Humphreys, **709**

Words for the Wind (Roethke), 522

Wovoka (Jack Wilson), 261

wrang-wrang, 372, **709**

Wright, Bert, 502, **709–10**

Wrinkled Old Family Retainer, The, 199, **710**

Wu, Sam, **710**

Wyandotte College, 73, 95, 224, 226, 299, 658, **710**

Wyatt, Radford Alden, **710**, 711

Wyatt, Sarah, 348–49, 357, 467, 584, 597, 606, **710–11**

Wyatt Clock Company, 468, 710, **711**

Wysocki, Mary Ann, 156, **711**

X, Mohammad Daffodil-11, **712**

Xanadu Writers' Retreat, 12, 85, 96, 169, 191, 204, 229, 305, 334, 465, 482, 493, 546, 554, 593, 596, 607, 608, 609, 622, 681, 710, **712–13**

Ximénez, Eduardo, 359, **713**

Yadin, Yigael, 425, **714**

Yamashiro, Hiroshi Raspberry-20, **714**

Yarmolinsky, Adam, 342, 675–76, **714**

Yarmolinsky, Jane Cox, 342, 675,
714–16
  see also Vonnegut, Jane Marie Cox
Ying, Pi, 17, 43–44, 363, **716**
Yonson, Yon, 584, **716**
Young, Buck, 298, **716–17**
Young, Ida, 342, 572, **717**
Young, Mary, 635, **717**

young man and woman, unnamed,
648
Young Men's Christian Association,
138

zah-mah-ki-bo, **718**
Zamiatin, Eugene, 490, **718**
Zappa, Lee Razorclam-13, **718**

Zappa, Vera, Chipmunk-5, 206, **718**
Zeltoldimar, 317, 359, 488, **718–19**
Zerbe, Gwen, 59, **719**
Zerbe, Mr., **719**
Zine, Clara, **719**
Zinka, 84, 314, 338, 340, **719–20**
Zircon-212, 58, **720**
Zog, 188, 423, **720**

PERMISSION CREDITS

ABOUT THE AUTHOR

MARC LEEDS is a graduate of the University at Buffalo, New York University, and Brooklyn College, and directed computer-based writing programs at East Tennessee State University and later at Shawnee State University in Ohio. He is the co-founder and founding president of the Kurt Vonnegut Society and a founding board member of the Kurt Vonnegut Museum and Library in Indianapolis. He is the author of *The Vonnegut Encyclopedia* (first edition) and numerous other publications about Vonnegut as well as composition studies.

ABOUT THE TYPE

This book was set in Electra, a typeface designed for Linotype by renowned type designer W. A. Dwiggins (1880–1956). Electra is a fluid typeface, avoiding the contrasts of thick and thin strokes that are prevalent in most modern typefaces.